*Special Edition*

# USING NETSCAPE COMMUNICATOR 4

que®

*Special Edition*

# USING NETSCAPE COMMUNICATOR 4

*Written by Mark R. Brown with*

*Tom Fronckowiak • Galen Grimes • Jerry Honeycutt
Allen Hutchison • Ted Lesley • Mike Logan • Mike Morgan
Andrew Bryce Shafran • Joe Simmons • Todd Stauffer • Paul Wallace*

QUe®

# Special Edition Using Netscape Communicator 4

Copyright© 1997 by Que® Corporation.

All rights reserved. Printed in the United States of America. No part of this book may be used or reproduced in any form or by any means, or stored in a database or retrieval system, without prior written permission of the publisher except in the case of brief quotations embodied in critical articles and reviews. Making copies of any part of this book for any purpose other than your own personal use is a violation of United States copyright laws. For information, address Que Corporation, 201 W. 103rd Street, Indianapolis, IN 46290. You may reach Que's direct sales line by calling 1-800-428-5331.

Library of Congress Catalog No.: 09805-6

ISBN: 0-7897-0980-5

This book is sold *as is*, without warranty of any kind, either express or implied, respecting the contents of this book, including but not limited to implied warranties for the book's quality, performance, merchantability, or fitness for any particular purpose. Neither Que Corporation nor its dealers or distributors shall be liable to the purchaser or any other person or entity with respect to any liability, loss, or damage caused or alleged to have been caused directly or indirectly by this book.

99 98 97      6 5 4 3 2 1

Interpretation of the printing code: the rightmost double-digit number is the year of the book's printing; the rightmost single-digit number, the number of the book's printing. For example, a printing code of 95-1 shows that the first printing of the book occurred in 1995.

All terms mentioned in this book that are known to be trademarks or service marks have been appropriately capitalized. Que cannot attest to the accuracy of this information. Use of a term in this book should not be regarded as affecting the validity of any trademark or service mark.

Screen reproductions in this book were created using Collage Plus from Inner Media, Inc., Hollis, NH.

# Credits

**PRESIDENT**
Roland Elgey

**SENIOR VICE PRESIDENT/PUBLISHING**
Don Fowley

**PUBLISHER**
Joseph B. Wikert

**GENERAL MANAGER**
Joe Muldoon

**MANAGER OF PUBLISHING OPERATIONS**
Linda H. Buehler

**PUBLISHING MANAGER**
Jim Minatel

**MANAGING EDITOR**
Thomas F. Hayes

**DIRECTOR OF ACQUISITIONS**
Cheryl D. Willoughby

**ACQUISITIONS EDITOR**
Jane K. Brownlow
Stephanie J. McComb

**PRODUCT DIRECTORS**
Mark Cierzniak
Henly Wolin

**SENIOR EDITOR**
Elizabeth A. Bruns

**EDITORS**
Kelli M. Brooks
Sean Dixon
Patricia Kinyon
Jeanne Terheide Lemen
Sean Medlock

**PRODUCT MARKETING MANAGER**
Kourtnaye Sturgeon

**ASSISTANT PRODUCT MARKETING MANAGERS**
Gretchen Schlesinger
Christy Miller

**TECHNICAL EDITORS**
Kyle Bryant
Dan Harris
Sunil Hazari
Troy Holwerda
Jim O'Donnell
Tony Schafer
Mark Totleben
Scott Warner
Ed Willett

**SOFTWARE SPECIALIST**
Benjamin Milstead

**ACQUISITIONS COORDINATORS**
Michelle R. Newcomb
Chantal Mees Koch

**SOFTWARE RELATIONS COORDINATOR**
Susan D. Gallagher

**EDITORIAL ASSISTANTS**
Jennifer L. Chisholm
Travis Bartlett
Jeff Chandler

**BOOK DESIGNER**
Ruth Harvey

**COVER DESIGNER**
Dan Armstrong

**PRODUCTION TEAM**
Julie Geeting
Brian Grossman
Sossity Smith
Staci Somers

**INDEXER**
Craig Small
with Nadia Ibrahim

Composed in *Century Old Style* and *ITC Franklin Gothic* by Que Corporation.

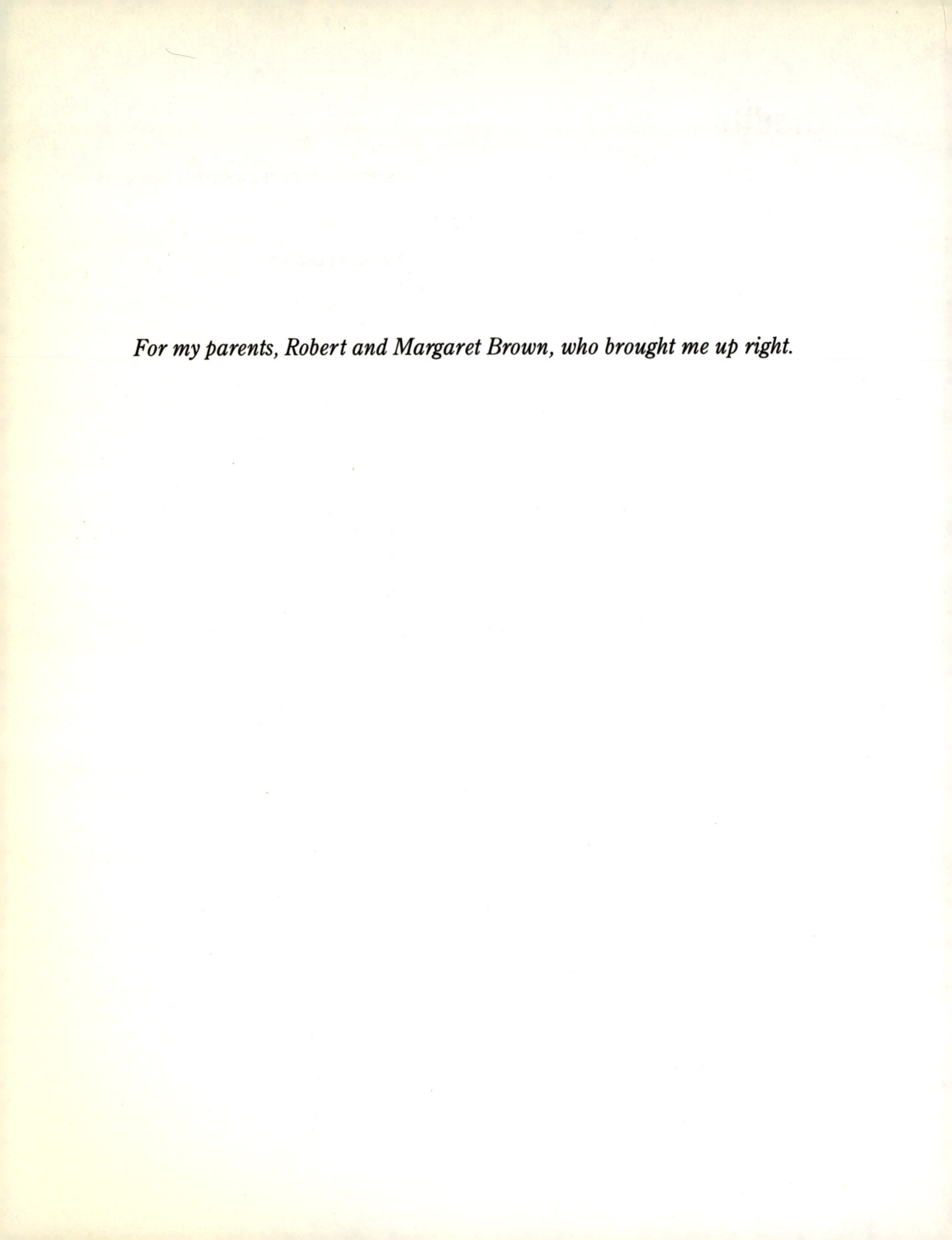

*For my parents, Robert and Margaret Brown, who brought me up right.*

# About the Authors

**Mark R. Brown** has been writing computer books, magazine articles, and software manuals for over fourteen years. He was Managing Editor of *.info magazine* when it was named one of the Best Computer Magazines by the Computer Press Association in 1991, and was nominated by the Software Publisher's Association for the Software Reviewer of the Year award in 1988. He's now a full-time freelance writer who has contributed to over a dozen Que books, and is the author of Que's *Special Edition Using Netscape* series, *Special Edition Using HTML 3.2*, and *WWW Plug-ins Companion*. He is Webmaster of a Web site devoted to the topic of airships at **http://www2.giant.net/people/mbrown**, and can be reached via e-mail at **mbrown@avalon.net**.

**Galen A. Grimes** has been working with computers since 1980, when he purchased his first PC, an Apple II+. Since then he has worked on PCs using DOS, Windows (3.1/95/NT 4.0), and UNIX and has programmed in about a dozen different programming languages including C/C++, Assembler, Pascal, BASIC, and xBase. Galen has a master's degree in Information Science from the University of Pittsburgh and is currently a computer systems project manager at Mellon Bank in Pittsburgh, PA.

Galen has worked as an author for several Macmillan Computer Publishing divisions for the past six years and has written *Teach Yourself Netscape Communicator in 24 Hours, 10 Minute Guide to Netscape With Windows 95, 10 Minute Guide to the Internet With Windows 95, 10 Minute Guide to Novell NetWare, 10 Minute Guide to Lotus Improv, Windows 3.1 Hyperguide, 10 Minute Guide to the Internet and World Wide Web, 2nd Ed., First Book of DR DOS 6,* and *10 Minute Guide to the Internet and World Wide Web, 3rd Ed.* Galen has also been a contributing author to *Special Edition Using Netscape 2, Special Edition Using CGI, Special Edition Using the World Wide Web, Special Edition Using Netscape 3, Netscape Navigator 3 Starter Kit,* and *WWW Plug-ins Companion*.

**Jerry Honeycutt** provides business-oriented technical leadership to the Internet community and software development industry. He has served companies such as The Travelers, IBM, Nielsen North America, IRM, Howard Systems International, and NCR. Jerry has participated in the industry since before the days of Microsoft Windows 1.0; and is completely hooked on Windows and the Internet.

Jerry is a leading author in the Internet field. He is the author of over a dozen books, each published by QUE, including *Special Edition Using HTML 3.2*; *Special Edition Using the Internet*; *Special Editon Using the Windows NT 4.0 and Windows 95 Registry*, *Using Netscape Composer*; *Using the Internet*; and *Windows NT 4.0 and Windows 95 Registry and Customization Handbook*. Many of Jerry's books are sold internationally and have been translated into a variety of foreign languages. Feel free to contact Jerry on the Internet at **jerry@honeycutt.com** or visit his Web site at **http://rampages.onramp.net/~jerry**.

**Michael Morgan** is founder and president of DSE, Inc., a full-service Web presence provider and software development shop. The DSE team has developed software for such companies as Intelect, Magnavox, DuPont, the American Biorobotics Company, and Satellite Systems Corporation, as well as for the Government of Iceland and the Royal Saudi Air Force. DSE's Web sites include the prestigious Nikka Galleria, an online art gallery. DSE's sites are noted for their effectiveness—one of the company's sites generated sales of over $100,000 within 30 days of being announced.

He holds a Master of Science in Systems Management from the Florida Institute of Technology, and a Bachelor of Science in Mathematics from Wheaton College, where he concentrated his studies on computer science. He has also taken numerous graduate courses in computer science through the National Technological University. Mike is a member of the IEEE Computer Society.

**Andy Shafran** has been writing computer books for several years. He enjoys working with the Internet, World Wide Web, and related information technologies such as Lotus Notes. Born in Columbus, Ohio, Andy recently graduated from The Ohio State University with a degree in Computer Science Engineering. He now lives in Cincinnati, the Queen City, and is an avid Reds baseball fan.

He has written several computer books including *Creating Your Own Netscape Web Pages*, *The Idiot's Guide to CompuServe*, and *Easy Lotus Notes (R3)*.

When he's not writing he enjoys live theater, particularly Broadway shows. He also loves traveling abroad and is constantly making excuses to buy yet another plane ticket to a foreign country. You can talk to Andy via e-mail at **andy@shafran.com** or visit his WWW page at **http://www.shafran.com**.

**Todd Stauffer** is a full-time freelance writer based in Colorado Springs, CO. He's written non-stop since graduation from Texas A&M University, where he studied English Literature and Management Information Systems. Since that time he's been an advertising copywriter, magazine columnist, and magazine editor, all in computing fields.

Todd is currently the Internet columnist for *Peak Computing Magazine*, and host of the Peak Computing Radio Hour on AM740 in Colorado. He's the author of *HTML By Example, Using the Internet With Your Mac, Using Your Mac, Easy AOL*, and co-author of a number of other titles, all published by Que. In his spare time he thinks of new and interesting ways to fund his health insurance and write off exotic vacations as tax deductible. He has no cats, although other people's cats are always bothering him.

Todd can be reached via e-mail at **tstauffer@aol.com** or through his personal Web site at **http://members.aol.com/tstauffer/**.

**Paul Wallace** lives in Knoxville, Tennessee, where he is pursuing a Ph.D. in Instructional Technology at the University of Tennessee. He is also an Internet consultant and developer specializing in content development, interface design, and interactive programming for the World Wide Web.

In his diminishing free time, Paul can be found relaxing with friends in one of Knoxville's coffee shops, swimming laps, or patiently awaiting the next Dinosaur Jr. album. Paul is an accomplished surfer who has traveled to many of the world's best point breaks and hopes to someday visit the coast of South Africa. Paul can be reached via his homepage at: **http://www.clever.net/wallace/**.

**Thomas Fronckowiak** is a computer engineer graduate from Rochester Institute of Technology and a native of Buffalo, New York. He's spent the last five years city-hopping his way up and down the east coast, working computer contracts, and searching for the perfect atmosphere for his character inventing. He currently resides in Huntsville, Alabama and when he's not dodging tornadoes or skiing the placid Tennessee, he finds time to work on his Internet and military techno-thrillers.

**Allen Dale Hutchison** is a staff member with Indiana University in charge of maintaining the Network R&D lab. Allen is also a part-time student at IU, and is majoring in Cognitive Science. Allen has contributed to many Que books as a technical editor, including *Special Edition Using CGI*, *Special Edition Using Java*, and *Special Edition Using Perl5 for Web Programming*.

**Ted Lesley** is the managing partner of the consulting firm Springside Communications based in Bluemont, VA (**http://www.springside.net**). He has offered technical support and consulting services to customers ranging from basement entrepreneurs to international bankers. Ted currently divides his time between his Northern Virginia clients and the most perfect baby in the world, daughter Laurel Lynne Lesley.

**Mike Logan** is a personal computer technician for State Farm Insurance's regional office in Columbia, MO. One of his primary duties is to create State Farm's Missouri regional office intranet. Mike's personal computing experience dates back to the early 1980's when the CPM operating system was popular.

**John Simmons** is a full-time writer and Web Designer living in Toronto, Canada. Besides writing technical manuals and creating interesting Web sites, he writes fiction. After first being exposed to the World Wide Web in early 1995, John quickly realized that it could revolutionize the way people communicate. He sees it as an ideal medium for individuals to reach a mass audience in a way never before possible. To this end, he encourages people to learn about the Web and become involved in this wonderful new opportunity in global communications.

# Acknowledgments

Writing is generally a pretty thankless game (except for the occasional paycheck), but an extra special pat on the back goes to the writers associated with this project. They put forth a tremendous effort to get this book out in spite of many delays by Netscape in releasing Communicator, and the many product changes associated with those delays. In essence, we planned this book a half-dozen times and wrote it twice.

The editors and staff at Que books certainly earned their kudos as well. Special thanks go to Cheryl Willoughby, Jim Minatel, Stephanie McComb, Elizabeth Bruns, Jane Brownlow, and Mark Cierzniak for their invaluable assistance and infallible guidance.

Of course, we wouldn't have a book at all if it weren't for the excellent products produced by the programmers, planners, and management of Netscape Corporation. Thanks to all—even the millionaires.

Then there "are all those wonderful people out there in the dark" who make up the World Wide Web. Certainly, to the people at CERN in Switzerland who first conceived and implemented the Web, our thanks. But the Web is made up of the efforts of literally millions of people, many of whom selflessly contribute, gratis, the thoughts, ideas, articles, stories, graphics, movies, sound clips, and all of the other elements that make up the multinational, multilingual, multimedia stew that is the World Wide Web. To all of them, our thanks for making Web surfing such an entertaining, enlightening, and engaging activity!

Writing's tough, but being a writer's spouse means spending lots of lonely nights near deadline. That's why this last line is always reserved for saying, "Thanks, Carol."

-Mark R. Brown

## We'd Like to Hear from You!

As part of our continuing effort to produce books of the highest possible quality, Que would like to hear your comments. To stay competitive, we *really* want you, as a computer book reader and user, to let us know what you like or dislike most about this book or other Que products.

You can mail comments, ideas, or suggestions for improving future editions to the address below, or send us a fax at (317) 581-4663. For the online inclined, Macmillan Computer Publishing has a forum on CompuServe (type **GO QUEBOOKS** at any prompt) through which our staff and authors are available for questions and comments. The address of our Internet site is **http://www.mcp.com** (World Wide Web).

In addition to exploring our forum, please feel free to contact me personally to discuss your opinions of this book: I'm **mcierzniak@que.mcp.com** on the Internet

Thanks in advance—your comments will help us to continue publishing the best books available on computer topics in today's market.

Mark Cierzniak
Product Development Specialist
Que Corporation
201 W. 103rd Street
Indianapolis, Indiana 46290
USA

**NOTE** Although we cannot provide general technical support, we're happy to help you resolve problems you encounter related to our books, disks, or other products. If you need such assistance, please contact our Tech Support department at 800-545-5914 ext. 3833.

To order other Que or Macmillan Computer Publishing books or products, please call our Customer Service department at 800-858-7674.

# Contents at a Glance

Introduction 1

## I | Communicator Quick Start

1 Overview 11
2 What's New in Netscape Communicator 27
3 Navigator Quick Start 39
4 Messenger Quick Start 51
5 Collabra Quick Start 71
6 Composer Quick Start 79
7 Conference Quick Start 95

## II | In-Depth Communicator

8 Navigator In-Depth 109
9 Using Bookmarks1 45
10 Interacting with Plug-ins, Java Applets, and JavaScript 163
11 Messenger In-Depth 199
12 Using the Address Book 231
13 Collabra In-Depth 245
14 Composer In-Depth 273
15 Conference In-Depth 301
16 Setting Preferences 319
17 Security Options 349

## III | Communicator Professional

18 Calendar 369
19 IBM Host-on-Demand 389

## IV | Netcaster

20 Setting Up Your WebTop 405
21 Channels 411

## V | For Webmasters

22 HTML Primer   435
23 Adding Links and Graphics   467
24 Organizing Content with Tables and Frames   487
25 Building Navigational Imagemaps   519
26 Creating Forms and Server Scripts   537
27 Dynamic HTML   561
28 Using Layers   573
29 Using Style Sheets   599
30 Embedding Multimedia   627
31 Adding Java Applets   641
32 Enhancing Your Documents with JavaScript   653

## VI | For Developers

33 Netscape Servers   667

## VII | Appendixes

A Getting Online   679
B Installing Communicator for Windows 3.1   689
C Installing Communicator for Windows 95   711
D Installing Communicator for Macintosh   727
E Installing Communicator for UNIX   741

# Table of Contents

**Introduction   1**
    Who Should Use This Book?   2
    How This Book Is Organized   3
    Conventions Used in This Book   6

## 1 | Communicatore Quick Start

### 1   Overview   11
    The World Wide Web and Netscape Navigator   12
    The Rise of the Corporate Intranet   15
    Navigator's Future in Application Development   17
    Electronic Mail and Netscape Messenger   18
    News and Netscape Collabra   19
    Creating Documents with Netscape Composer   21
    Netscape Conference   22
    Netcaster   23
    Communicator Integration   25

### 2   What's New in Netscape Communicator?   27
    Toolbars and Menus   28
        The Component Bar   28
        Changes to Toolbars   29
    Improved Document Features   30
        Additions to HTML   31
        Changes in Plug-Ins   31
        Changes in Java   32
        Other Document Improvements   32
    Mail and News   32
    Composer   33
    Conference   34
    Netcaster   35
    Preferences and Security   37
    Other New Features   38

### 3 Navigator Quick Start 39

    A First Look at Netscape Navigator 40
        Setting Your Own Home Page 41
    Jumping to Your Own Locations 42
    Using Navigational Links 43
    Navigation Using the Toolbar Buttons 44
        Basic Bookmarks 45
    Searching for Sites 47
    Moving to Other Communicator Applications 48
    Getting Additional Help 49

### 4 Messenger Quick Start 51

    Accessing Messenger 53
    Configuring Messenger 54
    Checking Your E-Mail 55
        Reading Your Messages 56
    Composing an E-Mail Message 58
        Sending Carbon and Blind Copies 61
        Adding Recipients to E-Mail Messages 62
        Checking Your Spelling 63
    Sending Your Message Now 64
        Choosing HTML or Plain Text Format 64
        Sending the Message 66
    Sending All Your Messages Later 66
    Replying to E-Mail Messages 67
        Quoting the Sender in Your Reply 68
        Sending the Reply 70

### 5 Collabra Quick Start 71

    Setup 72
    Basics 73
        Subscribing to a Newsgroup 73
        Reading Newsgroup Messages 75
        Filing a Newsgroup Message 76
        Replying to a Newsgroup Message 77

## 6  Composer Quick Start   79

Setup   80

Basics   81
- Create a Blank Page   81
- Add Text to Your Web Page   82
- Add an Image to Your Web Page   84
- Working with Links on Your Web Page   87
- Save Your Web Page   88
- Publishing Your Web Site with Composer   89

## 7  Conference Quick Start   95

Launching Conference   96

Configuring Conference   97

Making an Internet Phone Call   100

Text Chat   102

File Exchange   102

Collaborative Browsing   103

The Whiteboard   104

Integration   105

# II | In-Depth Communicator

## Navigator In-Depth   109

Communicator Preferences   110

Reviewing Navigator Basics   111

Bringing Up a New Navigator Window   113

Opening and Saving Pages   114

Printing Pages   115

Navigator Integration   117

Adjusting Look and Feel   120
- Fonts and Colors   120
- Toolbar Control   122

Navigation Tips and Tricks   123

Copy, Paste, and Find   125

Controlling Page Downloading   126
About This Page   127
Setting Up Multiple Users   131
Communicator Command-Line Options   132
The History List   133
The Status Bar   135
The Pop-Up Menu   136
Searching for Sites   137
Working with FTP, Gopher, and Telnet   138
    FTP   138
    Gopher   140
    Telnet   140
Other Navigator Features   140
NetHelp   141

## 9  Using Bookmarks   145

Adding and Referencing a Bookmark   146
More Ways to Create Bookmarks   147
More Ways to List Bookmarks   150
Organizing Your Bookmarks   151
    Creating and Using Folders   153
    Organizing Files and Folders   154
    Adding, Editing, and Deleting Bookmarks   154
Changing Points of View   156
Finding Bookmarks   156
Special Folder Features   157
Bookmark Tricks and Tips   158
Working With Multiple Bookmark Lists   160
Automatically Updating Bookmarks   161

## 10  Interacting with Plug-Ins, Java Applets, and JavaScript   163

Who's Who and What's What   164
Automated Pages   165
Imagemaps   166

Using Forms   167
   What Are Forms Good For?   167
   An Online Shopping Trip   170
   Form Elements   177
   Automatic Mail with Mailto   179
   Enough About Forms Already!   179

Frames   180
   Netscape's DevEdge Site   180
   The CyberDungeon   181
   Resizing Frames   182
   Frame Navigation   182
   The File Menu and Frames   183

Java   183

JavaScript and Dynamic HTML   184

Plug-Ins   185
   Navigator's Bundled Plug-Ins   186
   Third Party Plug-Ins   194
   Shockwave for Macromedia Director   196

OLE Integration   198

## 11  Messenger In-Depth   199

Organizing the Message List   200
   Sort Quickly with the Columns   201
   View Only New Messages   202
   Customize the Message Pane   202
   Change the Message's Appearance   204

Using Threads to Follow a Conversation   205
   Viewing Threads   206
   Expanding and Reading Threads   207
   Watching Threads   208
   Ignoring Threads   209

Create and Manage New Folders   210
   Create Subfolders   210
   Expand and Collapse Folders   211
   Move Folders   211
   Rename Folders   212
   Delete Folders   213

File Messages 213
Copy Messages 213
Deleting Messages 214

Emptying the Trash 215
Compressing Folders 215

Searching Through Folders 217

Creating a Filter 218

Attaching Files or Documents to Messages 219
Attaching a Web Page 220

Adding HTML to Documents 221
Using Basic Styles 222
Changing the Typeface 222
Changing Font Size and Color 223

Organizing Your Message 224
Adding Headings 224
Alignment 226
Creating a Hyperlink 226
Adding an Image 226
Making Your Image a Link 228

## 12 Using the Address Book 231

Working with the Address Book 232
Sorting the List 235
Display Fewer or More Fields 236
Searching for a Person 237

Adding a New Address Card 238
Changing an Address Card 239
Removing an Address Card 239
Creating a Card from a Directory 240

Creating a Mailing List 241

Contacting People from Your Address Book 242
Addressing an Internet Mail Message 242
Making a Call with Netscape Conference 243

## 13 Collabra In-Depth 245

Understanding UseNet Newsgroups 246
UseNet Is About Variety 246

Newsgroup Organization 246
news.newusers.questions 247

Working with Newsgroups 249
    Subscribing to a Newsgroup 252
    Unsubscribing from a Newsgroup 253
    Searching for a Newsgroup 253
    Watching the New Newsgroups 254
    Using Multiple News Servers 255

Browsing and Reading Newsgroup Messages 256
    Getting Around the Discussion Folder 262
    Filing a Newsgroup Message 263
    Replying to a Newsgroup Message 264
    Saving a Message's File Attachments 265

Posting Messages to a Newsgroup 266
    Attaching Files to Your Message 268
    Adding a Signature to Your Messages 268

Using Collabra to Read Newsgroups Offline 269
    Going Offline 269
    Setting Up the Startup Mode 270

## 14 Composer In-Depth 273

Working with Your HTML Document 274
    Search for Text 274
    Check for Spelling Errors 274
    Preview the Final Result 275
    Work with Raw HTML 276

Formatting Your HTML Document 278
    Character Formatting 278
    Paragraph Formatting 280

Adding Images to Your HTML Document 284
    Provide Alternative Text 284
    Align Your Image 285
    Position the Image 285
    Add a Margin 286
    Create a Background 286

Adding Links to Your HTML Document 287
    Change a Link 287

Remove a Link   287
Change a Link's Colors   287
Create Internal Links   288

Adding Tables to Your HTML Document   290
Add a Table to Your HTML Document   290
Change an Existing Table   292
Change Rows and Cells   293

Using Composer Plug-Ins to Enhance Composer   296
Plugging In to Plug-Ins   296
Downloading Sample Composer Plug-Ins   297
Using a Composer Plug-In   299

## 15 Conference In-Depth   301

System Requirements   302

Configuring Conference   303

Making an Internet Phone Call   307

Receiving a Call   310

Text Chat   311

File Exchange   312

Collaborative Browsing   313

The Whiteboard   314
Getting a Background Image   315
Using Markup Tools   316
The Whiteboard Options Menu   317
Other Whiteboard Functions   317

Conference's Limitations   318

## 16 Setting Preferences   319

Appearance   320
Fonts   322
Colors   323

Navigator   324
Languages   326
Applications   327

Mail & Groups   330
Identity   331

Contents | xxiii

    Messages 333
    Mail Server 335
    Groups Server 336
    Directory 337
  Composer 338
    Publishing 339
  Offline 340
    Download 341
  Advanced 342
    Cache 343
    Proxies 344
    Disk Space 346

## Security Options 349

  Configuring for Multiple Users 350
  Security Button 352
  Viewing Security Info 354
  Certificates 356
    Your Certificates 357
    Other People's Certificates 358
    Web Sites' Certificates 359
    Certificate Authorities 359
  Private Key Passwords 361
  Applications 362
    SSL Browsing 363
    S/MIME E-Mail 364
    Java Applet Privileges 365
  Cryptographic Modules 365
  Help 366

# III | Communicator Professional

## Calendar 369

  Getting Up and Running with Calendar 370
  Entering Information in Your Agenda 371
    Going Online When You Are Working Stand-Alone 373

Going Offline from Your Host Agenda  373
Learning Netscape Calendar from Soup to Nuts  373
Changing Calendar's Default Settings  374
Becoming Familiar with Calendar's Toolbar  376
Adding New Entries to Your Agenda  377
Responding to a Meeting Request  381
Creating Tasks in Your Agenda  383
    Viewing Your Task List  383
Entering Notes in Your Agenda  384
    Viewing Your Notes  385
Working with Your In-Tray  385
Designating Access Rights to Other Calendar Users  386

## 19 IBM Host On-Demand  389

Overview of TN3270 and the 3270 Family of Products  390
    Understanding SNA  390
    The 3270 Family of Terminals  392
    Function Keys  392
    Operator Information Area  393
    VM, MVS, and Mainframe Applications  393
Understanding IBM Host On-Demand  394
    What Do You Need?  394
    Setting Up a Connection  396
    Reading the OIA Messages  398
    Changing the Default Connection  400
    Starting a Session  401
    Ending a Session  402

# IV | Netcaster

## 20 Setting Up Your Web Top  405

Netcaster Quick Start  406

## 21 Channels  411

Starting Netcaster  412
Finding Channels  412

My Channels   416

The Netcaster Menu Bar   417
    Add   417
    Options   418
    Help   420
    Exit   421

The Netcaster Toolbar   421

Web Tops   422
    Web Tops in Brief   423
    Web Top Design   423

Channels   426

Marimba Castanet   427

Offline Browsing   429

Security   430

Netscape Netcaster versus Microsoft Active Desktop   431

# V  For Webmasters

## HTML Primer   435

Adding the *<HTML>* Tag   436

HTML Section Tags   436
    Using the *<HEAD>* Tag   437
    Using the *<BODY>* Tag   437

Titling a Document   437
    Using the *<TITLE>* Tag   438
    Choosing an Effective Title   438

Adding Headings to a Document   438

Organizing Paragraphs of Text   440
    Paragraph Breaks with *<P>*   441
    Line Breaks with *<BR>*   442
    The Horizontal Rule—*<HR>*   443
    Predefined Text with *<PRE>*   444

Basic Formatting Tags   445
    Strengthening Text with *<B>*   445
    Italicizing Text with *<I>*   447

Underline and Strikethrough Text  447
Blinking Text with *<BLINK>*  448
Centering Text—*<CENTER>*  449
Additional Formatting Tags  450

Advanced Text Formatting Tags  451
Controlling Font Size Dynamically  451
Changing the Displayed Font Color  453
Other Ways to Change Color  454
Color by Hexadecimal  455

Creating Lists  456
Adding an Unordered List  458
Adding a Numbered List  458
Adding a Definition List  459

Nesting Lists Within One Another  461

Including Comments  463

Building a Sample HTML Page  463

## 23 Adding Links and Graphics  467

Explaining HTML Links  468
Using Links  468
Dissecting an URL  469

Creating Your First Link  470
Using Absolute and Relative Links  470

Other Types of HTML Links  471
Using FTP Links  472
Using Gopher Links  472
Using UseNet Links  473
Using Mailto Links  473

Understanding HTML Anchors and Named Targets  475
Creating Named Targets  475
Linking to Named Targets  475

Tips to Consider When Developing Links  476

Adding Graphics with HTML  476

World Wide Web Image File Formats  477
GIF: Graphics Interchange Format  477
JPEG: Joint Photographic Expert Group  478

Using the *<IMG>* Tag   479
    Alternative Text   480
    Alignment and Image Placement Options   481
    Using the *<IMG>* Tag with *Height* and *Width* Attributes   481
    Vertical and Horizontal Alignment   482
    Borders   483

Using Images as HTML Links   484

## 24  Organizing Content with Tables and Frames   487

Creating a Simple Table   488

Using Advanced Table Features   490
    Lines Spanning Multiple Rows   490
    Spanning Multiple Columns   492
    Embedding Lists into Tables   493
    Setting Your Text Alignment   493
    Table Colors   495

Table Alternatives   497
    Lists Can Replace Tables   497
    Preformatted Text   498

Using Frames   498
    Useful Navigational Tools   500
    Organizing a Lot of Information   501
    Playing Tic-Tac-Toe: A Unique Frame Experience   501
    Frames Are Not Perfect for Every Situation   502

Building Simple Frames   503
    The First Step: Planning the Framed Site   504
    Next, Add the *<FRAMESET>* Tag   504
    Using Pixels Instead of Percentages   505
    Using the Asterisk   506
    Including the *<FRAME>* Tag   508
    Creating Links to Each Frame 511
    Other Target Keywords   511

Advanced Frame Features   512
    Working with Multiple Frames   512
    Another Example Using Multiple Frames   513
    Frames Within Frames   514
    Designing for Non-Frame-Capable Browsers   515

Borderless Frames   515

Alternatives to Frames   516
  Tables   516
  Navigation Button Bars   517
  Well-Organized Web Sites   517

## 25   Building Navigational Imagemaps   519

How Do Imagemaps Work?   520
  Imagemaps Are Not New Technology   521
  Server-Side and Client-Side Imagemap Differences   522

Creating an Imagemap   523
  Finding a Good Image   523
  Planning the Map   525
  Adding the Image to Your Web Page   525
  Mapping Your Image   526

Understanding the Imagemap Shapes   532
  Rectangles   533
  Circles   533
  Polygons   533
  How Do Overlapping Regions Work?   534
  Adding a Default Link   534

Test the Imagemap with Netscape   535

Providing a Textual Alternative   535

## 26   Creating Forms and Server Scripts   537

Creating Web Interactivity   538

CGI Scripting   539
  Setting Up for CGI   540
  CGI URLs   540
  Sample CGI Scripts   541

Creating HTML Forms   543
  *FORM*   544
  *TEXTAREA*   545
  *SELECT*   547
  *INPUT*   549

Bringing CGI and Forms Together   553
  *GET* and *POST*   555

Parsing   555
Encoding   556

Protecting Yourself and Your Users   556
Using Secure Forms   557

Using the Public Domain   557
Available Resources   558

## 27   Dynamic HTML   561

Cascading Style Sheets (CSS)   562

Classes Of Styles   565

Layers   566

Visibility   568

Scripting in Layers   570

## 28   Using Layers   573

Creating a Basic Layer   574
Position a Layer on the Web Page   576
Change the Size of a Layer   578
Display a Background Image or Color   580

Overlapping Multiple Layers   582
Change a Layer's *Z-INDEX*   584
Overlap Two Layers with *ABOVE* and *BELOW*   585

Nesting Layers to Create a Group   587

Creating Content for Browsers that Don't Do Layers   589

Attaching Scripts to Layers   589
Hide and Show a Layer Using a Script   591
Move a Layer with a Script   594

Putting Layers to Practical Use   596

## 29   Using Style Sheets   599

Understanding the Cascade in Cascading Style Sheets   600

Attaching a Style Sheet to Your HTML Document   600
Link to a Style Sheet   600
Embed a Style Sheet   601
Define Styles Inline   602
Importing Style Sheets   603

Understanding What Style Sheets Look Like (Syntax)   603
   Set Multiple Properties for a Style   603
   Set Styles for Multiple Tags (Grouping Selectors)   604
   Create Context Specific Styles (Contextual Selectors)   604
   Apply Style Classes to HTML Elements   604
   Override a Style's Importance in the Cascade   605
   Comment Your Style Sheet to Make It Readable   605

Hiding Styles from Non-Style-Enabled Browsers   606

Adding Style to Your Web Page   606
   Changing the Background of an HTML Element   607
   Work with an Element's Box Properties   610
   Float Elements on the Web Page   616
   Format Lists with Your Own Style   618
   Change the Properties of Text   619

## 30 Embedding Multimedia   627

Getting to Know Plug-Ins   628
   Embedded Plug-Ins   629
   Full-Page Plug-Ins   629

Inserting Plug-Ins into Your Web Page   630
   <EMBED>   630
   <OBJECT>   631

Adding Content to Your Web Page   633
   Audio   634
   Video   636

Rewarding the User (Bandwidth)   638

Finding Other Useful Plug-Ins   639

## 31 Adding Java Applets   641

Learn About Java   642
   Understanding How It Works   642
   Comparing Java to Plug-Ins   643
   Securing Java Applets   643
   Creating Your Own Java Applets   644

Embed a Java Applet into Your Web Page   645
   <APPLET>   645
   <OBJECT>   647

Use These Examples in Your Web Page  649
    Ticker Tape Navigation  649
    Fly-Over Buttons  650

## 32  Enhancing Your Documents with JavaScript  653

Introducing JavaScript  654
    Examples of What You Can Do with JavaScript  654
    Recognizing JavaScript When You See It  655
    JavaScript Details You Need to Know  656

Adding a Script to Your Web Page  658
    Hiding Scripts from Scriptless Browsers  658
    Connecting Scripts to Events  659

Sprucing Up Your Web Page with Scripts  661
    Fly-Over Help for a Link's Destination  661
    Using Forms and JavaScript for Navigation  662

# VI  For Develpers

## 33  Netscape Servers  667

SuiteSpot Servers  668

Netscape's Server Test Drive Program  671
    Enterprise Server  671
    Catalog Server  672
    Directory Server  672
    Proxy Server  673
    Mail Server and Messaging Server  673
    News Server and Collabra Server  674
    Calendar Server  674
    Media Server  674
    Certificate Server  675

FastTrack Server  675

# VII  Appendixes

## Getting Online  679

Getting Started  680
    Selecting a Modem  680

Internet Service Providers   681
    Internet Service Provider User Account Information   682
Creating a PPP Connection in Windows 95   683
    Installing Dial-Up Networking Components   683
Configuring TCP/IP Network Properties   685
    Setting Up a Connection Icon   687
Technical Issues of Making an Internet Connection   687
    Transmission Control Program/Internet Protocol   688
    IP Address   688
    Domain Name Server   688
    Point-to-Point Protocol or PPP   688

## B   Installing Netscape Communicator for Windows 3.1   689

Installation Requirements   690

Beginning the Installation   691

Creating Your First User Profile   698

Testing Netscape with Your New User Profile   702

Configuring Netscape   703
    Configuring Mail and Discussion Settings   703

## C   Installing Communicator for Windows 95   711

Installation Requirements   712

Beginning the Installation   712

Creating Your First User Profile   716

Testing Netscape with Your New User Profile   719

Configuring Netscape Communicator Mail and Discussion Settings   720
    Configuring Netscape Messenger to Handle Incoming Messages   722
    Configuring Netscape Messenger to Handle Outgoing Mail   723
    Configuring Netscape Collabra to Access Newsgroups   725

## D   Installing Communicator for Macintosh   727

Installation Requirements   728

Beginning the Installation   728

Creating Your First User Profile   731

Testing Netscape with Your New User Profile 733
Configuring Netscape 733
Configuring Mail and Discussion Settings 734

### E  Installing Communicator for UNIX 741

Hardware Requirements 742
Obtaining the Netscape Binaries 742
Downloading Communicator Using Netscape Navigator 744
Installing Netscape from an Archive File 745
Installing Netscape from a CD-ROM 746

# Introduction

*by Mark R. Brown*

The latest, and perhaps greatest, computer revolution started a scant couple of years ago, when Netscape Navigator—a friendly, quirky Web-browsing program—triggered an overnight explosion in the growth of the World Wide Web. Suddenly, people everywhere were using their computers to access a worldwide store of information that was presented in a new, fun, easy-to-understand way.

These same people soon found out that you could also access data on local networks and individual PCs using the Web's friendly hypertext/hypermedia graphical user interface (GUI). Corporate computer administrators eventually realized that, if they would only organize their corporate data into user-friendly Web-like intranets, people would actually begin to use all that information languishing in the company databases. Suddenly, there were almost as many people browsing corporate intranets as were browsing the Web.

Then Netscape Communications Corporation—and their archrival in the "browser wars," Microsoft—had a sudden inspiration: Why not use a browser as the GUI for applications development, too? Microsoft's ActiveX and Netscape's Java (developed by Sun) burst upon the scene, and people suddenly found they needed a browser to run applications as well.

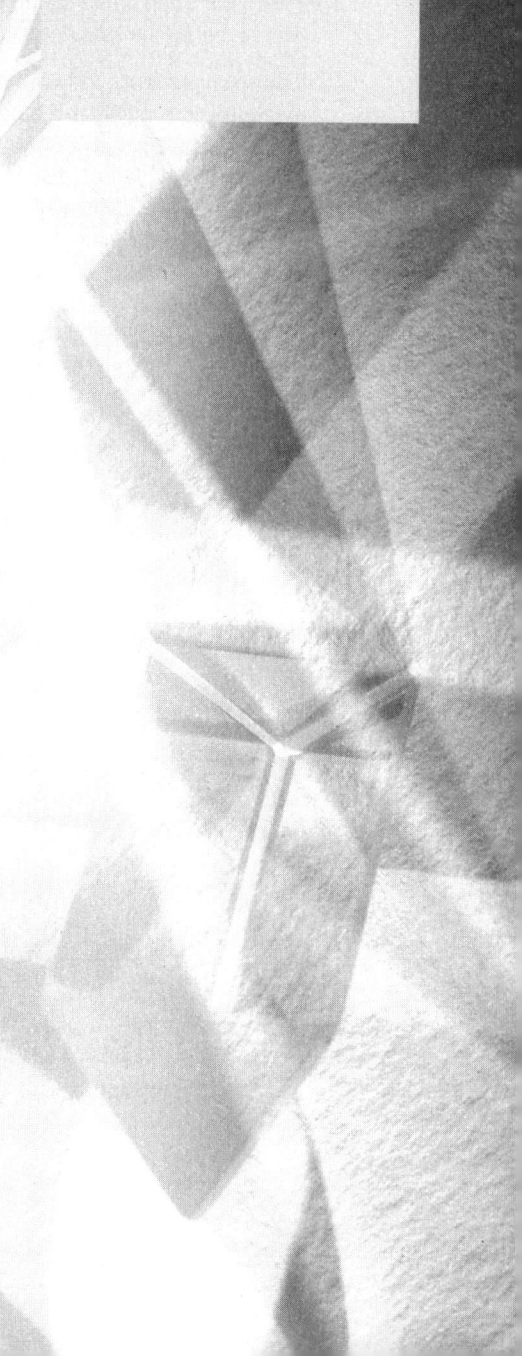

Such a paradigm shift almost invariably requires a redesign of the "tools of the trade," and so it is that the latest version of Netscape Navigator—the tool that started it all—is not a version of Navigator at all. It's a totally new software package called Netscape Communicator.

Oh, Navigator is still in there, but it's not the main thing anymore. Now it's one of a set of tools organized under the umbrella of the new Communicator taskbar. Presented alongside Navigator are a full set of tools—some familiar, some new—for exchanging e-mail, interacting with newsgroups, composing documents, and sharing information online.

All those changes are the *raison d'être* for this book. *Special Edition Using Netscape Communicator* gently guides you to a thorough understanding of how all this reorganization has helped Netscape Navigator grow into a multi-functional, multi-purpose communications and collaboration toolbox that is more than just a Web browser. Netscape Communicator (see Figure I.1) is a tool you can use to do almost everything you need to do at your computer. You can still browse the Web with Netscape Communicator, but that's just the beginning. This book explains the parts and pieces that make up Communicator, and takes you through all the steps to get Communicator set up and working to its full potential on your machine.

**FIG. I.1**
If not for its dockable taskbar (upper right), one might at first glance mistake Netscape Communicator for its predecessor, Netscape Navigator 3.

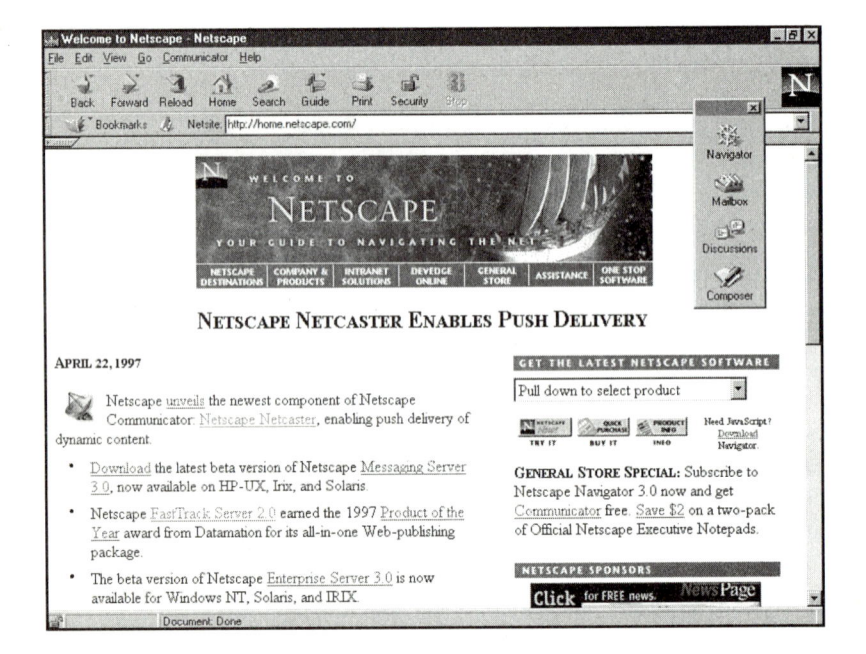

# Who Should Use This Book?

This book is intended for anyone and everyone who wants to get the most out of Netscape Communicator, whether accessing data on the World Wide Web, a corporate intranet, or a personal computer.

Novices will find information on how to install and configure Communicator, and how to begin using all of its components. If you haven't installed Communicator yet, you should turn to the Appendixes and follow the installation instructions for your particular computer. Then check out Chapter 1, "Overview," for an explanation of what this program does. Finally, move on to the "Communicator Quick Start" chapters to get up and running quickly with each of Communicator's component applications.

Intermediate users will discover tips, tricks, and techniques to make Communicator more useful and fun to use. Part II, "In-Depth Communicator," provides you with all the details of how to use each of Communicator's components to its fullest. There are also chapters on how to set all of Communicator's Preferences and Security options for optimum performance.

Advanced users will learn the nuts and bolts of Communicator operation. The "For Webmasters" section shows you how to create world-class Web pages that take advantage of powerful features like plug-ins, Java, JavaScript, style sheets, and layers. The "For Developers" section provides an overview of Netscape Communication Corporation's line of server software.

# How This Book Is Organized

*Special Edition Using Netscape Communicator* is organized into six logical sections (plus appendixes) that cover the entire Communicator package. These sections are:

- Part I: Communicator Quick Start
- Part II: In-Depth Communicator
- Part III: Communicator Professional
- Part IV: Netcaster
- Part V: For Webmasters
- Part VI: For Developers
- Part VII: Appendixes

### Part I: Communicator Quick Start

Chapter 1, "Overview," outlines Communicator's new role as a universal client. It explains how Navigator is used for Web browsing, Messenger for e-mail, Collabra for newsgroups, Composer for document creation, and Conference for conferencing.

Chapter 2, "What's New in Netscape Communicator," brings you up to speed on the additions and changes that Netscape made when morphing Netscape Navigator 3 into Netscape Communicator. In this chapter you'll find an explanation of what Communicator's new taskbar is and how to use it to switch quickly between applications. You'll also find information on new toolbar icons and menu items, changes in setup and preferences options, and an overview of Communicator's support for new Web page features like style sheets and layers.

Chapter 3, "Navigator Quick Start," helps you to quickly set up and begin using Communicator's Navigator application for hooking up to and browsing the World Wide Web. You'll learn how to navigate the Web using links and how to begin searching for topics of interest.

Chapter 4, "Messenger Quick Start," covers the basics of configuring Messenger so you can immediately begin receiving, reading, responding to, and sending your own e-mail.

Chapter 5, "Collabra Quick Start," explains how to subscribe to newsgroups so you can read online news postings. From there, it leads you through posting your own messages and responses, too.

Chapter 6, "Composer Quick Start," introduces you to the buttons, menu items, and processes you need to know to get started composing your own HTML Web pages, e-mail, and newsgroup posts with Netscape Composer.

Chapter 7, "Conference Quick Start," tells you how you can begin using Netscape Conference to collaborate online with your fellow workers using voice, text, file exchange, and a universal "white board."

**Part II: In-Depth Communicator**

Chapter 8, "Navigator In-Depth," begins where Chapter 3 left off, examining in detail how to wring the most out of Netscape Navigator. In this chapter you learn how to control Navigator's caching of data, how to interact with frames and fill out online forms, how to customize and use Navigator's toolbars to your best advantage, and more.

Chapter 9, "Using Bookmarks," shows you how to go beyond simple page bookmarking and use Navigator's built-in bookmark feature as an editable database to enable quick and easy navigation of HTML documents on the Web, on intranets, or on your own PC.

Chapter 10, "Interacting with Plug-Ins, Java Applets, and JavaScript," provides you with a plethora of examples of how these advanced technologies are enriching HTML documents with new interactive and multimedia content. Along the way, you learn what to expect from these technologies and how to interact with new applications you may encounter.

Chapter 11, "Messenger In-Depth," follows up Chapter 4 with in-depth information on managing e-mail folders, adding HTML and attachments to your messages, how to filter out "spam" messages, and other advanced topics.

Chapter 12, "Using the Address Book," focuses on using Communicator's built-in Address Book to add, delete, and manage lists and "card" entries, as well as how to interact with Web-based address databases like Four11 and Bigfoot.

Chapter 13, "Collabra In-Depth," builds on the knowledge you gained in Chapter 5. This chapter shows you how to use Communicator's Message Center, and makes clear the differences between e-mail and discussion groups. You find out how to find and subscribe to groups, manage messages, use attached files, and even create your own public or secure message groups.

Chapter 14, "Composer In-Depth," starts with what you learned in Chapter 6, then delves into using Composer to create ever more complex and detailed HTML documents. You find out how it works within Messenger and Collabra, as well as how to compose documents for viewing with Navigator.

Chapter 15, "Conference In-Depth," goes beyond the elementary information presented in Chapter 7 to explore in detail how you can collaborate with coworkers using all the options of Conference's built-in voice, text, file exchange, and white board tools.

Chapter 16, "Setting Preferences," organizes and recaps the full palette of preference options offered by Netscape Communicator. Though individual chapters of this book cover the preference options for each of Communicator's component parts, this chapter provides a detailed examination of all of Communicator's preferences in one convenient spot.

Chapter 17, "Security Options," does for Security settings what Chapter 16 does for Communicator Preferences—it steps through all of Communicator's Security options, so you can be sure you don't miss something important!

## Part III: Communicator Professional

Chapter 18, "Calendar," covers the first of the three additional components that Netscape includes in the Professional version of Communicator: Netscape Calendar. Calendar is a multi-user scheduling application that can be used over a corporate intranet or over the Internet to schedule meetings and projects. This chapter explains how to use all of Calendar's many options.

Chapter 19, "IBM Host On-Demand," shows how this third component of Communicator Professional provides full-screen IBM 3270 terminal emulation for mainframe-connected intranets.

## Part IV: Netcaster

Chapter 20, "Setting Up Your Web Top," introduces Netscape Communicator's built-in "push" technology interface, Netcaster. It goes on to show you how to set up your own Webtop to display custom information automatically on any computer you log into.

Chapter 21, "Channels," tells you how to subscribe to online channels of information that download to your system automatically. You find out how to locate and subscribe to these channels, and how to personalize your Netcaster setup.

## Part V: For Webmasters

Chapter 22, "HTML Primer," introduces you to the process of creating documents with HTML. In this chapter you learn about basic HTML tags for building pages and formatting text.

Chapter 23, "Adding Links and Graphics," advances your HTML document creation skills by adding links and graphic images to your pages.

Chapter 24, "Organizing Content with Tables and Frames," explains how you can create compelling, easily navigated, documents by incorporating HTML frames and tables.

Chapter 25, "Building Navigational Imagemaps," shows you how you can create your own visual imagemaps to enhance and simplify your viewers' browsing experiences.

Chapter 26, "Creating Forms and Server Scripts," introduces the topic of creating online forms, including creating forms that interact with server scripts.

Chapter 27, "Dynamic HTML," covers Communicator's new Dynamic HTML capabilities, and shows you how to create animated, interactive documents using them.

Chapter 28, "Using Layers," explains Communicator's new ability to layer and precisely position elements on a page.

Chapter 29, "Using Style Sheets," delves into Communicator's new capability to interpret and display HTML documents with attached style sheets. This new technique separates page content from presentation.

Chapter 30, "Embedding Multimedia," talks about using the EMBED and OBJECT tags to incorporate audio, video, interactive multimedia, and other exciting elements into your pages.

Chapter 31, "Adding Java Applets," explores the creation of Java applets, which literally allow you to add custom inline programs to your documents.

Chapter 32, "Enhancing Your Documents with JavaScript," explains how you can use JavaScript to tie together all of the elements that comprise your documents with interactivity and intercommunication.

### Part VI: For Developers

Chapter 33, "Netscape Servers," walks you through a menu of Netscape's server software products, including FastTrack and the entire SuiteSpot server family.

### Appendixes

Appendix A, "Getting Online," guides you gently into getting your computer connected to the Internet.

Appendixes B-E, "Installing Netscape Communicator," are a set of four appendixes, each of which covers installing Communicator on a different computer platform: Windows 3.1, Windows 95, Macintosh, and UNIX.

# Conventions Used in This Book

This book uses various stylistic and typographic conventions to make it easier to use.

Keyboard shortcut key combinations are joined by + signs; for example, Ctrl+X means to hold down the Ctrl key, press the X key, then release both.

Menu items and dialog box selections often have a mnemonic key associated with them. This key is indicated by an underline on the item on screen. To use these mnemonic keys, you press the Alt key, then the shortcut key. In this book, mnemonic keys are underlined, like this: File.

## Conventions Used in This Book

This book uses the following typeface conventions:

| Typeface | Meaning |
|---|---|
| *Italic* | Variables in commands or addresses, or terms used for the first time |
| **Bold** | Text you type in, as well as addresses of Internet sites, newsgroups, mailing lists, and Web sites |
| `Computer type` | Commands, HTML tags |

**N O T E** Notes provide additional information related to the topic at hand.

**TIP** Tips provide quick and helpful information to assist you along the way.

**CAUTION**
Cautions alert you to potential pitfalls or dangers in the operations discussed.

**TROUBLESHOOTING**
Troubleshooting boxes address problems that you might encounter while following the procedures in this book.

*Special Edition Using Netscape Communicator 4* uses marginal references like this one to point you to other places in the book with additional information relevant to the topic. Right-pointing arrows guide you forward; right-pointing arrows guide you to previous chapters.

▶ **See** "Navigator In-Depth," **p. 109**

PART I

# Communicator Quick Start

1  Overview   11

2  What's New in Netscape Communicator   27

3  Navigator Quick Start   39

4  Messenger Quick Start   51

5  Collabra Quick Start   71

6  Composer Quick Start   79

7  Conference Quick Start   95

CHAPTER 1

# Overview

*by Mark R. Brown*

Netscape Communications Corporation created Netscape Navigator so that we could all browse the World Wide Web. They created Netscape Communicator so that we'd never have to stop.

That's a bit of an overstatement, really. The actual purpose of Communicator is not to make us spend all of our time on the Web, but to make sure that we spend all (or at least, most) of our time in Netscape Communicator.

You see, Communicator is much more than just a Web browser. It's also an intranet client, and an e-mail program, and a news reader, and a collaboration tool, and an applications platform, and… well, in short, Communicator is now the base from which you can do just about anything you want to do with a computer.

If you examine what Communicator can do, it seems—perhaps somewhat surprisingly so—like it could actually deliver on its promises. It might really, truly make computers easier and more fun to use, while saving everyone lots of time and money along the way. ■

■ **Netscape Navigator has moved beyond the Web**

Netscape Navigator was originally used only for browsing pages on the World Wide Web, but it's grown way beyond its original boundaries.

■ **Netscape Messenger is the Net's most popular e-mail client**

E-mail was one of the first applications to use the Internet, and it's still the most-used.

■ **Netscape Collabra means news is not just for UseNet anymore**

Newsgroups grew out of e-mail, and still function in a similar manner.

■ **Netscape Composer makes creating HTML documents easy**

Netscape wants you to use HTML everywhere, not just on the Web, and they've provided a new editor that can add rich HTML content to e-mail and news, too.

■ **Netscape Conference lets you work online with others**

Need to share files, images, and ideas with collaborators online? Then Conference is the tool for you.

## The World Wide Web and Netscape Navigator

Communicator began its existence as Navigator, and Navigator is still the core component around which Communicator is built. (In fact, it's quite likely that browsing the Web will remain your main use for Communicator, at least for the next few months.) Netscape Navigator made the Web so ubiquitous and useful that the evolution of Communicator was almost inevitable. Here's how it happened:

There were a plethora of different data-indexing and retrieval experiments in the early days of the Internet, but none was all-pervasive until, in 1991, Paul Lindner and Mark P. McCahill at the University of Minnesota created *Gopher*. Though it suffered from an overly cute (but highly descriptive) name, its technique for organizing files under an intuitive menuing system won it instant acceptance on the Net. The direct precursor in both concept and function to the World Wide Web, Gopher lacked hypertext links or graphic elements (see Figure 1.1).

**FIG. 1.1**
Though Netscape Navigator was created for Web browsing, it can also display information on Gopher sites like this.

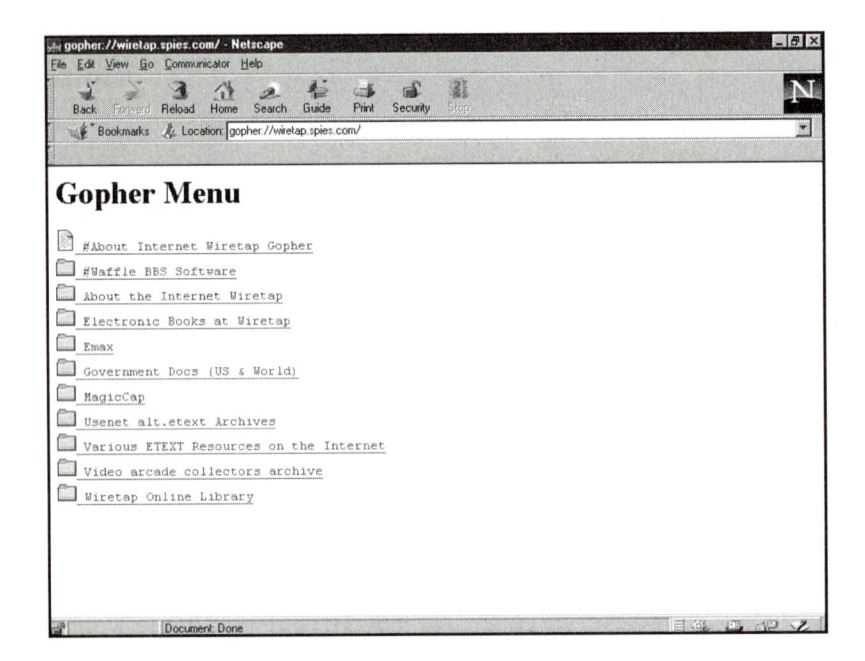

> **TIP** If you're curious about the origins of the Internet itself, read Bruce Sterling's excellent article on the subject at **gopher://oak.zilker.net:70/00/bruces/F_SF_Science_Column/F_SF_Five_**.

Although Gopher servers sprung up quickly all over the Internet, it was almost immediately apparent that something more was needed.

By the time "Gopherspace" began to establish itself, the European High-Energy Particle Physics Lab (CERN) had become the largest Internet site in Europe and was the driving force in getting the rest of Europe connected to the Net. To help promote and facilitate the concept of distributed computing via the Internet, CERN's Tim Berners-Lee created the World Wide Web in 1992.

The Web was an extension of the Gopher idea, but with many, many improvements. Inspired by Ted Nelson's work on Xanadu and the hypertext concept, the World Wide Web incorporated graphics, typographic text styles, and—most importantly—hypertext links.

**NOTE** The hypertext concept predates personal computers. It was first proposed by computer visionary Ted Nelson in his ground-breaking, self-published book *Computer Lib/Dream Machines* in 1974.

In a nutshell, electronic hypertext involves adding links to words or phrases. When selected, these links jump you to associated text in the same document or in another document altogether. For example, you could click an unfamiliar term and jump to a definition, or add your own notes that would be optionally displayed when you or someone else selected the note's hyperlink.

The hypertext concept has since been expanded to incorporate the idea of *hypermedia,* in which links can lead to and from graphics, video, and audio clips.

The World Wide Web introduced three new technologies:

- HTML (Hypertext Markup Language), used to write Web pages.
- HTTP (Hypertext Transport Protocol), to transmit those pages from a Web server computer.
- A Web browser client program to receive the data, interpret it, and display the results.

Using HTML, almost anyone with a text editor and access to an Internet site can build visually interesting pages that organize and present information in a way seldom seen in other online venues. In fact, Web sites are said to be composed of *pages* because the information on them looks more like magazine pages than traditional computer screens.

HTML is a markup language, which means that Web pages can only be viewed by using a specialized Internet terminal program called a *Web browser.* In the beginning, the potential was there for the typical computing "chicken and the egg problem": no one would create Web pages because no one owned a browser program to view them with, and no one would get a browser program because there were no Web pages to view.

Fortunately, this did not happen, because shortly after the Web was invented, a killer browser program was released to the Internet community—free of charge!

In 1993, the National Center for Supercomputing Applications (NCSA) at the University of Illinois at Champaign-Urbana released Mosaic, a Web browser designed by Marc Andreessen and developed by a team of students and staff at the University of Illinois (see Figure 1.2). It spread like wildfire though the Internet community; within a year, an estimated two million users were on the Web with Mosaic. Suddenly, everyone was browsing the Web, and everyone else was creating Web pages. Nothing in the history of computing had grown so fast.

**FIG. 1.2**
NSCA Mosaic, the browser that drove the initial growth of the World Wide Web, is now just a part of history.

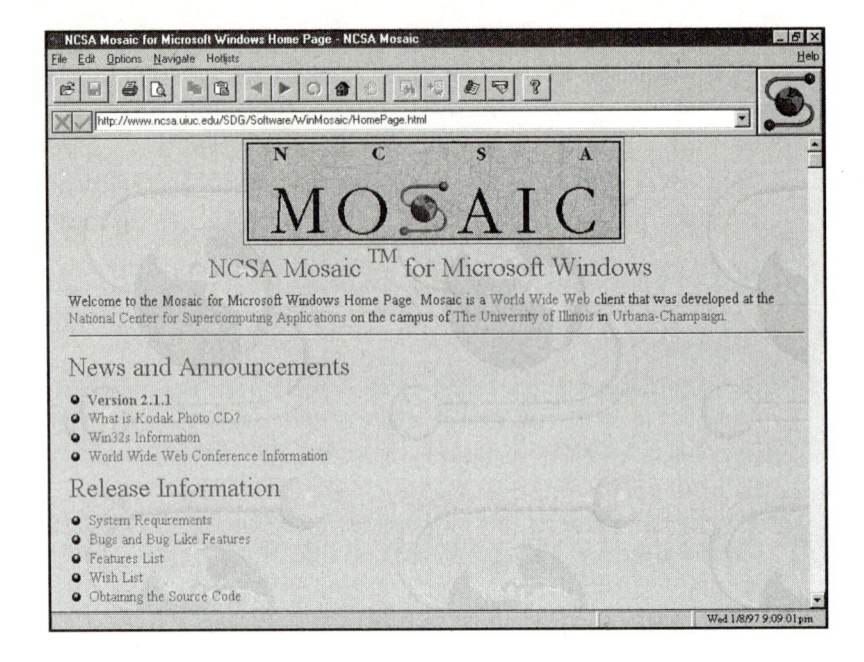

By mid-1993, there were 130 sites on the World Wide Web. Six months later, there were over 600. Today, there are over a quarter of a million Web sites in the world (more or less, depending on whose figures you believe).

Mosaic's success—and the fact that its source code was distributed for free—spawned a wave of new browser introductions. Each topped the previous by adding new HTML commands and features. Marc Andreessen moved on from NCSA and joined with Jim Clark of Silicon Graphics to found Netscape Communications Corporation. They took along most of the NCSA Mosaic development team, which quickly turned out the first version of Netscape Navigator for Windows, Macintosh, and UNIX platforms. Because of its many new features and free trial preview offer, Netscape Navigator rapidly became the most popular browser on the Web. The Web's incredible growth even attracted Microsoft's attention, and in 1995, they introduced their Internet Explorer Web browser to coincide with the launch of their new online service, the Microsoft Network (MSN).

Established online services like CompuServe, America Online, and Prodigy scrambled to meet their users' demands to add Web access to their systems. Most of them quickly developed their own versions of Mosaic, customized to work in conjunction with their proprietary online services. This enabled millions of established commercial service subscribers to spill over onto the Web virtually overnight; "old-timers" who had been on the Web since its beginning (only a year and a half or so before) suddenly found themselves overtaken by a tidal wave of Web-surfing *newbies*. Even television discovered the Web, and it seemed that every other news report featured a story about surfing the Net.

http://www.quecorp.com

The World Wide Web didn't get its name by accident. It truly is a web that encompasses just about every topic in the world. A quick look at Netscape's Search page on the Web lists topics as diverse as art, world news, sports, business, libraries, classified advertising, education, TV, science, fitness, and politics (see Figure 1.3). You can't get much more diverse than that! There are literally thousands of sites listed here through the services of WebCrawler, Yahoo!, and other online indexes and search engines.

**FIG. 1.3**
If you really want to know what's on the Web, just click the Search button on the Navigator toolbar to visit Netscape's Web Search page.

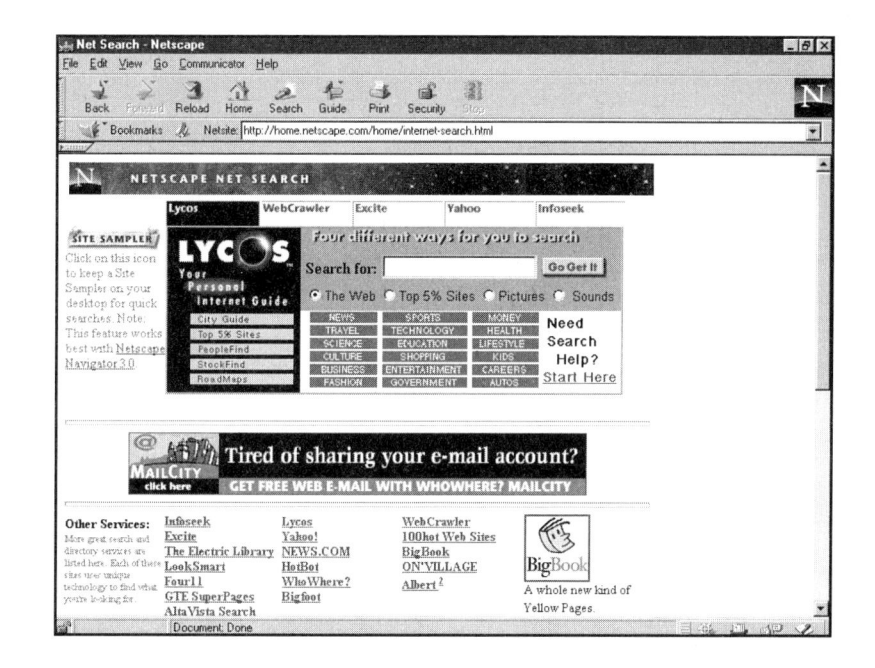

> **TIP** For more information about the World Wide Web, consult the latest edition of the WWW FAQ at **http://www.boutell.com/faq/**.

▶ To begin using Netscape Navigator to browse the World Wide Web, turn to Chapter 3, "Navigator Quick Start," on **p. 39**

▶ If you want to delve deeper into Navigator's features and functions, turn instead to Chapter 8, "Navigator In-Depth," on **p. 109**

## The Rise of the Corporate Intranet

The World Wide Web explosion still shows no signs of slowing down, and it has proved so intuitive and so much fun to use that people almost immediately began to see other uses for the Web browsing metaphor.

One of the first and most obvious was to build Webs that didn't communicate over the Internet at all, but were confined within the computer systems of individual companies and institutions. A term was quickly coined to distinguish these internal Webs: *intranets*.

The major difference between an intranet and a Web site—besides the obvious fact that the former is constrained to an individual institution, while the latter is worldwide—is the audience. On a Web site, the content is aimed at the public, while an intranet addresses the needs of an organization's own employees.

This means that intranets are more likely to contain company-specific—even confidential—data, such as sales reports, customer databases (see Figure 1.4), training materials, and employee manuals.

**FIG. 1.4**
Corporate intranets like this example at the Netscape Web site can give employees quick and easy access to company databases and resources.

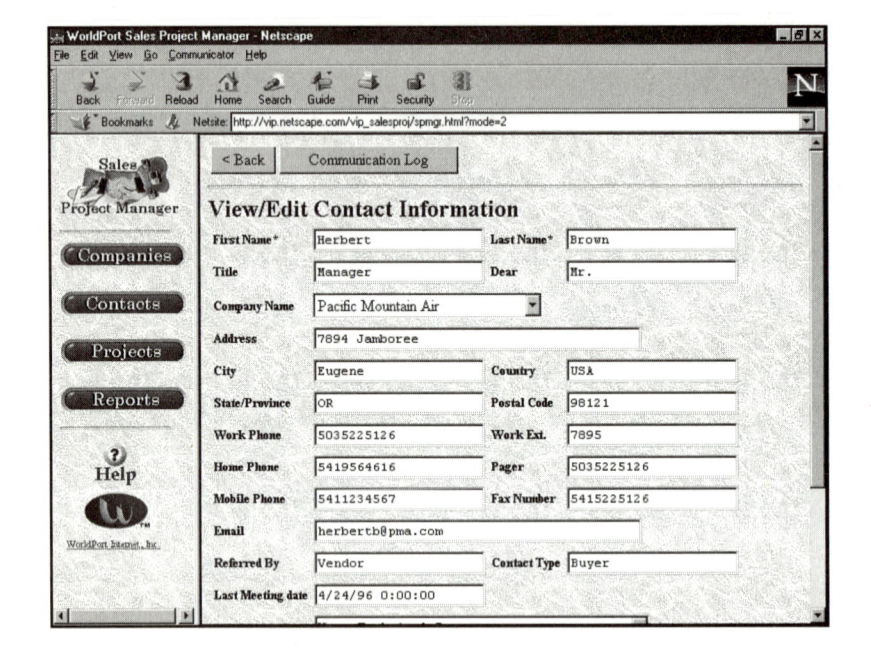

Though these kinds of data have been available on internal corporate networks for years, the difference with intranets is in the presentation. An HTML document browser like Navigator makes such information as fun and easy to use as that on most World Wide Web sites. Data which might have previously been locked up in difficult-to-use corporate databases can be made easily accessible to even computer novices.

Even with only a year or two of real-world usage, the utility of corporate intranets is already proven beyond the shadow of a doubt. Netscape Communications Corporation says that a resounding majority of their intranet customers report substantial cost savings after installing corporate intranets. Some have claimed 1000% returns on their investments, according to Netscape. In the world of business, this is a phenomenal rate of return, and a claim which has grabbed the attention of the majority of Fortune 500 companies—as well as many that are much, much smaller.

> **TIP** To read Netscape Communication Corporation's study on intranet return-on-investment, go to **http://home.netscape.com/comprod/announce/roi.html**.

In fact, interest in intranets is so great that HTML server and client publishers like Netscape and Microsoft predict that the majority of their HTML-related income over the next few years will be generated by intranet development, not the World Wide Web.

Companies have even begun to open their intranets to customers and suppliers outside the corporate network to create an amalgam of Internet and intranet called an *extranet*.

# Navigator's Future in Application Development

But that's not the end of Navigator's potential. Both Microsoft and Netscape are advocating that HTML and associated technologies—Java, JavaScript, ActiveX controls, plug-ins, et al.—be used as the basis for creating stand-alone applications.

HTML-based user interfaces are friendly and easy-to-use, a fact which has certainly been well-established on the Web and corporate intranets. But because HTML documents can also incorporate *active objects* like ActiveX controls and Java applets, HTML pages can act as *universal containers* for applications. HTML tags can be used to format text, graphics, interactive buttons, forms, and other objects on-screen which interact with the user just as any other GUI (Graphical User Interface) would. Incorporated into the HTML page are objects such as a plug-in or a Java applet (see Figure 1.5).

**FIG. 1.5**
This JavaScript-based online calculator is just a simple example of using HTML to create the user interface for an application program.

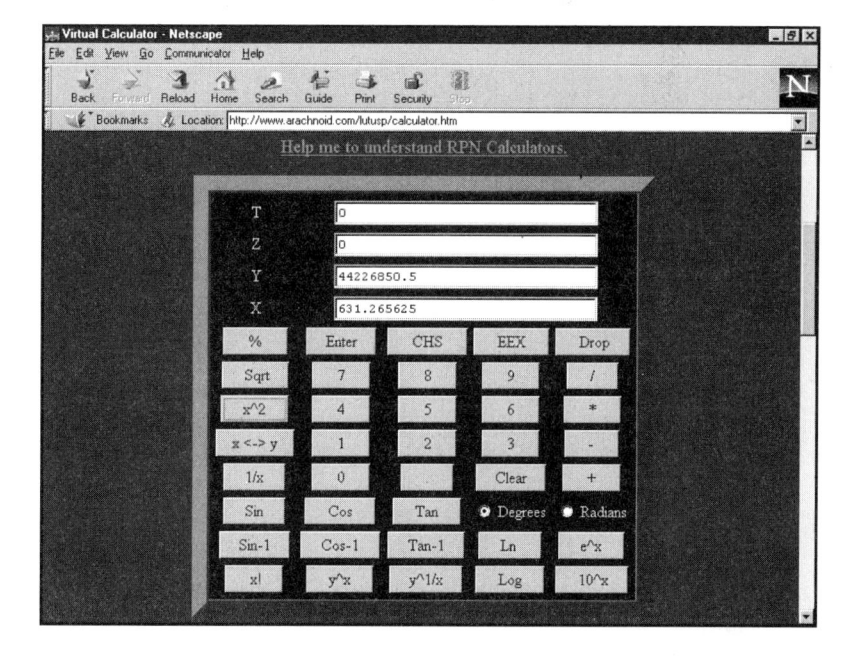

Netscape is actively pushing Sun's Java as its development language of choice, while Microsoft would like to see developers using their Windows-specific ActiveX controls. But each supports the other and—most importantly—both use a browser client to host applications.

We are already beginning to see complex, high-level applications that are written totally in Java, which can be run entirely in Netscape Navigator. Corel Office for Java (see Figure 1.6), for example, recreates Corel's popular Office suite (which includes the WordPerfect word processing program, Quattro Pro database manager, a calculator and PIM (Personal Information Manager), and other modules) as a Java application that runs within Communicator's Navigator component. In time, we may see the majority of special-purpose software and shareware written in this way, and even a substantial percentage of commercial applications may eventually be developed in this manner.

**FIG. 1.6**
Corel Office for Java is a complete commercial application, written entirely in Java, that runs from within Netscape Navigator.

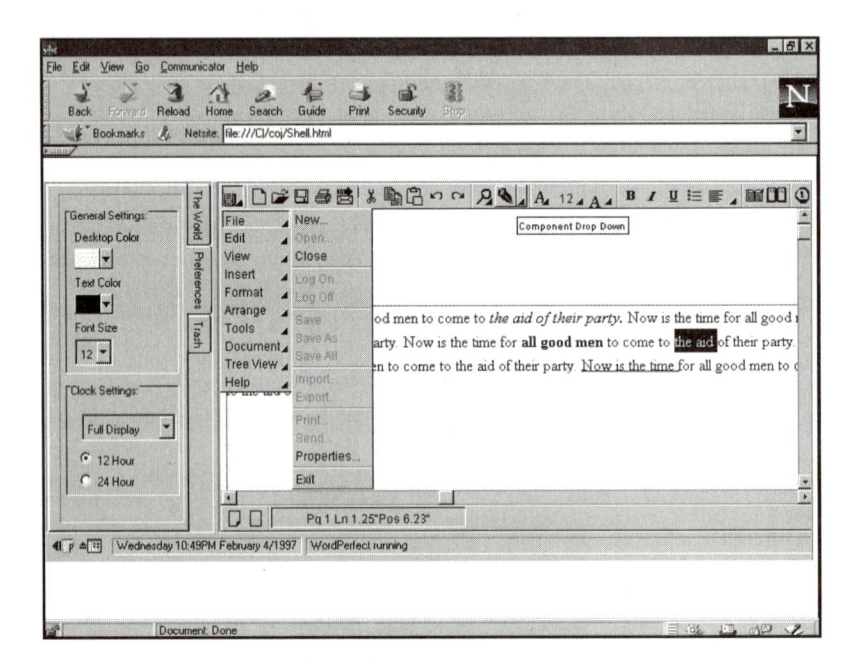

# Electronic Mail and Netscape Messenger

The Internet had its origins in the military's ARPAnet. Collaboration among scientists and researchers was the number one use of this system, so it is not surprising that the first major application developed for use on the old ARPAnet was electronic mail. With the advent of Ray Tomlinson's e-mail system in 1972, researchers connected to the Net could exchange ideas and research at a pace never before imagined.

E-mail has proven its value over time and has remained one of the major uses of the Net. In fact, you can now read and respond to your e-mail using Communicator's Messenger component (see Figure 1.7), so a separate e-mail program is not required.

http://www.quecorp.com

**FIG. 1.7**
Reading or sending e-mail with Netscape Communicator is done via the Messenger e-mail client, shown here.

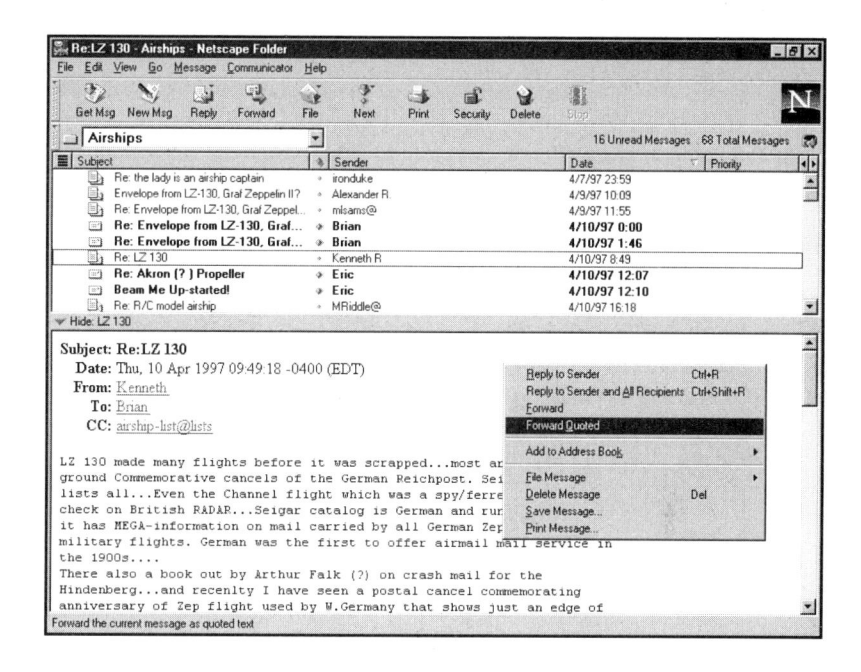

▶ To begin using Netscape Messenger to send and receive e-mail, turn to Chapter 4, "Messenger Quick Start," on **p. 51**

▶ If you want to explore Messenger's advanced features and functions, turn instead to Chapter 11, "Messenger In-Depth," on **p. 199**

> **TIP** You can find answers to most of your questions about Internet e-mail in the directory of e-mail FAQs at **ftp://ftp.uu.net/usenet/news.answers/mail/**.

## News and Netscape Collabra

E-mail eventually added the ability to send mail to multiple recipients. This precipitated the birth of "mailing lists" dedicated to specific topics, and users began open discussions on a multitude of subjects.

> **TIP** There are thousands of mailing lists you can subscribe to on the Internet today, covering topics as diverse as PERL programming and dog breeding. For a list of some of the many mailing lists available on the Net, check out Stephanie de Silva's list of Publicly Accessible Mailing Lists, updated monthly, at **http://www.neosoft.com/internet/paml/**, the list of LISTSERV lists at **http://tile.net/listserv/**, or the forms-searchable Liszt database of 25,000 mailing lists at **http://www.liszt.com/**.

A logical extension of the mailing list is the interactive conference, or *newsgroup*. The concept of interactive conferencing actually predates the existence of the computers to do it on; it was

## Chapter 1 Overview

first proposed by Vannevar Bush in an article titled "As We May Think" in the *Atlantic Monthly* in 1945 (v196[1], p. 101-108).

The first actual online conferencing system was called *Delphi* (after the Greek oracle), and it debuted in 1970. Though slow, it did enable hundreds of researchers at multiple locations to participate in an organized, ongoing, international discussion group. It is not an exaggeration to say that it revolutionized the way research is done.

In 1976, AT&T Bell Labs added *UUCP* (UNIX-to-UNIX CoPy) to the UNIX V7 operating system. Tom Truscott and Jim Ellis of Duke University and Steve Bellovin at the University of North Carolina developed the first version of UseNet, the UNIX User Network. Usenet quickly became the online conferencing system of choice on the Net. In 1986, the Network News Transfer Protocol (NNTP) was created to improve UseNet news performance. Since then, it has grown to accommodate more than 2.5 million people a month and is available to over ten million users at over 200,000 sites. There are over 10,000 active Usenet newsgroups.

Usenet is *not* the Internet or even a part of the Internet; it may be thought of as operating in parallel to and in conjunction with the Internet. While most Internet sites carry Usenet newsfeeds, there is no direct or official relationship between the two. However, Usenet news has become such an important part of computer Internet-working that a compatible newsreader is built into Communicator; it's called Collabra (see Figure 1.8).

**FIG. 1.8**
Collabra is Communicator's integral newsreader for reading and posting to newsgroups.

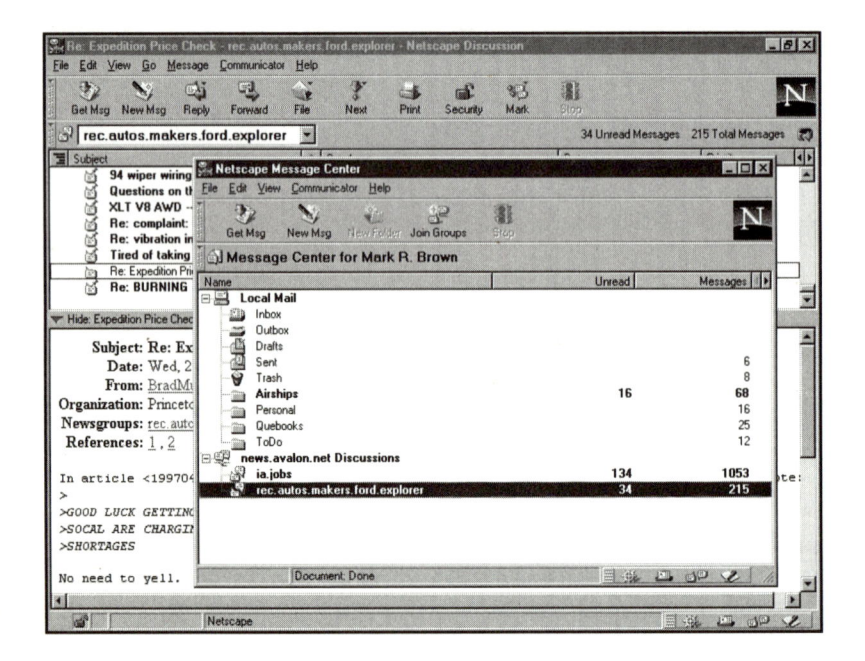

**TIP** The definitive online guide to Usenet is the comprehensive list of Usenet FAQs archived at **http://www.cis.ohio-state.edu/hypertext/faq/usenet/usenet/top.html**.

But UseNet isn't the only source for news these days. Many corporations, universities, and other organizations have set up internal newsgroup servers on which users can set up their own discussion groups, both public and secure. In many organizations, such newsgroups are coming to replace traditional meetings for many internal procedural, management, and collaborative design functions.

▶ To begin using Netscape Collabra to read Usenet newsgroups, turn to Chapter 5, "Collabra Quick Start," on **p. 71**

▶ To learn about Collabra's extensive features, turn instead to Chapter 13, "Collabra In-Depth," on **p. 245**

## Creating Documents with Netscape Composer

Today, HTML is not only the language of the Web, but of intranets, applications, and even e-mail and news. While you can certainly learn HTML and code your own HTML documents, Communicator's Composer application makes it much, much easier (see Figure 1.9).

**FIG. 1.9**
Netscape Composer lets you create rich HTML documents for viewing on the Web or via e-mail and newsgroups.

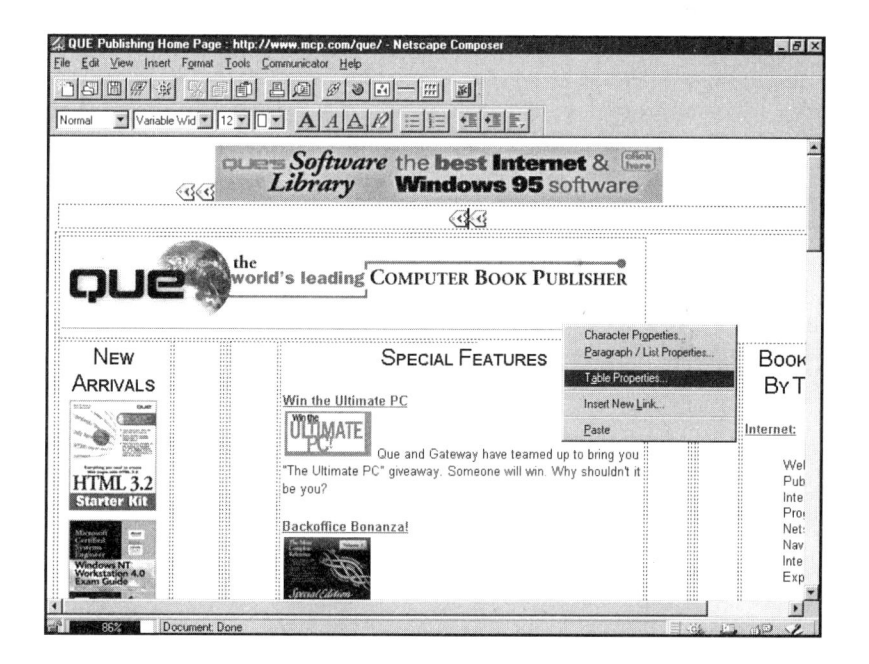

> **TIP** The non-profit governing body that defines the HTML standard is the World Wide Web Consortium, commonly referred to as the W3C. You can find out all you want to know about HTML on their Web site at **http://www.w3.org/pub/WWW/**.

Composer lets you click buttons and make menu selections to format text, create links, add graphics, and add all the other cool widgets and gadgets that make HTML pages so much more compelling than plain text. With Composer, you can create Web and intranet pages that are second to none.

Of course, HTML affords the same benefits to e-mail and news as it does to Web pages or intranets, such as an easy and fun-to-use interface, integration of text and graphics, hyperlinks, and the ability to integrate video, sound, and applications inline.

Where e-mail is just a way to exchange text, HTML-enhanced e-mail can enhance and reinforce text messages with graphics or other "rich" information. After all, sometimes a picture—or sound bite, or video clip—is worth a thousand words, or more.

Hyperlinks mean the ability to link an e-mail message to Web sites or intranet information. Integrated applications mean the ability to include even "live" spreadsheets or other data into e-mail messages.

Extend this concept to newsgroups, and you have the capability to turn static, all-text news postings into truly collaborative works. One worker can post an HTML message which contains an AutoCAD drawing, for example, and all the other members of the group can comment on it, adding notes or even making changes to the drawing itself.

Clearly, HTML in messages—both e-mail and newsgroups—may have as much of an impact on the way people communicate and collaborate online as the Web or intranets have already had. And Composer is the tool that will let you add HTML content to all of your communications.

▶ To begin creating HTML documents with Composer, turn to Chapter 6, "Composer Quick Start," on **p. 79**

▶ To use Composer to create fancier documents, turn instead to Chapter 14, "Composer In-Depth," on **p. 273**

## Netscape Conference

E-mail and newsgroups are fine as far as they go, but there is a recent demand on the Net for more interactive forms of collaboration. Communicator's Conference component supplies that functionality.

Conference lets you chat with others on the Internet via voice. At the same time, you can exchange files, type live messages back and forth, and work together on a common "whiteboard" (see Figure 1.10).

There's currently a television commercial which shows a pajama-clad woman telecommuting to work from home, participating in a boardroom conference while actively marking up charts and graphs being projected in the boardroom via a live connection from her home office. In this commercial the woman repeatedly asserts to the audience, "and I don't have to shower." With tools like Netscape Conference, big corporations may be able to see a major increase in the number of pajama-clad (and perhaps somewhat aromatic) workers they employ.

▶ When you're ready to start using Conference, turn to Chapter 7, "Conference Quick Start," on **p. 95**

▶ To wring the most out of Conference, turn instead to Chapter 15, "Conference In-Depth," on **p. 301**

**FIG. 1.10**
Netscape Conference features an Internet telephone, text chat, file sharing, and an interactive whiteboard.

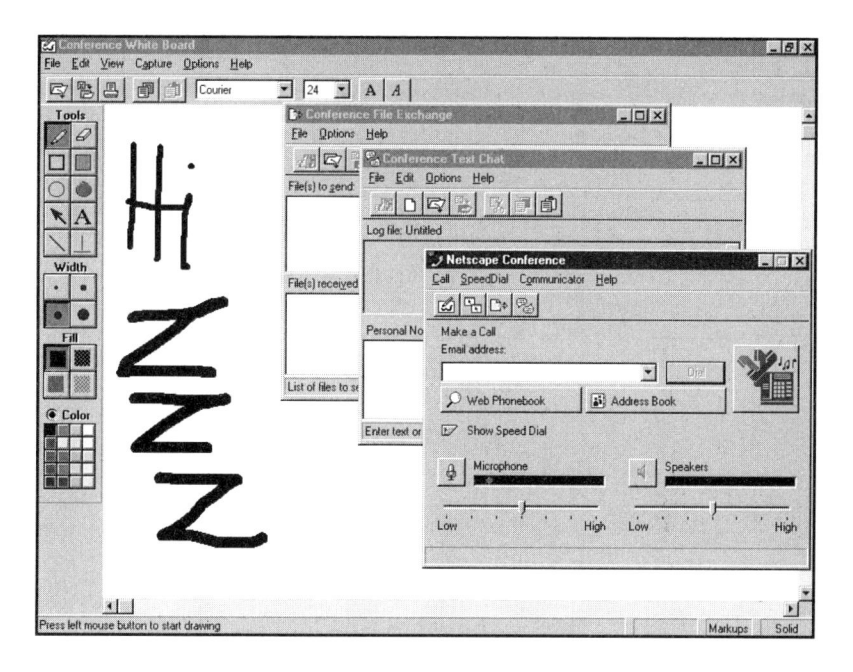

# Netcaster

The Web is becoming bigger by the second. It's already way too large for any single human being to comprehend, much less use in a meaningful manner. What's the solution?

Most Internet experts seem to think that the answer lies in "push" technology. Rather than surfing to Web sites on your own volition, you'll specify the topics you're interested in and that information will be "pushed" to your desktop for you to peruse at your leisure.

Though still in its infancy, Netscape is banking on push technology to drive much of the future development of the Web. Netscape began their experiments with push technology with In-Box Direct (see Figure 1.11).

You can surf to Netscape's In-Box Direct site at **http://form.netscape.com/ibd/html/ibd.html** and subscribe to any of a number of news services that will e-mail you daily or weekly news on topics as diverse as stocks and bonds, sports, and technology. There are dozens of services currently available, with more coming online all the time.

In-Box Direct services are delivered to your e-mail box. The information it provides is HTML-enhanced, so it can supply pictures, audio clips, and links to Web sites. You need to read them with an HTML-savvy mail client like Communicator's Messenger, giving you one more reason not to leave the program.

But push technology is destined to advance quickly beyond this relatively simple level. Netscape is already developing the next step, called Netcaster (see Figure 1.12).

**24** Chapter 1 Overview

**FIG. 1.11**
Netscape's In-Box Direct service is only the tip of what is almost certain to become an iceberg of push services.

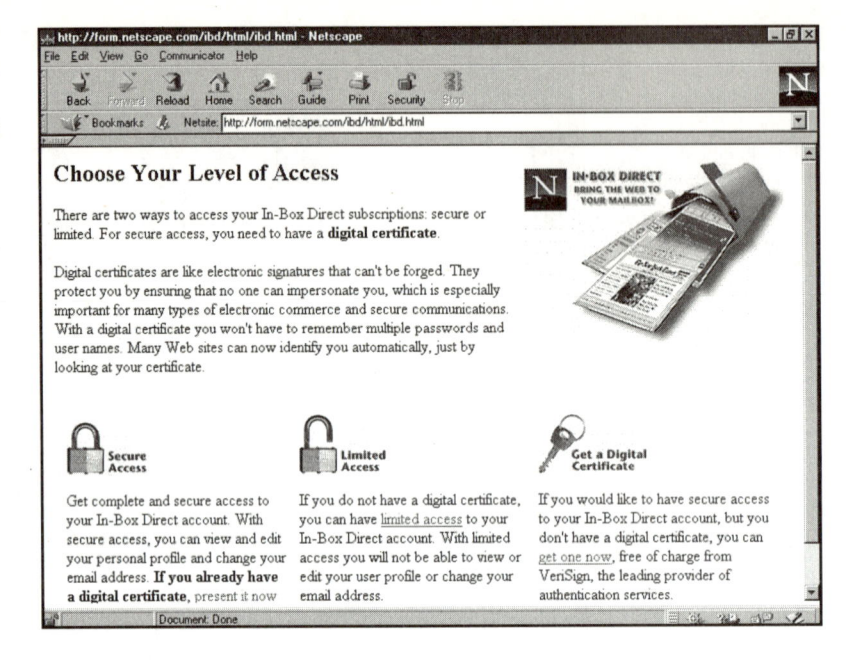

**FIG. 1.12**
Netcaster provides channels of "push" information as well as a universal desktop which acts as the host for everything you need to do on your computer.

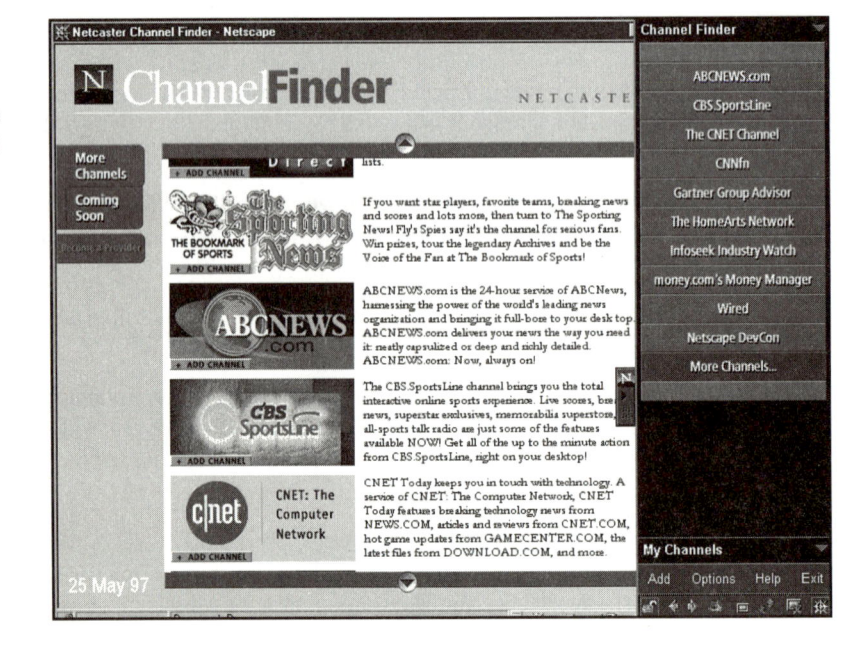

http://www.quecorp.com

Netcaster is a technology for delivering multiple channels of information to a customized platform-independent workspace or desktop environment. Tightly integrated with Communicator, it lets you create a work environment with links to stand-alone applications, news, Web sites, and everything else you use your computer for. It promises no more switching around to get all your work done; you can stay in the Netcaster *WebTop* to do everything you want to do.

Not only can you run Communicator components from your WebTop, you can also run stand-alone applications like Word and Excel. You can even access files and network resources, no matter what your system's underlying platform or operating system. Netcaster even provides familiar services like drag-and-drop editing between applications and file management.

In addition, your WebTop serves as a receiver for push information—a feature Netscape calls LiveSites. The source for this information can be the Web or a corporate intranet. Another feature called InfoBlocks keeps continuously updated information, like stock quotes, active and available on your WebTop desktop all the time. Real-time *Notifications* can also be sent to your system for time-critical information such as meeting reminders.

Perhaps Netcaster's most impressive feature is its location independence. Once you set up your WebTop, you can log into it from any computer system anywhere in the world and see your familiar WebTop user interface. Your Mac at home, your UNIX workstation at work, and your Windows PC at school will all look alike, work alike, and reflect the current version of your WebTop setup.

## Communicator Integration

Netscape talks a lot about integration—how all of its components work together to create an environment that is integrated, useful, and compelling. They've got a point. Thanks to HTML integration, you can link to Web pages from e-mail and newsgroup posts as easily as you can from other Web pages. You compose e-mail, posts, and pages with the same tool: Composer. You read and respond to e-mail and newsgroup messages from the same Messenger window. You run applications and read news from a ubiquitous WebTop interface.

Is this a better way to work? Well, you'll have to be the judge of that. But in the following chapters, you can at least find out how to use Netscape Communicator Netcaster to its fullest. Let's get started. ●

CHAPTER 2

# What's New in Netscape Communicator?

*by Mark R. Brown*

There really isn't a screen you can point to and say, "This is Netscape Communicator." Communicator is a suite of components which includes the latest version of Netscape Navigator along with applications that handle e-mail, newsgroups, HTML document editing, online conferencing, and much more. So the question, "What's New in this version of Netscape?" might easily be answered, "Everything!"

Of course, that's a bit of an exaggeration, but not much. Netscape Navigator 4.0, for example, looks familiar, but differs in dozens of subtle ways from Navigator 3.0. Composer is based on the HTML document authoring tool in Navigator Gold, but adds many new features, sports a redesign, and is now the editor for e-mail and news as well as Web pages. On the far end of the "What's New" spectrum, Messenger and Collabra combine e-mail and news into a totally new user interface. And Netcaster is a completely new application.

The biggest change in Communicator from previous versions of Navigator is reflected in its name. *Communicator* not only tells you that this is a brand new product, it states immediately that you're not just looking at Navigator anymore. Before, Navigator was the main component from which you launched other applications; now it's just one component in the Communicator suite.

### Navigator has changed in dozens of ways from previous versions

Though outwardly similar to previous versions, Communicator sports many changes both subtle and radical.

### E-mail and newsgroups now share a common user interface

Though quite different in function, e-mail and news are composed and managed identically in Communicator.

### HTML is no longer confined to Web pages only

HTML-enhanced e-mail and news posts can include graphics, links, and even embedded video and multimedia!

### Netcaster's Push technology brings news and information to your WebTop

You no longer have to browse for information on the Web—now it can find you.

This idea is further promulgated by a new level of integration and cooperation among Communicator's components. You can click a link in an e-mail message and launch Navigator to scan a Web page. You use Composer to create e-mail and newsgroup messages. Select a name in the Address Book and you can send someone e-mail, post a message to a discussion group, or call someone using the Internet phone in Netscape Conference. With all of its new capabilities, you might never have to drop out of Communicator to run another program. At least, that's what Netscape hopes.

Central to this new philosophy is Netscape's concept of "HTML Everywhere." No longer relegated only to the World Wide Web, Communicator lets you add HTML to intranets and extranets, e-mail, news, applications, and just about anything else you can think of. ■

## Toolbars and Menus

On a more mundane level, there are literally dozens of changes in Communicator that affect the way you work with the program. For example, Navigator 4.0 removes some lesser-used features, like the Open button and the row of directory buttons that used to be under the Location toolbar.

### The Component Bar

The most obvious new addition is the Component Bar (see Figure 2.1). It is the pivot point of Communicator, around which its major components—Navigator, Messenger, Collabra, and Composer—revolve.

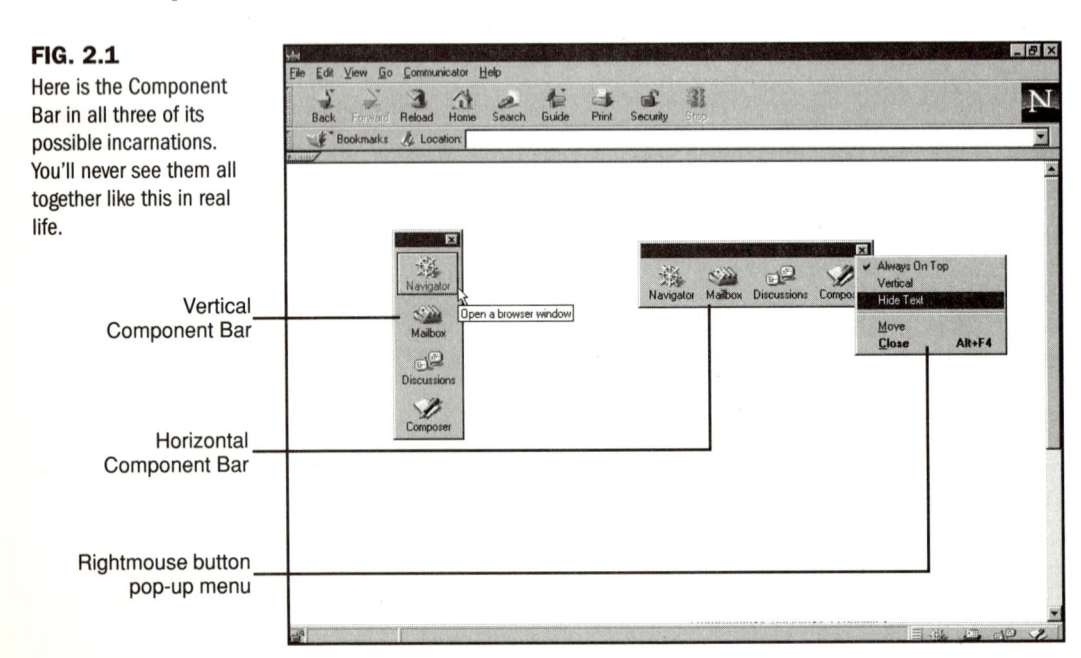

**FIG. 2.1**
Here is the Component Bar in all three of its possible incarnations. You'll never see them all together like this in real life.

Vertical Component Bar

Horizontal Component Bar

Rightmouse button pop-up menu

http://www.quecorp.com

The Component Bar can appear as a floating horizontal or vertical toolbar, or in its "docked" position in the lower-right corner of just about any Communicator component window. Clicking a Component Bar icon takes you to Navigator, Messenger, Collabra, or Composer instantly. Double-clicking the docked Component Bar turns it into a floating taskbar. Right-clicking a floating taskbar pops up the menu shown in Figure 2.1, and hovering over a button shows you a tooltip for that button.

> **TIP** When we say *right-click* we mean on Windows, Windows 95, and UNIX platforms. If you're running Communicator on a Macintosh, click and hold instead.

## Changes to Toolbars

Navigator's toolbars have also changed in many ways (see Figure 2.2).

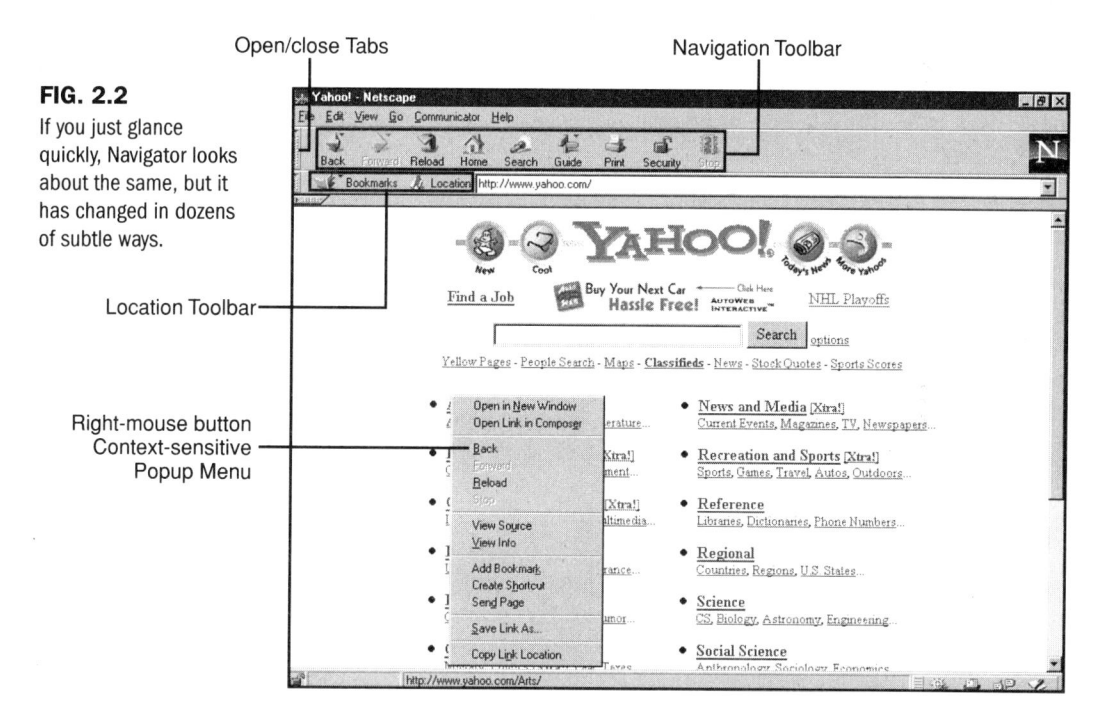

**FIG. 2.2**
If you just glance quickly, Navigator looks about the same, but it has changed in dozens of subtle ways.

Open/close Tabs
Navigation Toolbar
Location Toolbar
Right-mouse button Context-sensitive Popup Menu

Toolbars now come equipped with open/close tabs on their left ends. Click one and the toolbar disappears. Click again and it comes back. Figure 2.2 shows the Navigation and Location toolbars open, but the Personal toolbar closed. These tabs are great for temporarily freeing up a bit more room on the screen.

On the Navigation toolbar, the Back and Forward buttons have been enhanced with new tooltips and drop-down menus. Hover over a button and you'll see a tooltip with the address of the page you'll go to if you click it. Click and hold and you'll get a drop-down menu of all available Back and Forward sites, so you can go directly where you want to go without having to hit either button repeatedly and wait for the screen to update.

The Images button is now "smart." It only shows up on the toolbar if you've turned Autoload Images off in Preferences.

A new Search button replaces the old Find button. Where Find found text on the displayed page, Search is a shortcut to Netscape's own Web search page where you can search for information on the Web. (The Find command is now located on the Edit menu.)

On the Location toolbar, there's a new Bookmark Quickfile button. Click it and you'll get your bookmark list—*much* handier than having to go to the menus for it (though Bookmarks are available under the Communicator menu, too).

You can now create a bookmark by clicking the Location icon and dragging it to the Bookmark Quickfile icon. You can then drop it into place wherever you want. Slick and quick.

A new Personal (Custom) toolbar replaces the old and seldom-used Places toolbar. You can add your own custom location icons to this toolbar by simply dragging and dropping the Location icon onto it. (If you miss the old toolbar, check out the new Places button on the Navigation toolbar.)

Right-clicking just about anywhere in a Communicator display screen brings up a context-sensitive pop-up menu like the one shown in Figure 2.2. These have been improved with many new added functions, including the added ability to open a document being displayed in a frame in its own browser window. Links, graphics, bare spots, and other document elements each have their own individual pop-up menus.

**NOTE** There's also a new enhanced version of Communicator called Communicator Professional. It includes three new applications: Calendar, for scheduling; AutoAdmin for system administration; and IBM Host-on-Demand, for connecting to mainframe systems. Part III, "Communicator Professional," beginning on pg. XXX, covers these applications.

There are other, more subtle changes in Communicator such as the fact that Windows, Macintosh, and UNIX versions of Communicator now have the same default window size, which makes creating cross-platform friendly pages easier. You're sure to discover many other subtle changes as we cover Communicator's features throughout this book.

▶ You can get started with Navigator in Chapter 3, "Navigator Quick Start," **p. 39**, or dig in deep in Chapter 8, "Navigator In-Depth," **p. 109**

# Improved Document Features

Because Communicator now does so much more than just browse the Web, it has added many improvements to HTML, Java, and plug-ins; these improvements enable you to create more robust documents that go beyond mere Web page design.

▶ HTML, Java, JavaScript, and plug-ins are explored in detail in Part V, "For Webmasters," beginning on **p. 433**

## Additions to HTML

Besides supporting all HTML 3.2 specifications, Communicator has added a few semi-controversial additions to HTML.

First and foremost is Dynamic HTML, which Netscape describes as "a set of technologies" for transforming static HTML pages into dynamic, animated pages. Central to this philosophy is the interaction of JavaScript with two new features: Style Sheets and new HTML layering and positioning tags.

Style Sheets represent an attempt to divorce HTML document content from presentation. For example, a page might contain text and graphics discussing new cars, and be associated with a style sheet that defines an appropriate auto-related wallpaper and color scheme. Non-graphic browsers could display the page as easily as Navigator, and the page designer could change the look and feel of the page—or a group of pages—by simply changing the style sheet.

Navigator actually supports two different style sheet specifications: Cascading Style Sheets (CSS), which have been approved as an official Web standard, and JavaScript-accessible Style Sheets (JASS), which are still under standards consideration.

Dynamic fonts are also a part of this new setup; you can send a font along with a page if you want to.

Positioning and layering tags let you layer graphics and other elements and place them anywhere on the page. These elements can be made transparent at will and, under the control of JavaScript, their positions, layering, and visibility can be altered on-the-fly. These new capabilities should make for some very interesting new Web sites. In combination with JavaScript's ability to read and respond to user input, it means you can now develop interactive, animated pages without resorting to Java or Shockwave.

Microsoft and Netscape are still duking out the standards for these new technologies, so be prepared for them to experience some extreme changes over the next few months. They are, for now, anything but "standard."

## Changes in Plug-Ins

Beginning with Communicator, plug-ins can now be invoked using the OBJECT tag as well as the EMBED tag. The OBJECT tag is more universally useful, as it can also be used to insert applets and other objects.

A new feature called AutoInstall lets users automatically download a plug-in when they encounter a page that requires one. Plug-ins can now also be digitally "signed" so that users will be able to know they can trust the origin of the download for improved security.

Netscape has also made available a new plug-in API (Applications Programming Interface) which will allow developers to create new windowless, transparent plug-ins.

## Changes in Java

Java has a new JIT (Just In Time) compiler in Communicator, which is much faster than the previous one. (Thanks, Symantec!) There is also now support for Sun's JDK version 1.1, which means developers can add many new features to Java applets. New Java classes built in to the IFC (Internet Foundation Classes) also means additional new features in Java and JavaScript applications. The addition of Macromedia's Fireworks API improves and simplifies Java's ability to manipulate text, images, animation, and audio data.

Security has also been improved with the addition of extended system access for secure signed Java applets. Java applets can now read and/or write to disks and networks, depending on their level of "trustworthiness." The user still retains the right to refuse any of these levels of access at will, of course.

## Other Document Improvements

Communicator has improved its integration with OLE applications under Windows 95 and Windows NT. Office documents can now be edited in place, for example.

The addition of the Internet Inter-ORB protocol means Communicator can easily communicate with any CORBA-compliant networked object. If you run on a legacy mainframe system, that means better access to your system and your data.

# Mail and News

E-mail and news are totally different in Communicator than they were in previous versions of Navigator. Messenger, Communicator's e-mail client, and Collabra, its news client, share the same user interface (see Figure 2.3).

The integrated Message Center gives you a central repository for reading, organizing, and responding to mail and news. The user interface sports a user-customizable split-screen with button-based access to most-used functions, from downloading messages to creating new ones to filing old ones.

E-mail and news are now both fully HTML-compliant, which means you can include active links, graphics, and other HTML components in your messages, and read them when others send them to you. (See Figure 2.3 for an example HTML-based message from *Wired* magazine.)

This also means that you use Composer to create your mail and news messages. Though the mail and message composition window displays address and other information you don't see when you run Composer in stand-alone mode, all of its features and functions are available to you when you compose e-mail and news posts.

Sorting, following threads, hierarchical folders for organizing messages, automatic header expansion—there are so many useful features in the e-mail and news window that it's mind-boggling.

http://www.quecorp.com

**FIG. 2.3**
Messenger e-mail and Collabra newsgroups share a common user interface and toolset.

Toolbars
Message Center

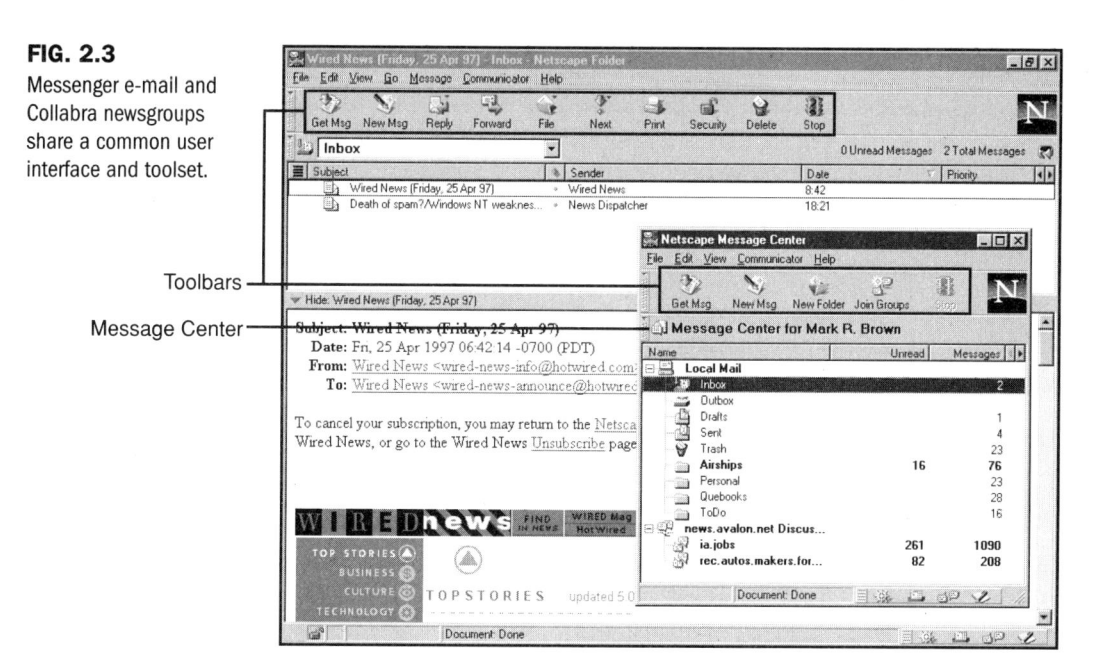

You can bookmark discussion group posts. You can filter mail a dozen ways from Sunday. You can drag and drop links into messages. To tell you all about Communicator's extensive new e-mail and news features would take several chapters. Fortunately, several chapters of this book are devoted to exactly those topics.

▶ For quick introductions to Communicator's e-mail and news applications, see Chapter 4, "Messenger Quick Start," **p. 51**, and Chapter 5, "Collabra Quick Start," **p. 71**

▶ For an exhaustive exploration of all the features of Messenger and Collabra, turn to Chapter 11, "Messenger In-Depth," **p. 199**, and Chapter 13, "Collabra In-Depth," **p. 245**

## Composer

You used to have to buy a special version of Navigator called Netscape Navigator Gold to get built-in WYSIWYG HTML editing. No more. Communicator now includes Composer, the latest version of the Navigator Gold editor (see Figure 2.4).

As we've said previously, perhaps the most surprising change to this HTML editor is that it is now also used for editing HTML-capable e-mail and news. But there are functional changes, as well.

Composer is more WYSIWYG than before. If you position things with spaces and paragraph marks, for example, those elements don't simply disappear when translated into HTML code. Composer is now smart enough to figure out what you really wanted to do, and will modify the HTML appropriately.

**34** Chapter 2 What's New in Netscape Communicator?

**FIG. 2.4**
Its roots are in the Netscape Gold HTML editor, but Composer also handles e-mail and news composition.

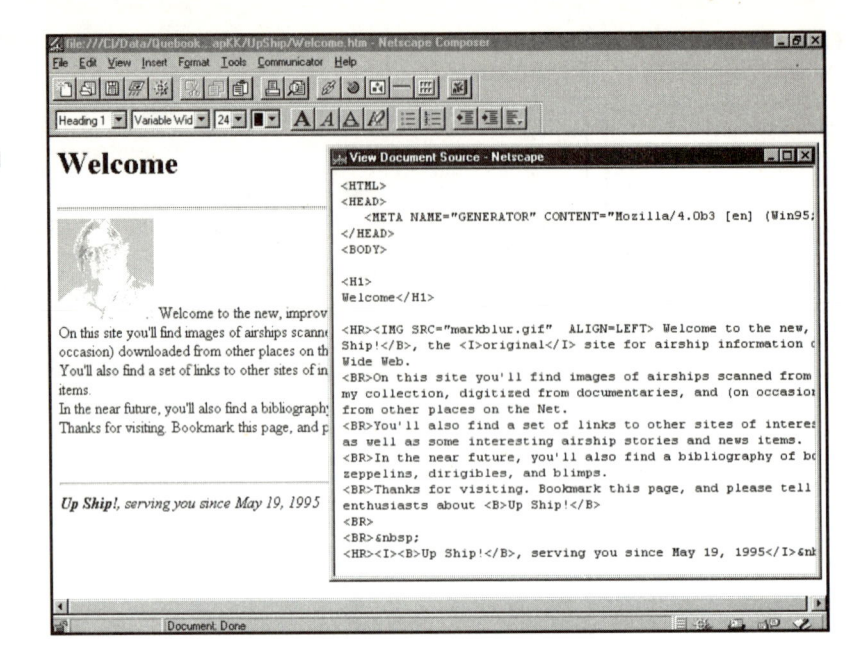

New Page Wizards and Page Templates are just a mouse click away, though they are located on the Netscape Web servers, so you'll have to be online to use them. A single click is also now all it takes to begin editing a displayed page.

Spell-checking is now built in, making Composer feel even more like a word processor than an HTML editor.

Composer is also smart enough to deal with editing table columns—you can modify the formatting of an entire column at once. Imported graphics are automatically converted to a Web-friendly format. One-Button Publish has been improved.

Most interesting of all is Netscape's new editor plug-in API, which will allow third parties to create functionality improvements for Composer. Built-in photo enhancing, anyone?

▶ Chapter 6, "Composer Quick Start," **p. 79**, provides a gentle introduction to using Composer. Chapter 14, "Composer In-Depth," **p. 273**, delves into all of its secrets.

# Conference

If you've used Netscape's stand-alone online conferencing suite, CoolTalk, then you've used the precursor to Netscape Conference. Of course, this version is more tightly integrated into the other components of Communicator.

Conference is an online communication tool that integrates full-duplex audio conferencing (sometimes generically called an "Internet phone"), text chat, file transfer, cooperative Web browsing, and a collaborative white board (see Figure 2.5).

http://www.quecorp.com

**FIG. 2.5**
Netscape Conference is a set of tools for online voice conferencing, text chat, file sharing, and whiteboard collaboration.

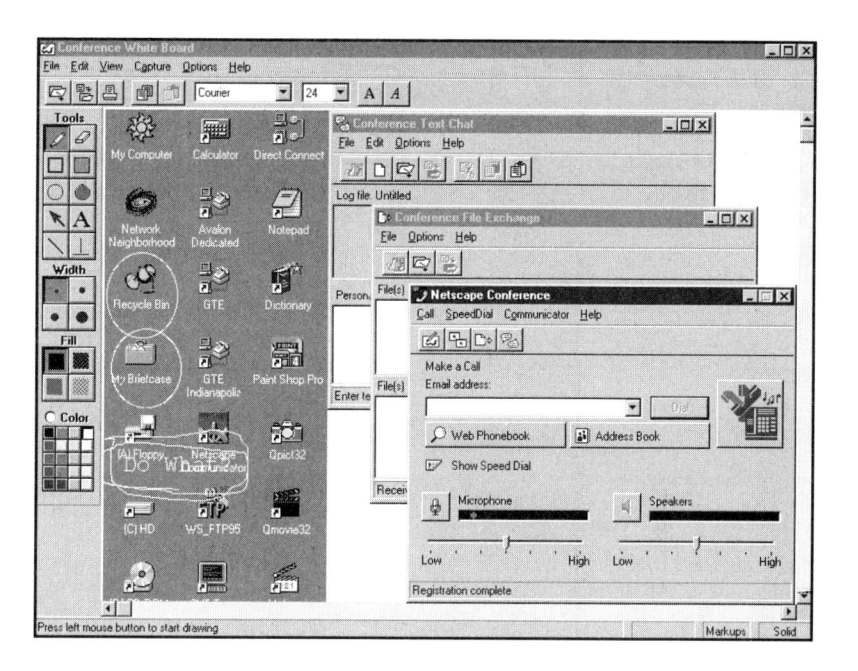

In a nutshell, Conference lets you collaborate with others over the Internet. (It's too bad the name "Collabra" was already taken by Communicator's news client....)

The phone portion of conference links to the Communicator address book, so you can initiate a call with a single click. There's also built-in voicemail, customizable speed dial buttons, caller ID for incoming calls, and much more. This module supports the H.323 audio conferencing standard for compatibility with other Internet phone programs, and also supports the use of multiple codecs (compression/decompression algorithms) for future improvements.

The text chat and file transfer functions are elementary, but essential. Cooperative Web browsing is fun, and could be very useful in many situations, especially over a company intranet.

The shared whiteboard lets you snapshot a work screen or import a picture and mark it up as you talk. If you've never done this, try to imagine an online game of tic-tac-toe, then expand the concept to importing and drawing anything you want. I think you'll see the possibilities.

Again, Netscape has developed an SDK (Software Development Kit) so that third parties can develop add-ons and improvements to Conference. It seems they're really going out of their way to make sure that Communicator never goes out of style.

▶ To begin using Conference, turn to Chapter 7, "Conference Quick Start," **p. 95**. For additional information, turn to Chapter 15, "Conference In-Depth," **p. 301**

# Netcaster

*Push* technology is all the rage on the Net, and Netcaster is Netscape's tool for incorporating push technology into Communicator (see Figure 2.6).

**FIG. 2.6**
You've probably been hearing a lot lately about *push* technology—Netcaster brings push information to your desktop.

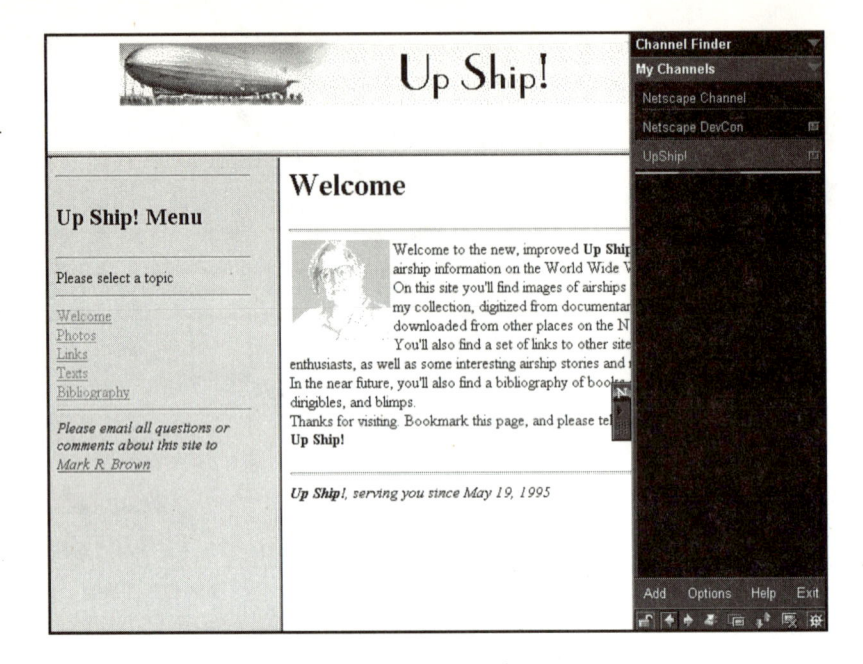

The concept of push is easy to understand—instead of searching for information on the Web, it comes to you automatically. In real-world implementations, of course, there's a bit more to it.

Netcaster lets you subscribe to *channels* of information that are analogous to TV channels. You define the kinds of information you want to receive, and these channels download to your computer in the background while you work. They are displayed full-screen to take advantage of more screen area. Because these channels are often rich with HTML, Java, and other flashy content, they need the extra space.

The Netcaster interface uses a Channel Finder to make it easier to find the kinds of content you want to see. Channels can be subscribed to or dropped at will. I'm sure we'll see a great deal of heated competition for users' subscriptions to online channels—maybe even as much as we now see on television.

Each channel has its own cache space and is accessed locally after downloading at a user-specified time. This lets you get information during off-peak hours and browse it offline at your leisure. (Though I'm not sure there will be such a thing as "off-peak hours" if push technology catches on like everyone says it will.)

Also part of Netcaster is a *Web Top* mode, where you can anchor your favorite channel to your desktop and have it launch automatically when you start your computer. You can even access the same WebTop from different systems. Magic.

http://www.quecorp.com

Corporate network administrators will be able to control all this to keep their workers from becoming addicted to frivolous channels during daytime hours.

▶ Netcaster is covered in great detail in Part IV, "Netcaster," starting on **p. 403**

## Preferences and Security

All of Communicator's absolutely required setup preferences are handled when you install the program, thanks to the Intelligent Setup Wizard. But when you want to start customizing the program to your liking, you'll find that Communicator has a new Preferences dialog box (see Figure 2.7).

**FIG. 2.7**
Netscape's Preferences are totally revamped, with an easy-to-use all-in-one dialog.

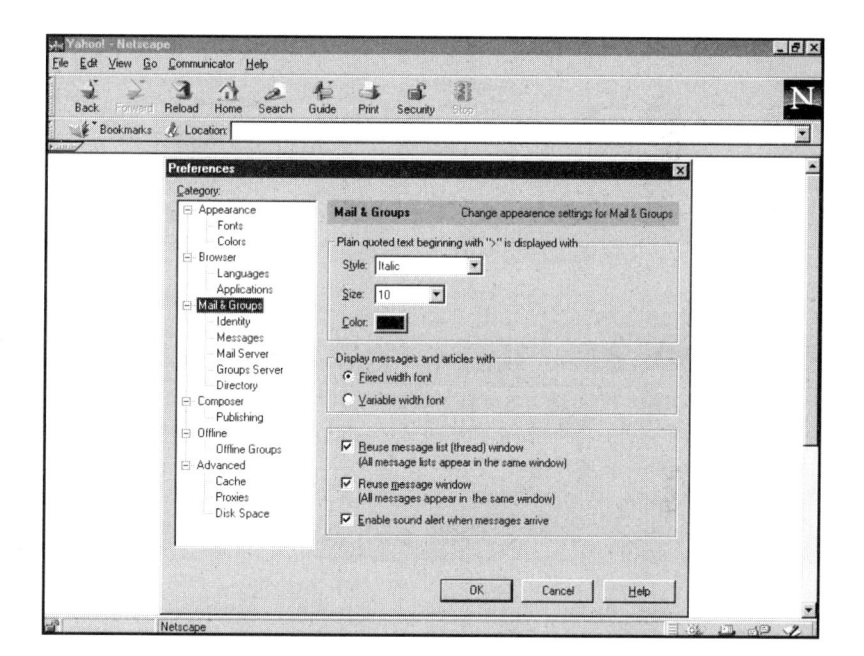

To go to this new dialog box, choose Edit, Preferences. This dialog box incorporates an expandable menu on the left and an ever-changing information window on the right. All Preference options are available from this single interface.

There's also a new Security Advisor window (see Figure 2.8). This isn't a dialog; it's implemented in HTML. Perhaps this is Netscape's first experiment at showing that interfaces that used to require custom programming can now be implemented in enhanced HTML, just as they're promoting to developers. It's a start! You invoke the Security Advisor by clicking the Security icon on the Navigation toolbar.

▶ Chapter 16, "Setting Preferences," **p. 319** covers the new Preferences dialog box. Chapter 17, "Security Options," **p. 349**, does the same for the Security Advisor.

**FIG. 2.8**
Communicator's Security button brings up this HTML-based security information window.

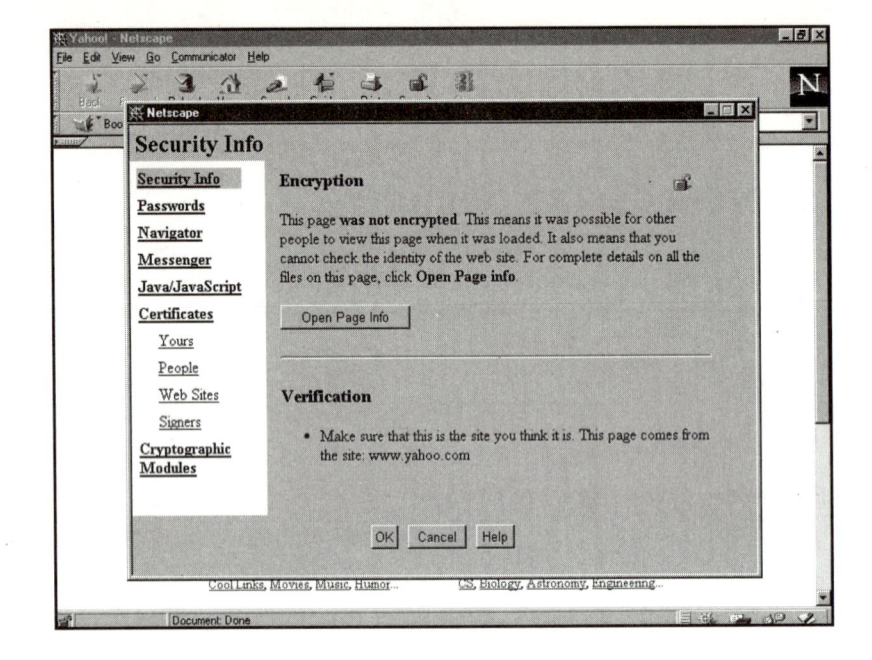

## Other New Features

There are other new features in Communicator, of course. For example, modular installation allows you to pick and choose which plug-ins and other features you want to install. There are lots of new keyboard navigation shortcuts. NetHelp takes you to help pages on Netscape's Web site. You can set up multiuser profiles, each with its own preferences and security settings. A new Canvas Mode makes it easy to create kiosk-type applications. Unicode browsing gives you international characters for easier internationalization of Web sites. We could go on and on.

But for now, we're going to wrap up this overview of what we believe are the most visible new features in Netscape Communicator. To list all of "What's New in Communicator" would probably take a thousand-page book. Hey! Come to think of it…. ●

http://www.quecorp.com

CHAPTER 3

# Navigator Quick Start

*by Mark R. Brown*

As a stand-alone product, Netscape Navigator made Netscape Communications Corporation both famous and successful. Now Navigator is just one of the many components that make up Netscape Communicator. But if you've used previous versions of Navigator, the odds are good that you're planning to spend a good deal of your Communicator time browsing the Web, and that means you'll still be using Navigator.

Sure, Navigator has changed from previous incarnations. But it has also stayed the same. For simple Web browsing, you may not even notice what's different. And if you're a brand new Communicator user, you'll find that browsing the Web with Navigator is not only simple, it's fun!

- **Navigator is the tool you use for surfing the World Wide Web**
  But it's not just for Web surfing anymore.

- **Navigator offers a multitude of different tools and methods for navigating HTML documents**
  You start out by using the Back and Forward toolbar buttons.

- **Links make the World Wide Web what it is**
  Click a link to jump to a new page anywhere in the world.

- **Searching for sites isn't something Navigator does by itself—it relies on Web-based search engines**
  The Navigator toolbar provides a link to Netscape's own search engine Web site.

> **See** Chapter 2, "What's New in Netscape Communicator," **p. 27** for an overview of all the changes Navigator has undergone in this release.

What is Navigator? Technically speaking, it's an HTML document interpreter and navigation tool. In other words, it lets you "navigate" to sources of HTML documents—on the Web, a corporate intranet, or stand-alone files stored on your system—and then interprets and displays those documents.

> **NOTE** HTML is the "HyperText Markup Language." It's the language that's used to create World Wide Web pages and other hypertext documents. You can find out more about HTML in Chapter 22, "HTML Primer," on **p. 435**

Of course, these days HTML documents contain much more than just HTML. They are also made up of Java applets, JavaScript scripts, videos, sound files, and much more. Navigator can interpret and display these components, and more.

Navigator performs three basic functions:

- Navigation—the ability to locate HTML documents
- Display—formatting and displaying various page elements like graphics, buttons, and text
- Linking—letting you click text or graphic links that take you to other HTML documents

# A First Look at Netscape Navigator

You don't have to do anything special to find Netscape Navigator. By default, when you run Communicator, Navigator is the first screen you see (see Figure 3.1).

Navigator isn't put together much different than most other programs these days; it appears in a window which includes a menu bar, several icon-laden toolbars, and a large display window (see Figure 3.1).

> **NOTE** Note the new Open/Close tabs on the left end of the Navigator toolbars. Clicking any of these tabs expands (opens) or hides (closes) its respective toolbar. Hovering over one with the mouse pointer displays a tooltip that indicates which toolbar you're on.

It's only necessary to learn to use a few of the menu selections and toolbar icons in order to start browsing the Web with Navigator.

> **TIP** Clicking the Netscape Logo button (see Figure 3.1) always takes you directly to the Netscape home page at **http://home.netscape.com**.

**FIG. 3.1**
Though intrinsically similar to earlier versions, Netscape Navigator 4.0 incorporates some subtle differences.

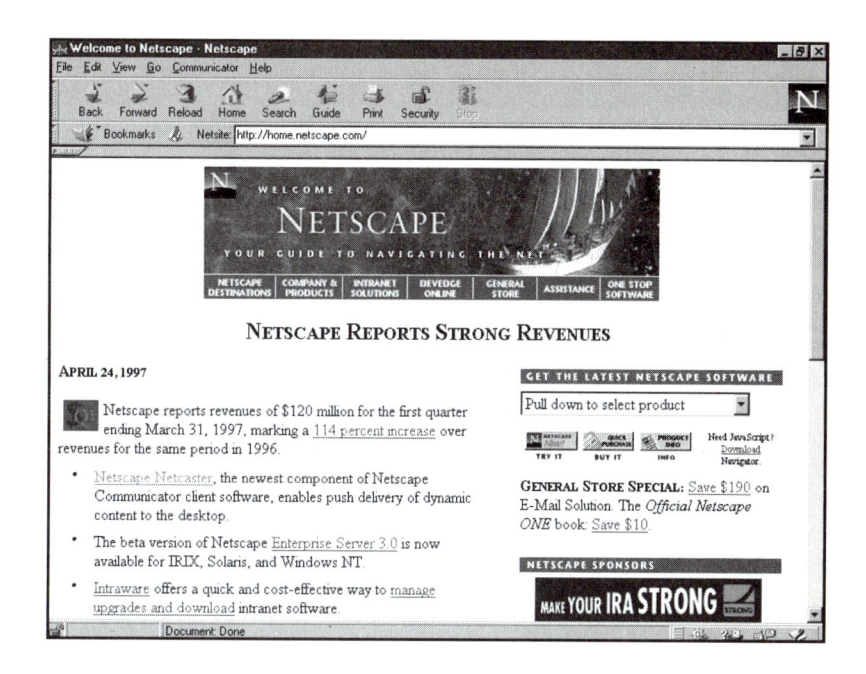

## Setting Your Own Home Page

The first document that Navigator displays when it starts up is your "home page." The address—or URL (Uniform Resource Locator)—of your home page is initially displayed in the Location toolbar (see Figure 3.2). Your home page is also displayed whenever you click the "Home" button on the Navigator toolbar, which is also shown in Figure 3.2.

By default, your home page is set to Netscape's home page at **http://home.netscape.com**. But many people set up Navigator to display their own home page of choice. (Mine is set to Yahoo! at **http://www.yahoo.com**.)

You can set your own home page location by following these steps:

1. Choose Edit, Preferences from the Navigator menu. The Preferences dialog box will appear (see Figure 3.2).

2. Click "Navigator" in the left-column menu of the dialog box. The word "Navigator" will become highlighted and you'll see the Preferences choices shown in Figure 3.2.

3. In the "Navigator starts with" section of this dialog box, make sure the "Home page" button is selected.

4. In the "Home page" section, enter the URL (address) of your desired home page in the Location box.

5. If the page you want to use as your home page is currently displayed, you can instead click the "Use Current Page" button to automatically set it as your home page.

# 42  Chapter 3  Navigator Quick Start

6. If you want to use a file on a network or hard drive as your home page, you can click the Browse button to look for it.

7. When you have your home page set, click the "OK" button to finish.

   ▶ There are many other interesting Preference options available from this dialog box. They are examined in detail in Chapter 17, "Setting Preferences," **p. 349**

**FIG. 3.2**
This dialog box lets you set your own home page.

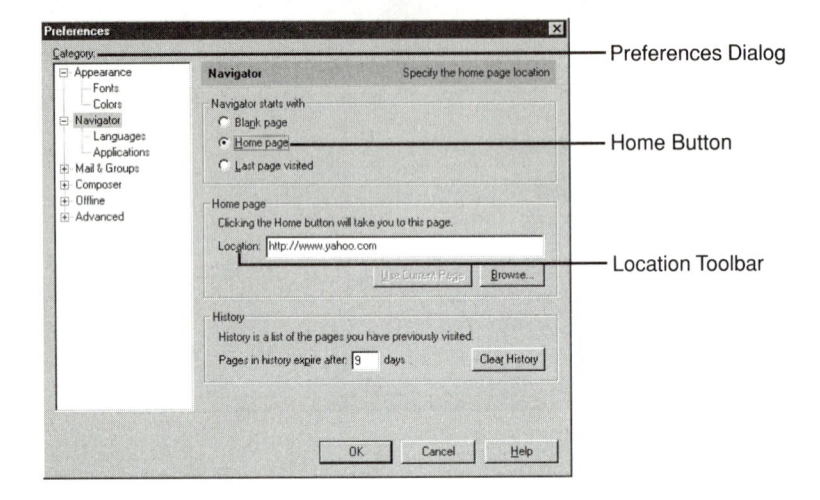

— Preferences Dialog
— Home Button
— Location Toolbar

## Jumping to Your Own Locations

Every TV commercial and magazine ad these days seems to include the Web address of the advertiser. You can easily surf directly to these locations—indeed, to any address on the Internet—by typing the URL directly into the Location toolbar. Here's how:

1. First, make sure you have the full address of the Web site you want to visit. It *must* begin with "http://" and will usually look something like this: **http://www.someplace.com**. (Actually, Navigator is smart enough to add the "http://" automatically if you don't type it in.)

2. Now click the text box in the "Location" toolbar, as shown in Figure 3.2. The existing text will be highlighted, indicating it will be replaced when you type.

3. Type in the address you want to visit. Be sure you type it *exactly*!

4. Press Enter and—if the address exists—you'll be instantly transported to the location you specified.

> **TIP** What if you want to display a document on your hard drive or network, instead of one from the Internet? Select File, Open Page from the menu (or type Ctrl+O) and you'll get a dialog box from which you can search for your file.

# Using Navigational Links

Links are what make the Web the Web. You click a link to jump from one Web page to another. Links on the next page jump to other pages, and this creates a "World Wide Web" of interlinked documents.

Figure 3.3 shows how text links usually look in HTML documents: highlighted in a contrasting color and underlined. Though this look can be changed both by page authors and by reconfiguring Navigator's Preferences, by default this is how you'll usually recognize text links.

> **TIP** Text links to sites you've visited recently are usually a different color than those for sites you haven't visited. This can provide an important visual clue when you're trying to get back to a site you've seen before, but can't quite recall exactly how you got there.

Links aren't limited to text, though; graphics and other elements can also incorporate links. How can you recognize when a non-text element on the page contains a link? Just keep an eye on the Navigator pointer. As shown in Figure 3.3, the pointer changes to a hand with a pointing finger when it's over a link. Not only that, if the link points directly to a specific document, Navigator displays the linked address in the status bar at the bottom of the window.

**FIG. 3.3**
Yahoo!'s pages are composed of almost nothing but lots and lots of links.

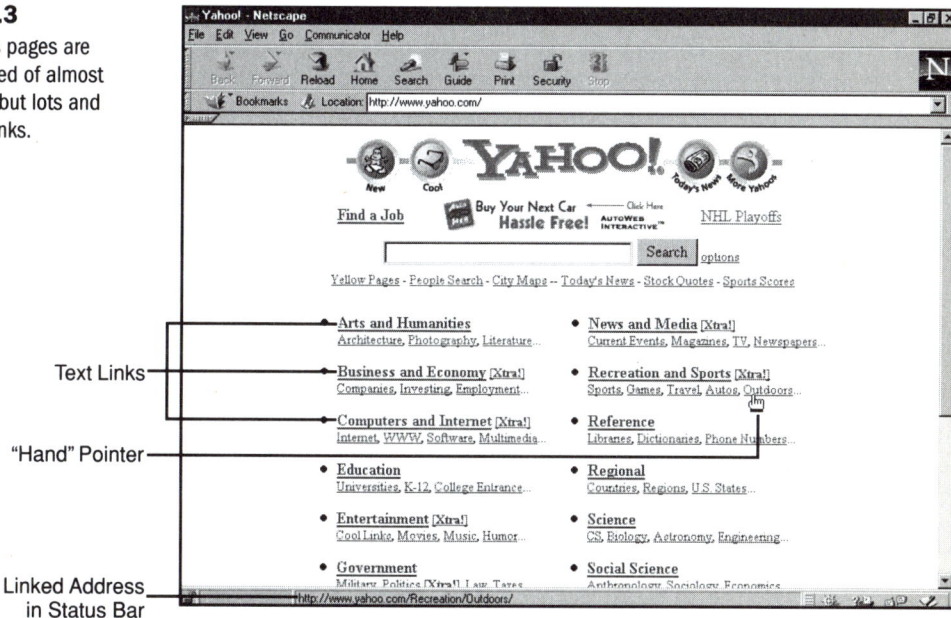

Text Links
"Hand" Pointer
Linked Address in Status Bar

> **TIP** Sometimes graphics don't link to a single location, but form an imagemap that links to different locations depending on where you click. Though you won't see a specific address shown in the status bar, if the imagemap is well designed it should provide you with clues as to where the link will take you.

## Navigation Using the Toolbar Buttons

What if you want to go where you've been before, but can't remember the address? Fortunately, Netscape has built in a couple of handy toolbar buttons to help you out in this very, very common situation.

The Back button (see Figure 3.4) takes you back to a previously visited page. Click it once and you go back one page. Click it twice and you go back two.

Hover the pointer over the Back button for a few seconds and you'll get a popup hint box that tells you what page you'll go to if you click it. (This "hover" trick also works with the Home page and Forward buttons.)

> **NOTE** The Go menu also takes you back where you've been before. The Back button keeps a list of sites you've visited in linear order, throwing away references that are outside the current string of visits. But the Go menu tracks a longer list of visited sites, and doesn't care much when or how you got there. The Go menu is a better choice than the Back button if you're trying to get somewhere you visited a few hours ago. The Back button is best for sites you went to a few minutes ago.

Right-click with the pointer over the Back button and you'll get a list of previously visited pages, as shown in Figure 3.4. Select one and you'll go there instantly, without having to wade through all the intermediate pages.

After you use the Back button, the Forward button is available. You can use it to move to the pages you came from before you used the Back button.

> **NOTE** The Web can often be very, very slow, so here's a neat trick that can sometimes help: If a page seems to be taking forever to load, with very little activity, click the Stop button to stop the transfer. Then click Reload to try again. You'll often get a faster connection and the page will load in like a dream. If it doesn't work, you can try this trick two or three times and still beat the *Waiting for Godot* tedium of a slow connection.

Of course, if 2-3 times doesn't do it, just content yourself to sit and wait, or choose another, faster, destination.

http://www.quecorp.com

## Navigation Using the Toolbar Buttons | 45

> **TIP** Not sure if a page is done loading? Navigator gives you two clues:
> - The Netscape logo is animated if it is still trying to transfer data.
> - The status bar at the bottom of the Navigator window says "Document: Done" when the page has finished loading.

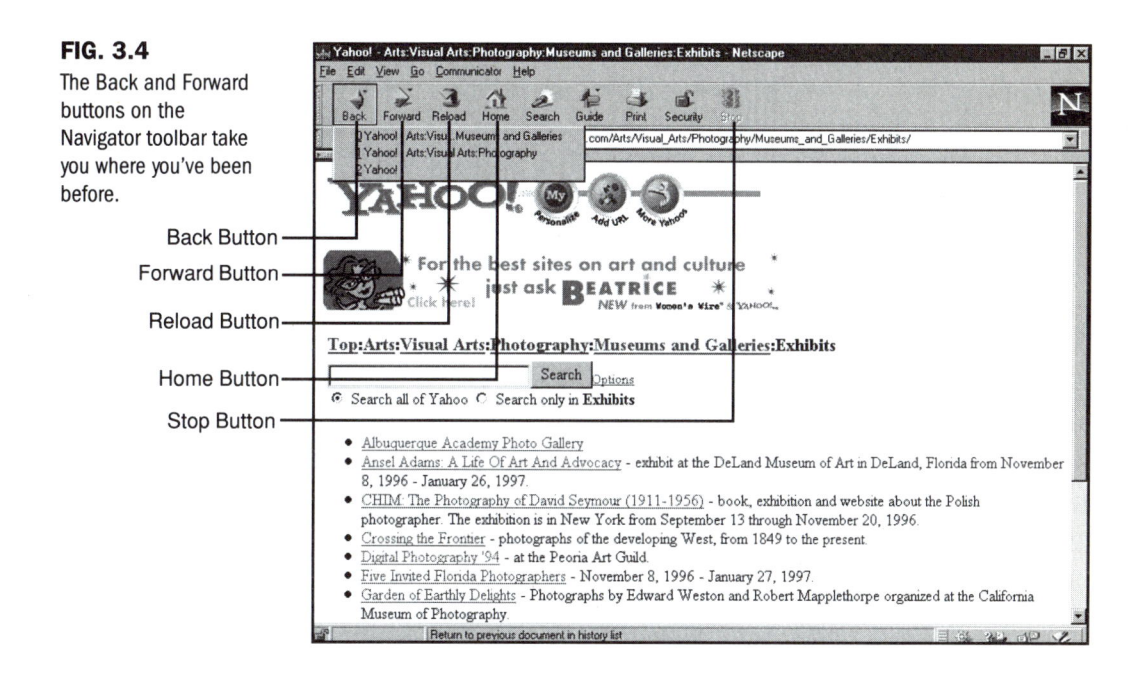

**FIG. 3.4**
The Back and Forward buttons on the Navigator toolbar take you where you've been before.

- Back Button
- Forward Button
- Reload Button
- Home Button
- Stop Button

## Basic Bookmarks

The Web would be a daunting place indeed if Navigator didn't give you the ability to bookmark your favorite places so you can quickly and easily come back to them. With millions of sites already online, and thousands more coming on every month, you'd soon lose track of all but that small handful of sites you visit daily.

Bookmarking a site is easy—with the page you want to bookmark displayed, click the right mouse button and select Add Bookmark from the pop-up menu (see Figure 3.5). Even easier is to press the hotkey combination Ctrl+D. (Unfortunately, you get no immediate feedback that your bookmark has been added to the list, so you might want to check your bookmark list to make sure.)

Your bookmark list is immediately available by clicking the Bookmarks Quickfile button on the Location toolbar (see Figure 3.6). Once the bookmark list is displayed, click the listing for the page you want to revisit.

▶ **See** Chapter 9, "Using Bookmarks," **p. 145**, for the complete story on bookmarks.

**FIG 3.5**
Clicking the right mouse button on a page brings up this handy pop-up menu. Adding a bookmark is only one thing you can do from this menu.

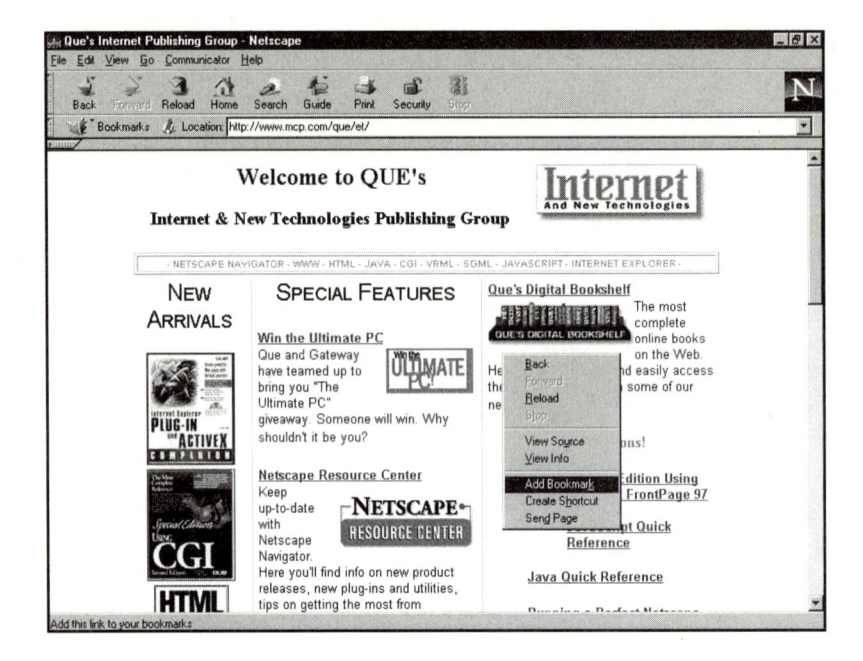

**FIG. 3.6**
The new Bookmark Quickfile button gives you instant access to your bookmark list.

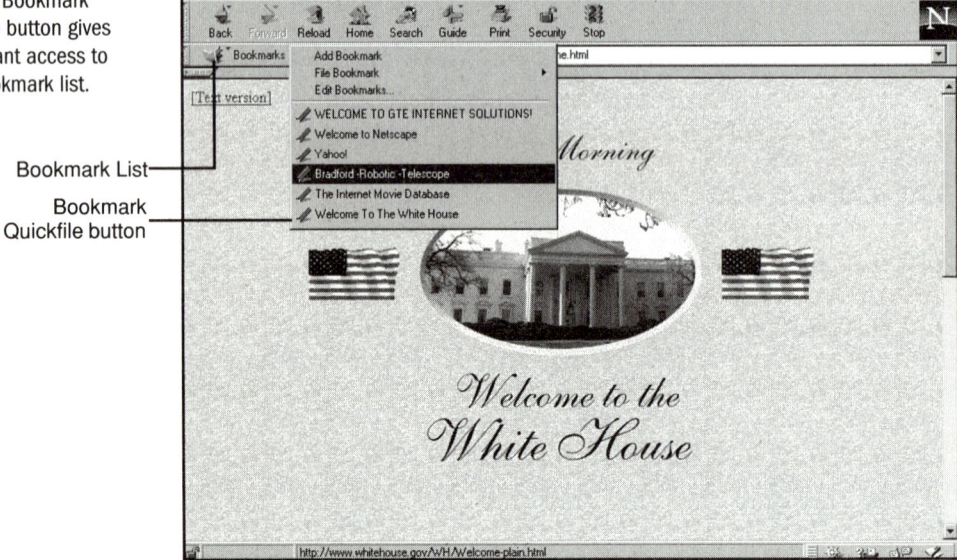

Bookmark List

Bookmark Quickfile button

http://www.quecorp.com

# Searching for Sites

So far, you've only found out how to navigate around Web pages for which you know the addresses. What if you know what you want to know about something, but don't know where it is? Say, for example, you desperately need to know about Dalmatians?

The answer is right there on the Navigator toolbar—the Search button (see Figure 3.7).

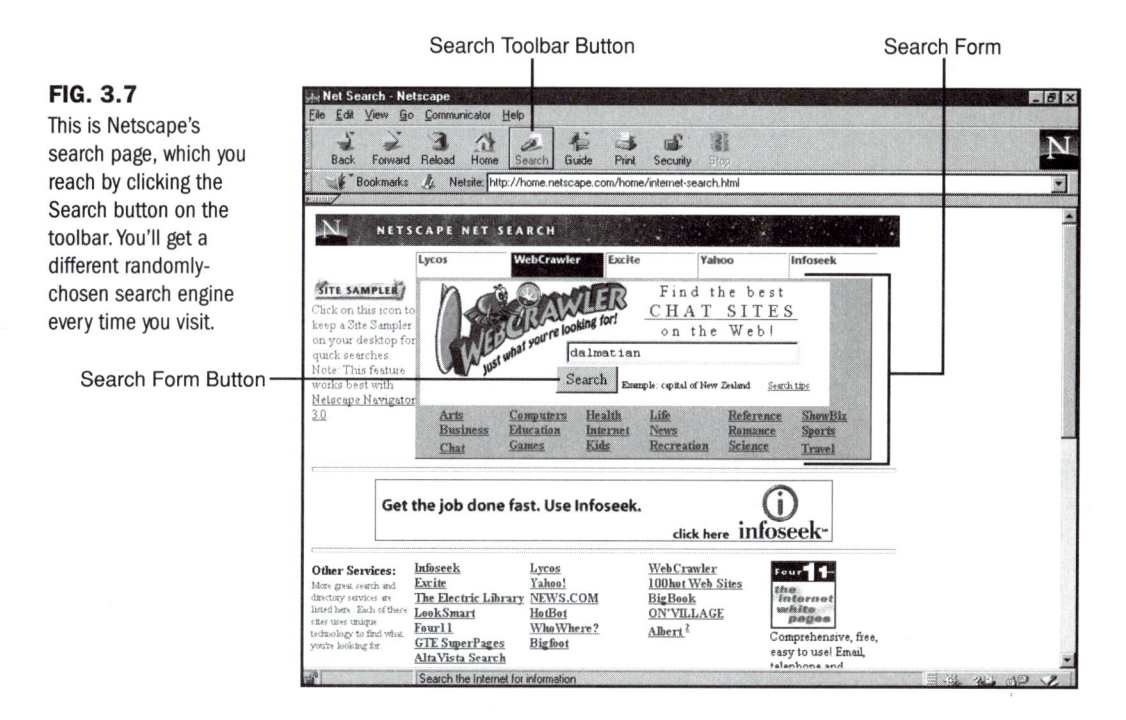

**FIG. 3.7**
This is Netscape's search page, which you reach by clicking the Search button on the toolbar. You'll get a different randomly-chosen search engine every time you visit.

Search Toolbar Button

Search Form

Search Form Button

> **TIP** Note that there are many other search sites listed on Netscape's search page. Chapter 8, "Navigator In Depth," on p. **109**, discusses search engines at greater length.

When you click on the Search button on the toolbar, you'll be whisked away to Netscape's search page. What you're interested in on this page is the Search form at mid-page. You type in your search word—in our example, **dalmatian**—then click the search form button below the form field. After a few seconds, you'll get a page of *hits*, which are links to Web pages that may have information pertinent to the subject of interest (see Figure 3.8).

**FIG. 3.8**
Our search for information on Dalmatians resulted in this list of links.

Minimized Communicator Component Bar

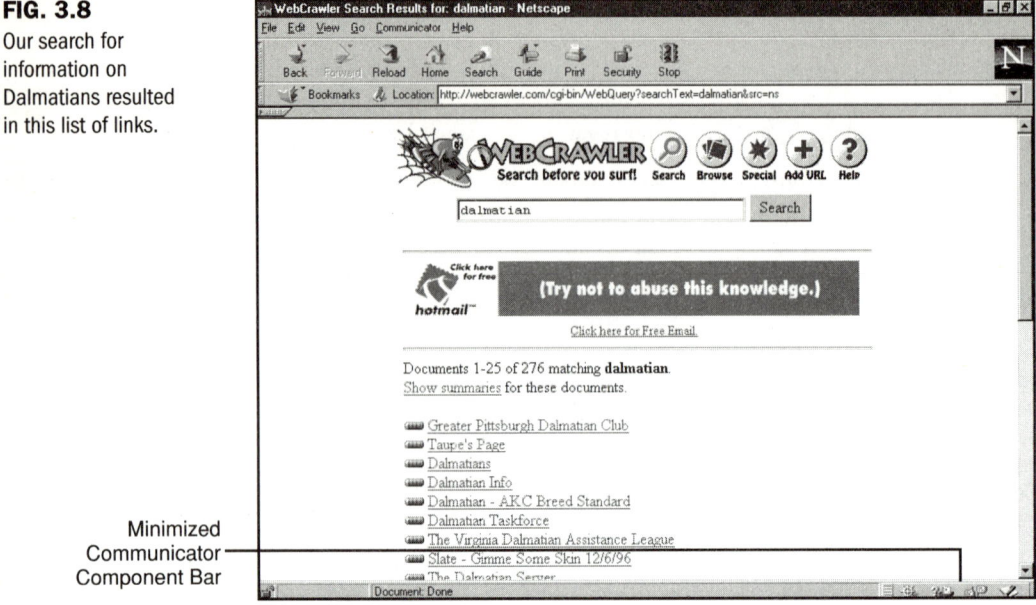

## Moving to Other Communicator Applications

Even though Navigator is the heart and soul of Communicator, you'll eventually want to try out the other applications in the suite. The quickest and easiest way to move around in Communicator is to use the dockable Component Bar (see Figure 3.9).

**FIG. 3.9**
Click the Communicator Component Bar icons to move to the other Communicator applications.

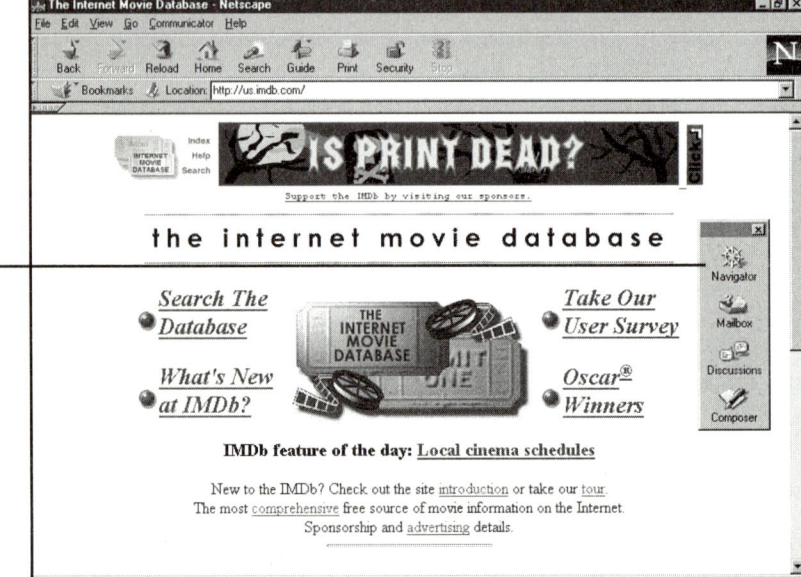

Floating Communicator Component Bar

When minimized, the Component Bar appears as a miniature version of itself in the lower right (see Figure 3.8). But it works the in the same manner.

## Getting Additional Help

We're far from through discussing the capabilities of Netscape Navigator. This was just a Quick Start chapter to get you going. Chapter 8, "Navigator In-Depth," delves into all of Navigator's capabilities and functions in great detail.

But if for some reason you want to know even more, you can turn to Navigator's NetHelp. Clicking the Help button on the Navigator toolbar or pressing function key F1 brings up a new Navigator window displaying Netscape's built-in HTML-based help pages for Communicator (see Figure 3.10).

**FIG. 3.10**
NetHelp is just a keystroke away—the F1 function key, to be specific.

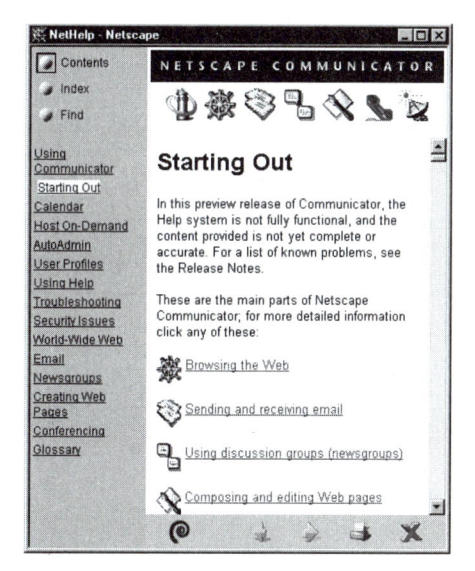

NetHelp is really just a Navigator window; all the menu items are links to HTML help documents included with the Communicator package. Because it's HTML-based, it's easy for Netscape to make sure the NetHelp information is always fresh and up-to-date with each release of the program. ●

CHAPTER 4

# Messenger Quick Start

*by Todd Stauffer*

**N**etscape Messenger is the component of Netscape Communicator that makes it possible to read, write and manage *electronic mail*, or e-mail. Electronic mail is one of the *services* on the Internet, requiring its own servers (special computers designed to transmit e-mail messages to and from different points on the Internet) and e-mail applications in order to work properly. It's useful to think of the Internet and e-mail as separate entities.

The Internet is the wiring and computers that make up the various connections around the world. The Internet is also the software programs and standards used for transmitting data. It's a lot like the international telephone system, which is also a network of wires and computers designed to let people talk using telephones. And, like the Internet, the phone system is there, and it works, but it's not terribly useful until you make a call.

For instance, if you've dealt with word processors from different companies, you're aware that these companies use different formats for their documents—Microsoft Word's files are different from WordPerfect's files. In Internet e-mail, all programs use the basic, universally-understood ASCII format for messages, as shown in Figure 4.1.

These days, e-mail can send special formatting, images, and even attached files and documents, all through a process called encoding. The best part is that Netscape Messenger and other modern e-mail programs perform

### Accessing and configuring Messenger
The first time you access Messenger, you're required to enter certain parameters, like your e-mail address and the addresses for your e-mail server computers.

### Checking your e-mail
Once you've configured Messenger, you can sign onto the Internet and check for new e-mail messages.

### Reading e-mail messages
When you receive e-mail messages, they automatically appear in your Messenger Inbox. Using the Inbox interface, you can quickly identify and read your new messages.

### Composing e-mail messages
Using a business memo-style interface, you can create your own e-mail messages, which can then be sent to one or more recipients. You can also carbon copy (CC) and blind carbon copy (BCC) messages to your recipients.

### Creating e-mail replies
Replying to an e-mail message you've received is similar to composing a new message, only easier. Messenger automatically fills in the e-mail addresses of your recipient(s). It also allows you to quote the original message, so that your recipient understands exactly what ideas you're replying to.

## Chapter 4  Messenger Quick Start

these encoding and decoding tasks without requiring much input from you. Using the tools in the program, it's fairly easy to format your text to be more interesting looking, add images, and have a good time at it, as shown in Figure 4.2.

▶ Encoding technologies are discussed in more detail in Chapter 11, "Messenger In-Depth," **p. 199** ■

**FIG. 4.1**
On top is a text document shown in NotePad, on the bottom, an MS Word document in NotePad. All the funny little codes and characters are part of Word's exclusive document format.

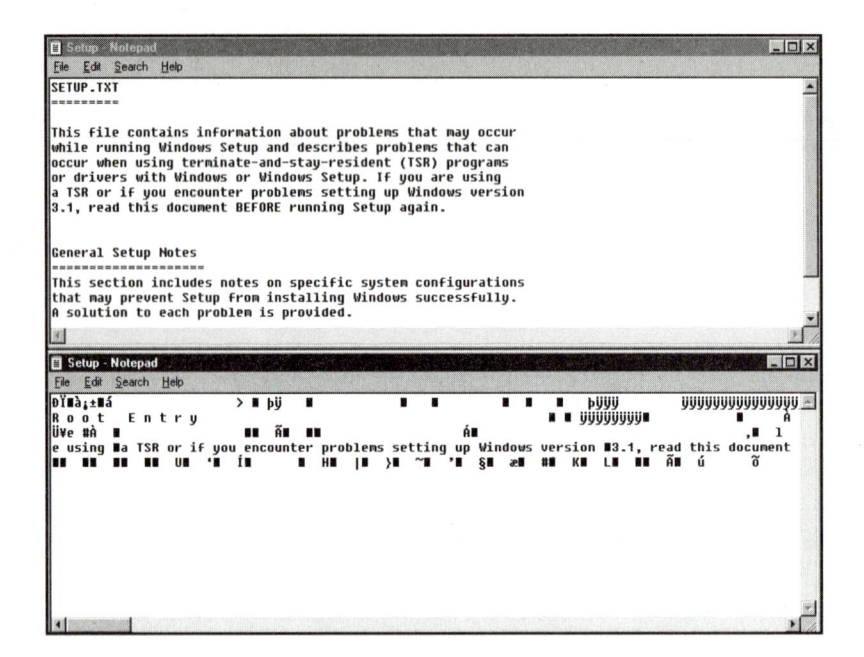

**FIG. 4.2**
Netscape Messenger is part of a new generation of e-mail programs that let you create attractive, easier-to-read e-mail messages.

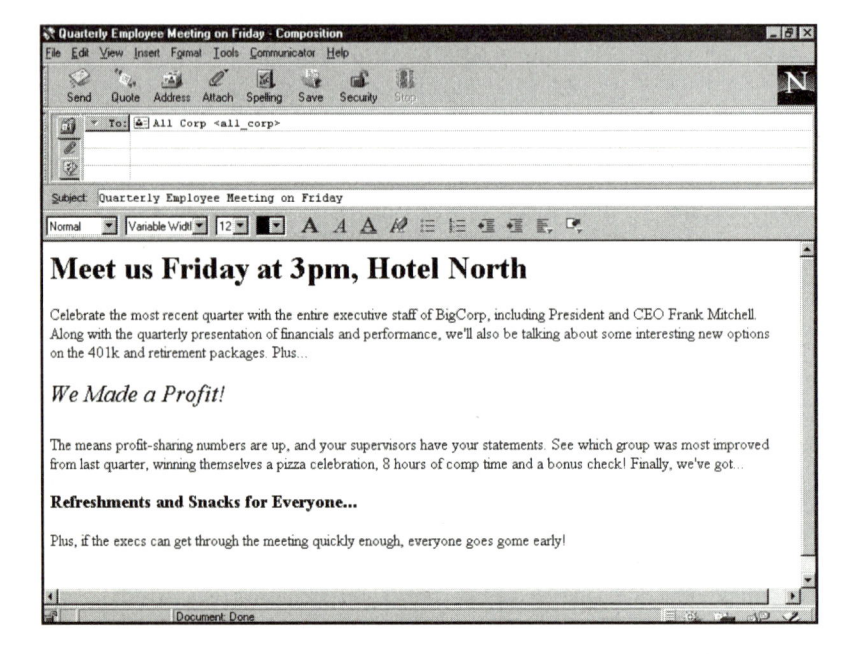

http://www.quecorp.com

## Accessing Messenger

To begin working with e-mail messages, you can access Messenger in a number of different ways:

- Double-click the Netscape Messenger icon in the Netscape or Netscape Communicator folder. Use the Program Manager in Windows 3.1 to find the Messenger icon, or open the Netscape Communicator folder in the Mac OS to find the Netscape Communicator icon. (There is no Messenger icon in the Mac OS version, so launch Communicator and then use option #3 or #4 to access Messenger.)

> **TIP** In Windows 95, a shortcut to the Communicator program appears on the desktop after a standard installation. Double-click that shortcut to open the folder and gain access to the Messenger icon.

- In Windows 95, choose Start, Netscape Communicator, Netscape Messenger.
- From the Netscape Navigator window in any OS version (or from other Communicator windows), choose the Inbox icon at the bottom of the Communicator window (see Figure 4.3).
- Choose Messenger Inbox from the Communicator menu when you're running any other Netscape Communicator module.

**FIG. 4.3**
Here are two of at least four ways to start Messenger.

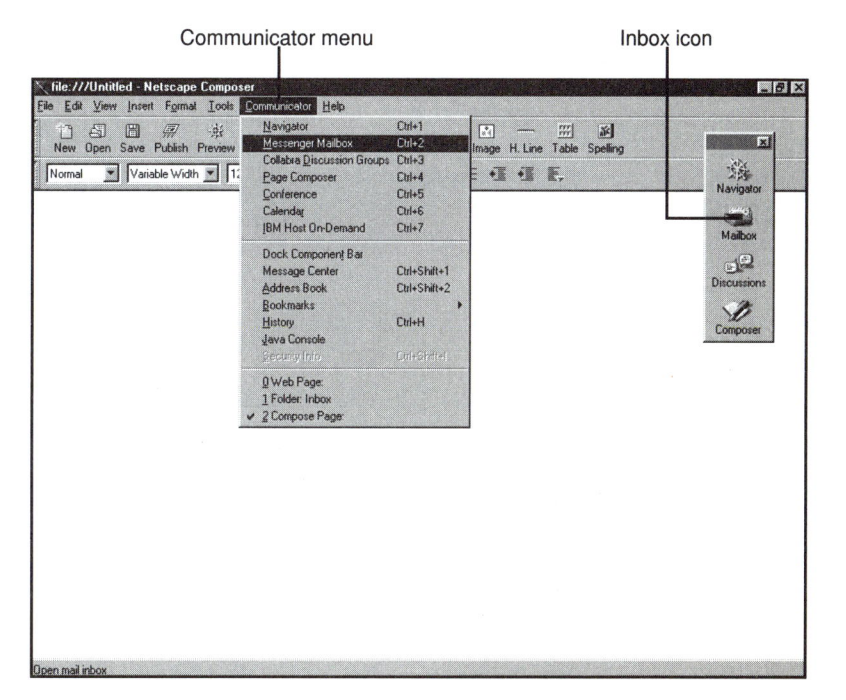

## Configuring Messenger

The first time you try to access your Messenger Inbox, you'll be presented with another series of setup screens. These are used to set the preferences specific to e-mail and *discussion groups*.

> **NOTE** As the Messenger setup screen points out, you can get back to these mail server and e-mail account settings by choosing Edit, Preferences in the main Messenger window if you've already been through them once. ■

Discussion groups? That's right—the Message Center in Communicator enables you to access not only your personal e-mail account, but also the UseNet discussion groups available over the Internet. These functions are generally accessed by choosing Communicator, Collabra Discussion Groups, which loads the Message Center, which then allows access to both e-mail and Internet discussions.

▶ For more on reading UseNet discussion groups in Communicator, see Chapter 5, "Collabra Quick Start," **p.71**

To set your preferences for e-mail and discussion groups, do the following:

1. Click the Next button after reading the first screen, which simply tells you that you need to configure your e-mail and newsgroup server addresses.

2. Enter or correct the personal information on this next screen, shown in Figure 4.4 (notice that Netscape fills in some of the info from your previous entries.) When you've filled in everything that's appropriate (entries like the Reply-To and Organization aren't necessary unless they're important to you), click Next.

**FIG. 4.4**
Your name and e-mail address are already entered—if you want to include your organization or specify a different Reply-To address, you can do so here.

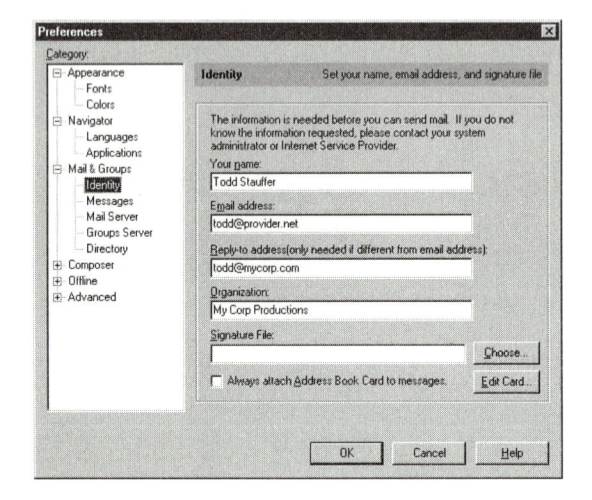

> **TIP** Your ISP or administrator should be able to tell you the address for your mail server. If whichever one you use doesn't, you can usually guess the server from your e-mail address—just take off everything before the @ symbol and substitute "mail." So, if your e-mail address is **you@yourcorp.com,** then my mail server is probably **mail.yourcorp.com**. It doesn't always work, but it's a good start.

3. Now you enter your mail user name (usually the user name for your ISP connection or your e-mail name) and the address for the incoming mail server (often, but not always, the same as your outgoing mail server). Figure 4.5 shows these entries.

**FIG. 4.5**
Here's where you enter the complete Internet addresses for your e-mail account.

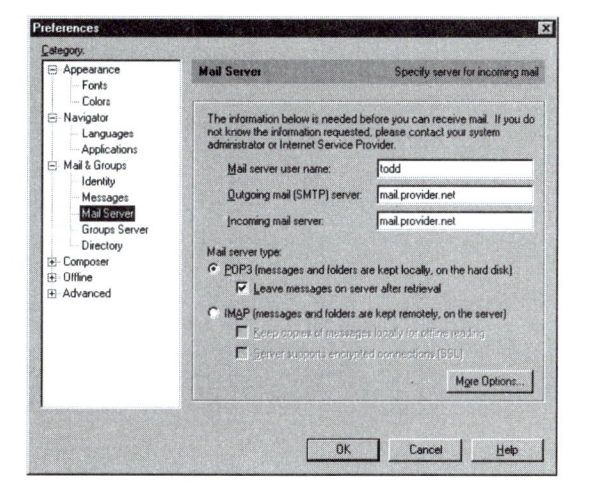

4. Then, choose the mail protocol your server uses and how you'd like mail stored. (Most ISPs uses POP3 and prefer that you store mail on your own PC, but your mileage may vary.) Click Next.
5. Finally, the last screen asks you simply to enter your ISP's news (discussion group) server address. This almost always works the same way mail server addresses do—substitute the word "news." for everything before the @ symbol in your e-mail address. In the previous example, it would be **news.yourcorp.com**. Click Finish.

## Checking Your E-Mail

Messenger should be running if you just finished setting it up. If it's not, go ahead and double-click its icon (in Windows Explorer or in the Mac's Finder) or choose Messenger in the Start menu. You should see the mail Inbox screen that allows you to download and read your mail.

To check for new mail, click the Get Msg button in the toolbar or choose File, Get Messages, New from Messenger's menu. You'll be asked for your e-mail account password; enter it and click OK. (The password is usually the same password you use for your ISP account.) If all

**56** | Chapter 4  Messenger Quick Start

goes well, Messenger will either present you with a message in the status bar that tells you there are no new messages or your new messages will begin downloading and appear in your Inbox, as shown in Figure 4.6.

> **TIP** If you're the only one who uses your computer (or you don't care if others have the ability to check your e-mail) you can have Netscape save your password for future mail checks. Select Edit, Preferences from the Messenger menu, then choose Mail Server. Click More Options, which is toward the bottom of the dialog box. Now check Remember my mail password and click OK.

**FIG. 4.6**
Messenger displays new messages in the Inbox interface. Click the name of a message in order to read it in the lower window.

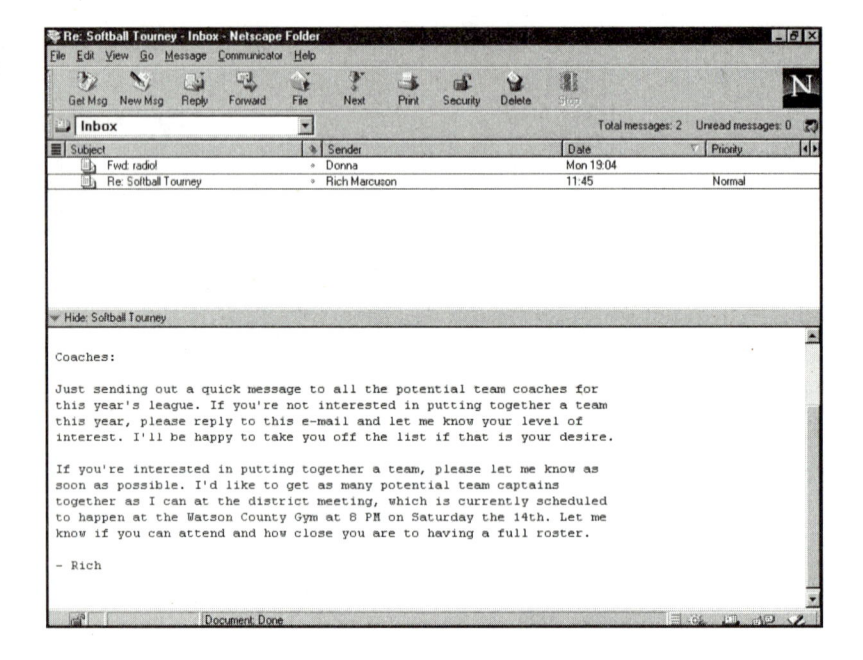

> **NOTE** If for some reason the connection fails, make sure of the following: First, check that your Internet connection is active and working correctly. Next, be careful that you're entering the correct password. Finally, go to Edit, Preferences and select Mail Server. Look these settings over and correct them if necessary.

## Reading Your Messages

If you have new messages waiting on the server, then they'll be downloaded to your computer and displayed in the Inbox. New messages have all of their information in boldface; messages you've already read but haven't yet moved from the Inbox appear in regular-style text, as shown in Figure 4.7.

Checking Your E-Mail   57

**FIG. 4.7**
Messenger makes clear what you have read and what still awaits your attention.

Old messages appear in regular text

New messages appear in bold

Click a message to read it

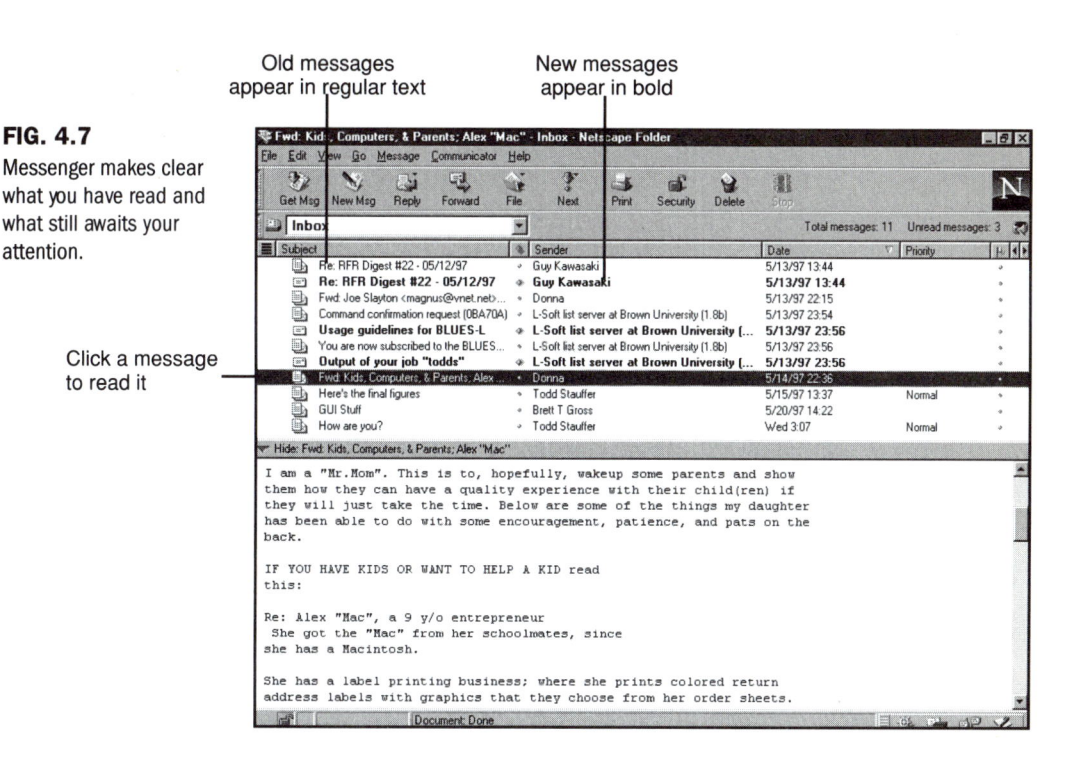

True to form, Messenger even offers you a couple of ways to read your messages. The basic interface, with its two different window panes for choosing and reading messages, can be very convenient for reading many messages in a quick sitting. Simply single-click a message you want to read and the text for that message appears in the bottom portion of the window. To move to the next message in the Inbox, you can simply hit the "down" arrow on your keyboard or you can choose Go, Next Unread Message from the menu.

> **TIP** In fact, if you read messages while they're in the Inbox, you can use the up and down arrow keys on your keyboard to move back and forth between messages, while the left arrow key moves you back to the top of your Inbox.

The other way to read messages is to double-click a message in the Inbox menu (or press Enter if the message is already highlighted). This brings up a full-sized window that includes the entire message text, which may make reading a particularly long message a bit easier, like in Figure 4.8.

To close the message and return to the Inbox, simply click the Close box in the upper-right corner (upper-left on Macs) when you're done reading.

Part
I

Ch
4

**58** Chapter 4 Messenger Quick Start

**FIG. 4.8**
You can bring up the full text of a message in its own window by double-clicking the message entry in the Inbox.

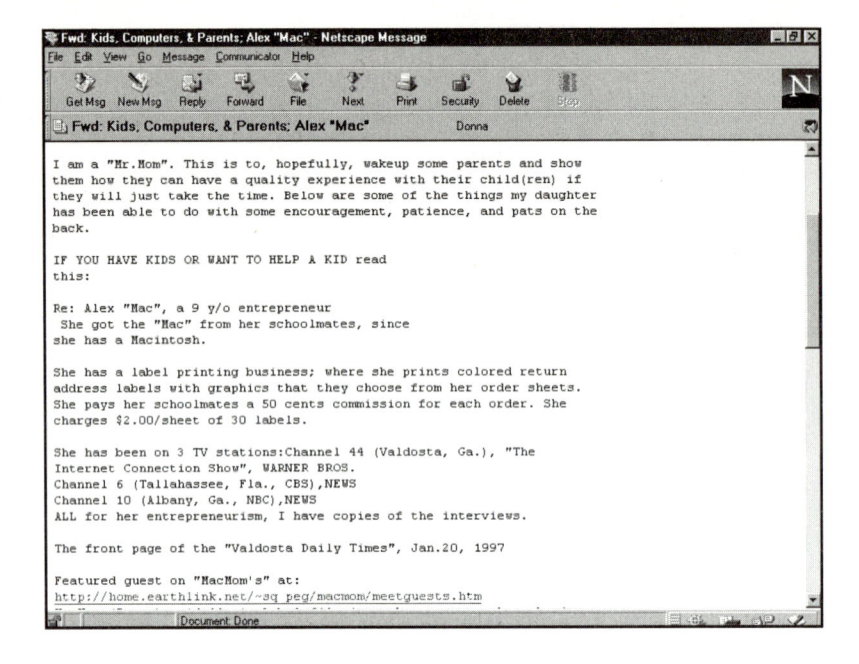

## Composing an E-Mail Message

Messenger uses a standard business memo-style interface to make creating an e-mail message straightforward. If you've ever written a formal memo, you have enough experience to create an e-mail message.

You can begin a new message one of two ways:

- Click the New Msg icon in the toolbar at the top of the screen, and choose File, New, Message from the Messenger menu.
- Choose Message, New Message from the menu.

Either way, the result will be a new Message Composition window, as shown in Figure 4.9.

**NOTE** In some versions of Communicator, the Message Composition window is called the Send Mail/Post News window. The two are basically identical, so don't let the name confuse you.

The first step is to enter an address for your main recipient—the person in the To: section of your e-mail memo. Enter an e-mail address for the recipient and press the Tab key.

**TIP** To begin, you need to enter the entire e-mail address for your recipient, in a form that follows the example: **friend@mycorp.com**. There are other more convenient ways to enter addresses, most of which involve the Address Book.

http://www.quecorp.com

Composing an E-Mail Message | 59

▶ Using the Address Book for saving addresses is discussed in Chapter 12, "Using the Address Book," **p. 731**

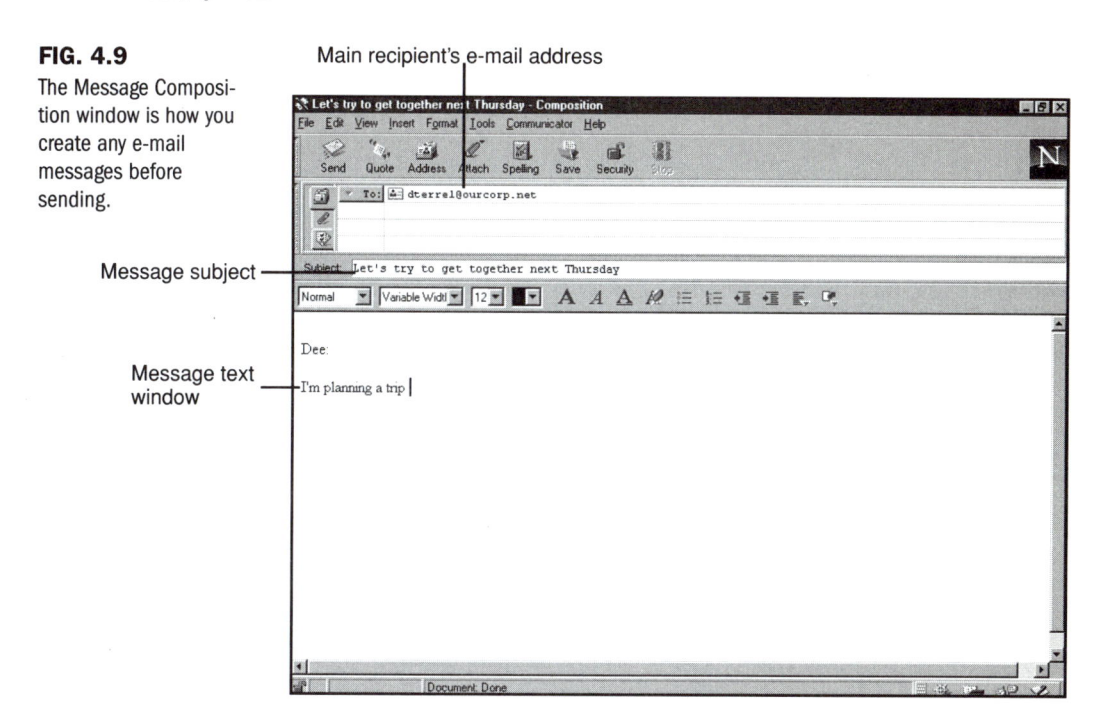

**FIG. 4.9**
The Message Composition window is how you create any e-mail messages before sending.

Main recipient's e-mail address

Message subject

Message text window

The insertion point (cursor) should now appear in the Subject line. Type a suitable subject for this e-mail message. Subjects should be reasonably short, but convey the matter and urgency of your message. "Hi!" is a pretty bad subject, while "Read now: Rumor Has It You're Fired" is a much better, clearer subject line. The best subject lines would fare well as newspaper headlines, including as many "who, what, when, where, why" elements as possible.

When you've finished your subject, press the Tab key.

**NOTE** If you try to send a message without a subject line, Netscape will prompt you to enter one.
If you refuse and send anyway, your recipient will get a message with the subject "No Subject."

Now's your chance to enter the message text. (There are certain etiquette conventions for creating e-mail messages—see the "Netiquette for E-Mail" sidebar later in this chapter.) Just start typing the message you want to send. Don't press Return at the end of each line—the text will wrap the same way it does in a word processing program. You only need to press Return (or Enter) when you want to start a new paragraph, as shown in Figure 4.10.

Just about everything you can type on your keyboard will work in a typical e-mail message, aside from special characters like typographer's (curly) quotes and non-English letters (in the English-language version of Netscape Communicator).

**FIG. 4.10**
You can decide whether to include "to" and "from" names in the message—some folks do, others don't.

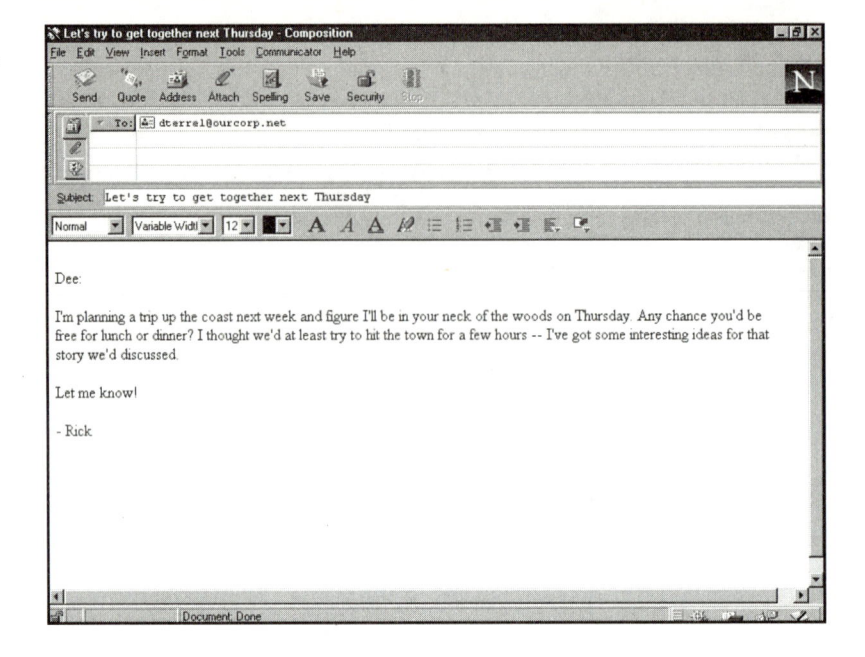

> **CAUTION**
>
> For now, you probably just want to leave your text as it is—plain. Using Netscape Messenger's special formatting features requires that you know something about your recipient's e-mail program and that you set some special preferences. A discussion of formatting e-mail messages appears in Chapter 11, "Messenger In-Depth."

### Netiquette for E-Mail

Over the years, people have figured out that it's possible to have a very curt, negative, or even misinterpreted "e-mail voice" that hampers communication between people, even if that isn't your intention. To avoid this, a couple of "Netiquette" rules—etiquette on the Internet—have been developed.

**Don't type in all-capitals.** In e-mail messages, typing in all caps is considered screaming. If you prefer, it's acceptable to type in all lowercase letters.

**Make your subject meaningful and your message brief.** If your message is unavoidably long, put "[Long]" after your subject; for example, "Notes on Recent Council Meeting [Long]." Also, remember to break longer messages into paragraphs, just as you would a business memo.

**Avoid spamming.** On the Internet, sending one message to thousands of people who haven't asked for it is called *spamming*. People tend to see "junk e-mail" messages as more intrusive and annoying than regular junk mail sent through the postal service. Most people pay for their e-mail service, and often don't want to pay to receive junk e-mail.

http://www.quecorp.com

> **Don't test your e-mail on unsuspecting book authors.** For that matter, don't test your e-mail on any public e-mail address. Instead, choose a friend who's willing to play "test the e-mail," or ask your ISP if they have a special test account. Some ISPs set up an account that will auto-respond to your test message, letting you know it was successful.

## Sending Carbon and Blind Copies

You may have noticed that you haven't actually sent that message you wrote a while ago. Well, you have a few more decisions to make before you send it off, including the possibility that you'd like to send it to some people in addition to the original addressee.

Just like a corporate memo, it's possible to "carbon copy" or CC your e-mail message to others. It's important to note that as far as your computer is concerned, the message is not changed when sent to your CC recipients. The only difference is in the message's appearance—CC recipients can view their name in the CC: header of their message, not in the To: section, as shown in Figure 4.11.

As far as you and your recipients are concerned, when you receive a CC'ed copy of an e-mail, it generally suggests that you're not required to respond. Instead, a CC is sent just "for your information."

> **TIP** You can also have more than one To recipient (either on their own lines in the header or separated by commas), which may suggest that both recipients (or more) should answer the message.

**FIG. 4.11**
The ability to send the message as a CC is more for humans than computers. If you want someone to see the message, but it's not directed toward them, send it as a CC.

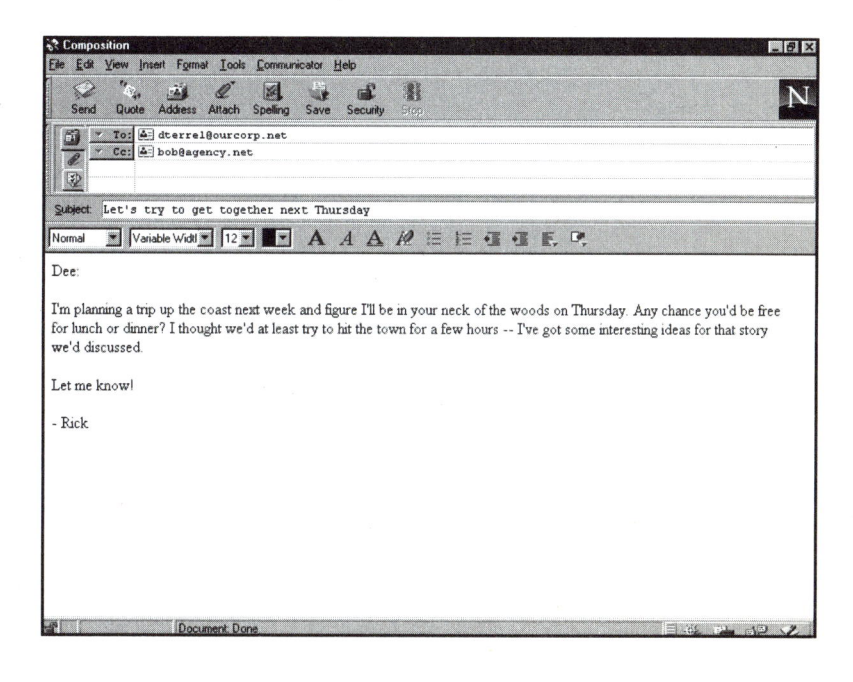

**62** Chapter 4 Messenger Quick Start

Blind Carbon Copy (BCC) does send the message in a slightly different way than CC. With a CC, anyone who receives the message will be able to see who the message was sent to and was CCed. BCC allows you to send a copy of the message to someone secretly.

For example, if you send a message to Jim, but BCC it to Mary, then Jim won't know Mary got a copy. If you just CC it to Mary, then Jim will be able to see Mary's e-mail address in the recipient header of the e-mail he receives.

> **CAUTION**
> Chances are you won't have a problem, but you should be aware that not all mail servers support BCC, instead turning them into CC addresses. That can be a problem if you're trying to keep your BCC recipients secret. You'll need to ask your system administrator for details.

## Adding Recipients to E-Mail Messages

To add recipients to your message, you can click the mouse pointer in the blank box directly below the last To: or CC: that currently appears. That should create a new line in the address header that allows you to enter another e-mail address. You can change the recipient's status (To, CC, BCC) by using the pull-down menu that appears when you click the current status (see Figure 4.12).

> **NOTE** To add an addressee in the Mac version of Messenger, click the Add button next to the address header box.

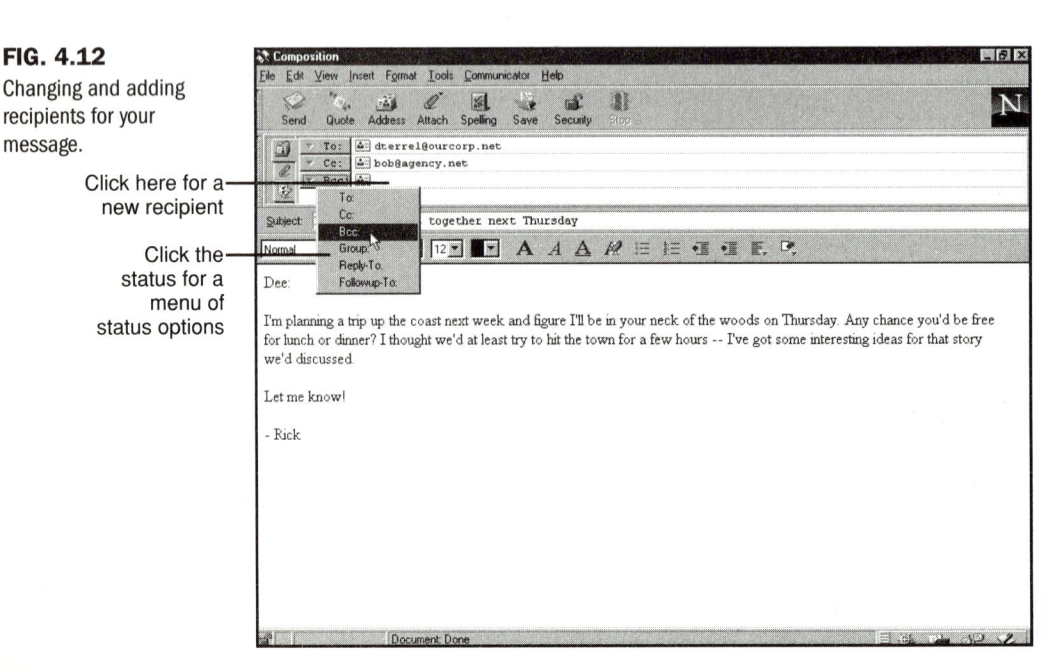

**FIG. 4.12**
Changing and adding recipients for your message.

Click here for a new recipient

Click the status for a menu of status options

http://www.quecorp.com

You can also delete a recipient that you've mistakenly created or no longer want to send a message. First, highlight the entire recipient address, then hit the Backspace key on your keyboard. This should delete the entire line. (On the Mac, the backspace key is generally labeled Delete.)

> **TIP** If the address disappears but the line remains, try pressing the Backspace key again. That should clear the entire line and place you on the line above it.

## Checking Your Spelling

Now that you've decided to CC your boss on all your work-related correspondence, it's probably important that you spell check your messages as well. (You might be able to come up with other reasons for "well-spelt" messages.) To do this, you simply select the Tools, Spelling command from the Message Composer menu. Messenger will automatically check the spelling of the text in your document.

> **CAUTION**
> Some versions of Messenger don't spell check the message subject. Realize that yours may not either—check your subject line carefully.

When the spelling checker encounters a word it believes is misspelled, it will present a dialog box that includes suggestions for changing the word (see Figure 4.13).

**FIG. 4.13**
You can select Spelling from the Tools menu at any time to check the spelling in the body of your message.

> **TIP** Some versions of Netscape Messenger also include a Spelling icon in the toolbar.

This works just like many of the spelling checkers in popular word processing programs. If one of the suggested spellings is correct, highlight it in the dialog box and click Change. If you know the correct spelling, you can edit the word at the top of the dialog and click Change to apply it. If you think you may have misspelled this word repeatedly, you can click the Change All button to correct every instance of this misspelling.

You can also choose to Ignore this word (and check the rest of the document), Ignore All occurrences of this misspelling, or Add the word to your custom dictionary. The menu next to the Add button can be used to change the custom dictionary you want to use for this message.

## Sending Your Message Now

Once your message is complete, and spell checking (along with any other final thoughts) has been done, you're ready to send. How you send, though, depends on whether or not you're currently connected to the Internet or if you're working "offline"—while you're not connected to the Internet.

> **TIP** Want a return receipt? Netscape can work with some other e-mail programs (and other copies of Netscape) so that you receive a quick e-mail receipt when your addressee downloads and reads your message. Choose the Options tab in the addressing area (just below the Attachment tab) and click the check box for Return Receipt.

If you're ready to fire this message off to its destination, then it's a simple matter. You can do one of the following:

- Click the Send icon in the toolbar
- Pull down the File menu and choose Send Now
- Press Ctrl+Enter (in Windows)

If you've added any HTML elements (special formatting, such as bold or list-formats) to your message, Messenger will ask you whether or not this message should be sent with the formatting intact. Make your decision and click OK (see the next section, "Choosing HTML or Plain Text Format" for help in making that decision).

## Choosing HTML or Plain Text Format

Whenever you send a message that has HTML text formatting in it (if you use the Bold, Font or List commands, for instance), Netscape will ask you if you really want to send the message with the formatting intact. The problem is that not everyone can read HTML-formatted messages in their e-mail program—only now are e-mail programs like Messenger being written to recognize HTML, the formatting language used to create World Wide Web pages.

> **NOTE** Messenger will not offer these options if you haven't used any HTML formatting commands in your message. Don't be alarmed if you don't see an HTML warning, especially if you haven't added any text emphasis or other HTML elements to your e-mail message.

So you have a number of options:

- You click Don't Send and re-edit the document so that it doesn't use any HTML formatting commands.
- You can choose to convert the message to plain text, an option that will allow anyone to read the message, but the message will no longer have the special text emphasis (bold, italics, and so on). This is probably the most basic choice, and the one you should choose if you're not sure of your recipient's e-mail capabilities. To do this, select the `Send in Plain Text Only` option and click Send, as shown in Figure 4.14.

http://www.quecorp.com

- You can send the HTML anyway, which is sure to annoy people who don't have the latest e-mail programs. HTML places many little codes (like `<b>these words are bold<b>`) to create the formatting. Reading a message filled with these codes is difficult. Choose the `Send in HTML Only` option and click Send.
- If you'd just like to stop worrying about it, go ahead and send the message as both plain text and HTML. The recipient will get two sets of the message body, one with HTML codes and one without them. Choose `Send in Plain Text and HTML` (it's the default setting) and click Send.

**FIG. 4.14**
Messenger gives you a number of options for how your messages will be formatted.

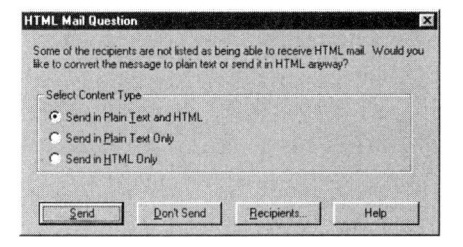

- If you happen to be sending the message to a user that you know has HTML e-mail capabilities, you can record their address as HTML-friendly. Click the Recipients option, then select their e-mail address and click the Add button shown in Figure 4.15. Click OK when you're done.
- Or, if you know that an entire company or organization can handle HTML-enabled e-mail, you can choose to have the entire group recognized as HTML-capable. Click Recipients, then select the `everybody@domain.ext` entry and click Add. Any message you send to this group (for instance, **aol.com** for the America Online service) will receive HTML-style e-mail messages (if you create them) without further prompting.

  ▶ HTML formatting is discussed at length in Chapter 11, "Messenger In-Depth," **p. 199**

**FIG. 4.15**
The Recipients dialog box allows you to store HTML-capable addressees and e-mail address domains.

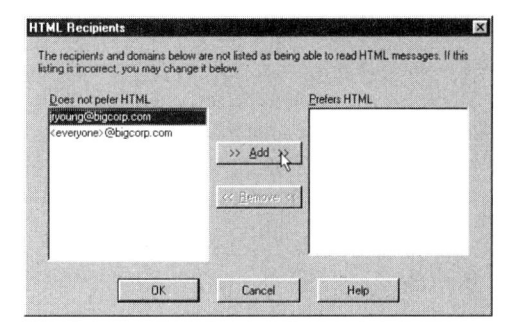

## Sending the Message

If you're using a modem-based PPP connection to access the Internet, it's possible to set your PPP software so that it connects to your ISP automatically whenever a software program (like Netscape Messenger) asks to be connected to the Internet. If you choose the Send Now command and you hear your modem fire up, your connection is already set this way.

That's all you have to do. Netscape will warn you if there's some trouble with your connection or with sending the mail. If you receive a `Netscape is unable to locate the server` error for instance, it probably means that your TCP/IP connection isn't running (see Figure 4.16). Invoke the connection (usually through a Dial-Up Networking shortcut on the Windows 95 desktop or through a PPP control panel on a Mac) and choose to send the message again once your connection is running.

**FIG. 4.16**
Messenger generates an error message if you can't get on the Internet—check to make sure your modem is on and your PPP connection has been activated.

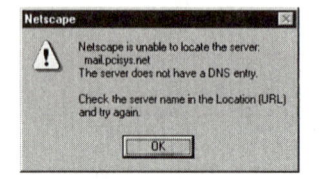

## Sending All Your Messages Later

Occasionally you find use for reading and writing your e-mail messages while you're not connected to the Internet—especially if you use a modem-based service that charges for the time that you're connected. If that's the case, it's a simple matter to bring up your PPP connection, check your e-mail, then close the PPP connection to avoid extra charges. Then you can read the mail in your Inbox at your leisure and even create new e-mail messages while you're disconnected.

The process is the same for writing an e-mail message whether you're online or offline—the only difference is in how you send the message. To place the messages in your Outbox in order to send them later (once you've connected), simply choose File, Send Later. If you've added any special formatting, you'll be asked the same questions about HTML formatting that are asked if you Send Now (see the section, "Sending Your Message Now," earlier in this chapter). Make your choice and click OK; your message is saved to the Outbox pictured in Figure 4.17.

To view messages in the Outbox, first return to the Inbox interface (using the Communicator, Messenger Inbox command or the Inbox icon at the bottom right of any screen). Then, in the pull-down menu below the toolbar, you can select the Outbox for viewing. Your screen should change to a listing of messages that are waiting to be sent. You can view them in the bottom window on the screen (just select the message with a single mouse click) or double-click the name of the e-mail to re-edit it.

**FIG. 4.17**
If you choose to Send Later, your message will be stored in the Outbox until you decide to sign onto the Internet and send it.

Choose Outbox here

Messages to be sent

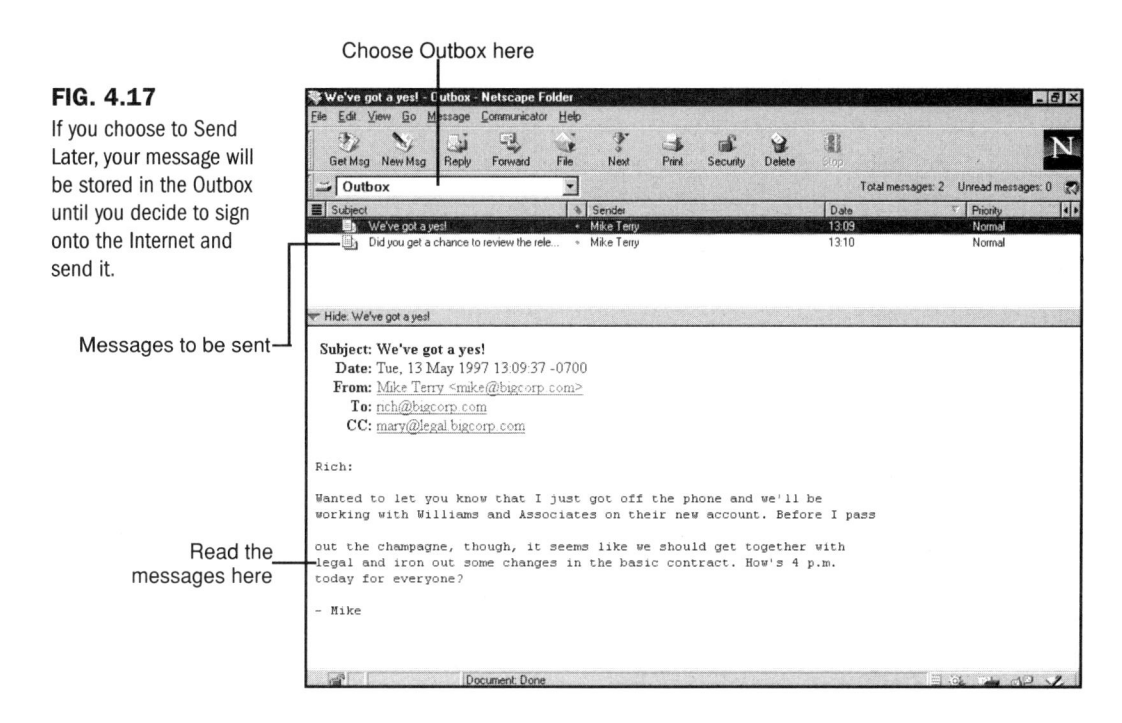

Read the messages here

If you're happy with what's to be sent, make sure your Internet connection is running (unless you know your PPP connection is set to be automatically invoked by Netscape) and choose the File, Send Messages in Outbox command from Messenger's menu. All your messages will be whisked away over the Internet to their destinations.

> **TIP** Since you're already online, you might as well check to see if any new messages have come in. Switch to the Inbox (use the pull-down menu) and click the Get Msg icon in the toolbar. (You can also use the Netscape Mail Notification utility, included with Communicator, which gives you the ability to check mail from an icon on the taskbar.)

Next stop: replying to messages. Hopefully you've gotten one or two—if not, create a message and send it to yourself (just type your own e-mail address on the To: line).

## Replying to E-Mail Messages

If you see a message in your Inbox that you feel warrants a response, it's easy enough to send one. Replying to an e-mail message is essentially the same as sending a regular e-mail message—the difference is, if done correctly, sending a reply is much simpler.

Begin by selecting the message in your Inbox by clicking the subject once. (If you've already double-clicked the message and you're reading it in a separate window, that's okay, too.) Now click the Reply button in the toolbar or select <u>M</u>essage, <u>R</u>eply, then choose to Sender or to Sender and All Recipients from the drop-down menu. What you choose depends on how many replies you want to send:

**Reply to Sender.** This reply will only go to the e-mail address listed in the From: or Reply-To: line of the original e-mail.

**Reply to Sender and all Recipients.** This reply will be sent not only to the originating party, but anyone else they sent the message to or CCed on the message.

> **TIP**
> You can also find the Reply commands in a context-sensitive menu (in Windows 95) that appears when you right-click a message in the Inbox.

After you choose how to reply, you're presented with the Composition window. It's just as if you were creating a new e-mail message, except the To: section is already filled in, as is the Subject line and some of the body of the message.

Why does Messenger fill in some of the body of the message? It's quoting the original text to which you plan to reply.

## Quoting the Sender in Your Reply

Quoting is an important part of e-mail netiquette, because it allows conversations to flow comfortably in e-mail without forcing your sender to call up his or her previous message and compare it with your answer (see Figure 4.18).

**FIG. 4.18**
When you choose to reply, Messenger quotes the entire original message for you.

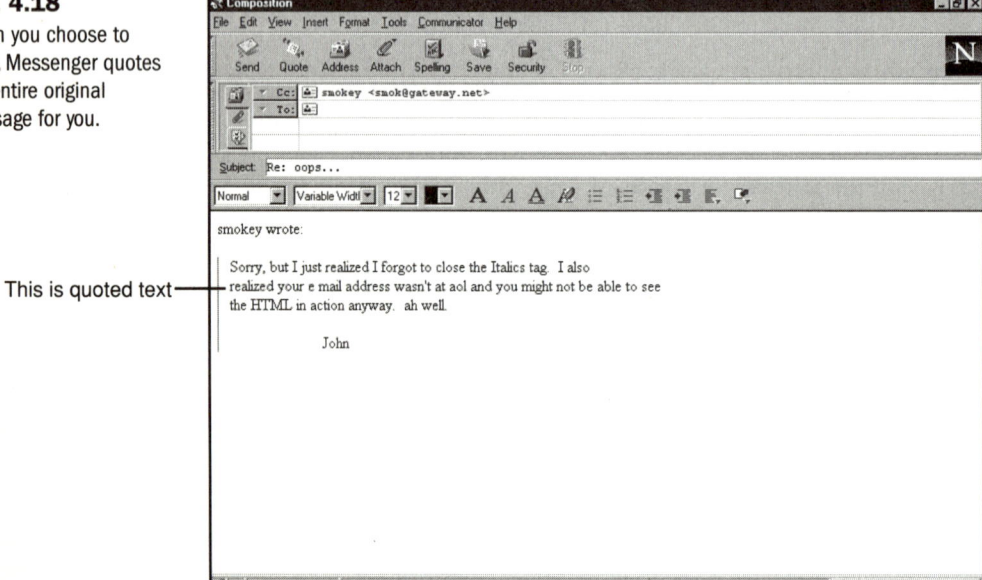

This is quoted text

Fortunately, with Netscape Messenger quoting is automatic by default. Whenever you hit the Reply button, the message originally sent is *quoted* in your reply—everything your recipient sent is copied into the reply, along with a special character that's placed at the beginning of each of their lines. Although they don't appear when you're editing your reply, the recipient will see a > in front of everything he or she originally wrote. They will also see the XX wrote: message at the beginning of their quote.

Now your job is to edit the quoted message so that the minimum to which you're interested in responding remains. Remember one of the main rules of netiquette: Keep it brief. It's not always useful or necessary to include the entire original message, even though Messenger does by default. If you take a moment or two to edit the quote down to its key points, life will be a lot better for your recipient.

> **TIP** You don't want to edit other people's work too much, but if you want to add a new Return in the message, try hitting Shift+Return. That will include the special "quote" mark and keep from adding too much space between the lines of quoted text.

Once you've formatted the quoted portion, you're ready to enter your reply. Simply type your reply after the end of the quoted material (see Figure 4.19). This is probably the most common and the most intuitive method. In English, people generally expect to read from top-to-bottom and see old-to-new information progress in that fashion. No need to confuse anyone.

**FIG. 4.19**
The typical e-mail reply. Quote the interesting bits, then type your reply below them.

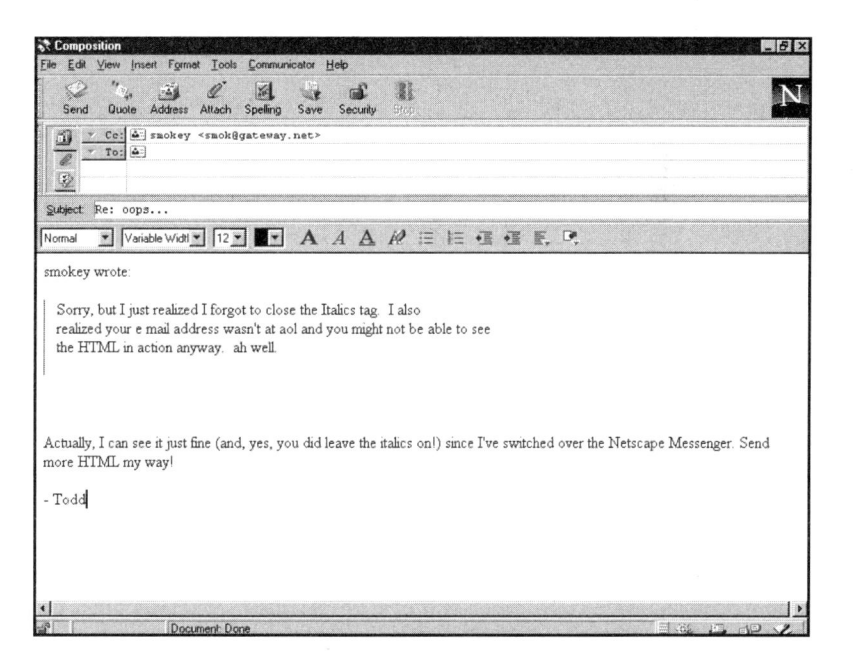

## Sending the Reply

You send a reply the same way you send a new e-mail message: It's as simple as clicking the Send button in the toolbar. If you don't want to send the message immediately, you can choose File, Send Later. The message will be sent the next time you sign on to the Internet. ●

CHAPTER 5

# Collabra Quick Start

*by Jerry Honeycutt*

Netscape designed Collabra to support workgroup discussions on a corporate intranet. In combination with Collabra Server software, Netscape says that Collabra provides "a powerful collaboration tool for corporations."

Collabra works quite well for browsing UseNet newsgroups, however. In fact, for this purpose, Collabra beats a majority of the newsreaders available today. It fully supports *NNTP* (Network News Transport Protocol), the protocol that newsreaders use to talk with news servers. Collabra provides the advanced features that UseNet junkies have grown accustomed to, such as offline reading and posting, advanced navigation, and much more.

This chapter introduces you to Collabra. It shows you how to set it up, how to download a list of newsgroups, and how to subscribe to your favorite newsgroups. It also shows you how to read, file, and reply to messages. You learn about Collabra's other features in Chapter 13, "Collabra In-Depth."

- **Set up Collabra so you can read UseNet messages**

  You can use Collabra to read UseNet newsgroups, or discussion groups, as Netscape calls them. Setting up Collabra to do this is a snap.

- **Subscribe to your favorite newsgroups**

  Your news server might contain thousands of newsgroups. This chapter shows you how to create a short-list of your favorite newsgroups.

- **Read and file newsgroup messages**

  Working with newsgroup messages is little different than working with Internet mail messages in Messenger.

- **Reply to newsgroup messages**

  Don't hoard all that information in your head. If you have something to add, share it with the other folks who frequent the UseNet newsgroups.

# Setup

Collabra has a few preferences that you must set before you can use it to browse the UseNet newsgroups. In most cases, you will have provided this information when you first started Communicator or when you set up your user profile. If you haven't yet supplied this information or you want to double-check the values that you have already supplied, use the steps in this section to set those required preferences. You learn about other preferences you can use to customize Collabra in Chapter 13.

To set up your preferences for Collabra, follow these steps:

1. Choose Edit, Preferences from Navigator or Collabra's main menu. Select Identity, under Mail & Groups on the left side of the Preferences dialog box (the Category), and you see the window shown in Figure 5.1.

**FIG. 5.1**
You use the Identity category to supply your name and mail address for Messenger and Collabra.

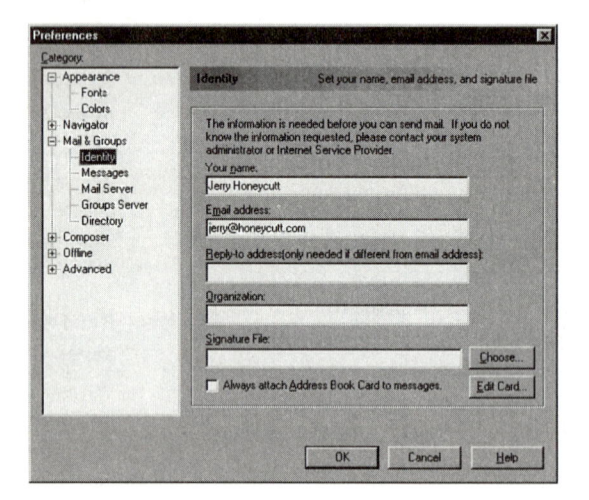

2. Type your full name in Your Name. The name you type in this field is what other users on UseNet see when they read your messages.

3. Type your Internet mail address in E-mail Address. Your Internet mail address looks something like *name@server.dom*. For example: jerry@honeycutt.com.

4. Select Groups Server, under Mail & Groups on the left side of the Preferences dialog box, and you see the window shown in Figure 5.2.

5. Type the Internet address of your news server in Discussion Groups (News) Server. This address looks something like *news.server.dom*. For example: news.onramp.net. If you don't know the address, contact your ISP or network administrator.

6. Click OK to save your changes.

**FIG. 5.2**
The Groups Server category specifies the NNTP news server with which Collabra will communicate.

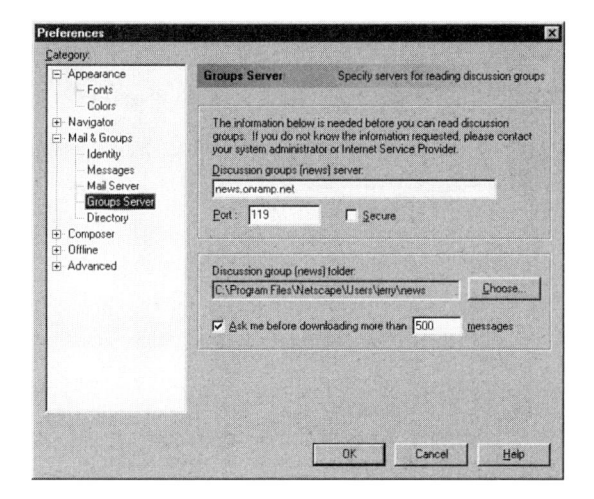

## Basics

When you start Collabra, you see the Message Center. This window is very similar to the windows in other Communicator components. However, it has a different Navigation toolbar, and the location toolbar works a bit differently. It's separated into several areas, which are identified in Figure 5.3 and discussed in the following list:

| | |
|---|---|
| **Menu** | You have access to all of Collabra's features using its menu. |
| **Navigation toolbar** | You use Collabra's Navigation toolbar to work with newsgroups, folders, and messages. |
| **Location toolbar** | The Location toolbar describes the user profile with which you're working. |
| **Status line** | Collabra uses the status line to display informational messages and one-line help about each menu entry and toolbar button. |
| **Progress indicator** | The progress indicator lets you know that Collabra is working. |
| **Component bar** | You use the Component bar to switch between Communicator modules. |

## Subscribing to a Newsgroup

Your news server can carry more than 16,000 newsgroups. You're probably only interested in repeatedly visiting a handful of those. That's like a needle in a haystack. If you had to wade through thousands of newsgroups to find those few that you're interested in, you'd quickly give up on UseNet and move on to something easier, like cork boards.

Fortunately, Collabra lets you subscribe to the newsgroups that you frequent. Then you can see the newsgroups to which you subscribe in a list separate from the thousands of other newsgroups. Here's how to subscribe to newsgroups:

**Chapter 5** Collabra Quick Start

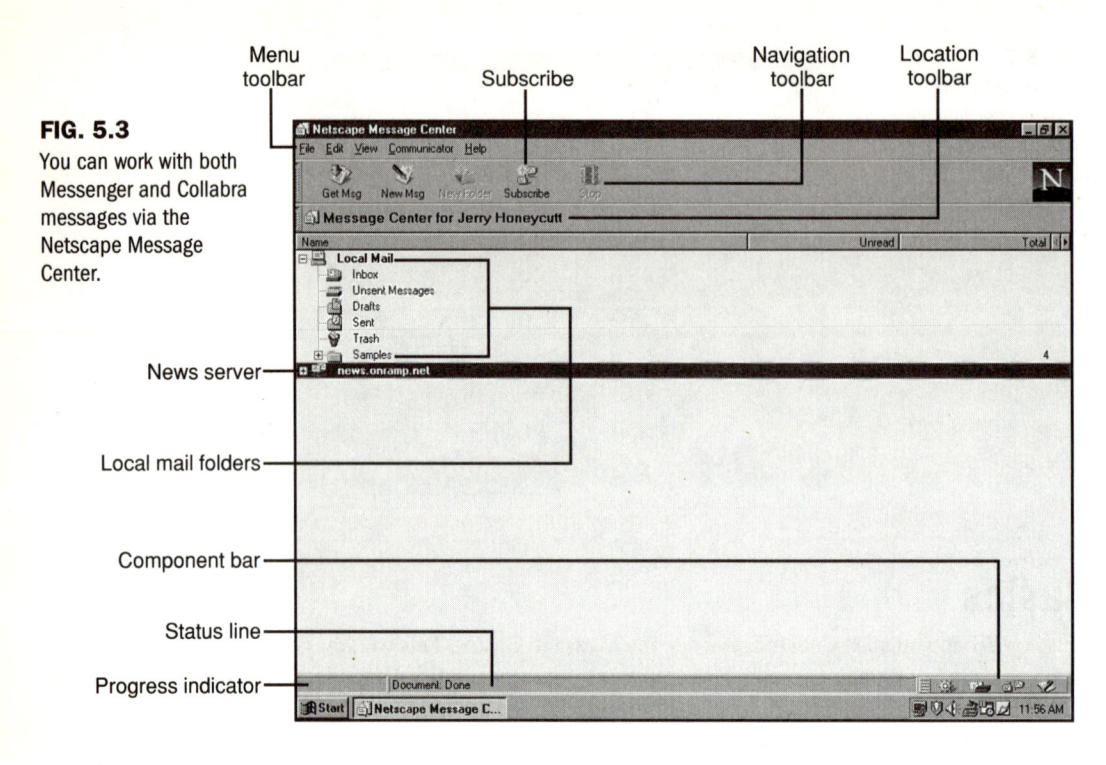

**FIG. 5.3**
You can work with both Messenger and Collabra messages via the Netscape Message Center.

Labels on figure: Menu toolbar, Subscribe, Navigation toolbar, Location toolbar, News server, Local mail folders, Component bar, Status line, Progress indicator.

1. Click the Subscribe button in the Navigation toolbar. Collabra displays the Communicator: Subscribe to Discussion Groups dialog box and immediately starts downloading the list of newsgroups available on your news server. After Collabra is finished, the Communicator: Subscribe to Discussion Groups dialog box looks similar to Figure 5.4.

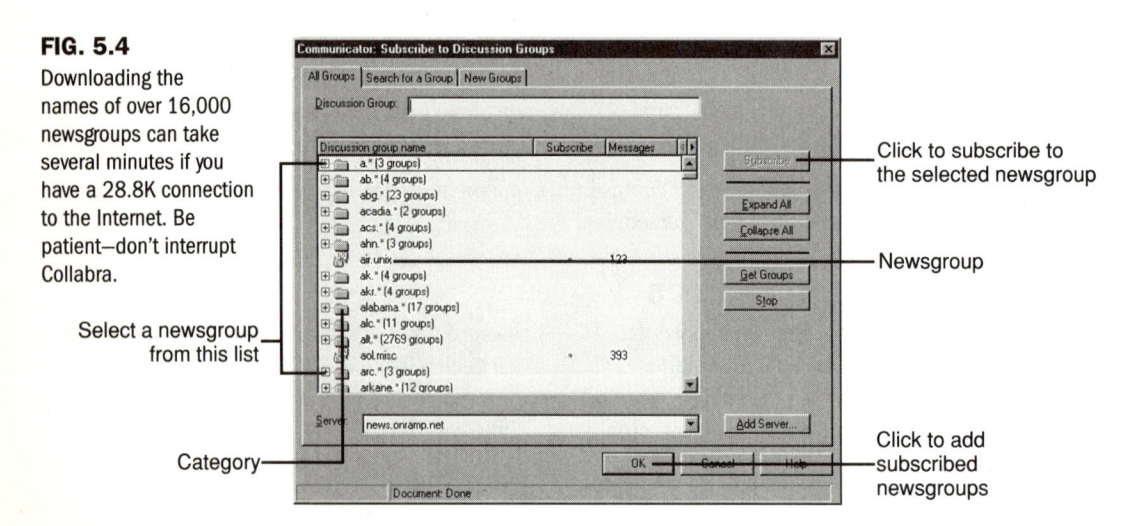

**FIG. 5.4**
Downloading the names of over 16,000 newsgroups can take several minutes if you have a 28.8K connection to the Internet. Be patient—don't interrupt Collabra.

Labels on figure: Select a newsgroup from this list, Category, Click to subscribe to the selected newsgroup, Newsgroup, Click to add subscribed newsgroups.

http://www.quecorp.com

2. Select a newsgroup to which you want to subscribe. Collabra displays the list of newsgroups in a hierarchical list. Click the plus sign (+) next to a category to see the subcategories and newsgroups available underneath it. Collabra displays a folder icon next to a newsgroup category and a discussion icon next to actual newsgroups.
3. Click Subscribe and Collabra places a check mark next to the newsgroup to which you've subscribed.
4. Click OK and Collabra adds the newsgroup to which you subscribed to the Message Center. In the Message Center, you see a plus sign (+) next to the news server in the Message Center. Click the plus sign to see the newsgroups to which you've subscribed.

**TIP** You can subscribe to more than one newsgroup at a time by repeating Steps 2 and 3 before completing Step 4.

**NOTE** The list of newsgroups you see on your UseNet server will most likely be different from the ones you see in these instructions. Every news server carries a different set of newsgroups, depending on the choices made by the administrators. Also note that downloading a list of newsgroups this large can take quite a while: several minutes if you're using a 28.8K connection.

## Reading Newsgroup Messages

To see the messages contained in a newsgroup, you have to open that newsgroup in a discussion window. To do this, double-click the newsgroup name in the Message Center. As a result, you see the discussion window shown in Figure 5.5. This window is organized much like Communicator's other windows. It has the Navigation and Location toolbars, the status line, the progress indicator, and the Component bar.

The discussion window is organized so that you can browse newsgroup messages quickly. It's separated into two portions, each of which is called a pane. The top pane (message pane) shows a list of message *headers*, which describes the subject, author, and date, for each message in the newsgroup. You can scroll this list up and down to see the message headers that aren't visible in the list. Select a newsgroup in the top pane, and Collabra displays the contents of the message in the bottom pane (body pane).

Notice that some of the message headers have plus signs (+) next to them or have message headers indented underneath them. This indicates that replies have been posted to that message. To see the replies, click the plus sign next to a message header and select one of the replies. Note that all of the messages indented under a message, including the original messages, are called a *thread*. By indenting the messages in a thread, Collabra makes following the conversation easier.

After you've read the message, you can select another message or you can use the Next button in the Navigation toolbar to get around. When you click the Next button, Collabra displays a drop-down menu that gives you several choices. Table 5.1 describes the most useful choices.

**FIG. 5.5**
The buttons in the Navigation toolbar apply to the message that's selected in the window's top pane.

Message headers — Message thread — File button — Next button

Contents of selected message

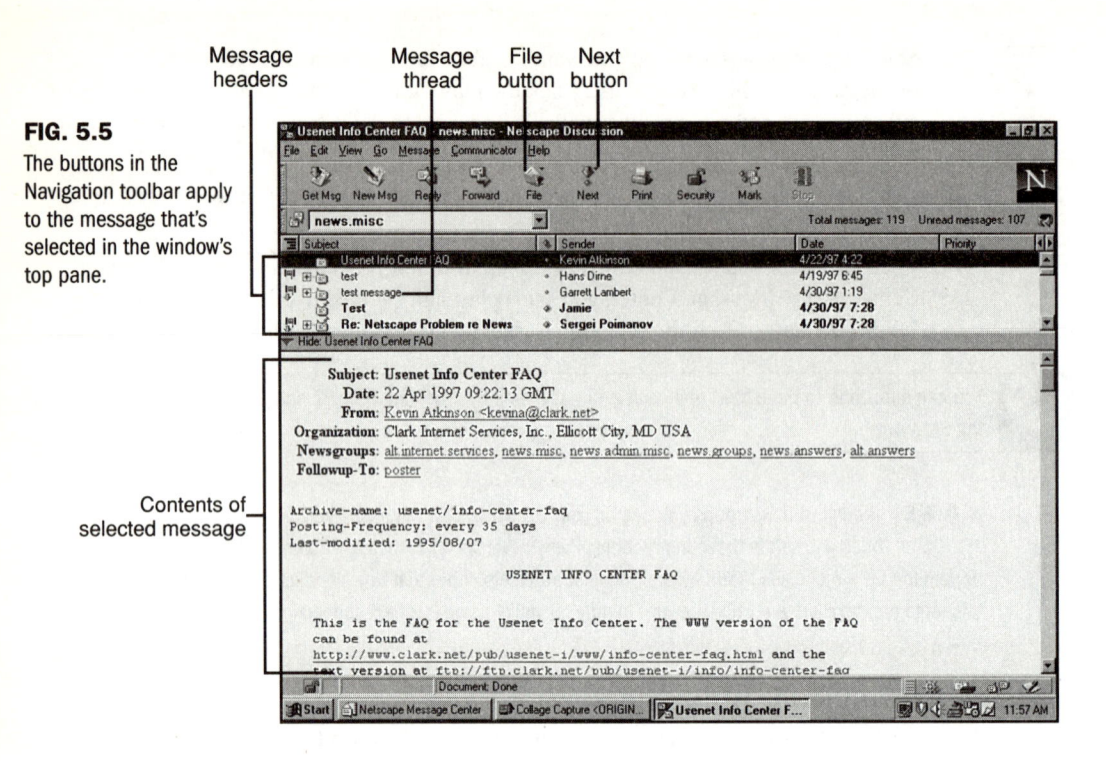

### Table 5.1  The Next Button's Drop-Down Menu

| Item | Description |
| --- | --- |
| Next Message | Reads next message |
| Next Unread Message | Reads next unread message |
| Next Unread Thread | Reads next unread thread |
| Next Group | Opens next subscribed newsgroup |
| Next Unread Group | Opens next unread subscribed newsgroup |

> **TIP** The best newsgroup in which to start out is **news.newusers.questions**. You can get your questions answered and try your hand at posting messages without anyone flaming (sending you a nasty message) you for doing so.

## Filing a Newsgroup Message

You might encounter newsgroup messages that you want to save in your local mail folders. You store newsgroup messages in the same folders that you use for Internet mail. To save a message in your mail folder, follow these steps:

http://www.quecorp.com

1. In the discussion window, select the message you want to file.
2. Click the File button in the Navigation toolbar and choose the local mail folder to which you want to file the message. If a mail folder has subfolders, selecting that mail folder drops down a submenu that contains an entry for each subfolder.

## Replying to a Newsgroup Message

If you have something to add to someone else's newsgroup message, you can post a reply. You might want to be helpful and answer someone's question. You're just as likely to find an interesting discussion to which you want to contribute. Either way, you can reply to a message two different ways: to the group or to the sender.

**Reply to Group**   If you want your reply to be read by everyone who frequents the newsgroup, post a follow-up message. Your reply is added to the thread. To post a follow-up message, follow these steps:

1. Click Reply in the Navigation toolbar, and you see a drop-down menu.
2. Choose Reply to Group or press Ctrl+D. Notice that the message is preaddressed to the newsgroup.
3. Type your reply in the body of the Composition window and click the Send button in the Message toolbar.

**Reply to Sender**   If your reply benefits only the person who posted the message, respond with an Internet mail message instead. That person gets the message faster, and the other newsgroup readers aren't annoyed. To reply to a message with an Internet mail message, follow these steps:

1. Click Reply in the Navigation toolbar, and you see a drop-down menu.
2. Choose Reply to Sender or press Ctrl+R. You see the same Composition window, except that Collabra preaddresses the message to the individual instead of the group.
3. Type your reply in the body of Composition window and click the Send button in the Message toolbar.

---

### Stay out of Trouble—Follow the Rules

Etiquette, as Miss Manners will tell you, was created so that everyone would get along better. Etiquette's rules are not official rules, however; they're community standards for how everyone should behave. Likewise, *netiquette* is a community standard for how to behave on the Internet. It's important for two reasons. First, it helps keep the frustration level down. Second, it helps prevent the terrible waste of Internet resources by limiting the amount of noise. Keep these points in mind while you're posting messages:

- Post your articles in the right place. Don't post questions about Internet Explorer, for example, to a newsgroup dedicated to Netscape Communicator.

*continues*

*continued*

- NEWSGROUP READERS REALLY HATE IT WHEN YOU SHOUT BY USING ALL CAPS. It doesn't make your message seem any more important.
- Don't test and don't beg for e-mail. There are a few places where that is appropriate, but this behavior generally gets you flamed (a *flame* is a mean or abusive message).
- Don't spam. *Spamming* is posting an advertisement to several, if not hundreds, of newsgroups. Don't do it. It's a waste of Internet resources.
- Don't cross-post your article. This is a waste of Internet resources, and readers quickly tire of seeing the same article posted to many newsgroups.

CHAPTER 6

# Composer Quick Start

*by Jerry Honeycutt*

You use Composer to write Web pages. It's a simple HTML editor that supports all of the basic Web publishing capabilities, such as text, lists, images, tables, and so on. If you've ever written HTML, you'll appreciate that Composer frees you from the tedium of countless brackets and obscure acronyms. If you've never seen a line of HTML in your life, open a Web page in Navigator, and choose View, Page Source from the main menu. You then get a perspective on how complicated HTML can be. For example, you use the <B> and </B> tags to format text using bold characters.

Composer works much like a word processor. You type text in the editor, format text using a variety of tools, and create links using a simple dialog box. Composer provides other tools, too, which you use to accomplish a variety of publishing tasks. Whereas creating a Web page by hand might take several hours, you can create the same Web page in a few minutes with Composer. ■

### Set up Composer for the first time
This chapter shows you how to get your Composer configuration just right—the first time.

### Work with text and images in your Web page
You don't have to know a lick of HTML in order to create simple Web pages with Composer.

### Create links to other Internet resources
Link your Web page to other Internet resources so you can be a part of the World Wide Web.

### Save and publish your Web page to the Internet
No one can see your handy work if you don't publish your page on the Internet. This chapter shows you how to upload your page to an ISP (Internet Service Provider).

# Setup

Composer has a small number of preferences that you can set in order to personalize it. You'll learn about some of those preferences here, and you'll learn about the rest later in this chapter.

1. Choose Edit, Preferences from Navigator or Composer's main menu. Select Composer on the left side of the Preferences dialog box (the Category), and you'll see the window shown in Figure 6.1.

**FIG. 6.1**
You can access Composer preferences from any module in Communicator.

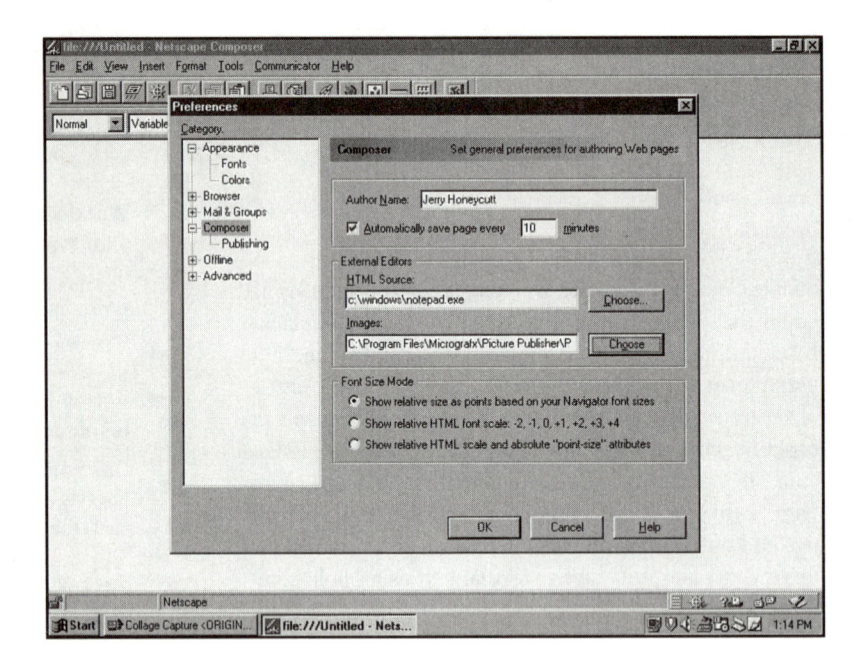

2. Type your full name in Author Name. This is your name as you want it to appear inside of the HTML files that Composer generates.

3. Select Automatically save page every if you want Composer to automatically save your work, or deselect it if you don't want Composer to automatically save your work. If you choose to have Composer automatically save your work, in the space provided, type the number of minutes you want Composer to wait between each time it saves your work.

4. Type the path of your favorite text editor in HTML Source. This is the editor you'll use to edit the HTML source by hand in those cases where Composer doesn't support an HTML feature you want to use. You can click Choose to pick a file from the Choose HTML Editor Application dialog box.

5. Type the path of your favorite image editor in Images. This is the image editor you'll use to edit the graphical images in your Web page. You can click Choose to pick a file from the Choose Image Editor Application dialog box.

http://www.quecorp.com

6. Select a font size mode, as described in the following list:

   **Show relative size points based on your Navigator font sizes**—Displays font sizes in points, such as 10pt or 12pt.

   **Show relative HTML font scale: –2, –1, 0, +1, +2, +3, +4**—Displays font sizes in a relative scale, where 0 is normal, +1 is a bit bigger, -1 is a bit smaller, and so on.

   **Show relative HTML scale and absolute "point-sizes" attributes**—Displays font sizes using both points and a relative scale.

7. Click OK to save your changes.

# Basics

To explorer Composer's window, make sure that you have opened it on your desktop so you can follow along. It wouldn't hurt if you maximized the window, too. Take a look at Figure 6.2, which shows the full Composer window. This window is separated into several areas, which are identified in the figure and discussed in the following list:

| | |
|---|---|
| **Menu Bar** | You can access all of Composer's features using its menu bar. |
| **Composition Toolbar** | You use the Composition toolbar to perform ordinary tasks such as saving and printing a file, or inserting a picture into a Web page. |
| **Formatting Toolbar** | You use the Formatting toolbar to manipulate the format of the text on the Web page. For example, you can change the text's font or center it on the page. |
| **Status Line** | Composer uses the status line to display informational messages, and to display online help about each menu entry and toolbar button. |
| **Progress Indicator** | The progress indicator lets you know that Composer is working. For example, while saving a file, you'll see an image move across the progress indicator. |
| **Component Bar** | You use the Component bar to switch between Communicator modules as described earlier. |

## Create a Blank Page

The easiest way to create that first Web page is to create a blank page in Composer. Little did you know, you create a blank Web page every time you start Composer.

However, you can create a blank page any time, even if you have a Web page already open in Composer. Click the New Page button on the toolbar and then click **B**lank Page; or choose **F**ile, New, Blank **P**age from Composer's main menu. You'll see a new, blank Web page as shown in Figure 6.2.

**82** Chapter 6  Composer Quick Start

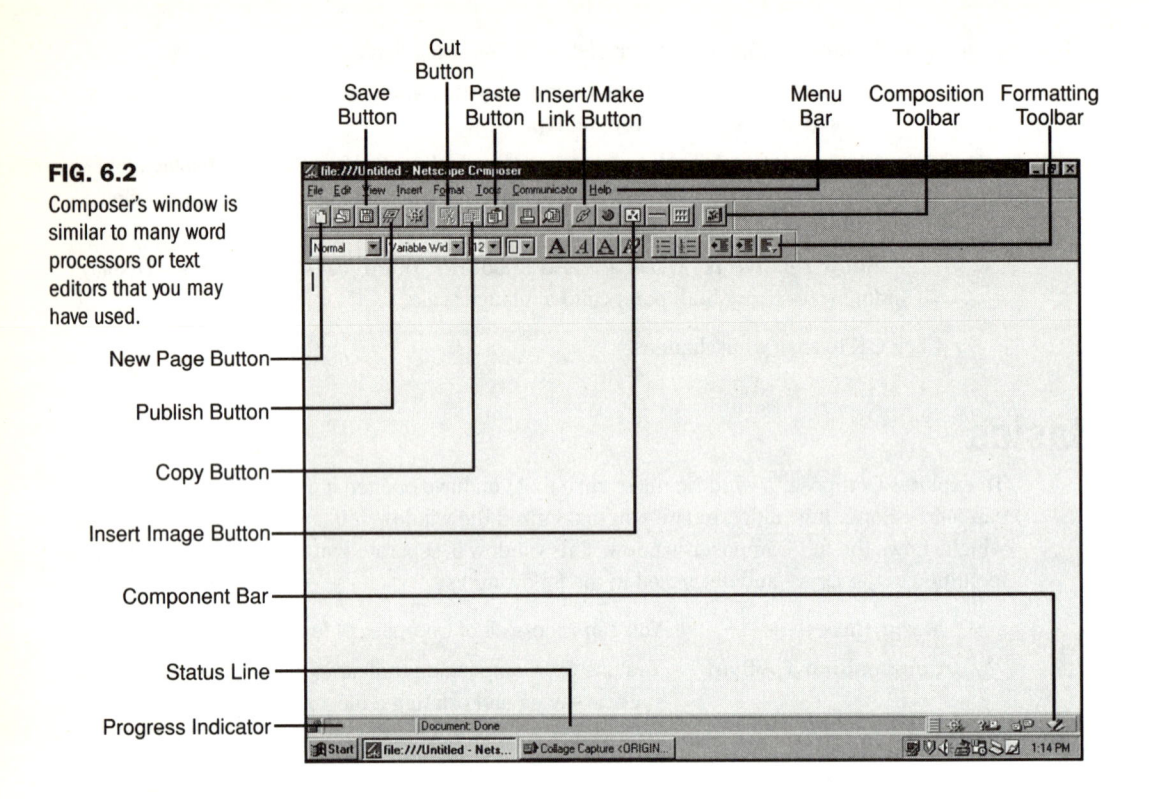

**FIG. 6.2**
Composer's window is similar to many word processors or text editors that you may have used.

Labels on figure:
- Save Button
- Cut Button
- Paste Button
- Insert/Make Link Button
- Menu Bar
- Composition Toolbar
- Formatting Toolbar
- New Page Button
- Publish Button
- Copy Button
- Insert Image Button
- Component Bar
- Status Line
- Progress Indicator

## Add Text to Your Web Page

To add text to your Web page, just start typing. You'll notice a blinking cursor in the editor window. This is the *insertion point*, which indicates the location at which Composer will insert any text you type. You're not limited to adding text at the current insertion point. That is, you can move the insertion point by clicking anywhere in the Composer window. For example, type some text in the Composer window; then, move the mouse cursor into the middle of the text. You'll notice that the mouse pointer changes to an I-beam, which indicates that you can click to move the insertion point to that location.

While you're editing text in Composer, you can use a variety of keys to move the insertion point, too. Table 6.1 describes many of the keys that you'll use.

**Table 6.1  Keys that Move the Insertion Point**

| Key | Description |
| --- | --- |
| Up-arrow | Move one line up |
| Down-arrow | Move one line down |
| Left-arrow | Move one character left |

http://www.quecorp.com

| Key | Description |
| --- | --- |
| Right-arrow | Move one character right |
| Ctrl+left-arrow | Move one word left |
| Ctrl+right-arrow | Move one word right |
| Home | Move to the beginning of the line |
| End | Move to the end of the line |
| Ctrl+home | Move to the beginning of the file |
| Ctrl+end | Move to the end of the file |
| Page-up | Move one screen up |
| Page-down | Move one screen down |

Aside from the keys that you can use to move the insertion point, you can use a few other keys to not only move the insertion point, but also to break lines or add tabs. Table 6.2 describes these keys.

**Table 6.2   Other Keys You Can Use in Composer**

| Key | Description |
| --- | --- |
| Enter | Break the line at the insertion point |
| Tab | Insert a tab at the insertion point |

**Deleting Text**   You won't want to keep everything you type in the Composer editor. You'll need to correct spelling mistakes, or you'll change your mind about a bit of text you typed in haste. If you're only going to delete a few characters or a few words, the easiest thing to do is to position the insertion point to the left of the first character you want to delete, and then press the Delete key to delete each character until you're done.

Deleting a larger chunk of text character by character is pretty tedious, though. So you'll want to do a block delete. Select the block of text you want to delete. Then, press the Delete key once to remove the entire block. That's all there is to it.

> **TIP** You can let Composer automatically check your Web page for spelling errors. See Chapter 14, "Composer In-Depth," for more information.

**Changing Text**   Changing text works just like deleting text. You can delete the text as described in the previous section and then start typing at the insertion point. Alternatively, you can highlight the block of text you want to change, and then just start typing. The text you type will replace the highlighted block of text.

**TIP**  Composer doesn't have an overtype mode (as do word processors such as Microsoft Word) in which each character you type replaces the character immediately to the right of the insertion point.

**Moving Text**   Remember the first time you ever used a word processor? I bet you were amazed that you could just move blocks of text around on the screen, instead of having to retype or rewrite the entire document. You can do the same thing in Composer, using two different methods:

**TIP**  If you right-click (Windows 95 users only, by the way) on a text selection, you can choose Cut or Copy from the pop-up menu. Likewise, you can right-click anywhere on your Web page and choose Paste to paste the contents of the clipboard at that location.

- You can drag-and-drop text from one location in your Web page to another. You can also drag-and-drop text from other applications into your Web page.
- Cut-and-paste works very similar to drag-and-drop, except that you don't have to have a mouse. Instead, you cut or copy the text you want to the clipboard, and then paste the clipboard where you want to insert the text.

**Undo and Redo Changes**   After you've been editing your Web page for a while, you're bound to make a change that you regret. It happens all the time. You can undo any change you make by pressing Ctrl+Z, or by choosing Edit, Undo from Composer's main menu.

Undo only reverses the most recent action. That is, if you just deleted a block of text, undo will replace the text. If you just typed a block of text, undo will remove it. If you just replaced a block of text, undo will replace the new text with the previous text.

**TIP**  If you've made a whole bunch of changes that you regret, you won't be able to use Undo to reverse them. The easiest way out is to quit Composer without saving the file.

Once in a while, you'll undo something and then regret it. In those cases, you can redo your changes by pressing Ctrl+Shift+Z, or by choosing Edit, Redo from Composer's main menu.

## Add an Image to Your Web Page

Images add a lot of pizzazz to a Web page. They make a dull, uninteresting, text-only Web page have more appeal by giving the reader's eyes something to look at.

Most of the time, you'll want to insert an *inline* image into your Web page (as opposed to linking to an image). A Web browser displays inline images on the Web page, right there with the Web page's text. Figure 6.3, which itself is an inline image, shows you a Web page that uses inline instead of linked images.

http://www.quecorp.com

**FIG. 6.3**
Inline images are better than linked images because the user can see the image in relation to the text.

Inline image

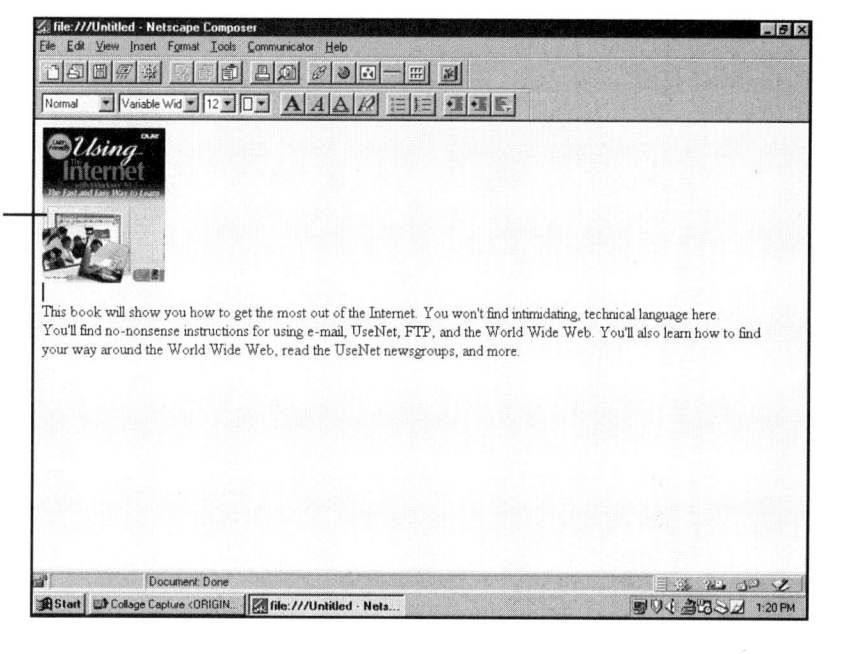

> **TIP** Linked images do have one really good use. You can put a small version of an image, called a thumbnail, on the Web page and then link the thumbnail to a larger version of the image. This helps users see the image faster, while those users who have faster Internet connections can see the larger image if they want to.

Ready to learn how to insert an image into your Web page? Make sure you have an image ready to insert (use GIF or JPEG images), and follow these steps:

1. Position the insertion point at the location where you want to insert an image.
2. Click the Insert Image button on the Composition toolbar, or choose Insert, Image from the main menu. You'll see the Image Properties dialog box shown in Figure 6.4.
3. Type the path and file name of the image in Image location; or, click Choose File to browse your computer for an image file.
4. Click OK, and Composer will insert the image at the insertion point, as shown in Figure 6.5.

**86** | Chapter 6  Composer Quick Start

**FIG. 6.4**
When you insert an image that's in a location other than the folder containing the Web page, Composer makes a copy of the image in the Web page's folder.

Path or URL of the image

Select if you don't want Composer to copy the image

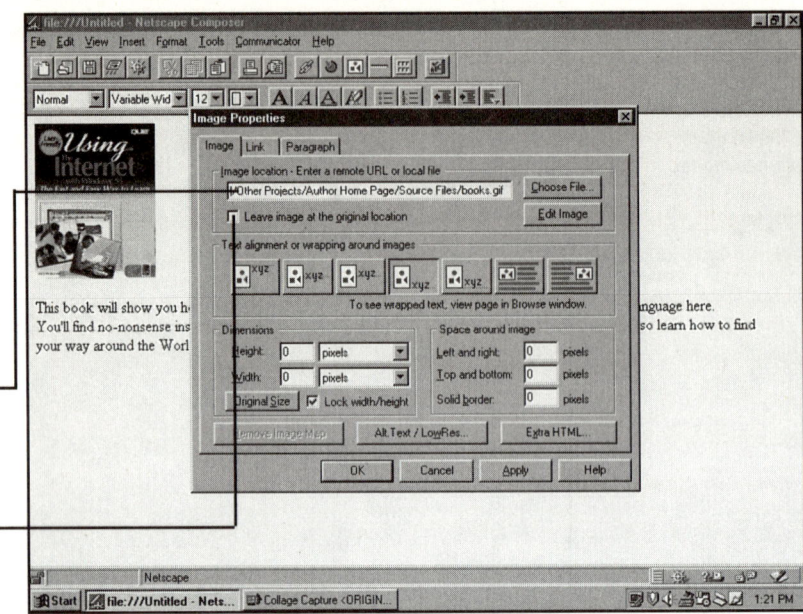

**FIG. 6.5**
Composer, and most Web browsers, align the bottom of the text with the bottom of the image.

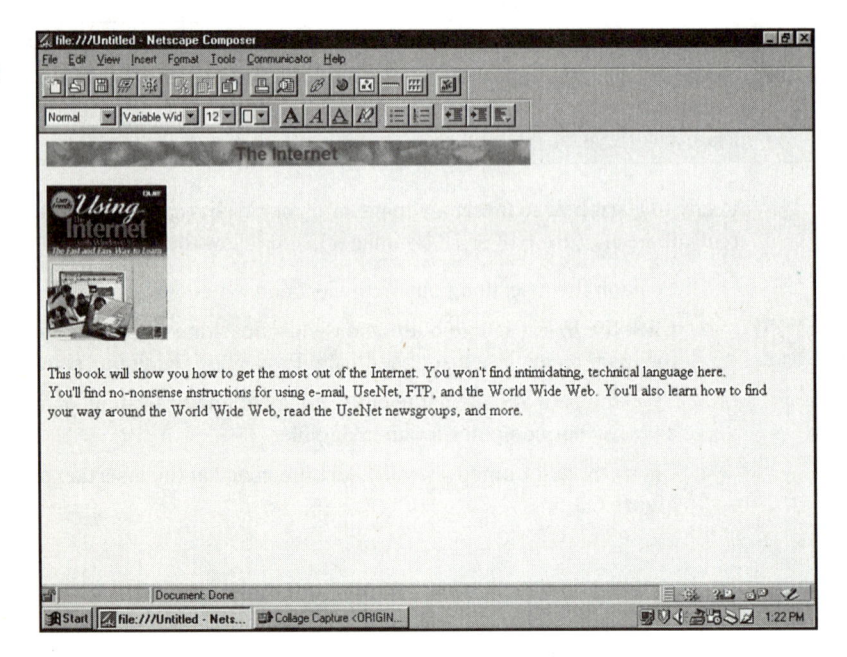

http://www.quecorp.com

## Working with Links on Your Web Page

With Composer, you don't have to write any HTML in order to add a link to your Web page. A few mouse clicks are all it takes to get things going; then, you type the URL of the Web page to which you're linking and click OK. That's all:

1. Select the text or image that you want to use as the anchor for a link.
2. Choose Insert, Link from Composer's main menu; or click Insert/Make Link in the Composition toolbar. You'll see the dialog box shown in Figure 6.6.

**FIG. 6.6**
The Link tab on the Character Properties dialog box shows you the text that you're using as the anchor.

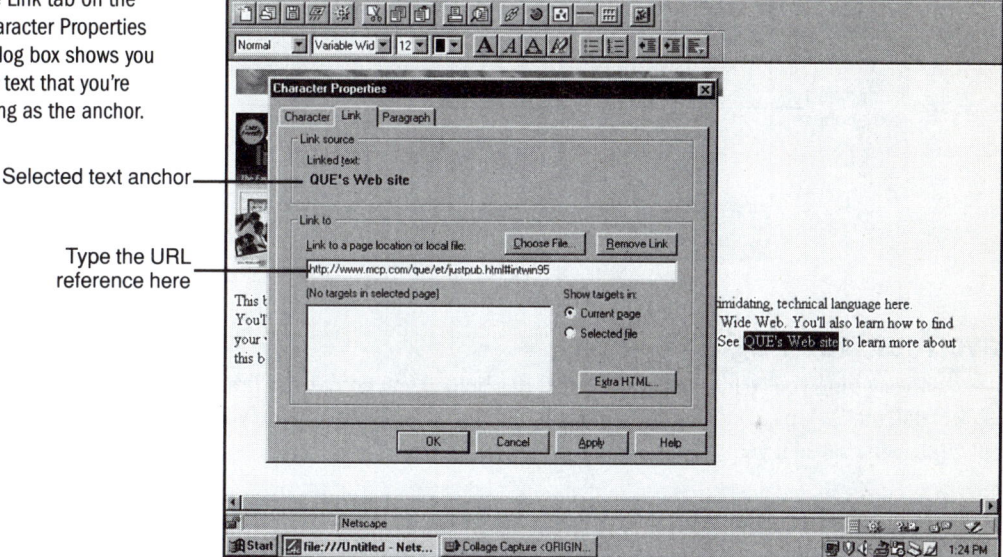

Selected text anchor

Type the URL reference here

3. Type the URL reference for the link in Link to a page location or local file. An URL looks something like **http://www.server.com/webpage.html**. Remember that an URL reference can refer to another Web page, an e-mail address, an FTP site, and so on.
4. Click OK, and you'll notice that the text anchor is now underlined (see Figure 6.7).

You can try out your new link in Composer by right-clicking it, and choosing Browse to. You'd be better off trying this example in Navigator by using the Preview option in Composer, so you can make sure the browser opens the specified Web page as expected.

**FIG. 6.7**
The user's Web browser will also underline the text anchor so that she can recognize it as a link.

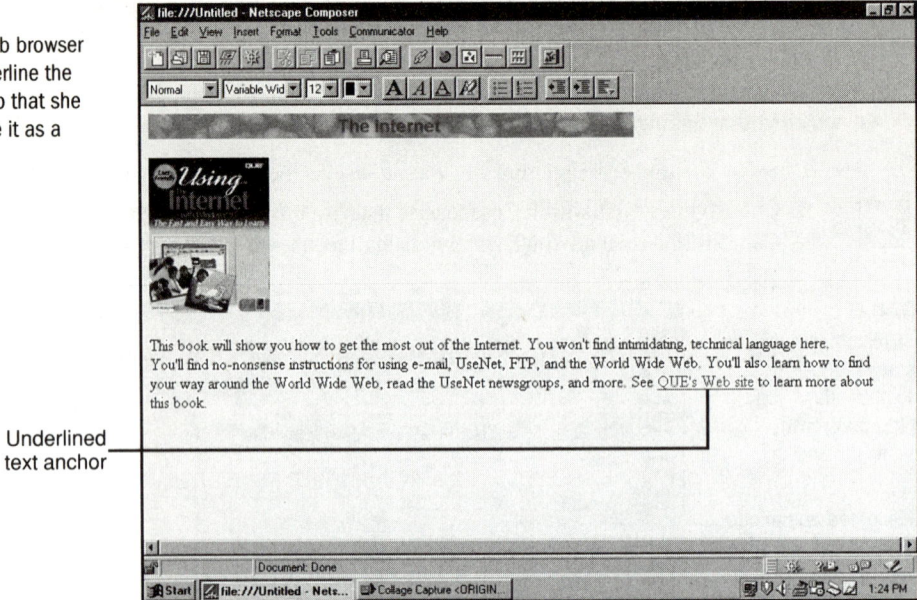

Underlined text anchor

## Save Your Web Page

Everything you've learned to this point has helped you create that first Web page. When you did, the Web page existed in Composer, but not as an HTML file on your hard disk because you haven't saved it yet.

Saving a Web page you create in Composer works like saving a document you create in Notepad or most other programs. In this case, however, you save your Web page as an HTML file on your computer. You choose File, Save As from the main menu. You probably already know how to do it. Just in case, however, the following steps show how to save your Web page:

1. Click the Save button in the Composition toolbar; or, choose File, Save As from Composer's main menu. You'll see a dialog box that looks like Figure 6.8.
2. Choose the folder in which you want to save the file, and type the file name you want to give to your Web page in File name.
3. Click Save; then, type a title for your Web page (as seen in the browser's title bar), and click OK to save your Web page. Composer saves the Web page, and copies any images that you inserted from a different location.

> **TIP** If you've been working on your Web page for a while without saving it, Composer will eventually ask you if you want to save your work (refer to "Setup," earlier in this chapter). Click Yes to save your work, or click No to continue working without saving your work.

http://www.quecorp.com

**FIG. 6.8**
Composer saves files using the HTM file extension; even though it says HTML in Save as type.

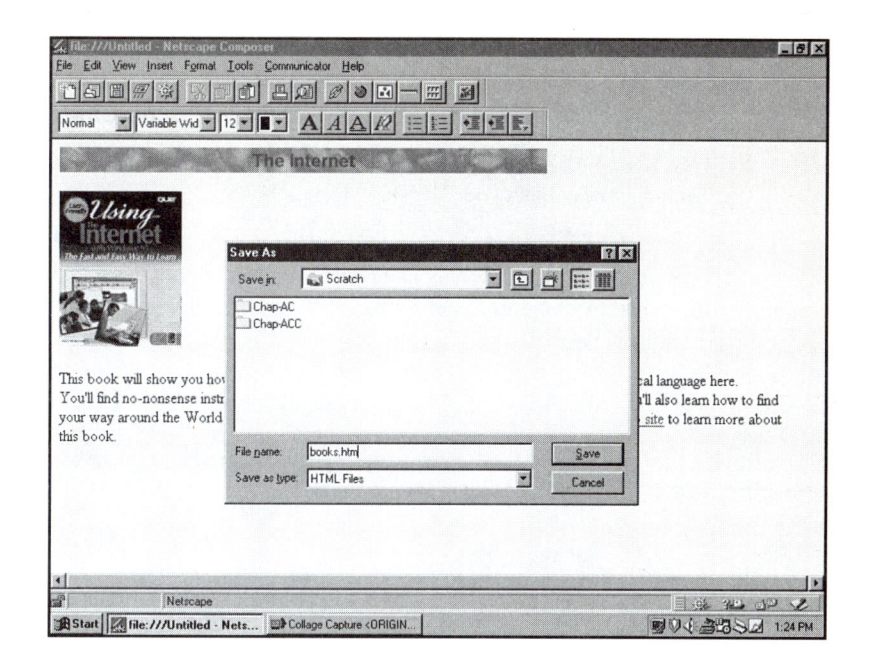

## Publishing Your Web Site with Composer

Now that you have a Web page, you're ready to publish it on the Internet. You first need to contact your ISP to find a home for your Web page and you need to configure Composer to publish your Web site. You can then actually use Composer to upload the files to the ISP's Web server.

**Find a Home**   Contact your ISP to make sure that you have Web space available. You can check your ISP's homepage or you can ring the support line (most ISPs don't like these types of calls, though). As well, your ISP might have sent you instructions when you first signed up for service; check those.

Your ISP is probably using UNIX. This is important for five reasons:

- You'll probably use FTP to upload your Web site to the Web server.
- You'll probably use your PPP username and password to access the FTP server. Your PPP username is the name you type when you first log onto the ISP.
- You'll probably upload your Web to the path `/public_html`.
- You'll probably give your homepage the file name `index.html`.
- You'll probably browse your Web at **http://*www.isp.com/~name***, where ***www.isp.com*** is the host name of your ISP's Web server and ***name*** is the username you use to log onto the ISP (your PPP username).

Just to make sure, though, you should verify each of the above items with your ISP. That is, you need to make sure you know the FTP address to which you'll upload files, the username and password you'll use to access the FTP server, and the URL you'll use to browse your Web.

**Set the Publishing Preferences** Once you've gathered all of this information, you can configure Composer to publish your Web site. Here's how:

1. Choose <u>E</u>dit, P<u>r</u>eferences from Composer's main menu, and select Publishing in the left list (<u>C</u>ategory). Publishing is under Composer so you might have to click the plus sign (+) next to Composer in order to see it. As a result, you'll see the dialog box shown in Figure 6.9.

**FIG. 6.9**
Don't change the settings under Links and Images as they're set to support remote publishing.

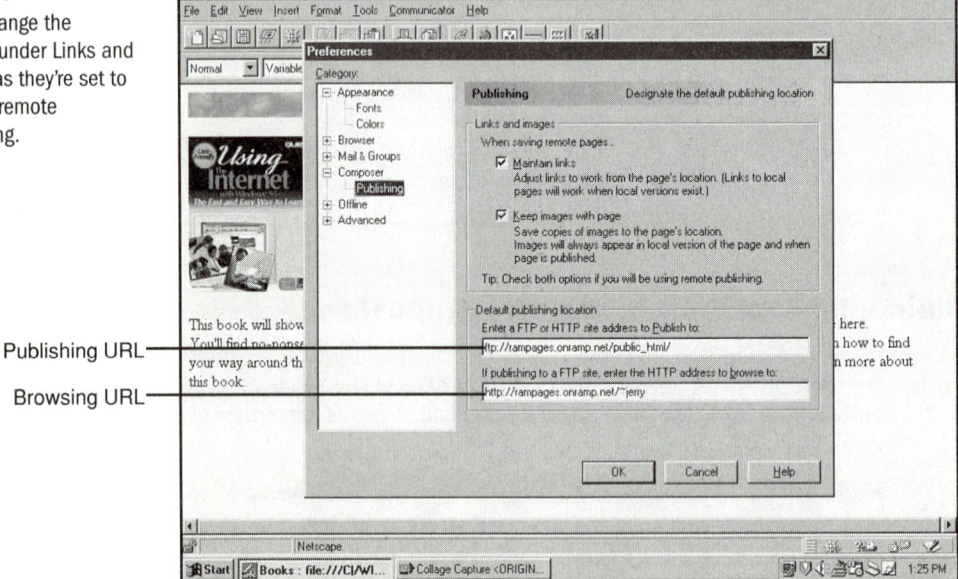

Publishing URL
Browsing URL

2. Type the URL to which you'll upload files in Enter a FTP or HTTP site address to <u>P</u>ublish to. This is usually an FTP address. Make sure that you include the full path and end the path with a forward slash (/). Look at Figure 6.9 to see an example that uses the path /public_html.

3. Type the URL that you'll browse to view your Web site in If publishing to a FTP site, enter the HTTP address to <u>b</u>rowse to. This is an HTTP address and probably includes your username as shown in Figure 6.9.

4. Click OK to save your changes.

**Upload Your Web Site to the ISP** After all that, you're now ready to upload your Web site to the Internet (can you hear the drum roll?). You've already configured the address to which you're publishing. The only thing left to do now is follow these steps:

http://www.quecorp.com

1. Open the Web page that you want to publish in Composer. You can only upload one Web page at a time, including all of its images, so you have to repeat these steps for each.
2. Click the Publish button on the Composition toolbar; or choose File, Publish from the main menu. You'll see the Publish Files dialog box shown in Figure 6.10.

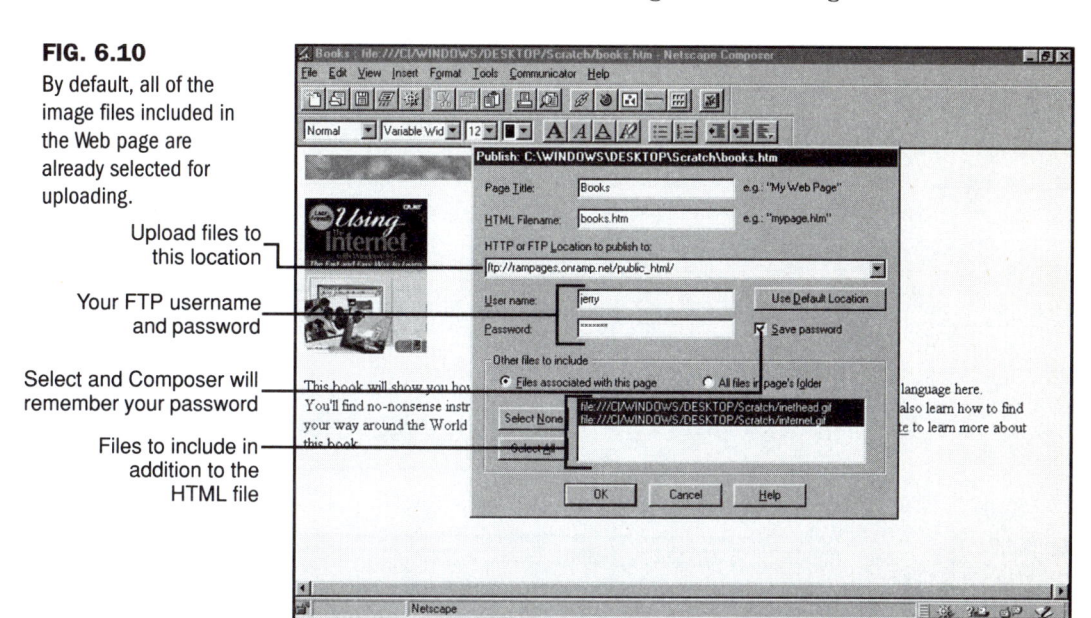

**FIG. 6.10**
By default, all of the image files included in the Web page are already selected for uploading.

- Upload files to this location
- Your FTP username and password
- Select and Composer will remember your password
- Files to include in addition to the HTML file

3. Type the title of the Web page in Page Title if you want to use a different title than you specified when you saved the page.
4. Type the file name of the HTML in HTML Filename. If you've already saved the file, Composer prefills this field with the current file name.

**TIP** If you called your homepage HOME.HTM on your computer, you can use `index.html` on the Web server by changing the file name in HTML Filename.

5. Click Use Default Location, and Composer will enter the publishing URL in HTTP or FTP Location to publish to.
6. Type your username and password in the space provided, and click OK. You'll see the Security Information dialog box shown in Figure 6.11.
7. Click Continue to close the Security Information dialog box and start uploading your files to the FTP server. As Composer uploads each file, you'll see the Publishing Document dialog box shown in Figure 6.12. After Composer finishes uploading your files, it will report that it finished successfully.
8. Click OK to close the successful completion report.

**FIG. 6.11**
If you don't ever want to see this dialog box again, deselect Show This Alert Next Time.

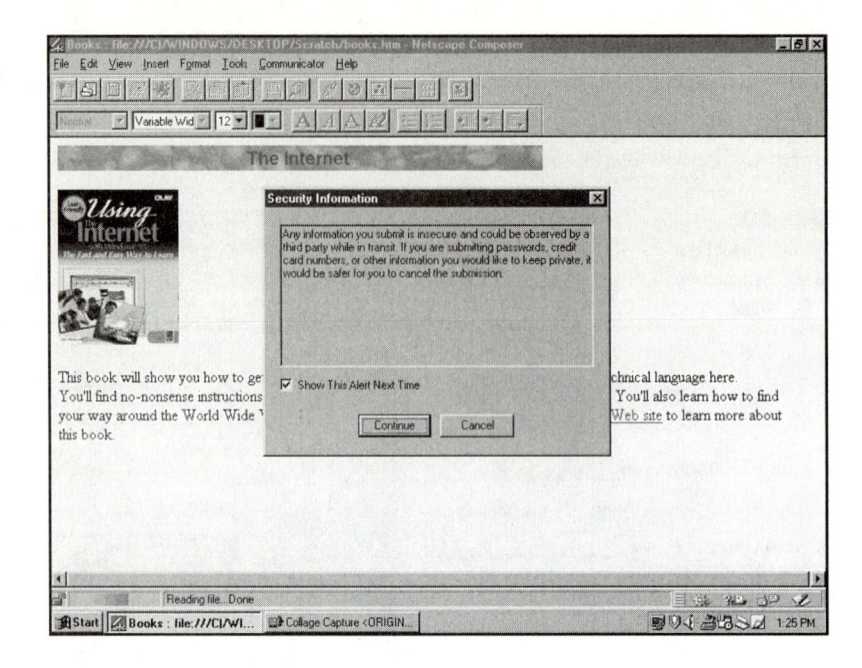

**FIG. 6.12**
If your Web site is small, this dialog box might appear and disappear so fast that you miss it.

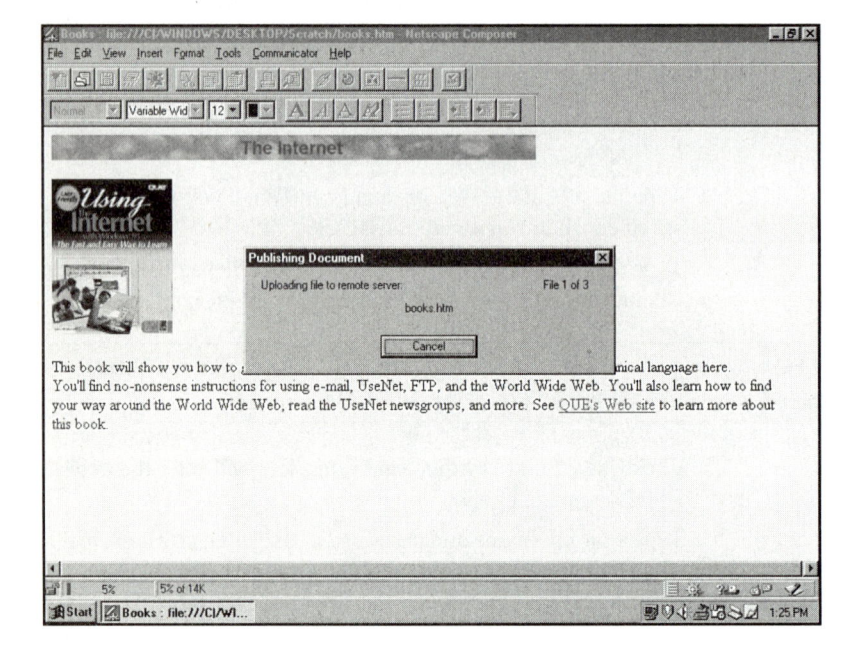

Now you've successfully published your Web page. You can repeat these steps to upload more Web pages.

◆ **TROUBLESHOOTING**

**I tried to open my Web page by typing an URL that looks like http://www.server.net/~name, but the browser can't find my homepage. Why do I have to explicitly provide the file name?** Make sure that your home page is named `index.html`. UNIX Web servers typically look for a file called `index.html` when a user opens an URL without giving an actual file name. For example, you can browse my Web by opening **http://rampages.onramp.net/~jerry** in your Web browser. Because you haven't specified a path, the Web server will return a file called `index.html`—my homepage.

CHAPTER 7

# Conference Quick Start

*by Mark R. Brown*

The Internet has been hailed as "a totally new way to do business." But some have sniggered that if the Emperor is wearing clothes, they must be mighty skimpy. Truth is, before the Net can be of much use to business, some new tools need to be developed.

For doing business on the Web, for example, there need to be new ways of securing online transactions. Methods need to be worked out for paying for online purchases. Security and "electronic cash" standards are still being worked out, and real-world solutions may be a year or two down the line yet. In the meantime, the number of electronic business transactions online is a mere fraction of what it could be if satisfactory security and e-cash systems were in place.

Another widely-promised potential use of the Net for business—interactive collaboration—has also been awaiting the arrival of the necessary tools. With Netscape's inclusion of Netscape Conference in Communicator, that wait may be over.

- **Netscape Conference has its origins in Netscape's stand-alone CoolTalk conferencing application**
  But Conference is integrated into Communicator.

- **Conference is Communicator's built-in Internet phone client**
  It is compatible with phone software from many other vendors.

- **Conference offers five distinct ways in which you can collaboratively share information with others on the Net**
  In addition to an Internet phone client, you have access to text chat, file sharing, collaborative browsing, and a shared white board.

- **Conference is the only Communicator application you can't reach from the Component Bar**
  You have to launch it using a hotkey combination or menu selection.

The concept of collaboration over the Net is intriguing, with the potential to save a great deal of time and money. For example, let's say you're the CEO of a computer software company in Ontario and your Vice President of Marketing is on a 3-week vacation in Canberra. Your major competitor suddenly announces a new product that sounds exactly like the new product you were going to announce next week. Besides the obvious question as to why you allowed your VP of Marketing to go on vacation at such a crucial time, you're asking yourself how you can somehow take advantage of the situation. You could exchange a flurry of phone calls and e-mail with your marketing VP, but the time frame is so tight you really need a way to brainstorm together.

You could rent one of those videoconference suites and have your VP rent one in Canberra and try to work things out at a rate of hundreds of dollars an hour. Or you could just fire up Netscape Conference. Conference lets you do five very handy things:

- Talk to someone anywhere in the world via an Internet phone client without incurring long-distance charges.
- Exchange files.
- Engage in text chat.
- Browse the Web together.
- Work together on an electronic "white board."

What's more, it lets you do all these things simultaneously.

So you dial up your Marketing VP and start discussing the situation. You send along the Word file containing your proposed press release and ad copy. You browse your competitor's Web site together, examining their product claims. You load up a copy of your own proposed ad in the white board. Your VP of Marketing marks up changes to your ad and simultaneously tosses new copy ideas to you in the text chat window. She cuts and pastes the things you mutually agree on into the original Word document, transferring the new file to you as soon as you're done. In less than an hour, you have done a major bit of damage control, you have a new ad campaign in hand, and your Marketing VP can go back to the beach. And you haven't even paid a penny in long-distance charges!

You can use the same Netscape Conference tools to collaboratively design new products, chat with Grandma (complete with pictures of the grandkids), or pick out a wedding dress from a shop halfway across the world. Pretty exciting stuff.

## Launching Conference

Netscape Conference began its life as a stand-alone program called CoolTalk. CoolTalk had many of the same features (and, indeed, the same "look and feel") as Netscape Conference, but it wasn't integrated into Netscape. Though Conference is a part of Communicator, it seems that it's still somewhat of a red-headed stepson—it's the only Communicator tool not accessible from the Component Bar. To launch Conference, you must select the Communicator menu, then the Conference menu item, or use the Ctrl+5 hotkey combination. When you do, you see the Conference window shown in Figure 7.1.

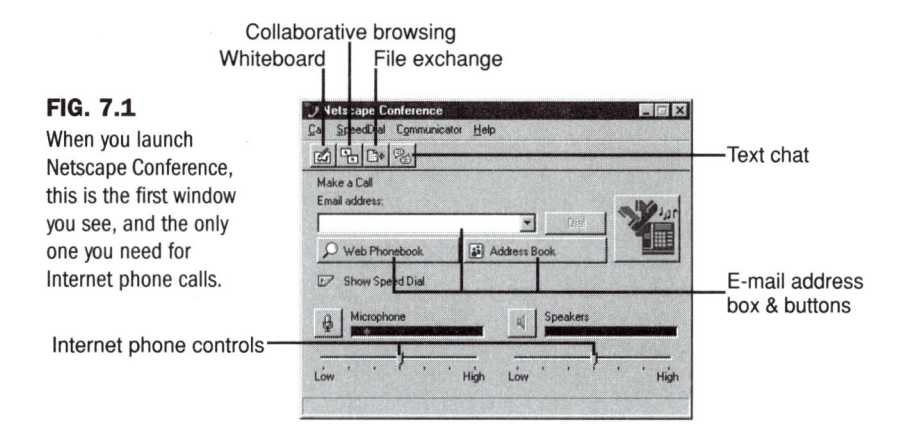

**FIG. 7.1**
When you launch Netscape Conference, this is the first window you see, and the only one you need for Internet phone calls.

Labels on figure: Collaborative browsing, Whiteboard, File exchange, Text chat, E-mail address box & buttons, Internet phone controls

## Configuring Conference

When you installed Netscape Communicator, you may have already run the Conference Setup Wizard. If not, you can run it now by choosing Help, Setup Wizard. The dialog box shown in Figure 7.2 appears.

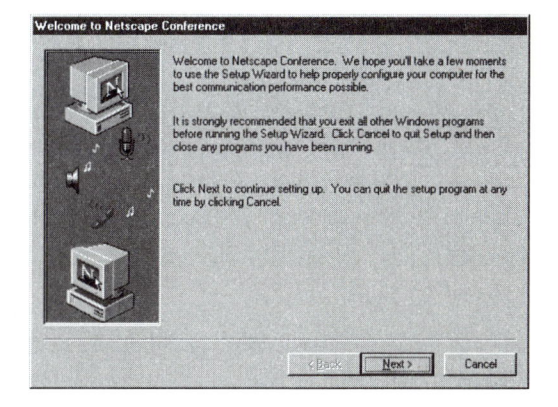

**FIG. 7.2**
The Conference Setup Wizard takes you through the options for configuring Netscape Conference.

> **CAUTION**
> Before proceeding with the Conference Setup Wizard, make sure your sound card is set up and operating properly. Conference uses your sound card to record and play back audio during an Internet phone call. Plug a microphone into the sound card and set the microphone recording and audio playback levels for your sound card using your system options setup program (i.e., Control Panel in Windows 95). Once you're sure that your sound card is configured properly, you may begin Netscape Conference setup.

The Setup Wizard performs three tasks:

- Registers you with your directory server
- Identifies your network connection
- Tests your audio levels

In order to perform these functions, you need three important pieces of information:

- Your name
- Your e-mail address
- Type of network connection (modem, T1, and so on.)

If you press the Next> button twice, you get to the dialog shown in Figure 7.3.

**FIG. 7.3**
This dialog box sets up Netscape Conference.

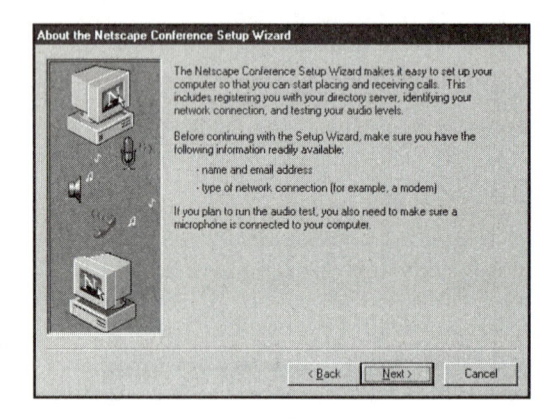

You need only fill in the Name and E-mail fields of this screen, which Netscape calls your "Business Card." If these fields are already filled in properly, you can press the Cancel button to quit; you've already gone through this Wizard when you installed Communicator.

▶ Creating your own Business Card is explained in "Configuring Conference," **p. 97**

Once your Name and E-mail address are filled in, click the Next button to continue. When you do, you see the dialog box shown in Figure 7.4.

This dialog box defines your Dynamic Lookup Service (DLS) and Phonebook servers. The DLS server routes calls to and from other users. The Phonebook lets you look up other users' addresses so you can call them. By default, the DLS server is set to Netscape's site, while the Phonebook is set to Four11. Unless you have access to custom servers, leave these settings alone.

You'll also note that there's a check by an item that says "List my name in phonebook." If you want people to be able to find you in the Four11 phonebook, leave this checked. If you prefer to be "unlisted," then uncheck the box.

**FIG. 7.4**
This part of the Setup Wizard lets you set up your user "Business Card."

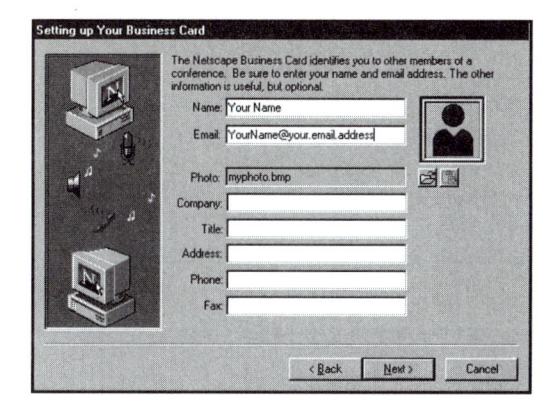

When you click Next this time, you go to a dialog box that sets your connection speed (see Figure 7.5). Select the appropriate radio button and click Next again.

**FIG. 7.5**
Connection speed is all-important when making Internet phone calls. This dialog box ensures that Conference is configured correctly for your connection.

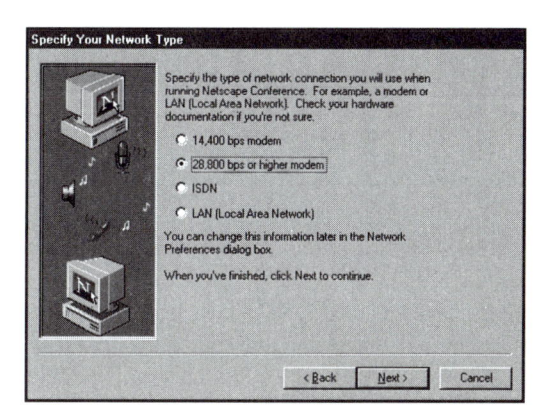

You select your sound card in the next dialog box (see Figure 7.6). If you don't have a sound card, you can't use Conference's Internet phone capabilities. The Microphone and Speakers selections are taken from your system setup. If your sound card is configured properly, you should be able to simply click the Next button.

Now you need to plug in a microphone, because the Wizard wants to take a sound level reading. Click Next and you see the dialog box shown in Figure 7.7.

**FIG. 7.6**
From here, you can set up your sound card and proceed to the test phase.

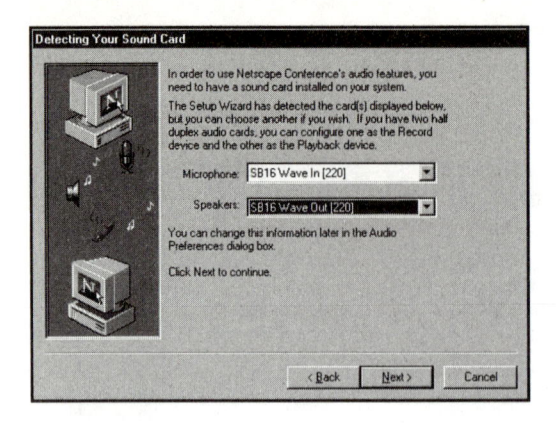

**FIG. 7.7**
Slide the "Silence Sensor" until you lock out background noise.

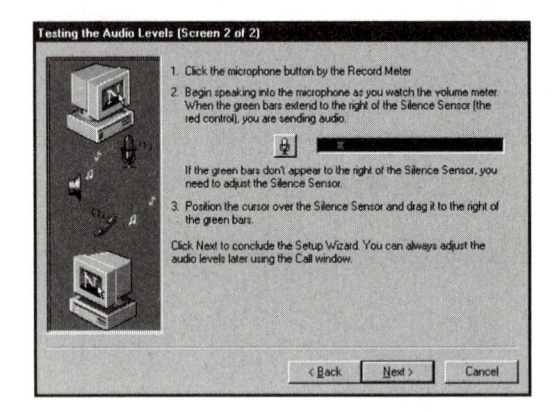

You see a green bar that represents the sound level output from your microphone. Slide the red "Silence Sensor" until it is slightly beyond the left side of the green bar when you are speaking. The "Silence Sensor" sets the VOX (voice activation) level of your microphone so you don't send long stretches of background noise, but only broadcast when you are actually speaking. Once this is adjusted correctly, select Next again. Then select Finish> to end the setup.

Communicator should now be set up for use.

> **NOTE** At any time, you can modify the settings you made with the Setup Wizard by choosing Call, Preferences from the Conference menu.

## Making an Internet Phone Call

You initiate an Internet phone call from the main Netscape Conference window, shown in Figure 7.8.

http://www.quecorp.com

**FIG. 7.8**
Enter an e-mail address to make an Internet phone call.

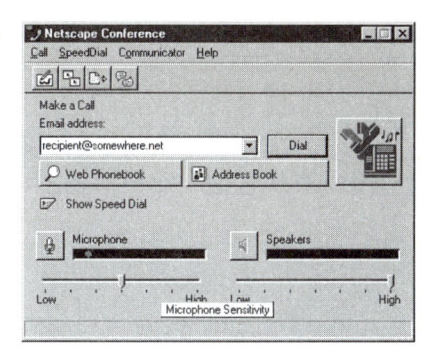

To call someone, simply enter their e-mail address in the E-mail address field and press the Dial button. If they're online, and if they're running Communicator, and if they've made themselves available through a DLS server, and if they haven't turned on "Do Not Disturb" mode, you'll be connected. That seems like a lot of "ifs," doesn't it? Needless to say, it's best to contact your intended recipient and establish a date and time beforehand if you intend to successfully connect to someone using this technology, unless you know for sure that the person you're calling always has Conference running and ready to go.

▶ What if you don't know someone's e-mail address? Netscape Conference can help you find e-mail addresses in several handy ways. "Making an Internet Phone Call," **p. 301**, in Chapter 15, "Conference In-Depth," explains these techniques.

If your call is unsuccessful, you see a dialog box that tells you so. If you do get through, the Dial button changes to a Hang Up button (see Figure 7.9).

**FIG. 7.9**
If your call is unsuccessful, you see a dialog that tells you so; this window indicates a successful connection.

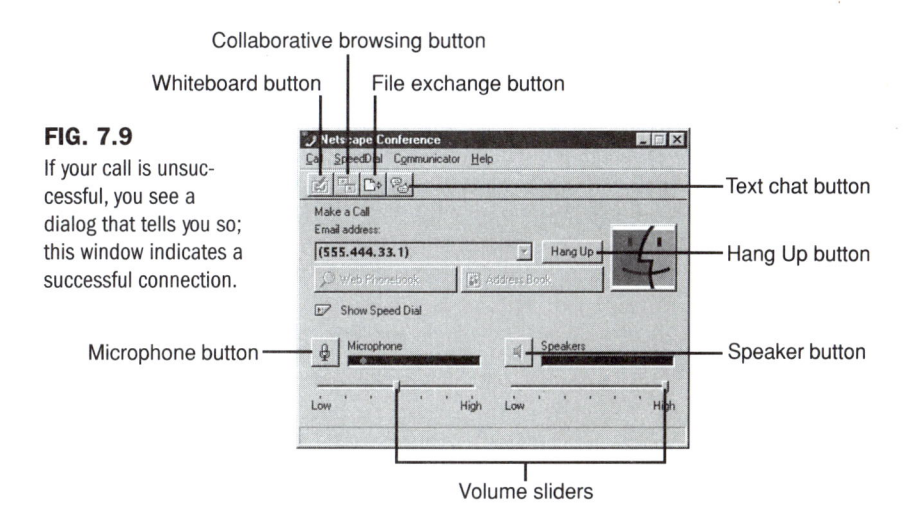

Once connected, you should be able to hear the call's recipient and be able to speak into your microphone to talk to him or her. If necessary, you can adjust the microphone or speaker volume by adjusting the volume sliders that appear below the microphone and speaker icons (refer to Figure 7.9).

When you are finished with your call, just click the Hang Up button.

▶ You can do much more with audio conferencing, including setting up Speed Dial buttons, sending voice mail, and so on. For more information on these topics, **See** "Making an Internet Phone Call," **p. 307,** in Chapter 15.

## Text Chat

Of course, there are other tools you can use in place of or in addition to audio chat. In fact, you don't have to use audio chat at all. Text chat might be more useful to you, especially if you have a slow or unreliable modem connection. To initiate text chat, choose the Text Chat button on the Conference toolbar (refer to Figure 7.9). When you choose text chat, you see the window shown in Figure 7.10.

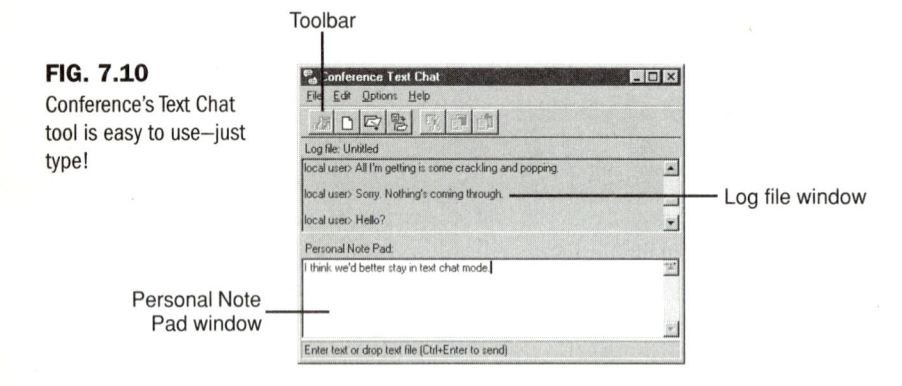

**FIG. 7.10**
Conference's Text Chat tool is easy to use—just type!

Toolbar

Log file window

Personal Note Pad window

The Text Chat window comes up with a blinking cursor in the Personal Note Pad window. To send text, just type, and end with a Ctrl+Enter key combination. What you type appears in the Log File window, along with anything typed by your conversation partner.

When you're done conversing this way, just hit the window's close button to get rid of the chat window.

▶ The Text Chat tool has many more options. For the full story on the Chat window, **See** "Text Chat," **p. 311,** in Chapter 15.

## File Exchange

You click the File Exchange button (see Figure 7.9) to send a file from your computer to your collaborator's computer.

Though it seems at first glance to be a simple function, Conference's built-in File Exchange client is actually the heart and soul of performing real collaborative work over the Internet. You can talk, and chat, and draw pictures all day long, but if you have no way to exchange the actual work files involved in a project, the process quickly degenerates into a swapfest of handwritten notes, guesses, and trial-and-error. But when you can send your collaborator a copy of the actual Word document, or AutoCAD drawing, or PowerPoint presentation file you're working on, online collaboration becomes a precision process with real-world usefulness.

Once you click the File Exchange button from the Conference window, you see the window shown in Figure 7.11.

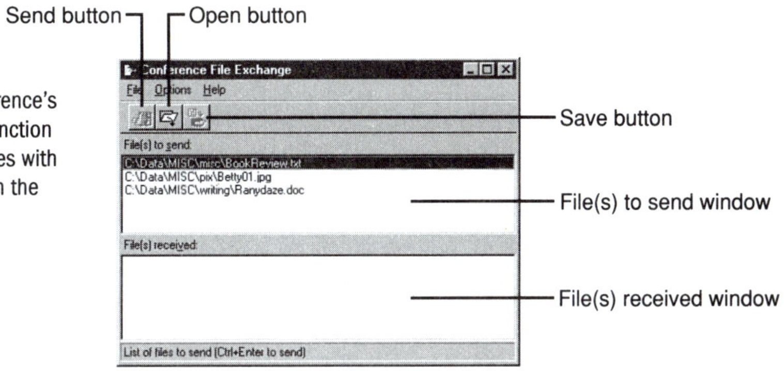

**FIG. 7.11**
Netscape Conference's File Exchange function lets you trade files with a collaborator on the Net.

- Send button
- Open button
- Save button
- File(s) to send window
- File(s) received window

You can queue up a list of files to send to your collaborator by choosing the Send button on the File Exchange window toolbar (refer to Figure 7.11). This brings up your system's standard file requester, from which you can select the files to send. As each is selected, it is listed in the File(s) to Send window. Once you've chosen all the files you want to send, clicking the Send button sends them off to your collaborator.

Receiving files is automatic. Any files sent to you by your collaborator are listed in the File(s) Received window, and you can save them by clicking the Save button.

To get rid of the File Exchange window, just click the window's Close button.

▶ Though File Exchange is a simple tool, it incorporates a few subtleties. To learn about them, **See** "File Exchange," **p. 312**, in Chapter 15.

## Collaborative Browsing

I first saw collaborative Web browsing almost two years ago in a program called PowWow, and I must confess I was very impressed by it. The concept is simple—while you browse the Web, others come along for the ride. In Netscape Conference, collaborative browsing is easy to do.

To start, you press the Collaborative Browsing button on the Conference toolbar (refer to Figure 7.9). You see the simple dialog box shown in Figure 7.10.

**FIG. 7.12**
Collaborative browsing is as easy as clicking two buttons.

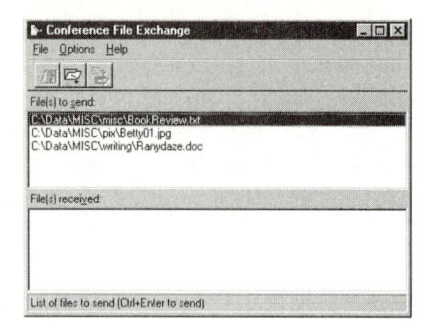

To get your collaborator's browser pointed to the same Web address as yours, press the Sync Browsers button. Then press the Start Browsing button to begin. Wherever you go on the Web, your collaborator goes, too. When done, go back to the Collaborative Browsing dialog box and press the Close button.

This tool is fantastic when you need to share information from a Web site with your partner, or if you are discussing the design of a Web site. If your Web designer is in California and you're in Chicago, it's a great way to discuss changes, ideas, and details. If your competitor just put up a new site, it lets you examine every nook and cranny together.

▶ For a few more ideas concerning collaborative browsing, **See** "Collaborative Browsing," **p. 313**, in Chapter 15.

## The Whiteboard

The standard, cliché brainstorming session looks something like this: a dozen people, sleeves rolled up, yellow legal pads and coffee cups in front of them, all seated around a conference table. Somebody stands in front of a white board making numbered lists and drawing diagrams while everyone throws out ideas and makes remarks on the ideas of others.

Though you have to provide your own coffee, Netscape Conference's Whiteboard tool provides much of the same functionality. With it, you can load in graphics and mark them up in real-time, all the while discussing the pros and cons of your mutual ideas.

You launch the Whiteboard by selecting the Whiteboard icon from the Conference toolbar (refer to Figure 7.9).

It's important to note that the Whiteboard works with two completely different kinds of on-screen graphics: the "white board" image, and markups. It is helpful to think of these as two separate layers: the image behind, and the markup layer in front. Each is independently changeable and erasable.

A BMP, GIF, TIF, or JPEG image can be loaded into the image, or background layer from disk by selecting the Open File button on the toolbar. If you're working on a project using any graphics program, you can save an image in any of these formats so that you can later load it up to collaborate online using the Whiteboard.

http://www.quecorp.com

However, you can also grab an image directly from your desktop as you work. To do so, clear your desktop of all but the windows you want to grab, except for the Whiteboard window itself. Arrange the windows the way you want them, then select one of the choices from the White board Capture menu. You can grab a Region by dragging a rectangle on the screen, grab the whole Desktop, or grab a single Window by clicking it.

Of course, the Whiteboard image can also be a blank screen. To clear the screen, select Edit from the Whiteboard menu, then choose the Clear Whiteboard menu item.

Once you have a background image you want to work with, you can use the WhiteBoard tools to add elements to the markup layer, like freehand scribbles, text, rectangles, and so on. There is even a repositionable arrow pointer you can use to emphasize points as you discuss various graphic items.

If you've used any graphics drawing program before, the operation of the WhiteBoard should be relatively intuitive. For example, to draw a rectangle, choose the rectangle tool. To choose a new color, simply pick it from the palette.

> **TIP** Don't forget you can get helpful pop-up Tooltips by hovering over a button or icon if you can't figure out what it does.

You can clear off all your markups at any time, leaving the underlying image undisturbed, by choosing Edit, Clear Markups from the menu.

The Conference Whiteboard is not only the most "fun" tool in the Conference toolbox, it's also arguably the most useful. There's nothing like sharing and scribbling on an image to focus the creative juices.

▶ The White Board tool has many, many more options. For the full story, **See** "The Whiteboard," **p. 314**, in Chapter 15.

# Integration

Remember that each of the Conference tools can be used in conjunction with all of the others. You can be speaking with your collaborator using the Conference Internet phone while drawing on the Whiteboard. You can send files to him or her in the background at the same time. You can use the Text Chat tool to keep notes on important points for saving or printing out at the end of your conference. And you can browse important Web sites together to prospect for information as you brainstorm.

In this chapter we've only scratched the surface of what you can do with Netscape Conference. For the complete story on Conference's many options, features, and functions, turn to Chapter 15, "Conference In-Depth," p. 301. ●

PART II

# In-Depth Communicator

- **8** Navigator In-Depth   109
- **9** Using Bookmarks   145
- **10** Interacting with Plug-Ins, Java Applets, and JavaScript   163
- **11** Messenger In-Depth   199
- **12** Using the Address Book   231
- **13** Collabra In-Depth   245
- **14** Composer In-Depth   273
- **15** Conference In-Depth   301
- **16** Setting Preferences   319
- **17** Security Options   349

CHAPTER 8

# Navigator In-Depth

*by Mark R. Brown*

By this point, you already know what Navigator is—a tool for viewing and interacting with HTML documents—and Chapter 3, "Navigator Quick Start," familiarized you with Navigator's basic functions and controls. In this chapter, we tear Navigator apart and wring every bit of performance and functionality out of it.

You learn how to customize Navigator so the "look and feel" matches your preferences and personality. You find out how to navigate documents and sites in dozens of innovative ways. You discover how to save links and graphics for later access. And you develop a deep understanding of how Navigator is organized and how it works.

Let's begin by finding out how to customize Navigator.

- **Learn about Navigator's features**
  Navigator is an extremely powerful program with many advanced features.

- **Customize Navigator in dozens of ways**
  Accommodate your native language, your personal preferences, and your system configuration.

- **Navigator is not just for displaying HTML documents**
  Navigator can analyze HTML documents in many ways.

- **Navigator's NetHelp**
  Navigator's built-in Help is extensive and also occasionally fun.

## Communicator Preferences

The key to customizing Navigator lies in the Preferences settings. You bring up the Communicator Preferences dialog box by selecting Edit, Preferences from the Navigator menu bar.

The left menu in the Preferences dialog box gives you access to dozens of customizable options. By default, the Navigator preferences item is selected and the right panel displays options for changing your home page and history settings. But by highlighting other selections in the left menu, you can change everything from background color to cache behavior.

> **TIP** The left menu in the Preferences dialog box is a collapsible hierarchical menu. To expand a topic, click the plus (+) sign next to the header. To collapse an expanded topic, click the minus (-) sign. By default, the Appearance and Navigator headers are expanded and the rest are collapsed.

> **NOTE** Chapter 16, "Setting Preferences," explains the workings of the entire Preferences dialog box in detail. For information on how to set individual Navigator options, please turn to that chapter.

What follows is a quick overview of what can be changed and which panel you need to access to make those changes.

The Appearance panel lets you choose which of the Communicator applications is launched when you start the program. By default, this is Navigator, but you can choose any of the other Communicator components instead. This panel is also where you can select whether the Navigator toolbar icons are displayed as text, graphics, or both.

The Fonts panel is where you select the default fonts for the Navigator display and whether your fonts or page-defined fonts are displayed. You can also choose to turn off Navigator's new Dynamic Fonts feature here.

From the Colors panel you define the colors for text, links, and background display, and you can choose whether your colors or the page's own colors are used.

As stated earlier, the Navigator panel selects what kind of page Navigator displays on startup and allows you to define the address of your home page. This panel also controls how long pages are kept in your history list.

The Languages panel specifies which languages Navigator will request from servers that provide multilingual versions of their pages.

You use the Applications panel to define helper applications for files that Navigator can't display natively.

The Mail & Groups and Composer panels (and associated subpanels) control how Messenger, Collabra, and Composer work. These panels are discussed in other chapters (we're concentrating on the Navigator client here).

The Offline panel lets you tell Navigator whether you usually work online or offline, so that it can adjust its behavior accordingly. (Offline's associated Download selection is related to how newsgroups work, so you can ignore it here.)

The final main panel, Advanced, lets you choose whether or not to automatically load images; whether to enable Java, JavaScript, Style Sheets, and AutoInstall of Communicator upgrades over the Net; and how to handle cookies.

The Advanced panel has three subpanels. The first, Cache, controls how disk and memory caching of pages is handled. This panel is especially important because it includes buttons to clear the memory and disk caches immediately, which can be important if your system is becoming "waterlogged" from holding too much cache information and you want to temporarily free up some system resources.

The Proxies panel is used to configure your proxy setup if you are behind a corporate firewall.

Finally, the Disk Space panel is associated with message downloading and is outside the topic at hand, Navigator.

Each of these Preferences panels is discussed in-depth in Chapter 16, "Setting Preferences," and many are mentioned again in context later in this chapter.

# Reviewing Navigator Basics

In Chapter 3, "Navigator Quick Start," you learned the basics of how to use Navigator to view and navigate HTML documents. You learned how to use the Back and Forward buttons on the Navigator toolbar and how to use links to jump to other documents.

In this chapter, we go beyond those techniques and make full use of all of Navigator's features and functions. But first, let's review the tools that are available in the Navigator window (see Figure 8.1). Later in this chapter, we examine each of these tools in-depth.

The menu bar is often not the quickest way to access Navigator's features and functions, but it is always the most complete. If you can't remember how to do something another way, the odds are good that you can find a menu selection to perform the same task.

There are three toolbars. By default, the top one is the Navigation toolbar, the middle one is the Location toolbar, and the bottom one is the Personal, or custom, toolbar. At the left of each toolbar is an Open/Close tab which can be used to compress or expand that toolbar. In Figure 8.1, the Personal (bottom) toolbar has been closed by clicking the Open/Close tab.

The Navigation toolbar is made up of nine buttons. The first two are for moving Back or Forward in a session. Clicking once on either moves one page forward or back, while clicking and holding creates a drop-down menu from which you can select any available page. The Reload and Stop buttons let you reload the data for a page or stop a page from downloading, respectively. The Home and Search buttons take you to your defined home page or to Netscape's search site on the Web. Clicking the Guide button creates a drop-down list just like the Back and Forward buttons, but, in this case, it's a fixed list of five "starting point" sites on the Web.

**Chapter 8** Navigator In-Depth

Clicking the Print button brings up a dialog box that prints the currently displayed page. And finally, selecting the Security button launches the Security Info window, which not only displays security information for the current page, but also gives you access to all of your security options.

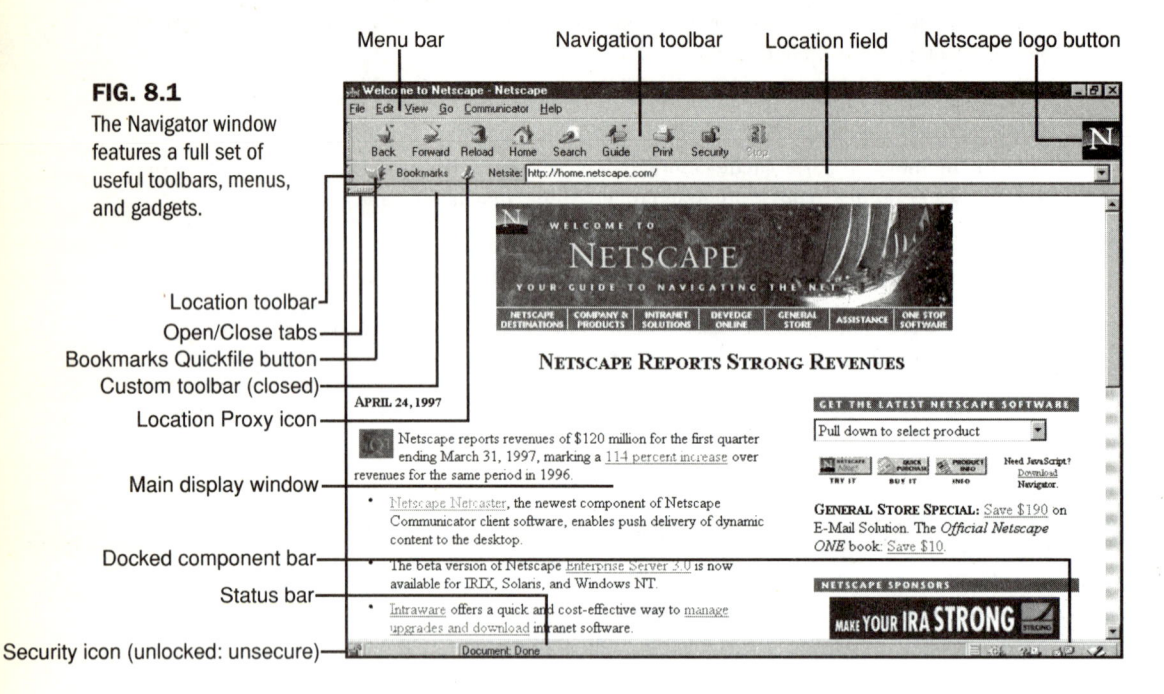

**FIG. 8.1**
The Navigator window features a full set of useful toolbars, menus, and gadgets.

Labels on figure: Menu bar, Navigation toolbar, Location field, Netscape logo button, Location toolbar, Open/Close tabs, Bookmarks Quickfile button, Custom toolbar (closed), Location Proxy icon, Main display window, Docked component bar, Status bar, Security icon (unlocked: unsecure)

At the far right of the Navigation toolbar is the Netscape logo icon. Clicking this icon takes you directly to Netscape's Web site at **http://home.netscape.com**.

The Location toolbar features two useful tools. Clicking the Bookmarks QuickFile button drops down a menu of all your bookmarked locations; selecting an item from this list takes you immediately to the bookmarked page. The Location field is where you can type in the URL of any location; press the Enter key when you're done and that page is loaded. There is a down-arrow button on the right end of the Location field; press it and you get a drop-down list of visited locations. To the left of the Location field is the Location Proxy icon, which you can drag-and-drop anywhere you want to duplicate the URL of the current page address. It's particularly useful for drag-and-drop page bookmarking (just drop it on the Bookmark QuickFile button).

The third toolbar, the Personal toolbar, is user-customizable. You can drag-and-drop the Location Proxy icon here to create a button for the currently displayed page. This toolbar is also customizable via the Edit Bookmarks window, where it shows up as a separate folder.

▶ **See** "Organizing Your Bookmarks," **p. 151**

The main display window is where you actually view HTML documents.

http://www.quecorp.com

The status bar appears at the bottom of the display window. At its left end is the security icon for the page. When the padlock is unlocked, the page is not secure; when locked, the page is secure. Next is the status line display, a line of text that tells you what's going on in the main display window. Messages here can tell you what percent of a file is loaded, when the document is done loading, when a Java applet is running, and much more. Finally, if the component bar is docked, it appears on the right end of the status bar. You can click the icons in the component bar to instantly bring up Navigator, Messenger, Collabra, or Composer at any time.

Now that we've refamiliarized ourselves with the major features of the Navigator window, let's dig into what these tools can do for us.

## Bringing Up a New Navigator Window

Sometimes you want to investigate a new site, but you still want to keep tabs on the site you're currently viewing. Fortunately, Navigator makes it easy to bring up a new window—just press Ctrl+N. (You can also select File, New, Navigator Window from the menu bar.)

This new window comes up with all the same options as when Navigator is first launched—colors, fonts, home page, and so on.

Navigator 3.0 only lets you open four viewing windows (unless you increased that number in Preferences). Navigator 4.0 seems to be limited only by the capabilities of your system. I've had eight windows open with no problem.

> **CAUTION**
>
> If you have too many windows open while they are still downloading data, each will take a proportionately longer time to load (1/2 the speed for 2 windows, 1/3 the speed for 3, and so on). But once a window has finished downloading, it can remain open without straining your connection. However, it will still take up system memory and processing power. As a rule of thumb, open extra windows while still downloading only if you have a fast direct connection to the Internet. Leave extra browser windows open only if you have plenty of system memory and a fast processor.

HTML links can automatically launch a new Navigator window containing the page linked to, so keep your eyes open when clicking away. Sometimes a new window comes up so fast you don't notice that you've changed windows. Your only clue might be the sudden and unexpected ghosting of your Back button. If this happens to you, you might be in a new, automatically launched browser window.

Some pages are now also bringing up a second, "mini" browser window that contains additional information, special offers (see Figure 8.2), or even a special "remote control" menu. Though reduced in size, and sometimes lacking toolbars and menus, don't be fooled—these are fully functional Navigator windows.

You can kill an unwanted "bonus" browser window by clicking the window's Close button. Ctrl+W also does the job, as does choosing Close from the File menu.

114 | Chapter 8  Navigator In-Depth

**FIG. 8.2**
The United Airlines home page brings up a bonus mini browser window that displays a special offer.

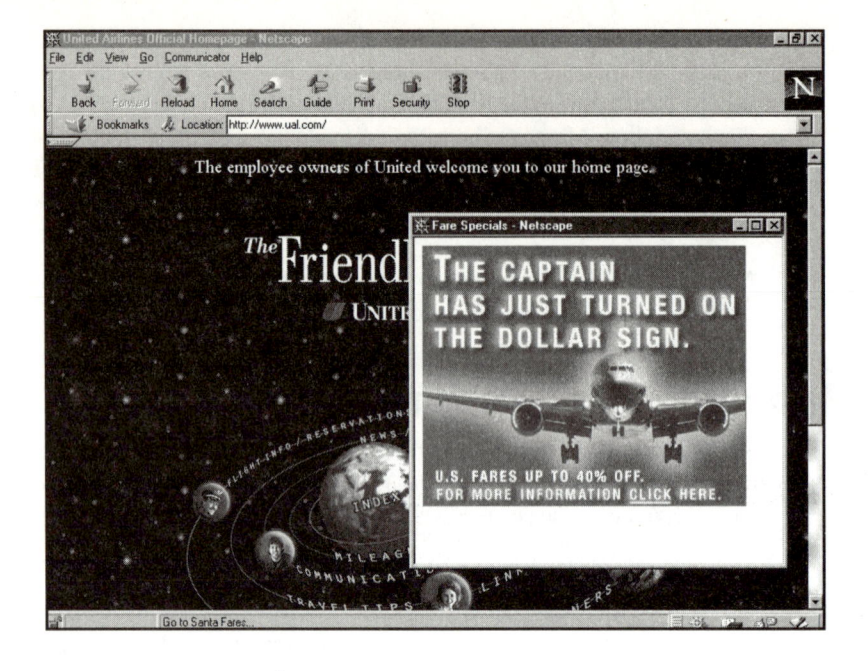

## Opening and Saving Pages

You can open any page by typing its address (URL) into the Location field on the Location toolbar. This works not only for pages on intranets and the World Wide Web, but also for pages stored on your hard drive or local area network.

But, if you'd like to load a page from disk or network using your system's standard file requester dialog box, you can do so by typing Ctrl+O (or by selecting Open Page from the File menu). When you do, you get the dialog box shown in Figure 8.3.

**FIG. 8.3**
This simple dialog box lets you load pages from your hard disk into Navigator or Composer.

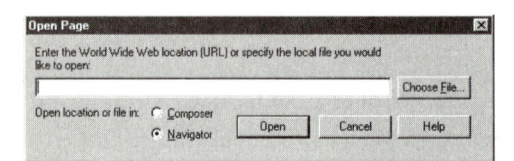

Click the Choose File button and you get the file requester dialog box for your computer. By default, the dialog box lists only HTML files, with the file name extension .htm or .html. However, you can also choose to view or load any registered file type that Navigator, its plug-ins, or its helper applications understand (.avi, .au, and so on). This makes it easy to use Navigator as a sort of "universal file reader" for graphics, audio files, video animations, and even Java applets (see Figure 8.4).

http://www.quecorp.com

**FIG. 8.4**
You can choose to load just about any type of file into Navigator.

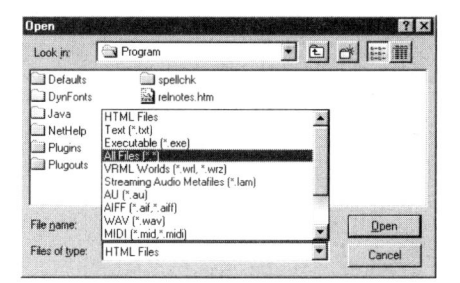

> **TIP** Note that, by clicking the appropriate option button, you can choose to load your page into Composer for editing instead of into Navigator for viewing. Click OK to load the page.

To save the currently displayed page, type Ctrl+S (or choose Save As from the File menu). Again, you get your system file dialog box. By default, the page is saved as an HTML file (with the file extensions .htm or .html) but you can also choose to save the page as a text file, with the extension .txt. The save routine strips out all HTML codes if you choose this option.

> **TIP** If the currently displayed page is composed of frames, you can also choose the currently active frame by choosing Save Frame As from the File menu. Note also that if frames are displayed, the Save As menu selection saves only the document that defines the outer frameset.

> **CAUTION**
> Don't save files using a colon (:), slash (/), or pound sign (#) in the file name. These characters are interpreted in a unique way when Navigator tries to access a Web address. When you try to load in a file with these characters in its name, they will confuse the browser into trying to access an Internet address instead.

## Printing Pages

Before you print a displayed page, you want to make sure your page printing preferences are correctly set. You do this by selecting File, Page Setup. You get the dialog box shown in Figure 8.5.

If the sample page in the upper-right corner isn't the proper page size and orientation, you need to close this dialog box and instead choose File, Print to adjust your printer to the correct page settings. But if the sample is correct, you can go ahead and check the boxes to adjust the look of your page output.

The Page Options section has four options. Beveled Lines gives your page lines a 3-D look. Black Text and Black Lines are good options to pick if you're printing on a black-and-white printer and you sometimes run into colored text and lines that look too light when printed out. Choose Last Page First if your printer collates printed pages backwards.

**FIG. 8.5**
The Page Setup dialog box lets you define how your printed pages will look.

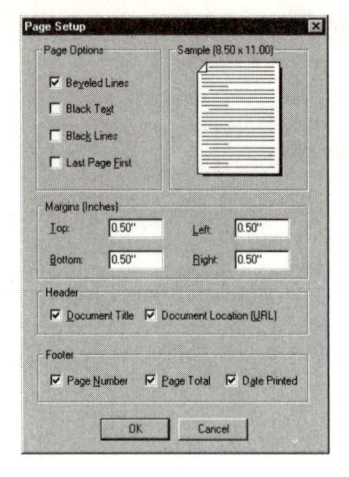

The Margins section lets you define Top, Bottom, Left, and Right margins for your pages. These all default to 1/2 an inch.

The Header and Footer sections let you choose what information you want to appear in each page's header and footer. By default, the header includes the Document Title in the upper-left and the Document Location (URL) in the upper-right. The footer defaults to printing the Page Number in the lower-left, the Page Total right after the page number (for example, 1 of 5), and the Date Printed (and time) in the lower-right. Any of these bits of information can be removed by unchecking the appropriate check box. Click OK when you're done.

After the Page Setup options are set, you can select Print Preview from the File menu to see how your page will look when printed out (see Figure 8.6).

The pointer looks like a little magnifying glass, and clicking anywhere on the displayed page gives you three different successive "zoom levels" of detail. (You can do the same thing with the Zoom In and Zoom Out buttons on the toolbar.) The Next Page and Prev Page buttons let you step through the entire preview. If you want to see two pages at once, the Two Page button lets you do so. When you're done previewing, clicking the Print button brings up the Print dialog box. Or you can just choose the Close button to quit.

> **TIP** Looking at a huge Web page, but only want to print out the little bit of information you really need? Choose Print Preview and see which page the information you want falls on, then click the Print button and choose the proper Print Range to print only the page or pages you need. Even then, the results may be a little different than displayed.

You can bypass all the preliminaries and go straight to the printing process by selecting File, Print from the menu bar (Ctrl+P). No matter how you get there, you see your system's Print dialog box. Figure 8.7 shows the dialog box for Windows 95. Make your choices and click OK to print your page.

http://www.quecorp.com

**FIG. 8.6**
The Print Preview window lets you see what your printout will look like.

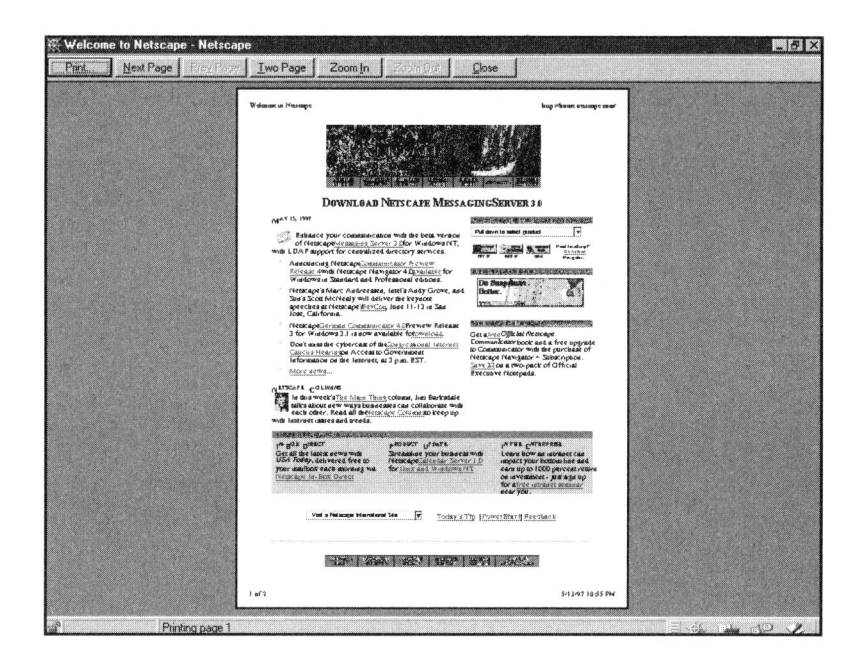

**FIG. 8.7**
Window's 95's print dialog box lets you choose which pages to print and how they are collated, among other things.

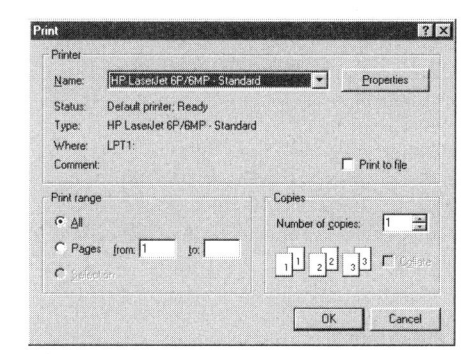

> **CAUTION**
> When you are displaying a page created using frames, the Print menu item changes to Print Frame, and it only prints the currently active frame.

## Navigator Integration

In Communicator, all of the tools are tightly integrated. From Navigator, you can perform many integrated tasks that call up Communicator's other clients—Messenger, Collabra, and Composer—that you would otherwise have to do independently.

## Chapter 8  Navigator In-Depth

For example, if you want to edit the currently displayed page in Composer, you only have to select Edit Page from the File menu. You don't first have to save the page, launch Composer, then load the page back in.

> **TIP** If the currently displayed page is composed of frames, Edit Page sends the page comprising the outer frameset to Composer. File, Edit Frame (which is otherwise a ghosted menu selection) lets you edit a selected frame.

Likewise, to e-mail a page or post it to a newsgroup, you simply select Send Page from the File menu and the message composition window is automatically launched, with the currently displayed page already included as an attachment. The message's Subject line is even conveniently set to the text of the page title (see Figure 8.8).

**FIG. 8.8**
Sending a page via e-mail or posting it to a newsgroup takes only a single selection from the Navigator File menu.

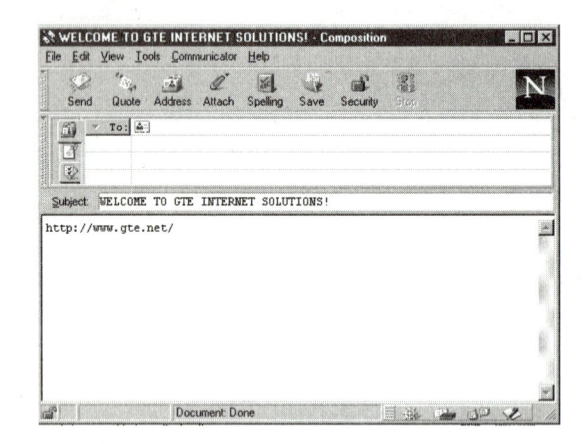

Another bit of Communicator integration is shown in the File, Go Offline selection, which brings up the dialog box shown in Figure 8.9.

**FIG. 8.9**
Download mail and messages, then go offline using this handy dialog box.

From this dialog box (which is available from most Communicator menus), you can choose to download mail and newsgroup messages, send any waiting mail messages you've composed offline, then go offline for reading. If you're paying by the minute for online access, this feature is a godsend.

http://www.quecorp.com

All of the previously mentioned features provide direct integration between components. If all you want to do, however, is bring up one of the other Communicator applications, the quickest way is to use the Component bar (refer to Figure 8.1). Whether docked in the lower-right corner of the status bar or floating as a stand-alone toolbar, the Component bar gives you direct access to Navigator, Messenger, Collabra, and Composer by simply clicking the appropriate icon.

Of course, there are many other components to Communicator besides these four. To bring them up, you can use the selections available from the Communicator menu (see Figure 8.10).

**FIG. 8.10**
The Communicator menu launches any Communicator component.

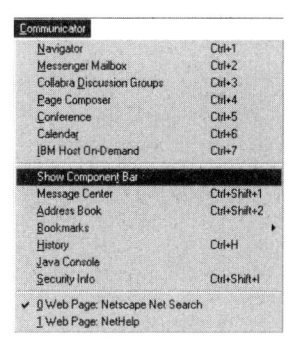

Each menu item also has an associated Ctrl key combination. Table 8.1 lists all of the hotkeys for launching Communicator components.

**Table 8.1 Communicator Application Hotkeys**

| Application | Ctrl Key Combination |
| --- | --- |
| Navigator | Ctrl+1 |
| Messenger Mailbox | Ctrl+2 |
| Collabra Discussion Groups | Ctrl+3 |
| Page Composer | Ctrl+4 |
| Conference | Ctrl+5 |
| Calendar (Pro version only) | Ctrl+6 |
| IBM Host On-Demand (Pro version only) | Ctrl+7 |
| Netcaster | Ctrl+8 |
| Message Center | Ctrl+Shift+1 |
| Address Book | Ctrl+Shift+2 |
| Bookmarks/Add | Ctrl+D |

*continues*

**Table 8.1 Continued**

| Application | Ctrl Key Combination |
|---|---|
| Bookmarks/Edit | Ctrl+B |
| History | Ctrl+H |
| Security Info | Ctrl+Shift+I |

**NOTE** On the Macintosh and PowerMac, use the Command (Apple) key instead of the Ctrl key.

# Adjusting Look and Feel

The person who designed the page you're looking at has a great deal of control over its look and feel. She can define colors, fonts, and even designate a wallpaper background graphic.

But, if you want, you can set your own preferences for those occasions when the designer has chosen to leave those options up to you. You can even choose to have your settings override hers.

## Fonts and Colors

The key to setting your own colors and fonts is in the Preferences dialog box, which is available as an item on the Edit menu (see Figure 8.11).

**FIG. 8.11**
The Fonts panel lets you define your own font choices for viewing HTML documents.

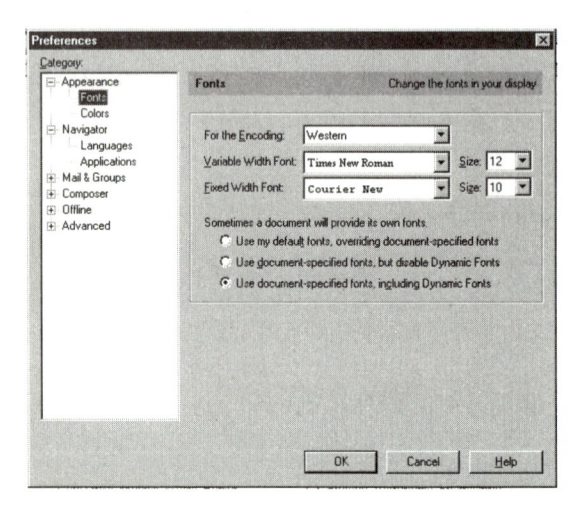

The Fonts panel lets you pick your own screen fonts. The first selection, For the Encoding, chooses which language character set you want to use as the default. This is set to European, but you can pick Japanese, Chinese, Cyrillic, or some other character set from the drop-down menu. The next two settings, Variable Width Font and Fixed Width Font, allow you to select the system fonts you want to use for your screen displays. Each is accompanied by a field for setting the font size. (Of course, you must have the appropriate fonts installed on your system for the languages you choose.)

In the bottom half of the panel, you can choose when you want your font choices to be active. You can choose from these selections:

- Use my defaul**t** fonts, overriding document-specified fonts
- Use **d**ocument-specified fonts, but disable Dynamic Fonts
- Use document-specified fonts, in**c**luding Dynamic Fonts

▶ Dynamic Fonts are a new feature that works in conjunction with Dynamic HTML to create pages that can be changed on-the-fly. **See** Chapter 29, "Using Style Sheets," on **p. 599**

The third selection displays pages as defined by the designer, while the first displays them entirely according to your preferences. The second choice merely turns off Dynamic Fonts.

**N O T E** Though the Fonts panel (along with the Languages panel) controls much of how page text displays in Navigator, there's also a menu selection that works in conjunction with these preferences settings. Choose **V**iew, **E**ncoding to select a default international character encoding scheme to use when a scheme is not specified by the page you're viewing, or when it's temporarily unavailable—for example, if the fonts you specify in the Fonts panel are missing. If you want to set your own Font panel setting (from the For the **E**ncoding field) as the default instead of one of the specific languages listed in the pull-right menu, choose Set Default Encoding.

**TIP** If you merely need a temporary change in font size (because, say, the page designer has set the font at 6 points and you're viewing the page on a laptop with a 10.3 inch screen), you can do so from the **V**iew menu by selecting In**c**rease Font (Ctrl+]) or **D**ecrease Font (Ctrl+[).

You can change the screen's display colors by choosing the Colors panel (see Figure 8.12).

By default, the Use **W**indows Colors check box is selected, and the screen colors are taken from the system palette. If you uncheck this box, you can select your own **T**ext and **B**ackground colors by clicking the box next to either selection and choosing a color from the palette dialog box (see Figure 8.13).

The color of **U**nvisited Links and **V**isited Links can be changed in a similar manner. There's also a check box to choose whether or not to **U**nderline Links.

Finally, you can also select the lower check box to say **A**lways Use My Colors, Overriding Document.

By choosing your own settings for all of these options, you can give your version of Navigator your own unique look and feel. If you're a rugged individualist or if you have a special viewing situation (such as a monochrome screen or a small-screen laptop), you might want to do so. But, by and large, it's usually best to let the page designer control her page's look and feel.

**FIG. 8.12**
The Colors panel gives you several options for changing the way Navigator displays text and links.

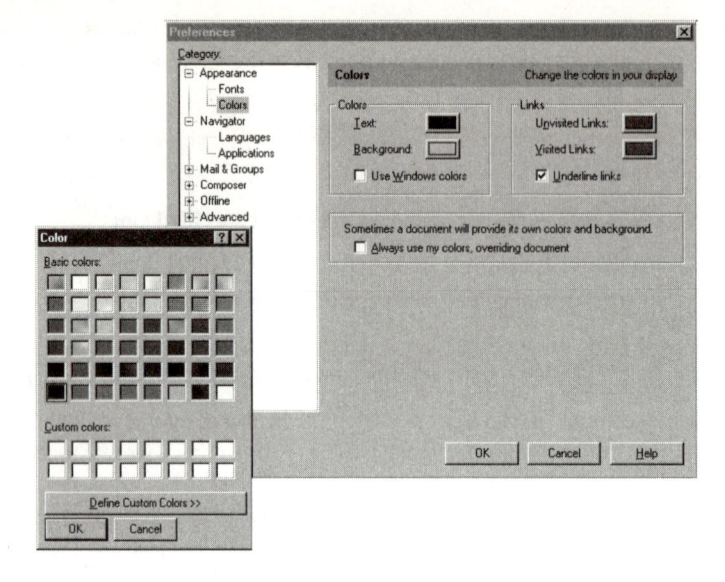

## Toolbar Control

Though Navigator's three toolbars are generally quite useful, sometimes you might like to get rid of them to free up some screen real estate—for viewing big pages or graphics, for example.

You can shrink any toolbar temporarily by clicking the Open/Close tab at the left end of the toolbar. The toolbar shrinks (closes) to a thin line, but a bit of the tab is still visible. Click this thin tab and the toolbar expands (opens) again.

A more permanent (but still reversible) solution is to choose the View menu, then pick Hide Navigation Toolbar, Hide Location Toolbar, or Hide Personal Toolbar. When any one of these is selected, the associated toolbar is taken completely off the screen, and the associated menu items change to Show Navigation Toolbar, Show Location Toolbar, and Show Personal Toolbar, respectively. Selecting any of these menu items brings that toolbar back.

If you don't like the toolbar order, that can be changed by clicking a toolbar, dragging it, and dropping it into its new location.

The Component bar can also be manipulated easily. When docked in the lower-right corner of the status bar, it can be turned into a floating toolbar by selecting Communicator, Show Component Bar. This menu item changes to Dock Component Bar when the Component bar is floating. You can also undock the Component bar by simply clicking the lined icon on its left end. To dock it when it's floating, right-click the window title bar and select Close from the pop-up menu, or use the Alt+F4 key combination.

> **NOTE** There are four other selections available from the Component bar pop-up menu: Always on Top, Horizontal, Hide Text, and <u>M</u>ove. When selected, Always on Top makes the Component bar the topmost window, no matter what. Horizontal changes the bar to a horizontal orientation and also changes the menu item to Vertical. Hide Text removes the text that appears below the icons. <u>M</u>ove lets you drag the bar wherever you want, though it's easier to just click and drag the window title bar.

## Navigation Tips and Tricks

After you get beyond the basics of clicking links and using the Back and Forward buttons (have you noticed that <u>B</u>ack and <u>F</u>orward are also available from the right-mouse button pop-up menu?), you might find that there are a lot of subtle ways you can improve document navigation.

Sometimes it's something as subtle as noting that the links you've visited recently are highlighted in a different color than links you haven't been to. If you're looking for a site that you've been to before, this alone can give you a real clue. (Visited links are those that are still included in your History List. You can change the number of days for the expiration of visited sites in the Appearance panel of the Preferences dialog box.)

Or maybe you've noticed that at the bottom of the <u>G</u>o menu there's a selectable list of the last few sites you've visited. Likewise, at the bottom of the <u>C</u>ommunicator menu is a selectable list of the open browser windows.

Maybe you even noted that the name of the Location: toolbar changes to Netsite: when you're connected to a Netscape server. Maybe you've decided that this is more of a curiosity than an actual help. Maybe it's just advertising for Netscape. Who knows?

> **TIP** Too lazy to point your mouse at a link? Use the Tab key to highlight successive links or the Shift-Tab key to cycle back through them. Press Enter when you're on a link you want to follow.

A more useful new feature of the Location field is its capability to automatically complete addresses for you. Type in **foo** and press Enter, for example, and after a few seconds Navigator figures out that you really want to be connected to http://www.foo.com. You can even type **foo/bar** and be whisked off to http://www.foo.com/bar. If the URL begins with ftp.*whatever*..., you'll be connected to ftp://ftp.whatever....

Even better, the Location field now gives you hints as you type, so you don't have to type the entire address. If, for example, you start to type http://www.yahoo.com, and, if that address is still in your history list, by the time you get to http://www.y, the entire address appears in the Location field. All you have to do is press the Enter key to accept it. If it guesses wrong—if, for example, you really wanted http:/www.yellostuff.com, you can hit the down-arrow key to step through all of its suggestions until you get the right one. This feature is absolutely indispensable for retyping in those excruciatingly long URLs that you have (naturally) forgotten to bookmark.

Even quicker, though, is the handy drop-down menu that you can access from the Location field by simply clicking the down-arrow to the right of the field. This isn't a complete list of all the addresses you've visited lately, though—only the ones you've typed into the Location field.

> **TIP**
> We've all seen that annoying dialog box that pops up and tells us "The server does not have a DNS entry" or the page that comes up as a cryptic "Not found—requested document does not exist." If you get the first message, try again. You might have just had trouble connecting to your Domain Name Server computer. A second try might get the page you want. (However, if other sites work but this one never does, it has probably disappeared.) In the second case, try entering the base URL without the page and/or path name—for example, not http://www.foo.com/bar.htm, but http://www.foo.com. The odds are good that you'll get the site's home page, and can search for the new location of the missing page from there.

If you're running Windows 95 or a Macintosh, you can drag and drop a link on the desktop to create a shortcut to that page. Click the shortcut and you automatically launch Navigator, pointed right at that page. Pretty slick.

On a final note, did you know that you can get Netscape to set up a home page for you—that is, if you lack the knowledge or inclination to do so yourself. Just point Navigator to **http://personal.netscape.com/custom/page/show_page.html** and follow the prompts.

### Understanding URLs

An URL, or Uniform Resource Locator, is a page's address. Web page addresses are on the Internet, though pages can also live on your disk drive, network, or corporate intranet. (Actually, each page element, such as images and applets, also has its own unique URL.)

Each URL takes the following form:

  Protocol://server/pathname/file

*Protocol* is the file transfer method. For Web pages, this is HTTP, or Hypertext Transfer Protocol. Other possible protocols include FTP (File Transfer Protocol), news, and gopher.

*Server* is the server computer's domain name. This is commonly something like www.foo.com. The part of the domain name after the last period (or dot, to use common Internet slang) indicates the type of host organization. Historical organization domain names have ended in .com for commercial businesses, .gov for federal government, .net for network service providers, and .org for non-profit organizations. However, new rules will open up a whole new list of potential server name suffixes.

*Pathname* is the path on the server computer in which the file is stored. If a file is stored in the server computer's root directory, no path name is required.

*File* is the file name you are requesting. For an HTML document, this file name will most often end in .htm or .html. However, you can request files of any type and they will be displayed if Navigator knows how to handle them.

A typical URL for an HTML document might look like this:

http://www.foo.com/stuff/index.htm

This indicates that the page should be transferred using HTTP protocol (in other words, it's an HTML document), and the server's name is www.foo.com. The file is stored on that computer in a directory named stuff, and the file's name is index.htm.

Documents stored on a local drive or network are accessed in the same manner, but the protocol designation is file:// and the server name is the drive number of the computer followed by a vertical bar. A typical local file might have this address:

file://C|/Data/tips.html

This file is on the C: drive in a directory named Data and is called tips.html.

## Copy, Paste, and Find

You expect just about every software program to have an Edit menu, and on this menu you'd expect to find the standard Cut (Ctrl+X), Copy (Ctrl+C), and Paste (Ctrl+V) commands. Navigator is no different. Though you can't edit on the screen, you can highlight text on the screen and copy it for pasting into other applications. (When text is highlighted, the Copy command is also available from the right mouse button pop-up menu.) The Cut and Paste commands are ghosted in Navigator, but can be used in Composer.

You can easily select and highlight all of the text in the current window or frame before copying by choosing Select All (Ctrl+A) from the Edit menu.

The Edit menu also includes a Find command, labeled Find in Page (Ctrl+F) to differentiate it from the Search button, which is for searching the Net, not the page. Selecting Find in Page brings up a pretty standard Find dialog box (see Figure 8.13).

**FIG. 8.13**
The Find dialog box is spartan, but utilitarian.

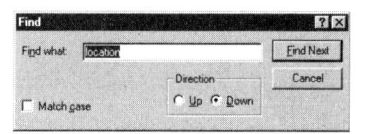

It allows you to specify a search word or phrase, whether to Match Case, and whether to search Up or Down from the current cursor position (which you can set by clicking in the display). After you've used the Find dialog box, you can Find Again by making that selection from the Edit menu, or by using the key combination Ctrl+G.

All of this is well and good for copying text, you say, but what if you want to save an image? No problem. Aim the mouse pointer at the graphic you want to save and click the right mouse button. The pop-up menu includes a selection labeled Save Image As, which brings up a dialog box from which you can save the selected image to disk.

## Controlling Page Downloading

The Web is a huge, lunkering beast and seems to be slowing down daily. If you're stuck with a slow dial-up connection, waiting for a big page to load can drive you nuts.

Fortunately, Navigator includes several tools to help you feel in control, though they do little to speed up actual loading.

First is the Stop button on the toolbar (or the Esc key, its keyboard equivalent). If a page is taking forever, click the button. The page stops loading and you're in control again. You can go elsewhere or click the Reload button (Ctrl+R) to try again and hope you luck onto a faster connection this time. (These options are also available as the Reload and Stop Page Loading selections on the View menu, and as Stop and Reload on the right mouse button pop-up menu.)

> **TIP** Are those clever GIF animations driving you nuts? You can turn them off by selecting View, Stop Animations.

If you have a really slow connection and it seems like you're always waiting for images to load, you can speed things up by turning off automatic image loading. You do this by selecting Edit, Preferences and selecting the Advanced panel. From here, uncheck the Automatically Load Images check box and click OK to finish. From here on out, you get placeholders instead of images, and the Navigation toolbar has a new Images icon you can click to selectively load in the images for the displayed page (see Figure 8.14).

**FIG. 8.14**
There are no graphics displayed on this page, only placeholders, but you can get them by clicking the Image button on the toolbar.

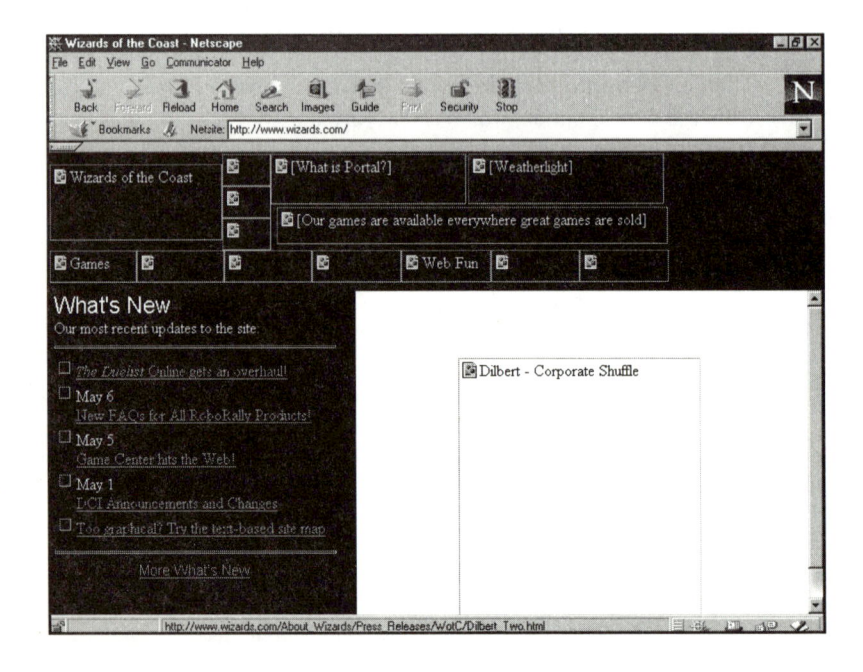

http://www.quecorp.com

If you have a slow connection but plenty of disk space and/or memory, you can speed up loading for frequently visited sites by adjusting your cache settings. You do this by choosing Preferences from the Edit menu and bringing up the Advanced/Cache panel (see Figure 8.15).

**FIG. 8.15**
Adjust your Cache settings to optimize overall Navigator performance, but watch your system resources when you do.

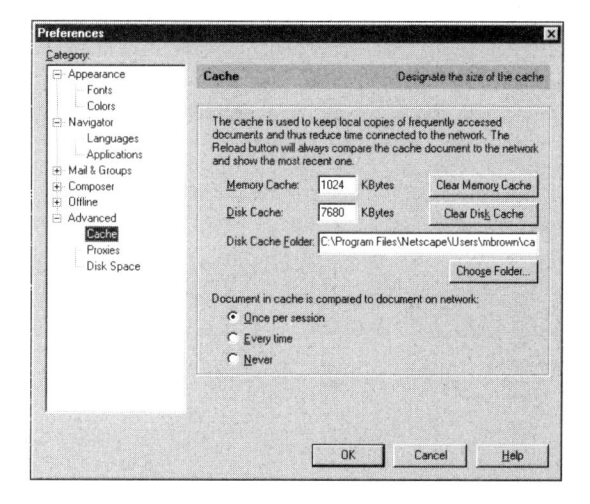

Set your Memory Cache and Disk Cache settings as high as your system resources allow. Perhaps even more important than the size of your caches, though, is the setting you choose using the three option buttons in the section labeled "Document in cache is compared to document on network:." By default, this is set to Once Per Session. This means that every time you boot up Navigator and go to a site for the first time in that session, Navigator compares the site data to the data already stored in the cache. This is slow, but worse than that is the second setting, Every Time, which makes the comparison every time you visit a site! For a very slow connection, you should choose Never. This setting always uses the data in your cache.

So how do you know when a site has been updated? You have to check manually. When a site you want to check is displayed, hold down the Shift key and click the Reload button. (Surprise! When used by itself, Reload just reloads from cache! The Shift key forces a "super reload.")

▶ **See** "Automatically Updating Bookmarks," **p. 161**

# About This Page

Some people are content to just get into a car and drive it away. Others just absolutely cannot enjoy the experience unless they know what's going on under the hood.

If you're the type who has to understand the underpinnings of everything before you can sit back and enjoy the experience, you'll be glad to know that Navigator provides a full set of tools for peeking "under the hood" of the pages you're viewing.

## Chapter 8  Navigator In-Depth

The easiest of these tools to get to are on the View menu: Page Source (Ctrl+U) and Page Info (Ctrl+I). These viewers are also available from the right mouse button pop-up menu, where they are mysteriously renamed View Source and View Info.

The first, Page Source or View Source, depending on where you launched it from, brings up a view window that displays the HTML source for the currently displayed page (see Figure 8.16).

**FIG. 8.16**
The Page Source window lets you examine the HTML code that makes up the displayed document.

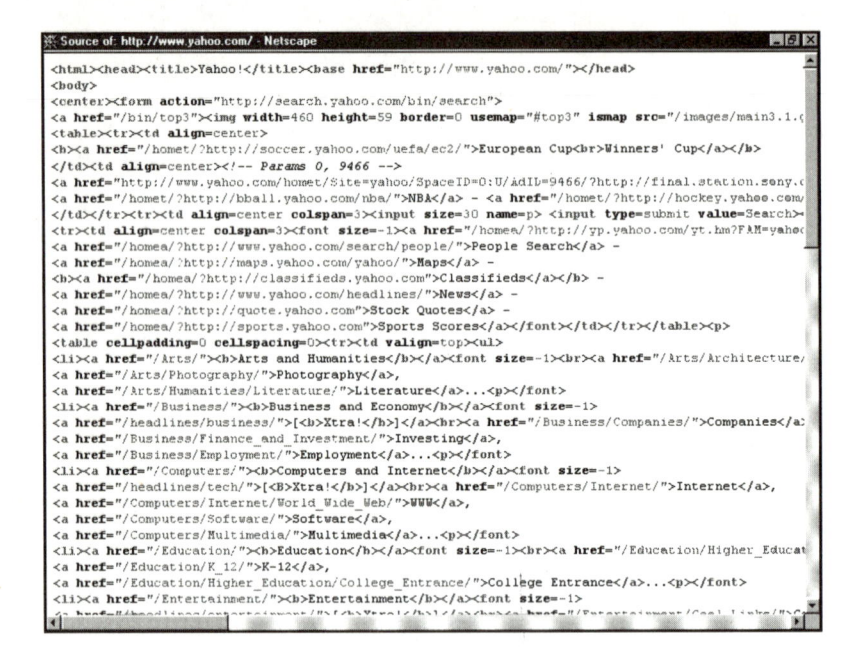

There's nothing fancy about this screen—it just shows you the HTML (and JavaScript) code for the current page. You can drag the mouse to highlight text, but to copy it for pasting into another application you have to use the Ctrl+C key combination. There's no edit menu on this screen. When you're done, you can click the window's Close button or use the Communicator close window hotkey combination Ctrl+W.

You can view the source to a page without first displaying the document by entering the page's URL into the Location bar in this format:

view-source:www.foo.com/page.htm

This leaves the page you're currently viewing alone and just loads the source of the target page. When you close the View Source window, you go right back to the Navigator window with your previous page intact, though the newly typed URL is still in the Location field. (If you type **about:document** into the Location toolbar, it's as if you typed **view-source:URL** for the currently displayed page.)

> **TIP**  Hung up? Want to show the current page transfer status? Press Ctrl+Alt+T.

View, Page Info (Ctrl+I, or View Info on the right mouse button pop-up menu) brings up the page information window shown in Figure 8.17.

**FIG. 8.17**
Everything you ever wanted to know about a page, but didn't know how to ask—it's all in the Document Info window.

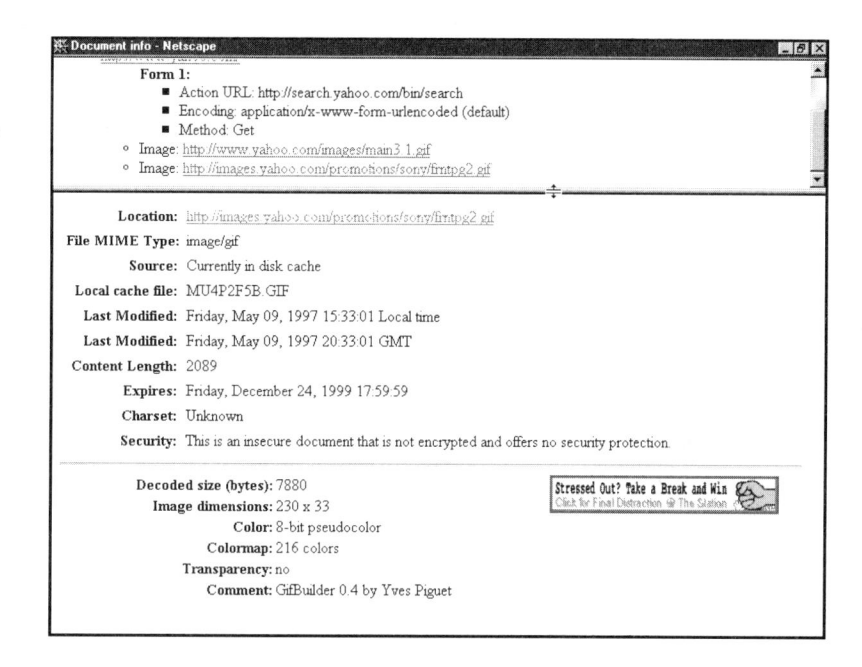

I won't bother to go through all the information displayed on this page. Suffice it to say that just about everything you'd ever want to know about a page is here somewhere. If there's enough information shown that you get scroll bars on the right side, you can click the center dividing bar and drag it up and down to make more room one way or the other.

> **TIP** If you're in a page that uses frames, the View menu's Page Source and Page Info selections only show you information for the outer frameset of the page. To view information for an individual frame, click in the frame, then right-click to bring up the pop-up menu. It lists menu items for View Frame Source and View Frame Info.

Among other things, the top frame lists the URLs of all page elements, such as graphics. The bottom frame initially lists information for the page itself. But if you click one of the URLs in the top frame, the bottom frame displays the chosen item and gives you information about that item only. Quite handy for analyzing a page in-depth—for example, in Figure 8.18, the bottom frame shows information about an advertising graphic on the Yahoo! home page.

As with the Page Source window, you can drag and use Ctrl+C to copy text to paste in other applications, and you can close the window by using the window's close button or the Ctrl+W key combination.

Is there a Java applet running on the current page? Then you might want to take a look at the Java Console, which is available from the Communicator menu, as shown in Figure 8.18.

**FIG. 8.18**
The Java Console displays messages that the applet programmer wants you to see.

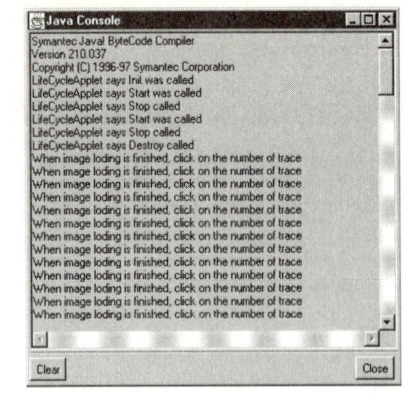

The Java Console only shows you messages that are programmed in by the applet creator. Many Java applets display no console messages at all. Some display instructions or status information. Most of the time, if the applet programmer wants you to look at the Java Console, she tells you somewhere on the applet's host page to launch the Java Console. You can still bring it up even if you're not told, but it's likely to remain blank except for some initial information about the Symantec Java JIT compiler that's built into Communicator.

Finally, if you want to know all about the Security Info for the current page, you can find out all you need to know by making that selection from the Communicator menu. But it's easier to just click the big padlock Security icon in the Navigator toolbar or use the hotkey combination Ctrl+Shift+S. You see a window similar to that shown in Figure 8.19.

**FIG. 8.19**
The Security Info window not only provides security information for the current page, it also serves as a menu for all Communicator security issues.

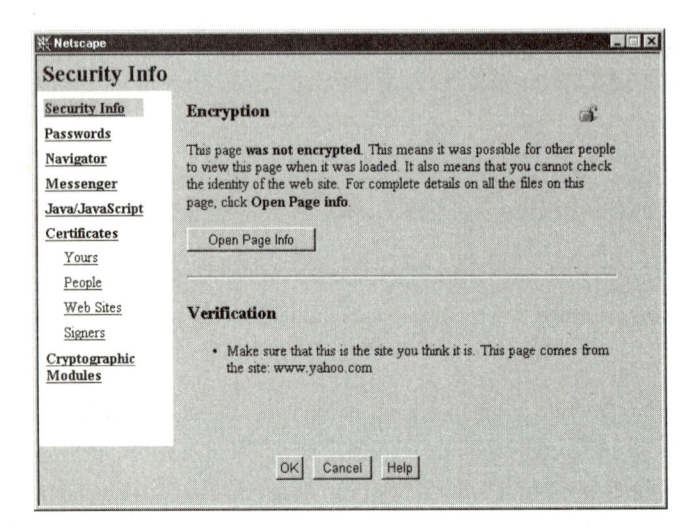

The unlocked lock icon in the upper-right, along with the accompanying text, verifies that the current page is not encrypted and is therefore not secure. If you want more information, you can click the Page Info button to bring up that screen, which we've already talked about.

http://www.quecorp.com

The left side of the Security Info window is taken up by a menu that has little or nothing to do with the current page. It's actually a menu for all the Communicator security options, and it's so important that we've dedicated an entire chapter to it—see Chapter 17, "Security Options."

## Setting Up Multiple Users

From the beginning, Netscape users have requested—nay, demanded—that Navigator be modified to accept multiple user profiles. With the introduction of Communicator, Netscape has complied with this request.

Individual user profiles means that you can set up multiple means of access for yourself, or for several individuals using the same computer. I use two profiles for my copy of Communicator, one for my primary ISP and one for my backup ISP. Each profile has separate settings for my e-mail and newsgroup servers and even different home pages.

You set up different user profiles through a stand-alone program called the Profile Manager. When you installed Communicator, it was installed in the same menu or icon group as Communicator itself. When you run it (you must shut down Communicator first), you see the screen shown in Figure 8.20.

**FIG. 8.20**
Profile Manager is a separate program that lets you create multiple user profiles.

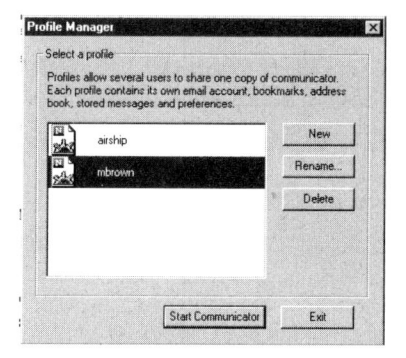

The central window lists profiles you've already created—in this case, airship for my secondary ISP, and mbrown for my primary ISP. I can rename either of these by highlighting the profile and clicking the Rename button, or I can get rid of the profile by choosing Delete. Instead, let's create a new user profile by clicking the New button.

You enter into a setup wizard that takes you through a sequence of dialog boxes. These ask you for your full name, e-mail address, and the name you want to use for the new profile. (You are also allowed to change the location of the directory that your new profile will be stored in, though that's not recommended.) You are asked for e-mail information for your new profile, including the URL of your SMTP (outgoing) mail server. You also need the name of your incoming mail server and whether it's a POP3 or IMAP server. (If you don't know the answers to these questions, you need to contact your ISP or system administrator and ask.) You also need the URL for your news (NNTP) server, its port number, and whether it is a secure server.

After entering all that, you click the Finish button to end and are dropped back to the dialog box shown in Figure 8.20. Your new profile is listed in the central window. At this point, you can choose to Exit or you can run Communicator.

# Communicator Command-Line Options

You can set up the Communicator icon to launch directly into any of its applications by setting it that way in the Appearance panel of the Preferences dialog box (Edit, Preferences). But that's the easy way. You can also do it by fooling around with its desktop shortcut icon. This method even gives you a couple of extra added secret goodies you can initiate on launch.

First, take a look at Table 8.2, which lists the Communicator command-line options.

**Table 8.2   Communicator Command-Line Options**

| Option | Action |
| --- | --- |
| -address | Opens Address Book |
| -compose | Opens Message Composition window |
| -edit [URL] | Opens Composer [URL optional] |
| -h URL | Opens URL in browser [-h optional] |
| -k | Navigator kiosk mode |
| -mail | Opens Messenger |
| -netcaster | Opens NetCaster |
| -new_profile | Launches New Profile Wizard |
| -news | Opens Message Center |
| -profile_manager | Launches Profile Manager |

Now perform the following steps:

1. Go to the desktop and right-click the Communicator shortcut icon.
2. Pick Properties from the pop-up menu.
3. Select the Shortcut tab.
4. The Target field is highlighted. Use the right-arrow key to place the cursor at the end of the line of text that is already in the field. DO NOT TYPE OVER ANY EXISTING TEXT!
5. At the end of the line, type a space followed by the command-line option you want to use. For example, to launch Messenger, add **-mail**.
6. Click OK to finish.

http://www.quecorp.com

The next time you double-click the Communicator icon, it comes up in Messenger (or whatever other option you chose) rather than Navigator.

Note that there are two command-line options that are not for simply switching the application that launches when you start up. If you add **-h URL**, Communicator launches Navigator with the page at the designated URL already loaded. In fact, the **-h** part is totally optional. If you just place an URL in the command line, Navigator finds the page and launches it. You can even use Location bar shortcuts. For example, if you add microsoft, Navigator launches with the page **http://www.microsoft.com**.

> **CAUTION**
>
> Watch out! If you mistype anything where you intended to add an URL or command-line option, Navigator launches and tries to interpret your mistyping as an URL. While this isn't disastrous (you just get a site-doesn't-exist-type message), it certainly isn't what you intended. This will happen every time you run Communicator until you fix the problem, so it becomes more than just a minor annoyance.

The other interesting command line option is -k. This launches Navigator in "kiosk mode"—that is, it leaves off the menu bar. You still get toolbars and a status bar, so the effect isn't complete. But if you want to eliminate the menu bar, toolbars, and status bar, do the following:

1. Run Navigator.
2. From the View menu, turn off all three toolbars.
3. Exit Navigator.
4. Now add the -k option to the Communicator shortcut icon, as outlined earlier.
5. Run Communicator from the icon.
6. You get a Navigator window with no menu and no toolbars. It displays your home page.
7. Press the Ctrl+Alt+S key combination. The status bar disappears.

You now have Navigator running without menu, toolbars, or status bar—true "kiosk mode."

# The History List

If you're the type who worries about Big Brother spying on you—or even if you're simply concerned that your spouse might find out what kinds of Web sites you've been browsing—you're going to hate the Navigator History List. If, on the other hand, you've browsed to a great site one night only to find out that you have lost it the next, the History List is bound to become your best friend.

To display the History List, select Communicator, History (Ctrl+H) from the Navigator menu. You see a window similar to that shown in Figure 8.21.

## Chapter 8  Navigator In-Depth

**FIG. 8.21**

Navigator's History List is your complete database of recently visited sites.

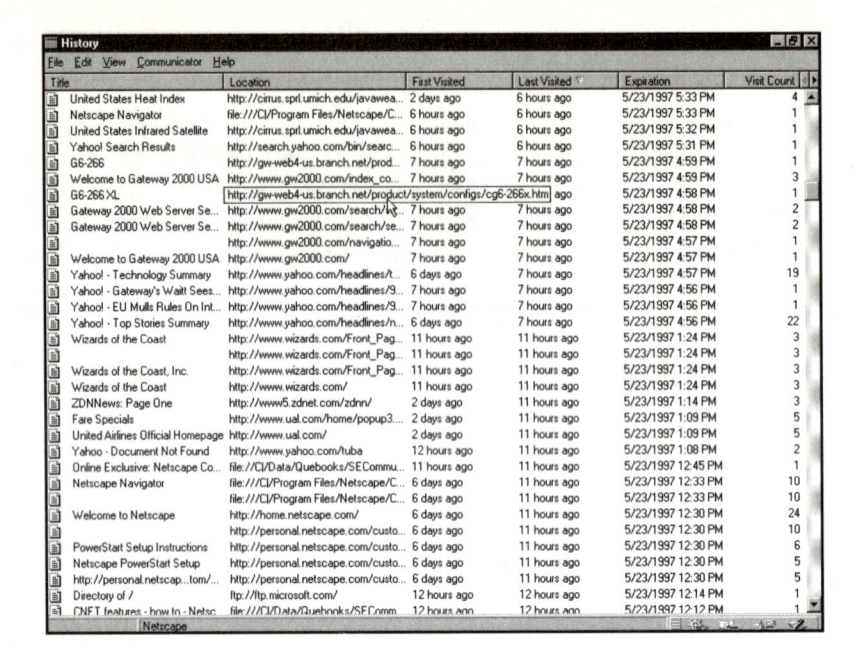

The History List shows the title of each site visited, its location, the time you last visited the site, when the entry is due to expire, and how many times you visited. Whew! Don't you wish you had records that good at tax time?

Clicking any column title sorts the list by that criteria. (You can do the same thing by selecting any of the View by options on the View menu.) Clicking the same title again sorts by descending, rather than ascending, order. (There are selections for these options, too, on the View menu.)

> **TIP** You can use multiple selection in the History List. To choose multiple contiguous entries, click one entry, then hold down the Shift key and click the entry at the other end of the group. To highlight multiple noncontiguous entries, hold down the Ctrl key as you click individual entries.

Double-clicking an entry takes you directly to that page in Navigator. Right-clicking an entry brings up a pop-up menu with options to Go to Page, Add to Bookmarks, Cut, Copy, or Delete the entry. Cut and Copy put only the URL of the entry into the Clipboard. Delete and Cut both remove an entry permanently from the list, though Delete doesn't put the URL into the Clipboard.

The File menu also contains the Go to Page and Add to Bookmarks options, but it also features Add Page to Toolbar and Create Shortcut. The former adds a button to the Personal Toolbar for the selected page; the latter creates a shortcut icon on the desktop.

The File menu also has a Save As item, which lets you save the entire History List as an HTML file, which you can later load as a page into Navigator.

http://www.quecorp.com

From the Edit menu, you can choose the Search History List option, which brings up the search dialog box shown in Figure 8.22.

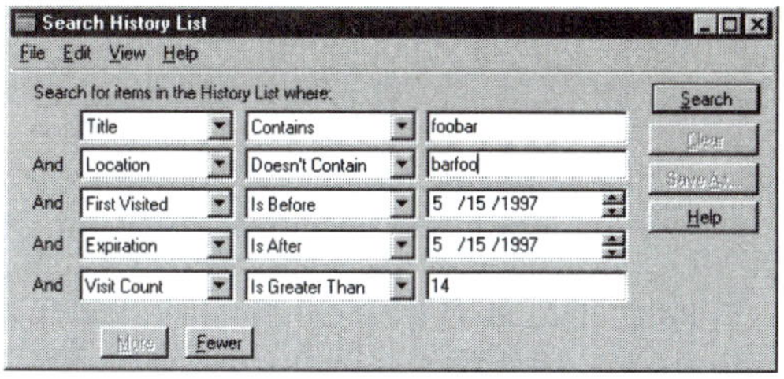

**FIG. 8.22**
The Search History List dialog box gives you plenty of ways to find a page.

From this dialog box, you can search for the page you want in dozens of different ways.

You can clear the entire History List by choosing Select All (Ctrl+A) from the Edit menu, then pressing the Delete key. But that's using the brute force method. There is a Clear History button on the Navigator panel of the Preferences dialog box. To get to it, select Edit, Preferences, then highlight the Navigator menu selection on the dialog box. While you're here, note the control next to the button, which lets you set the number of days until a visited page expires. That's where the History List gets its Expiration listing. You can, of course, change this if you want to. It defaults to nine days.

## The Status Bar

You probably pay a lot of attention to the Navigator status bar without even realizing it. The status bar (see Figure 8.23) tells you all about how page elements are loading. Its most common messages seem to be "Looking Up [host]" and "Contacting [host]". These are followed by messages reporting various percentages of page elements downloaded until you finally reach that Holy Grail of browsing: "Document: Done".

But the message area isn't the only useful part of the status bar.

At its left end is the security icon. This is displayed as an unlocked padlock when a page is unencrypted and a locked padlock when a page is encrypted. It mirrors the function of the Security icon on the Navigator toolbar and has the advantage of being smaller and of being visible even when the Navigation toolbar has been closed or hidden. You can even double-click it to bring up the Security Info window, just as you can with the larger toolbar icon.

To the padlock's right is the gas gauge area. This displays a constantly moving gray bar while page elements are being requested and downloaded, occasionally showing a percentage inline (refer to Figure 8.23) when it has some idea how much of an element has been downloaded.

The message area itself is likely to tell you just about anything. It says when it's looking up a host, when it's actually talking to one, what percentage of some particular page element has just been downloaded, when a document is done downloading, and even when a Java applet is running. Sometimes a particularly nasty site takes over this message area and displays an annoying scrolling message. You see how to take care of that in a moment.

**FIG. 8.23**
The status bar can tell you a lot about what's happening with your page.

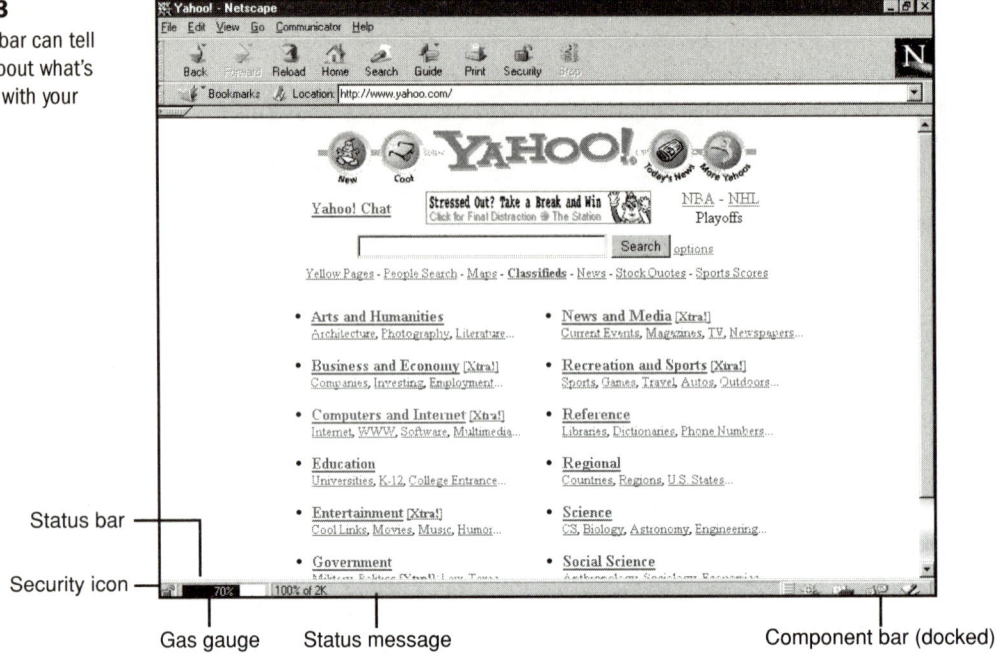

*Labels on figure:* Status bar, Security icon, Gas gauge, Status message, Component bar (docked)

> **TIP**
> Hover the mouse pointer over a link, and you see the URL it points to displayed in the status bar message area.

First we should discuss the final element on the right side of the status bar. If the Component bar is minimized and docked, this is where it lives. You can undock and expand the Component bar by clicking the box on its left end.

If you need to see just a little bit more screen real estate, or if that scrolling advertising message is just driving you nuts, you can evaporate the status bar by pressing Ctrl+Alt+S. And you can always bring the status bar back by pressing it again.

## The Pop-Up Menu

Time and again throughout this book we have been and will be mentioning the right mouse button pop-up menu. Wherever you are, whatever you want to do, always try pointing your cursor at the item you are interested in, and then click the right mouse button. Ninety-nine times out of 100, you get a very compact and extremely useful context-sensitive pop-up menu. That "context-sensitive" part is very, very important.

Bring up the pop-up menu over a blank area of the display, and the pop-up menu can help you save a background graphic, bookmark a page, and mimic a half dozen of the most useful Navigator menu options.

http://www.quecorp.com

Bring it up when you're over a graphic, and you can save that graphic to disk, or even set it as your system wallpaper.

Invoke the pop-up menu over a link, and you can bookmark the page it points to without even having to look at it.

When you're inside a set of frames, the pop-up menu lets you reload a single frame, or view its source, or…. Well, you get the idea. Don't forget the pop-up menu. It's handy, it's useful, and sometimes it's the only way to accomplish something in Navigator.

## Searching for Sites

Need to find a good place to go on the Web, but not quite sure how to start? If you're just curious, click and hold the Guide button on the Navigator toolbar. You get a drop-down menu with the following selections:

- *The Internet*—Selecting this takes you to the Netscape Guide by Yahoo!, an index to interesting sites organized by categories like Business, Computers, Entertainment, and Finance.
- *People*—This choice takes you to the Four11 "white pages" search page, where you can look up just about anybody's e-mail address or phone number.
- *Yellow Pages*—This is like the People choice, but it's for business information.
- *What's New*—Choosing this item takes you to a frequently-updated page that lists about two dozen hot new Web sites. You're sure to find something of interest.
- *What's Cool*—Please do not suspect that these companies pay Netscape for the privilege of being listed on this page. I'm sure that's just a nasty rumor. Really. (Actually, the sites listed on this page do seem to be pretty cool.)

The Guide button might get you started, but after you crawl, you want to learn to walk. That's what the Search button is for. Click it and you are whisked off to Netscape's multi-site search page, shown in Figure 8.24. (Choosing Edit, Search Internet also takes you there.)

One of the resident search engines is selected at random every time you go to this site, or you can click the Customize tab to select one you'd like to use every time you go there.

If that's too slow for you, you can initiate a search using Netscape's search page directly from the Location toolbar. Just type your search words into the Location toolbar, separated by spaces, and press Enter. You are taken directly to a search results page, bypassing the search engine home page. What could be quicker or cooler? (Oh, if you only have one search term, put a space and a period (.) after it, like this: item . That keeps the Location bar from trying to interpret your search item as a page address.)

> **CAUTION**
> Note that this auto-search feature means that if you mistype an URL, putting a space in it, you go to a very strange search results page instead of the site you had in mind.

**FIG. 8.24**
Netscape's search page brings together the top search engines on the Web.

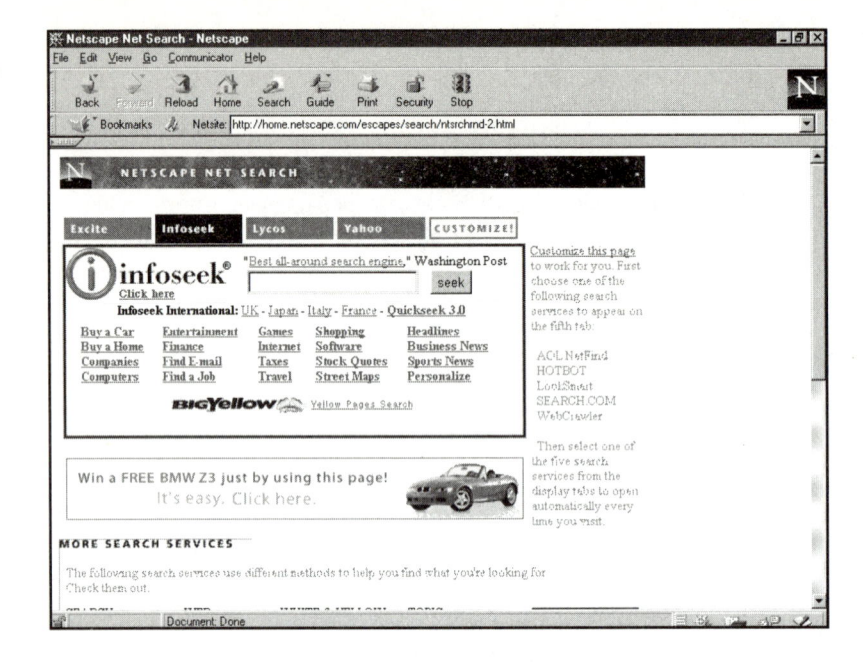

## Working with FTP, Gopher, and Telnet

HTTP isn't the only Internet protocol that Navigator understands, which is just another way of saying that it can handle more than just HTML documents. What interests us most in this context is that Navigator can also handle FTP file transfers, Gopher sites, and even Telnet sessions.

### FTP

Lots of sites are set up with huge libraries of files that you can download for your own use. Some have fancy Web page interfaces, though some just let you browse through their raw directories. It doesn't matter to you. Either way, it's the FTP Internet protocol that Navigator uses to transfer those files quickly and safely to your computer.

Oh, sites don't have to use FTP, but it's much faster than using standard Web HTTP protocol. If the site has a Web interface, the only thing you might notice is that the URL of the file starts with ftp:// rather than http://. But if the site doesn't have a Web interface, you might find yourself browsing through a file structure not unlike the one on your hard disk. Figure 8.25 shows the interface for a "raw" FTP site.

To download a file from an FTP site, you just click the linked file name (shown underlined in Figure 8.25). Your system brings up a file requester dialog box from which you can choose the location on your hard drive in which to save the file.

http://www.quecorp.com

Working with FTP, Gopher, and Telnet | 139

**FIG. 8.25**
Navigator displays the files on an FTP site.

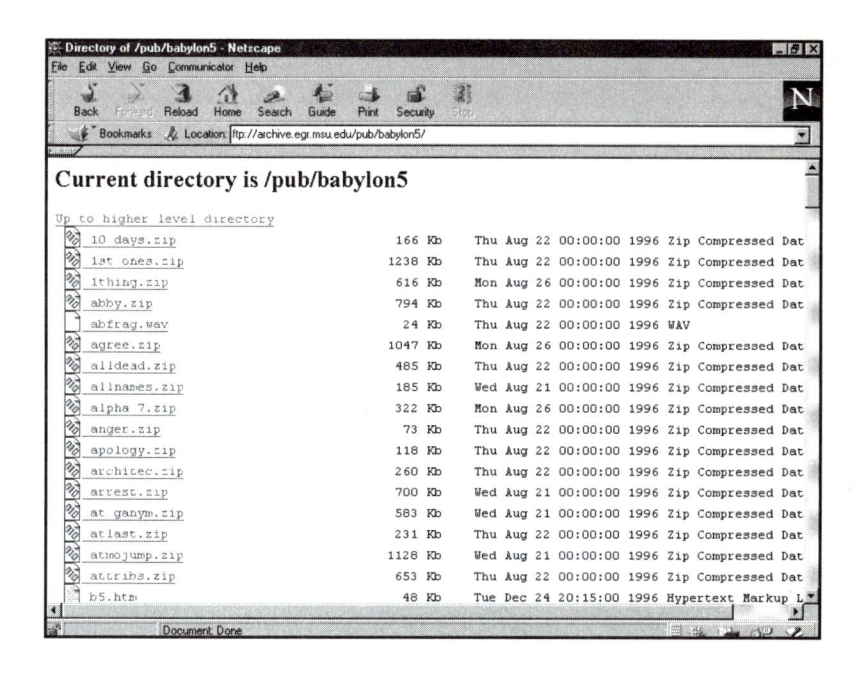

Most sites accept "anonymous" FTP; some require a user name and password. If a user name and password are required, you see a dialog box that asks for them when you try to connect to the site. You can bypass this dialog box by typing in your assigned user name and password as part of the address, like this:

ftp://user:password@ftp.site.com

Because many FTP sites insist that you use your real e-mail address as a password for anonymous downloading, there's a provision for doing that automatically. Just select Preferences from the Edit menu and choose the Advanced panel. You see a check box, Send Email Address as Anonymous FTP Password. Make sure this box is checked, then click the OK button to end.

Some FTP sites also allow you to upload files. If this is allowed, you can use the File, Upload File menu selection.

> **TIP** A great place to find FTP sites is the Monster FTP Sites List at **http://hoohoo.ncsa.uiuc.edu/ftp/**.

Communicator has one fantastic FTP feature that was commonplace in terminal programs, but has been conspicuously absent from browsers until now: FTP smart resume. All this means is, if an FTP transfer is interrupted, you can go back to the site and resume downloading from where you left off. Not only does this reduce frustration when you're 99 percent done with a two-hour download and lose your connection, it's also totally automatic.

## Gopher

Gopher was the precursor to the World Wide Web, and there are still many useful Gopher sites out on the Internet. Navigator can display Gopher information, which is organized in a file structure not unlike an FTP site. However, Gopher sites don't transfer files to your computer; instead, you display them on-screen, just as you do with a Web site.

Gopher sites contain most of the same files types that Web sites do: graphics, text files, and so on. These display just as they do when you encounter them on Web sites. About the only difference is the files-and-folders site structure, and the fact that the URL of a Gopher site begins with gopher:// instead of http://.

## Telnet

When you're talking Telnet, you're talking old, old Internet technology. In fact, you're talking text terminal window. The only good use for Telnet is in communicating with mainframes and minicomputers that are still hooked up to the Internet, such as big universities and scientific research sites.

Still, Navigator provides a way to interact with these sites, though not natively—you use a terminal helper application. The odds are good that a terminal helper application was automatically set up to work with Navigator when you installed Communicator. You can see by accessing a Telnet site, which has an address in the form of telnet://URL. If you don't have a Telnet address to connect to, it's best to just stop here and skip to the next heading. If you don't have an immediate need for Telnet, there's not much use setting it up. There are much better online resources available on the Web, or even via FTP or Gopherspace.

But if you try Telnetting to a location that you must access and it doesn't work, you have to set up a Telnet helper application. First make sure you have a program on your computer that's capable of establishing a text-only Internet connection. On Windows 95, for example, the Telnet.exe application in the Windows folder does just fine.

Choose Edit, Preferences from the Navigator menu and open the Applications panel. In the Description window, scroll down to the entry URL:Telnet Protocol. (If this entry doesn't exist, you have to make a New Type for it first.) Click the Edit button to set the path name to your Telnet program, and you should be in business.

# Other Navigator Features

That's not the nearly the end of what Navigator can do. There's the whole issue of bookmarks, for example. How about style sheets and dynamic HTML? And then there are plug-ins, and Java, and JavaScript, and…well, there's just a lot more territory to cover. But this chapter is already too long, so you'll have to refer to other chapters for those topics: Chapter 9, "Using Bookmarks," Chapter 10, "Interacting with Plug-ins, Java Applets, and JavaScript," Chapter 27, "Dynamic HTML," and Chapter 29, "Using Style Sheets." This one we wrap up with a look at the Help menu.

http://www.quecorp.com

# NetHelp

With Communicator, Netscape has moved all its help onto the Web. It makes sense. After all, it's much easier to create HTML help files and keep them up-to-date on the Web. And if anyone's going to extol the virtues of keeping things Web-centric, it's going to be Netscape!

The F1 key always brings up the context-sensitive NetHelp window, shown in Figure 8.26. (You can also find it by choosing Help Contents from the Help menu.)

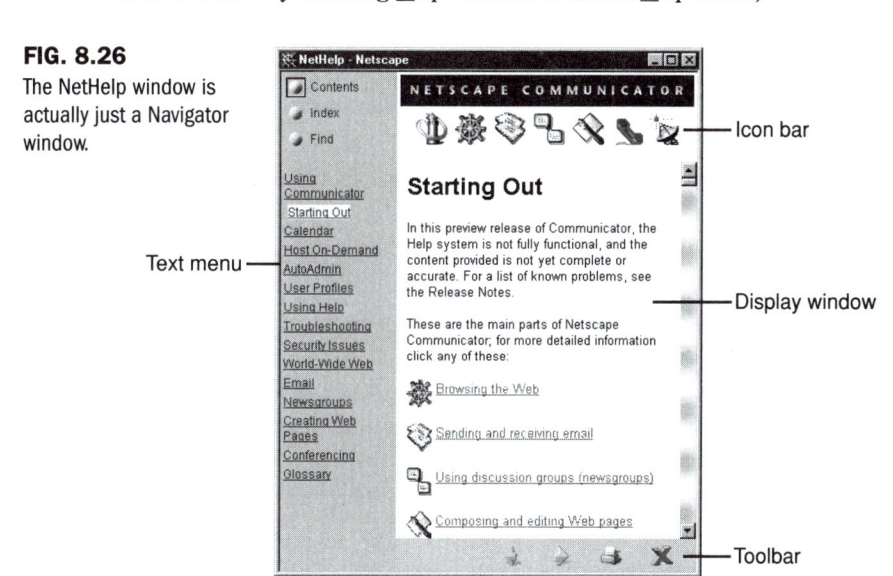

**FIG. 8.26**
The NetHelp window is actually just a Navigator window.

If NetHelp looks familiar, it should—it's actually just another instance of the Navigator browser. The toolbar has been customized and placed along the bottom of the window, but there are more similarities than differences. Along the left margin is an expandable/collapsible menu of available help topics, and along the top is an icon menu for each of the Communicator applications. The bottom-mounted toolbar is equipped with Back and Forward buttons as well as a Print button. The big X in the lower-right corner closes the window, though the window's close button or Ctrl+W does just as well.

In the upper-left corner are three buttons labeled Contents, Index, and Find. The first is for the menu shown in Figure 8.26. The Index button brings up a list of all available topics, in alphabetical order. It includes a search field called Look for:, but the Find button brings up an actual Find dialog box.

The Help menu includes almost a dozen other help selections, each of which takes you to a different page of information on the Netscape site. Here's a quick rundown of their functions:

- *Release Notes*—This takes you to a page that lists the latest features and known bugs for the version of Communicator you're running.

- *Product Information and Support*—Choosing this menu item brings up an informative page with links to FAQs (Frequently Asked Questions lists) and other product support information.
- *Software Updates*—This is the page where Netscape tries to sell you a copy of Communicator, if you haven't bought one already.
- *Register Now*—On this page, you can register your copy of Communicator if you have a valid digital certificate.
- *Member Services*—When I last checked, this link displayed the same page as Software Updates. Maybe Netscape has something else in mind later down the line?
- *International Users*—This selection displays information specific to non-U.S. users of Communicator.
- *Security*—This is the page to visit if you have questions about Communicator security issues.
- *Net Etiquette*—If you're a new UseNet user, you should check out this page before you post any messages. Trust me.
- *About Plug-Ins*—Choosing this menu item generates a custom page internal to Navigator, which shows you information about your installed plug-ins.
- *About Font Displayers*—This selection creates a dialog box that shows you information about Communicator's installed Dynamic Font displayers. Chapter 27, "Dynamic HTML," covers this window.
- *About Communicator*—If you want to see all the copyrights and credits for the Communicator program, take a look at this page.

Of course, not all the help is built into the Help menu. If you hover the cursor over a button, for example, a ToolTip pops up momentarily to explain what it is. Hover over a graphic, and you see the alternate text for that graphic. Hover over a link, and the URL that it points to is displayed in the status bar message area.

Navigator's strangest built-in help feature, though, has got to be the about: location. Type **about:** and the proper associated text into the Location toolbar, and you are treated to a weird and wonderful array of information—not all of it necessarily about Communicator.

Table 8.3 lists these strange about: URLs.

**Table 8.3  About: URLs**

| About: label | Information Displayed |
| --- | --- |
| about: | The Page Info window |
| about:blank | A blank Navigator page |

| About: label | Information Displayed |
|---|---|
| about:[name] | The home page of the Netscape-associated individual named. Names that work are: ari, atotic, blythe, chouck, dmose, dp, ebina, hagan, jeff, jg, jsw, jwz, karlton, kipp, marca, mlm, montulli, mozilla, mtoy, paquin, robm, sharoni, terry, timm |
| about:cache | Lists all files in disk cache |
| about:global | HTML page of global History List |
| about:image-cache | Lists all images in disk cache |
| about:memory-cache | Lists all files in memory cache |
| about:mozilla | Displays a quote from the Book of Mozilla |
| about:whatever | Displays "whatever" you type |

> **TIP** Just too weird to leave out: Type Ctrl+Shift+F to go directly to Netscape's "FishCam" page. Don't ask why, just do it!

In addition to the about: feature, there are a handful of other strange special-purpose URLs worth mentioning, just for the sake of completeness, if nothing else. These are listed in Table 8.4, which is where we end this chapter.

**Table 8.4  Miscellaneous Special URLs**

| Special URL | Action |
|---|---|
| mocha:[JavaScript Command]<br>javascript:[JavaScript Command]<br>livescript:[JavaScript Command] | These three commands are interchangeable. Each brings up the same JavaScript debugger window, which includes a field into which you can type JavaScript commands. If you include a JavaScript command on the line with the URL, it is immediately executed (see Figure 8.27). |
| view-source:URL | Displays the source code for the page |
| news:newsgroup | Launches Messenger and gets news in named group |
| pop3:URL | Opens Message Center |
| mailbox:boxname | Launches Messenger with named folder active |

**FIG. 8.27**
The strange (and perhaps even useful) JavaScript debugger window.

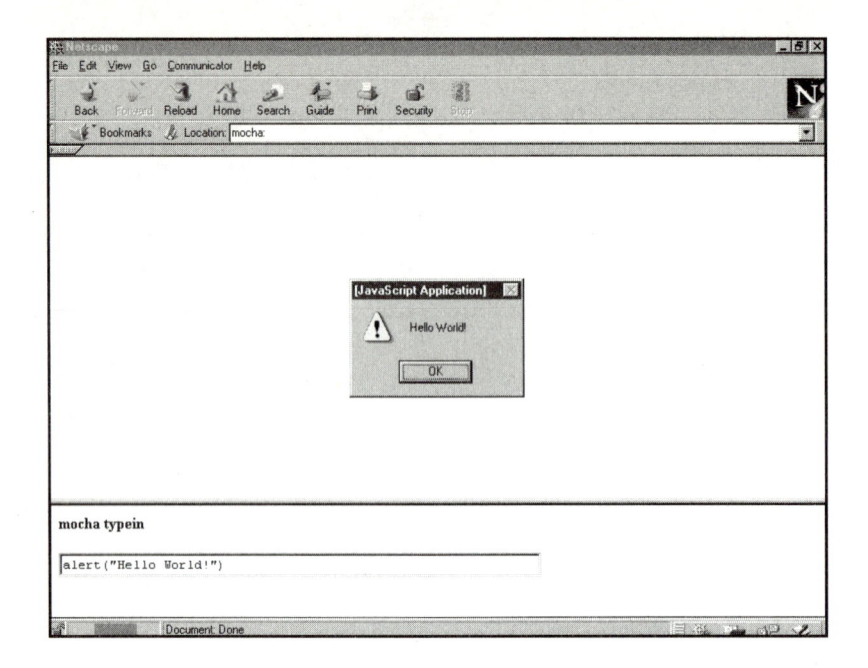

CHAPTER 9

# Using Bookmarks

*by Mark R. Brown*

Nobody really knows how many Web sites are on the Internet, but it's one of those shadowy statistics where you can say "a million" and not be too far wrong. While that number represents a huge potential well of information (and misinformation), it raises the question of how you can ever hope to find anything you're looking for on the Web.

Thankfully, that question is answered by the many index sites and search engines on the Web itself—useful entities like Yahoo!, Alta Vista, and Lycos.

But once you've found a useful (or entertaining) site on the Web, how are you supposed to find it again? You might be able to remember the URL for your favorite Web site, or your four or five most-visited sites, but most of us would be hard-pressed to remember the addresses of our personal "Top 10" sites, much less the most useful 50, or 100, or 1000 sites.

The answer to this dilemma is built into most Web browsers, and it's called *bookmarks*. By bookmarking pages, you create an index of sites you know you'll want to visit again, all listed by (hopefully) useful headings that lead you back again and again, without taxing your memory and overloading your brain with dozens of cryptic URLs.

- **Bookmarks tame the unruly Web**
  Bookmarks distill and organize your own list of Web pages into an intuitive, personalized index.

- **Your Bookmark list is similar to a personal address book**
  You can add to, delete from, edit, and reorganize your bookmark list at will.

- **Good bookmark organization is a must**
  A bookmark list can grow to a huge, unruly size in a short time.

- **Using Netscape Communicator**
  Bookmarking was once a weak spot in Navigator. Netscape even sold a supplementary bookmark management program called SmartMarks. Communicator now provides a full set of tools and features for creating, organizing, and accessing your bookmark list.

## Adding and Referencing a Bookmark

The easiest way to add a bookmark is to go to the page you want to bookmark and press the Ctrl+D key combination. Though easy, you get no feedback that your bookmark has actually been added to the list. When I create a bookmark this way, I always feel that I have to go check my bookmark list to make sure it's there.

A better way, I think, is to click the right-mouse button (click-and-hold on the Macintosh) and select Add Bookmar<u>k</u> from the popup menu (see Figure 9.1). Sirens don't go off, but it does feel more like you've really done something.

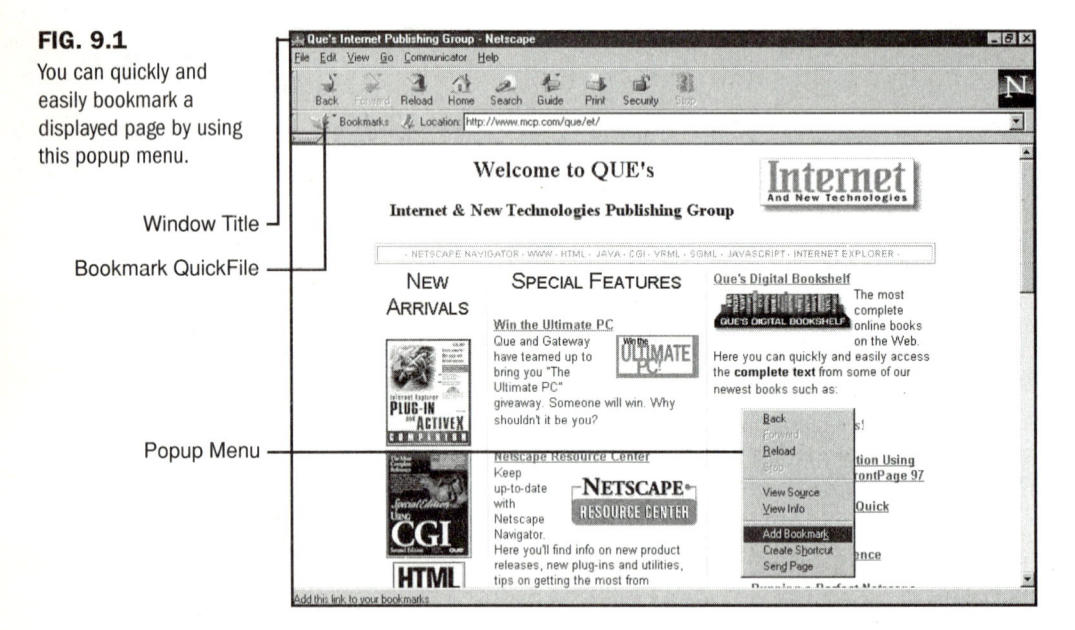

**FIG. 9.1**
You can quickly and easily bookmark a displayed page by using this popup menu.

- Window Title
- Bookmark QuickFile
- Popup Menu

So how can you check and see if the page is really bookmarked? The easiest thing to do is to look at the bookmark list by clicking the Bookmark QuickFile button on the Location toolbar (see Figure 9.1). If this is the first bookmark you've created, your list will only have a single entry, like the one shown in Figure 9.2.

The first thing you'll probably note about a bookmark listing is that the text in the bookmark list is taken from the window title of the page you bookmarked. In Figure 9.1, the window title displays "Que's Internet Publishing Group," and that's exactly how our bookmark is listed in Figure 9.2. Later, we'll see how you can edit your listings, but this is how all bookmarks are initially listed.

To return to the bookmarked page, all you have to do is click the Bookmark button to display the bookmark list, then click the entry of the page you want to go to.

http://www.quecorp.com

**FIG. 9.2**
If you're like most Web surfers, your bookmark list won't be this short for long!

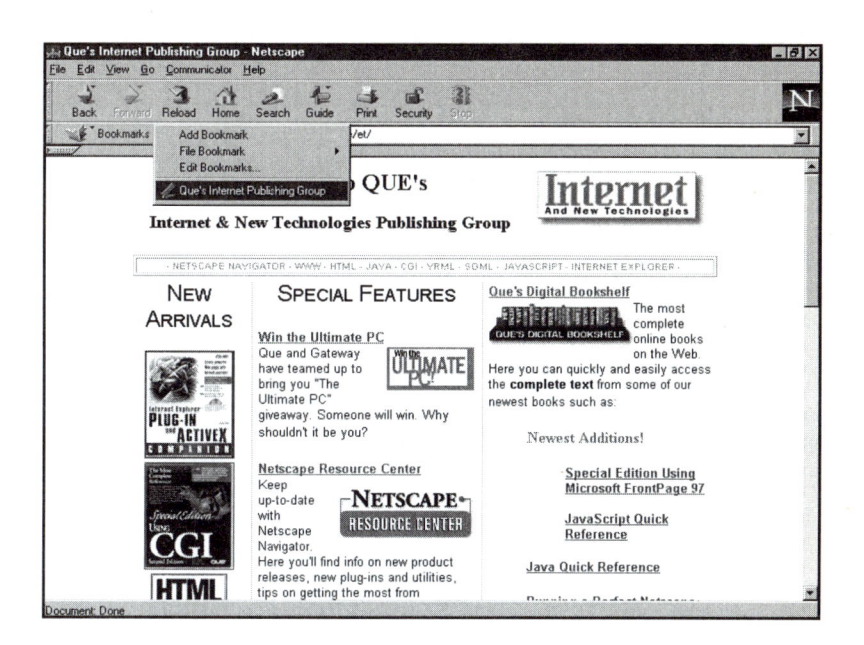

> **TROUBLESHOOTING**
>
> **I bookmarked a page a few weeks ago, but now when I click its name in my bookmark list, all I get is a Document not found error.** The Web is an ever-changing environment—every day, thousands of new pages go online, and thousands of old pages are taken down. The odds are good that the page you bookmarked has been deleted or moved. That's why it's generally best to bookmark a site's home page, which is less likely to disappear, rather than pages that contain specific information, and which are therefore more likely to become dated and obsolete.

If your needs are simple, that's all you really need to know about bookmarks. But if you plan to use more than 20 bookmarks or so, or if you think you're likely to ever want to delete, change, or update your bookmark listings, read on.

## More Ways to Create Bookmarks

Besides the two methods already mentioned (Ctrl+D and right-mouse button, Add Bookmar<u>k</u>), there are several other relatively easy ways to add bookmarks to your bookmark list.

One is via the Communicator menu. Choose <u>C</u>ommunicator, <u>B</u>ookmarks, Add Bookmar<u>k</u>, and the current page will be added. This is probably the most long-winded way to add a bookmark.

## Chapter 9  Using Bookmarks

A quicker method is to click the Bookmark QuickFile button on the Location toolbar and select Add Bookmark from the top of the bookmark list. It's one step shorter than using the menu bar method.

But here's perhaps the most fun way to add a bookmark: drag and drop. Here's how you can drag and drop a location into your bookmark list:

1. Display the page you want to bookmark.
2. Move your pointer over the Page Proxy icon to the left of the Location: window on the location toolbar Your mouse pointer will change into the hand shown in Figure 9.3.

**FIG. 9.3**
You can easily drag and drop the Location icon into your bookmark list.

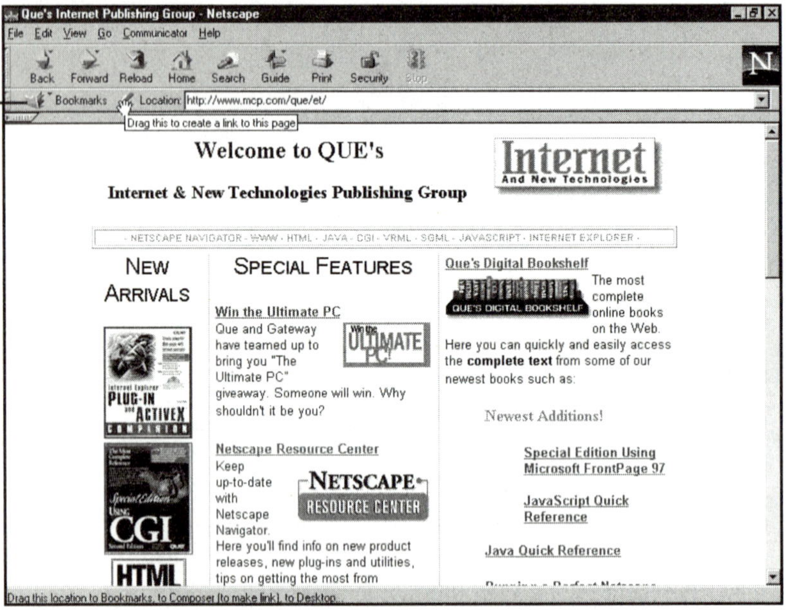

3. Click the location icon and drag the pointer (which will now appear as an arrow with a "chain link" graphic attached) onto the Bookmark QuickFile button right next door. The bookmark list will display, as shown in Figure 9.4.
4. Move the pointer up and down in the list, and you'll see a horizontal line between bookmark entries like that shown in Figure 9.4. When the line is in the spot where you'd like your bookmark to be placed, let go of the mouse button.

The advantage of this method is that it places your bookmark exactly where you want it in your list. Bookmarks created using the other methods simply appear at the end of the bookmark list.

http://www.quecorp.com

**FIG. 9.4**
Drop your link anywhere you want in your bookmark list.

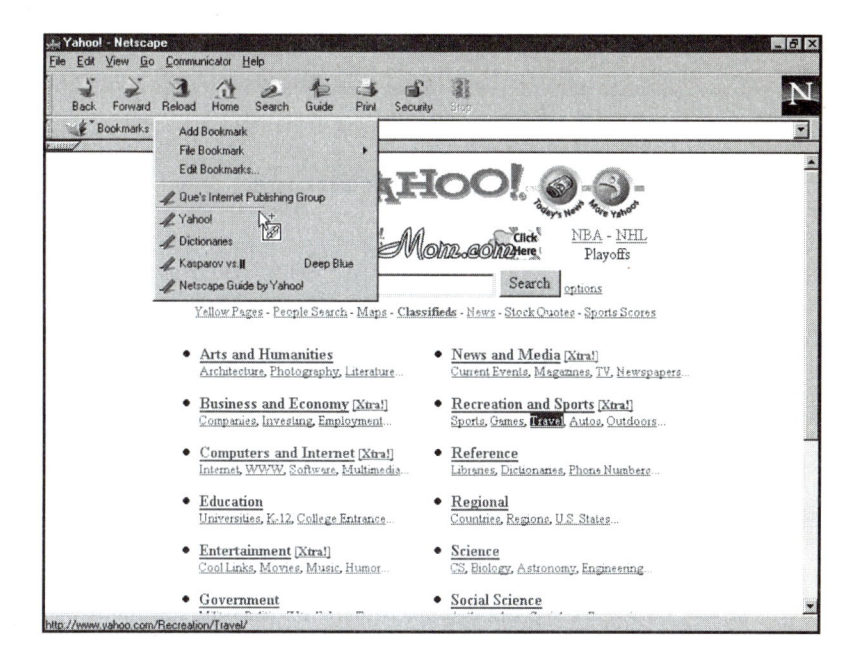

> **TIP** Drag-and-drop bookmarking also works with links displayed on a page. Just click a link, drag it, and drop it into your bookmark list just as you did with the Location icon. This is really slick for bookmarking links that look interesting, but that you don't have the time or inclination to visit right now. You can drag and drop the links into your bookmark list and check them out later.

### Creating Bookmarks from the History List

Well, you goofed up. You visited a great site last night and really meant to bookmark it, but—duh—you forgot. Too late now, right? Not necessarily. Navigator thoughtfully provides a list of the sites you've visited in the last few days, and even gives you a way to create bookmarks from that list. Here's how:

1. Bring up the History List by selecting Communicator, History (Ctrl+H) from the Navigator menu bar. Scroll through the list to find the site that interested you. If you can't find the site right away, it might be helpful to try some of the eight different ways you can list entries through various selections on the View menu.

2. Click and highlight the History List entry you want to bookmark.

3. Select File, Add to Bookmarks from the menu bar, or bring up the right-mouse button popup menu and select Add to Bookmarks (see Figure 9.5).

**FIG. 9.5**
Forget to bookmark an important page? Don't worry—you can add a bookmark later from your History List.

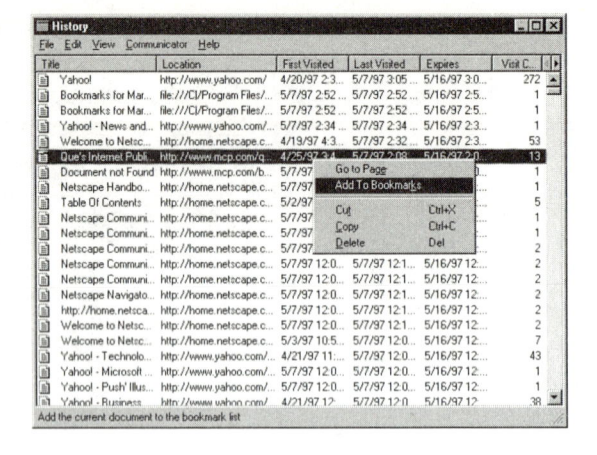

## More Ways to List Bookmarks

The Bookmark QuickFile button on the Location toolbar always provides the handiest access to your bookmark list. But if your Location toolbar is minimized and for some reason you don't feel like making it visible, you can access your list from the Communicator menus by choosing Communicator, Bookmarks. The list you get using this method adds a submenu that includes the destinations normally accessed using the Guide button on the Navigator toolbar (see Figure 9.6).

**FIG. 9.6**
A slightly enhanced Bookmark list is available from the Communicator menu bar.

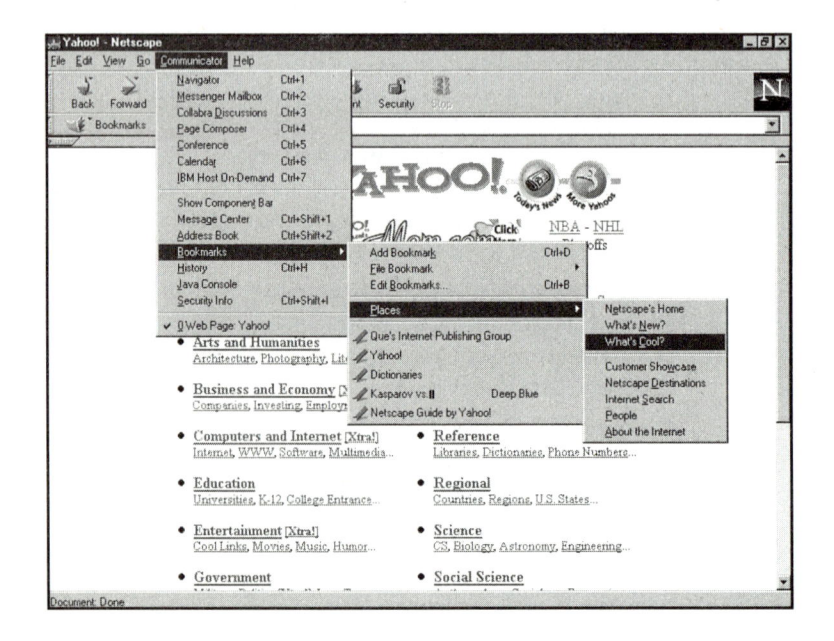

http://www.quecorp.com

Organizing Your Bookmarks | 151

The strangest and arguably most interesting way to display your bookmark file is to load and display it in the Navigator window (see Figure 9.7).

**FIG. 9.7**
A bookmark file is really just an HTML document which can be loaded and displayed in the Navigator window.

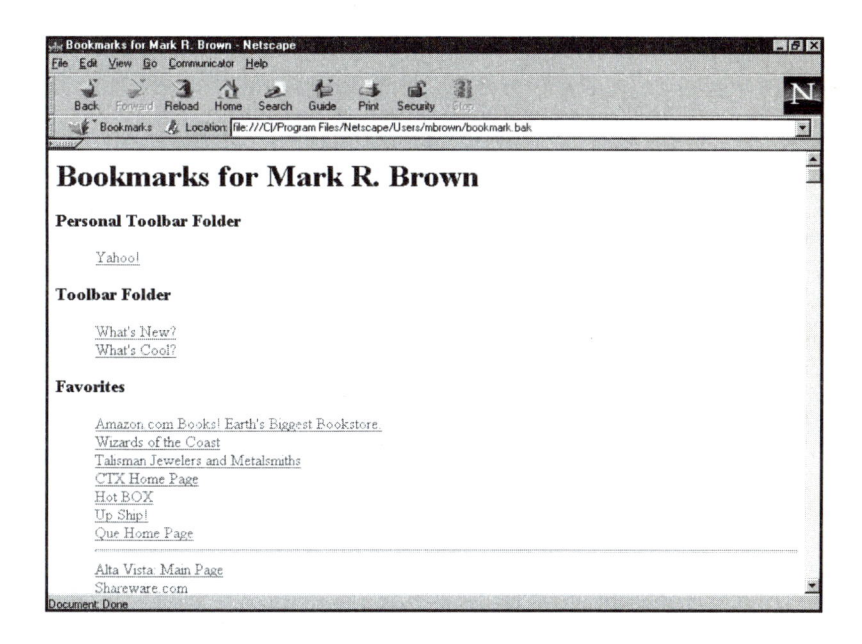

Your bookmark file is stored as an HTML document, and can be loaded and displayed just like any other HTML document. The key is in knowing where it's stored. With Communicator, that would be as a file called bookmark.htm in your user directory. On my Windows 95 system, that's C:/Program Files/Netscape/Users/mbrown/bookmark.htm. Depending on how you installed Communicator and what type of system you're running, your pathname might be something else.

> **TIP** You load an HTML document into Navigator from disk by selecting File, Open Page (Ctrl+O) from the menu. Use the Choose File button to browse your file directories for the file you want.

## Organizing Your Bookmarks

When you start bookmarking pages, the first thing you notice is that your list starts getting very long very quickly. It's obvious right from the start that what you really need is not a simple list, but some kind of hierarchical filing system, a directory-tree or folder-based system like your computer uses for storing program and data files.

Fortunately, that's exactly what Navigator's bookmark list is: a folder-based bookmark filing system (see Figure 9.8).

**FIG. 9.8**
You can create folders like these for storing your bookmarks and keeping them from becoming a disorganized mess.

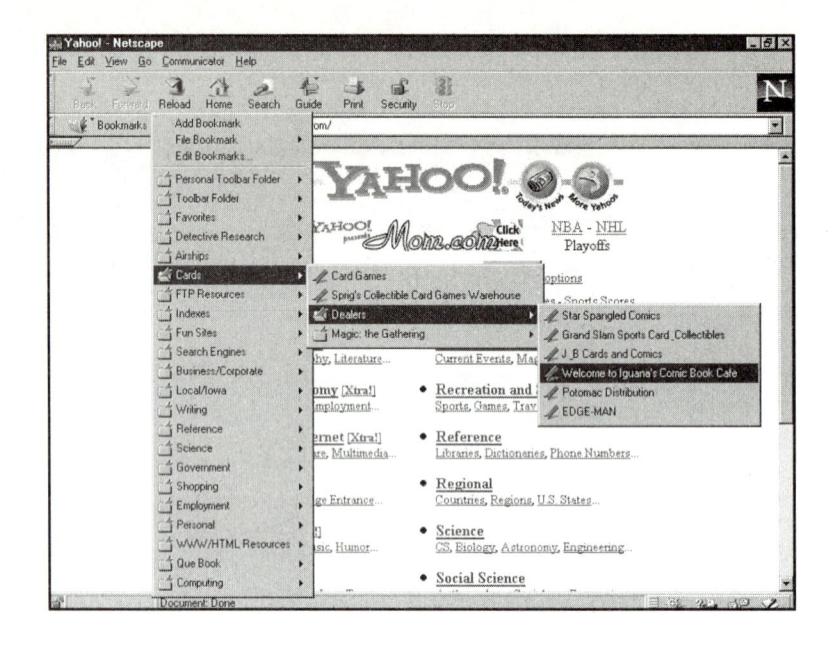

You create folders and store bookmarks in folders using the Edit Bookmarks window. You can bring up the Edit Bookmarks window by choosing Communicator, Bookmarks, Edit Bookmarks (Ctrl+B), but it's easier to click the Bookmark QuickFile button on the Location toolbar and select Edit Bookmarks. You'll see a window similar to the one shown in Figure 9.9.

**FIG. 9.9**
The Edit Bookmarks window is where you change, delete, and organize your bookmark entries.

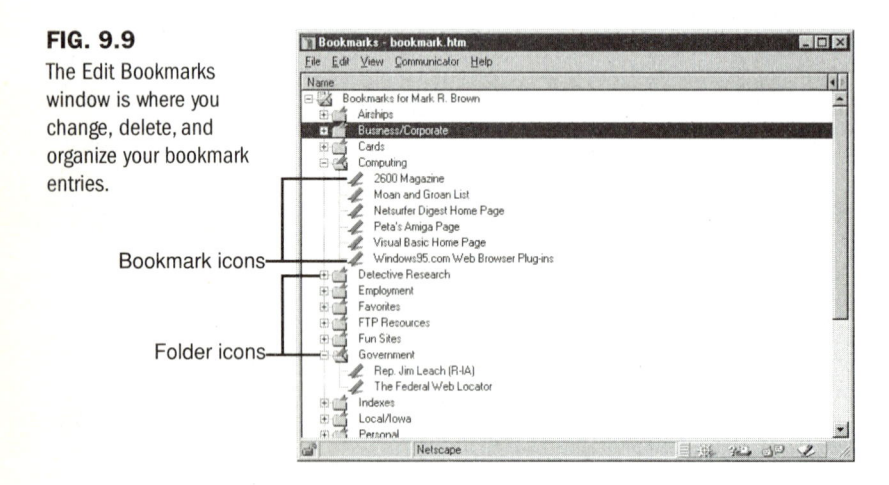

Bookmark icons

Folder icons

The Edit Bookmarks window is what makes Navigator bookmarks a true URL database rather than just a simple list. From here, you can add, delete, move, organize, edit, and otherwise control all of the entries in your bookmark list.

http://www.quecorp.com

Organizing Your Bookmarks | 153

> **TIP** With the Edit Bookmarks window open, you have yet another way to add a bookmark—just drag a link from the Navigator display window and drop it into the Edit Bookmarks window. Wherever you drop it, that's where it will appear in your bookmark list.

## Creating and Using Folders

Perhaps the most obvious and useful function of the Edit Bookmarks window is its ability to allow you to create folders in which to store your bookmarks. Figure 9.8 shows my personal bookmark list, which is organized into dozens of topical folders by topics.

To create a bookmark folder, you select File, New Folder, or you can invoke the right-mouse button popup menu and select New Folder. In either case, you'll see the Bookmark Properties dialog box shown in Figure 9.10.

**FIG. 9.10**
Creating bookmark folders is easy, and it's the key to proper bookmark organization.

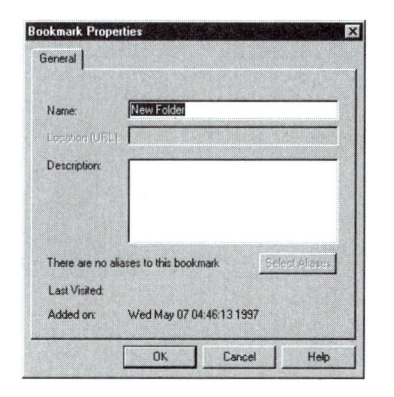

You must enter a Name for your folder (the default is New Folder, so you'll want to create something more descriptive and imaginative than that). You can also enter a description, which can come in handy later if you find you have dozens of folders and are a little foggy as to your original intentions for each of them. Once you've entered this information, click the OK button and you'll see your new folder among your bookmarks, easily identified by a folder icon (see Figure 9.9).

To place a bookmark in a folder, click the bookmark and drag and drop it into the folder.

To see what's in a folder, click the + sign to the folder's left and it will expand, displaying the bookmarks it holds. In Figure 9.9, the Computing and Government folders have been expanded to show the bookmarks they contain.

> **TIP** When you don't want to use a folder, but feel that you need some kind of visual indicator to help organize your bookmarks, you can add a simple separator, a horizontal line, to your bookmark list. To do so, click the bookmark or folder immediately above where you want the line to appear and select File, New Separator from the menu. The line will not be displayed in the Edit Bookmarks window, but will show up as a bookmark entry called `<separator>` which can be moved just like any other bookmark.

## Organizing Files and Folders

You can create a hierarchical, or multi-level, file system by putting folders inside of other folders. For example, you might create a top-level folder called Government and place separate folders inside of it called Federal, State, and Local.

You can do this by dragging and dropping one file into another, or you can click the top-level folder first before creating the second-level folder. The new folder will appear inside the selected folder rather than at the top level.

When you drag and drop a bookmark entry into a folder, it appears as the first (top) bookmark listed in that folder. If you want to change the order of bookmarks, you can drag and drop them into any position you want. As you move the file, a line will appear as a placeholder (see Figure 9.11).

**FIG. 9.11**
Dashed lines surround the Visual Basic Home Page bookmark to show that you're dragging it into position after the 2600 Magazine entry, as shown by the solid line by the pointer.

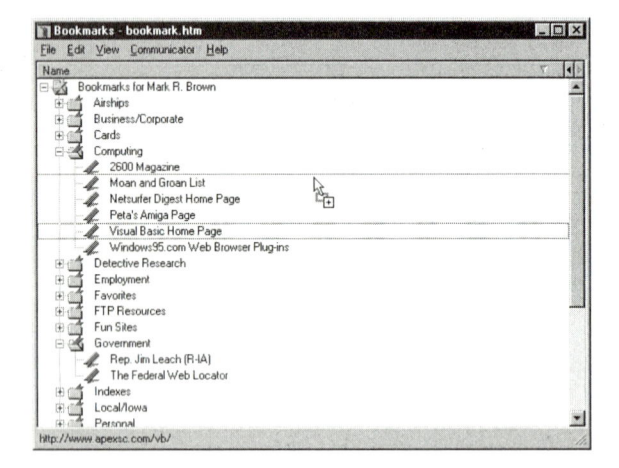

Using this simple drag-and-drop system, you can create as elegant or as simple a system of bookmark files and folder as you desire.

> **TIP** You should try to keep the number of bookmarks and folders on any level small, as long lists can quickly overwhelm your screen. While Navigator bookmark lists behave politely, wrapping when they must, they are easier to work with if you keep them short and under control.

## Adding, Editing, and Deleting Bookmarks

So far, we've talked only about creating bookmarks for pages you have visited which are currently displayed. What if you know the URL of a page and want to create a bookmark for it, but are offline or simply don't want to waste time visiting it just to create a bookmark for it?

No problem. You can create a bookmark for any page you want, whether or not its currently displayed in Navigator, by selecting File, New Bookmark from the Edit Bookmarks window

http://www.quecorp.com

menu, or New Bookmark from the right-mouse button popup menu. You'll get the dialog box shown in Figure 9.12.

**FIG. 9.12**
You add a new bookmark using this dialog box.

You must add a Name and Location (URL) for your bookmark, and may also add a Description. When done, click the OK button. Your new bookmark will appear at the location which was highlighted when you selected the New Bookmark option.

Editing a bookmark or folder is just as easy. Highlight the bookmark or folder you want to change, and select Edit, Bookmark Properties, or just Bookmark Properties from the right-mouse button popup menu. You'll get the very same dialog box you used to add a new bookmark, and you can edit any of the information fields for that bookmark.

Deleting a bookmark or folder is as easy as highlighting it and pressing the Delete key on your keyboard. Of course, you can also select Edit, Delete, or Delete Bookmark from the popup menu, but using the Delete key is quicker and easier.

> **TIP** You can select multiple contiguous bookmarks and folders as you're working in the Edit Window by holding down the Shift key while you make your selections. You can do the same with non-contiguous items by holding down the Ctrl key as you choose.

**CAUTION**
Be careful when deleting bookmark entries and folders. You are *not* asked "Are you sure?"—the bookmark or folder simply disappears. Be especially careful with folders, as all of the bookmarks stored in a folder also disappear along with the folder, without chance of recovery. If you do delete something accidentally, you can recover if you immediately choose Undo from the Edit menu. But that doesn't work if you've gone on to perform another action.

## Changing Points of View

It's often useful to look at things from a different perspective. Sometimes a fresh point of view can give you new insights into how to approach the topic at hand, such as how to organize your bookmarks.

You can look at your bookmark list in a variety of different ways by using the options under the View menu (see Figure 9.13).

**FIG. 9.13**
The View menu lets you dissect and examine your bookmarks in a multitude of different ways.

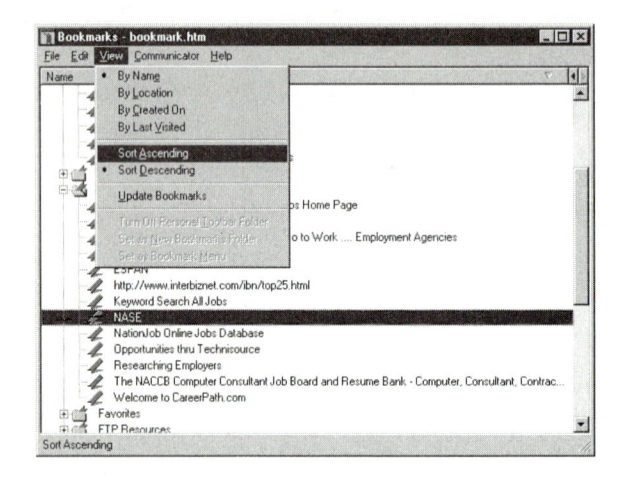

You can sort bookmark entries By Name, By Location, By [time and date] Created On, and By [time and date] Last Visited. By Name is the default listing method, but sometimes an alternate method of sorting your bookmark list has obvious advantages.

Figuring out exactly how sorting works can sometimes be a challenge. By Name is the easiest to figure out—folders and bookmarks on the top level are sorted alphabetically, then sublevels are each also sorted alphabetically. When you view By Location you get the same sort of organization, only by URL. Viewing By [time and date] Created On sorts not by the time of the creation of the page referenced—as you might believe if you didn't think about it too hard—but by the time and date when you created the bookmark. By Last Visited is the way to view pages you know you've seen recently.

Each viewing order can be supplemented by the Sort Ascending and Sort Descending methods. A bullet is shown on the View menu beside the currently selected sort order and method.

## Finding Bookmarks

Sometimes a site name just isn't enough to clue you in as to which bookmark you want to find. Is that Speed City link in your bookmark list the one about racecars, juicing up your browser, or the dangers of illegal amphetamines?

That's where the Description field and the Edit Bookmarks' Find function come in handy. You can use the Description field to create a detailed description of a bookmarked site. This Description isn't normally displayed, except when you're editing a bookmark's properties. However, it can be searched using the Edit, Find in Bookmarks (Ctrl+F) menu selection. When you select the Find function, you'll see the dialog box shown in Figure 9.14.

**FIG. 9.14**
The Find dialog box can save you a lot of time when sifting through a long list of bookmarks for a specific site.

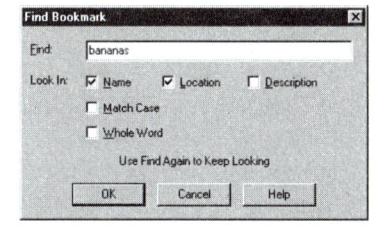

Type the word or phrase you want to find into the Find field. Note that you can choose to search in the Name, Location, or Description fields, or in any two, or even all three at once. If you make copious notes in the Description field for each of your bookmarks, searching there can be the most comprehensive way of finding your lost bookmarks. However, if you think you remember a word or two from the title, or even the URL of the site you want, you can use the Find dialog box to find those, too.

If you're looking for an exact match including capitalization, make sure the Match Case check box is selected. Likewise, check the Whole Word box if you want to exclude partial matches. Clicking OK will start your search, and the dialog box will disappear. If a bookmark is found that isn't the one you're looking for, pressing Ctrl+G (or choosing Edit, Find Again) will continue searching through the bookmark list.

## Special Folder Features

If you select a folder entry from the Edit Bookmarks window and then bring up the right-mouse button popup menu (see Figure 9.15), you'll find that there are three interesting options available that are unique for folders. (These options are also located under the View menu.)

The first option is Set as Toolbar Folder. When selected, this menu item creates a set of buttons on the Personal Toolbar that are based on the bookmarks in the selected folder. Only the first few entries are used, just as many as will comfortably fit on the toolbar based on window size. (For the common 800×600 window size, this is eight buttons, or six buttons for a 640×480 window.)

**TIP** To get rid of a set of Personal Toolbar buttons you've created using the Set as Toolbar Folder option, select the folder that is currently designated at the Toolbar Folder, then choose Turn Off Personal Toolbar Folder from the View menu, or pick Remove as Toolbar Folder from the popup menu.

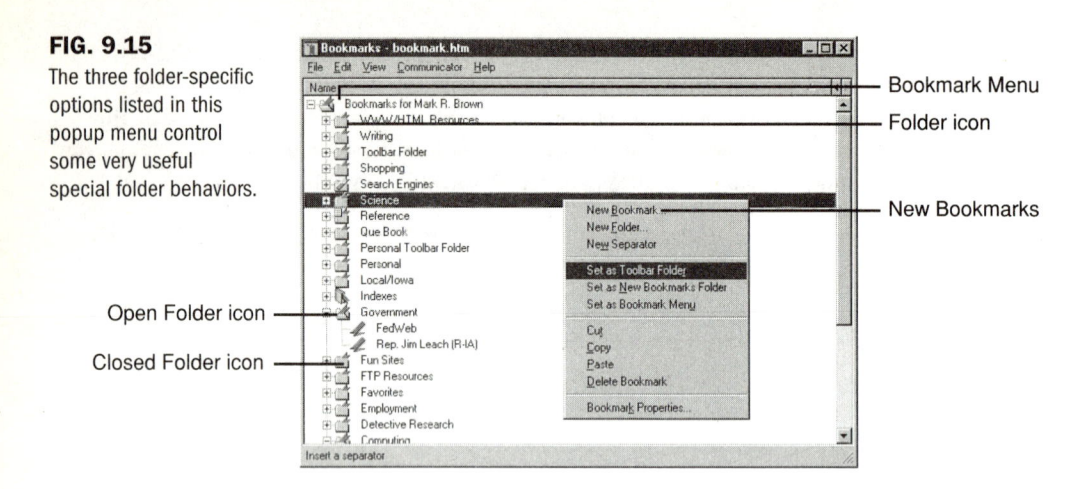

**FIG. 9.15**
The three folder-specific options listed in this popup menu control some very useful special folder behaviors.

Bookmark Menu
Folder icon
New Bookmarks
Open Folder icon
Closed Folder icon

> **NOTE** If you've created a Personal Toolbar of your own before designating another folder as your toolbar folder, you'll have a special folder in your bookmark file called Personal Toolbar Folder. You can redesignate it as your toolbar folder by using the Set as Toolbar Folder option on it, just as you would with any other folder. But if you simply turn off the toolbar folder setting you've set for another folder, the Personal Toolbar Folder again becomes your Personal Toolbar by default.

The second option is Set as New Bookmarks Folder. This option sets the selected folder as the place for new bookmarks to go. By default, new bookmarks go into the "top level" directory. But by using this selection, you can make new bookmarks go into the directory of your choice. This one might work really well if you created a folder called "New Bookmarks" and designated it as your new bookmarks folder. Then your newer, disorganized links would all go to a common place from which you could, at your leisure, move them into some semblance of order.

The third and final folder option on the popup menu is Set as Bookmark Menu. This option changes both the Bookmark Quicklink button on the Location toolbar and the Bookmark item on the Communicator menu to point to the folder you've chosen. If your bookmark file is huge, you can use this to restrict your bookmark list to a single folder hierarchy.

# Bookmark Tricks and Tips

There are several interesting miscellaneous features relating to bookmark entries in the Edit Bookmarks window, none of which is particularly spectacular, but each of which is useful in certain circumstances. Many of these features are available when you highlight a bookmark entry and invoke the right-mouse button popup menu (see Figure 9.16).

**FIG. 9.16**
This popup menu controls many of the more interesting bookmark features.

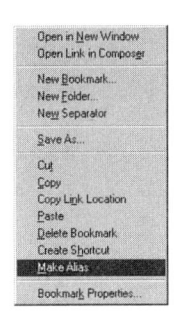

- Double-clicking a bookmark entry switches you over to the Navigator window and takes you to that page. It's much, much quicker than choosing File, Go to Bookmark. While this is certainly not the best way to use the bookmark list to get around the Web, it's a good way to check out entries that you're curious about while you're editing your list.
- When you click a bookmark, it is highlighted, and the URL it points to is displayed in the status bar at the bottom left of the Edit Bookmarks window.
- From the popup menu associated with a bookmark entry, you can choose to open the bookmarked page for viewing in a new browser window, or in Composer for editing.
- You can select Save As… from the popup menu if you want to save a page to disk without having to actually look at it. A file requester dialog box will be displayed; choose a file name from the dialog box, and Navigator will download the selected page from the Web and save it directly to disk without displaying it. Neat trick. (Be aware that you only get the referenced page, not any associated graphics or other files that might be a part of the page.)
- You can create a duplicate of a bookmark entry by selecting Make Alias from the popup menu. This entry will be identical in every way to the original, but it will be listed in italics instead of normal type. Any changes made to an entry will affect all of its aliases. Aliases are useful for putting the same bookmark entry into multiple folders.
- You might be confused by the Copy and Copy Link Location entries in the popup menu. The Copy, Cut, and Paste selections are to be used only for moving entries around within the Edit Bookmarks window. Use Copy Link Location if you want to copy the URL of the bookmark to paste into a document or other application.
- Highlight a bookmark entry and choose File, Add Bookmark to Toolbar to create a button on the Personal Toolbar for the highlighted bookmark.
- In Windows 95, and on the Macintosh, you can create a desktop Shortcut to a bookmarked page by selecting Create Shortcut from the popup menu. You'll get a dialog box that lets you redefine the Shortcut's name and URL if you want to. (You can also create a Shortcut by simply dragging a link from the Edit Bookmarks window or from an HTML document directly onto the desktop.)

**NOTE** You can move around in the Edit Bookmarks window using the standard cursor movement keys. Page Up, Page Down, Home, End, and the Up and Down cursor keys all work as expected. But the Right and Left arrow keys expand and contract folder entries, respectively. The Space bar toggles folders between their expanded and contracted states, as does double-clicking a folder.

## Working With Multiple Bookmark Lists

We've already revealed that the bookmark list that loads automatically when you run Communicator is called bookmark.htm and lives in your configuration directory. But you can actually create and use as many custom bookmark files as you want. The secret to doing so are the Open Bookmarks File, Import, and Save As... selections on the File menu (see Figure 9.17).

**FIG. 9.17**
It's easy to create and use many different bookmark files.

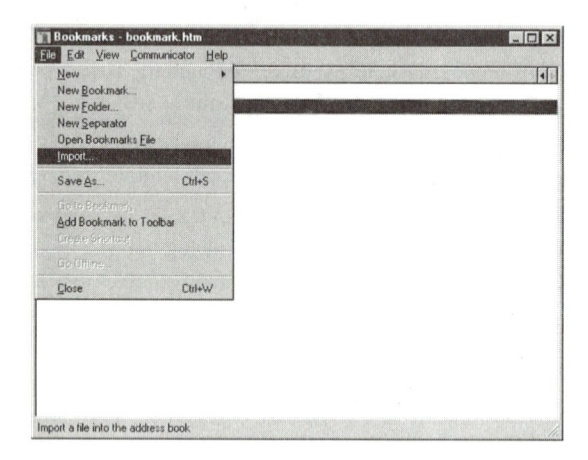

Save As... (Ctrl+S) lets you save any bookmark file you're working on with a file name of your choice. To use that file in the future in place of your default bookmark file (bookmark.htm), you can load it back into Navigator using the Open Bookmarks File menu selection (from the File menu in the Edit Bookmarks window, which you can open with Ctrl+B). You can display the new bookmark list immediately by clicking the Navigator Bookmark QuickFile button on the Location toolbar, or by choosing Communicator, Bookmarks. In addition, the Personal Toolbar and New Bookmark options change to those defined in the new bookmark file.

If you often use your browser for completely different purposes—for example, sometimes for doing research for scientific papers, and sometimes for pursuing a hobby—keeping different bookmark lists makes a lot of sense.

However, what if a friend of yours wants to share a select list of killer Web sites with you? You might want to merge her list with yours. That's where the Import option comes in. She can e-mail you a file, or make it available over your mutual network, or even give you a floppy disk—any means by which you can get it into your system—and you can select Import (from the File menu in the Edit Bookmarks window, which you can open with Ctrl+B) to merge her list with yours. Her entire bookmark list will come into your list as a folder labeled Bookmarks for [*her name*]. From there, you can move, edit, or delete her imported bookmarks and folders just as if you'd entered them yourself.

## Automatically Updating Bookmarks

Perhaps the most advanced (and scariest) feature built into the Edit Bookmarks window is the Update Bookmarks selection on the View menu. Select it and you'll get the deceptively ascetic dialog box shown in Figure 9.18.

**FIG. 9.18**
The two radio buttons in this dialog box control one of the Edit Bookmarks window's most powerful features.

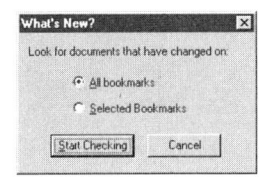

If you highlighted a few bookmarks or folders before selecting Update Bookmarks, you can choose the Selected Bookmarks radio button to update only those selected items. Otherwise, you can select the All Bookmarks button to update every site in your bookmarks file.

> **CAUTION**
> Checking all of your bookmarks can take a very, very long time! Use the All Bookmarks button only if you're absolutely positive you want to do so. I strongly recommend using the Selected Bookmarks option, and then only on a very short list of select sites.

When you click Start Checking, Navigator will begin querying all the sites you selected to find out if any of them have changed since you last visited them. Navigator displays a dialog box to let you know it's still checking, and will mark any sites that have changed since you last visited so that you can visit them at your leisure (see Figure 9.19).

The dialog box on the right in Figure 9.19 shows which site is currently being checked, and how much time remains before all selected sites are checked. As each is updated, its icon is changed in the Edit Bookmarks window to show its status. A plain icon beside a listing indicates the site is unchanged. An icon penetrated by a ribbon indicates that the site has changed since you last viewed it. An icon accompanied by a question mark shows that Navigator was unable to reach that site. This may mean that a site is gone, but it may also simply indicate network access difficulties.

# Chapter 9 Using Bookmarks

**FIG. 9.19**
Let Navigator's Bookmarks feature scan for changed sites for you!

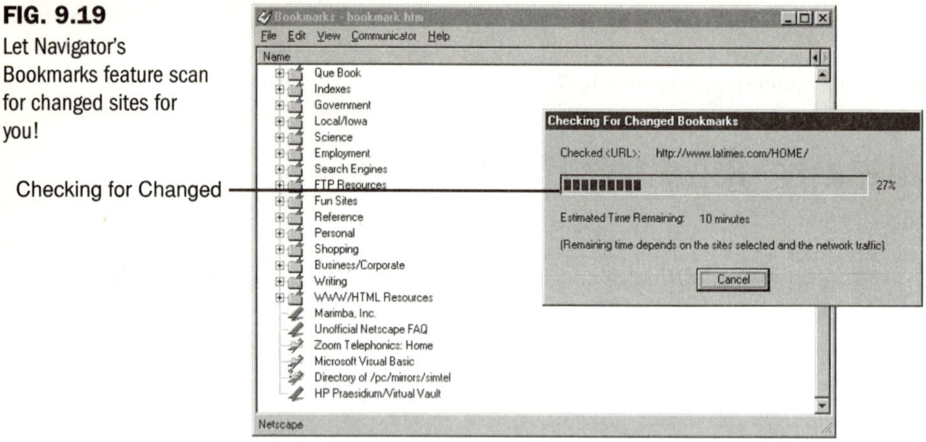

Checking for Changed

CHAPTER 10

# Interacting with Plug-Ins, Java Applets, and JavaScript

*by Mark R. Brown*

- **HTML tricks can create surprising page behavior**
  For example, server push and client pull can automate page downloading.

- **Imagemaps, frames, and forms are just a few of the available advanced HTML elements**
  They make pages more interesting and easier to use.

- **Java and JavaScript are actually programming languages**
  They are often used to make pages more interactive.

- **Plug-ins let page developers add enhanced content to pages**
  You'll see multimedia, video, audio, and much more.

In the beginning, Web pages consisted of a little HTML code, some text, a few text-based links, and maybe a small graphic or two. This was not because of some great design philosophy or bias against making pages fancy—there simply were no other tools for creating pages.

You can still create HTML documents using nothing more than HTML, text, and graphics—in fact, many of the most popular sites on the Web use nothing more than these simple elements. Take Yahoo!, for example. Though it's the most popular search and indexing site on the Web, Yahoo!'s pages are almost exclusively simple HTML documents filled with text links, descriptions, and simple graphics (which are mostly used for advertising). There's good reason for this—Yahoo! wants to make sure that everyone who visits can view its pages, and not all browsers support frames, Java, and all those other fancy new page-viewing capabilities. Besides, Yahoo! knows that it's still perfectly acceptable to create HTML-only pages.

But today's HTML document developer (who may no longer even have a desire, much less a need, to produce pages only for the World Wide Web) needn't restrict herself to using only HTML. She now can choose to add interactive Java applets, multimedia content that calls plug-ins, and even advanced HTML-based elements like clickable imagemaps, forms, frames, and pages that load automatically.

Though this makes for a much richer browsing experience, it also makes browsing more complex. While it is easy to find a text link to click, what are you supposed to do with all those on-screen slider bars, buttons, and blinking, scrolling interactive graphics?

In this chapter, you learn what all of these new page-development technologies are, what they're being used for, and how to interact with them. Along the way, you might discover ways in which you want to use these techniques in your own HTML documents. ■

## Who's Who and What's What

You've probably heard most of the new buzzwords: Java, plug-ins, Dynamic HTML…but what exactly are they? In a nutshell, they are all new ways in which page developers can add rich new content to HTML documents. No longer do pages have to be static. They can be animated, noisy, and interactive—and be all of these things all at once, if necessary.

In this chapter, we take a look at the following page-development technologies, which go beyond basic HTML:

- Automated pages
- Imagemaps
- Forms
- Frames
- Java
- JavaScript and dynamic HTML
- Plug-ins
- OLE integration

Each of these techniques and technologies is discussed in Section V, "For Webmasters," p. 433, from a page developer's point of view, but in this chapter, we concentrate on how you interact with these elements when you run into them in HTML documents.

The first thing I should say is that, in many ways, these technologies are interchangeable and transparent to you, the user. That is, when you run into an animated interactive button on a page, you don't really need to know or care which of these technologies was used to create it (see Figure 10.1). All you need to know is how to recognize that the element in question is a clickable button, or text-entry box, or volume control slider, and then be able to figure out how to use that element to accomplish the task at hand. That's what this chapter is all about.

http://www.quecorp.com

**FIG. 10.1**
Is this page an example of a Java applet, imagemap, plug-in, or some combination? It really doesn't make much difference from the user's perspective.

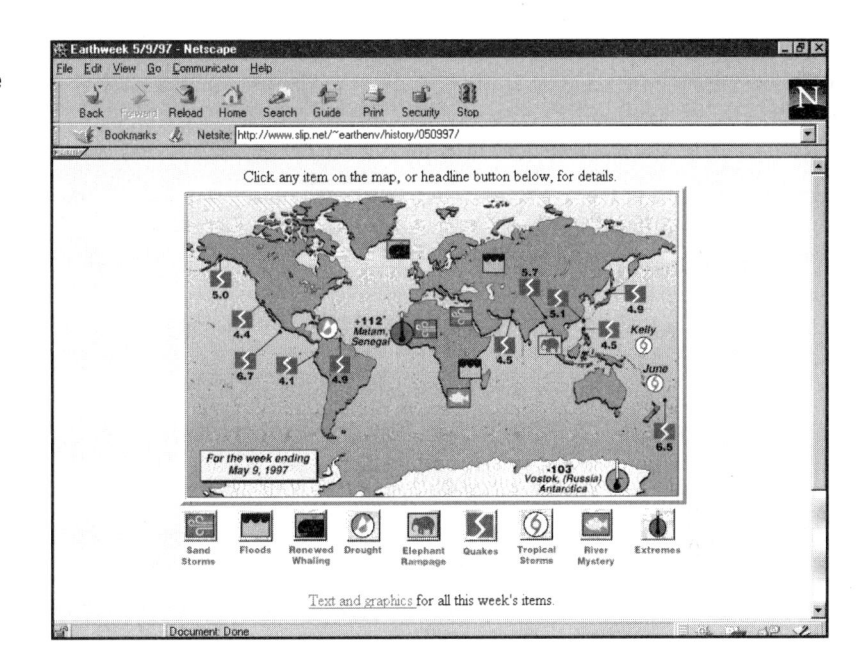

## Automated Pages

You usually have to click a text or graphic link to load a new page into Navigator. But there are two very similar features built in to Navigator that let pages seem to load by themselves. One is called Server Push, and the other is Client Pull. Though one is, as the names suggest, performed automatically by the server computer you are connected to, and the other is initiated by your client computer, the end result is the same: A page is automatically loaded after a preset time interval without your intervention.

This technique is often used when a site moves—a placeholder page is put up on the old site announcing that the page has moved, and this page then automatically (after 15 seconds or so) loads the new page from the new site (see Figure 10.2).

Server push or client pull can even be used to create an automated slide show of a sequence of pages.

▶ Server push and client pull are implemented through use of the HTML META tag. You can find out how to use them on your own pages by turning to Chapter 22, "HTML Primer," **p. 435**

A closely related feature is called *autoscroll*. An autoscroll page lets the server computer keep sending information to a page, without having to open a new page. The difference is that server push and client pull both send new pages, whereas autoscroll adds information to the bottom of the currently displayed page.

Don't let these automatic page-updating methods fool you—they're just tools that let page developers control your browser briefly.

**FIG. 10.2**
The All-in-One Search page has moved since I last visited it, but this placeholder page takes me to the new site automatically after 15 seconds.

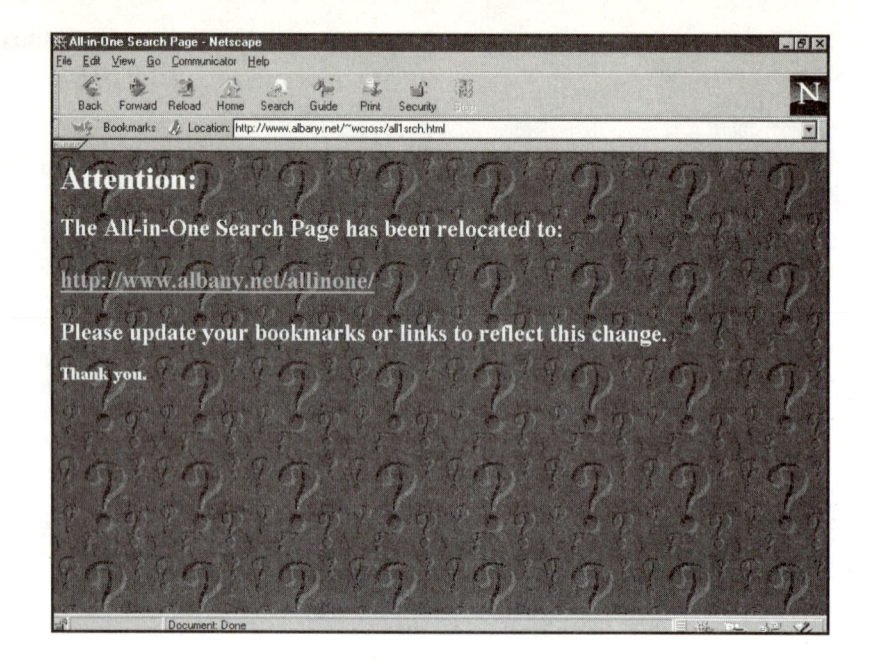

## Imagemaps

Sometimes a page designer wants a more unified look to his page than simple text links and static graphics can give. To make navigation simpler and to provide an intuitive map to his site, he might choose to provide a navigational imagemap.

An imagemap does exactly what its name implies—it provides a graphical map of a site. What's more, clicking any part of an imagemap takes you to the indicated section of the site (see Figure 10.3).

An imagemap is usually just a single GIF or JPEG image that is linked to a server script or a bit of client-side HTML code that associates the position of a mouse click with the appropriate page. Using an imagemap is easy—just point at what you want and click. The magic is invisible.

> **TIP** How can you tell an imagemap from a Java applet or other advanced page element? Right-click the map and, if it's an imagemap, you see a selection in the pop-up menu called View Image, along with the image's file name.

▶ You can create imagemaps to use on your own site. For details, see Chapter 25, "Building Navigational Imagemaps," **p. 519**

http://www.quecorp.com

**FIG. 10.3**
This imagemap at the United Airlines Web site whisks you away to different areas with a single mouse click.

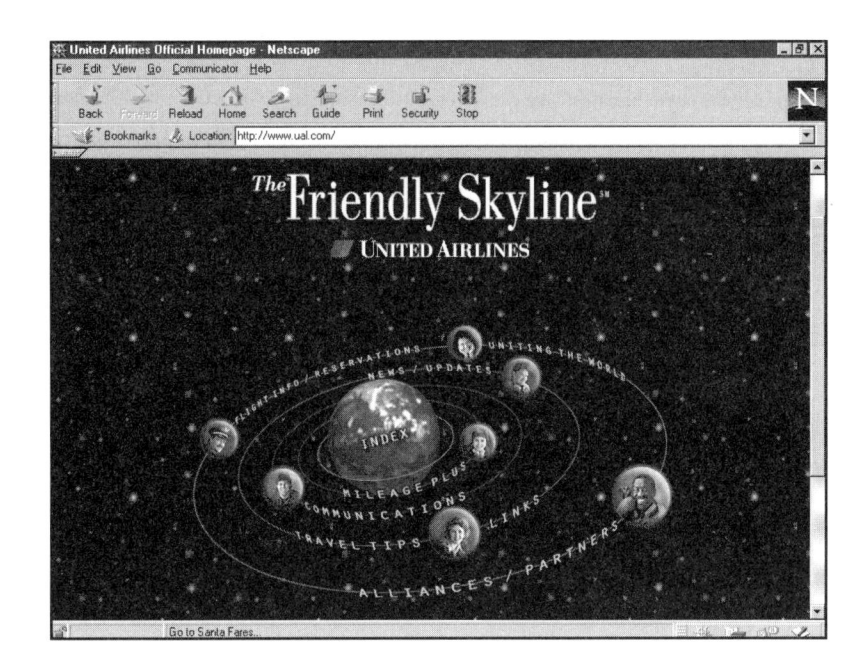

## Using Forms

Browsing the Web is mostly a matter of downloading files from a Web server to view with your browser. But when you fill out an online form, you're sending data the other way—from your computer back to the server you're connected to.

Web forms are like paper forms; they are comprised of data entry fields, check boxes, and multiple-choice lists. They open the electronic door to all kinds of exciting transactions on the Web. You can sign a guest book, sign up for a service, ask to be added to a mailing list, join an organization, request a catalog or brochure, and even make purchases by submitting forms over the World Wide Web.

A form is created using HTML commands, but the data sent back in response to a form request is generated by a program that runs on the host server computer.

▶ You can find out how to create your own HTML document forms and server programs in Chapter 26, "Creating Forms and Server Scripts," **p. 349**

### What Are Forms Good For?

Forms are the Web's standard method for letting you submit information to a World Wide Web server. They are used for the following four major functions:

- Searching for information in an online database
- Requesting a user-customized action, such as the creation of a custom map or table

- Registering for a service or group
- Online shopping

In each of these cases, forms give you the means to send specific information to the server you're connected to, so that you can receive a customized response back.

In contrast, normal page links only allow you to click a link from a list to retrieve a "canned" response from the server. Forms let Web page creators send you information and services that are tailored to your specific needs, rather than broad, generic responses built for an audience constrained by "least common denominator" considerations.

Let's take a quick look at four real-world examples from the Web, one for each of these common uses of forms.

**Searching with Forms**   The most popular site on the World Wide Web is Yahoo! at **http://www.yahoo.com**. Yahoo! is a combination Web index/search engine that lets you find just about any site on the Web in seconds. There are two different methods built into Yahoo! for finding specific Web sites.

One search method is a standard hierarchical index built up of text links (see Figure 10.4). While you can find a site by following the index through its ever-narrowing lists of topics and subtopics, this is definitely the brute-force approach, especially when you consider the tens of thousands of sites that are contained in Yahoo!'s index space!

The superior way to search Yahoo! is to let it build a custom index to your personal specifications. You do this by filling out and submitting the simple one-line form near the top of the page (see Figure 10.4). You just click in the data entry field and type a list of keywords, then click the Search button. Yahoo! then searches its database of Web site information and builds a custom index composed only of the entries that contain your keywords. This takes only a few seconds. Finally, Yahoo! builds and transmits a custom Web page that contains an index that has been generated on-the-fly just for you.

There are literally thousands of sites like Yahoo! on the Web that let you use forms to search online databases and retrieve custom pages containing information on a myriad of topics. Just about every kind of information you can imagine (and some you *can't* imagine!) is available on the Web somewhere in a forms-searchable database.

**Requesting with Forms**   Forms can also be used to ask a server to run a program to perform a specific task for you (see Figure 10.5). This is one of the most open-ended (and fun!) examples of interactivity on the Web.

Because a Web server is a computer just like any other, it is fully capable of running any program that any other computer can run. So the types of actions you can request of a Web server are limited only by what the server is willing to let you do.

**Registering with Forms**   You can use online forms to sign up for just about anything on the Web (see Figure 10.6). You can enter contests and sweepstakes, join organizations, apply for credit cards, subscribe to e-mail lists on hundreds of different topics, and even sign a guest book at some of the sites you visit.

## Using Forms    169

**FIG. 10.4**
Yahoo! lets you search for Web sites in two very different ways. The best is to use its online form to search for keywords.

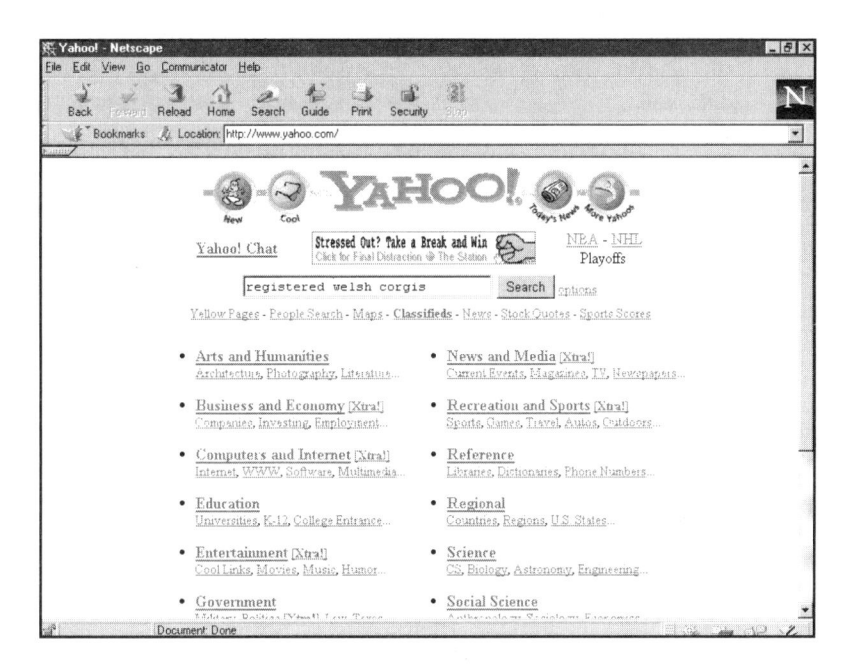

**FIG. 10.5**
The Earth Viewer form lets you specify latitude and longitude for your point of view, as well as which satellite data to use. You can even generate a custom view from the sun or the moon!

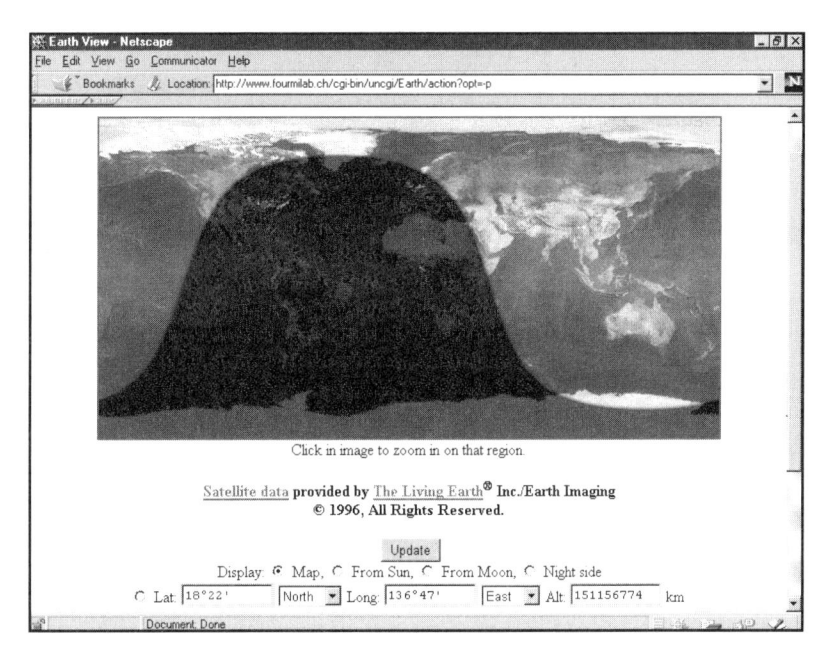

Most online registration forms ask you for the same information you'd supply on a paper registration form: name, address, phone, and—since this *is* the Internet, after all—e-mail address.

Many places also require user registration before they allow you into the deeper, and, hopefully, most interesting, regions of their Web site. (Some might charge you for this privilege, some not.)

**FIG. 10.6**
Apply for a credit card online? It's only one of many things you can do by filling out an online form.

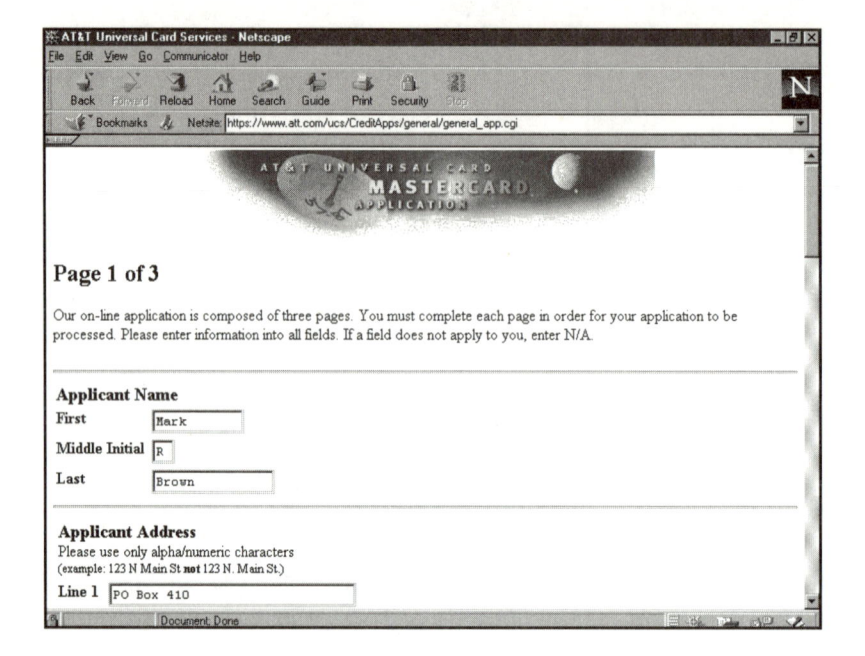

**Shopping with Forms**   You can shop 'til you drop without ever leaving home by cruising the electronic malls on the World Wide Web.

Web shopping generally involves filling out an order form (or registering as a shopper) with your name, address, and credit card information. Many sites now even include an electronic shopping cart. This allows you to browse a site, reading product descriptions and price information; when you find something you like, you just click the check box (an online form, of course) next to the item you want and it is added to your cart. When you get ready to leave the online store, you go through a checkout where your items are totaled and you are presented with a bill, which you can then pay with your credit card or even electronic cash.

By shopping, we really mean the process of requesting goods, hard copy information like catalogs or brochures, or services that require either the action of human beings or the transfer of physical objects through delivery services. Though this certainly can involve buying things, it also includes many other services.

## An Online Shopping Trip

As a real-world example of how to interact with online forms, let's take a virtual shopping trip on the World Wide Web. In fact, let's go to the online bookstore Amazon.com and buy a copy of the previous edition of this book. (We'd buy the current edition, but it hasn't been published yet—I'm still writing it.)

First, go to the bookstore site at **http://www.amazon.com** (see Figure 10.7).

**FIG. 10.7**
The Amazon.com bookstore is just one of thousands of stores now doing business on the World Wide Web.

Note that Amazon.com's home page is a nice-looking but simple, old-fashioned Web page composed of text, text links, and conservative graphics. No forms here! But I'll bet you find a form if you click one of the links under the Search By header. Let's pick Author, Title, Subject. Voilà! You get the online form shown in Figure 10.8.

You know the author name so you click the field labeled Author: and type **Mark R. Brown**. You could click the option button by *Exact* Name but Last Name, First Name (or Initials) is already selected, and it seems like that will do as well.

> **TIP** Easy as it might seem, the quickest way to figure out how to use any on-screen control is to *read the screen*. There are almost always instructions, labels, or other clues close at hand.

You also enter **Special Edition** in the Title: field, because you know that the book title begins with those words.

If you were to scroll down the screen, you'd find another field you could fill out for Subject:, but this seems like enough for now.

> **TIP** When conducting any search using an online form, only enter as much information as you need to narrow your search sufficiently. Don't give too much information, or you may not match anything at all!

**172** Chapter 10 Interacting with Plug-Ins, Java Applets, and JavaScript

**FIG. 10.8**
You search for a book using this simple online form.

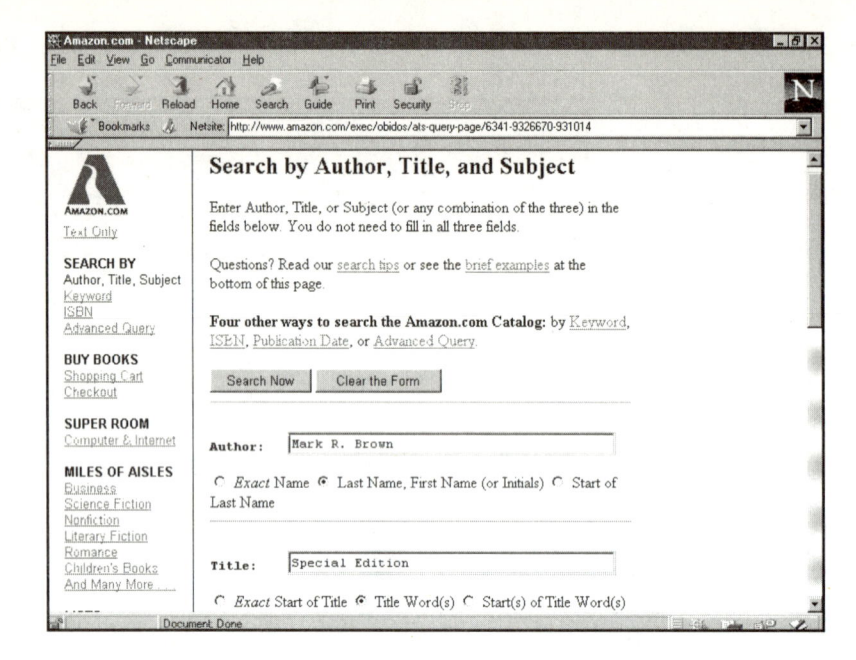

After you've filled out any form, you must send it to the server computer for processing. Every form has an associated Submit button. Sometimes, this button actually says Submit. But usually it says something else just as informative. In this case, the button says Search Now. There's another button labeled Clear the Form, but this is something you do not wish to do. (It might have come in handy if you had messed up, however.) Clicking the Search Now submit button results in a short wait followed by the screen shown in Figure 10.9.

In response to your request, the server has created a custom page just for you. On this page are listed the books that match your search criteria. You want a copy of *Special Edition Using Netscape 3* so you click that link and get the screen shown in Figure 10.10.

Because this is the book you want, you click the button labeled Add This Book to Your Shopping Cart. Note that there aren't any fields to fill in before pressing this version of the submit button. That's because the data is already predetermined by your choice of buttons. The server already knows what This Book is by the page it's displaying, so you don't have to fill in any fields to tell it that information. This is an example of a hidden form.

Clicking the button brings you to the page shown in Figure 10.11.

The shopping cart page lists the item you've decided to purchase and gives you the opportunity to change the quantity of items desired. If you're happy with one copy and don't want to buy any more books, click one of the Proceed to Checkout buttons and move on to the screen in Figure 10.12. If you want to buy more books, you can click the browser's Back button or one of the menu links on the left side of the screen to continue shopping.

http://www.quecorp.com

Using Forms | 173

**FIG. 10.9**
This screen of information never existed before you asked for the specific information displayed.

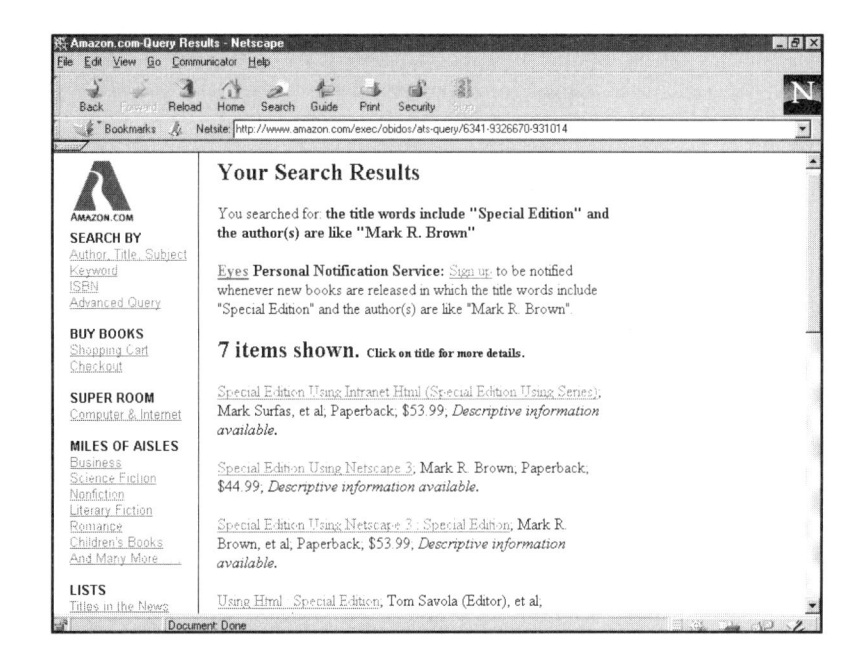

**FIG. 10.10**
This is the book you want. You can click a button to add it to your shopping cart.

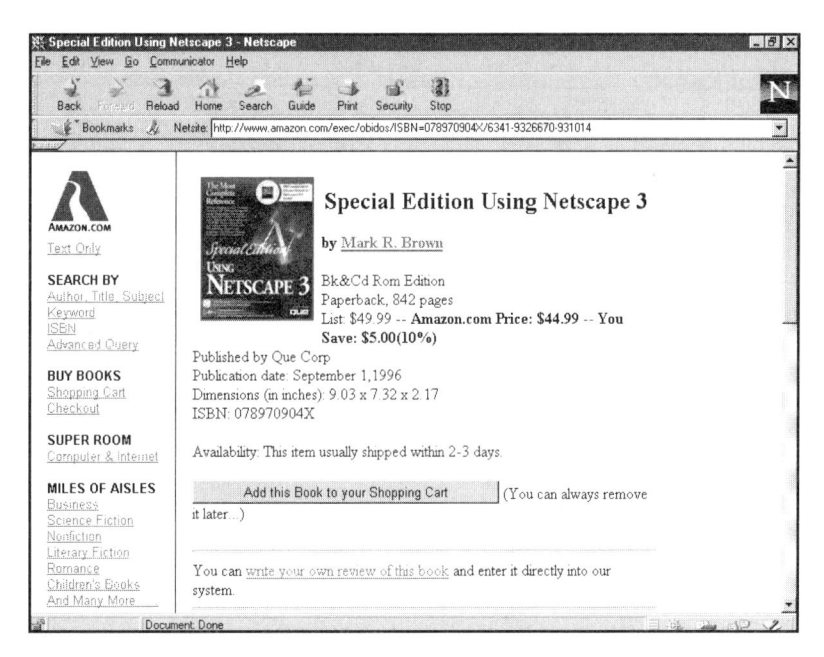

**Chapter 10** Interacting with Plug-Ins, Java Applets, and JavaScript

**FIG. 10.11**
The shopping cart turns out to be a form, too.

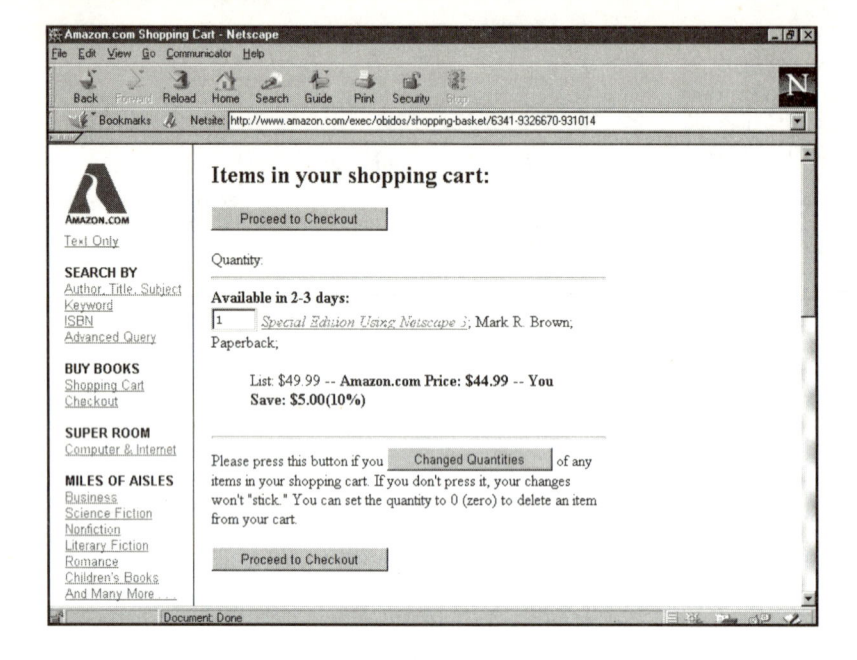

**FIG. 10.12**
Here's where you pay for your purchase.

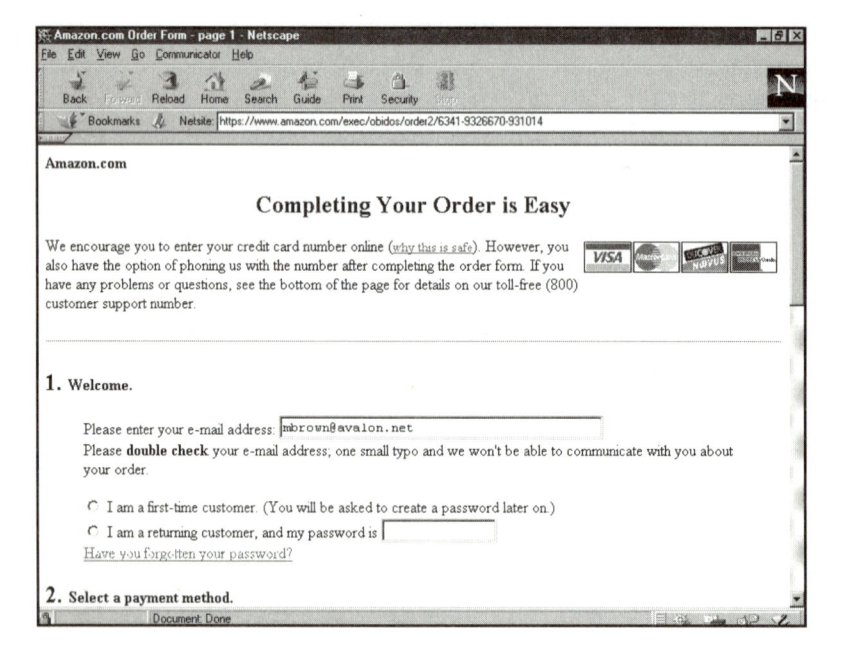

There are several more pages of forms to fill out with credit card and shipping information before your order is completed, but you get the idea.

http://www.quecorp.com

There are two more important elements of online shopping that we should discuss before moving on, though. These are cookies and security.

**Cookies** You can leave a shopping session on Amazon.com and when you return a few days later, your shopping cart will still contain all the books you placed in it in your previous session. This is something you certainly wouldn't expect at a local store, where they'd have the stock back on the shelves within minutes of your departure. How do online stores manage to do this?

Well, they get your computer to do it for them, by storing your shopping cart data in a *cookie file*.

Briefly, a cookie is a small amount of data sent back from the server to be stored on your computer, which the server can then access later. All cookies are concatenated into a single cookie file on your computer. This file contains all the active cookies from all the sites you've visited. Your cookie file might contain account information, or any other information associated with a specific session, which a server doesn't want to keep on hand, but needs to refer to again later.

Cookies (individual data packets) can be sent to the cookie file on your computer and back to the server in a secure or insecure manner. (So security with your cookie file is, as with any data transfer, a separate issue to itself.) It's all done invisibly, without your knowledge.

Communicator keeps your cookie file in your personal information folder. Just as an example, for Windows 95, this is, by default, in c:\program files\netscape\users\yourname\cookie.txt. You can load and read your cookie.txt file just like any other text file, though it's likely to consist of a wad of semi-intelligible words and numbers that only make sense to the server computers that created it in the first place.

If cookies make you nervous, you can turn them off (or at least control them) via Preferences. Follow these steps:

1. Select Preferences from the Edit menu.
2. In the Preferences dialog box, select Advanced in the left menu. You get the dialog box shown in Figure 10.13.
3. By default, the Accept All Cookies option button is selected. Leave this alone if you don't want any control over your cookie file.
4. If you don't mind cookies, but don't think any third party should be able to snoop and see what kinds of cookies you have on your system, select Accept Only Cookies That Get Sent Back to the Originating Server.
5. Click the Disable Cookies option button if the whole idea of cookies scares you. Of course, this will disable cookie-based features like online shopping carts and other custom user services.
6. Check the Warn Me Before Accepting a Cookie check box if you just want to be informed when your cookie.txt file is written to. Note that this selection can be chosen in conjunction with any of the other cookie options, while each of the others is mutually exclusive.
7. When you have your cookie options set to your liking, click OK.

**Chapter 10** Interacting with Plug-Ins, Java Applets, and JavaScript

**FIG. 10.13**
You can set your cookie file options from this Preferences dialog box.

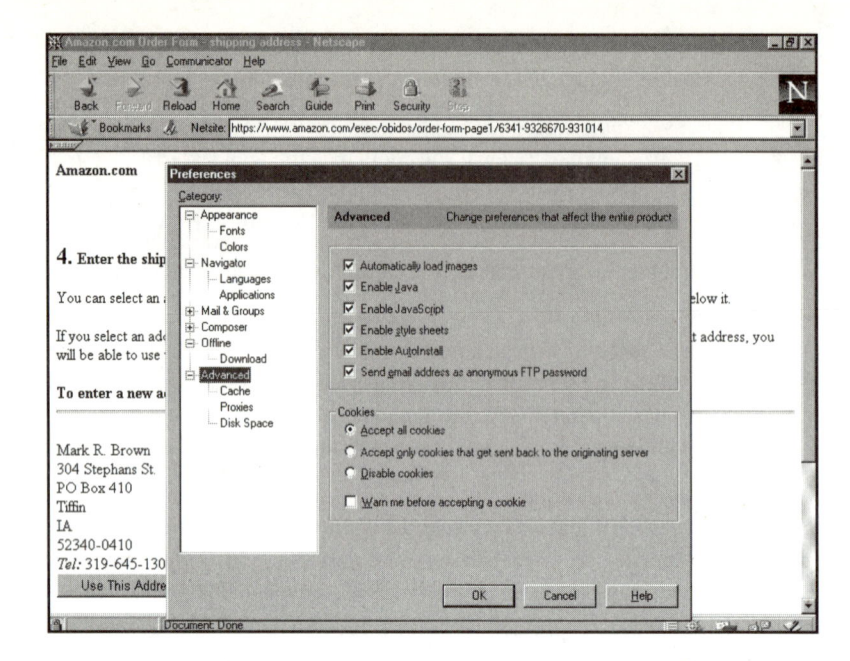

**Security**  How do you know that the credit card and other personal information you send over the Net is secure from prying eyes? Navigator gives you a visual cue—the padlock icons in the toolbar (labeled Security) and in the lower-left corner of the status bar (see Figure 10.14).

**FIG. 10.14**
Navigator's security lock icons show you that the current page is being sent via a secure server.

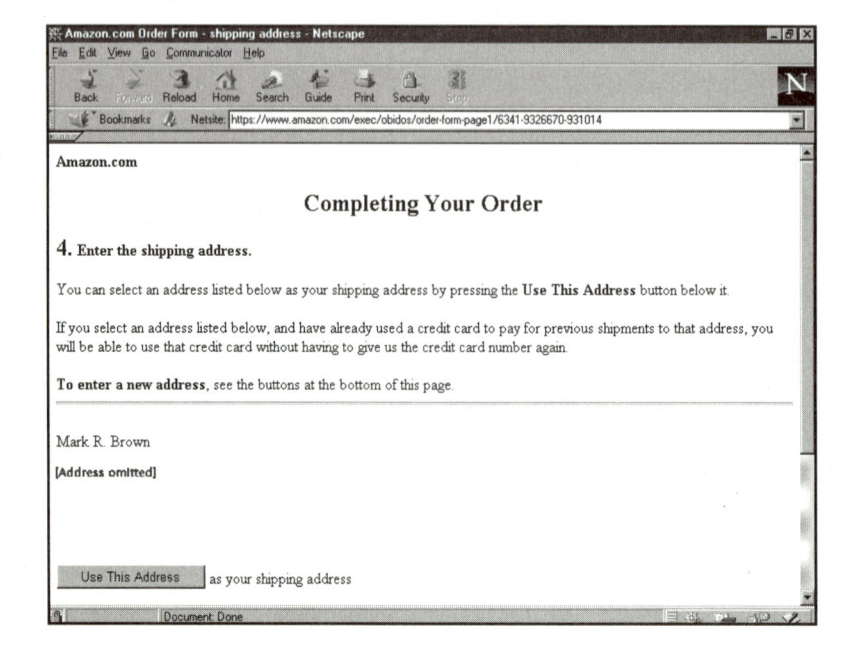

http://www.quecorp.com

Though usually displayed in an unlocked state, these padlock icons are shown locked when you are connected to a secure server. In addition, note that the Location: toolbar says Netsite:, and the Web address, which usually begins with http:, says https:. The extra s is for secure. Still not convinced? You can click the toolbar Security icon and bring up a Security Info window that fills you in on all the details.

Bottom line? Look for the locked padlock. Without it, your transactions are open to hackers. With it, you're sure your information is being transmitted safely.

▶ For the complete story on Communicator's built-in security features, see Chapter 17, "Security Options," **p. 349**

## Form Elements

Many options are available to Web forms designers to create a wide range of form elements. Online forms can include many different kinds of data entry fields, as shown in Figure 10.15.

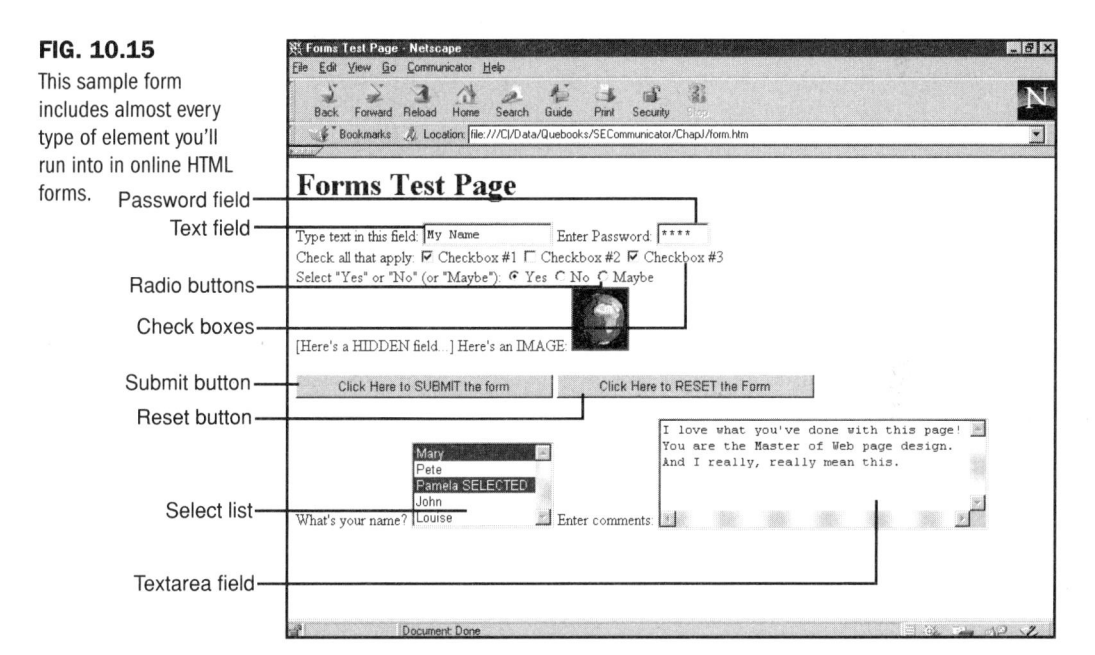

**FIG. 10.15**
This sample form includes almost every type of element you'll run into in online HTML forms.

Password field
Text field
Radio buttons
Check boxes
Submit button
Reset button
Select list
Textarea field

A *text* field is used for entering a single line of text. The size of the field and the maximum number of characters that can be input can both be set by the page designer. The designer can also set the default text that appears in the field, or the field can be left blank. To fill in a text field, you point and click in the field, then type.

> **TIP** You can move from one form field to the next by using the Tab key. You can back up using Shift+Tab.
>
> When any form field is active (that is, after you've clicked in it), your cursor and page up and down keys no longer work to scroll the Navigator window. Instead, they work to move around in the form field. To use them for scrolling the window again, just click anywhere in the window background.

A *Password* field is the same as a text field, but for security purposes the screen doesn't display what you type; instead, you see a string of asterisks (*). You fill in a password field the same way you fill in a text field.

*Check boxes* are for Boolean variables, variables that can take only one of two values. When a box is selected, its output is true; when unselected, it's false. (The actual values depend on how they are set by the Web page designer.) You check a check box by clicking it; you uncheck a checked check box by clicking it again.

*Option buttons* are for variables that can take any one of several different specified values. Selecting one of the buttons automatically causes any previously selected button in the group to be deselected. You select an option button by clicking it.

When you are done filling out a form, you generally click a *Submit* button to send all the data you've input into the form back to the server for processing.

However, the page designer can choose instead to use an *Image* button. This lets him substitute a graphic for the Submit button and gives him the added advantage of sending along the actual graphic coordinates that were clicked.

> **TIP**
> Submit buttons are often labeled something else, like Done or Send. Don't let labels fool you. If it's a pushbutton and it sounds like something you should only click when you're finished, it's probably a Submit button.

### CAUTION
Web pages can include several separate forms on a single page. If there are multiple forms on one page, they are totally independent of each other, and each will have its own individual Submit button.

### TROUBLESHOOTING

**I pressed the Submit button, but all I got back was some weird error message that I couldn't interpret. What gives?** There are a number of things that can happen when you press the Submit button that result in an error message. The following are just a few:

- Between the time you received the form and the time you submitted it, the server you were connected to might have gone down.
- The server you're connected to might submit its CGI scripts to another server to be run, and that server might be down. (Hey—nobody said this would be easy!)
- The CGI program (the program on the server that processes the form) might be buggy and might have choked on your particular data.
- The CGI program might be telling you that you filled out the form incompletely or incorrectly. Read the error message carefully to see if it's specific about the problem.

The fix is often no more complicated than pressing the Back button on the Navigator toolbar and filling out the form correctly. If you continue to get errors, your only solution might be to e-mail the Webmaster of the site where you're experiencing the problems. There's usually an address or link on most home pages for this purpose.

The page designer can also include a *Reset* pushbutton; selecting it resets all of a form's fields to their initial values. If you've totally mucked up filling out a form, you click the Reset button to reset all the fields to their default values so you can start over. (Like the Submit button, the Reset button can also have a custom name.)

The *Select* element can be used to produce a neat multiple-choice field in the form of a pull-down list. A default value can be defined by the page designer as being auto-selected, and multiple selections can also be enabled. To choose a Select list element, just click it. To select more than one option in a multiple-enabled list, click one option and drag to select more. To select non-contiguous options, hold the Ctrl key when you click additional items. Selected items are highlighted; if you can only highlight one option, then you can safely assume that the multiple attribute isn't enabled.

Finally, the TEXTAREA HTML tag lets a designer create a scrolling text box into which you can type multiple lines of text. Default text can be included. To fill in a Textarea field, just click in it and type. You can use all of the standard editing keys (arrows, delete, page up/down, and so on) to move around and edit in the Textarea box.

**N O T E** The page designer might give you the ability to upload a data file to fill out a form, rather than having to fill it all out by hand. This can save you lots of connect time when filling out long online forms. Look for on-screen instructions to see if and how you can upload a form data file, and for information on what format your file should take.

## Automatic Mail with Mailto:

When you press a form's Submit button, the form data is usually uploaded to the server for action. However, the page designer can choose to have you e-mail the data yourself, using a format known as Mailto:. All this does is bring up your own e-mail client (Messenger, if you're running Communicator) and start you into an e-mail editing session.

## Enough About Forms Already!

We've spent an inordinate amount of space in this chapter discussing forms. Why? Because they serve as a model for all the other topics in this chapter. Most of what you can do with forms, you can also do, to some degree or another, with Java, plug-ins, and JavaScript. If you understand how forms work and how to use them, the other technologies covered in this chapter will also make sense to you.

# Frames

First introduced in Netscape Navigator 2.0, HTML frames create independently changeable and (sometimes) scrollable windows that tile together to break up and organize a display so that it is not only more visually appealing, but easier to work with. Frames not only organize data, they organize your browser's display window, too. In fact, they break up the window into individual, independent panes or frames. Each frame holds its own HTML file as content, and the content of each frame can be scrolled or changed independently of the others. In a way, it's almost as though each frame becomes its own mini-browser.

Perhaps the best way to get a feel for what you can do with frames is to look at a couple of real-world examples.

## Netscape's DevEdge Site

As you might expect, Netscape—the inventor of frames—has some excellent examples of frames on their Web sites. Figure 10.16 is taken from their DevEdge developer's site (**http://developer.netscape.com**) and shows a window that is broken into four separate frames.

**FIG. 10.16**
Netscape's DevEdge site at **http://developer.netscape.com** showcases some excellent examples of using frames to separate information from navigation.

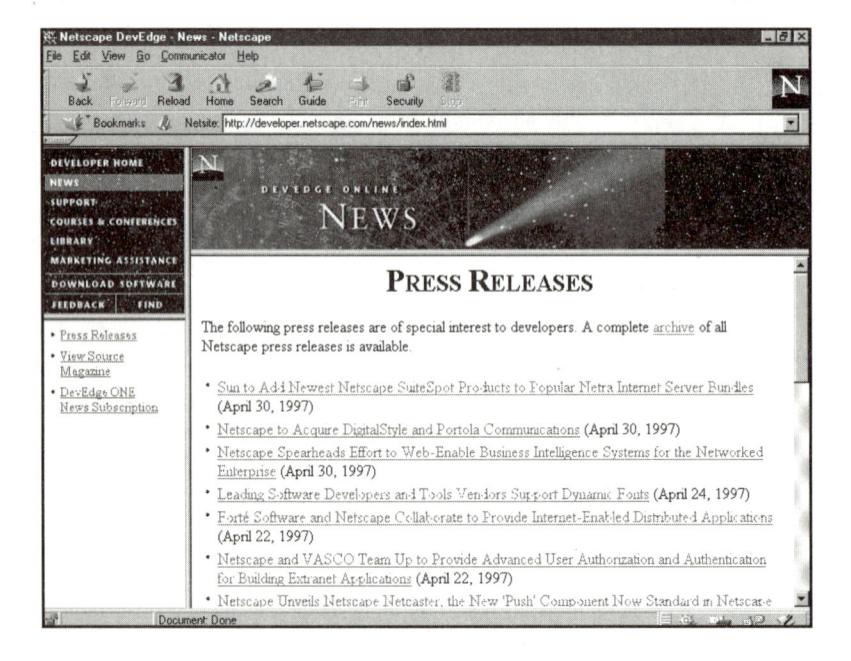

The frames on this page show how Netscape has split the information display into two frames on the right, while reserving navigation functions for the two frames on the left.

This page, or "frameset," features a title graphic to show you where you are, a topic menu in the upper left, a more specific menu in the lower left, and a large content window. The menus remain stable and available while you browse through the site's various content pages, which makes for a reassuring and easy-to-use browsing experience.

> **TIP** Note how Netscape has saved themselves a great deal of time and development work by making only the category-level menus graphic, while using much easier-to-create text-only lists of links for the more numerous sub-category menus.

This site can definitely serve as a template for good frames-based HTML document design for any information that is hierarchically organized by category. You'll see many sites that mimic this sort of frames-based organization, with a slender menu at the side and a content window taking up the majority of the screen's real estate.

## The CyberDungeon

Frames aren't just for business documents. Take a look at Figure 10.17, which depicts the online CyberDungeon adventure game.

I doubt that you will ever find 10 frames used as gracefully as they are on this site. (Usually it's bad practice to use more than four frames at a time.) This artfully done Web site anticipates the recent mantra of both Microsoft and Netscape, who are now encouraging developers to use HTML to create graphical user interfaces (or GUIs) for application programming.

**FIG. 10.17**
The CyberDungeon game can be accessed from its home page at **http://www.cyberdungeon.com**. It uses a set of 10 frames to create a familiar and friendly adventure game interface.

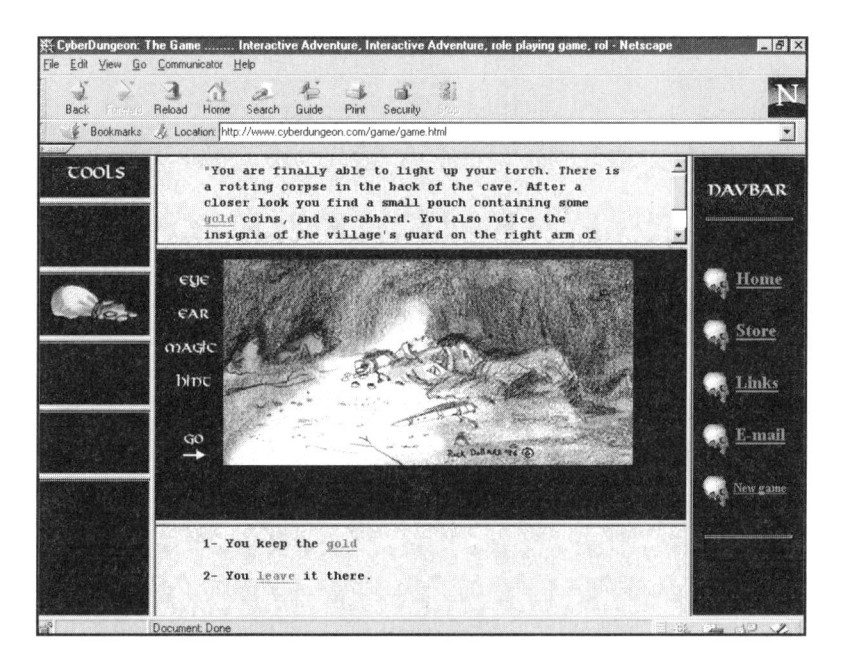

The CyberDungeon site uses a set of frames down the left side of the screen to hold graphical icons of objects that you (the resident adventurer) pick up in your explorations. The top frame of the center set of three displays the text description of your current location, while the larger frame below it shows a picture of the same scene. The bottom frame gives you choices to make along the way.

Finally, the tall right-hand frame keeps the navigational menu for the CyberDungeon site handy as you play.

This site provides a wonderful example of how a well-designed HTML document using frames can replicate applications that previously had to be written in high-level languages like C or C++.

## Resizing Frames

Usually, you won't find any need to have to manipulate a set of frames. If the page designer did his work well, the frameset will be pleasing to the eye and will display the site's data gracefully.

If, however, your browser is set to a non-standard size, you might find that you want to resize the frames. When you move over a resizable frame border with the mouse cursor, it changes to a double-arrow, indicating that the frame can be resized. (If you don't get the double-arrow, it means that the page designer has turned off the frame resizing feature.) To resize a resizable frame, grab the frame border by clicking and dragging it with your mouse to a new position.

**NOTE** The page designer also has control over the color, width, and other attributes of the frame margins. She can choose to include or exclude scrollbars and even has the option of making frames invisible, which can make it difficult for you to even know when a page is composed of frames.

If you stay keenly aware of how a page is laid out and how it is functioning, you should be able to recognize a page built up of frames no matter how its look and feel are altered. ■

## Frame Navigation

One major advantage of pages built using frames is that you can click in a link in one frame and it will update the information in another. For example, in Figure 10.16, you can click in the menu on the left side of the screen and it will change the data in the window on the right.

A page designer might sometimes choose to have a link update more than one frame at once or even the entire screen. A link can even launch a new browser window. Pay close attention when navigating pages built with frames and you won't be fooled by any of these tricks.

**NOTE** In Netscape Navigator 2.0, the toolbar's Back button didn't back you out of a frame, it backed you out of the whole frameset to the previous page.

With versions 3.0 and later, pressing the Back button (or selecting Back from the right-mouse button pop-up menu) returns you to the previous state of the currently selected frame. You only back out of the whole frameset when you get back to your original starting point.

To navigate forward or backward within a frame, make sure you make the frame active first by clicking in it somewhere, then use the Forward or Back buttons or menu selections to navigate within that frame. ■

▶ To discover how to use frames in your own documents, see Chapter 24, "Organizing Content with Tables and Frames," **p. 487**

## The File Menu and Frames

When you're viewing a page with frames, you might notice a few minor changes to the Navigator File menu. Click a frame to activate it, then select the File menu. You see four new or changed selections: Save Frame As, Send Frame, Edit Frame, and Print Frame.

The new Save Frame As selection lets you save the HTML file that is associated with the selected frame. (Save As saves only the outer frameset document, which usually just defines the structure of the display window.)

Send Page changes to Send Frame, which lets you e-mail the frame to someone. A new Edit Frame item launches Composer with the frame content ready for editing. Finally, Print Page becomes Print Frame, which means you can't print an entire frameset; you have to print it frame-by-frame.

> **TIP** There's also a minor change in the Edit menu: Find in Page (Ctrl+F) becomes Find in Frame. Subtle, but important.

## Java

Java is the new darling of the Web. There are even those who go so far as to predict that it will soon come to replace HTML completely.

Don't believe it. Java is great for what it is intended to be—a cross-platform application development language. You write programs in Java, then you can run them on any computer platform that understands Java. At last count, this was almost every computer currently manufactured.

Communicator has a built-in understanding of Java, so Java programs (or *applets*) can be included in HTML documents, and they run when the page is loaded. This means that Web pages, intranet documents, and even e-mail can contain actual running programs.

While this is not an insignificant development, Java remains a programming language. As such, it is difficult to learn and requires that you create an entire program every time you want it to do anything for you. It's still much easier to say "Hello World!" with HTML than it is with Java, and that situation is likely to remain unchanged for the near future.

Still, Java is unquestionably the master at doing what it was designed to do—integrating applications into HTML documents. Some are more impressive than others, of course. I'm sure we're all sick of seeing those annoying scrolling LED marquees on Web sites, and there are signs that the novelty has begun to wear off even for Java programmers. (Thank goodness!)

However, Java is flexing its muscles and might become the language of choice not only for document creation on the Web and intranets, but even for stand-alone application development. Corel, for example, has released a version of WordPerfect written in Java. It can run in the Navigator window.

Because it is a programming language, the form it takes in documents is varied and ever-changing. Java applets can be as simple as the aforementioned LED marquee, and as complex as Corel's inline version of Corel Office Suite, which includes WordPerfect.

You can easily recognize Java applets when you encounter them, though. Before they run, the Navigator status bar displays the message `Loading applet`, and, as they run, you see `Applet [name] running` (see Figure 10.18).

**FIG. 10.18**
This Java applet displays various up-to-the-minute weather maps.

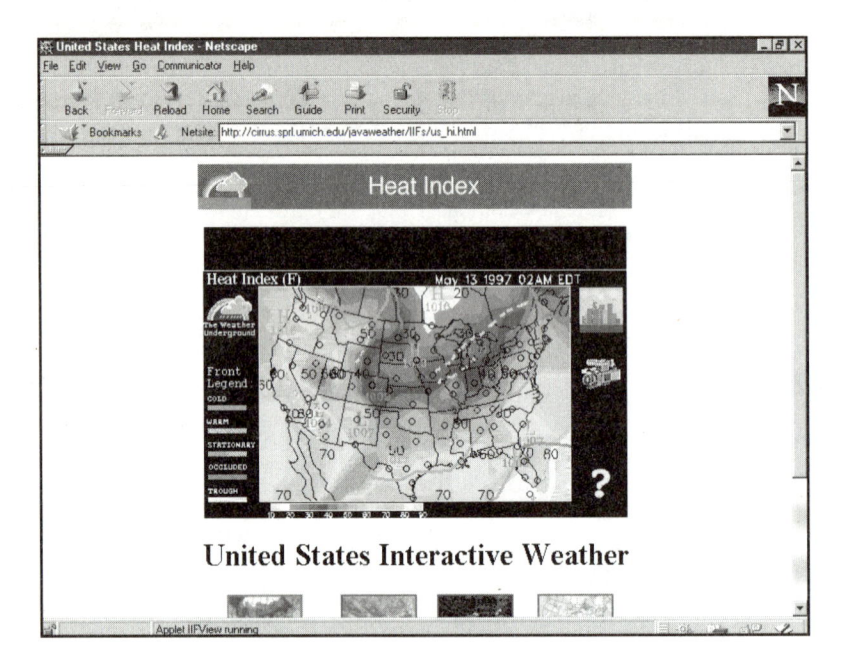

Interacting with Java applets is exactly like running any stand-alone computer program, because that's essentially what they are. The applet programmer can create any controls, buttons, input fields, or other interactive devices she wishes. Polite programmers include on-screen instructions and nice labels to help you figure out the interface. Nasty ones leave you to fend for yourself.

▶ If you're serious about high-level page design, you might want to learn all you can about Java. A good place to start is Chapter 31, "Adding Java Applets," **p. 641**

## JavaScript and Dynamic HTML

JavaScript is a lot like Java, only it's a scripting language not a programming language. JavaScript scripts are actually included as text inside HTML documents. Ostensibly easier to figure out than Java (and much less powerful), JavaScript scripts are meant to serve as a sort of glue to tie together other page elements. JavaScript can be used to tie together HTML forms, Java applets, and plug-ins to create powerful pages that combine the best of all these different page-construction tools.

For example, the page shown in Figure 10.19 uses JavaScript to create an on-screen calculator out of a set of form fields and buttons.

http://www.quecorp.com

- The LiveAudio plug-in plays audio files.
- The LiveVideo plug-in displays Video for Windows (AVI) videos.
- For playing QuickTime videos and QuickTime VR 3-D scenes, there's the QuickTime plug-in.
- The Media Player plug-in is for streaming audio in real-time and coordinating audio with other multimedia elements.
- The Cosmo plug-in lets you display and navigate 3-D VRML (Virtual Reality Modeling Language) worlds.

Each plug-in is assigned one or more file types that it can play or display. For example, the LiveAudio plug-in plays four unique sound file formats. Navigator is aware of which plug-ins are installed and which is assigned to each type of file. You can see a list of these file-to-plug-in assignments by selecting Help, About Plug-Ins from the Navigator menu (see Figure 10.20). Navigator displays a list of installed plug-ins and their assigned files in the main display window.

**FIG. 10.20**
You can display a list showing what plug-ins are installed in Navigator by selecting Help, About Plug-Ins from the menu.

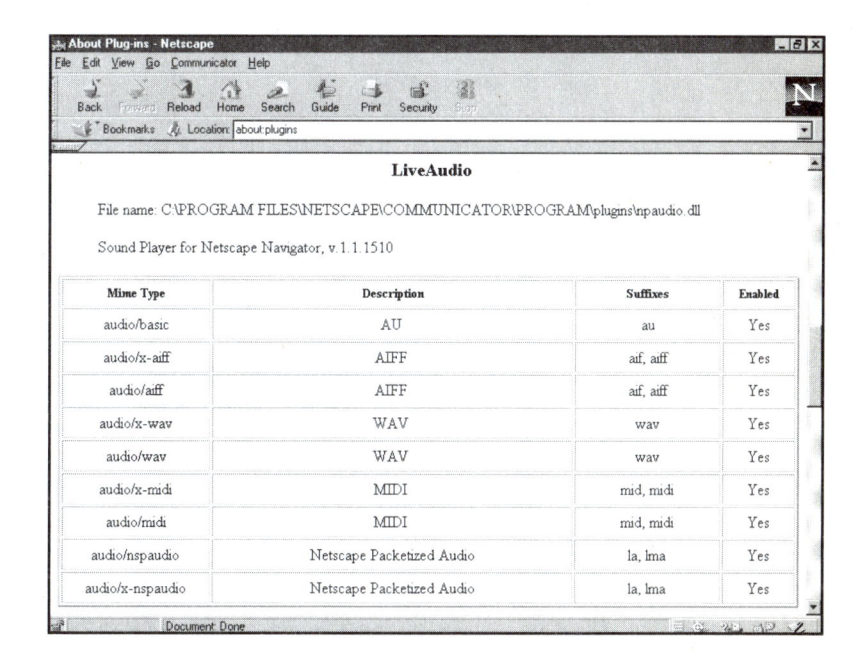

**CAUTION**
Navigator only displays plug-in information if Java and JavaScript are enabled. (The list is generated by an internal Java applet.) If you don't get a list of installed plug-ins when you select Help, About Plug-Ins from the Navigator menu, select Options, Network Preferences from the Navigator menu; then make sure the Enable Java and Enable JavaScript check boxes are selected on the Languages tab.

**188** Chapter 10 Interacting with Plug-Ins, Java Applets, and JavaScript

**LiveAudio**  Because it ships with Communicator, the LiveAudio plug-in is essentially the official Netscape audio player. Unlike many other audio plug-ins, LiveAudio doesn't use a proprietary sound file format, but instead plays standard AIFF, .AU, MIDI, and WAV files. LiveAudio features an easy-to-use console with play, pause, stop, and volume controls.

If you scroll down through the plug-ins list displayed when you select Help, About Plug-ins from the Navigator menu, you should find the entry shown in Figure 10.20. Similar entries should exist for all of the bundled Navigator plug-ins.

If your system is equipped with a sound card, LiveAudio enables you to listen to audio tracks, sound effects, music, and voice files embedded in Web pages. You can also use LiveAudio to listen to stand-alone sound files both on the Web and on your own computer system.

When you encounter a LiveAudio-compatible sound file embedded or linked into a Web page, LiveAudio generally creates the onscreen control console shown in Figure 10.21.

**FIG. 10.21**
The LiveAudio plug-in appears as a minimalist inline audio-player control console, shown here on a Netscape Web site demo page. The LiveAudio audio player control box features four manual controls and a simple drop-down menu.

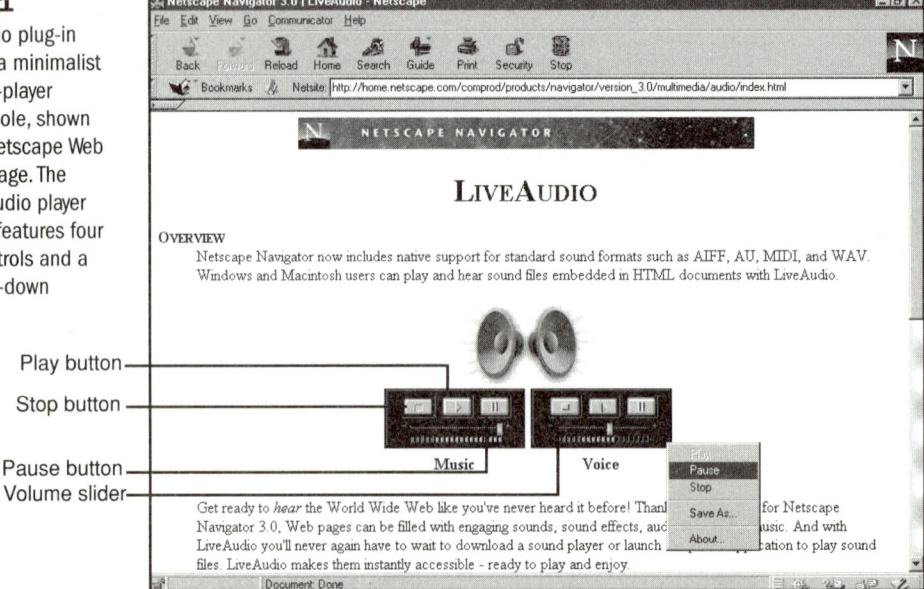

The LiveAudio console controls are intuitive and easy to use (see Figure 10.21). The Stop, Play, and Pause buttons work just as they do on a tape or CD player. You click the Play button to play the sound, the Stop button to stop it, and the Pause button to pause audio playback. If you click the Pause button a second time, play resumes from the point at which you paused the sound.

Click to the right or left of the Volume slider knob to increase or decrease volume. The volume can be jumped only in increments of 20 percent—you can't slide the volume smoothly from 0 percent to 100 percent. The light-emitting diode (LED) bar graph below the Volume slider indicates the current volume level. The dark green LEDs are for the 0–40 percent range; light green LEDs take over for 40–100 percent.

http://www.quecorp.com

Right-clicking the LiveAudio console displays the pop-up menu shown in Figure 10.21. This menu includes selections that duplicate the Play, Stop, and Pause buttons. The menu also provides a selection to display the program's About dialog box and a final non-selectable menu item that tells you the volume level as a percentage of the maximum.

The LiveAudio player has a single keyboard hot key: the spacebar. Pressing the spacebar reactivates whichever button you pressed last (Stop, Play, or Pause). Restopping an already stopped playback is of limited use, but if you last pressed Pause, the spacebar becomes an unpause/repause toggle. If you last pressed Play, the spacebar becomes a handy replay key.

The page designer has the option of including any or none of the on-screen controls and can also specify playback volume, start position into the sound file, and whether or not the sound file autoplays on startup.

**Media Player**   Streaming audio and video content is all the rage these days, but what does it mean? Simply put, streaming content is audio or video that is delivered continuously, in real-time. It doesn't suffer from the jerk-and-stop qualities that plague audio and video content delivered by standard Internet data-delivery methods (such as HTTP).

Netscape's new Media Player is a plug-in for delivering streaming audio content that can be synchronized with other content, including HTML documents, Java applets, and JavaScript. Netscape aimed to make it compatible even with slower dial-up Internet connections.

The Media Player plug-in launches automatically when it encounters a page containing a file in its proprietary LAM (Live Audio Metafile) format.

Media Player is unusual among plug-ins in that it has its own stand-alone configuration program. Look for it in the folder that contains the Communicator components. When you run the Media Player Configuration program, you get the window shown in Figure 10.22. By and large, you can get by with Media Player's default settings just fine. It's not necessary to make adjustments. But if you aren't getting the performance you think you should or if you need to adjust for special circumstances (such as being stuck behind a corporate firewall), you need to run the Configuration program. Click the Help button for assistance in adjusting its wide range of specialized settings.

**LiveVideo**   There are three standard video formats on the Web: Video for Windows, QuickTime, and MPEG. Video for Windows is the standard for PC platforms; QuickTime is used extensively on the Macintosh; and MPEG is the standard for high-end video.

A Video for Windows driver is built in to the Windows 3.1, Windows 95, and Windows NT operating systems. Windows' Media Player is the system-supplied stand-alone application for playing Video for Windows movies within the Windows operating systems; these files are identified by the file name extension .AVI. Not surprisingly, .AVI format movies have also become popular on the Web. With the right Netscape plug-in, you have no problem viewing them inline in Web pages.

**FIG. 10.22**
The Media Player Configuration Program allows you to adjust a wide range of Media Player operating parameters.

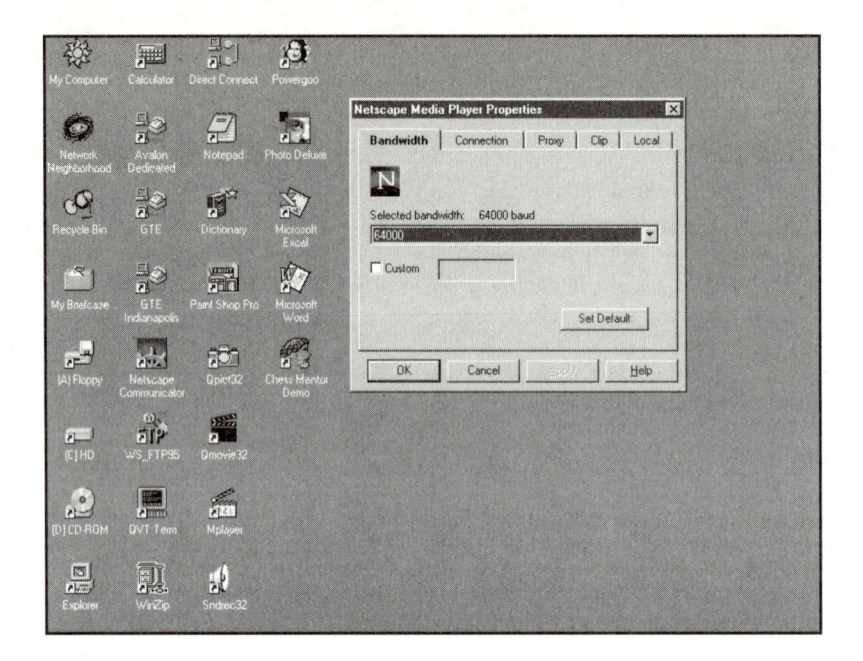

Netscape's official bundled plug-in for displaying .AVI videos is LiveVideo, which is included with the Netscape Communicator distribution. LiveVideo automatically installs and configures as your Video for Windows player of choice. You click a movie image displayed in the Navigator main window to play the plug-in and click again to stop it. Right-clicking an image pops up a complete menu of controls, including Play, Pause, Rewind, Fast Forward, Frame Back, and Frame Forward.

◆ **TROUBLESHOOTING**

**When I try to play an online .AVI file using a plug-in, I get a message saying** `Cannot find "vids:msvc" decompressor.` **What's wrong?** Your Windows 95 MS Video 1 video compressor, which is required for playing any .AVI file, might not be loaded. In the Windows 95 Control Panel, select Add/Remove Programs, click the Windows Setup tab, and then double-click Multimedia. Scroll down to Video Compression and make sure there is a check mark in the box. If there isn't, click the check box and you are prompted to insert your Windows 95 system CD or diskettes.

Figure 10.23 shows LiveVideo in action.

You simply click the embedded video frame to start it playing. Click again to pause the video if needed, and then click to resume.

To access the LiveVideo player controls, right-click the displayed video frame. You get the pop-up menu shown in Figure 10.23.

http://www.quecorp.com

**FIG. 10.23**
LiveVideo plays .AVI videos inline in the Netscape window. To display this pop-up menu, right-click.

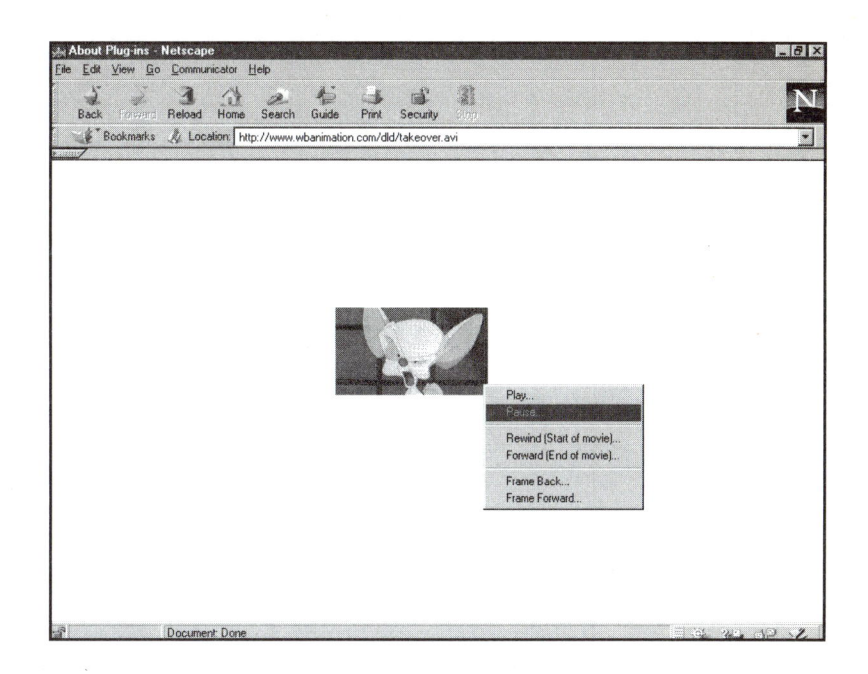

There are six basic controls available from the LiveVideo pop-up menu. You can Play, Pause, or Rewind to the start of the movie and Fast Forward to the end. Like on a VCR, when you've played a video through to the end, you have to rewind it before you can play it again. You can also select Frame Back or Frame Forward to step backwards or forwards through the movie a frame at a time.

The page designer can control whether or not you see any controls and whether the video autoplays on loading.

**QuickTime Plug-In** QuickTime is the video format used on the Apple Macintosh. However, because it was one of the first movie formats, and because it is so widely used by the art community that favors the Mac, QuickTime .MOV movie files are in ample supply on the Web.

Apple's QuickTime plug-in is also included with Navigator. It lets you view QuickTime content directly in the browser window (see Figure 10.24). The QuickTime plug-in works with existing QuickTime movies, as well as with movies prepared to take advantage of the plug-in's fast-start feature. The fast-start feature presents the first frame of the movie almost immediately and can begin playing even before the movie has been completely downloaded.

All flavors of the Apple Macintosh ship QuickTime-enabled, but if you want to play QuickTime movies on your Windows computer, you need the proper version of QuickTime for Windows in addition to the QuickTime plug-in. You can download versions for Windows 3.1, Windows 95, and Windows NT from **http://quicktime.apple.com**.

**192** | Chapter 10  Interacting with Plug-Ins, Java Applets, and JavaScript

**FIG. 10.24**
The Apple QuickTime plug-in features an integrated control toolbar and a pop-up menu that displays when you right-click.

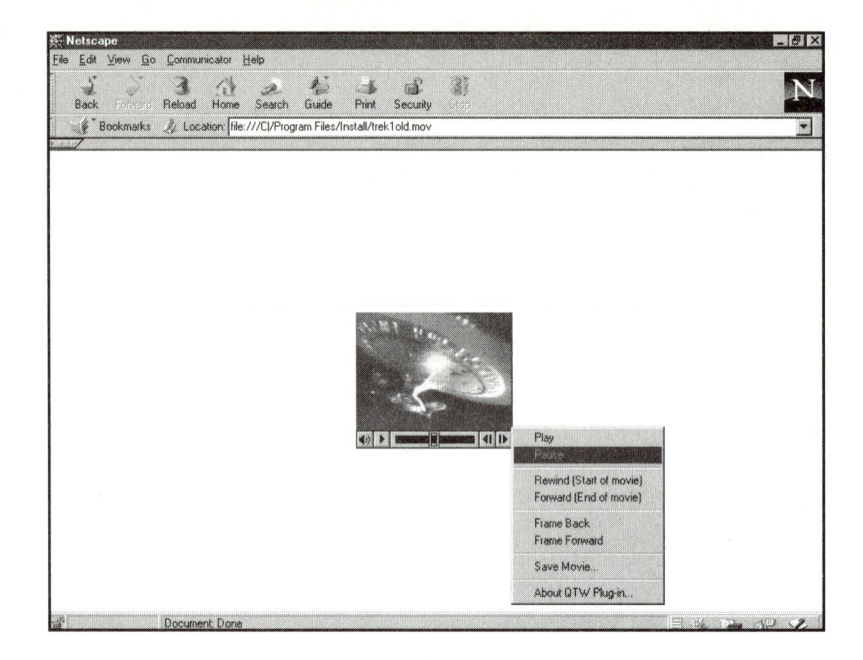

The plug-in can play many kinds of QuickTime movies (.MOV files), including movies with text, MIDI, and other kinds of data. The QuickTime plug-in supports a wide set of embedded commands, allowing changes in user interface and background content—for example, music. You can also interact with QuickTime VR Panoramas and Objects. QuickTime VR stitches together a series of images into a panorama or scene (see Figure 10.25).

**FIG. 10.25**
To view a QuickTime VR panorama, you just click and drag the mouse.

> **N O T E**  If you're interested in creating QuickTime movies to play back on your site, you can find tools for Webmasters (like the Internet Movie Tool for the Mac) at **http://quicktime.apple.com/sw/**. You can also check into **http://quicktime.apple.com/dev/** for more information on how to use QuickTime on the Web.

http://www.quecorp.com

**Cosmo**  VRML, the Virtual Reality Modeling Language, lets you create navigable 3-D worlds almost as easily as you create HTML pages. Many Web sites have sprung up featuring these 3-D worlds, and true believers in VRML believe it will eventually evolve into Hollywood-type virtual reality.

With a VRML viewer plug-in, you can use Navigator to display and move around in VRML worlds. Paper Software developed one of the first VRML viewer plug-ins, called WebFX. Netscape liked WebFX so much that it bought the company, renamed it Live3D, and bundled it with Navigator 3.0. However, with Communicator, Netscape is bundling Silicon Graphics' Cosmo VRML viewer.

Cosmo shows several improvements over WebFX, including integration with scripting languages, built-in object animation and interaction, and compliance with the latest VRML standards.

Navigating through a virtual environment using Cosmo is straightforward. The plug-in is shown in Figure 10.26.

**FIG. 10.26**
Cosmo is the "official" VRML plug-in for Navigator.

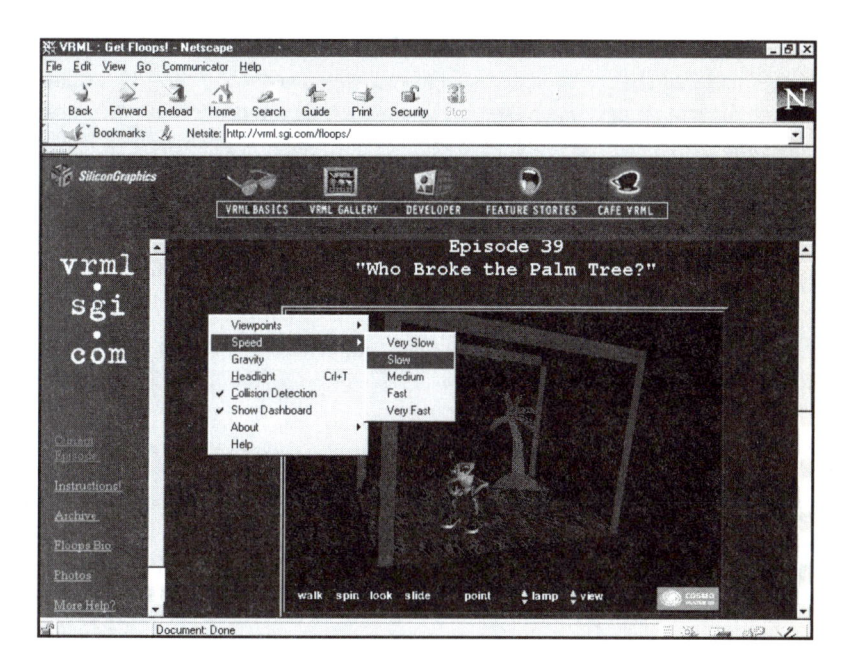

Along the bottom of the screen is a toolbar that enables you to perform various simple operations.

By holding down the left mouse button, you can walk through the world. Moving the mouse forward moves you forward, moving it backward moves you backward. Sideways motion of the mouse lets you turn left or right, and you can combine this motion with the forward or backward motion.

Holding down the Ctrl key with the left mouse button enables you to *look* in different directions without moving at all. Moving the mouse forward and backward enables you to look up and down, for example. Holding down the Alt key makes the left mouse button slide you around, both left/right and up/down.

Holding down the right mouse button spins the world around, so that you can look at it from different angles. Holding down the Ctrl key and clicking an object once moves your camera until it looks right at the object.

The toolbar enables you to modify the action that your left mouse button performs. If you click Spin, the left mouse button does the same as the right mouse button does—it spins the world. If you click Look, the left mouse button does the same as when you hold down the Ctrl key—it lets you look around. Clicking Slide makes the left mouse button behave the way that it does when you hold down the Alt key. When you click the Point button, left mouse clicks have the same effect as holding down Ctrl while left-clicking—you go to the object that you clicked.

The toolbar also enables you to turn your headlight (the light source attached to your viewpoint, like the lamp on a miner's helmet) on and off (which you can also do by pressing Ctrl+T) and adjust the overall scene brightness up or down (which you can also do by pressing Ctrl+1 and Ctrl+2). The toolbar also lets you cycle between several Viewpoints in the file or return to the most recently selected Viewpoint (which you can also do by pressing Ctrl+V).

The Cosmo pop-up menus duplicate much of the toolbar's functionality, but also enable you to do such things as navigate to a particular Viewpoint by name, turn gravity off, and so on. You can also control display speed and the visibility of various controls.

To access the menus, right-click anywhere in the main window. Figure 10.26 shows a typical set of menus.

By using the menus and the toolbar, you have considerable control over the Cosmo plug-in's features.

> **TIP** Go to Silicon Graphics' Web site at **http://www.sgi.com/Products/cosmo/** to find out more about Cosmo, as well as their VRML authoring tools.

## Third Party Plug-Ins

Netscape's built-in suite of plug-ins handles many file types that Communicator itself doesn't display. But there are hundreds more that its built-in plug-ins won't handle. Fortunately, a multitude of other companies are also producing plug-ins for Communicator—well over a hundred at last count.

Adding third-party Navigator plug-ins couldn't be much easier. Netscape maintains a page that lists many of the currently available plug-ins, with links to the pages from which you can download them. You can find the page at the following address:

> http://home.netscape.com/comprod/products/navigator/version_2.0/plugins/index.html

(Note that Netscape hasn't adjusted the version number in this URL since version 2.0. Of course, that doesn't mean they won't someday.)

The Plug-Ins Plaza site (see Figure 10.27) seems to be even more consistently up-to-date than Navigator's own site. You can find the Plug-Ins Plaza at the following address:

**http://browserwatch.iworld.com/plug-in.html**

**FIG. 10.27**
A trip to the Plug-Ins Plaza site gives you the latest scoop on all the hot new plug-ins.

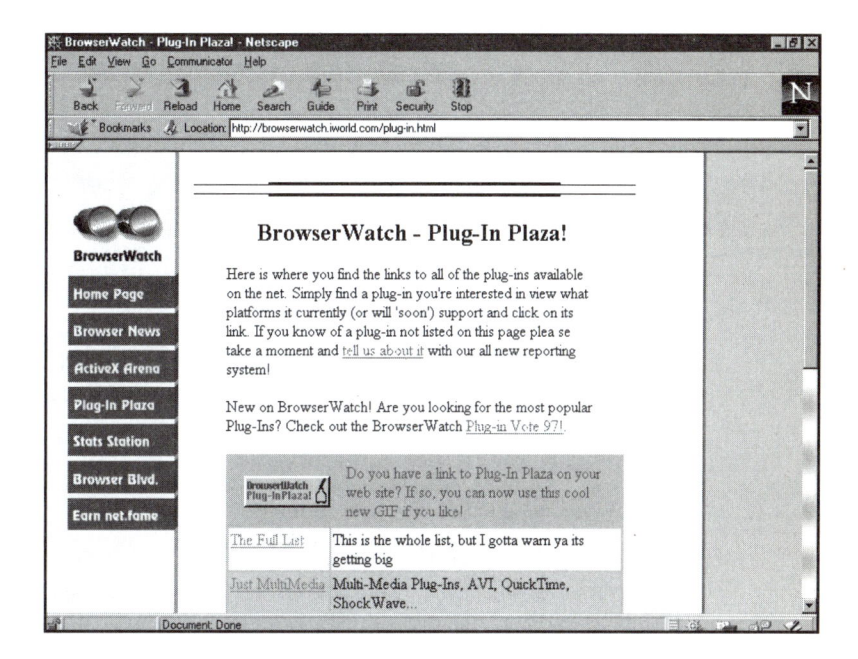

The biggest problem you might run into when you install third-party plug-ins is learning how the controls work. Each plug-in comes with its own custom controls. Many of these programs provide on-screen controls for zooming, printing, panning, scrolling, and so on. Each plug-in comes with detailed documentation explaining its specific controls and how they work. (In some cases, you might have to download a separate manual file, or the plug-in's documentation might be online in the form of Web pages. Make sure that you get your plug-in's documentation.) Read the documentation so that you know all about a plug-in *before* you encounter any files that it will display. Then you don't have to spend valuable online time trying to figure out your plug-in's behavior.

Let's take a look at a few of the most popular third-party Navigator plug-ins.

**RealAudio**   Progressive Networks' RealAudio plug-in (see Figure 10.28) provides live, on-demand, real-time audio over 14.4 kilobytes per second (Kbps) or faster Internet connections. Though Netscape's own Media Player is obviously intended to go head-to-head with RealAudio, you'll still run into many sites that feature RealAudio content.

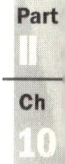

**FIG. 10.28**
RealAudio is the most popular audio program on the Web right now. You can sample it via free download or buy it boxed at a software dealer near you.

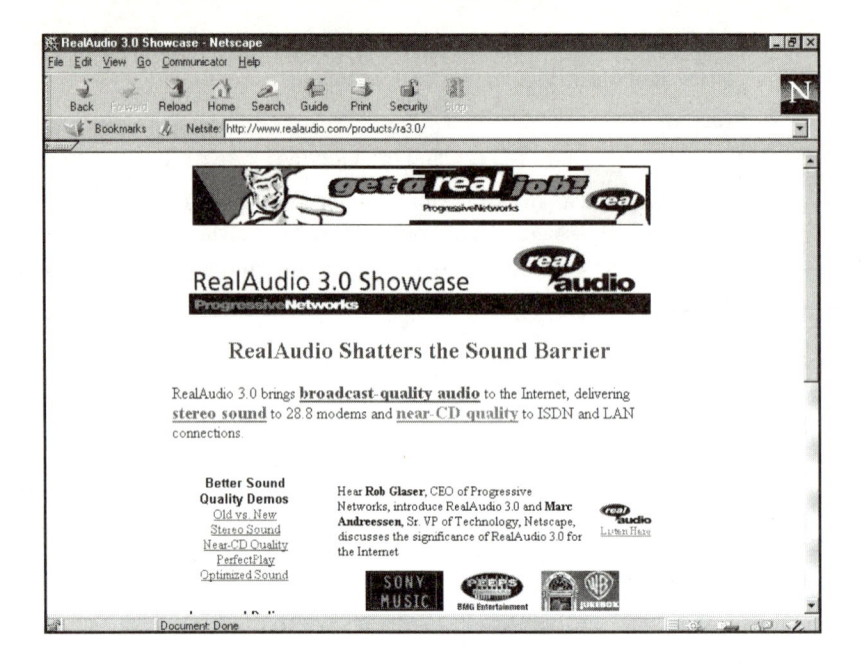

You can download RealAudio from the following site:

   http://www.realaudio.com/products/ra3.0/

**MPEG Plug-Ins**   MPEG is currently the bright and shining star of multimedia. The MPEG2 movie compression standard is destined to provide full-screen, full-motion movies on a highly compressed CD-ROM, among other things. Because of its high compression ratios, MPEG is also a good choice for delivering movies over the Internet.

MPEG works best with a video board capable of doing hardware decompression. But even running in software on fast Pentium systems, MPEG shows promise.

Though Netscape doesn't provide an MPEG plug-in, several Navigator plug-ins are available for playing inline MPEG videos.

InterVU's PreVU plug-in, for example, plays streaming MPEG video without specialized MPEG hardware or a proprietary video server. This plug-in gives you a first-frame view inline, streaming viewing while downloading, and full-speed cached playback from your hard drive. You can download PreVU from the following site:

   http://www.intervu.com/player/player.html

## Shockwave for Macromedia Director

Multimedia is a good buzzword, but what does it really mean? Literally translated as "more than one medium," most people use the term as a presentation that includes some combination of sound, graphics, animation, video, and even interactivity.

Interactivity is an important part of multimedia. It's the part that puts the flow of the whole thing under the user's control. While this can be as simple as an onscreen button that you click to move to the next slide, more often it involves making selections from multiple choices.

One of the most-used, most significant, and most awe-inspiring third-party plug-ins for Navigator is Macromedia Shockwave for Director. With this plug-in, you can view Director movies directly on a Web page. (Don't confuse Director movies with other file types of the same name, such as QuickTime movies.) To create Director movies, you use Macromedia's Director, a cross-platform multimedia authoring program that enables multimedia developers to create fully interactive multimedia applications, or *titles*. Because of its interactive integration of animation, bitmap, video, and sound media, and its playback compatibility with a variety of computer platforms including Windows, Macintosh, OS/2, and SGI, Director is now the most widely used professional multimedia authoring tool.

The Shockwave for Director plug-in is available from:

http://www.macromedia.com

**Adobe Acrobat Reader**   Adobe's Acrobat Reader enables you to view and print Acrobat Portable Document Format (PDF) files. In a nutshell, PDF files are viewable documents that have the visual integrity of a desktop-published document that has been printed on paper. PDF viewers are available for UNIX, Macintosh, and Windows platforms, and each displays PDF documents identically. If the integrity of your documents is important to you (as it is, for example, to the Internal Revenue Service, which uses Acrobat to distribute accurate tax forms over the Web), PDF files are for you.

When activated, the Acrobat plug-in creates a dockable toolbar in the Navigator window. The toolbar provides controls for zooming, printing, and navigating the Acrobat document.

The Acrobat plug-in is available for Windows 3.1, Windows 95, and Macintosh; a UNIX version is in the wings. You can download it from the Adobe Web site:

http://www.adobe.com/

**ActiveX**   Microsoft is actively promoting its Windows-based ActiveX control technology as an alternative to Sun's platform-independent Java. Who will "win" this battle remains to be seen, but, in the meantime, there are many sites that are using ActiveX controls in their pages.

Though Navigator can't make use of ActiveX controls by itself, ExCITE's NCompass division has created a Navigator plug-in for Windows 95 called ScriptActive with which you can view and use embedded ActiveX controls.

You can download NCompass's ScriptActive plug-in from the following site:

http://www.ncompasslabs.com

## OLE Integration

Built in to the Windows 95 and Windows 3.1 versions of Communicator is the capability to have Communicator components (Messenger, Navigator, and so on) interact with other Windows programs though the OLE (Object Linking and Embedding) capabilities built in to Windows itself.

What this means is that Navigator can load an inline version of Word into its display to work on a Word document (see Figure 10.29), or Excel can include an instance of Navigator in a spreadsheet as an embedded Web browser. Though it sounds strange, it works quite well in many instances.

**FIG. 10.29**
A Word document being edited inline in a Navigator window, thanks to Windows 95's built-in OLE capabilities.

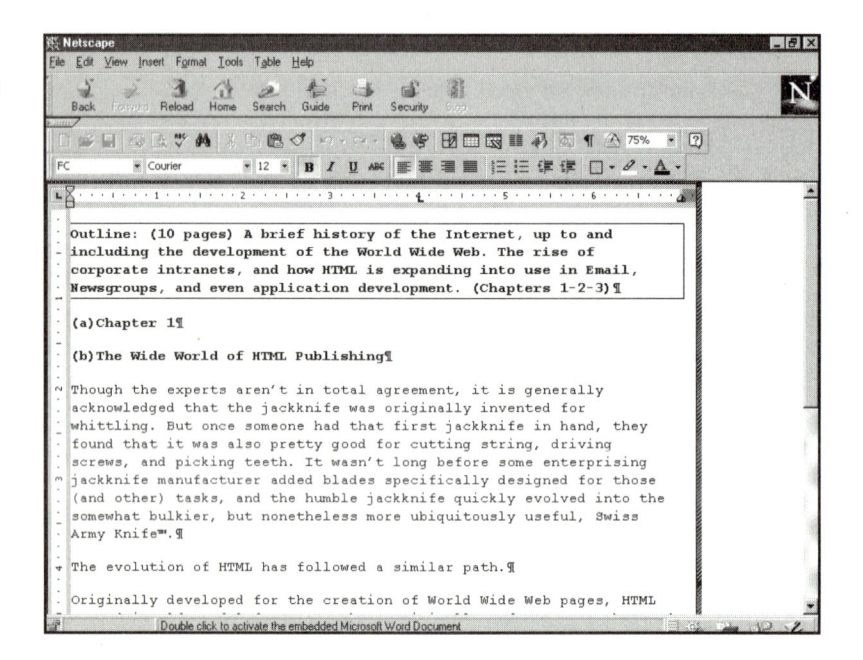

Note that the Word toolbars appear beneath the Navigator toolbars. The document is fully editable in the Navigator window thanks to OLE. This tight integration is a real boon to those who have to share documents over a corporate intranet, for example.

http://www.quecorp.com

CHAPTER 11

# Messenger In-Depth

*by Todd Stauffer*

**W**ith a program as powerful as Messenger, it's possible to be overwhelmed by all the features and options. But part of the power of Messenger is in its flexibility. After you learn a few of the tricks to organizing your Inbox, you'll be a fan of Messenger's power.

In this chapter, you learn the various ways to customize and configure Messenger to make the experience of reading larger quantities of e-mail more palatable. You also see some organizing methods that make Messenger a delight to work with in business. You see how you can attach documents, programs, Usenet messages, and even Communicator Address Book cards to your outgoing e-mail messages. And, just in case you aren't getting enough e-mail, you see some interesting ways to add mailing list discussion groups and Netscape's In-Box Direct service to your e-mail accomplishments.

### Organizing the message list

Messenger's interface makes it easy to read as much mail as you can receive. Sort your messages, hide messages that you don't want to read, or mark them for reading later.

### Reading threaded messages

Messages that continue the same topic can be arranged by thread, allowing you to selectively read or ignore those message threads, depending on what you feel like reading.

### Managing e-mail

Messenger gives you a lot of control over the system you use to store e-mail messages. It's a good idea to create a solid system if you'll be dealing with a lot of messages.

### Searching and filters

Messenger gives you the ability to search through all your stored messages to find particular messages you need to retrieve. You can also create filters that automatically file, reply to, or delete messages as they come into your Inbox, based on criteria you establish.

**Chapter 11** Messenger In-Depth

## Organizing the Message List

To resize a column in the Message List, move the mouse pointer over the black line that separates the two column headings (the gray title bars for each column). This changes the look of your mouse pointer to two little arrows that point left and right, as shown in Figure 11.1. After the pointer changes, click and hold. Moving the mouse left and right resizes the column to the left of your pointer.

> **NOTE** Two things to watch out for here: The rightmost column cannot be resized without first being moved (which is discussed next), and the two icon-based columns can't be resized at all. ■

**FIG. 11.1**
Resizing columns is more art than science. Just get the columns wide enough that you can read everything and be done with it.

Click here to resize

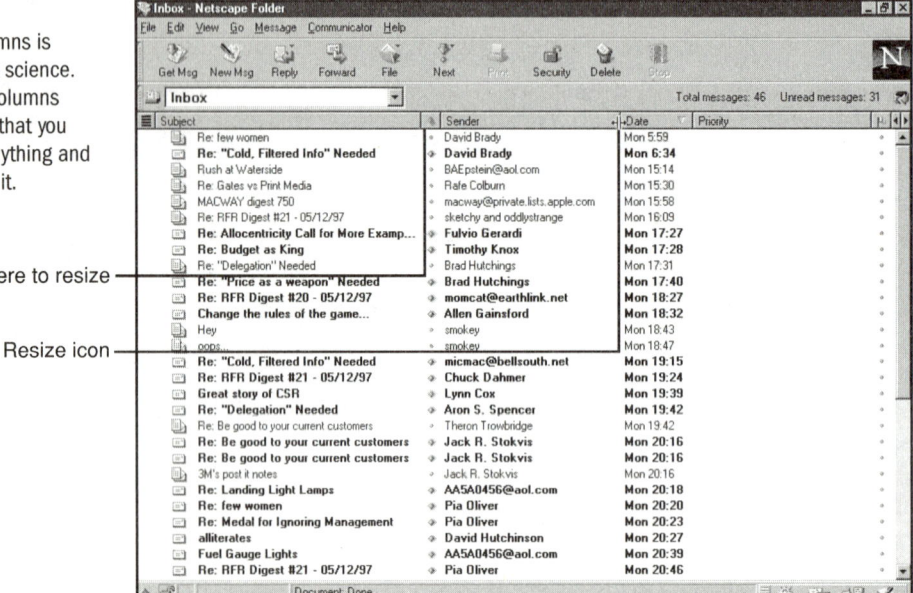

Resize icon

Moving columns is even easier than resizing them. Just click the column heading and hold the mouse button down while moving the mouse left or right. As the selected column heading passes over another, they switch places. Release the mouse button when you're happy with the column's new location.

> **TIP** Most of these columns are self-explanatory, but what are the little green dots? They're the read/unread indicators. Click the dot for a message you've already read and it becomes unread, which is great way to remind yourself to read the message again.

http://www.quecorp.com

## Sort Quickly with the Columns

Sorting your messages in the Message List is possible by simply clicking the column headings in the Message List. To sort by a particular column heading, click that heading once to select it. You see a little arrow appear, indicating the direction in which the sort is taking place, as in Figure 11.2.

> **NOTE** In the column headings, an up arrow means the sort is taking place from the bottom to the top; a down arrow means the column is sorted from the top toward the bottom.

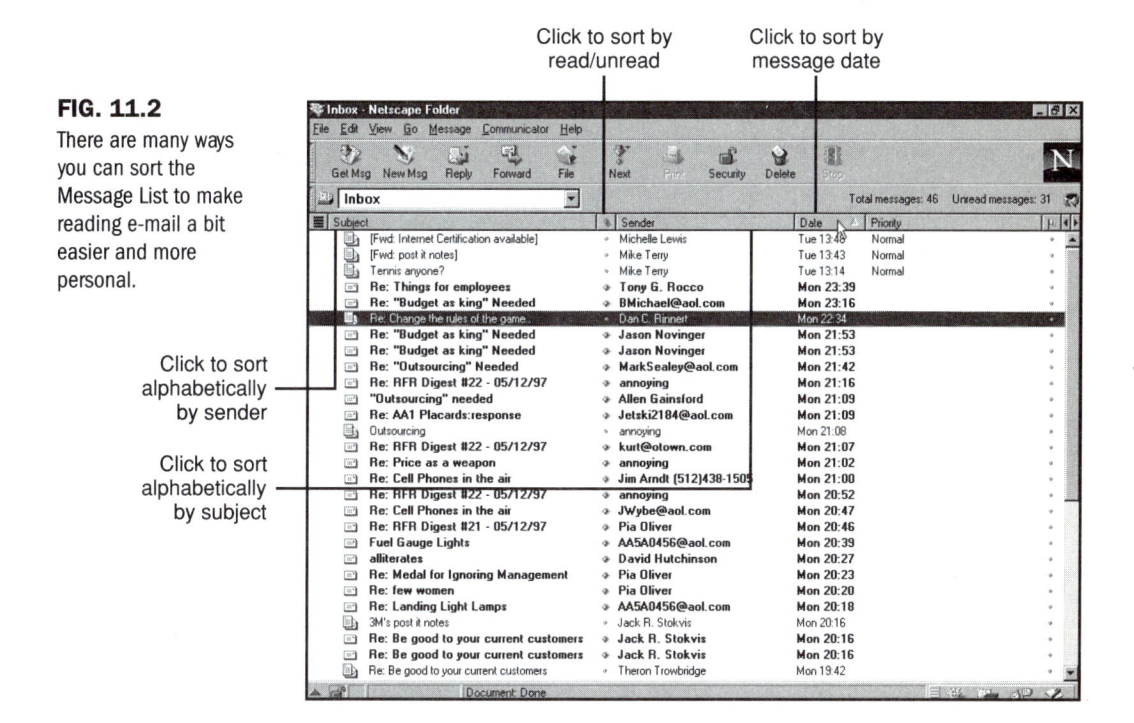

**FIG. 11.2**
There are many ways you can sort the Message List to make reading e-mail a bit easier and more personal.

Click to sort by read/unread
Click to sort by message date
Click to sort alphabetically by sender
Click to sort alphabetically by subject

To change the order of a particular sort, simply click the column heading that has the arrow again. The arrow changes directions and all the messages in the Message List change their positions accordingly.

> **NOTE** All of these sorting functions are duplicated in the Messenger menu under the View, Sort command.

## View Only New Messages

It's possible to view only the New messages in your Message List using Messenger. This doesn't delete older messages; it just hides them from view. To do this, select View, Messages from the menu and choose New. Now your Message List changes to reveal only the messages that you haven't yet read, as shown in Figure 11.3.

**FIG. 11.3**
You can choose to view only new messages, but watch out. After you've read the message, it's no longer displayed.

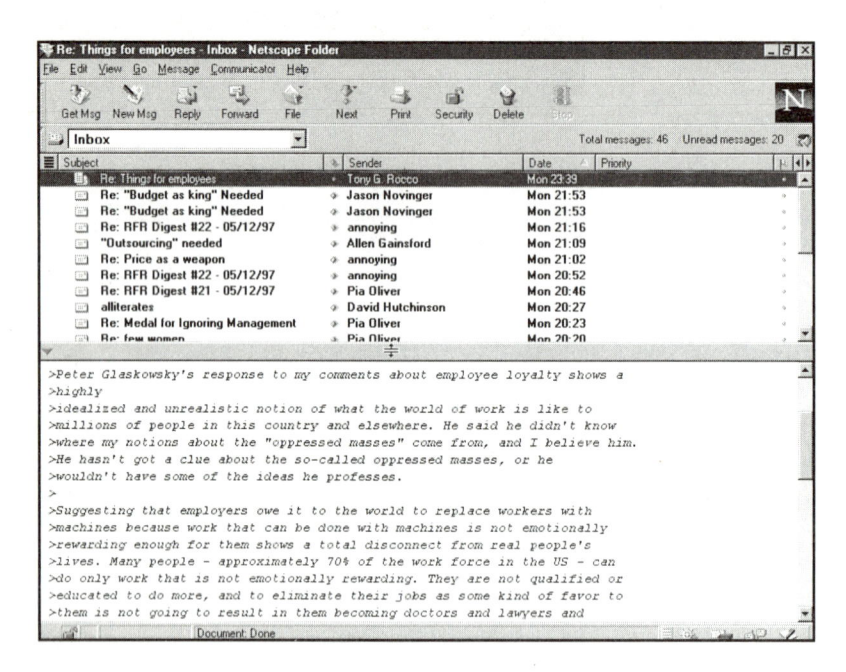

This setting should be considered a temporary setting, because it only allows you to view messages for as long as they're left unread. It might be a good idea to invoke this setting right after you've received new mail. After all the new mail has been read, you can switch back to View, Messages, All so you can see all the messages you've received.

## Customize the Message Pane

You can make the message pane smaller or larger, hide it completely, or choose to have more or less information appear in that pane, as shown in Figure 11.4. If you can't see enough of the message when you're reading—or if you can't see enough of the Message List columns—resizing the interface is a simple matter. Simply select and hold down the mouse button on the large gray bar between the two panes. Drag up or down until the panes are more appropriately placed and release the mouse button.

If you'd prefer to hide the message pane completely (assuming, perhaps, that you'd rather double-click the messages to see them in a full-sized window), then click the down arrow in the

# Organizing the Message List | 203

resizing bar once. Figure 11.6 shows how clicking the down arrow collapses the message pane so that only the Message List columns are showing. To get the message pane back, click the up arrow that appears at the bottom of the entire Message List window.

**FIG. 11.4**
Resizing or hiding the message pane can make it easier to manage your Message List.

Resizing bar
Hide/Show arrow

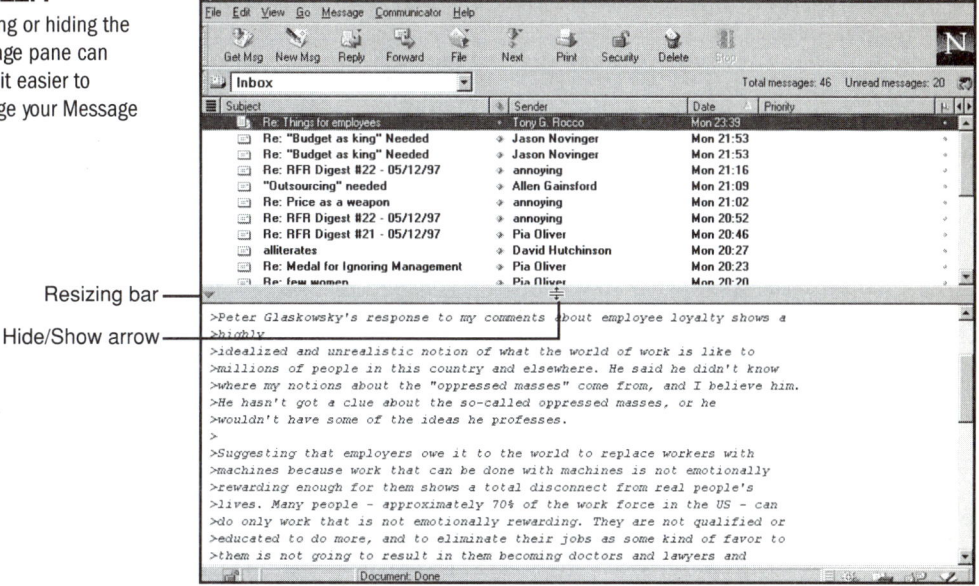

**FIG. 11.5**
Collapsing the message pane leaves you with nothing but an up arrow at the bottom of the screen.

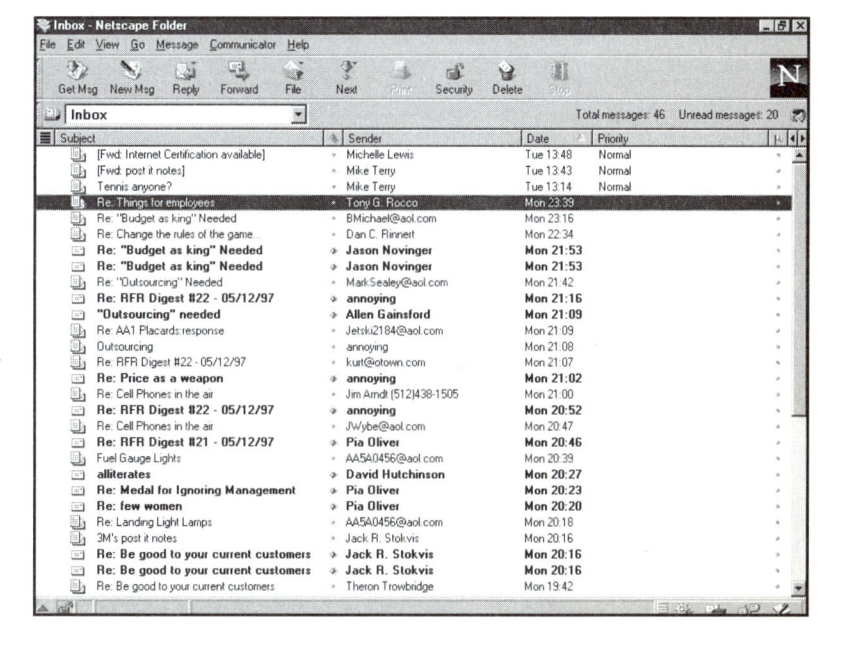

## Change the Message's Appearance

You also have control over how much information appears in that message pane when you're trying to read e-mail. If you're not a big fan of Internet headers (all the To, From, and Subject information), then you can elect to change the level of information presented by Messenger.

> **N O T E** All of these different options affect e-mail messages whatever way you read them—whether that's in the Message List window or by double-clicking the message to view it in its own window. ∎

To change the level of information shown, select View, Headers from the Messenger menu. This results in another menu, where you can choose from the following:

- **All**. Allows you to see all of the Internet e-mail headers for a message (including fascinating reading such as routing information, MIME version, and X-Mailer entries).
- **Normal**. Now the only headers you see are the To, From, Subject, and CC headers, which are things that are nice to print but that duplicate what's in the Message List columns.
- **Brief**. A quick one-liner, including the subject and who sent the message, shown in Figure 11.6.

**FIG. 11.6**
If you choose to view Brief headers, you get to move directly into the interesting parts of the e-mail message.

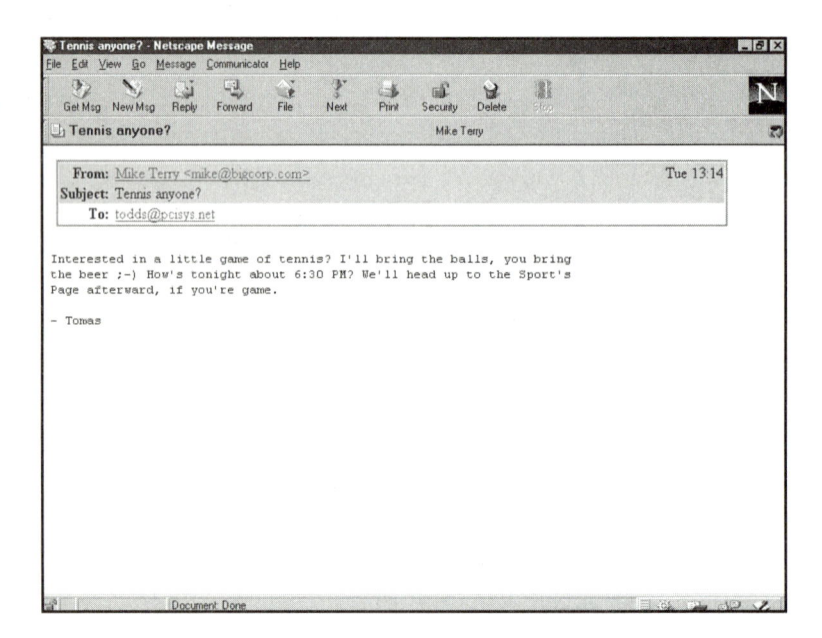

Your other option for viewing e-mail is to decide whether you want to view attachments as part of your e-mail message or if you want only to see a link to the attachment in your e-mail message. Some attachments (like word processing documents) are linked regardless, because Netscape is only designed to display certain types of files. But others, like Web pages, can be shown directly within an e-mail message.

To choose how you view attachments, select View, Attachments from the Messenger menu. If you want to see the attachments within the e-mail message, choose Inline. If you'd rather see a link every time, like in Figure 11.7, choose As Links.

**FIG. 11.7**
Here's an image file viewed inline in an e-mail message.

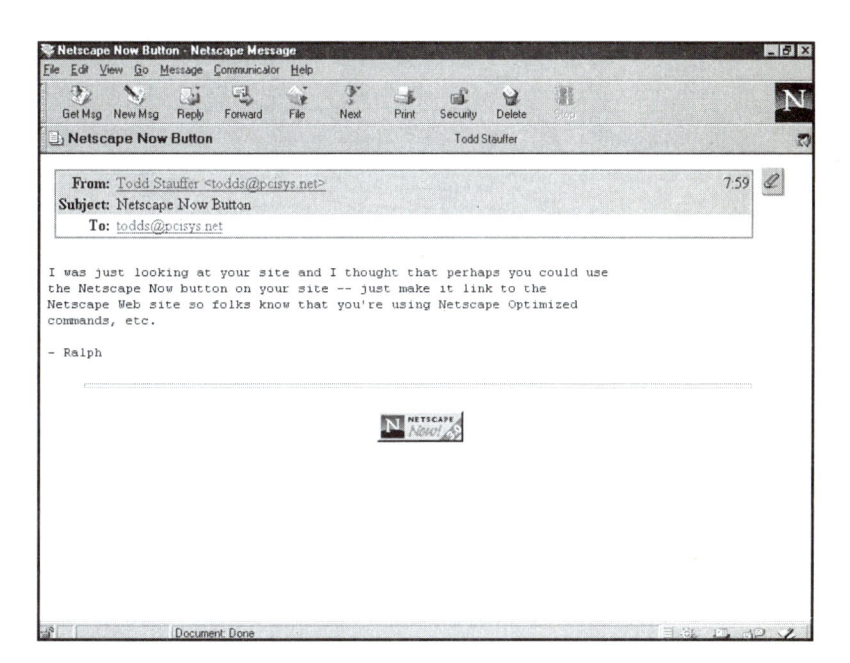

## Using Threads to Follow a Conversation

For quite some time now, people reading Usenet discussion groups have found it useful to have their messages organized into *threads*, or related messages (grouped by subject). Picture a common thread running through each of the messages (ideally, all on the same subject) that binds them together. If you regularly read e-mail from mailing lists, for instance, or if you like to have long discussions that go through many replies (or have many recipients), you'll learn to love the threaded nature of Messenger.

But how does Messenger know when to group messages together in a thread? For the most part, it uses the messages' subject in your Message List to determine what messages are in a particular thread. It uses the dates (and times) on those messages to put them in order. As shown in Figure 11.8, Messenger is also clever enough to know that a message titled June Report has replies titled Re: June Report, or something similar.

**FIG. 11.8**
Message threads are another clever, commonsense way to organize your Message List.

A regular message

A message thread

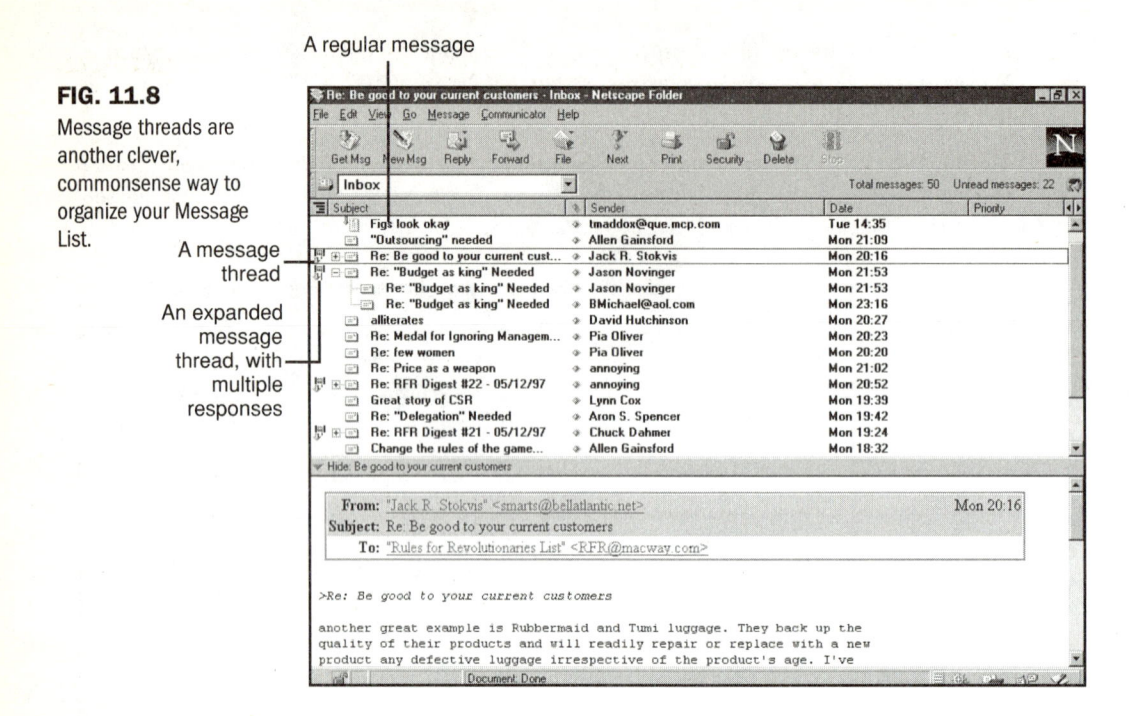

An expanded message thread, with multiple responses

## Viewing Threads

To get started, you need to tell Messenger to organize your Message List by threads. It's easy enough to do—just a mouse click or a menu command. You might even have noticed that we skipped a particular column heading when they were discussed earlier in this chapter. Go click the Thread column heading—it's the one that's probably on the far left (unless you've moved it) and looks like four black lines.

Click that heading once and suddenly the thread icons pop up for some of your messages. You might also notice that any duplicate subject lines have disappeared from your Message List, as shown in Figure 11.9.

You can also change the sorting order (alphabetical) by clicking the Thread column heading again. The column heading is too small to see an arrow (as you can in the Subject or Sender column headings), so you have to reason out the direction for yourself.

> **NOTE** If you prefer, you can also make the threads appear by using the View, Sort command and choosing By Thread. This is the same as clicking the Thread column heading in the Message List window.

**FIG. 11.9**
Sorting by threads takes little more than a click of the mouse.

The Thread icon

The tread column heading

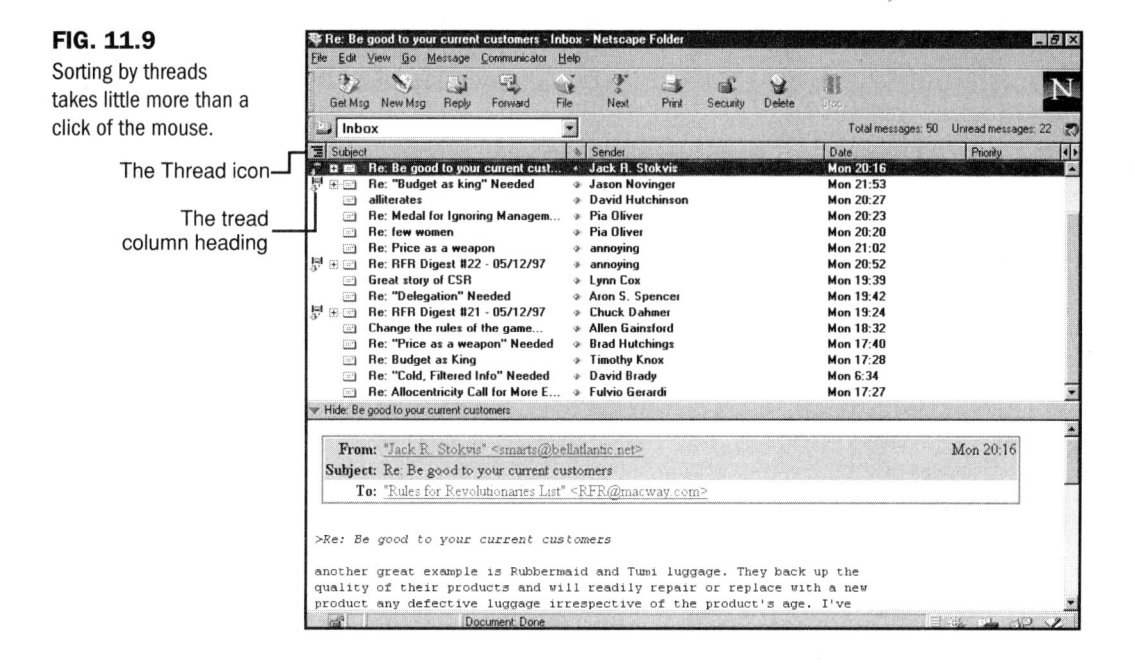

## Expanding and Reading Threads

If you click the little plus sign next to the Thread icon, the thread is expanded so that all of the reply messages can be seen along with the original message (or original reply, as the case may be). See Figure 11.10 for an example of this.

> **TIP** If you want, you can temporarily view just the discussion threads in your Message List; choose View, Messages from the menu and change the setting to Threads with New. Make sure you change it back to All before getting new messages, though (see the "Caution" in the next section).

You can read threads the same way you'd read any other message—just select the message in the Message List and its text appears in the pane below. You can use keyboard commands (such as the up and down arrows) to move to the next message in the thread, or you can move on to the next message in the thread by selecting the Go, Next Unread Message command from Messenger's menu.

**FIG. 11.10**
With a thread expanded, you can see and read all the messages that thread contains. Click the minus sign to collapse the thread to a single message again.

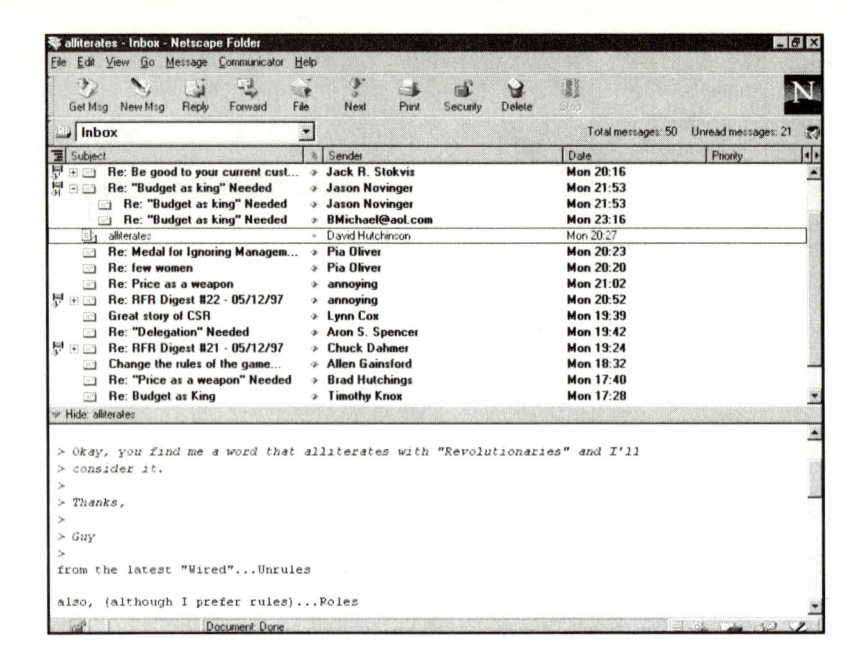

## Watching Threads

If you discover a message thread that you find particularly interesting, you can mark that thread as *watched*. Now, when you choose to view your watched threads, you get only those you've marked previously as worth your time. It's just another way to sort your Message List.

To mark a thread as Watched, select the thread's first message (or a collapsed thread's only message) and choose the Message, Watch Thread command. Do that for any threads you want to watch closely.

> **TIP** You can also invoke this command (and other thread commands) by right-clicking a particular thread in the Message List and choosing Watch Thread from the menu.

Now comes the cool part. To view only your watched threads, select the View, Messages command and choose Watched Threads with New from the menu. This causes your Message List to display only the threads that you've marked as interesting (or watched) that happen to contain new messages. On top of that, you can download new mail, and the screen changes to reflect any additions to your watched threads, as shown in Figure 11.11.

> **CAUTION**
> This should be treated as a temporary setting. If you leave your Message List set this way, you can miss important new messages that aren't part of a watched thread. It is best to only use this setting for reading mailing lists or e-mail conversations offline; when you reconnect to the Internet, you should switch immediately back to View, Messages, All so you don't miss any important new messages.

http://www.quecorp.com

**FIG. 11.11**
This cleans up the old Message List considerably. Now, with only watched threads showing, you can jump into the conversations you find most interesting.

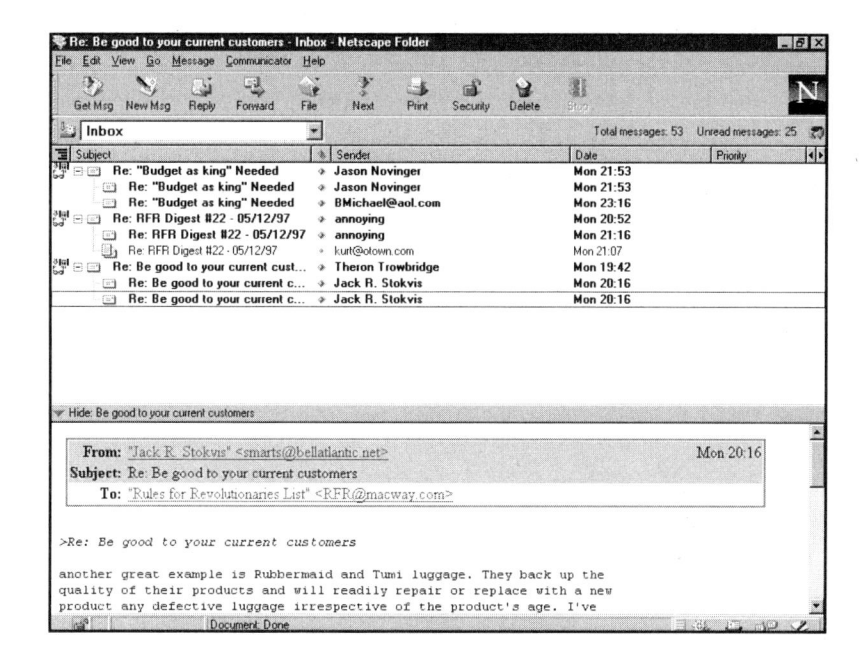

## Ignoring Threads

To ignore a thread, select the first message in the thread (or the collapsed thread's only message) and choose Message, Ignore from the Messenger menu; then choose Thread. The newly ignored thread disappears from view in the Message List. The best part is that messages in this thread continue to be downloaded and sorted by Messenger. They're just not shown. Of course, there's a way to show the ignored threads again, if you want or need to.

Why not just delete the boring thread? Because more messages might come in for that thread the next time you check your e-mail, which you'd also have to delete. (That is, you'll just keep seeing messages in that thread, even if you delete them as they arrive.) Instead, even *new* messages in the ignored thread subject will be downloaded and sorted by Messenger, but hidden from view. (Of course, you can also set up a *killfile*, which automatically deletes new messages with a particular subject or author.)

To view a previously ignored thread, choose the View, Messages command from Messenger's menu, and then choose Ignored. This doesn't switch the View to only the Ignored threads; it just includes them again in the Message List. To stop viewing the Ignored files, repeat the View, Messages, Ignored procedure and they disappear from the Message List again.

While you're viewing all of the ignored messages, that's your chance to un-Ignore a particular thread that you're ready to start dealing with again. To do that, choose the currently ignored thread and select Message, Watch Thread from Messenger's menu. Now this thread is no longer ignored and shows up even if you have the command for viewing ignored threads (View, Messages, Ignored) toggled off.

# Create and Manage New Folders

Creating a folder is simple and straightforward, and after you've designed a system for storing your e-mail, you'll find plenty of instances where creating a folder comes in handy. Messenger also makes it simple to create subfolders, move folders around, rename them, and generally spend a good deal of time managing e-mail.

Following is the basic process for creating a folder:

1. Open the Netscape Message Center by going to the Communicator menu and choosing Message Center.

> **TIP** If you're already looking at the Message List window, you can choose Mail from the pull-down menu in the Location toolbar to open the Message Center.

2. After you're in the Message Center, click the New Folder icon in the toolbar. (You can also choose File, New, Folder from the Message Center menu.) This opens the Create New Folder dialog box, shown in Figure 11.12.
3. In the dialog box, enter the name for your folder. Then, in the pull-down menu, choose Mail (chances are it's already chosen for you). Click OK when you're done.

**FIG. 11.12**
If you're creating a main-level folder, just enter a name for it and click OK.

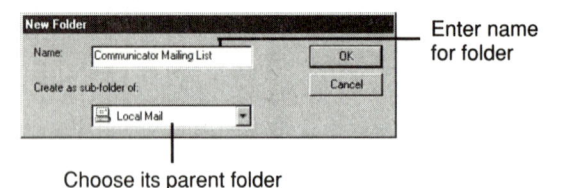

Enter name for folder

Choose its parent folder

If all goes well, you should have a new folder that appears just below the Trash under the Mail hierarchy in the Message Center (assuming you made it a main-level folder, which means it's a subfolder of Local Mail).

## Create Subfolders

The process for creating subfolders is the same as for creating any other type of folder—with one difference. Instead of choosing Mail in the Create New Folder dialog box, choose one of your other folders from the pull-down menu. Click OK when you've chosen one.

> **TIP** You can also create subfolders in Windows 95 by right-clicking the parent folder (the folder that will hold the new subfolder) and choosing the New Subfolder command.

It's generally a good idea to create subfolders only for other folders you create; there's not much point in creating a subfolder for the Outbox, for instance, because messages in that subfolder aren't sent along with the messages in the regular Outbox. Depending on the system you create, you might want to create subfolders for your Inbox, but doing so is pretty much the same as creating a main-level folder.

http://www.quecorp.com

> **CAUTION**
>
> Messenger allows you to create subfolders of any of its default folders, including the Trash. If you do create a subfolder for the Trash, however, recognize that Messenger deletes that folder whenever you elect to "throw out" the Trash (detailed in "Emptying the Trash," later in this chapter).

Can you create subfolders within subfolders? Yes, you can, as long as you don't go over 19 subfolders under a particular main folder (at least, in my testing).

## Expand and Collapse Folders

If you've created subfolders in your Message Center hierarchy, you might notice that you can't always see those folders under their parents. Even if all you're seeing is the first level of folders, however, you can tell if any of them have subfolders—just look for the plus sign to the left of the folder name. If you see a plus sign, subfolders exist in this folder. Click the plus sign to expand that folder and view its subfolders, as in Figure 11.13.

**FIG. 11.13**
If you see a plus sign, it means you can expand that folder to view its subfolders.

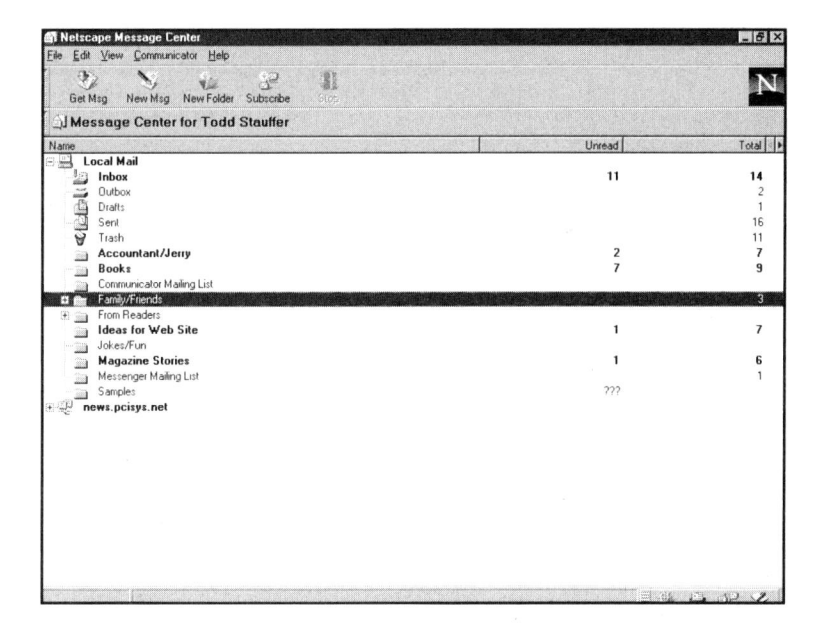

To collapse a folder (so that its subfolders are no longer visible), click the minus sign next to the expanded mail folder.

## Move Folders

Subfolders don't have to live their entire lives as subfolders, and main-level folders can be downgraded to subfolders at any given moment. All you have to do is move them to their new homes in the Messenger Center. To do this, click the name of the folder you want to move and

**212** Chapter 11  Messenger In-Depth

hold down the mouse button. Drag the mouse up or down the list of folders and subfolders. The highlight bar moves in synch with the mouse movement. When the highlight bar is over the folder in which you want the selected folder, release the mouse button (see Figure 11.14).

> **TIP** If you want the selected folder to become a main-level folder, then select the Mail folder with the highlight bar and drop the selected folder there.

**FIG. 11.14**
The Friends' e-mail folder will be a subfolder of Personal E-mail from now on.

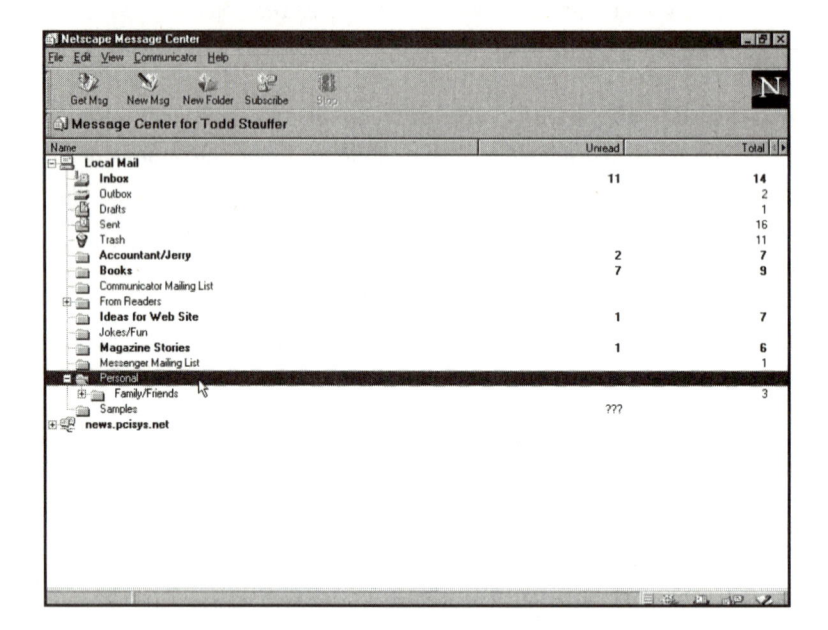

Of course, if you want the selected folder to become the subfolder of a subfolder that's not currently shown, you need to expand the folder that's holding the targeted subfolder. Then you can see the subfolder in the Message Center (check out the previous section "Expand and Collapse Folders").

## Rename Folders

Sick of what you named a particular folder or subfolder? You can change it. Select the folder name in the Message Center, then choose File, Rename Folder from the Message Center menu, which brings up the Rename Folder dialog box. Enter the new name for your folder, then click OK. That folder is now renamed in the Message Center.

> **TIP** In Windows 95, you can also rename folders by right-clicking the folder and choosing Rename Folder.

http://www.quecorp.com

## Delete Folders

To delete a folder, select it in the Message Center and press the Delete key on your keyboard. (You can also right-click the folder in Windows 95 and choose **D**elete Folder from the menu.) When you delete a folder (just as when you delete a message), you actually make it a new subfolder underneath the Trash folder. The folder can be recovered by moving it back out into the hierarchy the same way you move any other folder.

## File Messages

You can file your messages from the Message List window (even if you're looking at folders other than the Inbox) or when reading a message in its own window. Either way, the procedure's pretty much the same.

> **NOTE** Most of the time, you'll probably file messages from the Inbox, but you can use the Message List window to re-file any message while you're viewing any of the available folders.

If you're reading messages in the Message List, you can file those messages by simply selecting the message in the Message List window and clicking the File icon in the toolbar. A menu appears, allowing you to choose the folder (and then subfolder) in which you'd like your message to appear. Choose that folder from the menu by clicking it. Your message is moved (see Figure 11.15).

If you're using Windows 95, you can right-click a particular message, then choose **F**ile Message from the contextual menu that appears.

> **TIP** To select more than one message, hold down the Shift key while clicking each message (or, in Windows, hold down the Control key to add messages that aren't right next to each other) in the Inbox window. You can then use the File icon to move all of those messages at once.

If the message you want to file is currently being displayed in its own window, the procedure is still the same—click File in the toolbar and select the folder you want the message stored in from the menu that appears.

## Copy Messages

At times, you might find it useful to have the same message in two different folders at once—perhaps one is used for important archiving (placed in a special folder so you can copy it to a backup device or a network) while another is the regular folder for saving the file on your own computer.

**214** | Chapter 11  Messenger In-Depth

**FIG. 11.15**
You can also use Message, File Message to accomplish the filing pictured here.

Click the File button

Select message(s) in the Inbox window

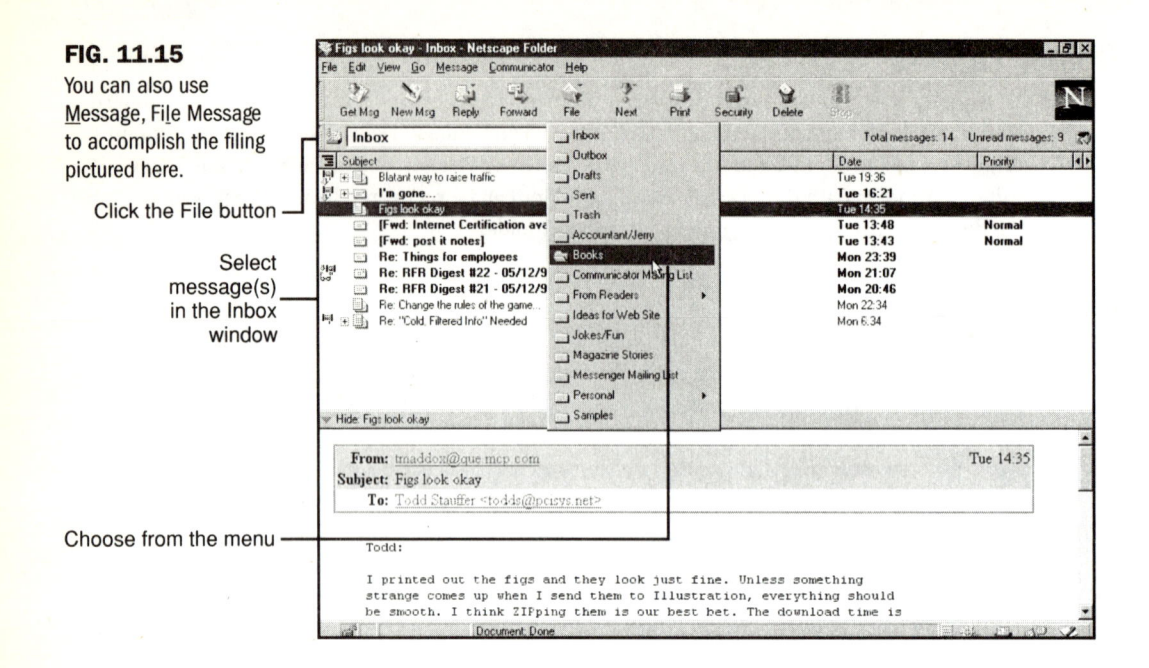

Choose from the menu

Whatever the reason, you can copy messages from the Inbox interface by selecting the message, then choosing Message, Copy Message in the Messenger menu. Then choose the folder to which you want the message copied. After you've done that, the copy is made.

> **TIP** You can also copy multiple messages at one time (holding down the Shift or Control keys while you select them with the mouse). For example, this allows you to copy many messages at once to your backup folder.

## Deleting Messages

Deleting messages follows many of the same steps as filing or copying—in fact, one way to delete messages is to simply "file" them in the Trash folder. This is essentially what any of the other delete methods are doing, anyway.

To delete, select the unfortunate message and click the Delete icon in the toolbar. You can also choose Edit, Delete Message from the Messenger menu; or, with the message selected, simply press the Delete key on your keyboard. The message disappears from its current folder and is moved to the Trash folder, as shown in Figure 11.16.

> **TIP** You guessed it. Another alternative is right-clicking a message in Windows 95, then choosing Delete Message from the menu that appears.

http://www.quecorp.com

**FIG. 11.16**
Here's a folder in the Trash; notice that it appears as a subfolder of the Trash folder.

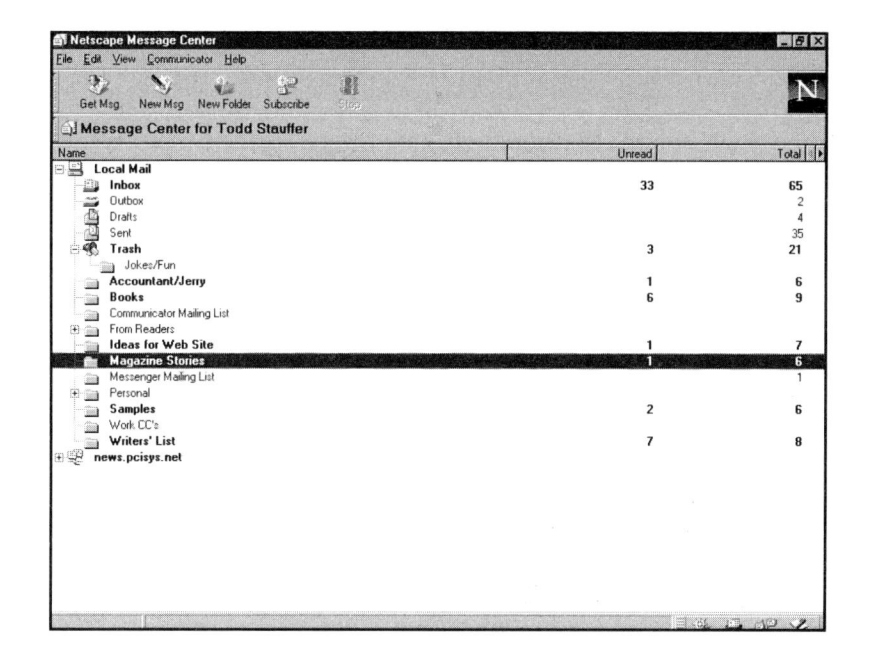

Remember, Messenger never really deletes something from your hard drive when you select delete in the program; instead, it moves and stores everything in the Trash folder. To make a message go away forever, you need to empty the trash…which is discussed in the next section.

## Emptying the Trash

If you feel like it's time you did something about those messages in your Trash folder, you can toss out the trash manually in Messenger. To do this, switch to the Netscape Message Center, then head up to the File menu, and select the Empty Trash folder command. The messages that were once in the Trash are no more.

> **NOTE** Messenger generally doesn't ask you if you're sure that you want to empty the trash—after you choose the command, the files are gone. The exception to this rule are folders in the Trash. If a folder you've deleted still has files in it, Messenger asks you if you're sure that you want to delete the folder. Click OK if you are sure.

## Compressing Folders

Odd as it might seem, moving files to the Trash folder and then throwing away the Trash doesn't make the files that store your folders' contents any smaller. Huh? The problem is, you're not throwing away actual e-mail *files* when you throw away the messages—you're just throwing away references to those messages in your Messenger folders. You can't read the messages anymore, but they're still there.

**216** | Chapter 11  Messenger In-Depth

To solve this problem, you need to compress the folders so that the deleted material is actually taken out of the folders. Please don't ask why—unless it's in an e-mail message to Netscape.

> **NOTE** After a message has been deleted and the Trash has been emptied, you'd think it would be impossible to recover the message. Well, it's not. You can dig into your personal user directory (on your hard drive), open the Mail subdirectory, and double-click the text-file associated with a particular Messenger folder. (The text file is the one that doesn't have a file extension.) Associate the file with Netscape and—voilá—you're reading every message in that folder, including deleted messages that just haven't yet been compressed. Maybe it's been left in for nosy system administrators?

To compress all folders manually, switch to the Message Center and choose File, Compress Folders from the menu. This compresses all the folders to their smallest possible size by eliminating any text that might be lingering from previously Trashed messages. In Windows 95, you can manually compress individual folders by right-clicking the folder, then choosing Compress Folder from the menu that appears, as in Figure 11.17.

**FIG. 11.17**
You can compress folders easily by choosing the command from a Windows 95 contextual (right-click) menu.

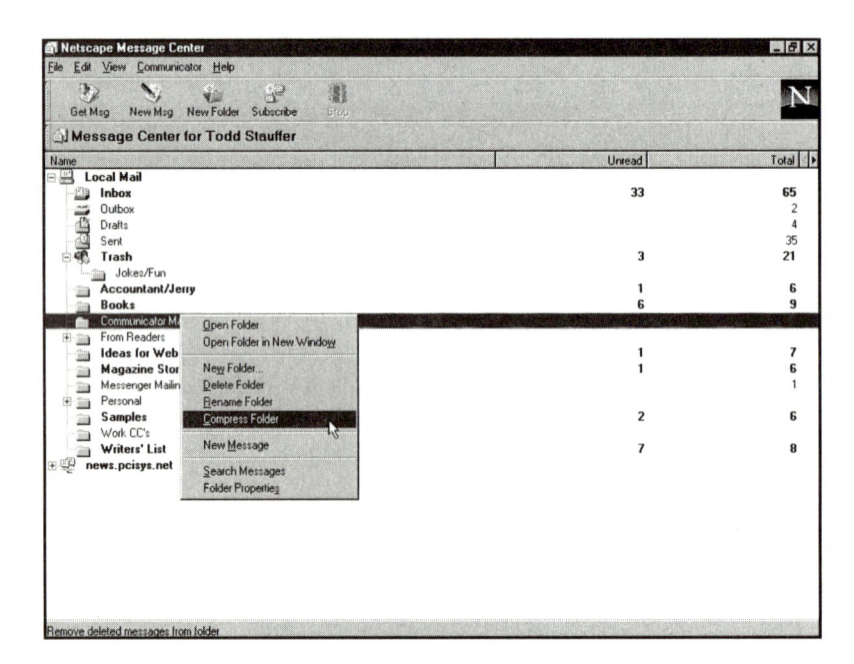

You can also force Messenger to compress folders automatically; just follow these steps:

1. In the Message Center, choose Edit, Preferences.
2. Expand the Advanced menu item by clicking the plus (+) sign.
3. Choose the item called Disk Space.
4. In the dialog box, click the box marked Automatically Compact Folder when It Will Save Over and enter the amount of disk space it should wait for before it prompts you. 50K is a

http://www.quecorp.com

reasonable number, but you can make it lower if you want to remove deleted messages from your system more often.

5. Click OK for the Preference changes to take effect.

## Searching Through Folders

Sometimes a message is simply going to get away from you. Perhaps it's been misfiled or filed in a folder filled with hundreds of other messages. In this case, it's best to try out Messenger's search commands to see if you can locate the message. At least it beats spending hours shoveling through your folders trying to find a particular message.

To search for a particular message, you use the Search Messages dialog box, shown in Figure 11.18. To access and use this dialog box, follow these steps:

1. Choose Edit, Search Messages.
2. In the Search Messages dialog box, choose the top-level folder you want to search in. For all your mail folders, choose the Local Mail option in the pull-down menu.
3. Choose the portion of the message you want to search from the pull-down menu that appears after the word the. (By default the menu shows sender.)
4. In the next pull-down menu, choose the type of search. You can tell Messenger to find entries that contain, don't contain, match, begin with, or end with the search text.
5. Now enter the search text you want Messenger to find in the text box at the end of the row of pull-down menus. You can enter text that you think could help identify the message.
6. If you'd like to enter more than one search parameter (for instance, to search for messages that have the subject New File and the date 5/21/1998), click the More button. You can click the Fewer button to take out search parameters if you have more than one.

**N O T E** Some of the search type options change the subsequent menus and the text box. For instance, choosing to search the Date entry in e-mail message changes the text box to a date-entry control, as shown in Figure 11.18.

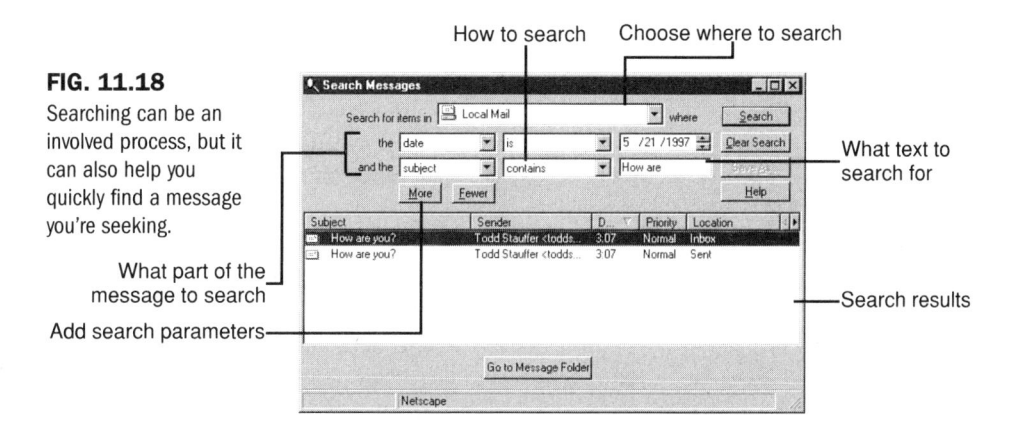

**FIG. 11.18**
Searching can be an involved process, but it can also help you quickly find a message you're seeking.

When you've finished adding parameters, click the Search button to see the e-mail messages that result. To read one of the resulting messages, double-click the message in the dialog box. If you simply want to open the folder holding the message, select it in the dialog box and click the Go To Message Folder button.

## Creating a Filter

A filter is simply a small bit of Messenger-specific scripting that allows you to compare incoming e-mail messages against certain criteria—things like the From portion of the address or the subject of the message. It's possible to create fairly simple scripts that compare against one criterion ("Is the message from don@isp.net?") or more complex scripts that compare a number of different criteria.

In either case, creating the filter is fairly straightforward because all of the scripting is done using pull-down menus and English-style sentence construction. To build a filter, follow these steps:

1. Choose New from the Mail Filters dialog box (Edit, Mail Filter Rules in the Messenger menu). Give the new filter a name.

2. Enter your first criteria. Begin by looking at the From portion of the e-mail message, for addresses that contain the domain for your workplace—*company*.com.

3. Click the More button to enter a second criterion, shown in Figure 11.19.

> **NOTE** The Fewer button appears when you click the More button. Clearly, this button allows you to do away with the extra filtering criteria, one line at a time. Even if you've entered new information, clicking the Fewer button does away with the second level of filtering and returns the filter to its original, one-level checking. The good news is that if you click the More button again, you don't have to reenter your criteria, unless you've closed and reopened the filter.

4. Create the second level of the filter using the menus and text box. Have the filter check to see if the CC section of the e-mail includes your own e-mail address.

5. Complete the filter by choosing Move to Folder and the name of the folder any matching message should be moved to. Call the folder CC Messages.

> **CAUTION**
> You need to create the folder before creating the mail filter or the folder won't appear in the pull-down menu next to the Move to Folder command. If you haven't yet created the folder, set up the rest of the filter and point to the Inbox. Then click OK to get out of the Filter Rules dialog box. Return to Messenger, create a new folder, then choose the Edit this filter in the Mail Filters dialog box. Now you can choose the folder.

6. Enter a description for the folder and click OK. The filter is complete (see Figure 11.20).

Those are the two different criteria within a message. You can set up a filter that checks up to five different parts of the message before putting an action into effect.

**FIG. 11.19**
Clicking the More button in the Filter Rules dialog box allows you to check more than one part of an e-mail message.

**FIG. 11.20**
The filter is complete.

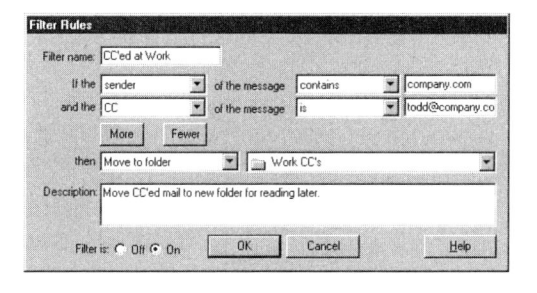

## Attaching Files or Documents to Messages

If you've created a standard e-mail message (or replied to someone else's) and you're ready to attach a document or program to that message, it's a simple matter. You start by clicking the attachment tab in the Message Composition window (the tab appears just below the address tab—see Figure 11.21). You can also click the Attach icon in the toolbar.

> **TIP** Using the same process you can attach your personal Address Book card or a particular Web page to an e-mail message as well.

There are two ways you can attach a file to your message and both net the same result:

1. If you choose the Attachment tab, double-click in the attachment header space to bring up a standard Open File dialog box. Now hunt down the file you want to attach. Select it and click Open to attach it to the document.

2. If you choose the Attach icon, you'll be given the choice of attaching a file or a Web page. For now, choose to attach a file. An Open File dialog box appears. Find the file you want to attach, select it in the dialog box, and click Open. You'll see that it's attached to the document by clicking the Attachment tab. In the attachment header, the filename appears.

**FIG. 11.21**
Attaching a file to a message is as simple as opening a file in any other application.

The Attachment tab

Attachment icon

Double-click to add a file

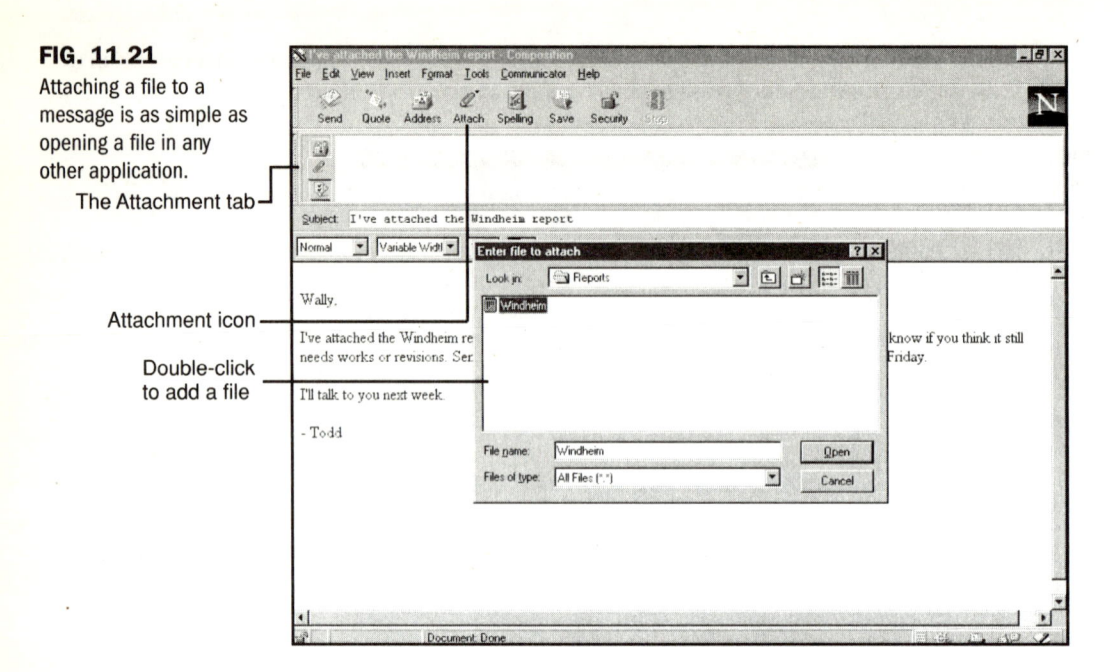

The next step: Send as usual. The file will be sent along with your message; When the file arrives at your recipient's computer, he or she will be able to open and work with it as if you'd transferred it over a corporate network or by disk.

> **CAUTION**
> Your recipient may not be able to use the attachment if their e-mail program isn't capable of reading MIME-encoded attachments. You should also consider compressing large files (or groups of files) with PKZip for StuffIt Expander (for Mac) before sending attachments over the Internet.

## Attaching a Web Page

In isolated cases, you might come up with a reason to send an entire page—perhaps your user only has access to e-mail, or is traveling and can't afford to spend much time online.

The interesting thing about sending a Web page is that the raw, basic HTML document is sent to your recipient, but all of the associated graphics and other elements remain on the original Web server.

For instance, if Netscape's home page is "attached" to an e-mail message and sent to you, then you'll receive only the HTML document—not the graphics and animations. Instead, when you view the page, your e-mail program (Messenger, in this case) will send the page to your browser program, and the browser will go out on the Internet to gather the images from Netscape.

http://www.quecorp.com

That's a cool way to do it, but it means two things. First, it means you won't tie up your recipient's e-mail program while they download a huge file, but they'll still get the full benefit of viewing the Web page (as long as they're reading it while they're connected to the Internet). If they're not connected, or if the page has changed, it means they may not be able to see all of the multimedia elements associated with that page.

> **CAUTION**
>
> Notice that, although the entire page appears in the message, the user has no way of knowing the page's original URL. It's a good idea to send the URL along, in case they can't read the whole page or want to investigate the site further.

Here's how you attach a Web page to an e-mail message:

1. Create a typical e-mail message, including subject, a To: recipient and a message in the body.
2. Click the Attach button once, then select Web Page from the drop-down menu.
3. In the dialog box, enter the complete URL to the page you want to attach to this message. Click OK.

> **CAUTION**
>
> It's best to send a complete URL, including the name of the individual page you want to send to your recipient, just to avoid confusion. An address such as **http://www.netscape.com/** may work, but it's better to send something like **http://www.netscape.com/index.html** whenever possible.

4. Complete your message and click the Send button. Your page is ready to go!

> **N O T E** Messenger doesn't ask you if you want to send a page with a Web page attachment as HTML or Plain Text (unless you've also included a link or formatted text in the message itself). Non-HTML mail editors simply allow the user to detach the page and save it to his or her hard drive. They can then use their Web browser to view the document

# Adding HTML to Documents

You add HTML elements to your messages by selecting them from the menus or the formatting toolbar in the Message Composition window. This makes it simple to add rather complex HTML tags to your documents.

HTML formatting involves the better part of two entire menu choices in the Message Composition window. Basic text emphasis sticks mostly to the Format menu, which allows you to change how your text is emphasized, organized, and displayed. The Insert menu, on the other hand, is used more to add links, tables, and images to your e-mail messages.

## Using Basic Styles

You often use *styles* in Messenger to change the way recipients see your text. The style commands are the typical text emphasis commands, like italics and bold.

The most common styles are available from the Formatting toolbar in the Message Composition window, shown in Figure 11.22. Just click one of the formatting buttons for bold, italic, or underlined styles, then begin typing.

> **TIP** You can also choose these styles with the typical keyboard shortcuts: in Windows, use Ctrl+B for bold, Ctrl+I for italics, and Ctrl+U for underline. Using the Mac OS, these shortcuts are [ap]+B, [ap]+I, and [ap]+U, respectively.

**FIG. 11.22**
Basic text emphasis is available from the formatting toolbar, as well as from Format, Style in the Messenger menu.

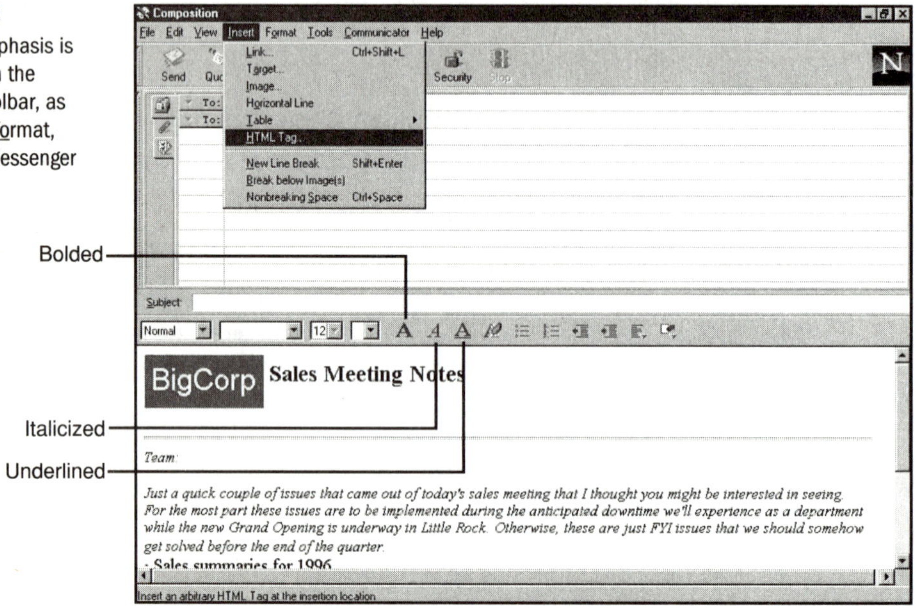

## Changing the Typeface

Netscape makes it simple to change the typeface for your document (or parts of your document) by selecting the new typeface from the pull-down menu in the Formatting toolbar.

Note that your options are somewhat limited. Choosing the default font is pretty much the same as choosing no font in HTML—this message will use the recipient's Web browser's default font. Choosing "Fixed Width" is the same as using the F_ormat, _Style, _Fixed Width command, which was discussed in the previous section, "Other Styles". You also have some other, more specific font choices, as shown in Figure 11.23.

**FIG. 11.23**
The pull-down menu in the Formatting toolbar gives you access to a few different font options.

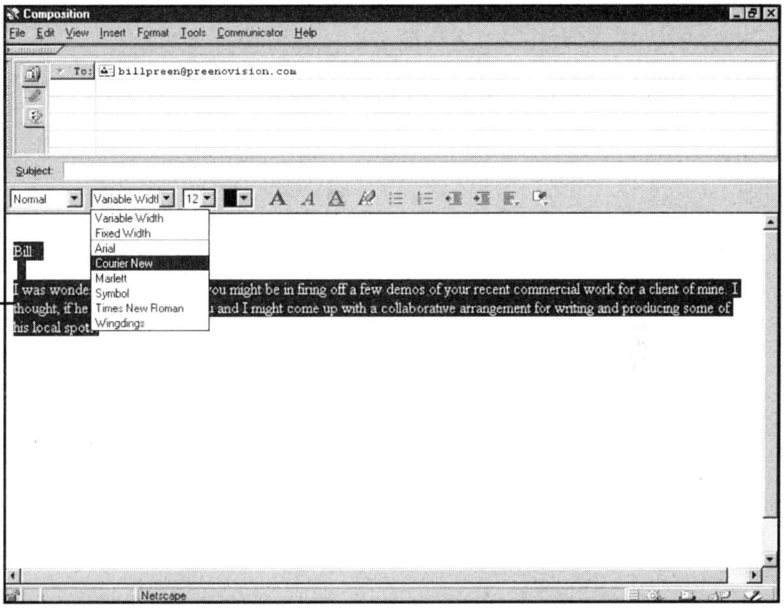

The font menu

## Changing Font Size and Color

Both of these changes can also conveniently be made from the Formatting toolbar. To change the text's size, highlight the text in the message composition window, then choose a new size from the pull-down menu in the Formatting toolbar (see Figure 11.24). You can also change the size first, then begin typing your text—everything you type will remain at that size until you change the font size again (or select some of the other formatting options, like a Heading, discussed later in this chapter).

You can also set the default font size for paragraphs by heading once again to the Character Properies dialog box (F_ormat, _Font). With the Character tab selected, you can choose the default font size from the Size pop-down menu.

To change font colors, choose the new color from the pull-down menu in the Formatting toolbar. When you begin typing, notice that your words have changed to the new color. (You can also highlight previously-typed text and change it with the color menu.) Other options for changing the font color include the menu command F_ormat, _Color, which brings up the Color dialog box, where you can select colors and create new colors.

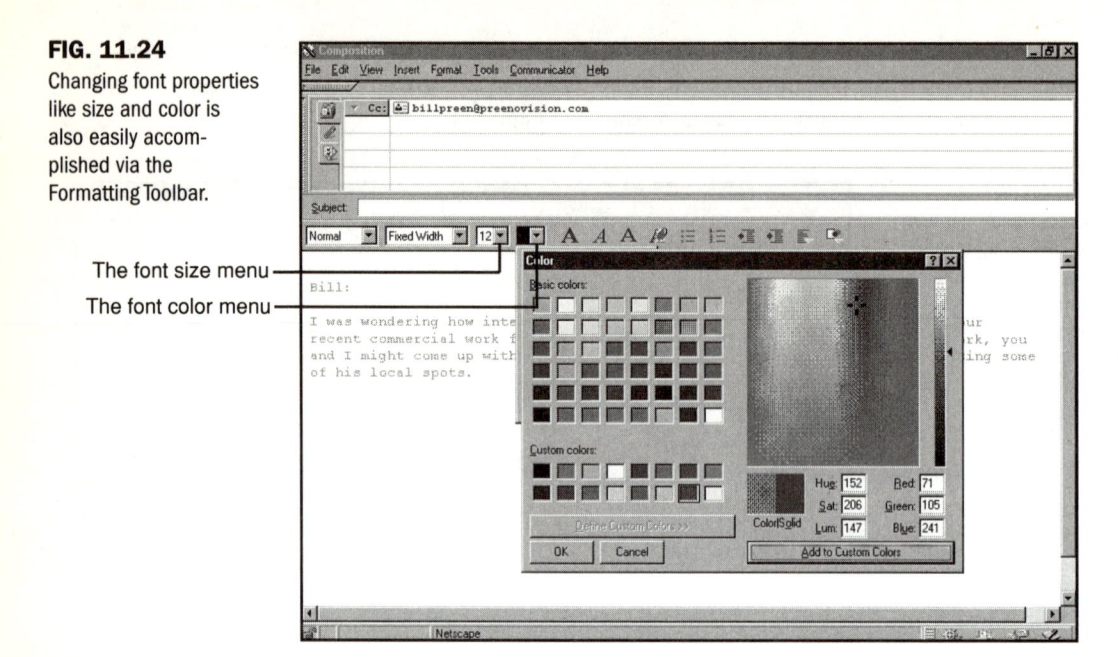

**FIG. 11.24**
Changing font properties like size and color is also easily accomplished via the Formatting Toolbar.

The font size menu
The font color menu

## Organizing Your Message

HTML was originally designed for the purpose of disseminating academic research and reports over the Internet. To that end, many of the conventions are commands built for the creation of formal, text-oriented documents instead of, for instance, page-layout designs. Obvious extensions of this "document" approach are some of the tags available for organizing HTML documents—Headings, Paragraph styles, and Lists. Each is useful and easy to add—you might find that the more formal the e-mail, the more useful these features will be.

> **NOTE** All of the commands described in this section are on until turned off (unless you invoke them after selecting text with the mouse). To switch back to regular text, choose Normal from the Paragraph menu in the Formatting toolbar.

## Adding Headings

Headings are designed to be used as section titles and subheadings for your e-mail message. You might not find much use for them in regular e-mail communications, but they can be valuable for formatting an important proposal or business report.

http://www.quecorp.com

> **CAUTION**
> Using font size commands can interfere with the way headings appear in your document. If you've assigned text a certain size, and then find that changing the heading size has no affect on that text, select the text and choose Format, Clear All Styles from the menu. Now you can use the Heading commands to change the text's size.

Headings also have the distinction of being the original way to change the size of the text in your document or message. While the font size commands (discussed in the last section) are the newer, more flexible way of doing this, headings can be used to change the size of text just as easily (see Figure 11.25).

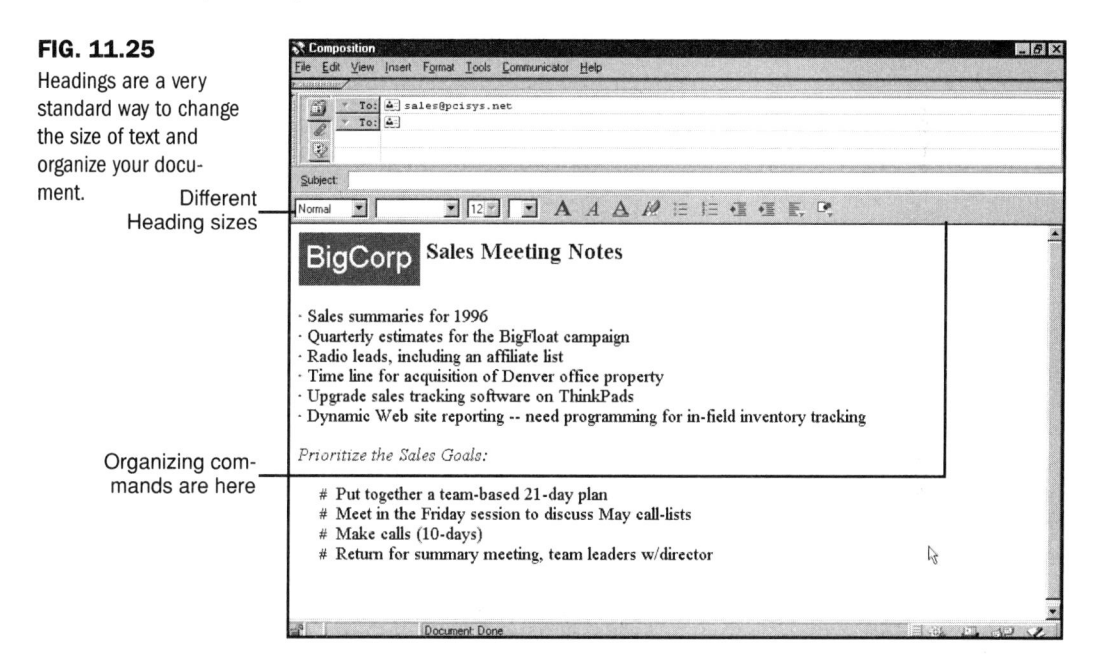

**FIG. 11.25**
Headings are a very standard way to change the size of text and organize your document.
Different Heading sizes
Organizing commands are here

To change the Heading level you use for a particular line of text, pull down the list of paragraph commands in the Formatting toolbar and choose a Heading level, 1 being the largest, 6 being the smallest. You can also choose headings from the Messenger menu by selecting Format, Heading, and the number of the heading you want to use.

> **NOTE** Using a Heading command on a line of text (or selecting text and changing it to a Heading) automatically enters a line return at the end of the line.

## Alignment

You can place the cursor in that line of text, then click and hold the mouse button down on the Align button in the Formatting toolbar to force an entire line or paragraph to change its alignment. (Align is just to the right of the Indent buttons.) This causes a pull-down menu to appear, allowing you to choose Left, Center, or Right alignment.

You can also access this command through the Messenger menu at F<u>o</u>rmat, <u>A</u>lign.

## Creating a Hyperlink

Type the link's text in the Message Composition window to get started, then highlight all the text with your mouse that you want made "clickable" for the recipient is the next step. With your descriptive text selected, adding a hyperlink is as easy as pulling down the <u>I</u>nsert menu and choosing <u>L</u>ink. That brings up the Character Properties dialog box, shown in Figure 11.26.

**FIG. 11.26**
With the Link tab selected, all you need to do in order to make the selected text a hyperlink is enter an URL and click OK.

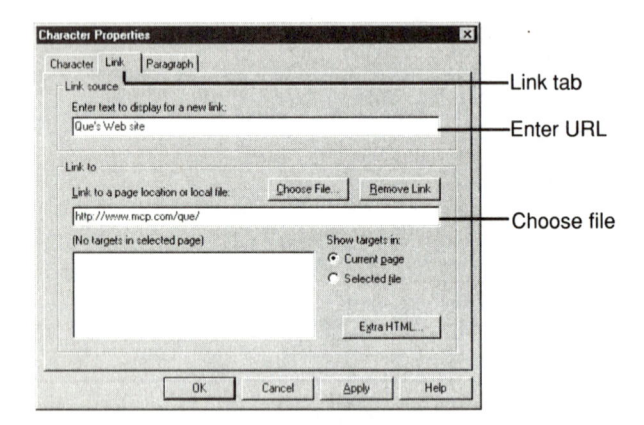

You have two choices for creating this hyperlink, although it's difficult to understand why Netscape offers both options. The first makes complete sense—just enter an URL for a page that's somewhere on the Web and click OK in the dialog box.

The other option allows you to click the Choose File button and create a link to a file on your hard drive. This really isn't useful, unless you happen to be composing the message from a computer that's also a Web server. Since you're probably not composing mail on a Web server computer, your recipient won't be able to access the linked document over the Internet, since the linked file is sitting on your hard drive.

## Adding an Image

Adding a JPG or GIF formatted image to your e-mail program is a fairly straightforward process, although there are a good deal of options that make the Image Properties dialog seem a bit crowded. To start, choose <u>I</u>nsert, <u>I</u>mage from the menu. That brings up the Image Properties dialog box shown in Figure 11.27.

> **CAUTION**
> You should realize that any image you add to an e-mail message is going to add considerably to the size of that message. And that translates to an increase in the amount of time it takes you to upload your message and for your recipient to download the message.

**FIG. 11.27**
Inserting an image requires only an image file to work with—but there are plenty of options for tweaking, too.

Choose file from hard drive
Align image
Enter URL to image on the Web
Choose Height and Width

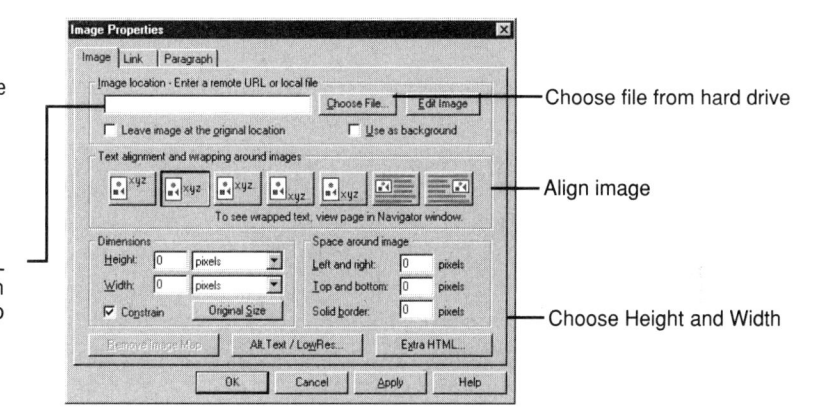

If the image you want to add is on your hard drive, make sure the Leave Image at the Original Location box in unchecked, and click the Choose File button. Now, search your hard drive for the image. When you find it, select it in the Open File dialog box and click the Open button. Its name is added in the Image Properties dialog.

> **NOTE** Your other option is to simply enter an URL in the Image Location box—but it needs to be a complete URL that points directly to an image file on the Internet. If you click Leave Image at Original Location, your recipient's e-mail program will attempt to access the image when they read your e-mail message. Otherwise, with the option unclicked, Messenger will attempt to download the image from the Web, then send it along with your e-mail message. Sending the image makes your e-mail messages take much longer to transmit, but it also ensures that the recipient will be able to view the image. If the image is left on the Web, it may become inaccessible before your recipient can see it.

From here, you have a number of options:

> **Text alignment.** Each button in this section of the dialog box shows you how the text around the image will be aligned—click the button that most resembles the way you want text to appear. Note that the last two buttons actually wrap text around the image while forcing it to *float* at the left or right border of the window. When an image is floating, it's not anchored to a particular part of the text, so the text flows naturally around the image, like you might see in a magazine layout.

**Dimensions**. Here you can enter new dimensions (in pixels or percentage of the window) for the image. You can also click the Original Size button to return the height and width to the image's actual pixel size. Checking the Lock width/height option forces the image to maintain the same aspect ratio (ratio of height-to-width).

> **CAUTION**
> Changing an image's dimensions so that it appears smaller than it actually is will not affect the amount of time it takes to transmit the file over the Internet. To make the actual file itself smaller, you need to resize it in an image-editing program.

**Space around image**. Numbers in these boxes add space to the vertical or horizontal sides of the image, so that text doesn't butt right up against the image. You can also choose to have a border around the image.

**Alt. Text/LowRes**. Click this button for another dialog box that allows you to enter alternate text or a link to a low-resolution file for this image. You can enter some Alt text if you prefer (so that viewers with non-graphical programs still get the idea of your image), but because this is an e-mail message, neither of these is really necessary. Both are geared toward the Web and Web browsers.

**Extra HTML**. Click this button if there's any other HTML codes you'd like to hand-enter for this image.

Click OK and your masterpiece appears in the e-mail document, ready to show the world (or, at least, your recipients. See Figure 11.28.

## Making Your Image a Link

You can easily turn an image in your e-mail message into a clickable image link. To do this, double-click the image in the e-mail window. This brings back the Image Properties dialog box. Now, click the tab marked Link at the top of the dialog box (see Figure 11.29).

With the Link tab's dialog box showing, you see that the image is already the *link source* (the image will be clickable, instead of the descriptive text you'd usually use for a hyperlink). Now, enter an URL in the Link To textbox. When you're finished with the URL, click OK. The image appears with a special border around it, back in your e-mail program. When your recipient receives the message, he or she will be able to click this image, which in turn will send a link to their browser (assuming they're properly equipped).

http://www.quecorp.com

Organizing Your Message | 229

**FIG. 11.28**
After all that work, an image finally appears in your e-mail message.

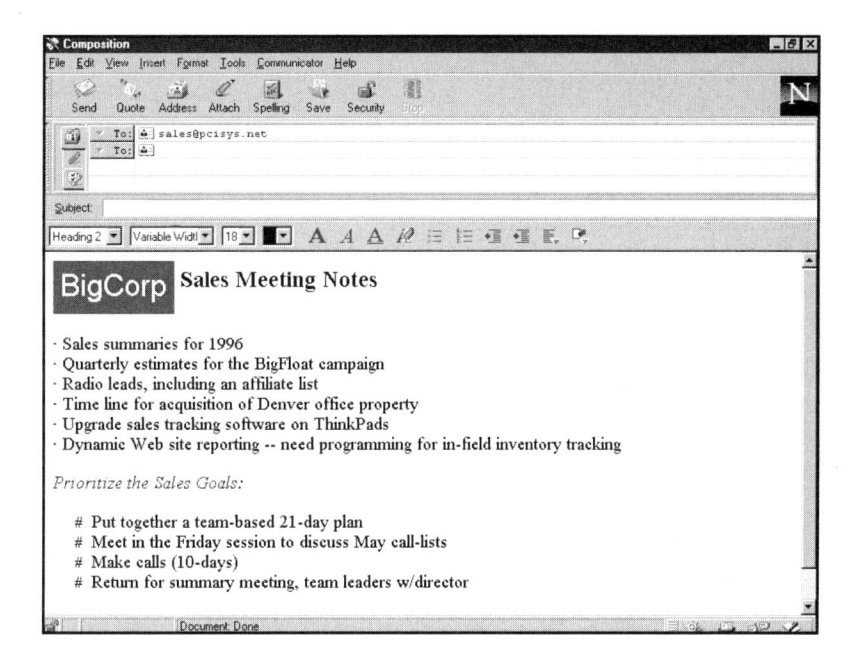

**FIG. 11.29**
The Link tab allows you to make an image a hyperlink as well, so users can click it to move to a Web page.

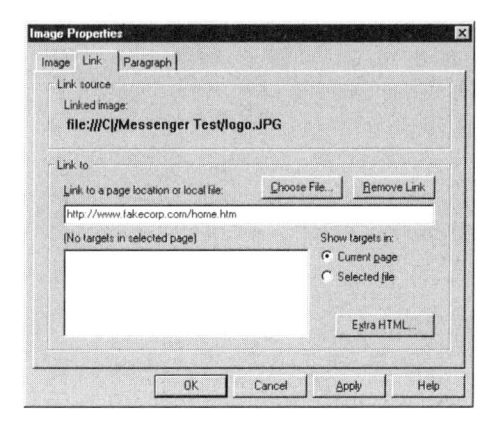

Part
II
Ch
11

CHAPTER 12

# Using the Address Book

*by Jerry Honeycutt*

The Address Book works just like the tiny, old, black address book your grandmother used to use (the one with all the green stamps hanging out of it). You look up a person's name, and you get plenty of contact information in return. You can keep track of an individual's address, phone number, and so on. In that regard, the Address Book is good as a day-to-day contact manager.

Instead of just associating names, addresses, and phone numbers, however, it associates Internet addresses with individuals as well. You use it to keep track of all the people to whom you send Internet mail messages. If you had to remember and type all those Internet mail addresses, for example, you'd go nuts. You also use it to keep track of those with whom you call using Netscape Conference. ∎

### Learn how to use the Address Book
This chapter shows you how to get around the Address Book, how to sort its contents, and how to search for address cards in it.

### Add address cards to the Address Book
Adding a new address card to the Address Book is easy. And if you don't know the Internet mail address of an individual, you can find it online.

### Create your own personal mailing lists
You can create a personal mailing list that lets you blast out messages to a crowd of eager recipients.

### Integrate the Address Book with other components
The Address Book is completely integrated with the other components in Netscape Communicator. This chapter shows you where to look and how to use it.

# Working with the Address Book

The address book displays a simple list of all the address cards that it contains. The main window should look oddly familiar to you as it has the same parts as the other Communicator components: a menu, the toolbar, progress indicator, status line, and Component bar. The Search bar, which you use to look up address cards in the list, is unique to the Address Book (see Figure 12.1).

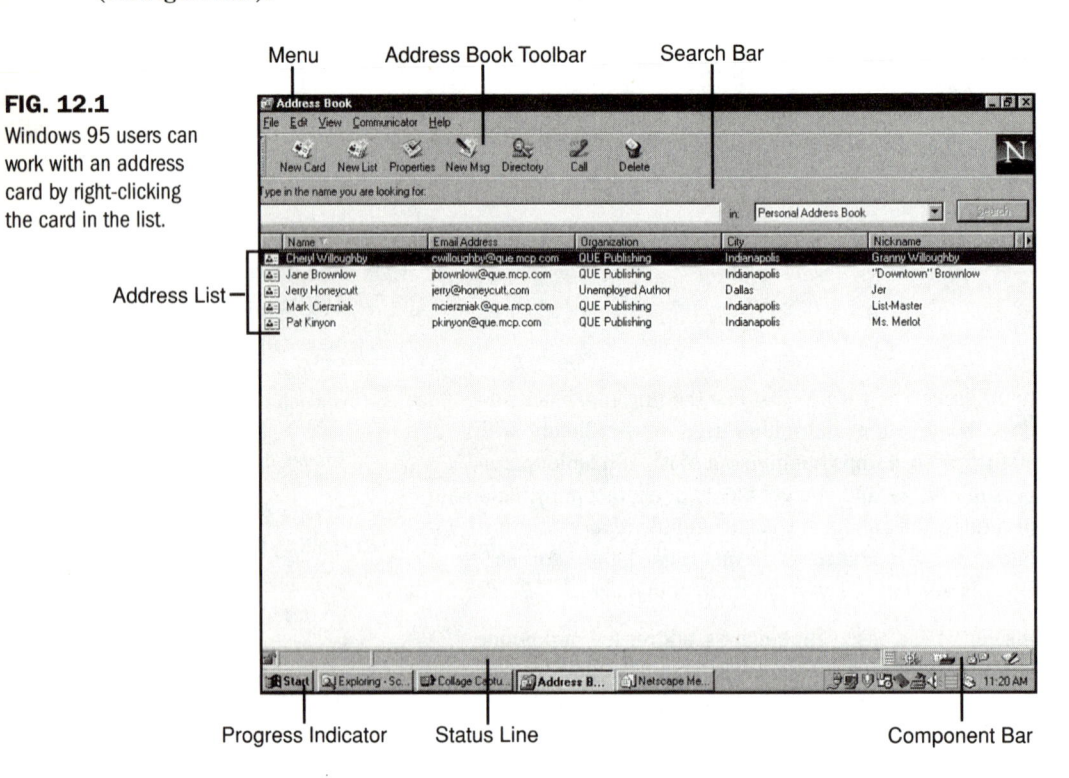

**FIG. 12.1**
Windows 95 users can work with an address card by right-clicking the card in the list.

You can access all of the Message Center's features through its menus. Table 12.1 describes each menu option.

**Table 12.1  Address Book Menu Options**

| Option | Description |
| --- | --- |
| **File Menu** | |
| New | Create a new Web page. |
| New Card | Create a new address card. |
| New List | Create a new mailing list. |
| Import | Import address cards from an external file. |

http://www.quecorp.com

| Option | Description |
|---|---|
| **File Menu** | |
| Save As | Save an address card to disk. |
| Call | Place a call to the selected address card using Conference. |
| Close | Close this Address Book. |
| Exit | Exit Communicator. |
| **Edit Menu** | |
| Undo | Undo the last change. |
| Redo | Redo the last undone change. |
| Delete | Delete the selected address card. |
| Search Directory | Search an LDAP directory for an individual. |
| HTML Domains | Specify domains that can receive HTML formatted messages. |
| Card Properties | Change an address card. |
| Preferences | Set personal preferences. |
| **View Menu** | |
| Hide Address Book Toolbar | Hide the Address Book toolbar. |
| By Type | Sort by card type. |
| By Name | Sort by the person's name. |
| By Email Address | Sort by the Internet mail address. |
| By Company | Sort by the company. |
| By City | Sort by the city. |
| By Nickname | Sort by the person's nickname. |
| Sort Ascending | Make sort order ascending. |
| Sort Descending | Make sort order descending. |
| My Address Book Card | Open your personal address card. |
| **Communicator Menu** | |
| Navigator | Open Navigator. |
| Messenger Mailbox | Open Messenger. |
| Collabra Discussions | Open Collabra. |

*continues*

**Table 12.1 Continued**

| Option | Description |
| --- | --- |
| **Communicator Menu** | |
| Page Composer | Open Composer. |
| Conference | Open Conference. |
| Show Component Bar | Dock/Undock Component bar. |
| Message Center | Open Message Center. |
| Address Book | Open Address Book. |
| Bookmarks | Open Bookmark list. |
| History | Open History list. |
| Java Console | Open Java Console. |
| Security Info | Open security settings. |
| **Help Menu** | |
| Help Contents | Display help contents. |
| Release Notes | Display release notes. |
| Product Information and Support | Display support information. |
| Software Updates | Display update information. |
| Register Now | Registry Communicator. |
| Member Services | Extend Communicator. |
| International Users | Display international help. |
| Security | Display security information. |
| Net Etiquette | Display netiquette issues. |
| About Plug-ins | Display list of plug-ins. |
| About Font Displayers | Display list of displayers. |
| About Communicator | Display version information. |

You can also access some of Address Book's features using the Address Book toolbar. See Table 12.2 for a description of each button in this toolbar.

http://www.quecorp.com

## Table 12.2 Address Book Toolbar Buttons

| Button | Name | Description |
| --- | --- | --- |
| New Card | New Card | Create a new address card. |
| New List | New List | Create a new mailing list. |
| Properties | Properties | Change an address card. |
| New Msg | New Msg | Address a new Internet mail message. |
| Directory | Directory | Look up a person in an LDAP directory. |
| Call | Call | Call using Netscape Conference. |
| Delete | Delete | Delete the selected address card. |

## Sorting the List

If you're trying to find a particular address card, but you don't know enough about the entry in order to be able to search for it, you might want to trying sorting the list by various fields so you can pin that card down. You can easily sort the Address Book by clicking one of the list's headings; each time you click a heading, the sort order switches between ascending and descending order. The pointer next to the field's name shows the order in which that field is sorted. If it's pointing down, the list is sorted in descending order by the field. If it's pointing up, the list is sorted in ascending order.

Alternatively, you can use the Address Book's menu to sort the list. Choose View from the main menu, then choose the field by which you want to sort the list:

By Type
By Name
By E-mail Address
By Company
By City
By Nickname

**Chapter 12  Using the Address Book**

After you've selected a field by which to sort the list, you can change its sort order:

- Choose View, Sort Ascending to sort the list ascending by the chosen field.
- Choose View, Sort Descending to sort the list descending by the chosen field.

## Display Fewer or More Fields

By default, the Address book displays the Name, E-mail Address, Organization, City, and Nickname for each address card. You can display fewer fields by clicking the right-arrow in the header (see Figure 12.2). You can display more fields by clicking the left-arrow. By default, the Address Book displays all of the available fields.

**FIG. 12.2**
If you display all of the fields that are available, you'll have a hard time reading the list.

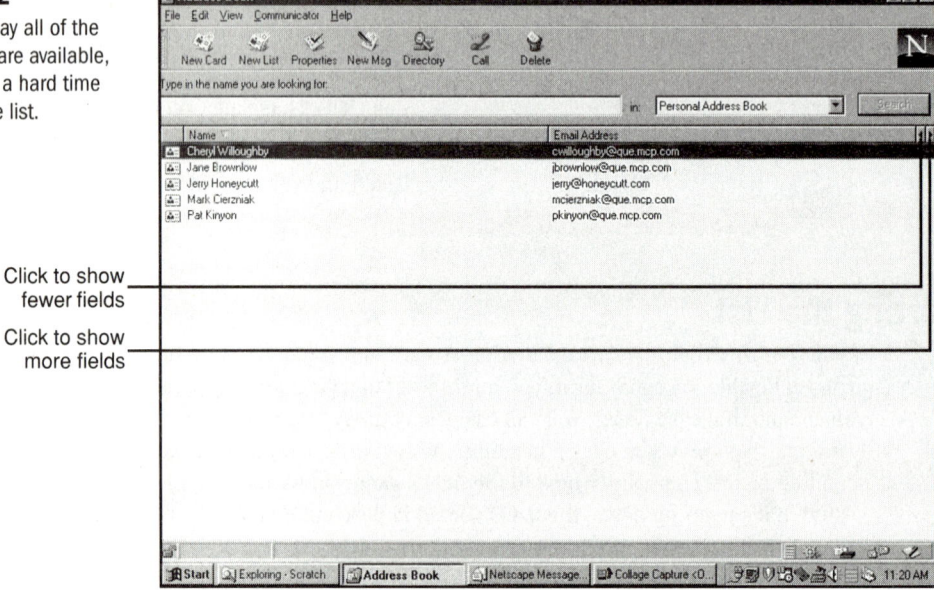

Click to show fewer fields
Click to show more fields

The available fields include:

Name

E-mail Address

Organization

City

Nickname

> **TIP** You can customize which fields the Address Book displays. Display all the fields that are available; then, drag the fields you're most interested in to the far, left side of the list. When finished, click the right-arrow to hide the fields on the right side.

http://www.quecorp.com

## Searching for a Person

If the Address Book doesn't contain many entries, you'll have no problem finding the one you want. If it contains over a few dozen, however, you'll find the address card you want faster by searching for it. After you've found the address card for which you're looking, you can contact that person directly from the Address Book.

**In Your Address Book**  You can search for an address in your Personal Address Book using an incremental search. In the Type in the Name You Are Looking For text box, type the person's name. Because the Address Book uses an incremental search technique, it matches the letters you've typed with the beginning of each full name. Thus, you want to start typing the person's first name, followed by a space, then the person's last name. The Address Book will probably highlight the address card for which you're looking before you've completely typed that person's name.

For example, assume you have two Address Book entries: one for Jane Brownlow and one for Jane Seymour. Also assume that you sorted the list by Name in ascending order. If you start typing the letters **jane**, the Address book highlights the first occurrence of an address card whose name begins with **Jane**; in this case, Jane Brownlow. If you continue typing a space, followed by **s**, the address book will highlight the first occurrence of an address card whose name begins with **Jane S**; in this case, Jane Seymour.

> **TIP** The Address Book also looks for a match in the Nickname field. If you know the person's nickname, you might find a match much faster this way.

**In a Directory**  You're not likely to know the Internet mail address for every individual to whom you want to send a message. You might have long lost friends you'd like to contact. Worse, you might need to send an Internet mail message to an associate at 2 a.m. and not have access to a company directory.

You can search for an Internet mail address using one of the available LDAP directories, which are Internet services you use to find a person's Internet mail address. The Address Book is already configured to use six different LDAP directories:

- Bigfoot Directory
- FedEx Package Trace
- Four11 Directory
- InfoSpace Directory
- Switchboard Directory
- WhoWhere Directory

> **TIP** Because each of the directories in which you can search use different methods to get their data, try searching all of them for a match. You will get different results with every search directory.

**238** | Chapter 12  Using the Address Book

Here's how to look up directory entries using your keywords:

1. In the Search bar, choose the directory you want to use (my personal favorite is Four11) from the drop-down list.
2. Type the person's first and last name in the Type in the Name You Are Looking For text box.
3. Click Search, and the Address Book displays all the matches in the list. If it doesn't find any matches, it displays a dialog box that reports No matches.
4. Work with the list as necessary: addressing Internet mail, making calls using Conference, and so on.
5. When you're finished with the list, don't forget to return to your Personal Address Book by choosing Personal Address Book from the drop-down list in the Search bar.

## Adding a New Address Card

When you add an address card, you can stick with the Internet fields, or you can opt to fill in the physical address fields and phone numbers. If you'll be initiating calls to this person using Netscape Conference, don't forget to fill in the Netscape Conference tab, either. Here's how to create a new address card:

1. Click the New Card button in the Address Book Toolbar. You see the New Card dialog box shown in Figure 12.3.

**FIG. 12.3**
The only fields on this tab that show on the list are First Name, Last Name, Organization, Email Address, and Nickname.

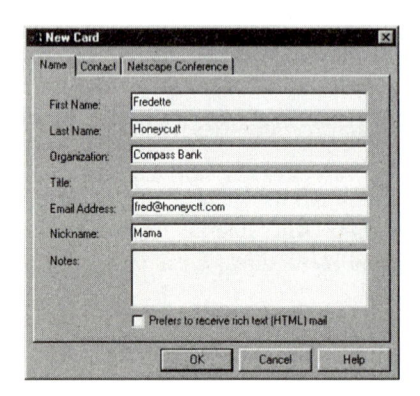

2. Fill in the fields that you can provide. Make sure that you at least provide the person's first and last name, as well as his Internet mail address. If the person uses an Internet mail client that can handle HTML mail messages, select Prefers to Receive Rich Text (HTML) Mail.
3. Click the Contact tab, and the New Card dialog box will look like Figure 12.4.
4. Fill in the fields that you can provide.
5. If the person you're adding to the Address Book uses Netscape Conference, click the Netscape Conference tab. The New Card dialog box will look like Figure 12.5.

**FIG. 12.4**
The only field on this tab that shows in the list is the City.

**FIG. 12.5**
The conference server is the Internet host with which the person you're adding to the Address Book registers themselves.

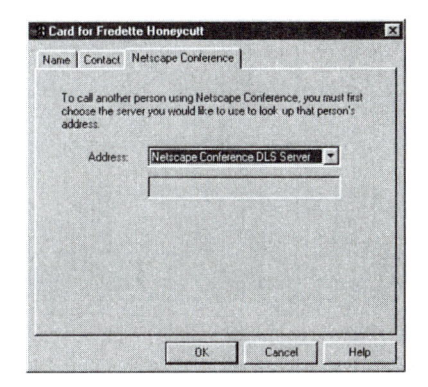

6. Specify the address of the conference server that the person uses. Select the type of address from the Address drop-down list. If you select Specific DLS Server or Hostname or IP Address, provide the actual address in the space provided.
7. Click OK to save your changes.

## Changing an Address Card

Double-click an item in the Address Book's list to change it. You'll see the same dialog box you saw in the previous section, except that the person's name will be in the dialog box's title bar. Make any changes you require, and click OK.

## Removing an Address Card

Remove an address card when it's no longer useful to you. However, you might want to keep around address cards that are invalid just as a reminder to get more current information for that person. To remove an address card, select it in the Address Book's list, and click the Delete button in the Address Book toolbar.

> **TIP** You can undo a delete by choosing Edit, Undo.

## Creating a Card from a Directory

When you search for an address in the Address Book's list using one of the search directories, you can't easily add that address to the Address Book. It only displays a list of matching address cards to which you can address an Internet mail message or initiate a call using Netscape Conference. You won't find a menu option for adding that address card to your Personal Address Book, however.

You can still search the directories, using a different method, and then add the result to your address book:

1. Click the Directory button in the Address Book toolbar. You see the Search dialog box shown in Figure 12.6.

**FIG. 12.6**
Maximize the Search dialog box, and you'll have more space to type.

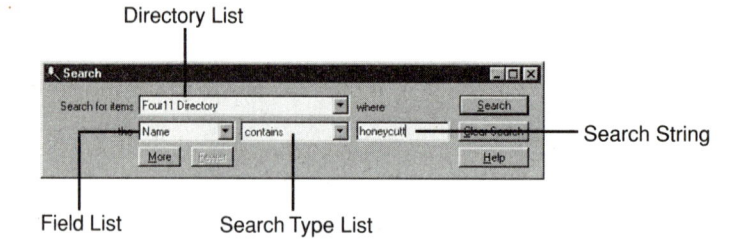

2. Select the directory you want to search from the directory list.

3. Select the field in which you want to search from the field list. You can choose Name, Email, Phone number, Organization, City, or Street.

4. Select the type of search you want to perform from the search type list: *contains*, *doesn't contain*, *is*, *isn't*, or *begins with*. In most cases, you want to use *contains* so that you'll find all directory entries that contain the text you type.

5. Type the text for which you're searching in the search string field.

6. If you want to search in more than just one field, click More, and repeat Steps 3 through 6 for the new field.

7. Click Search, and the Address Book contacts the search directory. A moment or two later, the Address Book will display the results, as shown in Figure 12.7.

8. If you located the right directory entry, select it. Then, click Add to Address Book to add that entry to your Personal Address Book. You can also address an Internet mail message to that person by clicking Compose Message.

9. When you're finished with the list, close it by clicking the Close button in the title bar of the window.

**FIG. 12.7**
The Address Book truncates fields that are too big to display. Hold your mouse pointer over such a field for a moment, and you'll see the entire field.

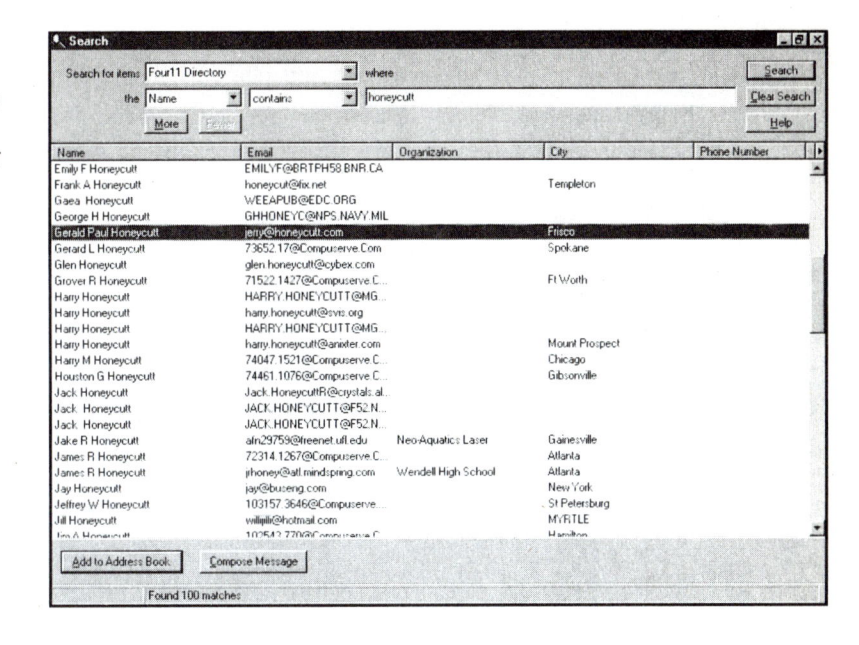

## Creating a Mailing List

You use a mailing list to address an Internet mail message to a group of individuals. That is, instead of typing each mail address in the Address area of the Composition dialog box, you can just provide the mailing list name.

To add a mailing list to the Address Book, you create a new list and then add address cards to it one at a time:

1. Click the New List button in the Address Book's toolbar. You see the Mailing List dialog box shown in Figure 12.8.

**FIG. 12.8**
The only required field is the list name.

2. Type a brief description of the list in List Name. You can also give the list a nickname by typing it in List Nickname and a description by typing it in Description.

3. In the space provided for list names, begin typing the name of an individual as it appears in the Address Book. As soon as the Address Book finds a match, it completes the entry for you.

4. Press Enter to move to the next line in the list.

5. Repeat Steps 3 and 4 for each name you want to add to the mailing list. To remove a list entry, select the entry and click Remove.

6. When finished, click OK to save your changes.

In the Address Book, a mailing list looks like yet another address card. It's almost indistinguishable from regular Address Cards, as shown in Figure 12.9, except for the fact that the icon in the first column shows two cards and the remaining fields on the line are blank.

**FIG. 12.9**
You address Internet mail messages to a mailing list the exact same way that you address a message to an individual.

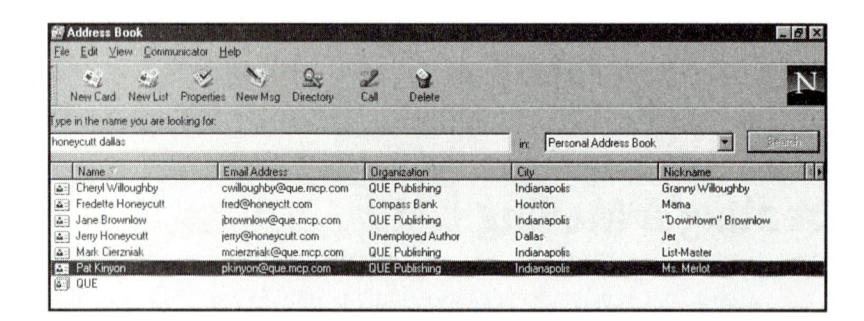

> **NOTE** Mailing lists you create in the Address Book are personal mailing lists. They aren't the same as Internet mailing lists like Major Domo or Listserv.

# Contacting People from Your Address Book

An Address Book is pretty worthless unless you can use it to contact people. In general, you can invoke the address book while addressing a message, or you can address a message directly from the Address Book.

## Addressing an Internet Mail Message

There are two ways you can address an Internet mail message using the information contained in the Address Book. First, you can select an address card in the Address Book's list, and click the New Msg button in the Address Book toolbar. You'll see the Composition dialog box you learned about in Chapter 11, "Messenger In-Depth." Compose your message and click Send to post the message.

http://www.quecorp.com

Second, you can pick an Internet mail address while actually addressing a message:

1. Click the Address button in the Message toolbar, and you'll see the Select Addresses dialog box shown in Figure 12.10.

**FIG. 12.10**
The Select Addresses dialog box is a slimmed-down version of the Address Book.

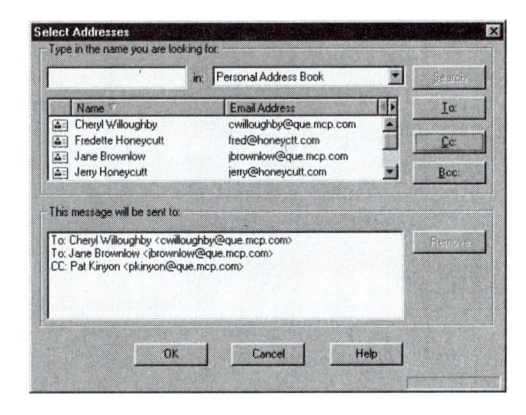

2. Search for or select the names of the individuals to which you want to address the message, and click To:. The Select Addresses dialog box adds the addresses to the address list at the bottom of the dialog box and shows that these are the primary recipients by prefixing their names with To:.

3. Add the recipients to which you want to copy the message by selecting them in the top list and clicking either Cc: or Bcc:. Again, the Select Addresses dialog box adds the addresses to the bottom list and indicates that they're receiving a copy of the message.

**TIP** Any addresses that you add to the Bcc: list will receive a blind carbon copy of the message. The primary recipients of the message won't know that you sent the other folks a carbon copy because you sent it blind.

4. Click OK to finish addressing your message.

**NOTE** In both Messenger and Collabra, you can search the LDAP directories as described in "Creating a Card from a Directory," earlier in this chapter. In the Message Center or a folder, choose Edit, Search Directory.

## Making a Call with Netscape Conference

Unlike addressing Internet mail messages, there's really only one way you can initiate a call to an individual in your Address book. Select an address card in the Address Book's list, and click the Call button in the Address Book toolbar. You'll see the Netscape Conference window described in Chapter 15, "Conference In-Depth." Conference will immediately initiate the call to that individual.

**244** | Chapter 12  Using the Address Book

If your Netscape Conference is open on your desktop, you can quickly open the Address Book by clicking the Address Book button in the middle of the window (see Figure 12.11).

**FIG. 12.11**
After you've initiated a call using the Address Book, add it to your speed dialer so that you don't have to open the Address Book again.

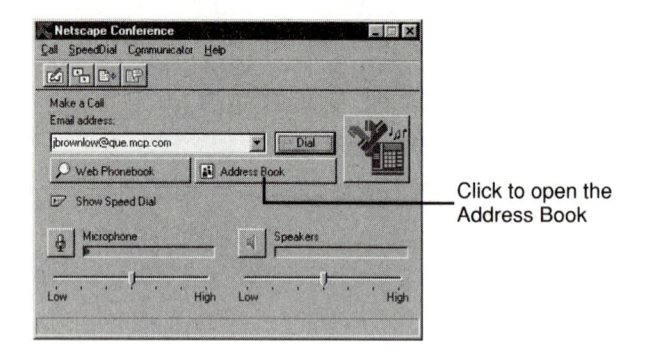

Click to open the Address Book

http://www.quecorp.com

CHAPTER 13

# Collabra In-Depth

*by Jerry Honeycutt*

You have access to millions of other people on more than 16,000 UseNet newsgroups. UseNet covers a tremendous variety of subjects, including gossip, gripping, fan clubs, gardening, Web browsers, and programming tools. You'll find newsgroups for any and every topic imaginable. You need a newsreader to access UseNet newsgroups; Netscape Communicator offers Collabra. There are plenty of newsreaders available on the market, but few have the features you'll find in Collabra—like offline reading, for example.

You can also use Collabra in combination with Collabra server software, which provides workgroup collaboration (thus the name Collabra, eh?). You can create new discussion groups for a variety of topics and facilitate an exchange among various people in an organization.

This chapter focuses primarily on using Collabra with UseNet newsgroups; however, you'll also find material on using Collabra in the corporate environment.

### Learn what UseNet newsgroups are all about
This chapter gives you a brief overview of what you can expect from UseNet and how UseNet newsgroups are organized.

### Work with newsgroups in the Message Center
The Message Center is newsgroup central for Netscape Communicator. You subscribe to, unsubscribe from, and search for newsgroups here.

### Browse and read newsgroups with discussion folders
Collabra's discussion folders provide an easy-to-use interface between you and the messages in a newsgroup.

### Post your own messages to a newsgroup
If you're in the mood for good conversation, advice, or even a scrappy argument, post your own messages to a UseNet newsgroup.

### Collabra supports reading newsgroups offline
One of the best features in Collabra is the ability to read and compose newsgroups messages while you're not connected to the Internet.

# Understanding UseNet Newsgroups

If you've ever used a forum or BBS on a commercial online service, you're already familiar with the concept of a UseNet newsgroup (newsgroup for short). A user *posts* messages (*articles* in Net-speak) to a newsgroup for other people to read. A user can also reply to messages that he reads on a newsgroup. It's one way for people like you to communicate with millions of people around the world.

Behavior on newsgroups is a bit looser, however. A newsgroup doesn't necessarily have a watchdog—besides the readers themselves. As a result, the organization is a bit looser and the content of the messages is often way out of focus. The seemingly chaotic nature of newsgroups, however, produces some of the most interesting information you'll find anywhere.

> **NOTE** *Moderated* newsgroups are a bit more civil and the articles are typically more focused than unmoderated newsgroups. Moderators look at every article posted to their newsgroup before making it available for everyone to read. If they judge it to be inappropriate, they don't post it.

## UseNet Is About Variety

The variety of content is exactly what makes newsgroups so appealing. There are newsgroups for expressing opinions—no matter how benign or radical. There are other newsgroups for asking questions or getting help. And, best of all, there are newsgroups for those seeking companionship—whether they're looking for a soul mate or longing to find someone with a similar interest in Microsoft bashing.

To illustrate the diversity you'll find on UseNet, here's a sample of some newsgroups:

- **alt.tv.simpsons** contains a lot of mindless chatter about the Simpsons.
- **comp.os.ms-windows.advocacy** is one of the hottest Windows newsgroups around. You'll find heated discussions about both Windows 3.1 and Windows 95.
- **rec.games.trading-cards.marketplace** is the place to be if you're into sports trading cards.
- **rec.humor.funny** is where to go to lighten up your day. You'll find a wide variety of humor, including contemporary jokes, old standards, and bogus news flashes.

## Newsgroup Organization

UseNet organizes newsgroups into a hierarchy of categories and subcategories. Take a look at the **alt.tv.simpsons** newsgroup discussed earlier. The **top-level** category is **alt**. The subcategory is **tv**. The subcategory under that is **simpsons**. The name goes from general to specific, left to right. You'll also find other newsgroups under **alt.tv**, such as **alt.tv.friends** and **alt.tv.home-imprvment**.

> **TIP** **alt.tv.*** means all the newsgroups available under the **alt.tv** category.

http://www.quecorp.com

There are many different top-level categories available. Table 13.1 shows some that probably are available.

**Table 13.1  Internet Top-Level Newsgroup Categories**

| Category | Description |
| --- | --- |
| alt | Alternative newsgroups |
| bit | BitNet LISTSERV mailing lists |
| biz | Advertisements for businesses |
| clarinet | News clipping service by subscription only |
| comp | Computer-related topics: hardware and software |
| k12 | Educational; kindergarten through grade 12 |
| misc | Topics that don't fit the other categories |
| news | News and information about UseNet |
| rec | Recreational, sports, hobbies, music, games |
| sci | Applied sciences |
| soc | Social and cultural topics |
| talk | Discussion of more controversial topics |

These categories help you nail down exactly which newsgroup you're looking for. A bit of practice helps as well. If you're looking for information about Windows 95, for example, start looking at the **comp** top-level category. You'll find an **os** category, which obviously represents operating systems, right? Under that category, you'll find an **ms-windows** category.

> **TIP** If you're using Collabra in combination with Collabra server software, you can use plain English newsgroup names such as **Widget Design Discussion**.

### TROUBLESHOOTING

**I don't see all these categories you talked about. Where are they?** Exactly which newsgroups are available on your news server is largely under the control of the administrator. Some administrators filter out regional newsgroups that don't apply to your area. Some also filter out the **alt** newsgroups because of their potentially offensive content.

## news.newusers.questions

Whenever I go someplace new, I first try to locate a source of information about that place. Likewise, the first few places that you need to visit when you get to UseNet are all the newsgroups that are there to welcome you. It's not just a warm and fuzzy welcome, either. They provide useful information about what to do, what not to do, and how to get the most out of the newsgroups. If you are a new user, Table 13.2 shows you the newsgroups that you need to check out.

**Table 13.2  Newsgroups for the UseNet User**

| Newsgroup | Description |
| --- | --- |
| **alt.answers** | A good source of FAQs and information about **alt** newsgroups. |
| **alt.internet.services** | This is the place to ask about Internet programs and resources. |
| **news.announce.newsgroups** | Announcements about new newsgroups are made here. |
| **news.announce.newusers** | Articles and FAQs for the new newsgroups user. |
| **news.newusers.questions** | This is the place to ask your questions about using newsgroups. |

> **TIP** Don't post test messages to these newsgroups. Also, don't post messages asking for someone to send you an Internet mail message. This is a waste of newsgroups that are intended to help new users learn the ropes.

### news.announce.newusers

The **news.announce.newusers** newsgroup contains a lot of great articles for new newsgroup users. In particular, look for the articles with the following subject lines:

- A Primer on How to Work with the UseNet Community
- Answers to Frequently Asked Questions About UseNet
- Emily Postnews Answers Your Questions on Netiquette
- Guidelines on UseNet Newsgroup Names
- Hints on writing style for UseNet
- How to find the right place to post (FAQ)
- Rules for posting to UseNet
- Welcome to UseNet!
- What is UseNet?
- What is UseNet? A second opinion

## Working with Newsgroups

You work with newsgroups in the Netscape Message Center (see Figure 13.1). This is the same window that you learned about in Chapter 11, "Messenger In-Depth." However, this window has features you use to access newsgroups that are specific to Collabra. You'll learn how to use those features specific to reading newsgroups in the sections that follow. But first you'll take a tour of the window, its menus, and its toolbars.

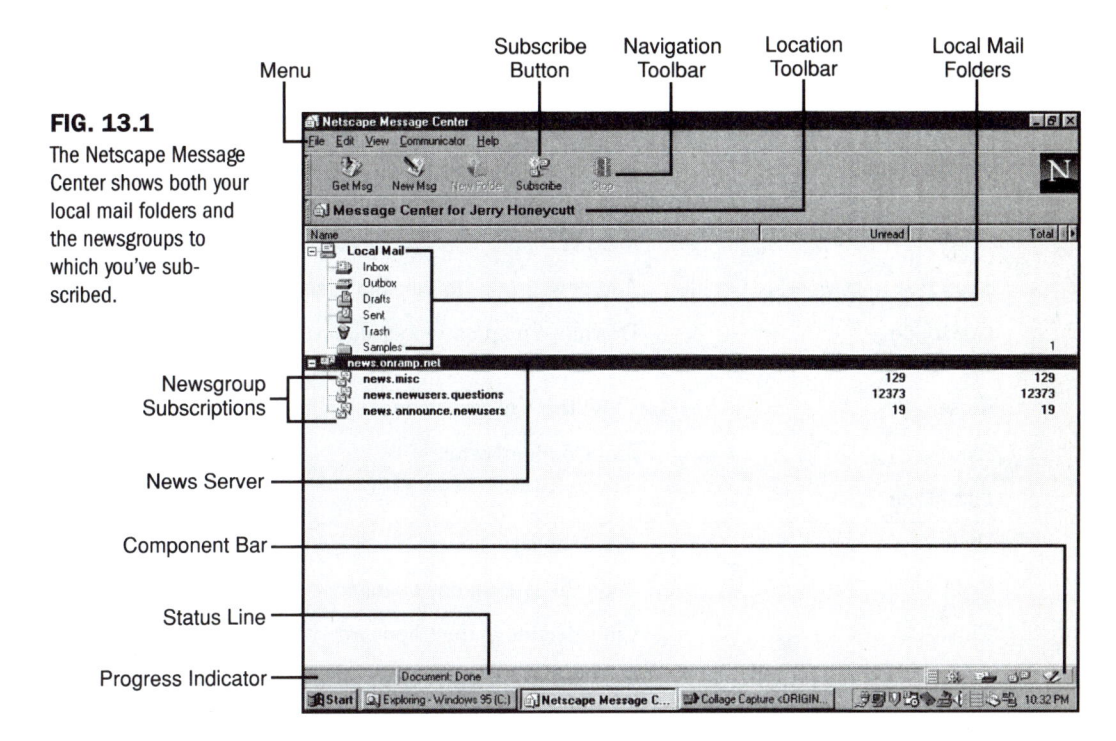

**FIG. 13.1**
The Netscape Message Center shows both your local mail folders and the newsgroups to which you've subscribed.

You can access all of the Message Center's features through its menus. Table 13.3 describes each menu option.

### Table 13.3  Collabra Menu Options

| Option | Description |
| --- | --- |
| **File Menu** | |
| New | Create a new Web page. |
| New Folder | Create a new mail folder. |
| New Discussion Group Server | Add a new news server to the Message Center. |

*continues*

**Table 13.3   Continued**

| Option | Description |
| --- | --- |
| **File Menu** | |
| Open Folder | Open the selected mail folder or newsgroup. |
| Rename Folder | Rename the selected folder. |
| Empty Trash Folder | Permanently delete all items in the Trash folder. |
| Compress Folders | Compress the mail folders by getting rid of dead space. |
| Get Messages | Retrieve Internet mail messages from the mail server. |
| Send Unsent Messages | Post new newsgroup messages after working offline. |
| Update Message Count | Update counters that indicate unread newsgroup messages. |
| Subscribe to Discussion Groups | Add newsgroups to the short-list of favorite newsgroups. |
| Go Offline | Download marked newsgroups and messages; and disconnect. |
| Close | Close this Collabra window. |
| Exit | Exit Communicator. |
| **Edit Menu** | |
| Undo | Undo the last change. |
| Redo | Redo the last undone change. |
| Cut | Cut selection to the Clipboard. |
| Copy | Copy selection to the Clipboard. |
| Paste | Paste selection to the Clipboard. |
| Delete Discussion Group Server | Delete the selected news server from Message Center. |
| Select All | Select all mail folders. |
| Search Messages | Search for messages. |
| Search Directory | Search for a mail address. |
| Manage Mail Account | Change mail settings. |
| Manage Discussion Group | Change newsgroup settings. |
| Mail Filters | Filter incoming messages. |
| Discussion Group Properties | Change newsgroup settings. |
| Preferences | Set personal preferences. |

| Option | Description |
| --- | --- |
| **View Menu** | |
| Hide Navigation Toolbar | Hide the Navigation toolbar. |
| Hide Location Toolbar | Hide the Location toolbar. |
| Move Folder | Move folder to a subfolder. |
| Stop Loading | Stop loading from the Web. |
| **Communicator Menu** | |
| Navigator | Open Navigator. |
| Messenger Mailbox | Open Messenger. |
| Collabra Discussions | Open Collabra. |
| Page Composer | Open Composer. |
| Conference | Open Conference. |
| Show Component Bar | Dock/Undock Component bar. |
| Message Center | Open Message Center. |
| Address Book | Open Address Book. |
| Bookmarks | Open Bookmark list. |
| History | Open History list. |
| Java Console | Open Java Console. |
| Security Info | Open security settings. |
| **Help Menu** | |
| Help Contents | Display help contents. |
| Release Notes | Display release notes. |
| Product Information and Support | Display support information. |
| Software Updates | Display update information. |
| Register Now | Registry Communicator. |
| Member Services | Extend Communicator. |
| International Users | Display international help. |
| Security | Display security information. |
| Net Etiquette | Display netiquette issues. |
| About Plug-ins | Display list of plug-ins. |
| About Font Displayers | Display list of displayers. |
| About Communicator | Display version information. |

You can also access some of Message Center's features using the Navigation toolbar. See Table 13.4 for a description of each button in this toolbar.

**Table 13.4  Navigation Toolbar Buttons**

| Button | Name | Description |
| --- | --- | --- |
| | Get Msg | Download new messages. |
| | New Msg | Create a new message. |
| | New Folder | Create a new mail folder. |
| | Subscribe | Subscribe to a newsgroup. |
| | Stop | Stop current activity. |

## Subscribing to a Newsgroup

Before you can read the articles in a newsgroup, you have to *subscribe* to it. When you subscribe to a newsgroup, you're telling Collabra that you want to read the messages in that newsgroup. Collabra displays only the newsgroups to which you've subscribed. Subscribing to a handful of newsgroups keeps you from having to slog through a list of 16,000 newsgroups to find what you want. Use these steps to subscribe to a newsgroup:

1. Click the Subscribe button in the Navigation toolbar. Collabra displays the Communicator: Subscribe to Discussion Groups dialog box, and immediately starts downloading the list of newsgroups available on your news server. After Collabra is finished, the Communicator: Subscribe to Discussion Groups dialog box looks similar to Figure 13.2.
2. Select a newsgroup to which you want to subscribe. Collabra displays the list of newsgroups in a hierarchical list. Click the plus sign (+) next to a category in order to see the subcategories and newsgroups available underneath it. Collabra displays a folder icon next to a newsgroup category and a discussion icon next to actual newsgroups.
3. Click Subscribe, and Collabra places a check mark next to the newsgroup to which you've subscribed.
4. Repeat Steps 2 and 3 for each newsgroup to which you want to subscribe.
5. Click OK, and Collabra adds the newsgroup to which you subscribed to the Message Center. In the Message Center, you'll see a plus sign (+) next to the news server in the Message Center. Click the plus sign in order to see the newsgroups to which you've subscribed. When you open a news server this way, Collabra automatically connects you to the Internet in order to update the message counts for each newsgroup.

Working with Newsgroups | 253

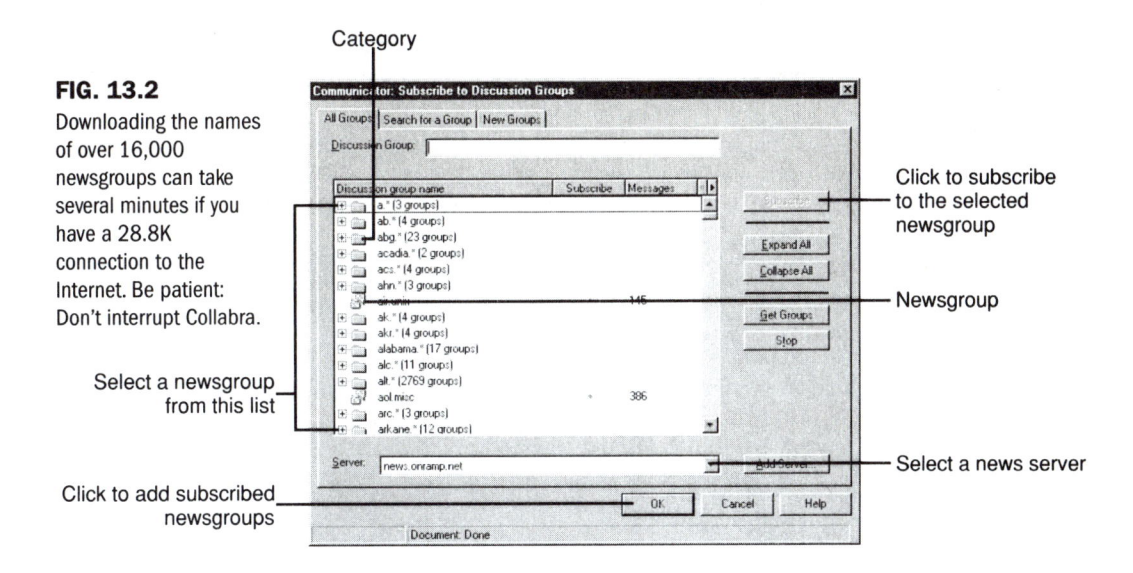

**FIG. 13.2**
Downloading the names of over 16,000 newsgroups can take several minutes if you have a 28.8K connection to the Internet. Be patient: Don't interrupt Collabra.

Callouts on figure:
- Category
- Click to subscribe to the selected newsgroup
- Newsgroup
- Select a newsgroup from this list
- Select a news server
- Click to add subscribed newsgroups

> **TIP** If you don't like how Collabra organizes the newsgroups to which you subscribe, and you use Windows 95 or Windows NT, you can create shortcuts to your favorite newsgroups and stash them in a folder. You can then organize them any way you like.
>
> Here's how to create a shortcut to a newsgroup:
>
> 1. Right-click in a folder, and choose New, Shortcut.
> 2. Type the URL for your newsgroup such as **news:alt.tv.simpsons** (don't forget to prefix the newsgroup name with "news:").
> 3. Click Next, and then type a plain English name for your shortcut. Click Finish to save your shortcut.
>
> If Collabra doesn't start automatically when you double-click the shortcut, make sure that Netscape Communicator is your default browser.

## Unsubscribing from a Newsgroup

If you're no longer frequenting a particular newsgroup to which you've subscribed, you can remove it from your short-list. In the Message Center, select a newsgroup from which you want to unsubscribe, and choose Edit, Delete Discussion Group from the main menu. The Message Center will ask you to confirm this activity; click OK to go ahead and remove the newsgroup from the list.

## Searching for a Newsgroup

Your news server probably has so many newsgroups that it's sometimes hard to find the right one. Collabra lets you do an *incremental search* (the search narrows in after each character you type) to limit the list to those newsgroups that match the search string you've typed in the search field. For example, if you start to type **news.a** in the Discussion Group field, Collabra displays all the newsgroups that begin with that string of characters.

> **TIP** Type a top-level category name followed by a space to quickly open that folder without having to find it in the list. For example, type **alt.** followed by a space in the Discussion Groups field to quickly open the folder for the **alt** top-level category.

Collabra also provides a more advanced search feature. You can use this feature to search for newsgroups using multiple keywords. Here's how:

1. In the Communicator: Subscribe to Discussion Groups dialog box, click the Search for a Group tab. You'll see the dialog box shown in Figure 13.3.

**FIG. 13.3**
Collabra limits its search to newsgroup names. It doesn't search newsgroup descriptions as well.

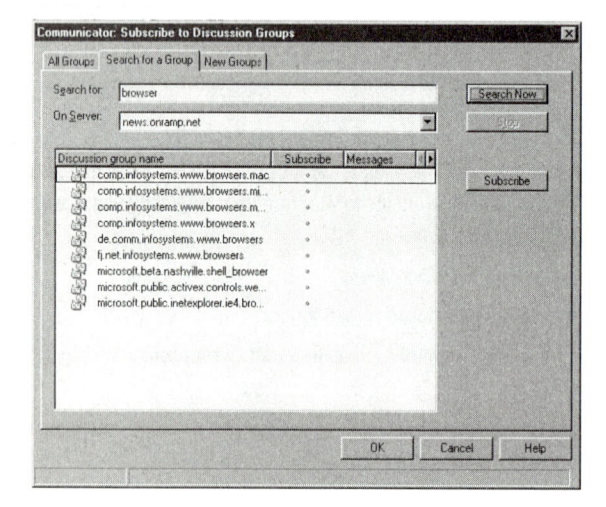

2. Type the keywords for which you're searching in Search For, and click Search Now. Collabra quickly displays a list of all the matching newsgroup names.
3. Select a newsgroup from the list, and click Subscribe to add the selected newsgroup to the Message Center. You can repeat this step for each newsgroup to which you want to subscribe.

## Watching the New Newsgroups

Your news server receives new newsgroups almost every day. Collabra is able to detect these new newsgroups, too, and it gives you the chance to subscribe to them before they disappear forever in the big list. Here's how:

1. In the Communicator: Subscribe to Discussion Groups dialog box, click the New Groups tab. You'll see the dialog box shown in Figure 13.4.

Working with Newsgroups | 255

**FIG. 13.4**
Collabra displays all of the newsgroups that are new since the last time you clicked Clear New.

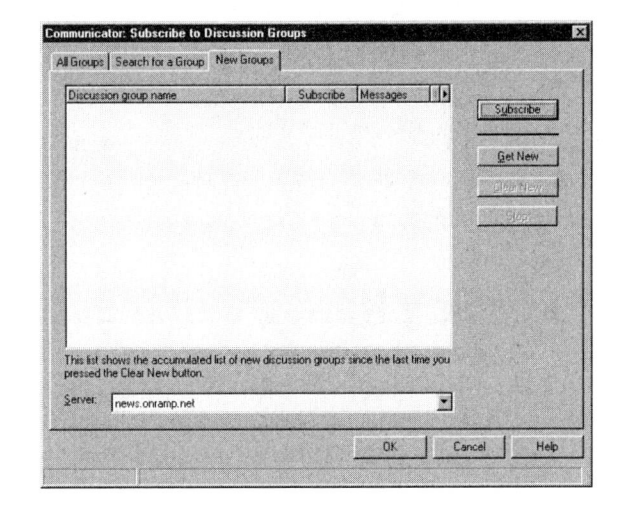

2. Click Get New, and Collabra displays a list of new newsgroups.
3. Select a newsgroup from the list, and click Subscribe to add the selected newsgroup to the Message Center. You can repeat this step for each newsgroup to which you want to subscribe.

## Using Multiple News Servers

Tracking multiple news servers is now an absolute requirement for any serious newsreader. First, you might want to monitor newsgroups within your own organization, as well as on UseNet. Second, many companies have moved their support forums from online services such as CompuServe to UseNet. They've done so by creating their own news servers. You don't want to have to change your configuration and download a new batch of newsgroups every time you want to get product support.

It just so happens that Collabra supports multiple news servers. You add a new news server to the Message Center, and then work with all your news servers together:

1. In the Communicator: Subscribe to Discussion Groups dialog box, click Add Server. You'll see the New Discussion Groups Server dialog box shown in Figure 13.5.

**FIG. 13.5**
Select Always use name and password only if you're using a secure news server.

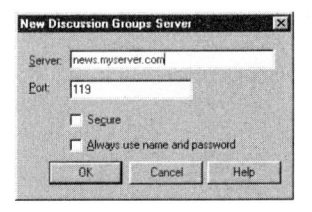

2. Type the Internet address of the new news server in Server, and click OK to save your changes.

**256**   Chapter 13   Collabra In-Depth

> You see all of the news servers that you've added in the Message Center. In order to subscribe to newsgroups in a specific news server, select that news server before clicking Subscribe in the Navigation toolbar. You can also choose a different news server in each tab of the Communicator: Subscribe to Discussion Groups dialog box:
>
> - In the All Groups and New Groups tabs, select a server from Server.
> - In the Search for a Group tab, select a server from On Server.

## Browsing and Reading Newsgroup Messages

In order to read the messages within a newsgroup, double-click a newsgroup name in the Message Center. Collabra opens a discussion folder that contains the current messages for that newsgroup (see Figure 13.6). This window is organized much like Communicator's other windows. It has the Navigation and Location toolbars, the status line, the progress indicator, and the Component bar.

**FIG. 13.6**
With few differences, discussion folders work exactly like the mail folders you learned about in Chapter 11, "Messenger In-Depth."

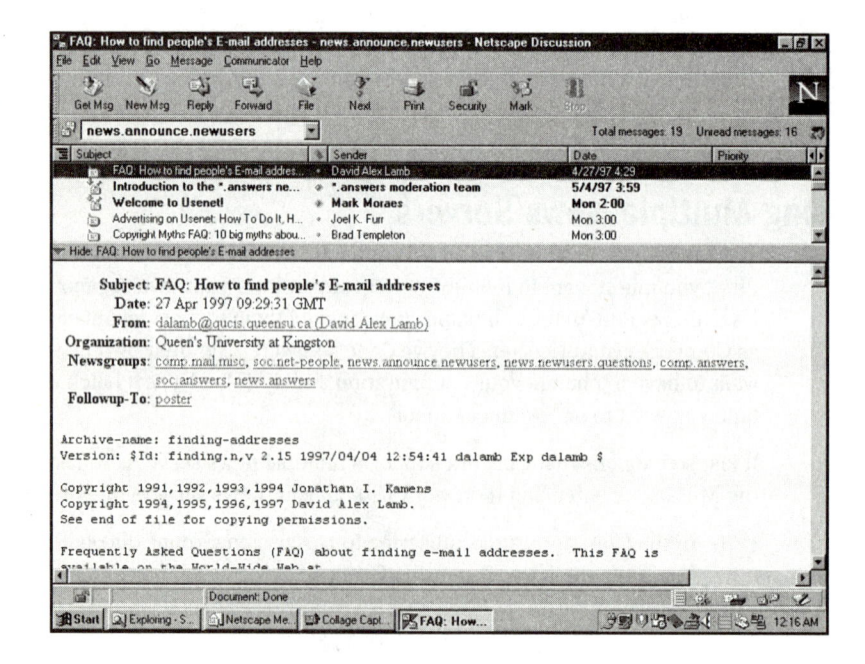

Table 13.5 describes each menu option in the discussion folder.

http://www.quecorp.com

### Table 13.5 Discussion Folder Menu Options

| Option | Description |
| --- | --- |
| **File Menu** | |
| New | Create a new Web page. |
| New Discussion Group | Create a new newsgroup. |
| Open Message | Open the selected message. |
| Open Attachments | Open any attached files. |
| Save As | Save the message to your disk. |
| Edit Message | Change the message. |
| Rename Folder | Change the newsgroup's name. |
| Empty Trash Folder | Permanently delete all items in the Trash folder. |
| Compress Folders | Compress the mail folders by getting rid of dead space. |
| Get Messages | Retrieve Internet mail messages from the mail server. |
| Send Unsent Messages | Post new newsgroup messages after working offline. |
| Subscribe to Discussion Groups | Add newsgroups to the short-list of favorite newsgroups. |
| Go Offline | Download marked newsgroups and messages and disconnect. |
| Page Setup | Set up your printer for printing newsgroup messages. |
| Print Preview | Preview before printing the selected message. |
| Print | Print the selected message. |
| Close | Close this Collabra window. |
| Exit | Exit Communicator. |
| **Edit Menu** | |
| Undo | Undo the last change. |
| Redo | Redo the last undone change. |
| Cut | Cut selection to the Clipboard. |
| Copy | Copy selection to the Clipboard. |
| Paste | Paste selection to the Clipboard. |

*continues*

**Table 13.5  Continued**

| Option | Description |
| --- | --- |
| **Edit Menu** | |
| Cancel Message | Cancel the selected message. |
| Select Message | Select all messages, those in a thread or those flagged. |
| Find in Message | Search for text in the selected message. |
| Find Again | Repeat the last text search. |
| Search Messages | Search for messages. |
| Search Directory | Search for a mail address. |
| Manage Mail Account | Change mail settings. |
| Manage Discussion Group | Change newsgroup settings. |
| Mail Filters | Filter incoming messages. |
| Properties | Change newsgroup settings. |
| Preferences | Set personal preferences. |
| **View Menu** | |
| Hide Navigation Toolbar | Hide the Navigation toolbar. |
| Hide Location Toolbar | Hide the Location toolbar. |
| Show Categories | Display available categories. |
| Hide Message | Hide the message pane. |
| Sort | Sort the message headers. |
| Messages | Choose to view all messages or unread messages only. |
| Headers | Select a header style. |
| Attachments | Choose to display attachments inline or as links. |
| Increase Font | Make text bigger. |
| Decrease Font | Make text smaller. |
| Reload | Reload the message headers. |
| Show Images | Show images in the message. |
| Refresh | Reload the selected message. |
| Stop Loading | Stop loading message headers. |
| Unscramble (ROT13) | Unscramble a ROT13-encoded message. |

| Option | Description |
| --- | --- |
| **View Menu** | |
| Wrap long lines | Break long lines at the window border. |
| Page Source | View the raw text for the message. |
| Page Info | Display statistical information about the message. |
| Encoding | Change the selected language. |
| **Go Menu** | |
| Next Message | Select the next message. |
| Next Unread Message | Select the next unread message. |
| Next Flagged Message | Select the next flagged message. |
| Next Unread Thread | Select the next unread thread. |
| Next Category | Select the next category. |
| Next Unread Category | Select the next unread category. |
| Next Group | Select the next newsgroup in the Message Center. |
| Next Unread Group | Select the next unread newsgroup in the Message Center. |
| Previous Message | Select the previous message. |
| Previous Unread Message | Select the previous unread message. |
| Previous Flagged Message | Select the previous flagged message. |
| First Flagged Message | Select the first flagged message. |
| Back | Move backward in the history list. |
| Forward | Move forward in the history list. |
| **Message Menu** | |
| New Message | Post a new message. |
| Reply | Reply to the selected message. |
| Forward | Forward the selected message. |
| Forward Quoted | Forward the selected message, quoting it in the new message. |
| Add to Address Book | Add sender's mail address to the address book. |
| File Message | File message in a local mail folder. |

*continues*

**Table 13.5  Continued**

| Option | Description |
| --- | --- |
| **Message Menu** | |
| Copy Message | Copy the message to a local mail folder. |
| Mark | Mark the selected message or group of messages as read. |
| Flag | Flag the message. |
| Unflag | Remove the flag from a message. |
| Ignore Thread | Ignore the selected thread. |
| Watch Thread | Keep track of the selected thread. |
| **Communicator Menu** | |
| Navigator | Open Navigator. |
| Messenger Mailbox | Open Messenger. |
| Collabra Discussions | Open Collabra. |
| Page Composer | Open Composer. |
| Conference | Open Conference. |
| Show Component Bar | Dock/Undock Component bar. |
| Message Center | Open Message Center. |
| Address Book | Open Address Book. |
| Bookmarks | Open Bookmark list. |
| History | Open History list. |
| Java Console | Open Java Console. |
| Security Info | Open security settings. |
| **Help Menu** | |
| Help Contents | Display help contents. |
| Release Notes | Display release notes. |
| Product Information and Support | Display support information. |
| Software Updates | Display update information. |
| Register Now | Registry Communicator. |
| Member Services | Extend Communicator. |
| International Users | Display international help. |

http://www.quecorp.com

# Browsing and Reading Newsgroup Messages | 261

| Option | Description |
|---|---|
| **Help Menu** | |
| S<u>e</u>curity | Display security information. |
| Net Etiq<u>u</u>ette | Display netiquette issues. |
| Abou<u>t</u> Plug-ins | Display list of plug-ins. |
| About Font <u>D</u>isplayers | Display list of displayers. |
| <u>A</u>bout Communicator | Display version information. |

You can also access some of the discussion folder's features using the Navigation toolbar. See Table 13.4 for a description of each button in this toolbar.

### Table 13.6   Navigation Toolbar Buttons

| Button | Name | Description |
|---|---|---|
| Get Msg | Get Msg | Download new messages. |
| New Msg | New Msg | Create a new message. |
| Reply | Reply | Reply to selected message. |
| Forward | Forward | Forward selected message. |
| File | File | File the selected message; select a local mail folder from the drop-down menu. |
| Next | Next | View the next message; select next message, unread message, unread thread, and so on from the drop-down menu. |
| Print | Print | Print the selected message. |
| Security | Security | Display security information. |
| Mark | Mark | Mark the selected message; select unread, read, thread unread, and so on from the drop-down menu. |
| Stop | Stop | Stop current activity. |

**NOTE** When you open a newsgroup that contains more than 500 message headers, Collabra gives you the choice of downloading all of the headers or just the first 500 headers. If you choose to download the first 500 headers, you can download the next 500 headers by choosing G*e*t Messages, Next 500 from the discussion folder's main menu.

## Getting Around the Discussion Folder

The discussion window is organized so that you can browse newsgroup messages quickly. It's separated into two areas. The top area (the header area) shows a list of message *headers* that describe the subject, author, and date for each message in the newsgroup. You can scroll this list up and down to see the message headers that aren't visible in the list. Select a newsgroup in the header area, and the discussion folder displays the contents of the message in the bottom area (the message area).

Notice that some of the message headers have plus signs (+) next to them or have message headers indented underneath them. This indicates that replies have been posted to that message. In order to see the replies, click the plus sign next to a message header, and then select one of the replies. Note that all of the messages indented under a message, including the original message, are called *threads*. By indenting the messages in a thread, Collabra makes following the conversation easier.

### TROUBLESHOOTING

**What happened to the messages that were here a few days ago?** It's not practical to keep every message posted to every newsgroup indefinitely. Your service provider deletes the older messages to make room for the newer ones. Another way of saying this is that a message *scrolled off*. The length of time that a message hangs around varies from provider to provider, but is usually between three days and one week.

**I opened an message, but its contents were all garbled.** You've probably opened an message that is ROT13-encoded. ROT13 is an encoding method that has little to do with security. It allows a person who is posting a potentially offensive message to place the responsibility for its contents on you—the reader. It essentially says that if you decode and read this message, you won't hold me responsible for its contents. To decode the message, select the message and choose View, Unscramble (ROT13).

After you've read the message, you can select another message, or you can use the Next button in the Navigation toolbar to get around. When you click the Next button, Collabra displays a drop-down menu that gives you several choices. Table 13.7 describes the most useful choices.

http://www.quecorp.com

### Table 13.7 The Next Button's Drop-Down Menu

| Item | Description |
| --- | --- |
| Next Message | Read next message. |
| Next Unread Message | Read next unread message. |
| Next Unread Thread | Read next unread thread. |
| Next Group | Open next subscribed newsgroup. |
| Next Unread Group | Open next unread subscribed newsgroup. |

> **TIP** To open a message in its own window, double-click it, or choose File, Open Message from the discussion folder's main menu. This makes reading the message a bit easier.

**Changing the Sort Order** You can change the order in which the discussion folder sorts messages. If you're looking for multi-part attachments, for example, you might want to sort the message headers by subject. If you're looking for a message from a particular author, you can sort message headers by sender. Here's how:

1. Choose Sort from the discussion folder's main menu. You see a submenu that contains a list of fields by which you can sort.
2. Choose the field by which you want to sort from the submenu.
3. Choose Sort, Ascending to sort in ascending order or choose Sort, Descending to sort in descending order.

**Viewing All or Only New Messages** By default, Collabra displays every message header that you've ever downloaded. Unread message headers are set in bold text, while read message headers are set in normal text. There is also a larger green diamond in the message header of a read message than in an unread message.

You can also choose to show only those messages that are new. Choose View, Messages, New from the main menu. In this case, Collabra displays only the message headers that are more recent than the time you last downloaded message headers from the newsgroup.

Alternatively, you can choose Threads with New. If you're following any threads in a newsgroup, this is the best choice. Why? Because if you only display new messages, you won't be able to see the message that originally started the thread. Choosing this option displays an entire thread, even though you've already read the first few messages in the thread.

## Filing a Newsgroup Message

You're going to encounter newsgroup messages that you'll want to save in your local mail folders. You store newsgroup messages in the same folders that you use for Internet mail. Here's how:

1. In the discussion window, select the message that you want to file.
2. Click the File button in the Navigation toolbar, and choose the local mail folder to which you want to file the message. If a mail folder has subfolders, selecting that mail folder drops down a submenu that contains an entry for each subfolder.

## Replying to a Newsgroup Message

If you have something to add to someone else's newsgroup message, you can post a reply. You can reply to a message two different ways: to the group or to the sender.

**Reply to Group**  If you want your reply to be read by everyone who frequents the newsgroup, post a follow-up message. Your reply is added to the thread. Here's how:

1. Click Reply in the Navigation toolbar, and you'll see a drop-down menu.
2. Choose Reply to Group. You'll notice that the message is preaddressed to the newsgroup.
3. Type your reply in the body of the Composition window shown in Figure 13.7, and click the Send button in the Message Toolbar.

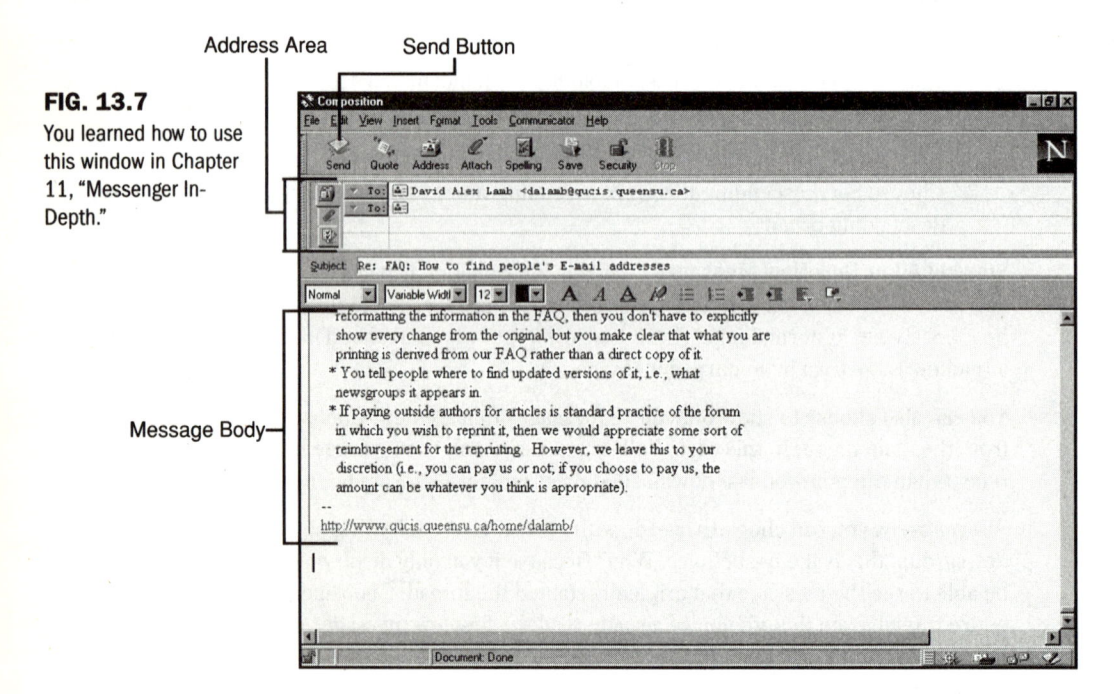

**FIG. 13.7**
You learned how to use this window in Chapter 11, "Messenger In-Depth."

**Reply to Sender**  If your reply would benefit only the person who posted the message, respond with an e-mail message instead. That person gets the message faster, and the other newsgroup readers aren't annoyed:

http://www.quecorp.com

1. Click Reply in the Navigation toolbar, and you'll see a drop-down menu.
2. Choose Reply to Sender. You'll see the same Composition window shown in Figure 13.6, except that Collabra will preaddress the message to the individual instead of the group.
3. Type your reply in the body of Composition window, and click the Send button in the Message Toolbar.

## Saving a Message's File Attachments

Collabra makes saving a newsgroup message's attachments about as easy as saving an Internet mail message's attachments. If you've configured Collabra to display attachments inline—by choosing View, Attachments, Inline from the discussion folder's main menu—you'll see most images embedded within the text. If you've configured Collabra to display attachments as links—by choosing View, Attachments, As Links—you'll see a paperclip icon in the message header and a list of attachments at the bottom of the message.

Collabra provides three different ways you can work with the attachments in a newsgroup message:

- Click the paperclip icon that's in the message header, and Collabra will display an attachment area that contains an icon for each attachment in the message (see Figure 13.8). You can double-click the icon to open it in the associated application, or you can drag it to a folder on your computer.

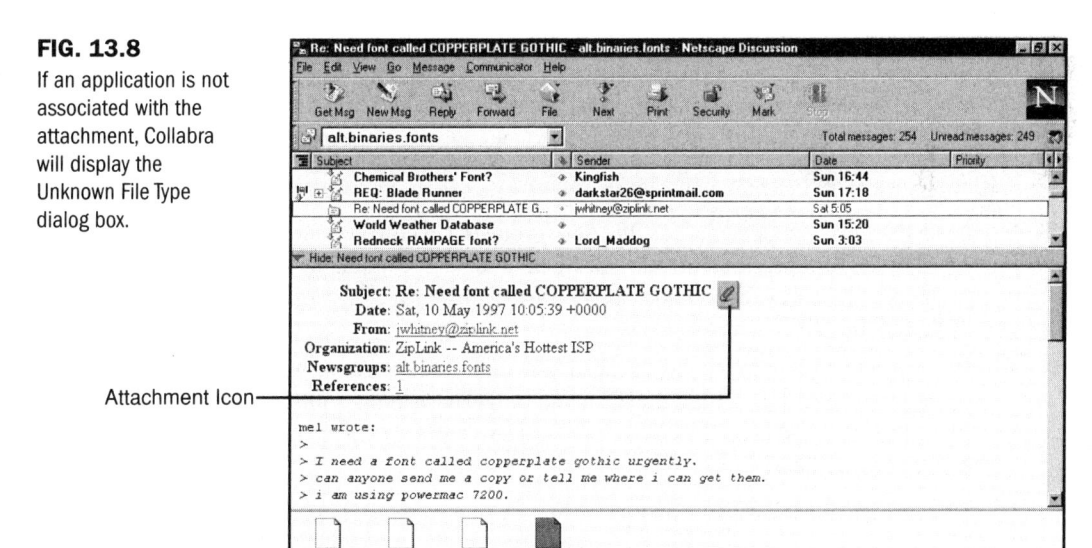

**FIG. 13.8**
If an application is not associated with the attachment, Collabra will display the Unknown File Type dialog box.

Attachment Icon

- Click one of the links that you see at the bottom of the message to open it in the application associated with that file type. You'll find one link for each file attachment.

- Choose File, Open Attachments from the discussion folder's main menu, and you see a submenu that contains an entry for each attachment in the message. Choose one of the attachments to open that file in the associated application.

While you're browsing a newsgroup, you might notice a few articles with subject lines that look like the following example (headings are provided for your convenience). These articles are three parts of the same file. The first article is probably a description of the file because it is part zero, and because there are only five lines in it. The next two articles are the actual file.

| Lines | File Name | Part    | Description              |
|-------|-----------|---------|--------------------------|
| 5     | HOMER.GIF | [00/02] | Portrait of Homer Simpson |
| 800   | HOMER.GIF | [01/02] | Portrait of Homer Simpson |
| 540   | HOMER.GIF | [02/02] | Portrait of Homer Simpson |

In most cases, Collabra will detect the multi-part attachment and handle it automatically. Just make sure that you select the first newsgroup message representing the file, either [00/02] or [01/02]. If Collabra can't find all the parts of the attachment, however, you won't be able to view or save the attachment.

## Posting Messages to a Newsgroup

Posting a newsgroup message with Collabra is just like posting an Internet mail message with Messenger. You use the exact same window. That's probably why Netscape has gone against UseNet convention and used the term *message* instead of *article*. The only difference between sending a mail message with Collabra and posting a message with Collabra is that you don't address it to a mail address—you address it to a newsgroup name instead.

Here's how to post a message to a newsgroup:

1. In the Message Center, select the newsgroup to which you want to post a message, and click the New Msg button in the Navigation toolbar. You can also click the New Msg button in the discussion folder for a newsgroup. You see the Composition window shown in Figure 13.9.
2. Type a brief description of your posting in Subject. If you're attaching a file to your message, consider putting the file name somewhere in the subject line so that other folks can see it easily.
3. Type your message in the message area.
4. Click Send in the Navigation toolbar to post your message to the newsgroup.

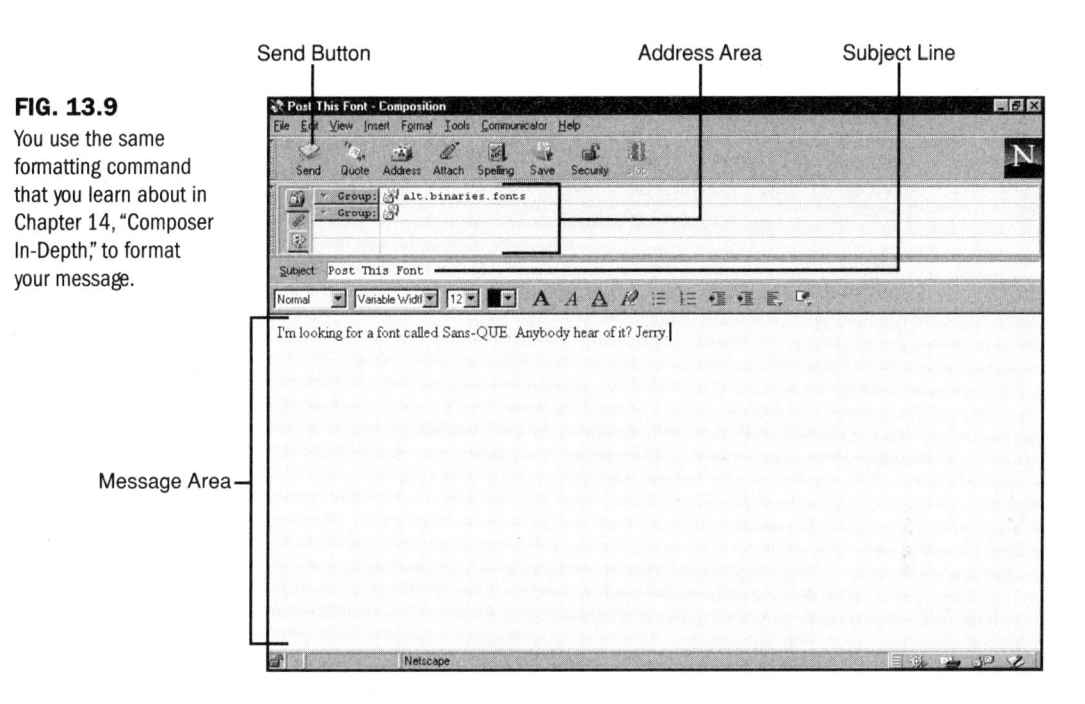

Posting Messages to a Newsgroup | 267

**FIG. 13.9**
You use the same formatting command that you learn about in Chapter 14, "Composer In-Depth," to format your message.

*Labels on figure: Send Button, Address Area, Subject Line, Message Area*

> **CAUTION**
> When posting to a UseNet newsgroup, don't format your message using HTML, because this really annoys those folks who don't have an HTML-enabled newsreader. If you do format your newsgroup message, Collabra will ask you to confirm how you want to post the message (see Figure 13.10). Make sure you select Send in Plain Text Only so that other users can easily read your message.

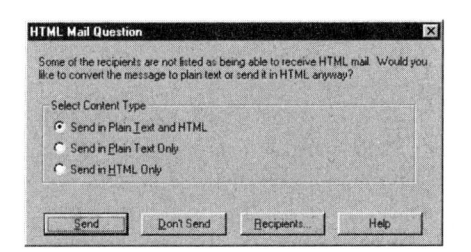

**FIG. 13.10**
If you choose Send in Plain Text Only, Collabra strips out all of the HTML tags that it finds in the message; possibly messing up your format a bit.

> **TIP** If you feel an overwhelming need to post a test message to try out these instructions, post it to **alt.test**. This is the only UseNet newsgroup in which posting test messages is acceptable usage.

Part II
Ch 13

## Attaching Files to Your Message

Like retrieving attachments from a newsgroup message, Collabra provides different ways to attach a file to your message. You can use the menu, toolbar, or the address area:

- Choose Attach, File from the Composition window's main menu (shown earlier in Figure 13.9). Select a file from your computer or type a file name in File Name, and then click Open.

- Click the Attach button in the Composition window's toolbar, and choose File from the drop-down menu. Select a file from your computer or type a file name in File Name, and then click Open.

- Click the paperclip icon in the addressing area to change to the attachment tab (see Figure 13.11), and click anywhere within the attachment tab. Select a file from your computer or type a file name in File Name; then, click Open.

**FIG. 13.11**
The paperclip icon changes to a sheet of paper with a paperclip when you add attachments to the message.

## Adding a Signature to Your Messages

Signatures are bits of plain text that you add to the end of every message you send. They're a substitute for your real signature in that they allow you to personalize your message. Signatures express something interesting about you such as a favorite quotation or hobby. Many people put the URL of their home page in their signature. Others use fancy ASCII artwork for their signature. Here's what my mail signature looks like:

```
Jerry Honeycutt ------------------------------------------+
Author of QUE's Using the Internet, Second Edition        |
For more information, see http://rampages.onramp.net/~jerry  <-+
```

You can have Collabra automatically add a signature to every outgoing newsgroup message or you can choose to insert it only when you feel that it's appropriate. Regardless, you have to configure Collabra so that it knows about your signature:

1. Choose Edit, Preferences from Navigator or Collabra's main menu. Select Identity, under Mail & Groups on the left-hand side of the Preferences dialog box (the Category), and you'll see the window shown in Figure 13.12.

**FIG. 13.12**
You use a signature to tell people more about you, such as how to contact you or how you're feeling about life.

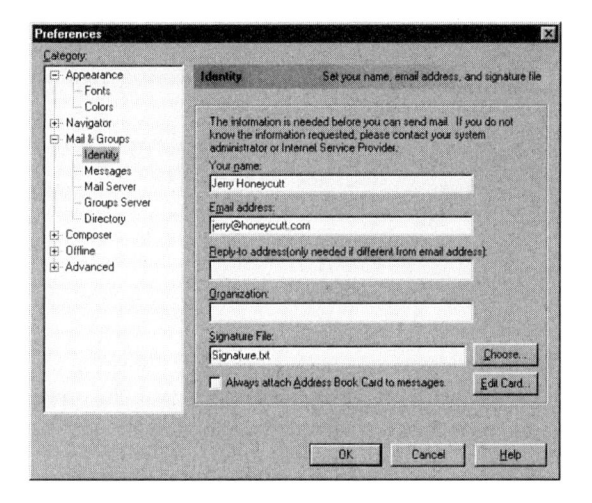

2. Type the name of the text file that contains your signature in Signature File, or click Choose to pick a file from your computer.
3. Click OK to save your changes.

Collabra will now paste your signature into every new message that you create. If you don't want the signature in a particular message, just delete it from the message.

> **CAUTION**
> Unless you know exactly who is going to read your mail, I don't recommend putting your home address or telephone number in your signature. You don't want unexpected guests or strange telephone calls, do you?

## Using Collabra to Read Newsgroups Offline

One of the hottest features in Collabra is the ability to read newsgroups offline, while you're not connected to the Internet. That means that Collabra will download all of the message headers and the contents of each message so that you can read the messages at your own leisure. You save connect time by reading messages offline. Collabra works with local messages much faster than with online messages; thus, your overall experience will be more satisfying.

### Going Offline

Here's how to work with newsgroup messages offline:

1. From either the Message Center or a discussion group folder, choose File, Go Offline from the main menu. You see the Download dialog box shown in Figure 13.13.

**FIG. 13.13**
If you're interested only in downloading newsgroup messages, deselect Download Mail.

2. Click Select Items for Download, and you see the Discussion Groups dialog box. Select the newsgroups that you want to download by clicking the green diamond next to each until the diamond turns into a check mark. Alternatively, you can click Choose All to select all of the newsgroups to which you subscribe. Click OK.

> **TIP** Collabra remembers the newsgroups you selected for offline reading between sessions. Thus, you don't need to reselect the newsgroups unless you want to download a different set from session to session.

3. In the Download dialog box, click Go Offline and Collabra will download all of the messages in the selected newsgroups, and then disconnect from the news server.
4. Read the messages in the newsgroups that you downloaded as though you were connected to the news server.
5. When you're ready to go back online, choose File, Go Online. You see the Download dialog box shown in Figure 13.13, again. Click Go Online to upload any messages that you created while offline and download any new newsgroup messages.

> **NOTE** An alternative approach is to flag each message that you want to read offline by selecting the message and choosing Message, Flag from the main menu. Then, choose File, Get Messages, Flagged for Offline Reading.

## Setting Up the Startup Mode

By default, Collabra connects you to the Internet and updates your message counters each time you open a news server in the Message Center. If you want to work offline, however, that's not the best behavior for a newsreader. You can change this behavior:

1. Choose Edit, Preferences from Navigator's or Collabra's main menu. Select Offline on the left-hand side of the Preferences dialog box (the Category), and you'll see the window shown in Figure 13.14.

http://www.quecorp.com

Using Collabra to Read Newsgroups Offline | 271

**FIG. 13.14**
If you choose Ask Me, Collabra will annoy you every time you open a news server by asking you if you want to connect.

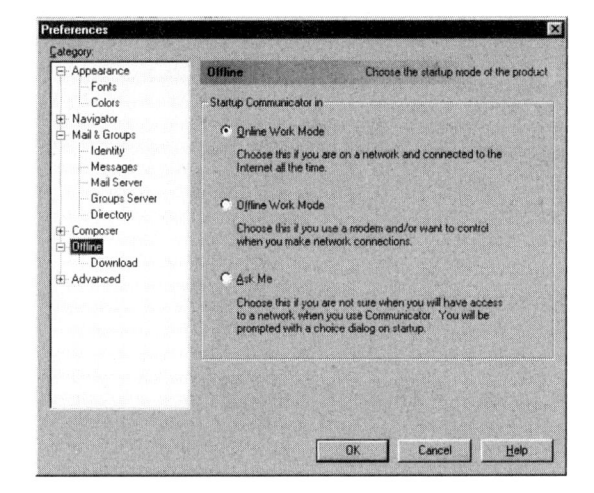

2. Choose Online Work Mode if you want Collabra to connect to the Internet whenever you open a news server in the Message Center. Choose Offline Work mode if you want Collabra to connect to the Internet online when you choose File, Go Online from the Message Center's or discussion folder's main menu.
3. Click OK to save your changes.

CHAPTER 14

# Composer In-Depth

*by Jerry Honeycutt*

In Chapter 6, "Composer Quick Start," you learned the Composer basics. You learned how to create a new HTML document, add text and images, add links, and publish your HTML document. Not a bad start.

This chapter shows you the more advanced features in Composer. It starts off by introducing you to every menu option and toolbar button that Composer has. Then, it shows you how to use those menu options and toolbar buttons to perform common, but advanced, tasks like adding a table or creating a target link. ■

### Use Composer's advanced features
This chapter shows how to use Composer's more advanced features such as spelling check. You also learn how to work with raw HTML.

### Format your HTML document's text and paragraphs
You can easily apply both character and paragraph formatting to your HTML document using Composer's menus or toolbars.

### Work with images, links, and tables like a pro
Advanced HTML doesn't have to elude you. Composer makes adding images, links, and tables to your HTML document as easy as using a word processor.

### Expand Composer via Composer plug-ins
Composer plug-ins add features to Composer that it didn't originally include. Learn how to download, install, and use plug-ins.

# Working with Your HTML Document

In Chapter 6, you learned how to edit text in Composer's window. This section shows you how to do the following things with your HTML document:

- Search for text
- Check for spelling errors
- Preview your HTML document
- Work with raw HTML

## Search for Text

Some of your HTML documents might get pretty big. If so, you might appreciate the ability to search your HTML document for a particular word or phrase. Composer makes it easy to search for text; just follow these steps:

1. Click the Find button on the Composition toolbar. You see the Find dialog box shown in Figure 14.1.

**FIG. 14.1**
This dialog box is identical to the Find dialog box in Windows Notepad.

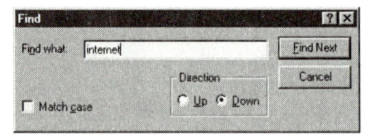

2. Type the word or phrase you want to find in Find what.
3. Click Find Next, and Composer highlights the next occurrence of the search phrase immediately after the insertion point. Note that Composer doesn't close the Find dialog box.
4. Click Find Next again to continue searching the remainder of your HTML document, or click Cancel to close the Find dialog box.

> **TIP** After Composer highlights a block of text as a result of your search, you can drag and drop or cut and paste that block of text just as if you had selected it yourself.

## Check for Spelling Errors

The spelling checker is a marvelous invention. It saves folks like you and me a tremendous amount of embarrassment. Truth be told, if I didn't have a spelling checker while working on this book, the editors would beat me to a pulp. Keep in mind, though, that spelling check isn't a substitute for proofing your HTML documents. There are plenty of errors that it won't catch. You don't have to subject yourself to that kind of embarrassment, either. You can use Composer's spelling checker to make sure that you got everything just right. To use it, follow these steps:

Working with Your HTML Document | 275

1. Click the Check Spelling button on Composer's toolbar. Composer scans your HTML document for any spelling errors. If it doesn't find any, it displays a dialog box that says `Finished checking this page for spelling errors`. If it does find errors, however, you see the Spelling dialog box shown in Figure 14.2.

**FIG. 14.2**
Composer's spelling checker highlights the offending word in the HTML document so that you can see it in context.

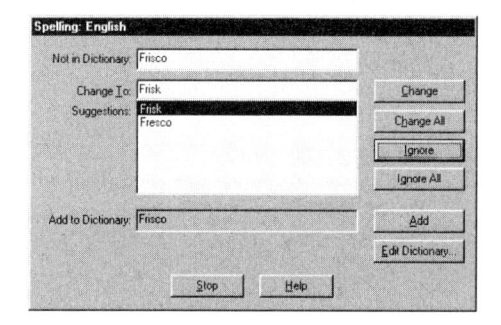

2. After Composer has identified a misspelled word, you can click one of the buttons on the right-hand side of the Spelling dialog box to act on it. The following table describes each button:

| Button | Description |
| --- | --- |
| Change | Makes the suggested change and continues |
| Change All | Changes every occurrence of this spelling |
| Ignore | Ignores the spelling error and continues |
| Ignore All | Ignores every occurrence of this spelling |
| Add | Adds this word to the custom dictionary |
| Edit Dictionary | Adds custom words to the dictionary |
| Stop | Stops spell checking the HTML document |

After Composer has finished spell checking the HTML document, it closes the Spelling dialog box and displays a dialog box that reports `Finished checking this page for spelling errors`. You can, of course, stop the spelling checker at any time by clicking the Stop button.

> **TIP** If you're creating an HTML document that contains a lot of industry-specific keywords, add those keywords to the custom dictionary the first time you use the spelling checker so that it doesn't nag you about them every time.

## Preview the Final Result

There is no sense at all in publishing your HTML document if you don't know what it looks like in real life. Certainly, viewing the HTML document in Composer gives you an idea of what the page looks like, but that's no substitute for the real thing. First of all, you have no guarantee that the combinations of tags you've used work well in Navigator, especially if you're adding your own HTML to the HTML document.

You can easily take a look at your HTML document in Navigator by clicking the View in Browser button on the Composition toolbar. When you browse your new creation in Navigator, you don't see any of the special formatting symbols such as paragraph marks or gridlines.

You can also print your HTML document to get a better look at it. Click the Print this Page button on the Composition toolbar. You see the Print dialog box shown in Figure 14.3.

**FIG. 14.3**
You can change how Composer prints your HTML document by choosing File, Page Setup from the main menu.

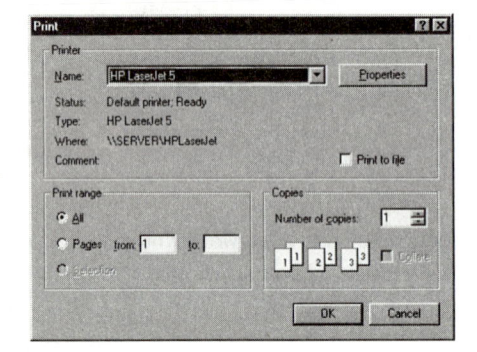

> **TIP** Choose File, Print Preview from Composer's main menu to preview your printout before actually printing it. Then, while previewing the output, click the Print button at the top of the window to actually print it, or press Esc to close the preview window.

## Work with Raw HTML

You probably want to know what your HTML document looks like in raw HTML. Choose View, Page Source from Composer's main menu, and you see the window shown in Figure 14.4. Click the window's Close button to get rid of it.

> **TIP** You can learn how to read raw HTML in *Special Edition Using HTML,* Third Edition, published by Que.

**Insert an HTML Tag**   Composer is a great product, but it has some limitations. It doesn't do frames, style sheets, or layers, for example. To use these HTML features, you're going to have to insert some HTML directly into your HTML document. To do so, follow these steps:

1. Choose Insert, HTML Tag from Composer's main menu, and you see the HTML Tag dialog box shown in Figure 14.5.

http://www.quecorp.com

Working with Your HTML Document | 277

**FIG. 14.4**
This window is actually a Navigator window that is in canvas mode.

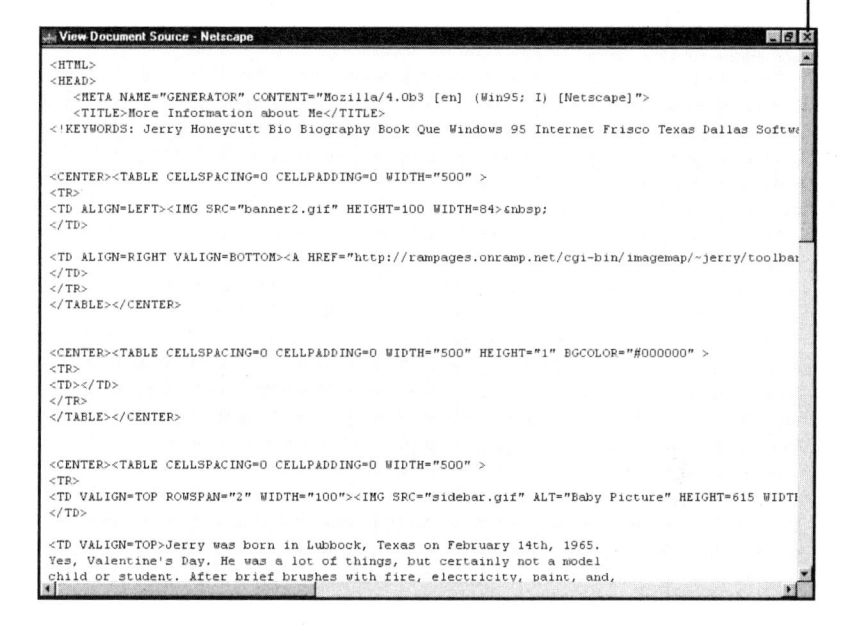

Click to close window

**FIG. 14.5**
You can insert more than one HTML tag at a time using this dialog box.

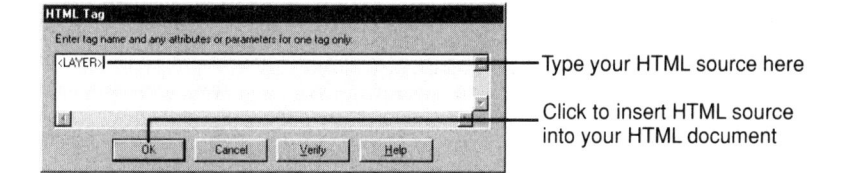

Type your HTML source here

Click to insert HTML source into your HTML document

2. Type your HTML tag in the dialog box, as shown in the figure, and click Verify to make sure that the tag is properly formed.
3. Click OK and Composer adds your HTML tag to the HTML document. Notice that Composer displays a special icon in your HTML document to indicate you've inserted a custom HTML tag (see Table 14.1).

**Table 14.1 Icons Representing Tags**

| Icon | Description |
| --- | --- |
|  | Represents an opening HTML tag |
|  | Represents a closing HTML tag |

Part
II
Ch
14

**NOTE** Composer doesn't do <P> tags; if you insert a paragraph tag into your HTML document, Composer translates it into two <BR> tags.

**Edit the HTML File** If you'll be inserting more than a handful of HTML tags, or the HTML that you're adding to your HTML document is a bit complicated, you can work with your HTML document's HTML file in a text editor. Make sure that you've configured a text editor as described in Chapter 6, "Composer Quick Start"; then, use these steps:

1. Choose Edit, HTML Source from Composer's main menu. If you haven't yet saved your HTML document, you see the Save New Page dialog box; click Save to save your work to an HTML file.
2. If you've made changes to your HTML document since you last saved it, Composer prompts you to save the file. Click Yes to save the file.
3. Composer opens the HTML document's HTML file in the text editor. Make any changes you require, save them, and close the text editor.
4. Composer automatically detects that you changed the HTML file and asks you if you want to reload the page. Click Yes to reload the page. If you're not exactly sure about the changes you made, click No, and resave the file.

**CAUTION**
Don't try to work with your HTML document in both Composer and the text editor at the same time. You'll very likely become confused about what changes you've made in which program and, as a result, will lose some of the changes that you've made.

# Formatting Your HTML Document

You've probably worked with a word processor before in which you formatted text and paragraphs. Composer provides the same two types of formatting as those you've worked with in the past. They are as follows:

- *Character formatting*, with which you format how each character looks on the HTML document.
- *Paragraph formatting*, with which you format how blocks of text called paragraphs look.

You learn about both types of formatting in this section—beginning with character formatting.

## Character Formatting

You can make a stylish, but subtle, impact on your HTML document's appearance using character formatting. A typical example, from the world of publishing, is to use a font face like Arial (a *sans serif* font, which has very straight lines in each character) for headings and a font face

http://www.quecorp.com

# Formatting Your HTML Document 279

like Times (a *serif* font because it has "feet" that hang off the edges of each character) for body text. Then, you make the headings bold and a few points larger than the body text to make sure they stand out.

At first, you might be taken aback because Composer provides three different ways to change a font's face, style, size, and color. You can use the Formatting toolbar, the Format Menu, or the Character Properties dialog box. Don't let all these alternatives throw you, though, because they all do the exact same things. You can use each interchangeably.

Whereas you have to use different menus or toolbar buttons to apply different types of character formatting, you can apply all of the available character formats via the Character Properties dialog box; just follow these steps:

1. Select one or more characters that you want to format. You can use the mouse or the keyboard.
2. Choose Format, Character Properties from the main menu (Windows 95 users can right-click the selected text and choose Character Properties), and you see the dialog box shown in Figure 14.6.

**FIG. 14.6**
The changes you make in the Character Properties dialog box apply to the selected text you see behind it.

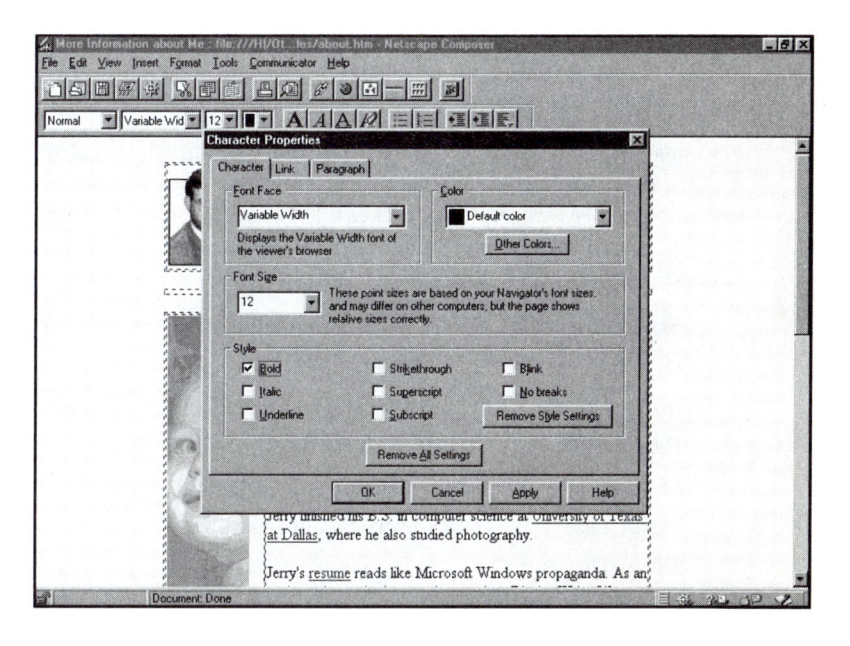

3. Select a font face from Font Face. If you set it to Default Font, that text uses the HTML document's default font face.
4. Select a color from the Color list. Again, set it to Default if you want to use the HTML document's default text color.

5. Select a size from Size. Set it to Default if you want to use the current paragraph style's default font size (you learn about paragraph styles in "Paragraph Formatting," later in this chapter). Note that this isn't the same as using the HTML document's default font size.

6. Select one or more font styles by clicking the box next to each font style until you see a check mark beside it.

7. Click OK to save your changes.

**TIP** You can apply the bold, italic, and underline character formatting using the Ctrl+B, Ctrl+I, and Ctrl+U key combinations, respectively. You can also click the Bold, Italic, and Underline buttons in the Formatting toolbar.

**NOTE** When you move the insertion point, any text you type at that point has the same character formatting as the text immediately to the left of the insertion point. Thus, you can apply formatting on-the-fly by positioning the insertion point anywhere in the HTML document, changing the character formatting in the Character Properties dialog box, and typing any text that you want to use that format.

## Paragraph Formatting

In Composer, you can assign a format to an entire paragraph that affects how it looks. You can assign a format to a paragraph that makes it look like a heading, for example. You can assign a format to another paragraph that makes it look like a citation in a high-school term paper. Composer provides other paragraph formats, such as lists, addresses, and preformatted text, as described here:

| | |
|---|---|
| **Normal** | Normal paragraph text |
| **Heading 1-6** | Heading levels 1 through 6 |
| **Address** | E-mail or physical address |
| **Formatted** | Preformatted text |
| **List Item** | Bulleted, numbered, directory, menu, or description list |
| **Desc. Title** | Description list entry's title |
| **Desc. Text** | Description list entry's text |

**NOTE** For all you HTML hand-coders, a Composer paragraph is any block of text separated by two <BR> tags or enclosed within one of the paragraph formatting tags, such as <H1>, <ADDRESS>, <LI>, and <PRE>. Composer doesn't use the <P> tag to separate paragraphs.

Just like character formatting, you might have gathered that Composer provides three different ways you can apply paragraph formatting. You can use the Formatting toolbar, the Format menu, or the Character Properties dialog box. To change a paragraph's style using the Formatting toolbar, follow these steps:

1. Place the insertion point inside of the paragraph that you want to format.
2. Choose a paragraph style from the Paragraph Style list in the Formatting toolbar, as shown in Figure 14.7.

**FIG. 14.7**
If you're working with lists, you can choose a list format by clicking the Bullet List or Numbered List buttons in the Formatting toolbar.

**Aligning Text**   Composer lets you change how a paragraph is aligned on the page. You can align the text with the left edge of the HTML document or right edge. You can also center the text on the HTML document. You can't use Composer to justify your text on the left and right edges of the HTML document, though. To align a paragraph, follow these steps:

1. Place the insertion point inside the paragraph you want to align.
2. Click the Alignment button in the Formatting toolbar and you see three more buttons drop down, as shown in Figure 14.8.

**FIG. 14.8**
You can choose Align from Composer main menu, and you can choose Left, Center, or Right.

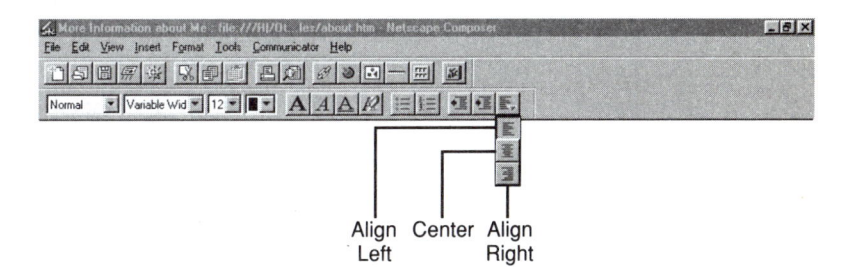

3. Choose Align Left, Center, or Align Right.

**Indenting Text**   You can use Composer to indent the text on your HTML document so that it's offset underneath the preceding text. It shows the middle paragraph indented underneath the first paragraph. To indent text, place the insertion point inside the paragraph you want to indent and click the Increase Indent button on the Formatting toolbar. You can also decrease an indent by clicking the Decrease Indent button.

> **TIP** Composer uses the <UL> (unordered list) tag to indent text.

**Organizing with Headings**   Headings help you organize your text into bite-size pieces that the reader can focus on (look closely at the headings in this chapter for an illustration). They provide a roadmap for the reader so that he can understand the organization and contents of the document. Headings also help the reader immediately find information that's relative to him.

Traditionally, headings are set apart from the body text using white space, or blank lines. The characters in the heading are a bolded sans serif font and are usually a few points larger than the body text. You don't have to worry about these details, however, because you can use the Composer paragraph styles to format a paragraph as a heading. Then, the user's Web browser figures out the best way to display the heading on the screen.

> **TIP**   You can view marks in Composer that make seeing the division between each paragraph easier. Choose View, Paragraph Marks from the main menu.

Creating a heading is quite easy. Place the insertion point inside the paragraph that you want to make a heading and choose one of the heading styles from the Paragraph Style list in the Formatting toolbar.

**Making Lists**   You make lists almost everyday. Shopping lists. To Do lists. Honey Do lists. You even keep a list in your checkbook. The instructions in this book are lists. Lists are an important way in which you keep your thoughts organized.

Likewise, you can use lists on your HTML document to organize your thoughts and present them to the user. You might give the user a series of instructions, for example, or list the top ten castles to visit in Scotland. Composer provides several different types of lists you can use, but only the following two are very useful:

| | |
|---|---|
| **Bulleted** | A bulleted list is an unordered list that uses a special symbol (a bullet) to start each entry. |
| **Numbered** | A numbered list is an ordered list that uses a number to start each entry. |

> **NOTE**   There is little use for directory and menu lists, because most browsers don't implement these lists any differently than bulleted lists.

Creating a list is as easy as indenting text. You click the Bullet List button to create a bulleted list or the Numbered List button to create a numbered list. Then, you start typing. Composer creates a new list item, with its own bullet or number, each time you press the Enter key. To end the list, click the Bullet List button again.

http://www.quecorp.com

> **TIP** Composer doesn't display numbers in numbered lists. To see how your list is actually numbered, you must preview the HTML document in Navigator; click the View in Browser button on the Composition toolbar.

**Dividing the Page** Composer provides many different ways you can create white space on the HTML document. The most common, and the ones you learn about in the rest of this section, are by using line-breaks, non-breaking spaces, and dividing lines.

A line-break does just that—it breaks the line. You can use a line-break to increase the distance between two paragraphs. The easiest way to add a line-break to your HTML document is to just press the Enter key. Composer adds the <BR> (break) tag to your HTML file so that the rest of the text starts on the next line. The more times you press the Enter key, the more blank lines you see before the text starts again.

Spaces don't mean much in HTML, as most browsers compress multiple spaces down to a single space. You can add one or more spaces to your HTML document, however, that a Web browser won't remove. Press Shift+Spacebar, instead of Spacebar, and Composer inserts a non-breaking space into your HTML document. You can press Shift-Spacebar five times, for example, and the Web browser displays five spaces instead of one.

You use a dividing line to break up your HTML document into smaller chunks that the reader can easily absorb. A dividing line marks the end of something and the beginning of something else. It's the perfect element to use to put a not-so-subtle division on your HTML document. To insert a dividing line in your HTML document, place the insertion point at the location you want the dividing line and click the Insert Horiz. Line button from the Composition toolbar.

**Preformatting Text** The paragraph styles that you've learned about in this chapter let you tell Composer how to format a paragraph of text. The user's Web browser displays that text in the best manner possible. It might wrap lines a bit differently than you'd expect; it compacts spaces; and it otherwise controls how each paragraph lays out on the HTML document.

You *can* get control of how the Web browser displays some text, however. While you don't want to make a habit of this, you can format a block of text with all the line breaks, spaces, and tabs that you want and then tell the browser not to touch a single thing. When the browser encounters such a block of text, it doesn't collapse spaces or rewrap any lines of text. It displays the text just as you typed it. Want to know how? Well, follow these steps:

1. Position the insertion point at the location where you want to insert preformatted text.
2. Select the Formatted paragraph style from Composer's Formatting toolbar. You should select this style before you start typing—as opposed to changing an existing paragraph's style—so that you can control the layout of the text as you type.
3. Type the text you want to format. You can use as many spaces, tabs, and line breaks as you need. Figure 14.9 shows what preformatted text looks like in Composer.

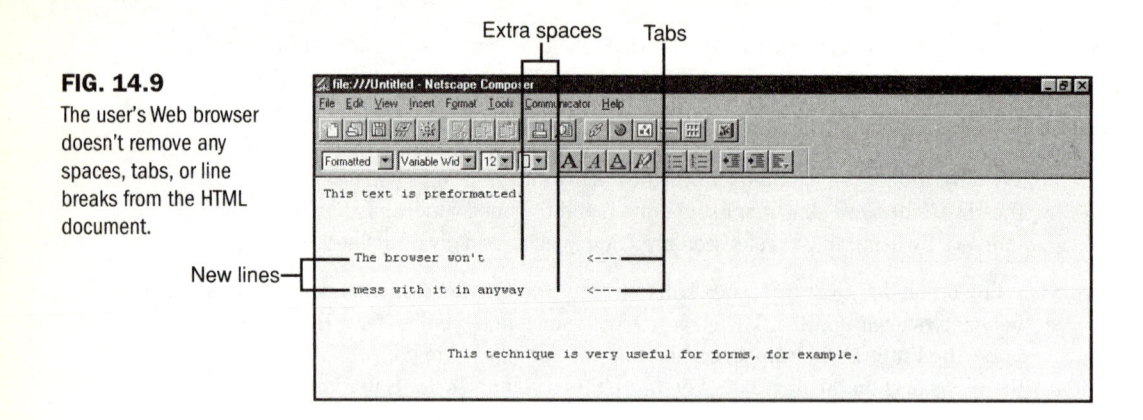

**FIG. 14.9**
The user's Web browser doesn't remove any spaces, tabs, or line breaks from the HTML document.

Extra spaces   Tabs

New lines

# Adding Images to Your HTML Document

In Chapter 6, you learned how to add an image to your HTML document. There's more to an image than just inserting it in the page, however. You can provide alternative text for users who can't see images, for example, or you can better position the image on the HTML document.

## Provide Alternative Text

Many people are using text-only browsers, such as Lynx. As well, folks who have very slow Internet connections might use a graphical browser with images disabled. Doing so allows them to see an HTML document faster because the browser doesn't download the HTML document's image files.

Even though these folks can't see the image itself, you can tell them what they're missing. You use alternative text, which most Web browsers display if they can't display the actual image. Composer doesn't just invent this text, you have to provide it. Follow these steps:

1. Double-click the image for which you want to provide alternative text. You see the same Image Properties dialog box.
2. Click Alt. Text/LowRes and you see the Alternate Image Properties dialog box, as shown in Figure 14.10.

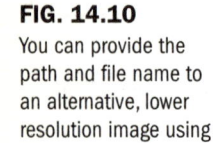

**FIG. 14.10**
You can provide the path and file name to an alternative, lower resolution image using this dialog box.

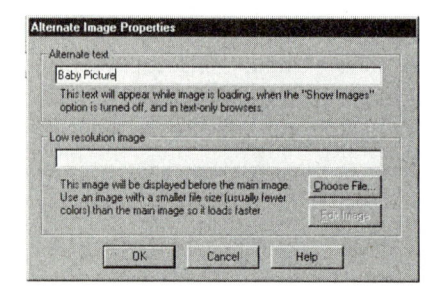

http://www.quecorp.com

3. Type a very brief description of the image in Alternate Text. This should give the user of a text browser an idea of what the image is in as few words as possible.
4. Click OK to save your changes to the alternate text. Click OK again to save your changes to the image properties.

> **TIP** If the image is a very large image, you can provide a much larger alternate description because there is more room to display the text within the dimensions of the image.

## Align Your Image

By default, the Web browser aligns the bottom of the image with the bottom of the text in which it's embedded. If this isn't suitable, you have a variety of alternatives. For example, to align the top of the image with the top of the text, follow these steps:

1. Double-click the image you want to align and you see the dialog box shown in 14.11.

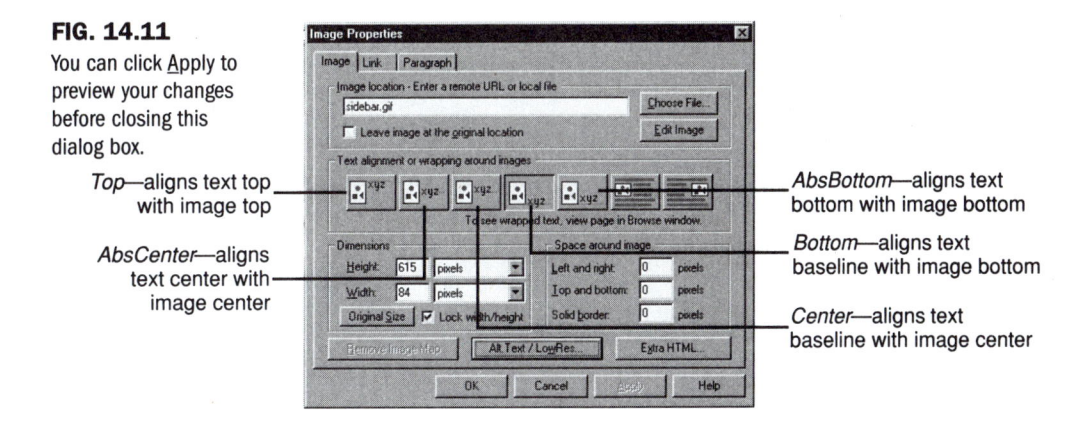

**FIG. 14.11**
You can click Apply to preview your changes before closing this dialog box.

*Top*—aligns text top with image top

*AbsCenter*—aligns text center with image center

*AbsBottom*—aligns text bottom with image bottom

*Bottom*—aligns text baseline with image bottom

*Center*—aligns text baseline with image center

2. Click one of the buttons representing an alignment, as described in Figure 14.11.
3. Click OK to save your changes.

## Position the Image

You can cause the Web browser to wrap text around an image by setting its alignment to left or right. Setting it to left causes the image to float to the left side of the browser window and the text to wrap around the image's right side. Setting it to right causes the image to float to the right side of the browser window and the text to wrap around the image's left side.

The instructions for floating an image to the left or right side of your HTML document are very similar to the instructions in the previous section; they are as follows:

1. Double-click the image you want to align and you see the Image Properties dialog box.
2. Click the Left button to float the image to the left side of the browser window or click the Right button to float the image to the right side of the browser window.
3. Click OK to save your changes.

> **TIP** You can get more complete control over how a Web browser displays an image by using tables to format your HTML document. Add a table to your HTML document and then insert images into each cell of the table. That way, you have control over where the image lands on the page and how it's positioned in relation to the content around it.

## Add a Margin

By default, there's not much room between the text and the image. Publishing-wise, that's not good. The user's eyes need someplace to rest, and they're not going to get any rest that way. You can add some space around each image, called a margin, so that they're not quite as crowded. To add a margin, follow these steps:

1. Double-click the image around which you want to add space. You see the Image Properties dialog box.
2. Type the width, in pixels, of the left and right margins for the image in Left and Right.
3. Type the width, in pixels, of the top and bottom margins for the image in Top and Bottom.
4. Click OK to save your changes.

## Create a Background

You can also use an image as a background. Then, everything on the HTML document displays over the background—kind of like a fancy watermark on stationary. You need to find a suitable image to use as a background, because the Web browser tiles the image. That is, the Web browser repeats the image horizontally and vertically to fill the entire browser window. Keep that in mind so the right side of the image matches the left side, and the top of the image matches the bottom.

After you select an image, you can use these steps to use it as a background image:

1. Choose Format, Page Colors and Properties from Composer's main menu and click the Colors and Background tab. You see the dialog box shown in Figure 14.12.
2. Type the path and file name to the background image in Use Image or click Choose File to browse your computer for an image file.
3. Click OK to save your changes.

http://www.quecorp.com

**FIG. 14.12**
You can also use this dialog box to change the colors used for links.

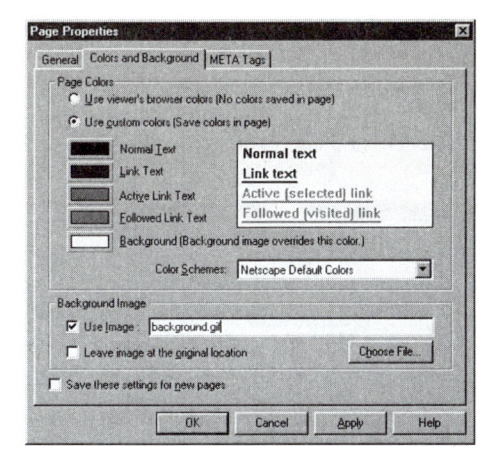

## Adding Links to Your HTML Document

You learned about creating links in Chapter 6. This section shows you a bit more about links, such as how to change or remove a link. It also shows you how to create links that point to locations within an HTML document.

### Change a Link

You use the same dialog box that you used to create a link to change a link. Place your insertion point anywhere within the text anchor or select the graphical anchor, and click the Insert/Make Link button on the Composition toolbar. You see the same dialog box that you used to create the link. You can make any changes to this link's URL reference that you like. Click OK to save your changes.

### Remove a Link

To remove a link from your HTML document, place the insertion point anywhere within the text anchor or select the graphical anchor, and choose Edit, Remove Links. Composer removes the URL reference from the link.

> **TIP** You can remove more than one link at a time (a great way to start over). Highlight a block of text that contains multiple links. Then, choose Edit, Remove Links, and Composer removes all of the selected links. Composer doesn't remove any of the text or images, however.

### Change a Link's Colors

Links have three different colors that describe what the link looks like at different times. These three colors specify what the link looks like before you've clicked it, while you are clicking it, and after you've clicked it (visited links).

In most cases, you want to use the default colors for links. If you do want to change the colors used for links, however, use these steps:

1. Choose F_ormat, Page Colors and Properties from the main menu and click the Colors and Background tab. You see the Page Properties dialog box shown in Figure 14.13.

**FIG. 14.13**
You can also use this dialog box to change the color of normal text and the HTML document's background.

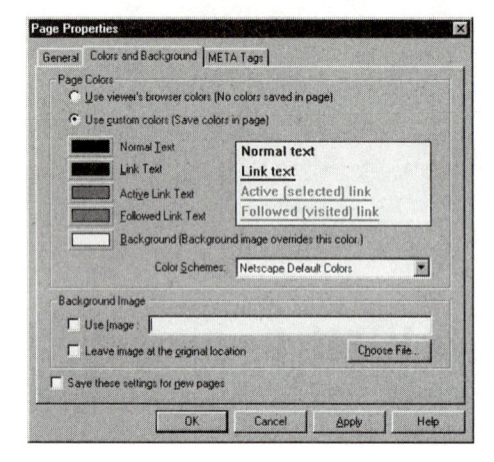

2. To change the color used for unvisited links, click Link Text; choose a color from the palette; and click OK. Likewise, click Active Link Text to change the color that links use while they're being clicked. Followed Link Text changes the color that links use after they've been visited.
3. Click OK to save your changes to the HTML document.

> **TIP** You can also change the color for normal text and the background by clicking Normal Text and Background on the Page Properties dialog box, respectively.

## Create Internal Links

You've seen how to create a link to another HTML document or resource on the Internet. You can also create a link that jumps to the middle of any of your own HTML documents. For example, you can put a brief outline of an HTML document at the top of the page, and then when the user clicks one of the links in the outline, the Web browser jumps down to that section.

You perform two steps to link to locations within a HTML document. First, you create a named anchor. Then, you link to that named anchor. The rest of this section shows you how to do both steps.

**Create a Named Anchor**   Named anchors are similar to the anchors you've already learned about. They don't have an URL reference, however, and the browser doesn't underline them in the HTML document. Instead, they give a name to a certain location within an HTML document (as the name implies).

http://www.quecorp.com

After you create a named anchor, you can use it as a target of a link. While you're trying out these steps for the first time, use an HTML document that's more than one page long. Otherwise, you see the Web browser jumping to the named anchor because the page contains both the link and the named anchor. To add a named anchor to your HTML document, follow these steps:

1. Position the insertion point at the location where you want to add a named anchor. In this case, position the insertion point at the end of the HTML document so that the example is more dramatic.

2. Click the Insert Target button in the Composition toolbar. Composer displays the dialog box shown in Figure 14.14.

**FIG. 14.14**
Keep your names short and simple so that you can easily remember them.

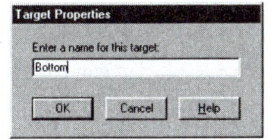

3. Type a name for the named anchor and click OK. You see the named target icon, which marks the location of the named anchor.

> **TIP** Composer displays an icon in the HTML document to represent a named anchor (the browser doesn't, by the way). Thus, you can make the HTML document easier to work on if you insert named anchors at the beginning of a line instead of in the middle of a line. The effect is the same.

**Create a Link to that Anchor**  After you've added a named anchor to your HTML document, you're ready to link to it. Follow these steps:

1. Select the text you want to use as a link to the named anchor.

2. Click the Insert/Make Link button in the Composition toolbar and you see the dialog box shown in Figure 14.15.

**FIG. 14.15**
You can also link to named anchors in other HTML documents by typing the URL of the HTML document in the space provided.

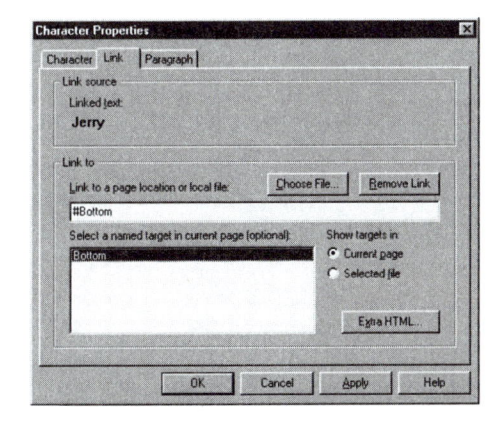

3. Select one of the named anchors from the bottom list.
4. Click OK to save your changes.

You can try this out in Composer by right-clicking the new link and choosing Browse To. You are better off trying this example out in Navigator, however, so that you can see the effect of clicking the link to jump to another location in your HTML document.

> **TIP** Professional Web developers typically put links at the bottom of the HTML document that point to a named anchor at the top of the page. This way, the user has a quick and easy way to get back to the top of the page.

# Adding Tables to Your HTML Document

What can you do with HTML tables in Composer? A lot. You can use tables to present tabular data. You can correlate, compare, and analyze information—not just numbers, either. You can use tables to organize your thoughts in a visual manner. However, the most common use for HTML tables is as a formatting tool. For example, take a look at the HTML source for most of the well formatted HTML documents on the Internet. You'll notice that they're formatted with tables.

## Add a Table to Your HTML Document

The easiest way to add a table is to use Composer and accept all of its defaults. That's where you begin in this section. Ready? Use these steps to add a basic table to your HTML document:

1. Position the insertion point at the location where you want to add your table.
2. Click the Insert Table button on the Composition toolbar. You see the New Table Properties dialog box shown in Figure 14.16.

**FIG. 14.16**
You can control every single facet of how your table appears using this dialog box.

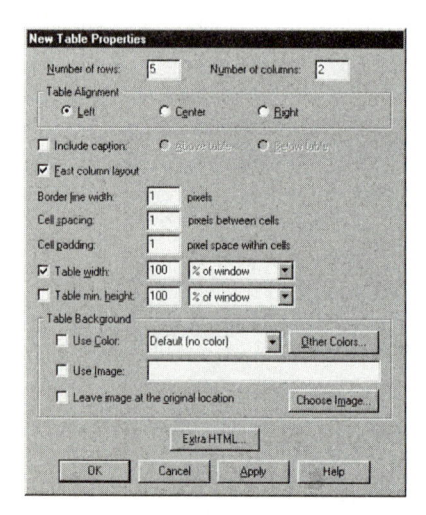

3. Type the number of rows you want in Number of Rows and the number of columns in Number of Columns. For example, to create a table with five rows and three columns, type **5** in Number of Rows and **3** in Number of Columns.
4. Click OK to create the table in your HTML document.

**Creating a Borderless Table**   If you're going to use a table as a formatting tool, you don't want any borders around the table. After all, the table is just a layout guide for the HTML document. Borders would look kind of tacky. You can make your table borderless when you create it. Change Border Line Width to 0 in the New Table Properties dialog box you learned about earlier.

**Choosing a Background Color**   If you are using a table to present data, you might want to color it in. To add color to your table, follow these steps:

1. In the New Table Properties dialog box, select Use Color.
2. Pick the color you want for the table to be by selecting a standard color from the list, or click Other Colors to pick a color from the Color dialog box.
3. Click OK to save your changes.

**Aligning the Table on the Page**   By default, the user's Web browser positions tables at the left margin of the HTML document. This isn't always the most attractive place to position a table, however, particularly if the table doesn't fill in the entire width of the HTML document. You can choose to align your table in the center of the HTML document or on the right margin. Choose Left, Center, or Right at the bottom of the New Table Properties dialog box.

**Changing the Width of the Table**   By far, the most frustrating part of using a table in your Web is getting the width of the table just right. Composer's default is to let the table occupy 100 percent of the HTML document's width. That's fine in many cases; in other cases, you might want a bit more control. You can specify a table's width either in percentages or in screen pixels. To do this, follow these steps:

1. In the New Table Properties dialog box, make sure Table Width is selected.
2. Select Pixels or % of Window from the list that's to the right of Table Width. If you want to specify an exact width in pixels, use Pixels. If you want the size of the table to be relative to the width of the Web browser's window, choose % of Window.
3. If you selected Pixels in Step 2, type the number of pixels wide that you want the table to be in the space provided. If you selected % of Window in Step 2, type the percentage of the browser window that you want the table to occupy in the space provided.

**N O T E**   This section has showed you how to control the width of the entire table. You can also control the width of each individual cell in the table. Combining control of the table's width and each cell's width gives you a lot of formatting flexibility.

## Change an Existing Table

After you create a table, you'll no doubt want to make a few changes. Left out a column? Don't worry, you don't have to start from scratch. You can change any portion of the table at any time. To change your table, follow these steps:

1. Place the insertion point anywhere within the table and choose Format, Table Properties from the main menu. Then, click the Table tab and you see the Table Properties dialog box shown in Figure 14.17.

**FIG. 14.17**
You can change any of the table properties that you initially set when you first added the table to your HTML document.

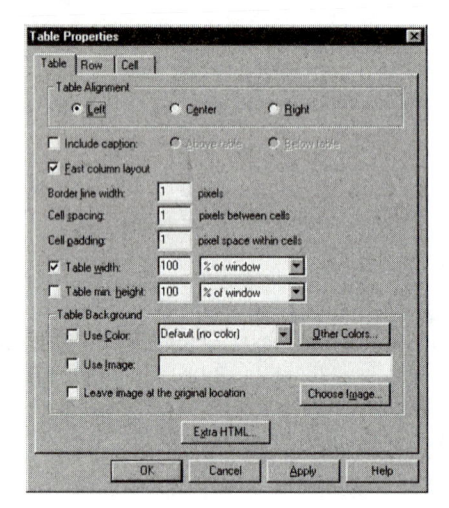

2. Change the properties of the dialog box as you require. You might find that you often use this dialog box to change the alignment or width of the table.
3. Click OK to save your changes.

**Adding Rows or Columns** You don't have to start your table over from scratch to add a row or column to it. You can use Composer to insert a new one by following these steps:

1. Position the insertion point in the row or column after which you want to insert a new row or column. For example, if you want to add a column to the end of the table, put the insertion point in any cell in the last column of the table.
2. Choose Insert, Table, Row to add a new row to the table. Choose Insert, Table, Column to add a new column to the table.

**Deleting Rows or Columns** Not only will you occasionally want to add a row or column, but you might want to delete a row or column, too. Just remember that when you delete a row or column, you lose the content in that row or column. To nuke a row or column, follow these steps:

Adding Tables to Your HTML Document | 293

1. Position the insertion point in the row or column you want to delete. You can put the insertion point in any cell within that row or column.
2. Choose Edit, Delete Table, Row to remove the row. Choose Edit, Delete Table, Column to remove the column.

## Change Rows and Cells

You can't avoid it. At some point, you're going to get down to the nitty-gritty and start working with each individual row and cell in your table. Maybe you want to format a row or a few cells differently than the others. If your table is going to have headings, for example, you need to format the cells in the first row as headings.

You work with a table's rows and cells using the Table Properties dialog box that you saw earlier. Instead of using the Table tab, however, you use the Row and Cell tab. To format a row or cell, follow these steps:

1. If you want to format a row, place the insertion point in any cell of that row. If you want to format one or more cells, select each cell using the mouse (just like selecting text).
2. Choose Format, Table Properties from the main menu.
3. Click the Row tab to format the selected row and you see the dialog box shown in Figure 14.18. Click the Cell tab to format the selected cell and you see the dialog box shown in Figure 14.19.
4. Make your changes to the Row or Cell tabs and click OK.

**FIG. 14.18**
The Row tab lets you choose how text is formatted within each row.

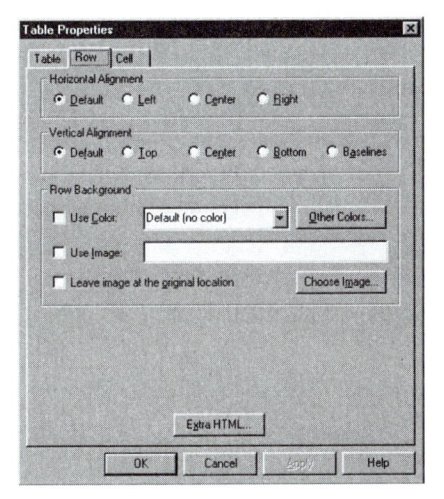

**FIG. 14.19**
You can also apply cell formatting to an entire row of cells.

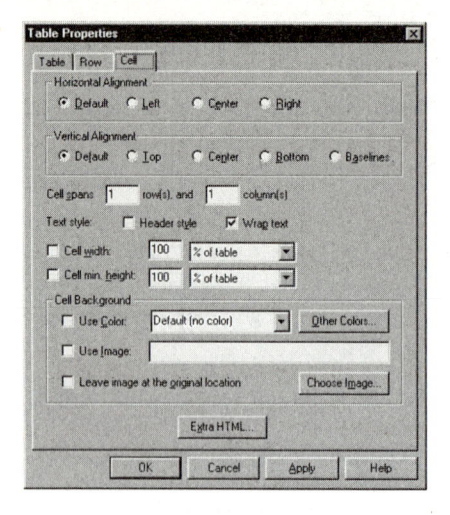

**Using Color with Rows or Cells**  There are a lot of reasons you might want to change the color of a row or cell. For example, many folks use a different color for the first row of the table, which contains the table's headings. You can also change a cell's color to highlight a particular value. To change a cell's or row's color, follow these steps:

1. In the Table Properties dialog box, click the Row tab if you want to change the color of a row; otherwise, click the Cell tab.
2. In either the Row or Cell tab, select Use Color and select a standard color from the list. You can also click Other Colors to pick a color from the Color dialog box.
3. Click OK.

**Aligning Text within a Row or Cell**  If you look at many tables that are used to present data, you might notice that different cells are aligned differently. For example, a column of numbers might be right aligned, while a column of product names might be left aligned or centered. To align the text in your tables, follow these steps:

1. To align the text within a row, click the Row tab of the Table Properties dialog box. To align the text within one or more cells, click the Cell tab of the Table Properties dialog box.
2. Select how you want the content within each cell aligned horizontally and vertically, as described in Table 14.2.
3. Click OK to save your changes.

**Table 14.2  Row and Cell Alignment Options**

| Option | Description |
| --- | --- |
| **Horizontal Alignment** | |
| Left | Aligns the content to the left |
| Center | Centers the content within the cell |
| Right | Aligns the content to the right |
| **Vertical Alignment** | |
| Top | Aligns the top of the content with top |
| Center | Aligns the center of the content in the cell |
| Bottom | Aligns the bottom of the content at the bottom |
| Baselines | Aligns the baselines of the text across cells |

**Changing the Size of a Cell**   Working with the size of individual cells in raw HTML can be very frustrating but because Composer is a WYSIWYG editor, it's a lot easier. To change the size of a cell, follow these steps:

1. In the Cell tab of the Table Properties dialog box, make sure Cell Width is selected.
2. Select Pixels or % of Window from the list that's to the right of Cell Width. If you want to specify an exact width in pixels, use Pixels. If you want the size of the table to be relative to the width of the Web browser's window, choose % of Window.
3. If you selected Pixels in Step 2, type the number of pixels wide that you want the table to be in the space provided. If you selected % of Window in Step 2, type the percentage of the browser window that you want the table to occupy in the space provided.

**N O T E**   You can specify the width of a single cell in the table, and then let the Web browser figure out the best size for the remaining cells. For example, you might want the first column to be exactly 120 pixels width, while you don't care about the size of the remaining columns. In that case, set the width of the first cell in the first column to 120 pixels and let the browser figure out the rest.

**Merging Table Cells (Spanning)**   The most difficult table concept to grasp, even for seasoned HTML pros, is cell spanning. Cell spanning allows you to join two or more cells so they become one cell. For example, if you have a table with two rows and two columns, you can join the top two cells so that there's one cell in the first row and two cells in the bottom row. This type of technique is important if you're going to use tables to lay out your HTML document. To span cells, follow these steps:

1. Position the insertion pointer in the upper-left cell of the block of cells you want to span.
2. In the Cell tab of the Table Properties dialog box, type the number of rows you want to span in the Row(s) and the number of columns you want to span in Column(s).

# Using Composer Plug-Ins to Enhance Composer

A Composer plug-in is a component that you add to Composer. You can think of plug-ins like you think of the components of your stereo system. When you want to add features to your stereo, such as the ability to play music CDs, you drop in another component, like a CD player. When you want to add a feature to Composer, you drop in a plug-in that provides that feature.

## Plugging In to Plug-Ins

Composer plug-ins work with the HTML in your HTML document, but they do their work outside of Composer. You need to understand this concept, so we'll walk through it step-by-step. Here's what happens when you start a plug-in:

1. Composer runs the plug-in and hands it all of the HTML that makes up your HTML document.
2. You interact with the plug-in in its own window. That is, the plug-in opens its own window outside of Composer's window (see Figure 14.20).

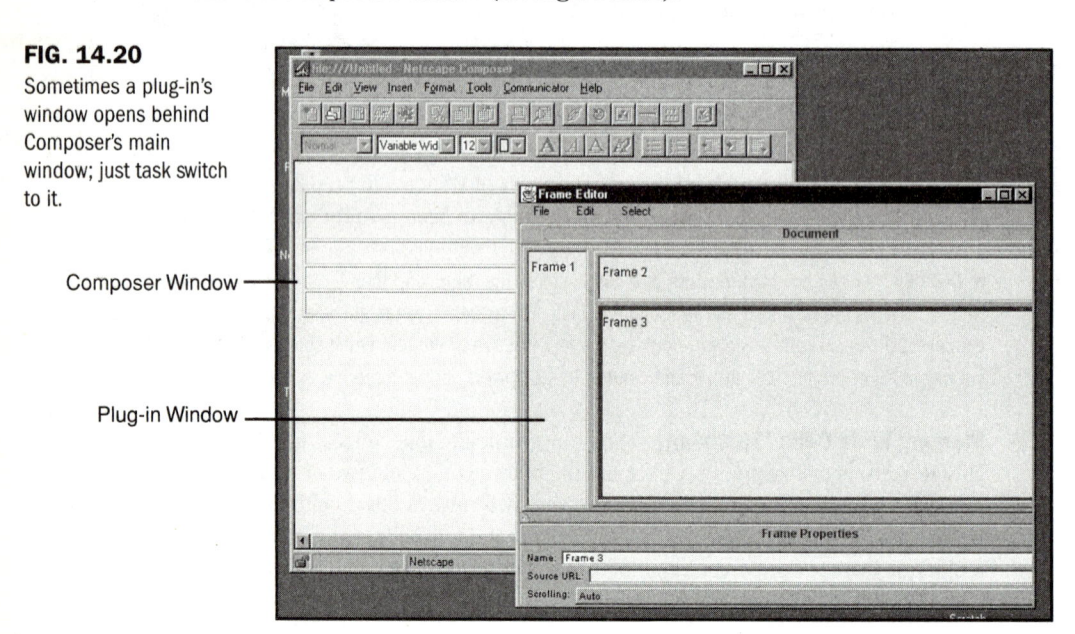

**FIG. 14.20**
Sometimes a plug-in's window opens behind Composer's main window; just task switch to it.

Composer Window

Plug-in Window

3. The plug-in changes the HTML to reflect your input as you interact with it.
4. The plug-in hands all of your HTML document's HTML back to Composer when you close it so that you can continue editing the HTML document.

http://www.quecorp.com

Using Composer Plug-Ins to Enhance Composer | 297

> Due to the way Composer plug-ins work, you might notice an interesting side effect. Because Composer plug-ins don't work within Composer, Composer doesn't always display the HTML document correctly after the plug-in has done its trick. In cases like these, you see the HTML tag icons that represent any HTML tags Composer can't handle. For example, Composer doesn't know how to display the <STYLE> tag. If you use a plug-in to add styles to your HTML document, Composer doesn't display the layers correctly; it displays the HTML tag icons instead.

## Downloading Sample Composer Plug-Ins

What kinds of Composer plug-ins exist? Well, anyone and everyone who can write a Java applet can create a Composer plug-in. So, you can expect to find a variety of sources for plug-ins. Try searching your favorite Web index, for example, for interesting and useful plug-ins.

Until third-party Composer plug-ins start popping up here and there, you can download and try the handful of plug-ins that Netscape provides. The sections that follow describe the types of plug-ins you can find on Netscape's Web site, as well as how to download and install them.

**Where to Find Plug-Ins**  You can find Netscape's Composer plug-ins at **http://developer.netscape.com/library/examples/plugins/composer/index.html**. Table 14.3 describes each file that you can download from this HTML document and the plug-ins that each file contains.

**Table 14.3  Composer Plug-Ins from Netscape**

| Plug-In Name | Description |
|---|---|
| **cpTest.zip** | |
| Colorize | Makes selected text very colorful |
| Document Info | Displays document statistics |
| Edit HTML | Allows you to edit the raw HTML |
| Netscape Button | Adds a Netscape Now button |
| Small Caps | Changes font style to small caps |
| Tableize | Makes a table from selected text |
| Tag Stripper | Removes all HTML tags from selection |
| Test Applet | Adds a NervousText Java applet |
| **cpMapEdt.zip** | |
| Image Map Editor | Creates client-side imagemaps |

*continues*

### Table 14.3 Continued

| Plug-In Name | Description |
| --- | --- |
| **cpFrames.zip** | |
| Frame Editor | Creates framesets and frames |
| **cpGIFEnc.zip** | |
| GIF Encoder | Converts images to GIF89a |
| **cpInSpec.zip** | |
| Special Character | Inserts a special character |
| **cpTOC.zip** | |
| Table of Contents | Generates a table of contents |

**Downloading a Plug-In** Each time Netscape Communicator starts, it looks in the Plug-In folder for any plug-in files. Each plug-in is stored in either a JAR or ZIP compressed file. You don't have to decompress them, however, just drop them in the Netscape Plug-In folder. To download and install a plug-in, follow these steps:

1. Open the HTML document that contains the Composer plug-in you want to download.
2. Click the link to the plug-in's JAR or ZIP file and, after a few moments, you see the Unknown File Type dialog box.
3. Click Save File to save the plug-in to your Plug-In folder and you see the renowned Save As dialog box.
4. Type the path to the Netscape Plug-In folder in the space provided. Alternatively, browse your computer for the Plug-In folder. Table 14.4 shows the folder for which you're looking, depending on the platform you use.

### Table 14.4 Netscape Plug-In Folders

| Platform | Folder |
| --- | --- |
| Mac | Plug-ins, directly under the Netscape folder |
| Windows | Plug-ins, directly under the Netscape folder |
| UNIX | /usr/local/netscape/plug-ins |

4. Click Save and Netscape downloads the file to the Plug-In folder.
5. Close and restart Netscape Communicator.

## Using a Composer Plug-In

Each time you start Composer, it takes a peek in the Plug-In folder and loads each plug-in file it finds. Each file might contain a single plug-in that adds a menu option to Composer's Tools menu. Menu options specific to each plug-in are on that plug-in's submenu. Figure 14.21 shows you what the Tools menu looks like after installing the files shown in Table 14.5.

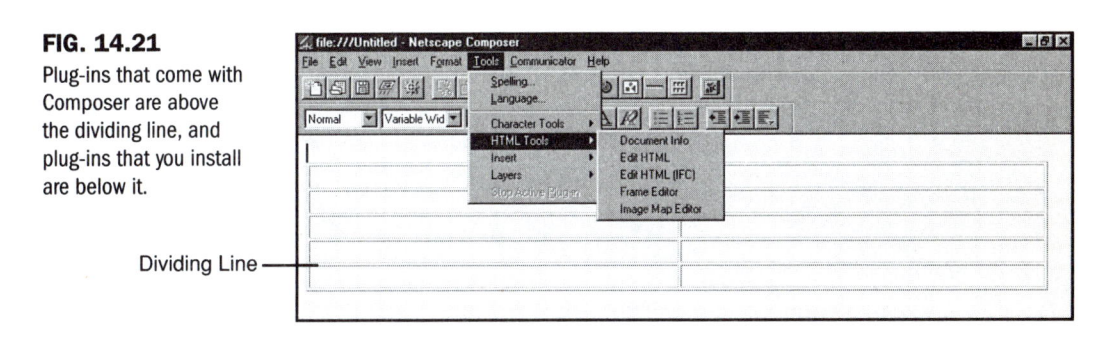

**FIG. 14.21**
Plug-ins that come with Composer are above the dividing line, and plug-ins that you install are below it.

Dividing Line

> **N O T E** Most plug-ins drop a menu option on the Tools menu. These plug-ins are called *menu option plug-ins*. Other plug-ins, called *event handler plug-ins*, work behind the scenes. You don't interact with them at all.

CHAPTER 15

# Conference In-Depth

by *Mark R. Brown*

How would you like to have free long-distance telephone service for life? "Wow! Is this a prize in the lottery?" you ask. Not exactly. All you need is Internet access and a sound card to be able to call anyone, anywhere, anytime, for free.

Of course, there are a few catches. The people you call also have to have Internet access and a sound card. They need to be connected to the Internet when you try to call. They have to be running compatible Internet telephony software. It's not as easy as just picking up a phone and dialing. (Though if you think about it, the requirements are similar—you can't call someone on the phone if they're not connected to the phone system or don't own a telephone.) If you have a cousin in France, a fiancé in Alaska, or just like to call your Mom back home in Biloxi for a couple of hours every night, these shortcomings might not mean much compared to the savings you'll realize.

This free (except for ISP charges) telephone magic is accomplished by using Netscape Communicator's built-in collaboration tool, Conference. But Conference lets you do more than just make free phone calls. Its Chat Tool lets you converse with another Conference user by typing in text. Built-in File Transfer lets you share files online. Collaborative browsing lets you surf the Web together. But the Whiteboard is probably Conference's coolest option—it lets you load up graphics (even snapshots of

- **You can use Conference to call anyone, anywhere for free**

  Even over a dial-up connection, it's realistic to use the Internet for voice communications.

- **The hardware and software requirements for Internet voice communications are low**

  If you have a sound card, you can probably use your computer to talk on the Internet.

- **Conference's tools expand and enhance its voice chat capabilities**

  Text chat, file exchange, collaborative browsing, and the conference Whiteboard are useful real-world tools.

- **You can use Conference in a corporate environment or at home**

  Though it has some limitations, Netscape Conference is a thorough and useful collaboration tool.

your work screens) and share them over the Net. Better yet, you can both mark up the screen and see the comments you both make. This sort of functionality is called *collaborative software* by groupware developers, and it's currently one of the hottest areas of software development.

## System Requirements

If your computer is capable of connecting to the Internet, the odds are excellent that you already have the one additional component that you need to be able to digitize your voice to transmit, and then to convert the data you receive from the Net back into voice—a sound card.

You also have to have the following:

- At least a 50 MHz 486 CPU or comparable Mac or UNIX system
- 12M to 16M of RAM
- A set of self-amplified speakers
- A microphone, preferably with an on/off switch
- A reliable connection to the Internet (14.4Kbps dial-up or better)

> **CAUTION**
> Real-time voice communication on the Internet is a real system hog. It uses lots of CPU time, hardware resources, and RAM. If you're going to be talking on the Internet, it's best to refrain from running any other tasks. Otherwise, your audio feed is likely to break up.

> **NOTE** Contrary to popular belief, you don't have to have a direct TCP/IP connection to the Internet to use Conference. You can talk just fine over a SLIP or PPP dial-up connection via a 14.4 or 28.8Kbps (Kilobits per second) modem. Voice communications don't use nearly the bandwidth that graphics and video do, so chatting over the Internet on a dial-up connection is not only realistic, but, under ideal conditions, is indistinguishable from communicating over a direct connection.

All sound cards can convert digital data to audible audio, and most can also digitize audio in real-time from a microphone input. Almost any sound card that can do both can be used with Conference.

A 16-bit stereo sound card is best; though an 8-bit card will work okay, a 16-bit card will give you better sound quality and trouble-free compatibility. Creative Labs' Sound Blaster 16 is the industry standard; if you have a Sound Blaster card or compatible hooked up to a microphone and a set of speakers or headphones, you're all set for holding conversations on the Internet with Conference.

> **CAUTION**
> Windows 95 multitasking doesn't mean you can use two programs that use the sound card at the same time. For example, you can't play MIDI music files while chatting on the Internet.

Most sound cards operate in *half duplex* mode—that is, you can record audio or play audio, but you can't do both simultaneously. This means that your Internet conversations are limited to a one-way-at-a-time mode. Most people have experienced this type of conversation when using a CB radio or speakerphone; while one person is talking, the other listens. Participants in a conversation must take turns.

There are a few sound cards on the market that support *full duplex* mode—that is, they can record and play sound simultaneously. With such cards, Conference supports full telephone-style two-way conversations.

## Configuring Conference

When you select Conference from the Communicator menu, you get the small window shown in Figure 15.1. Before you can use Conference, though, you need to set some Preference options.

**FIG. 15.1**
From the main Communicator window, you can easily make an Internet phone call or launch one of the other Conference tools.

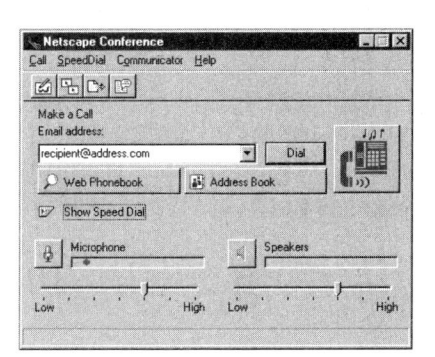

In Chapter 7, "Conference Quick Start," you walked through the Conference Setup Wizard, which sets up the information that's necessary to run Conference. But if you later need to change or add configuration information, you can do so via the Call menu—just select the Preferences menu item and you get the dialog box shown in Figure 15.2.

This dialog box has three tabs labeled Network, Business Card, and Audio. The Network tab is, by default, the one that is displayed first.

The DLS (Dynamic Lookup Service) Server field lists the public server on which you are listed when you're online and Conference is running. It defaults to the Netscape/Four11 server at **netdls.four11.com**. If you know of another server and prefer to be listed on it, enter the URL for that server in this field (omit the http://).

**FIG. 15.2**
The Network preferences tab is the first thing you see in the Preferences dialog box.

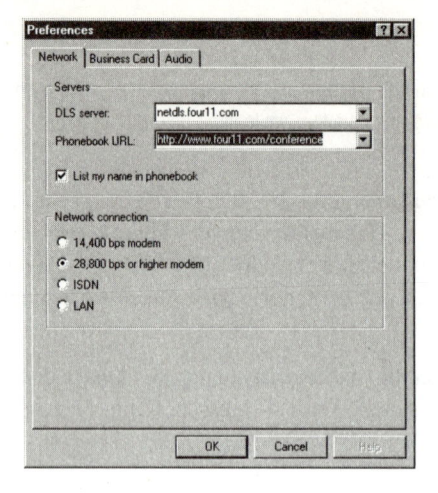

The Phonebook URL field lists the Web phonebook that you access when making calls using the Web Phonebook button in the Conference window. Again, this defaults to the Four11 server, whose lookup address is **http://www.four11.com/conference**. If you prefer to use another, you can enter its URL.

Both of these fields feature drop-down menus of any servers you've entered previously. The DLS Server field also allows you to select <None> if you prefer not to make Conference calls. You must have a valid entry in the DLS Server field to make Conference calls. However, if you prefer not to be listed publicly in an online directory, you should uncheck the check box labeled List My Name in Phonebook. This essentially gives you an unlisted number.

The Network Connection area of this dialog box lets you specify your connection speed. You should pick one of the following four choices:

- 14.4Kbps modem
- 28.8Kbps or higher modem
- ISDN
- LAN

Choose LAN if you are connected to a corporate intranet or a direct Internet connection like a T1 line.

Clicking the Audio tab brings up the panel shown in Figure 15.3.

Conference automatically detects whether your audio card is half duplex or full duplex, and tells you which you have at the top of this panel beside the label Operation Mode.

If your card is half duplex, you cannot send and receive audio at the same time. The Recording/Playback Autoswitch check box lets you indicate that you want Conference to automatically switch into send mode when you speak. If this box is unchecked, you have to manually switch between microphone and speaker modes by clicking the mike and speaker buttons in the Conference window.

**FIG. 15.3**
The Audio panel (right) lets you make minute adjustments to match your audio card and drivers to the Conference software. The Advanced panel (left) lets you fine-tune your settings.

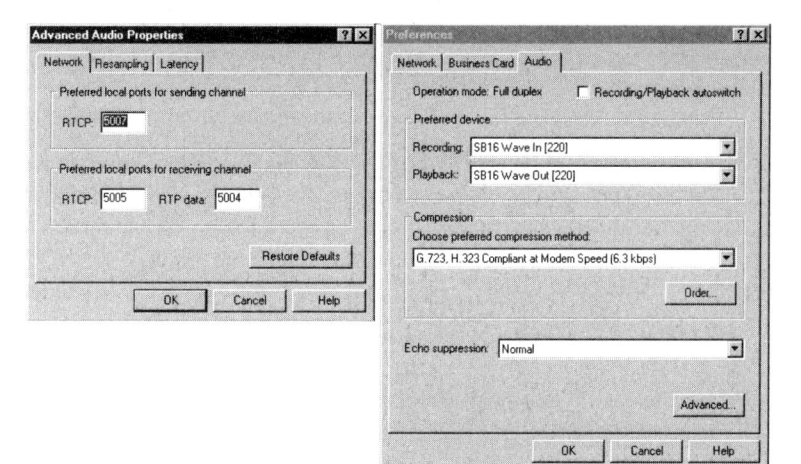

> **TROUBLESHOOTING**
>
> **I've got a half duplex sound card. Why is it that sometimes I can't hear the other person or they can't hear me?** You probably need to adjust the Silence Sensor. It's the movable button on the sound level meter next to the microphone button. Turn on your mike, but don't speak, and adjust the button until it's just beyond the noise level indicated by the moving bar. This sets it so that your mike only kicks in when you talk, and your speakers kick in when you're not talking. You might have to do this a couple of times to get it to work well. For this setting to automatically switch your mike in when you talk, you have to have selected the Autoswitch check box in the Audio Preferences setting, as explained earlier.

If you have more than one audio card installed in your computer, you can use the Preferred Device fields to specify which is used for Recording and which for Playback.

The Compression field chooses which audio codec (compression/decompression) method Conference uses for audio communications. When you connect to another Internet phone application, the programs try to find a codec in their list that they both understand. You can find three codecs listed in the drop-down list. You can choose the order on which they are tried by clicking the Order button and using the Up and Down arrows to move the entries in the list.

**N O T E** Though Conference uses the H.323 phone communication "standard," this standard uses several different codecs. Just because an Internet phone program claims to be H.323-compliant doesn't necessarily mean that you can speak to it. For example, at this writing, both Netscape's and Microsoft's Internet phones are H.323-compliant, but they share no codec, so they can't speak to one another.

If you have a full duplex sound card, your microphone and speakers can conspire to create an echo when you speak, but you can make a choice in the Echo Suppression field to minimize this problem. Leave it set to Normal unless you have problems; set it to Off if you're using a headset or Maximum if you get a lot of echo.

Clicking the Advanced button brings up the dialog box shown on the left in Figure 15.3.

The Network tab of this dialog box lets you configure Conference to work inside a corporate firewall. You have to get port numbers for these settings from your system administrator.

### TROUBLESHOOTING

**I've tried to call someone who is outside of my company and can't. Why?** System administrators set up firewalls to keep outsiders from accessing your network. But if you're to hold a conversation with someone outside of your organization, data must be transferred through the corporate firewall. Netscape Conference uses the following ports, which must remain open:

| Service | Port Number | Packet Type |
| --- | --- | --- |
| Audio data | 2327 | UDP |
| Data transfer | 6502 | TCP |
| DLS | 6498 | TCP |
| H3.23 call setup | 1720 | TCP |

Your system administrator can help you configure Conference so that you can use it for voice conversations, file transfer, text chat, collaborative browsing, or Whiteboard, depending on your company policy.

The Resampling tab lets you fix a problem that sometimes occurs where sounds are played back at the wrong pitch. If this happens to you, click the Enable resampling check box and pick one of the two resampling rates. (Try one, and then the other.)

Finally, the Latency tab provides two sliders that control the number of packets and the size of the queue that your audio board can handle at once. Increasing the queue size improves sound quality, but causes longer delays. You can safely experiment with these settings to get the performance you want. You can always click the Restore Defaults button to set things back as they were.

The middle tab of the main Conference Preferences dialog box sets your Business Card information (see Figure 15.4).

This dialog box lets you set up the information you want to make known to your conversation partners. You can include the following:

- Name
- E-Mail
- Photo
- Company

http://www.quecorp.com

- Title
- Address
- Phone
- Fax

**FIG. 15.4**
Your Business Card identifies you to your conversation partner. (My photo is blurred on purpose.)

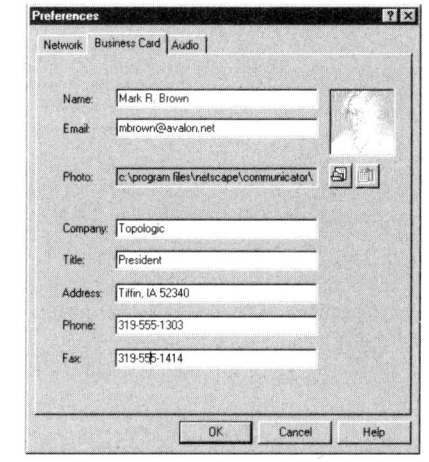

Name and e-mail address are required, but if you want to keep any other item of information private, just leave that field blank.

Use the Photo field to define an ID image for yourself. While this can be a picture of yourself, you can also use an image of your company logo or product, a universal symbol, or just about anything else. You can enter the file name or URL of an image directly into the field or click the Load Bitmap button to bring up a file requester dialog box. You can also cut an image into your system Clipboard and paste it using the Paste Bitmap button.

The Photo image can be a BMP, GIF, TIF, or JPEG file.

**TIP** For some inexplicable reason, some .BMP files display upside down when used as a business card image. If this happens to you, just load the image into a paint program and flip, then save the upside-down image. When you load it into Conference, it flips back over and looks right-side up. In computer terminology, this is known as a workaround.

## Making an Internet Phone Call

From the small main Conference window, you can initiate a phone conversation by entering an e-mail address in the center field, then clicking the Dial button (see Figure 15.5). (Inexplicably, the Dial button function is mirrored on the Call menu, though you have to enter the recipient's address in the E-Mail Address field before you can use it.)

**308** Chapter 15 Conference In-Depth

**FIG. 15.5**
Enter an e-mail address to make an Internet phone call.

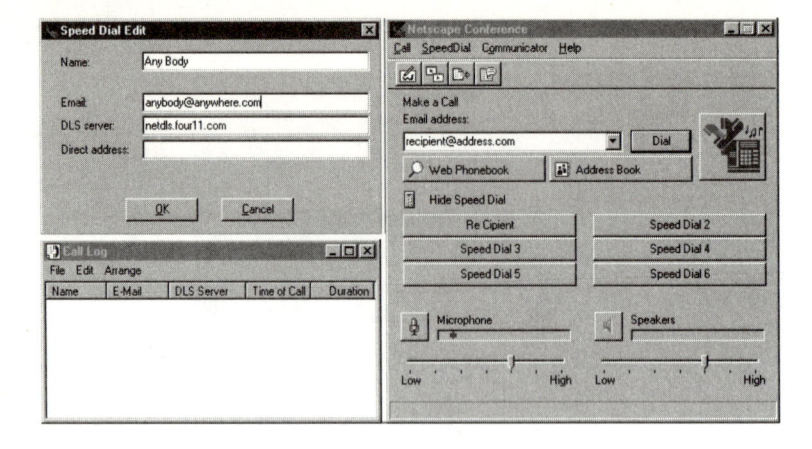

> **N O T E** Don't plan to use voice? You still need to make the call from here first. Even if you plan on using only the Chat Tool, Whiteboard, or some other Conference feature, you must still place a call from this window before you can use any of those tools.

You can click the Web Phonebook button to bring up a Web page in Navigator from which you can initiate a call. Using the Communicator, Web Phonebook menu selection does the same thing. (The Web directory you are transported to is the one you set under the Network tab of the Preferences dialog box in the Phonebook field.) Double-click the entry for the person you want to talk to, then click the Dial button back in the Conference window.

You can even click the Address Book button to bring up the Address Book and make a phone call from its listings. (Or choose Communicator, Address Book from the menus.) Highlight the entry you want and click the Call button to start your call.

If you call someone frequently, you can create a Speed Dial button for him. To do so, click the Show Speed Dial tab in the middle of the Conference window to display the six Speed Dial buttons. Right-click one and you are put into an Edit dialog box from which you can enter the recipient's Name, E-Mail Address, DLS Server, and Direct Address. (You can accomplish the same thing by making selections from the SpeedDial menu.) You must enter the recipient's Name and either his DLS Server or Direct Address. The rest is optional.

> **TIP** To update the information in someone's Speed Dial button automatically, just select the entry from the SpeedDial menu and choose Replace while you're online with the person.
>
> To remove a SpeedDial entry, choose Clear from the same menu.

The Direct Address field is for the specific IP address or Domain Name of the machine of the person you're calling, if you know it. This information allows you to directly connect to the recipient's computer over the Internet without having to go through a directory server.

http://www.quecorp.com

> **TIP** If you know the recipient's specific IP address or Domain Name, you can use the Call, Direct Call menu selection to connect to him directly. You can also enter a direct address into the main E-Mail Address field, but you must enclose it in parentheses.

Conference sends your intended recipient an invitation to accept your call, and you see the Pending Invitation dialog box. This dialog box displays the recipient's name while you wait, and you can click its Cancel button to bail out.

When a call is unsuccessful, you get a dialog box telling you so. This can happen if the recipient isn't running the phone client, isn't online, or has selected Do Not Disturb mode. If this is the case, you are invited to record a Voice Mail message for him. (You can also choose Voice Mail from the Communicator menu.)

If you choose to leave Voice Mail, you see the dialog box shown in Figure 15.6.

**FIG. 15.6**
Recording Voice Mail is just one more useful function of Conference.

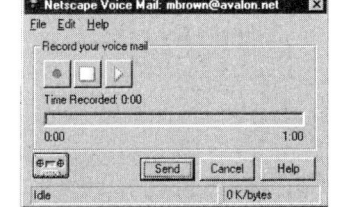

Click the red button to record, the white square to stop, and the white triangle to preview what you've recorded. Clicking the Send button transmits your message. (Not satisfied? Choose Edit, Preferences from the menu to adjust recording quality.)

If your call goes through successfully, the Icon in the right center of the window changes into the recipient's photo, if he's defined one in his Business Card. (If he doesn't have a photo, you see the Netscape Conference logo instead.) Clicking the image (or the default icon) displays his Business Card Information.

The little microphone icon is, as you'd expect, a push-to-talk button. Click it to begin talking. If you're not running a full duplex modem, or if you've declined to use Automatic Mode with a half duplex modem, the microphone icon is your push-to-talk button, and you must push it every time you want to speak.

Press the speaker icon to listen to the party you're conversing with. Press it every time you want to listen if you're not running automatically.

The sliders below the bar graph displays let you set amplification for microphone (left) and speaker (right) sound levels. It's important to adjust these properly for each conversation, as you're likely to run into a wide variety of quality in your connections. I've had good quality hookups with people overseas who are connected with a 486 computer and a 14.4 dial-up connection, and bad-to-the-point-of-unintelligible talks with folks hooked up with a T1 line and a Pentium 166. A lot of external factors can affect your connection, including the other person's Conference settings. If you're both willing to play with these a bit, you can usually achieve a very good connection.

When you complete a call successfully, the Dial button changes to a Hang Up button. Click this to end your call or use Hang Up from the Call menu.

# Receiving a Call

When you're running Conference, you can set it up to handle incoming calls in one of three different ways—all are available from the Call menu.

Always Prompt brings up a dialog box telling you who's calling and asking if you want to accept the call. This is the default and is just like having a phone with caller ID.

Auto Answer always accepts all incoming calls, no questions asked. If you're gregarious, or if you're expected to be available all the time—for example, on a company intranet—this might be your choice.

Do Not Disturb keeps you from being disturbed by any incoming calls, though you can still receive Voice Mail.

When you're not participating in a conference, the photo icon displays an icon that indicates which answer mode you're in.

> **TIP** You can improve performance if you turn off Auto Answer mode when you're already in a conference.

When you run Conference, you also get an icon in the Start menu tray called the Netscape Conference Attendant (see Figure 15.7).

The Attendant is what watches for incoming calls. It also provides you with a handy menu with some of the most-used Conference menu commands, including all three answer modes. Selecting Hide Window from Conference's Call menu puts Conference away, but leaves the Attendant in the tray to listen for calls. You can always bring the Conference Window back again by choosing Show Conference from the Attendant's right mouse button pop-up menu.

When you close Conference, the Conference Attendant goes away as well.

> **NOTE** For more information on the topic of voice communications on the Internet, check out the Internet Phone FAQ (Frequently Asked Questions) file on UseNet. This file is posted on the 5th and 19th of each month to the UseNet newsgroups **alt.internet.services, alt.bbs.internet, alt.culture.internet, alt.winsock.voice, alt.winsock.ivc, comp.sys.mac.comm, comp.os.ms-windows.apps.comm, alt.answers, comp.answers,** and **news.answers.** The latest version is also available on the World Wide Web at **http://www.northcoast.com/~savetz/voice-faq.html**.

**FIG. 15.7**
The Netscape Conference Attendant acts as your online watchdog.

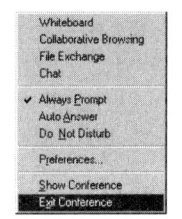

## Text Chat

Conference's Chat Tool is easy to bring up—you just press the Chat Tool button in the Conference toolbar or select Chat from the Communicator menu. You see the Chat Tool window shown in Figure 15.8.

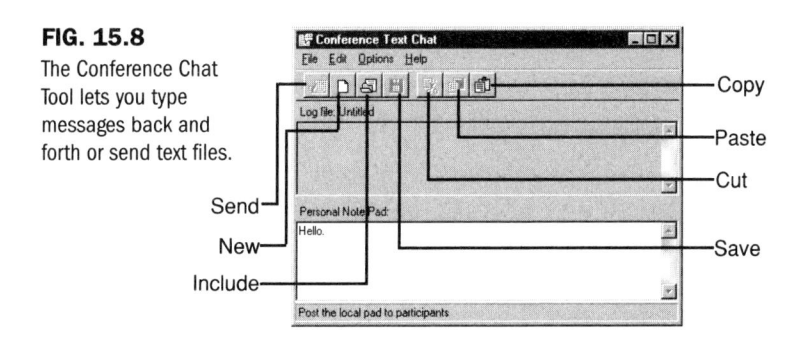

**FIG. 15.8**
The Conference Chat Tool lets you type messages back and forth or send text files.

You simply type your messages into the lower text box. (You can also paste text in from the Clipboard.) Send them by pressing Ctrl+Enter, clicking the Send button, or selecting File, Post NotePad from the menu. These notes appear on your conversation partner's screen, as well as in the upper Log file window of your Chat Tool window. Messages sent from the other party appear in your Log file window too, of course. Messages from both parties are mixed in the order in which they are sent or received.

You can save the Log file of your Chat session by selecting Save (Ctrl+S) or Save As from the File menu, or by clicking the Save button. Clicking the New button or selecting File, New, (Ctrl+F) clears the text windows and starts a new Log file—you are asked if you want to save the old one first. Picking File, Include (Ctrl+I), or clicking the Include button, brings up a file requester dialog box that lets you send along a text file (though unfortunately not binaries). There are buttons and menu selections for cut, copy, and paste, and the File menu includes Print Setup and Print options.

There are just two selections under the Options menu in the Chat Tool. The first is Pop Up On Receive. If checked, this option automatically launches the Chat Tool when a text message is transmitted to you.

The second is Font, which results in a dialog box that lets you define the display font, size, and style for the Chat window.

The Chat Tool is great for exchanging pre-written notes, meeting minutes, and so on, and is a handy backup means of communication if you're having problems with voice transmissions.

## File Exchange

You click the File Exchange button (see Figure 15.9) to send a file from your computer to your collaborator's computer. When you select the File Exchange button from the Conference window, you see the window shown in Figure 15.9.

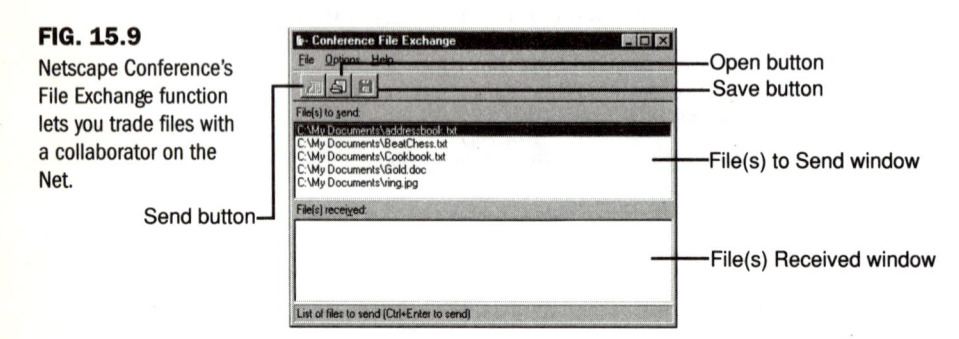

**FIG. 15.9**
Netscape Conference's File Exchange function lets you trade files with a collaborator on the Net.

Send button — Open button — Save button — File(s) to Send window — File(s) Received window

You can queue up a list of files to send to your collaborator by choosing the Send button on the File Exchange window toolbar or by selecting File, Add to Send List (Ctrl+A) from the menu. This brings up your system's standard file requester, from which you can select the files to send. As each is selected, it is listed in the File(s) to Send window. After you've chosen all the files you want to send, clicking the Send button sends them off to your collaborator. If you put a file into the Send window and change your mind, highlight it and press the Delete key or choose Delete from the File menu.

Receiving files is automatic. Any files sent to you by your collaborator are listed in the File(s) Received window, and you can save them by clicking the Save button or choosing Save (Ctrl+S) from the File menu. If you prefer to delete a file without saving it, highlight the file name and press the Delete key or select Delete from the File menu.

To get rid of the File Exchange window, just click the window's Close button or choose Exit from the File menu.

As with the Chat Tool, the File Exchange window has a Pop Up on Receive selection on the Options menu. When selected, the File Exchange window automatically launches when an incoming file is detected.

The Options menu also lets you choose whether files are sent in ASCII or Binary mode. If you are transferring text files, choose ASCII mode to ensure cross-platform compatibility. Choose Binary for all other file types.

Checking the Options, Compress menu item turns on File Exchange's built-in compression algorithm. File compression and decompression is automatic and invisible. This increases file processing time, but decreases transmission time. Check your own system to see which setting best improves overall file transfer time.

Many people think that file sharing is more important than simply exchanging files and point to this as one of Conference's major shortcomings. After all, other conferencing programs—for example, Microsoft's NetMeeting—let you actually load up applications software and work on file changes interactively. Proponents of Netscape's approach say it's much safer to simply exchange files and comments.

Choose Close (Alt+F4) from the File menu to exit File Exchange or just click the window's Close button.

## Collaborative Browsing

Conference's Collaborative Browsing tools let you and your conversation partner browse the Web together. This feature is great for discussing Web site design with an absent collaborator, for mutually browsing a client's or competitor's site for information, or even for making presentations on the other coast. You can put your slide show on the Web, have another party fire up Communicator, call in, and narrate using Conference's voice phone while browsing your slides on your Web site. Saving plane fare, hotel bills, taxi fare, meals, and a couple of days of your time can make it worth the effort.

To start, you press the Collaborative Browsing button on the Conference toolbar. You see the simple dialog box shown in Figure 15.10.

**FIG. 15.10**
Collaborative browsing is as easy as pressing two buttons.

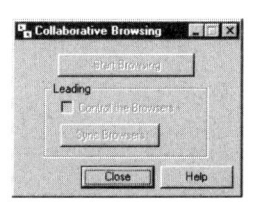

Click the Start Browsing button to begin, and your partner sees an invitation dialog box that invites her to start browsing with you. If she declines, you get a dialog box that tells you so. Otherwise, Navigator launches on both computers. Where you browse to, your partner browses to as well. If she should move to some other site on her own, click the Sync Browsers button to bring her back to the location you're viewing.

If you decide not to be the leader anymore, uncheck the Control the Browsers check box. The other party can then check the Control the Browsers check box on her machine to take over leadership, if she wants.

You can click the Close button to quit the Collaborative Browsing client. Each of you must then exit from Navigator manually.

**314** | Chapter 15   Conference In-Depth

# The Whiteboard

The Conference Whiteboard tool lets you share graphic information with your online collaborator. Each of you can load graphics into the Whiteboard screen and mark them up as you exchange ideas. You can draw arrows and circles on a screen shot of a new product, for example, or examine art for an ad campaign. You'll each not only see the same picture, but you can modify it together.

You launch the Whiteboard by selecting the Whiteboard icon from the Conference toolbar or by choosing Whiteboard from the Conference menu. When you do, you see a window similar to the one shown in Figure 15.11.

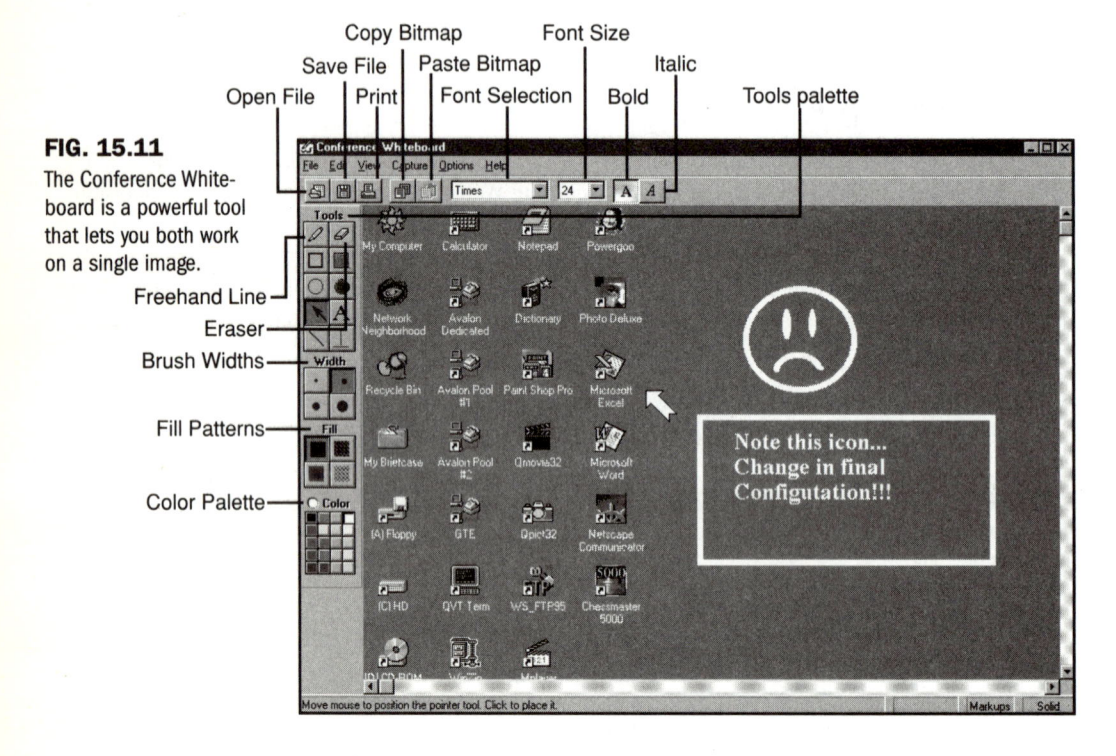

**FIG. 15.11**
The Conference Whiteboard is a powerful tool that lets you both work on a single image.

There are many collaborative Whiteboard programs out there, some stand-alone and some built into online conferencing suites like Communicator. The concept is simple—you can load up a background graphic, and participants can type comments or mark up changes on the Whiteboard. The background graphic and markup image are two separate elements. You can load in a new background at any time or leave the background intact and only erase markups.

http://www.quecorp.com

## Getting a Background Image

You can load a bitmap image into the Whiteboard's background, or you can grab all or part of your system screen. You can even use a blank screen, if you want.

The Conference Whiteboard can load the following seven varieties of bitmapped images:

- Windows Bitmap BMP
- CompuServe GIF
- TIFF Revision 5.0
- JPEG
- Truevision TARGA
- Sun Raster
- Zsoft Paintbrush PCX

An image can be loaded into the image, or background, layer from disk by selecting the Open File button on the toolbar or by choosing File, Open (Ctrl+O) from the menu. If you've been working on a project using any graphics program, you can save an image in any of these formats so that you can later load it up to collaborate online using the Whiteboard.

You can also choose to grab an image directly from your desktop as you work. To do so, clear your desktop of all but the windows you want to grab. Arrange the windows the way you want them, then select one of the choices from the Whiteboard Capture menu. You can grab a Region by clicking one corner of a rectangle on the screen and then clicking the opposite corner; you can grab the whole Desktop; or you can grab a single Window by clicking it.

> **TIP** Want the Whiteboard window to politely get out of the way when you use one of its capture functions? First, check the Hide on Capture selection in the Options menu.

> **TIP** Want to see what you captured before you paste it down? Hold down the Shift key as you move the selection rectangle to preview the image.

Finally, the Whiteboard image can be a blank screen. To clear the screen to blank, select Edit from the Whiteboard menu, then choose the Clear Whiteboard menu item.

There are several interesting Paste options available from the Edit menu. If you have a bitmap image in the Clipboard, choose Paste Bitmap (Ctrl+V) and you see a position rectangle. Move this into position, click the left mouse button, and the bitmap in the Clipboard is pasted into the background layer, overwriting existing images in both the background and markup layers.

If there is text in the Clipboard, choose Paste Text from the Edit menu. The text is pasted in the currently selected font, size, and style, which is displayed on the Whiteboard toolbar. As with a bitmap, the text overwrites everything it is positioned over.

Paste Picture pastes text as an image. It also overwrites the selected area.

Choose Paste Owner Display from the Edit menu to paste image display data from the Clipboard onto the image layer of the Whiteboard.

Clear the entire screen, background, and markups at any time by choosing Edit, Clear Whiteboard. There is no provision for clearing the background and leaving the markups, which makes some sense.

## Using Markup Tools

After you have a background image you want to work with, you can use the Whiteboard markup tools to add elements to the markup layer, like freehand scribbles, text, rectangles, and so on. There is even a repositionable arrow pointer you can use to emphasize points as you discuss various graphic items.

> **TIP** Don't forget, you can get helpful pop-up ToolTips by hovering over a button or icon if you can't figure out what it is for.

You can clear off all your markups at any time, leaving the underlying image undisturbed, by choosing Edit, Clear Markups from the menu.

You can clear the entire Whiteboard by choosing Edit, Clear Whiteboard from the menu. To clear markup only, choose Edit, Clear Markups. The Eraser tool can be used to erase bits of either. In the lower-right corner of the Whiteboard status bar is a Layer indicator. If it says Markup, the eraser erases only markup elements. Double-click the indicator and it switches to say Image, and the Eraser tool erases both background image and markup elements. Options, Erase Image or Erase Markups also switch modes. There is no way to erase background only.

To the right of the Layer indicator in the status bar is a Fill style indicator. Double-clicking this swaps between Solid and Clear fill modes. When you pick a pattern fill from the Tool Palette, this selection chooses whether the lighter color in the fill pattern is white or transparent. (Fill Solid and Fill Clear are also available as selections from the Options menu.)

The Tools Palette lets you choose from a variety of drawing tools.

The Freehand tool lets you draw free lines. The Eraser erases according to the schemes explained earlier. Open Rectangle and Open Oval tools let you draw outlined geometric shapes, while the Filled Rectangle and Oval tools create versions filled according to the fill selection.

> **TIP** To draw a perfect circle with the Oval tools, or a perfect square with the rectangle tools, hold down the Shift key as you drag-and-draw.

Clicking the arrow pointer creates a big, mobile arrow that you can draw around. It's the only non-permanent item on the Tool Palette. When you move the arrow and click, it moves to a new position. You can click-and-drag the arrow to have it move in real-time on your partner's screen.

The Text tool is for typing text onto the screen in the currently selected font and color. Pick these before you type anything on the screen. Press Enter to finish and send the typed text to your collaborator.

The last two drawing tools draw a straight Line at any angle or a Constrained Line at 90-degree increments.

You have your choice of four different brush Widths, and four different Fill patterns, which apply to all of the drawing tools except the pointer and text.

Finally, you can choose any of 20 available colors to use with each tool.

## The Whiteboard Options Menu

The Options menu lets you control several aspects of the Whiteboard's operation.

Choose Floatin g Toolbox (Ctrl+T) to turn the toolbox into a floating, repositionable window. This gives you a little more work room and lets you drag the toolbox into a convenient working position.

The Dither Screen Capture menu item lets you capture screens using fewer colors. Though this takes more time to capture, it takes less time to transmit dithered screen images.

The Compress option is similar to compression in the File Exchange window. If selected, files are automatically compressed when sent and decompressed when received. This saves transmission time, but takes some processing time at either end.

As with the Chat Tool and File Exchange windows, if you select Pop Up on Receive, the Whiteboard automatically runs when your collaborator starts a Whiteboard session.

Click the Canvas Size menu item to bring up a dialog box that allows you to specify the height and width (in pixels) of the Whiteboard canvas. Note that any new setting does not take effect until you close and run Communicator again.

## Other Whiteboard Functions

The View menu offers seven zoomed views of the Whiteboard canvas, from a 1:8 tight zoom to a 9:1 wide angle view. In between is Original Size. When you specify a zoom mode, the cursor appears as a magnifying glass—click the point on the canvas that you want to be the zoom center. Also on the View menu is the Refresh (Ctrl+R) option, which can straighten out a garbled display.

The File menu contains standard application tools such as Save (Ctrl+S), Save As, Print Setup, and Print. To exit the application, choose Close (Alt+F4) from the File menu or click the window Close button.

## Conference's Limitations

Conference is a great collaboration tool, but it's not without a few shortcomings. When people compare Internet conferencing programs, inevitably three major criticisms of Conference crop up.

First, they say, Conference doesn't allow true application collaboration. You can transfer work files using the File Transfer application, you can mark up graphics using the Whiteboard, and you can discuss changes using Text Chat or Voice Chat. But you can't load up an Excel spreadsheet and both work on it, making real changes to the actual spreadsheet. Everything is done in a one-level-removed manner. Any changes discussed must be made offline, then files must be transferred again. And each participant must make changes individually, which means that the current file is always in the possession of one participant, and the other must wait for it to be transferred back before making additional changes.

Proponents of Netscape's way of doing things argue that Conference provides an additional level of security, because no one else can make and save changes to a file without going through an offline process.

Secondly, Conference doesn't handle video conferencing, just audio. The value of video conferencing depends mostly on your point of view. If you need it, Conference doesn't have it. But if you prefer working from home in your pajamas, you probably prefer to avoid video conferences, anyway. You can still sound quite professional whether you've showered or not.

Finally, critics say that conferencing between two people is just too restrictive. If you have three people at one location and seven at another who want to share ideas, you have to all gather around two computers. Worse, if you have any people at a third location, they can't participate at all. This is probably Conference's biggest limitation, and Netscape must address it before large, multi-operation corporations take Conference seriously. ●

http://www.quecorp.com

CHAPTER 16

# Setting Preferences

*by Mark R. Brown*

After using the setup wizards to install Communicator, it generally works fine. But over time, you may find some things just aren't the way you'd like them to be. Maybe you're bored with the default home page. Maybe the screen colors just don't have enough contrast for your laptop screen. Maybe your slow dial-up connection is driving you nuts, and you'd like to find a way to speed things up a bit.

Never fear. By adjusting the Communicator Preferences, you can fix all of these minor annoyances, and many more. You bring up the Netscape Preferences dialog box (shown in Figure 16.1) by choosing Edit, Preferences.

- **You can use the Preferences panel to customize Communicator**

    Communicator is the most user-configurable product ever produced by Netscape.

- **An intuitive menu guides you to the options you want to modify**

    The left-side collapsible menu gives you access to 20 different Preferences panels.

- **Preferences panels are categorized under six major headings by functionality**

    You have control over Appearance, Navigator, Mail & Groups, Composer, Offline, and Advanced options.

- **More powerful program control means more user responsibility**

    Before making a change to any Preferences setting, make sure you understand all the implications of changing that setting.

**FIG. 16.1**
The Communicator Preferences dialog box lets you set preferences for the entire Communicator suite.

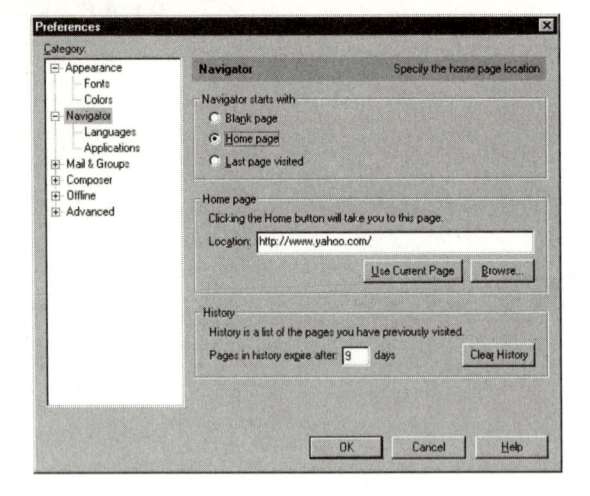

Note that there are six upper-level areas for which you can modify Communicator Preferences settings. They are listed in the menu along the left side of the Preferences dialog box. These six areas are

- Appearance
- Navigator
- Mail & Groups
- Composer
- Offline
- Advanced

Each of these main levels has associated sub-levels that can be displayed by expanding the menus. To do so, you click on the "+" sign next to the appropriate header. The Appearance and Navigator items are, by default, already expanded, though clicking the "-" sign next to these headers collapses them.

In this chapter, we examine each of these preference settings in detail.

> **TIP** Like all Communicator components, the Preferences panel is equipped with context-sensitive NetHelp. If you get stuck, click the Help button and the NetHelp window will pop up, pointed to information relevant to the task at hand.

# Appearance

Click the Appearance item in the left menu, and the Appearance panel appears in the right window (see Figure 16.2). This panel is labeled Appearance—Change the Appearance of the Display, but this description is somewhat broad. This panel actually only controls which

http://www.quecorp.com

application(s) launch when you start up Communicator, and how items appear on the toolbar. (The Appearance sub-categories Fonts and Colors control other aspects of Navigator's appearance.)

**FIG. 16.2**
From the Appearance panel you can control the look of the toolbar and what launches when you run Communicator.

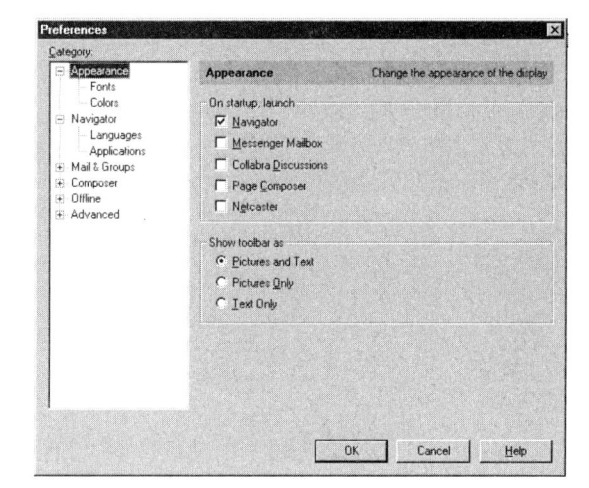

The first portion of the Appearance panel is labeled, On Startup, Launch, and includes five check boxes, one for each of Communicator's major applications:

- Navigator
- Messenger Mailbox
- Collabra Discussions
- Page Composer
- Netcaster

You can select as many or as few of these check boxes as you wish. Each application that is checked runs automatically on startup whenever you run Communicator.

> **TIP** Throughout the Communicator Preferences panels, you can select as many square check boxes in a set as you wish, and all will be considered selected. In a set of round "radio buttons," however, each button is exclusive—that is, when you select one button in a set, all of the others become grayed, or unable to be selected. Only one option in a set of radio buttons can be active.

The bottom portion of the Appearances panel is labeled, "Show Toolbar As." You have three radio button selections:

- Pictures and Text
- Pictures Only
- Text Only

These selections control how you view the buttons on the Navigation toolbar. When you begin, you'll probably want to keep the default Pictures and Text selection, to remind you what each button does. Later, you can choose one of the other selections. Text Only takes up the least screen space and is best if you prefer a large display window.

## Fonts

Highlight the Fonts selection in the Category section and you'll get a panel called Fonts—Change the Fonts in Your Display (see Figure 16.3). From this panel you can exert complete control over the font choices Communicator makes when displaying HTML documents.

**FIG. 16.3**
You define display fonts from the Fonts panel.

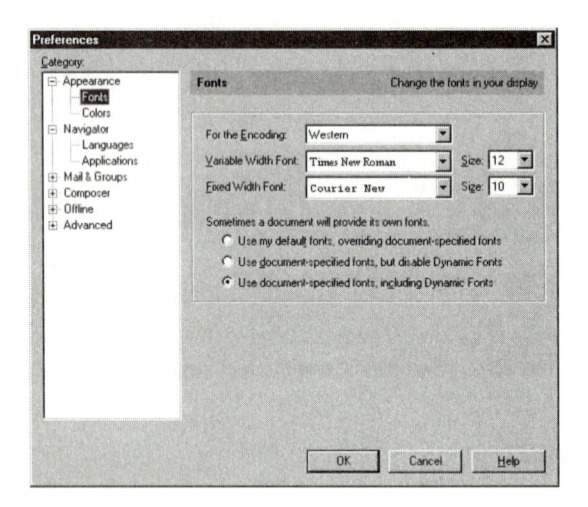

The first field, For the Encoding:, is a drop-down list of available language encoding schemes. Encoding basically determines which character is assigned to which hexadecimal digit in a file. Different encoding allows a stream of digital data to represent English characters, Japanese, Korean, or any language you choose. Of course, you can't turn Japanese data into English merely by changing the encoding—what you get is a mess! But you must have the correct encoding set for the language you are viewing, or all you'll get is gobbledygook. (I'm sure you've noted this effect if you've ever tried to view a Japanese site by using your English browser settings.)

Each encoding scheme has its own associated variable width and fixed-width fonts. These can also be set for the currently selected encoding scheme by using the Variable Width Font: (Size:) and Fixed Width Font: (Size:) fields.

The next group, called Sometimes a Document Will Provide Its Own Fonts, enables a page designer to control which system fonts are used to display a page. In the past, that type of control was system-specific. For example, a page designer could specify a certain Windows system font, but if a user was viewing the page on a Unix system that didn't have that font available, the page would default to the fonts that were set in the user's system and browser.

http://www.quecorp.com

A new feature of Communicator called *Dynamic Fonts* changes all that. A page designer can now define and download the fonts he or she wishes to use, and they are displayed on every browser and every system in the same manner—that is, they are displayed as long as the viewer's browser is able to make use of Dynamic Fonts.

The three radio buttons in this section enable you to define how you want fonts to be used:

- Use My Defaul*t* Fonts, Overriding Document-Specified Fonts
- Use *D*ocument-Specified Fonts, but Disable Dynamic Fonts
- Use Document-Specified Fonts, In*c*luding Dynamic Fonts

If you want to define the look of all pages yourself, choose the first button. If you simply want to avoid Dynamic Fonts, choose option two. (Turning off Dynamic Fonts can improve download times.) The third option defaults to all the settings chosen by the page designer, thus guaranteeing you'll see all pages in the format he or she intended.

> **N O T E** Variable-width fonts are used to display most page text, while fixed-width fonts are used for form input fields and some preformatted text.

## Colors

Select Colors from the Category section and you'll get a panel labeled: Colors—Change the Colors in Your Display (see Figure 16.4). From here, you define screen, text, and link colors.

**FIG. 16.4**
The Colors panel makes use of the brilliant Color dialog box.

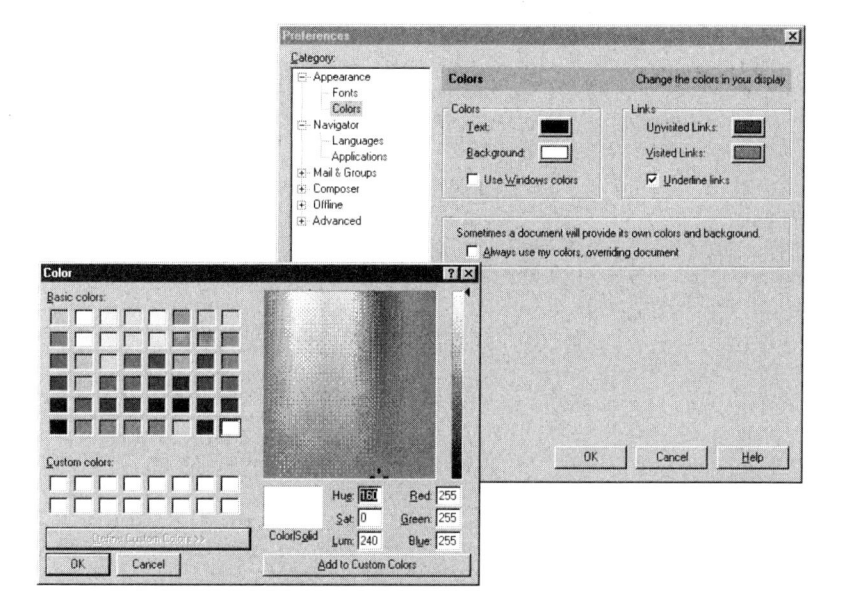

The Colors area of this panel lets you set Text: and Background: colors. (Black and White are the default text and background colors, respectively.) Click the color button to the right of either of these selections and you get the Color dialog box shown in Figure 16.4. From this dialog box, you can select a color or define one of your own, then click OK to finish. The color button on the Colors panel changes hue to reflect your new choice.

You can also click the check box next to Use Windows Colors and Communicator simply uses the system colors.

There are two other "text" colors, though, and you can set them in the Links portion of the dialog box. You set the colors for Unvisited Links and Visited Links by using the same Color dialog box. (Blue is default for unvisited links, purple for visited ones.) You can also choose to Underline Links: by clicking the associated check box.

As the panel says, Sometimes a Document Will Provide Its Own Colors and Background. If you prefer to, you can select to Always Use My Colors, Overriding Document by choosing this item's check box.

Using your own colors is a particularly good idea if you use an unusual display setup, such as a monochrome monitor or a laptop with a small screen.

# Navigator

By default, the Communicator Preferences dialog menu comes up with the "Navigator" item highlighted. Netscape must think you'll want to change the Navigator preferences. They're probably right.

This panel is labeled Navigator—Specify the Home Page Location. This dialog box also enables you to specify how the History window behaves (see Figure 16.5).

**FIG. 16.5**
The Navigator Preferences dialog box sets Home Page and History options.

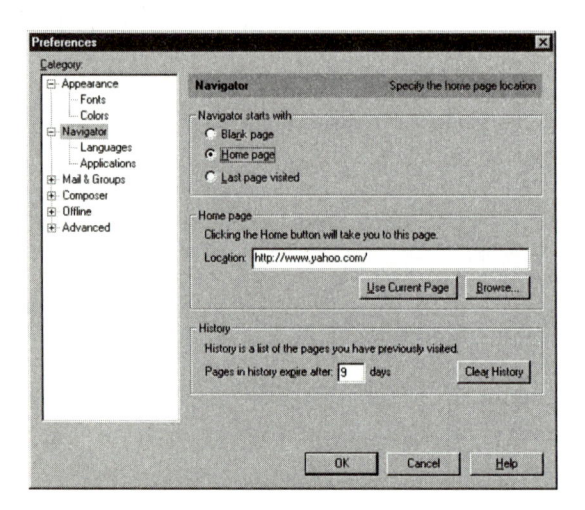

The first section is labeled Navigator Starts With and displays three option buttons that let you select whether, on startup, Navigator displays:

- Bla**n**k Page
- **H**ome Page
- **L**ast Page Visited

The first selection, Bla**n**k Page, is especially useful if you regularly launch Navigator when you're not online. Instead of spinning its wheels looking for a Web page that simply isn't available, Navigator instead politely displays a blank screen and waits for you to select a destination.

The second selection, **H**ome Page, is the default. If you are usually connected before you launch Navigator, or if your home page is stored on your disk drive or network, this is where you generally want to start out.

The final selection, **L**ast Page Visited, is useful if you spend a lot of time searching for information and generally want to be able to pick up right where you left off.

The second section is labeled Home Page and lets you define the URL of your home page. This is not only the page that Navigator starts with (if you have the Home Page option button selected), it's also the page you jump to if you click the Home button on the Navigator toolbar. By default, the home page is defined as Netscape's page, but most people prefer one of these other options:

- A personal home page
- An official company intranet page
- A useful Web search engine or index

A personal page is especially useful if it is located on your computer's hard drive. Then you don't need to be online to run Navigator. It's also a great place to organize your favorite links.

An "official" company page is a great place to start if you are connected to an office intranet and need to keep up on corporate announcements and news.

But the most popular home page is probably a Web search engine or index page like Yahoo! (**http://www.yahoo.com**) or Lycos (**http://www.lycos.com**).

If you know the URL of your intended home page, you can simply type it into the Location field. If the page you want to use is on your hard drive or network, you can click the **B**rowse button to find it. If you want to display your intended home page in Navigator before you launch Preferences, you can click the **U**se Current Page button to set it as your home page.

Both of the Navigator Preferences we've set so far have to do with configuring how Navigator acts on startup. The History setting controls how long Navigator keeps a previously listed page listed in the History window.

## 326   Chapter 16   Setting Preferences

You can type any number you want in the Pages in History Expire After: X Days field. The default is 9, but if you find your history list becoming cluttered too quickly, you may want to reduce that number. If, on the other hand, you are a light user, you may find you want to be able to reference previously visited sites up to several weeks later.

You can also immediately clear the entire history list by clicking the Clear History button. Remember where this button is located, because you may find it useful to use this button on occasion to clear your history list before starting certain projects.

> **TIP** When a page reference disappears from the history list, any link referring to that page then appears as an "unvisited link." Whether or not a page has been visited is determined solely by whether it is still listed in the history list.

## Languages

Many U.S. citizens will never have to use the Languages Preferences dialog box (see Figure 16.6). But if your native language is something besides English, you'll want to visit this dialog box to set your language preference. If you're multilingual, or if you regularly visit many foreign sites, you can set several languages.

**FIG. 16.6**
The Language Preferences dialog box lets you set your native tongue.

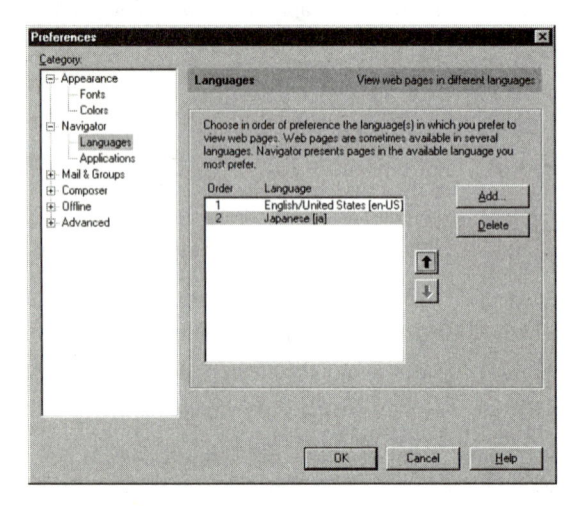

To display the panel in Figure 16.6, choose Navigator, Languages. This dialog box is labeled Languages—View Web Pages in Different Languages. By default, the only language listed is English/United States. But by clicking the Add button you can bring up a list of additional available languages (see Figure 16.7).

Click the language you want to add and then the OK button; the language selected is added to your language preference list. In Figure 16.6, we've already added Japanese. When requesting a Web page, Navigator first requests a page in U.S. English then, if that's not available, in Japanese.

**FIG. 16.7**
Navigator is truly an international product; it can handle all of the most-used world languages.

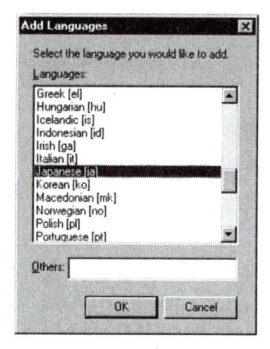

Note that these requests mean nothing unless the server we're contacting has multiple language versions of its pages available, and unless it understands Navigator's request. The actual request code is shown in the preference panel in brackets. For U.S. English, the code is "[en-US]"; for Japanese, it's "[ja]".

What if your language isn't listed in the Add dialog box? You can type it into the Others field in the format "Language[code]" (see Figure 16.7). Of course, your code must correspond to a valid ISO (International Standards Organization) language code or it will be ignored. One site that lists these codes is **http://www.de.relator.research.ec.org/mlhtml/ISO-lg-codes.mlhtml**.

What if you prefer a different order to your list? Highlight the name of the language you want to move, then click the Up or Down arrow buttons to increase or decrease the priority of that language by one position. In our example in Figure 16.6, Japanese is highlighted; you could move it ahead of U.S. English in the list by clicking the Up arrow button once.

## Applications

Though Communicator displays text, HTML documents, and even inline GIF and JPEG images all by itself, there are a huge number of other types of files that you may want Communicator to display. These range from hundreds of other graphics file types to audio files to video and multimedia presentation files. Somewhere, someone has put each of these types of files into an HTML document. Eventually, you're going to run into dozens—even hundreds—of files that Navigator can't display by itself. Fortunately, Netscape has made provisions. You can extend Navigator's file display capabilities through the use of plug-ins and helper applications. What's the difference? Simply put, plug-ins work hand-in-hand with Navigator, generally displaying a new file type right in-line in the browser window. On the other hand, helper applications are exactly what they claim to be—separate, stand-alone applications that help Navigator when it doesn't know how to display a file. Navigator launches the helper application and it displays the file in its own window.

▶ For information on installing and using plug-ins, **see** "Plug-Ins," **p. 185**. [in Chapter 10, "Interacting with Plug-Ins, Java Applets, and JavaScript."]

## Chapter 16  Setting Preferences

You install helper applications by using the Preferences panel labeled: Applications—Specify Helper Applications for Different File Types (see Figure 16.8).

**FIG. 16.8**
The Applications panel lets you investigate how Navigator handles various file types.

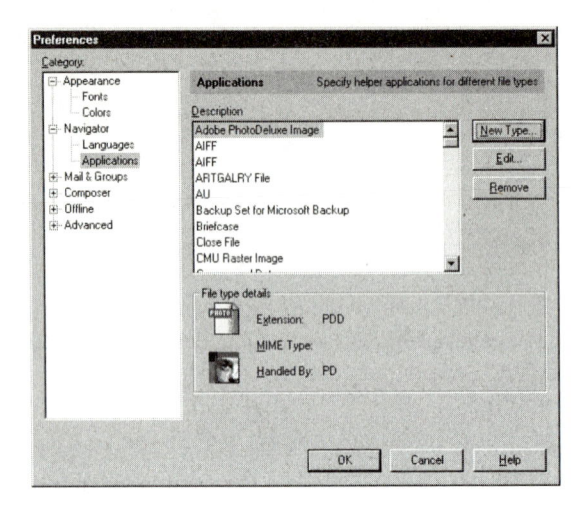

The upper Description window provides a scrolling list of the file types recognized by Navigator, and shows how each is displayed. Highlight an entry and the bottom File type details section lists three important items of information:

- Extension:—This is the file name extension, usually the last three characters after the "." in a file name. For example, in the text file "sometext.txt" the file name extension is "txt."

- MIME Type:—The MIME type tells Navigator what sort of information will be sent to it by a server to identify the file type.

- Handled By:—Finally, this field identifies the application that is used to display the file. This says "Netscape [internal]" if the file type is handled by Navigator itself; "Plugin" if displayed by a plug-in; and it displays the name of a program if a helper application has been defined for that file type.

**NOTE** About MIME Types—Before a server computer sends a file to Navigator, it sends along a little snippet of information that isn't displayed. This information packet tells Navigator (among other things) the MIME type of the file that is to follow. MIME stands for "Multipurpose Internet Mail Extensions," but it has come to be used for much more than just mail.

In a nutshell, a MIME type definition consists of a simple text string like "text/ascii."

The part before the slash is a generic definition, while the part after the slash is more specific. There are only a handful of generic MIME type definitions, like: application/, video/, audio/, image/, and text/.

There are dozens of more specific official definitions for after the slash. Some real-world MIME types are image/jpeg for JPEG images, video/mpeg for MPEG compressed movies, and text/html for HTML markup documents.

http://www.quecorp.com

Besides the "official" definitions, you can make up your own if you prefix them with an "x-." For example, you might define a new MIME type of "image/x-poofit" if you invented a new image compression filetype that uses "poofit" compression technology.

When you use the Applications Preferences panel, you are actually assigning which application will respond when a file of that MIME type is sent to Navigator.

All the file types displayed natively by Navigator are automatically displayed in the Description list, as are file types handled by installed plug-ins. Any file types registered with the operating system are also automatically included in the list, and the programs assigned by the operating system to handle those file types are also automatically registered as helper applications for Navigator.

However, if you wish to define new file types and associated helper applications, you can do so by choosing the New Type button. When you do, you'll see the dialog box shown in Figure 16.9.

**FIG. 16.9**
From this dialog box you can define new file types and associate helper applications to display them.

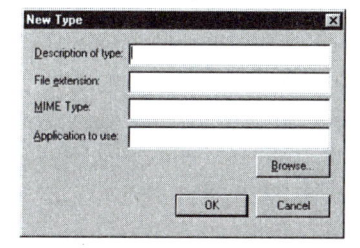

The Description of Type field produces the information that is shown in the Description window, while File extension:, MIME Type:, and Application to Use: all define the information that appears below it in the File type details section. You can click the Browse button to pick a helper application. Choose OK to finish.

The Edit button brings up the dialog box shown in Figure 16.10. (Highlight a listing first, then click the Edit button.)

**FIG. 16.10**
In this dialog box, you can choose to be warned or even to save a file to disk rather than have it displayed.

You can change the MIME type for a file by using this dialog box. You can also choose to have the file displayed by Navigator (if Navigator supports this type of file). You can Save to Disk if you don't want to automatically display this file type, or you can pick an Application to display the file by clicking the Browse button to do so. Finally, the Ask Me Before Opening Downloaded Files of This Type check box lets you choose to be alerted before a file of this type is handled in the manner you've chosen. (This check box is only active if you've chosen an Application as your display option.)

Finally, the Remove button deletes an entry from the Description field, and takes away all associated display functions. This is a welcome change from earlier editions of Navigator—once you set a helper application in them, it was set in stone for all eternity. If you do choose to remove a filetype, you'll be asked for confirmation before your choice is obliterated for good.

## Mail & Groups

Choose Edit, Preferences, Mail & Groups to bring up the Mail & Groups panel, which is labeled: Mail & Groups—Change Appearance Settings for Mail & Groups (see Figure 16.11).

**FIG. 16.11**
Modify fonts and window behavior with the Mail & Groups panel.

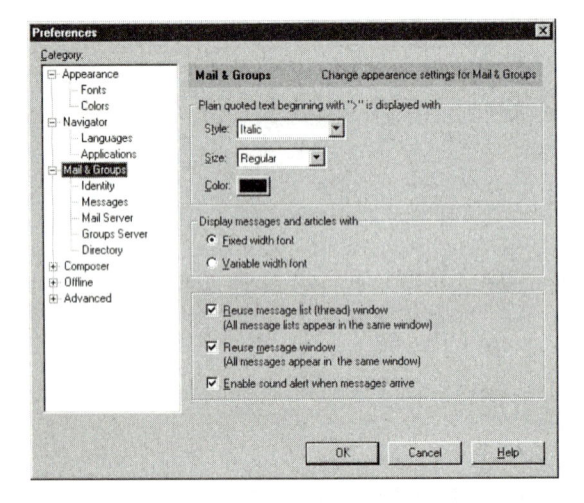

The upper section of the Mail & Groups panel says Plain Quoted Text Beginning with ">" Is Displayed With, and it defines the Style, Size, and Color used to display quoted text in mail messages. There are three drop-down settings each for Style and Size, and the Color is chosen from the standard color dialog box.

You can also choose the Display Messages and Articles With option either a Fixed Width Font or a Variable Width Font. (The actual fonts used are selected in the Fonts panel.)

Window behavior is controlled by using two check box options. These are

- Reuse Message List (Thread) Window. (All message lists appear in the same window.)
- Reuse Message Window. (All messages appear in the same window.)

http://www.quecorp.com

Finally, you can choose to Enable Sound Alert When Messages Arrive. This option works only if you are using the Netscape Mail Notification program.

▶ For information on the Netscape Mail Notification program, **see** "Messenger In-Depth," **p. 199**

## Identity

The Identity panel is labeled Identity—Set Your Name, E-mail Address, and Signature File (see Figure 16.12).

**FIG. 16.12**
Let people know who you are with the Identity panel settings.

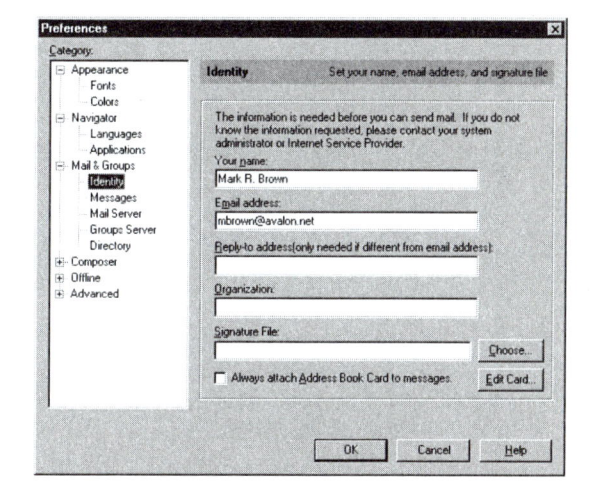

The first two selections on this panel—Your Name and Email Address—are required items. You can't send or receive e-mail without them, so make sure they're accurate.

The Reply-to Address only needs to be set if you regularly receive mail at a different address than the one from which you send mail.

Organization is completely optional, but a necessity if you want to be recognized as speaking with the combined voice of a company or other entity.

You can also choose to define and send a Signature File with every e-mail. If you want to use a signature file, create the file separately by using Notepad or any other application that can save your creation as an ASCII text file, then select it here by clicking the Choose button.

Instead (or even in addition) you can choose the Always Attach Address Book Card to Messages check box. If you do, all your e-mail will be accompanied by your own sort of personalized electronic business card. You create this card by clicking the Edit Card button and filling in the fields on the associated dialog box (see Figure 16.13).

There are three tabs to choose: the Name tab, the Contact tab, and the Netscape Conference tab.

**Chapter 16** Setting Preferences

**FIG. 16.13**
The Edit Card dialog box lets you define a personalized electronic business card.

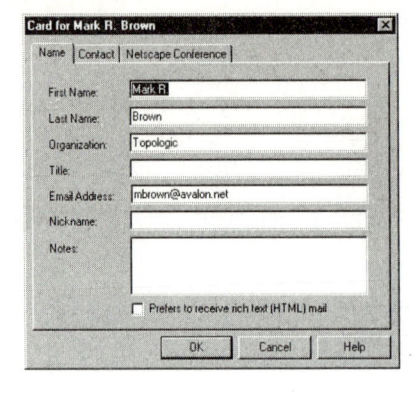

The Name tab asks you for the following information. You can fill out as much or as little of it as you wish.

- First Name
- Last Name
- Organization
- Title
- Email Address
- Nickname
- Notes

A check box tells your recipients that you prefer to receive rich text [HTML] mail messages.

The Contact tab continues with additional personal information:

- Address1
- Address2
- City
- State
- Zip
- Country
- Work Phone
- Fax
- Home Phone

The final tab, Netscape Conference, tells your recipients where you are listed if they wish to contact you by using the Conference client built into Communicator. The drop-down Address field has three choices:

- Netscape Conference DLS Server

Mail & Groups | 333

- Specific DLS Server
- Hostname or IP Address

If you choose the first, the recipient will look for you on Netscape's directory. The second and third choices give you the opportunity to list your own custom server or IP address.

To get started using Conference, turn to Chapter 7, "Conference Quick Start," which introduces the Conference application. Then move on to Chapter 15, "Conference In-Depth."

> **NOTE** The card you define by using the Edit Card dialog box is just your own personal entry in the Communicator Address Book. Your card is listed in your Address Book and can be edited there, and when your card is attached to your outgoing e-mail messages, others can add it to their Address Books. Very handy, but make sure you never store any personal information in your own Address Book entry that you want to keep private!

## Messages

Choosing Messages from the Category section brings up a panel labeled "Messages—Choose settings for outgoing messages" (see Figure 16.14).

**FIG. 16.14**
The Messages panel controls the behavior of all the messages you send.

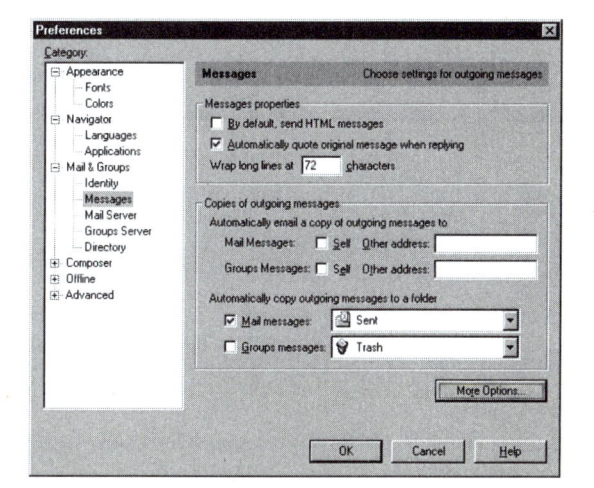

The Messages Properties section of this panel includes a check box called, By default, Send HTML Messages. Check this box only if you send mail exclusively to others who can display HTML in their e-mail clients; for example, if all your e-mail is on a corporate intranet to other Communicator users.

You can choose the check box to Automatically Quote Original Message When Replying if you generally like to send back a copy to the sender.

Adjust the width of your screen display by typing in a number for Wrap Long Lines at XX Characters to match your display.

The Copies of Outgoing Messages section lets you choose to automatically e-mail a copy of outgoing messages to yourself or to another address. There are separate selections for Mail Messages (Self and/or Other address) and Groups Messages (Self and/or Other address).

Likewise, you can automatically copy outgoing messages to a folder. For Mail messages, this defaults to the Sent folder, but for Groups messages, the default is Trash.

Clicking the More Options button displays the dialog box shown in Figure 16.15.

**FIG. 16.15**
Radio buttons galore under More Options for Messages Preferences.

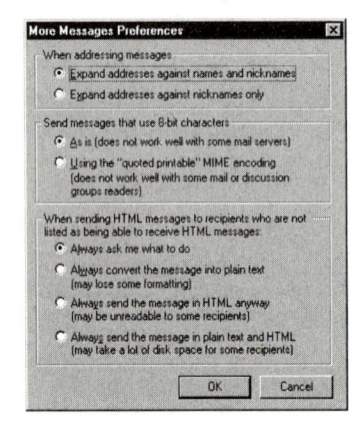

The When Addressing Messages section lets you choose how addresses appear in the To: box. You can select:

- Expand Addresses Against Names and Nicknames
- Expand Addresses Against Nicknames Only
- Send Messages that Use 8-bit Characters
- As Is (Does Not Work Well with Some Mail Servers)

Leave this alone unless you have problems. If your mail comes across as garbage, try using the other setting:

- Using the "Quoted Printable" MIME Encoding (Does Not Work Well with Some Mail or Discussion Groups Readers)

The last section says: When Sending HTML Messages to Recipients Who Are Not Listed as Being Able to Receive HTML Messages. The first selection is the default and gives you the most flexibility. The dialog box explains the possible complications with other selections:

- Always Ask Me What to Do
- Always Convert the Message into Plain Text (May Lose Some Formatting)
- Always Send the Message in HTML Anyway (May Be Unreadable to Some Recipients)
- Always Send the Message in Plain Text and HTML (May Take A Lot of Disk Space for Some Recipients)

## Mail Server

Before you can send mail, you must make sure that your Mail Server preferences are set correctly. This panel is labeled: Mail Server—Specify Server for Incoming Mail (see Figure 16.16).

**FIG. 16.16**
If you don't know what to put into the Mail Server panel fields, contact your Internet Service Provider.

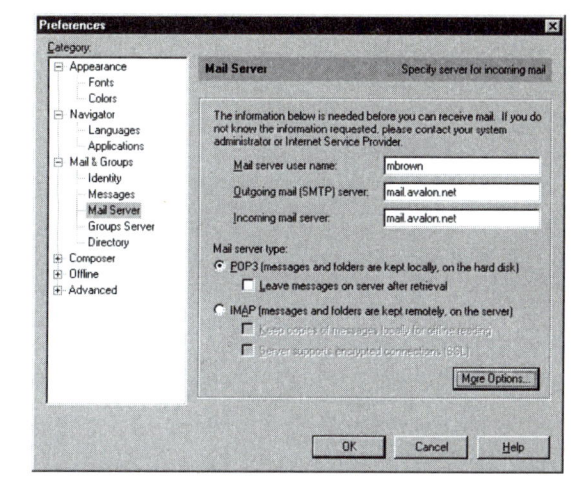

Your Mail server user name is usually the part of your e-mail address that comes before the "@" sign. The Outgoing Mail (SMTP) Server and Incoming Mail Server fields are often the same, but they may be different.

Your Mail Server Type is either POP3 or IMAP. If POP3 (Messages and Folders Are Kept Locally, on the Hard Disk), you can choose a check box to Leave Messages on Server After Retrieval. If IMAP (Messages and Folders Are Kept Remotely, on the Server), you can check to Keep Copies of Messages Locally for Offline Reading, and to indicate that the Server Supports Encrypted Connections (SSL).

Click the More Options button to display the dialog box shown in Figure 16.17.

Here, you can set a Local Mail Directory by clicking the Choose button and an IMAP Mail Directory if you have an IMAP server.

You can select the Check for Mail Every XX Minutes option to have Communicator automatically check mail for you. You can also select the Remember My Mail Password option, if you have no fears about prying eyes on your system.

Finally, there's a check box that says you can Use Netscape Messenger from MAPI-based Applications. In other words, programs that can send e-mail by using a MAPI client will choose to use Messenger to do so.

# 336 Chapter 16 Setting Preferences

**FIG. 16.17**
More Options for your Mail Server settings.

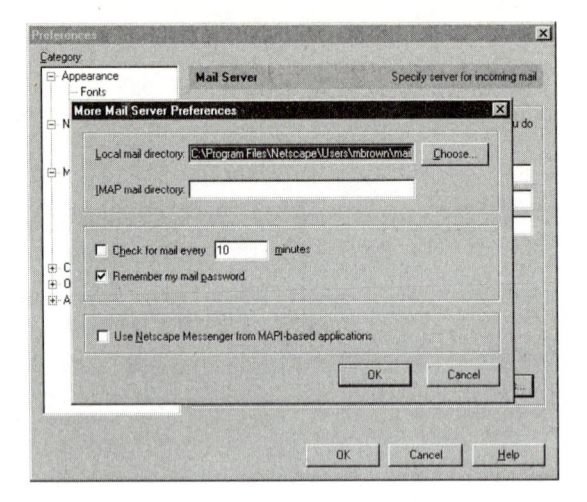

## Groups Server

The Groups Server Preferences panel is labeled Groups Server—Specify Servers for Reading Discussion Groups (see Figure 16.18).

**FIG. 16.18**
You must include the topmost information in this panel if you want to engage in newsgroup discussions.

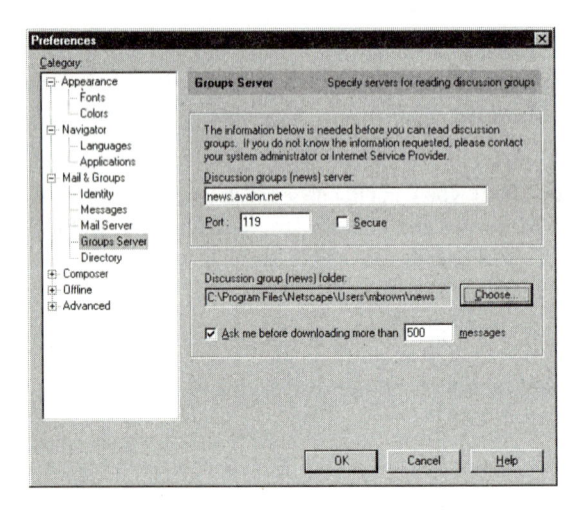

The Discussion Groups (News) Server field should contain the URL of your news server computer. The Port: selection is automatic, and changes if you select the Secure check box. (If your news server uses non-standard ports, you need to get the correct port numbers from your system administrator or Internet Service Provider.)

http://www.quecorp.com

You can set your Discussion group (news) folder by clicking the Choose button.

If the newsgroups you subscribe to fill up fast, you might also want to choose an appropriate setting for Ask Me Before Downloading More than XXX Messages.

## Directory

The Directory panel is labeled Directory—Choose Directories for Searching Addresses (see Figure 16.19).

**FIG. 16.19**
You can search for people in a wide variety of places by using Communicator.

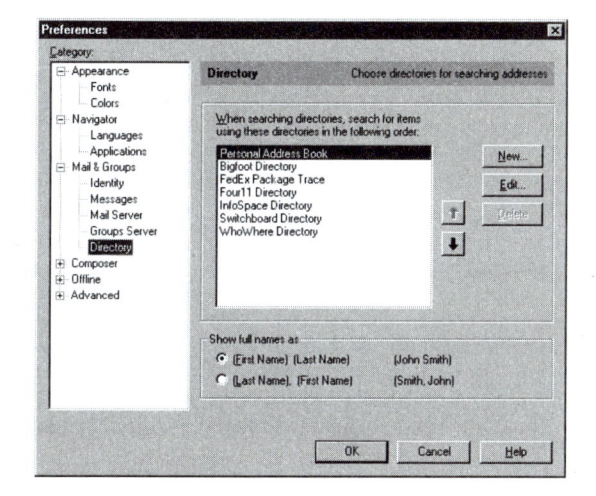

In the Message Composition window, you can click the Address button to search for an address. The search engines you use, and the order they appear in the drop-down list there, is determined by the settings in this preferences panel.

The scrolling list of directories is labeled When Searching Directories, Search for Items Using These Directories in the Following Order:, and the following entries appear there:

- Personal Address Book
- Bigfoot Directory
- Four11 Directory
- InfoSpace Directory
- Switchboard Directory
- WhoWhere Directory

By highlighting an entry and clicking the Up or Down arrow buttons, you can move an entry's position in the list.

Click the New button and you get the dialog box shown in Figure 16.20.

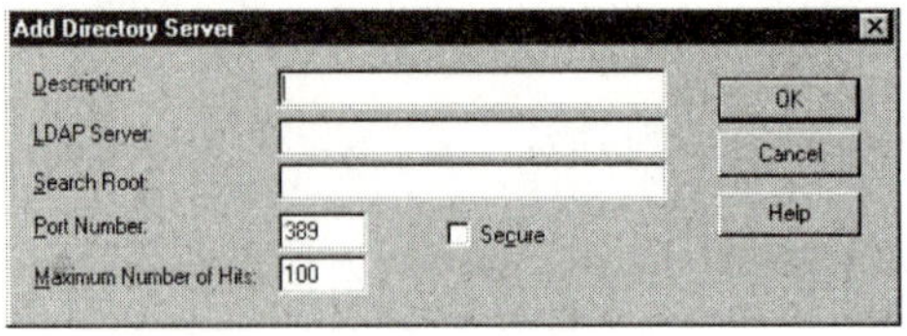

**FIG. 16.20**
The New entry dialog box for the Directory panel.

This dialog box asks for the following information:

- Description
- LDAP Server
- Search Root
- Port Number
- Secure
- Maximum Number of Hits

You must obtain this information from the directory server before attempting to create an entry for a new server. The last entry selects how many entries to download when you do a search.

The Edit button brings up the same dialog box, but filled with information for the currently selected entry.

The Delete button deletes an entry from the list.

Finally, the last two radio buttons choose how an entry is displayed: Show full names as

(First Name) (Last Name) (John Smith)

(Last Name), (First Name) (Smith, John)

# Composer

There are three sections in the panel labeled Composer—Set General Preferences for Authoring Web Pages (see Figure 16.21).

In the first section, you set your Author Name and can select a check box to Automatically Save Page Every XX Minutes.

> **CAUTION**
> If you don't select to auto-save, make sure you save manually every few minutes!

**FIG. 16.21**
The Composer Preferences Panel controls how Netscape Composer works and acts.

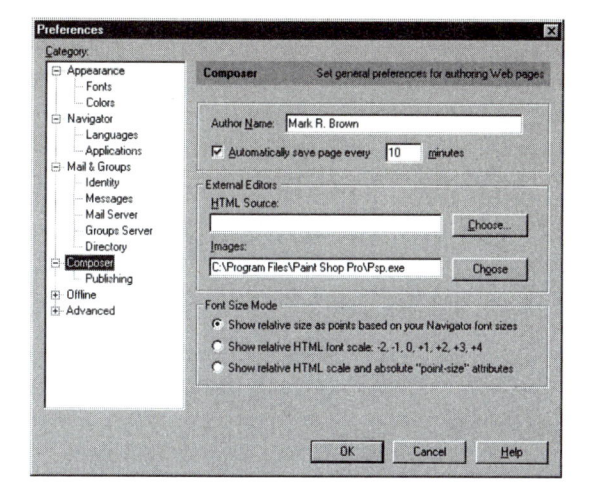

The second section lets you pick External Editors for HTML Source and/or Images. Each has a Choose button for selecting an application from disk.

The final section sets Font Size Mode, and it has three mutually exclusive radio button choices:

- Show Relative Size As Points Based on Your Navigator Font Sizes
- Show Relative HTML Font Scale: -2, -1, 0, +1, +2, +3, +4
- Show Relative HTML Scale and Absolute "Point-Size" Attributes

Choose the first if you are used to working with point sizes, and the second if you prefer to see relative sizes based on HTML settings. The third choice shows both.

## Publishing

Where does a page go, and how, when you publish it using Composer? That's determined by the settings in the Preferences panel labeled Publishing—Designate the Default Publishing Location (see Figure 16.22).

The Links and Images section of the Publishing panel determines how these elements behave when you move your page from the place where it was edited to the place where it will be viewed. When saving remote pages, you can choose two behaviors: Maintain Links and Keep Images with Page. You should select each if the pages linked to and the images you use will both be transferred to the new location. You should uncheck each if the images and links are absolute—that is, if they exist offsite.

The final section sets the Default Publishing Location. You should Enter a FTP or HTTP Site Address To Publish To, and If Publishing to a FTP site, Enter the HTTP Address to Browse to, If Different Than the FTP Address.

**FIG. 16.22**
Link and image behavior and publishing location are both set through this panel.

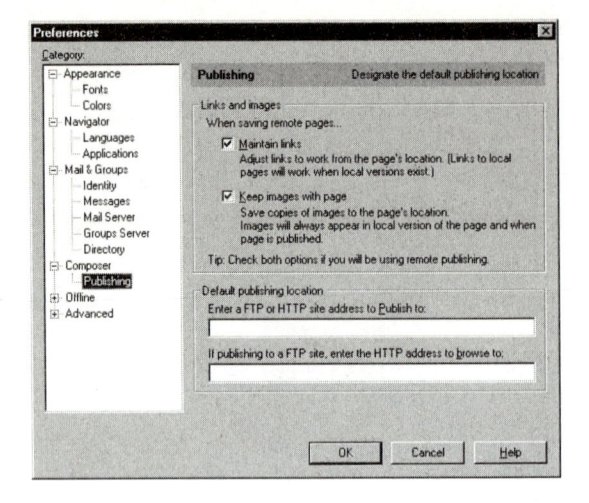

## Offline

If you often work offline, you'll want to make some settings in the Preferences panel labeled Offline—Choose the Startup Mode of the Product (see Figure 16.23).

**FIG. 16.23**
Use a laptop? Then you may want to call up the Offline Preferences panel.

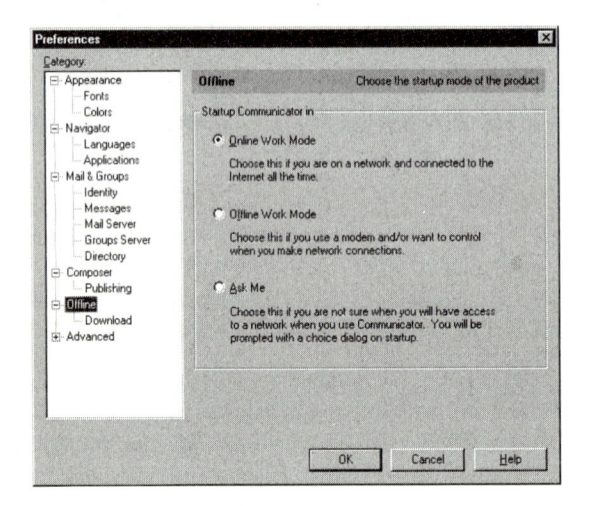

This panel has just three radio button selections that let you Startup Communicator in:

- Online Work Mode
- Offline Work Mode
- Ask Me

Choose the first if you are usually connected to a network. Choose the second if you are usually working without a network connection. Choose Ask Me if your situation often changes.

http://www.quecorp.com

## Download

If you do a lot of work offline and also access newsgroups, you'll need to make some choices in the Preferences panel labeled Download—Choose Settings for Reading Messages Offline (see Figure 16.24).

**FIG. 16.24**
Control over newsgroup message downloading is imperative if you're going to work offline.

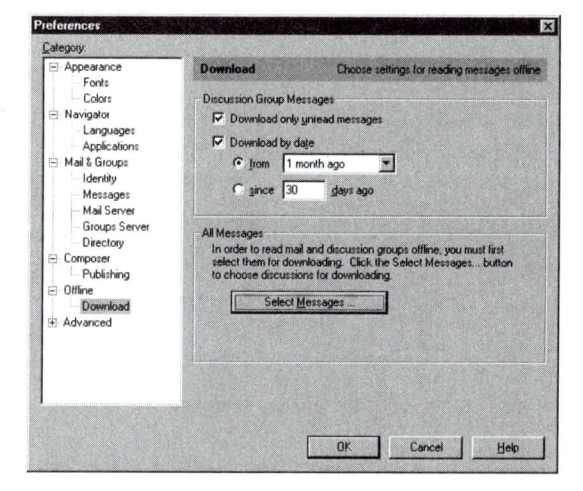

The Discussion Group Messages section of this panel lets you choose to Download Only Unread Messages and/or Download By Date from a Certain Date, or Since XX Days Ago.

The All Messages section lets you select messages you would like to download. Clicking the Select Messages button brings up the dialog box shown in Figure 16.25.

**FIG. 16.25**
This dialog box lets you choose which message groups to download.

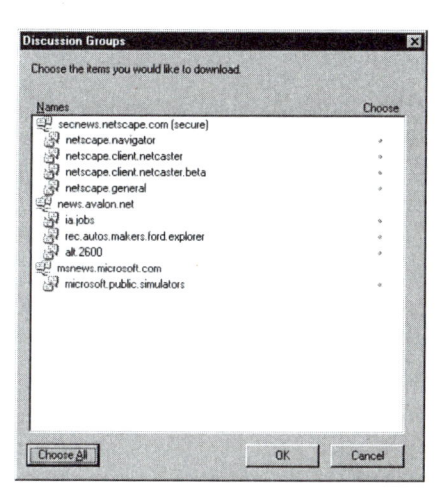

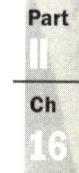

Newsgroup Names are listed on the left; you can click the dot to a name's right to choose that group for downloading. If you want to select all groups, click the Select All button; click OK to finish.

Choose wisely from both these dialog boxes; your hard drive can quickly become overwhelmed if you download too many messages for offline viewing.

## Advanced

Choosing the Advanced menu selection brings up the panel labeled Advanced—Change Preferences That Affect the Entire Product (see Figure 16.26).

**FIG. 16.26**
You should understand what each option listed here controls before you change it.

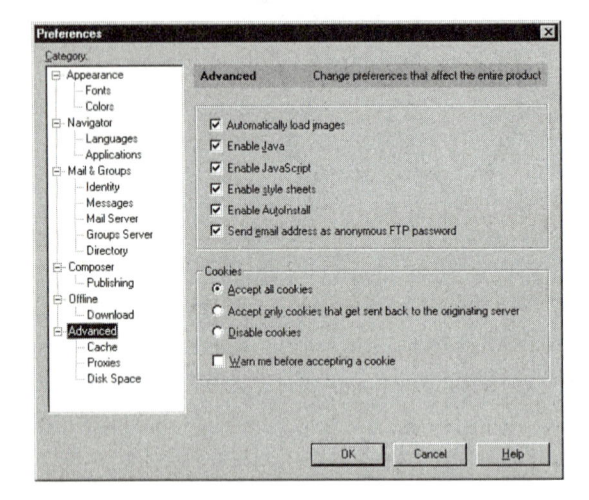

There are six check box selections in the top half of this panel:

- Automatically Load Images—This choice should be deselected to disable image loading, thus speeding up page loading over slower connections. However, images will be shown with placeholders instead of pictures. If you disable Automatic Image Loading, you'll get a new button on the Navigation Toolbar called "Images" that you can click to selectively load images. If connection speed isn't a problem for you, leave this box checked for normal image display.
- Enable Java—Keep this box checked to automatically run Java applets. Uncheck it if Java downloads are a time or security concern to you.
- Enable JavaScript—This does for JavaScript what the above selection does for Java.
- Enable Style Sheets—If you want to see pages with Communicator's new style sheet capability turned on, leave this box checked. If this makes your pages too slow, or if you prefer your own page style settings, deselect it.

- Enable Au*t*oInstall—If checked, Communicator can be automatically updated on disk from the Netscape site. If unchecked, you will have to manually update Communicator when new releases are made available.
- Send *E*-mail Address as Anonymous FTP Password—If you regularly download files from anonymous FTP sites, check this option. If you prefer to keep your e-mail address a secret, by all means leave this box unchecked.

Cookies are short bits of information added to a file on your computer's hard drive by systems you visit. For example, you might visit an online store, add some items to an electronic shopping cart, then bail out to return later. Information stored by that site in your "cookie file" will enable you to continue shopping with all the items in your cart intact.

Some users prefer not to allow sites to write to their cookie file. The Cookies section of this panel gives you three mutually exclusive cookie options:

- *A*ccept All Cookies
- Accept *O*nly Cookies that Get Sent Back to the Originating Server
- *D*isable Cookies

Choose the first option if you don't care who creates or reads your cookies, and the second option if you want only the originator to be able to read back the information in your cookie file. Choose the third option if you want no one to be able to read or write to your cookie file.

No matter which option you choose, you can also select the check box next to the selection *W*arn Me Before Accepting a Cookie to be informed when a site tries to write a cookie. Cookies are covered in depth in Chapter 17, "Security Options."

## Cache

The Cache panel is labeled, Cache—Designate the Size of the Cache (see Figure 16.27).

Navigator uses both your computer memory and hard disk space to save information from the sites you visit. That way, multiple visits are quicker, because text, images, and other page elements can be loaded locally instead of from the network.

You can control how much is cached in memory or on disk by using the *M*emory Cache and *D*isk Cache settings at the top of this panel. Each is set in kilobytes (1,024 byte blocks). If your system has little memory and a small hard disk, set these low. If your system is fully decked out, set them high. The default setting is 1024K for the *M*emory Cache, and 7680K for *D*isk Cache.

You can immediately clear out the contents of the memory cache by clicking the Clear Memor*y* Cache button; you can do the same for the disk cache by clicking the Clear Dis*k* Cache button.

You can select where you want to store the disk cache by filling in the Disk Cache *F*older field, or by clicking the Choo*s*e Folder button.

**FIG. 16.27**
This panel lets you control how much memory and disk space are used by Navigator.

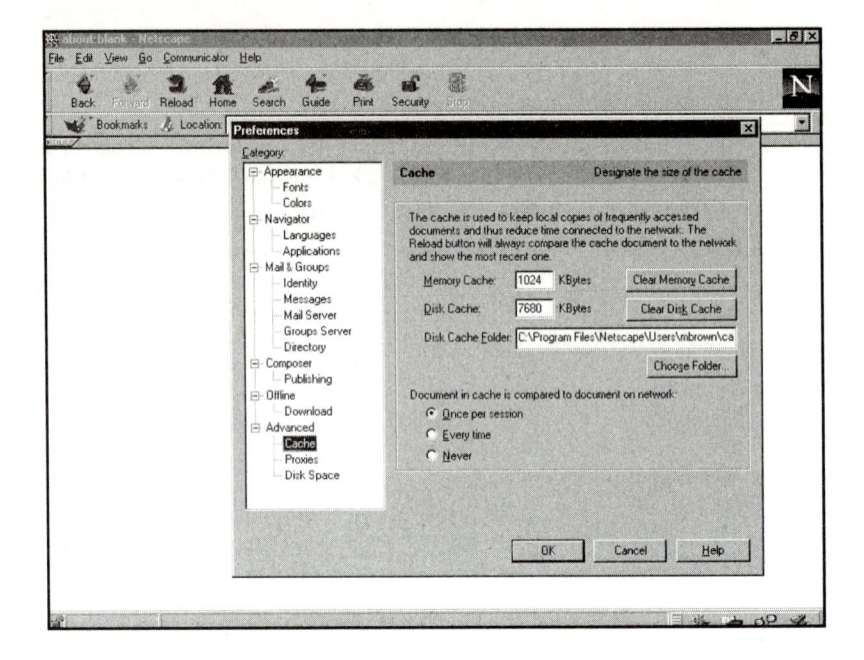

Finally, the Cache panel lets you control how the document in the cache is compared to the document on the network. You can choose

- Once Per Session
- Every Time
- Never

Choose the first selection to give you maximum throughput combined with very good accuracy—any page you try to load will only be compared against the version in the disk cache the first time you try to load it in each session. Choosing Every Time makes sure that the version of the page you view is the latest revision, but costs you a lot of time making comparisons to the cached version every time you access a page. The final choice, Never, means that you always use a cached version of a page if it is available. While fast, you may not always get the latest version of a page this way.

> **TIP** You can always compare the latest version of a page from cache to one stored on the network by clicking the Reload button on the Navigation toolbar. To forcibly reload a page from the network, hold down the Shift key when you click the Reload button.

## Proxies

If your computer is secure behind a corporate firewall, you'll need to make some changes in the Proxies panel, labeled Proxies—Configure Proxies to Access the Internet (see Figure 16.28).

http://www.quecorp.com

Advanced | 345

**FIG. 16.28**
Get the settings for your Proxies Preferences from your system administrator.

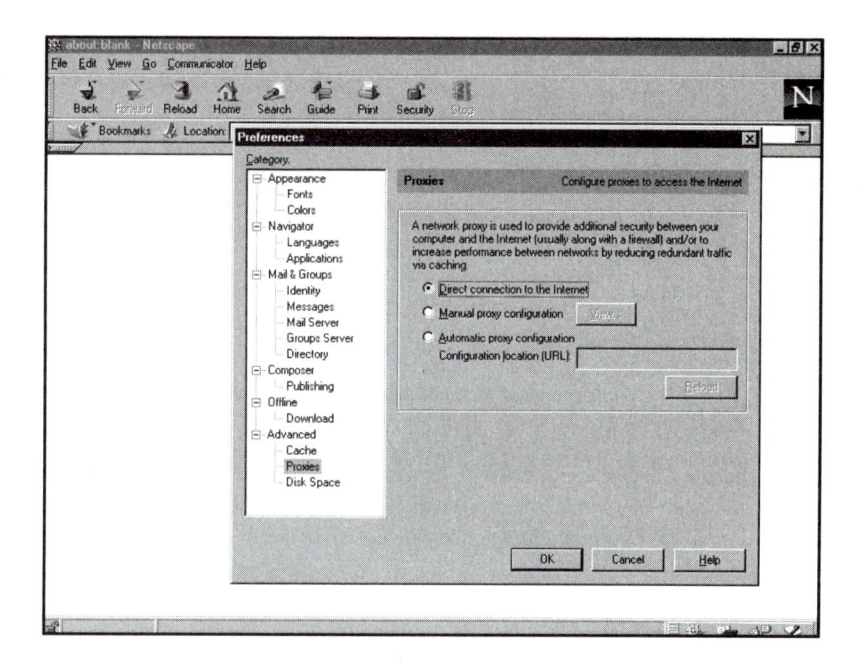

There are three option buttons for your proxy settings. Direct Connection to the Internet is the default, and you should leave this setting alone if you're not behind a firewall.

The second selection, Manual Proxy Configuration, requires you to click the View button to bring up the dialog box shown in Figure 16.29.

**FIG. 16.29**
The Proxy Settings dialog box lets you configure proxy settings for six common Internet functions.

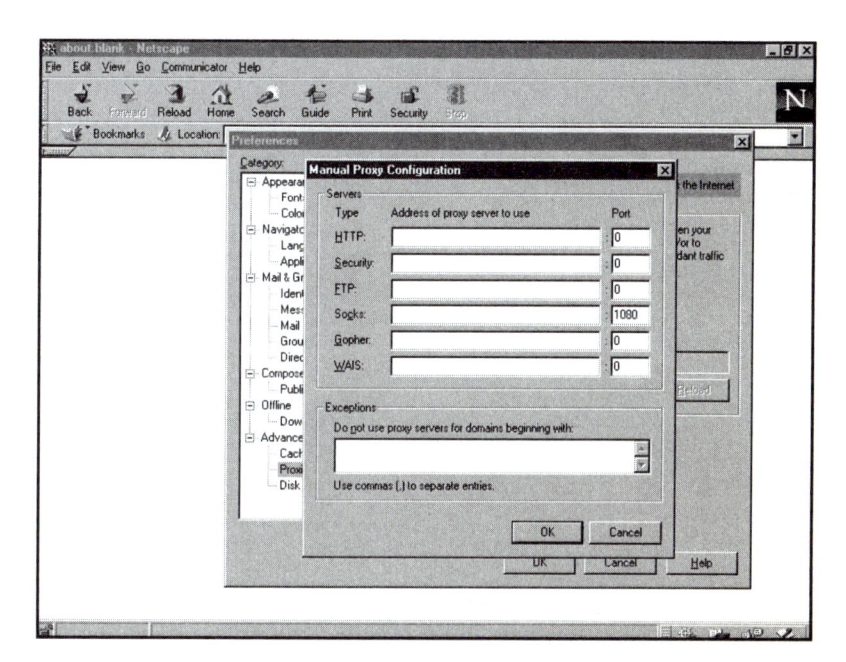

Part II
Ch
16

From this dialog box, you can set the URL and port number for servers to handle:

- **H**TTP
- **S**ecurity
- **F**TP
- So**c**ks
- **G**opher
- **W**AIS

All of these address and port settings should come from your system administrator.

You can also enter a list of domain exceptions that will be accessed without going through a proxy server. This can be handy if you operate with a corporate intranet inside the firewall, for example. Use commas (,) to separate entries.

The final selection allows you to enter an URL for **A**utomatic Proxy Configuration. The information on the designated page must be set up by your system administrator. But if your system administrator has set up such a page, it can save you a lot of work. If the settings (but not the URL) are ever changed by your system administrator, you can update your proxies by clicking the **R**eload button.

## Disk Space

The final selection in the Preferences panel settings is labeled Disk Space—Manage the Amount of Disk Space Taken By Messages (see Figure 16.30).

**FIG. 16.30**
E-mail and discussion group messages can quickly overwhelm your hard drive. This panel lets you keep them under control.

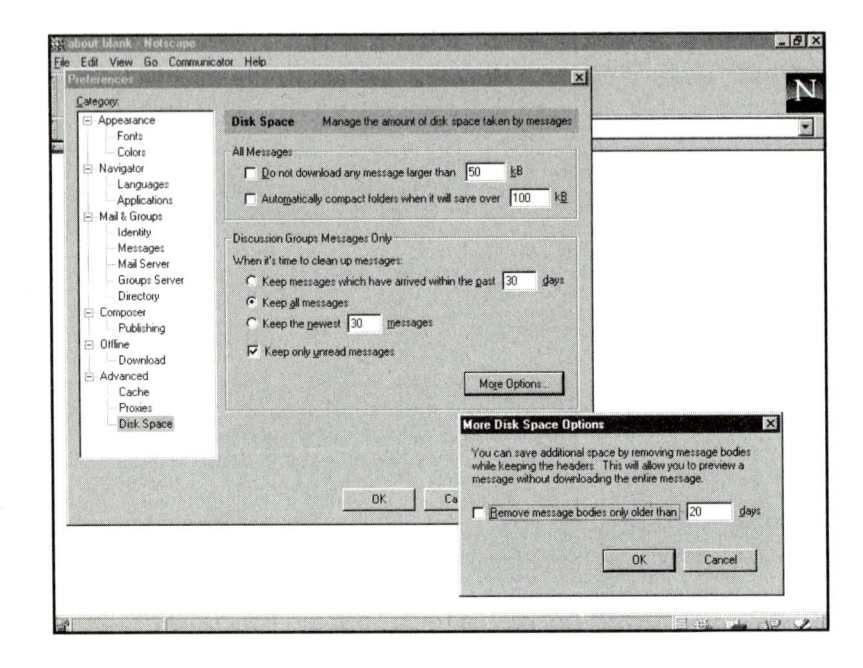

http://www.quecorp.com

There are two settings that affect all messages—that is, both e-mail and discussion groups. Check the Do Not Download Any Message Larger Than XX kB check box to designate a maximum download size for e-mail and group messages. Select Automatically Compact Folders When It Will Save over XXX kB to allow folder compression when you can free up the designated amount of disk space.

The second section sets options for Discussion Groups Messages Only. You can have Communicator clean up messages by using one of three options:

- Keep Messages Which Have Arrived Within the Past XX Days
- Keep All Messages
- Keep the Newest XX Messages

The first allows you to designate that files should be kept for a certain time period. The second chooses to keep all messages, and is obviously the most wasteful of disk resources, but the most cautious approach. The last option keeps only a specified number of the newest messages.

A final check box works in conjunction with your choice above, and designates that, whatever other option you've chosen, you will actually Keep Only Unread Messages that also meet the other criterion.

Clicking the More Options button brings up a dialog box that lets you select a check box to Remove Message Bodies Only Older Than XX Days. This lets you keep headers, but remove the actual messages, which can be re-downloaded by clicking on their headers. ●

CHAPTER 17

# Security Options

*by Tom Fronckowiak*

The word *security*, when transplanted from common usage into Internet vernacular, assumes a number of additional meanings—privacy, confidentiality, authenticity, and non-repudiation, to name a few. The word even extends to the services that provide these requirements—password protection, public key encryption, digital signature, and strong authentication. Netscape Communicator has a number of security features that ease the fear of transacting over the unsecured (and often unfamiliar) bandwidths of the Internet.

- **How to configure Communicator for multiple users**

  Allow a profile for more than one person or multiple profiles for a single person.

- **How to understand Communicator's security information**

  Comprehend the basics of certificates and how they're used in secure transactions.

- **How to password-protect your private keys**

  Make sure no one can send messages pretending to be you.

- **How to manage certificates**

  Learn the difference between user, site, and signer certificates, and how to control access to your machine.

- **How security is applied to e-mail and Web browsing**

  What SSL and S/MIME provide in the way of secure transactions.

# Configuring for Multiple Users

Netscape allows you to configure Communicator for a multiuser environment by creating a profile for each user. Each profile contains its own set of user-specific data including e-mail accounts and address books. This is also useful if you wear a number of different hats during the day. You can create a profile for each of your personalities and reduce the chance of doing something careless, like erroneously sending out a top secret, official document to all the guys in your string quartet. To create multiple profiles, follow these steps:

1. Open the Profile Manager by clicking the User Profile Manager icon in your Netscape Communicator folder. It might have been installed in the Utilities subdirectory.

2. Examine your current profiles and determine what users or personalities you want to add, delete, or rename (see Figure 17.1).

**FIG. 17.1**
Allow multiple users to share one copy of Communicator by creating profiles for each person.

3. To add another personality, click the New button. You see the New Profile Setup dialog box (see Figure 17.2). Click Next.

**FIG. 17.2**
Profiles can be used to distinguish between multiple people or to separate different identities of a single person.

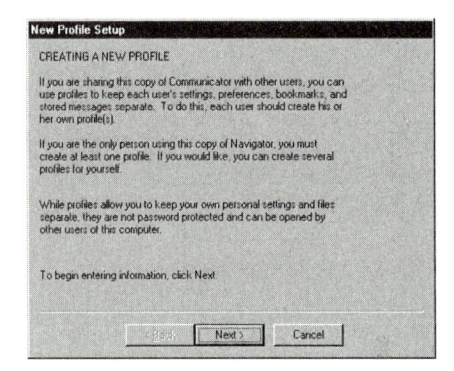

4. Enter the full name of the user and the user's e-mail address as shown in Figure 17.3. Click Next.

**FIG. 17.3**
Enter the user's full name and e-mail address.

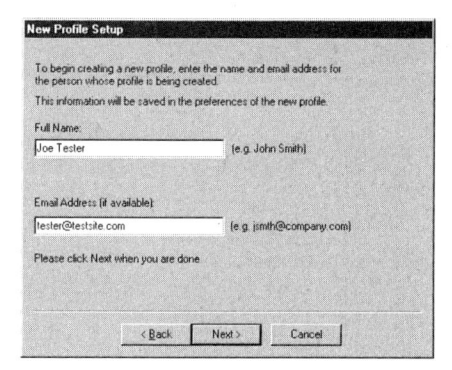

5. Figure 17.4 shows the default name given for the profile. Change this or keep the default, whichever you want, remembering that profile names should be unique. The second input box allows you to choose the directory where the user settings and preferences are stored. The default path is recommended. Click Next.

**FIG. 17.4**
Choose a unique profile name, one that identifies the user.

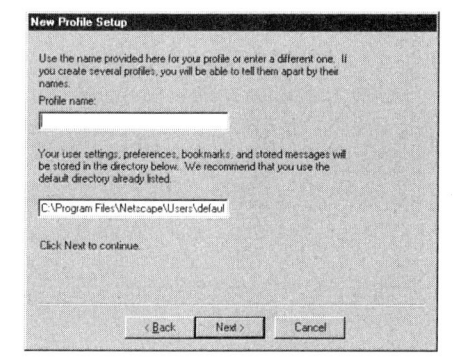

6. The next three input dialog boxes retrieve information for use in setting up mail and discussion groups. You are asked for the following input: Outgoing Mail Server, Mail Server User Name, Incoming Mail Server, Mail Server Type (POP3 or IMAP), News Server, and Port. These are needed for sending and receiving mail and reading discussion groups. If you do not know these values, ask your system administrator or leave these fields blank. You can enter them at a later time.

7. The last of the Mail and Discussion Groups Setup dialog boxes is shown in Figure 17.5. The Secure option button can be turned on to allow a private connection to your News Server. When you feel the information has been entered adequately, click Finish. Your new profile is created.

**Chapter 17** Security Options

**FIG. 17.5**
Select the Secure option button to ensure confidential news transmissions.

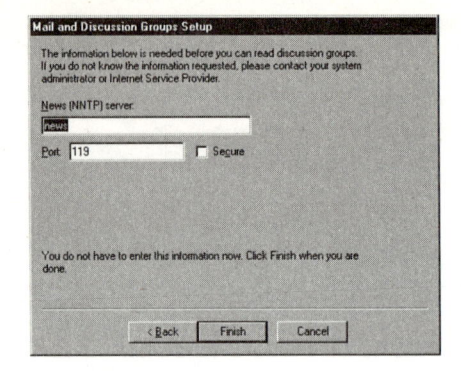

You can now use the Profile Manager to keep tabs on the Jekylls and Hydes of your machine. In the "Private Key Passwords" section later in this chapter, you see how passwords restrict access to your private encryption keys.

---

**New Netscape Administration Kit**

Netscape has a new administration kit called Mission Control, available separately, which allows central administration of its products.

Targeted at cutting ownership costs, Mission Control lets managers configure user interfaces and set security policies from a centralized location. This means a reduction in installation costs and maintenance travel.

In addition to company-wide customization, Mission Control can also serve to restrict e-mail and discussion server access, allow distribution of new software, and administer parts the Netscape Communicator suite, such as Netcaster.

---

## Security Button

No doubt by the time you've gotten to this chapter, you've already been experimenting with your browser and have managed to casually work your way through some of the less understood menus. If you haven't already guessed, the button with the brown padlock in the toolbar is the security button. It serves two purposes. First and most obvious, it's the button you click to get to the security dialog box. Second, it's a visual cue that tells you whether your connection is secure. Unless you're connected to a secure server using SSL, or viewing a security-enhanced Messenger message, the lock is open and dull. Figure 17.6 shows an insecure connection to **http://www.verisign.com**. Notice the padlock icon present at the lower-left corner of the screen. These padlocks remind you that any information traveling to and from your machine is being transmitted in an unsecured manner.

http://www.quecorp.com

**FIG. 17.6**
An insecure connection—the brown padlock on the security button in the toolbar and the smaller lock in the lower-left corner are open.

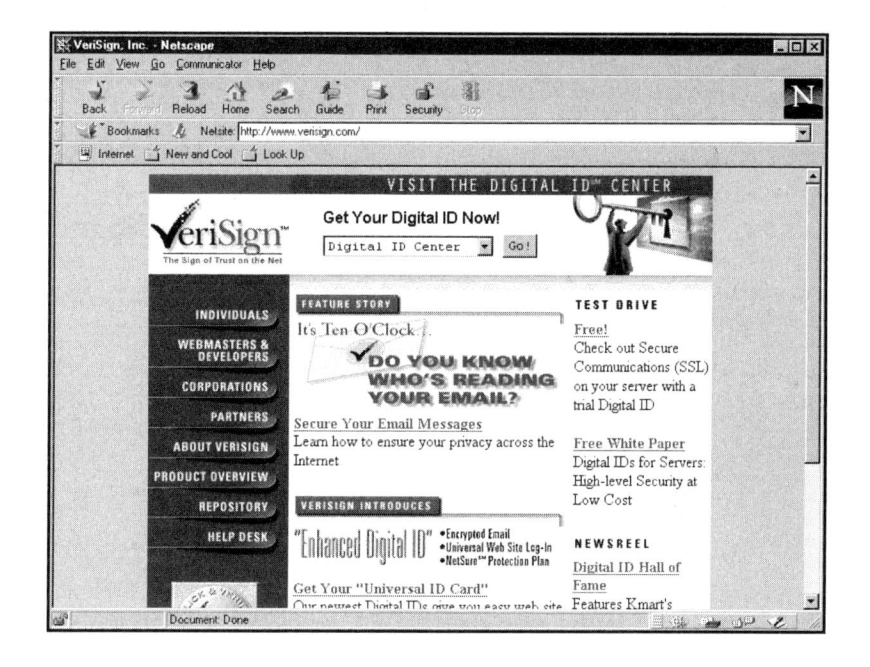

**N O T E** Previous versions of Netscape Navigator used a skeleton key to denote the presence and absence of security.

The Internet community and surrounding organizations have feverishly been developing new protocols and specifications in the interest of privacy, while at the same time enhancing existing protocols; SLDAP, S/MIME, SNEWS are some examples. But regardless of whether these protocols are secure sisters of pre-existing standards or new kids on the block, chances are their acronyms carry an *s*; and chances are that *s* stands for *secure*.

HTTP is no exception. URLs for secure servers begin with https instead of http. Figure 17.7 shows such a connection—**https://www.verisign.com**. The suffix for the Verisign URL is the same; we've just changed to a secure protocol. Notice how the padlock on the security button is now completely closed and surrounded by a yellow corona.

By clicking the padlock button, you can display security information about your current connection or modify the security options within Communicator. (The small padlock in the bottom left corner also opens the security dialog box.) The left side of the security dialog box (see Figure 17.8) shows the following list of topics:

- Security Info
- Passwords
- Navigator
- Messenger
- Java/JavaScripts
- Your Certificates

- Other People's Certificates
- Web Site Certificates
- Signer Certificates
- Cryptographic Modules

**FIG. 17.7**
For secure connections, https is used in place of http. The padlock on the security button tells you that the connection is secure.

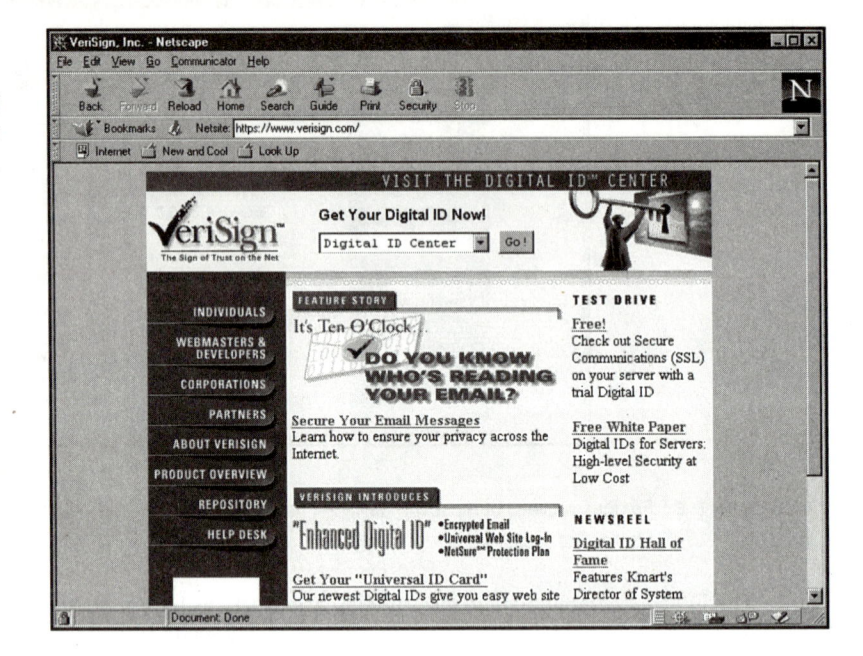

The rest of this chapter deals with manipulating the settings of these categories, and how they enhance the security of your Web browsing and e-mail messages.

## Viewing Security Info

When you first enter the security dialog box—by clicking the padlock button or selecting Communicator, Security Info from the pull-down menu—the Security Info topic is highlighted by default. Figure 17.8 shows the information for a secure link to Verisign. The text tells you that, in fact, the page was encrypted and you're operating in a secure environment. The small padlock next to the scroll bar is lit and locked. Another thing to notice is the presence of the View Certificate button. Figure 17.9 shows the information on an e-mail message in Messenger that did *not* have security applied to it. Because the message was not encrypted, the View Certificate button is absent, and the padlock is surrounded by a blue haze.

**FIG. 17.8**
Displaying information about a secure connection presents a View Certificate button.

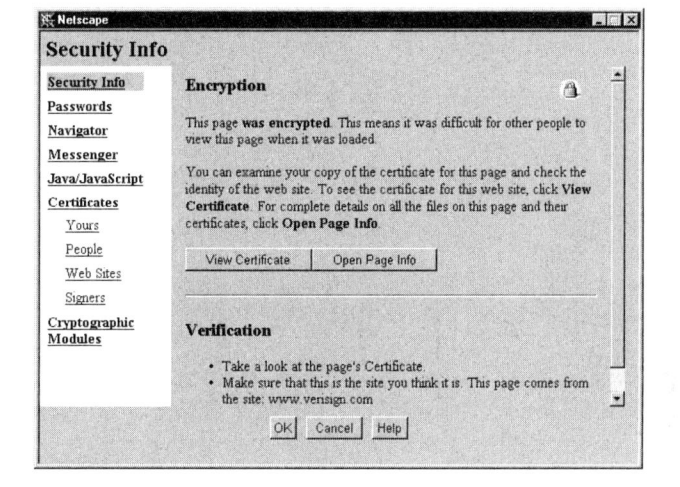

**FIG. 17.9**
Remove the security and the View Certificate button disappears.

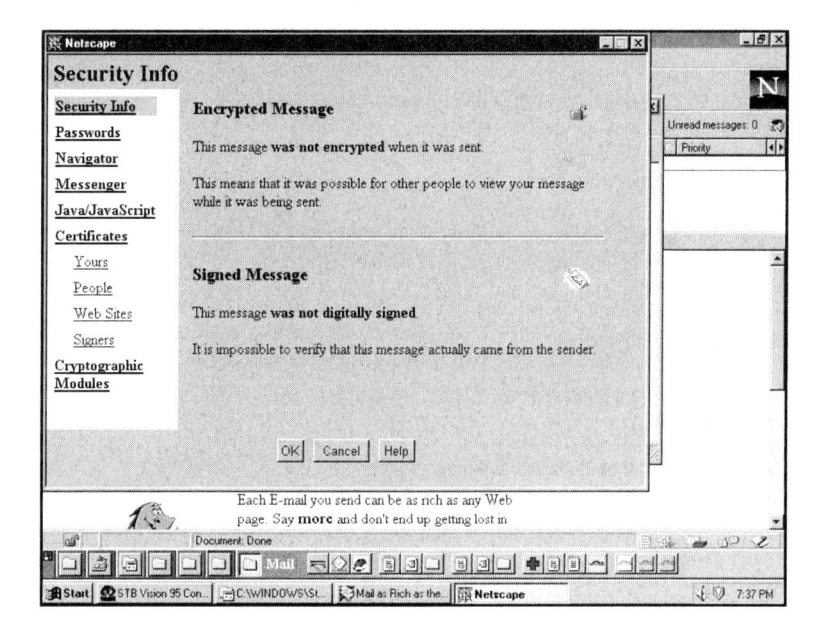

Now you know how to tell if a document was sent and received privately. But what does that tell you about its authenticity? Do you know that it came from whom you think sent it? Clicking the View Certificate button shown in Figure 17.8 shows you. Figure 17.10 is the Verisign Site Certificate.

**FIG. 17.10**
Certificates identify you to secure servers, and secure servers to you.

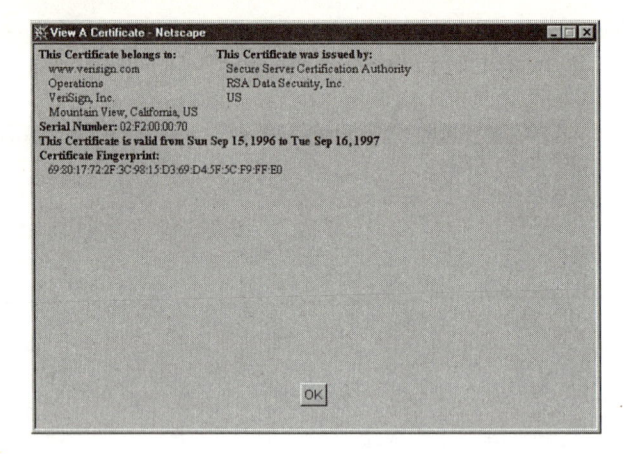

Look at the subject (who the certificate was issued to) and the issuer of this certificate. Is this who you expected to see? The answer is yes! We're connected to Verisign's Web page; we expected to see Verisign's name in the certificate.

Authenticity relies mainly on a level of trust. Quite often you don't know who or when to trust, simply because the person or organization you're communicating with is unfamiliar to you. You must depend upon an authority—a Certificate Authority—to vouch for that person. But sometimes you don't even recognize the Certificate Authority. Then what? In the next section, you see how to control who to trust and not to trust.

# Certificates

In the grand scheme of public key cryptography, certificates are used to identify people and entities by binding them to a particular public key. It's like taking a house key and carving your name into it, except house keys are for your own use. Public keys are for anyone who wants to encrypt something to you and wants to be certain that only you can read it. Whenever anyone locks data with the public key in Honest Oscar's certificate, they can be quite certain that only Honest Oscar's private key can unlock it. He owns that certificate!

### What Is Public Key Cryptography?
Historically, encryption was performed using a single key (symmetric encryption). One key to encrypt, the same key to decrypt. This is analogous to locking a letter in a key vault. The key used to unlock the vault had to be the same key that originally locked it. The problem presented was, how do you transmit the key without compromising it? And if you have the secure means to do so, why even encrypt the letter in the first place? Why not just send it through the secure means?

Public key cryptography fixed that dilemma by utilizing a public/private key pair. Two keys—one to encrypt, one to decrypt (asymmetric encryption). Anyone can encrypt the message using the public key, but only the person holding the private key can decrypt it. Because the public key is made readily available, there need not be a secure channel between sender and receiver. This is analogous to a key vault with a mail slit on the top. Anyone can slip in a letter, but only the one with the private key can open the vault and remove it.

When you view a certificate, as you did in the previous section, the following fields are displayed (refer to Figure 17.10):

- *The certificate belongs to*—This is the subject of the certificate. It can be a person, an organization, a Web site, or some other entity.
- *The certificate was issued by*—This is the issuer of the certificate. He vouches for the subject by digitally signing this certificate.
- *Serial Number*—The serial number, along with the issuer's name, uniquely identifies a certificate.
- *This certificate is valid from*—This is the validity period of the certificate. When it expires, a new certificate is needed.
- *Certificate Fingerprint*—This helps identify a certificate.

You might notice that the public key is not displayed as part of the certificate. That's fine. Because it's a string of binary data, you wouldn't be able to read it anyway.

**NOTE** The names that describe the subject and issuer are a hierarchical list of elements, not unlike your postal mail address. They start at the most specific element, a name or organization, and regresses to the most general, a state or country.

Communicator supports the following three types of certificates:

- User certificates, which include your certificates and other people's certificates
- Web Site Certificates
- Signer Certificates

## Your Certificates

Being a multi-faceted, dynamic, independent person, you might have the need to keep and maintain numerous certificates. You're known as the PTA president to members of the school board. To the hardware competitors across town, you'd like to be addressed as chief engineer of development. And to everyone else, you're happy with the role of neighborhood watch chairman.

On the left margin of the security dialog box, under Certificates, click Yours. The Your Certificate display appears, as shown in Figure 17.11. The certificates you obtain are listed in this dialog box.

**FIG. 17.11**
People and Web sites use your certificates to encrypt data to you and to verify digitally signed messages from you.

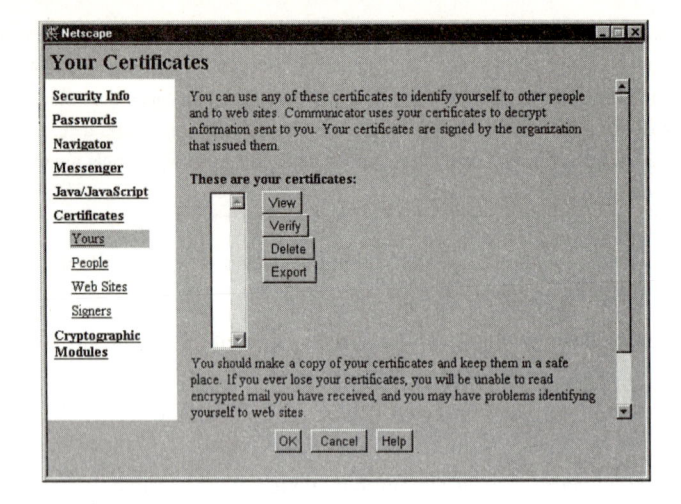

## Other People's Certificates

Besides keeping a list of your certificates, Communicator keeps a list of all the certificates you collect when other people send you secure mail. Click the People option on the left margin of the security dialog box to use the Other People's Certificate dialog box. From here, you can manage certificates obtained from friends, co-workers, and even strangers. Figure 17.12 shows the Other People's Certificate dialog box.

**FIG. 17.12**
You can send encrypted e-mail to people whose certificates are listed under Other People's Certificates.

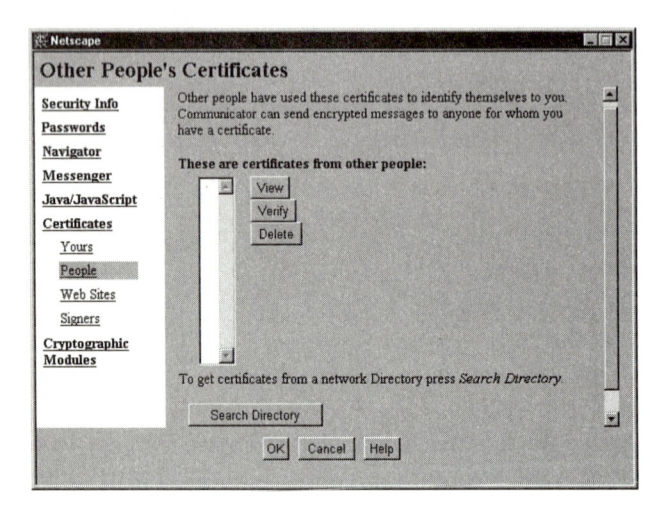

To encrypt to someone, you must first have that person's certificate. He can send it to you by way of a digitally signed message, or if he has an entry in a network directory, you can click the Search Directory button and search for it by his e-mail address.

http://www.quecorp.com

## Web Sites' Certificates

Web Sites' Certificates are certificates signed by a Certificate Authority just like user certificates, but are only issued to operators of a Web site. Like user certificates, they provide proof of identity and can be verified against the Certificate Authority. In addition, they allow secure connections to the Web site. Figure 17.13 shows the Web Sites' Certificate dialog box. Clicking the Sites option in the left margin of the security dialog box gets you there. Site certificates that you collect are listed in this dialog box.

**FIG. 17.13**
Web Sites' Certificates, like other people's certificates, are subject to the scrutiny of your personal discretion.

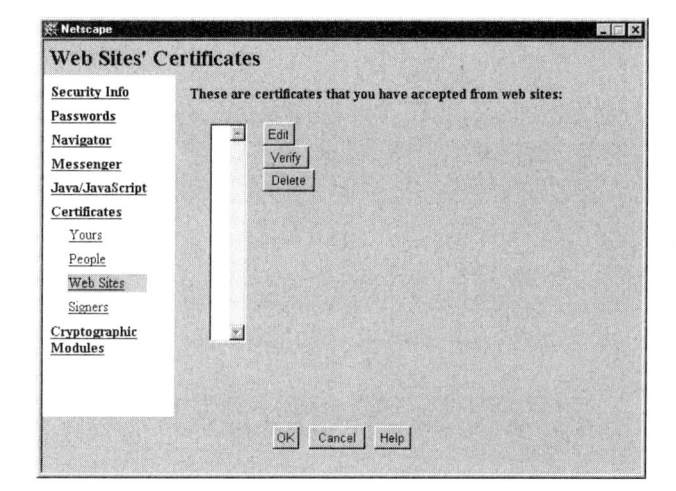

## Certificate Authorities

Now is a good time to talk about trust and the certificate issuer. I mentioned earlier how certificate issuers (a.k.a. Certificate Authorities) vouch for users and sites who might be, and usually are, unfamiliar to you.

You know that a certificate is an encoded blob of data containing a person's name and public key, among other things. The way a Certificate Authority (CA) vouches for this person is by digitally signing his certificate. What's created is a digital signature that can be traced back up the CA and provides not only an identity of the signer, but also integrity of the data being signed. If the certificate is tampered with, the signature is broken.

Trust, then, is siphoned up to the Certificate Authority level. I can trust a certificate only as long as I can trust the CA who signed it. It then falls on the shoulders of the CA to ensure that the subject of the certificate is exactly who he claims to be. CA's have detailed policies that define how they verify a certificate holder's identity.

To view all the certificate signers whose certificates you currently accept, click Signers in the left margin of the security dialog box. Figure 17.14 shows this.

**FIG. 17.14**
Keep a current and accurate list of certificate signers by using this dialog box.

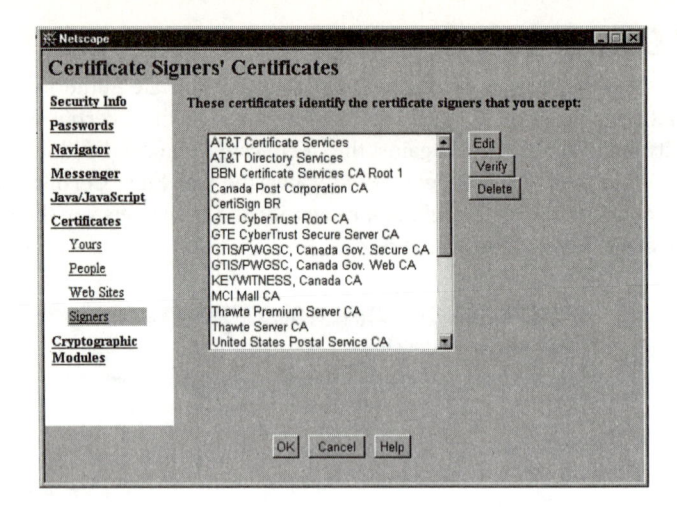

If Certificate Authorities sign user certificates and Web site certificates, who then signs the Certificate Authority's certificate? By choosing a CA certificate and clicking the edit button, you can find out. Figure 17.15 shows the edit dialog box.

**FIG 17.15**
Signer's certificates are usually self-signed.

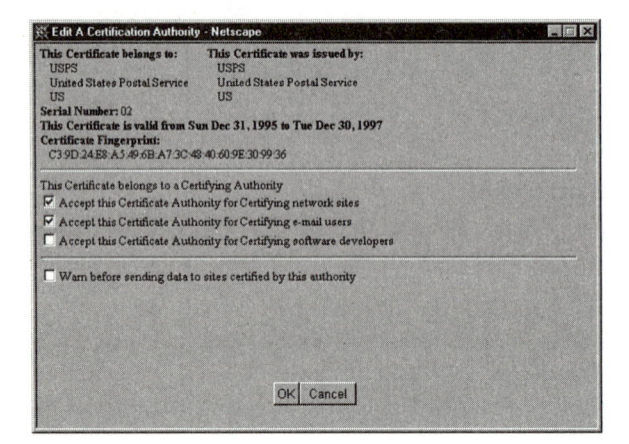

The following four options are available to control trust for a particular certificate signer:

- *Accept this Certificate Authority for Certifying network sites*—Select this to accept the CA while browsing the Web.
- *Accept this Certificate Authority for Certifying e-mail users*—Select this option to accept the CA while verifying e-mail.
- *Accept this Certificate Authority for Certifying software developers*—Select this option to accept the CA while downloading software.

http://www.quecorp.com

■ *Warn before sending data to sites certified by this authority*—Select this option to display a warning message when you're about to send data to this CA.

Clicking OK returns you to the Certificate Signers' Certificates window. By highlighting an entry and clicking the Verify button, you digitally confirm the authenticity of any of these certificates. In the same manner, you can delete Certificate Authorities you find untrustworthy. Highlight that certificate from the list and press the Delete key.

Now that you've seen how to manage your certificates, let's see how you can protect them.

## Private Key Passwords

In the first section, "Configuring for Multiple Users," you saw the need for two or more people to use the same computer and why access control is important in a multiuser environment. While sharing machines might not be the norm in today's highly personalized computer world, there are many reasons why an isolated user puts himself in jeopardy by not keeping his private keys, well, private. Think about how many people have access to your computer at work. At home? And what about the laptop you lug to business meetings? Anyone who can access your private keys has cryptographic authority to send and receive messages as if they were you. And it's not limited to physical tampering. Computers connected to networks are just as susceptible.

Communicator allows you to password-protect your private keys; follow these steps:

1. Click the passwords option on the left side of the security dialog box. Figure 17.16 shows the Passwords window.

**FIG. 17.16**
A password allows you to control access to your certificates.

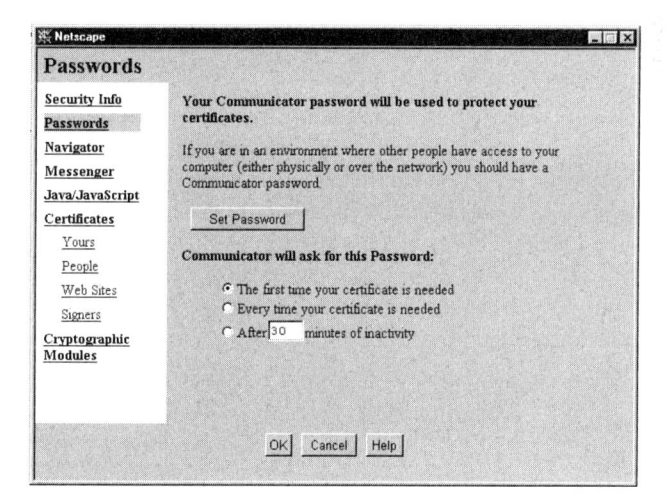

2. Click the Set Password button. The Setting Up Your Communicator Password window appears, shown in Figure 17.17.

3. Type and re-type your password. Remember that your password is the only thing standing between your privacy and a would-be attacker. Weak passwords like names, dates, and dictionary words should be avoided. A good rule of thumb is to mix numbers with upper and lowercase letters.

**FIG. 17.17**
Passwords are displayed as a string of asterisks, hiding them from nosy coworkers.

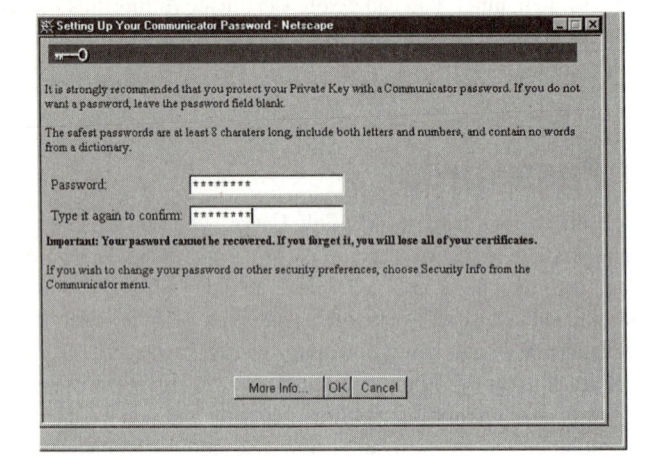

> **CAUTION**
> Commit your password to memory. And don't forget it. Ever. If you need to write it down, keep it in a safe place. If you forget or lose your password, you'll need to have your certificates reissued.

5. When you're finished, click OK and you're returned to the Passwords window shown back in Figure 17.16.
6. Finally, determine how often you want Communicator to prompt you for your password by choosing one of the "Communicator will ask for this Password" options. This depends on the amount of trust you have in your particular environment. For a lax security environment, choose The First Time Your Certificate Is Needed option button, and you only need to bother with it, at most, once per session. Choosing Every Time Your Certificate Is Needed causes Communicator to prompt you whenever a certificate is required. After *N* Minutes of Inactivity is a good choice if you find yourself away from your desk often and you want your security privileges to time out after a certain time of idleness.

## Applications

Certificates are electronic passports to private and exotic islands. But how do you get there? You need a vehicle that lets you travel as smoothly as you did before, but without the danger of being mugged on the way. Communicator offers you your choice of rides. Preferences for all three applications are listed in the security dialog box and are as follows:

http://www.quecorp.com

- *Navigator*—Allows secure connections servers via the Secure Sockets Layer (SSL).
- *Messenger*—Allows security-enhanced e-mail, including digital signatures and encryption, using S/MIME.
- *Java/JavaScript*—Restricts access to applets attempting to write to your machine or network.

## SSL Browsing

SSL stands for Secure Sockets Layer and allows secure transmissions across the Internet using public key encryption. Logically, it lies between TCP/IP and the application protocols, allowing it to be application protocol independent. To initiate and maintain a secure link, both the server and client must exchange credentials, which involves identifying themselves to each other. This gives either one a chance to bow out and deny service—for instance, a client was late paying his access fee and he was blacklisted.

After the strong link is established, information is transmitted under the cover of encryption—no longer susceptible to unauthorized disclosure.

You can bring up the Navigator options (see Figure 17.18) by clicking Navigator in the left side of the security dialog box.

**FIG. 17.18**
Select your security preferences for browsing the Web.

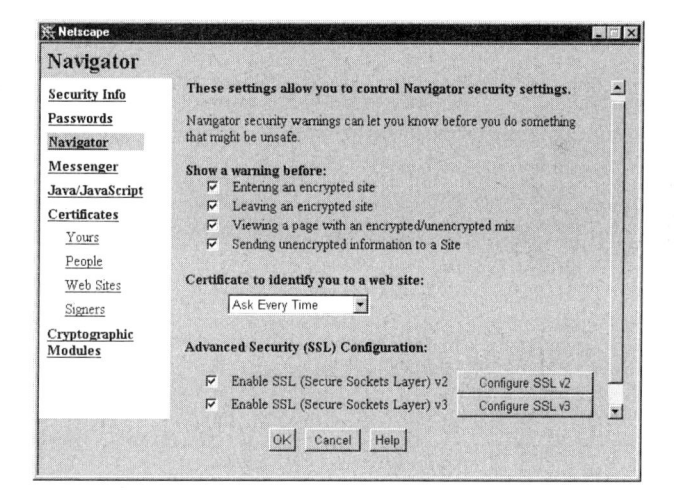

For the Show a Warning Before settings, choose a configuration that you feel most comfortable with. The following are your choices:

- *Entering an encrypted site* tells Navigator to remind you when you make a secure connection. You can tell by the padlock locking and turning yellow.
- *Leaving an encrypted site* tells Navigator to remind you when you move from a secure server to an insecure server. Again, the padlock tells you by unlocking, but make sure you pay close attention! It's far worse to send data in the clear that's supposed to be encrypted than it is to encrypt something that's supposed to be clear.

**Chapter 17  Security Options**

- *Some pages might have a mix of encrypted and unencrypted links.* View a Page with an Encrypted/Unencrypted Mix gives you control over whether Navigator warns you about these mixes or not.
- *Sending Unencrypted Information to a Site* tells Navigator to warn you when sending data to an insecure server.

An insecure warning message is shown in Figure 17.19.

The next setting, Certificate to Identify You to a Web Site, allows you to control whether Navigator asks for your certificate when accessing a Web site. Ask Every Time gives you the assurance of knowing which certificate is used. Selecting Automatic removes the hassle.

**FIG. 17.19**
Security Information gives an additional measure of comfort by continuing only at the user's discretion.

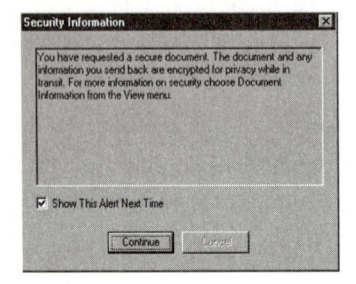

## S/MIME E-Mail

S/MIME was developed by RSA and allows encryption and digital signatures of electronic mail. You can bring up the Messenger options (see Figure 17.20) by clicking Messenger in the left side of the security dialog box.

**FIG. 17.20**
Select your security preferences for sending electronic mail.

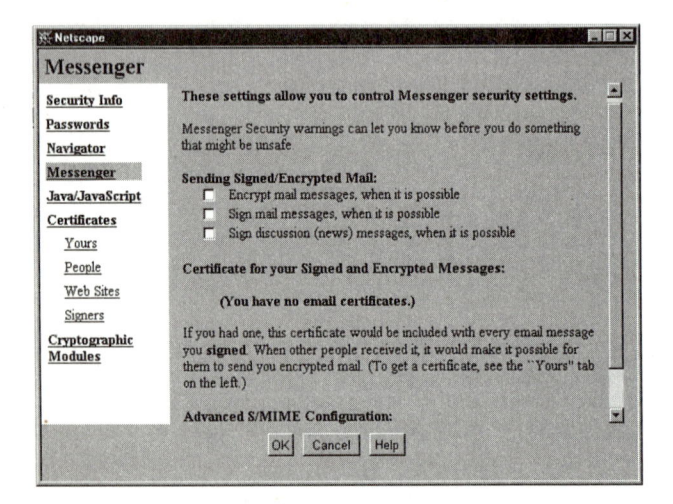

http://www.quecorp.com

Messenger allows you to select defaults for the security applied to your e-mail messages. Listed below are the Sending Signed/Encrypted Mail options shown in Figure 17.20:

- *Encrypt mail messages, when it is possible*—This automatically encrypts messages for recipients whose certificates you have on file.
- *Sign mail messages, when it is possible*—This automatically signs messages if you're cryptographically able to do so.
- *Sign discussion (news) messages, when it is possible*—This automatically signs discussion messages if you're cryptographically able to do so.

## Java Applet Privileges

Figure 17.21 appears when you click Java/JavaScript on the left side of the security dialog box. By maintaining a list of valid certificates and configuring the privileges for these, you can ensure that unwanted applets and scripts are restricted from gaining access to your computer.

**FIG. 17.21**
Control access to your computer or network by keeping only desirable certificates.

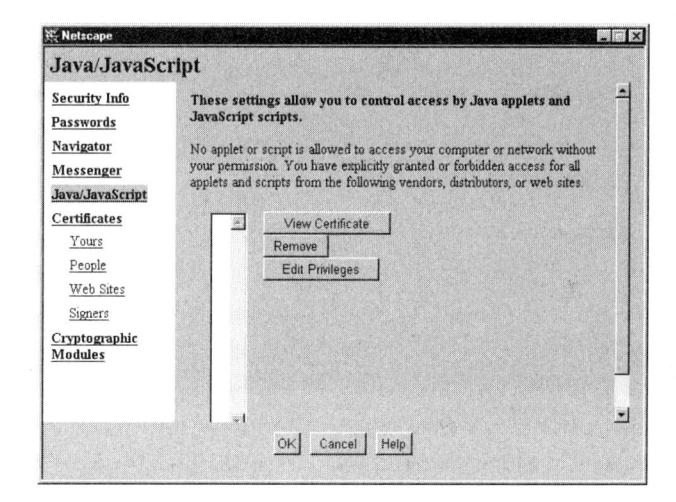

# Cryptographic Modules

Clicking Cryptographic Modules on the left side of the security dialog box brings up Figure 17.22. By using cryptographic modules, the application is isolated from the details of the cryptography.

**FIG. 17.22**
The Netscape Internal PKCS #11 Module is currently loaded.

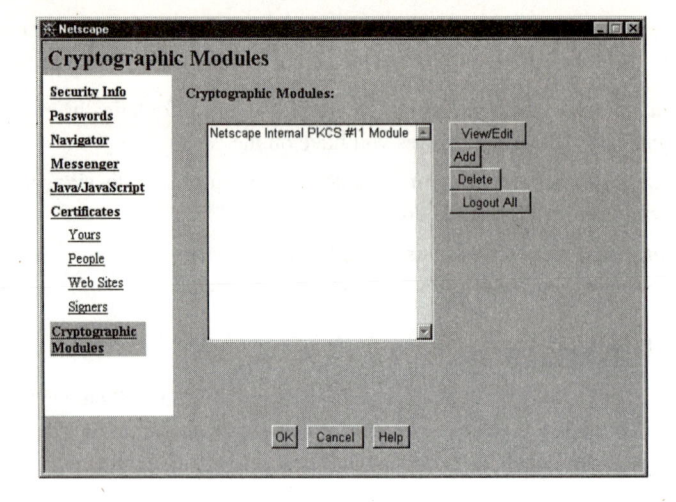

## Help

The topics covered in this chapter deal with security options, most of which are found on dialog boxes which contain Help buttons at the bottom. These buttons can give you additional information for specific questions you might have.

Communicator also has a security Web page that covers general topics relating to Internet security. It can be opened from the main pull-down menu through Help, Security. Following is a brief glance of what you can find there:

- *SSL*—Netscape's data security protocol
- *S/MIME*—RSA's standard for digitally signing and encrypting e-mail
- *Fortezza*—NSA's PCMCIA-based security services
- *Access Control and Single-User Login*

If you're interested in cryptography, RSA has a FAQ document at **http://www.rsa.com/rsalabs/newfaq/home.html** that has everything from DNA computing to elliptic curve cryptosystems to attacks based on the birthday paradox. ●

**PART III**

# Communicator Professional

**18** Calendar 369

**19** IBM Host-on-Demand 389

CHAPTER 18

# Calendar

*by Galen A. Grimes*

For the average corporate user of Netscape Communicator, the most useful component in the software suite is probably Netscape Calendar. Calendar is a Web-based PIM—Personal Information Manager—what most of us call an appointment book, a scheduler, or, more simply, a date book. What sets Netscape Calendar apart from other PIMs is its capability of operating over the Internet. The capability to function over the Internet means that corporate users who travel extensively can now plan meetings over the Internet just as easily as their office-bound counterparts can over their LAN-based PIMs and schedulers.

But just because Netscape Calendar can be used over the Internet doesn't mean you can only use it over the Internet. Calendar functions in both online and offline modes. In its offline mode, Netscape Calendar allows you to enter information on your own schedule and prepare your own To Do tasks list. When you go online with Netscape Calendar, you can query other Calendar users' schedules and prepare meetings or schedule the use of corporate-wide resources such as conference rooms or video conferencing facilities. Imagine being able to check schedules and plan a conference call or video conferencing meeting with managers in a dozen different cities in just a few seconds.

### Using Netscape Calendar as your corporate-wide calendar
This chapter will show you how to use Netscape Calendar as your scheduling client and post your information on a corporate-wide Netscape Calendar server.

### Scheduling meetings with other Calendar users
You'll learn how to schedule meetings between yourself and other Calendar users and check each participant's calendar for their availability.

### You don't always have to be connected to your corporate Calendar server
You'll also learn that you can use Calendar in both its offline and online modes. The offline mode is used primarily when you are traveling.

### Some operations in Calendar become easier and less redundant if users you schedule activities with are placed in groups
If you find yourself scheduling meetings or other activities with the same group of Calendar users repeatedly, you will learn how to create working groups of Calendar users and schedule the group and not just individuals.

# Getting Up and Running with Calendar

If you've already installed the Netscape Communicator Professional Edition, then Calendar is already installed on your computer and you don't have to spend any time on configuration settings to begin using Calendar to keep track of your schedule. You can use Calendar in one of two operational modes—offline on a stand-alone computer or online logged in to your corporate Netscape Calendar server. In this section, you learn the basics of what you need to quickly get up and running with Calendar.

To start Calendar and create your first Agenda, follow these steps:

1. Start Calendar by clicking the Netscape Calendar icon. The Sign-In dialog box appears (see Figure 18.1).

**FIG. 18.1**
When you start Calendar, you have to sign in whether you are in offline or online mode.

2. Enter your User Name, Password, and select offline for Server Name. The user name you enter depends on whether you are using Calendar strictly as a stand-alone application or in conjunction with a corporate Calendar server. If you are using Calendar as a stand-alone system, you can enter any user name you want. But if you are using Calendar in conjunction with a corporate Calendar server, you need to enter the user name assigned to you by your Calendar server administrator. Select OK.

3. If this is the first time you have started Calendar, you are prompted to create an offline *Agenda*. Select Yes to create your offline Agenda.

   **NOTE** An Agenda in Calendar is your schedule, the list of your appointments by date and time.

4. After you read the information screen explaining the two operational modes for Calendar, select OK to continue.

5. Calendar displays its Offline Agenda Configuration dialog box (see Figure 18.2). Enter or change your user name. Enter your Time Zone, Region, and the directory where your offline Agenda will be stored on your computer. Select OK to create your Agenda.

   Your new Agenda is created and appears on your screen.

   **NOTE** The first view of your Agenda might be the In-Tray view. To see the scheduling view of your Agenda, open the Communicator menu and select the menu item after In-Tray.

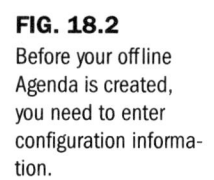

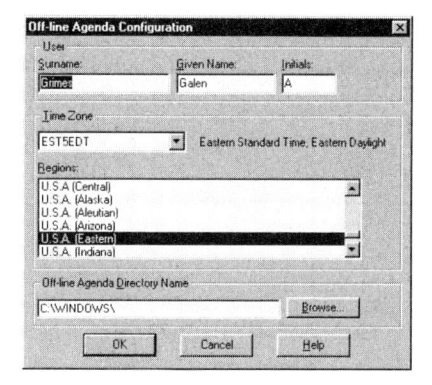

**FIG. 18.2**
Before your offline Agenda is created, you need to enter configuration information.

If you prefer to enter Calendar in its online mode (which means you have a corporate Calendar server up and running), the only difference in the sign-on procedure is that, in step 2, you enter the name of the Calendar server instead of selecting offline for the Server Name.

## Entering Information in Your Agenda

Now that you have your Agenda created, you can start entering your schedule. Keep in mind that, if you are working offline, you can only enter scheduling information for yourself. You cannot query the Agendas of other Calendar users, nor can you query how *resources* in your system have been scheduled.

> **NOTE** In Calendar, a resource is an inanimate object that has its own Agenda. Examples of resources you might see in Calendar are conference rooms, videoconference rooms, and equipment.

To enter information into your Calendar Agenda:

1. With your Agenda displayed on your screen, double-click a time slot for the time and date when you want the activity to begin. This opens the New Agenda Entry dialog box (see Figure 18.3).

2. In the Title text box, enter a name for this activity, such as Meeting with Finance Dept. Mgr.

3. Set the Duration or End Time for (approximately) how long you expect this activity to last. If this activity only involves you, skip to step 6.

4. If you are planning a meeting and you're working online, you can now add people or resources to this activity. In the Add text box, enter the names of the persons or resources you want to add to this entry.

5. When you have finished entering all the names or resources you want to include in this entry, select Check Conflicts to see if any of the people or resources you have included in this entry have previously scheduled activities. If no conflicts exist, Calendar confirms

## Chapter 18 Calendar

the time and date for your meeting by placing a check mark next to your activity entry displayed just below the Check Conflicts button. If a conflict does exist, you can select the Suggest date/time button to have Calendar identify the next available date/time with no conflicts.

**FIG. 18.3**
You use the New Agenda Entry dialog box to enter new activities in your Agenda.

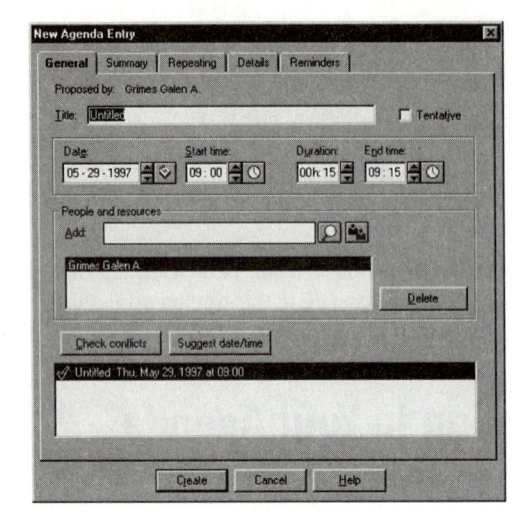

6. When you have resolved any possible conflicts and Calendar has confirmed your activity, select Create to enter this entry in your Agenda (see Figure 18.4).

**FIG. 18.4**
Calendar displays your newly entered activity in your Agenda.

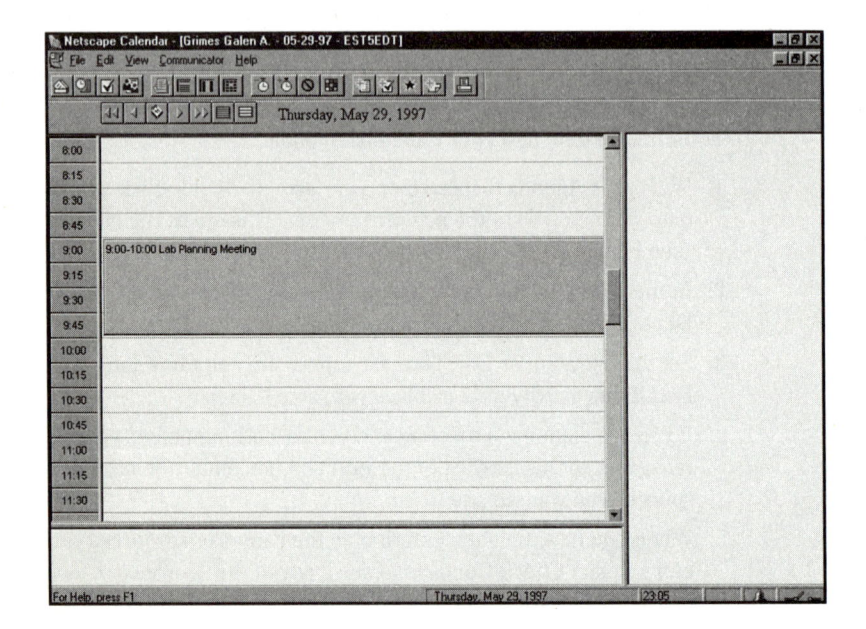

http://www.quecorp.com

## Going Online When You Are Working Stand-Alone

As mentioned earlier, you can use Netscape Calendar in either its online mode, which means you are logged in to your company's corporate Netscape Calendar server, or in its offline mode, which means you are running Calendar on a stand-alone computer. Calendar also allows you to easily switch between the two modes. For example, suppose you are returning from a two-week business trip, you just finished updating some Agenda entries offline and now you want to connect to your corporate Calendar server so you can upload your stand-alone Agenda. To do this, follow these steps:

1. Select File, Go Online. The Sign-In dialog box appears.
2. Enter your User Name, Password, and Calendar Server Name. Select OK to log in to your Calendar server.
3. A dialog box appears informing you that Calendar has detected that your offline Agenda has updated entries not contained in the Agenda stored on your Calendar server and asks if you would like to update your Host (Calendar server) Agenda. Select Yes to begin the update.

Depending on the number of entries you have entered in your offline Agenda, the update can take anywhere from a few seconds to a few minutes. While your Host Agenda is being updated, Calendar displays its progress.

## Going Offline from Your Host Agenda

Calendar also lets you move your Agenda in the opposite direction. If you frequently travel for your company and need to update your offline Agenda with the information stored in your Host Agenda, follow these steps to copy your Agenda to a stand-alone computer:

1. Select File, Download to Local file. Calendar displays the Downloading Host Agenda dialog box.
2. When you are ready to begin the download, select Start, and your offline Agenda is updated with the information contained in your Host Agenda. Depending on how much information you need to copy to the stand-alone computer, the update can take anywhere from a few seconds to a few minutes.

# Learning Netscape Calendar from Soup to Nuts

Now that we've covered the basics of using Netscape Calendar and you are feeling pretty comfortable with it, it's time to move into a more detailed coverage of what you can do with this Internet-based PIM. As stated earlier, you can use Netscape Calendar "right out of the box," without making any configuration changes. But there are a few configuration changes you will likely want to make to increase the overall functionality of the program.

If you prefer to enter Calendar in its offline mode (which means you are not connected or don't have a corporate Calendar server), the only difference in the sign-on procedure is that you select offline for the name of the Calendar server instead of the actual server Name.

# Changing Calendar's Default Settings

As mentioned earlier, you do not have to make changes to Calendar's default settings to use the program, but there are a few changes you will probably want to make.

To change Calendar's default configuration:

1. Select Edit, Preferences, Agenda to open the Agenda Preferences dialog box (see Figure 18.5).

**FIG. 18.5**
The first configuration changes you will likely want to make are with the way your Agenda is displayed.

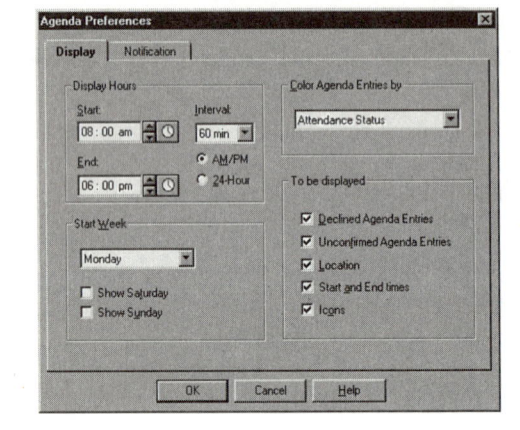

2. Reset your Start and End times to reflect when you actually begin and end your workday.
3. Unless you plan your schedule and activities in 15-minute intervals, change the time Interval from 15 to 30 minutes. Unless you operate on military time change 24-Hour to A.M/P.M.
4. If your workweek typically begins on a day other than Monday, make that adjustment in the Start Week section. You can also set whether you need Saturday and Sunday to be shown on your Agenda. Select OK to save your changes and close the dialog box.

Next, you might want to make a few changes in the way Calendar notifies you when you have been included in scheduled meetings on another user's Agenda.

To change Calendar's default notification settings:

1. Select Edit, Preferences, Agenda to open the Agenda Preferences dialog box. Select the Notification tab to display the Notification sheet (see Figure 18.6).
2. In the Entries Received section, select to Receive notifications of new Entries by e-mail. If your e-mail program is not set to periodically check your mailbox for messages, also select to Check for New Entries Every *n* Minutes. You can change the time interval from 15 minutes to whatever time interval suits your needs. Select OK to save your changes and close the dialog box. Select OK again to save your changes and close the last dialog box.

http://www.quecorp.com

## Changing Calendar's Default Settings | 375

**FIG. 18.6**
You will likely want to also make changes to how you are notified about meetings you are invited to.

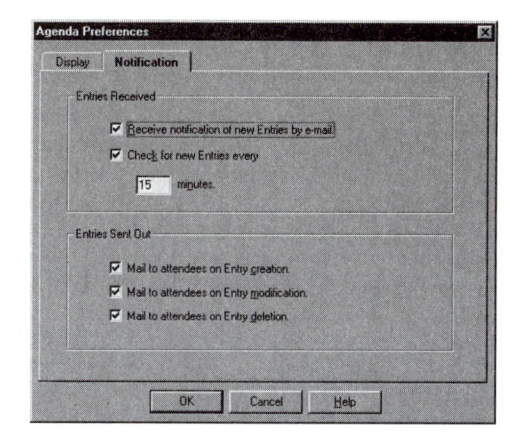

> **TIP** Some preference changes do not take effect until you restart Calendar.

You might also want to change certain entry defaults. Under entry defaults, you can set whether you want reminders on or off by default and set certain access, importance, and priority levels for your Agenda entries, notes, tasks, and events.

To change the default settings for how Agenda entries are made:

1. To set your entry defaults, select Edit, Preferences, Entry Defaults. This opens the Entry Defaults dialog box (see Figure 18.7).

**FIG. 18.7**
You don't have to accept the default method of entering entries into your Calendar agenda.

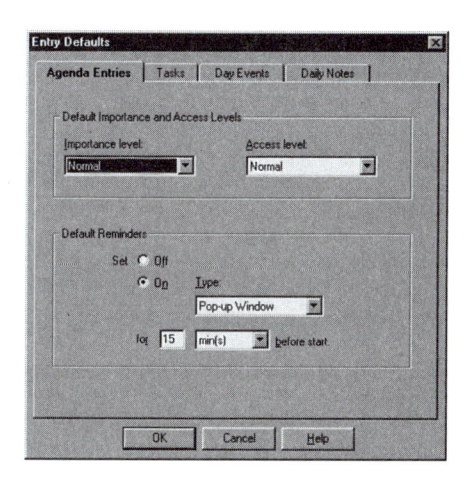

2. Select each of the tabs (Agenda Entries, Tasks, Day Events, and Daily Notes) and set the respective Importance, Access, and Priority levels and whether the reminder for each type of entry is turned On or Off.

Part III
Ch 18

3. When you have changed or set all of the entry defaults, select OK to save your changes and close the dialog box.

Keep in mind that there are numerous other configuration changes you can make so that Calendar suits your personal needs and likes. After you become more familiar with Calendar, take some time to look through the other Preferences dialog boxes to see what changes might be beneficial or desirable.

One more change you might want to make is to display your Agenda one week at a time rather than one day at a time. Click the seventh icon on the toolbar from the left. Toolbar functions are covered in the next section.

## Becoming Familiar with Calendar's Toolbar

While Calendar does not use the most intuitive icons on its toolbar, you still might want to become familiar with some of them in the event that you find yourself using a particular function regularly. Table 18.1 lists the icons on the Calendar toolbar and explains what function each icon performs.

**Table 18.1  The Netscape Calendar Toolbar**

| Icon | Function |
| --- | --- |
| **Upper Toolbar** | |
| Open In-tray | Displays your in-tray |
| Open an Agenda | Displays your Agenda |
| Open tasks | Displays your task list |
| Open Group Agenda | Opens a group Agenda |
| Go to Entry | Displays particular entry |
| View day | Displays daily view of your Agenda |
| View week | Displays weekly view of your Agenda |
| View month | Displays monthly view of your Agenda |
| Decrease time slot | Decreases the size of time slots |
| Increase time slot | Increases the size of time slots |
| Icons on/off | Turns icons on or off in the Notes section |
| Agenda Entry colors | Allows you to change colors of Agenda entries for Importance Level, Attendance Status, and Entry Ownership |
| New Agenda Entry (meeting) | Opens New Agenda Entry dialog box |

| Icon | Function |
| --- | --- |
| **Upper Toolbar** | |
| New Task | Opens New Task dialog box |
| New Day Event | Opens New Day Event dialog box |
| New Daily Note | Opens New Daily Note dialog box |
| Print | Prints your Agenda |
| **Lower Toolbar** | |
| Backward one month | Advances your Agenda back one month |
| Backward one week | Advances your Agenda back one week |
| Display calendar | Displays a standard calendar of current month |
| Forward one week | Advances your Agenda forward one week |
| Forward one month | Advances your Agenda forward one month |
| Decrease time slot | Reduces the size of your Agenda time slots |
| Increase time slot | Increases the size of your Agenda time slots |

# Adding New Entries to Your Agenda

Obviously, most of what you will be using Calendar for is keeping track of your daily activities, which include meetings, tasks, and reminders.

To use Calendar to plan a meeting and check for potential scheduling conflicts:

1. With your Agenda displayed on your screen, double-click a time slot for the time and date when you want the activity to begin. The New Agenda Entry dialog box opens (see Figure 18.8).

2. In the Title text box, enter a name for this activity, such as Meeting with Finance Dept. Mgr. or Reminder: Set Up New Computer.

3. Set the Duration or End Time for (approximately) how long you expect this activity to last. If this activity only involves yourself, such as a reminder, skip to step 7.

4. If you are planning a meeting, you can now add people or resources to this activity. In the Add text box, enter the names of the persons you want to add to this entry. If you want to add a resource, preface the name with r, re:, or res:. If you are inviting a group to your meeting, preface the name of the group with g:, gr:, or grp:. If you need to search for a person, resource, or group (possibly because they are on a different Calendar server), select the Search icon (the first of the two icons to the right of the Add text box) to open the Directory Search dialog box (see Figure 18.9).

**FIG. 18.8**
You use the New Agenda Entry dialog box to enter new activities in your Agenda.

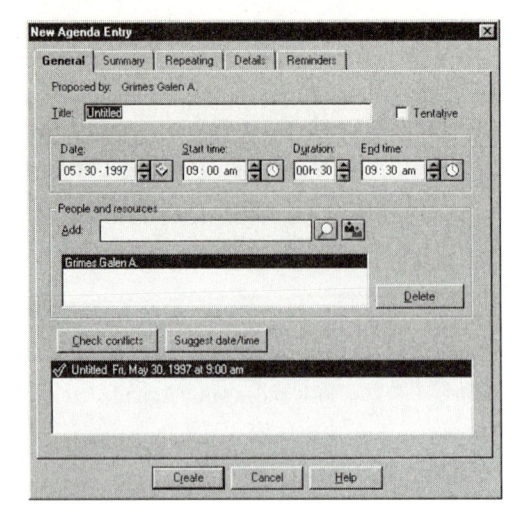

**FIG. 18.9**
To search for people, resources, or groups to add to your activities, you can use the Directory Search dialog box.

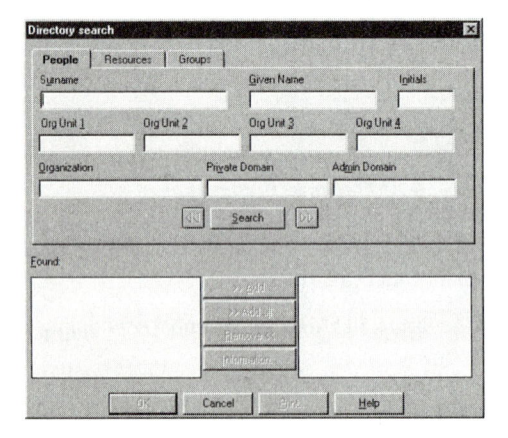

5. Enter the name of the person, resource, or group you want to search for. If your company makes use of organizational units or domains, you can also conduct your search by these classifications. When you have added all of the people and resources needed for this activity, select OK to close the Directory Search dialog box.

6. When you have finished entering all the names or resources you want to include in this entry, select Check Conflicts to see if any of the people or resources you have included in this entry have conflicting meetings or activities scheduled.

> **CAUTION**
> If you do not have access rights to view the Agenda entries of the people or groups you are adding, you cannot detect conflicts in scheduling. Calendar will notify you when you do not have the needed access

http://www.quecorp.com

> rights to check for conflicts. Check with your server administrator to make sure the proper access rights have been set.

If no conflicts exist, Calendar confirms the time and date for your meeting by placing a check mark next to your activity entry displayed just below the Check Conflicts button. If a conflict does exist, you can select the Suggest date/time button to have Calendar identify the next available date/time with no conflicts.

7. If you want to specify a location for this activity, select the Summary tab (see Figure 18.10).

**FIG. 18.10**
When you plan a meeting or other activity, you can also specify a location for this activity on the Summary sheet.

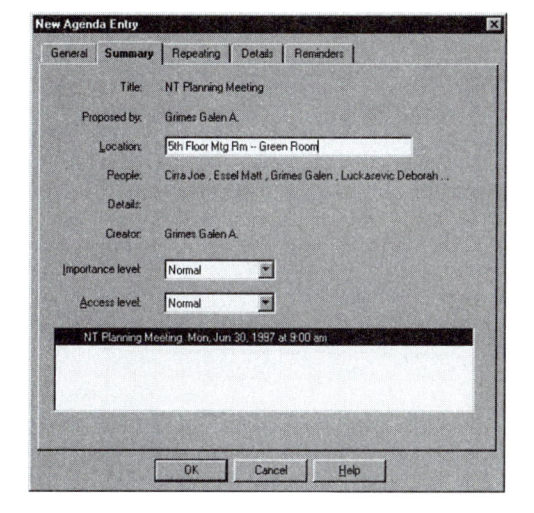

> **N O T E** Besides setting a location for this activity, you can also indicate its level of importance (high, normal, low, or lowest).

8. If this is a recurring activity, you can specify its repeating status by selecting the Repeating tab (see Figure 18.11).
9. Finally, if you want to set a reminder for this activity, select the Reminders tab (see Figure 18.12).

> **N O T E** Calendar lets you set reminders minutes, hours, days, weeks, months, or even years before a scheduled activity.

**Chapter 18** Calendar

**FIG. 18.11**
You can also add repeating activities.

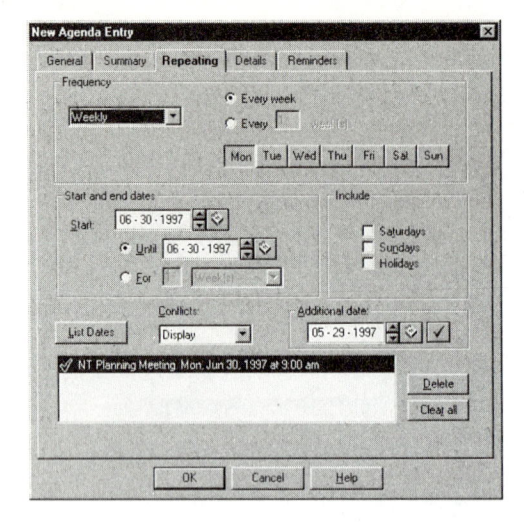

**FIG. 18.12**
Calendar also lets you set reminders for your Agenda activities.

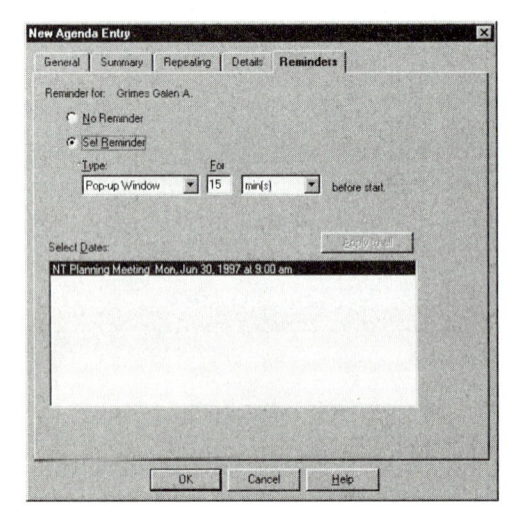

10. When you have resolved any possible conflicts, set a reminder, location, and so on, and Calendar has confirmed your activity, return to the General tab and select Create to enter this entry in your Agenda (see Figure 18.13).

http://www.quecorp.com

**FIG. 18.13**
Calendar displays your newly entered activity in your Agenda.

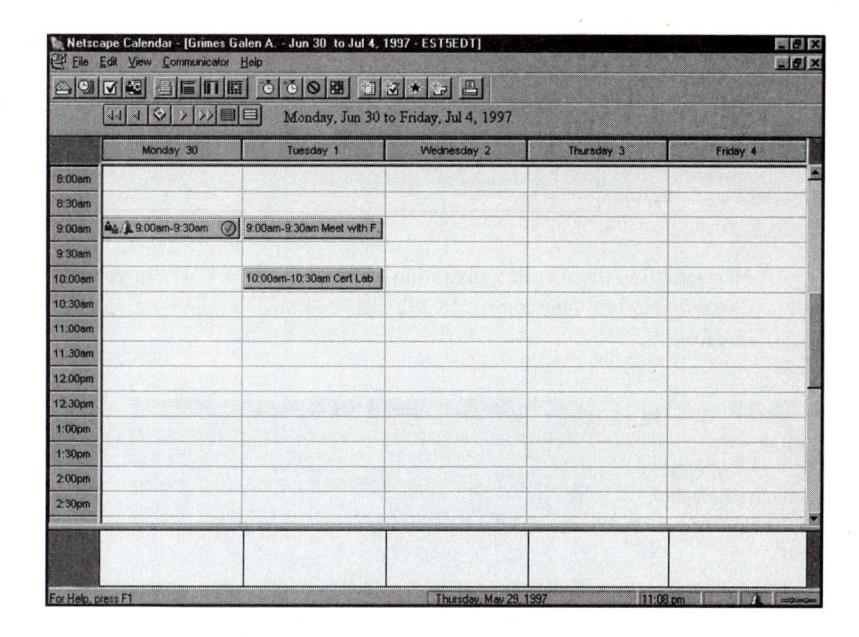

## Responding to a Meeting Request

When one of your coworkers uses Calendar to plan a meeting, all invited attendees receive an invitation, which appears both in your Agenda (see Figure 18.14) and in your In-Tray (see Figure 18.15).

**FIG. 18.14**
When you are invited to a meeting, the invitation appears in your Agenda...

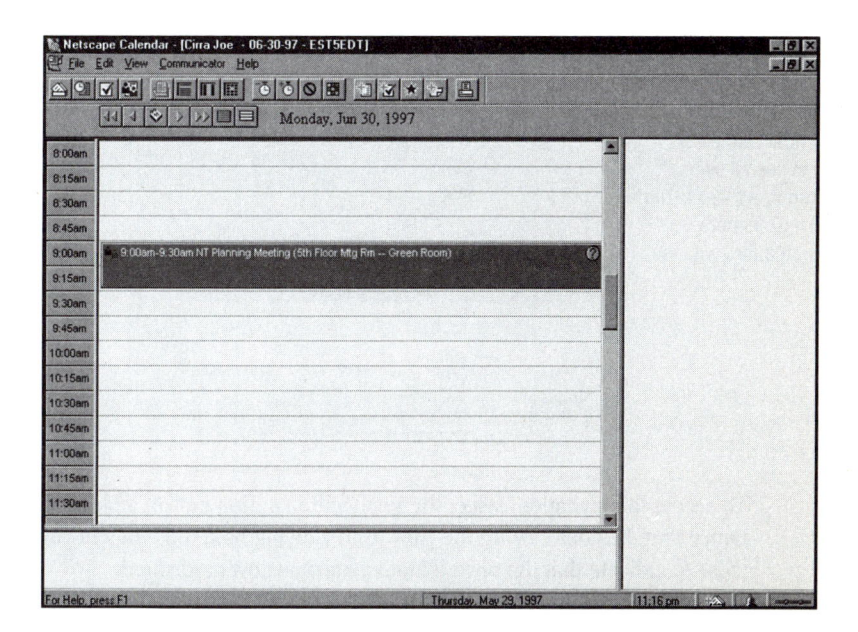

**FIG. 18.15**
...and in your In-Tray.

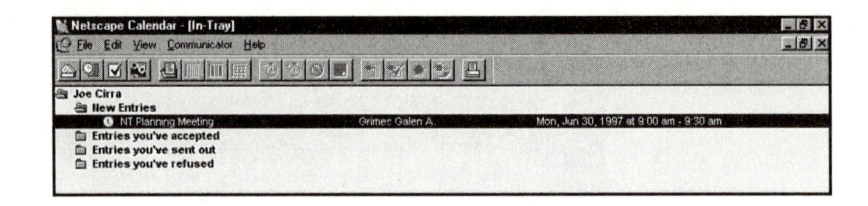

To respond to the meeting invitation, double-click the entry in your Agenda to open the View Entry dialog box (see Figure 18.16) and see more detailed information about the planned meeting.

**FIG. 18.16**
You can view the invitation in your Agenda to get more information about the planned meeting.

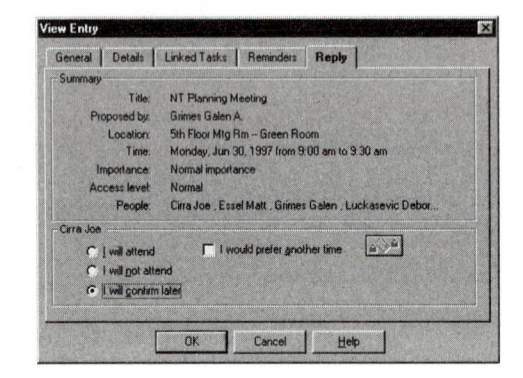

Besides learning when, where, and how long the meeting will be, you can also check to see who else has been invited to the meeting and whether the other people have accepted the invitation (see Figure 18.17).

**FIG. 18.17**
Calendar also allows you to see all users invited to a meeting and which users have accepted the invitation.

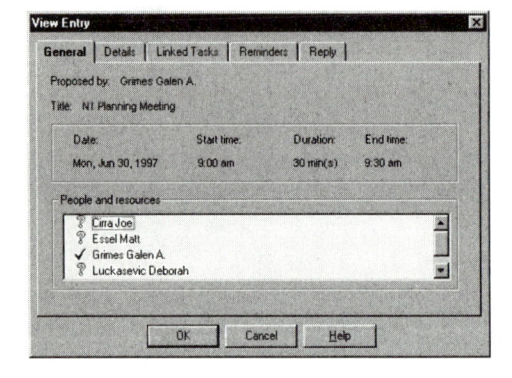

To accept the invitation, select the I will attend option button and then select OK. You might notice that, besides closing the View Entry dialog box, the entry in your Agenda has changed color to indicate that the once tentative entry is now confirmed.

http://www.quecorp.com

# Creating Tasks in Your Agenda

Besides activities, such as meetings, you can also use Calendar to track tasks you need to perform. Netscape Calendar doesn't replace project management software, but you can use Calendar to prompt you when certain tasks are due and use the program to plant reminders in your scheduling calendar.

To create a task entry, follow these steps:

1. Select File, New, Task or press F7 to open the New Task dialog box (see Figure 18.18).

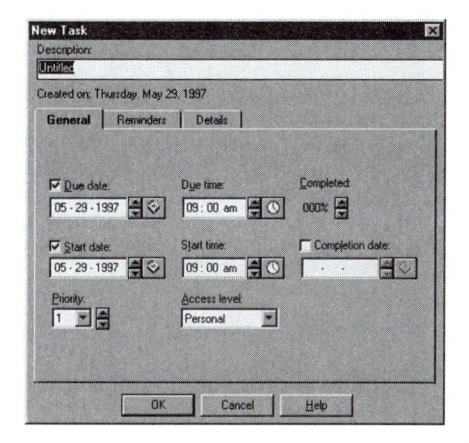

**FIG. 18.18**
You can also create a task, or "to-do" list in Calendar.

2. Give your task a name and (optionally) set a due date and time. You can also enter a starting date and time, the priority you want to set for this task, and an access level to grant others (who might have access to view your Agenda) the ability to view this task.
3. Select OK to close the dialog box and add the new task to your task list.

## Viewing Your Task List

As you work on your tasks, you can adjust the percentage complete of each task in increments of five percent. At any time, you can view the tasks on your task list to see the status of each task. To view your task list, select File, Open Tasks, Your Tasks (see Figure 18.19).

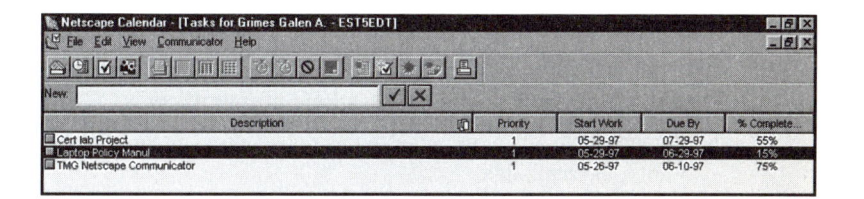

**FIG. 18.19**
You can keep track of various tasks and To Do items on your task list.

## Entering Notes in Your Agenda

Calendar also provides an excellent means of creating daily notes for yourself. If you look at your Agenda, you might notice that near the bottom of the screen is a framed-in area about twice the size of a time slot. This is your note area. You can use Calendar's Daily Note function to leave yourself notes.

> **NOTE** If it's starting to look like some of the functions in Calendar (for example, reminders, notes, tasks, and so on) seem a little redundant, what you are actually seeing is just several ways of accomplishing certain tasks or operations in Calendar. Rather than look at these functions as redundant, think of it as Calendar offering you more flexibility in being able to perform certain tasks.

To create a note to yourself, follow these steps:

1. Select File, New, Daily Note or press the F3 key to open the New Daily Note dialog box (see Figure 18.20).

**FIG. 18.20**
You can use the New Daily Note function to create notes for yourself.

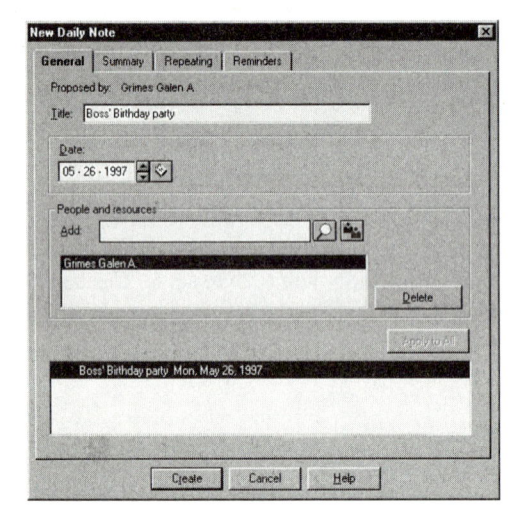

2. Enter a Title for your message, which appears in your Note area.
3. You can also Add other people, and they get a copy of your note on their Agenda.
4. If this is a repeating event, you can select the Repeating tab and select the frequency with which you want this note to appear in your Agenda.
5. If you want to add a reminder to this note, select the Reminder tab and set when you want to be reminded.
6. When you've entered all of the information you want to enter for this note, select Create on the General sheet to create your note and close the dialog box. Your note is created and now appears on your Agenda on the date you specified.

## Viewing Your Notes

Anytime you want to view a note in the note area of your Agenda, simply double-click the note to open the Note entry (see Figure 18.21).

**FIG. 18.21**
Besides viewing your notes you can also make changes to your notes in the view mode.

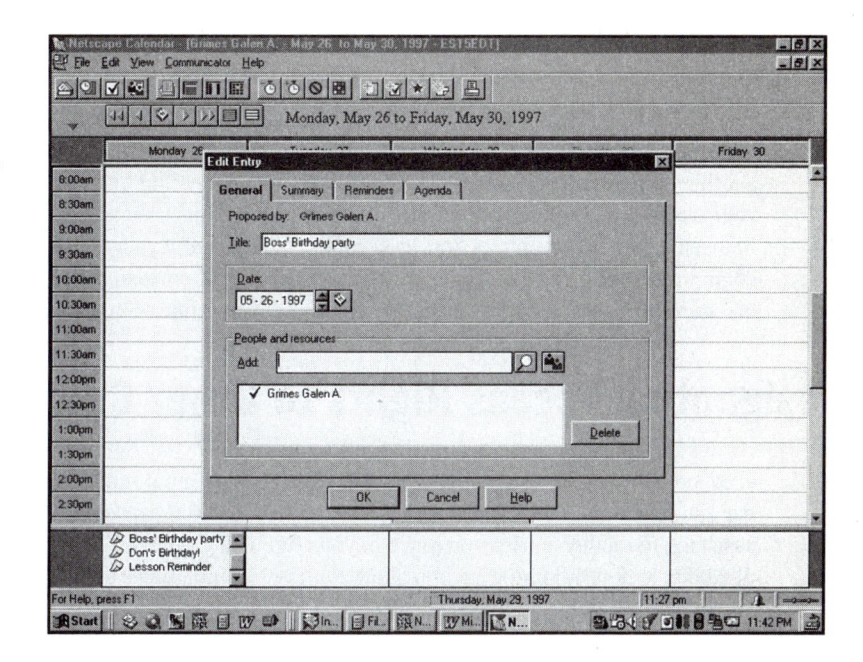

Besides viewing the note entry, you can also edit and make changes to the note. Select OK to close the dialog box.

# Working with Your In-Tray

The In-Tray is a very important feature in Netscape Calendar. Your In-Tray is where you receive all Agenda entries (for example, meeting invitations, Daily Notes, Day Events, and so on) from other Calendar users. Your In-Tray is also a place where you can keep track of the entries you send out to other Calendar users.

When you open your In-Tray (by choosing File, Open In-Tray or pressing Ctrl+I), you see a folder labeled with your name. Double-click this folder to open it, and you see four sub-folders (see Figure 18.22) labeled as follows:

- New Entries
- Entries you've accepted
- Entries you've sent out
- Entries you've refused

**FIG. 18.22**
This is how your In-Tray initially appears with the four default sub-folders.

The In-Tray is more than just a handy place to check your Agenda entries. You can edit and make changes to entries you have created as well as drag and drop entries from one folder to another. For example, if you decline an invitation to a meeting but later change your mind (or your plans) and decide to attend the meeting, you can move the entry from the Entries You've Refused folder to the Entries You've Accepted folder. And if your Calendar administrator has configured your Calendar system for e-mail replies, you can also automatically send an e-mail message to the entry originator informing him of your change in plans.

# Designating Access Rights to Other Calendar Users

By default, all users possess some limited rights to view your Agenda. These limited rights allow others to invite you to meetings and check for potential scheduling conflicts. But Calendar allows you to grant greater access to your Agenda. You can allow others, like a secretary or assistant, to modify entries you make in your Agenda. Calendar does give you a fair amount of flexibility in determining what you allow another Calendar user to view or modify.

To grant or change access rights, or what are called designate rights, follow these steps:

1. Select Edit, Access rights to open the Access Rights dialog box (see Figure 18.23).

**FIG. 18.23**
You grant or change another user's access rights to your Agenda through the Access Rights dialog box.

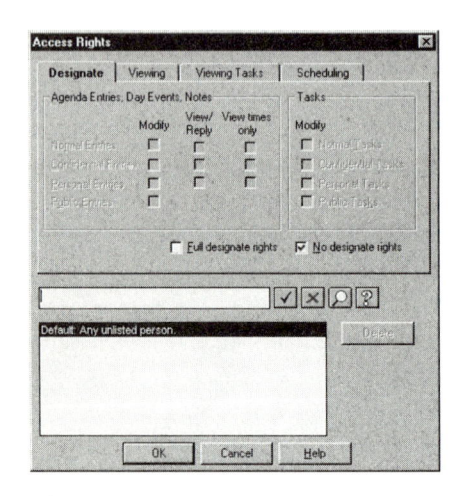

http://www.quecorp.com

2. Step through the four sheets of this dialog box (Designate, Viewing, Viewing Tasks, and Scheduling) using the tabs and decide what level of access you want others to have to your Agenda.
3. After you decide what level of access you want to grant to another user, enter that user's name in the text box. The text box has a search feature to allow you to search for users in case you are not sure how their names are entered into your system.

**CAUTION**
Be careful that you do not remove all access rights for a user. If you do, that user cannot invite you to meetings.

4. When you have completed your changes for access rights, select OK to save your changes and close the dialog box.

CHAPTER 19

# IBM Host On-Demand

*by Mike Morgan*

**B**ecause you're running Netscape Communicator, you know about the cutting edge of information technology—the Internet, Local Area Networks, and the World Wide Web. If you work in a large organization, you also know about *legacy applications*. Many organizations have hundreds of thousands of lines of code running on IBM mainframes. The cost of converting these applications to intranet or desktop applications is staggering, and unnecessary. These applications work just fine and, thanks to IBM Host On-Demand, are available from your desktop and even your Web page.

You might have accessed hosts running UNIX, VMS, or other operating systems by using Telnet over the network. You cannot Telnet to IBM mainframes; they use a different protocol that is not compatible with Telnet. IBM Host On-Demand is software designed to connect to IBM mainframes from inside a Web browser such as Netscape Navigator.

Many organizations have a significant investment in legacy applications. By adding that information to the range of information you can access through Communicator and display on a Web page, your organization can continue to reap benefits from that legacy code for years to come. ∎

- **Learn how IBM came to use a networking standard that is incompatible with the Internet**

  IBM uses SNA, a system of protocols that cannot be sent over the Internet without using special gateway software.

- **See how IBM 3270 terminals differ from other "dumb" terminals**

  IBM's dumb terminals are more sophisticated than the VT-100 family popular in the Internet community.

- **Learn how to establish a connection with an IBM mainframe through Host On-Demand**

  You need the name and port number of a communications server that can serve as a gateway between SNA and the Internet.

- **Learn to read the status messages in the Operator Information Area**

  You can tell at a glance whether you have a communications problem if you know the codes.

- **Learn how to use HTML to embed a Host On-Demand session into a Web page**

  You can present a mainframe application in context with other information from a Web server.

# Overview of TN3270 and the 3270 Family of Products

Not too many years ago, IBM set the standards for quality and reliability in computing. In those days, IBM was able to define its own protocols and proprietary standards. Today, the industry is broader, and IBM has had to move closer to the mainstream, including the protocols of the Internet. IBM Host On-Demand allows an Internet or intranet user to access applications on IBM mainframes, bridging the gap between IBM's technology and the Internet's open standards.

> **ON THE WEB**
>
> http://www.hursley.ibm.com/cics/internet/index.html   One of the broadest classes of mainframe applications is based on the IBM Customer Information Control System (CICS). If you need to connect to CICS from the Internet, consider using the CICS Gateway for Java, described on this page.

This section describes the IBM way of communication—a communication architecture called *SNA* and a terminal called the *IBM 3270*.

## Understanding SNA

During the 1970s, the computer industry developed several networking standards. One standard, based on UNIX and some work funded by the Defense Advanced Research Projects Agency (DARPA), became the basis for the Internet. Another standard, called Systems Network Architecture, or SNA, was developed by IBM and is the basis for communications with an IBM mainframe.

Compared with the Internet protocol (called TCP/IP, for Transmission Control Protocol/Internet Protocol), SNA is highly reliable with excellent error reporting. This design is not surprising because IBM built its reputation on reliability and excellent support. Unfortunately, SNA also has a reputation for high maintenance and complex administration.

SNA was designed for user sessions in which a user on a simple terminal (typically a member of the Model 3270 family) established a relatively long-term connection with a mainframe. This design decision is a major distinguishing factor of SNA compared to TCP/IP; the two parties must establish a *session* before any messages can be sent.

In recent years, SNA has been updated to take advantage of new technology. IBM supports Advanced Peer to Peer Networking (APPN) for SNA communications over Local Area Networks (LANs). IBM also offers a technology called Logical Unit 6.2 (LU6.2) which affords Advanced Program to Program Communication (APPC). As its name implies, APPC is used when both ends of the conversation are software.

Most frequently, one end of an SNA conversation is a 3270-family terminal (or a desktop computer running IBM Host On-Demand), and the other end is an IBM mainframe. You can establish an SNA session, however, with any computer that supports the protocol, including UNIX machines (running IBM's AIX operating systems) or IBM's mid-range machine, the AS/400 (although the 5250-family of terminals are more frequently used with that machine).

> **ON THE WEB**
>
> http://www.networking.ibm.com/pcf/pcfprod.html  If you need to communicate with an IBM AS/400, your best choice is to emulate a model 5250 terminal. IBM offers TN5250 emulators, described on this page.

Figure 19.1 illustrates a typical SNA installation. Each network controller is responsible for managing its attached terminals, printers, and workstations—a collection known as the *Subarea SNA*. When a user presses the ENTER key on the terminal, the terminal sends a message (that includes any data the user has entered) to the network controller. (Unlike the character-based terminals common in the UNIX environment, IBM's terminals send an entire form's worth of data at a time.)

**FIG. 19.1**
In SNA, each set of terminals and other devices gets its own network controller to reduce the load on the host.

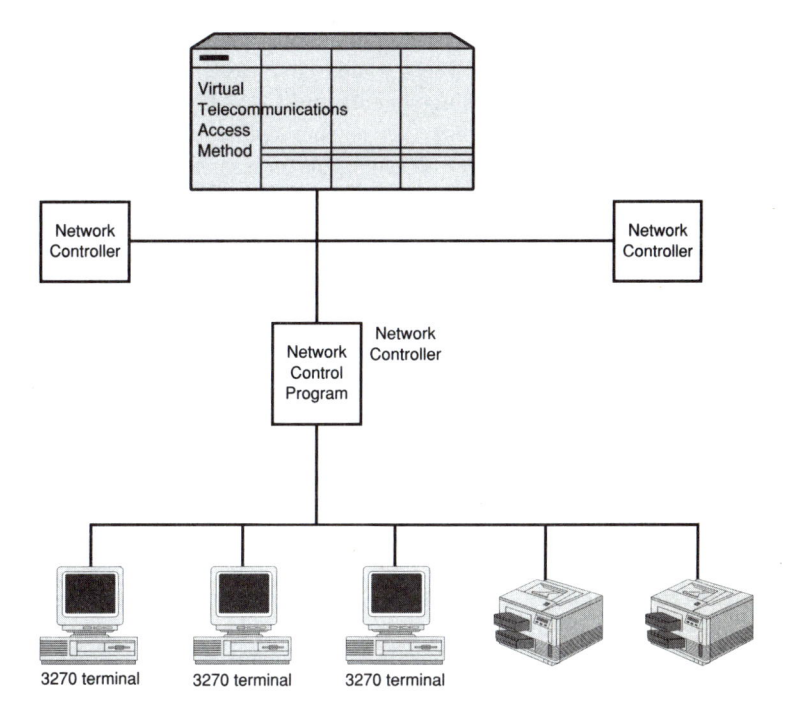

The network control program in the network controller picks up messages from the terminals and other devices and sends them to the mainframe. The mainframe keeps track of where each device is located on the network and how to access it with a program called *VTAM*, the Virtual Telecommunications Access Method.

**NOTE** In an APPN environment, each device keeps track of the addressing of the virtual devices with which it communicates. This method is much simpler than VTAM.

## The 3270 Family of Terminals

Members of IBM's 3270 family of terminals are often called dumb terminals, because they do not have the intelligence of a full desktop computer. They have no local disk drive or other storage mechanism and do no processing of the data. Compared to a desktop computer running Netscape Communicator, these dumb terminals are simple communications devices.

At about the same time that IBM was introducing the 3270, Digital Equipment Corporation (DEC) was introducing the VT-100 terminal in the environment that includes UNIX as well as DEC's proprietary operating systems. DEC designed the VT-100 to connect directly to the computer with a simple *serial* protocol—when the user presses a key, the code associated with that key is sent to the computer one bit at a time over a simple cable with just a few wires. The character encoding is called *ASCII*—the American Standard Code for Information Interchange.

By contrast, SNA uses coaxial cables and a character encoding mechanism called *EBCDIC*—Extended Binary Coded Decimal Interchange Code. EBCDIC and ASCII are completely different encodings. When you press a key on your keyboard, you send an ASCII character. The software in the TN3270 server is responsible for translating that character into EBCDIC before passing it on to the host. Of course, EBCDIC characters must be translated into ASCII on their way back to your desktop.

When computer networks became popular, the UNIX community (which was still making heavy use of VT-100-family terminals) developed an ASCII-based protocol that allows a networked computer to contact a server computer and emulate a character-based dumb terminal. (The emulated terminal looks suspiciously like a VT-100.) The protocol is called *Telnet*.

With the growing popularity of the Internet and in-house intranets, and the continued success of IBM mainframes, many organizations felt the need for a Telnet-like protocol that would allow them to emulate a 3270 terminal. This software is more complex than Telnet, since SNA is a more complex protocol than the simple character-based transmissions used by VT-100s. The 3270-emulation protocol is called TN3270 and is the basis for IBM Host On-Demand.

When you press a key on your desktop computer's keyboard, you send an ASCII character. The software in the TN3270 server is responsible for translating that character into EBCDIC before passing it on to the host. Of course, EBCDIC characters must be translated into ASCII on their way back to your desktop.

## Function Keys

The IBM 3270 terminal has 24 function keys, a SYS ATTN key, a REQuest key, a CLEAR key, PA1 and PA2 keys, and a SEND or ENTER key. These additional keys do not appear on standard PC keyboards. Some TN3270 emulators provide a template for the keyboard or stickers for the keys to show which keys are used for these special keys. IBM Host On-Demand solves this problem in a much nicer way by putting buttons along the bottom of the screen to provide these special keys.

## Operator Information Area

At the bottom of the 3270's screen is an Operator Information Area, often called the *OIA*. In this part of the screen, the host can display status information about the SNA session. These status displays can appear rather cryptic until you know the codes.

In general, if you see a message in the OIA, you cannot communicate with the host. You should not type on the keyboard or press the ENTER key. The terminal is said to be *input-inhibited*. The next section, "Understanding IBM Host On-Demand," contains a list of status messages that Host On-Demand can display in the OIA.

## VM, MVS, and Mainframe Applications

IBM mainframes run the Virtual Machine (VM) and Multiple Virtual Storage (MVS) operating systems. These are multitasking multiuser systems—ancestors of Windows NT and OS/2, but without the graphical user interface.

**ON THE WEB**

http://www.vm.ibm.com/    Nine million people log on to a machine running the VM operating system every day. Learn more about this important product on-line.

**NOTE**  IBM has also announced plans to support OS/390, an integrated mainframe operating system. From OS/390, you can access the services of MVS, UNIX, LANs, distributed computing, and application enablement services. This operating system runs on the S/390, IBM's new multiprocessor-based mainframe.

**ON THE WEB**

http://www.s390.ibm.com/    Read more about the S/390 machine and its operating system at this Web site. OS/390 is more fully described at **http://www1.pok.ibm.com/os390/index.html**.

Before you can communicate with an application, you must establish a session with the host operating system. For each session that is started, the host sets up a separate environment. This design gives the user the impression the he has the whole host all to himself. As more and more sessions are added and more applications are running, the system's resources are being drained. As a result, you see that your response time (after you press the SEND or ENTER key) gets longer. The solution, of course, is to add more resources to the host (by upgrading the mainframe or adding an additional machine) or move some people out to LANs.

# Understanding IBM Host On-Demand

IBM Host On-Demand is a Java program written by IBM. It can run in any environment that provides a Java Virtual Machine, or JVM. IBM Host On-Demand offers two sessions of TN3270 emulation. If you want to use Host On-Demand to offer the equivalent of a 3270 terminal on your desktop computer, these two sessions mean that you have *two* 3270s available to you.

> **NOTE** When you run IBM Host On-Demand, you are running Java in your browser. If Host On-Demand won't load, choose Edit, Preferences from Communicator's menu. Then click the Advanced element and be sure that Enable Java is selected.

If you prefer, you can use IBM Host On-Demand to "embed" a 3270 in a Web page. This design allows you to place host applications, such as public catalogs and databases, in the context of other Web data.

### ON THE WEB

**http://www.raleigh.ibm.com/hex/hexprod_en.html**   This page is the home page for Host On-Demand. You might also want to visit **http://www.raleigh.ibm.com/hex/defects_v1.0.0_en.html**, which shows the latest usage notes and known defects in Host On-Demand.

# What Do You Need?

Because IBM mainframes are essentially SNA devices, and the Internet is based on TCP/IP, you need a gateway to convert back and forth between the two protocols. IBM (and other companies) sells software and dedicated controllers that sit between the Internet or your intranet and the mainframe, as shown in Figure 19.2. You need to know the Internet host name or IP address of that gateway. For many host applications, you also need a user name and password to gain access to the mainframe.

### ON THE WEB

**http://www.networking.ibm.com/csn/csnprod.html**   Learn about IBM's Communications Server for Windows NT, which can provide the gateway between TCP/IP and SNA. Similar products for OS/2 and AIX are described at **http://www.networking.ibm.com/cm2/cm2prod.html** and **http://www.networking.ibm.com/asf/asfprod.html**, respectively.

**http://iamg.novell.com/iamg/products/saa/nwsaatoc.htm**   If you prefer Novell's products, evaluate NetWare for SAA, another product that can provide TN3270E services.

> **NOTE** In Host On-Demand, this gateway is called the TN3270E Server. In some of IBM's documentation, it is called the Communications Server. These two terms refer to the same software, which runs on a computer somewhere on your network, bridging the gap between TCP/IP and SNA.

**FIG. 19.2**
You must use a communications server (also known as a TN3270E server) as a gateway between SNA and TCP/IP.

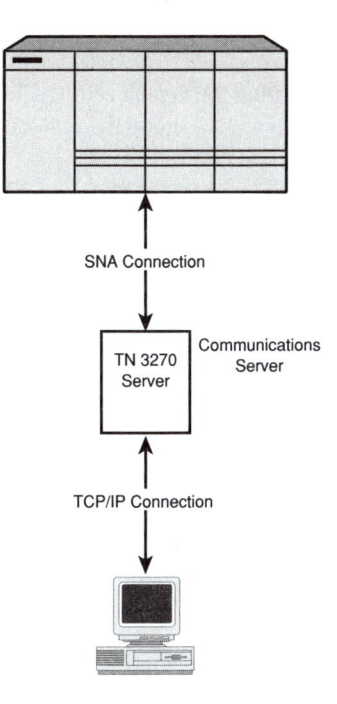

In addition, you need a browser that is capable of running Java and displaying frames. IBM has tested Host On-Demand with the following client software:

- On Windows 95 or Windows NT 3.51 or later:
    - Lotus Notes 4.5 or later
    - Netscape Navigator 3.0 or later
    - Microsoft Internet Explorer 3.0 or later
- On IBM AIX 4.1.4   Netscape Navigator 3.0 or later
- On IBM OS/2 4.0 (with the latest Java Developers' Kit):
    - Netscape Navigator for OS/2 2.02 or later
    - AppletViewer

> **TIP** If you browse IBM's Web pages that discuss Host On-Demand, you see a toll-free support number mentioned. If you obtained Host On-Demand as part of Communicator, you should call Netscape's Technical Support to obtain any help you need. The IBM number is for customers who obtained Host On-Demand directly from IBM.
>
> The version of Host On-Demand offered by Netscape differs somewhat from the version available directly from IBM. Netscape's version is self-contained; IBM's version is tightly integrated with their Communications Server products (as well as Novell's NetWare for SAA) and will not work with other TN3270E servers.

## Setting Up a Connection

The easiest way to connect to a host is by using the default settings. In Communicator, choose Communicator, IBM Host On-Demand. Figure 19.3 shows the resulting page.

**FIG. 19.3**
If you start your connection with the default settings, you need to enter an Internet address for the TN3270E server.

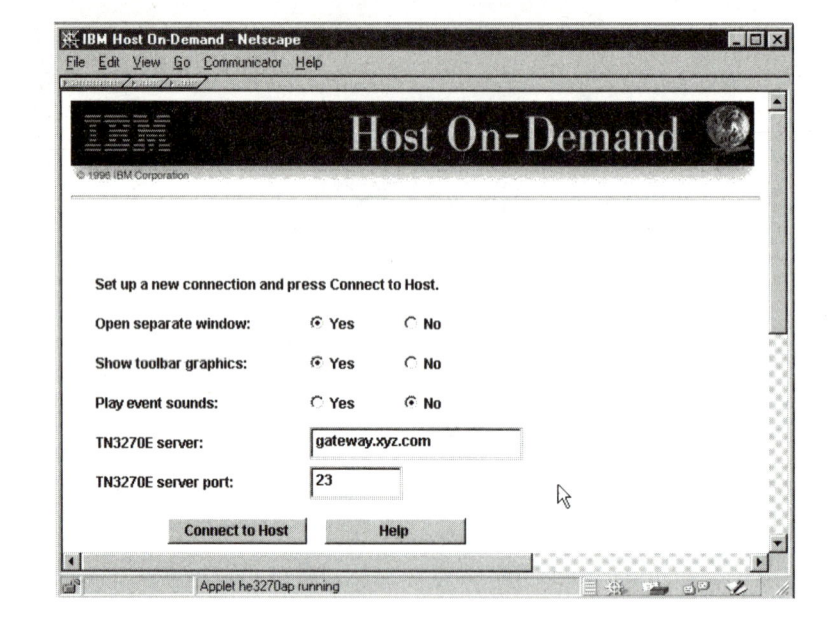

Set the radio buttons as you see fit and enter the Internet address of your TN3270E server. If the server is using a non-standard port, change the port from the default value of 23. When you're ready, click Connect to Host. You get a terminal emulation screen similar to the one shown in Figure 19.4.

Notice that you have an operator information area near the bottom of the screen and special 3270 function keys below it. Within a few seconds, you should see the logon screen of the IBM host that is connected to the communications server. If you don't, you see a status code in the Operator Information Area. Use the list of codes given later in this section to determine why your connection has not yet succeeded.

> **TIP** If you find the function keys cumbersome, click Keypad in the toolbar to toggle them off. You can access many of these special keys from a conventional keyboard; Table 19.1 shows the correspondence between 3270 function keys and conventional keyboard keys.

http://www.quecorp.com

**FIG. 19.4**
IBM Host On-Demand uses a Java applet as a 3270-emulator.

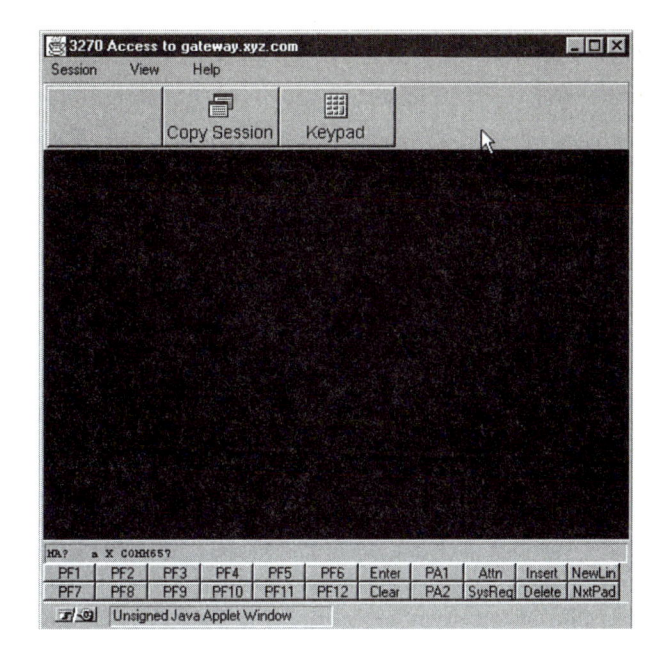

Table 19.1  3270 Function Keys

| 3270 Function Key | Keyboard Key | Notes |
| --- | --- | --- |
| F1-F9, F11, F12 | F1-F9, F11, F12 | |
| F10 | | The keyboard F10 is reserved. |
| F13-F24 | Shift+F1-F12 | |
| Cursor left | Left arrow | |
| Cursor right | Right arrow | |
| Cursor up | Up arrow | |
| Cursor down | Down arrow | |
| Del | Delete | |
| Backspace | Backspace | |
| Forward Tab | Tab | |
| Back Tab | Shift-Tab | |
| Enter | Enter | |
| Clear | Esc | |

*continues*

**Table 19.1 Continued**

| 3270 Function Key | Keyboard Key | Notes |
|---|---|---|
| PA1 | Home | |
| End | End | |
| Character keys | Character keys | |

> **CAUTION**
>
> Some implementations of the JVM do not pass all keyboard characters to the Java program. If some of the special keys do not appear to work from the keyboard, use the keypad equivalents.

## Reading the OIA Messages

Recall from the first section, "Overview of TN3270 and the 3270 Family of Products," that the IBM 3270 terminal has an Operator Information Area (OIA) at the bottom of the screen. This section reviews the messages you see in IBM Host On-Demand. If you see a message in that area, your terminal is input-inhibited—you cannot send data to the host. If the message does not clear within a short time, look up the message to see why you are unable to communicate.

### TROUBLESHOOTING

**How can I see what Host On-Demand is doing, so that I can debug a connection?** Start by reading the messages that appear in the OIA. If you need additional information, set the Debug parameter (described later in this section) in the HTML code to YES. You then can choose Help, Debug, and select components you want to trace.

Be sure to turn the Debug parameter off after you're finished tracing Host On-Demand; using some aspects of the debug utility can significantly impact performance.

> **TIP**
>
> You can print the debug log by selecting the text you want to print and copying it to the Clipboard. Open an editor, paste the text into the document, and print from the editor.

**X []** In general, if you see an X in the OIA, you know that the system has disabled the keyboard of your 3270. The symbols X[ ] in the OIA mean that the host is processing the data you just sent. You should wait until these symbols disappear.

> **NOTE** If you were using an actual 3270 terminal, you would see an X and a clock icon in the OIA under these circumstances. The [ ] in this message is IBM's stand-in for the clock.

http://www.quecorp.com

**X SYSTEM** The message X SYSTEM means that the host has locked your keyboard while communications are taking place. If this message remains on for an extended period, there might be a communications problem or a problem with the host. You should wait to see if the problem clears by itself. If it does not, contact the help desk that supports the host application.

**X <-o->** Many applications are organized as a series of forms. You can enter data into some fields; other fields are read-only. When the host downloads the form into the terminal, it also downloads information about which fields can be changed.

If you try to change the contents of a read-only field, you get the X <-o-> message.

**Comm 654** The word Comm in the OIA means that the terminal or, in this case, IBM Host On-Demand, is unable to communicate with the host. The error number gives you more specific information. Error 654 is displayed by IBM Host On-Demand when it is unable to establish a connection with the communications server. Check to be sure you have the correct host name and port for that server and that the server is running.

If you're connecting to a host through this particular server for the first time, it's possible that IBM does not support the TN3270 software running on your gateway.

### ON THE WEB

http://www.networking.ibm.com/hex/faq_v1.0.0_en.html#comm_servers   Check the latest list of supported communication servers to be sure you're accessing through a supported program.

Host On-Demand version 1.0 has been tested with the following TN3270 software:

- IBM Communications Server for AIX V4R2
- IBM Communications Server for OS/2 Warp V4R1
- IBM Communications Server for Windows NT V5.0
- Novell NetWare for SAA V2R2

**Comm 655** Error 655 is a status message that says that Host On-Demand is talking to the TN3270 server, attempting to negotiate a common set of options. This message should only be displayed briefly and is then replaced with a different code.

**Comm 657** If you direct IBM Host On-Demand to connect you to the IBM host that is serviced by the communications server at, for example, gateway.xyz.com, Host On-Demand must look that name up in the Domain Name Service (DNS) to obtain an *IP address*—a four-byte code usually written as four numbers separated by dots (for example, 207.2.80.1). During the fraction of a second or so that your desktop machine is talking to the nameserver to resolve the server's name, you'll see Comm 657. If you see this message for a longer period, there might be a problem with your nameserver, or the name you entered might not be valid.

> **TIP**
>
> You can get the IP address of the machine itself by using `ping` or other utilities you might have on your desktop machine, or you can get it from your system's administrator. If you get a prolonged Comm 657 error, replace the symbolic name of the machine with the IP address. If you're now able to connect, but couldn't when you used the symbolic name, you should report a problem with the nameserver.

**Comm 658**    IBM Host On-Demand establishes a TCP/IP connection to the communications server. While it is establishing this connection, it displays code 658. If you see this code for more than a second or so, there might be a problem with the network, or you might have entered an invalid address for the TN3270 server.

**Comm 659**    After Host On-Demand has established the TCP/IP connection (as evidenced by code 658 clearing from the OIA) any TCP/IP communications lost is evidenced by code 659. If you're on a dial-up link, you might have lost the modem connection.

If this code appears before you've established a session with the IBM host, the server name and port that you entered might not have been correct, or your network connection might be down. It's also possible that Host On-Demand established a connection with the machine and port that you named, only to discover that the server it had connected to was not running TN3270.

If you have not connected through this communications server before, be sure the software on the communications server is supported by IBM.

**Prog 755**    If the Host On-Demand program detects an incompatibility with the communications server software that is running on the gateway, it displays `Prog 755`. Double-check the server's name and port and any customizations you have made to the connection parameters. If you still cannot connect, contact your system administrator; it's possible that the server software is not compatible with IBM Host On-Demand.

## Changing the Default Connection

If you examine the source of the IBM Host On-Demand default connection page, you'll see the HTML shown in Listing 19.1.

**Listing 19.1   Code Telling the Browser to Load the IBM Host On-Demand Java Applet**

```
...
<APPLET ARCHIVE="he3270ap.zip" CODE="he3270ap.class" WIDTH=900
➥HEIGHT=600 ALIGN=Center>
<PARAM NAME=CABBASE VALUE=he3270ap.cab>
<PARAM NAME=AUTO_CONNECT VALUE=NO>
<PARAM NAME=DEBUG VALUE=NO>
<PARAM NAME=SEPARATE_WINDOW VALUE=YES>
<PARAM NAME=TN3270E_SERVER_PORT VALUE=23>
<PARAM NAME=GRAPHICS VALUE=YES>
<PARAM NAME=AUDIO VALUE=NO>
...
```

http://www.quecorp.com

You can change some of these parameters by clicking the radio buttons in the applet; others can only be changed by editing the HTML and reloading the applet. This section describes the impact of each of these parameters.

**CABBASE**  The CABBASE parameter points to a cabinet file that contains a set of platform-specific parameters. Do not change this parameter.

> **TIP**  If you're also using Host On-Demand with Microsoft Internet Explorer 3.0, you should consider digitally signing the he3270.cab file with your organization's credentials. Visit **http://www.microsoft.com/intdev/security/authcode/sixsteps.htm** for information on digitally signing a file.

**AUTO_CONNECT**  If you set AUTO_CONNECT to Yes, the emulator contacts the host through the specified TN3270 server as soon as the applet is loaded. This option can be used in conjunction with SEPARATE_WINDOW set to No to embed a 3270 window in a Web page.

**DEBUG**  By default, DEBUG is set to No. If you set it to Yes, the Debug item on the Help menu is enabled, and you can get a trace of Host On-Demand as it runs.

Be sure to set DEBUG back to No when you're done tracing. Some elements of tracing cause severe performance degradation.

**SEPARATE_WINDOW**  Use SEPARATE_WINDOW to run the emulator in a new window. Experienced 3270 users often prefer to set this option to Yes so they can move or resize the window. If you are supporting less experienced users, consider setting this parameter to No so that the applet appears in the browser window.

This parameter is set to Yes by default.

**TN3270_SERVER_PORT**  By default, TN3270 is offered on port 23. If your communications server uses a different port, override it by setting this parameter.

**GRAPHICS**  Many users prefer the look and feel of a graphical toolbar. By default, GRAPHICS is set to Yes so that toolbar graphics are on. If you set GRAPHICS to No, the program runs faster and uses less memory.

**AUDIO**  IBM 3270 terminals can emit a variety of beeps to give feedback to the operator. For example, if you're using OfficeVision, an IBM integrated desktop product, your terminal will beep when a message comes in. If you're filling out a form in a mainframe application, the terminal will beep if you press a key that cannot be accepted in the current field. (For example, you'll get a beep if you attempt to enter an alphabetic character into a numeric field.)

By default, this audio is off, which helps improve program performance and reduces memory requirements. If you want audio feedback, set this parameter to Yes.

## Starting a Session

When you connect to an IBM mainframe, the emulator opens the first session for you and displays the host's welcome screen. Typically, you log in by entering a user name and password.

If you need to start another session, choose Session, Copy Session from the menu, or Copy Session on the toolbar.

After you've got two sessions running, you can switch from one to the other by choosing Session, Next Session from the menu, or Next Session from the toolbar.

If you press the keyboard's F10, the Java Virtual Machine intercepts the keystroke. The JVM's use of the machine is specific to your implementation of Java; in general, the keystroke is not passed to Host On-Demand. If you need to send an F10, use the PF10 key on the keypad.

**NOTE** If you establish a session and leave it open for an extended period, both Host On-Demand and the IBM mainframe release some of the resources associated with the session. When you resume activity in the session, you might experience a slight delay while both ends of the session reallocate resources.

## Ending a Session

To end a session, log off of the host application. If you have a command prompt, type **LOGOFF**. If you're in an application and can't see the command prompt, type **=LOG** or **LOFF**—one of those will usually log you off.

**NOTE** Each session requires about one megabyte of RAM on your desktop computer. When you end the session, Java frees up about 128K immediately. The rest of the memory is released gradually.

If you start and end several sessions in rapid succession, you can use up available memory. Java releases this memory, but the system can appear to hang while Java frees the necessary resources.

http://www.quecorp.com

PART IV

# Netcaster

**20** Setting Up Your Web Top   405

**21** Channels   411

# CHAPTER 20

# Setting Up Your Web Top

*by Mark R. Brown*

Once upon a time, you probably heard a lot of hoopla about "push" technology and a new Netscape product called Constellation. With the introduction of the Netscape Communicator suite, Constellation is now a real product. Of course that was just its working title. It's now called Netcaster.

Netcaster implements Netscape's vision of push technology, which is the next generation concept for Web pages. Instead of having to search for and "pull" Web pages down when you want to read them, "push" technology lets you select Web-based information that you can schedule for automatic delivery to your computer so that you can read it at your leisure.

It's a little like the difference between watching TV without a VCR and watching with one. Without a VCR, you channel surf until you find something you think you might want to watch, then watch it for a little while and stay with it until the end of the show if it's interesting. When you're done, or when you've determined that the show really doesn't interest you, you surf on to another channel. But if you own a VCR, you look up programs in the TV Guide and program your VCR to record them for you. Then you can watch them whenever you want to, and you know you'll probably like what you see because you made an informed viewing decision ahead of time.

- **Netscape Netcaster lets you subscribe to Web-like channels**

  They bring timely information directly to your desktop—or "Webtop."

- **The Web top is a compelling new kind of user interface**

  It could change the way people interact with the Web for good.

- **Netcaster gives you incredible control over the kinds of information you receive**

  You also control how that information is downloaded and handled.

- **Netcaster itself reflects Netscape's application design vision**

  It's one of the first truly useful real-world applications to be developed using only Java, HTML, and JavaScript.

On the Web, you surf to find Web sites that you think might interest you, then look around them for a bit to see if you do. If a site suits you, you'll spend a bit of time reading pages and poking around. If not, you'll surf on. But with Netcaster, you study a list of Web-based "channels," then tell the program to download these channels at intervals you specify. The content files are saved on your computer's hard drive, ready for you to view when you want to.

Because push technology is a new paradigm for viewing Web pages, Netscape also came up with a new look and feel for it. You can still see Netcaster content in the Navigator Web browser window if you want to, but Netscape has devised a new viewing window called the Web top that's much more compelling.

The Web top is basically a borderless Navigator window with no "chrome" (that's industry parlance for the borders and buttons that usually adorn a system window). Instead of using the regular browser menus and buttons to navigate Web pages, the site creator has to implement her own set of custom controls. This usually involves creating menus, buttons, and other navigational tools using Java or JavaScript. The resulting full-screen "Web top" essentially replaces your system's desktop screen, running under any other application windows you may have open. If done well, Web top channels look a generation ahead of even the best-looking Web site. ■

> **CAUTION**
> Netcaster was not included in the first public release of Communicator, upon which this book is based. Therefore, the information in the Netcaster section is based on preliminary beta-test information. The final release version of Netcaster may differ from this beta version in subtle or even significant ways.

## Netcaster Quick Start

You launch Netcaster from within any Communicator application by choosing the Netcaster (Ctrl + 8) menu item on the Communicator menu. When you do so for the first time, you'll see the Java Security window shown in Figure 20.1.

**FIG. 20.1**
If you do things right, you'll only see this window once.

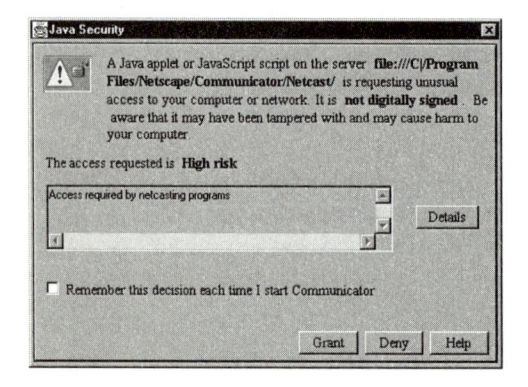

Netcaster, it turns out, is entirely implemented using Web-centric development tools like Java, JavaScript, HTML, and so on. Since it needs to write to your hard disk, the Java security system asks you to grant it permission to do so. But before you click the Grant button, check the box labeled Remember this decision each time I start Communicator. That will keep you from having to see this dialog again. (The initial implementation of Netcaster brings up three of these dialogs the first time it is run, though this may change in later versions.)

> **NOTE** Curious as to how a complex application like Netcaster could be created without using compiled C++? All of the source files for Netcaster—Java, images, and HTML with JavaScript—are stored on your system in C:Program Files/Netscape/Communicator/Netcast (Win95). Check them out—but don't change any of them!

Once you've granted permissions, the Netcaster menu comes up over any other windows you have open, on the right side of the screen (see Figure 20.2).

The Netcaster interface slides out over any windows you may have open, as it does over the Navigator window in Figure 20.2. You can slide it out of the way to the right by clicking once on the Netcaster tab. You might want to do so when you start up, so you can close your open windows. Since many channels use a Web top display, and Web top displays normally go behind all other open windows, minimizing your other windows gives you the best view when you're just starting out with Netcaster. Later, when you're used to how Web tops and the Netcaster interface behave, you can bring your windows back.

> **NOTE** You can change the Netcaster interface's position to the left side of the screen by adjusting a setting in the Options menu, and you can control the layering of Web tops using the Toolbar. Both of these topics will be covered later in this chapter.

At the top of the Netcaster interface is a bar labeled Channel Finder. The Channel Finder is a list of channels that you can subscribe to. The Channel Finder list is constantly and automatically updated from Netscape's Web site, so you'll often find new listings here.

To preview a channel, click its listing once in Channel Finder. The list will expand to show you a thumbnail image representation of the chosen channel (see Figure 20.3). This thumbnail has a small button in its lower left corner that's labeled Add Channel. Click the Add Channel button and you'll get a Channel Finder preview window.

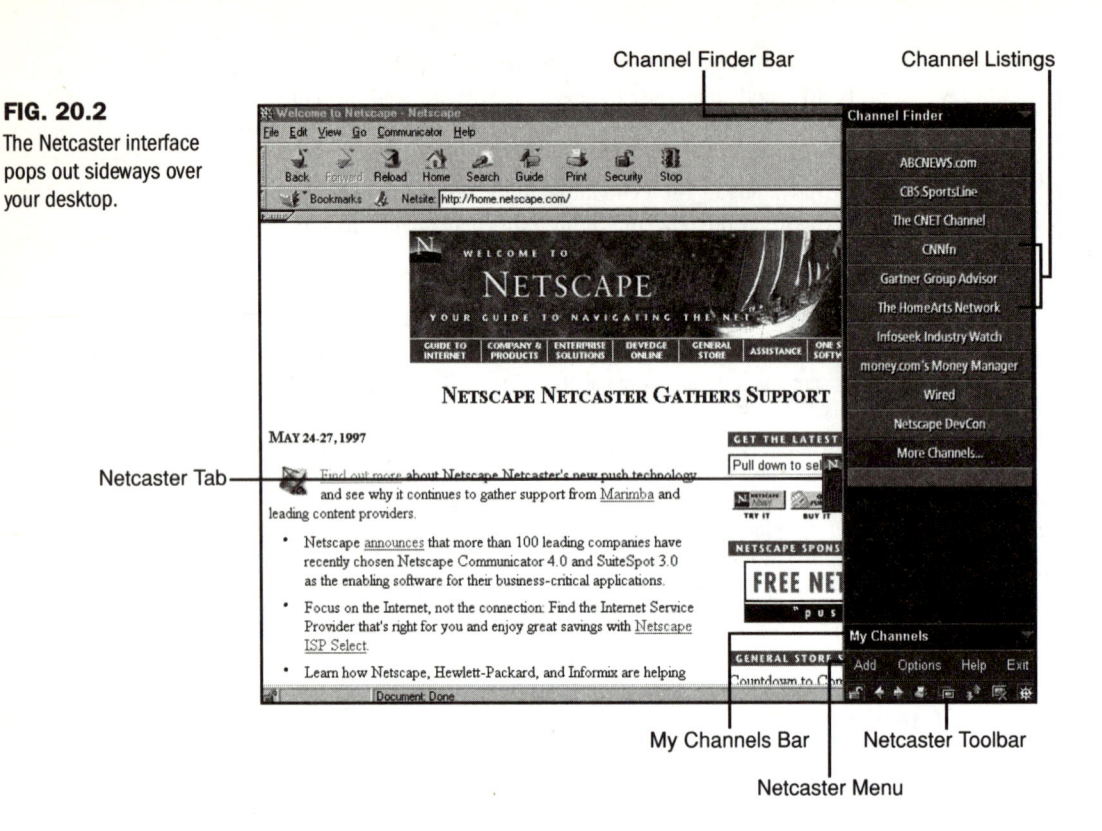

**FIG. 20.2**
The Netcaster interface pops out sideways over your desktop.

*Callouts on figure:* Channel Finder Bar, Channel Listings, Netcaster Tab, My Channels Bar, Netcaster Menu, Netcaster Toolbar

Most previews are animated, and will step through some of the major features of the channel you chose. If you decide you want to subscribe to that channel, click Add Channel in the preview window. Otherwise, click the Cancel button.

If you do add the channel, you'll get the Channel Properties dialog box shown in Figure 20.4. All of the default settings are set for you by the channel creator, so you can just click the OK button to accept her settings for now.

The channel you subscribed to is now listed under the My Channels heading, which is compressed. To expand it, click anywhere on the bar. The My Channels list will expand and cover all but the title bar of the Channel Finder section. You'll see the channel you just subscribed to listed there (see Figure 20.5).

You'll probably see a thin gray line below your subscribed channel listing, with a small red line moving back and forth in it. This is the download status bar, and it's indicating that Netcaster is currently downloading information from that channel.

Click the entry for your subscribed channel, and Netcaster will launch that channel. If the channel is in Web top mode, it will (usually) appear without borders and behind all other windows. If not, it will appear in a "normal" Navigator window, perhaps with some or all of the toolbars missing. That depends on how the channel creator set things up.

http://www.quecorp.com

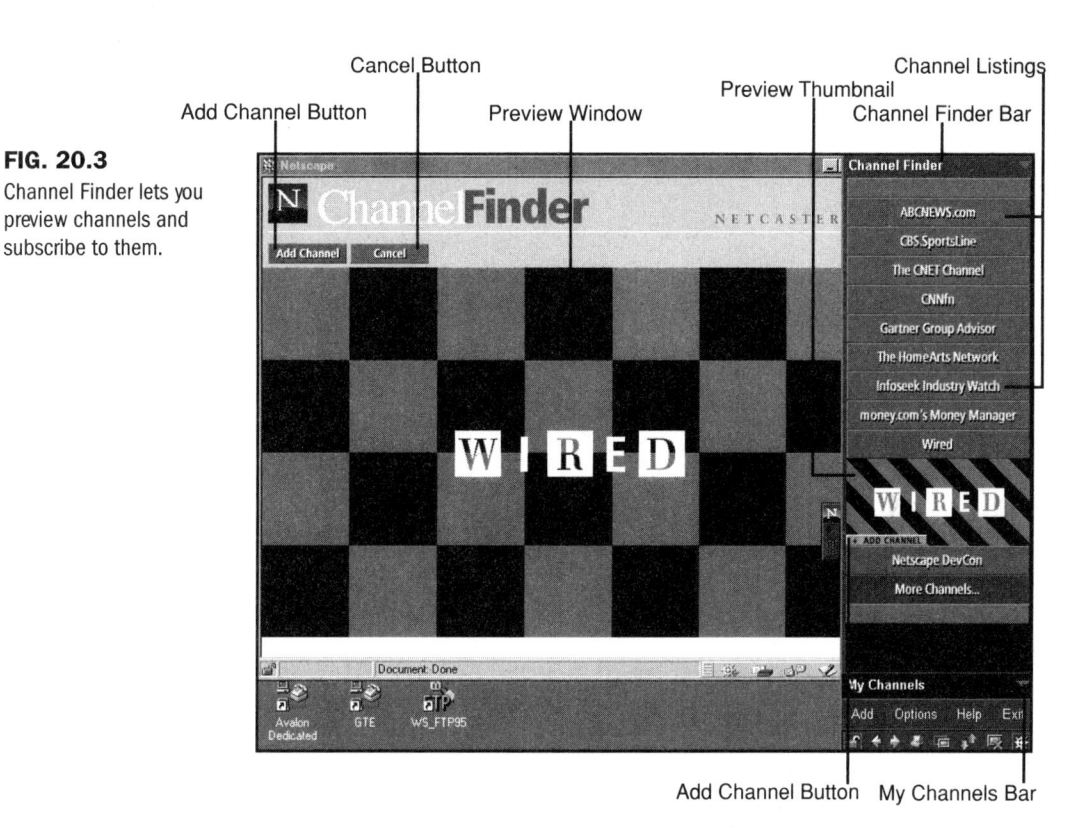

Netcaster Quick Start | 409

**FIG. 20.3**
Channel Finder lets you preview channels and subscribe to them.

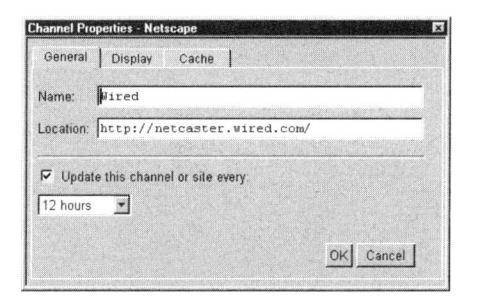

*Labels: Add Channel Button, Cancel Button, Preview Window, Preview Thumbnail, Channel Listings, Channel Finder Bar, Add Channel Button, My Channels Bar*

**FIG. 20.4**
You can make a lot of adjustments to a channel using the Channel Properties dialog box.

Viewing channel content is mostly a matter of figuring out what the channel designer had in mind when designing the channel controls. There will generally be buttons to click, menus to select, and maybe even tabs to drag. Many channels exhibit a high degree of animation and interactivity, all driven by underlying JavaScript and Dynamic HTML elements.

In any event, when you're done you can quit the channel by clicking the window's Close button (if it's in a window), or by clicking the Close the Web top button in the Netcaster toolbar.

Part IV
Ch 20

**FIG. 20.5**
My Channels lists the channels you've subscribed to.

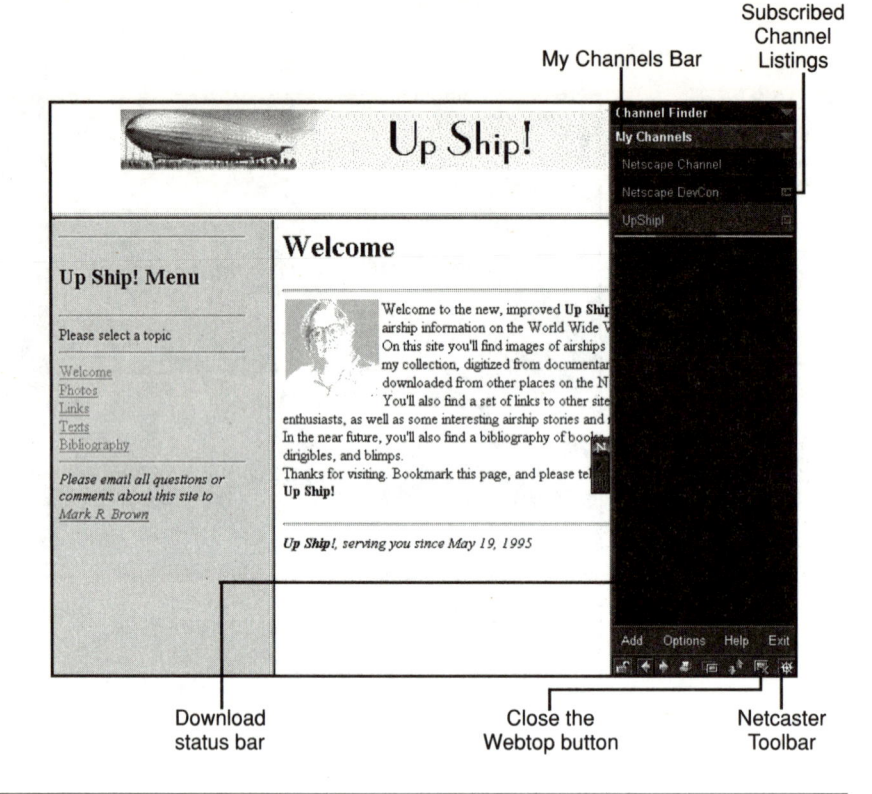

Subscribed Channel Listings

My Channels Bar

Download status bar

Close the Webtop button

Netcaster Toolbar

> **TIP** Hover the mouse pointer over a toolbar button to get a Tooltip that describes the button.

Those are the basics, but Netcaster has a lot of extra features and options. These are covered in the next chapter.

CHAPTER 21

# Channels

*by Mark R. Brown*

You're probably already used to the way you get information on the World Wide Web—you search for it. Sometimes you search, and search, and search. Often you never do find quite what you're looking for, and in the meantime you've wasted hours browsing off into sidetracks that looked promising and interesting, but weren't really what you needed.

"Push" technology is designed to change that way of gathering information. The concept is simple, really—instead of browsing for Web sites that might be of interest, you subscribe to "channels" that promise to deliver content you really want to see.

It's similar to the way television changed when cable came into being. Broadcast TV channels delivered a thoroughly mixed soup of programs—comedy, drama, variety, and documentaries were delivered in a format that was convenient to the way TV networks wanted to do business. You had to channel surf to find something worth watching. But when cable TV was installed, many focused channels were offered. Suddenly, you could get a channel of just nature shows, or history documentaries, or even romance movies. It became much easier to find something you wanted to watch.

▬ **Netcaster's Channel Finder helps you find interesting content**

Once you find a channel of interest, it's easy to subscribe.

▬ **Netcaster channels deliver timely, focused content to your own Web top**

Sports, news, entertainment, and even software updates can be automatically downloaded to your computer.

▬ **Netcaster can "tune" Castanet channels as well as its own**

There are already over a hundred Castanet channels available.

▬ **Who will win the "Channel Wars"?**

Netscape, Microsoft, and even third party providers like PointCast are squaring off for a battle over standards.

The Web is organized according to what is convenient for developers. Each site offers its own content, and you have to Web surf to find anything of interest. But you pick and choose to subscribe to Netcaster channels. The content is focused. It means you no longer have to surf to find information you want. It's delivered directly to you. ■

## Starting Netcaster

As mentioned in the previous section, you can start Netcaster by selecting Communicator, Netcaster (Ctrl + 8) from the menu bar of any Communicator component. If you want to run Netcaster from the desktop, you can find the Netcaster icon in your Communicator program group and double-click it.

You can also choose to have Netcaster run when you run Communicator. To do so, select Edit, Preferences from the menu bar, and choose the Appearance panel (see Figure 21.1). Check the checkbox next to Netcaster in the On startup, launch section, and click the OK button. The next time you start up Communicator, Netcaster will launch automatically.

**FIG. 21.1**
This dialog box lets you tell Communicator that you want Netcaster to run automatically.

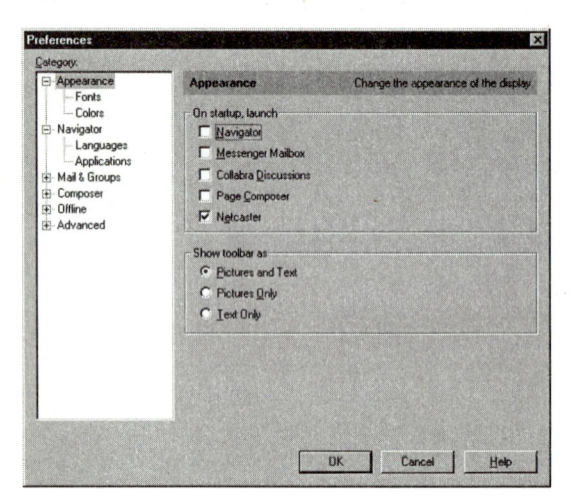

## Finding Channels

Think of Channel Finder as a sort of *TV Guide* for push content. It not only provides convenient listings for the best and most popular Netcaster channels, it lets you preview them before you subscribe. Channel Finder even lets you turn normal Web sites into push channels!

When you launch Netcaster, Channel Finder automatically occupies most of the Netcaster user interface (see Figure 21.2).

http://www.quecorp.com

**FIG. 21.2**
Channel Finder is your jumping off point for finding great channels to subscribe to.

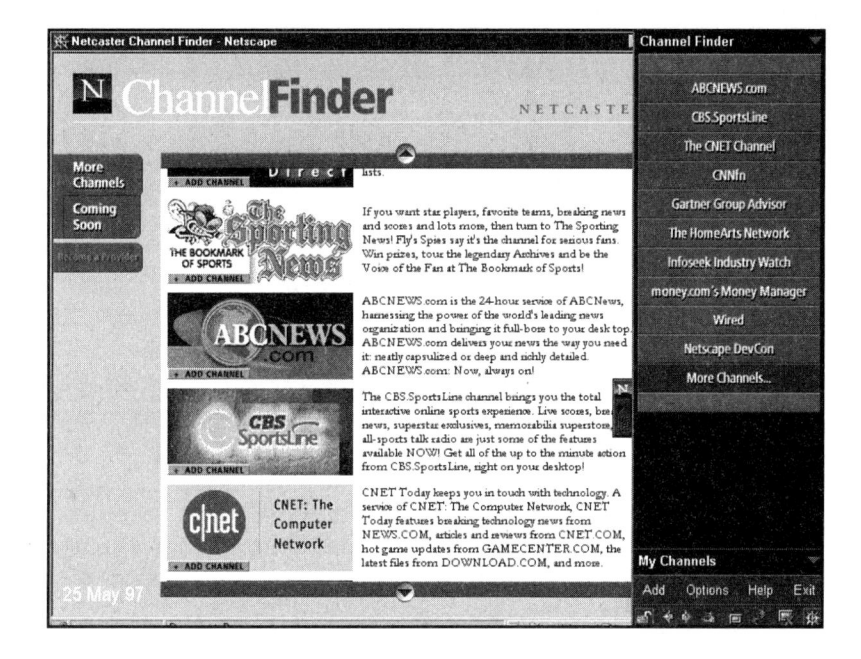

Channel Finder lists ten channels. If you're an individual user, you see a different list than that seen by a user at a corporate site. A system administrator can even define a custom list of up to ten channels to be listed in Channel Finder. This is a great option for companies that want to create their own in-house channels on a corporate intranet.

The personal and default enterprise ten-channel lists are kept on the Netscape site and are periodically (and automatically) updated from the Internet, so the Channel Finder list changes often. Don't take it for granted—check it occasionally to see if the channel list has changed.

> **TIP** If Channel Finder is hidden by the My Channels bar, just click the Channel Finder bar to bring it back.

Move your mouse pointer over a channel name to see a brief description of that channel. As described in the previous section, you click a channel name to bring up a thumbnail "card" representing the channel, then click the Add Channels button on the card to launch a channel preview window. Clicking the Add Channels button on the preview window brings up the Channel Properties dialog box (see Figure 21.3).

> **N O T E** There's also a selection in Channel Finder called More Channels (see Figure 21.2, above). Clicking this tab launches a Navigator window that takes you to the Channel Finder Web site. This site lists hundreds more Netcaster channels. Each is shown with its own preview card and blurb. Adding a channel from this list is identical to adding one from the Channel Finder menu. Just click the preview card's Add Channel button.

**FIG. 21.3**
The General panel of the Channel Properties dialog box sets a channel's identity and update information.

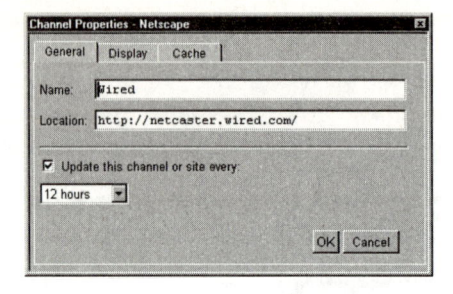

There are three tabs in the Channel Properties dialog box, labeled General, Display, and Cache. These control all the settings for the selected channel. All of the fields under each of these tabs will contain the default information for the channel you're subscribing to, as defined by the channel provider.

> **TIP** If you select the Add Channel button in the preview window for a site that you already subscribe to, the Channel Properties will be updated to the latest values for that channel. If you suspect that the way a channel works has changed substantially since you subscribed, this is a quick shortcut to bringing that channel up to date.

The first tab, General (see Figure 21.3), asks for four bits of information. The Name: field contains the name of the channel as it will be shown in the My Channels list after you subscribe. This will generally be the same as the name you selected in its Channel Finder listing, though that may not always be so. The Location: field contains the URL of the channel. This should not generally be changed by the user.

The whole idea of push technology is to let channels be downloaded and updated automatically for later viewing. The final two fields under the General Channel Properties dialog box control download timing. First, the checkbox labeled Update this channel or site every: must be checked for automatic updates to occur. The drop-down list box lets you choose a frequency for timed downloads. A channel provider will usually set this value to correspond approximately to how often information on the site changes, but you can set it to check more or less often if you wish.

The second tab is labeled Display (see Figure 21.4). It has only two mutually exclusive option buttons. If the top one (Default Window) is selected, the channel is displayed in a Navigator window. If the bottom option button (Web top Window) is chosen, the channel is displayed in Web top mode. The preview area to the right of the buttons is there to remind you which is which.

> **NOTE** If the Default Window is selected, the Navigator window used to display the channel will still conform to the window definition used by the channel developer. For instance, the menu bar and toolbars may be turned off.

The third and final tab is labeled Cache, and is shown in Figure 21.5.

http://www.quecorp.com

# Finding Channels    415

**FIG. 21.4**
The Display tab chooses Web top or window mode display.

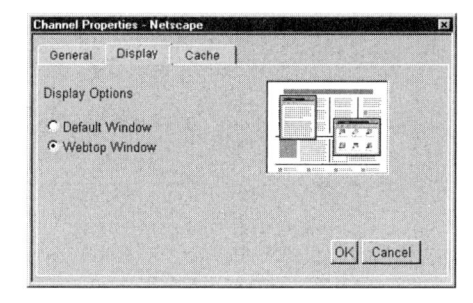

**FIG. 21.5**
The Cache tab determines how much time and disk space are taken up by downloading a channel.

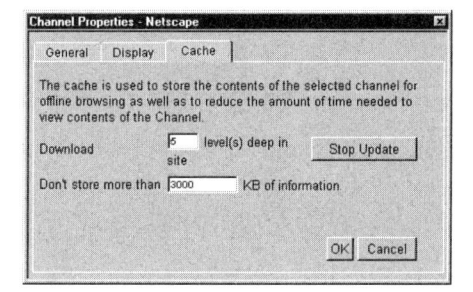

Download "x" levels deep in site controls how many link levels are downloaded. For example, if you type in "3" for this value, Netcaster will download the channel's home page, any pages referenced by the home page, and any pages referenced by those pages. Many channels will set this value to only 1 or 2, to minimize download times. That way, you only get the updated home page and maybe the first level of links.

The downside to this is that any further links have to be retrieved in real-time when you view the pages; they can't be cached from your hard disk because they were never downloaded. Make sure this setting matches the way you view a channel. If you find you're constantly trying to view deeper than the levels you download, set the value for this field higher. If you consistently only skim a site's top level or two, set this value to just one or two to save system resources and download times.

The second field under the Cache tab is labeled Don't store more than "xxx" KB of information. The value in this field serves to set an absolute limit on how much information is downloaded, no matter how many levels are set in the other field.

> **TIP** Try to keep track of the total number of KB you've specified for the total of all your subscribed channels to make sure that downloaded Netcaster channels don't take over all the free space on your hard drive.

Finally, the Cache panel includes a Stop Update button, which can be pressed to stop the current download-in-progress for the selected channel. This can be handy if you need to disconnect your system from your network, and so on.

Clicking OK ends the Add Channel process. At any time, you can click the Cancel button to drop out and leave the channel unsubscribed.

## My Channels

Once you've subscribed to some channels, you view them using the My Channels menu. Click on the My Channels bar to move it up over the Channel Finder menu, revealing your list of subscribed channels (see Figure 21.6).

**FIG. 21.6**
The My Channels menu gives you a simple point-and-click interface to your subscribed channels.

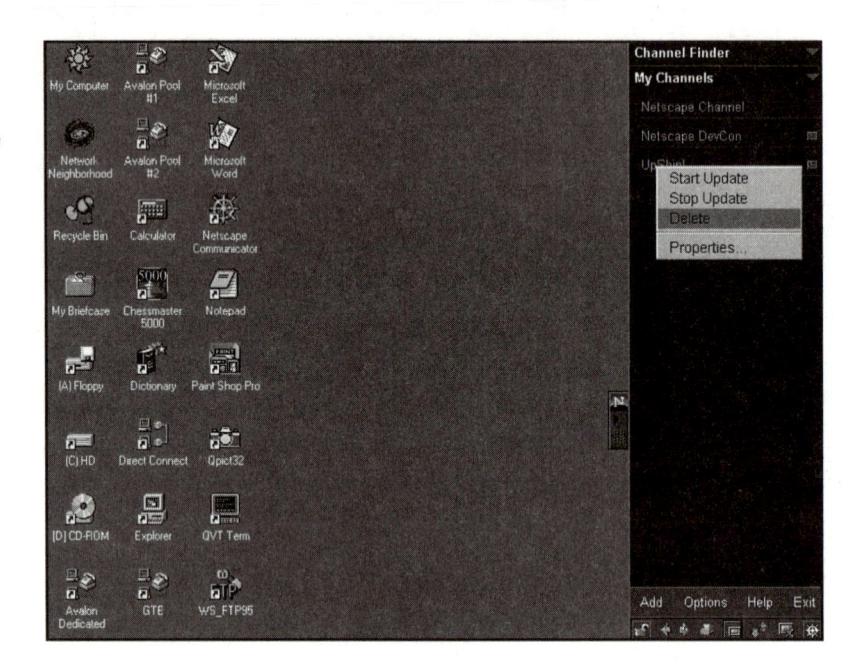

> **TIP** Notice the right-mouse button pop up menu over the My Channels menu in Figure 21.6. This menu gives you quick access to Start Update, Stop Update, Delete, and Properties settings for any subscribed channel.

If a channel is designated as a Web top, its title bar will show a small monitor icon. As you move the pointer over each channel title, it is highlighted. Hover the pointer over a title to see the last time it was updated. Click the title to view the channel.

If a channel is displayed in a normal Navigator window, you may or may not have the usual Navigator menus and toolbars to work with, depending on how the channel provider set up the window. There may be custom controls instead. You'll have nothing but custom controls if the channel is designated for Web top display.

http://www.quecorp.com

> **TIP** If a channel display window has the Navigator menu enabled, you can always turn on the toolbars from the View menu. If the status bar is missing from the bottom of the window, you can toggle it on by pressing Ctrl + Alt + S.

> **TIP** Whether a channel is displayed in normal or Web top view, the right mouse button can always be used over the window background or over any object to bring up the normal Navigator pop-up menu for that context.

## The Netcaster Menu Bar

Near the bottom of the Netcaster user interface is a menu bar containing four selections. Click Add to add a channel or Web site to My Channels. Choose Options to bring up a dialog box from which you can change the Netcaster window. If all else fails, you can click Help to open the NetHelp window. Exit closes Netcaster.

### Add

There are actually three ways to add a channel to your My Channels menu. The first is to use Channel Finder, of course. The second is to browse to a Web site that includes a special Netcaster icon, and click the Add Channels button on that icon. The third is to select Add from the menu bar.

When you click Add, you get exactly the same Channel Preferences dialog box that you get when you subscribe to a channel using Channel Finder. The only difference is that all the fields are blank. You have to fill them in by hand. This means that you have to know the values for all of the boxes before you start.

We won't go through all the settings and what they do—they were all explained back in the section on using Channel Finder.

The Name: and Location: fields in the General Channel Preferences dialog box are the only fields that are absolutely required for you to fill in. Make the name something appropriate and short enough to fit nicely in the Subscribed Channel list under the My Channels menu. The Location: field must contain a valid URL.

> **NOTE** Note that any valid URL can be used in the location field. This means that you can turn a regular Web site into a channel! Just enter the page's URL into the Location: field, pick an appropriate Name:, and set the Display and Cache values to your specifications. The result is practically indistinguishable from a "real" channel.

All of the other fields have defaults set for you. In the General panel, the automatic update box is checked, with a time interval of 12 hours. The Display setting is Default Window. The Cache settings are to download two levels with a maximum download size of 5000kb. If any of these settings aren't to your liking, change them. Choose OK to finish, or Cancel to bail out at any time.

## Options

Choose the Options button on the Netcaster menu and you'll get the dialog box shown in Figure 21.7.

**FIG. 21.7**
The Options dialog box controls the look and feel of both the Netcaster interface and all of your subscribed channels.

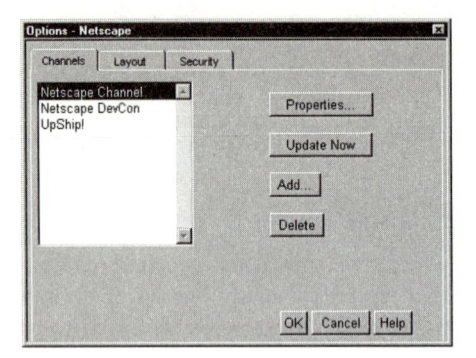

There is only one Preferences setting for Netcaster that you can make from the Edit, Preferences dialog box—choosing whether Netcaster should be launched when you start Communicator. (This is set from the Appearance panel, by the way.) All other Netcaster preferences are set from the Options dialog box.

There are three tabbed panels available in the Options dialog box: Channels, Layout, and Security.

**The Channels Panel**   The Channels panel (see Figure 21.7, above) controls the properties of all of your subscribed channels.

On the left is a scrollable list of all the subscribed channels that are listed in the My Channels menu. You can modify the place that a listed channel occupies in this window (and, therefore, in the My Channels menu) by highlighting it and moving it up or down by clicking the Up or Down arrow.

If you highlight a channel name and click the Properties button, you'll bring up the Channel Properties dialog box, from which you can make any changes.

Clicking the Update Now button causes Netcaster to begin downloading updated information from the highlighted channel immediately. You'll see the download update bar for that channel appear in the My Channels menu as soon as you click this button.

> **TIP**   If you click the Update Now button and then change your mind, you can choose Preferences and select the Cache tab from the Preferences dialog, then click the Stop Update button.

You can delete a highlighted channel by clicking the Delete button. You'll get a dialog box that asks you if you're sure.

http://www.quecorp.com

Finally, this panel includes a highly redundant Add button, which acts exactly like the Add button on the Netcaster menu. That is, clicking it brings up the General Preferences dialog for setting up a new channel.

**The Layout Panel** The Layout panel controls the general look and feel of Netcaster (see Figure 21.8).

**FIG. 21.8**
The Layout panel lets you move Netcaster elements and specify a Web top.

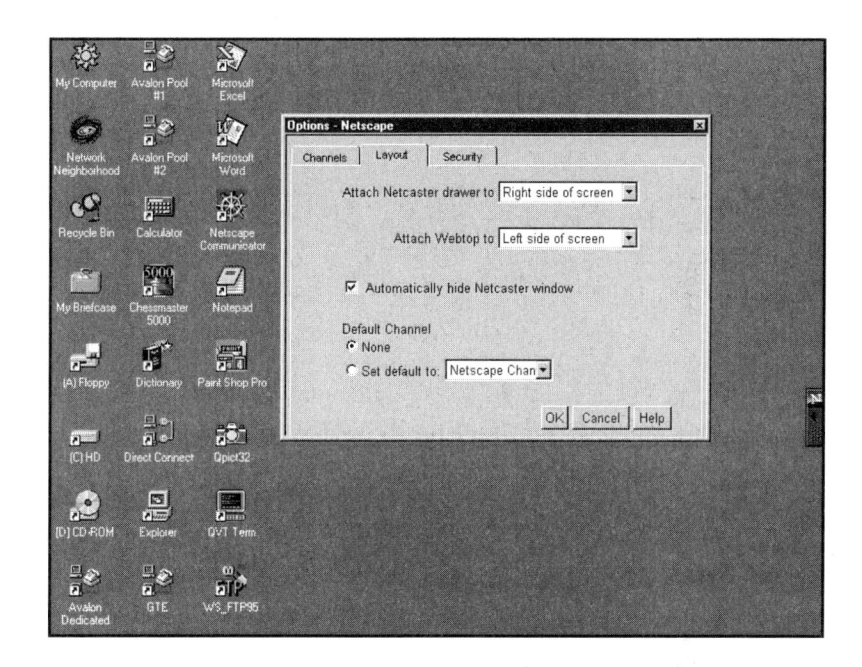

The Netcaster user interface appears on the right side of your screen by default. If you wish, you can change this to the left side by making that selection from the drop-down menu.

Likewise, the Web top itself is generally attached to the left side of the screen. This fact often goes unnoticed because the Netcaster Web top is usually full-screen. However, if your Web top is smaller, it will, by default, appear on the left. This panel lets you switch that to the right side if you wish. You usually want to specify the drawer on one side and the Web top on the other.

You can check the Automatically hide Netcaster window checkbox if you want the Netcaster drawer to slide politely out of the way whenever you open a Web top. Odds are that the channel designer has told it to get out of the way anyway, but this is nice if you have some old-fashioned Web pages designated as channels.

If you like, you can specify a channel to display automatically when you run Netcaster. The radio button labeled None is checked by default—check the other and choose a channel if you want one. It's cooler to pick a channel that displays as a Web top, of course, but you can also choose one that shows up in a Navigator window if you wish.

**The Security Panel**   Netcaster has its roots in Marimba's Castanet, and can display Castanet channels as easily as it displays its own. (More about this later.) But Castanet channels pull some interesting tricks that may compromise your system security. Just to put your mind at ease, Netscape has included a Security panel that lets you turn off these Castanet goodies if you wish (see Figure 21.9).

**FIG. 21.9**
Control Castanet Security settings with this Options panel.

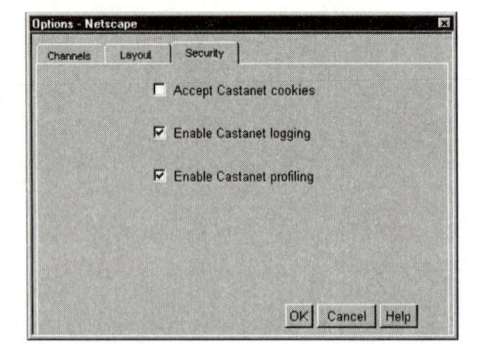

There are three checkboxes on this panel. Check the first if you want to Accept Castanet Cookies. This is normally off. Check the second to Enable Castanet logging, and the third to Enable Castanet profiling. These are normally selected "on."

> **TIP**  You can find out all the details about Castanet security by browsing to Marimba's Web site at **http://www.marimba.com**.

> **NOTE**   One more note about Netcaster configuration: On a LAN, the system administrator can use Netscape Mission Control (formerly Administration Kit 4.0) to control what kinds of information can be pushed over Netcaster channels. The system administrator has full control over options like update intervals, cache size, and so on.

# Help

Like all Communicator applications, Netcaster is equipped with context-sensitive NetHelp. Clicking the Help button from any dialog box brings up NetHelp displaying pertinent information about that dialog box. Choosing Help from the Netcaster menu displays the full NetHelp menu for Netcaster (see Figure 21.10).

Choose the topic you need help with from the left-side menu, click the Find button to search for a specific topic, or just scroll through the information window for clues. You can jump to help for other Communicator applications at any time by clicking the appropriate icon on the upper toolbar. Print what's in the display window by choosing the printer icon from the bottom toolbar.

**FIG. 21.10**
Netcaster's NetHelp window is searchable and menu-driven.

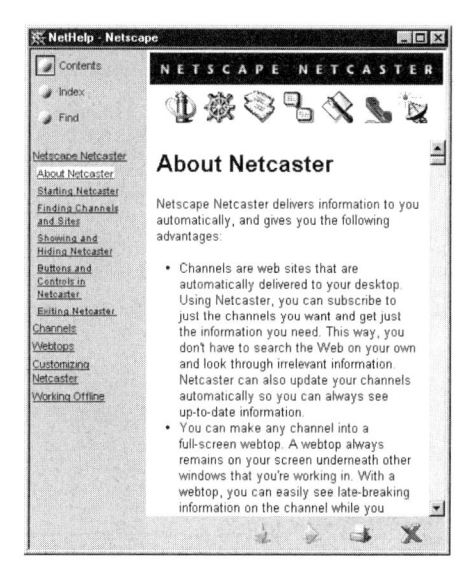

## Exit

Click the Exit button to quit Netcaster at any time. Open Web tops will also close, though channels displayed in "normal" Navigator windows stick around.

## The Netcaster Toolbar

The Netcaster Toolbar floats above all other windows on your desktop. If a Web top channel isn't being displayed, it pops in and out of view with the rest of the Netcaster interface when you click the Netcaster "N" tab. But if a Web top is displayed, the Toolbar "tears off" of the Netcaster menu and remains with the Web top when the interface slides offscreen.

There are eight icon buttons on the Netcaster Toolbar (see Figure 21.11).

The Security padlock icon serves the same purpose as the similar icon on a Navigator window's status bar. If unlocked, it indicates the displayed Web top is not encrypted. If locked, it shows the Web top is secure. Clicking the padlock icon brings up the Security Information window for the Web top.

The Go to previous page on Web top icon serves the same function as the Back button in a Navigator window. If you've jumped to a linked page, clicking it takes you back to the previous page.

The Go to next page on Web top mirrors Navigator's Forward button. It only comes into play if you've first moved forward a page, then back to where you started.

To print the displayed page, choose the Print the Web top icon to bring up the system Print dialog box.

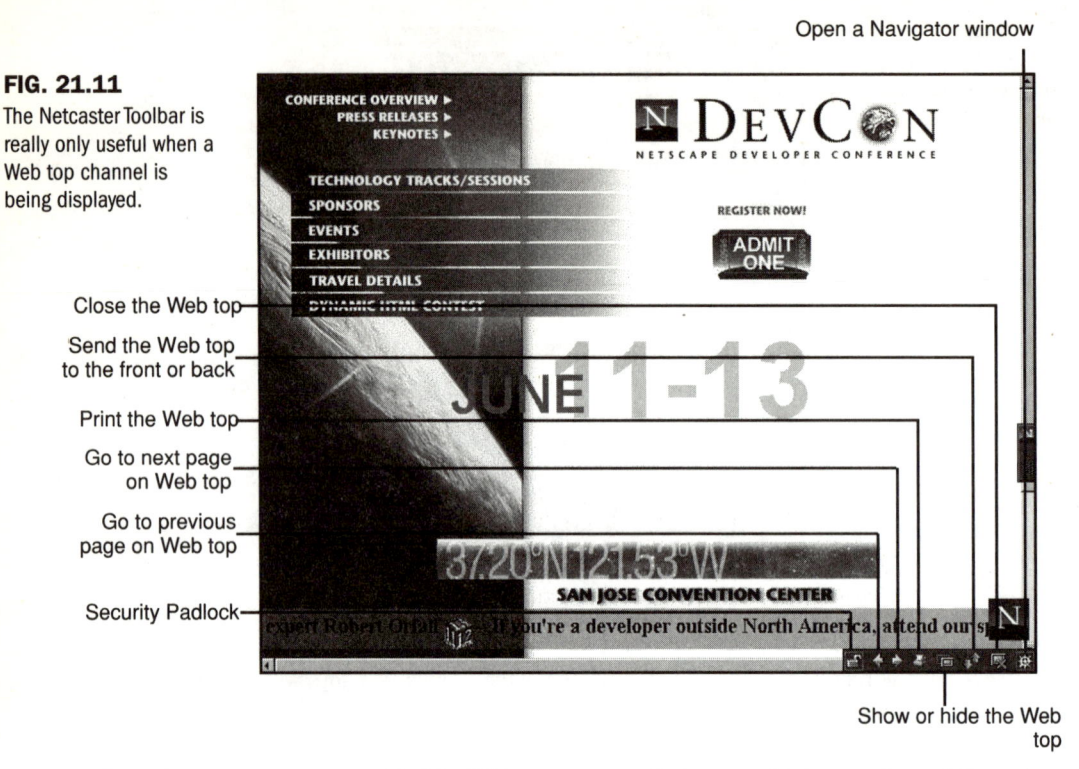

**FIG. 21.11**
The Netcaster Toolbar is really only useful when a Web top channel is being displayed.

Callouts on figure:
- Open a Navigator window
- Close the Web top
- Send the Web top to the front or back
- Print the Web top
- Go to next page on Web top
- Go to previous page on Web top
- Security Padlock
- Show or hide the Web top

Sometimes you want to get rid of the Web top temporarily because it's in your face while you're trying to do something else. Clicking the Show or hide the Web top button will toggle the displayed Web top off, leaving only the Toolbar. Clicking it again will redisplay the Web top.

A Web top page is normally displayed behind all other open windows, emulating your desktop. However, the Send the Web top to the front or back button toggles its position. Clicking it once moves the Web top in front of all open windows; clicking it again moves it to the back.

When you're done viewing a Web top, clicking the Close the Web top button gets rid of the Web top completely.

While Netcaster doesn't have the full Communicator Bar, it does have the Open a Navigator window button. If you find yourself in sudden need of a Navigator window, clicking this button will bring up a new one, pointed to your home page.

# Web Tops

We've talked a lot about Web tops, but what is a Web top, really?

A Web top is the same thing as a channel. A channel is a Web site that is specially designed or configured to be downloaded automatically (or "pushed") to your computer. A Web top is just a special way of displaying a channel.

The short explanation is that a Web top is a windowless display area. It is usually full-screen size, but it can be smaller. It has no borders, no menus, and no toolbars. A Web top locks to the left or right edge of your desktop, depending on your Options setting, and can appear in front of or behind all of your open applications windows, depending on how it was created and whether or not you have clicked the Toolbar button to flip it to the front or back of your display.

## Web Tops in Brief

Many channels are set up to run as Web top displays. If they are, they appear in the My Channels menu with a small monitor icon to the right of their name.

You can only have one Web top display. If you have a Web top open and then open another, it takes the place of the first Web top. When you open a Web top, it initially appears in front of all other windows, then moves behind (if it is designed to do so—most Web tops are). Upon opening, most Web tops also automatically slide the Netcaster interface window off the screen. The Toolbar stays behind.

You can temporarily hide the displayed Web top by clicking the Hide Web top toolbar button. Click it again to restore the Web top display. You click the Close Web top button on the Toolbar to close the current Web top.

You can choose a Web top to open automatically when Netcaster is run. This was explained in the Options section of this chapter, but the short form is that you click the Options button, choose the Layout tab, select the Set Default to: option button, and choose the channel you want from the drop-down list.

If the Web top channel you're viewing seems stale, or if it seems it didn't download properly, you can update it immediately by choosing Options from the menu bar, selecting its title from the scrolling list, and clicking the Update Now button. (Click OK to finish.)

## Web Top Design

Because the Web top eliminates all of Navigator's normal controls, the Web top designer has to carefully consider how her site is going to look and feel to the user. All of the normal functions have to be replicated somehow in a proprietary format. While this means extra work for the designer, it also means extra rewards, because the channel will have a unique design that totally reflects the needs of the site design.

The main idea in Web top design is to create a replacement for the user's desktop (see Figure 21.12). The Web top is supposed to sit in the background as a user works, displaying updated information in a compelling and pleasing manner. The Web top becomes an integral and indispensable part of the user's system.

This is why a Web top display usually covers the entire screen. It obliterates the operating system screen and changes the whole functionality of the computer. All application windows appear on top of the Web top, just as they would over the desktop. The desktop is, of course, still there, and is immediately accessible any time the user needs it.

**FIG. 21.12**
You'd expect Netscape to provide a good example of clean, compelling Web top design, and their Netscape channel is just that.

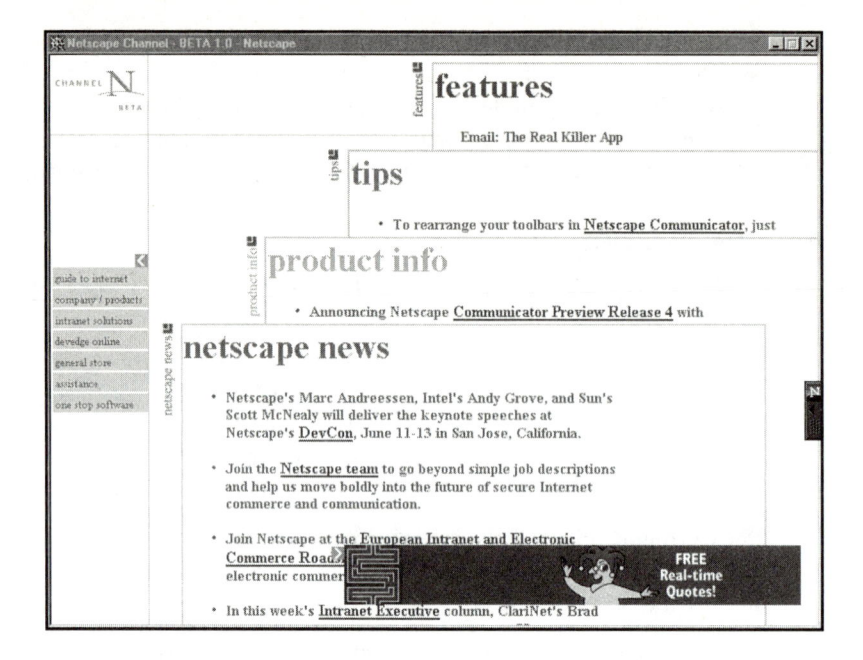

A link from the Web top generally opens a new, separate window over the Web top. The idea is to make the Web top an anchor page or launching point from which the user jumps off to pertinent information.

Web tops often incorporate rich animated features like auto-highlighting Java menus, layered moving windows created using dynamic HTML (see Figure 21.13), and interactive buttons powered by JavaScript. Seen on a full-screen Web top display, such features are twice as awesome as when used in a boxed-in Navigator window.

Web top displays also lend themselves well to the display of continuously updated dynamic information, such as scrolling stock ticker displays. By setting the update interval to 15 minutes or so, and scrolling the information as it is updated, a Web top can provide an immediacy that is completely missing from a static desktop background.

Perhaps the most variable and personality-prone part of a Web top is the user interface. Because the Web top has no access to the Navigator toolbars and menus, the Web top channel designer has to create a complete set of controls for her site. These controls can be as simple or as complex as she desires. They can also be staid and traditional, or wild, colorful, and animated. I imagine we will see Web tops that cover the entire spectrum from unimaginative and stuffy to outrageous and incomprehensible. In between there will be some very, very good designs. And that's the test of a real art form, isn't it?

**FIG. 21.13**
Click a tabbed window on the Netscape channel and it slides neatly into a prominent position.

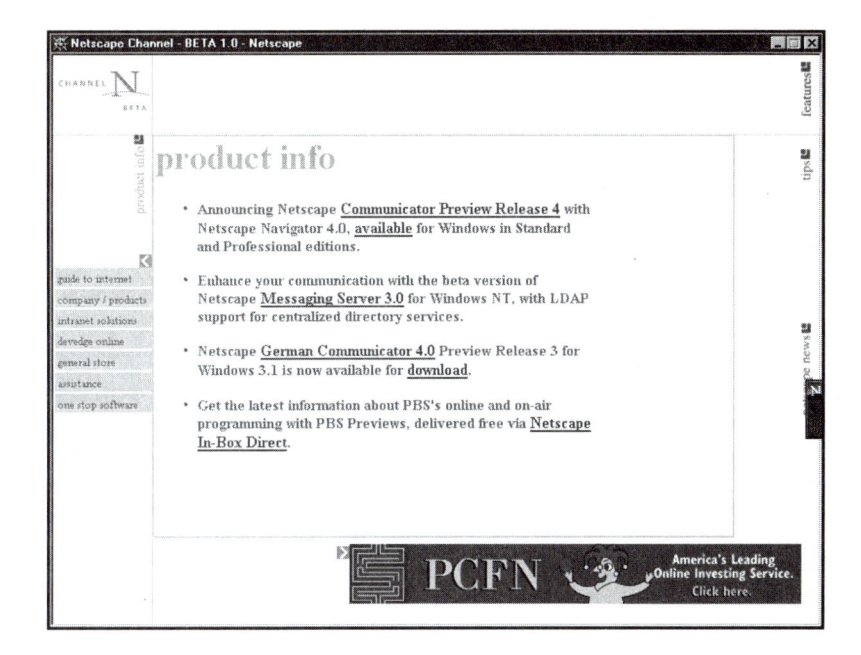

One of the major challenges facing Web top designers comes from the fact that the Web top exists behind all other open application windows. The Web top has to work with the rest of a user's applications. If its too intrusive, the user will reject the Web top design and find another, or move back to his old desktop paradigm. It is incumbent on Web top designers to remember that the user will usually want to live with his Web top all the time, just as he currently lives with his desktop.

The best Web top designs will allow the user some degree of customization, even if only being able to choose from among a number of different Web tops from the same site. It's also important that the Web top remain consistent from session to session. Cookies will probably be used by many sites to store user preferences and settings.

It will be very, very easy for people to create Web tops (and, indeed, any kind of channel) that are overly data-heavy, requiring exorbitant download times and way too much hard drive space. That is the real challenge—to create compelling a Web top interface for a content-rich channel and still keep the download frequency, time, and size under control.

As one example, remember that the user has control over how many levels are downloaded. If a Web top links to sub-menus and these sub menus link to content pages, and those pages link to more content pages, a channel designer has already lost the majority of Netcaster users, who will limit their downloads to two or three levels at the most.

If you are considering developing your own channel with a Web top interface, use Channel Finder to guide you to some good examples first. Channels and Web tops are cool, but they aren't just pushed Web pages. They have their own subtle design challenges and rewards.

# Channels

On the Web, you have to go find information, but Netcaster channels find you. That's the basic, fundamental difference between Web pages and Netcaster channels.

Channels and Web sites have lots of similarities, of course. They are both built of the same components—HTML, Java, JavaScript, graphics, links, and so on. They are built using the same tools—HTML editors, Java and JavaScript development tools, and so on.

But the types of content that lend themselves to delivery via Netcaster channels are usually somewhat different than what you'll find on Web sites. Channel content is usually time-intensive. It's information you want while it's timely and fresh. That's why most Netcaster channels are set to be automatically updated every 12 hours, or every week, or even every 15 minutes. They contain information that you just don't have time to surf the Web for—stock quotes, business news, and sports scores, for example.

You subscribe to a Netcaster channel for the same reasons you subscribe to a newspaper, business magazine, or pay cable TV channel—because you're convinced that channel will deliver the information (or entertainment) you need on a regular schedule and in a timely manner. You may get more leisurely information by surfing the Web or even by visiting bookmarked sites, but you trust the sites you have listed in My Channels to bring you what you need without further thought or intervention on your part. In short, you expect the channels you subscribe to will make your life a little easier.

Presentation is still important, sure (see Figure 21.14); nobody wants to read a badly written newspaper or watch a badly produced TV special, and no one wants to have to look at a badly presented Netcaster channel, either. But content is what makes push technology work. If the content isn't solid, each "push" is more like a "shove".

Of course, if you've got a favorite Web site that you've just got to see every day (or week, or month), it's easy to turn that site into a channel. If your favorite news site, for example, doesn't have a Netcaster channel set up yet, you can click the Add button and create one for it. The channel you set up won't be optimized for channel delivery, of course, but if you set your Cache and other Preferences wisely there's no reason why you can't keep up-to-date this way. Turning your favorite news site into a channel has many advantages over browsing the same site. For one, you can download your news during off-peak hours and have it available on your hard drive for viewing when it's convenient. For example, you could have the news come in at 6:00 a.m. and have it waiting for you on your Web top when you start work at 8:00 a.m. You don't have to log on to the net and wait for the pages to download. You're ready to go, and can probably get caught up on the day's news in half the time it would have taken you to download it in real-time.

But the odds are good that your favorite timely Web sites are already working on push pages. Netscape has started out Netcaster with an impressive list that includes ABCNEWS.com, CBS SportsLine, CNNfn, Gartner Group Advisor, Hearst's HomeArts Network. Companies in the "second wave" include heavy hitters like Astrology.com, Charles Schwab, CitySearch Inc.,

http://www.quecorp.com

Corel, EarthWeb Gamelan, Excite, Federal Express Corp., go2net, Kaplan Educational Centers, Knight-Ridder, MapQuest, N2K, Pencil Me In, Planet Out, Playsite.com, Sesame Street, and Wire Networks (Producers of Women's Wire, Healthy Ideas, and Beatrice's Web Guide). And Netscape hopes that Netcaster will quickly grow to include millions of users.

**FIG. 21.14**
Not all channels appear as a Web top. This site from Infoseek provides useful and timely information in a standard Navigator window, complete with menus and toolbars.

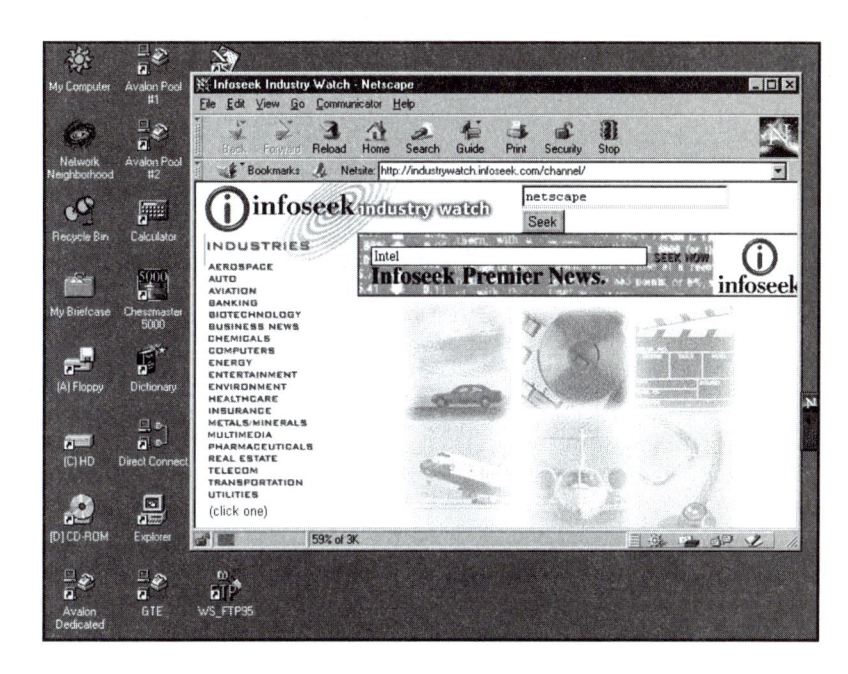

## Marimba Castanet

One of Netcaster's great strengths is that it incorporates Castanet technology from Marimba (see Figure 21.15), which already has hundreds of channels available for it. Netcaster doesn't require Castanet's proprietary "Transmitter" server, but it can handle Castanet channels just fine because it includes a built-in Castanet channel tuner.

Castanet provides some interesting features that Netcaster channels don't intrinsically offer (though they could be added through custom Java and JavaScript applets). For example, Castanet channels offer user feedback and polling, logging, cookies, and a distributed server architecture with support for UNIX and Windows NT.

> **NOTE** Castanet has its own proprietary protocol, which looks like this in the Navigator Location toolbar: **castanet://trans.marimba.com**

Companies that are already set up with the Castanet Transmitter server and Castanet Tuner clients can immediately switch to Communicator and Netcaster with no problem and no system changes. Even better, they can increase the audience for their channel immediately without creating new versions of their content pages. Netcaster users can view them just fine.

**FIG. 21.15**
The Marimba site provides a wealth of information about Castanet, as well as links to over a hundred Castanet channels.

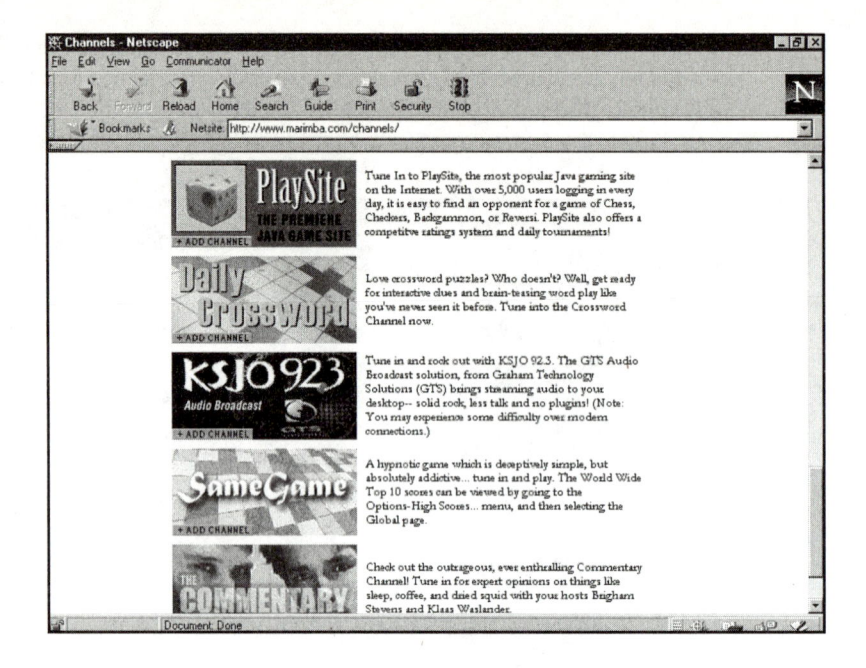

Netscape says that Channel Finder will list the best Castanet channels as well as native Netcaster channels. Even more Castanet channels will be listed under the More Channels bar. If that's not enough, you can browse to the Marimba site at **http://www.marimba.com**.

> **NOTE** Logically enough, the above Web site is also a wonderful source of additional information about Castanet.

One thing that Castanet does easily is automatically distribute and maintain software applications. This makes it a good choice for companies wishing to automatically update employee's software installations, or those wanting to distribute their software products over the Internet.

A Castanet channel can consist of a few HTML pages, an entire Web site, or even a Java application or applet. Existing Java code can be turned into a Castanet channel with few modifications.

If a Castanet channel incurs some small changes, it can instruct Netcaster to selectively download just the changes instead of the entire site, inserting changes on-the-fly, an incredible download time-saver.

If you want to create Castanet channels, Marimba offers a visual tool called Bongo for doing so with Java. It includes many pre-written visual controls and gives you a drag-and-drop interface. Once channel pieces are in place, Bongo lets you create JavaScripts to control your creation. When you're done, you can publish your Castanet channel with the push of a button.

http://www.quecorp.com

# Offline Browsing

The whole idea of push technology is to let channels download invisibly in the background while you're doing something else so you can view them at your leisure.

You can view channels while you're still connected to the Internet, and there are many good reasons for doing so. A Web top might have links to "foreign" sites that aren't cached automatically. Or you might find an interesting series of links that extend beyond the 3 or 4 levels you've instructed Netcaster to cache.

But offline browsing has its appeal, too. If you're on the road with your laptop during the day, for example, it makes a lot of sense to have Netcaster download your favorite channels and Web sites for viewing while you're offline in your car. If you pay by the minute for your Internet connection (does anyone still do this?) you can certainly download a site and scan it offline for less money than you would spend to sit there and stare at the screen while the meter ticks away your hard-earned money.

Effective offline browsing is based on making sure that your Channel Preferences are set correctly for the channels you're subscribed to, and making sure that the information is downloaded and cached before you go offline.

We've discussed the first concern in the Channel Finder section of this chapter. The second, while elementary, is fundamental to a good offline browsing experience.

There are really two things to watch. The first is easy: bring up My Channels and make sure that there are no red lines moving before you shut down your computer. While a channel is being downloaded this red line indicates that the transfer is not done yet. If you go offline while the red line is still moving, your download will be incomplete.

The second point is to make sure that your computer is connected to the Internet at all times designated as update times for your subscribed channels. Open Options and check the Preferences for every channel to see what time you've chosen. If they don't match your schedule, change them so they're more convenient. If you don't pay for Internet access by the minute, you might want to set your update times for the middle of the night, so you can take advantage of off-peak download speeds.

If nothing else, you can manually select a channel from the Options dialog and click the Update Now button to update a channel just before you log off the Net.

To view a Netcaster channel while you're offline, you'll need to use Communicator's offline mode. Just load up Communicator and select the File menu, then Go Offline. Launch Netcaster and you're in business.

If you're in offline mode when Netcaster is supposed to update a channel, it won't. But if you're in Communicator's online mode but otherwise disconnected from the Internet, Netcaster will try to connect and do the scheduled download. It's best to let Communicator know when you're offline by choosing that mode from the File menu.

## Security

We've already discussed how you can set the way that Netcaster handles security issues related to Castanet through the Options, Security panel. But there are other security issues related to Netcaster, mostly involving Java.

A large portion of Netcaster is written in Java, which would not have been possible just a few months ago. Java originally operated in a security "sandbox" which didn't allow it access to vital system resources, such as writing to disk. Since writing to disk is what Netcaster is all about (caching channel information), it had to have some way to get permission to do so.

This is why you have to "grant" Netcaster Java permissions the first time you start it up, as explained early in this chapter (see Figure 21.16). In fact, if you don't tell those Java Security dialog boxes to remember your settings, you have to grant permissions every time you run Netcaster.

**FIG. 21.16**
Though scary-looking, Java Security dialog boxes like this one are really your best friend.

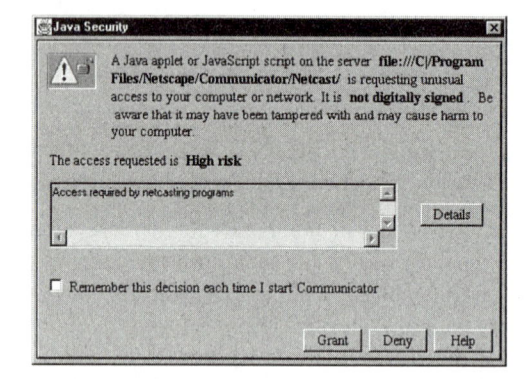

Likewise, many channels you subscribe to will be composed of Java applets and JavaScripts. The odds are good that you'll have to grant permissions for some of them some of the time. Fortunately, you don't have to do so blindly.

Most of this system is based on trust. The creator of a Java applet has a signed certificate that identifies her as a trustworthy soul. When her page loads you see a Java Security window asking if you want to grant permission. You can click a button to examine her certificate and make sure she's trustworthy. Then you can click another button to grant her applet permission to run on your computer. Or you can click cancel and skip viewing her channel.

Though those Java Security dialogs look scary, there's really no need to fear them. They tell you exactly what kind of access the applet is requesting, so you won't be surprised by unwanted intrusions into your system.

You must grant an application permission before it can perform any of the following actions:

- Writing to the hard disk
- Creating windows smaller than 100x100 pixels

http://www.quecorp.com

- Creating chromeless windows without controls or border elements
- Creating offscreen windows
- Creating dependent windows
- Accessing scripts across domain boundaries, including other frames within a single frameset
- Turning off the title bar
- Performing certain actions using LiveConnect

There's also a three-level risk classification system. The presumed risk of a signed applet will be rated as High risk, Medium risk, or Low risk depending on Netscape's assessment of the situation.

Just make sure the applets you grant permission to really do come from a reliable source and you'll be okay.

# Netscape Netcaster versus Microsoft Active Desktop

Netscape wasn't the first-to-market with push technology. That prize probably goes to the PointCast Network, which has been delivering information channels for months. Castanet also beat them to market, and did so very successfully, which is why they incorporated Castanet technology into Netcaster.

But Netscape beat Microsoft to market. Microsoft's Active Desktop is still months away from delivery as this is being written, but I'm running Netcaster on my desktop right now.

Is being fast good enough, though? Will Netcaster really beat out Active Desktop? Or is its integration into the Windows 95 operating system going to be such a strong selling point that Netcaster will fade into oblivion? Maybe, just maybe, it's even possible that the push market will prove to be broad enough to support both "standards"?

Who knows? But Netcaster has a few points in its favor.

The first is its compatibility with Castanet, which gives Netcaster a huge jump in installed channel base. There are over a hundred existing channels available in Castanet format, and it's sure to take a bit of time for Netcaster and Active Desktop to catch up. In the meantime, Netcaster can play those Castanet channels just fine, thank you very much.

Second is the fact that Microsoft's Active Desktop is based on a new "standard" called the Channel Definition Format (CDF). Netcaster is based on existing standards like HTML, Java, and JavaScript. In fact, you can turn an existing Web page into a Netcaster channel with zero effort, if you want to. Active Desktop channels will require special preparation.

Netscape claims that channel updating under CDF is akin to rocket science, whereas channel updates under Netcaster are easy and user-definable. It even requires a special server-side process, they say. If true, that's an important point.

CDF also requires a configuration file, whereas Netcaster doesn't. And who likes configuration files? ●

# PART V

## For Webmasters

- **22** HTML Primer  435
- **23** Adding Links and Graphics  467
- **24** Organizing Content with Tables and Frames  487
- **25** Building Navigational Imagemaps  519
- **26** Creating Forms and Server Scripts  537
- **27** Dynamic HTML  561
- **28** Using Layers  573
- **29** Using Style Sheets  599
- **30** Embedding Multimedia  627
- **31** Adding Java Applets  641
- **32** Enhancing Your Documents with JavaScript  653

CHAPTER 22

# HTML Primer

*by Andrew Shafran*

▬ **Use basic HTML formatting tags to create basic HTML documents**

▬ **Understand how to use the <P> tag to separate paragraphs of displayed text**

▬ **Include several types of lists in your HTML document. Text lists allow you to organize and structure multiple pieces of information effectively.**

▬ **Build a sample HTML document from scratch. Put all the HTML basics together to create a sample file.**

**A**s you've worked with the World Wide Web, you've most likely come across HTML, the underlying programming language that the WWW is based upon. While not as difficult to understand or use as other computer languages out there, HTML has its own quirks and idiosyncrasies that require you to spend some time learning about it. Unlike standard programming languages, HTML is a formatting language. You start with a page of pure text, and then add special HTML attributes that tell Netscape how to display that information on-screen.

This chapter takes you right into HTML and serves as an introduction to build your own Web pages. In addition to learning all the basic markup tags, you become familiar with using horizontal lines, tables, and other popular HTML attributes. ■

## Adding the <*HTML*> Tag

Through a comprehensive set of formatting tags, Netscape knows which text to display as a headline, where to separate two paragraphs, and how to highlight and format vital information. Typically, these formatting tags come in pairs, surrounding the text they intend to mark up. For example, marking a title on a Web page looks like this:

<TITLE> This is my Netscape title </TITLE>

When used in pairs, HTML tags are always related. The closing tag is just the initial tag with a / added within it.

While most tags come in pairs, you'll also encounter some HTML tags that appear alone, without a closing tag. These tags tend to separate paragraphs of text, or embed graphics on-screen, and don't change how text is formatted. For example, to add a horizontal line on-screen (often used to separate two paragraphs of text), you'd simply use this tag: <HR>.

In this chapter, when a new tag is introduced, you'll always learn whether it has a corresponding closing tag, and if so, how to use the pair correctly.

The first set of tags that you use in your HTML document is <HTML> and </HTML>. Add this set of tags so they appear like this:

<HTML>
</HTML>

WWW browsers use the <HTML> tags to recognize that they are reading an HTML document. Without them, a WWW browser might not recognize the other markup tags that you've included in your document. As a rule, most browsers don't require the <HTML> tag, but using it is considered good practice. While Netscape is smart enough to recognize other HTML tags without <HTML>, future versions and other WWW browsers might require it to recognize standard formatting tags.

**N O T E** With the advent of VRML (Virtual Reality Modeling Language), Java (Sun Microsystems advancements for the Web), and future WWW enhancements on the way, using the <HTML> and </HTML> tags is really a must. Without them, Netscape may not understand which programming language is used in a WWW document, or how to display information correctly. The <HTML> and </HTML> tags are how Netscape definitively recognizes an HTML file if it is missing a .HTM or .HTML file extension.

## HTML Section Tags

With your initial tag in place, you can start typing text and information into the HTML document. Using additional tags, you should organize WWW pages into two different sections: the header and body.

Using these section tags allows Netscape to take a quick snapshot of a document and recognize that it is separated into two components. This makes it easier to display information and keep the file organized.

## Using the *<HEAD>* Tag

The <HEAD> tag marks an HTML document's heading. By default, the heading contains the document title, indexing information, and important settings for that specific page.

Also, container tags, <HEAD> and </HEAD>, surround only a few lines of your file.

Netscape uses the information contained within the <HEAD> tags as a quick reference of the page while it is downloading the complete text and graphics. This allows Netscape to display the title before the rest of the document appears on-screen.

Include the <HEAD> tags within the main <HTML> tags, as follows:

```
<HTML>
<HEAD>
</HEAD>
</HTML>
```

## Using the *<BODY>* Tag

Used hand-in-hand with the <HEAD> tags, the <BODY> and </BODY> tags signify the rest of an HTML document. These tags surround most of your file. While the <BODY> tags don't affect how information is displayed within Netscape, they help keep the text file organized and indicate the main meat of a document.

By adding the <BODY> and </BODY> tags to your page, you have three sets of tags with no information to display, as follows:

```
<HTML>
<HEAD>
</HEAD>
<BODY>
</BODY>
</HTML>
```

# Titling a Document

The first bit of text you type into your HTML document is the title. Like a book title, your document title is a concise statement that accurately reflects the contents of the document.

Your HTML title is the first piece of information people see when they visit your WWW page. In Netscape, the title appears in the title bar at the top of the screen while the rest of the page is loading.

In addition to appearing in the Netscape title bar, the HTML title is also the information saved when a Netscape user adds a page to his list of bookmarks.

## Using the *<TITLE>* Tag

Adding a title to an HTML document requires using the <TITLE> and </TITLE> tags. Embedded within the document's header, titles can be any length desired. The <TITLE> tags should be within your <HEAD> and </HEAD> tags on your Web page. To name a document Andy's Home Page, add the following line of HTML to your WWW document:

```
<TITLE> Andy's Home Page </TITLE>
```

## Choosing an Effective Title

Like any good book title, an HTML document's title should be focused, concise, and well thought-out to pique curiosity and attract attention. When choosing a title, follow these tips:

- *Describe the page accurately*—The title should be a complete phrase that describes what appears in that file. If the HTML document is a particular scene within *Hamlet*, then a good title would be Shakespeare's *Hamlet*: Act I, Scene ii.
- *Keep the title short*—Long titles may not fit in the Netscape title bar and are difficult to read and digest quickly.

# Adding Headings to a Document

Similar to using a document title, headings are also used to introduce a WWW page. Coming in six different sizes, headings are eye-catching bits of information that stand out when looking at a page with Netscape.

Add a size 1 heading by surrounding text with the <H1> and </H1> tags. Figure 22.1 shows how the following tag appears within Netscape:

```
<H1> Dewey beats Truman!</H1>
```

Heading sizes range from 1 (the largest) to 6, and can be added by using the corresponding number tag. For example, a size 3 heading uses the <H3> and </H3> tags to mark specific text.

Figure 22.2 compares the six different sizes of headings and how they are displayed within Netscape.

### TROUBLESHOOTING

**Is there any way I can add a more pronounced heading to my HTML file to make sure people always see the proper headline?** As a standard procedure, many WWW developers include a size 1 heading as the first piece of displayed text within an HTML document. Similar to the document's title, this heading is much larger, more noticeable, and easier to read than the small title that is included in the Netscape title bar. To avoid being redundant, make sure you don't use the exact same text in the large heading and title.

http://www.quecorp.com

Adding Headings to a Document | 439

**FIG. 22.1**
Headers are the real eye catchers of a WWW document.

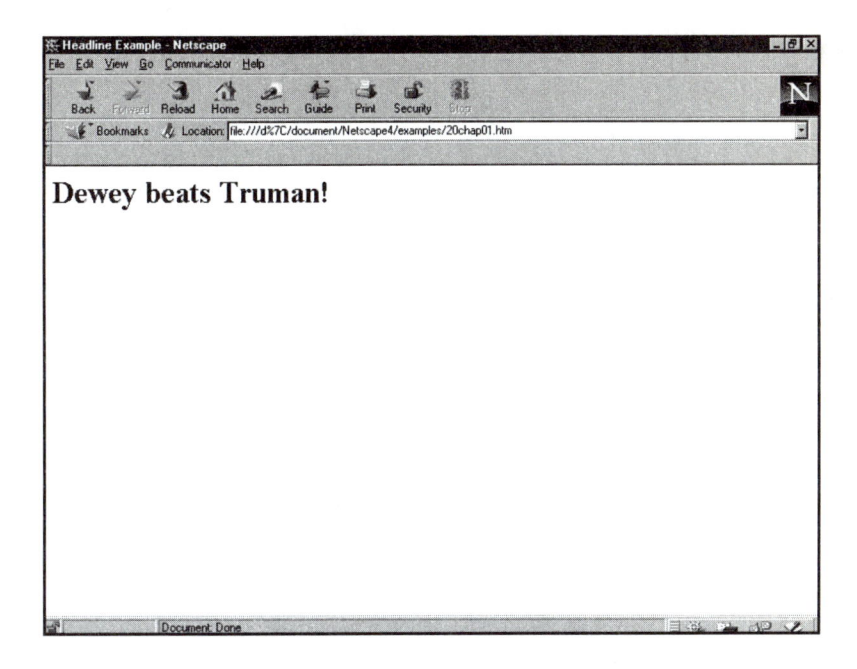

**FIG. 22.2**
Headlines come in all sizes.

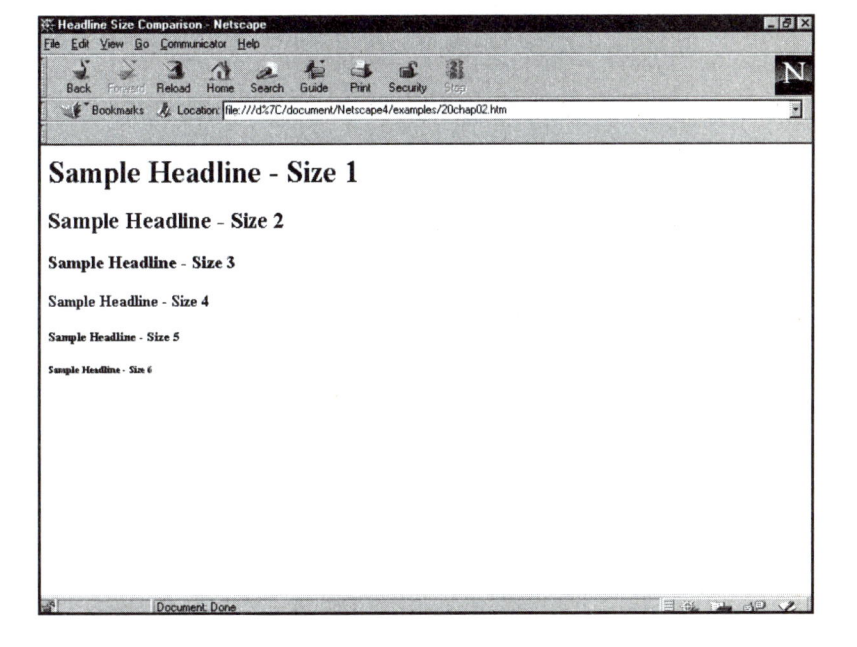

# Organizing Paragraphs of Text

You're probably familiar with how a word processor works. After typing several sentences of information, you hit the Enter key and then start typing on the next line. This way, you can organize your thoughts into separate paragraphs, making it easy for readers to browse through your document.

Formatting HTML doesn't work quite the same way. In an HTML file, you can use the spacebar and the Tab and Enter keys to make the source file easily readable, but without using HTML in paragraph-formatting tags, Netscape displays a jumbled mess.

Figure 22.3 shows how Netscape displays several paragraphs of text without using paragraph tags. Figure 22.4 is the same text, only formatted in a readable manner with a few simple HTML tags, such as the <H1> tag described earlier.

**FIG. 22.3**
Not even Wordsworth could read this mess.

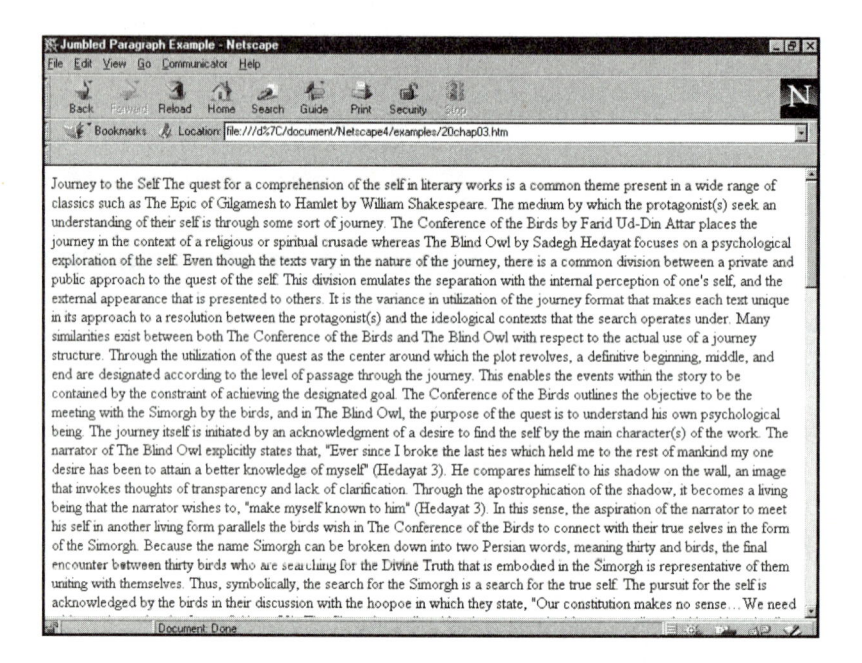

With these paragraph-organizing HTML tags, you can do the following:

- Organize and separate paragraphs of text on WWW pages
- Group pieces of related information together in an easy-to-read format
- Create itemized lists of information
- Focus attention on certain pieces of information on Web pages

**FIG. 22.4**
A few short tags make quite a readability difference.

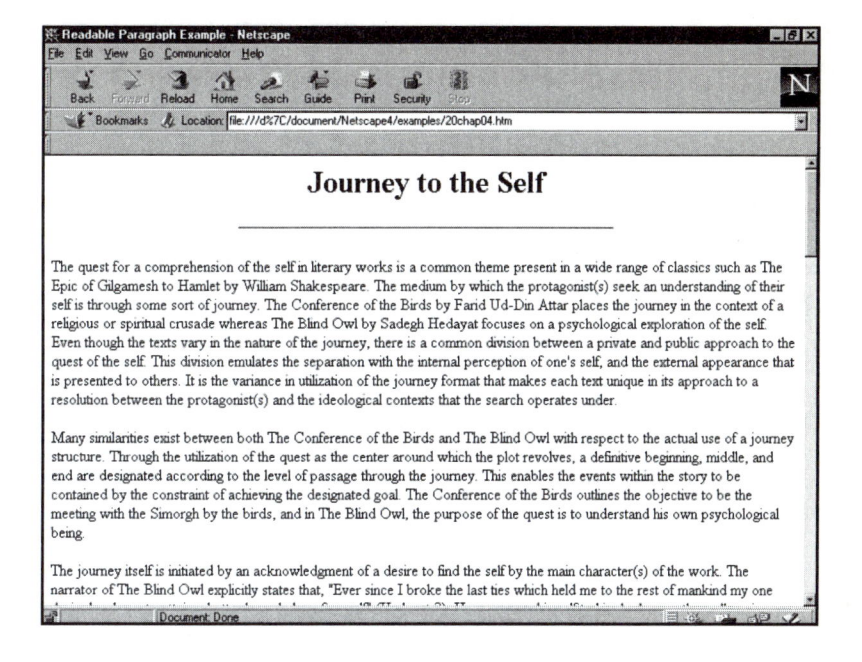

## Paragraph Breaks with <P>

The most common paragraph tag used on WWW pages is the <P> tag. This tag separates two paragraphs of information with a blank line. To use the paragraph tag, simply add <P> to your HTML file where you want to separate two lines of text. This tag isn't a container tag and can be added anywhere within your HTML document.

Figure 22.5 shows how the <P> tag formats the following information:

```
Typically, you'll want to separate paragraphs of information with the HTML
paragraph tag.
<P>
However, sometimes you want to use the <P> Paragraph <P> tag <P> to <P>
really <P> separate <P> pieces <P> of <P> text.
```

> **N O T E** Unlike most HTML tags, the <P> tag works both as a container tag (with the closing </P> tag) and as a separate stand-alone tag. Initially, WWW browsers (including Netscape) required that each separate paragraph of text was surrounded by the <P> and </P> tags. This was quite a hassle because the closing tag was often forgotten or not used. Nowadays, Netscape allows you to separate two paragraphs of text by only using the <P> tag.

**FIG. 22.5**
The <P> tag is the most popular paragraph separation tag.

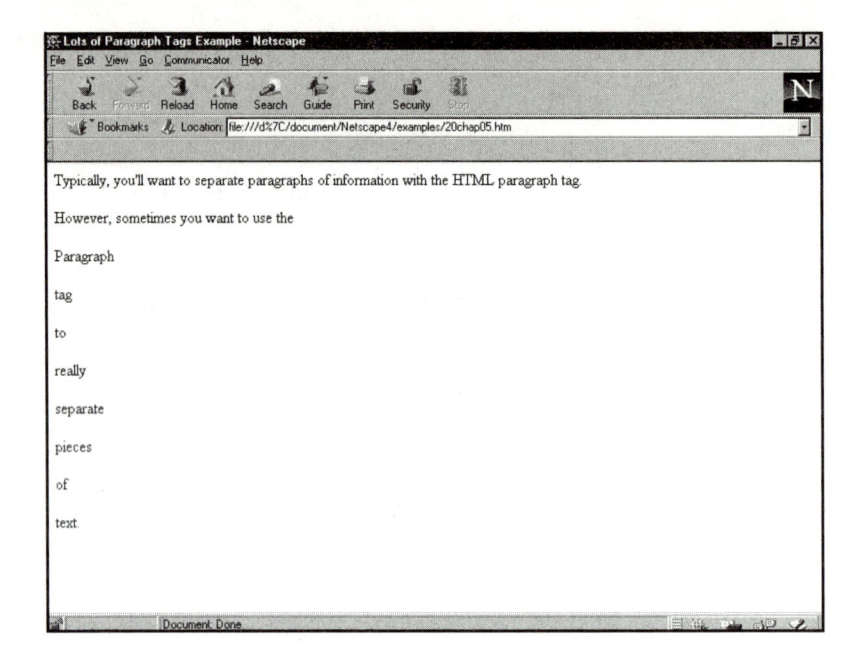

## Line Breaks with <BR>

Similar to the paragraph tag, the line break tag is also used to correctly place text on a page. The only difference is that the <BR> tag places text on the next line, without a blank line between two lines of text.

Think of the <BR> tag as hitting a carriage return on a typewriter. Whenever Netscape spots one, it automatically zings to the next line when displaying information. This tag is useful in telling Netscape where it can break up lines of text that are displayed on-screen. Figure 22.6 shows how the following snippet of HTML code appears in Netscape:

```
<H2>College Student Grocery List</H2>
Milk <BR>
Brownies <BR>
Frozen Pizza <BR>
Spaghetti <BR>
Beer <BR>
```

> **TIP** The heading tags automatically include a carriage return and blank line after text surrounded with the <Hn> and </Hn> tags (where the n stands for the header level as described previously) without worrying about using the line break or paragraph tags.

http://www.quecorp.com

**FIG. 22.6**
The <BR> tag is popular for listing several items on subsequent lines.

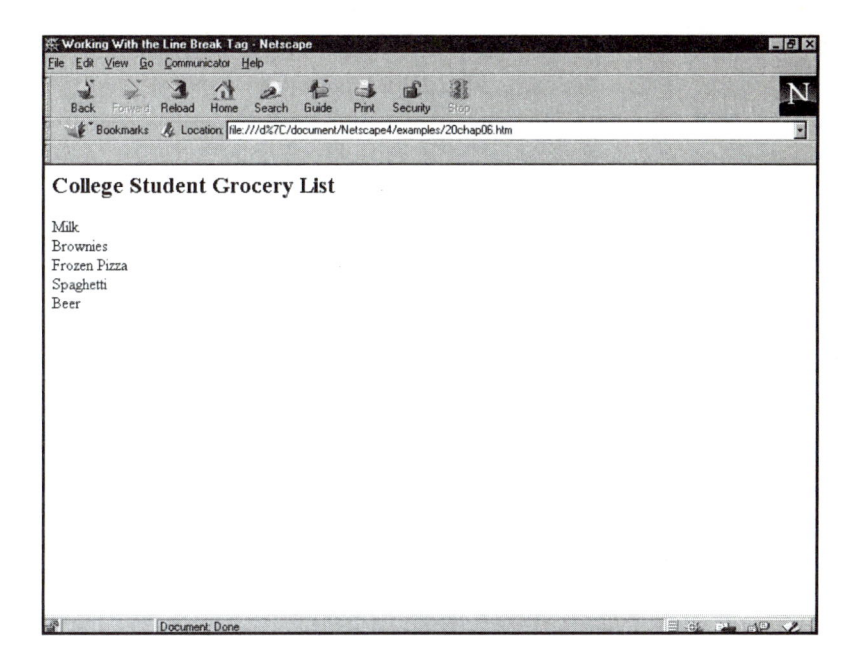

> **N O T E** HTML also includes two derivations of the <BR> tag.
>
> The word break tag, <WBR>, marks where Netscape should break up a specific word, should it need to wrap to a following line (particularly useful for long and extended medical terminology).

The opposites of <BR>, <NOBR> and </NOBR>, surround text that should never be wrapped on subsequent lines automatically by Netscape. The no break tag disables automatic word wrapping and is useful when you need to ensure a group of text always appears on the same line. The effect of using the <NOBR> and </NOBR> tags is that text never scrolls to the next line, just continues on to the right, off the screen.

## The Horizontal Rule—<HR>

A different way to separate and organize paragraphs of information with HTML is using the <HR>, or horizontal rule tag. The <HR> tag inserts a solid line that goes completely across the Netscape screen to separate different parts of an HTML document.

Not a container tag, adding a horizontal rule to a WWW page is as simple as typing <HR> into the HTML file. Netscape supports a variety of options that enable you to customize the appearance of horizontal lines on-screen, including the length, thickness, and alignment.

Often, the <HR> tag is used to separate the main body of a document from the title and footer. A footer is a standard set of text that appears at the bottom of all the pages in a particular site. Figure 22.7 shows an example of how the solid horizontal lines clearly define the different areas of the WWW document.

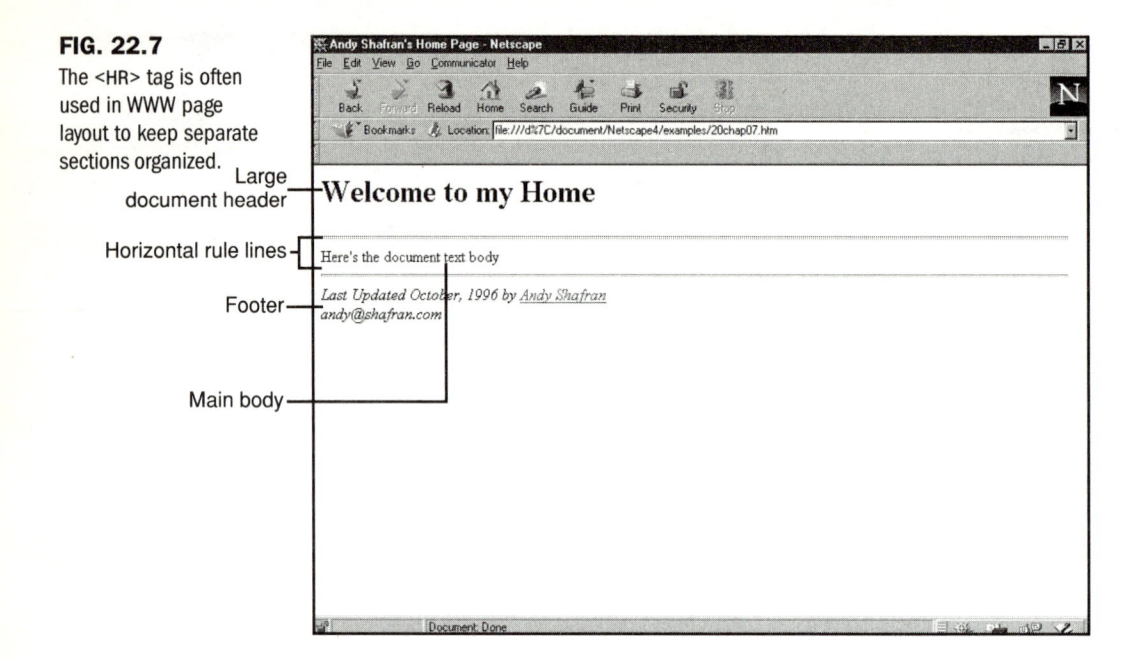

**FIG. 22.7**
The <HR> tag is often used in WWW page layout to keep separate sections organized.

- Large document header
- Horizontal rule lines
- Footer
- Main body

## Predefined Text with *<PRE>*

Usually, Netscape ignores how text is placed within the actual HTML text file without paragraph formatting tags. Tabs, extra spaces, and carriage returns are all ignored by Netscape when deciding how to format a WWW page.

To circumvent this, use the <PRE> and </PRE> container tags to specifically arrange preformatted text to appear in a distinct manner within Netscape.

All tabs, carriage returns, and extra spaces are displayed exactly as they appear within the <PRE> and </PRE> tags. By allowing users to predefine how text appears on-screen, Netscape lets WWW page creators create lists, tables, and specially formatted bits of information without hassling with learning advanced HTML tags.

Figure 22.8 shows how the following text appears, tabs and all, in Netscape:

```
<PRE>
<H2>How to pay for a wedding</H2>
<B>         Bride's Family    Groom's Family </B>
Reception    xxx
Alcohol                        xxx
Flowers      xxx               xxx
</PRE>
```

Other formatting tags such as headlines, italicizing, and bolding work within the preformatted text tags.

**FIG. 22.8**
Preformatted text lets you format text on-screen without using several different HTML tags.

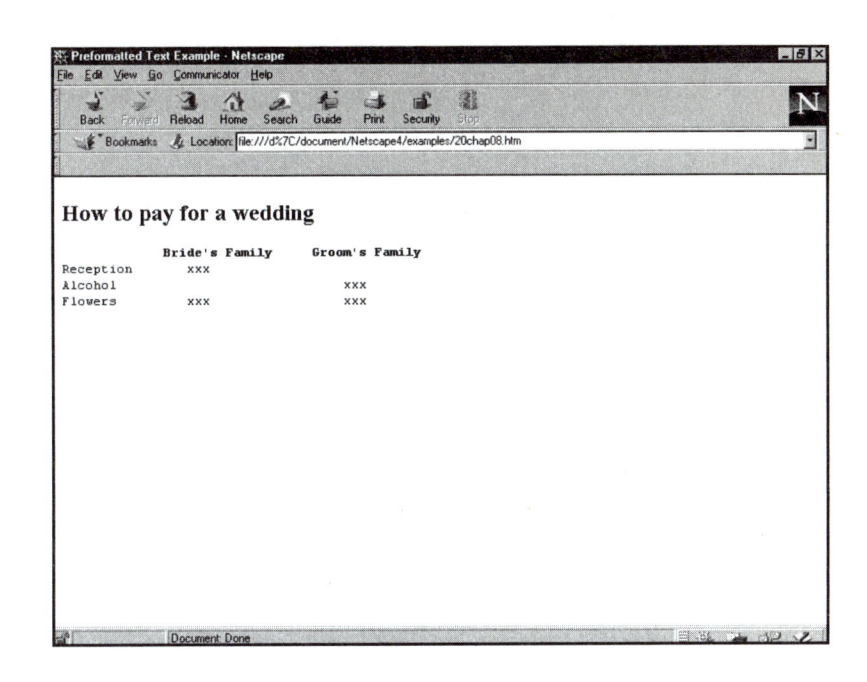

> **N O T E** When displaying preformatted text, Netscape uses a monospace font to ensure that each letter and character is the same width when displayed on the screen. This is so Netscape can guarantee that the text you type within the <PRE> tags lines up correctly.

## Basic Formatting Tags

Formatting paragraphs and chunks of text on-screen can be a harrowing task at best. In addition to organizing paragraphs of information, you worry about how to make certain pieces of text stand out by using boldface, italic, underline, strikethrough, text centering, and other formatting characteristics.

This section describes the popular HTML formatting tags and how they are used.

### Strengthening Text with <B>

How often have you typed an entire paragraph, but wanted to make a single word or phrase stand out from the rest of the text? Maybe it's a special term, or the main focus of the paragraph. Either way, you want that word to jump out and catch a reader's eye on your WWW page.

Using the <B> and </B> container tags, surrounded text is displayed in boldface, making the letters appear thicker and darker on-screen compared to regular text.

Figure 22.9 shows how Netscape uses the <B> tag to make important text stand out on a WWW page. Notice how Netscape tends to display the logical and physical tags in a virtually identical fashion.

**FIG. 22.9**
Boldfacing text adds significant character to specific words within paragraphs.

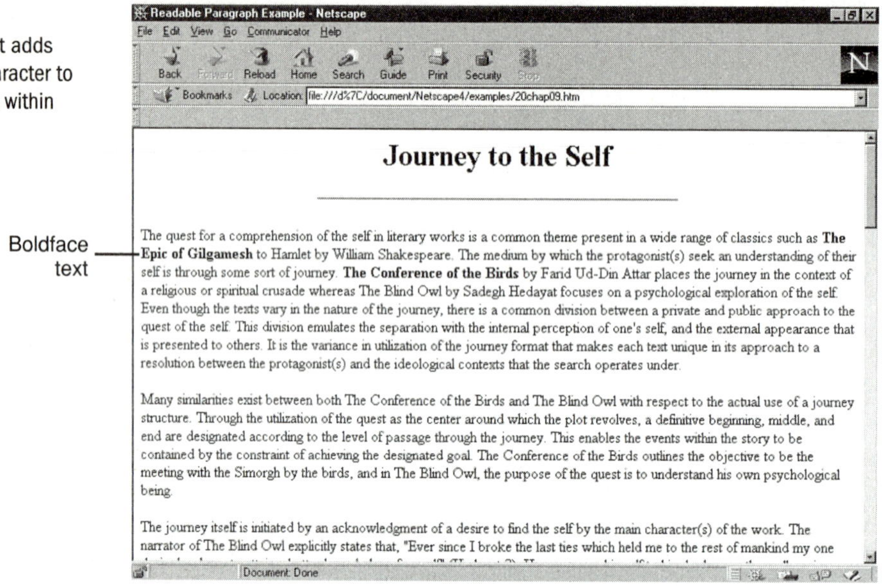

Boldface text

**Logical versus Physical Tags**  Logical versus physical formatting is a common debate among HTML programmers. Nowhere can this debate be better witnessed than in deciding how to make specific pieces of text stand out in bold or italic. The physical answer to this question is to use the <B> and <I> container tags to mark text as bold or italic. These physical tags tell Netscape that you want this text to be displayed in bold type. Bold type is commonly associated as thicker and darker text than regular text.

On the flip side, logical proponents suggest using the <STRONG> and <EM> (emphasis) tags to make text stand out. These two tags are used to describe how text should appear relative to normal text on-screen. Typically, the <STRONG> tag bolds surrounded text while the <EM> tag italicizes it, but this interpretation depends on each WWW browser's interpretation. For example, another browser might decide that <EM>phasized text should be bright red and in huge letters, while there's a much more standard approach to displaying <I>talic text—slightly slanted towards the right. With logical formatting tags, you're at the mercy of a WWW browser to interpret them however it likes.

Nowadays, most HTML programmers tend to use the physical tags (<B> and <I>) because of the underlying uncertainty of exactly how WWW browsers will display text marked with logical tags. The reality is that all common browsers such as Netscape display logical and physical tags in identical fashion. In Netscape, <EM> text looks just like that marked with the <I> tag and <STRONG> is the same as marking information with <B>.

http://www.quecorp.com

## Italicizing Text with </I>

Another way to enhance the appearance of text within Netscape is by using the <I> and </I> tags. These tags indicate that text should appear italic.

Italic can be used for highlighting a certain word or phrase, citing a published work, or for simply making a WWW page more readable. Look at Figure 22.10 for an example of italic (<I>) and emphasized text (<EM>) as listed:

```
After reading <I>The Body Farm</I> by Patricia Cornwell, I immediately had to go
out and buy her other best selling books. <EM>Postmortem</EM> and <I>All that
Remains</I> are among my favorite hair raising whodunits!
```

**FIG. 22.10**
Italic comes in handy when referring to other printed works, and for highlighting certain words in a paragraph.

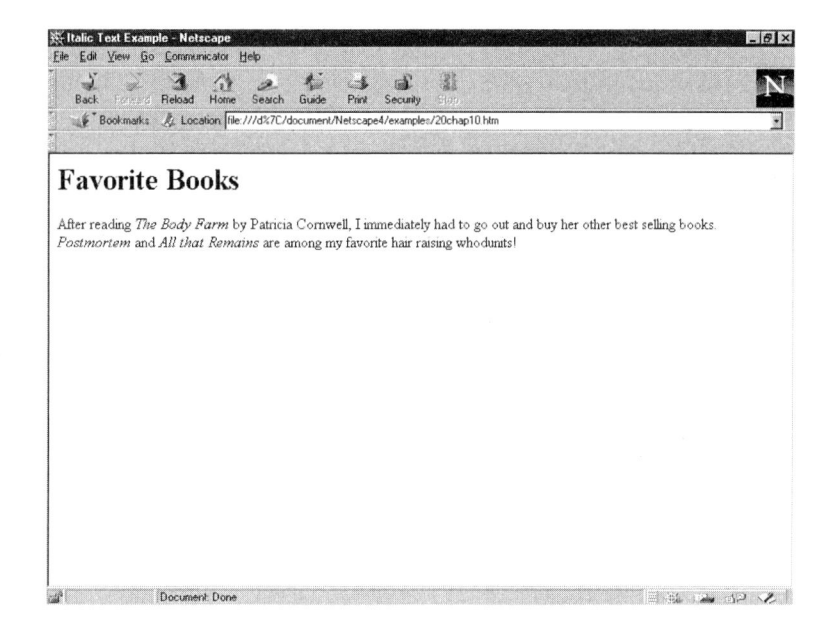

**N O T E** You can use the italic tags alone, or in conjunction with other text-formatting tags. For example, you can make some text appear boldface and italic by surrounding it with <B><I> YOUR TEXT </I></B>. When embedding tags within one another, make sure you close the most recently opened tag first. Otherwise, you're more likely to forget to close a tag and have unwanted side effects.

## Underline and Strikethrough Text

Two more methods for making text appear different on the screen are underlining text or making it appear with a line striking through it. You can underline text with the <U> and </U> tags. Underlined text is often used to depict a book or magazine title, as an example.

**448** Chapter 22 HTML Primer

In contrast, strikethrough text is often used to x something out on the screen. Using the `<S>` and `</S>` tags, often strikethrough text means that a word or phrase should be erased, but you are just documenting that it originally existed. Figure 22.11 shows an example of both these tags in action with the sample HTML code listed below:

```
The quest for a comprehension of the self in literary works is a common theme
present in a wide range of classics such as <B>The Epic of Gilgamesh</B> to
<U>Hamlet</U> by William Shakespeare.  The medium by which the protagonist(s)
seek an understanding of their self is through some sort of journey.  <STRONG>The
Conference of the Birds</STRONG> by Farid Ud-Din Attar places the journey in the
context of a religious or spiritual crusade whereas The Blind Owl by Sadegh
Hedayat focuses on a psychological exploration of the self.  Even though the
texts vary in the nature of the journey, there is a common division between a
private and public approach to the quest of the self.  This division emulates the
separation with the internal perception of one's self, and the external appear-
ance that is presented to others. <S>The variance of being used </S>It is the
variance in utilization of the journey format that makes each text unique in its
approach to a resolution between the protagonist(s) and the ideological contexts
that the search operates under.<P>
```

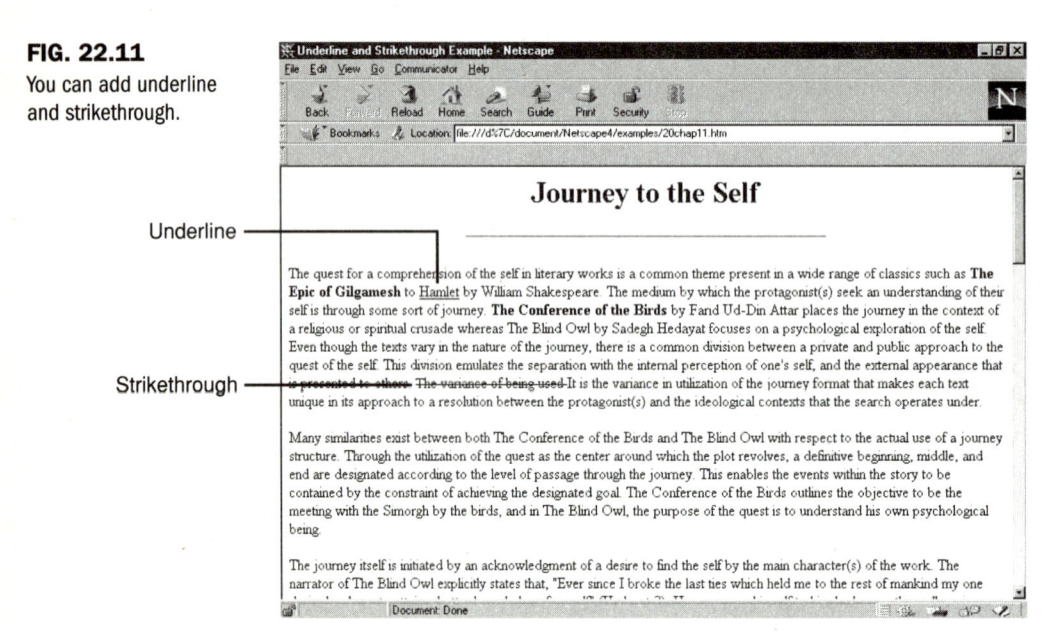

**FIG. 22.11**
You can add underline and strikethrough.

Underline

Strikethrough

## Blinking Text with `<BLINK>`

Another lesser-used text formatting feature is the `<BLINK>` HTML tag. Using this set of container tags, displayed text intermittently blinks on and off, quickly attracting the attention of someone visiting that WWW page.

http://www.quecorp.com

Adding blinking text to a WWW page is as simple as surrounding text with the `<BLINK>` and `</BLINK>` keywords as shown in the following example:

```
<BLINK> <H1> On the Road Yet Again </H1> </BLINK>
```

> **CAUTION**
> At best, blinking text should be used extremely sparingly as a text formatting feature. Prudent use of the `<BLINK>` tag is required unless you want to create an unwelcome eyesore on the WWW. Visitors will not be impressed nor will they want to return to a page that has hundreds of blinking words, making a WWW page difficult to read.

## Centering Text—*<CENTER>*

One of the most often used HTML tags allows you to center headlines and text in Netscape. Using the `<CENTER>` and `</CENTER>` container tags, marked text always appears horizontally in the middle of Netscape's screen. Regardless of how skinny or wide your Netscape window is, text is automatically centered for visitors.

This flexibility allows WWW page creators to practice more page layout and design techniques, as well as use more of the available Netscape window.

Figure 22.12 shows how a previous example changes when the main header is centered.

**FIG. 22.12**
You may want to take advantage of centering text on-screen to make headlines and information stand out more distinctly.

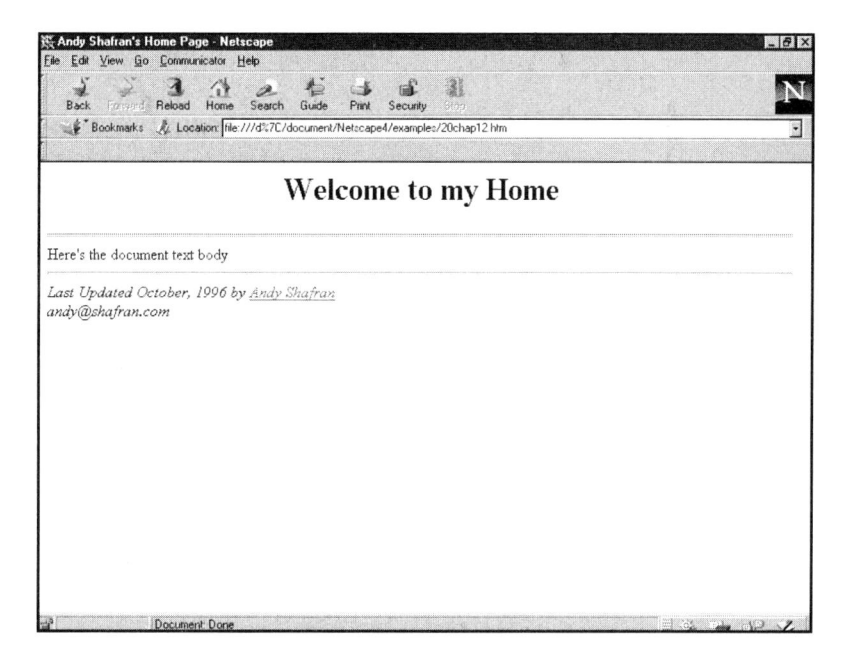

## Additional Formatting Tags

In addition to bolding and italicizing text, HTML also supports several other popular text formatting tags. Table 22.1 outlines these additional HTML tags and how they make text appear in Netscape. These tags are used less often and are not always supported by other non-Netscape browsers. Figure 22.13 shows several of these tags being used.

**Table 22.1  Additional Logical Tags**

| HTML Tag | Tag Description |
| --- | --- |
| <SUB> </SUB> | Makes selected text appear smaller and slightly below other text on a line, in a subscript manner |
| <SUP> </SUP> | Makes selected text appear smaller but raised slightly, in a superscript manner |
| <BIG> </BIG> | Makes selected text appear logically bigger than surrounding pieces of text |
| <SMALL> </SMALL> | Makes marked text smaller in comparison to other text on-screen |
| <TT> </TT> | Fixed width font that resembles a typewriter |
| <BLOCKQUOTE> </BLOCKQUOTE> | Used to make references of blocks of text from another reference. It indents text on both the left and right side of the screen, centering its left and right side text wrapping boundaries. |

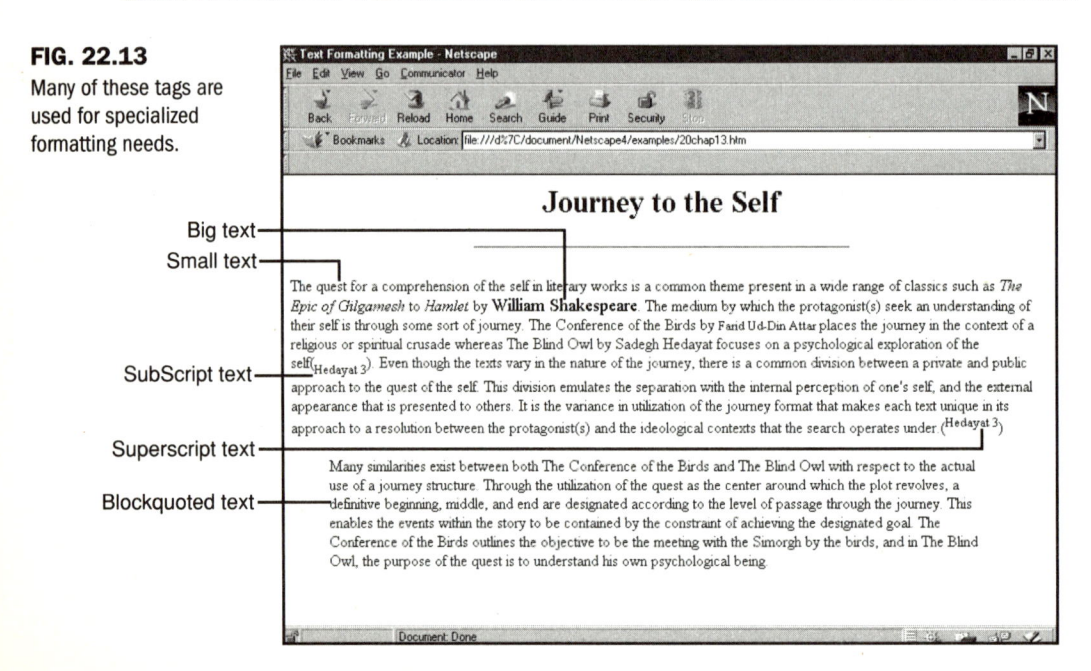

**FIG. 22.13**
Many of these tags are used for specialized formatting needs.

# Advanced Text Formatting Tags

The last section introduced you to several popular and common ways to control how text appears on-screen. Realizing that Web developers wanted more control over font size and color, Netscape added several new tags that let you control these attributes. This section will show you how to control the color and relative size of text on screen, and change the colors of "hot" or linked text.

## Controlling Font Size Dynamically

The most flexible new Netscape tag is <FONT>. Using the <FONT> tag, you can set specific text size and color for a specific piece of text. You'll appreciate the new flexibility that <FONT> gives you when creating Web pages. Text color can be controlled on-the-fly and you can mark certain phrases as important by increasing the size on-screen, and much more. This section introduces you to the three different ways you can customize text appearance using the <FONT> and </FONT> tags.

**Setting Actual Font Size**   Earlier in this chapter in the section labeled, "Titling a Document," you learned how to control the size of headings on-screen using six different sets of tags ranging from <H1> to <H6>, you could specify exactly how a heading should appear on-screen. The only drawback was you only used the <H1> tags for headlines. You didn't have that kind of flexibility with regular text on the screen.

Now, with the <FONT> tag you have the same flexibility with regular text. Text can appear in seven different sizes on screen ranging from 1 (the smallest) to 7 (the largest). Normally, without using the <FONT> tag, text appears in size 3. That means Netscape gives you four new settings to make text larger (4–7) and two to make text smaller (1–2). All you have to do is surround the text whose font size you want to change, and add the SIZE= keyword like the following example:

```
<FONT SIZE=5> Here's text displayed in Size 5 </FONT>
```

The previous <FONT> tag sets the surrounded text to be of size 5, two steps larger than text normally appears on-screen. Figure 22.14 shows you how all seven font sizes compare against one another.

> **TIP**   Just like using headings, make sure you change font sizes step-by-step. Jumping from size 1 to size 6 on subsequent lines makes a Web page look odd and out of place. Differentially sizing text should be used carefully and scrutinized closely.

**Setting Relative Font Sizes**   The <FONT> tag also has slightly more flexibility when setting the actual size of your text on-screen. Instead of setting your text size to be a specific number, you can instead give it a relative size, such as +3 or –1. Netscape takes your relative size tag and adds to (or subtracts it from) the default font size being used (size 3). Take a look at the following examples:

```
<FONT SIZE=+3> A Relative Font Size Example </FONT>
<FONT SIZE=-2> Another Font Size Example </FONT>
```

**FIG. 22.14**
This figure compares the multiple text sizes with one another.

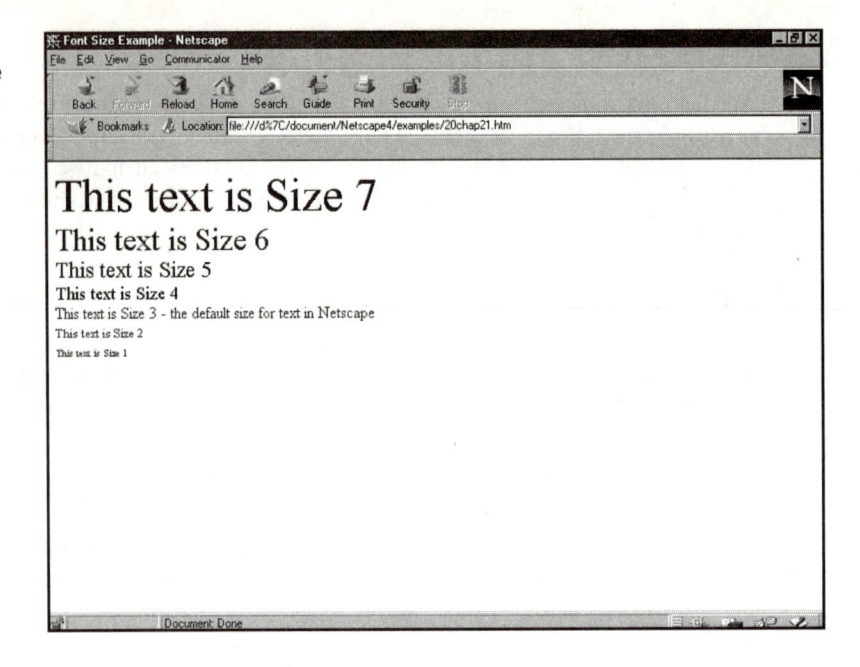

> This text is Size 7
> This text is Size 6
> This text is Size 5
> This text is Size 4
> This text is Size 3 - the default size for text in Netscape
> This text is Size 2
> This text is Size 1

Since the normal font size of text is size number 3, the first line above makes the surrounded text display on screen in size 6 (3 + 3 = 6) while the second line displays text in size 1 (3 – 2 = 1). Figure 22.15 shows how Netscape interprets the previous two lines of HTML.

**FIG. 22.15**
Relative font sizes let you tell Netscape to increase or decrease the size of fonts on a step-by-step basis.

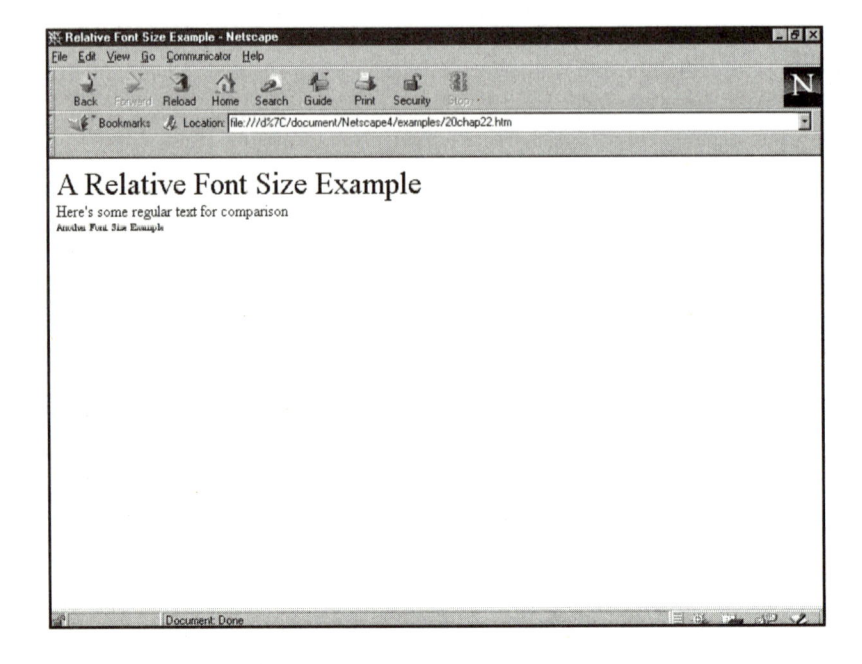

> **A Relative Font Size Example**
> Here's some regular text for comparison
> Another Font Size Example

http://www.quecorp.com

One popular way of using relative font sizing is to make the first character in a phrase appear larger than the rest of the sentence. This method helps draw attention to this particular part of your Web page because it uses a larger-than-average first character. You can make the first letter appear larger by placing the <FONT> and </FONT> tags only around the one specific letter:

```
<FONT SIZE=+6>B</FONT>aseball Season
```

**Embedding <FONT> Tags** You can also embed <FONT SIZE> tags within one another—but they don't work as you might assume. Let's say you wanted to make three words appear subsequently larger, like this:

Big Bigger Biggest

Your first reaction might be to embed three <FONT> tags inside of each other, like the following:

```
<FONT SIZE=+1> Big <FONT SIZE=+1> Bigger <FONT SIZE=+1> Biggest </FONT> </FONT>
</FONT>
```

That way the first word, *Big*, would be enlarged by one size; then *Bigger* is enlarged another size; and *Biggest* is enlarged for a cumulative total of three sizes—but that's not how Netscape works. <FONT> tags are not cumulative in nature. Each of the <FONT SIZE=1> tags sets the surrounded text to be one size larger than regular—the result being that all three words are the same size.

To make cumulative changes in font size, you'd have to create your HTML like this:

```
<FONT SIZE=+1> Big <FONT SIZE=+2> Bigger <FONT SIZE=+3> Biggest </FONT>
</FONT> </FONT>
```

> **TIP** If you change the relative size of text to be larger than +4 or smaller than -2, Netscape just assumes you want to display the information in the largest (or smallest) size available.

## Changing the Displayed Font Color

One of the most popular ways to customize text is changing the color of any piece of information being displayed. Now, you can set a word or sentence in a paragraph, item in a list, or snippet of text to automatically appear in any of millions of different colors. Netscape lets you choose from 16 different default colors, or you can create your own particular color creation by mixing and matching different shades of red, green, and blue.

Changing the color of displayed text is one of the easiest things you can do to spice up and enhance your Web page. Using the COLOR= keyword in the <FONT> tag, you can specify several different colors for your text to appear, like the following:

```
<FONT COLOR=RED>Some Red Text</FONT>
```

You have 16 different default colors at your fingertips that are named and recognized within Netscape. You can use them as often as you'd like on your Web page—just be careful not to make your text unreadable.

The 16 colors you can identify directly by name are as follows:

| Black  | Maroon  | Green | Olive  |
|--------|---------|-------|--------|
| Navy   | Purple  | Teal  | Gray   |
| Silver | Red     | Lime  | Yellow |
| Blue   | Fuchsia | Aqua  | White  |

Besides using the 16 named colors, Netscape allows you to specify colors by mixing different shades of red, green, and blue. This gives you literally millions of different colors to choose from. See the section "Color by Hexadecimal" later in this chapter for more information.

> **TIP** Use the <FONT> tag to change text color for a small piece of your Web page. If you want to modify the text color for the entire page, see the following section.

## Other Ways to Change Color

Changing text color on-screen is an advanced feature that you'll want to take advantage of. Primarily, the <FONT> and </FONT> tags are used to change the color of a small piece of text on your Web page. You can also change the default text color for the entire page by adding new keywords to your <BODY> tag. Each of these keywords uses the exact same color formula as described above—where you name the color you want to use from the 16 listed colors.

You'll want to customize these options when you start using images and colors on your Web page. By default, the Netscape text color is black, and the background is gray or white. But if you set your background color to become black using the <BODY BGCOLOR=> tag, then you won't be able to read any text on the screen. In this case, you need to change the color of text to something light—like white. Figure 22.16 shows one of my sample Web pages that has a black background and white text.

**Text Color**   To change the default color of text of your screen, add the TEXT= keyword to your <BODY> tag, like the following:

<BODY TEXT=Lime>

The above tag sets all text on a Web page to lime green.

> **NOTE** Colors specified using the <FONT> tag as described above override your default color setting from the <BODY> tag.

**Link Color**   You can also change the color of "hot" text that links your Web page to another spot on the World Wide Web. Use the LINK= keyword just as you used the TEXT= tag previously. The following is an example:

<BODY TEXT=LIME LINK=AQUA>

All linked text on my page now appears in aqua to match the lime green specified for regular text.

Advanced Text Formatting Tags | 455

**FIG. 22.16**
This Web page uses a black background and white text for contrast.

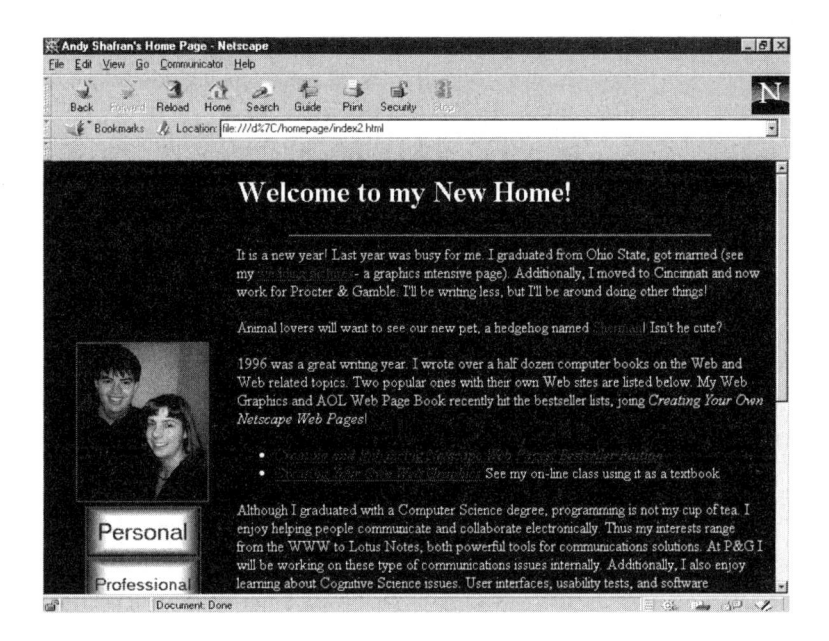

**Visited Link Color**   You may have noticed that sometimes linked text appears in a slightly different color, indicating that you've already traveled that particular thread of the WWW.

You can change the color of Visited Link text on your Web page with the VLINK= keyword, like the following:

`<BODY TEXT=LIME LINK=AQUA VLINK=SILVER>`

The color of links on this Web page becomes silver once you've visited them.

**Active Link Color**   The final color customization you can make is what color text appears as it is being clicked. This text is signified as Active Link text and uses the ALINK= keyword. When someone visits your Web page, the color of linked text is set with LINK=. But when it is clicked, for a brief moment it changes to the color you specify with ALINK=:

`<BODY TEXT=LIME LINK=AQUA VLINK=SILVER ALINK=YELLOW>`

Now, Active Linked text is set to bright yellow.

## Color by Hexadecimal

Many times, you might want to use other colors not specified in the default named 16 provided. Just like a painter, you want to mix and match different hues and shades to come up with your own color concoction.

Another way to set your COLOR= keyword inside of the <FONT> tag is by using the six-character hexadecimal equivalent. Specific colors are indicated by a six-character hexadecimal combination which tells Netscape how it should mix red, blue, and green together to get your specified color. Hexadecimal numbers range from 0–9 and A–F.

All colors are a mix of red, green, and blue. Each of these three primary colors controls two of the six hexadecimal characters. By mixing and matching different shades of these colors, you have literally thousands of different possibilities to choose from. For example, let's say you wanted to use a pure shade of red on your Web page. For this, you'd use <FONT> in the following manner:

`<FONT COLOR=FF0000>Some Red Text</FONT>`

Notice the six-character color tag. Each primary color—red, green, and blue—is assigned to two characters correspondingly. So the above tag, interpreted, says to mix 100 percent full vibrant red with zero percent of green, and zero percent of blue. Similarly, true green and blue are defined below:

`<FONT COLOR=00FF00>Some Green Text</FONT>`

`<FONT COLOR=0000FF>Some Blue Text</FONT>`

For a more complete listing of hexadecimal colors and examples, visit **http://www.infi.net/wwwimages/colorindex.html**.

Table 22.2 is a short table of several popular colors in hexadecimal format.

**Table 22.2—Hexadecimal Color Formats**

| Color | Six-Digit Code |
|---|---|
| Black | 000000 |
| White | FFFFFF |
| Yellow | FFFF00 |
| Gray | C0C0C0 |
| Maroon | 8E236B |
| Hunter Green | 215E21 |
| Pink | BC8F8F |
| Navy Blue | 23238E |
| Violet | 4F2F4F |

# Creating Lists

Every day you make a list to organize various pieces of information in a specific order. Whether it's creating a grocery list to go shopping or a to-do task list, keeping track of a lot of information is vital. Within HTML, lists are one of the most widespread and powerful tools used to display text with Netscape. The following is a list of several popular reasons to include a list in your HTML document:

Advanced Text Formatting Tags | 457

- You can organize a lot of different types and pieces of information in one structured, easy-to-read format.
- You can describe a complicated step-by-step process in edible chunks of information.
- Create highlights of information in a table-of-contents fashion that points to other more general pieces of information.

Using the several different types of built-in lists, you can handle virtually any situation. You'll learn the differences among ordered, unordered, and definition lists, as well as learn the important syntax for displaying a list within Netscape.

Figure 22.17 shows an example of what a list looks like within Netscape.

**FIG. 22.17**
This simple unordered list could appear on any WWW page listing personal interests.

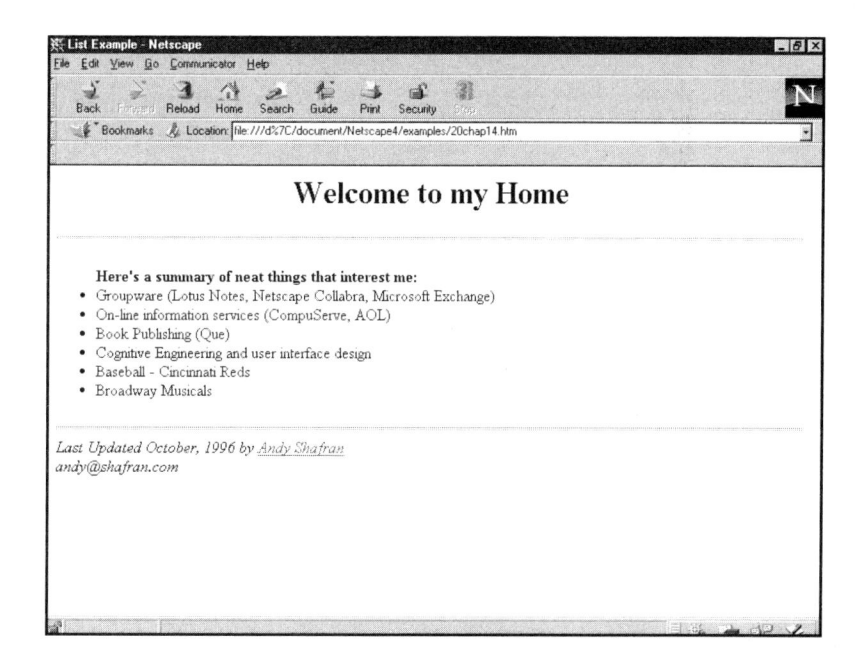

In HTML, adding a list is not as easy as using a simple container tag. Several related HTML tags work together to allow you to select which type of list you want to display, how to delineate among different items within a list, and how to include a title for the list. For example, the HTML source code for the previous list is shown:

```
<UL>
<LH><B>Here's a summary of neat things that interest me:</B></LH>
<LI>Groupware (Lotus Notes, Netscape Collabra, Microsoft Exchange)
<LI>On-line information services (CompuServe, AOL)
<LI>Book Publishing (Que)
<LI>Cognitive Engineering and user interface design
<LI>Baseball - Cincinnati Reds
<LI>Broadway Musicals
</UL>
```

The <UL> and </UL> tags select the list type (unordered). The <LH> and </LH> tags markup the list header, or title, and the <LI>, or list item tag, separates each list item from one another. Together, these three parts make up a complete list. By adding each tag in a step-by-step process, your list is finished.

Next, you learn how to include three different types of lists within HTML documents.

## Adding an Unordered List

On the WWW, the unordered list is most commonly used. This list displays each list item with a bullet preceding each item of information.

To add an unordered list, follow these steps:

1. First add the <UL> and </UL> tags to your HTML document.
2. Within the unordered list tags, type in the text you want to appear as the list's header, and surround it with the <LH> and </LH> tags:

    ```
    <UL>
    <LH>Saturday Night Live Guest Hosts</LH>
    </UL>
    ```

3. Add the list item tag, <LI>, and type in that piece of information.

    ```
    <LI> Chevy Chase
    ```

4. Repeat step 3 until you have every list item typed in and accounted for. Figure 22.18 shows the final unordered list created with the following text:

    ```
    <UL>
    <LH>Saturday Night Live Guest Hosts</LH>
    <LI> Chevy Chase
    <LI> Steve Martin
    <LI> Jim Belushi
    <LI> Dan Akroyd
    </UL>
    ```

## Adding a Numbered List

Similar to an unordered list, the numbered list presents separate items displayed in an organized order. The main difference between the two list types is that the numbered list automatically numbers each list item according to its order of appearance within the list.

Creating a numbered list is virtually identical to creating an unordered one. Follow these steps to build a numbered list:

1. First add the <OL> and </OL> tags to your HTML document.
2. Within the numbered list tags, type in the text you want to appear as the list's header, and surround it with the <LH> and </LH> tags:

    ```
    <OL>
    <LH>Favorite baseball teams</LH>
    </OL>
    ```

http://www.quecorp.com

3. Add the first list item tag <LI> and type in that piece of information. Remember that this first item will be numbered with a 1:

   ```
   <LI>Cincinnati Reds
   ```

4. Repeat step 3 until you have every list item typed in and accounted for. Figure 22.19 shows the final numbered list created in the following example:

   ```
   <OL>
   <LH><B>Favorite baseball teams</B></LH>
   <LI>Cincinnati Reds
   <LI>Seattle Mariners
   <LI>Chicago Cubs
   </OL>
   ```

**FIG. 22.18**
This simple unordered list depicts data that doesn't require any specific ordering.

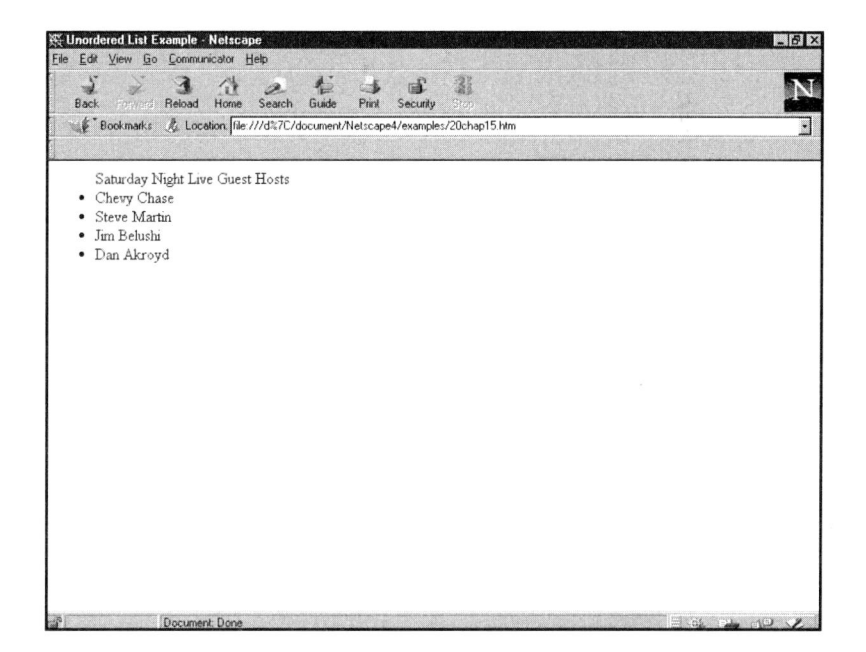

> **TIP** If you don't want to display the numbered list in straight numeric format, you can also number items with a letter (upper- and lowercase) or a Roman numeral. To change this Netscape-only feature, add the TYPE= keyword to the <OL> tag. To use Roman numerals, your <OL> tag becomes the following:
>
> `<OL TYPE=I, II, III...>`
>
> To list elements with a letter instead of a number, try the following:
> `<OL TYPE=A, B, C...>`

## Adding a Definition List

Unlike the other common types of lists, definition lists have two parts to each item. Much as dictionary entries have two elements, the word and the definition, the definition list has two separate terms.

**FIG. 22.19**
This simple numbered list is a good example of how numbered lists prioritize list items.

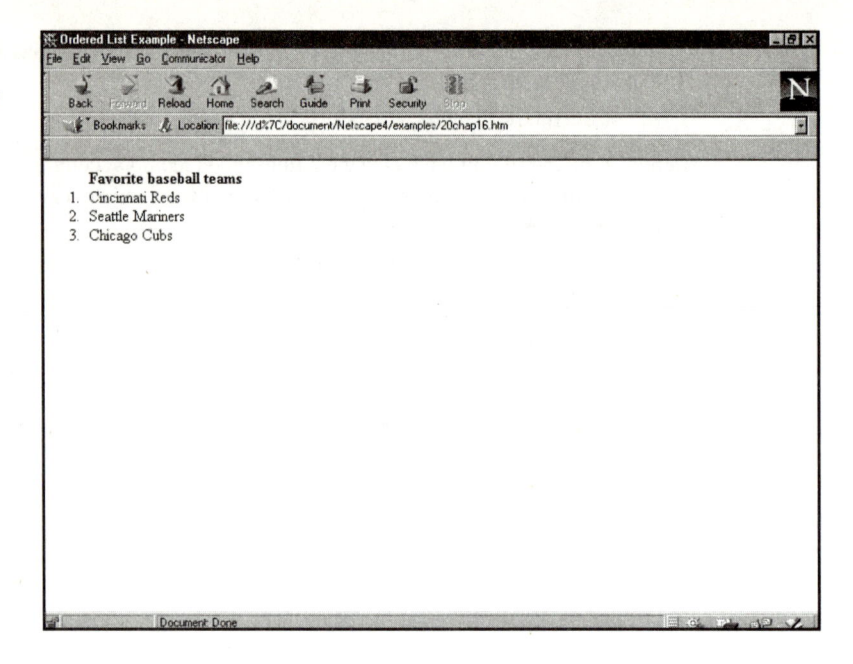

To add a definition list to your HTML document, follow these steps:

1. First add the `<DL>` and `</DL>` tags to your HTML document.

2. Within the numbered list tags, type in the text you want to appear as the list's header, and surround it with the `<LH>` and `</LH>` tags:

   ```
   <DL>
   <LH><B>Important Web terms</B></LH>
   </DL>
   ```

3. Unlike the other lists, which had a single component for each list item, the definition list has two. First type `<DT>` (short for definition term) and type in the term you want to define.

   ```
   <DT> HTML
   ```

4. Next type `<DD>` (definition definition) and type in the term's definition.

   ```
   <DD> Hyper Text Markup Language
   ```

5. Repeat the previous steps until you have every term and definition listed. Figure 22.20 shows the final definition list created in the following example:

   ```
   <DL>
   <LH><B>Important Web terms</B></LH>
   <DT> HTML
   <DD> Hyper Text Markup Language
   <DT> WWW
   <DD> World Wide Web
   <DT> VRML
   <DD> Virtual Reality Markup Language
   </DL>
   ```

**FIG. 22.20**
This definition list is only a sample of the flexibility lists provide.

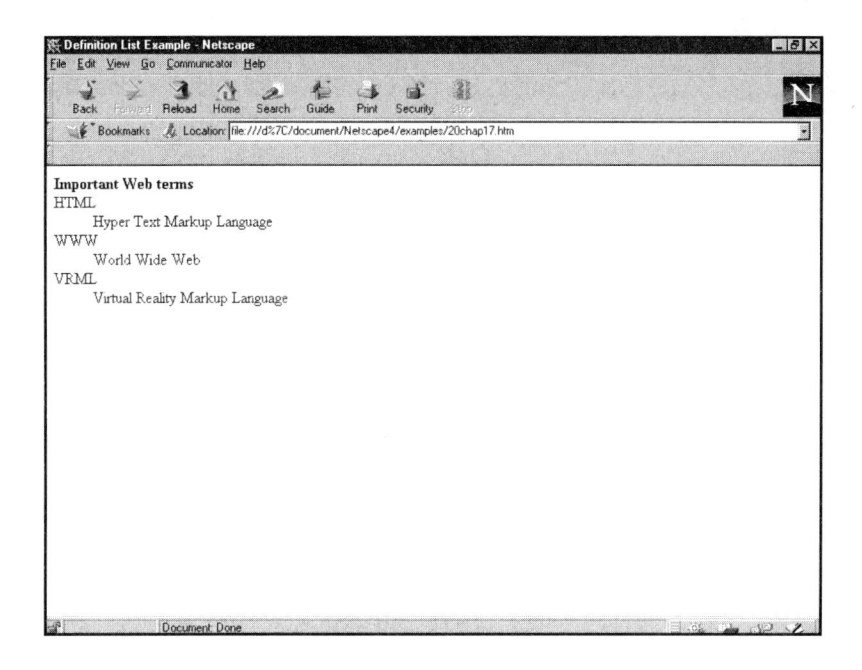

[Screenshot: Definition List Example - Netscape, showing:
**Important Web terms**
HTML
   Hyper Text Markup Language
WWW
   World Wide Web
VRML
   Virtual Reality Markup Language]

Notice how the definition term appears on one line, with the subsequent definition indented and on the following line.

## Nesting Lists Within One Another

Like most other HTML elements, you can have lists within lists, allowing you to subcategorize a single list into many different pieces. Mixing and matching lists is permitted, although be careful when embedding a list within the definition list because of the separate types of list elements.

To embed a list within another list, first create the initial list:

```
<OL>
<LH><B>Favorite baseball teams</B></LH>
<LI>Cincinnati Reds
<LI>Seattle Mariners
<LI>Chicago Cubs
</OL>
```

Then, embed the <UL> </UL> (or whichever type of list you want to use) within the original list tags. For example, an expansion of the following initial list appears in Figure 22.21:

```
<OL>
<LH><B>Favorite baseball teams</B></LH>
<LI>Cincinnati Reds
<UL>
<LH>Favorite Players </LH>
<LI>Smiley
```

```
<LI>Larkin
<LI>Santiago
</UL>
<LI>Seattle Mariners
<UL>
<LH>Favorite Players </LH>
<LI>Johnson
<LI>The Kid
<LI>Buhner
</UL>
<LI>Chicago Cubs
<UL>
<LH>Favorite Players </LH>
<LI>Sosa
<LI>Grace
</UL>
</OL>
```

> **TIP** Notice how I used the <B> tags in the preceding list header. This draws eyes to the description of the list before people start perusing it so they know what they are reading. Using formatting tags such as <B> or <I> are common within list headers and list items.

**FIG. 22.21**
Nested lists follow the same rules as single-level lists.

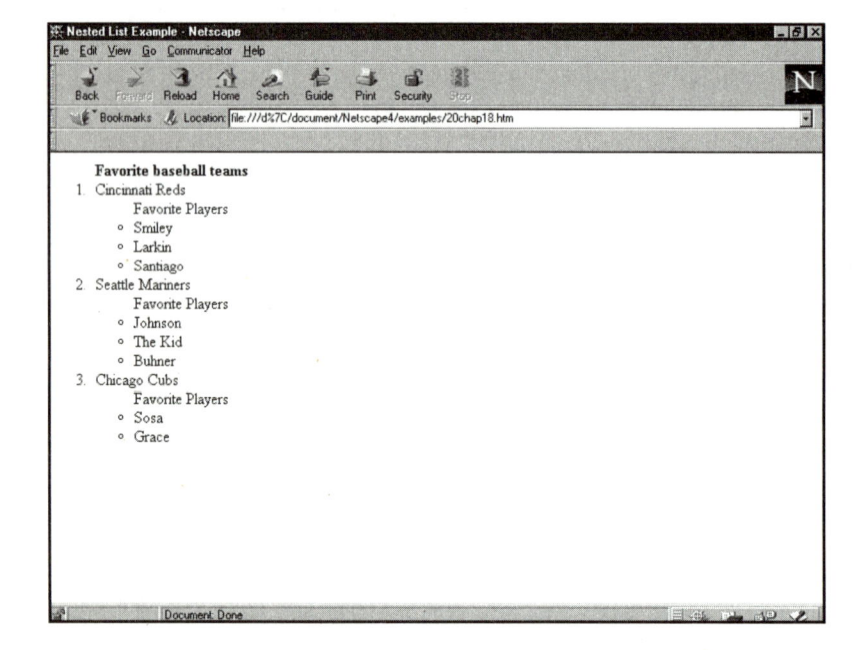

## Including Comments

In the world of programming, commenting sections of a program are virtually a required task. It is difficult to look back at work done several months ago and exactly remember the reasons you decided to display information in a certain format, or why you ignored specific conventions. Commenting within HTML is just as important.

Comments are typed bits of information that can only be seen when a visitor chooses to specifically view the page's source code. Standard comments should include the last time a file was updated, who made the modifications, and a description of recent changes. While HTML is usually straightforward, some tags can be deceptive. Commenting on how the tag works and why you chose to use that tag is useful for future maintenance of that HTML document.

To add a comment to your document, surround the commented code with <!- and ->, as in the following:

```
<!- My baseball Numbered list ->
<OL>
Favorite baseball teams</LH>
<LI>Cincinnati Reds
<LI>Seattle Mariners
<LI>Chicago Cubs
</OL>
```

> **CAUTION**
> Make sure you don't include private or confidential information within source code comments. Anyone who visits the page can see the original HTML text, if they want.

## Building a Sample HTML Page

Now that you're finished with the HTML crash course, let's take a moment and review many of the different tags you've learned. Let's build a sample HTML document for a fictional local restaurant, trying to incorporate the many different HTML lessons learned. These are the steps to follow:

1. The first step is adding the important tags that must be in all HTML documents:
    ```
    <HTML>
    <HEAD>
    </HEAD>
    <BODY>
    </BODY>
    </HTML>
    ```

2. Within the <HEAD> and </HEAD> tags, add a title to HTML document:
    ```
    <TITLE> OrangeBee's American Cuisine </TITLE>
    ```

3. Along the same lines as the title, add a large and bold header to the document:

   ```
   <BODY>
   <H1> OrangeBee's Fabulous American Cuisine on the Web </H1>
   </BODY>
   ```

4. Type in some basic information about the restaurant. Take care to separate the paragraphs of text using the proper tags. So far your sample HTML document looks like this:

   ```
   <HTML>
   <HEAD> <TITLE> OrangeBee's American Cuisine </TITLE> </HEAD>
   <BODY>
   <CENTER><H1> OrangeBee's Fabulous American Cuisine on the Web </H1>
   </CENTER>
   <HR>
   Since 1991, OrangeBee's has been the fastest growing chain of American
   cuisine and affordable eating. We offer a wide variety of menu items,
   including several that contain under 5 grams of fat. <P>
   <B>Stop by our nearest restaurants at: </B><BR>
   Morse Road <BR>
   Great Southern Shopping Center <BR>
   Bexley <BR>
   <HR>
   <!- Created by OrangeBee's 1995 ->
   </BODY>
   </HTML>
   ```

5. Now the final step to this fictitious restaurant is to add a few menu items using a definition list. Try this list as an example:

   ```
   <DL>
   <B>OrangeBee's famous menu</B></LH>
   <DT> Shrimp Cocktail
   <DD> <I>This succulent platter of shrimp served with a tangy sauce. </I>
   <DT> Fat-free Caesar
   <DD> <I>Our homemade fat-free Caesar dressing makes this salad ideal. </I>
   <DT>Steak and Eggs
   <DD> <I>Our cholesterol killer. This combo is everything the '90s doctors say not to eat.</I>
   </DL>
   ```

Figure 22.22 shows the final result of this sample WWW page. Read on to the next chapter to learn how to spice it up with graphics and links.

> **TIP** When creating a lot of HTML files, most developers tend to create and use a standard template. This template has all the basic and necessary tags (such as <HTML> and <BODY>) already typed in, and follows a standard format (such as an unordered list). After a template is created, all you have to do is fill in the blanks by typing the needed text, and the page is finished. Using a template saves you from always worrying about miscellaneous tags that are commonly forgotten. Many popular Editors such as HotDog (**www.sausage.com**) and Microsoft FrontPage (**www.microsoft.com**) include the ability to work with and create your own custom HTML templates.

**FIG. 22.22**
OrangeBee's Web page has a simple and nice-looking Web page that shows several different types of lists put together.

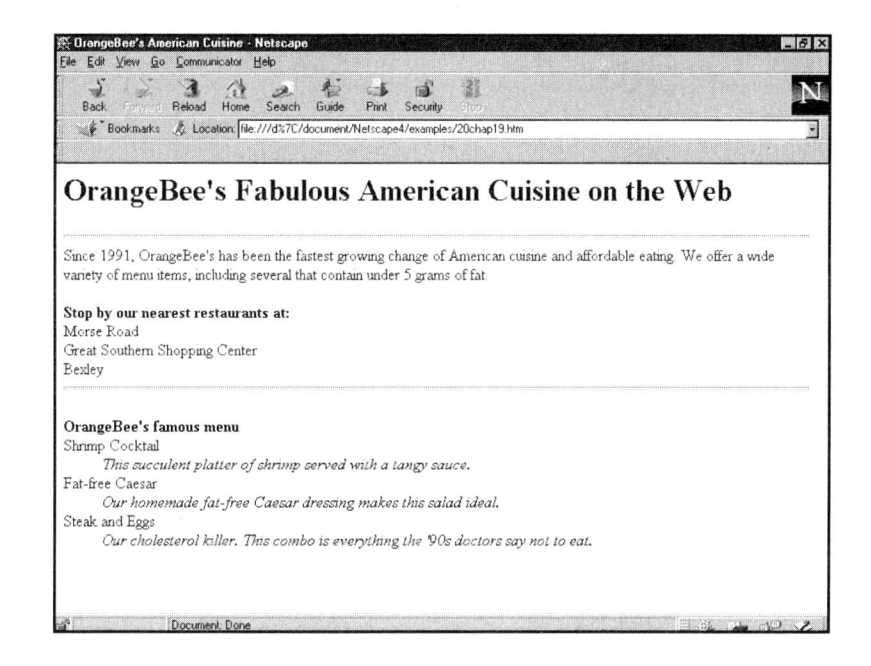

# OrangeBee's Fabulous American Cuisine on the Web

Since 1991, OrangeBee's has been the fastest growing change of American cuisine and affordable eating. We offer a wide variety of menu items, including several that contain under 5 grams of fat.

**Stop by our nearest restaurants at:**
Morse Road
Great Southern Shopping Center
Bexley

---

**OrangeBee's famous menu**
Shrimp Cocktail
  *This succulent platter of shrimp served with a tangy sauce.*
Fat-free Caesar
  *Our homemade fat-free Caesar dressing makes this salad ideal.*
Steak and Eggs
  *Our cholesterol killer. This combo is everything the '90s doctors say not to eat.*

CHAPTER 23

# Adding Links and Graphics

*by Paul Wallace*

You're now probably familiar with how to use hyperlinks to jump from site to site on the WWW. In this chapter, you learn how to create and include hyperlinks in your own HTML documents. As you'll see, links come in all different shapes, sizes, and formats. We show you how to make hyperlinks to documents within your own World Wide Web site, as well as to resources available elsewhere on the Internet.

Graphics help spice up WWW pages, making them more interesting and informative to visit. HTML allows you to include a wide variety of graphic files in your WWW pages. This chapter introduces you to the basic file formats used for Web images. We also cover the specific tags used to customize image size and placement in Netscape Communicator.

### How to create hypertext links on your Web pages

Hypertext links allow visitors to jump from page to page within your site or to other resources on the Web.

### Relative and absolute links

We will clarify the meaning of the terms *relative* and *absolute* links, and explain when it is best to use each of these when linking to other WWW pages.

### Linking to Internet resources

In addition to linking to other HTML pages, you will learn how to create links to Internet resources like Gopher, FTP, UseNet newsgroups, and e-mail.

### How to use the <IMG> tag

This chapter introduces you to the <IMG> tag and its many alignment attributes, thereby allowing you to add a variety of images to your pages with HTML.

### Using images as links

We tie the ideas of links and images together and show you how to use graphics as hyperlink "buttons" within your Web site.

## Explaining HTML Links

The underlying premise behind the World Wide Web is the capability to link information from all over the globe together in a single accessible format. People browsing the WWW in Moscow, for example, can have immediate access to information located on a server in Tennessee. To accomplish this formidable task, every file and document on the Internet is given its own unique *URL* (Uniform Resource Locator), or World Wide Web address. Similar to a mailing address, the URL tells an Internet browser where to go when looking for specific information.

After you know a document's URL, you can easily create a *hypertext link* directly to that spot on the Internet. By linking documents and files together around the world, you create a virtual "Web" of links back and forth—thus, inspiring the name World Wide Web.

## Using Links

In Netscape, hypertext links typically appear as underlined blue text (see Figure 23.1). Using your mouse, you can click the underlined text and the linked document is brought to your computer. HTML authors can link to other HTML files, specific spots within an HTML file, WWW sites elsewhere on the Web, or even additional Internet resources such as UseNet newsgroups, Gopher, and e-mail addresses.

**FIG. 23.1**
In general, blue underlined text on a World Wide Web page indicates a hypertext link.

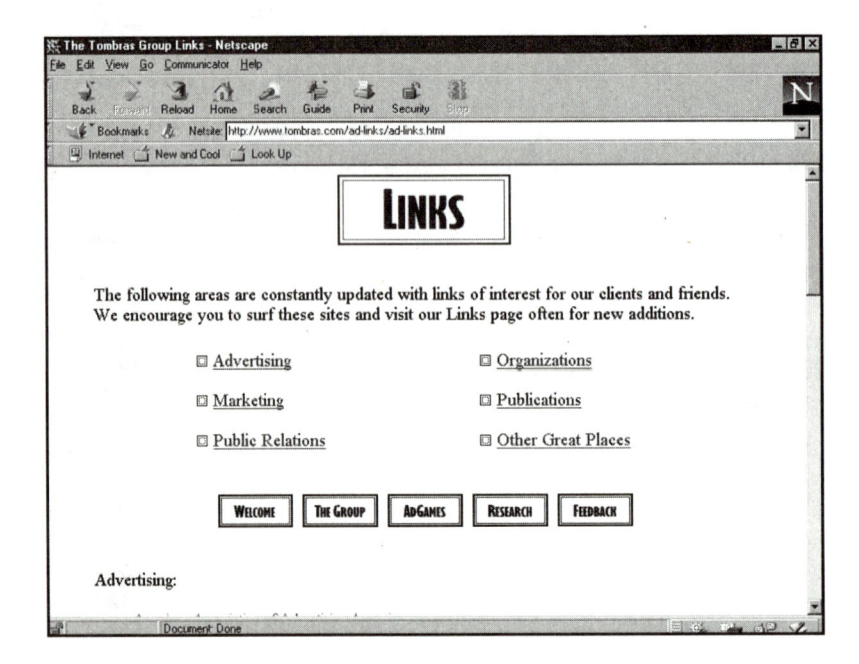

After you visit a page, the text that links you to that page changes color, indicating that you've already traversed that specific strand of the WWW. This serves as a useful reminder of where you've been and where you have yet to visit.

http://www.quecorp.com

**NOTE** Not all hypertext links appear underlined or in blue. Web designers can change the color of links on their pages. Typically though, hypertext links are formatted in a different color than passages of text—indicating that they are "hot" hypertext links.

There are no technical limitations to the number of links available from a single HTML document. Web designers should be careful not to overwhelm their visitors with too many hypertext links.

The most important links to include in your pages give visitors access to similar or supporting information elsewhere within your site or in someone else's site on the Web. Remember that the more external (outside your Web site) links you provide, the more opportunity you give visitors to leave your site altogether. It is a time-consuming process to regularly check all your links to see if they still work, and then re-write your HTML code each time one of your links moves or leaves the Web entirely. Therefore, only include those links that are most pertinent to your subject.

## Dissecting an URL

A Uniform Resource Locator (just think of it as a Web address) is made of several distinct elements. Much like a mailing address is made up of a street address, city, state, and ZIP code, an URL has its own unique collection of identifiers. In general, all URLs contain the following components:

**Protocol://Host_Name/path/and/filename**

- Protocol—The Internet Protocol Netscape uses when connecting to the specified server. Most often, you use http to link to other World Wide Web HTML documents, but e-mail, UseNet, FTP, and Gopher all have their own special identifiers (we get to those later in this section). HTTP stands for Hypertext Transport Protocol and tells Netscape how to handle this type of linked information.

- Host Name—The Internet domain name (IP name or number) of the server to which you are connecting. Domain names are unique to each server on the Internet. They are registered through InterNic—a non-profit organization.

- /path/and/filename—The complete file name of the HTML document you want to access, and the directory path required to reach it. If no file name is specified, Netscape automatically looks for a *default* HTML file in the directory specified. If this default file (usually titled "index.html" or "default.html") is not found, Navigator will return a list of files that are contained in that directory.

Combining all the pieces, here's the URL for Que, the publisher for this book:

http://www.quecorp.com

## Creating Your First Link

After you know the URL of a document, creating the link in HTML is a relatively simple process. As with everything else in HTML, adding links requires a special tag to tell the browser what to do. HTML uses the anchor tag, <A>, to create a link. You may recall from the previous chapter that most HTML tags require a beginning and an ending tag. The anchor (<A>) tag conforms to this rule, and encloses the hot hyperlink text between the <A> and </A>.

Follow these steps to add a hypertext link to an HTML document:

1. First identify the unique URL that you want to link to, for instance:

    **http://www.quecorp.com**

2. Add the HTML anchor tags (<A> </A>) to the URL in the following fashion:

    ```
    <A HREF="http://www.quecorp.com"> </A>
    ```

    The HREF attribute indicates that you are creating a link to the Hypertext Reference URL that you provide; in this case, **http://www.quecorp.com**. You should include the quotation marks before and after the URL—type it in just as it is written in the preceding line of code.

3. Indicate the text that you want to identify as hot (that is, appearing underlined and in blue) between the <A> and </A> tags. For instance, to make the line "Link to Que Publishing" the hot text for this example, type the following:

    ```
    <A HREF="http://www.quecorp.com">Link to Que Publishing</A>
    ```

## Using Absolute and Relative Links

Linking your HTML pages to other documents on the World Wide Web is as simple as knowing the complete URL to the desired location. This type of link is known as an *absolute link*, because it includes the absolute address on the Internet to another document. The URL to the Que Web site (used in the preceding section) is an example of an absolute link. It contains all the information that will link you to the Que Publishing World Wide Web site (**http://www.quecorp.com**).

If you only want to link to HTML documents that are located within your own site, you can take advantage of several shortcuts.

When linking to files on the same server, a *relative link* allows you to type an URL that is relative to the original document's location. For example, to link to an HTML file named moreinfo.html that is located in the exact same directory as the file you are linking from, you can just type the file name as the following URL:

```
<A HREF="moreinfo.html">Link to More Information</A>
```

Because keeping every HTML file in the same directory can be confusing, relative linking can indicate files within subdirectories as well. To do this, however, you first need to know a little bit about navigating through directories.

UNIX machines (most of the servers on the World Wide Web) use the forward slash (/) to indicate a directory. To move deeper into *nested* directories you must type the / character between the names of the subdirectories. You also type the / between names of directories and the names of files contained within them.

So, to link to a file named evenmore.html in a subdirectory named INFORMATION, you type the following:

```
<A HREF="INFORMATION/evenmore.html">Link to Even More Information</A>
```

Similarly, you can link to files in *parent* directories (one level higher than the current subdirectory in the server's hard drive structure) by using the sequence ../, which translates to "move up a directory." For instance:

```
<A HREF="../themost.html">The Most Information</A>
```

This example links to a file named themost.html, which is located one directory up, or in the parent directory, of the server's hard drive.

In general, you should always use relative links when creating links within your Web site. Relative links have the following good selling points:

- Relative links allow you to test your complete site from your personal computer before you upload it to an Internet Web server.
- With relative links, you can easily move HTML documents from one server to another without having to change all the URLs in your links.
- Using relative links makes it easier when typing in your links, because you don't have to type the complete URL for every linked document.

> **CAUTION**
> Most HTML documents reside on servers that are case sensitive. Always type in an URL link exactly as given to you, or exactly as you see it printed in Netscape's Location window.
>
> For instance, the URLs **http://www.mcp.com/que/bookshelf/** and **http://www.mcp.com/que/Bookshelf/** are not the same. The first will take you to a listing of online books, the second (with an uppercase "B") will tell you that the file could not be found.

## Other Types of HTML Links

Besides linking to other hypertext pages, HTML also handles several other popular Internet resources that exchange and share information—UseNet newsgroups, e-mail, FTP, and Gopher. Each of these different Internet services can be linked directly from your Web page with the HTML anchor (<A>) tag simply by specifying their unique URL components.

## Using FTP Links

FTP, which stands for File Transfer Protocol, enables users to log on to an Internet domain, search through the file listings, and download a file to their personal computer. FTP is commonly used to access and download shareware programs, program updates, and ASCII text files. With the anchor(<A>) tag in HTML you can directly link to files on an FTP site from your WWW page. This lets visitors download these files simply by clicking the underlined hypertext link.

An FTP URL looks similar to a standard URL except that it uses the Internet service protocol ftp://. To create a link to a file named f1040.pdf on the ftp server, ftp.fedworld.gov, type the following:

`<A HREF="ftp://ftp.fedworld.gov/pub/irs-pdf/f1040.pdf">Download This Tax Form</A>`

When you click the text, Download This Tax Form, your browser automatically logs on to the specified ftp server, finds the file to download, and begins downloading it. If this is a text file, it is displayed in Netscape's window; binary files (like software programs) are downloaded directly to your hard drive.

> **NOTE** A strategy often used when linking to files via the FTP protocol is to link to a directory listing instead of a specific file. By linking to a directory, Netscape brings up a list of files in that directory instead of downloading a single file. This is a particularly useful feature, because Internet files and software programs tend to change names as newer versions are released. Using just the directory listing saves you the hassle of constantly updating your HTML documents each time a file changes names.

To link to an FTP directory instead of a file, simply leave off the file name within the URL, as follows:

`<A HREF="ftp://ftp.fedworld.gov/pub/irs-pdf/">Tax Form List</A>`

## Using Gopher Links

Gopher menus link to worldwide resources in much the same way as HTML links. Over the years, enormous libraries of information have been placed on Gopher servers; most of these are not yet available in HTML format. Thousands of Gopher servers exist worldwide, with topics ranging from Cub Scout meetings to the United States State Department Travel Advisories.

Fortunately, you can add links to any Gopher server via HTML as long as you know the proper URL. Gopher links use gopher:// as the Internet service protocol. They also tend to include a server port number and extended file and directory names. The following is an example of a Gopher URL link:

`<A HREF="gopher://thisweek.chronicle.com:70/11/">Academe This Week</A>`

Clicking the hypertext link, Academe This Week, tells Netscape to connect to the chronicle.merit.edu server and retrieve the current edition of *Academe This Week*.

## Using UseNet Links

UseNet URLs are simpler than most other types of URLs. They require the prefix news:, then the full name of the particular newsgroup. For instance, a UseNet URL link to a popular newsgroup would be:

**news:www.authoring.images**

UseNet URLs work differently than most Internet services because there is no one central news server. The URL tells Netscape to connect to the news server selected by the user in Communicator's Preferences (located in the Edit Menu).

The following is a complete HTML link to a newsgroup:

<A HREF="news:www.authoring.images">Newsgroup for Web Designers</A>

Figure 23.2 shows the Communicator window opened to a UseNet URL.

**FIG. 23.2**
Newsgroups are another service accessible from links within Communicator.

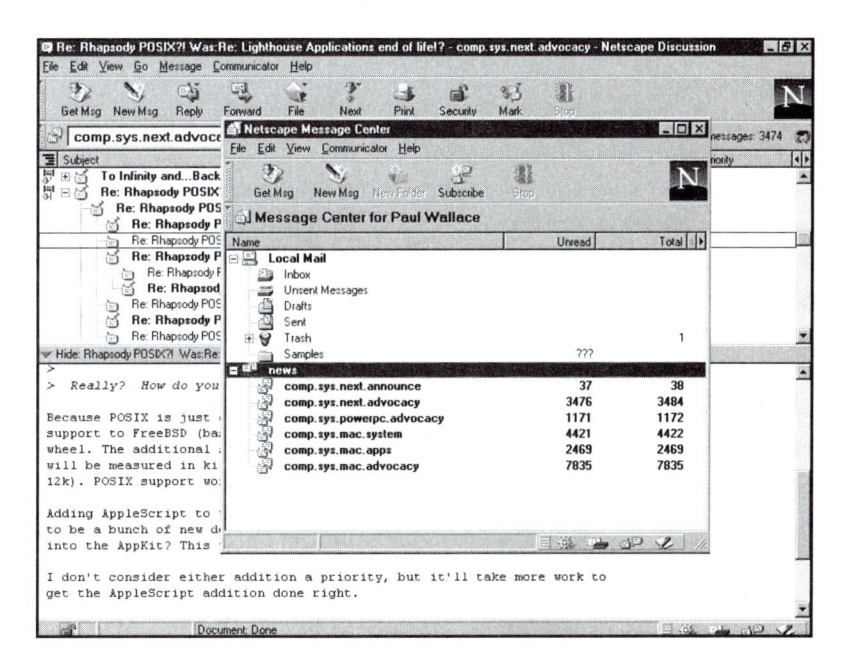

## Using Mailto Links

One of the most important communication tools on the Internet is electronic mail. E-mail allows people to send personal messages to other individuals all across the world quickly and efficiently. With HTML, you can include an e-mail link on a WWW page that lets visitors easily send mail to a specific address.

Using the : prefix, building an e-mail URL merely requires knowing the full e-mail address of the recipient. For example, to build a link to **president@whitehouse.gov**, you would use the following URL:

**mailto:president@whitehouse.gov**

**Chapter 23** Adding Links and Graphics

The full HTML for the e-mail link looks like the following:

```
<A HREF="mailto:president@whitehouse.gov">president@whitehouse.gov</A>
```

When you click the hot link text, `president@whitehouse.gov`, Netscape brings up a pre-addressed Netscape mail window. Here users can type a subject and message, and then send the e-mail on its way (see Figure 23.3).

> **NOTE** The hot text of an e-mail link should *always* be the recipient's e-mail address—the same e-mail address used in the URL. This makes it clear to everyone that this is an e-mail link, and not a link to another World Wide Web page.
>
> This practice is also useful for those visitors who print out your page. They are then able to see your e-mail address on the printout, not just underlined text that says `click here to send me e-mail`.

> **TIP** In addition to pre-addressing the e-mail, you also can specify a subject in an e-mail link. This is shown in the following example:
>
> ```
> <A HREF="mailto:president@whitehouse.gov?subject=Question About Foreign Policy">president@whitehouse.gov</A>
> ```
>
> When this e-mail link is clicked, Netscape will open a Messenger window pre-addressed to **president@whitehouse.gov** with the line, Question About Foreign Policy, inserted in the subject field.

**FIG. 23.3**
Links in Communicator can be used to automatically send e-mail.

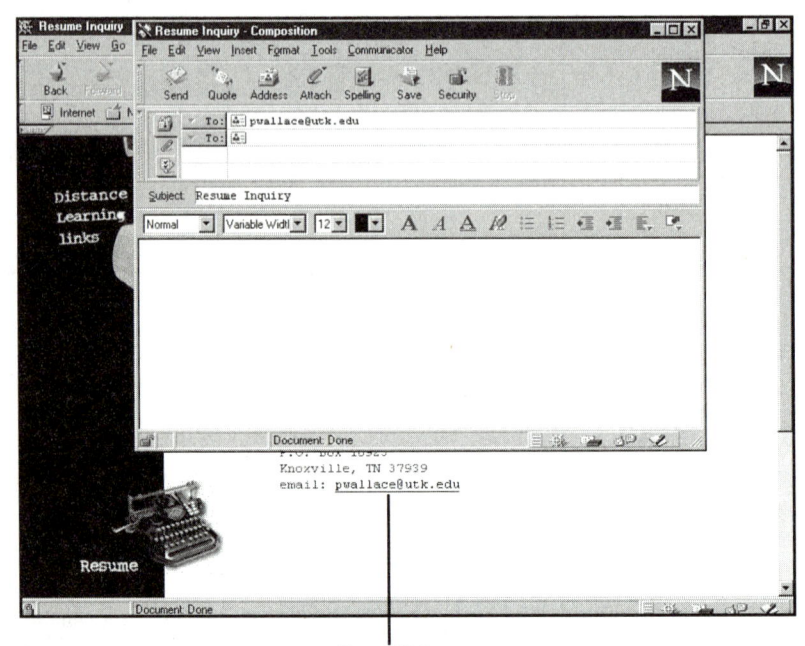

E-mail link

http://www.quecorp.com

# Understanding HTML Anchors and Named Targets

In addition to linking to other WWW files and Internet resources, HTML has the capability to link to internal points within HTML documents. This can function like a table of contents, because you can place multiple text targets within an HTML document and create a centralized index of links at the top of the page. By clicking the hyperlinks in the index, visitors aren't taken to a separate document, but to a specific spot called a *named target* within the same HTML file.

This type of link is used primarily for lengthy files or dated material. The HTML coding requires two separate steps. First, you have to create the named targets within the HTML file, then you must build the index of links to each of those specific targets.

## Creating Named Targets

Follow these steps to add named targets to your HTML document:

1. Choose a different name for each of your targets. This name should be succinct and to the point, yet not too cryptic to be confusing. For example: Mammals.

2. Use the <A> and </A> tags to mark the text as a target, but instead of using the HREF keyword, use NAME instead:

   ```
   <A NAME="Mammals"></A>
   ```

3. Type in the corresponding text that you want associated with the named target. This is the text the target is attached to. Notice that other tags can be included within the named anchor tags:

   ```
   <A NAME="Mammals">
   <H3>Warm Blooded Creatures</H3>
   </A>
   ```

After your named target is added, you're ready to move on to the next step, creating an index of links to these named targets.

## Linking to Named Targets

Linking to a named target within the same document is similar to linking to other WWW documents, with one minor difference: Instead of typing a complicated URL, you simply type in the target name with a hash symbol (#) in front of it.

The following is an example of how to link to a named target called Mammals:

```
<A HREF="#Mammals">Find out about Mammals</A>
```

Links to named targets appear the same in Netscape's window as links to other HTML files—they are underlined and blue.

You can also link to specific named targets in other HTML files elsewhere within your Web site, or somewhere else on the WWW. Within your own site, simply type the relative link URL, followed by the # and anchor name. For instance, to link to a named anchor, Insects, in a file in the same directory named lifeforms.html, type:

```
<A HREF="lifeforms.html#Insects">Now find out about Insects</A>
```

To find and link to a target name on another Internet site, view that page's HTML source code and manually pick out the target name.

> **CAUTION**
> Don't forget the hash symbol (#) in front of the target name. Without it, Netscape doesn't know to look for a named target, and attempts to link to a separate file (located in the current directory) with that target name.

## Tips to Consider When Developing Links

There are several important tips to consider when linking HTML documents to one another. The following is a simple checklist to help you evaluate your WWW links:

- Test and re-test every HTML link. Make sure that there are no typos or incorrect URLs included within your HTML documents.
- Periodically check your HTML file for outdated links. On the World Wide Web, files occasionally move, are renamed, or even are deleted. Regularly checking WWW links ensures that they are current and still exist.
- Organize your lists of links. If you need to include many links within a single document, use an alphabetical list, table, or other organization technique to keep the list usable and readable.
- Associate relevant information to your hyperlink text. Avoid using the phrase "click here" or other trite expressions. Pretend that you are only looking at the hot text; you should be able to understand where that link takes you before clicking it. The phrase "click here" is vague, and does not indicate where the link goes.

## Adding Graphics with HTML

Creating HTML files wouldn't be complete without learning how to add exciting and colorful images and graphics. On the World Wide Web, graphics are important design elements; they can be used to liven up a bland page.

For reasons beyond aesthetic purposes, graphics can play an important role in the navigation and communication of your WWW content. Images serve as hyperlinks to other WWW pages, formatting tools to organize text, or interesting visual replacements for complex information.

This section introduces you to *inline images*—images that are displayed along with text in the Netscape browser window. While adding a simple image to your page is easy, HTML also offers a multitude of advanced customization techniques that allow you to precisely lay out your WWW documents.

# World Wide Web Image File Formats

On the WWW, there are two popular image file formats that are widely supported and in use today: GIF and JPEG. Of these two file formats, each has its own advantages and disadvantages for certain situations, as discussed in the following:

## GIF: Graphics Interchange Format

The Graphics Interchange Format, or GIF, was developed by CompuServe to provide an efficient way of storing and exchanging image files across platforms (see Figure 23.4). A file in this format can contain a maximum of 256 colors, or 8 bits per pixel. GIFs are the most popular images to use as inline images because they are supported by all graphical browsers. They are also the only format for the Web that supports transparent backgrounds and multi-file animations.

The GIF format is best suited for the following types of images:

- Black-and-white line art and text
- Images with a limited number of distinct colors
- Graphics that have sharp or distinct edges—most menus, buttons, and graphs
- Graphics that are overlaid with text

**FIG. 23.4**
GIF is the best graphics format to use for images such as buttons and menus.

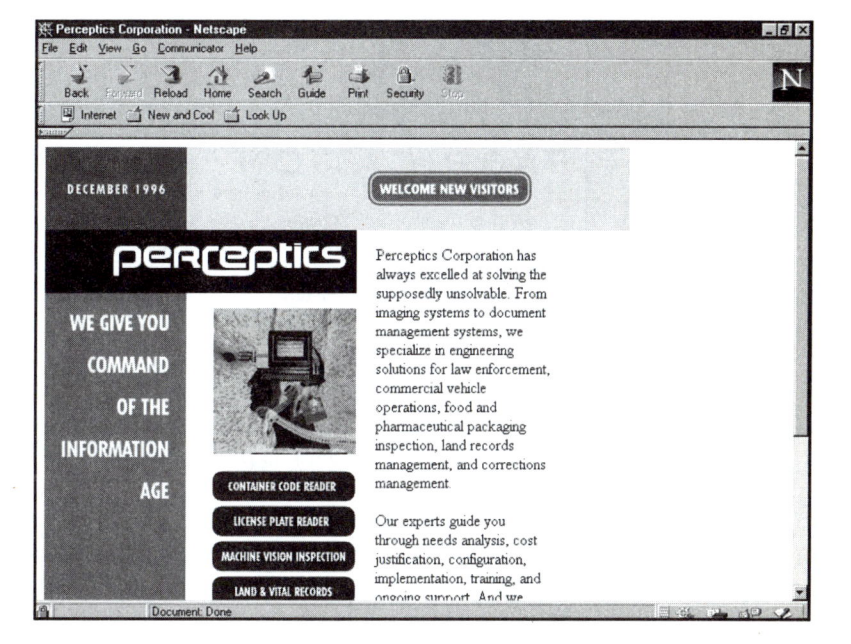

## JPEG: Joint Photographic Expert Group

JPEG compression and the JFIF format (commonly know as a JPEG or JPG image) was developed by the Joint Photographers Expert Group as a means of compressing images with a color palette of 24 bits per pixel, or 16.7 million possible colors (see Figure 23.5).

JPEG compression is best suited for the following types of images:

- Scanned photographs and ray-traced renderings
- Images that contain a complex mixture of colors
- Any image that requires more than a 256-color palette

**FIG. 23.5**
JPEG is the best type of file for photographs and any image that contains a complex mixture of colors.

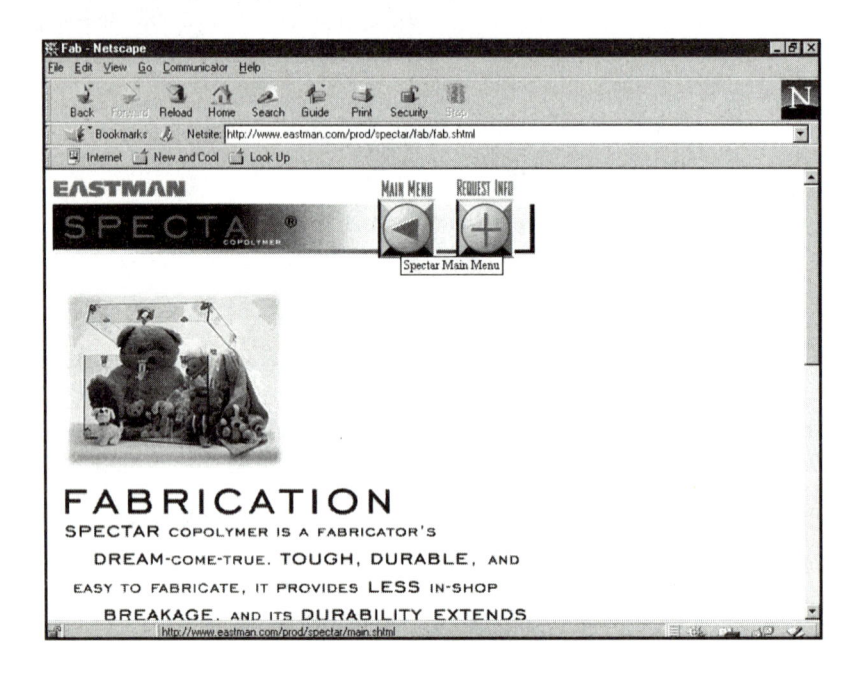

Initially, only GIF graphics were supported in the early WWW browsers. Nowadays, however, you should feel free to use whichever of the two image types best suits the nature of your original graphics. For more information on GIF, JPEG, and other image formats, consult the World Wide Web FAQ at **http://www.boutell.com/faq/**.

> **N O T E** Be careful when including other popular image formats. such as .TIF, .PCX, .PIC, or .BMP. in your HTML pages. To view these images, individuals must have an external helper application to assist Netscape.

# Using the <IMG> Tag

In HTML the image (<IMG>) tag allows you to select which graphics to include within a Web page. In addition to <IMG>, there are a number of HTML tag *attributes* (sub-tags) that are used to allow you control over image size and layout on the screen.

Without any special formatting attributes, adding a graphic is relatively easy. For example, the inline image seen in Figure 23.5 uses the following tag:

```
<IMG SRC="toybox.jpg">
```

When placed in an HTML document, the *source* (SRC) portion of the <IMG> tag tells Netscape to retrieve the graphic entitled parrot.jpg (which, in this case, is located in the same directory as the HTML file), and position it on-screen at the point where the tag is located in the document.

When adding inline images to Web pages, you do not actually place the image in your HTML document. The <IMG> tag is used to tell the browser where the image is located, and where it is to be positioned on the viewer's screen. If you're accustomed to working in a page layout program where the image becomes part of the document along with the text, this type of image placement may take a little getting used to.

However foreign this concept may seem, the fact that images are not stored *in* HTML documents allows you to include images on your Web pages that exist on other servers on the WWW. For example, because the file parrot.jpg is stored on an accessible World Wide Web server, you could add the following tag to include that image in your own Web page:

```
<IMG SRC="http://www.coe.utk.edu/images/parrot.jpg">
```

Simply, when Netscape finds this tag, it connects to **www.coe.utk.edu**, retrieves the selected image from a directory named images, then displays it on your WWW page.

> **CAUTION**
>
> Linking images from other Web sites to your own pages can cause performance problems for your visitors. That's because a visitor has to wait for the information to be retrieved from another site, then be sent to his PC before he can see it. Sometimes, the other server may be slower than your own, or may even be offline!
>
> For best performance, ensure that displayed images are saved on the same Internet server as the HTML file.

Another popular way to include images within HTML documents is the use of thumbnail images. Thumbnail images are miniature versions of a larger image that take up less screen size and, thus, have a much smaller file size.

Thumbnail images are usually linked to a full-size version of the same image. This allows individuals the option of viewing the full-size image; or simply being satisfied with the smaller, thumbnail version (see Figure 23.6).

**FIG. 23.6**
Thumbnails are an efficient use of screen size and bandwidth.

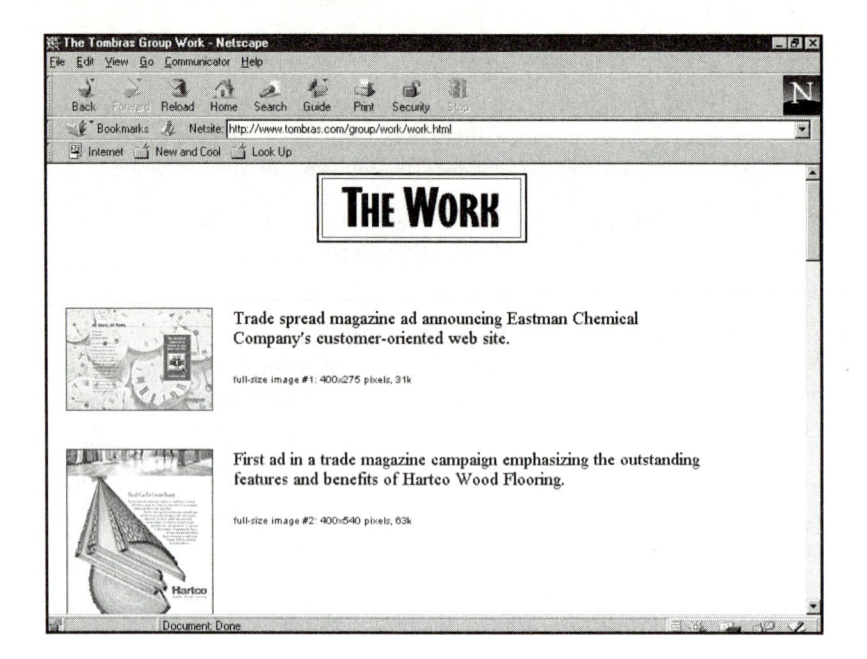

> **N O T E** Graphics can be stored and organized in separate directories just like HTML files. Using the *relative link* method outlined previously in this chapter, you can direct Netscape to retrieve graphics stored in directories both higher and lower in your server's hard drive.
>
> As with using relative links within your own Web site, using relative path names for your images allows you to test the complete site without having to be online.

When placing graphics on WWW pages, the <IMG> tag offers a great deal of flexibility regarding how the image appears and is formatted on-screen. The following sections explain the most popular <IMG> attributes that allow you to customize image placement and size in Netscape's window.

## Alternative Text

Not all WWW browsers are created equal. While Navigator is by far the most robust and popular, others, such as Lynx, are text only, and don't have the capability to display graphics and images.

Additionally, Netscape Communicator allows users to customize whether or not to display graphics when visiting new WWW pages, because sometimes it takes a long time to download and display all inline images.

To handle non-graphical browsers and Communicator's flexibility, it is standard practice to include an alternative text name for each inline image within the `<IMG>` tag. This text is displayed in Communicator's screen when the specific image doesn't load.

Use the `ALT="name"` attribute to specify the alternative text to display instead of a graphic.

## Alignment and Image Placement Options

When including graphics on a WWW page or within an e-mail message, you have several different choices as to where they are placed in the Communicator window. These alignment options are set with the `ALIGN="attribute"`. With this `<IMG>` tag attribute you can specify not only where the image is aligned on-screen, but also how text appears in relation to displayed images.

Table 23.1 lists the five unique `ALIGN` attributes and how they display images and text accordingly.

**Table 23.1  HTML Alignment Options**

| Attribute | Result |
| --- | --- |
| ALIGN=Left | Aligns an image on the browser's left margin |
| ALIGN=RIGHT | Aligns an image on the browser's right margin |
| ALIGN=TOP | Aligns an image with the top of the tallest item on the same line, whether it is text or another image |
| ALIGN=MIDDLE | Aligns the top of the text to the middle of a placed graphic |
| ALIGN=BASELINE | Aligns the bottom of the graphic with the bottom of the line of text |

Although there are other `<IMG>` `ALIGN` attributes, they are often repetitive and not commonly accepted. For example, the `BASELINE` keyword is interchangeable, and virtually identical, with the `BOTTOM` and `ABSBOTTOM` attributes—just a different syntax for the same effect.

Getting your images to align where you want them to takes some practice. Figure 23.7 helps show how graphics are displayed on-screen using the following attributes of the `<IMG>` tag:

```
<IMG SRC="parrot.jpg" ALIGN="LEFT"> Left Alignment
<IMG SRC="parrot.jpg" ALIGN="RIGHT"> Right Alignment
<IMG SRC="parrot.jpg" ALIGN="TOP"> Top Alignment
<IMG SRC="parrot.jpg" ALIGN="MIDDLE"> Middle Alignment
<IMG SRC="parrot.jpg" ALIGN="BASELINE"> Baseline Alignment
```

## Using the *<IMG>* Tag with *Height* and *Width* Attributes

One way to reduce the amount of time someone waits for your inline graphic to load is to tell the browser the size of the image in advance. Netscape uses this information when interpreting the final page layout. When the browser receives an HTML document, it spends a bit of time deciphering where to place the different elements on the screen. By knowing the exact dimensions of an incoming image, Netscape can immediately begin to lay out the text areas relative to where the image will eventually be.

**FIG. 23.7**
With recent graphic alignment options, HTML designers have significant control over the appearance of their WWW pages.

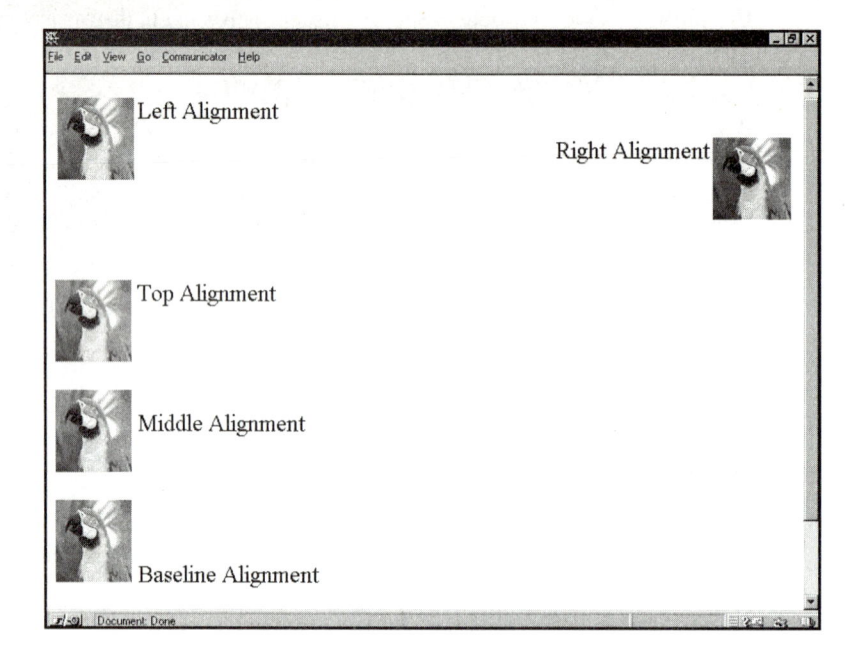

Netscape can take advantage of the `<IMG>` tag appended with the height and width of the inline image to which it refers. This is done by adding `HEIGHT` and `WIDTH` attributes to the `<IMG>` tag. The height and width of an image are measured in pixels. The use of this tag for the example image parrot.jpg, with a height of 300 pixels and a width of 100 pixels, would be written like this:

`<IMG SRC="parrot.jpg" HEIGHT="300" WIDTH="100">`

It doesn't matter whether the `HEIGHT` or `WIDTH` attribute comes first, but they both must be included along with the `IMG` and the `SRC` elements.

Adding `HEIGHT` and `WIDTH` attributes to your images does not make them load any faster, but these attributes allow Netscape to leave the correct amount of room for where those images will be placed on the page—before the browser actually receives the image file. This gives the *illusion* of a faster-loading overall page.

## Vertical and Horizontal Alignment

Another of the image placement attributes are `HSPACE` and `VSPACE`. These two attributes specify the amount of blank space that is placed around an image in respect to horizontal and vertical distance. This ensures that text and other HTML elements remain a reasonable distance from the image.

http://www.quecorp.com

Similar to the HEIGHT and WIDTH attributes, VSPACE and HSPACE require numeric values in the form of pixels. As good practice, try to keep at least a 10-pixel border between an image and associated text. The following HTML example shows how to use the HSPACE and VSPACE attributes to provide a standard 10-pixel radius around an image:

```
<IMG SRC="parrot.jpg" VSPACE="10" HSPACE="10">
```

**NOTE** Using the VSPACE and HSPACE attributes with images adds the designated amount of space to all sides of your images, not just the edge adjacent to the text.

## Borders

The last image customization technique to cover is the BORDER=*"width"* attribute. With this setting, you can tell Netscape to automatically create a thick (or thin) border around any image included on your WWW pages.

Using the BORDER attribute, you can have a border thickness ranging from 0 to 10 pixels. The following example sets your image border thickness to 5 pixels:

```
<IMG SRC="parrot.jpg" BORDER="5">
```

Figure 23.8 shows a sampling of five different border sizes ranging from 1 to 9 pixels. The border color is determined by the text color of your document.

**FIG. 23.8**
Adding an outline border to your images frames them in the Communicator window.

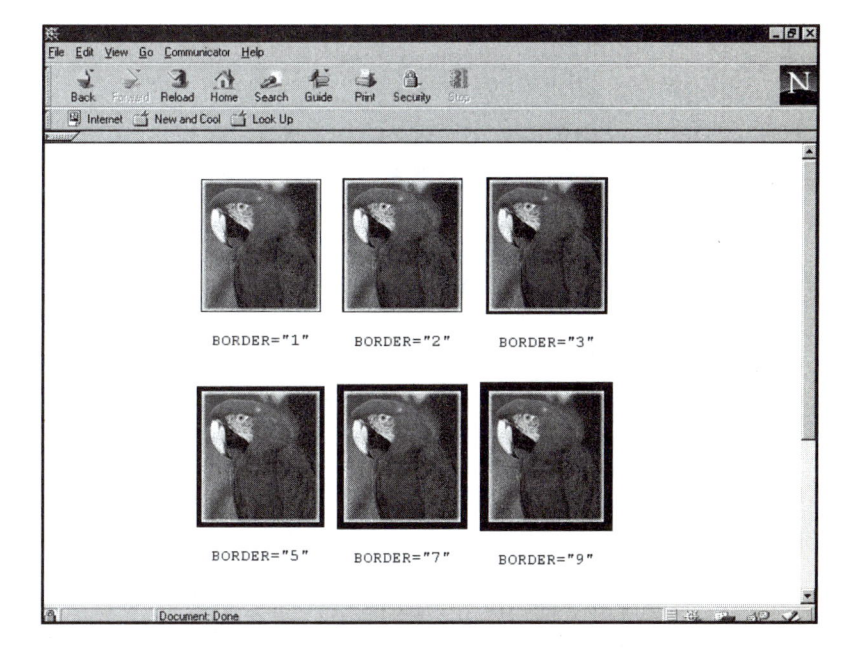

## Using Images as HTML Links

Not only do graphics serve an aesthetic purpose, they can also be used as navigational buttons and menus. By adding the proper HTML tags, inline images can serve as links to other WWW documents in your own site and to sites around the world.

Making an image serve as a link is a two-step process. First, you add the `<IMG>` tag, along with any appropriate attributes, into the HTML document:

`<IMG SRC="info.gif" ALIGN="LEFT">`

After you add the image, you must make it a hyperlink in the same manner as you did with text links earlier in this chapter. However, instead of using a text phrase surrounded by the `<A>` and `</A>` tags, surround the `<IMG>` tag with `<A>` and `</A>` like so:

`<A HREF="information.html"><IMG SRC="info.gif" ALIGN="LEFT"></A>`

You can also include text along with the `<IMG>` elements, so both the image and a text phrase link you to the same HTML document:

`<A HREF="information.html"><IMG SRC="arrows.gif" ALIGN=LEFT> <H2>More Information<H2></A>`

Figure 23.9 shows how graphics can be used to link to different HTML documents. A blue outline border surrounds the graphics that are linked to other documents. By clicking the graphic, users are hyperlinked to the associated file.

**FIG. 23.9**
HTML flexibility allows images to serve as links to other WWW documents.

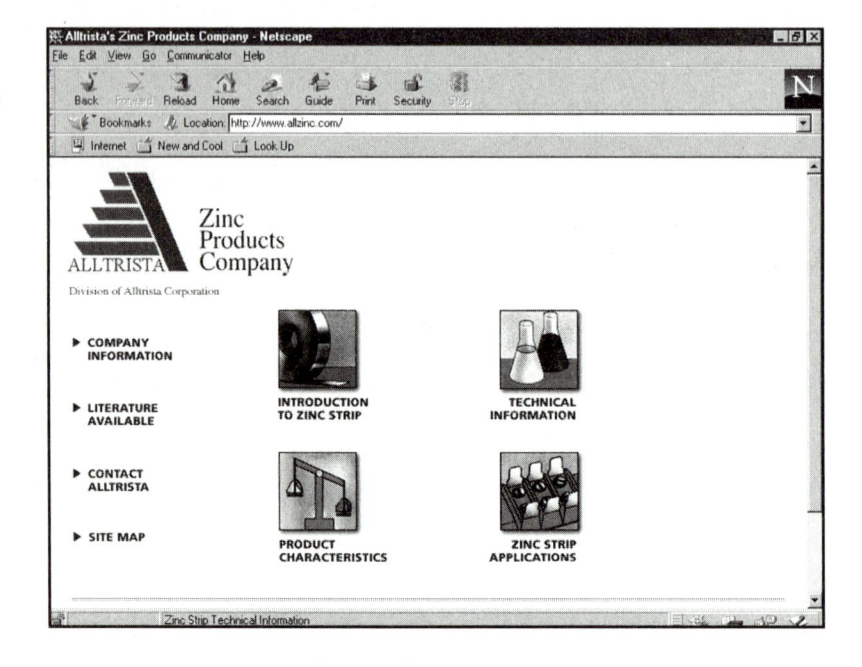

http://www.quecorp.com

## TROUBLESHOOTING

**I have added some images to my Web page that are links to other documents. Mine all have a blue border around them, yet I've seen sites on the Web where the images' links have no border. How do they do that?** Simple, just set the BORDER attribute of your image links to 0. For instance, to take off the border in the previous example, type:

`<A HREF="information.html"><IMG SRC="info.gif" ALIGN="LEFT" BORDER="0"></A>`

CHAPTER 24

# Organizing Content with Tables and Frames

*by Andy Shafran*

- Working with basic Table tags to build simple tables
- Deciding when to use frames
- Using advanced table formatting techniques for complicated tables
- Creating a simple frame layout for your Web page
- Using advanced keywords and characteristics when designing with frames
- Evaluating practical alternatives to frames and tables on your Web page

The HTML language is geared toward logically deciding how information will appear through the eyes of a Web browser, such as Communicator. Different HTML tags control the size, color, and attributes of text and graphics on the screen.

Beyond these fundamental HTML snippets, there are many more advanced tags that allow even greater flexibility in how your information appears and is organized on-screen. One important set of HTML tags allows you to create tables—simple columns and rows—of HTML information so that you can organize your information in a logical manner.

Frames, on the other hand, allow you to separate your single Netscape window into multiple panes. By dividing the screen into multiple frames, you can display many different pages of HTML at one time.

This chapter introduces you to both of these powerful Web techniques and steps you through the HTML specifics of including them in your Web pages.

# Creating a Simple Table

Besides using standard lists and formatting tags, tables are another powerful tool for displaying information within HTML documents. Emulating the look and feel of a spreadsheet, tables allow you to specify rows and columns of information to be organized and displayed in Netscape.

Tables are similar to lists because they allow a lot of information to be easily displayed in a small area. The main difference is that tables allow multiple columns of information, making it easier to compare data. This flexibility of working with two dimensions instead of one is a powerful concept when building Web pages.

A good table can make your Web page look very neat and organized, while offering a lot of information to the viewer. A bad, or inappropriate, table splits up your page and introduces confusion to the point you're trying to convey. Figure 24.1 shows a sample table done well.

**FIG. 24.1**
This table organizes information in a straightforward and comparable manner that might come in handy for baseball fans.

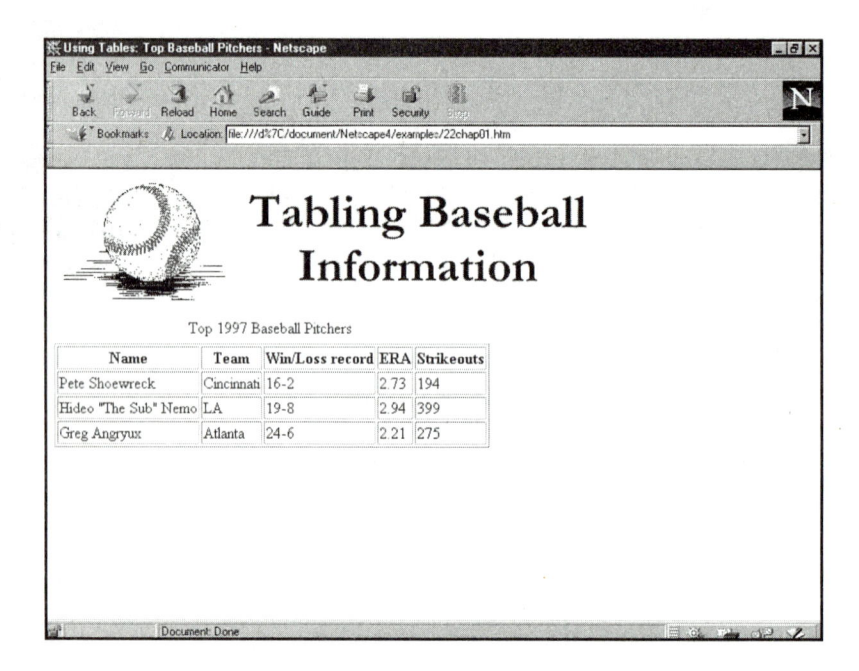

> **NOTE** Although the pitchers in the table in Figure 24.1 aren't in any particular order, it's easy to see how listing them in a certain way makes using tables a powerful feature for Web pages. The pitchers could be listed in order of ERA or Wins and Losses so you know that the best (or worst) are listed at the top of the table. Organizing your table in a specific order provides even more information to visitors who see your page because it automatically provides a comparison and contrast.

http://www.quecorp.com

Adding tables to your Web page isn't difficult, but there are several new HTML tags to learn. First off, there's the overall surrounding table tag—<TABLE>. <TABLE> and </TABLE> surround the entire table, and several other tags define how the table should appear.

Within the <TABLE> tag, you can specify the thickness of the lines separating each cell with the BORDER= keyword. The default border thickness is 1, but you can change it to any value you want:

```
<TABLE BORDER=3>
```

The lines on the table are three pixels thick. To specify no lines you can set BORDER=0. Visitors won't see any lines separating table rows and cells and might not even notice a table exists unless they view the document's source code when BORDER=0.

After your generic <TABLE> and </TABLE> tags are added, the next step is to build a table title, or caption. Use the <CAPTION> and </CAPTION> tags to designate information that labels this particular table:

```
<CAPTION>Top 1997 Baseball Pitchers</CAPTION>
```

Next, it's time to start creating each item in the table. Information is added to a table one row at a time, starting from left to right.

To add a new row to your table, add the <TR> and </TR> tags:

```
<TABLE>
<CAPTION>Top 1997 Baseball Pitchers</CAPTION>
     <TR>
     </TR>
</TABLE>
```

After the Table Row tags are added, it's time to start building the meat of the table. Most tables have some sort of header columns, or individual labels for each column, so that visitors know what they are looking at. Table Headers are specially formatted tags that appear in bold and serve as column or row labels in your table. The Table Header tags <TH> and </TH> are used for each specific cell of information you want to mark as a header. A single row of five separate header columns looks like this:

```
<TR>
     <TH>Name</TH>
     <TH>Team</TH>
     <TH>Win/Loss record</TH>
     <TH>ERA</TH>
     <TH>Strikeouts</TH>
</TR>
```

After the Header columns are created, you can build each cell of information with the Table Data container tags—<TD> and </TD>. Each cell must be individually added within the <TR> and </TR> tags, just like the Table Header tags:

```
<TR>
     <TD>Pete Shoewreck</TD>
     <TD>Cincinnati</TD>
     <TD>16-2</TD>
```

```
            <TD>2.73</TD>
            <TD>194</TD>
    </TR>
```

Make sure that your columns of information match up with the appropriate Table Header you give so that your information is lined up correctly. Repeat this step until you have created all of your rows of information. Following is the complete set of HTML for the image shown in Figure 24.1:

```
<TABLE>
<CAPTION>Top 1997 Baseball Pitchers</CAPTION>
    <TR>
            <TH>Name</TH>
            <TH>Team</TH>
            <TH>Win/Loss record</TH>
            <TH>ERA</TH>
            <TH>Strikeouts</TH>
    </TR>
    <TR>
            <TD>Pete Shoewreck</TD>
            <TD>Cincinnati</TD>
            <TD>16-2</TD>
            <TD>2.73</TD>
            <TD>194</TD>
    </TR>
    <TR>
            <TD>Hideo "The Sub" Nemo</TD>
            <TD>LA</TD>
            <TD>19-8</TD>
            <TD>2.94</TD>
            <TD>399</TD>
    </TR>
    <TR>
            <TD>Greg Angryux</TD>
            <TD>Atlanta</TD>
            <TD>24-6</TD>
<TD>2.21</TD>
            <TD>275</TD>
    </TR>
</TABLE>
```

# Using Advanced Table Features

Now that you can create a good-looking, simple table, let's try adding a little flavor to it. Netscape offers several impressive ways to customize your tables.

Each of these techniques requires that you carefully calculate the number of rows and columns used in your table so that the information is appropriately organized.

## Lines Spanning Multiple Rows

When you start using tables more often, you'll occasionally find situations where you want your information to span multiple rows. That's where the ROWSPAN keyword is useful.

ROWSPAN is a special keyword that you add to the <TD> tag for a specific cell. To have a cell span 2 columns instead of the default 1, replace something like <TD>Your Cell's Text Here</TD> with the following:

<TD ROWSPAN=2>Your extended Text HERE</TD>

When your table displays, the cell you added ROWSPAN to now takes up two rows. Here's how ROWSPAN changes the baseball table:

```
<TR>
<TD>Pete Shoewreck </TD>
<TD ROWSPAN=2>Cincinnati</TD>
<TD>16-2</TD>
<TD>2.73</TD>
<TD>194</TD>
</TR>
<TR>
<TD>Jose Rio</TD>
<TD>28-2</TD>
<TD>1.92</TD>
<TD>199</TD>
</TR>
```

Figure 24.2 shows the changed table in Netscape.

**FIG. 24.2**
Here's how ROWSPAN can shape up a table to spread information into multiple rows of data.

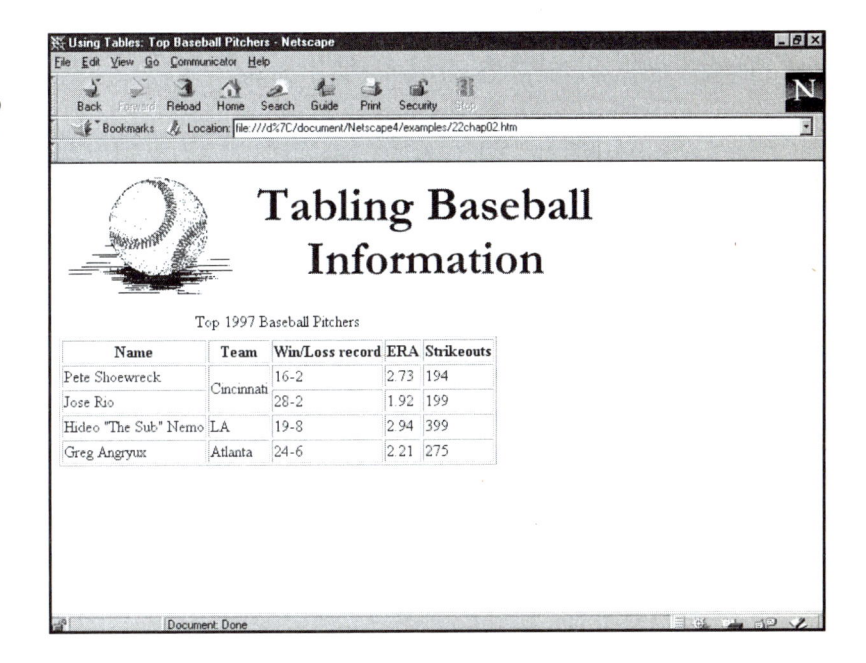

> **CAUTION**
> When you use ROWSPAN (or COLSPAN, described in the next section), make sure that you take into account the reduced number of rows or columns you need to fill for other table entries. For example, one less column of information for Jose Rio was needed when his row of information was typed into the HTML file.

## Spanning Multiple Columns

Just as ROWSPAN enables specific cells to span multiple rows, COLSPAN enables specific cells to span multiple columns. Using the COLSPAN keyword, you can instruct your table to span across as many cells as you want. Consider the following example:

```
<TR>
<TH COLSPAN=2>Personal Information</TH>
<TH COLSPAN=3>Statistics</TH>
</TR>
<TR>
<TH>Name</TH>
<TH>Team</TH>
<TH>Win/Loss record</TH>
<TH>ERA</TH>
<TH>Strikeouts</TH>
</TR>
```

Figure 24.3 shows the results of this use of COLSPAN.

**FIG. 24.3**
Similar to ROWSPAN, COLSPAN gives more control to Web developers when working with HTML tables.

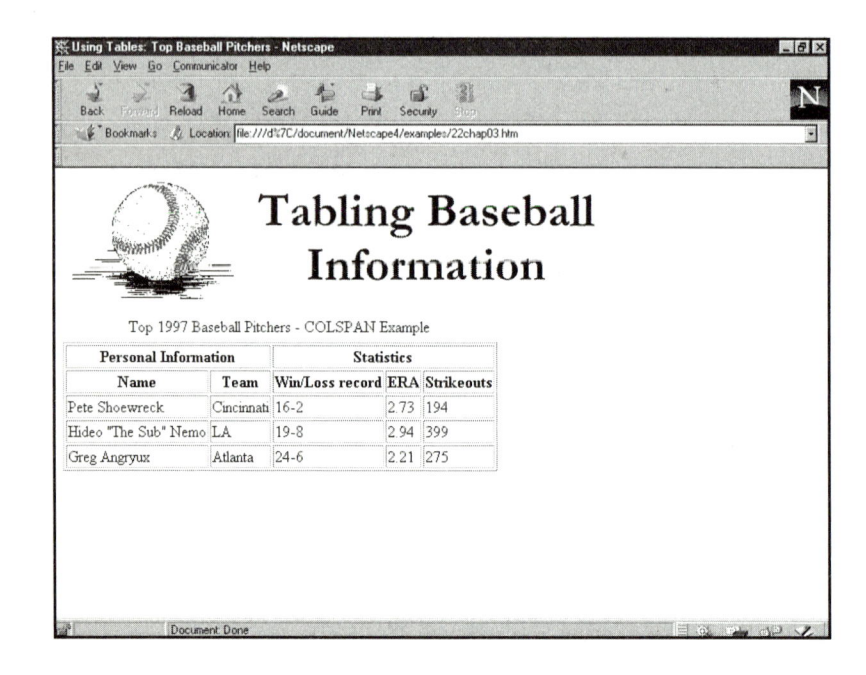

http://www.quecorp.com

## Embedding Lists into Tables

Tables can be combined with other HTML elements and can contain any of the list types described in Chapter 22, "HTML Primer." All three list types perform the same when embedded within a table. Make sure that you carefully add all necessary closing tags whenever you add a list to your table—they're easy to lose track of.

In Figure 24.4, a simple unordered list is included in the baseball table.

**FIG. 24.4**
Lists allow you to incorporate multiple pieces of information into a specific table cell.

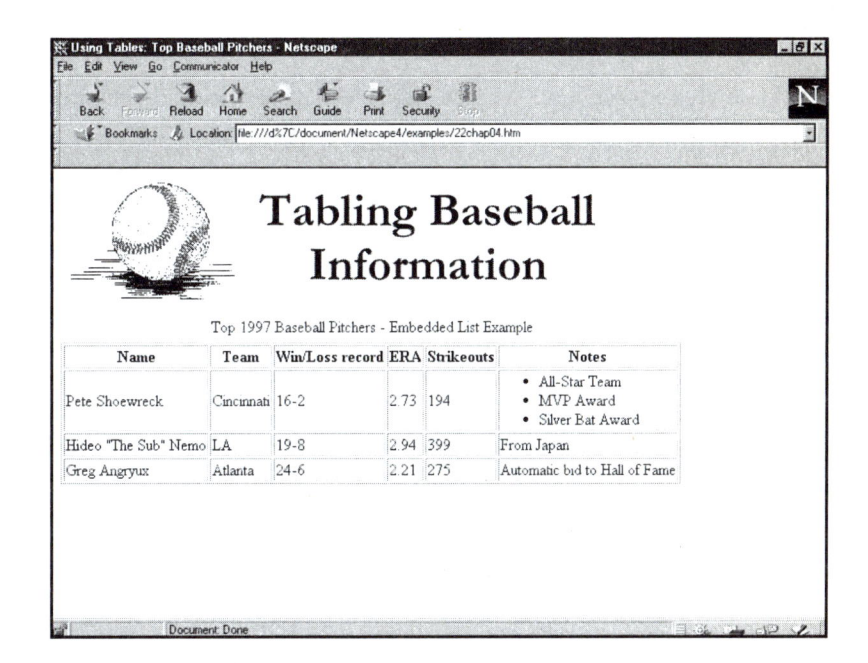

**N O T E** If you're looking for a challenge, try embedding a table within a table. The effects are worthwhile, but keeping track of your HTML can be a bear! You've got to make sure that you use all the </TABLE> closing tags properly, and lining up each element is difficult. Embedded tables often don't need any headers or borders.

## Setting Your Text Alignment

Netscape tables let you customize the alignment of each cell both vertically and horizontally. Set by special keywords—ALIGN and VALIGN—these alignment settings offer you increased flexibility for how your table looks. You can set table alignment within the entire table (in the <TABLE> tag), in a specific row (in the <TR> tag), or in a single cell (in the <TD> tag).

The ALIGN and VALIGN keywords each have three possible settings and are used in the same spot as the COLSPAN and ROWSPAN keywords described in the previous section—within the <TD> tag. Table 24.1 details the use of these two keywords.

**Table 24.1  Keyword Setting Descriptions**

| Keyword Setting | Description |
| --- | --- |
| ALIGN=LEFT | Left-justifies text in the cell (the default setting). |
| ALIGN=CENTER | Centers text horizontally within the cell. |
| ALIGN=RIGHT | Right-justifies text in the cell. |
| VALIGN=TOP | Starts text at the top of the cell (particularly useful when information in the row has multiple lines of information). |
| VALIGN=MIDDLE | The default setting; centers text vertically within the cell. |
| VALIGN=BOTTOM | Positions text at the bottom of the cell. |

Continuing with the baseball example, VALIGN=TOP has been added to the entire row that has the list in it so text doesn't appear to float in the middle of that cell. The new <TR> tag looks like this:

`<TR VALIGN=TOP>`

Figure 24.5 shows how this setting affects the baseball table.

**FIG. 24.5**
The information on one of the pitchers has been moved to the top of the cell with the VALIGN keyword.

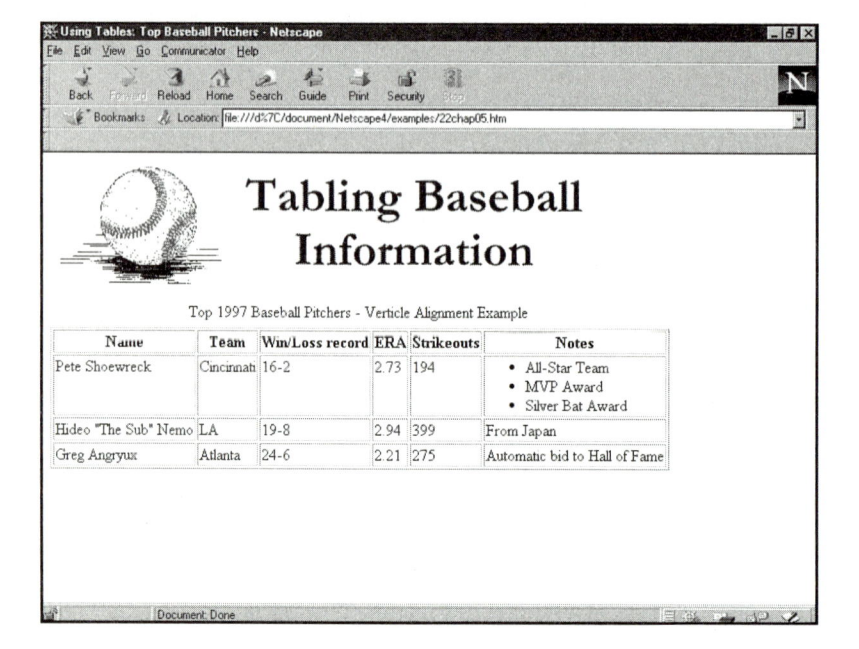

> **TIP** Some Web pages use ALIGN and VALIGN to organize graphics within a table. By removing the table's border, you can perfectly line up sets of graphics in an organized fashion.

http://www.quecorp.com

## Table Colors

Until recently, you haven't been able to control the colors of the tables on your Web page. Table borders had to be black, and the background color of each and every cell had to be whatever was used for the rest of the Web page. This made it difficult to add spot color to a particular cell that had important information, or to use a variety of colors when developing your Web pages.

With several new HTML tags, you can now control the color of your table's background and borders. Most importantly, you can add the BGCOLOR keyword to your standard <TABLE> tag, as follows:

```
<TABLE BORDER BGCOLOR=YELLOW>
</TABLE>
```

Figure 24.6 shows a sample table with the background color set to yellow.

**FIG. 24.6**
Color breathes new life into tables.

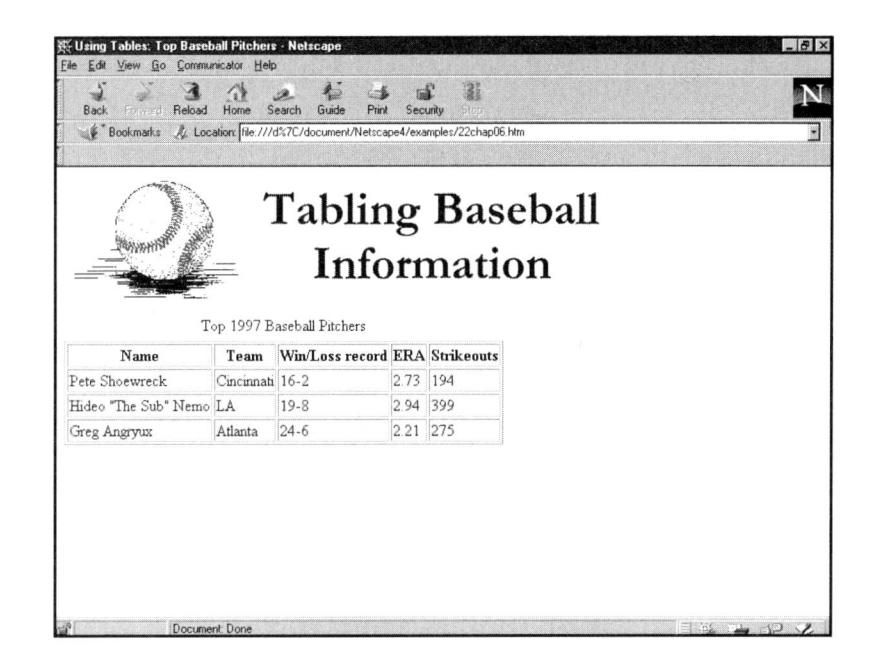

Now the background color of the entire table is set to yellow. You can set your background color to any of these 16 default colors by specifying the color name. These are the same 16 colors listed in Chapter 22, "HTML Primer," and can be used to control text colors as well:

| Black | Maroon | Green | Olive |
| Navy | Purple | Teal | Gray |
| Silver | Red | Lime | Yellow |
| Blue | Fuchsia | Aqua | White |

**496** Chapter 24 Organizing Content with Tables and Frames

Besides the BGCOLOR keyword, there are several other new color enhancements you can choose from, as follows:

BORDERCOLOR          Sets the lines of the table border to the color you specify.

BORDERCOLORDARK/     Used to change the colors BORDERCOLORLIGHT of your table border to give a three-dimensional effect. By setting both attributes, it creates the appearance that your table is in 3-D. Try experimenting with it and use a thick table border (BORDER=6).

The following is a simple example of the new table keywords in action:

```
<TABLE BORDER BGCOLOR=YELLOW BORDERCOLOR=RED BORDERCOLORDARK=BLUE
BORDERCOLORLIGHT=GREY>
</TABLE>
```

As you can see, these new keywords add a lot of flexibility to the appearance of your tables. You can also add these keywords to each individual cell or row of data to control the color of that particular element. The following HTML code customizes each cell color individually (see Figure 24.7):

```
<TABLE BORDER=2 WIDTH=300>
<TR>
    <TD BGCOLOR=YELLOW> Don't you think</TD>
    <TD BGCOLOR=BLACK><FONT COLOR=YELLOW>That this Table</FONT></TD>
</TR>
<TR>
    <TD BGCOLOR=BLACK><FONT COLOR=YELLOW>Looks similar to</FONT></TD>
    <TD BGCOLOR=YELLOW>A BUMBLEBEE!!!</TD>
</TR>
</TABLE>
```

**FIG. 24.7**
Color can be assigned to each cell and row within a table.

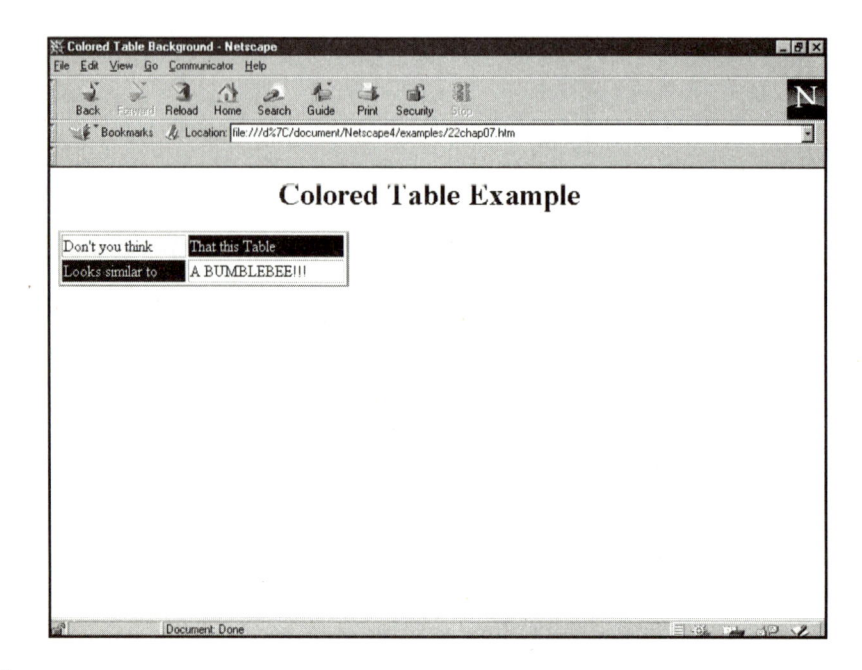

http://www.quecorp.com

You can also add these new keywords to the <TR> tag to control an entire row's color coordination. Notice also how the color of the text was changed using the <FONT> tag. This is to ensure that the background and text colors contrast so the text is readable.

## Table Alternatives

If you are concerned that non-Netscape browsers cannot display your tables, find tables too bulky to use, or prefer not to use them at all, you'll be pleased to know that there are a few popular alternatives to using tables.

The two most popular options are using extra lists, or using the <PRE> and </PRE> HTML tags. These two workarounds offer table-like functionality, but are limited in nature.

### Lists Can Replace Tables

Even though lists are one-dimensional displays of information, you can replace virtually any table with a couple of lists, if you use them properly.

Let's return to the baseball player table. You can replace that table with a few lists (see Figure 24.8). Of course, these lists aren't as easy to read as a table, and they make the user scroll through the screen because of the way the information is presented. In general, lists tend to be more spread out than tables and make it more difficult to compare information between the items.

**FIG. 24.8**
Although they present the same amount of information, lists aren't as flexible as tables.

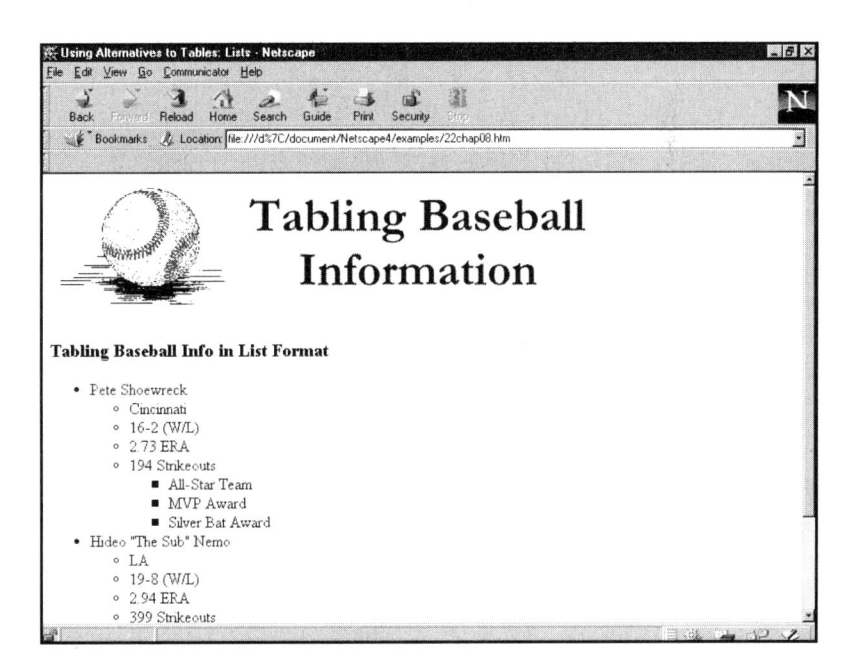

## Preformatted Text

Another way of replacing tables is using the `<PRE>` and `</PRE>` tags. This set of tags causes Netscape to display information on your Web page exactly as you type it, without any Netscape interpretation of how the information should be presented.

You can use these tags to emulate a table. The result is not as flashy as a table, and you cannot have graphical borders, but most people don't notice the difference. Using carriage returns, spaces, and tabs, preformatted text presents the same baseball information (see Figure 24.9):

```
<PRE>
<B>Name               Team            (W/L)   ERA     Strikeouts</B>
Jon Happy            Cincinnati      16-2    2.73    194
Hideo "The Sub" Nemo Los Angeles     19-8    2.94    399
Greg Angryux         Atlanta         24-6    2.21    275
</PRE>
```

**FIG. 24.9**
The `<PRE>` tag lets you present this simple "table" with no problems.

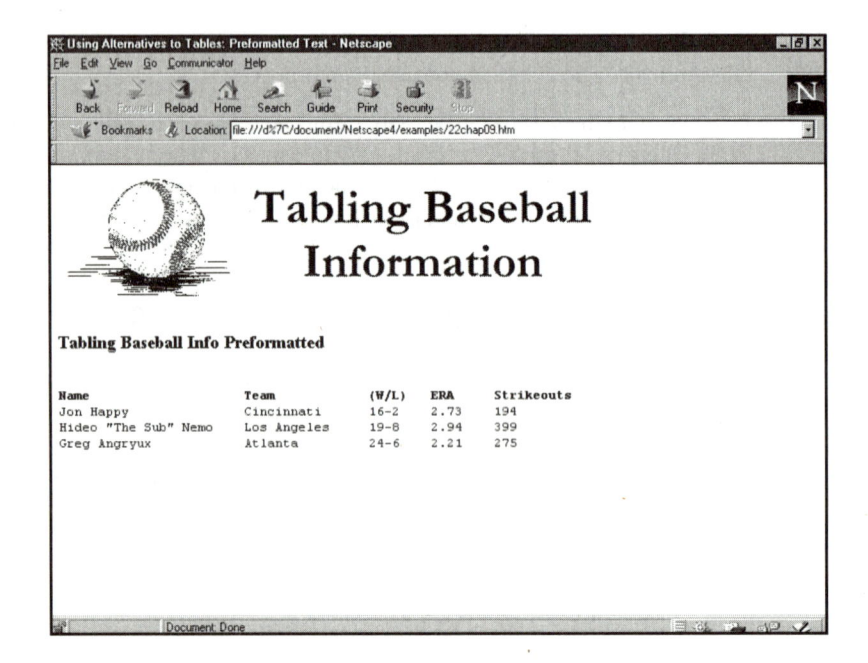

> **TIP** Notice that you can use text formatting tags within your preformatted text to add bold or italic to parts of the table.

## Using Frames

If you're like most people, you can do more than one thing at a time. Some people can type while talking on the phone, and almost everyone can listen to the radio while driving. In the computer world, operating systems now multitask, letting you run two (or more) programs at

http://www.quecorp.com

once. The latest televisions have picture-in-picture support, letting you watch two shows simultaneously.

Not wanting to be left behind, Netscape now allows you to display multiple HTML files on-screen at the same time. Using frames, you can create different areas within the Netscape window that display separate HTML files. You can link to many different sites across the world at once.

This section introduces you to frames and shows how you can use them in your Web pages. You'll learn the proper HTML for frames, useful techniques for adding them, and when you should (and shouldn't) use frames for your Web pages.

Netscape frames give you significantly more control over how your Web page appears to visitors. By using special HTML tags, you can create multiple independent frames within your Netscape screen, with each frame pointing to a different HTML file and linking to different sites on the Web. This allows you to control the presentation of your page and makes it easier for users to navigate through your site.

However, by using frames on a Web page, you can freeze the header and footer information into separate frames—because they never change—and let people browse through a Web site with that default information always on-screen. Figure 24.10 shows a Web page broken into several frames (**http://www.whitlock.com**).

**FIG. 24.10**
This framed site always has a header and footer available.

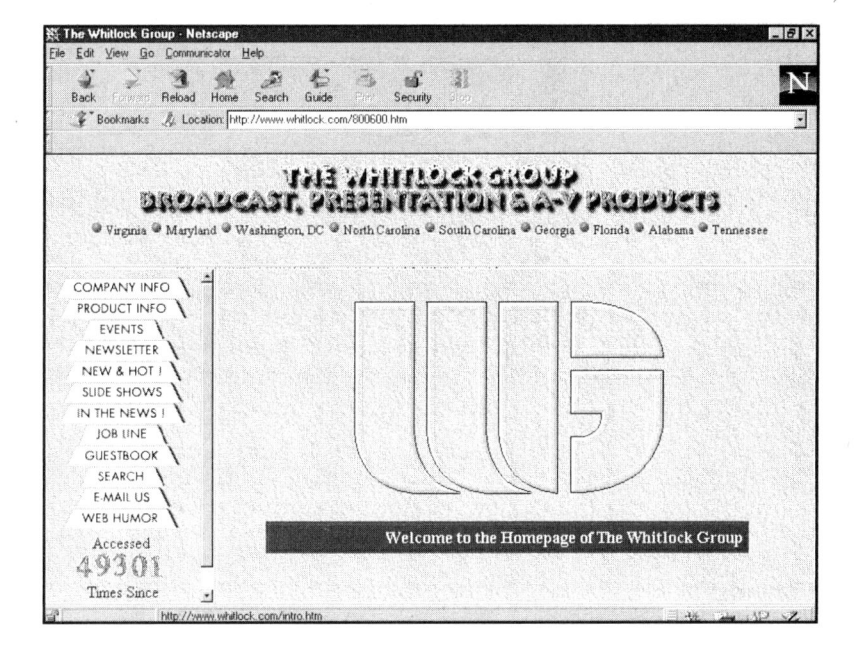

Each of the four frames points to a different HTML document, so you're actually seeing three separate files at once.

Freezing standard text is just one use of frames. In this section, you'll learn several other ways you can use frames on your Web page. You'll see that frames can be used for informational purposes, navigational reasons, or to keep material organized.

## Useful Navigational Tools

Probably the most useful way to implement frames is as a navigational tool. You can create a frozen set of icons that appears at the bottom or side of the Netscape screen and lets users work their way through your Web site.

A great example of this is at the Piper Studios Web site (**http://www.piper-studios.com/knw/knw.htm**) shown in Figure 24.11. The icons appear on the top and center of the screen and take you to a different part of the site. They always remain there while exploring this site.

**FIG. 24.11**
Piper Studios uses frames to make a standardized navigation bar on the left side of the window.

http://www.quecorp.com

## Organizing a Lot of Information

Another good use for frames is to sort and organize a lot of information. Figure 24.12 shows Bill Gerrard's home page (**http://www.gerrard.org/billnpam/**). Bill had a lot of information to put on his Web page. He decided to use frames to keep track of that information and tie it all together.

**FIG. 24.12**
Visit Bill and Pam's site to take a look at how individuals can use frames on their personal Web pages.

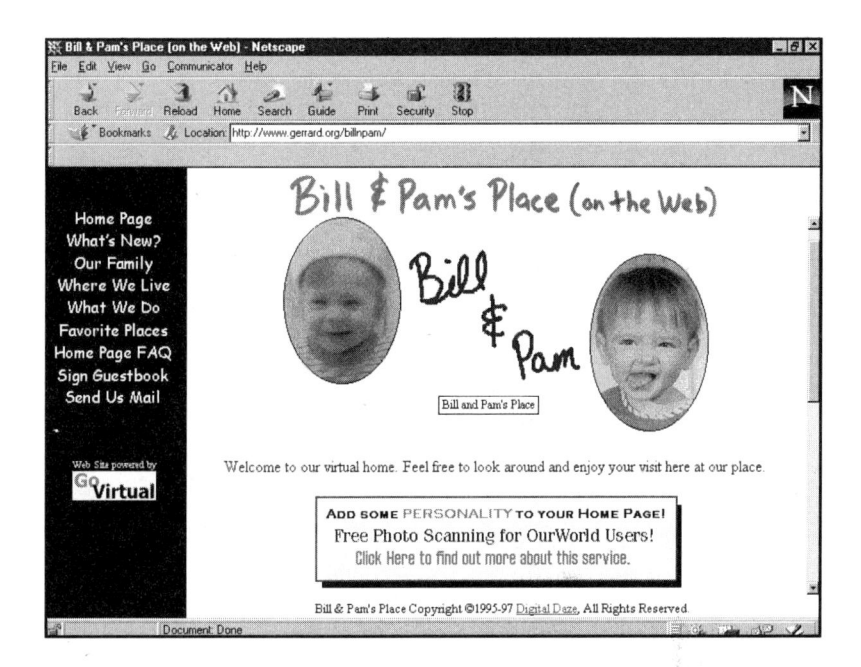

> **TIP** If you like how Bill's page is organized, choose View, Document Source from the Netscape menu bar to see exactly how his HTML code is structured.

On the left side of the screen, Bill has created a simple table of contents for the information available on his Web page. When you click an item from the TOC, that information appears in the window on the right. The TOC is always there (like the navigation bar at the Netscape home page), but is structured in a different format. Bill's home page also has a standard header and footer that never change.

## Playing Tic-Tac-Toe: A Unique Frame Experience

The impressive thing about frames is that they are extremely flexible and allow you to structure Web pages in just about any way you choose.

For example, one innovative way to use Netscape frames is to create a tic-tac-toe board. Using nine separate frames, Figure 24.13 shows how you can play a quick game of tic-tac-toe from Netscape.

**FIG. 24.13**
The Netscape window is divided into nine equal sections.

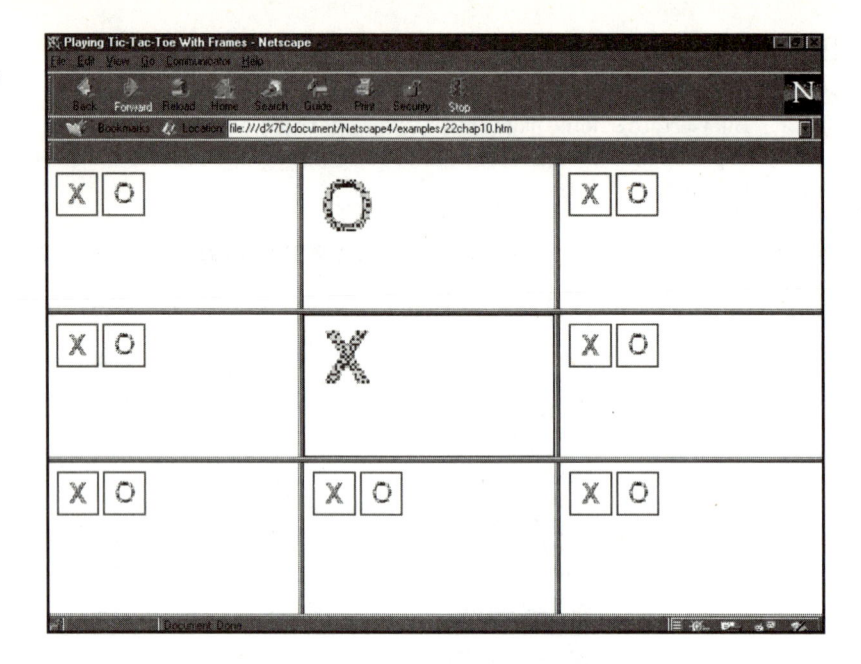

This example of frame use is interesting because each frame points to the exact same HTML file. All that's in the file is two small image tags, one for an X and another for an O. When you click one or the other, Netscape redraws the frame with a large X or O. There are not separate HTML files for each frame. Because all nine frames work the same way, there only needs to be a single HTML file, of which as many as nine separate instances can be open at once.

## Frames Are Not Perfect for Every Situation

As with all new technology, you need to be careful where you choose to use Netscape frames. As you can see, there are a lot of different places where frames let you build custom interfaces to your Web site and make it more exciting and interesting. But don't add frames to your Web page just because you can. For an example of a bad Web page, take a look at the fictitious Web page shown in Figure 24.14.

There are a lot of Netscape enhancements used in this parakeet Web page, including a colorful image and tables. Now, notice the two frames at the top of the page; they seem to logically divide the two types of headlines for Polly's Web page. Unfortunately, they don't succeed. The headlines are not sized correctly to fit in the frames. Actually, these two frames serve no purpose. This same information could just as easily be incorporated without using frames, and be simpler to read. Also, notice the copyright symbol in the bottom frame—another bad use of frames. This simple frame is too small to display all of the information on-screen, and generally isn't useful to visitors.

**FIG. 24.14**
There's no point to the frames on this Web page—it needs a better design.

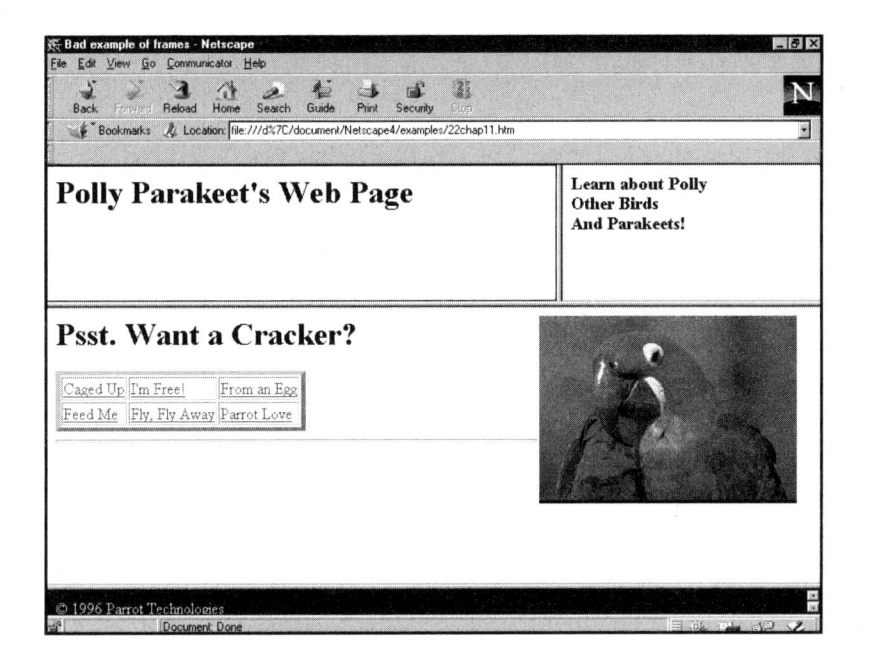

Frames aren't necessarily a bad idea for this particular page, but they should certainly be better thought out. Don't use frames just because they are available. Test and evaluate a Web page interface to make sure it is usable and presentable.

> **N O T E** Using frames on your home page tends to significantly increase the required time to download and see the entire page. That's because visitors must download a whole set of HTML files before they can see the Web site.

Netscape itself learned this painful lesson early in 1996. Its site was redesigned to take advantage of new frame capabilities. Unfortunately, instead of streamlining the interface to its site, its use of frames was difficult to use and required visitors to wait several minutes before the entire home page was downloaded. So, Netscape removed frames off its Web pages in order to rethink and re-engineer how to use them effectively. Using frames on a large site—especially one as big as Netscape's—can be a daunting task.

## Building Simple Frames

Now that you're familiar with how frames can be used, let's start learning how to create them. There are just a couple of simple tags to learn; the tricky part is using them properly so that the frames appear the way you want them to make your Web page look better.

This section takes you through creating a simple Web page that is divided into two frames. You'll learn what the HTML tags are, how to use them, and what files you need to create.

## The First Step: Planning the Framed Site

When you want to add frames to your Web page, the first step is to think about how you want the frames organized, and how they should be displayed. After you have a model in your mind, creating the actual HTML is relatively simple.

This example creates a two-paned frame system that uses one frame as a navigational tool, while using the main, larger frame for displaying information. The first step is to map out exactly how the framed site should operate.

This enables you to visualize how the site will work and what HTML files must be created.

## Next, Add the *<FRAMESET>* Tag

The first file you must create tells Netscape how to divide the screen logically using some new tags. The first pair consists of the <FRAMESET> and </FRAMESET> tags. In your Web page, this pair of tags replaces the <BODY> and </BODY> tags.

When you use <FRAMESET>, you need to use additional keywords to signify whether you are splitting the Netscape window into different rows or columns. For example, to split your Netscape window into two columns of equal width, use COLS= as follows (see Figure 24.15):

```
<FRAMESET COLS="50%,50%">
</FRAMESET>
```

**FIG. 24.15**
These two columns of frames are of equal width.

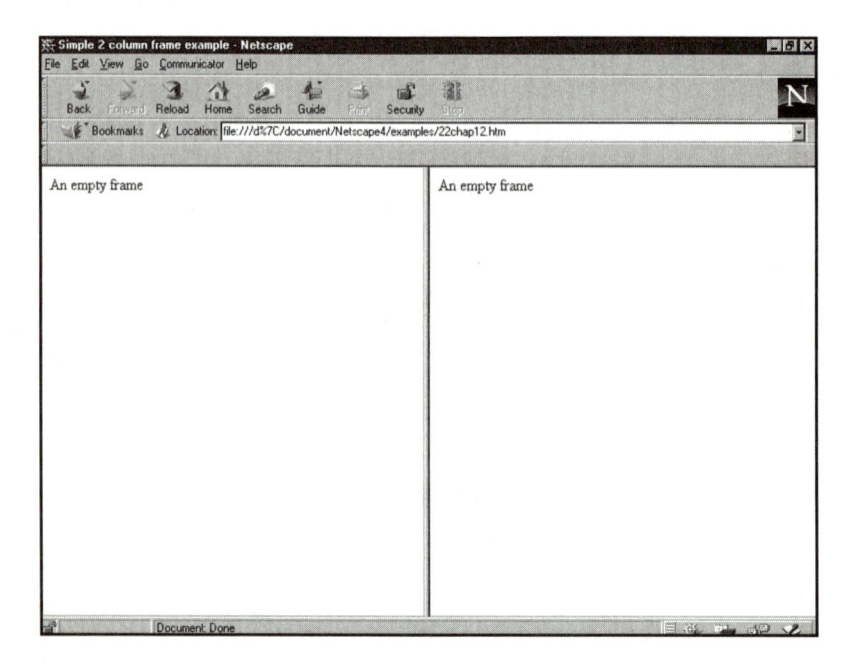

Likewise, to create two distinct rows on your Web page, use ROWS= as follows (see Figure 24.16):

```
<FRAMESET ROWS="60%,40%">
</FRAMESET>
```

**FIG. 24.16**
These two rows of frames are of different height.

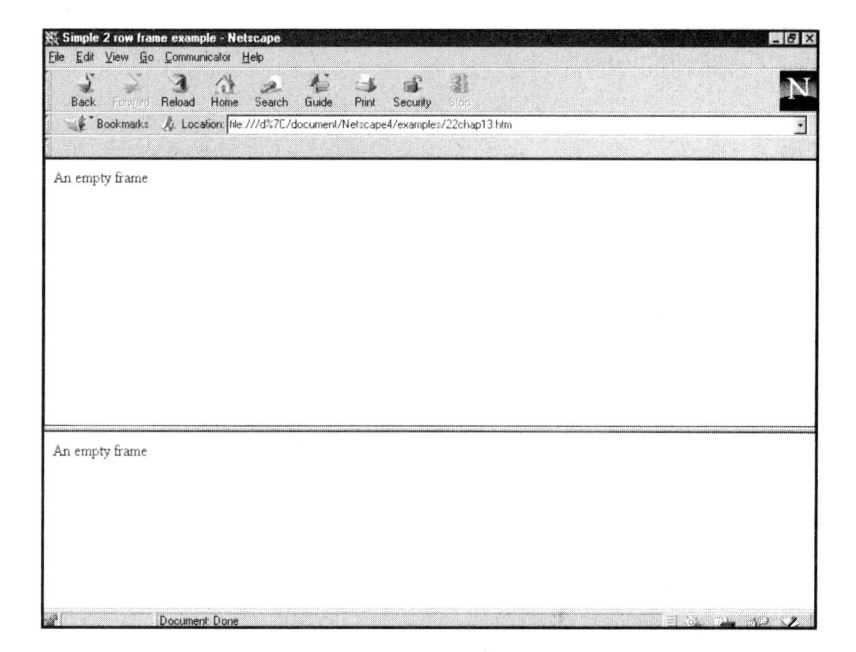

You are telling Netscape that you want to split the screen into two rows that take up 60 and 40 percent of the screen, respectively. You can tell Netscape to create as many rows and columns as you want, as long as the total percentage adds up to 100 percent.

> **TIP** In case your percentages don't quite add up to 100 percent, Netscape recalculates the proportions for you. For example, you might accidentally use the following:
>
> ```
> <FRAMESET COLS="33%,33%,33%,33%">
> </FRAMESET>
> ```
>
> Netscape assumes that you want to have four columns of 25 percent each. Although Netscape tries its best to figure out what you mean, you should spend extra time to make sure that your numbers add up, to avoid surprises on the finished page.

## Using Pixels Instead of Percentages

Instead of using percentages, you have other options when creating the dimensions of frames. You can indicate specific pixel counts. On standard VGA screens, the monitor displays 640 pixels horizontally and 480 pixels vertically. Super VGA dimensions are 800×600, and

## 506   Chapter 24   Organizing Content with Tables and Frames

extremely high-resolution monitors can display 1024×768 or higher. If you use actual pixel counts on your Web pages, it's best to assume that everyone is using a standard VGA monitor at 640×480.

Thus, to create four even rows of frames on-screen using pixel coordinates, you can use the following pair of tags (see Figure 24.17):

```
<FRAMESET ROWS="120,120,120,120">
</FRAMESET>
```

> **TIP** Notice in the HTML code listed (and shown in Figure 24.11) that the total pixel amount adds up to 480—this implies that you are using a VGA screen whose screen size measures 640×480 pixels. Netscape automatically interprets the meaning of this for SuperVGA and higher resolutions. In this example, you are actually using 800×600 resolution to divide your screen.

**FIG. 24.17**
Four frames of exactly the same pixel height.

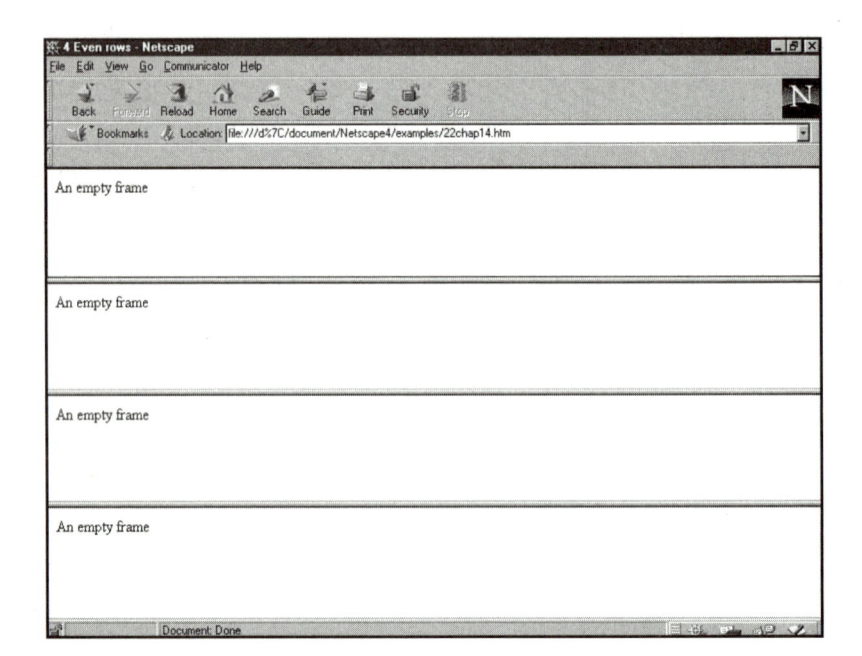

## Using the Asterisk

When telling Netscape to divide your screen, you can also use the asterisk (*) as a wild card when specifying the height or width. Consider the following example:

```
<FRAMESET ROWS="100,*,100">
</FRAMESET>
```

These tags create three rows of frames. The top and bottom rows are exactly 100 pixels tall, and the middle frame is the leftover amount. This method is extremely useful when building frames, because you can disregard whether the visitor's screen resolution is 640×480 or

http://www.quecorp.com

1024×768. The top and bottom frames are always the same size, and the browser makes sure that the variable number adds up correctly. Figure 24.18 shows this example on-screen that has a resolution of 800×600.

**FIG. 24.18**
The asterisk can create a "remainder" frame size so you don't have to worry about the exact numbers in pixels or percentages.

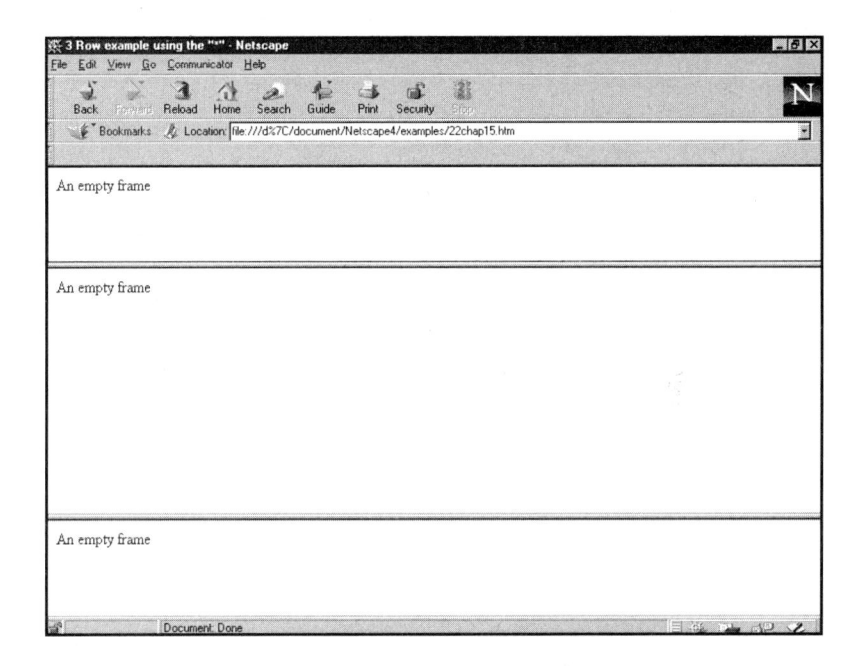

> **N O T E** The asterisk also can be used to create frames of relative sizes. Consider the following example:

```
<FRAMESET ROWS="*,2*,*">
</FRAMESET>
```

Here, you are requesting three frames. The first gets 25 percent of the screen, the second gets 50 percent, and the third gets 25 percent.

How does Netscape figure this? It creates a simple algebraic equation using * as a variable, and using 100 percent for the total screen height (for rows) or total screen width (for columns). In this example, the equation is:

`* + 2* + * = 100%`

When this equation is solved—* = 25%—Netscape replaces * with 25 percent to figure out the frame sizes, and ends up allocating frames of 25 percent, 50 percent, and 25 percent.

Using an asterisk this way lets you develop frames that work for every visitor regardless of screen resolution.

> **CAUTION**
>
> Be careful not to divide your screen into too many frames, lest they become unusable. Consider this pair of tags:
>
> ```
> <FRAMESET COLS="10%,10%,10%,10%,10%,10%,10%,10%,10%,10%">
> </FRAMESET>
> ```
>
> The preceding tag does add up to 100 percent, but displaying 10 separate frames on a single Web page is overkill. As a general rule, more than five rows or columns on a single page tends to be too much—and even fewer frames than that can be overwhelming, depending on what's in them.

## Including the <FRAME> Tag

After you've decided how to split up your screen into multiple frames, the next step is to tell Netscape which HTML file to display in each frame, and set several options for how the file should appear on-screen. The syntax of the <FRAME> tag is similar to incorporating an image on your Web page, and this tag must appear within the <FRAMESET> and </FRAMESET> tags.

The number of <FRAME> tags must correspond to the number of frames indicated by the <FRAMESET> tag. Consider this example:

```
<FRAMESET COLS="30%,70%">
<FRAME SRC="cartoon.htm" NAME="Navigation Window">
<FRAME SRC="welcome.htm" NAME="Cartoon Window">
</FRAMESET>
```

Here, you tell Netscape to divide the screen into two frames (columns). The left frame displays the HTML file named cartoon.htm and the right frame displays welcome.htm. Figure 24.19 shows these frames in Netscape.

Notice the NAME= keyword within the <FRAME> tag. This keyword names each frame for Netscape's benefit, and lets you access the frames separately. You'll learn more about NAME= in a moment. With the new frame setup in this example, the TOC always stays on the left, while the frame on the right changes, depending on which link is selected. Figure 24.20 shows the Netscape window after clicking Winnie the Pooh.

> **NOTE** When completing the SRC="" portion of the <FRAME> tag, you can insert any valid URL between the quotation marks. This example simply referenced two local files that are stored in the same subdirectory as the file for the page.

To access a file within the CARTOON sub-directory, for instance, you use the following tag:

```
<FRAME SRC="CARTOON/cartoon.htm">
```

To access a directory one level above the current directory you use .., as follows:

```
<FRAME SRC="../cartoon.htm">
```

You can use this concept to access files several directories above the current directory. The following example points to a file three directories above:

```
<FRAME SRC="../../../cartoon.htm">
```

http://www.quecorp.com

Building Simple Frames | 509

You can even link to other Web pages on the Internet. For example, with this tag, you link to a foreign WWW site that has this cartoon file:

```
<FRAME SRC="http://www.shafran.com/enhancing/cartoon.htm">
```

**FIG. 24.19**
These two frames are the backbone for this cartoon Web page.

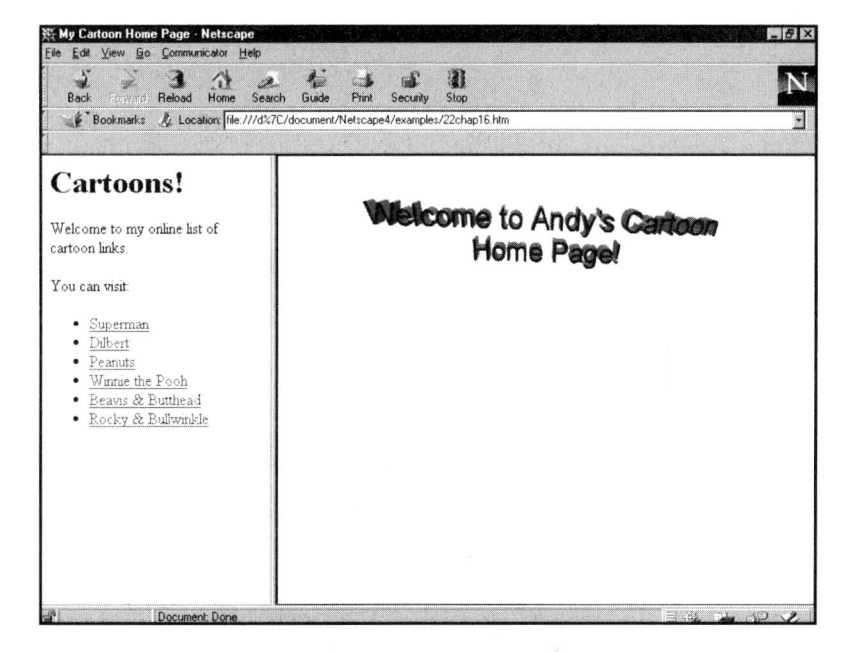

**FIG. 24.20**
These two frames let you easily visit every cartoon site within moments.

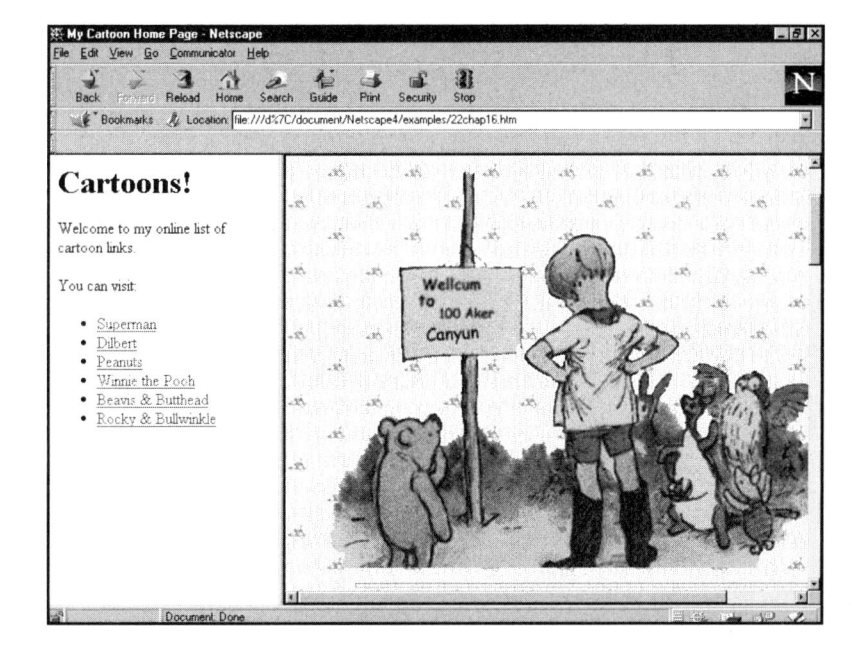

**The *NORESIZE* Keyword**   Several other keywords can be added to the `<FRAME>` tag, including `NORESIZE`. Without this keyword, visitors to your Web page can shift and move the column and row boundaries if they want. People can simply move the frame boundaries by moving their mouse over a frame border and dragging it up and down or left and right to set it for their preferences.

To ensure that your frames appear exactly as you've specified, add `NORESIZE` to the `<FRAME>` tag:

```
<FRAME SRC="cartoon.htm" NAME="Navigation Window" NORESIZE>
```

In most situations, you don't need to add this keyword. People generally don't resize frames. Think carefully before adding this tag, because it means that visitors with different screen resolutions will not be able to make your page work better for them by changing how the frames appear.

**Control Scrolling**   Another keyword you can add is `SCROLLING`. This keyword indicates whether or not scroll bars should be added to frames in which some text or image is too big to fit, given the frame size specification. You can set `SCROLLING` to `YES`, `NO`, or `AUTO`. By default, it is set to `AUTO`, meaning that Netscape adds scroll bars when it deems them necessary.

Usually, you don't bother with the scroll bar settings, but sometimes you might want to permanently suppress them by adding `SCROLLING=NO` to your tag. Figure 24.21 shows you an example of scroll bars that get in the way.

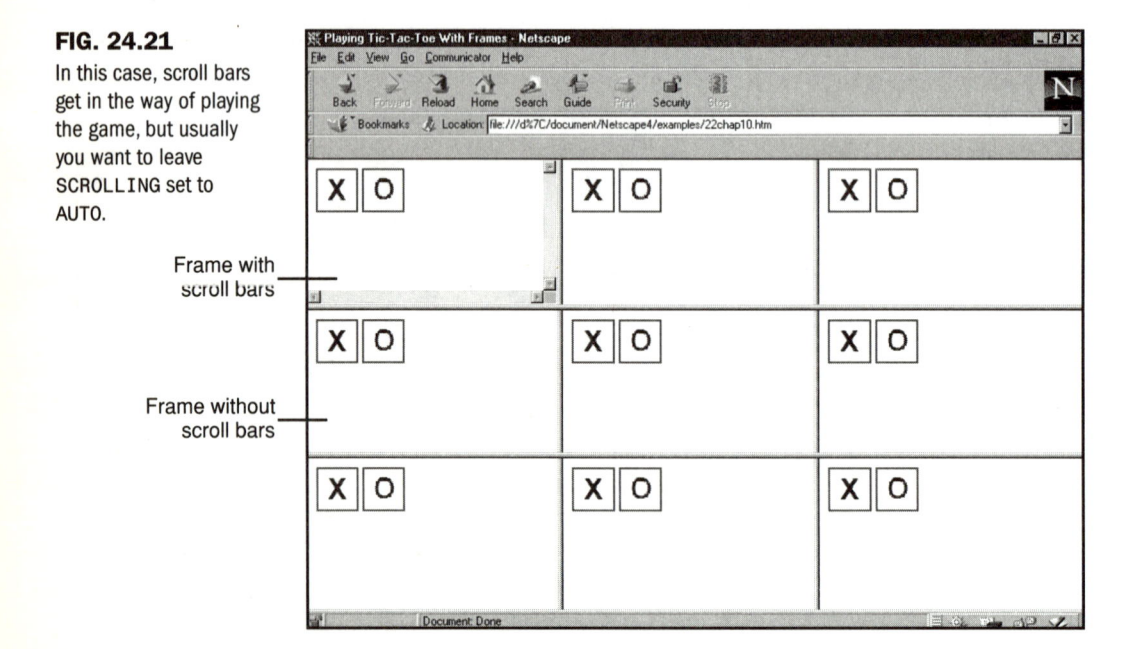

**FIG. 24.21**
In this case, scroll bars get in the way of playing the game, but usually you want to leave SCROLLING set to AUTO.

## Creating Links to Each Frame

After your frame is built, you're almost finished. The last step is to learn another keyword that Netscape recognizes when creating hypertext links. With the <A HREF= > tag you can use the TARGET= keyword to tell Netscape which frame you want the linked text to appear in; the default is the current frame that's selected. Remember how you named the frames earlier in the section "Including the <FRAME> Tag"? Use those names to explain to Netscape which frame you want to use for loading certain things.

For the cartoon example, the left frame remains on-screen as a TOC. When a visitor clicks a specific cartoon in the left frame, therefore, the appropriate linked HTML file appears in the right frame. When building the list of links on the left, each one uses TARGET=. Here's a snippet of HTML from the cartoon.htm file:

```
<UL>
<LI><A HREF="http://www.unitedmedia.com/comics/dilbert" TARGET="Cartoon
Window">Dilbert</A>
<LI><A HREF="http://www.unitedmedia.com/comics/peanuts" TARGET="Cartoon
Window">Peanuts</A>
<LI><A HREF="http://www.midtown.net/~olen/pooh" TARGET="Cartoon Window">Winnie
the Pooh</A>
<LI><A HREF="http://mindlink.net/charles_ulrich/frostbite.html" TARGET="Cartoon
Window">Rocky & Bullwinkle</A>
</UL>
```

Whenever one of the links is selected from the TOC listing, Netscape goes out and retrieves the linked text, then displays it in the frame named "Cartoon Window," leaving the TOC frame unchanged.

> **TIP** Make sure that the value you use for the target is exactly the same as the value you typed when naming the window.

## Other Target Keywords

When building links and targets, there are a few other options you should know. Netscape recognizes certain values that always work the same with TARGET=, regardless of how you have named your frames:

- TARGET="_blank"—This brings up an entirely new window of Netscape to display the linked information.
- TARGET="_self"—This tells Netscape to display the linked information in the frame where this URL is displayed (useful for the tic-tac-toe example).
- TARGET="_parent"—This tells Netscape to display the linked information in the frame previous to the current document; this is seldom used.
- TARGET="_top"—This tells Netscape to load the linked information into a completely new screen of Netscape, not divided into any frames.

> **TIP** Remember to add `TARGET="_top"` to any links that take the user away from your Web site. If you don't specify this, the frame characteristics you set for your screen remain the same as users go on to browse other parts of the Web.

# Advanced Frame Features

Now that you're familiar with adding simple frames to your Web page, you're ready to learn some advanced ways that frames can be used.

This section shows you how to include both rows and columns on your Web page (like the tic-tac-toe board), and how to build recursive frames. This section shows you how to set up your page so that users without a current version of Netscape don't see a bunch of gibberish when visiting your frame-enabled site.

## Working with Multiple Frames

So far, you know how to add rows or columns to your home page, but sometimes you may want to use both. All you need to do is to embed additional `<FRAMESET>` tags within the first pair of tags, and make sure that they work together.

Let's say you want to add two new rows to the cartoon screen: one across the top and one across the bottom. The top one is a standard header that is included on every Web page at this site, and the bottom one is the footer that includes an e-mail address and other valuable information.

First, define the number of rows that you want on-screen: three. Next, to split the middle row into two columns, build two levels of `<FRAMESET>` tags:

```
<FRAMESET ROWS="70,*,50">
    <FRAME SRC="myheader.htm" NAME="Header Window">
    <FRAMESET COLS="30%,70%">
        <FRAME SRC="cartoon.htm" NAME="Navigation Window">
        <FRAME SRC="welcome.htm" NAME="Cartoon Window">
    </FRAMESET>
    <FRAME SRC="myfooter.htm" NAME="Footer Window">
</FRAMESET>
```

Figure 24.22 shows the new cartoon Web page after clicking Superman.

> **CAUTION** Every time you embed tags within tags, make sure you have the appropriate closing tags in your HTML file. In this example, for instance, two `</FRAMESET>` tags are needed or Netscape doesn't display the frames correctly.

http://www.quecorp.com

**FIG. 24.22**
With four frames, this cartoon Web page is just about finished.

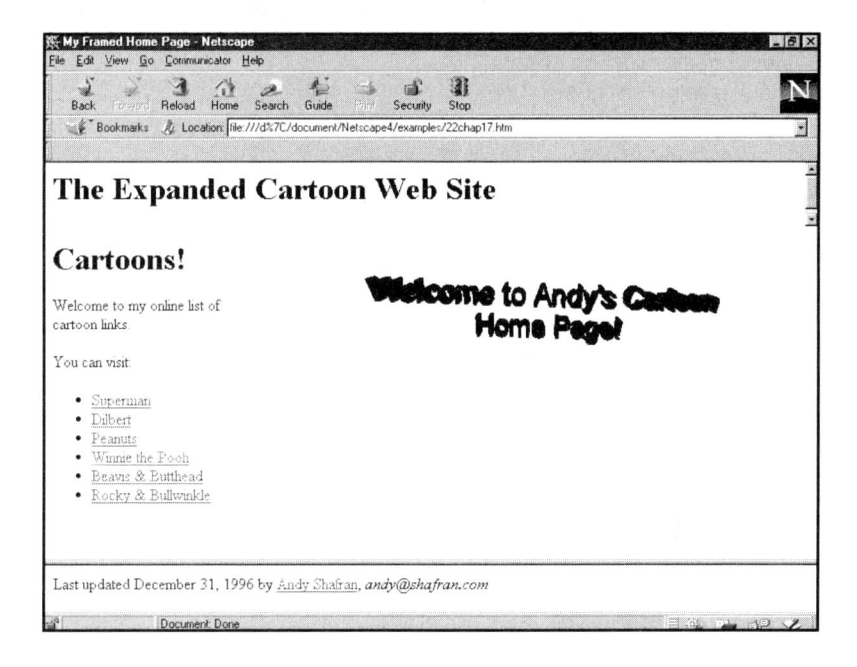

## Another Example Using Multiple Frames

For the tic-tac-toe game shown earlier, the screen was divided equally into spaced rows. Then, each row was equally divided into three columns per row. The HTML is still relatively simple, and you can see how each frame is specified:

```
<FRAMESET ROWS="33%,33%,33%">
     <FRAMESET COLS="33%,33%,33%">
          <FRAME SRC="choose.htm">
          <FRAME SRC="choose.htm">
          <FRAME SRC="choose.htm">
     </FRAMESET>
     <FRAMESET COLS="33%,33%,33%">
          <FRAME SRC="choose.htm">
          <FRAME SRC="choose.htm">
          <FRAME SRC="choose.htm">
     </FRAMESET>
     <FRAMESET COLS="33%,33%,33%">
          <FRAME SRC="choose.htm">
          <FRAME SRC="choose.htm">
          <FRAME SRC="choose.htm">
     </FRAMESET>
</FRAMESET>
```

This section of HTML produces the table that you saw earlier in this chapter in Figure 24.13. The HTML within choose.htm is extremely similar:

```
<BODY>
<A HREF="bigx.gif"> <IMG SRC="littlex.gif"> </A>
<A HREF="bigo.gif"> <IMG SRC="littleo.gif"> </A>
</BODY>
```

All this file does is displays two small images for each frame—a small x and a small o. If the small x is clicked, for example, then the frame links to an image of a larger X.

> **NOTE** You may have noticed that NAME= isn't used for these nine individual frames. It's unnecessary. Because they're not named, Netscape automatically replaces the frame that has the file linked to it. So, as the game is played, the big X or O replaces the two smaller letters in whichever frame is clicked.

## Frames Within Frames

Another innovative way to include frames on your Web pages is by recursively adding frames within frames. You can build frames within frames within frames, and so on. All you have to do is add the appropriate `<FRAMESET>` and `<FRAME>` tags.

For example, in the tic-tac-toe file, each of the nine frames displays an X or an O. Figure 24.23 shows how Netscape appears when each of the nine tic-tac-toe frames are told to build another set of nine frames inside of itself.

**FIG. 24.23**
This super tic-tac-toe board has two levels of recursive frames so that 81 separate areas appear on-screen.

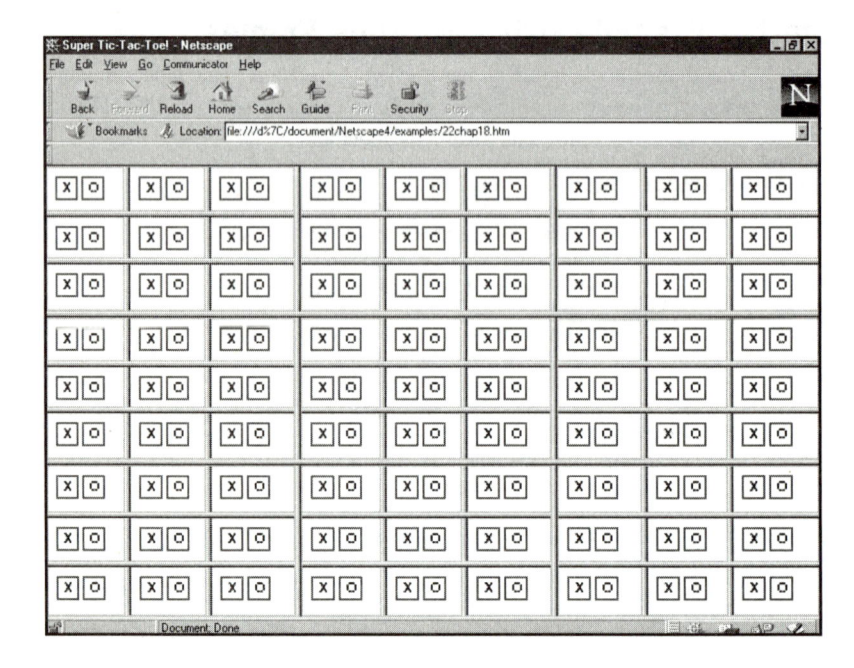

Use recursive frames carefully, because too many different frames on-screen can easily confuse visitors to your Web site, and they can also slow down performance. It takes about 30 seconds to load this Super Tic-Tac-Toe example to see all of the 81 frames and 162 little images, even when all the files are on your local computer.

## Designing for Non-Frame-Capable Browsers

Realizing that not all Web browsers are created the same, Netscape has built in an additional tag to make sure your Web pages look good to non-frame-capable users. Using <NOFRAMES> and </NOFRAMES>, you can mark text that appears only when a visitor stops by your Web site with a browser that doesn't support frames.

When a Netscape 2.0 (or Internet Explorer 3.0) or better browser stops by, it automatically ignores the text specified in the <NOFRAMES> tag. When a non-Netscape 2.0 browser stops by, it ignores the commands within the <FRAMESET> and <FRAME> tags, and only displays the information specified by <NOFRAMES>.

With the <NOFRAMES> tag pair, you can create regular HTML files, including lists and tables, and even link to images and other sites. Some sites spend time creating two sites—a frame and non-frame site—but this can be difficult and time consuming.

Alternatively, use the <NOFRAMES> tag to display a short message to non-Netscape 2.0 users urging them to get a newer version of Netscape and then return back to this Web page:

```
<NOFRAMES>
<H1> This page is no fun for you. </H1>
<HR>
Because I use frames on my Web page, you won't be able to experience my page as
I've designed it. Try downloading Netscape 2.0 or better and then coming back
here to see my site in its full glory.
<P>
<B>Andy Shafran</B>
</NOFRAMES>
```

Make sure that your <NOFRAMES> tags appear between the <FRAMESET> and </FRAMESET> tags in order to work correctly with current versions of Netscape.

The decision to exclude non-Netscape users or to work twice as hard for a simple Web page is yours.

## Borderless Frames

One of the biggest complaints with using frames to organize a Web site is the creation of separate frames in a single browser. Many times you might want to achieve the effect of using frames on a site, but don't want bothersome columns interfering with how your Web page appears.

Realizing this, Netscape added a new specialized keyword that can be used within the <FRAME> or <FRAMESET> tags. By adding FRAMEBORDER=NO to either of these tags, visitors do not see the

**516** Chapter 24 Organizing Content with Tables and Frames

separating pane between individual frames. Figure 24.24 shows an example of an online book at Que which uses borderless frames. There are actually three frames on this site (**http://www.mcp.com/que/developer_expert/lotus45/lotus45.html**).

**FIG. 24.24**
No one can tell where each frame ends and the next one begins.

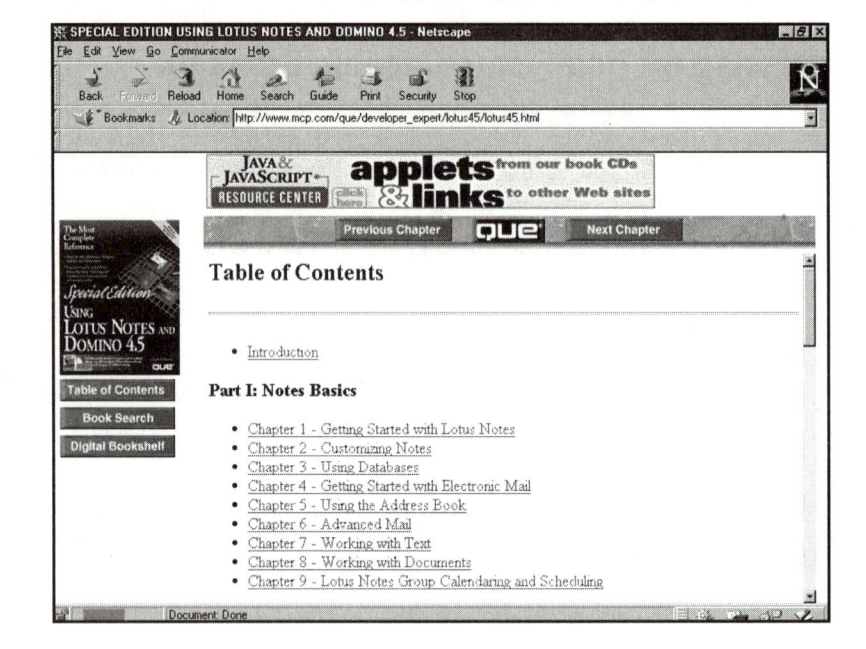

## Alternatives to Frames

The presentation possibilities with frames are spectacular. With this Netscape enhancement, you have significantly more control over how your page appears, and can make it easier for people to peruse your whole site.

Frames are not, however, the perfect solution to every situation. Sometimes you want to design Web pages for people who use a non-frame-capable browser, and other times frames just don't fit the purpose you are trying to achieve. This section takes a quick look at some practical alternatives to frames, and shows you how they can be used in your Web pages.

### Tables

Tables and frames have a lot in common with each other. They both require a handful of HTML tags, help you to line up the correct number of rows and columns on-screen, and give you a lot of flexibility when displaying information.

http://www.quecorp.com

Tables let you split the parts of your screen into different cells of information. They work differently than frames because tables don't link to separate HTML files to be displayed in the corresponding cells. All the information for building a table is in a single file.

The cartoon page could easily be created using tables instead of frames, but it would have to be designed much differently. Because tables don't actually split the screen, you could never view two different sites at once. Whenever a cartoon listed in the table is clicked, the whole window would be replaced by the new site.

As a general rule, tables are a great idea for displaying information in Netscape. The cell display and formatting capabilities make them ideal for comparing information or listing it in a usable fashion—but not for creating an interface to your Web pages.

## Navigation Button Bars

The precursor to frames is the technique of creating a customized navigation bar at the top or bottom of the screen. Several icons are displayed, and, when clicked, each icon takes you to a different URL.

These bars are nice because you can use them to link from page to page easily. Such bars still make sense when letting users navigate your Web site, but these days many people are putting them in a frame that stays put at the bottom of the screen (recall the Netscape home page we looked at earlier). That way, no matter what information is displayed in the top window, the navigation bar stays put and is always available for clicking.

If you use a customized button bar, however, don't feel obligated to start including support for frames in your site. Think through how people will visit your Web site, and be sure it makes sense before you build a special frame for the navigation icons.

## Well-Organized Web Sites

The best alternative to using frames at your Web site is careful and thorough planning. Using frames introduces a different way to display Web pages that might not fit in with what your site already has available. For example, if the first thing visitors see is a big picture of you or your company's logo, then adding a frame to split up the page may distract the user from what you want him to see.

If you keep close track of how your pages link to each other, and make it easy for people to browse your site, then there may be no need to add frames. Test your Web page to see if there is an appropriate number of hypertext links, if information is displayed in a concise and simple format, and if your progression of links follows a logical order. These factors are usually enough to make a site successful. ●

CHAPTER 25

# Building Navigational Imagemaps

*by Andrew Shafran*

One feature you see in some of the more advanced home pages is imagemaps. These are simply Web graphics with certain designated areas that go to different URLs. Imagemaps are inherently easier to use than regular text links because there's no need to explain what the link does. A person doesn't have to read where a link might take him, he just sees it.

Though this might sound like imagemaps should be used everywhere, that's not true. There are some things to consider before using imagemaps. You also have to make sure it makes sense to put in imagemaps.

This chapter discusses the ins and outs of adding imagemaps to your Web pages, taking advantage of the Netscape technology that makes creating imagemaps easier than ever. Anyone can add an imagemap, called a *client-side imagemap*, to her Web page in a matter of minutes. ■

- **What imagemaps are and how they work**
  Visual imagemaps allow Web developers to graphically organize and design Web sites.

- **How to choose appropriate imagemap graphics**
  Understand what images make good imagemaps.

- **Tell the difference between client-side and server-side imagemaps**
  Imagemaps can be created in two different fashions that are both in use today.

- **Basic elements of laying out your imagemap**
  Create various shapes and sections on a graphic that link to different HTML files.

- **Decipher the new HTML tags that support client-side imagemaps**
  Work with the <MAP> tag that defines imagemaps to Netscape.

- **Build a simple imagemap for your Web page with a simple, free tool—MapThis!**
  Creating imagemaps is a straightforward process when you use the right tools.

## How Do Imagemaps Work?

You are already familiar with adding inline graphics to Web pages. By embedding the `<IMG>` tag inside a hypertext reference, you can create links from images, just as you would from text. Look at the following HTML example:

```
<A HREF="ROME.HTML"> <IMG SRC="ROME.GIF"> </A>
```

Shown in Figure 25.1, this example adds an image of the Coliseum in Rome to this Web page. When visitors click the image, Netscape automatically loads the file `ROME.HTML`.

**FIG. 25.1**
Linking an image to an HTML page is easy to do.

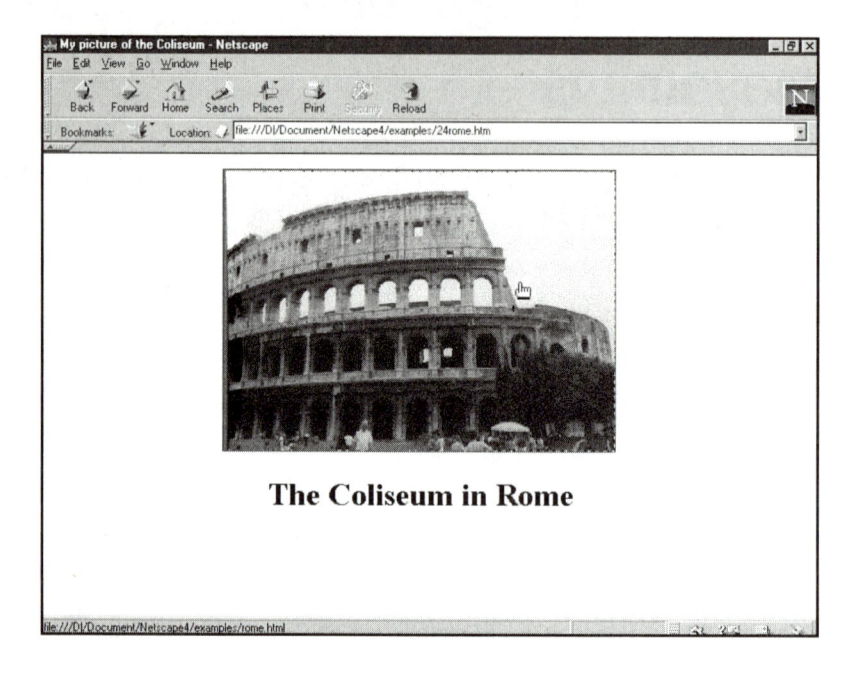

No matter where on the picture you click, Netscape always links to `ROME.HTML`. This is where an imagemap could come into play. Using an imagemap, you can link different areas of an image to different HTML files, based on what section of the image is clicked.

This is an extremely useful technique, because it lets visitors who see this Web page get accustomed to a single image and navigate from page-to-page by clicking different sections of that image.

Look at the Magnavox home page (**http://www.magnavox.com**) for an excellent example of an imagemap (see Figure 25.2). Here, the developers have included a picture of a remote control with several buttons drawn on it. Each section of the image brings you to a different spot on the Magnavox Web site. For example, clicking Company Info in the image brings up information about Magnavox, while you can easily imagine what kind of stuff appears when you click Fun & Games.

http://www.quecorp.com

## How Do Imagemaps Work? 521

**FIG. 25.2**
Magnavox's imagemap is smart—very smart.

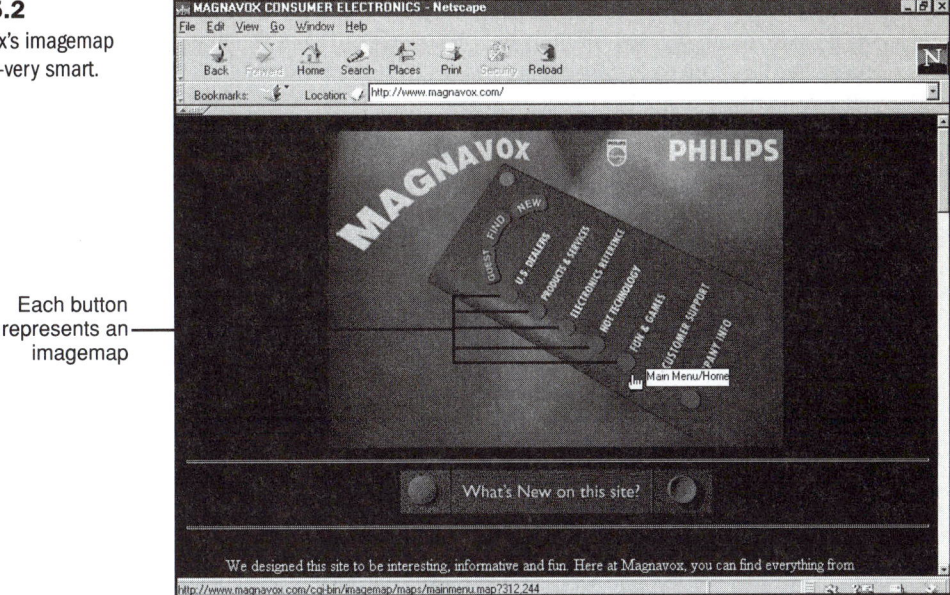

Each button represents an imagemap

There are many good uses for imagemaps. For example, Italy might place a virtual map online. Using your mouse, you would click whichever region or city in Italy you wanted to learn more about. Clicking Rome might bring up the Coliseum, and Pisa could link to the famous leaning tower. Or, as another example, Boeing might place a picture of its new 777 plane on the WWW. Visitors could click different parts of the cockpit to learn how the plane operates.

Virtually any image can become an imagemap—and they're easy to create. With the right tools, imagemaps can easily be designed and incorporated into a Web site within minutes.

▶ **See** Chapter 22, "HTML Primer," on **P. 435** for more information on basic HTML tags

## Imagemaps Are Not New Technology

Clickable imagemaps have been around for a long time—since the early versions of Netscape. You have always been able to add one to your Web page if you knew the right steps to follow. Recently though, adding imagemaps to your Web page has become significantly simpler.

Previously, to add a clickable imagemap to your Web page, you were dependent on your Web server software. Your server software controls all access to Web pages at a particular Internet site. To add an imagemap to your page, you had to find the right image, decide how each part of the image would link to a different HTML file, and then set up and customize your server properly. This was quite a hassle, even for those people who could understand every step; and some Web servers don't even *permit* imagemaps to run on them. Therefore, using imagemaps on Web pages was effectively limited to professional Web developers and larger companies; few individuals used imagemaps on personal Web pages.

Today, though, creating imagemaps is much easier. A new development called *client-side imagemaps* makes it easier for individual Web page developers—like you—to add a clickable imagemap to a Web page. More imagemaps are being created every day because of their relative ease-of-use.

▶ **See** Chapter 33, "Netscape Servers," on **P. 667** for more information on working with a Web server.

## Server-Side and Client-Side Imagemap Differences

As previously mentioned, server-side imagemaps have been around for a couple of years, but they were awkward to use and had several disadvantages. In this section, you learn exactly how server-side imagemaps run and why they've been pushed aside for newer technology.

Here's how a server-side imagemap works. When visiting a Web page, you might see a large image that has several different sections on it that are clearly delineated. Each section, when clicked, looks like it takes you to a different Web page. After looking at the image for a while, you click one area (such as one of the buttons on the Magnavox remote control in an earlier example in this chapter), presumably to take you to a corresponding page of HTML. Netscape stores the coordinates that you clicked in X,Y-pixel coordinates and then sends that information to the Web server. The server takes those coordinates and runs a separate CGI program that translates those coordinates into an URL—the file name of the linked area clicked. Then the Web server sends that file name back to Netscape, which goes and loads the correct file.

As you probably can gather, server-side imagemaps aren't very efficient and can be difficult to use for the following reasons:

- Server-side imagemaps cannot be used when running your site locally off a hard drive, because they require direct interaction with a Web server.

- Not everyone can use server-side imagemaps. To create this type of imagemap, you need access to execute a CGI program on your Web server. Many WWW sites do not permit CGI access, and, thus, you cannot include a server-side imagemap at your site.

- Because server-side imagemaps require a separate transaction with the Web server, they take a few extra moments to sync up the server and Netscape client before going to the selected HTML file.

- They can bog down Web servers. If you have a Web server that is extremely popular, it can spend all its time running the special program that translates pixel coordinates into an HTML file. This puts a heavier load on the Web server and slows access for everyone reading pages at that particular Web site.

Fortunately, a new type of imagemap has taken the WWW by storm. Client-side imagemaps (called CSIM, for short) are significantly simpler, easier to use, and are more efficient when interacting with Web servers. As far as users can tell, the same image appears on-screen, but what happens when they click the image is different. Instead of exchanging information with the Web server, Netscape automatically knows which HTML file to link to—and takes them there automatically. This process is significantly quicker to process (you don't have to wait for the Web server) and easier for Netscape to interpret. Each region in the image has its pixel coordinates defined within the same HTML file as the rest of the Web page; so Netscape can link to another page of HTML just as if it was using a normal <A HREF> tag.

Client-side imagemaps are more efficient, easier to create, and better for users who visit your Web pages. Eventually, client-side imagemaps will entirely replace imagemaps that are dependent on the Web server.

> **NOTE** You always can tell whether you are using a server-side imagemap or a client-side one. Take a look at the status bar at the bottom of the Netscape screen while you move your mouse over an imagemap. If you see scrolling numbers, then you know it's a server-side imagemap (those pixel coordinates are sent to the server when you click). If you see a file name instead of coordinates, then you're using a client-side imagemap.

> ▶ **See** Chapter 26, "Creating Forms and Server Scripts," on **P. 537** for more information on working with CGI scripts.

# Creating an Imagemap

Now that you understand the difference between the two types of imagemap technologies, it is time to see how to build an imagemap on a Web page. You'll see a step-by-step process for building and adding an imagemap. This chapter focuses almost entirely on creating client-side imagemaps for your Web pages.

This section creates an actual imagemap from start to finish. You'll learn how to select the right kinds of images, link the different areas to separate HTML files, and add the correct tags to your Web page.

## Finding a Good Image

When creating imagemaps, the first step is selecting a good image to use. You want to make sure that visitors who see the image understand that there are several different areas on the picture they can select to link to different items. You need to select definitive images that have different regions easily delineated on-screen and that make sense to visitors.

Figure 25.3 shows a sample image that makes for an excellent client-side imagemap for the ACME Block Company.

> **TIP** Images that are mapped tend to have larger file sizes because they usually appear larger on-screen than other graphics, such as icons and bullets, found on Web pages. Make sure that your image's file size isn't outrageous (for instance, above 100K); otherwise, visitors to your Web page might become impatient.

Imagemaps can be created from virtually any graphic you can add to your Web page. Icons, buttons, bars, pictures, and images of all types can be sectioned out and presented as an imagemap for visitors. Not all images, however, make sense for use as imagemaps. In general, pictures become difficult imagemaps because they often lack clearly defined areas for the user to click. Recall the picture of the Coliseum earlier in the chapter (refer to Figure 25.1)? That image wouldn't make a good imagemap because there aren't any well-defined areas other than the large image of the Coliseum.

**FIG. 25.3**
The big blocks make it easy for users to identify the different regions of the imagemap.

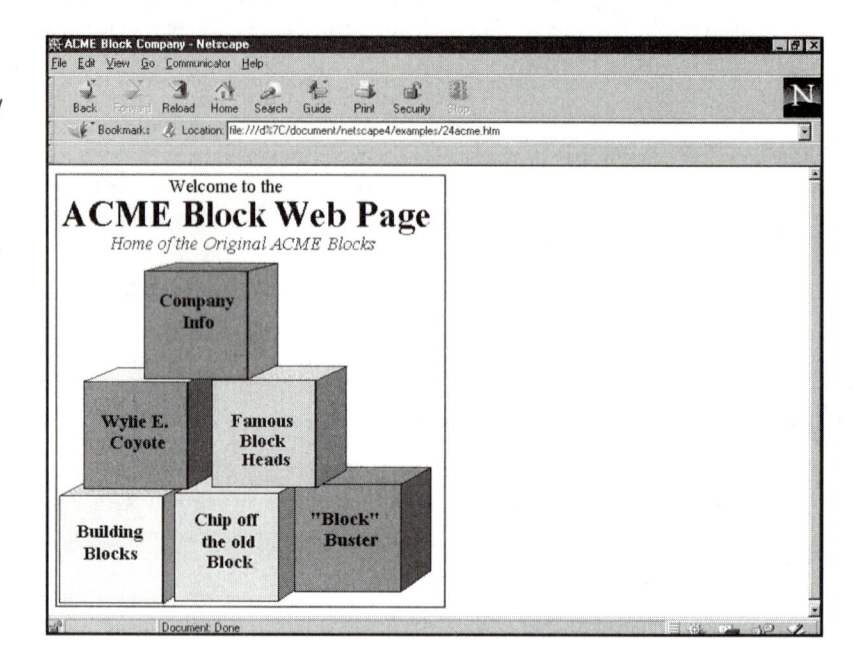

People and animals aren't always bad candidates for imagemaps, but you need to make sure that users understand they can access different Web pages by clicking different parts of the image (for instance, body parts). Visit **http://www.cs.brown.edu/people/oa/Bin/skeleton.html** for a prime example of how a picture of a person (in this case, a skeleton) can be used as an imagemap (see Figure 25.4).

You can use a graphics or paint program to create images that can serve as imagemaps. For example, the block image (refer to Figure 25.3) was created in Paint Shop Pro, a graphics editing application that allows you to customize, optimize, and modify images.

> **TIP** Use interlaced GIFs or Progressive JPEGs when working with imagemaps. Interlaced and Progressive images are those that load in multiple levels, starting out fuzzy and slowly becoming more detailed. These types of graphics are ideal for imagemaps because as soon as visitors recognize which area they want to click, they don't have to wait for the whole image to appear. Learn more about creating interlaced images in *Creating Your Own Web Graphics with Paint Shop Pro*, also published by Que.

http://www.quecorp.com

**FIG. 25.4**
Clicking various parts of this skeleton brings you to specific information about that particular bone.

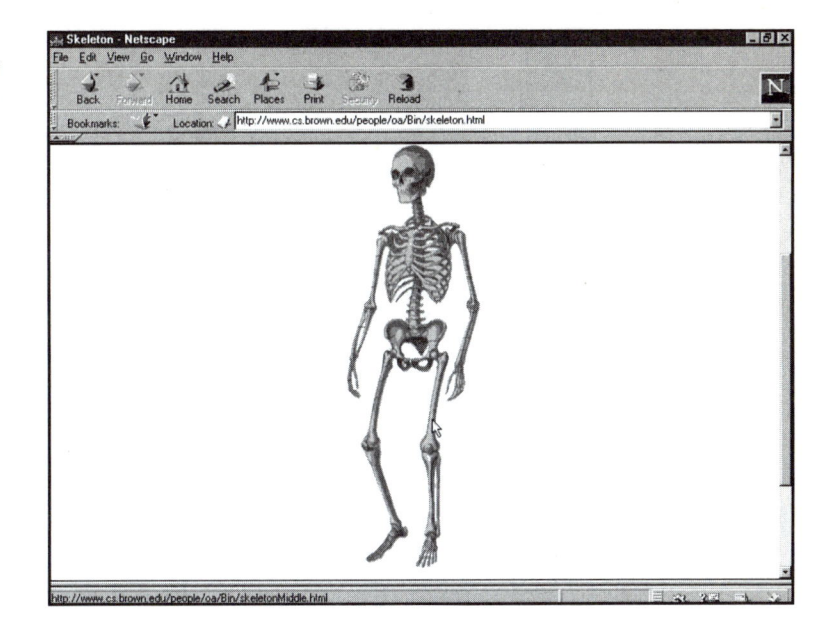

## Planning the Map

After you've selected an image, the next step is to logically divide it into different regions and define how you want the imagemap to work.

For this sample block graphic, each individual block should be linked to a separate Web page (see Figure 25.5).

After you have a good idea of how to divide your imagemap, you're ready to move to the next step—adding the necessary HTML tags to your Web page.

> **CAUTION**
> Make sure that each HTML file your image links to exists. It's easy to forget to create one or more of the HTML files if you create your imagemap when they don't all exist.

## Adding the Image to Your Web Page

With the correct image selected, it's time to start learning the new HTML tags that support client-side imagemaps. Adding imagemaps is similar to adding regular images except that you need a new keyword and a couple of new tags. Fortunately, you don't have to learn all the complicated HTML if you don't want to; this section focuses on a useful tool that avoids all that work.

**FIG. 25.5**
Planning each link from your imagemap is an important step.

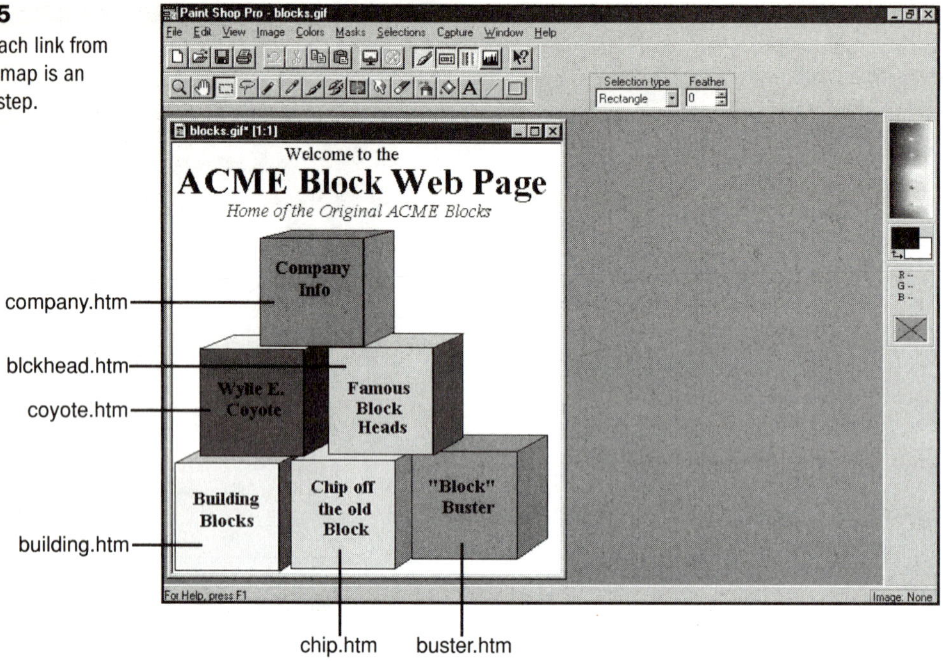

If you're going to add the proper HTML yourself, first embed the image into your Web page using the <IMG> tag with the USEMAP keyword:

<IMG SRC="BLOCKS.GIF" USEMAP="#ACME Block Image Map">

This tag tells Netscape to display BLOCKS.GIF on the Web page. USEMAP tells Netscape that the image is a client-side clickable imagemap and to look for the named section ACME Block Image Map in this HTML file. This named section of HTML tells Netscape how to interpret clicks on different coordinates of the image.

The # is very important because that's how Netscape recognizes named references within a file.

**N O T E** Netscape makes you name each set of imagemap coordinates so you can have multiple client-side imagemaps within a single page.

## Mapping Your Image

With the image embedded in your Web page, the next step is to define each region on the image graphically. Think of each image as a large piece of graph paper, where you have to identify the exact X and Y coordinates for each section that links to an HTML file. For images, coordinates are measured in pixels (the dot resolution of your computer monitor). You have to specify the pixel dimensions of each section for it to properly link to an HTML file.

http://www.quecorp.com

Fortunately, several easy-to-use tools exist that make it easy for you to specify each distinct section of the imagemap. With Map This!, you use your mouse to draw each section on the image, and thereby create a link to an HTML file.

This section uses Map This! to create a complete imagemap from start to finish. Map This! can be found online at **http://galadriel.ecaetc.ohio-state.edu/tc/mt/**. Just follow these steps:

1. Start Map This!. A blank screen appears.
2. Choose File, New to create a new imagemap from scratch. The Make New Image Map dialog box appears (see Figure 25.6).

**FIG. 25.6**
First you need to tell Map This! which image you're mapping.

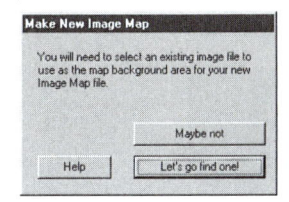

3. Click Okay to reach the Open Existing Image File dialog box (see Figure 25.7) where you can specify the image you want to map.

**FIG. 25.7**
Select your mapped image in the Open Existing Image File dialog box.

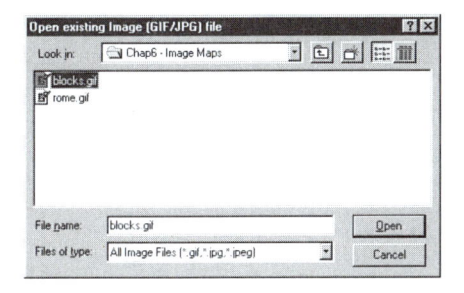

4. Select the image you want to edit (Map This! currently supports only GIF and JPEG image formats—not PNG) and then click Open to bring up the mapping window shown in Figure 25.8.
5. After the image is opened, you can draw three types of shapes to indicate sections on your image: rectangles, circles, and polygons. Click the shape you want to draw and then use your mouse to make your shape on the screen.
6. Draw as many different shapes and sections on your image as you need. For this sample image, there are six different sections, one for each of the blocks. Figure 25.9 shows the image with each section marked.

**FIG. 25.8**
From here, you can map the image with your mouse.

Use these icons to draw rectangles, circles, and polygons

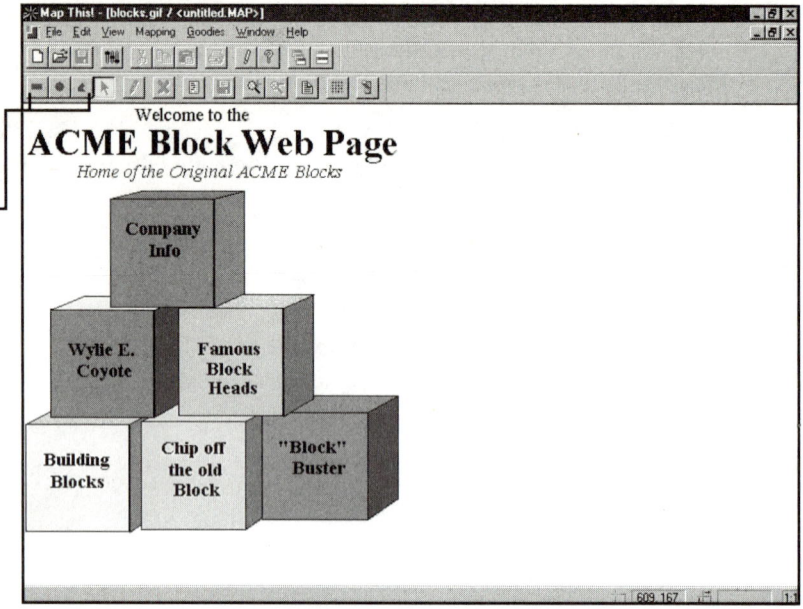

**FIG. 25.9**
Notice the six rectangles drawn around the significant blocks on the image.

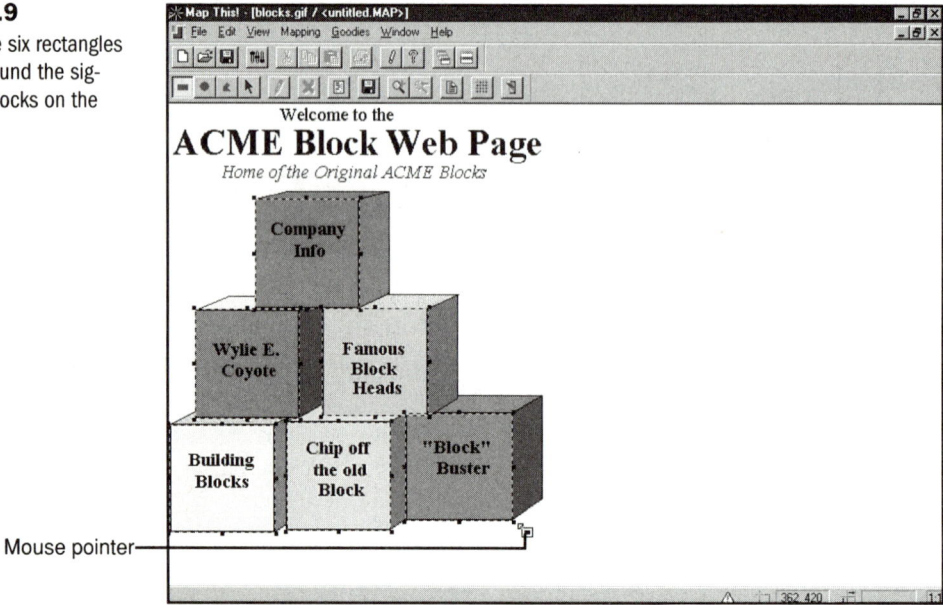

Mouse pointer

http://www.quecorp.com

Creating an Imagemap | 529

> **TIP** Define mapped areas clearly. Make sure you use an image that makes it easy for visitors to know which sections are mapped to other HTML files. It's easy for visitors to overlook small areas (or illogical areas) on an imagemap.

7. Now, click the Show/Hide Area List icon on the toolbar to bring up the Area List dialog box (see Figure 25.10).

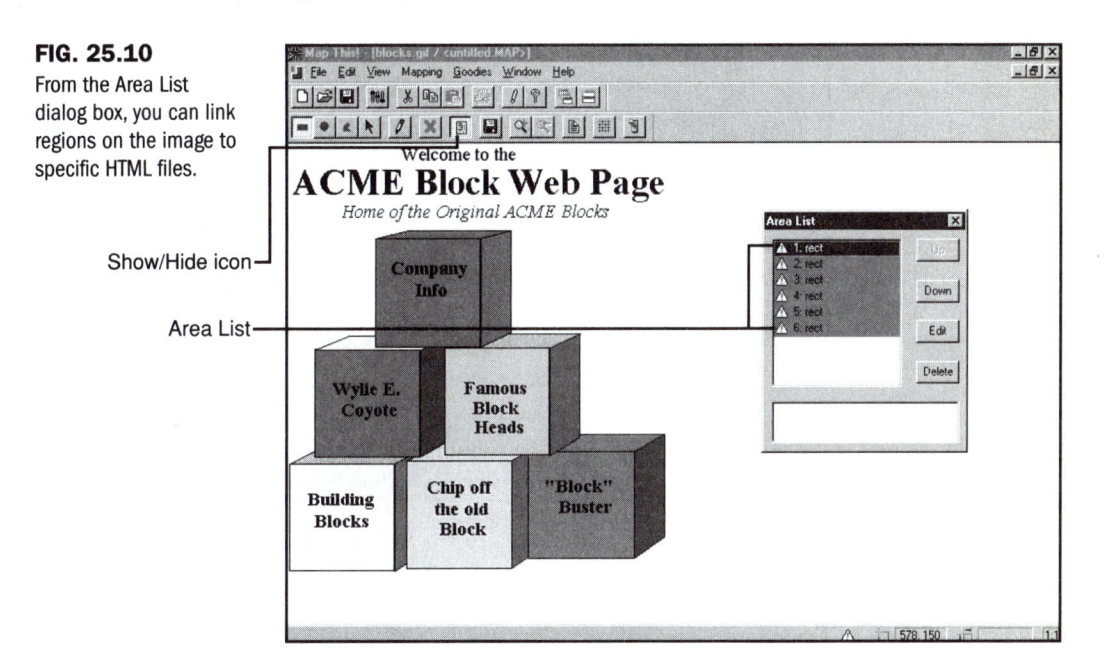

**FIG. 25.10**
From the Area List dialog box, you can link regions on the image to specific HTML files.

Show/Hide icon

Area List

8. Select a listed area, and then click Edit to bring up the Settings dialog box (see Figure 25.11). Here, type the URL of the file you want linked to this region. Click OK after you type the URL.

> **TIP** When entering the URL of the file you want to link to, remember that you have the option of typing in a full URL such as the following:
>
> http://www.shafran.com/ACME/block1.html
>
> or a relative URL and file name like this:
>
> ACME/block1.html
>
> Make sure that you correctly type the full path for the HTML file you want linked to this region.

Part V
Ch 25

**FIG. 25.11**
For each area, tell Map This! what you're mapping.

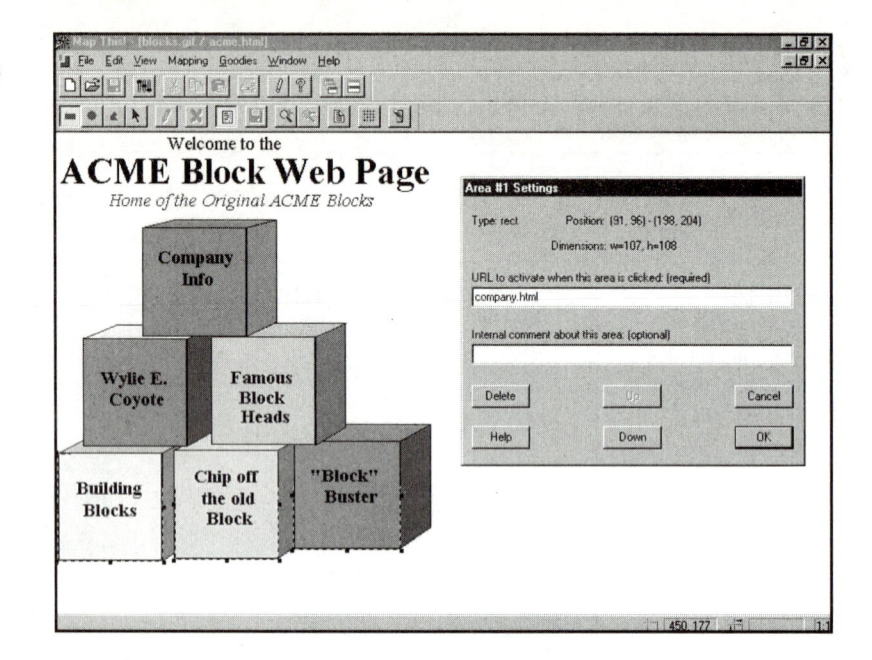

9. Repeat step 8 for every region defined on your image. After you finish, your Area List dialog box lists each region along with the corresponding linked file (see Figure 25.12).

10. Choose File, Save from the menu bar to bring up the Info About This Mapfile dialog box (see Figure 25.13).

**FIG. 25.12**
The finished Area List dialog box—every region on the image map is now properly linked.

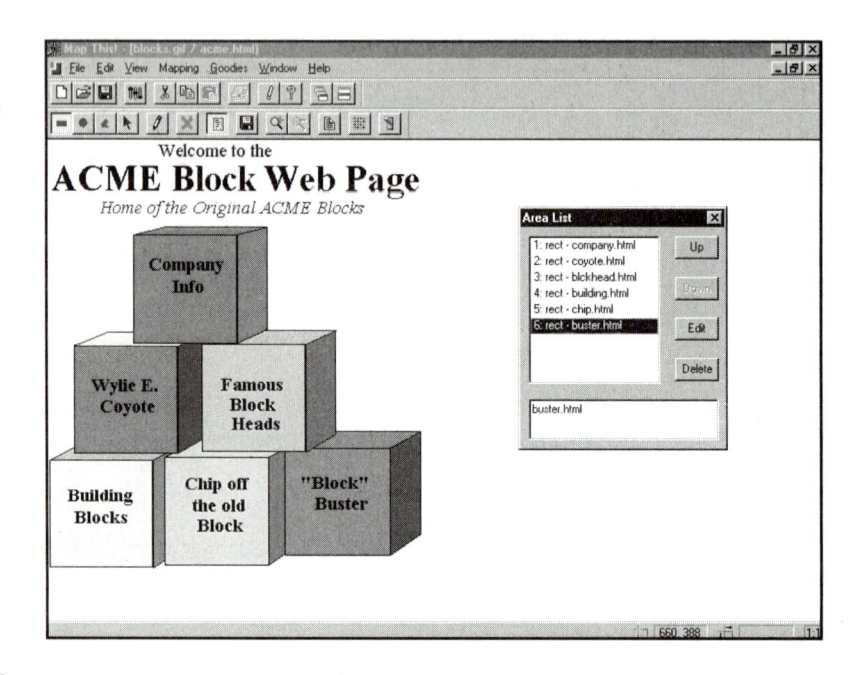

**FIG. 25.13**
Set your image map options here and you're nearly finished.

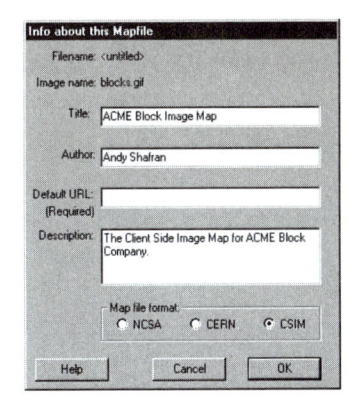

11. Enter the map's title and make sure that the CSIM option button is selected as the map file format. (Remember that CSIM stands for client-side imagemap.) You also can type in a default URL to link this image to if users click a part of the image outside of the regions you've defined.

> **CAUTION**
> For your imagemap to work properly, make sure that the title you type in the Info About This Mapfile dialog box corresponds exactly to what you entered following the USEMAP keyword earlier.

12. When you finish setting your imagemap options, click OK. Map This! prompts you to save the client-side imagemap to an HTML file.

Here's a copy of the finished file for the example being discussed:

```
<BODY>
<MAP NAME="ACME Block Image Map">
<!-- #$-:Image Map file created by Map THIS! -->
<!-- #$-:Map THIS! free image map editor by Todd C. Wilson -->
<!-- #$-:Please do not edit lines starting with "#$" -->
<!-- #$VERSION:1.20 -->
<!-- #$DESCRIPTION:The client-side Image Map for ACME Block Company. -->
<!-- #$AUTHOR:Andy Shafran -->
<!-- #$DATE:Mon Mar 29 21:38:26 1996 -->
<!-- #$PATH:C:\ -->
<!-- #$GIF:blocks.gif -->
<AREA SHAPE=RECT COORDS="91,96,198,204" HREF=company.html>
<AREA SHAPE=RECT COORDS="29,206,136,314" HREF=coyote.html>
<AREA SHAPE=RECT COORDS="2,322,110,428" HREF=blckhead.html>
<AREA SHAPE=RECT COORDS="124,319,230,426" HREF=building.html>
<AREA SHAPE=RECT COORDS="161,205,269,311" HREF=chip.html>
<AREA SHAPE=RECT COORDS="247,310,355,416" HREF=buster.html>
</MAP>
```

Now that you've successfully created your imagemap definition, all you have to do is add it to your HTML document (preferably just below the <IMG> tag), and you're all done. You've just created your own personalized client-side imagemap.

Figure 25.14 shows what the example imagemap looks like in Netscape 4.0. Notice how the status bar at the bottom of the screen indicates which HTML file will be linked to as the mouse hovers over a particular block.

**FIG. 25.14**
Here's the finished product—the ACME Block imagemap.

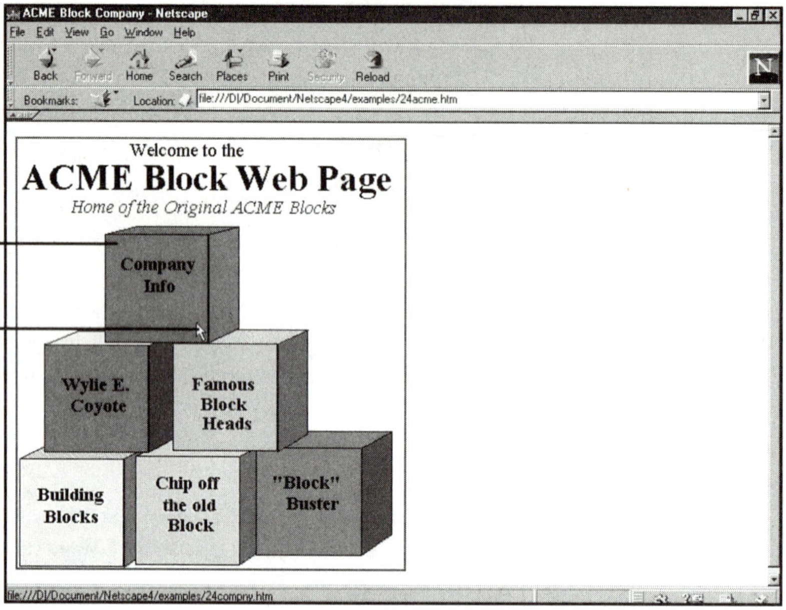

## Understanding the Imagemap Shapes

Although you'll probably only create an imagemap with Map This! or a similar program, this section describes the different aspects of creating an imagemap definition from scratch, so you can understand all the tags used in the file in the last section.

After you've added the image tag to the Web page, the next step is to add the <MAP> and </MAP> tags:

```
<MAP NAME="ACME Block Image Map">
</MAP>
```

These are new HTML tags used to tell Netscape where each region of the image is linked. Make sure that the value following NAME corresponds *exactly* to the value used with USEMAP earlier. Otherwise, Netscape cannot interpret the imagemap links correctly.

The <MAP> tag tells Netscape that this section of your HTML file describes how each region of the imagemap should work.

Within the <MAP> tag pair, you need to add an individual <AREA> tag for each section of the image you want mapped to another HTML file. You can have three different shapes: rectangles, circles, and polygons.

## Rectangles

To create a rectangular section on an image, you need to know the actual pixel coordinates of the upper-left and lower-right corners of the rectangle.

Pixel coordinates come in pairs, with the upper-left corner of an image always identified as 0,0. The first number is the horizontal measurement from left to right, and the second number is the vertical measurement from top to bottom. The pixel coordinates are labeled on this image. To add this section to your HTML file, therefore, your <AREA> tag would look like this:

```
<AREA SHAPE=RECT COORDS="70,45,210,90" HREF=rectangle.html>
```

The SHAPE keyword tells Netscape that you've defined a rectangular shape. The COORDS keyword requires four values: X and Y coordinates for the upper-left and lower-right corners of the rectangle. Finally, the HREF keyword tells Netscape which HTML file you want loaded when the user clicks this particular area.

> **TIP** In case you have forgotten, squares are rectangles with four equilateral sides. Therefore, to add a square shape to your image map, you still use AREA=RECT.

## Circles

Mapping circular shapes is almost as easy as rectangles, but there are a few differences. To map the shape of a circle, you only need three coordinates (as opposed to four for a rectangle). You need the X and Y coordinates of the circle's center, and the length of the circle's radius.

As you can see, the center of the circle is located at 200,100 and the circle has a radius of 50 pixels. The corresponding <AREA> tag looks like this:

```
<AREA SHAPE=CIRCLE COORDS="200,100,50" HREF="circle.html">
```

## Polygons

The final shape you can define on an imagemap is a polygon. By specifying a polygon, you can identify a shape of any size with any number of sides. Simply tell Netscape the coordinates of every corner of the shape.

Adding the appropriate <AREA> tag is simple; the only difference is that you need to list a pair of coordinates for each corner of the polygon. Thus, for this example we have six pairs of X,Y-coordinates:

```
<AREA SHAPE=POLY COORDS="40,75,10,100,60,100,60,200,120,10,40,75"
➥HREF="polygon.html">
```

The key to creating polygon regions on an imagemap is that the first and last pair of coordinates must be the same, so that Netscape can close the region. While there are six sets of coordinates in this example, notice that the first and last sets are identical.

> **CAUTION**
> Map This! only supports up to 64 sets of corners for a polygon when you draw the shape with your mouse.

## How Do Overlapping Regions Work?

When creating imagemaps, you can have two or more different areas that overlap.

In this example, there is a small *overlapping region* for the two rectangles. How does Netscape interpret a click in the overlapping region? The answer is simple—it links to the first region listed in the <MAP> tag. The example is coded this way:

```
<MAP NAME="Overlap Example">
<AREA SHAPE=RECT COORDS="70,45,210,90" HREF=rectangle1.html>
<AREA SHAPE=RECT COORDS="150,60,290,120" HREF=rectangle2.html>
</MAP>
```

Therefore, Netscape brings you to `rectangle1.html` if the overlapping region is clicked.

> **NOTE** Sometimes there are sections of the imagemap that are contained within two different shapes. How does Netscape know which link to follow? When Netscape registers a click an imagemap, it starts logically reading through the <MAP> tag. It checks each area, in sequential order, to see if the coordinates that have been clicked fit within that shape. As soon as it finds a match, it whisks you away to the linked page, not bothering to look at the rest of the areas in the <MAP> tag. So, when an overlapped section of an imagemap is selected, Netscape activates the first area that contains the selected coordinates.

## Adding a Default Link

Another concern besides overlapping regions is the issue of what happens when a user clicks outside of all established regions on your imagemap? You can specify a *default link* that is activated in this type of situation. Default links are nice because they make sure that visitors to your Web page are always linked to *some* page, regardless of where they click the image.

To add a default link to your imagemap, all you have to do is add one final region to your imagemap—a rectangle that spans the entire width and height of your image. For example, the ACME Block Company image is 300 pixels wide and 400 pixels tall, so add the following line to the end of the imagemap definition:

```
<AREA SHAPE=RECT COORDS="0,0,299,399" HREF=default.html>
```

> **TIP** The preceding code line uses 299 and 399 as the coordinates because the pixel count starts at 0,0. Thus, the 300th pixel across the screen is actually at X coordinate 299.

> **CAUTION**
> Make sure that this default area is the last item in your <MAP> tag! Otherwise it supersedes any areas that might follow.

Of course, you might want nothing to happen when a user clicks outside of your designated areas. In that case, you still should add an all-image <AREA> tag, but use the NOHREF keyword:

http://www.quecorp.com

```
<AREA SHAPE=RECT COORDS="0,0,299,399" NOHREF>
```

This informs Netscape that any clicks outside of the other defined regions should be ignored. This tag isn't really necessary; it just makes your imagemap definition more complete.

## Test the Imagemap with Netscape

After you're finished creating the imagemap, make sure that you test it thoroughly with Netscape. Use Netscape to test every region, one at a time, to make sure that your links have been created properly.

Many people overlook this step, assuming that there aren't any mistakes as long as they have followed the steps in creating an imagemap properly. However, typos, incorrect file names, and other mistakes can easily create flaws in your imagemap.

## Providing a Textual Alternative

Although virtually all new Web browsers support client-side imagemaps, it's always a good idea to provide some sort of textual alternative. This accommodates visitors to your page who are using a browser that doesn't read client-side imagemaps, or who don't want to wait for the entire image to download before selecting a region on the imagemap.

Figure 25.15 shows how the ACME Block home page is updated to have textual links as well as graphical ones. Using a two-column table with the left column displaying the main imagemap and the right column showing a simple list of links, this page balances Web graphics and text well.

**FIG. 25.15**
This simple table provides an alternative to using an imagemap.

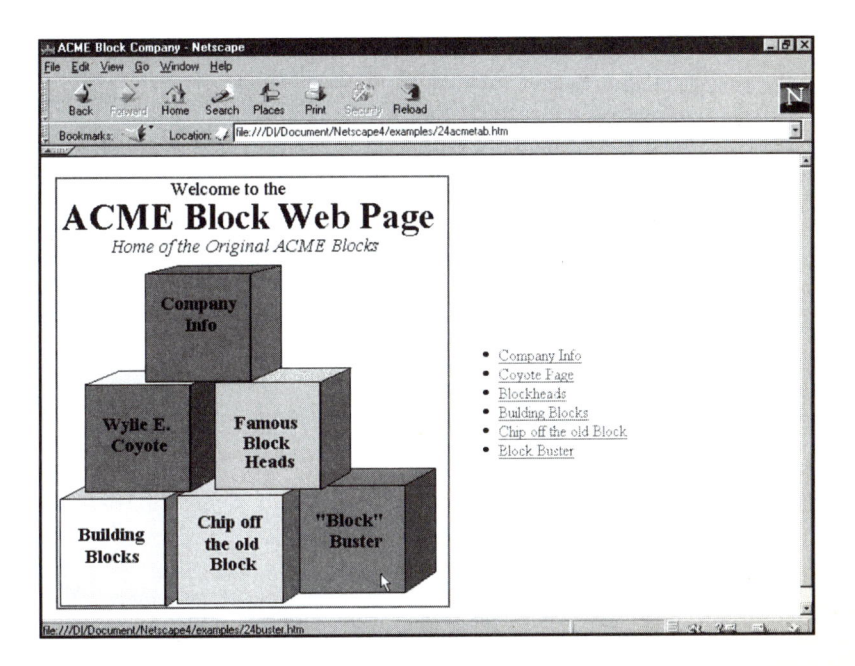

CHAPTER 26

# Creating Forms and Server Scripts

*by Paul Wallace*

The Web can seem a constantly changing, dynamic place. Netscape gives you a feeling of almost unlimited freedom and endless possibilities—a full tank of gas; wide, rough tires; and a wide, colorful horizon spreading off as far as you can see.

Sometimes it seems like there's something more. Some sites on the Web are thriving, somehow even more exciting than the usual. It's hard to pin down, but some outposts in cyberspace seem more alive. What is it? What's the thing that separates these Web sites from thousands of others?

They're interactive! You can enter data and receive customized responses. You can make choices and alter the site as you like. You aren't just reading information, you're controlling it.

True interactivity—sites that let users do more than just browse—is the one thing that sets one bus stop on the Information Superhighway apart from another; it really defines the World Wide Web as a new medium. ■

### Creating dynamic Web sites
How CGI scripts and forms interrelate to create dynamic Web sites. You receive specific examples for learning how to send dynamic messages through your Web site.

### An introduction to simple scripting
You receive an introduction to writing CGI scripts in Bourne shell, Perl, or other languages.

### Design the interface for your forms
Learn how to create sophisticated forms using specific HTML tags.

### Access ready-made programs on the Web
Find out about the best places on the Web to get publicly available code for creating your own interactive Web sites.

# Creating Web Interactivity

Two elements go into making interactivity on the Web possible: CGI scripts and HTML forms. While these elements are probably two of the least understood and most confusing aspects of creating a Web site, they are among the two most powerful. With them, you can do anything including asking the user to guess a number to offer comprehensive searches of your Web database, as shown in Figure 26.1.

**FIG. 26.1**
What makes The Internet Travel Network (**www.itn.com**) special? One thing is its capability to interactively search for flight information—something only CGI scripts and forms make possible.

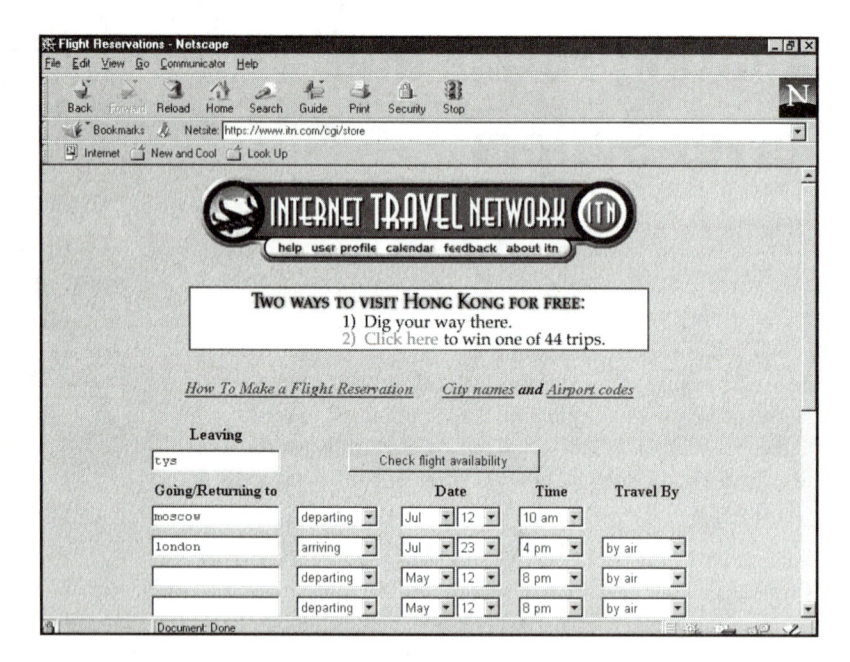

To get true interactivity on the Web, you need to understand and use both CGI scripts and HTML forms, because they make up two halves of the same coin. Forms allow the user to enter data—personal information, requests, purchase orders, or anything else—into Netscape and send it through the World Wide Web to your server. This is a *front end* that users see and interact with. Figure 26.2 is an illustration.

CGI scripts make up the *back end*. They take the information sent to the server through the Web and process it—querying databases, placing orders, or simply logging accesses. It all happens behind the scenes, but it's where the real work takes place. The results are then passed back.

Though it can seem confusing, CGI scripts and forms are worth the trouble. They can transform your site from something static and predictable to something dynamic and exciting.

**FIG. 26.2**
HTML forms allow users to enter data and send it through the World Wide Web back to your server.

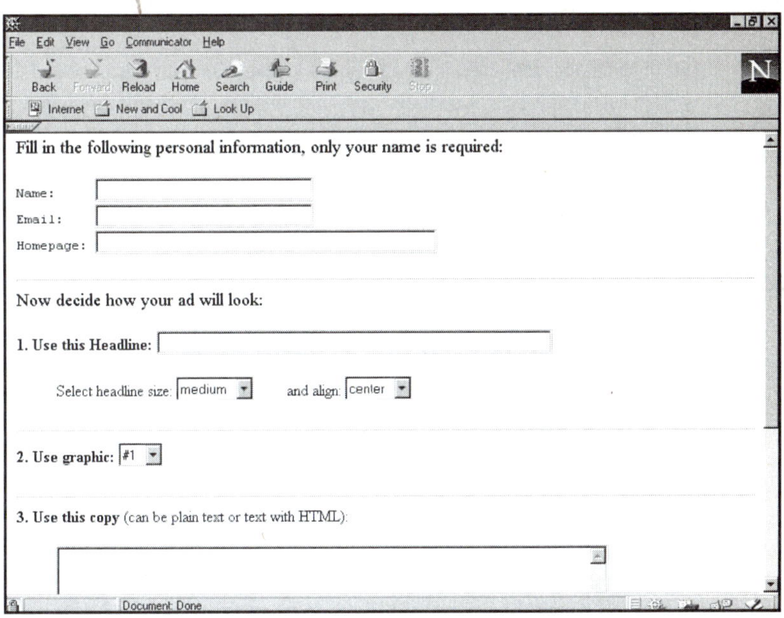

## CGI Scripting

The Common Gateway Interface is the full name of CGI. It is a way for your Web server to extend its capabilities by running external programs—much the way Netscape uses helper applications to display a Word document, for example. CGI is a gateway to functionality not pre-programmed into the server. It allows you to use all of your computer's capabilities, instead of just those that are already part of the HTTP server software.

To a user, a link to a CGI program looks like a link to any other URL. It can be clicked like any other link and results in new information being displayed, just like any other link.

But a CGI program, under the hood, is much more than a normal Web page. When a normal URL is selected, a file is read, interpreted, and displayed by Netscape. When a link to a CGI program is selected, it causes a program to run on the server system, and that program can do just about anything you want it to—scan databases, sort names, or send e-mail. CGI scripts allow for complex back-end processing.

CGI changes the definition of what Netscape can do. While normal HTML pages are static and unchanging, CGI programs allow a page to be anything you want it to be.

### Scripts versus Programs

What's the difference between a CGI script and a CGI program? Semantics, mostly. The term script is left over from the early days of the Web, when it ran exclusively on UNIX machines. A UNIX script is a

*continues*

*continued*

list of commands that are run in sequence, a lot like DOS batch files. The first CGI programs were written using these scripts, so the name CGI scripts caught on. Later, true programs (written in Perl or C, usually) were used to perform the same functions. There is no functional difference between scripts and programs—neither the user nor the server software can tell them apart—and both terms are used interchangeably in this chapter.

## Setting Up for CGI

Before you can begin to use CGI scripts, you must take care of a few preliminaries. Because what follows really has nothing to do with Netscape Communicator—CGI scripts live and run on the server—in this section, we just touch on the requirements. The following are some rudimentary requirements:

- You must have access to a Web server, or the ability to install and configure one. This can be a complicated, tedious job and you should ask your company's or school's system administrator or Webmaster if the facility is already set up.

- You must know a computer language. CGI scripts are not written in HTML like normal Web pages. Instead of HTML tags interpreted by the Netscape browser, CGI scripts are actual computer programs. This gives them a flexibility that normal Web pages don't have, but also increases their complexity. Before you can write CGI scripts, you must know how to program.

  While you can use almost any language to write your CGI scripts, the most popular are Bourne shell (on UNIX), batch files, Basic (on Windows NT and Windows 95), Perl, and C. Each has strengths and weaknesses, and while a discussion of each is beyond the scope of this book, there are many excellent references available.

- You must have permission to correctly install your script on the server. For UNIX Web servers, by default, there is a subdirectory where CGI access is allowed. This directory is called cgi-bin. On most servers, CGI scripts must reside in this directory, though you need specific UNIX permissions to access it. Again, talk to your system administrator or Webmaster for details.

## CGI URLs

After the Web server is installed and you have correct access, the CGI script can be accessed like any other URL. A script called DEMO.CGI, if placed right in the cgi-bin directory, would have an URL like this:

http://www.server.com/cgi-bin/demo.cgi

Subdirectories can be used for CGI scripts as well, allowing for URLs like this:

http://www.server.com/cgi-bin/marketing/demo/start.cgi

## Sample CGI Scripts

Now that all the preliminaries are out of the way, the best way to see what CGI scripts can actually do is to write a few and see how they perform. Following are four simple examples that demonstrate some of the power that CGI scripts give to Web pages.

**Sending a Simple Message**   While many CGI programs are extremely complex, they don't have to be. Probably the simplest example possible is the UNIX shell script in Listing 26.1. This code produces Figure 26.3.

### Listing 26.1   A Very Simple CGI Script

```
#!/bin/sh
echo "Content-type: text/html"
echo ""
echo "<HTML><HEAD><TITLE>Listing 26.1</TITLE></HEAD>"
echo "<BODY>This is a <EM>simple</EM> CGI script.</BODY></HTML>"
```

**FIG. 26.3**
Listing 26.1 creates a page that looks like normal HTML.

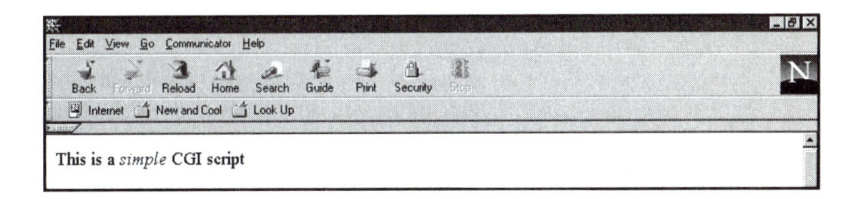

A lot is happening in this five-line CGI program, and all of it is vital for the script to work as intended.

The first line of this program tells UNIX that this script is to run in the Bourne shell, one of the many available in UNIX. Bourne is the most common and the only one that comes with every UNIX machine, so it is the most often used. If this program were a Windows NT or 95 batch file, this first line could be left off.

The second line tells Netscape what kind of information it is about to receive. The Content-type: is required for all CGI scripts and it must correspond to a valid MIME type.

MIME (or Multipurpose Internet Mail Extensions) is a method for delivering complex binary data over networks. Web browsers, like Netscape, use it to invisibly encode and decode that data. The two most common MIME types used by CGI scripts are text/html for HTML output, and text/plain for flat ASCII text.

The third line is simply an empty space to tell the server that what follows is the data described by the Content-type. You must include this empty line, or there is nothing to separate this header information from the main body of the message.

## 542  Chapter 26  Creating Forms and Server Scripts

> **CAUTION**
> One common error when writing CGI scripts is to have an incorrect Content-type for the type of data that is being sent. If your script sends HTML, as Listing 26.1 does, but the `Content-type:` is text/plain, none of the HTML tags are interpreted by Netscape, leaving your page looking like HTML source code.

The fourth and fifth lines are the actual HTML data that is to be sent to Netscape Navigator. These lines are passed through the server and interpreted, just as it would be if it been read from an HTML file.

◆ **TROUBLESHOOTING**

**I keep getting errors when I try to run my CGI program. What do they mean? And what's the best way to debug my script?** The most common error is `500 Server Error`, and it means that you either forgot to send the `Content-type:` line before your data, or your CGI program failed somehow while executing. Both cases mean you have some debugging to do.

If you get `403 Forbidden`, you might need to set certain permissions on your CGI script. When a Web server is installed, it is *owned* by a specific user on the system (usually root), and that user must be able to read and execute the CGI script itself, as well as traverse the directories that contain it. Talk to your system administrator or Webmaster to correct this problem.

The best way to debug a CGI program is to execute it from the command line instead of through the Web server. Set any appropriate environment variables by hand—environment variables are discussed later in the chapter—and simply run your program. This allows you to see any errors your script generates instead of the generic `500 Server Error` message.

**Sending a Dynamic Message**   Of course, the preceding simple CGI program only outputs static data—no matter how many times you call it, the output doesn't change—and a user wouldn't be able to tell it from a normal Web page. The real power of CGI scripts can be seen when your scripts go beyond this, when they start generating dynamic data—something that's impossible for a normal page to do.

The CGI script in Listing 26.2 displays a new fortune each time you jump to it. The output is shown in Figure 26.4.

**Listing 26.2   A Dynamic CGI Script**

```
#!/bin/sh
echo "Content-type: text/html"
echo ""
echo "<HTML><HEAD><TITLE>Fortune</TITLE></HEAD>"
echo "<BODY>Words of wisdom:<HR><PRE>"
FORTUNE=/usr/games/fortune
if [ "$FORTUNE" = "" ]; then
    echo "A wise system administrator installs 'fortune' for his
```

http://www.quecorp.com

```
           _users."
           echo "         -- Anon"
    else
           echo $FORTUNE
    fi
    echo "</PRE></BODY></HTML>"
```

**FIG. 26.4**
Web users are given new words of advice from the UNIX fortune command each time they execute this script.

## Creating HTML Forms

While CGI scripts are interesting in and of themselves and allow Web pages to come alive—through variation, personalization, and animation—their real power comes when they're combined with specific information received from the individual user. This is where creating HTML forms comes into play.

Forms allow you to pose specific questions to a Netscape user and send back an answer to him based on the processing done in a CGI script. A form can be as business-like or as informal as you need it to be (see Figure 26.5). They can even add to the flavor of your site by being professional, friendly, or full of attitude. Their design is all up to you.

**FIG. 26.5**
This site allows you to send an e-mail using HTML forms.

If CGI scripts are the back end of Web interactivity—taking care of the processing behind the scenes—forms are the front end—the pretty, GUI view that users see. CGI scripts and forms are two sides of the same coin, and, to get the maximum use out of either, you must understand both.

A form in Netscape is almost exactly like a form in a database program. It's made up of fields to enter text information, lists of choices to check, and options to select from. But while a paper form must then be turned in or mailed off, a Netscape form is instantly submitted—and can be instantly responded to.

There are a number of form tags that Netscape understands, and they're used just like any tags. The tag, `<FORM>`, simply defines the beginning and end of a form, and how and where the information collected in it will be sent. The other form attributes make up the part of the form the user sees and interacts with—text entry areas, menu selections, and push buttons.

## FORM

The `<FORM>` tag is used to mark the beginning of a form, while its compliment, `</FORM>`, is used to mark the end. All the other form tags are ignored outside of a `<FORM>` `</FORM>` pairing, so you must be sure to use these tags to define both the beginning and the end of your forms!

> **TIP** It's good practice to add a `</FORM>` tag immediately after you create a `<FORM>`, then go back and fill in the contents. This helps eliminate accidentally leaving the end form tag off after you've finished.

The `<FORM>` tag has three attributes, or sub-tags, that define how a particular form behaves. While the contents of the form are set by the form contents tags, these three `<FORM>` attributes determine where the information entered by the user goes and how it is sent there.

The first attribute is `ACTION`. A form's `ACTION` defines to what URL the information entered into a form is sent. It appears inside the `<FORM>` tag in the following format:

```
<FORM ACTION="URL">
...
</FORM>
```

URL can be any URL, though for the data entered into the form to be processed correctly, URL should point to a CGI script that is designed to handle that particular form. If an `ACTION` is omitted, the URL of the page containing the form is used by default.

The `<FORM>` tag's second attribute is its `METHOD`. The `METHOD` defines how the information collected by that form is sent to the `ACTION` URL. The `METHOD` can be one of two choices: `GET` or `POST`. The `GET` method is the simpler of the two, while `POST` allows far more data to be transmitted. The `METHOD` you choose depends entirely on how the CGI program that processes the form data is written, but a well-written CGI program can handle both. `METHOD` has no effect on the form itself, only how the gathered information is sent.

http://www.quecorp.com

Creating HTML Forms | 545

> **TIP** It is almost always a good idea, when writing CGI scripts, to use a library that parses form data automatically, no matter which METHOD you use. These libraries are covered later in the "Encoding" section.

The METHOD attribute is used inside the <FORM> tag like this:

```
<FORM METHOD="POST">
...
</FORM>
```

The third attribute—ENCTYPE—is rarely used. ENCTYPE defines the MIME content type that is used to encode the contents of the form when they are sent to the server. The default ENCTYPE is application/x-www-form-urlencoded, which is the standard URL encoding.

Of course, any or all of these attributes can be set for any particular form. For example, the following use of ACTION and METHOD is very common:

```
<FORM ACTION="http://my.server.com/cgi-bin/form.cgi" METHOD="GET">
...
</FORM>
```

After your form has defined how it will be used with the <FORM> tag, you must fill it with controls that the user can see and interact with.

## TEXTAREA

The <TEXTAREA> tag allows users to enter free-form text information in an open-ended edit field. This is useful for doing anything from sending comments to telling a story.

TEXTAREAs are defined with a beginning <TEXTAREA> and a closing </TEXTAREA>, with the default contents held between them, as follows:

```
<FORM ACTION="http://www.myserver.com/cgi-bin/form.cgi" METHOD="POST">
Type in your comments and suggestions:
<BR>
<TEXTAREA>
Type a message in this Textbox
</TEXTAREA>
</FORM>
```

This code sample produces Figure 26.6.

> **CAUTION**
> No HTML tags used inside a TEXTAREA pair are interpreted. For example, if you use the italics tag, <I>, you get three characters—the less-than symbol, capital I, and the greater than symbol—instead of the italics tag.

Like <FORM>, <TEXTAREA> also has a set of attributes that can be used inside the initial tag.

**FIG. 26.6**
A simple message text box can be created with the <TEXTAREA> tag.

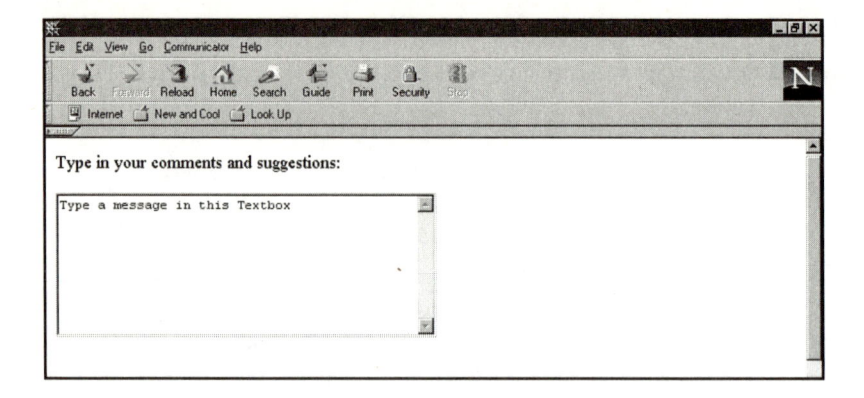

The first attribute is NAME, and it defines the name of the TEXTAREA. What you set a TEXTAREA's name to is paired with the contents of the area when the user finishes editing and submits the form. You must always give form contents a NAME, as this is how the control is identified and its value retrieved.

The next two attributes are ROWS and COLS, which define how large the TEXTAREA is to be in character heights and widths. If left off, Netscape sets ROWS to one (1) and COLS to twenty (20), only allowing a very small typing area. For example:

```
<TEXTAREA NAME="comment" ROWS=4 COLS=36>
This TEXTAREA is 4 rows high and 36 columns wide
</TEXTAREA>
```

This snippet of HTML results in the TEXTAREA shown in Figure 26.7.

**FIG. 26.7**
This TEXTAREA is named "comment," and is 36 columns wide and four rows high.

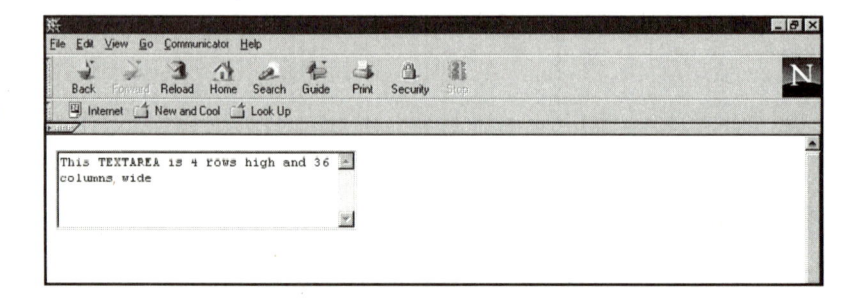

The final attribute is WRAP. WRAP affects how text appears within a TEXTAREA and can be set to OFF (which is the default) or to PHYSICAL or VIRTUAL.

If WRAP is omitted or set to OFF, the user must decide where each line entered into the TEXTAREA ends. If she continually types without pressing Return, the text remains confined to the first line and the TEXTAREA scrolls to accommodate it. If WRAP is set to PHYSICAL or VIRTUAL, the text wraps around to the next line, like it does when you type into a word processor.

The difference between PHYSICAL and VIRTUAL only becomes apparent when the data is sent to a CGI script. If WRAP is set to PHYSICAL, line breaks are added to the end of each line, as if the

Creating HTML Forms | 547

user had pressed Return there. If set to VIRTUAL, the text is delivered as if it had been entered all on one line.

## SELECT

While TEXTAREAS allow users to enter free-form text information, it's often more desirable to allow users to make limited choices from a pre-defined list—just what the SELECT tag was designed to do.

The SELECT tag itself is simple, just a <SELECT> </SELECT> pair with three attributes: NAME, SIZE, and MULTIPLE.

> ### TROUBLESHOOTING
>
> **What happened? All the selection options after my <SELECT> prompt text is gone!** You forgot to include a closing </SELECT> tag. If left off, no other HTML tags are interpreted until the </FORM>.

NAME, like it is used in the <TEXTAREA> tag, defines a name that is paired with whatever value the user selects.

SIZE defines the height of the list of selections to show the user. If it's left off, or if it's set to 1, the user is shown the selection choices in a pop-up menu, as seen in Figure 26.8.

**FIG. 26.8**
In this SELECT form content, only the current selection is shown when SIZE is set to 1.

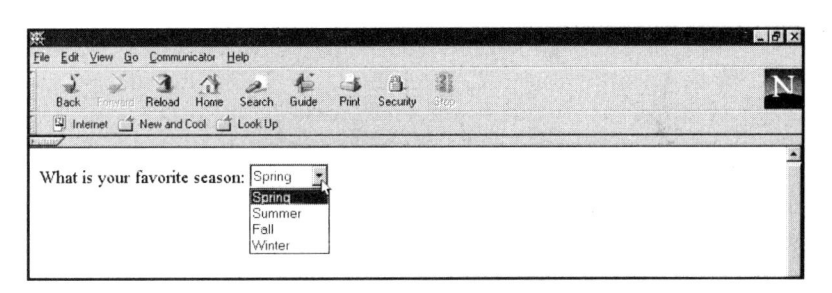

If SIZE is set to greater than one, the choices are shown as a list that the user can select from. If SIZE is greater than the number of actual choices available, empty spaces are displayed after the choices, as in Figure 26.9.

The next attribute, MULTIPLE, takes no value and simply defines if this SELECT group allows multiple selections at one time. If omitted, the user is only able to make one choice from the list; if included, the user is able to make any number of choices, including zero. Also, as a side-effect of specifying MULTIPLE, the list is shown as a scrollable list, even if SIZE is set to 1.

After the SELECT entity is defined, OPTIONs must be defined within it. The <OPTION> tag defines each individual choice that the user will see and is only recognized inside a <SELECT> </SELECT> pair. Like the <LI> tag in an HTML list, an OPTION's text does not need to be closed with </OPTION>. For example:

**548** Chapter 26 Creating Forms and Server Scripts

```
<FORM METHOD="GET">
Select your favorite food:
<SELECT NAME="food">
<OPTION>Cold pizza
<OPTION>Cold Chinese
<OPTION>Cold fried chicken
</SELECT>
</FORM>
```

The `<OPTION>` tag has two attributes: VALUE and SELECTED.

**FIG. 26.9**
With SIZE set to 7, the entire list—including empty spaces—is displayed.

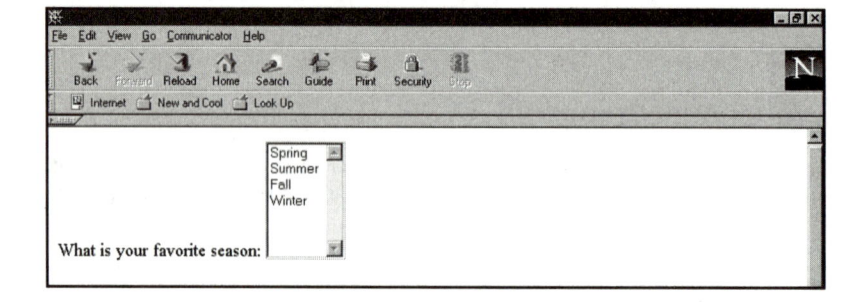

The VALUE of an `<OPTION>` is what is associated with the NAME, if that option is chosen by the user. This is used by the CGI script to identify the option, but does not need to correspond to the text the user sees. Creative use of this can make selections easier to deal with from the CGI side of a form. If VALUE is omitted, it is defaulted to the text that follows the `<OPTION>`.

The second attribute, SELECTED, simply defines which OPTIONs are selected by default when the choices are first displayed. If SELECTED is not sent on any OPTIONs, none of them are chosen; if more than one is marked as SELECTED, those are all marked. Usually, only the single most common selection should be set as the default.

> **CAUTION**
> The SELECT tag's MULTIPLE flag only comes into play if the user selects something other than the default selections you have defined. If your SELECT is not MULTIPLE, it is still possible to have multiple selections returned—if more than one OPTION is marked as SELECTED by default.

If you want to allow customers to rate your service people, you might use a selection similar to the following. Note that the VALUEs of the OPTIONs are related to your scoring system, rather than the actual text of the OPTION. For example:

```
<FORM ACTION="/cgi-bin/service_logger.cgi" METHOD="GET">
Please rate the service you received:
<SELECT NAME="service">
<OPTION VALUE="100">Excellent
<OPTION VALUE="75" SELECTED>Good
<OPTION VALUE="60">Fair
<OPTION VALUE="50">Poor
</SELECT>
</FORM>
```

The result of this is shown in Figure 26.10.

**FIG. 26.10**
Web sites can offer two-way communication, providing information to visitors and generating it for you.

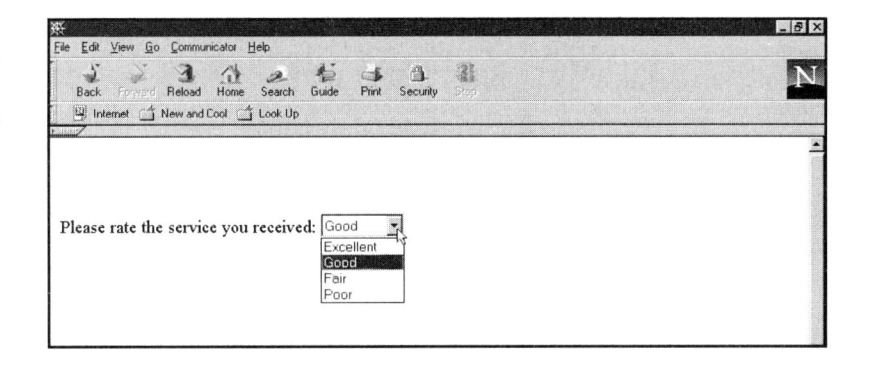

# INPUT

The final form content tag we discuss, <INPUT>, is far and away the most flexible and the most complex. While <TEXTAREA> produces editable text-box fields and <SELECT> produces lists of choices, the <INPUT> tag can be used to create six different input methods: TEXT, PASSWORD, CHECKBOX, RADIO, HIDDEN, RESET, and SUBMIT.

Each kind of input is specified by an attribute of <INPUT> called TYPE. All the other attributes related to <INPUT> are based on what TYPE is set.

**TEXT**   The TEXT attribute produces a single-line text entry field, like a single row TEXTAREA.

If the TYPE of an <INPUT> is set to TEXT, a NAME must be specified, along with three other optional attributes: SIZE, MAXLENGTH, and VALUE.

The SIZE of a TEXT INPUT is how many characters wide the text-entry field will be; MAXLENGTH specifies the maximum number of characters a user can enter into the field. If SIZE is bigger than MAXLENGTH, the text field scrolls to allow the user to enter more data. If SIZE is excluded, the default is 20 characters; if MAXLENGTH is excluded, there is no limit on the amount of text that can be entered.

The final attribute, VALUE, can be set to the default contents of the field, or left off entirely if there are none. For example:

```
Please enter your name, first then last:
<INPUT TYPE="TEXT" NAME="first" SIZE="15" MAXLENGTH="13" _VALUE="John">
<INPUT TYPE="TEXT" NAME="last" SIZE="20" MAXLENGTH="18" _VALUE="Smith">
```

This result is shown in Figure 26.11.

**PASSWORD**   PASSWORD is similar to TEXT—they share the same attributes—except that the characters typed into a PASSWORD TYPE are hidden. This, of course, allows passwords and other secret data to be entered without showing on Netscape's screen. For example:

```
Password: <INPUT TYPE="PASSWORD" NAME="pass" SIZE="8" MAXLENGTH="8">
```

**FIG. 26.11**
TEXT INPUT fields allow you to design online database entries.

If the user enters this form code, it appears as shown Figure 26.12.

**FIG. 26.12**
No matter what characters are typed into a PASSWORD field, they are hidden from prying eyes.

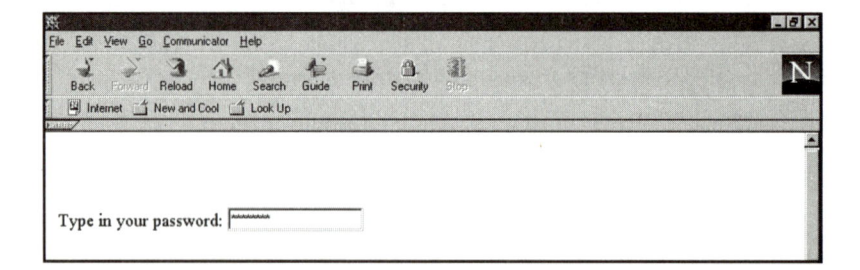

> **CAUTION**
> It is important to remember that even though a PASSWORD field prevents your secret data from being read off the screen, it is still passed over the network as plain, unencrypted text. It can even appear in the URL that way. Don't let PASSWORD lull you into a false sense of security.

**CHECKBOX**   A CHECKBOX form content is simply a toggle field; it can be either on or off. CHECKBOX is great for the simple, yes/no choices on your form.

CHECKBOX has three attributes: NAME, VALUE, and CHECKED.

NAME is the name that is delivered to the Web server, paired with the VALUE, if the check box is selected when the form is submitted. If VALUE is left off, it is automatically set to on. If the final attribute, CHECKED, is included, the default state of the box is on instead of off. For example:

```
Select the condiments you would like:
<INPUT TYPE="CHECKBOX" NAME="mayo" CHECKED> Mayonaise
```

```
<INPUT TYPE="CHECKBOX" NAME="mustard" CHECKED> Mustard
<INPUT TYPE="CHECKBOX" NAME="relish"> Sweet Relish
```

This HTML produces the check boxes shown in Figure 26.13.

**FIG. 26.13**
Checkboxes allow for yes/no choices that are independent of each other.

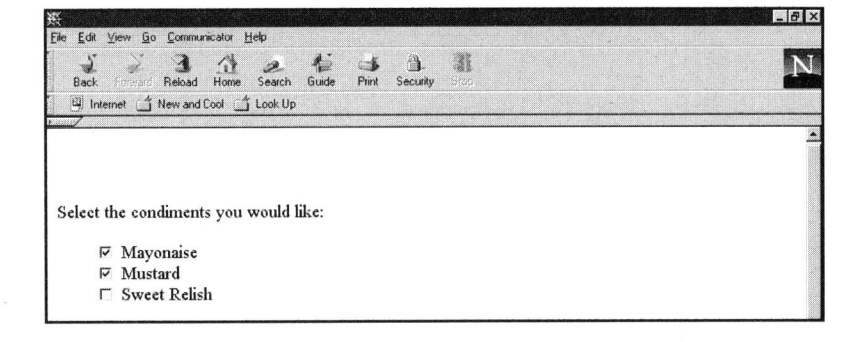

**RADIO**  RADIO is a lot like CHECKBOX, but only one toggle in a group can be selected at a time. All RADIO buttons in a single form that share a common NAME are considered members of the same group. If one is chosen by the user, any other selected button is cleared. Otherwise, RADIO functions exactly like CHECKBOX, even down to the attributes it uses.

You might notice that this functionality sounds a lot like a non-MULTIPLE SELECT, and they accomplish almost exactly the same thing. Which one you choose depends largely on the look and feel you want your World Wide Web page to have.

The following code demonstrates the RADIO TYPE:

```
Select the type of bread:
<INPUT TYPE="RADIO" NAME="bread" VALUE="white" CHECKED> White
<INPUT TYPE="RADIO" NAME="bread" VALUE="wheat"> Wheat
<INPUT TYPE="RADIO" NAME="bread" VALUE="roll"> French Roll
<INPUT TYPE="RADIO" NAME="bread" VALUE="rye"> Rye
```

The result is shown in Figure 26.14.

**FIG. 26.14**
The RADIO attribute is useful for when you want the user to be able to make only one selection from several choices.

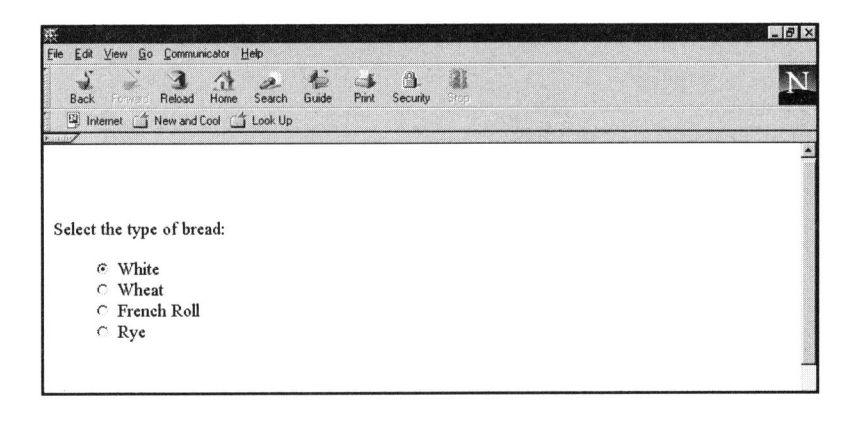

**552** | Chapter 26  Creating Forms and Server Scripts

> **CAUTION**
> As with `SELECT`s that are missing a `SELECTED` entry, it's possible that no member of a `RADIO` group will be `CHECKED` if you don't initially define a default. Always be sure to mark the most common choice as the default, with `CHECKED`.

**HIDDEN**  Different from all the other `INPUT TYPE`s, `HIDDEN` does not produce any graphics on the screen. It exists simply to allow the CGI script to receive a `NAME` and a `VALUE` that is guaranteed not to have been edited by the user.

There are several reasons to want to do this; the most common reason is to maintain a transaction number between server accesses. If, for instance, a CGI script generates a page that it wants to identify again, it inserts a `HIDDEN` element—containing some checksum, identification number, HTML Cookie, or password—that it can check for in the future.

**RESET**  The `RESET TYPE` creates a push button on the screen that clears the form and returns all the settings to their original default values. Its only attribute, `VALUE`, can be set to the text that you want the button to have. `VALUE` can also be left off, resulting in the text "Reset."

Consider the following small bit of HTML:

```
<INPUT TYPE="RESET">
<BR>
<INPUT TYPE="RESET" VALUE="Clear Choices">
```

Its result is shown in Figure 26.15.

> **CAUTION**
> The `RESET TYPE` is not a required element for HTML forms. There are times when it is handy to use, allowing users to reset the form to the default values, but if a user mistakenly clicks `RESET` instead of `SUBMIT`, he has to retype all fields in your form! Use the `RESET` sparingly and only where appropriate.

**FIG. 26.15**
The top button is the default text for the `RESET TYPE`.

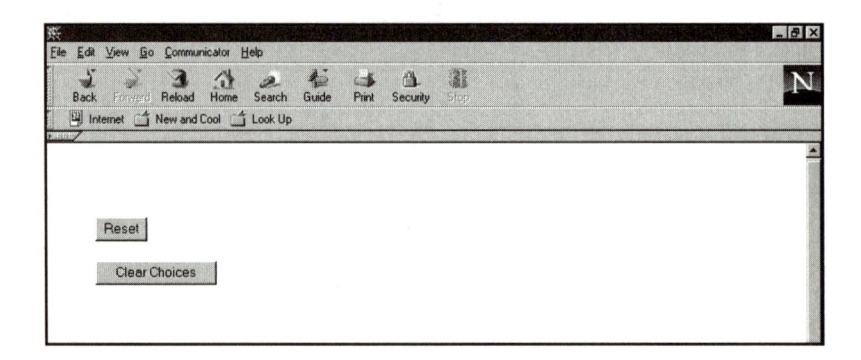

http://www.quecorp.com

**SUBMIT**  SUBMIT works a lot like RESET but achieves an entirely different result—exactly the opposite, as a matter of fact. While RESET clears a form of user-entered values, SUBMIT gathers them up and sends them off to the Web server for processing, to the URL specified back in the ACTION. A SUBMIT button is the Go switch that every form must have to let the user say when he is done editing.

The only attribute to SUBMIT is VALUE, which sets the text of the push button. If excluded, the default is "Submit Query." For example:

```
<INPUT TYPE="SUBMIT">
<BR>
<INPUT TYPE="SUBMIT" VALUE="     OK     ">
```

This code shows up as in Figure 26.16.

**FIG. 26.16**
The top button uses the default SUBMIT text; the bottom, a custom button message.

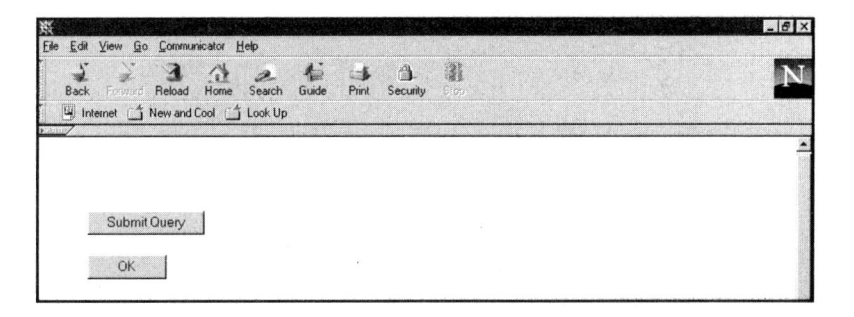

### CAUTION
If the text of a button is very short, like "OK," the button usually ends up looking ugly. You can avoid this by padding the VALUE of the button with an equal number of spaces on both sides to widen it.

# Bringing CGI and Forms Together

Now that you have some basic background on both CGI scripts and forms, you're ready to bring them together to allow true user interaction with your Web site. The combination of CGI scripts and forms can bring a Web page to life, turning what was a static display of information into a customized and dynamic experience.

The program in Listing 26.4 is a guestbook, an electronic version of the familiar visitor log used by hotels and museums. It first displays a list of signees, then uses a form to ask the current user to add his or her name. It is written in Perl and uses a form-input library called cgi-lib.pl to parse—untangle—the data sent from Netscape. The result of the program is shown in Figure 26.17.

**Listing 26.4   cgi-lib.pl   A CGI Program to Process Form Input**

```perl
#!/usr/local/bin/perl
print "Content-type: text/html\n\n";
# Load the library
require "cgi-lib.pl" || die "Fatal Error: Could not load cgi-bin.pl";
&ReadParse;
# Set the location of the guestbook
$guestbk = "guestbk.txt";
# Get the sign-ins name
$name = $in{'name'};
# Only add to the log if they entered something
if (length($name) > 0) {
    open(FILE,">>$guestbk");
    print FILE "$name\n";
    close FILE;
}
# Show the current sign-ins
print "<HTML>\n<HEAD><TITLE>Guestbook</TITLE></HEAD>\n";
print "<BODY>\n<H1>Guestbook</H1>\n<H2>Current signees:</H2>\n<HR>\n\n";
open(FILE,"<$guestbk") || print "You'll be the first\!\n";
while (<FILE>) {
    print "<LI>$_";
}
close FILE;
print "</UL>\n";
# Request new sign-ins
print "<HR>\n<FORM METHOD=\"GET\" ACTION=\"$ENV{'SCRIPT_NAME'}\">";
print "Your name: <INPUT TYPE=\"text\" NAME=\"name\" SIZE=\"20\">";
print "<INPUT TYPE=\"submit\" VALUE=\"Sign in\!\"></FORM>\n</BODY>\n</HTML>\n";
```

There are a few things to note about this CGI script. The first, and probably most important, is that it is not only a CGI script; it does processing, like a normal script, but it also generates its own form. The last three lines, in the Request new sign-ins section, generates the HTML to request more information from the user.

This neat trick, where a CGI script also generates a form, is becoming standard practice on many Web sites. It allows a single program to both request and process the data; it can even be expanded to generate its own error message pages, too.

Secondly, you should note that this program uses the cgi-lib.pl library to extract the information the user has typed into the form. By using this utility, the user-entered information is pulled out of the request, decrypted, and stored in a Perl table called $in, easily and conveniently. You can get the VALUEs of each form INPUT by asking $in for it, by referencing its NAME. For instance, if a form INPUT has the NAME "address," the following line of Perl code would return the value the user entered:

```perl
$addr_variable = $in{'address'};
```

Of course, before you can use $in, you must have loaded cgi-lib.pl and called the library routine that sets up the table (lines four and five in Listing 26.4).

**FIG. 26.17**
A guestbook is a simple way to make your site more personal.

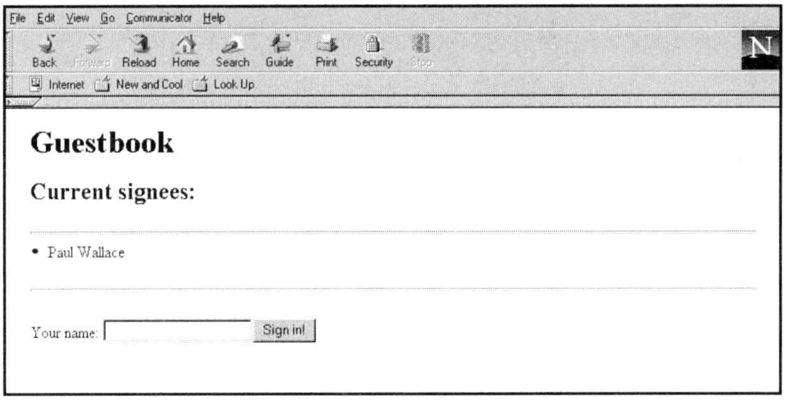

## GET and POST

There are two ways to read the form data submitted to a CGI script, depending on the METHOD the <FORM> uses. The type of METHOD the form uses—either GET or POST—is stored in an environment variable called REQUEST_METHOD. Based on that type, the data should be read in one of the following ways:

- If the data is sent from a GET METHOD FORM, the input stream is stored in an environment variable called QUERY_STRING. This input stream usually is limited to about one kilobyte of data, which is why the GET METHOD is losing popularity to the more flexible POST.

- If the data is submitted from a POST FORM, the input string waits on stdin, with the number of bytes waiting stored in the environment variable CONTENT_LENGTH. POST can accept data of any length, up into the megabytes, though this is not very common yet.

**CAUTION**
While the GET METHOD is simpler for CGI scripts to handle, it limits the amount of data that can be sent, usually to slightly less than one kilobyte. If there is any chance that your form will generate more data than that, you should use the POST METHOD.

## Parsing

After your CGI script has read the submitted data, it must parse it to pull out each NAME and VALUE that was sent from the form.

When a user clicks the SUBMIT button on a form, Netscape gathers all the user's choices and strings them together in NAME=VALUE pairs, each separated by an ampersand (&) character. For example:

```
<FORM ACTION="/cgi-bin/form.cgi" METHOD="POST">
<INPUT TYPE="TEXT" NAME="first">
<INPUT TYPE="TEXT" NAME="last">
```

```
<INPUT TYPE="SUBMIT">
</FORM>
```

This code snippet, if edited and submitted by Curly Howard, could produce the following data waiting on a CGI script's `stdin`:

`first=Curly&last=Howard`

For your CGI script to actually use this information, it first must search for each ampersand to get each NAME/VALUE pair, then split the pair at the equal sign.

## Encoding

There is more to getting the data that a user enters into a form than simply reading and parsing it. The submission is encoded to protect it from 7-bit network layers that might silently strip significant bits from the data, damaging it in the process.

> **CAUTION**
> You should be careful not to confuse encoding with encryption. When data is submitted from a normal form, it is encoded simply to protect the integrity of the data while it travels over the network. This does not prevent it from being discovered, and decoded, by prying eyes.

The encoding format used when Netscape submits a form to a CGI script is determined by the ENCTYPE of the <FORM>, by default the MIME content type `application/www-x-form-urlencoded`. This encoding format simply replaces spaces with the plus character and translates any other possibly troublesome character (control characters, the ampersand and equals sign, some punctuation, and so on) to a percent sign followed by its hexadecimal equivalent. So, using `application/www-x-form-urlencoded` style encoding, the string

`Here I am!`

becomes

`Here+I+am%21`

After your script has read the submitted data and parsed it into NAME and VALUEs, it must finally decode it into the actual data that the user entered into the form. Then it is ready to use.

# Protecting Yourself and Your Users

While programming CGI scripts and their forms is fun, the following are tips you should keep in mind—to protect yourself and your users:

- You should handle the submission of an empty form as elegantly as possible. For instance, if a user mistakenly presses the SUBMIT button without entering any information into your form, what does your CGI script do? A well-written program handles this situation gracefully, without even trying to process the submission.

When your script receives an empty request, it should be programmed to either return an error message telling the user what he or she did wrong, or, even better, return the contents of the form that need to be filled out. That way, as with the guestbook example, a single CGI script can both request and process the data, guaranteeing that both situations are handled. This is also handy for the first time the URL is jumped to, when the CGI script automatically presents the form to request data.

- Be mindful that your users might not have a secure connection, and warn them if you are requesting sensitive data. At the very least, you should be wary of requesting sensitive data—bank account numbers, passwords—and, if you must, explicitly warn the user of the possibility (no matter how remote) of the data being sniffed.

## Using Secure Forms

To ensure the security of any data submitted from a form, you must use Netscape's "secure HTTP" URL type, https.

If you know that a form will be sending data to a CGI script running on a Netscape Commerce Server, you simply need to change the http that starts the <FORM>'s ACTION URL to https, and the data will be encrypted and indecipherable to anybody "sniffing" the network. For example:

http://www.megaco.com/order.cgi

becomes

https://www.megaco.com/order.cgi

Any transactions made with the second URL are completely secure—the little "lock" icon in the lower-left corner of the Communicator window has become "secured" (see Figure 26.18). No other changes are needed, either to your form or CGI script.

# Using the Public Domain

Form and CGI programming can be frustrating in the beginning. There are many rules to follow, most of which can be obscure or complex. Even getting a simple script up and running can be a chore.

One of the best ways to get over these first few hurdles and start CGI programming is to look at existing code. By reviewing (or simply using) already existing CGI scripts, you can not only save yourself a lot of time, but teach yourself new techniques.

Existing code almost always makes a good base to expand from. Instead of implementing a new script from scratch, an older program can often be expanded (or shrunk) to suit your needs. The earlier guestbook program, for example, can be modified to automatically add the name of the computer the user is connecting from, if that's what you want your guestbook to do.

**FIG. 26.18**
When operating with a secure server, Communicator displays the lock icon.

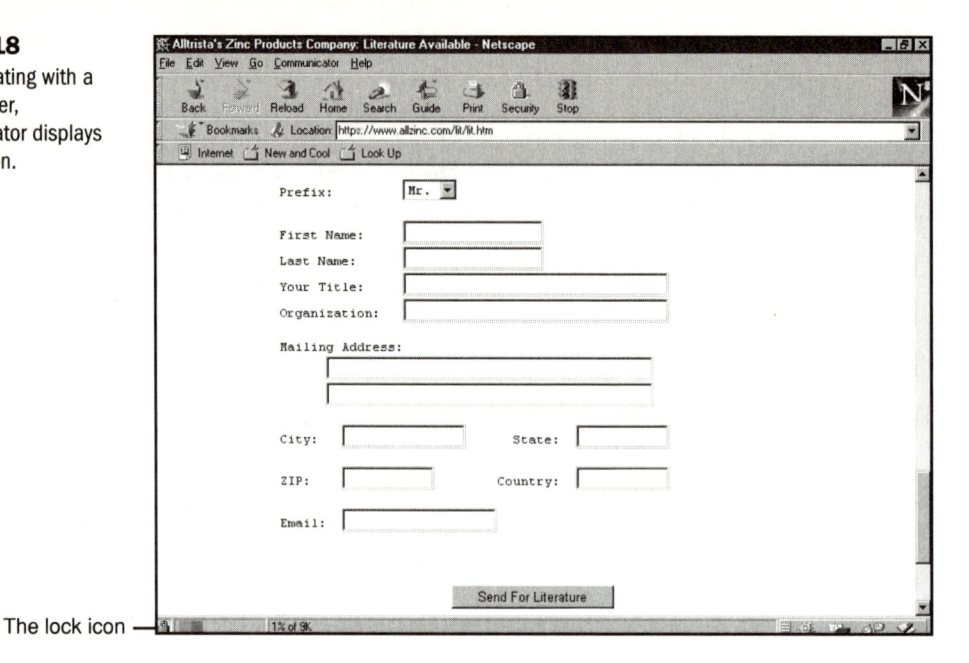

The lock icon

Experienced CGI programmers are almost always happy to share their code and talents with you. They've probably already solved any problem you might have and can save you hours of frustration with a word or a clue. Just ask. And be sure to return the favor when you become an expert!

## Available Resources

You can find many public domain CGI references and scripts on the Web itself. Good places to begin looking are the following:

- Selena Sol's Public Domain Script Archive: **http://www.eff.org/~erict/Scripts/**
- Yahoo's index of CGI programming resources: **http://www.yahoo.com/Computers_and_Internet/Internet/World_Wide_Web/CGI___Common_Gateway_Interface/**
- NCSA's introduction to CGI programming: **http://hoohoo.ncsa.uiuc.edu/cgi/**
- UseNet newsgroup on CGI programming: **news:comp.infosystems.www.authoring.cgi**

Because every CGI program that receives data from a form must go through the bothersome decoding and parsing steps to get the information the user entered, common libraries have been created to handle the trouble for you. It is much, much easier to use this existing code than to go to the trouble of writing your own decoding and parsing routines, because these existing libraries come tested and are free. Following are the addresses for two of the most popular CGI form libraries:

http://www.quecorp.com

- Perl library of routines to manipulate CGI input: **ftp://ftp.ncsa.uiuc.edu/Web/httpd/Unix/ncsa_httpd/cgi/cgi-lib.pl.Z**
- C library of routines for CGI: **ftp://ftp.ncsa.uiuc.edu/Web/httpd/Unix/ncsa_httpd/cgi/ncsa-default.tar.Z**

CHAPTER 27

# Dynamic HTML

*by John Simmons*

**H**TML is continually evolving along with the World Wide Web. What began as a tool for scientists to communicate over the Internet has very quickly evolved into a full-blown desktop publishing application.

With the pressure to meet the demands of Web creators, standards for Dynamic HTML have to be adopted internationally. These standards are determined by the World Wide Web Consortium (W3C) (**http://www.w3.org/**). Their members include MIT, (**http://www.ics.mit.edu**), the Institut National de Recherche in Informatique et en Automatique (INRIA, **http://www.innia.fr**), and Keio University in Japan (**http://www.keio.ac.jp**).

Microsoft and Netscape forge ahead with conventions not formally decided upon by the W3C. The results are that code that works perfectly well in Netscape Navigator is ignored by Internet Explorer. And the competing companies say they have no plans to support each other's features.

It is important to understand that codes which work in Netscape Navigator will not work in Microsoft's Internet Explorer and, according to Microsoft, will never be supported (**http://www.microsoft.com/workshop/author/dhtml/dhtmlcc.htm**). One of these is Netscape Navigator's <Layer> tag. In this chapter, we have followed the W3C's standards for creating layers, avoiding the necessity for learning two different code sets. Microsoft Internet Explorer and Netscape Navigator both conform to W3C standards. ■

### What is Dynamic HTML?

Dynamic HTML is the combination of new functionality of HTML and the increased capability of Web browsers.

### Defining Attributes with Classes

You can define a combination of colors, backgrounds, font styles, and weights to any block elements of HTML through the creation of a class definition.

### Cascading Style Sheets

Cascading Style Sheets define a group of Classes in the <STYLE> element of an HTML document. In effect, a series of document attributes can be defined by one word so that their use throughout the document can be activated by a few words of syntax, instead of a long string of script.

# Cascading Style Sheets (CSS)

Style sheets allow the Web developer to create stylistic templates in which to formulate his pages. They allow for precise control over font attributes such as style, weight, color, and size. They can be defined in the head of a document or in a separate file using the syntax shown in Listing 27.1.

**Listing 27.1  Hierarchical Listing of Styles**

```
<HEAD>
<TITLE>title</TITLE>
 <LINK REL=STYLESHEET TYPE="text/css"
 HREF="http://thestyleinfo.com/kewl" TITLE="Kewl">
 <STYLE TYPE="text/css">
 @import url(http://style.com/basic);
 H1 { color: blue }
 </STYLE>
 </HEAD>
 <BODY>
 <H1>This H1 headline would be blue</H1>
 <P STYLE="color: green">While this is all green until </P> ends it.
 </BODY>
 </HTML>
```

The example above contains three elements. The `<LINK REL=...>` statement refers this HTML page of a separate file through the `<...HREF="http://thesytleinfo.com/kewl">` URL. The file "kewl" will form the basis for the style definition of this page. The style information contained in the separate document "kewl" will provide all the necessary style information for this Web page.

Any documents that reference this file will have the same styles. Therefore, any change to the styles in the "kewl" document will effect all Web pages referencing that document.

The "@import url" statement allows for increased modularity, defining specific characteristics for any element such as tables, paragraphs, or heads.

It is similar to the "kewl" style in that it is a separate file that is called from the Web page containing it. Any changes to the "basic" file (in this example, it is called 'basic') will change all documents that reference it.

Finally, the "H1 { color: blue }" style defines for each occurrence of `<H1>` that the type will be blue only in the document that contains the code.

The priority here is important. The `<P STYLE="color: green">` on line 12 of Listing 27.1 will override any style for `<P>` defined in the head. Likewise, "H1 { color: blue }" will override anything in the "@import" statement. The "@import" statement will override anything from the `<LINK REL=...>` statement. The more specific the instruction, the higher the priority.

# Cascading Style Sheets (CSS) | 563

To briefly sum up:

- The LINK element refers to alternate style sheets (ASCII files) that the Web page refers to. They have the least priority.
- The @import url also refers to separate files. However, import automatically loads their values with the Web page. They have the next priority.
- H1 {color: blue } is the most basic style instruction. Every instance of <H1> following this will be blue. This instruction is more specific, so it has a higher priority.

**N O T E** An attribute definitions <u>must</u> be contained within the <STYLE> and </STYLE> commands.

If you use just the H1 { color: blue}, it is written as the following:

```
<STYLE TYPE="text/css">
H1 { color: blue}
</STYLE>
```

In this example, every instance of H1 is blue, unless it is overridden by a more specific (that is, closer) instruction. e.g.

```
<H1 STYLE="color = 'red'"> This heading would be red</H1>
```

This would override a "H1 {color: blue}" definition in the <STYLE> tags of the document because the instruction is on the same line as the heading: i.e. it is more specific or 'closer' to the text it is affecting.

**FIG. 27.1**
Cascading style sheet hierarchy.

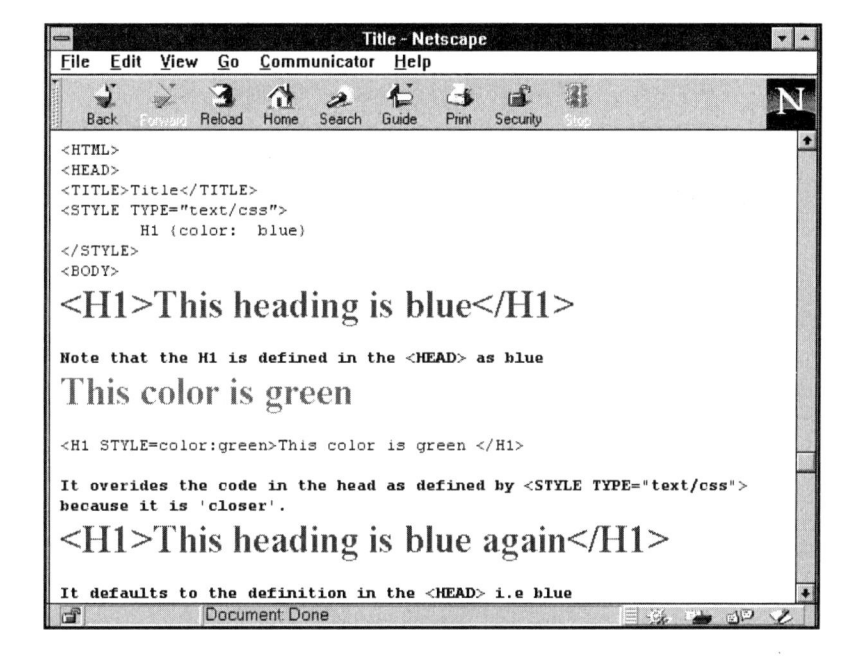

You will want to hide this command from browsers that do not recognize the `<STYLE TYPE="text/css">` tag. This is accomplished by the following:

```
<STYLE TYPE="text/css">
<!--
 H1 { color: blue}
-->
</STYLE>
```

All browsers will ignore everything between the `< >` brackets, but will include the text between the `<STYLE TYPE="text/css">` and `</STYLE>` if they do not recognize the `<STYLE>` tag. Without the `<!--` before `H1 {color: blue}` and the `-->` at the end, `'H1 {color: blue}'` would appear as text on your Web page.

Netscape interprets JavaScript code, as well as conforming to the standards set out by the W3C. The following two examples introduce cascading style sheets in JavaScript and CSS syntax.

```
<STYLE TYPE="text/css">
```

This can also be achieved in JavaScript, as follows:

```
<STYLE TYPE="text/javascript">
```

The following Listings 27.2 and 27.3 do exactly the same thing. Please note that the code following each `<STYLE TYPE=>` tag varies depending on whether you are using JavaScript or CSS syntax. The result is that `<H1>` is blue.

### Listing 27.2  Blue Headings with JavaScript

```
<HTML><HEAD>
<TITLE>Harold the Hamster's Kewl Homepage</TITLE>
 <STYLE TYPE="text/javascript">
 tags.H1.color = "blue"
 </STYLE>
</HEAD>
</BODY>
```

### Listing 27.3  Blue Headings using CSS Syntax

```
<HTML><HEAD>
<TITLE>Harold the Hamster's Kewl Homepage</TITLE>
 <STYLE TYPE="text/css">
 H1 {color: blue}
 </STYLE>
</HEAD>
</BODY>
<H1>This heading would be blue</H1>
```

Taking the preceding examples, all headings in the document are now blue unless you specifically override them. Overriding them can be done by using the following tag:

```
<H1 STYLE="color = 'red'">This heading would be red</H1>
```

```
<H1>Whereas this heading would revert to the style specified in the head, that is blue.</H1>
```

## Classes Of Styles

The CLASSES property is used within the <STYLE> tag and defines specific properties for each tag.

The following listing shows you how to create general to specific classes within your HTML documents in both JavaScript and 'CSS'.

### Listing 27.4 Classes Definition Using CSS Syntax

```
<HTML><HEAD>
<TITLE>A Title</TITLE>
<STYLE TYPE="text/css">
 all.magentaclass (color: magenta;}

 P.yellow1 {color: yellow; fontWeight: bold;}
 BLOCKQUOTE.yellow1 {color: yellow; fontWeight: bold;}
</STYLE}
<HTML><HEAD>
<TITLE>A Title</TITLE>
<STYLE type="text/javascript">
 classes.magentaclass.all.color="magenta";
 classes.yellow1.P.color = "yellow";
 classes.yellow1.P.fontWeight = "bold";
 classes.yellow1.BLOCKQUOTE.color = "yellow";
 classes.yellow1.BLOCKQUOTE.fontweight = "bold";
</STYLE>
```

The following describes what is happening in Listings 27.4 and 27.5. The results are exactly the same in both the `JavaScript` and `CSS` examples.

- The default for all tags is magenta.

    In JavaScript it is stated as classes.magentaclass.all.color="magenta;"

    In CSS it is stated as: all.magentaclass {color: magenta;}

- Any <P> tag will be magenta. With <P Class="yellow1">, any text following will be yellow and bold as defined by 'yellow1' above. The text will revert to the default (magenta) after the closing </p> tag in both the JavaScript and the CSS version.

- For `<BLOCKQUOTE>`, the default is defined by `classes.magentaclass.all.color` in JavaScript, or `all.magentaclass {color: magenta;}` in CSS. This is magenta for all elements of type. `<BLOCKQUOTE CLASS="yellow1">` will override the global magenta class and assume the properties defined by `classes.yellow1.BLOCKQUOTE.color="yellow"` and `classes.yellow1.BLOCKQUOTE.fontweight="bold"` above in JavaScript or `BLOCKQUOTE.yellow1 {color: yellow; fontWeight: bold;}` in CSS.

# Layers

Layers can be achieved with CSS and avoid the use of the Netscape Navigator exclusive `<LAYER>` tag altogether. As this has been formally adopted by the W3C and is a universal standard, we will use examples based on this CSS syntax where Layers are referred to as Positioned Elements.

There are two kinds of positioned elements: absolute and relative. They are placed in the `<body>` of the HTML document with the following `<SPAN>` tags:

**Listing 27.6  Use of *<SPAN>* Tags**

```
<body>
<p>The cat didn't come back</p>
<sp\an id=outer>Where is the cat?
<span id=inner>He isn't here.</span>
Or here</span>
</body>
```

`<SPAN>` in line tags indicate which text to apply the predefined styles 'outer' and inner', as shown in Listing 27.7.

**Listing 27.7  Definition of Styles Applied by *<SPAN>* Tags**

```
<STYLE TYPE="text/css">
<!--
  #outer {position:absolute; top: 150px; left: 150px; color: green;}
  #inner {color: red;}
-->
</style>
```

In Listing 27.7, the `outer id` has been given an absolute position (`position:absolute`) and the xy coordinates are defined in pixels (px) (`top: 150px; left: 150px;`). The green color is defined by `color: green;`.

By controlling the position and visibility of layers, you can create many kinds of interesting effects, as shown in Figure 27.2. But be careful. It may look great in the latest version of Netscape Navigator or Internet Explorer. In Figure 27.3, however, you can see what happens to Figure 27.2 when viewed through a browser not capable of displaying style sheets.

Figure 27.1 shows a Web page before disabling the style sheet. The drop caps using negative spacing are very effective. However, to a browser unable to understand layers and style sheets, the Web page shown in Figure 27.2 can result.

**FIG. 27.2**
File viewed through a dynamic HTML capable browser.

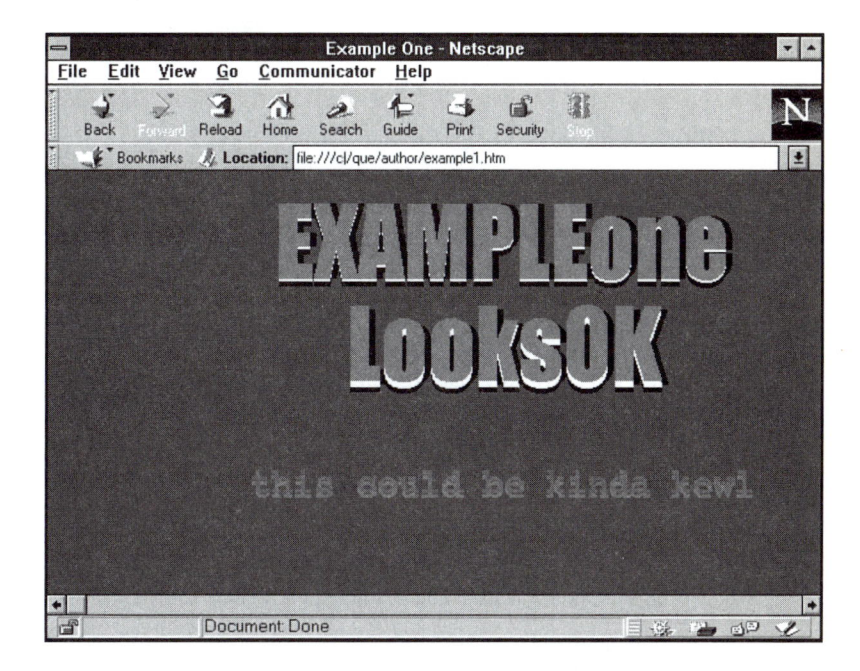

**FIG. 27.3**
Same file viewed with a browser incapable of viewing dynamic HTML.

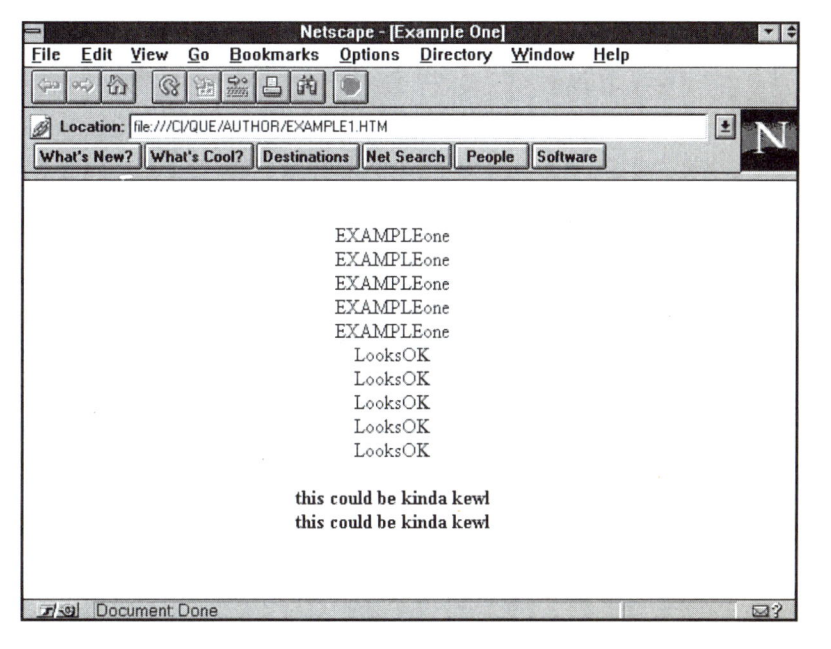

An incomprehensible page, stripped of its layers and style sheets, leaves an impression that certainly wasn't planned. Be sure to test your pages in earlier versions of Internet Explorer and Navigator to make sure they are legible.

By the use of scripts in layers, you can add all sorts of effects and even animations. Layers can be stacked above and below each other with Z-INDEX.

### Listing 27.8    Use of Positioned Elements (Layers)

```
<STYLE type="text/css">
<!--
.example {position: absolute; left: 1in; top: 1in; width: 2in; width:
2in; height: 3in; }
-->
</STYLE>
<IMG SRC="hammie.gif" CLASS="example" ID="image" STYLE="z-index: 1">
<DIV CLASS="example" ID="text1 STYLE="z-index: 3">
This text will overlay hammie the hampsters image.
</DIV>
<DIV CLASS="example" ID="text2 STYLE="z-index: 2">
This text will underlay text 1 but be on top of hammie's picture.
```

In the above example, the z-index order is from back to front. Since "hammie.gif" is z-index: 1, he is at the back. ID="text" 1 is z-index: 3 this text will be on top. ID="text2" is z-index: 2 it will overlay Hammie's picture but be underneath text 1.

The order of elements from back to front is:

- Hammie (back)
- text2 (middle)
- text1 (front)

You will notice that the "<!--" begins the code and the "-->" ends the ".example" code to hide it from browsers not capable of displaying CSS.

The <DIV CLASS="example"...> tag passes the parameters defined by '.example' in the <STYLE> tags to the Web page. This makes the <DIV> tag and <SPAN> tag similar. The <SPAN> tags works in line (i.e. on the same line) and the <DIV> tag works with block elements.

The best way to understand a block element is to look at an HTML document in a browser. Any element that has a line break before and after it is a block element. Examples are any <H> tags and <P> tags. Examples of tags that are not block elements, i.e in line tags, are <i> and <em> tags.

## Visibility

The visibility property determines what is displayed initially.

For example, see Listing 27.9.

### Listing 27.9  Layers and Visibility

```
<STYLE type="text/css">
<!--
#box1 { position: absolute; top: 1in; left: 1in;}
#box2 { position: absolute; top: 1in; left: 1in; visibility:hidden;}
-->
</STYLE>
```

This defines two layers: box1 and box2. When the document is loaded for the first time, only box1 will be visible (see Listing 27.10). Box2 visibility has been defined as hidden (visibility:hidden;).

### Listing 27.10  Using Positioned Elements (Layers)

```
<STYLE type="text/css">
<!--
#box1 { position: absolute; top: 1in; left: 1in;}
#box2 { position: absolute; top: 1in; left: 1in; visibility:hidden;}
-->
</STYLE>
<DIV ID="box1">
<IMG SRC="hammie.gif">
<p>Name: The Late Great Hammie the Hampster</P>
<P>Residence: A little plot in the garden</P>
</DIV>
<DIV ID="box2">
<IMG SRC="thecat.gif">
<P>Evil Cat, Slayer of Hampsters</P>
<P>Residence: Currently unknown, wanted, approach with caution</P>
</Div>
```

When loading this page, a picture of Hammie the Hampster will appear with the text "Name: The Late Great Hammie the Hampster," underneath which will appear the text "Residence: A little plot in the garden." The contents of "box2" will be hidden.

To activate this page you can add the following <FORM> tags underneath the above HTML creating buttons to show the hidden box.

### Listing 27.11  Form to Activate Hidden Box

```
<FORM NAME"deadhampster">
 <INPUT TYPE="button" VALUE="Hammie" onclick='show{"box1"};hide{"box2"}'>
 <INPUT TYPE="button" VALUE="Evil Cat" onclick='show{"box2"};hide{box1"}'>
</FORM>
```

When clicking the "Evil Cat" button, "Hammie" will be replaced by the cat picture and text. Likewise, clicking the "Hammie" button will show the Hammie picture and information, hiding the cat picture.

These layer elements are all handled in the above examples with syntax that has been standardized by the W3C, and therefore, will work in all Dynamic HTML capable browsers.

## Scripting in Layers

The following example makes use of the `<LAYER>` tag and JavaScript. By using simple scripts in your layers, you can make your pages come alive for Netscape Navigator users:

**Listing 27.12  Netscape Navigator Dynamic HTML**

```
<LAYER ID="layer1" BGCOLOR="red"
onMouseOver='changeColor ("red")'
onMouseOut='changeColor ("blue")'>
<P>It was a hot day...</P>
<SCRIPT>
function.changeColor (newcol) {
bgColor=newcol;
}
</SCRIPT>
</LAYER>
```

When the mouse moves into the layer, it turns red. When it moves out, the layer turns blue.

One advantage of layering is that it pre-loads all the elements (text and image files) from the Web page, even though they remain hidden to the viewer. When called, they appear instantly, eliminating the need for the client to keep accessing the Web server.

Borders can be three dimensional or solid. The padding area uses the same element as specified in `backgroundColor` or `backgroundImage`. The width of the box is the sum of its content (text or image), its border, and its padding.

It is also important to note that readers can define their own styles. The following lines:

```
H1 {color: black ! important; background: white ! important}
P { font-size: 12pt ! important; font-style: italic}
```

cause a prioritizing of color, background, and font size. You might notice that the font style of italic is not defined with the `! important` property.

If a reader has his or her own style sheet and needs to see very large type due to visual impairment, for example, the definition of `font-size: 12pt ! important;` would override the reader's `font-size: 48pt ! important;`.

An `! important` definition in a reader's style sheet overrides a normal definition in an author's style sheet. However, an `! important;` definition in a author's style sheet downloaded off the Web overrides a reader's personal style sheet residing on their own system.

Keep this is mind when using `! important` on your Web pages. This leads us to another caution.

HTML was created with this in mind, as a markup language that would adapt to operating systems of all sorts, from UNIX to the PowerPC. Certain elements introduced by browser vendors defeat this adaptability feature such as the `<font face=, size=, color=>` element.

By defining absolutely font sizes, colors, and face, thereby overriding personal preferences in the client browser, Web readers face unpredictable results when confronted with absolutes such as `<font color=white>`; it can lead to illegible text, text designed to compensate for color blindness, and so on. Relative commands `<FONT SIZE=+1>`, `<BIG>`, and `<SMALL>` adjust the reader's text relative to what he already has on his system.

The use of dynamic fonts addresses this by referencing font definition files. These font files may contain one font or many. You can use them in your Web page using `<LINK REL=fontdef SRC="Error! Bookmark not defined.">` where fontchoice.pfr is the font definition file. This font is automatically loaded with the Web page, thereby allowing complete control over font faces and attributes.

Unlike the printed page, which is static, Web pages are being displayed on different monitors across a myriad of operating systems. Each system makes its own demands on our HTML files. After all, the primary function of the World Wide Web is to communicate.

The introduction of style sheets addresses these concerns, letting the author post their Web page with confidence, and knowing that the browser and server can negotiate the best possible display on the user's system. Web page authors can communicate their ideas as closely as possible to their original intent. ●

CHAPTER 28

# Using Layers

*by Jerry Honeycutt*

In the desktop publishing world, layers are rectangular blocks of text and artwork that you can position anywhere on the page you like. Publishers overlap layers so that one is hidden behind another or one bleeds through another. They use layers to create some pretty awesome layouts. Take a look at a few advertisements in your favorite trade rag, for example. Chances are, the publisher used layers. For that matter, take a look at the cover of this book to see a great example of how a publisher uses layers.

Although desktop publishers take layers for granted (even the simplest desktop publishing programs enable you to create and overlap layers), HTML designers don't. They've never had the capability to overlap blocks of text and artwork because HTML is *streaming*. That is, each HTML element is displayed sequentially, one after the other, in order. HTML has never provided for the positioning of an HTML element, much less for overlapping HTML elements.

Until now.

Netscape Navigator 4.0 introduces the <LAYER> tag. You use this tag to create layers, which you can position anywhere on the HTML document, overlapping the HTML document and other layers. You can use it to create advanced layouts in your HTML document, to create simple

### Easily add layers to your HTML documents
The <LAYER> tag gives you real desktop publishing capabilities in a straightforward manner.

### Overlap multiple layers
You have complete control over how overlapped layers appear in your HTML document.

### Create groups by nesting layers
You can insert one layer within another. The nested layer always moves with the outside layer.

### Control your layers with scripts
The real power of layers comes from controlling them with scripts. This chapter shows you how.

### Master layers with this example: fly-over help
The example at the end of this chapter shows you how to create fly-over help for your link.

**574** Chapter 28 Using Layers

animation effects such as a curtain that unveils the contents of your document, or even to provide simple fly-over help for each link on the HTML document. Layers are even more useful when you use them in conjunction with JavaScript to control each layer's position and visibility. For example, you can overlap 10 layers and then peel them away, using a script, to create a simple animation. ■

## Creating a Basic Layer

Listing 28.1 shows the most basic layer possible—easy enough. You start off with the <LAYER> and </LAYER> tags, which define the beginning and end of the layer. Then, you put the HTML content of the layer between those two tags. In this case, no attributes are given. As shown in Figure 28.1, however, you can hardly tell the difference between this result and streaming HTML.

### Listing 28.1  A Simple Layer

```
<HTML>
<HEAD>
<TITLE>Layer 1</TITLE>
</HEAD>
<BODY>

<P>This example shows what a basic layer that contains an image looks like.
Note that the layer isn't positioned in any way whatsoever. Thus,
you can hardly tell it from in-line HTML.</P>

<LAYER>
   <IMG SRC=init.gif>
</LAYER>

</BODY>
</HTML>
```

**FIG. 28.1**
Without positioning the layer, you can't tell the difference between this result and streaming HTML.

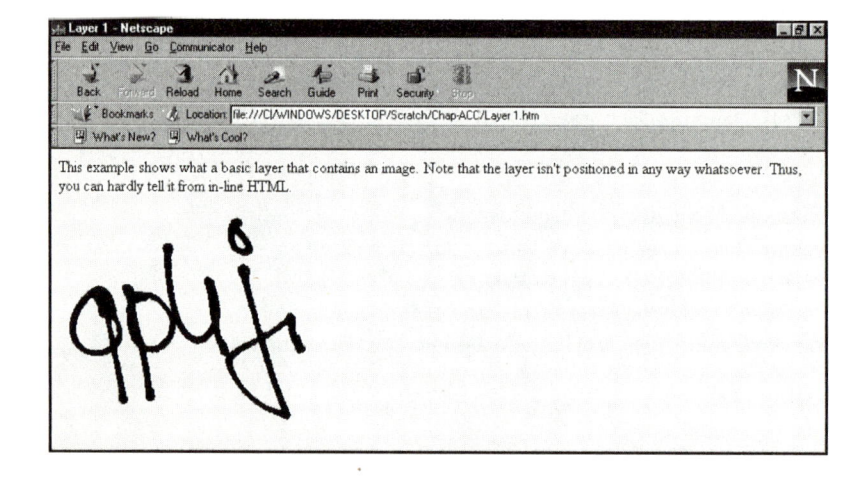

http://www.quecorp.com

> **TIP** You can put any valid HTML within a layer. You can even put plug-ins within a layer.

For your convenience, Table 28.1 describes all of the attributes that the <LAYER> tag supports; however, look to the rest of this chapter to see actual examples of tasks you can do with these attributes. You learn how to position a layer, for example, or overlap a layer with another layer.

**Table 28.1  <LAYER> Attributes**

| Attribute | Description |
| --- | --- |
| ABOVE=layername | Name of the layer that overlaps the target layer |
| BACKGROUND=URL | URL of the layer's background image |
| BELOW=layername | Name of the layer that the target layer overlaps |
| BGCOLOR=color | Color of the layer, which can be specified as an RGB color number or standard color name |
| CLIP="x1,y1,x2,y2" | Clipping rectangle—each dimension is specified as a number of pixels or percentage of the parent container |
| HEIGHT=height | Height, specified as a number of pixels or percentage of the parent container |
| LEFT=x | Horizontal position at which to position the layer relative to its container, specified as a number of pixels or percentage of the parent container |
| NAME=layername | Layer name used for references |
| PAGEX=x | Horizontal position at which to position the layer relative to the Web page, specified as a number of pixels or percentage of the window |
| PAGEY=y | Vertical position at which to position the layer relative to the Web page, specified as a number of pixels or percentage of the window |
| SRC=URL | URL of an HTML file that provides the HTML content of the layer |
| TOP=y | Vertical position at which to position the layer relative to its container, specified as a number of pixels or percentage of the parent container |
| VISIBILITY=option | Visibility of the layer, which can be SHOW, HIDE, or INHERIT |
| WIDTH=width | Width, specified as a number of pixels or percentage of the parent container |
| Z-INDEX=number | Z-index of the layer in relation to the other layers on the Web page |

## Position a Layer on the Web Page

Positioning a layer on your HTML document is real power. You no longer have to struggle to get just the look you want with HTML. Now you can create any look you like by positioning individual blocks of HTML, using the LEFT and TOP attributes of the <LAYER> tag, like this:

```
<LAYER TOP=100 LEFT=20>
```

LEFT and TOP are represented in pixels and are relative to the top-left corner of the containing area within the HTML document. That is, these attributes are relative to the area created if you remove the <LAYER> and </LAYER> tags. For example, to create a layer 10 pixels from the left edge of the browser window and 40 pixels from the top edge, use LEFT=10 and TOP=40. The browser draws the HTML document as though the entire <LAYER> container did not exist, and then the layer is overlapped with the Web page at the given offset. If you were to insert one layer within another layer (you'll learn about nesting layers later), the LEFT and RIGHT attributes of the inside layer would be relative to the top-left corner of the outside layer.

Listing 28.2 shows an HTML document with a layer positioned at 0, 0. Notice in Figure 28.2 how the contents of the HTML document show through the layer.

### Listing 28.2  Positioning a Layer

```
<HTML>
<HEAD>
<TITLE>Layer 2</TITLE>
</HEAD>
<BODY>

<P>This example shows what the same basic layer looks like.</P>

<P>This layer is positioned, however, so that it overlaps
the HTML document below it. Notice how this text displays
through the image's transparent background.</P>

<P>This layer is positioned, however, so that it overlaps
the HTML document below it. Notice how this text displays
through the image's transparent background.</P>

<P>This layer is positioned, however, so that it overlaps
the HTML document below it. Notice how this text displays
through the image's transparent background.</P>

<P>This layer is positioned, however, so that it overlaps
the HTML document below it. Notice how this text displays
through the image's transparent background.</P>

<LAYER TOP=0 LEFT=0>
  <IMG SRC=init.gif>
</LAYER>

</BODY>
</HTML>
```

http://www.quecorp.com

**FIG. 28.2**
Using a layer positioned at 0, 0, you can write HTML that fits snugly against the left border of the browser window.

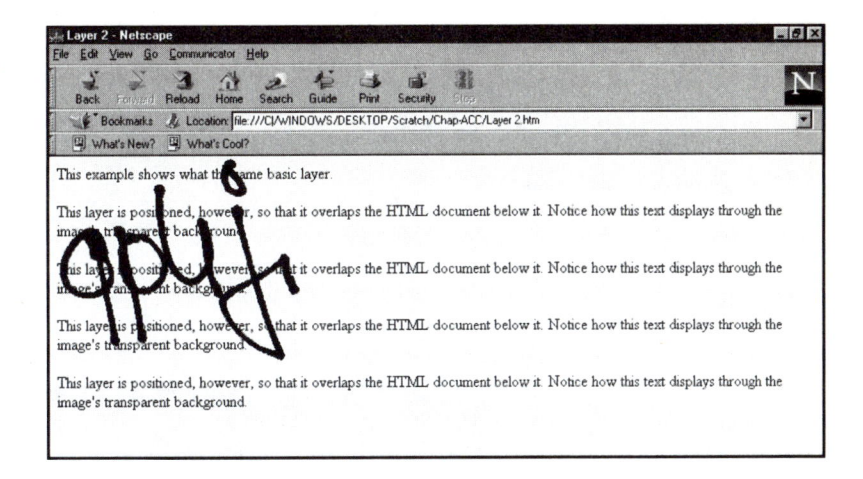

> **NOTE** Positioning a layer at 0,0 isn't the same as omitting the LEFT and TOP attributes from the <LAYER> tag. Positioning a layer at 0, 0 causes the layer to overlap the Web page at the top-left corner. Omitting the LEFT and TOP attributes causes the contents of the layer to appear inline.

Listing 28.3 is a similar example that positions the layer in the middle of the Web page. As shown in Figure 28.3, the contents of the HTML document show through the contents of the layer.

### Listing 28.3  Positioning a Layer in the Middle of the Web Page

```
<HTML>
<HEAD>
<TITLE>Layer 3</TITLE>
</HEAD>
<BODY>

<P>You can position the layer anywhere you like.</P>

<P>This layer is positioned, however, so that it overlaps
the HTML document below it. Notice how this text displays
through the image's transparent background.</P>

<P>This layer is positioned, however, so that it overlaps
the HTML document below it. Notice how this text displays
through the image's transparent background.</P>

<P>This layer is positioned, however, so that it overlaps
the HTML document below it. Notice how this text displays
through the image's transparent background.</P>
```

*continues*

### Listing 28.3 Continued

```
<P>This layer is positioned, however, so that it overlaps
the HTML document below it. Notice how this text displays
through the image's transparent background.</P>

<LAYER TOP=40 LEFT=100>
  <IMG SRC=init.gif>
</LAYER>

</BODY>
</HTML>
```

**FIG. 28.3**
If the layer doesn't entirely fit within the browser window, the browser clips the layer.

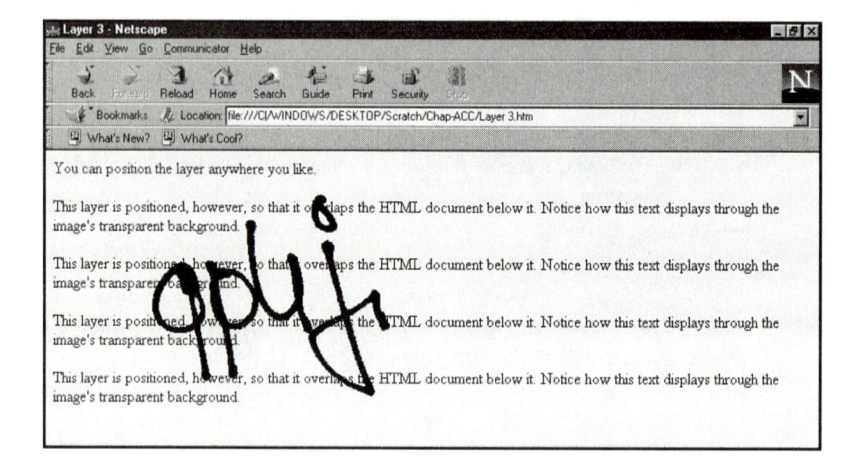

**N O T E** The <ILAYER> tag is very similar to the <LAYER> tag. Instead of positioning its content relative to its container (the window in most cases), it positions its content relative to the location at which the browser would normally position the content if it were inline. You can think of the <ILAYER> tag as a way to gently nudge a block of HTML in one direction or another. For example, if you set LEFT=5 and TOP=2 in the <ILAYER> tag, the browser will draw the layer 5 pixels from the left and 2 pixels from the top of the location where the browser would display the content if you hadn't used the <ILAYER> tag.

## Change the Size of a Layer

You can control the width of a layer, and let the browser determine the appropriate height. You can also control both the width and height. You use the <LAYER> tag's WIDTH and HEIGHT attribute to set the size of the layer in pixels:

```
<LAYER TOP=5 LEFT=5 WIDTH=300 HEIGHT=400>
```

You don't use these attributes to define the absolute size of the layer. Instead, these attributes are used to suggest a size for the purposes of wrapping the text contained within the layer. If the text doesn't completely fill the layer, however, the layer will not actually be as tall and wide

http://www.quecorp.com

as specified. If you're inserting an image (or another element that the browser can't wrap) inside of a layer and the image is bigger than the suggested size, the actual size of the layer will be bigger than the suggested value.

Listing 28.4 shows an example of a layer positioned 100 pixels from the top that is 60 pixels wide. As shown in Figure 28.4, the text wraps within the layer, just like it would wrap within a table cell that's 60 pixels wide.

### Listing 28.4 Specifying the Width of a Layer

```
<HTML>
<HEAD>
<TITLE>Layer 4</TITLE>
</HEAD>
<BODY>

<LAYER TOP=0>
  This text is contained within the first layer. It starts in the
  upper, left-hand corner of the browser window. Notice that the
  width of this layer isn't controlled.
</LAYER>

<LAYER TOP=100 WIDTH=160>
  This text is contained within the first layer. It starts in the
  upper, left-hand corner of the browser window. Notice how the width
  of this layer is controlled.
</LAYER>

</BODY>
</HTML>
```

**FIG. 28.4**
You can leave out either the TOP or LEFT attributes and the browser will position the layer as though the omitted attribute is 0.

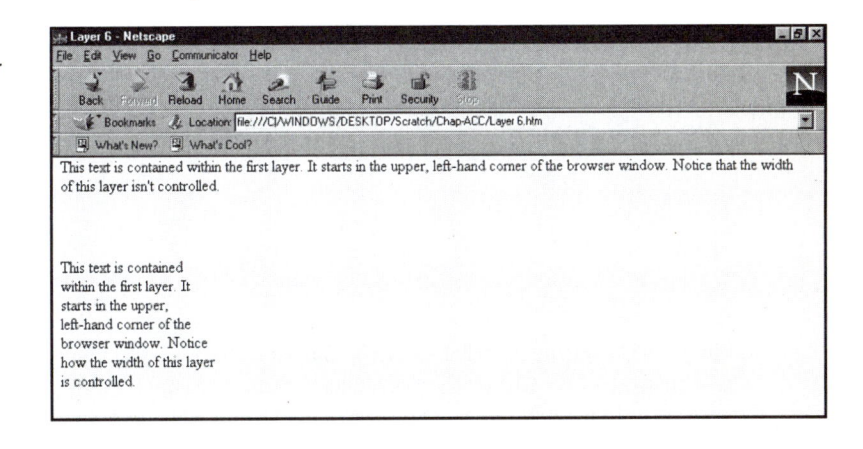

> **TIP** You can use a layer to do many of the same formatting tricks you've learned to do with the <TABLE> tag.

## Display a Background Image or Color

By default, the empty space in a layer is transparent. That is, if a pixel in the layer doesn't contain any rendered text, or it contains a portion of an image that's transparent, anything underneath the layer shows through at that point. You can use this to create some incredible effects.

You might want the layer to occupy a well-defined space on the Web page, however. If a layer contains mostly text and it's overlapped, the content of the layer might be hard to read. You can use a background image or background color with a layer so that what's behind the layer doesn't show through.

Listing 28.5 shows a layer that defines a background color for a layer using the BGCOLOR attribute. You can set this attribute to any valid color name or RGB color value (#FF0000, for example), just as you would with any other color attribute in HTML. As Figure 28.5 shows, the content behind the layer no longer shows through.

### Listing 28.5  Setting a Layer's Background Color

```
<HTML>
<HEAD>
<TITLE>Layer 5</TITLE>
</HEAD>
<BODY>

<P>Change the background color of a layer.
Notice that this text doesn't show through a layer
that uses the BGCOLOR attribute.</P>

qwerty. qwerty. qwerty. qwerty. qwerty. qwerty. qwerty. qwerty. qwerty.
qwerty. qwerty. qwerty. qwerty. qwerty. qwerty. qwerty. qwerty. qwerty.
qwerty. qwerty. qwerty. qwerty. qwerty. qwerty. qwerty. qwerty. qwerty.
qwerty. qwerty. qwerty. qwerty. qwerty. Qwert . qwerty. qwerty. qwerty.
qwerty. qwerty. qwerty. qwerty. qwerty. qwerty. qwerty. qwerty. qwerty.
qwerty. qwerty. qwerty. qwerty. qwerty. qwerty. qwerty. qwerty. qwerty.
qwerty. qwerty. qwerty. qwerty. qwerty. qwerty. qwerty. qwerty. qwerty.

<LAYER TOP=40 LEFT=100 BGCOLOR=GRAY>
   <IMG SRC=init.gif>
</LAYER>

</BODY>
</HTML>
```

Listing 28.6 shows you a similar example that sets a background image for the layer using the BACKGROUND attribute. You set the BACKGROUND attribute to the URL (relative or absolute) of the image you want to tile in the background of the layer. Unlike normal tiled backgrounds in

HTML, if a layer's background image has transparent areas, the content behind the layer shows through those areas. Figure 28.6 shows what this example looks like in the browser window.

**FIG. 28.5**
When you use a background color, the content behind the layer doesn't peek through.

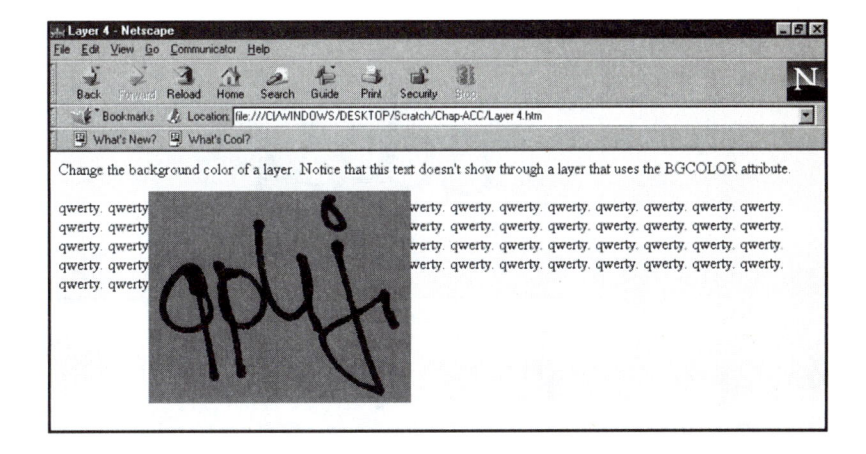

**Listing 28.6  Setting a Layer's Background Image**

```
<HTML>
<HEAD>
<TITLE>Layer 6</TITLE>
</HEAD>
<BODY>

<P>Use a background image with a layer.
Notice that this text doesn't show through a layer
that uses the BACKGROUND attribute.</P>

qwerty. qwerty. qwerty. qwerty. qwerty. qwerty. qwerty. qwerty. qwerty.
qwerty. qwerty. qwerty. qwerty. qwerty. qwerty. qwerty. qwerty. qwerty.
qwerty. qwerty. qwerty. qwerty. qwerty. qwerty. qwerty. qwerty. qwerty.
qwerty. qwerty. qwerty. qwerty. qwerty. qwerty. qwerty. qwerty. qwerty.
qwerty. qwerty. qwerty. qwerty. qwerty. qwerty. qwerty. qwerty. qwerty.
qwerty. qwerty. qwerty. qwerty. qwerty. qwerty. qwerty. qwerty. qwerty.
qwerty. qwerty. qwerty. qwerty. qwerty. qwerty. qwerty. qwerty. qwerty.

<LAYER TOP=40 LEFT=100 BACKGROUND=bg.gif>
   <IMG SRC=init.gif>
</LAYER>

</BODY>
</HTML>
```

**FIG. 28.6**
Use your favorite graphics editor to create a border and then insert it into the layer.

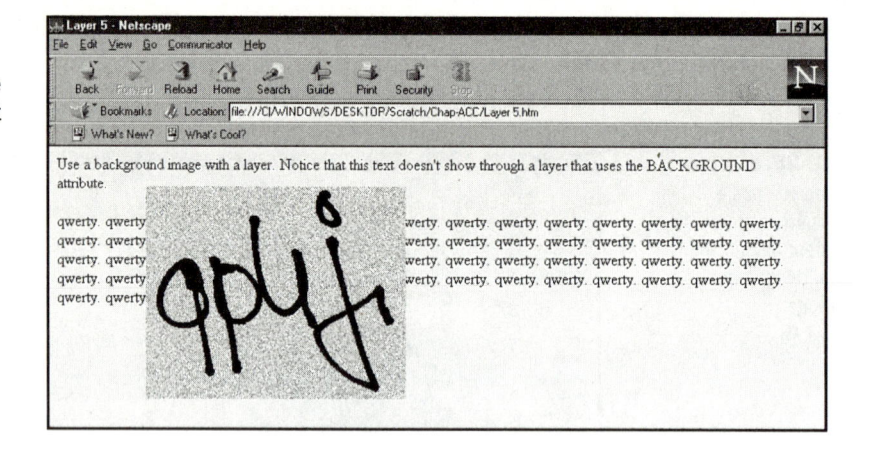

## Overlapping Multiple Layers

Thus far, you've seen examples that use a single layer. However, you can add as many layers as you like in your HTML document, as shown in Listing 28.7 and Figure 28.7. Each layer can contain any valid HTML, including images, text, and plug-ins. A good case for using multiple layers is to create layers that define different backgrounds for different areas of the Web page. You can add different layers to the Web page that might be visible at different times, based upon the user's interaction with the Web page.

**Listing 28.7  Using Multiple Layers**

```
<HTML>
<HEAD>
<TITLE>Layer 7</TITLE>
</HEAD>
<BODY>

<LAYER TOP=40 LEFT=60 BACKGROUND=bg.gif>
  <B>This is the first layer.</B><BR>
  <B>This is the first layer.</B><BR>
  <B>This is the first layer.</B><BR>
  <B>This is the first layer.</B><BR>
  <B>This is the first layer.</B><BR>
  <B>This is the first layer.</B><BR>
  <B>This is the first layer.</B><BR>
  <B>This is the first layer.</B><BR>
</LAYER>

<LAYER TOP=40 LEFT=220>
  <IMG SRC=init.gif>
</LAYER>

</BODY>
</HTML>
```

http://www.quecorp.com

**FIG. 28.7**
You can build your entire HTML document using layers and then arrange them as you like.

You can also cause layers to overlap by setting each layer's TOP and LEFT attributes so that one layer appears on top of another. Figure 28.8 shows two layers. The first layer contains a handful of text and has a background image. The second layer contains an image with a transparent background. The second layer is positioned so that it overlaps the first layer.

**Listing 28.8  Positioning Two Layers so that They Overlap**

```
<HTML>
<HEAD>
<TITLE>Layer 8</TITLE>
</HEAD>
<BODY>

<LAYER TOP=40 LEFT=60 BACKGROUND=bg.gif>
   <B>This is the first layer. It's behind the second layer.</B><BR>
   <B>This is the first layer. It's behind the second layer.</B><BR>
   <B>This is the first layer. It's behind the second layer.</B><BR>
   <B>This is the first layer. It's behind the second layer.</B><BR>
   <B>This is the first layer. It's behind the second layer.</B><BR>
   <B>This is the first layer. It's behind the second layer.</B><BR>
   <B>This is the first layer. It's behind the second layer.</B><BR>
   <B>This is the first layer. It's behind the second layer.</B><BR>
</LAYER>

<LAYER TOP=80 LEFT=200>
   <IMG SRC=init.gif>
</LAYER>

</BODY>
</HTML>
```

**N O T E**  By default, the browser draws overlapped layers in the order that it encounters them. That is, it draws the first layer, overlaps that with the second layer, and so on.

**FIG. 28.8**
Since the image in the second layer has transparent areas, the content behind this layer bleeds through.

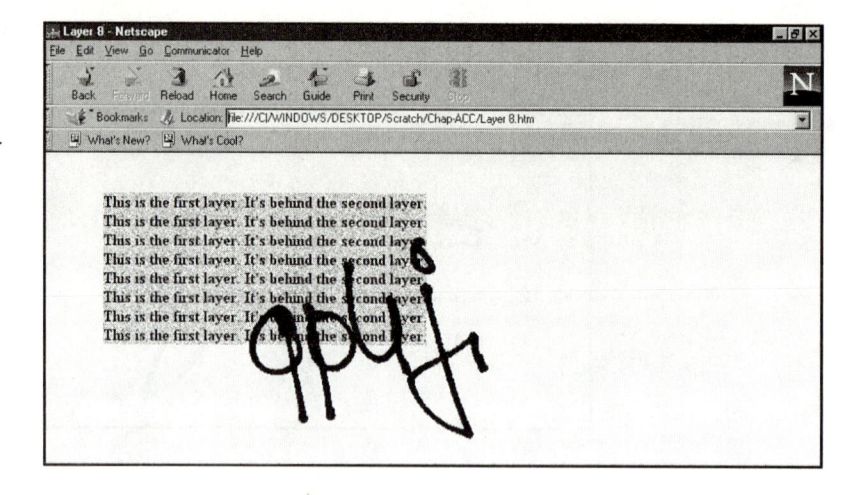

## Change a Layer's *Z-INDEX*

If you don't like the order in which the browser overlaps layers, you can easily change it. The most straightforward way to change the order in which layers overlap is by using the `<LAYER>` tag's `Z-INDEX` attribute, which you set to any positive integer value to define the stacking order for a layer:

`<LAYER Z-INDEX=1>`

Layers are drawn in increasing stacking order. For example, a layer with a stacking order of 10 overlaps a layer with a stacking order of 5. On the other hand, a layer with a stacking order of 3 is overlapped by a layer with a stacking order of 5. Still escapes you? Place your left hand down on a table, and put your right hand on top of it. The right hand covers the left hand, so it has a higher stacking order than the left hand.

Listing 28.9 is an example of three layers, each of which uses the `Z-INDEX` attribute to define its stacking order. The first layer has a stacking order of 2, the second has a stacking order of 1, and the third has a stacking order of 3. Thus, the browser draws the second layer first, the first layer second, and the third layer last, as shown in Figure 28.9.

### Listing 28.9  Using Z-INDEX

```
<HTML>
<HEAD>
<TITLE>Layer 9</TITLE>
</HEAD>
<BODY>

<LAYER TOP=40 LEFT=60 BACKGROUND=bg.gif Z-INDEX=2>
  <B>This is the first layer. It's in the middle.</B><BR>
  <B>This is the first layer. It's in the middle.</B><BR>
  <B>This is the first layer. It's in the middle.</B><BR>
  <B>This is the first layer. It's in the middle.</B><BR>
```

http://www.quecorp.com

```
        <B>This is the first layer. It's in the middle.</B><BR>
        <B>This is the first layer. It's in the middle.</B><BR>
        <B>This is the first layer. It's in the middle.</B><BR>
        <B>This is the first layer. It's in the middle.</B><BR>
    </LAYER>

    <LAYER TOP=80 LEFT=200 BACKGROUND=bg2.gif Z-INDEX=1>
        <B>This is the second layer. It's behind the first layer.</B><BR>
        <B>This is the second layer. It's behind the first layer.</B><BR>
        <B>This is the second layer. It's behind the first layer.</B><BR>
        <B>This is the second layer. It's behind the first layer.</B><BR>
        <B>This is the second layer. It's behind the first layer.</B><BR>
        <B>This is the second layer. It's behind the first layer.</B><BR>
        <B>This is the second layer. It's behind the first layer.</B><BR>
        <B>This is the second layer. It's behind the first layer.</B><BR>
    </LAYER>

    <LAYER TOP=100 LEFT=80 Z-INDEX=3>
        <IMG SRC=init.gif>
    </LAYER>

</BODY>
</HTML>
```

**FIG. 28.9**
The Z-INDEX attribute essentially defines the order in which each layer is drawn.

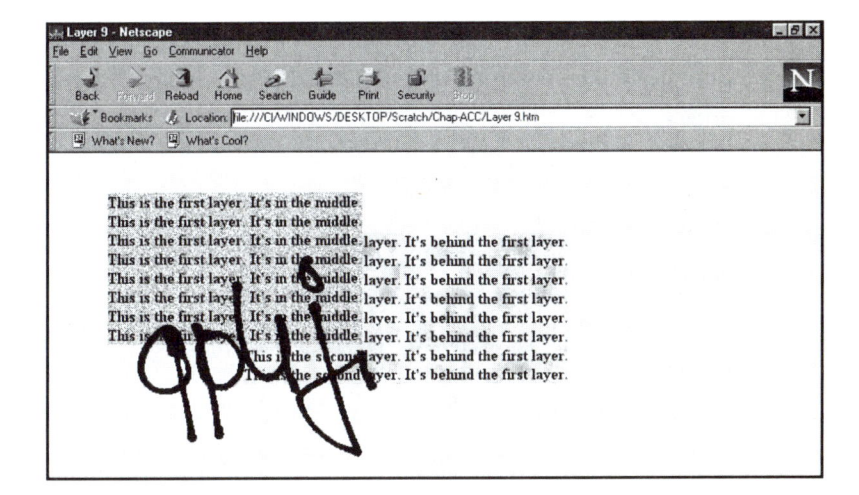

**TIP** You can overlap several layers at the same position, define each layer's stacking order in sequence, and then peel away the layers one at a time (using a script) to create a simple animation.

## Overlap Two Layers with *ABOVE* and *BELOW*

The Z-INDEX attribute specifies the order in which layers are drawn by ranking each layer. You can get much more specific than that, however, by defining exactly which layer you want to display above or below another layer. For example, if you have a layer containing an image, and you want to make sure that a specific layer containing text is displayed over it, you can tell the browser to specifically draw the text layer over the image layer.

Before you can do that, however, you have to give each layer a name. Use the NAME attribute, like this:

`<LAYER NAME=MYLAYER>`

Then, you use the `<LAYER>` tag's ABOVE or BELOW attributes to specify exactly which layer you want to draw above or below the current layer, referring to each layer by its name. For example, if you have an existing layer called MYLAYER, and you want to make sure that the browser draws it below a layer named YOURLAYER, you'd write a `<LAYER>` tag that looks like this:

`<LAYER NAME=YOURLAYER BELOW=MYLAYER>`

On the other hand, if you want to make sure that the browser draws MYLAYER on top of a layer named HERLAYER, you'd write a `<LAYER>` tag that looks like this:

`<LAYER NAME=HERLAYER ABOVE=MYLAYER>`

Listing 28.10 shows the example from Listing 28.9, rewritten to use the ABOVE and BELOW attributes. Instead of defining a Z-INDEX for each layer, it specifies that the layer called FIRST is above the layer called SECOND, and below the layer called THIRD (see Figure 28.10).

### Listing 28.10  Using *ABOVE* and *BELOW* to Specify Order

```
<HTML>
<HEAD>
<TITLE>Layer 10</TITLE>
</HEAD>
<BODY>

<LAYER NAME=FIRST TOP=40 LEFT=60 BACKGROUND=bg.gif>
  <B>This is the first layer. It's in the middle.</B><BR>
  <B>This is the first layer. It's in the middle.</B><BR>
  <B>This is the first layer. It's in the middle.</B><BR>
  <B>This is the first layer. It's in the middle.</B><BR>
  <B>This is the first layer. It's in the middle.</B><BR>
  <B>This is the first layer. It's in the middle.</B><BR>
  <B>This is the first layer. It's in the middle.</B><BR>
  <B>This is the first layer. It's in the middle.</B><BR>
</LAYER>

<LAYER NAME=SECOND TOP=80 LEFT=200 BACKGROUND=bg2.gif ABOVE=FIRST>
  <B>This is the second layer. It's behind the first layer.</B><BR>
  <B>This is the second layer. It's behind the first layer.</B><BR>
  <B>This is the second layer. It's behind the first layer.</B><BR>
  <B>This is the second layer. It's behind the first layer.</B><BR>
  <B>This is the second layer. It's behind the first layer.</B><BR>
  <B>This is the second layer. It's behind the first layer.</B><BR>
  <B>This is the second layer. It's behind the first layer.</B><BR>
  <B>This is the second layer. It's behind the first layer.</B><BR>
</LAYER>
```

```
<LAYER NAME=THIRD TOP=100 LEFT=80 BELOW=FIRST>
  <IMG SRC=init.gif>
</LAYER>

</BODY>
</HTML>
```

**FIG. 28.10**
The top layer doesn't use a background so it is transparent.

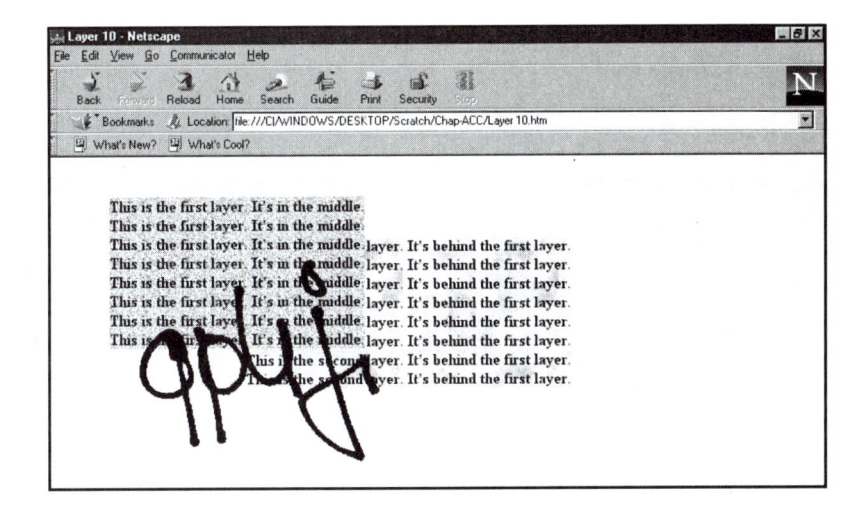

> **N O T E** If your layers get overly complicated, you can store the content of each layer in a separate HTML file, just as you do with frames. Create an HTML file for each layer. Then, within the <LAYER> tag, set the SRC attribute to the URL of the layer's HTML file, like this: `SRC=layer1.html`.

## Nesting Layers to Create a Group

So far, you've only seen cases where a handful of layers were added to the HTML document. They were siblings insofar as one was not contained within another. You can insert one layer inside of another layer, however, to create a parent-child relationship. In that case, the child (inside) layer is relative to the parent (outside) layer. Thus, if you create a layer called PARENT and locate it at 10, 10, and then nest a layer inside of PARENT called CHILD located at 5, 5, the child layer will actually be displayed at 15, 15 on the HTML document. If you move the parent layer to 20, 20, the child layer will move right along with it to 25, 25.

Listing 28.11 shows you an example of nested layers. The parent layer contains an image of a Christmas tree29. It contains a number of nested layers that represent bulbs. The coordinates of each nested layer are relative to the upper-left corner of the parent layer. If you move the Christmas tree to another location on the Web page, the bulbs will move right along with it.

### Listing 28.11  Nesting Layers

```
<HTML>
<HEAD>
<TITLE>Layer 11</TITLE>
</HEAD>
<BODY>

<LAYER TOP=0 LEFT=0 CLIP=300,400>
<IMG SRC=xtree.gif>

<LAYER TOP=160 LEFT=60>
</LAYER>

<LAYER TOP=150 LEFT=60>
<IMG SRC=ball1.gif>
</LAYER>

<LAYER TOP=20 LEFT=100>
<IMG SRC=ball2.gif>
</LAYER>

<LAYER TOP=130 LEFT=120>
<IMG SRC=ball1.gif>
</LAYER>

<LAYER TOP=170 LEFT=140>
<IMG SRC=ball2.gif>
</LAYER>

<LAYER TOP=200 LEFT=120>
<IMG SRC=ball2.gif>
</LAYER>

<LAYER TOP=80 LEFT=80>
<IMG SRC=ball3.gif>
</LAYER>

<LAYER TOP-90 LEFT=125>
<IMG SRC=ball3.gif>
</LAYER>

<LAYER TOP=200 LEFT=60>
<IMG SRC=ball3.gif>
</LAYER>

<LAYER TOP=200 LEFT=180>
<IMG SRC=ball3.gif>
</LAYER>

</LAYER>

</BODY>
</HTML>
```

http://www.quecorp.com

**FIG. 28.11**
By capturing the mouse events for each bulb, as described in "Attaching Scripts to Layers," you can allow the user to move the bulbs around on the Christmas tree.

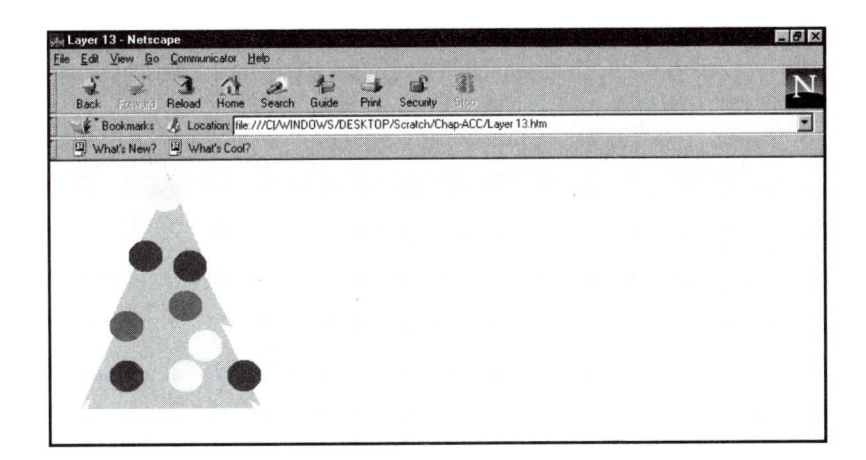

> **TIP** You'll frequently see the terms *reference* layer or *target* layer in Netscape documentation. When you're writing a layer that refers to other layers, such as a parent layer, the layer that you're writing is called the reference or target layer. This terminology is a bit confusing because you'd think that the reference layer is the one to which you're referring.

# Creating Content for Browsers that Don't Do Layers

<LAYER> is not part of HTML 3.2 and is only supported by Navigator 4.0. Thus, if you're concerned about compatibility with Internet Explorer or other browsers, you should avoid the <LAYER> tag or provide an alternate HTML document for those users. Note that you can also position content using Cascading Style Sheets, as described in Chapter 29, "Using Style Sheets."

If you want to provide additional content for those browsers that can't display the <LAYER> tag, add the content sandwiched between the <NOLAYER> and </NOLAYER> tags. Browsers that can't display layers won't display the contents of the <LAYER> container, but will display the contents of the <NOLAYER> container. On the other hand, Netscape Navigator will display the contents of the <LAYER> tag, while ignoring the contents of the <NOLAYER> tag.

# Attaching Scripts to Layers

The ability to position a layer anywhere in an HTML document and to overlap that layer with other layers gives you a wealth of publishing capabilities. Additionally, you can create a variety of special effects by attaching a script to a layer, which can then be used to hide, show, or move the layer within the browser window.

You can reference a layer by using its name, like this:

```
Layers.LayerName
```

*LayerName* is the name of the layer as defined by the `<LAYER>` tag's `NAME` attribute. You can also reference a layer by using the layers array: `document.layers`. You use an index with the layers array, or you reference a layer in the array by name:

```
document.layers[2]
document.layers["MyLayer"]
```

Layers have a variety of properties and methods. Properties of a layer are written as *LayerName.PropertyName* and *LayerName.MethodName(Parameters)*. For example, to make a layer invisible, you set its `visibility` property to `HIDE`, like this:

```
layers.MyLayer.visibility = "hide";
```

Table 28.2 describes the properties of the Layer object. These properties roughly correspond to the attributes you've already learned about in this chapter.

### Table 28.2  The Layer Object's Properties

| Property | Description |
| --- | --- |
| above | See `ABOVE` in Table 28.1 |
| background | See `BACKGROUND` in Table 28.1 |
| below | See `BELOW` in Table 28.1 |
| bgColor | See `BGCOLOR` in Table 28.1 |
| clip | See `CLIP` in Table 28.1 |
| layers | Array that contains all of the child layers that are nested within the referenced layer |
| left | See `LEFT` in Table 28.1 |
| name | See `NAME` in Table 28.1 |
| pageX | See `PAGEX` in Table 28.1 |
| pageY | See `PAGEY` in Table 28.1 |
| parentLayer | Name of the layer that contains the referenced layer, if the layer is nested |
| siblingAbove | Name of the layer displayed immediately above the referenced layer |
| siblingBelow | Name of the layer displayed immediately below the referenced layer |
| src | See `SRC` in Table 28.1 |
| top | See `TOP` in Table 28.1 |
| visibility | See VISIBILITY IN Table 28.1; set to `"hide"`, `"show"`, or `"inherit"` (note that these are strings, not keywords) |

http://www.quecorp.com

Table 28.3 describes the methods of the Layer object. Note that every method corresponds to a property, so that you can control layers by setting their properties or calling their methods (or both).

**Table 28.3  The Layer Object's Methods**

| Method | Description |
| --- | --- |
| load(URL,width) | Loads the given HTML file into the layer and sets the layer's width |
| moveAbove(layer) | Stacks the referenced layer above the layer called layer |
| moveBelow(layer) | Stacks the referenced layer below the layer called layer |
| moveBy(x,y) | Offsets the layer by the given deltas so that LEFT = LEFT + x and TOP = TOP + y |
| moveTo(x,y) | Changes the layer's position so that LEFT = x and TOP = y, relative to the layer's container |
| moveToAbsolute(x,y) | Changes the layer's position so that pageX = x and pageY = y |
| resizeBy(width,height) | Changes the height and width of the layer's clipping rectangle by the given delta |
| resizeTo(width,height) | Changes the height and width of the layer's clipping rectangle |

## Hide and Show a Layer Using a Script

You can use a script to hide and show layers in an HTML document. For example, you can create a layer that is only displayed when the user moves the mouse across an image. In that case, you set the layer's VISIBILITY attribute to "HIDE" so that it's not displayed initially. Then, in the image's OnMouseOver event, you set the layer's visibility property to "SHOW", like this:

```
Layers.MyLayer.visibility = "show";
```

You can also set VISIBILITY to "INHERIT". This causes the layer to inherit the VISIBILITY attribute of its parent container. For example, if you've nested one layer within another, setting "INHERIT" in the child layer causes it to inherit the VISIBILITY attribute of its parent layer.

Listing 28.12 shows you an example that does something similar. It contains three layers and three buttons. The script associated with each button toggles the visibility of each layer. Click a button associated with a visible layer and the script makes the layer invisible (see Figure 28.12).

Take a look at the function called ToggleFirst(). It toggles the state of the flag called ShowFirst, which indicates whether or not the layer called FIRST is visible. Then, it sets the layer's visibility property to "HIDE" if ShowFirst is false; otherwise, it sets the property to "SHOW".

### Listing 28.12   Hiding and Showing Layers

```
<HTML>
<HEAD>
<TITLE>Layer 12</TITLE>

<SCRIPT LANGUAGE=JAVASCRIPT>

ShowFirst = true;
ShowSecond=false;
ShowThird=true;

function ToggleFirst()
{
  ShowFirst = !ShowFirst;
  document.layers["FIRST"].visibility = ShowFirst ? "SHOW" : "HIDE";
}

function ToggleSecond()
{
  ShowSecond = !ShowSecond;
  document.layers["SECOND"].visibility = ShowSecond ? "SHOW" : "HIDE";
}

function ToggleThird()
{
  ShowThird = !ShowThird;
  document.layers["THIRD"].visibility = ShowThird ? "SHOW" : "HIDE";
}

</SCRIPT>

</HEAD>
<BODY>
<LAYER NAME=FIRST TOP=80 LEFT=60 BACKGROUND=bg.gif>
<B>This is the first layer. It's in the middle.</B><BR>
<B>This is the first layer. It's in the middle.</B><BR>
<B>This is the first layer. It's in the middle.</B><BR>
<B>This is the first layer. It's in the middle.</B><BR>
<B>This is the first layer. It's in the middle.</B><BR>
<B>This is the first layer. It's in the middle.</B><BR>
<B>This is the first layer. It's in the middle.</B><BR>
<B>This is the first layer. It's in the middle.</B><BR>
</LAYER>

<LAYER NAME=SECOND TOP=120 LEFT=200 BACKGROUND=bg2.gif Z-INDEX=1 BELOW=FIRST
VISIBILITY=HIDE>
<B>This is the second layer. It's behind the first layer.</B><BR>
<B>This is the second layer. It's behind the first layer.</B><BR>
<B>This is the second layer. It's behind the first layer.</B><BR>
<B>This is the second layer. It's behind the first layer.</B><BR>
<B>This is the second layer. It's behind the first layer.</B><BR>
<B>This is the second layer. It's behind the first layer.</B><BR>
<B>This is the second layer. It's behind the first layer.</B><BR>
<B>This is the second layer. It's behind the first layer.</B><BR>
```

Attaching Scripts to Layers | 593

```
</LAYER>

<LAYER NAME=THIRD TOP=140 LEFT=80 BELOW=FIRST>
<IMG SRC=init.gif>
</LAYER>

<LAYER TOP=0 LEFT=0>
<FORM NAME=TOGGLE>
  <TABLE ALIGN=CENTER>
    <TD>
      <INPUT NAME=FIRST TYPE=BUTTON VALUE="Toggle First Layer "
onclick="ToggleFirst();">
    </TD>
    <TD>
      <INPUT NAME=SECOND TYPE=BUTTON VALUE="Toggle Second Layer"
onclick="ToggleSecond();">
    </TD>
    <TD>
      <INPUT NAME=THIRD TYPE=BUTTON VALUE="Toggle Third Layer "
onclick="ToggleThird();">
    </TD>
  </TABLE>
</FORM>
</LAYER>

</BODY>
</HTML>
```

**FIG. 28.12**
As you click buttons to hide a layer, the browser peels that layer away, unveiling what's underneath it.

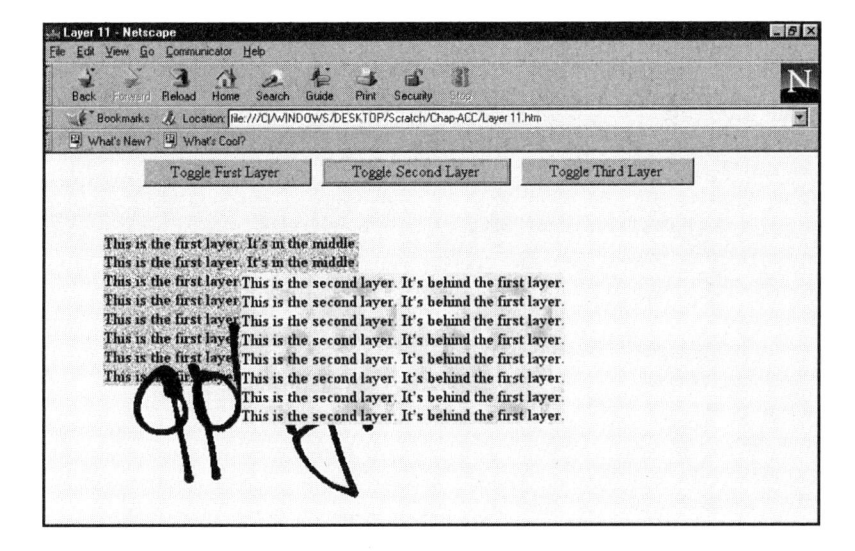

**TIP** In Windows 95, you've seen dialog boxes that contain a button with the text More>>. When you click that button, additional fields are presented. You can achieve the same effect in an HTML form by attaching a script to a form's button that shows another form hidden within a layer.

## Move a Layer with a Script

Besides showing and hiding a layer, you can also move it around on the Web page. You can use this to create some pretty fancy animation effects, such as a curtain that appears to open, unveiling the contents of the page. Moving a layer around is easy. You can either use the moveBy or moveTo methods; or you can set the value of the left and top properties, which is the approach taken in Listing 28.13; the result is shown in Figure 28.13.

This example contains two layers. It also contains four buttons labeled Up, Down, Left, and Right. Each button is associated with a function that moves the second layer in the appropriate direction. For example, the Up function subtracts 10 from the second layer's top property, which has the effect of moving the layer up 10 pixels. The Right function adds 10 to the second layer's left property, which has the effect of moving the layer right 10 pixels.

### Listing 28.13  Moving a Layer with a Script

```
<HTML>
<HEAD>
<TITLE>Layer 13</TITLE>

<SCRIPT LANGUAGE=JAVASCRIPT>

function Up()
{
  document.layers["SECOND"].top -= 10;
}

function Down()
{
  document.layers["SECOND"].top += 10;
}

function Left()
{
  document.layers["SECOND"].left -= 10;
}

function Right()
{
  document.layers["SECOND"].left += 10;
}

</SCRIPT>

</HEAD>
<BODY>

<LAYER NAME=FIRST TOP=200 LEFT=300 BACKGROUND=bg.gif>
<B>This is the first layer. It's always on top.</B><BR>
<B>This is the first layer. It's always on top.</B><BR>
```

## Attaching Scripts to Layers

```
    <B>This is the first layer. It's always on top.</B><BR>
    <B>This is the first layer. It's always on top.</B><BR>
    <B>This is the first layer. It's always on top.</B><BR>
    <B>This is the first layer. It's always on top.</B><BR>
    <B>This is the first layer. It's always on top.</B><BR>
    <B>This is the first layer. It's always on top.</B><BR>
    <B>This is the first layer. It's always on top.</B><BR>
</LAYER>

<LAYER NAME=SECOND TOP=180 LEFT=0 ABOVE=FIRST>
<IMG SRC=init.gif>
</LAYER>

<LAYER TOP=0 LEFT=0>
<FORM NAME=BUTTONS>
  <TABLE>
    <TR>
      <TD></TD>
      <TD ALIGN=CENTER>
        <INPUT WIDTH=100% NAME=UP TYPE=BUTTON VALUE="Up" onclick="Up();">
      </TD>
      <TD></TD>
    </TR>

    <TR>
      <TD ALIGN=CENTER>
        <INPUT NAME=LEFT TYPE=BUTTON VALUE="Left " onclick="Left();">
      </TD>
      <TD></TD>
      <TD ALIGN=CENTER>
        <INPUT WIDTH=100 NAME=RIGHT TYPE=BUTTON VALUE="Right" ➥
            onclick="Right();">
      </TD>
    </TR>

    <TR>
      <TD></TD>
      <TD ALIGN=CENTER>
        <INPUT WIDTH=100 NAME=DOWN TYPE=BUTTON VALUE="Down " ➥
            onclick="Down();">
      </TD>
      <TD></TD>
    </TR>

  </TABLE>
</FORM>
</LAYER>

</BODY>
</HTML>
```

**FIG. 28.13**
As you move the second layer relative to the first layer, it will disappear underneath. This is because the second layer's ABOVE property is set to FIRST.

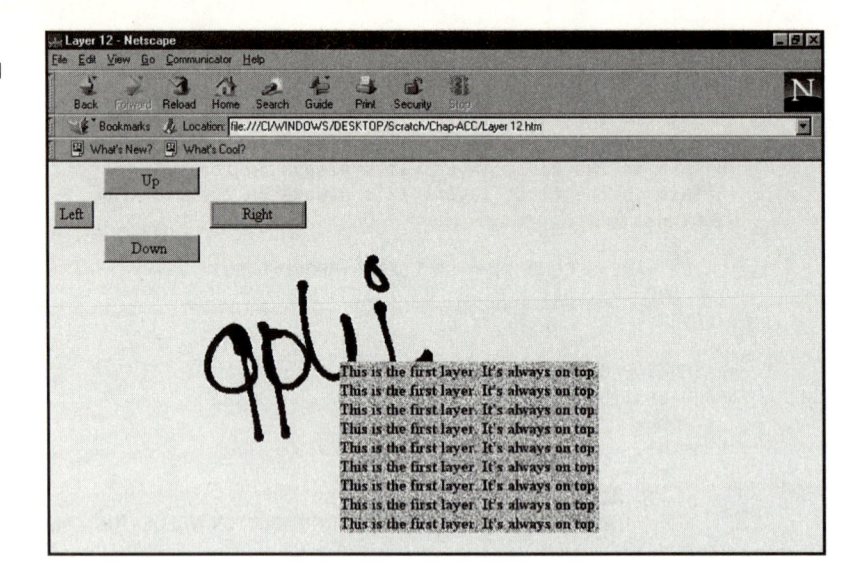

> **TIP** Resizing the Web browser causes the layers to return to their original position.

## Putting Layers to Practical Use

One of the practical uses for layers is to create fly-over help or tips for links and objects on the HTML document. For example, you can insert a number of art images on a page and then display more information about the image when the user moves the mouse across the image.

The example shown in Listing 28.14 gives the user additional information about each link on the HTML document. When the user moves the mouse over the second link shown in Figure 28.14, for example, the function associated with that link shows the appropriate layer, which contains additional information about the link.

**Listing 28.14  Providing Fly-Over Help for Links**

```
<HTML>
<HEAD>
<TITLE>Layer 14</TITLE>
</HEAD>
<BODY>

<SCRIPT LANGUAGE="JAVASCRIPT">

// Hide all of the layers (tips) in this HTML document
```

http://www.quecorp.com

## Putting Layers to Practical Use

```
function ClearHelp()
{
  for( i=0; i < document.layers.length; i++)
    document.layers[i].visibility = "HIDE";
}

// Clear all the displayed layers; then, display the layer by the
// given name. Set a timer to automatically clear the layers after
// five seconds.

function OnLink( Name )
{
  ClearHelp()
  document.layers[Name].visibility="INHERIT";
  window.window.setTimeout( "ClearHelp()", 5000 );
}
</SCRIPT>

<A OnMouseOver='OnLink("LINK1")' HREF="http://rampages.onramp.net/
~jerry">Jerry's Home Page</A>
<LAYER NAME=LINK1 VISIBILITY=HIDE>
<TABLE BORDER=1 BGCOLOR=YELLOW>
  <TD>
    Click on this link to jump to Jerry's home page.
  </TD>
</TABLE>
</LAYER>

<BR>

<A OnMouseOver='OnLink("LINK2")' HREF="http://www.netscape.com">Netscape's Home
Page</A>
<LAYER NAME=LINK2  VISIBILITY=HIDE>
<TABLE BORDER=1 BGCOLOR=YELLOW>
  <TD>
    Click on this link to jump to Netscape's home page.
  </TD>
</TABLE>
</LAYER>

<BR>

<A OnMouseOver='OnLink("LINK3")' HREF="http://www.yahoo.com">Yahoo!</A>
<LAYER NAME=LINK3  VISIBILITY=HIDE>
<TABLE BORDER=1 BGCOLOR=YELLOW>
  <TD>
    Click on this link to jump to Yahoo!
  </TD>
</TABLE>
</LAYER>
</BODY>
</HTML>
```

**FIG. 28.14**
Using a bordered table within a layer helps to better set it off from the underlying HTML document.

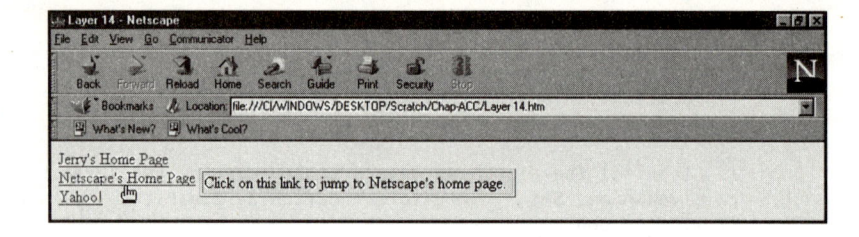

At the bottom half of the listing, you see three links. Each link uses the `OnMouseOver` attribute to associate a JavaScript function with that link. In this case, each link is associated with the function called `OnLink`. That `function` is passed the name of the layer to be shown. The first link calls `OnLink` like this:

`OnLink("LINK1")`

Just under each link, you see a layer. Each layer has a unique name and is hidden. Each layer also contains the help text associated with the preceding link.

At the top of the listing, you see two functions. Here's a description of each:

| | |
|---|---|
| `OnLink(Name)` | Hides all of the layers on the HTML document, then displays the layer called `Name`. Set a timer to call `ClearHelp()` in 5 seconds (5,000 milliseconds) so that the browser will hide the layer at that time. |
| `ClearHelp()` | Hide all of the layers in the HTML document. It uses the layers array to visit each layer and to set its `visibility` property to `"HIDE"`. Note that you can get the size of the layers array by using the property `document.layers.length`. |

CHAPTER 29

# Using Style Sheets

*by Jerry Honeycutt*

Style sheets are a W3C recommendation that defines a standard by which you can format Web pages using desktop publishing concepts. You can get more information about the W3C recommendation at its Web site: **http://www.w3.org/pub/WWW/TR/WD-css1.html**. Note that W3C uses the terminology *Cascading Style Sheets Level 1*. In this chapter, however, I use the simpler term *style sheet*.

Before you go any further, you need to understand what you can do with style sheets. Most word processors let you specify styles that describe how a block of text will be formatted. For example, you can specify a paragraph style that sets the line spacing to one, the font to Courier, and the left margin to one inch. Then you can assign this style to any number of paragraphs in your document. You can use HTML style sheets to do essentially the same thing. ■

### ▬ Attach style sheets to your HTML file
This chapter shows you four different ways to associate a style sheet with your HTML document and recommends one that you should stick with.

### ▬ Write style definitions like the pros
You'll learn the basic syntax of a style definition, as well as more advanced techniques such as grouping, classes, selectors, and so on.

### ▬ What about browsers without style sheet support?
If you follow a few simple rules, browsers that don't do style sheets won't choke on your page.

### ▬ Set a variety of properties within a style
Style sheets provide a large variety of properties you can set within your styles. You can control how text displays on the page, for example.

### ▬ Position HTML content anywhere on the Web page
You can use style sheets to achieve the same effect as you do with layers: You can position a block of HTML anywhere on the Web page.

# Understanding the Cascade in Cascading Style Sheets

W3C refers to style sheets as cascading style sheets because you can use multiple styles to control how your Web page looks; the browser follows a certain set of rules to determine the precedence and to resolve conflicts between styles (cascading order). For example, you can define a style sheet for your Web site, and the reader can have her own style sheet. The cascading rules determine who wins if both style sheets define a style for a particular type of text.

So how does this work? Each style is assigned a weight by the browser. When the browser is working with the occurrence of a particular tag, it finds all of the styles that apply to it (some can come from the user, others can come from the Web page). The browser then sorts those rules by their weight, applying the style with the greatest weight.

In general, there are just a few rules that you need to be aware of when dealing with competing style sheets:

- The author's style sheet overrides the user's style sheet, while the user's style sheet overrides the browser's default values.
- Inline styles take precedence over embedded style sheets, while embedded style sheets take precedence over linked style sheets.

# Attaching a Style Sheet to Your HTML Document

What's the big deal about style sheets? Here's the scoop: You separate the format of your Web page from its content. Sounds benign enough, but that simple act makes your job much, much easier. You specify how the text will look in a different location than the contents of the text itself. If you later decide that you want all your headings to be displayed in blue characters, you only have to change the style for those headings, instead of changing each heading within the HTML file.

The following are four methods you can use to attach a style sheet to your Web page:

| | |
|---|---|
| **Linking** | You can link an HTML file to a style sheet contained in a separate file. |
| **Embedding** | You can embed the style sheet within the HTML file by using the `<STYLE>` container. |
| **Inline** | You can define styles on-the-fly within an HTML tag such as `<P>`. |
| **Import** | You can use the `@import` keyword to import a style sheet into your HTML file. |

## Link to a Style Sheet

As I noted earlier, you can create a style sheet in a separate file and then apply that style sheet to all of the pages on your Web site. I recommend this method to you only because it makes creating a consistent Web site much easier. In fact, you can create a corporate style sheet and have everyone in your organization use it with their Web sites (imagine an intranet with a common look).

You store a linked style sheet in a text file with the CSS file extension. It's a plain text file that you can create with your favorite text editor. The format of the text file is readable by humans and is easy to understand. Thus, you don't have any trouble creating your style sheets by hand.

To link to a style sheet stored in a separate file, store all of the style definitions in the CSS file and link your HTML files to it through use of the <LINK> tag, like this:

```
<LINK REL=STYLESHEET HREF="http://www.myserver.com/mysheet.css"
➥TYPE="text/css">
```

Assign the URL of the style sheet to the HREF attribute. Set TYPE to "text/css" so browsers that don't support style sheets can avoid the download.

**TIP** Store your corporate style sheets in a common location on the Web server and then have everyone in the company who is creating Web pages reference that style sheet from their HTML files. Everyone can even use the same <LINK> tag. In this way, you can have a more consistent look across all of the Web pages on the server.

## Embed a Style Sheet

You don't have to store your style sheet in a separate file. You can embed the style sheet inside each HTML file. Note that the styles within an embedded style sheet only affect the HTML within that file. Thus, you can't embed a style sheet in an HTML file and expect to use that across multiple HTML files without copying and pasting it into each file (hence, my earlier recommendation that you use linked style sheets). You might prefer this method if you're not creating a large, corporate Web site, and you don't want to use the same style sheet in multiple HTML files.

You use the <STYLE> container to embed a style sheet in your HTML file. Put this container between the <HTML> and <BODY> tags of your file, like this:

```
<HTML>
<HEAD>
</HEAD>
<STYLE TYPE="text/css">
   Style definitions go here
</STYLE>
<BODY>
</BODY>
</HTML>
```

The following example shows you what a real <STYLE> tag looks like. You can ignore the actual style definitions for now—they are covered in "Adding Style to Your Web Page," later in this chapter.

```
<STYLE TYPE="text/css">
  H1 {color: BLUE}
</STYLE>
```

> **TIP** Indent your style definitions within the `<STYLE>` and `</STYLE>` tags so that your style sheet is easier to read.

## Define Styles Inline

Inline styles are styles that you define on-the-fly. You can use inline styles to quickly change the appearance of a single tag—on-the-run. You can also use inline styles to override a style for a particular tag. For example, if you've defined a style that sets the color of the H1 tag to blue, you can set the color of a specific element by setting its H1 tag to red.

Inline styles affect the individual tag for which it is defined; that is, you define a tag's style within the tag itself. You do this by using the STYLE attribute, which is supported by all the child tags of the BODY tag. To define an inline style, add the STYLE attribute to the tag whose style you want to change and set its value to the string representing the style definition, like this:

```
<H1 STYLE="color: blue">
```

> **NOTE** If an inline style conflicts with an embedded or linked style, the inline style wins. This enables you to change individual elements without modifying the overall style.

You can use inline styles with the `<DIV>` tag to set the style for an entire block of HTML within your document. This works because of the concept of inheritance. For example, if you want to change the text color of an entire block of tags to blue, you can put those tags in the DIV container and define a style for the `<DIV>` tag that sets the text color to blue. It looks like this:

```
<DIV STYLE="color: blue">
  <H1>This is a heading</H1>
  <P>This is a paragraph. It will look blue in the user's browser</P>
</DIV>
```

You can also use inline style sheets with the `<SPAN>` tag to change the formatting for a few words, or even just a few letters. For example:

```
This is a <SPAN STYLE="color: blue">simple</SPAN> block of text.
```

> **CAUTION**
> Don't rely on inline styles too much. They quickly clutter your HTML file so that it's harder to read and much harder to maintain. This obviously diminishes the greatest advantage of style sheets: separating format from content. However, if you don't want to take full advantage of style sheets but still want to add a bit of special formatting to just a few elements, go ahead and use inline styles.

## Importing Style Sheets

Earlier in the chapter, you learned about linking to a style sheet. You can also use the `@import` keyword to import a style sheet into your HTML file. Remember that you're just importing the text file, so you have to insert it in the `<STYLE>` container. In this manner, importing a style sheet works just like embedding a style sheet into your HTML file. For example:

```
<STYLE TYPE="text/css">
  @import url(http://www.myserver.com/style.css);
</STYLE>
```

# Understanding What Style Sheets Look Like (Syntax)

Style sheets are stored in text files that you can easily read and understand. They're also very easy to create by hand. Note that, in the future, you'll be able to create and use styles sheets with the more popular HTML editors.

Linked and embedded style sheets enable you to define styles for one or more individual tags. For example, you can create a style sheet that defines styles for the `<H1>`, `<H2>`, `<P>`, and `<EM>` tags. Each style definition is called a *rule* (you can use both terms interchangeably and not sound foolish). A rule contains a selector (the HTML tag), followed by the declaration (the definition of the style). The rule's selector is what ties the style's definition to tags you use in the HTML file. Here's an example of a rule that defines a style for each occurrence of the `<H1>` tag:

```
Rule   Declaration
 |         |
H1    {color: blue}
```

The declaration is enclosed in curly braces (`{}`). Each item in the declaration has two parts: the property name and the value you're assigning to the property, separated by a colon (`:`). In the previous example, `color` is the property name and `blue` is the value you're assigning to it. HTML predefines dozens of property names (`font-size`, `font-style`, `color`, `margin-right`, and so on), which you learn about in "Adding Style to Your Web Page," later in this chapter. Each property also accepts a predefined type and range of values.

## Set Multiple Properties for a Style

The examples you've seen so far only set a single property: `color`. You can also set multiple properties within a declaration. You do this by separating each assignment with a semicolon (`;`), like this:

```
H1 {color: blue; font-size: 12pt; text-line: center}
```

In this example, the browser displays each occurrence of the `<H1>` tag in the color blue, in a font size of 12 points, and centered in the browser window. For all other properties, the browser uses its default values. For example, it sets the `font-style` property to `normal`.

## Set Styles for Multiple Tags (Grouping Selectors)

If you want to define a similar style for several tags, you can list them individually in your style sheet, like this:

```
P {font-size: 12pt}
UL {font-size: 12pt}
LI {font-size: 12pt}
```

This is not the most efficient way to do this, however, considering that you can group the selectors together and define a rule for them as a group. The following example groups the selectors in the previous example on one line and defines a rule that sets the font-size property to 12pt:

```
P, UL, LI {font-size: 12pt}
```

Note the comma between each selector in the list. Leaving this comma out means a totally different thing, as you learn in the next section.

## Create Context Specific Styles (Contextual Selectors)

With HTML style sheets, you can get very specific about when a style is applied to a tag. For example, you might want to define two styles for the <LI> tag: one that's applied when it's a child of the <UL> tag and another when it's a child of the <OL> tag. You do this with contextual selectors.

Contextual selectors define the exact sequence of tags for which a style is applied. In other words, you can specify that a style applies to a particular tag, such as <LI>, only if it's a child of the <OL> tag, like this:

```
OL LI {list-style-type: decimal}
```

You can also specify that a particular style applies to the <LI> tag, only if it's a child of the <UL> tag, like this:

```
UL LI {list-style-type: square}
```

Note the list of selectors is not comma-separated. Separating each selector with a comma would cause all of the tags in the list to be assigned the rule.

**NOTE** In HTML, tags inherit certain properties from their parents. For example, all of the tags within the <BODY> tag inherit certain properties from it. Likewise, a <LI> tag inherits properties from the <UL> tag that contains it. As such, a child tag inherits any styles defined by the parent tag. For example, if you create a style for the <P> tag that sets the text color to blue, any <EM> tags you enclose within a <P> tag will also have blue text. ■

## Apply Style Classes to HTML Elements

A class defines a variation of style, which you refer to in a specific occurrence of a tag by using the CLASS attribute. Every HTML 3.2 tag now has the CLASS attribute. For example, you can define three variations of the H1 style and then use each one in the appropriate context. You define a class much like you normally define a style, only you add an arbitrary class name to the end of the tag, separating them with a period. For example:

```
H1.blue {color: blue}
H1.red {color: red}
H1.black {color: black}
```

Then, when adding the `<H1>` tag to your HTML document, you set the CLASS attribute to indicate exactly which style you're using:

```
<H1 CLASS=red>Red Heading</H1>
```

```
<H1 CLASS=blue>Blue Heading</H1>
```

A more common use for classes is to define a class that's not necessarily associated with a particular HTML tag, but that you can apply at will. If you leave off the name of the tag in a class, the class doesn't apply to any specific HTML tag. Instead, you can apply it using the CLASS tag. For example, you can define a class that changes color of the text to blue and indents the text by one inch, like this (note the period that begins the rule):

```
.BLUEINDENT {color: blue; text-indent: 1in}
```

Then, you can apply this class to the specific elements that you want to have a blue background with a one-inch indent. This method is common on sites such as CNET (**http://www.cnet.com**). Here's what an element looks like that uses the BLUEINDENT style class (the period isn't used when you apply the class):

```
<P CLASS=BLUEINDENT>This text is blue and indented one inch</P>
```

## Override a Style's Importance in the Cascade

At the beginning of this chapter, you learned how styles cascade from the browser to the user, then to the Web page. Any style defined by the Web page overrides the same style if defined by the browser. You can override the precedence for a style by using the `important` keyword. In the following example, the assignment of red to the property color and the assignment of sans-serif to the property font-family are marked as important:

```
H1 {color: red ! important font-weight: bold font-family: sans-serif ! important}
```

By doing this, the browser does not override these styles if the user has defined her own style for H1.

## Comment Your Style Sheet to Make It Readable

If your style sheet gets a bit complicated or you need to explain why you've made a particular design decision, you can add a comment to the style sheet. Comments only serve to document your style sheet, they don't have any impact on how the browser displays the HTML document.

Enclose your comments between /* and */. The following example shows you what a one-line comment looks like:

```
BODY {margin-left: 1in}              /* Create space for sliders */
H1 {font-size: 16; margin-left: -1in}    /* Out one inch */
H2 {font-size: 14; margin-left: -1in}    /* Out one inch */
```

You can also use the /* and */ characters to create block comments. This is useful to explain an entire portion of your style sheet. Like this:

```
/*---------------------------------------------------------------
  The margin-left property is set to one inch for the BODY tag.
  Since all of its enclosed tags will inherit this setting, the
  entire page will appear to be indented by one inch. The first-
  and second-level headings are indented to the left by one inch
  so that they slide out into the margin.
-----------------------------------------------------------------*/

BODY {margin-left: 1in}            /* Create space for sliders */
H1 {font-size: 16; margin-left: -1in}    /* Out one inch */
H2 {font-size: 14; margin-left: -1in}    /* Out one inch */
```

## Hiding Styles from Non-Style-Enabled Browsers

HTML style sheets are new. Netscape Communicator and Internet Explorer are the first browsers to support them. You still need to consider all those browsers that don't support style sheets.

Most browsers are designed to simply ignore the tags and attributes they don't understand. They ignore the <STYLE> tag, for example. They don't necessarily ignore what you put in the <STYLE> tag, though, and display its contents as text on the Web page. To get around this problem, you can use an HTML comment within the <STYLE> tag to hide the style definitions, like this:

```
<STYLE TYPE"text/css">
<!--
H1 {color: red}
-->
</STYLE>
```

Browsers that don't support style sheets display the HTML files with their default styles. They ignore the style definitions.

> **TIP** Take a look at your HTML documents without the associated style sheets so that you can verify how your Web pages look in browsers that don't support style sheets.

## Adding Style to Your Web Page

HTML style sheets define a wide variety of properties you can use to change how your HTML document looks in the browser—word-spacing and background-image, for example. Most of the names contain multiple words, each separated by a hyphen (-). In property names that contain multiple words, the first word usually indicates a category. As well, most categories also have a *shorthand* property name you can use to simplify your style sheet.

The remainder of this chapter describes all of the properties that are available, and, if appropriate, the shorthand property you can use to simplify your rules.

http://www.quecorp.com

## Changing the Background of an HTML Element

HTML style sheets provide you with the capability to decorate the background of an element with color and images. Using the properties described here doesn't define the background for the Web page as a whole. Instead, these properties set the background of an element on the Web page.

Table 29.1 describes the background properties. You learn more about the values you can assign to each property in the sections that follow.

**Table 29.1  Background Properties**

| Property | Description |
|---|---|
| background-color | Background color |
| background-image | URL of background image |
| background-repeat | Tile a background image |
| background-attachment | Fix or allow an image to scroll |
| background-position | Background position |

You can group the background properties you learn about in this section using `background`. You specify the background color, image, repeat, attachment, and position (separate each property with a space, not a comma), like this:

```
background: background-color background-image background-repeat
➥background-attachment background-position
```

**Background Color**  You can change the background color for an element by using the `background-color` property. You assign one of the standard color names to `background-color`; an RGB value like #808080 (white) can also be used. Listing 29.1 shows a style sheet that sets the background color of all `<H1>` and `<H2>` tags to yellow. Figure 29.1 shows what this looks like in the browser.

**Listing 29.1  Background Color**

```
<HTML>
<HEAD>
<TITLE>Style 1</TITLE>
</HEAD>
<STYLE TYPE="text/css">
  H1 {background-color: yellow}
</STYLE>
<BODY>
  <H1>Heading 1</H1>
  The above heading appears with a yellow background.
</BODY>
</HTML>
```

## Chapter 29 Using Style Sheets

**FIG. 29.1**
Changing the background color for certain types of tags is useful to highlight information on the Web page.

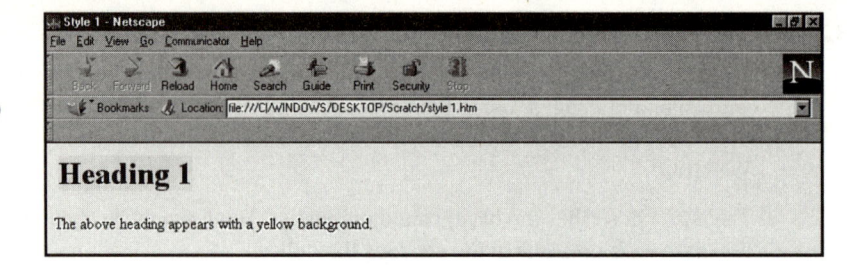

**Heading 1**

The above heading appears with a yellow background.

**Background Image**   You can display a background image in an element by setting the value of the `background-image` property to the URL of an image. This has the effect of a watermark displayed behind that element on the Web page (the element's content is displayed over the background image).

You set the URL by using the URL(address) format, like this:

H1 {background-image: URL(http://www.myserver.com/images/heading.gif)}

Listing 29.2 shows you the previous example, using a background image instead of color.

**Listing 29.2   Background Image**

```
<HTML>
<HEAD>
<TITLE>Style 2</TITLE>
</HEAD>
<STYLE TYPE="text/css">
  H1 {background-image: URL(background.gif)}
</STYLE>
<BODY>
  <H1>Heading 1</H1>
  The above heading appears with an image in the background.
</BODY>
</HTML>
```

You can cause the user's browser to tile the background image so that it fills the entire area of the containing element. This is only useful, however, if the image itself is smaller than the size of the element. The `background-repeat` property can have four values, as described in Table 29.2.

**Table 29.2   *background-repeat* Values**

| Value    | Description                                   |
|----------|-----------------------------------------------|
| repeat   | Repeats the image both vertically and horizontally |
| repeat-x | Repeats the image horizontally                |

http://www.quecorp.com

| Value | Description |
|---|---|
| repeat-y | Repeats the image vertically |
| no-repeat | Doesn't repeat the image |

When working with an image in the background of an element, you have control over how the browser treats the image when the user scrolls the Web page. The background-attachment property determines whether the background image is fixed in the browser window or if it scrolls as the user scrolls the window. You can use this to create a watermark behind your Web page that stays put regardless of which portion of the Web page the user is viewing. You can assign two possible values to background-attachment, as described in Table 29.3.

**Table 29.3** *background-attachment* **Values**

| Value | Description |
|---|---|
| fixed | Fixes image within the browser window |
| scroll | Image scrolls as user scrolls the window |

**Background Position**   You change the position of the background image by using the background-position property. The position is always relative to the upper-left corner of the element in which you're positioning the image. That is, if you're positioning an image for the <UL> tag, the image's position is relative to the upper-left corner of the unordered list.

The background-position property looks like this:

background-position: *x y*

*x* is the horizontal position and *y* is the vertical position of the image. *x* and *y* can be a percentage that is relative to the size of the element, a fixed amount such as 1in, or one of the keywords that indicate a relative position as described in Table 29.4.

**Table 29.4** *background-position* **Positions**

| Keyword | Description |
|---|---|
| top | Aligns the image with the top of the containing element; useful only when substituted for *y*. |
| left | Aligns the image with the left side of the containing element; useful only when substituted for *x*. |
| right | Aligns the image with the right side of the containing element; useful only when substituted for *x*. |

*continues*

### Table 29.4 Continued

| Keyword | Description |
| --- | --- |
| bottom | Aligns the image with the bottom of the containing element; useful only when substituted for *y*. |
| center | Centers the image within the containing element; when substituted for *x*, the image is centered horizontally; when substituted for *y*, the image is centered vertically. |

## Work with an Element's Box Properties

W3C's style sheet recommendation provides the capability to define borders, margins, and padding for elements on the Web page. You can wrap a border around a heading, for example, or change the margins of the <P> tag so that any occurrence of this tag is indented into the page. Here's an overview of the properties you can use to change the boxes that are associated with an element:

**Border**  You use the border properties to set the left, right, top, and bottom borders of an element. You can set the border's width, color, and style.

**Margin**  You use the margin properties to set the left, right, top, and bottom margins of an element. With these properties, you specify only the size of the margin.

**Padding**  You use the padding properties to specify how much space the browser displays between the border and the content of the element. With the padding properties, you specify only the size of the margin.

Figure 29.2 shows you how the border, margin, and padding properties work with the height and width properties to form the boxes around the element. The following list describes these in more detail:

- The height and width properties determine the overall size of the element's containing box.
- The margin properties determine the element's margins within its containing box.
- The border properties determine the position of the border within the element's margins.
- The padding properties determine the amount of space between the element's border and the contents of the element itself.

Table 29.5 shows you the properties available that you can use to control an element's box properties. You learn about the values you can assign to each property in the following sections.

**FIG. 29.2**
There are actually four boxes around each element.

*Labels on figure:* Height and Width, Padding, Border, Margin

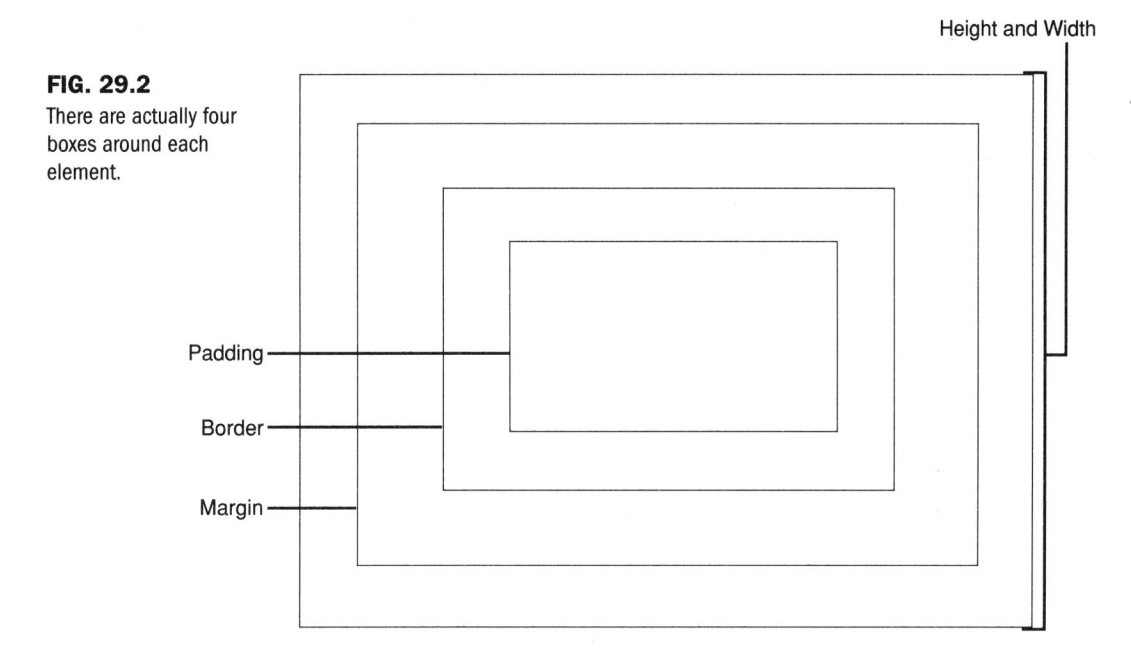

**Table 29.5  Box Properties**

| Property | Description |
| --- | --- |
| **Size Properties** | |
| height | Height of the element |
| width | Width of an element |
| **Border Properties** | |
| border-color | Color of the border |
| border-style | Style of the border |
| border-bottom-width | Width of the bottom line |
| border-left-width | Width of the left line |
| border-right-width | Width of the right line |
| border-top-width | Width of the top line |
| **Margin Properties** | |
| margin-bottom | Bottom margin |
| margin-left | Left margin |

*continues*

**Table 29.5 Continued**

| Property | Description |
|---|---|
| **Margin Properties** | |
| `margin-right` | Right margin |
| `margin-top` | Top margin |
| **Padding Properties** | |
| `padding-bottom` | Padding at bottom of element |
| `padding-left` | Padding at left of element |
| `padding-right` | Padding at right of element |
| `padding-top` | Padding at top of element |

You can group border properties in five different ways. You can specify the properties for a particular side of the element using `border-top`, `border-right`, `border-bottom`, or `border-left`. You can also specify all sides of the border at one time by using `border`. With any of these attributes, you specify the width, style, and color of the border, like this:

`border:` *border-width border-style border-color*

You can also group the margin and padding properties. For both, you specify the top, right, bottom, and left margins. The following two examples show you what margin and padding properties look like when grouped together:

```
margin: margin-top margin-right margin-bottom margin-left
padding: padding-top padding-right padding-bottom padding-left
```

**Box Size**  You set the total height of the element with the `height` property and the total width with the `width` property. You can set this property for text blocks or images. For example, you can use the `height` and `width` properties to create a special warning on the Web page that has a fixed size. You can set this property to any length, a percentage value, or `auto`, which lets the browser determine the best size for the element.

`height` and `width` are more useful with images. In fact, setting the height of a text element has virtually no effect, as the browser always resizes the box to fit the height of the text element. When you set the width of an element, the browser uses that width to determine where to break the text, and the browser properly sets aside that space for the element so that no other element can occupy it.

Listing 29.3 shows you an example that has five different blocks of text. The first three blocks of text use a style width of a different width. The last two blocks of text use a style with a differing height. Each style also sets a background color so that you can more easily see the change in size. Take a look at Figure 29.3 to see what the listing looks like.

http://www.quecorp.com

Adding Style to Your Web Page | 613

### Listing 29.3  Size Properties

```
<HTML>
<HEAD>
<TITLE>Style 3</TITLE>
</HEAD>
<STYLE TYPE="text/css">
  P.small  {background-color: yellow; height: 50; width: 100}
  P.medium {background-color: yellow; height: 100; width: 150}
  P.large  {background-color: yellow; height: 150; width: 200}
</STYLE>
<BODY>
  <P CLASS="small">Small Block of Text</P>
  <P CLASS="medium">Medium Block of Text</P>
  <P CLASS="large">Large Block of Text</P>
</BODY>
</HTML>
```

**FIG. 29.3**
Sizing an element makes more sense for images than for text; text better illustrates this example, however.

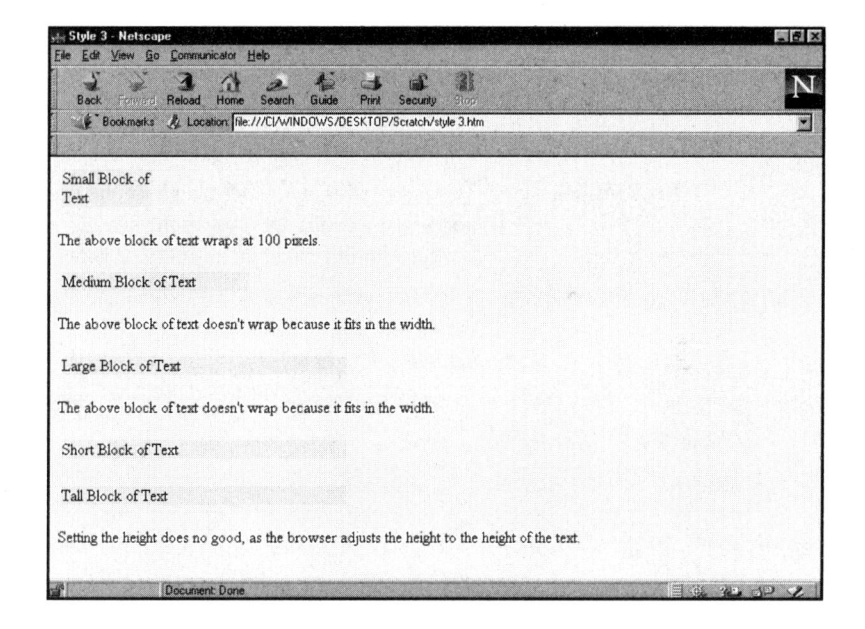

**Box Border**   You set the size of an element's border using the border-top-width, border-left-width, border-right-width, and border-bottom-width property. Each property changes only one side of the border. That is, it doesn't affect the other sides of the border. You can assign any of the values described in Table 29.6 to these properties.

### Table 29.6  Width Values

| Value | Description |
| --- | --- |
| thin | Thin line |
| medium | Medium line |
| thick | Thick line |
| length | Exact width of the border by using points (pt), inches (in), centimeters (cm), or pixels (px) |

The border-color property sets the color of the element's border. You can use a named color, such as RED, or you can use an RGB value, such as #FF0000.

The border-style property determines the style of the border that the browser displays. Table 29.7 describes the values you can use for a border's style. You can specify from one to four of the following values for this property:

| | |
| --- | --- |
| **One Value** | All four borders are set to the style. |
| **Two Values** | The top and bottom borders are set to the style in the first value; the left and right borders are set to the style in the second value. |
| **Three Values** | The top border is set to the style in the first value; the right and left borders are set to the style in the second value; and the bottom border is set to the style in the third value. |
| **Four Values** | The top border is set to the style in the first value; the right is set to the second value; the bottom is set to the third value; and the left is set to the fourth value. |

### Table 29.7  *border-style* Values

| Value | Description |
| --- | --- |
| none | No border |
| dotted | Dotted line |
| dashed | Dashed line |
| solid | Solid line |
| double | Double line |
| groove | 3-D groove |
| ridge | 3-D ridge |
| inset | 3-D inset |
| outset | 3-D outset |

http://www.quecorp.com

Listing 29.4 shows a style sheet that adds a border to the first- and second-level headings. In order to show precedence, the border around the first-level headings is heavier than the border around the second-level headings. Figure 29.4 shows you what this HTML looks like in the browser.

### Listing 29.4  Border Properties

```
<HTML>
<HEAD>
<TITLE>Style 3</TITLE>
</HEAD>
<STYLE TYPE="text/css">
  P.small   {background-color: yellow; width: 100}
  P.medium  {background-color: yellow; width: 200}
  P.large   {background-color: yellow; width: 290}
  P.shorty  {background-color: yellow; height: 10; width: 290}
  P.tall    {background-color: yellow; height: 290; width: 290}
</STYLE>
<BODY>
  <P CLASS="small">Small Block of Text</P>
  The above block of text wraps at 100 pixels.

  <P CLASS="medium">Medium Block of Text</P>
  The above block of text doesn't wrap because it fits in the width.

  <P CLASS="large">Large Block of Text</P>
  The above block of text doesn't wrap because it fits in the width.

  <P CLASS="shorty">Short Block of Text</P>
  <P CLASS="tall">Tall Block of Text</P>
  Setting the height does no good, as the browser adjusts the
  height to the height of the text.

</BODY>
</HTML>
```

### TROUBLESHOOTING

**I've set the width of my border but it still doesn't display. Why?** Setting the width of the border isn't enough. You also have to set the border style by using the `border-style` property. This is because the default style for every border is `none`.

**Box Margin**   You set the margins of an element using the `margin-bottom`, `margin-left`, `margin-right`, and `margin-top` properties. You can specify any valid length, a percentage value (relative to the `height` and `width`) of the element, or `auto`, which lets the browser determine the best margins to use for the element. You can also use a negative margin size.

**FIG. 29.4**
Apply borders to floating or positioned styles so that they stand ou.

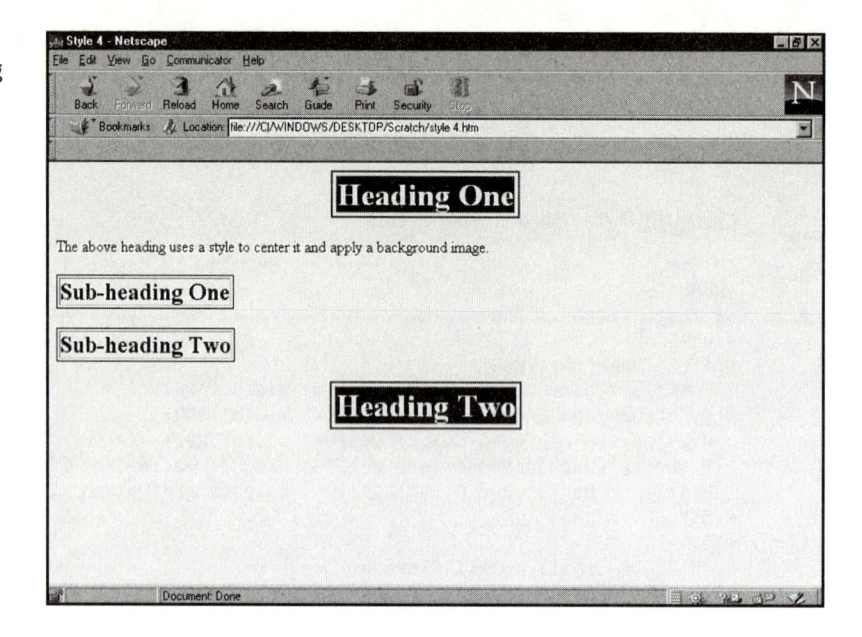

**Box Padding** The `padding-bottom`, `padding-left`, `padding-right`, and `padding-top` properties specify the amount of space to display between the element's bottom border and the element's contents. You can set this property to a valid length or a percentage value (relative to the `height` and `width`) of the element.

## Float Elements on the Web Page

You already know how to float images on the Web page. HTML style sheets let you do the same thing—to any element on the Web page. You can float a heading to the right side of the Web page and let the text wrap around it. You can create a text pull-out from a length article, draw a border around it, and let it float to the left side of the Web page.

You use two properties to control how elements float on the Web page: `float` and `clear`. The `float` property specifies that the element is floated to the left or right side, with the surrounding elements flowing around it. Table 29.8 describes the values you can assign to this property.

**Table 29.8  *float* Values**

| Value | Description |
| --- | --- |
| none | Displays the element where it is |
| left | Moves to the left and wraps text around it |
| right | Moves to the right and wraps text around it |

http://www.quecorp.com

Listing 29.5 shows you an example of a text box that floats to the right side of the Web page. The inline text wraps around the text box. Note that the floating element uses a style class, so that the floating style can be assigned at will, rather than to every occurrence of a particular tag.

### Listing 29.5 Float Properties

```
<HTML>
<HEAD><TITLE>Style 5</TITLE></HEAD>
<BODY>

<STYLE TYPE="text/css">
  .FLOAT {
        background-color: yellow;
        border-width: thin; border-style: solid; border-color: black;
        float: right
      }
</STYLE>

<P CLASS=FLOAT>This text floats to the right side of the Web page.</P>
qwerty. qwerty. qwerty. qwerty. qwerty. qwerty. qwerty.
qwerty. qwerty. qwerty. qwerty. qwerty. qwerty. qwerty.
qwerty. qwerty. qwerty. qwerty. qwerty. qwerty. qwerty.
qwerty. qwerty. qwerty. qwerty. qwerty. qwerty. qwerty.
qwerty. qwerty. qwerty. qwerty. qwerty. qwerty. qwerty.
qwerty. qwerty. qwerty. qwerty. qwerty. qwerty. qwerty.
qwerty. qwerty. qwerty. qwerty. qwerty. qwerty. qwerty.
qwerty. qwerty. qwerty. qwerty. qwerty. qwerty. qwerty.
qwerty. qwerty. qwerty. qwerty. qwerty. qwerty. qwerty.
qwerty. qwerty. qwerty. qwerty. qwerty. qwerty. qwerty.
qwerty. qwerty. qwerty. qwerty. qwerty. qwerty. qwerty.

</BODY>
</HTML>
```

**FIG. 29.5**
You can float an image using style sheets just like you can float the text shown in this figure.

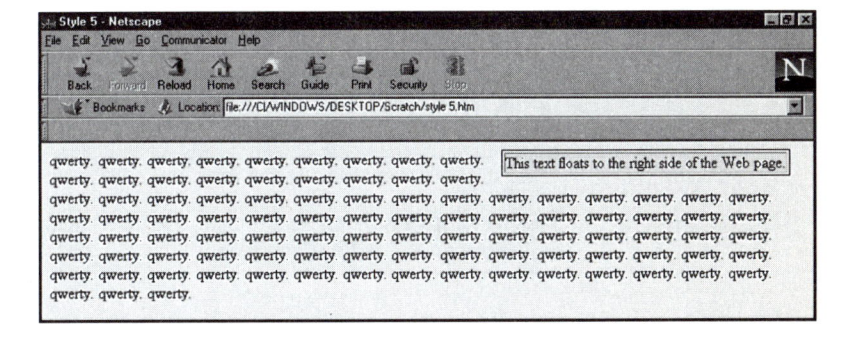

The `clear` property determines whether the browser can display floating elements on the sides of an element. The property's value indicates the sides on which floating elements are not allowed. For example, `clear: left` means that the browser can't float elements on the left side of the element. Table 29.9 describes the values you can assign to this property.

**Table 29.9  clear Values**

| Value | Description |
| --- | --- |
| none | Floating elements are allowed on all sides. |
| left | Floating elements are not allowed on the left. |
| right | Floating elements are not allowed on the right. |
| both | Floating elements are not allowed on either side. |

# Format Lists with Your Own Style

You use the list properties to specify how lists display in the browser window. You can change the position of the marker (`list-style-position`) and the style or image used for the marker (`list-style-type` and `list-style-image`). You can group the list properties using the `list-style` property. You specify the marker type, marker image, and position, like this:

`List-style: list-style-type list-style-image list-style-position`

> **NOTE** The list properties are inherited, so if you define a property for the <UL> tag, all of its enclosed <LI> tags inherit those properties. For example, if you define an image to use as the marker (bullet), you can define that image in the <UL> tag so that it applies to every list item within an unordered list. You can override a property on an item-by-item basis, however, by using inline styles.

The `list-style-position` property determines the relative position of the marker. Table 29.10 describes the possible values you can assign to this property.

**Table 29.10  list-style-position Values**

| Value | Description |
| --- | --- |
| Inside | The list item's text wraps to the next line underneath the marker. |
| Outside | The list item's text wraps to the next line underneath the start of the text on the previous line (hanging indent). |

You use the `list-style-image` property to specify an image that the browser displays as the marker for a list item. The property's only value is the URL, using the URL(*address*) format, of the image to use as the marker, like this:

`list-style-image: url(http://www.myserver.com/images/marker.gif)`

You use the `list-style-type` property to specify the type of marker the browser displays. Use this instead of a marker image. Table 29.11 describes each of the possible values you can assign to this property.

**Table 29.11  `list-style-type` Values**

| Value | Description |
| --- | --- |
| `disc` | Disc |
| `circle` | Circle |
| `square` | Square |
| `decimal` | Numbered (1, 2, 3, ...) |
| `lower-roman` | Lowercase roman numerals (i, ii, iii, ...) |
| `upper-roman` | Uppercase roman numerals (I, II, III, ...) |
| `lower-alpha` | Lowercase alphabet (a, b, c, ...) |
| `upper-alpha` | Uppercase alphabet (A, B, C, ...) |
| `none` | No markers |

## Change the Properties of Text

The text properties give you complete control over how the browser displays an element's text. You can change its color, size, font, spacing, and so on. Table 29.12 shows you the text properties that are available. The following sections describe in more detail the types of values you can assign to these properties.

**Table 29.12  Text Properties**

| Property | Description |
| --- | --- |
| **Character Spacing Properties** | |
| `letter-spacing` | Spacing between characters |
| `line-spacing` | Spacing between lines |
| `white-space` | Whether or not white space is collapsed |
| `word-spacing` | Additional space between words |
| **Font Properties** | |
| `font-family` | Name of the font family |
| `font-size` | Point or relative size of font |

*continues*

**Table 29.12 Continued**

| Property | Description |
|---|---|
| **Font Properties** | |
| `font-style` | Style to apply to the font |
| `font-variant` | Additional styles to apply |
| `font-weight` | Relative weight of the font |
| **Formatting Properties** | |
| `color` | Color of the text |
| `text-decoration` | Decorations such as underlining |
| `text-transform` | Transformations as all caps |
| **Paragraph Properties** | |
| `text-align` | Alignment of the text |
| `text-indent` | Indentation of the text |
| `vertical-align` | Vertical alignment of the text |

You can group the font properties (a subset of all the text properties) by using `font`. You specify the weight, style, size, and family, like this:

`font: font-weight font-style font-size font-family`

**Font Color** The `color` property determines the foreground color for the element. The browser displays the element's text using this color. You can set `color` to a named color or an RGB value. Named colors include those in the following list:

| | | | |
|---|---|---|---|
| black | silver | gray | white |
| maroon | red | purple | fuchsia |
| green | lime | olive | yellow |
| navy | blue | teal | aqua |

As shown in Listing 29.6, changing both the foreground color of a heading and its background color is an effective way to make the heading stand out on the Web page. This example, shown in Figure 29.6, creates headings that are white on black with a border.

**Listing 29.6  Color**

```
<HTML>
<HEAD><TITLE>Style 6</TITLE></HEAD>
<BODY>

<STYLE TYPE="text/css">
```

```
    H1 {
        background-color: black;
        color: white;
        border-width: thin; border-style: solid; border-color: black
    }
</STYLE>

    <H1>Heading 1</H1>
    The above heading is white on black.

</BODY>
</HTML>
```

**FIG. 29.6**
Create a style class that changes the font color and then apply that style on-the-fly by setting an element's CLASS attribute to the name of the class.

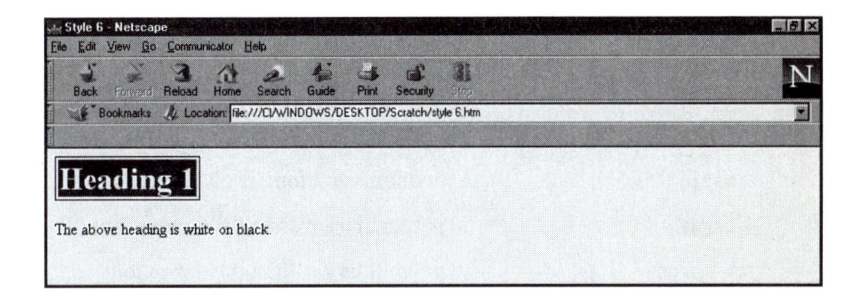

**Font Faces** `font-family` is a prioritized list of typefaces for an element. You can specify a single typeface or a list of alternatives, separated by commas. If you're using a font name that has multiple words, enclose the font name in quotes. For example:

`font-family: "Courier New", Times, Serif`

You can use a font name you expect to be on the user's computer, such as Courier or Helvetica, or you can use a generic font name. Table 29.13 shows you the generic font names and provides an example of a font that looks similar.

**Table 29.13  Generic Fonts**

| Name | Similar to |
| --- | --- |
| serif | Times |
| sans-serif | Helvetica |
| cursive | *Nuptial Script* |
| fantasy | COMICS CARTOON |
| monospace | Courier |

**NOTE** In case the font you've requested is unavailable, you should always use a generic font name as the last item in the list. In the previous example, `serif` is the last font in the list. If the user doesn't have `courier` or `times`, the browser uses the generic font instead.

`font-size` determines the size of the text in points (pt), inches (in), centimeters (cm), or pixels (px). You can also use a percentage, which is relative to the parent element's font size. Or you can use one of the values shown in Table 29.14.

**Table 29.14  font-size Values**

| Value | Description |
| --- | --- |
| xx-small | 50 percent smaller than the `x-small` font |
| x-small | 50 percent smaller than the `small` font |
| small | 50 percent smaller than the `medium` font |
| medium | A medium-sized font, probably 10 points |
| large | 50 percent larger than the `medium` font |
| x-large | 50 percent larger than the `large` font |
| xx-large | 50 percent larger than the `x-large` font |
| larger | 50 percent larger than the parent element's font |
| smaller | 50 percent smaller than the parent element's font |

**NOTE** The W3C recommendation that vendors use a scaling factor of 50 percent is only a recommendation. Vendors are free to use any scaling factor they want. Thus, the values in Table 29.13 are only guidelines.

You can change the style of the font by using the `font-style` property. Table 29.15 describes each of the possible values.

**Table 29.15  font-style Values**

| Value | Description |
| --- | --- |
| normal | Selects a normal face |
| oblique | Selects an oblique face |
| italic | Selects an italic face |

http://www.quecorp.com

You use the `font-variant` property to display text in small caps. Setting this property to `normal` causes the browser to display the text normally. Setting this property to `small-caps` causes the browser to display the text using small caps.

`font-weight` determines the thickness of the font. You can assign `normal`, `bold`, `bolder`, or `lighter` to this property. You can also assign one of the series of numbers from `100`, `200`, up to `900` to this property, with each successive number representing a weight that is thicker than the previous number. For example, `font-weight: 700` sets a thicker font weight than does `font-weight: 400`.

> **TIP** A font weight of 400 is roughly equivalent to that of a normal font.

Listing 29.7 shows a Web page that uses a combination of the properties described in this section. Figure 29.7 shows what the Web page looks like in Navigator.

**Listing 29.7   Text Properties**

```
<HTML>
<HEAD><TITLE>Style 7</TITLE></HEAD>
<BODY>

<STYLE TYPE="text/css">
  H1 {
        Background: black repeat-x fixed;
        text-align: center;
        color: white;
        border-width: medium; border-style: groove; border-color: black;
     }
  H2 { border-width: thin; border-style: solid; border-color: black }

  P {font-size: large; font-family: serif}
  EM {font-size: x-large; font-family: sans-serif; font-weight: bold}

</STYLE>

<H1>Heading One</H1>

<P>The above heading uses a <EM>style</EM> to center it and apply a background
image.</P>

<H2>Sub-heading One</H2>
<H2>Sub-heading Two</H2>
<H1>Heading Two</H1>

</BODY>
</HTML>
```

**FIG. 29.7**
HTML style sheets support most of the text-formatting capabilities that many word processors do.

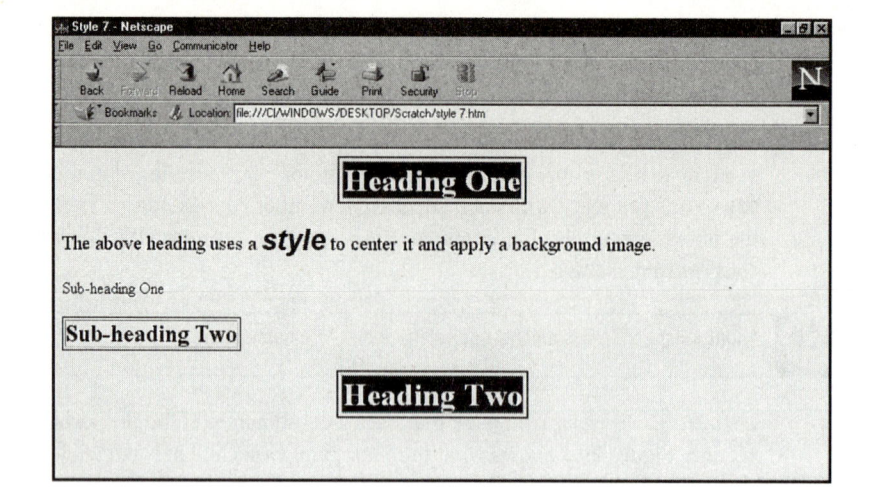

**Text Formatting** You can add special decorations, such as underlining, to an element by using the `text-decoration` property. Table 29.16 describes the values you can assign to this property. You can combine these values, too.

**Table 29.16  *text-decoration* Values**

| Value | Description |
| --- | --- |
| `none` | No decorations |
| `underline` | Underlined text |
| `overline` | Text with a line over it |
| `line-through` | Strikethrough |
| `blink` | Blinking text |

> **TIP** You can prevent the browser from underlining anchors by setting `text-decoration` to none for the `<A>` tag.

`text-transform` specifies that the text should be changed according to the values in Table 29.17.

**Table 29.17  *text-transform* Values**

| Value | Description |
| --- | --- |
| `capitalize` | Capitalizes first letter of each word |
| `uppercase` | Uppercases all letters in the element |

http://www.quecorp.com

| Value | Description |
|---|---|
| lowercase | Lowercases all letters in the element |
| none | No transformation |

**Text Spacing**   letter-spacing determines the spacing between each letter in a line of text. You can set this property to normal and let the browser worry about it, or you can set this property to any valid length, such as 1px.

You use the line-height property to set the leading for an element. An element's leading is the distance between the baselines of two text lines. You can use any valid length, a percentage (which is relative to the parent element's line-height property), or you can set this property to normal. Note that the spacing is added before each line, not after.

> **CAUTION**
> This setting doesn't work well on text lines that use multiple font sizes on the same line.

The white-space property defines how the browser handles white space within the element. You can leave things alone and let the browser collapse all of the white space, or you can specify that the browser treat white space as if you're within a <PRE> container. Table 29.18 shows you the values you can assign to this property.

**Table 29.18   *white-space* Values**

| Value | Description |
|---|---|
| normal | White space is collapsed. |
| pre | Handle white space like the <PRE> tag. |
| nowrap | Wrapping is only permitted with <BR>. |

word-spacing determines the spacing between each word in a line of text. You can set this property to normal and let the browser worry about it, or you can set this property to any valid length, such as 1px.

**Text Alignment**   You use the vertical-align property to change the vertical position of the element's text within the element itself. You can use one of the keywords described in Table 29.19.

**Table 29.19  vertical-align Values**

| Value | Description |
| --- | --- |
| baseline | Aligns the baseline of the element with the baseline of the parent |
| middle | Aligns the middle of the element with the middle of the parent |
| sub | Subscripts the element |
| super | Superscripts the element |
| text-top | Aligns the top of the element with the top of the parent element's text |
| text-bottom | Aligns the bottom of the element with the bottom of the parent element's text |
| top | Aligns the top of the element with the tallest element on the line |
| bottom | Aligns the bottom of the element with the lowest element on the line |

The `text-indent` property is used to indent the first line of an element's text. You can set this property to any valid length. For example, here's how to indent the `<P>` tag's text to the right by one inch:

`P {text-indent: 1in}`

**TIP** You can create a hanging indent by setting a tag's style `text-indent` to a negative value and `margin-left` to a positive value.

CHAPTER 30

# Embedding Multimedia

*by Jerry Honeycutt*

**W**hat comes to mind when you think of multimedia? Graphics? Video? Sound? While the exact definition of multimedia alludes many folks, I like to think of it more as an experience. That is, when you interact with your computer, anything that wows your senses is multimedia. An interactive, three-dimensional game uses multimedia video, audio, and input to give you that type of experience, for example.

How about your Web page? The same. You might consider anything you add to your Web page that tingles one of the user's senses multimedia. You can add sound to your Web page to give the user's ears an experience. You can add video or animation for the user's eyes, or add really cool interactivity to involve the user's sense of touch (let me know when you invent a scratch-and-sniff monitor). As you learn in this chapter, adding rich multimedia to your Web page isn't going to get much easier. You use either the <EMBED> or <OBJECT> tags to insert multimedia into your Web page, in the form of plug-ins, Java applets, ActiveX controls, and more. ■

**Learn how plug-ins work**

This chapter helps you understand plug-ins so that you can use them effectively in your Web page.

**Embed content using <EMBED> or <OBJECT>**

You can embed multimedia content using either the <EMBED> or the <OBJECT> tag. This chapter shows both and helps you choose between them.

**Add audio and video content to your Web page**

Adding audio and video content to your Web page is easy, because Netscape Communicator comes with plug-ins for both: LiveAudio and LiveVideo.

**Find and use third-party plug-ins**

You're not limited to Netscape's plug-ins at all. You can embed content for a variety of third-party plug-ins, too.

> **TIP** *Web Developer* magazine has a great FAQ on embedding multimedia in your Web page: **http://www.webdeveloper.com/frames/faqs/mmfaq.htm**.

## Getting to Know Plug-Ins

When a user starts Communicator on her desktop, it checks the appropriate folder (see Table 30.1) to see what plug-ins are installed. Communicator makes a note of each plug-in and its MIME type, which indicates the type of file with which the plug-in is associated.

**Table 30.1  Netscape Plug-in Folders**

| Platform | Folder |
| --- | --- |
| Mac | Plug-ins, directly under the Netscape folder |
| Windows | Plugins, directly under the Netscape folder |
| UNIX | /usr/local/netscape/plugins |

When the user opens a Web page that embeds a multimedia file, Communicator notes the MIME type of the file, finds a plug-in that can open that type of file (if available), and loads the plug-in, passing it the file. The drawing in Figure 30.1 illustrates this concept for you. The most important concept for you to understand is that you, as the HTML author, embed a multimedia file into your Web page, while a plug-in on the user's computer actually displays that file in the Web browser.

**FIG. 30.1**
You provide the data, and the user provides the plug-in.

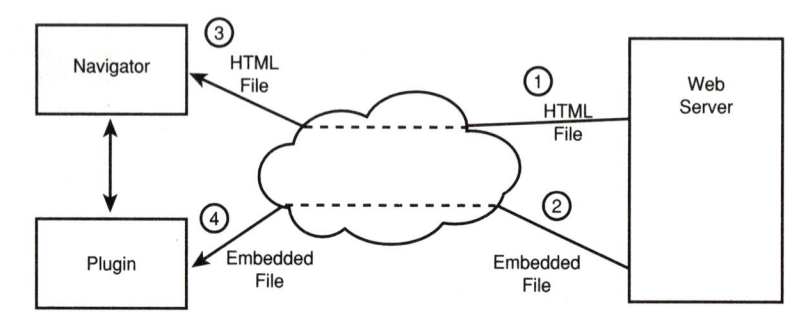

1. Web Page
2. Multimedia (or Embedded) File
3. Communicator
4. Plug-in

> **TIP** The information contained in this section is valid for all plug-ins, whether you use the <EMBED> tag or <OBJECT> tag to insert them.

## Embedded Plug-Ins

Embedded plug-ins are visible on the Web page and display inline with the rest of the Web page's content. Embedded plug-ins always occupy a rectangular area on the Web page (see Figure 30.2). You, as the HTML author, embed the multimedia file in the Web page, and the plug-in, on the user's computer, displays that file inside the Web page.

Embedded plug-ins can be hidden. That is, the HTML author can designate that the plug-in is not to display anything on the Web page. For example, you might not want to display anything on the Web page if you're embedding a sound file.

**FIG. 30.2**
Live3D is a Netscape plug-in that comes with Netscape Communicator; it is used to display VRML worlds.

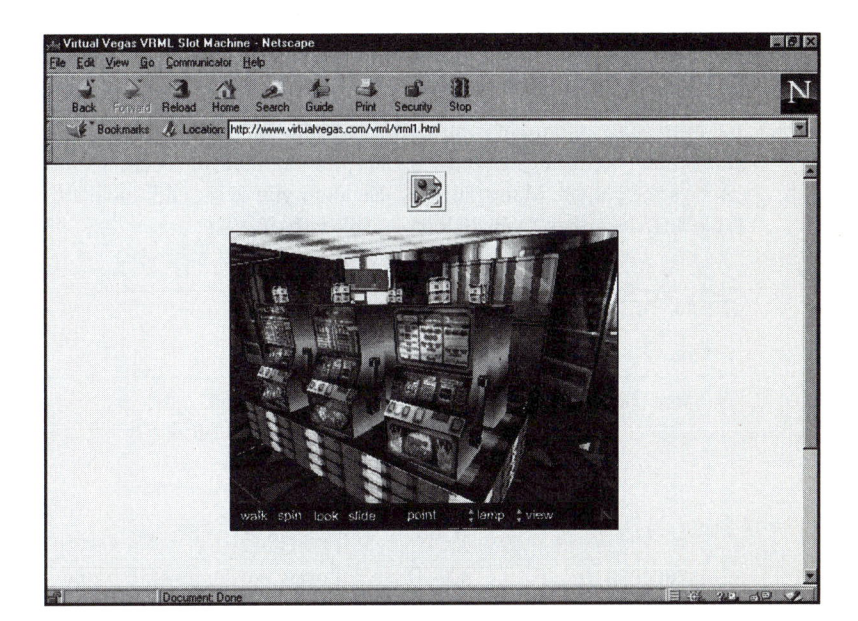

## Full-Page Plug-Ins

Other plug-ins are full-page; they don't occupy space in the Web page itself, but occupy the entire browser window.. After the user has finished interacting with the plug-in, he can click Back on Communicators Navigation toolbar to return to the original Web page.

# Inserting Plug-Ins into Your Web Page

With Communicator, and thanks to the efforts of W3C, you have two different ways to embed plug-ins into your Web page. You can use the old sturdy <EMBED> tag, or you can use the new-fangled <OBJECT> tag. Making this choice is a lot harder than actually writing the HTML for either. Here are some thoughts on the subject, though, that might help you:

- Use the <EMBED> tag if you're concerned with compatibility across a variety of Web browsers. This Netscape extension has been in place since Navigator 2.0, and many other Web browsers have adopted its use.

- Use the <OBJECT> tag if you want to be hip to the latest HTML technology, you want to conform to future HTML standards, or you want to use the <OBJECT> tag's apology section to supply content for those browser's that don't support plug-ins. The simple truth of the matter is that both Microsoft and Netscape are adopting the use of the <OBJECT> tag for this kind of work, so you might want to start doing it yourself.

## <EMBED>

You have a fair amount of control over any plug-in that you embed into your Web page using the <EMBED> tag. You can control its size, for example, or whether or not the browser actually displays the plug-in. Many plug-ins also allow you to set additional attributes that control them. Table 30.2 describes each attribute of this tag.

### Table 30.2  <EMBED> Attributes

| Attribute | Description |
| --- | --- |
| ALIGN=value | LEFT—Aligns text flush left<br>RIGHT—Aligns text flush right<br>TOP—Aligns text with top<br>BOTTOM—Aligns text with bottom |
| BORDER=num | Width of frame's border in pixels |
| FRAMEBORDER=value | NO—Does not draw border around frame |
| HEIGHT=num | Height of frame as defined by UNITS |
| HIDDEN | Makes the plug-in invisible on the page |
| HSPACE=num | Width of left and right margin in pixels |
| NAME=name | Name of the embedded object |
| PALETTE=value | FOREGROUND—Foreground colors<br>BACKGROUND—Background colors |
| PLUGINSPAGE=URL | URL of the Web page that contains instructions for installing the plug-in if the user does not have it installed |

| Attribute | Description |
|---|---|
| SRC=*URL* | URL that indicates the location of the embedded multimedia data file; if you don't use this attribute, use TYPE |
| TYPE=*type* | MIME type of the embedded object, which determines the plug-in that loads; use TYPE for plug-ins that require no data |
| UNITS=*value* | PIXELS—Use pixels for measurements<br>EN—Use half the point size, instead |
| VSPACE=*num* | Width of top and bottom margin in pixels |
| WIDTH=*num* | Width of frame as defined by UNITS |

Many plug-ins also have *private attributes*. Communicator looks for all of the attributes described in Table 30.2 when it parses the <EMBED> tag, but it ignores other attributes. When Communicator loads the associated plug-in, it passes the plug-in all of the attributes it found. For example, many audio plug-ins have a private attribute called AUTOSTART, which indicates whether or not you want the plug-in to immediately start playing the sound file when it loads.

## <OBJECT>

W3C is in the process of defining the <OBJECT> tag. It's a work in progress. Many vendors, however, including Microsoft and Netscape, have already adopted the <OBJECT> tag. As the working draft for this tag has not changed in quite some time, it's pretty stable and suitable for you to use. You can get the full details on this tag at W3C's Web site: **http://www.w3.org/pub/WWW/TR/WD-object**.

Using the <OBJECT> tag is just a bit more complicated than using the <EMBED> tag. You have to form the <OBJECT> tag as described in Table 30.3, specify any required parameters using the <PARAM> tag, and provide content for those users who have browsers with no <OBJECT> support or who don't have the required plug-in.

**Table 30.3  <OBJECT> Attributes for Plug-Ins**

| Attribute | Description |
|---|---|
| BORDER=*num* | Width of frame's border in pixels |
| CLASSID=*URL* | URL of the plug-in for installing the plug-in if the user does not have it installed |
| DATA=*URL* | URL of the object's data file |
| HEIGHT=*num* | Height of frame as defined by UNITS |
| HSPACE=*num* | Width of left and right margin in pixels |

*continues*

### Table 30.3 Continued

| Attribute | Description |
| --- | --- |
| ID=*name* | Name of the embedded object |
| TYPE=*type* | MIME type of the embedded object, which determines the plug-in that loads; use TYPE for plug-ins that require no data |
| TYPE=*type* | MIME type of the object's data file |
| VSPACE=*num* | Width of top and bottom margin in pixels |
| WIDTH=*num* | Width of frame as defined by UNITS |

**Sandwiching <*PARAM*> Tags**   You can provide additional properties to the plug-in, if the plug-in supports them, using the <PARAM> tag. You embed a <PARAM> tag between the beginning and ending <OBJECT> tags for each property you want to provide to the plug-in, like this:

```
<OBJECT definition>
  <PARAM NAME="LOOP" VALUE="TRUE">
</OBJECT>
```

Using the <PARAM> tag is similar to using private properties with the <EMBED> tag. The NAME attribute is the name of the property and the VALUE attribute is the actual value you want to assign to that name. Thus, the following PARAM tag is equivalent to the AUTOSTART attribute in the <EMBED> tag you see just below it:

```
<PARAM NAME=AUTOSTART VALUE=TRUE>
<EMBED blah-blah-blah AUTOSTART=TRUE>
```

**Providing Alternate Content (Apology)**   Not all browsers or users are created equal. Some browsers don't know what in the world to do with the <OBJECT> tag. Still, some users don't have access to a plug-in that you've embedded into your Web page. The authors of the <OBJECT> tag's working draft have created a way for you to handle this situation, however—alternative content. Some folks also call the alternative content the apology section. Here's how it works:

- If the browser can handle the <OBJECT> tag and it has a plug-in available for the specified data type, the browser parses the <OBJECT> tag and any <PARAM> tags contained within it. It ignores everything else.

- If the browser can handle the <OBJECT> tag, but it doesn't have a plug-in available for the specified data type, the browser ignores the <OBJECT> tag and the <PARAM> tags contained within it. The browser does parse any other content contained within the <OBJECT> tag.

- If the browser can't handle the <OBJECT> tag, it can't handle the <PARAM> tag, either. By design, the browser does not parse those tags, but parses anything else in its path, including content inside the <OBJECT> tag.

Consider Listing 30.1, for example, which is an example of inserting a multimedia file into a Web page. If the browser doesn't do the <OBJECT> tag, all it's going to parse is the <A>, <IMG>, and `</A>` tags. If the browser does support the `<OBJECT>` tag, but it doesn't have a plug-in for MOX files, it ignores the `<OBJECT>` and `<PARAM>` tags, parsing the same tags as in the previous case. Last, if the browser does support the `<OBJECT>` tag and it has a plug-in for MOX files, it parses the `<OBJECT>` and `<PARAM>` tags, ignoring everything else.

### Listing 30.1    Alternative Content

```
<OBJECT DATA=MYFILE.MOX WIDTH=100 HEIGHT=100>
  <PARAM NAME=AUTOSTART VALUE=TRUE>
  <A HREF="get-mox.htm">
    <IMG SRC=need-mox.gif WIDTH=100 HEIGHT=100>
  </A>
</OBJECT>
```

#### A Word with Our Lawyer, Please?

Copyright laws protect the author of a work from other folks making illegal copies of their work. You can't photocopy a magazine article or make a duplicate of a musical CD, for example, without violating the copyright law. If you do, the organization that owns the copyright can pursue the matter in court (translation: sue the pants off of you).

The copyright laws apply to electronic expression as much as they do to other forms. Thus, the Web pages and multimedia files you find on the Internet can have copyrights with just as much weight as the copyright on this book. Ignorance isn't an excuse, either. Just because you didn't know that a file was copyrighted doesn't protect you when the copyright hits the fan.

So, having scared you a bit, how do you know if an image is indeed copyrighted? It's not quite as cut-and-dry as looking for a copyright symbol (audio clips don't have one). In fact, there is no requirement that work contain a copyright symbol in order to be protected by the copyright laws. You can check a few other places for file's copyright status, however:

- Look for a copyright notice in the document that originally contained the file. This is the most likely place to find such a notice.
- If you're using a video from a library, check the library's license agreement to see what kind of rights you have for redistribution.
- Look for any comments embedded within the file that might include a copyright notice. Most audio and video editors allow you to edit and view embedded comments.

## Adding Content to Your Web Page

Before you can jazz up your Web page with multimedia, you have to make or find multimedia content. Making your own multimedia content isn't always practical, especially for a novice. You have to work within a third-party authoring environment such as a video editor and sometimes have to purchase additional hardware such as a video camera. You can learn more about creating your own multimedia content in *Special Edition Using HTML 3.2*, Third Edition.

Using free or store-bought multimedia libraries is the quickest route to multimedia bliss. Most multimedia libraries come with a combination of graphical images, sound clips, and video clips. Some libraries do include a handful of Shockwave files, too. While you can find a whole host of different plug-ins, you'll mostly use audio and video in your Web page. Sticking with audio and video is a reality for most HTML authors, and that's good for two reasons:

- Netscape Communicator, and most other Web browsers, have the built-in capability to play audio and display video files. Netscape has LiveAudio and LiveVideo, for example. Microsoft has ActiveMovie.

- Audio and video files are relatively easy to come by. You can download files from the Internet, or you can purchase CD-ROMs from your local computer retailer that contain a selection of both file types. Yes, you can also make these files on your own, which you learn how to do in Que's *Special Edition Using HTML 3.2*, Third Edition.

**NOTE** To see a list of the types of plug-ins with which Communicator comes, choose Help, About Plug-ins from Communicator's main menu. You see a list similar to that shown in Figure 30.3.

**FIG. 30.3**
Choose Click Here, at the top of this page, to see a list of plug-ins available at Netscape's Web site.

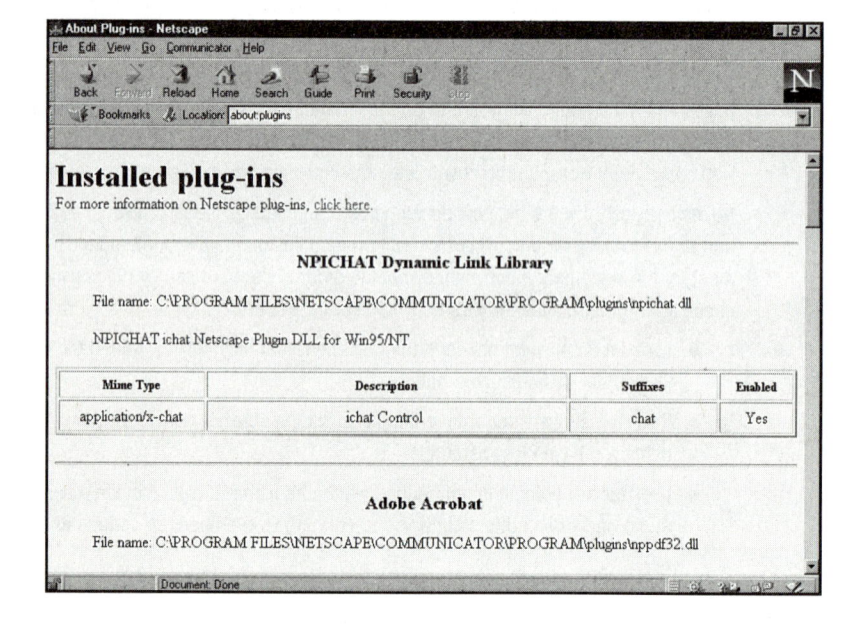

## Audio

Netscape Communicator comes with an audio plug-in called LiveAudio. As shown in Figure 30.4, LiveAudio has a very simple user interface that the user can interact with to stop, play, and pause the audio clip, as well as adjust the volume. LiveAudio handles a majority of the sound files you find on the Internet. It definitely handles WAV and MIDI files, which takes care of most of the audio content you'll embed into your Web page.

**FIG. 30.4**
LiveAudio sports controls that anyone who has ever used a tape-deck can understand.

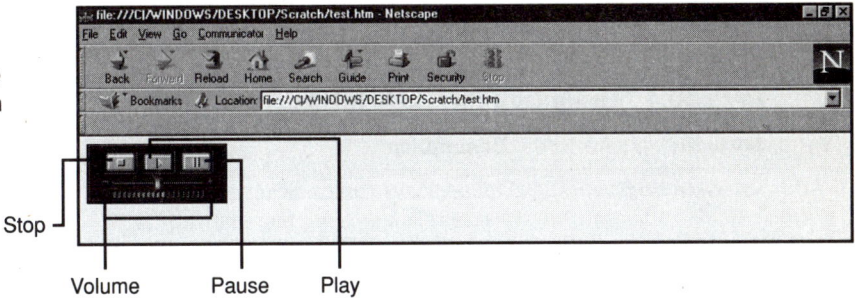

Stop — Volume — Pause — Play

**N O T E**  A user must have a sound card and speakers installed in his computer to hear any audio clips embedded in your Web page. Chances are good these days that most users have a sound card.

You can use either the <EMBED> or the <OBJECT> tag to embed an audio file into your Web page. Listing 30.2 shows you an example of a Web page that uses the <EMBED>. The SRC, WIDTH, and HEIGHT attributes are the same ones you learned about earlier in this chapter. If you want the user to see the audio controls, you must use the WIDTH and HEIGHT attributes. The best size for the controls is 144 pixels wide and 60 pixels high.

**Listing 30.2   Embedding Audio Using <EMBED>**

```
<HTML>
  <HEAD>
    <TITLE>Embedding using EMBED</TITLE>
  </HEAD>
  <BODY>
    <EMBED SRC=EXAMPLE.WAV HEIGHT=60 WIDTH=144>
  </BODY>
</HTML>
```

Listing 30.3 shows you the same example using the <OBJECT> tag. The parameters are the same as those for the <EMBED> tag, except that you use the DATA attribute instead of the SRC attribute to specify the source file.

**Listing 30.3   Embedding Audio Using <OBJECT>**

```
<HTML>
  <HEAD>
    <TITLE>Embedding audio using OBJECT</TITLE>
  </HEAD>
  <BODY>
    <OBJECT DATA=EXAMPLE.WAV WIDTH=144 HEIGHT=60>
    </OBJECT>
  </BODY>
</HTML>
```

LiveAudio supports several private attributes, each described in Table 30.4.

**Table 30.4  LiveAudio's Private Attributes**

| Attribute | Description |
| --- | --- |
| AUTOSTART=*value* | TRUE—Plays automatically<br>FALSE—Doesn't play automatically |
| AUTOLOAD=*value* | TRUE—Load clip automatically<br>FALSE—Doesn't load automatically |
| STARTTIME="*mm:ss*" | Starts time from beginning of clip |
| ENDTIME="30*mm:ss*" | Ends time from beginning of clip |
| VOLUME=*num* | Initial value as a percentage |
| CONTROLS=*value* | CONSOLE—Displays the console<br>SMALLCONSOLE—Displays small console<br>PLAYBUTTON—Displays Play button<br>PAUSEBUTTON—Displays Pause button<br>STOPBUTTON—Displays Stop button<br>VOLUMELEVER—Displays volume slider |

> **TIP** Choose MIDI files over WAV files every chance you get. It's more economical. For the same file size, you can get a much longer audio clip from a MIDI file than you can from a WAV file.

## Video

Like audio, you can use the <EMBED> or <OBJECT> tag to embed a video into your Web page. Listing 30.4 shows you an example of a Web page that uses the <EMBED> tag to embed an AVI file into a Web page. The SRC, WIDTH, and HEIGHT attributes are the same ones you learned about earlier in this chapter.

**Listing 30.4  Embedding a Video Using <*EMBED*>**

```
<HTML>
  <HEAD>
    <TITLE>Embedding a video using EMBED</TITLE>
  </HEAD>
  <BODY>
    <EMBED SRC=EXAMPLE.AVI WIDTH=150 HEIGHT=100>
  </BODY>
</HTML>
```

Listing 30.5 shows you the same example using the <OBJECT> tag. Note that the parameters are the same as those for the <EMBED> tag, except that you use the DATA attribute instead of the SRC attribute to specify the source file. In this example, you see the <IMG> tag sandwiched in the

Adding Content to Your Web Page 637

object, which provides alternative content for users who can't display videos. Figure 30.5 shows what this video looks like in Communicator.

**Listing 30.5 Embedding a Video Using <OBJECT>**

```
<HTML>
  <HEAD>
    <TITLE>Embedding a video using OBJECT</TITLE>
  </HEAD>
  <BODY>
    <OBJECT DATA=EXAMPLE.AVI WIDTH=150 HEIGHT=100>
      <IMG SRC=EXAMPLE.GIF WIDTH=150 HEIGHT=100>
    </OBJECT>
  </BODY>
</HTML>
```

**FIG. 30.5**
To access the controls when they're not visible on the Web page, right-click the video.

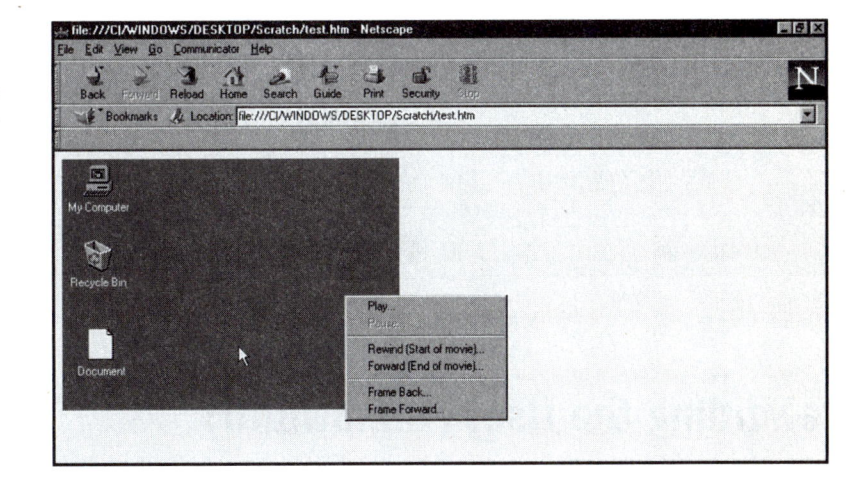

**AVI Files (LiveVideo)** LiveVideo, which is the plug-in for AVI files, has some additional private attributes that you can use to better control how the plug-in displays in the browser. You see those attributes in Table 30.5.

**Table 30.5  LiveVideo's Private Attributes**

| Attribute | Description |
|---|---|
| AUTOSTART=value | TRUE—Video starts automatically<br>FALSE—Video doesn't start automatically |
| LOOP=value | TRUE—Video plays repeatedly<br>FALSE—Video plays one time |
| CONTROLS=value | TRUE—Plug-in shows video controls<br>FALSE—Plug-in doesn't show controls |

**TIP:** Turn your favorite AVI video into an animated GIF. Download the GIF Construction Set from Ziff-Davis (http://www.hotfiles.com), which converts an AVI file into an animated GIF frame by frame. It cuts the size of the file in half and allows the user to see the animation as the file loads from the Web server.

**MOV Files (QuickTime)** The QuickTime plug-in, included with Netscape Communicator, also has some private attributes that you can specify to control how it displays in the browser. You see those attributes in Table 30.6.

**Table 30.6  QuickTime's Private Attributes**

| Attribute | Description |
| --- | --- |
| AUTOPLAY=value | TRUE—Automatically starts<br>FALSE—Doesn't automatically start |
| CONTROLLER=value | TRUE—Displays a toolbar<br>FALSE—Doesn't display a toolbar |
| LOOP=value | TRUE—Plays video repeatedly<br>FALSE—Plays video a single time |
| PLAYEVERYFRAME=value | TRUE—Plays while downloading<br>FALSE—Doesn't play while downloading |
| HREF=URL | URL to which the video is linked |
| TARGET=FRAME | Targeted link for the video |

# Rewarding the User (Bandwidth)

Be considerate of those users who have slow connections to the Internet. A user who has a 28.8K connection to the Internet, which is very common, waits over four minutes for a 1M video to download. A 1M video, on the other hand, only plays for a few seconds; thus, you're asking a user to wait four minutes to view a few seconds of video— the user might feel cheated unless it's a pretty spectacular video clip. Mark Brown, the lead author of this book, calls this the *wait/reward ratio*. Think of it this way: if the only reward you get after waiting seven hours for Thanksgiving dinner is leftovers, you'd feel a bit cheated.

The solution? Provide a link on your Web page to the video clip. If a user wants to see the video clip, she can click the link—it's her choice. For example, you might add a link to your Web page, with a warning, that looks something like this:

```
Take a look at this AVI video of my new Yorkie.
This video is 1M in size. At 14.4K, it takes over 9 minutes to download. At
28.8K, it takes over 4 minutes.
```

http://www.quecorp.com

# Finding Other Useful Plug-Ins

You're not limited to using the plug-ins that Netscape provides with Communicator. You can use a different plug-in from LiveAudio to play audio files, for example. You also need to use a third-party plug-in if you want to embed multimedia content into your Web page other than video, audio, and VRML—for example, Shockwave.

Netscape maintains a fairly comprehensive list of plug-ins. You can find this list at **http://home.netscape.com/comprod/products/navigator/version_2.0/plugins**. Click one of the six categories (3D and Animation, Business and Utilities, Presentations, Audio/Video, Image Viewers, and What's New), and you see a list of plug-ins. For each plug-in, you see a description and links to the vendor and example Web pages.

The ultimate resource for plug-ins is BrowserWatch (**http://browserwatch.iworld.com/plug-in.html**, shown in Figure 30.6). You can view this list by different categories: multimedia, graphics, sound, document, productivity, or VRML. You can also view the list of plug-ins by platform: Macintosh, OS/2, UNIX, and Windows.

**FIG. 30.6**
The BrowserWatch Web site provides links to each plug-in's vendor, as well as links to example Web pages.

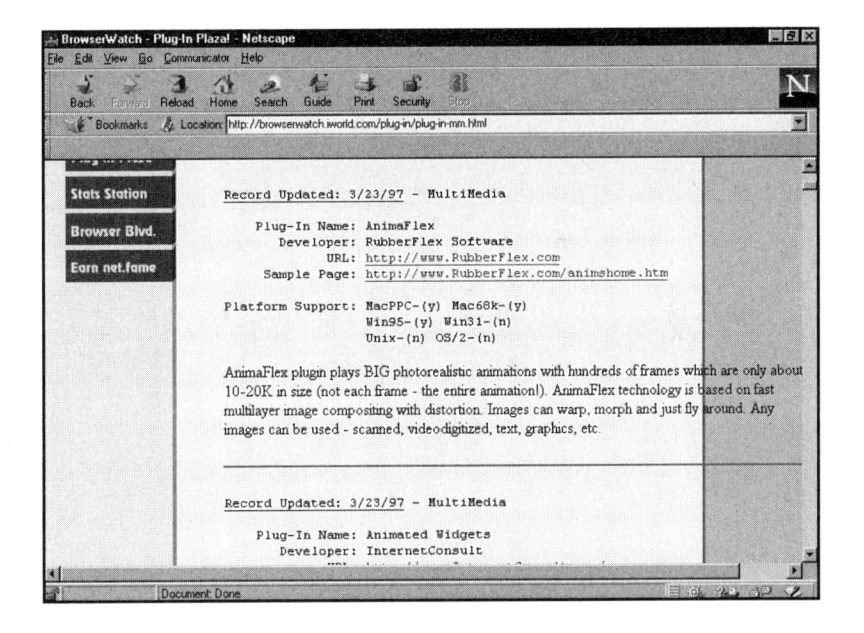

> **TIP** If you use a plug-in that the user isn't likely to have installed already, use the PLUGINSPAGE attribute to point Communicator to the download page for that plug-in. Doing so helps Communicator install the plug-in more or less automatically.

CHAPTER 31

# Adding Java Applets

*by Jerry Honeycutt*

The most common use for Java is as a simple enhancement to a Web page. The Web page is your primary focus, and you use Java applications to enhance it. For example, you might use a Java applet to create imagemaps that change as the user moves the mouse over them; in this way, the user knows that the mouse is passing over something that's clickable. The possibilities are endless.

This chapter doesn't teach you how to write Java applications; instead, it shows you how to use existing Java applications in your Web page. You can find thousands of Java applets on the Internet that you can use. Some of them are free, others cost a little loot. If you're interested in creating your own Java applications, though, take a look at Que's *Special Edition Using Java*. You might also look to Netscape for more information: **http://www.netscape.com**.

■ **Learn how Java applets are developed**

This chapter gives you the scoop on how developers create Java applets and how they work in the user's Web browser.

■ **Embed Java applets using <APPLET> or <OBJECT>**

You can use either tag for embedding Java applets into your Web page.

■ **Borrow Java applets from the Internet**

You can download a plethora of free Java applets from the Internet. This chapter shows you where to get them and provides a few examples to show you how to add them to your Web page.

## Learn About Java

Sun Microsystems' Java didn't get its start as Java. It started off as an embedded language called Oak that was used to build intelligent consumer electronics devices—you know, smart appliances like toasters that flush the toilet when your Pop Tarts catch fire. Sun even prototyped intelligent remote controls using Oak, but they just couldn't rally enough support for this technology. It died a slow and painful death.

The team responsible for Oak realized that their technology would work great on the Web (trying to save their jobs, I suppose). So, they changed its name to Java and built a Web browser called HotJava that would show off its capabilities. It was a hit. Netscape, followed by Microsoft, quickly embraced Java in its Web browser. Java has become so popular now that Sun has created a new business unit called Javasoft. Javasoft focuses on the further development of Java.

### Understanding How It Works

Java is a cross-platform development tool. The developer compiles a Java applet into intermediate code called *bytecodes*. When a browser opens a Web page that contains the Java applet, it downloads the bytecodes to the user's computer. The browser's Java interpreter interprets the bytecodes to execute the program. As a result, the same Java applet runs on any platform for which there is a Java interpreter. Figure 31.1 illustrates this concept.

**FIG. 31.1**
Java programmers can create Java applets on virtually any platform for which there exists a Java interpreter.

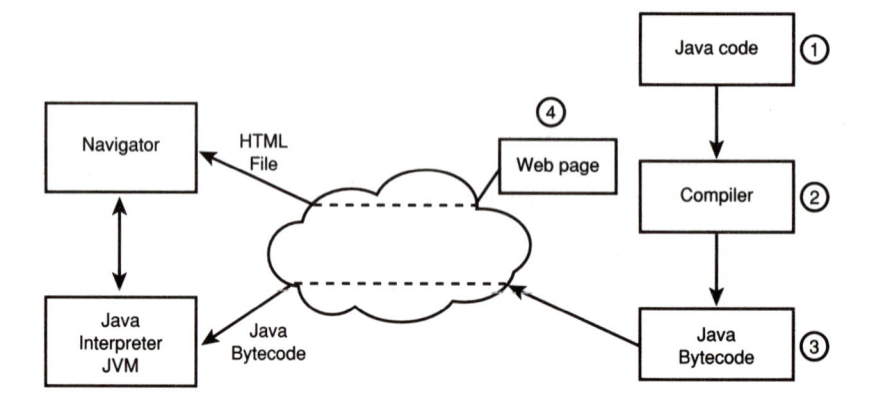

In some cases, a browser actually compiles a Java applet's bytecodes into machine code. Machine code executes much, much faster than interpreted code. This doesn't diminish Java's platform independence, though, because the compilation is actually occurring on the user's computer. This technology is also known as *Just in Time compilation* (JIT compilation).

> **NOTE** Whereas a Java *application* is a stand-alone program, a Java *applet* is a smallish program that you embed in a Web page. A Java applet can't run outside of the Web browser.

## Comparing Java to Plug-Ins

You can accomplish many of the same things with a Java applet that you can with a plug-in. You can create animations, buttons that glow when the mouse moves over them, ticker tape streams of text, and so on. You can even play complicated multimedia files such as video and sound files.

You're a bit constrained by plug-ins, however. The user has to install a plug-in before viewing a Web page that uses it. Not only that, but you can't be absolutely sure that a plug-in you embed in your Web page is going to be available for every user's platform.

Java doesn't constrain you in the same way that plug-ins do. The user doesn't have to preinstall the applet. The user's browser downloads the applet to her computer when it's referenced in a Web page. Not only that, a Java applet is cross-platform; thus, any user who opens a Web page containing a Java applet can run that Java applet on his computer. The only constraint here is that the user has to be using a Java-enabled Web browser.

The long and the short of it is that if you can accomplish the same task with either a plug-in or a Java applet, choose the Java applet every time.

## Securing Java Applets

There's not much chance that a Java applet can wreak havoc with a user's computer. Java has security devices that protect the user from errant Java applets. The Java class hierarchy prevents a Java applet from doing anything harmful, for example. Many folks call this approach to security the "Java sandbox." Here's what that means to you:

- Java applets can't read or write files on the user's computer. There is no risk of an applet tampering with the user's disk.
- Java applets can't read from or write to the computer's memory. An applet can't cause the user's computer to crash by tampering with memory and can't read information from the user's computer.
- Java applets can't launch applications on the user's computer. For example, an applet can't launch a command that deletes files from the user's disk.
- Java applets don't have direct access to the operating system. Thus, an applet can't call the operating system's API functions.

Java applets can create their own windows outside of the browser window, however. The only security risk this poses is Trojan horses that look reputable but have more devious ambitions. Fortunately, you can easily identify such a window because the Java interpreter labels them with the words `Unsigned Java Applet Window` at the bottom of the window (see Figure 31.2).

# 644   Chapter 31   Adding Java Applets

**FIG. 31.2**
Realize that any window labeled `Unsigned Java Applet Window` belongs to a program you downloaded from the Internet.

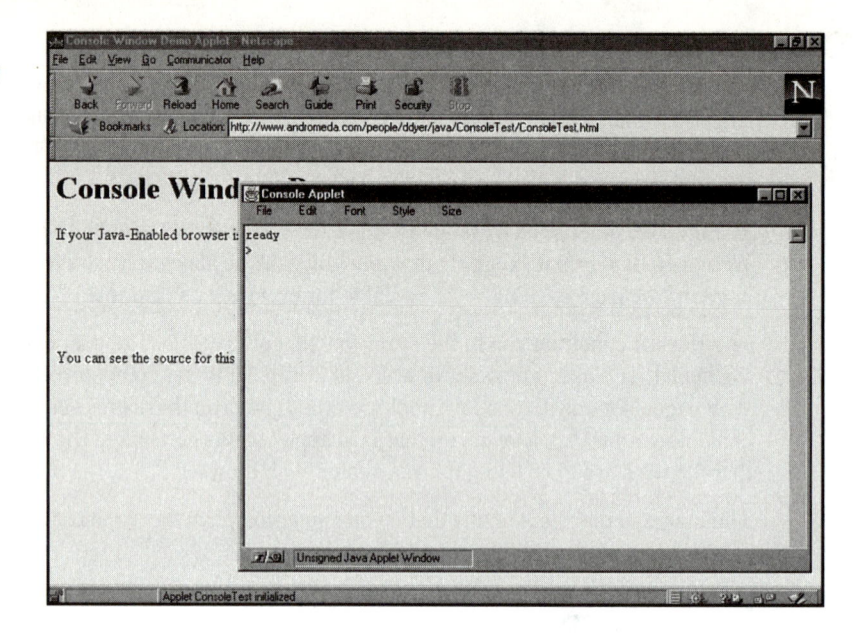

## Creating Your Own Java Applets

Java applets are not very easy for a nonprogrammer type to create. You have to be familiar with the Java language, first of all, which is loosely based upon the C++ language. You also have to be familiar with various programming concepts, such as event-driven programming and working with windows—not easy for a newcomer.

If you're determined to learn how to build your own Java applets, however, start with a good book such as Que's *Special Edition Using Java*. This book teaches you programming basics, such as conditional and looping statements. It also teaches you how to write event-driven and object-oriented programs.

*Special Edition Using Java* recommends some development environments for you to use, but following are some other suggestions:

- Javasoft, the ipso-facto Java development company, provides the Java Development Kit (JDK). You can download the JDK at **http://www.javasoft.com**.

- Symantec provides Symantec Café, which is a full-blown integrated development environment for Java. It has a Java class browser, debugger, editor, and compiler. You can get more information about this product at **http://cafe.symantec.com/index.html**.

- Microsoft has joined the fray, too. Visual J++ is a first-rate development environment for Java (see Figure 31.3). Like Symantec Café, Visual J++ is an IDE that includes all of the tools you need to write great applets. Visual J++ also comes with wizards that generate all of the basic code for you. You can get more information at Microsoft's site: **http://www.microsoft.com/visualj**.

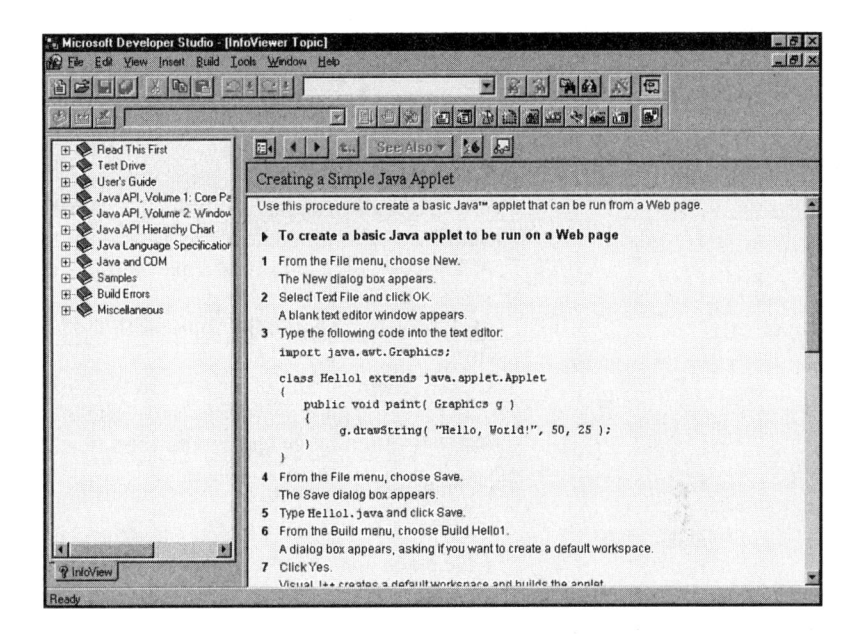

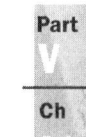

**FIG. 31.3**
Microsoft's Visual J++ integrates into Developer Studio.

# Embed a Java Applet into Your Web Page

With Communicator, and thanks to the efforts of W3C, you have two different ways to embed Java applets into your Web page. You can use the <APPLET> tag, or you can use the new <OBJECT> tag. Making this choice is a lot harder than actually writing the HTML for either. Following are some thoughts on the subject, though, that might help you:

- Use the <APPLET> tag if you're concerned with compatibility across a variety of Web browsers. This Netscape extension has been in place since Navigator 2.0 and, thus, many other Web browsers have adopted its use.

- Use the <OBJECT> tag if you want to be hip to the latest HTML technology or you want to conform to future HTML standards. The simple truth of the matter is that both Microsoft and Netscape are adopting the use of the <OBJECT> tag for this kind of work, so you might want to start doing it yourself.

## *<APPLET>*

You have a fair amount of control over any Java applet that you embed into your Web page using the <APPLET> container tag. You can control the amount of space the applet occupies, for example. Many applets also allow you to set additional properties that control how they execute. Table 31.1 describes each attribute of this tag.

### Table 31.1  <APPLET> Attributes

| Attribute | Description |
| --- | --- |
| ALIGN=value | LEFT—Align applet flush left<br>RIGHT—Align applet flush right<br>TOP—Align top of applet with the top of the tallest item on the line<br>ABSMIDDLE—Align middle of applet with the middle of the line<br>ABSBOTTOM—Align bottom of applet with the bottom of the lowest item on the line<br>BASELINE—Align bottom of applet with the baseline of text on the line<br>BOTTOM—Align bottom of applet with the baseline of text on the line<br>MIDDLE—Align middle of applet with baseline of text on the line<br>TEXTTOP—Align top of applet with the tallest text on the line |
| ALT=text | Alternate text to display |
| ARCHIVE=URL | The URL of the archive that contains the class referenced by CODE; its file extension must be .ZIP |
| CODE=class | The file name of the applet class to load; its file extension must be .CLASS |
| CODEBASE=URL | Folder that contains the Java class |
| HEIGHT=num | Height of frame in pixels |
| HSPACE=num | Width of left and right margin in pixels |
| MAYSCRIPT | Allows the applet to access JavaScript |
| NAME=name | Name of the embedded object |
| VSPACE=num | Width of top and bottom margin in pixels |
| WIDTH=num | Width of frame in pixels |

**Passing Parameters to the Applet**   You can provide additional properties to the applet, if the applet supports them, using the <PARAM> tag. You embed a <PARAM> tag between the beginning and ending <APPLET> tags for each property you want to provide to the applet, like this:

```
<APPLET CODE="text.class" HEIGHT=100 WIDTH=100>
  <PARAM NAME="ENABLED" VALUE="TRUE">
</APPLET>
```

Using the <PARAM> tag is similar to using the attributes of an HTML tag. The NAME attribute is the name of the property and the VALUE attribute is the actual value that you want to assign to that name.

**Providing Alternative Content**   Not all browsers support Java. Thus, some don't know how to interpret the <APPLET> tag. Still, other users have disabled Java in their Java-enabled Web browser. You can provide alternative content for those users, however, using the apology section of the <APPLET> tag, as follows:

Embed a Java Applet into Your Web Page | 647

- If the browser supports Java, it parses the `<APPLET>` tag and any `<PARAM>` tags contained within it. It ignores any other content contained in the `<APPLET>` container, though.
- If the browser doesn't support Java, or the user has disabled Java in the browser, the browser ignores the `<APPLET>` and `<PARAM>` tags. It parses everything else contained within the `<APPLET>` and `</APPLET>` tags, however.

Consider Listing 31.1, for example, which is an example of inserting a Java applet into a Web page. If the browser doesn't do Java, all it's going to parse is the `<A>`, `<IMG>`, and `</A>` tags. If the browser does support Java, it parses the `<APPLET>` and `<PARAM>` tags, ignoring everything else.

### Listing 31.1 Providing Alternative Content with the `<APPLET>` Tag

```
<APPLET CODE="applet.class" WIDTH=100 HEIGHT=100>
  <PARAM NAME=ENABLED VALUE=TRUE>
  <A HREF="get-mox.htm">
    <IMG SRC=need-mox.gif WIDTH=100 HEIGHT=100>
  </A>
</OBJECT>
```

## `<OBJECT>`

W3C is in the process of defining the `<OBJECT>` tag. It's a work in progress. Many vendors, however, including Microsoft and Netscape, have already adopted the `<OBJECT>` tag. As the working draft for this tag has not changed in quite some time, it's pretty stable and suitable for you to use. You can get the full details on this tag at W3C's Web site: **http://www.w3.org/pub/WWW/TR/WD-object**.

Using the `<OBJECT>` tag is no more complicated than using the `<APPLET>` tag. You have to form the `<OBJECT>` tag, as described in Table 31.2; specify any required parameters using the `<PARAM>` tag and provide content for those users who have browsers with no Java support or who have disabled Java in their browser.

### Table 31.2 `<OBJECT>` Attributes for Java Applets

| Attribute | Description |
| --- | --- |
| ALIGN=*value* | LEFT—Align applet flush left<br>RIGHT—Align applet flush right<br>CENTER—Center applet on Web page<br>TOP—Align top of applet with top of the tallest item on the line<br>ABSMIDDLE—Align middle of applet with the middle of the line<br>ABSBOTTOM—Align bottom of applet with the bottom of the lowest item on the line<br>BASELINE—Align bottom of applet with the baseline of text on the line |

*continues*

**Table 31.2  Continued**

| Attribute | Description |
|---|---|
|  | BOTTOM—Align bottom of applet with the baseline of text on the line<br>MIDDLE—Align middle of applet with the baseline of text on the line<br>TEXTTOP—Align top of applet with the tallest text on the line |
| ALT=*text* | Alternate text to display |
| BORDER=*num* | Width of frame's border in pixels |
| CLASSID=*URL* | URL of the Java applet in java:*URL* format—for example, java:applet.class |
| CODEBASE=*URL* | Folder that contains the Java class |
| CODETYPE=*type* | MIME type of the object in CLASSID; for Java applets, set to application/java-vm |
| HEIGHT=*num* | Height of frame in pixels |
| HSPACE=*num* | Width of left and right margin in pixels |
| ID=*name* | Name of the embedded object |
| VSPACE=*num* | Width of top and bottom margin in pixels |
| WIDTH=*num* | Width of frame in pixels |

**Passing Parameters to the Applet**   Passing additional properties to a Java applet using the <OBJECT> tag works exactly the same as using the <EMBED> tag. You use the <PARAM> tag as described earlier in this chapter. Here's an example:

```
<OBJECT CLASSID="java:applet.class" HEIGHT=100 WIDTH=100>
  <PARAM NAME="ENABLED" VALUE="TRUE">
</OBJECT>
```

**Providing Alternative Content**   Likewise, providing alternative content for users who don't have Java works the same for the <OBJECT> tag as it does for the <APPLET> tag. You sandwich the HTML you want such a user to see between the beginning and ending <OBJECT> tag. Listing 31.2 shows you an example.

**Listing 31.2  Providing Alternative Content with the <*OBJECT*> Tag**

```
<OBJECT CLASSID="java:mox.class" WIDTH=100 HEIGHT=100>
  <PARAM NAME=ENABLED VALUE=TRUE>
  <A HREF="get-mox.htm">
    <IMG SRC=need-mox.gif WIDTH=100 HEIGHT=100>
  </A>
</OBJECT>
```

http://www.quecorp.com

# Use These Examples in Your Web Page

The Internet is teeming with free Java applets you can use on your Web page. For example, Web Developer's Virtual Library (**http://www.stars.com/Multimedia/Java**) has a handful of Java applets that you can use to add multimedia effects.

By far, the most popular site for free Java applets is the Gamelan's site (**http://java.developer.com**). Gamelan indexes hundreds of Java applets and provides examples of each. You find games, multimedia, special effects, and more. Gamelan also maintains a large index of documentation you can use to learn how to write Java applets.

The sections that follow show you some examples. In each case, you learn how to add a particular Java applet to your Web page by nabbing it from the Internet and adding the appropriate HTML to your Web page.

## Ticker Tape Navigation

If you've logged on to C|NET's site recently, you've seen those ticker tapes that stream text past your eyes while you watch. When you click a word in the ticker tape, the browser opens an appropriate URL. You can accomplish this same feat using the Navigator Ticker found on its Web site (**http://163.121.10.41/java/applets/NavTickr**). Figure 31.4 shows you an example of this ticker tape found on the its Web site.

**FIG. 31.4**
Point at a scrolling phrase to see the URL reference; click the phrase to open that URL in the browser.

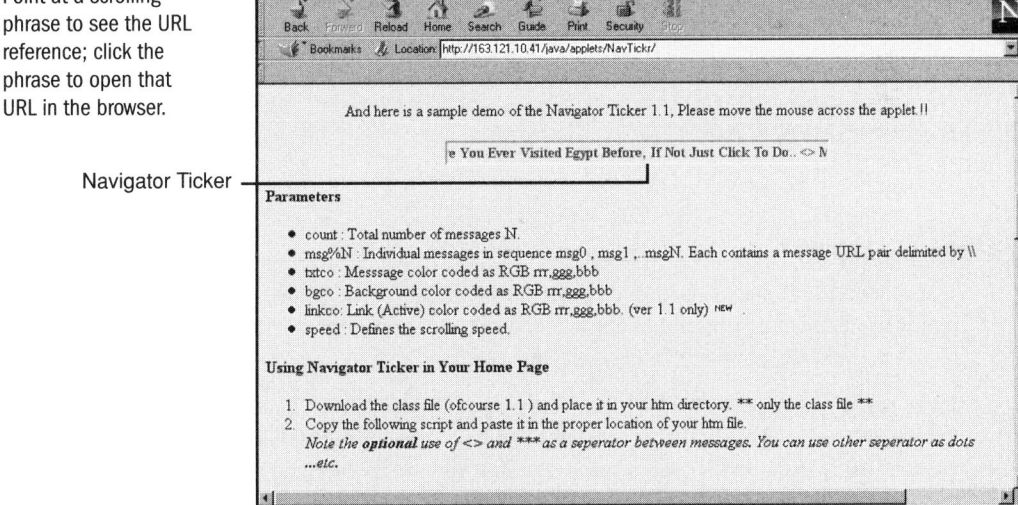

Using the Navigator Ticker is easy. Download the class file from this site by clicking the `Navigator Ticker class 1.1` link at the bottom of the page; save it in the folder that contains your Web page. Then use the following steps:

1. Add the beginning and ending <APPLET> tags to your HTML where you want it, like this:

   ```
   <APPLET CODE=NavigatorTicker11.class WIDTH=300 HEIGHT=28>
   </APPLET>
   ```

2. Add a <PARAM> tag to the <APPLET> container that indicates the number of messages you want to display in the ticker. The name is count and the value is the total number of messages you're displaying:

   ```
   <PARAM NAME=count VALUE=2 >
   ```

3. Add a <PARAM> tag for each message you want to display. The name of the first tag is msg0, the name of the second tag is msg1, and so on. The value of this parameter is the actual message that you want to display, followed by three asterisks (***) and the URL of the associated link. Here's an example of two messages:

   ```
   <PARAM NAME=msg0 VALUE="Check out Netscape's Site *** http://
   ➥www.netscape.com" >
   <PARAM NAME=msg1 VALUE="Jerry's site is brand new *** http://
   ➥rampages.onramp.net/~jerry">
   ```

Listing 31.3 shows the completed example.

### Listing 31.3  Using the Navigator Ticker

```
<APPLET CODE=NavigatorTicker11.class WIDTH=300 HEIGHT=28>
  <PARAM NAME=count VALUE=2 >
  <PARAM NAME=msg0 VALUE="Check out Netscape's Site *** http://www.netscape.com" >
  <PARAM NAME=msg1 VALUE="Jerry's site is brand new *** http://
  ➥rampages.onramp.net/~jerry">
</APPLET>
```

## Fly-Over Buttons

The latest craze, it seems, is buttons that change when the user moves the mouse over them. A button might become brighter or the actual image might change to let the user know that the button is clickable, as shown in Figure 31.5.

If this is the type of user interface you want on your Web site, you need to download the ButtonOnFly class from **http://rcr-www.med.nyu.edu/~zhaoh01/ButtonOnFly/ButtonOnFly.html**. Click The `.class file` link you see in the middle of the Web page. Listing 31.4 shows what the HTML you use to embed this applet looks like.

## Use These Examples in Your Web Page

**FIG. 31.5**
Move the mouse over one of the buttons to see the alternative image.

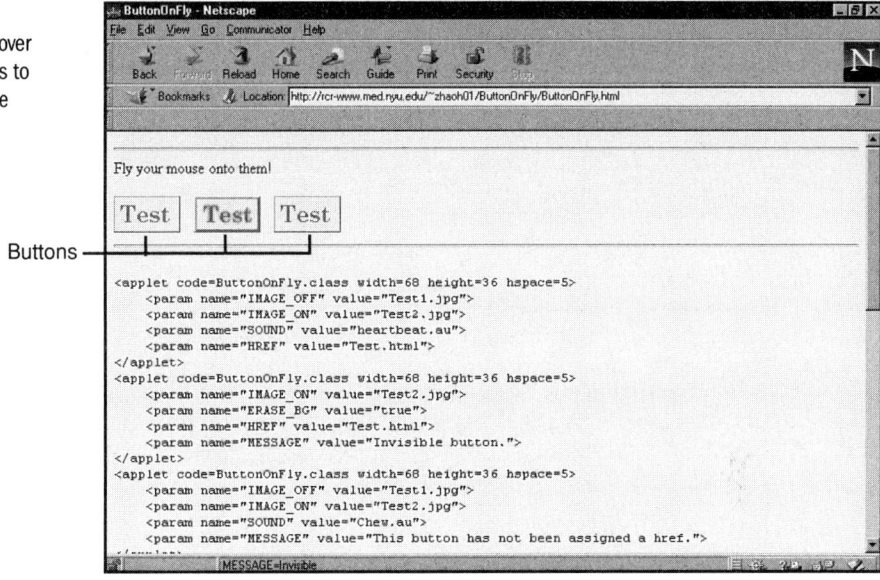

```
<applet code=ButtonOnFly.class width=68 height=36 hspace=5>
    <param name="IMAGE_OFF" value="Test1.jpg">
    <param name="IMAGE_ON" value="Test2.jpg">
    <param name="SOUND" value="heartbeat.au">
    <param name="HREF" value="Test.html">
</applet>
<applet code=ButtonOnFly.class width=68 height=36 hspace=5>
    <param name="IMAGE_ON" value="Test2.jpg">
    <param name="ERASE_BG" value="true">
    <param name="HREF" value="Test.html">
    <param name="MESSAGE" value="Invisible button.">
</applet>
<applet code=ButtonOnFly.class width=68 height=36 hspace=5>
    <param name="IMAGE_OFF" value="Test1.jpg">
    <param name="IMAGE_ON" value="Test2.jpg">
    <param name="SOUND" value="Chew.au">
    <param name="MESSAGE" value="This button has not been assigned a href.">
```

### Listing 31.4  *ButtonOnFly* Java Applet

```
<APPLET CODE=ButtonOnFly.class WIDTH=60 HEIGHT=40>
  <PARAM NAME=IMAGE_OFF VALUE=off.gif>
  <PARAM NAME=IMAGE_ON  VALUE=on.gif>
  <PARAM NAME=SOUND     VALUE=swish.au>
  <PARAM NAME=HREF      VALUE="http://rampages.onramp.net/~jerry">
  <PARAM NAME=MESSAGE   VALUE="Click to visit Jerry's Web site">
</applet>
```

The ButtonOnFly class takes five parameters. IMAGE_OFF is the file name of the image to display on the button while the mouse is not over it. IMAGE_ON is the file name of the image to display when the mouse is over the button. SOUND is the name of a sound file, in AU format only, that the applet plays when the mouse first moves onto the button. HREF is the URL you want the user's browser to open when she clicks the button. MESSAGE is a brief message that you want to display in the browser's status line. ●

CHAPTER 32

# Enhancing Your Documents with JavaScript

*by Jerry Honeycutt*

You use JavaScript to make your Web page dynamic, interactive, and, on the whole, a lot more exciting than a plain-old-ordinary Web page. You can validate a form before submitting it to the server, for example. Better still, you can control the data that the user inputs into a form as she enters it. Forms aren't the only HTML object you can control with a script, either. If you can put it on a Web page, you can attach a script to it or control it with a script. Imagine creating simple animations using JavaScript.

Want to know the best part? You don't have to know a lick of programming to use JavaScript on your Web page. This chapter doesn't even show you how to write scripts; for that, you can turn to Que's *Special Edition Using JavaScript* or Netscape's JavaScript Guide at **http://home.netscape.com/eng/mozilla/3.0/handbook/javascript/index.html**. This chapter shows you how to find useful scripts on the Internet, instead, and embed those scripts into your Web page. ■

### Familiarize yourself with JavaScript

This chapter gives you a bit of JavaScript background and teaches you that JavaScript is an interpreted language with many facets.

### Add JavaScript to your Web page with ease

You don't need to know how to program to use JavaScript. All you need to know is how to add scripts to your existing HTML.

### Connect scripts to objects in your Web page

This chapter shows you how to connect the scripts you drop into your Web page to the objects in it.

### Use scripts without writing any code

You can download scripts from a variety of sources, without charge, and include them in your Web page. This chapter shows you examples.

## Introducing JavaScript

JavaScript is loosely based upon Java. Originally, Netscape created a scripting language called *LiveScript* to tie Java applets together on the Web page. A script could change the properties of one applet due to an event that another applet caused, for example. LiveScript contained many of the same concepts and keywords that you find in Java; however, it omitted many concepts and keywords to better its performance and security. Over time, LiveScript evolved into JavaScript as you know it today.

Most of the scripts you use work in both Netscape Communicator and Internet Explorer 4.0. Microsoft's version of JavaScript is called *JScript*. JScript, as found in Internet Explorer 3.0, was not completely compatible with JavaScript. In fact, you couldn't open Netscape's home page without getting JScript error messages. In Internet Explorer 4.0, however, JScript and JavaScript are mostly compatible.

> **NOTE** You can get more information about Microsoft's flavor of JavaScript at **http://www.microsoft.com/jscript**.

## Examples of What You Can Do with JavaScript

You've already had a small taste of what JavaScript can do for you, but that's not enough. You know that you can control objects on the Web page with a script. You know that you can handle certain events on the Web page as they occur. That's pretty abstract, though. To give you a better idea of what you can do with JavaScript, take a look at the following real-world examples of how a script might be used:

- Validate forms before submitting them to the Web server. For example, you can make sure that a user enters her name and mail address before submitting the form.
- Control layers on the Web page. A prime example is overlapping a handful of layers onto the Web page and then peeling them away one at a time to create a simple animation. Another example, shown in Figure 32.1, is to display or hide a layer in response to clicking a button.
- Associate scripts with content on the Web page. For instance, you can associate a script with each heading in a document that displays summary information when the user moves the mouse over the heading.
- Build a Web page dynamically. You can build a Web page on-the-fly, making decisions about what to put on the Web page based upon the setting you store on the user's computer (a.k.a. *cookies*).
- Make Java applets and other objects play well together. The original intent of JavaScript was to glue together applets on the Web page so that they cooperate with each other.

> **NOTE** Netscape provides over a dozen, real-world example JavaScript Web pages on its Web site: **http://developer.netscape.com/library/examples/examples.html#javascript**.

**FIG. 32.1**
Click More>> to display a hidden form. Chapter 28, "Using Layers," shows you how to build a form like this using JavaScript and layers.

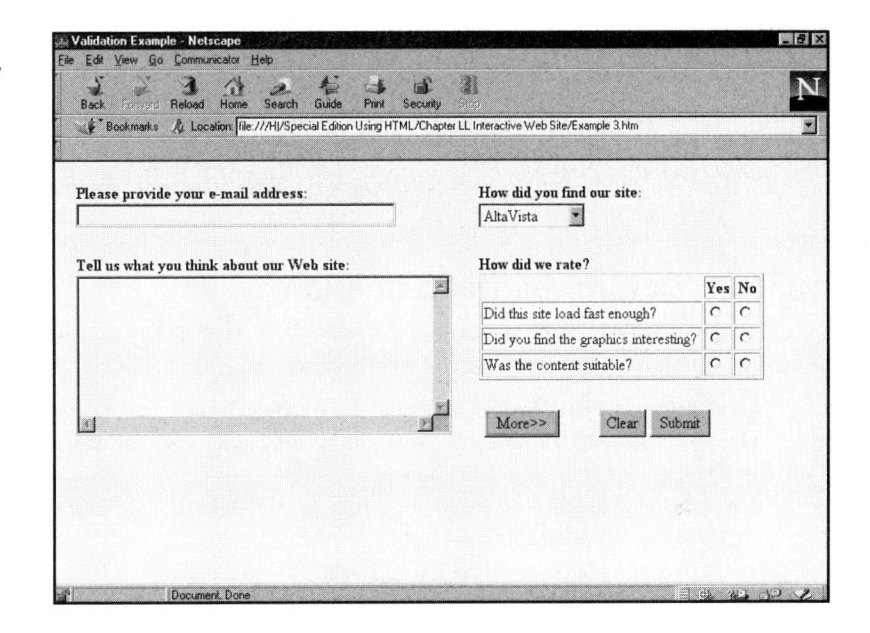

## Recognizing JavaScript When You See It

If you're at all familiar with C++ or Java, you'll easily recognize JavaScript when you see it (see Listing 32.1). JavaScript looks a lot like Java, which is loosely based on C++. In fact, JavaScript is based upon a subset of Java. It has the same keywords like `if`, `for`, and `return`. It has a subset of the same runtime library. It uses the concept of objects. It even uses the same syntax.

**Listing 32.1  Sample Script Using JavaScript**

```
function AddSeries( Last )
{
  intTotal = 0;
  for( j = 1; j <= Last; j++ )
  {
    intTotal += j;
    alert( intTotal );
  }
  return intTotal;
}
document.write( "Howdy" );
```

Listing 32.1 shows you an example of a JavaScript script, albeit a bit useless. You might note a few important characteristics of this script:

- The keyword `function` begins a JavaScript function. The first and last curly braces ({}) identify the beginning and ending of the function. In this case, the function name is AddSeries.

- Each statement in the script ends with a semicolon (;). The semicolon helps the interpreter know where one statement ends and another begins. Thus, `intTotal += j;` and `alert( intTotal );` are two separate statements.
- Inline JavaScript is not part of any function. The last line in the script, `document.write ("Howdy");`, is an *inline script*, which the Web browser executes when it loads the Web page.

## JavaScript Details You Need to Know

You don't have to know anything about JavaScript to use it. You can simply drop a borrowed script into your Web page and hope for the best.

You'll get more out of JavaScript if you understand a few basic concepts, though. First of all, you need to know that JavaScript is an interpreted language. You also need to know that JavaScript is event-driven, and you need to know when the browser actually executes a script. Last, you need to know where to put scripts in your HTML file. You'll read about each of these topics in the following sections.

**JavaScript Is an Interpreted Language**  JavaScript is an interpreted language, or scripting language, as opposed to a compiled language. Developers create programs using a compiled language such as C++. A *compiler* actually translates each instruction into *machine code* that the computer can execute directly. Whereas a computer executes a compiled program directly, a program called an *interpreter* interprets and executes a script line by line.

Obviously, an interpreted language is slower than a compiled language, but considering the usage of an interpreted language that's not really an issue. Your scripts are interpreted by the Web browser and are usually very small. As well, they probably only execute in response to something that the user does (clicking the mouse), instead of executing continuously as compiled programs sometimes do. Compiling a script is like owning a Ferrari when all you do is drive to work and back; it's overkill.

**NOTE**  In a compiled program, the CPU might execute three machine code instructions to perform a particular function. In an interpreted program, the CPU might end up executing hundreds of machine code instructions to perform the same function. Thus, you can easily understand the difference between the performance of each. ■

**JavaScript Is Event-Driven**  With JavaScript, you embed instructions into your Web page that describe how you want the browser to handle certain events. Events are things that happen on the Web page. For example, the user clicking a button is an event. Moving the mouse over a link is an event. Even the Web page itself causes an event when it loads. As you can surmise, most events are caused by mouse actions like clicking and moving, but many other types of events can occur on a Web page, such as a timer finishing its countdown.

Figure 32.2 illustrates this *event-driven* concept. There are three key parts in this figure: an object, the event itself, and the event-handler. The following list describes the three parts:

- An *object* can be anything on the Web page—a button will do nicely.
- Objects raise *events* in response to something the user does to them. For example, if the user clicks a button, the button raises a click event.
- *Event-handlers* take action on the event. To create an event-handler, you associate a JavaScript function with the event. Then, the browser executes that function whenever that event occurs.

**FIG. 32.2**
Events signal to the browser that an object on the Web page needs attention by a script. The browser determines which function to use.

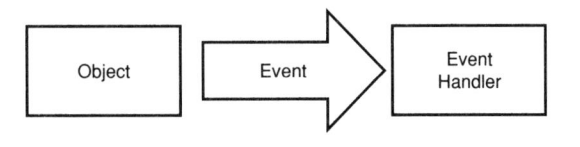

**When Scripts Are Executed** When a user opens a Web page that includes JavaScript, the browser makes note of every script in the page. It translates the scripts into an intermediate code that's a bit more efficient to execute. It also creates a table that contains the name of each JavaScript function in the Web page (called a *symbol table*).

The user's Web browser executes different types of JavaScript code at different times. It doesn't execute JavaScript functions as the Web page loads. It waits for an event, which you associate with a JavaScript function, to execute a particular function. The browser does execute inline JavaScript as it loads the Web page, though. Inline JavaScript is code you include in a script that's not actually inside a function. You can use inline JavaScript to affect how the browser draws the Web page.

Take another look at Listing 32.1, for example, repeated as Listing 32.2 for your convenience. The last line in the script executes as the browser loads the Web page, which creates the Web page shown in Figure 32.3, because it's not inside of a function. The remaining lines don't execute until some event causes the function called AddSeries to execute.

**Listing 32.2  Sample Script Using JavaScript**

```
function AddSeries( Last )
  {
    intTotal = 0;
    for( j = 1; j <= Last; j++ )
    {
      intTotal += j;
      alert( intTotal );
    }
    return intTotal;
  }

document.write( "Howdy" );
```

**FIG. 32.3**
document.write writes content to the Web page as the browser loads the HTML file.

Result of document.write ("Howdy")

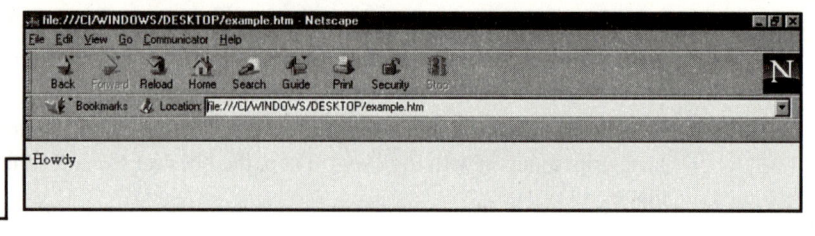

**Where to Put Your Scripts** In reality, you can put a script anywhere in your Web page. Many folks prefer to put their scripts inside the <HEAD> container, which means that all of the scripts are organized at the beginning of the HTML file. That way, it's easier to find a particular script in the HTML file.

The hardcore crowd prefers to organize their scripts near to the location where the scripts are actually used. They locate scripts associated with the events within a form near the form. They locate scripts associated with a Java applet near the applet's <APPLET> or <OBJECT> tag.

**N O T E** Organizing your scripts at the top of the HTML file can cause problems for some Internet search engines. For example, some search engines use the Web page's first handful of text lines to provide a description of the page. If you have 100 lines of script at the top of your home page, and you list your site with AltaVista, the only description of your Web site that a user will see is the script. ■

## Adding a Script to Your Web Page

Now that you have the basics under your belt, I bet that you're ready to add some JavaScript to your Web page. You use the <SCRIPT> tag to do just that. This tag has a single attribute called LANGUAGE. You set the value of this attribute to JAVASCRIPT to denote that the script uses the JavaScript language, as opposed to another language, such as Microsoft's VBScript. Because <SCRIPT> is a container, you end a script with the closing </SCRIPT> tag. Here's what this tag looks like:

```
<SCRIPT LANGUAGE=JAVASCRIPT>
   JavaScript Statements
</SCRIPT>
```

**T I P** You can leave out the LANGUAGE attribute if you like. If you don't specify a language, most Web browsers assume that you're using JavaScript. It pays to be specific, however, because this behavior is not specified by W3C or any other standards body.

## Hiding Scripts from Scriptless Browsers

A lot of users use a browser that can't interpret JavaScript. When one of these browsers encounters a script, it ignores the <SCRIPT> and </SCRIPT> tags because it doesn't know how to interpret them. The browser displays everything in between those two tags as HTML content, however, which is not exactly what you had in mind—is it? Figure 32.4 shows an example of what this looks like.

**FIG. 32.4**
You can see this example for yourself by mistyping SCRIPT in the <SCRIPT> tag, and opening the Web page in Communicator.

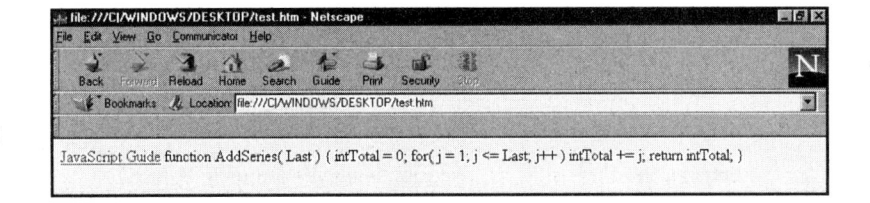

You use an HTML comment to hide scripts from those scriptless browsers. Make the opening HTML comment the first line within the script block. The closing HTML comment should be the last line in the script block. Note that you begin this line with a JavaScript comment (//), because after JavaScript starts interpreting code, it thinks that everything else in the script is actual JavaScript code. Script-enabled browsers ignore the comments, while scriptless browsers ignore all of the content between the comments. Listing 32.3 shows you an example.

**Listing 32.3   Hiding Scripts**

```
<SCRIPT LANGUAGE=JAVASCRIPT>
<!--
  function AddSeries( Last )
  {
    intTotal = 0;
    for( j = 1; j <= Last; j++ )
    {
      intTotal += j;
      alert( intTotal );
    }
    return intTotal;
  }

  document.write( "Howdy" );
//-->
</SCRIPT>
```

## Connecting Scripts to Events

You must learn how to connect scripts to the objects on your Web page. Before you're finished reading this chapter, you're going to learn how to download a script from the Internet and embed it into your Web page. Many times, though, you're going to actually have to hook up that script to the objects in your Web page. You don't just drop a new CD player in your stereo cabinet without plugging it in to your receiver, do you? The same is true for JavaScript—you have to plug it in.

Most of the objects on a Web page have events. Some of the events to which you attach scripts include those listed in Table 32.1.

### Table 32.1 Common HTML Events

| Name | Event Is Raised When: |
| --- | --- |
| onBlur | A form's field loses focus. |
| onChange | The contents of a field or list changes. |
| onClick | The user clicks an object. |
| onFocus | A form's field gains focus. |
| onMouseOut | The mouse moves out of an object. |
| onMouseOver | The mouse moves over an object. |
| onSelect | The user selects a form's field. |
| onSubmit | The user clicks a form's submit button. |

Recall from Figure 32.2 that objects, events, and event-handlers all work together. You have to associate an object with an event-handler via that object's event. You do that by adding the event's attribute to the object's HTML tag and setting its value to a single JavaScript statement that executes the function. For example, to associate a JavaScript function called MyFunction() with the onClick event of a button, you write the button's <INPUT> tag like this:

```
<INPUT TYPE=BUTTON NAME=BUTTON onClick="MyFunction()">
```

You can just as easily associate an event-handler with any other event in Table 32.1. In this case, the event attribute is onClick. Add another event attribute from the first column of Table 32.1 to the tag in the previous example to associate an event-handler with that event, like this:

```
<INPUT TYPE=BUTTON NAME=BUTTON onClick="MyFunction()" MouseOut="ByeMouse()">
```

Suppose, for example, you downloaded a really cool script that displays a message in the status line when the user moves the mouse over a link. You drop the script shown in Listing 32.4 into your Web page, but nothing happens. The problem is that you haven't plugged it in to your Web page. You do that by associating the function called Message() with the onMouseOver event of each anchor in your HTML file, as shown in Listing 32.5.

### Listing 32.4  New Script

```
<SCRIPT LANGUAGE=JAVASCRIPT>
<!--
  function Message()
  {
    window.status="You just passed over a link; wow!";
  }
//-->
</SCRIPT>
```

**Listing 32.5 Plugging in the New Script**

```
<HTML>
<HEAD>
  <TITLE>Plugging in the New Script</TITLE>
</HEAD>
<BODY>
  <A HREF="more.htm" onMouseOver="Message()">See more stuff</A>
  <A HREF="less.htm" onMouseOver="Message()">See less stuff</A>
</BODY>
</HTML>
```

## Sprucing Up Your Web Page with Scripts

The quickest way to add JavaScript flair to your Web page is by using a script that you download from a JavaScript gallery or library. For example, the Template Studio (**http://tstudio.usa.net**) is a comprehensive gallery that contains numerous scripts you can use in your Web page. The scripts you find on this site include scripts for detecting the user's browser, dynamically replacing an image, controlling a window, displaying messages, and setting cookies.

Gamelan (**http://javascript.developer.com**) also has a comprehensive site that you can use to find good JavaScript for your Web page. Tutorial examples, games, and other miscellaneous scripts are featured on this Web site. You'll also find documentation that helps a new JavaScript developer get up-to-speed in a heartbeat.

If you want even more immediate gratification, however, you can try out the scripts described in the following sections. These scripts help you add fly-over help for the links on your Web page.

### Fly-Over Help for a Link's Destination

Take a look at Communicator's status line when you hold the mouse pointer over a link. It shows the URL to which the link points. You can provide a more useful description of the link's destination by using a script (see Figure 32.5).

**FIG. 32.5**
Providing a more thorough description of a link can keep the user from visiting Web pages in which she isn't interested. Thus, you're saving Internet bandwidth.

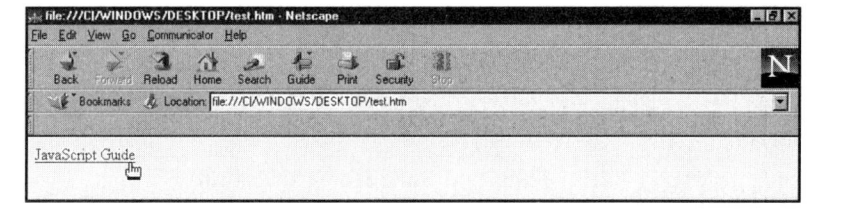

You use the `<A>` tag's `onMouseOver` event to display the help text and its `onMouseOut` event to remove the text. So, what do you assign to these two events? For every link on your Web page, add the following `onMouseOver` attribute to its `<A>` tag. Each time the user moves the mouse over the link's anchor, the two statements assigned to this event execute. The first statement, `self.status='The help text';` displays the text contained within the single quotes on the browser's status line. Change this text to a brief description of the link. The following shows the second statement, `return true;`, which prevents the browser from displaying the link's URL reference on the status line:

```
onMouseOver="self.status='The help text'; return true;"
```

Also add the `onMouseOut` event attribute to each `<A>` tag as you see in the following example. This works just like the `onMouseOver` attribute you just read about, except that it clears the status line when the user moves the mouse out of the link. The effect is that the user sees the help text as long as she holds the mouse over the link; but when she moves the mouse away from the link, the status line clears.

```
onMouseOut="self.status=''; return true;"
```

## Using Forms and JavaScript for Navigation

If you've been to Netscape's site recently, you've seen forms used for navigation. Here's how it works: you select an item from the drop-down list and click a button. The browser opens the URL associated with that list item (see Figure 32.6).

**FIG. 32.6**
Alternatively, you can create a CGI script that processes the user's choice on the server. This approach is more efficient, however, because it's done on the client.

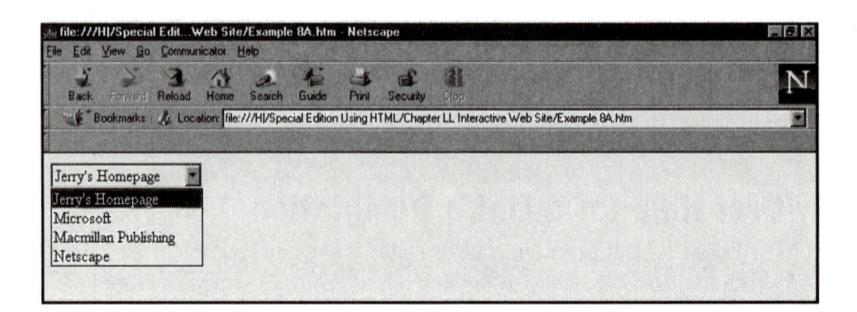

Take a look at Listing 32.6. It shows the HTML for a form with a single drop-down list. It opens the Web page that the user picks from the list. The function `OpenURL()` is associated with the `<SELECT>` tag's `OnChange` event. When the user selects an item from the form's list, `OpenURL()` sets `window.location` to the associated URL.

### Listing 32.6 Form and Script for Navigation

```
<HTML>

<SCRIPT LANGUAGE=JAVASCRIPT>
<!--
  function OpenURL( Index )
```

```
   {
     if( Index == 0 ) window.location = "http://rampages.onramp.net/~jerry";
     if( Index == 1 ) window.location = "http://www.microsoft.com";
     if( Index == 2 ) window.location = "http://www.mcp.com";
     if( Index == 3 ) window.location = "http://www.netscape.com";
   }
//-->
</SCRIPT>

<FORM NAME=NAVIGATE>
  <SELECT NAME=LIST SIZE=1 OnChange="OpenURL( document.
➥NAVIGATE.LIST.selectedIndex )">
  <OPTION NAME=JERRY>Jerry's Homepage
  <OPTION NAME=MS>Microsoft
  <OPTION NAME=QUE>Macmillan Publishing
  <OPTION NAME=NETSCAPE>Netscape
  </SELECT>
</FORM>
</HTML>
```

To make this work for you in your Web page, you need to update the form's list to contain an entry for each Web site to which you want the user to navigate. Then, you need to add a line to the `OpenURL` function that checks the index of the user's selection and opens the appropriate URL in the browser. The easiest thing to do is to copy one of the existing lines, change the bit index number so that it corresponds with the form, and then change the URL assigned to `window.location`. Just remember that the first item in the list has an index of 0, the second has an index of 1, and so on. ●

PART VI

# For Developers

**33** Netscape Servers 667

CHAPTER 33

# Netscape Servers

*by Mark R. Brown*

- **The SuiteSpot server family is Netscape's major product**
  It scales to handle Web sites from the obscure to the obfuscated.

- **The Enterprise Server is the centerpiece of SuiteSpot**
  It handles Web and intranet sites.

- **SuiteSpot servers control all site services**
  They handle directories, security, e-mail, news, and other site and administration services.

- **Netscape's FastTrack server is the Web server "for the rest of us"**
  It's inexpensive, easy to install and maintain, and runs on Windows 95 or NT.

Netscape Communicator forms just one end of a communication link. Whether you use it over the Internet or an intranet, Communicator has to talk to a server computer on the other end.

A server is simply a system that "serves up" data in a standardized format. On the Internet, those standards are called IP, or Internet Protocols. The most familiar of these is HTTP (Hypertext Transport Protocol), which is the protocol used for delivering HTML documents (Web pages) over the Internet or a corporate intranet. A computer configured with the proper software to deliver HTML documents is called an HTTP server, or simply a Web server.

But there are other network protocols and other types of server software, as well. Electronic mail is delivered by a POP server or an SMTP server. News is handled by an NNTP server. And there are directory services, catalog servers, and many more.

Each of these services is handled by a different server program. In many cases, all (or most) of the server programs are run on the same server computer in a multitasking environment. However, on larger systems, each server program might run on its own system. On large corporate intranet or Web sites, there might even be dozens of server computers running the same server software.

Not surprisingly, Netscape makes server software for most of the services you can imagine. After all, it practically gives away its browser client, Communicator. A vast majority of users use the trial versions without ever paying for them. Corporate users are the ones who pay the bills at Netscape Communications Corporation, through licensing of vast numbers of client programs and the purchase and licensing of server software programs. This helps explain why Netscape is concentrating so hard on developing its penetration into the corporate intranet market.

Netscape maintains a Web page full of information about all of its server products at **http://home.netscape.com/comprod/server_central/index.html** (see Figure 33.1).

**FIG. 33.1**
Netscape's Server Central Web pages provide complete information on all of their server products.

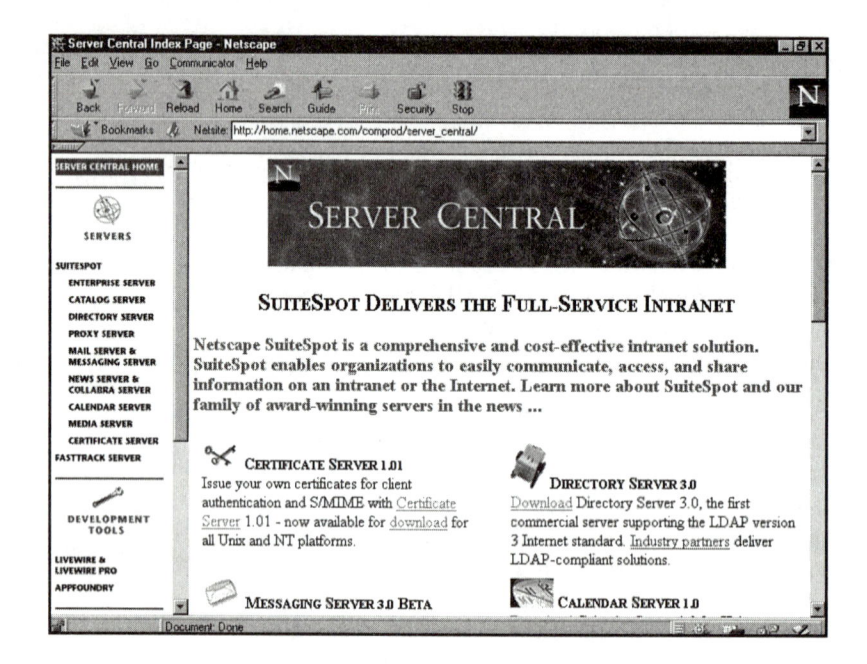

A quick perusal of the menu in the left column reveals a somewhat surprising fact—Netscape has only two server "families"—SuiteSpot and FastTrack. The SuiteSpot server suite comprises a complete collection of various server software programs. FastTrack is a simple Web server for individuals and very small businesses.

## SuiteSpot Servers

On closer inspection, it becomes immediately obvious why Netscape offers only two server solutions. The low-end product, FastTrack, is an unexpandable, introductory-level product aimed at those whose needs are few, or who are just getting started. The SuiteSpot family takes care of everyone else. Rather than provide multiple levels of server software of various complexities, Netscape offers a suite of full-powered server programs that are available as integrated components in a server suite. You can buy as many or as few servers as you need. If all you need is a high-powered HTML document server, you can buy just the Enterprise server. If you're setting up a heavily loaded corporate intranet site with full services for thousands of employees, you can purchase the full suite of all nine SuiteSpot servers, plus the LiveWire Pro database development tool.

Following are the nine SuiteSpot servers:

- *Enterprise Server*—SuiteSpot's Web (HTML document) server
- *Catalog Server*—Creates and maintains an online catalog of intranet documents
- *Directory Server*—An online "white pages" server that handles lists of names, associated e-mail addresses, and certificates
- *Proxy Server*—SuiteSpot's server that provides replication and filtering services behind a corporate firewall
- *Mail Server & Messaging Server*—Handles incoming and outgoing e-mail
- *News Server & Collabra Server*—The SuiteSpot news server for both UseNet newsgroups and specialized discussion groups
- *Calendar Server*—For scheduling people and resources
- *Media Server*—Serves streaming (real-time) audio
- *Certificate Server*—Issues and manages public-key certificates

The nine servers that make up the SuiteSpot family can be purchased individually, but Netscape has a bundle deal that lets you pick any five of them for a flat $4,995. Individual servers are priced in the $995–$1,995 range. SuiteSpot servers run on Windows NT or a wide variety of UNIX systems. If you buy the five-server pack, you also get Netscape LiveWire Pro 3.0, which assists in the creation of database-driven HTML documents and sites.

> **NOTE** You can find out all about LiveWire and LiveWire Pro at **http://home.netscape.com/comprod/server_central/product/livewire/index.html**.

The SuiteSpot servers together provide support for all the key Internet standards: HTML and HTTP, Java and JavaScript, SMTP and POP3 e-mail, MIME, NNTP and NNTPS news, and SSL security.

SuiteSpot also serves as the base from which developers can create applications based on Netscape ONE technology. Netscape ONE is a philosophy (which is supported by a collection of tools) based on creating applications that can be authored once to run on a wide variety of computer platforms.

> **NOTE** To find out all about Netscape ONE, point Communicator to **http://developer.netscape.com/library/one/index.html**.

Interested in becoming a Netscape developer? Then back up a couple of steps to the DevEdge home page at **http://developer.netscape.com** (see Figure 33.2). Even if you don't want to develop applications for Netscape, you'll find a wealth of useful information on this site.

**FIG. 33.2**
The DevEdge site holds multimegabytes of information about Netscape's products and programs.

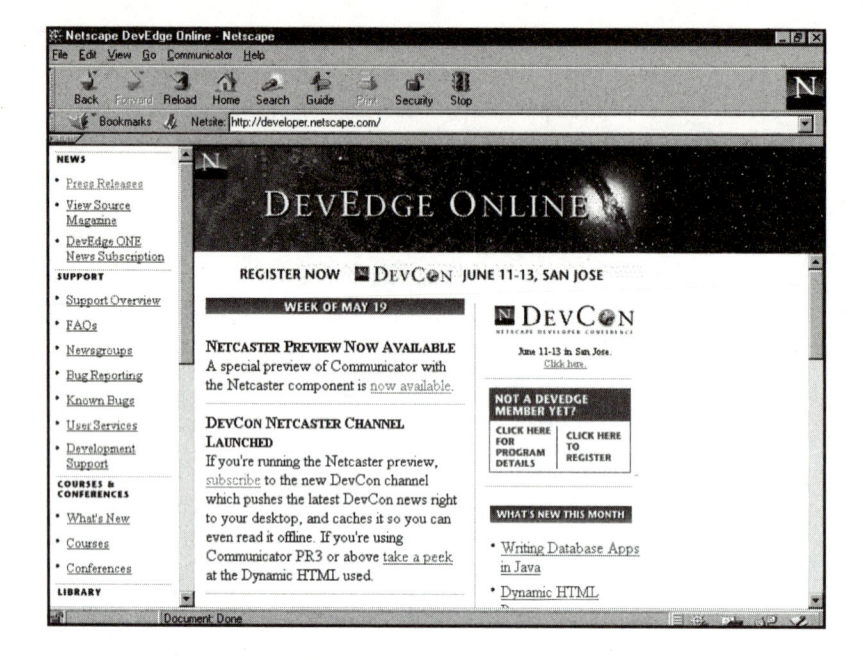

SuiteSpot incorporates many standardized functions that make it easy to manage and implement Web sites and corporate intranets. For example, administration is simplified through LDAP-based user and group management. LDAP—the Lightweight Directory Access Protocol—provides an easy means of organizing and updating users and groups from a central directory server. Because it is an Internet standard, incorporating LDAP makes SuiteSpot more integrated with other Internet products and applications, as well.

Also built into SuiteSpot are replication services that allow the content of newsgroups, databases, HTML documents, and so on to be duplicated across a network, making access easier and more efficient. SuiteSpot's replication services take into account the different needs of different types of data to maximize efficiency.

SuiteSpot server management is done from a common HTML-based management interface, which lets system administrators update servers and install applications from a central control point. One interface manages all servers, which makes administration easier and faster. The SNMP (Simple Network Management Protocol), which is built into SuiteSpot, means yet another industry standard is at work, which ensures compatibility with a wide range of server products from many different vendors.

This suite of servers also includes powerful, standard security features like robust SSL security and X.509 public-key certificates. SuiteSpot servers can be used for just about any secure application without fear of security breaches. All of SuiteSpot's built-in security functions are also industry standards.

> ### SuiteSpot Server Plug-Ins
> If the SuiteSpot server you're considering doesn't have quite the features you want, the odds are good that you can add a plug-in to add the functionality you're missing. All of the SuiteSpot servers support software plug-ins, and third-party companies have quickly jumped on the bandwagon to offer additional functions via plug-ins for the following:
>
> - Database Access
> - Development
> - Full-Text Search Engines
> - Information and Document Management
> - Intranet and Enterprise Applications
> - Legacy Systems Connectivity
> - Networking Connectivity
> - Remote Access
> - Site-Monitoring
> - User-Tracking and Log-Analysis
> - Workflow
>
> Netscape maintains a list of currently available SuiteSpot server plug-ins at **http://home.netscape.com/comprod/server_central/server_add_ons.html**.

# Netscape's Server Test Drive Program

Before we get into the features of individual SuiteSpot servers, you should know that all of them are available for downloading from the Netscape Web site for free 60-day evaluation. Just go to **http://home.netscape.com/comprod/mirror/server_download.html**, fill out the trial agreement form, pick the server you're interested in, and click the download link.

If you're daunted by the size of the download files, or if you want to try out the whole suite, a CD containing all the SuiteSpot servers is available for $10 (plus shipping) from the same address.

> **TIP** You can find out more about Netscape's SuiteSpot Servers on their Server Central Web pages at **http://home.netscape.com/comprod/server_central/product/suite_spot/index.html**.

# Enterprise Server

The Enterprise Server is the heart and soul of SuiteSpot. It is SuiteSpot's HTTP (Hypertext Transport Protocol) daemon, the server that serves up Web pages as well as HTML documents for other purposes.

Besides transferring HTML documents over the network, the Enterprise server also provides tools for content creation and management and enables application creation through CGI, Java, and JavaScript. It also includes support for Microsoft Office and legacy mainframe systems.

Enterprise Server supports custom content searches and the creation of custom pages. Automatic link management and document revision control are built in, making it easier for workgroups to develop and share documents. Built-in agents can track files and send out notices when content changes. Database support is provided for Informix, Oracle, Sybase, and ODBC-enabled databases.

This server is 100 percent compliant with Netscape ONE development tools and can serve as the platform for deploying applications developed with Netscape ONE tools and components, such as the Netscape Internet Foundation Classes.

## Catalog Server

Every site bigger than a gnat's whisker needs some way to keep track of documents, e-mail addresses, file archives, and the other data files that make up a Web or intranet site. The Catalog Server is SuiteSpot's tool for tracking these elements.

It builds and maintains an online catalog of documents and provides automated search tools for accessing those documents. Creating and sorting documents with Catalog Server is highly automated. After you set it up, it automatically updates its catalogs as a site's content changes. It can even create Yahoo!-like category-based hierarchical directories.

How does it work? Robots. Crawlers. These go out and search and report back the information you want them to, whether it's on your own intranet or on the Internet as a whole. They can bring back summaries or full-text versions, which means you get just the information you need. Based on rules you set up, the information is then indexed, classified, and served up as an HTML document.

The Catalog Server has a graphical interface that lets you make simple keyword searches or complex logical queries. Catalog Server even includes automatically updated What's New and What's Popular queries.

## Directory Server

Users. They're why you have an intranet. How do you keep track of them all? With SuiteSpot's Directory Server.

Directory Server tracks white pages information for a site's users—names, e-mail addresses, security certificate status, phone numbers, and more. It also incorporates LDAP (Lightweight Directory Access Protocol)—are you noticing a pattern here? Netscape beats the drum loudly for supporting Internet standards, but it also marches to the beat of its own drum. LDAP means that directories from any industry-standard applications can be mixed and matched.

Besides being a boon to network administrators, the Directory Server can provide public white pages services appropriate to both intranets and the World Wide Web. In fact, it can support large directories of up to a million entries and fast searches of up to 300,000 queries per hour.

Replication and security services are built in to Directory Server, and it provides a set of point-and-click administration tools. Its integration with other SuiteSpot servers means that an administrator can delete an entry from the company database and that user's mailbox will automatically be removed, and access to protected pages and groups will be denied. All with one change. Access to directory information can be controlled on an individual or group basis.

## Proxy Server

Sites behind a corporate firewall that still need access to Internet services can do so with SuiteSpot's Proxy Server.

Proxy Server replicates and filters Internet content, making Web access faster while allowing the system administrator full control over system security. The system administrator also gets a set of tools for controlling access to resources and monitoring network traffic.

With Proxy Server, sites can be enabled or blocked, URLs can be filtered, and viruses can be scanned for. SSL security and powerful logging features ensure system integrity.

Proxy Server can cache up to 128 gigabytes of Internet data and can handle over 70 million URLs. Its replication-on-demand feature means that frequently accessed Web sites can be accessed totally from within the firewall, with data updated only as it is changed. Entire sites, or just individual documents or directories, can be cached, and updates can be downloaded during off-peak hours.

Proxy Server also caches push traffic from Netscape Netcaster.

## Mail Server and Messaging Server

E-mail is handled by SuiteSpot's Messaging Server, which can control incoming and outgoing mail over the Internet and over proprietary LAN-based mail systems.

Standards? Messaging Server is based on a whole alphabet-soup-bowl full of standards—LDAP, SMTP, IMAP4, SNMP, X.509V3, and POP3. Suffice it to say that it'll work with just about anything else on the Net.

Messaging Server gives administrators centralized user control, of course, which is integrated with directory services. S/MIME and certificate support means secure e-mail is a given.

HTML support means the capability to send and receive "rich" HTML-enhanced e-mail, which can include multimedia elements, Java applets, and just about anything else you can put on a Web page.

## News Server and Collabra Server

The Netscape Collabra Server is SuiteSpot's newsgroup server. It not only provides an interface to UseNet news, it also lets you create and maintain private (and public) newsgroups for internal collaboration (hence the name).

Built-in SSL encryption and certificate support means you can create secure groups as well as open ones. Access can be controlled at the group level.

Replication provides for rapid distribution of groups, and support for moderated discussions can help keep them under control. Administration of group access is easy. Like e-mail, news posts can also include HTML and other elements.

Hierarchical organization, search, and notification tools mean users can find the topics they are interested in quickly.

## Calendar Server

Communicator Pro includes a Calendar tool, and SuiteSpot's Calendar Server is the back end for that tool. It lets an enterprise schedule personnel, groups, and even meeting rooms and other resources, via an integrated company-wide system.

Supporting dozens or thousands of users, Calendar Server allows scheduling in one building or around the world. Integration with LDAP directory access and SMTP Internet e-mail means everyone will get the message.

Administrators can set up scheduling on a single server or on many across the enterprise and have a single control point for granting viewing and modifying permissions for all users.

Event and task entries can include a wide variety of information, from notes, holiday notations, and reminders to text files, attachments, and due dates. Categories are included for classifying activities as personal, public, private, or normal, with priorities of high, normal, low, and lowest.

## Media Server

Multimedia is all the rage on the Net, especially real-time streaming multimedia. The Media Server is Netscape's first entry into this field and provides real-time streaming audio.

Scalable to both direct and slow dial-up lines, the Media Server provides real-time audio streams that can be synchronized with text, graphics, and other page elements.

Media Server's streaming audio format has been offered as an Internet standard and is supported by the Netscape Internet Foundation Classes, which means developers can easily incorporate these audio files when creating applications.

On the client end, the Media Player plug-in built in to Communicator plays the audio files delivered by Media Server.

## Certificate Server

Security is a hot issue on the Web. In fact, many claim it's the one stumbling block to the growth of business on the Internet. SuiteSpot's Certificate Server might help to change all that.

A certificate is an encoded security document issued to an individual or company which can serve as a sort of secure digital ID. When a document is delivered with a secure, tamper-proof certificate, the recipient can be sure that the document is safe.

Certificate Server lets an organization issue, sign, and manage security certificates. SSL (Secure Sockets Layer) encryption ensures the integrity of these documents. Certificates can be used to authenticate both clients and servers.

Open standards are again in evidence, as Certificate Server supports all of these Internet standards: X.509v3, SSL, HTML, HTTP, PKCS, S-MIME, and LDAP. A built-in database manages certificates and allows queries, and a Web-based interface means Communicator users can easily request certificate issuance and information.

Certificates can be used to encrypt access to secure servers, as well as to confirm and encrypt e-mail messages.

## FastTrack Server

SuiteSpot provides a complete set of servers and tools for managing a large site, but what if you're an individual or small company that doesn't need (or can't afford) all that horsepower? Never fear. That's why Netscape created the FastTrack Server. An all-in-one Web server, FastTrack Server is available for Windows 95, NT, or UNIX for only $295 complete. You can even download a free 60-day trial version from Netscape's site at **http://home.netscape.com/comprod/mirror/server_download.html**.

As the only Netscape server that can run under Windows 95, it's pretty obvious that Netscape had the individual and small business owner in mind when it designed this one. It's also easy to use, with a graphical user interface that controls all its setup and functions.

FastTrack is an HTML document server that is intended primarily for use as a Web server, though it can certainly handle a small intranet, as well. It's fully compatible with Enterprise Server, so you can start small and grow as needs dictate.

An Installation Wizard makes installing FastTrack a simple process of answering a few setup questions and pressing a few buttons. A configuration agent automatically detects network settings and configures FastTrack to work properly with them. If you get stuck in the installation process or any time during future system administration, built-in context-sensitive help is just a keystroke away.

SSL security, full reporting capabilities for Web stats, and performance optimization mean that FastTrack is suitable for real-world Web applications. There's even support for server-side Java, JavaScript, and CGI applications, as well as the capability to run applications created using Netscape ONE tools. Remote management means you can administer the server from anywhere on the network.

**NOTE** As this is being written, Netscape Navigator Gold is included with the FastTrack Server as its HTML document creation tool. With the release of Communicator, I'm sure that Communicator will probably be bundled with it in the future.

**TIP** You can find out more about FastTrack at **http://home.netscape.com/comprod/server_central/product/fast_track/index.html**.

PART VII

# Appendixes

- **A** Getting Online 679
- **B** Installing Communicator for Windows 3.1 689
- **C** Installing Communicator for Windows 95 711
- **D** Installing Communicator for Macintosh 727
- **E** Installing Communicator for UNIX 741

APPENDIX A

# Getting Online

*by Mike Logan*

**G**etting a connection to the Internet is often construed as an awesome task. I do not agree. If connecting to the Internet is such an insurmountable task, then why are there 50 million plus users today? "Getting Connected" is nothing more than a step-by-step process.

This appendix takes a step-by-step approach to connecting to the Internet. I assume you are using Windows 95. You can start at any step, so long as you have completed the previous steps. We'll discuss the following:

- What you need to get before connecting—a modem, an Internet service provider, and user account information the Internet service provider will assign to you.
- Installing Dial-Up Networking—step-by-step procedures to ensure Dial-Up Networking for Windows 95 is set properly.
- TCP/IP Networking Setup—step-by-step TCP/IP configuration information.
- Technical issues of making an Internet connection—a few of the more common Internet terms defined and explained.

## Getting Started

Let's make a list of what you need to connect to the Internet. Then we will discuss each item separately. For starters, you need the following:

- Modem, at least a 28.8Kbps or 33.6Kbps, or, if your ISP supports it, a 56Kbps model.
- An Internet Service Provider (ISP)
- User account and network information provided by your ISP

## Selecting a Modem

A modem is a device you connect to your telephone line to call the ISP. Modems come in various throughput speeds, like 9.6Kbps (kilobits per second) or 9,600bps (bits per second), 14.4Kbps or 14,400bps, and 28.8Kbps or 28,800bps. A modem manufacturer advertising a modem with the capability to transmit 28,000bps typically uses the term 28.8Kbps. You want to get the fastest throughput possible, so a 28.8Kbps modem is a must. Today, a 28.8Kbps modem is very common and most Internet service providers will have 28.8Kbps modems. Two newer and faster modems have just arrived on the market. These modems have a throughput of 33.6Kbps and 56Kbps, respectively. Two modems with different rated speeds can communicate with each other at the lower of the two speeds. If you want to connect to your Internet service provider at these higher speeds, make sure your Internet service provider also has the higher-speed modems. This is especially true if you want a 56Kbps modem.

If you have put off buying a 28.8Kbps modem because you cannot justify the expense or you are waiting for a faster modem to come out (which will undoubtedly happen), let me give you some numbers. An average Web page of 14,400 characters takes about 15 seconds to download at 9,600bps, and about 5 seconds to download at 28,800bps. You can see that a 28.8Kbps modem is three times as fast as a 9.6Kbps modem!

http://www.quecorp.com

> **TIP** To calculate throughput, you need to know that a character is 8 bits long, and the modem adds a start and stop bit to frame the character. So basically, to transmit a character, 10 bits are used. A 28,800bps modem transfers 2,880 characters per second (28,800/10=2,880). Now divide the size of the transfer—in our example, 14,400 characters—by the number of characters per second the modem can pass—2,880 for a 28.8Kbps modem. Your answer is 5 seconds.

Your connection speed can vary each time you call the ISP, due to telephone line quality. If you already have a 28.8Kbps modem, you may have noticed than on some occasions your connection speed is 26,400bps rather than 28,800bps. This throughput always depends on telephone line quality at the time of the call.

## Internet Service Providers

Internet Service Providers come in an almost limitless variety. There are undoubtedly several local and national ISPs in your area. I live in a small city in Missouri with a population of approximately 70,000. Believe it or not, I have no less than 10 ISPs to choose from! A complete list of ISP providers is available from **http://www.thelist.com**.

The Internet service provider is your way onto the Internet. How does this work? Well, when you call your Internet service provider with your 28.8Kbps modem, your Internet service provider also has a number of 28.8Kbps modems answering. As calls come in to the ISP, they roll over to the next available modem. The ISP's modems connect you to their computers, which are connected to the Internet through what is known as a T1 line. In the simplest terms, a T1 line is a special telephone line with the capability to carry 1.5M/sec! Or the Internet service provider could have a T3 line, which has a 45M/sec connection to the Internet. Today's Internet backbone, for instance, is built on T3 lines (45M/sec) operated by MCI. Local access from users to hosts and hosts to the backbone occurs at rates ranging from 2400bps to 33.6Kbps for dial-up, or via leased lines at multiples of 56Kbps or 64Kbps up to the T1 rate of 1.5M/sec.

Two new technologies, Asymmetric Digital Subscriber Line (ADSL) and cable modems, are now in trial markets in the United States. ADSL uses the standard telephone line presently in your house and can offer speeds up to 9M/sec. Cable modems, as name implies, will attach to your cable connection. These devices have speeds ranging from 500Kbps to 10M/sec.

So what should you look for in an ISP? This depends on your special needs. Most ISPs offer several service levels and connection pricing plans. These range from direct T1 access to leased lines to ISDN connections to the typical dial-up connection most of you use in your homes today. Typically, the dial-up connection is the cheapest access provided, and the direct T1 access is the most expensive.

Assess your situation before choosing an ISP. Following is a small sampling of questions to ask yourself and an ISP. Your answers to these questions will help you decide on the type of service you are likely to need. First, ask yourself the following questions concerning how you intend to use the Internet:

- How many hours a month will I need to connect to the Internet?
- Will I use the Internet for research or just surfing?
- Is a 28.8Kbps connection fast enough?
- What kind of technical assistance will I need?
- Do I want e-mail? How many e-mail accounts do I need?

Next, ask the following questions of the Internet Service Provider you are considering:

- Is the call to the ISP free?
- Does the ISP provide technical assistance?
- What hours is technical assistance available?
- Does the ISP have the services I need?
- Can I access the ISP during peak hours or do I get a busy signal?

I suggest that you ask friends and business associates, and contact computer users in your locale for recommendations.

## Internet Service Provider User Account Information

Typically, an Internet service provider will provide you with a User ID and a password, along with certain settings for Windows 95. However, many ISPs—like Earthlink, Concentric, and Netcom, to mention a few—provide software that makes the necessary configuration for you. You only provide your User ID and password. The user ID usually becomes part of your e-mail address.

After you have selected an Internet Service Provider, they may ask you for a user identification (user ID), also known as your user name. Other ISPs will assign a user ID to you. You use this to log on to their server. They will also provide you with the following information:

- Your password
- Their local access telephone number
- Your host name (usually your user name)
- Their domain name
- Their IP subnet mask
- Their gateway IP address
- Their DNS address

Keep all this information close by, as you use it to configure the TCP/IP settings, which are discussed later in this appendix. If you did not get this information, contact your Internet Service Provider and get it. These settings will be used in the section "Configuring TCP/IP Network Properties."

http://www.quecorp.com

# Creating a PPP Connection in Windows 95

You must set up Windows 95 so that it can communicate using the same protocols used on the Internet. Protocols can be simply defined as rules. The Internet uses a protocol known as Transmission Control Program/Internet Protocol, or TCP/IP; therefore, your computer must be set up with this same set of rules, or protocols. Windows 95 comes with all the protocols and components needed to connect to the Internet, including TCP/IP. The next step is to configure your Windows 95 networking capabilities.

> **NOTE** Netscape will continue to produce Communicator versions and components beyond the present 4.0. To keep you updated, Netscape offers a SmartUpdate feature allowing you to tune your present version of Communicator in less time than it would take to completely reinstall a newer program.
>
> In Navigator, click on the Software Update command under the Help menu. You will see the SmartUpdate web page where Netscape will tell you what version you are presentlky using and, if applicable, wjat version you could be running. If you need to upadate, simply click Begin SmartUpdate and the program will automatically begin downloading and installing the new components

## Installing Dial-Up Networking Components

Now that you have selected a modem and ISP of your choice, you can begin to set up Windows 95 to make your connection. At this time, make sure you have your Windows 95 CD-ROM at hand, as you may need to install additional programs from it.

In this step, you need to ensure the following components are installed on your computer:

- *Dial-Up Networking*—Allows Windows 95 to connect to other computers using a modem
- *Dial-up Adapter*—Enables the PPP for connections over a modem

To check for Dial-Up Networking installation, chose Start, Programs, Accessories. The Dial-up networking icon should be listed there if it is installed. If Dial-Up Networking is not installed, follow these steps:

1. Click the Start button and choose Settings, Control Panel.
2. Double-click the Add/Remove Programs icon.
3. Select the Windows Setup tab. Under the Windows Setup tab section of the Add/Remove Programs dialog box, you can install or change various components of Windows 95.
4. Select Communications, listed in the Components list box.
5. Click the Details button. The Communications dialog box is displayed, showing the current configuration of your Windows 95 communications system.
6. Make sure the Dial-Up Networking entry is checked. If it is not, select it and click OK.

**FIG. A.1**
The Communications dialog box for installing Dial-Up Networking.

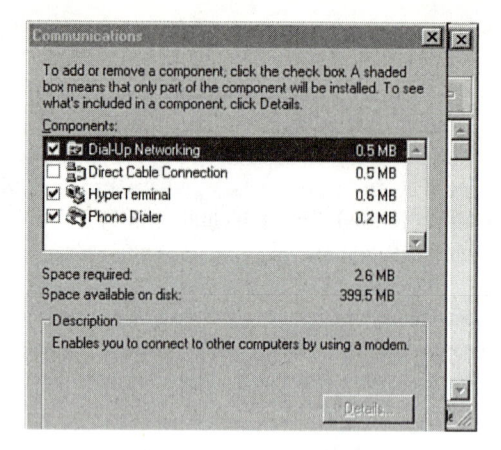

To check for Dial-Up Adapter installation, follow these steps:

1. Click the Start button, and select Settings, Control Panel.
2. Double-click the Network icon. The Network dialog box is displayed.
3. The Configuration tab is selected by default. This is where you select network protocols and adapters for your Windows 95 environment. Figure A.2 shows the Network dialog box.

**FIG. A.2**
The Network dialog box for setting your network environment, Dial-Up Adapter, and TCP/IP.

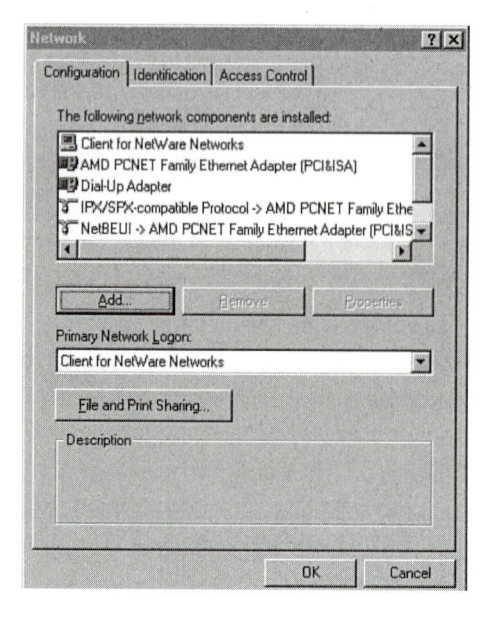

4. Both Dial-up Adapter and TCP/IP should be installed.
5. Click OK on the TC/IP Properties dialog box.
6. Click OK on the Network dialog box.

If Dial-Up Adapter is not present in the Network dialog box, follow these steps:

1. Choose Start, Settings, Control Panel, then double-click the Networking icon.
2. Click the Add button. The Select Network Component Type dialog box is displayed. Here you tell Windows 95 what networking components you want to add to your computer.
3. Double-click Adapter. The Select Network Adapters dialog box is displayed. Notice that there are two scroll boxes, one called Manufacturers and the other called Network Adapters.
4. In the Manufacturers scroll box, scroll until you see the Microsoft entry.
5. Select Microsoft. Choose Dial-Up Adapter from the Network Adapters scroll box on the right.
6. Click OK.

If TCP/IP is not present in the Network dialog box, follow these steps:

1. Click the Add button.
2. Double-click Protocol. TCP/IP is the networking protocol used on the Internet. The Select Network Protocol dialog box is displayed.
3. Again, there are two scroll areas, one called Manufacturers and the other Network Protocols. Scroll the Manufacturers scroll box until you see the Microsoft entry.
4. Select Microsoft. Choose TCP/IP in the Network Protocols scroll box.
5. Click OK. You should see both TCP/IP and Dial-Up Adapter in the Network dialog box.
6. With Dial-Up Adapter highlighted, click Properties, select the Bindings tab, and make sure the TCP/IP box is checked.
7. Click the OK button.

# Configuring TCP/IP Network Properties

The next step you must perform is to input all the information provided to you by your Internet Service Provider. Because the Internet uses TCP/IP, you must make these TCP/IP settings on your computer. The Internet is a network of networks, and this information virtually makes you part of the Internet when you log on to your Internet Service Provider's computer, commonly called a server. To enter your ISP information, follow these steps:

1. Click the Start button, and choose Settings, Control Panel.
2. Double-click the Network icon. The Network dialog box is displayed. Highlight the TCP/IP Protocol (see Figure A.3).

## Appendix A  Getting Online

3. In the Network dialog box, click the Properties button.
4. IP Address Tab is the default selection. Two option buttons allow you to Obtain an IP Address Automatically or Specify an IP Address. Select Obtain an IP Address Automatically if your Internet service provider generates an IP address for you when you log on. This is the most common kind of IP addressing used by ISPs. If you have a static IP, select the option button Specify an IP Address. Then you will need to type your IP address into the IP Address box and your subnet mask into the Subnet Mask box provided. If you have a static IP address, this information was given to you by your Internet service provider.

**FIG. A.3**
The Network dialog box with TCP/IP highlighted and Properties selected will bring up the TCP/IP Properties dialog box.

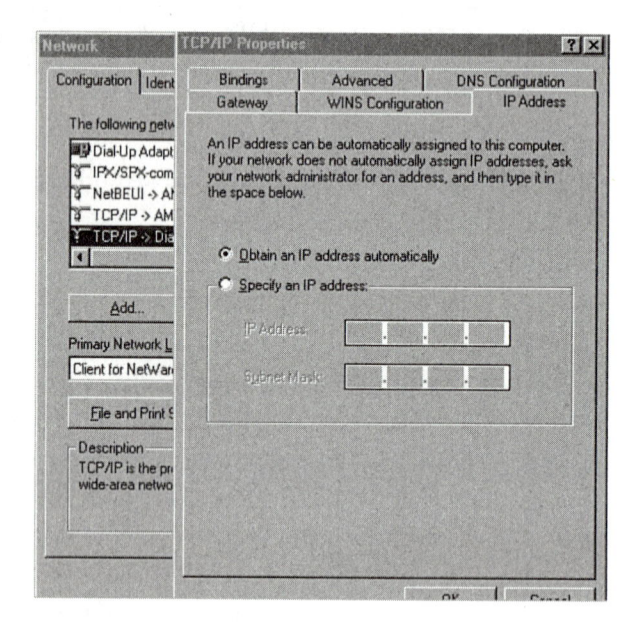

5. Select the WINS Configuration tab and disable WINS Resolution.
6. Select the Gateway tab, type the IP address for your ISP's gateway or router, and then click the Add button.
7. Select the DNS Configuration tab, select Enable DNS option, and enter the host name of your computer (your user ID) in the Host box.
8. Enter the domain name of your ISP in the Domain box.
9. In the DNS Server Search Order section, enter the IP address of your ISP's DNS server.
10. Enter the domain name for your ISP in the Domain Suffix Search Order section and click the Add button.
11. Double-check all your entries, and then click OK.
12. Windows 95 asks you to reboot your computer. Click Yes.

Congratulations, you have completed the Windows 95 environment setup. Dial-up Networking, Dial-up Adapter, and TCP/IP are ready for use. Next, you need to create an icon that places the call to your Internet Service Provider and starts a PPP connection to the Internet.

## Setting Up a Connection Icon

There are several things you must do to set up a Connection icon. First, you need to access the Make a New Connection Wizard. To do this, follow these steps:

1. Double-click the My Computer icon on your desktop.
2. Double-click the Dial-Up Networking icon.
3. Double-click the Make New Connection icon. A Make New Connection wizard box comes up that guides you through the remaining setup.

The Wizard then walks you through the following steps:

1. Name your connection. This name will appear on the new connection icon.
2. The modem you have installed through Control Panel, Modem appears in the Select a Modem box. Click Next.
3. Enter your Internet Service Provider's telephone number and click Next.
4. Click Finish. You should see a new connection icon with the name that you entered in the New Connection Wizard, in Dial-Up Networking.

Before you make your first call, let's double-check the Windows 95 default settings that the Wizard created. If these are not set to the default settings, you will not be able to log on to your Internet service provider server. To check the default settings for the Connection icon, follow these steps:

1. Click the right mouse button on your connection icon. A pop-up menu is displayed.
2. Choose Properties from the pop-up menu.
3. Click the Server Type button, and then select PPP from the list box.
4. Verify that the TCP/IP box in the Allowed Network Protocols section is checked, and make sure that the Log On to Network box is not selected.
5. Click OK.
6. Click OK again.

You are now ready to get connected to the Internet through your Internet service provider.

# Technical Issues of Making an Internet Connection

You have completed your setup of Windows 95. Now you can connect to your Internet Service Provider and explore the World Wide Web. But, what did you do exactly? To gain an understanding of all the settings you made, let's take a closer look at TCP/IP, IP address, DNS, and PPP.

## Transmission Control Program/Internet Protocol

Transmission Control Program/Internet Protocol, or simply TCP/IP, is a network protocol, a set of rules enabling networks of different types to connect to each other. TCP/IP was actually developed by the Department of Defense so it could tie together networks running different software.

TCP/IP actually has two separate pieces, TCP and IP. The TCP part of the protocol validates the delivery of data from client to server. It also provides support of error detection and initiates the retransmission of lost or destroyed data packets. The IP part moves packets of data from one point to another. IP forwards each packet based on a four-byte destination address.

Basically, you set up the Windows 95 TCP/IP so that you can connect to many different networks on the Internet.

## IP Address

An IP address is a 32-bit number divided into four 8-bit sections. For example, the IP address 204.170.120.101 has four sections, and each is 8 bits long. Each computer on the Internet has its own unique IP address. Your computer will have its own unique IP address when you connect to your Internet Service Provider. Remember, you selected Obtain IP Address Automatically in the TCP/IP Properties dialog box, which means that each time you log on to your Internet Service Provider, you will be assigned a different IP address.

## Domain Name Server

A Domain Name Server is just what its name implies. It is a computer with a database of IP addresses and the names associated with them. It is much easier to remember names than numbers, so the DNS provides this translation service for you. It translates the name into the IP address numbers. Therefore, you can request a name of a computer to connect to instead of using the IP numeric address. Connecting to Macmillan Publishing's Web site can be accomplished by typing the name convention **http://www.mcp.com/** into the Netscape Communicator Location box. If you did not have a DNS to translate **www.mcp.com**, you would have to enter the actual IP address for this computer. Using names instead of numbers is preferable any day. If your DNS is entered into Windows 95 incorrectly, using the name convention in Netscape Communicator Location box fails to connect you to Macmillan Publishing's Web site. The common name does not get translated into an IP address. However, typing in the IP address works! Obviously, no conversion is needed.

## Point-to-Point Protocol or PPP

PPP (Point-to-Point Protocol) is a very reliable dial-up protocol. It allows you to connect to other computers via a modem instead of using a network card and cabling. PPP is based on another, older protocol, SLIP, or Serial Line Interface Protocol. PPP is a more robust protocol having additional error detecting and authentication, making it more reliable than SLIP. Because PPP is more reliable, it is widely accepted to be the standard for connecting to the Internet. ●

APPENDIX B

# Installing Netscape Communicator for Windows 3.1

*Galen A. Grimes*

**B**efore you can begin using Netscape Communicator as your Internet application suite, you need to install the program on your computer. If you regularly install software on your computer, installing Netscape Communicator should be a piece of cake. There is nothing new or unusual about Netscape Communicator that might throw you a curve during the installation process.

But if you have never installed an application program on your computer or you've only installed a few applications, the installation process might appear somewhat confusing, especially with the choices presented during installation and the decisions you are forced to make regarding file directories and installation options.

- **Computer requirements**
  Find out the minimum computer hardware requirements to install and operate Netscape Communicator under Windows 3.1.

- **Installation decisions**
  How to install Netscape Communicator and what decisions you have to make if you are new to using Netscape, new to the Internet, and this is your first Web browser installation.

- **Upgrading to Netscape Communicator**
  How to install Netscape Communicator over a previous Netscape installation and how to preserve your previous settings and options.

## Installation Requirements

Before you begin, you need to make sure your computer is equipped to run Netscape Communicator. Following are the minimum requirements you need:

- 386 processor
- 8M of memory
- 6M of free disk space on your computer's hard disk drive
- VGA graphics card and monitor
- 9600 bps modem

Obviously, this is a bare bones set of requirements, but this computer configuration allows you to at least run Netscape Communicator. However, considering that most manufacturers ceased production on 386 computers and 9600 bps modems several years ago, you likely will be less than thrilled with the performance this configuration gives you.

A more realistic minimum computer configuration might look something like this:

- 486 or Pentium processor
- 16M of memory
- 40M–100M of free disk space on your computer's hard disk drive
- VGA graphics card and monitor
- 14.4 Kbps modem

In addition to this configuration, you need to have Windows 3.1 already installed on your PC and an account with an Internet Service Provider or direct connection to the Internet through a local area network. If you are connecting to the Internet through an Internet Service Provider, your provider should also supply you with a dial-in application that you use with your modem to dial in to your service provider. Your service provider should also supply you with a program called a *Winsock*. A Winsock (short for Windows Socket layer) is a program that loads the TCP/IP protocol on your computer.

Make sure, before you begin installing Netscape Communicator, that you can attach to the Internet. If you are attaching through a service provider, any questions you might have about a dial-in program or a Winsock need to be answered first.

If your PC exceeds these configurations in any way, all the better, especially if you have a modem that allows you to communicate faster than 14.4 Kbps (such as 28.8, 33.6, or 56 Kbps). Your enjoyment of the Internet and the World Wide Web will be much higher if you spend more time viewing Web pages as opposed to waiting for them to load.

▶ **See** Chapter 3, "Navigating HTML Pages," for more about downloading files using FTP.

http://www.quecorp.com

# Beginning the Installation

Because you are installing Netscape Communicator to run under Windows 3.1, you need to make sure you are installing the 16-bit version of the program and not the 32-bit version. The 32-bit version only runs under Windows 95 or Windows NT. It does not run under Windows 3.1.

To obtain your copy of Netscape Communicator you will need to download a copy from Netscape's FTP site. To perform the download you will need an FTP program or a previous version of Netscape Navigator. If you do not an FTP program you can obtain one either from your local Internet Service Provider or from your systems administrator.

Enter the following URL for Netscape's FTP site:

**ftp://ftp.netscape.com**

Follow the directory prompts to proceed to directory /pub/communicator/4.01/shipping/english/windows/windows3.1. At this point you will have to decide whether you want to download the base installation of Netscape Communicator or the complete installation. The difference between the two versions is that the complete installation contains numerous multimedia plug-ins pre-installed which saves you the trouble of having to download and install them yourself. If you want the base installation, select the directory /base_install, and then select the file cb16e401.exe to download. If you want the complete installation, select the directory /complete_install, and then select the file cc16e401.exe to download.

Before you begin the installation program, make sure you exit any programs you have running in Windows. The installation program writes to and updates some of your common Windows system files. If you have other programs running, the installation program might not have complete access to update these common system files.

To begin installing Netscape Communicator on your computer:

1. If you are installing Netscape Communicator from a purchased CD, go to the Windows Program Manager menu, select File, Run and then enter **cc16e401.exe** to start the installation program (see Figure B.1). Click OK to start the installation program.

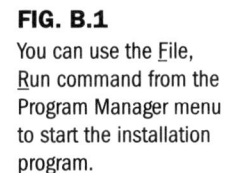

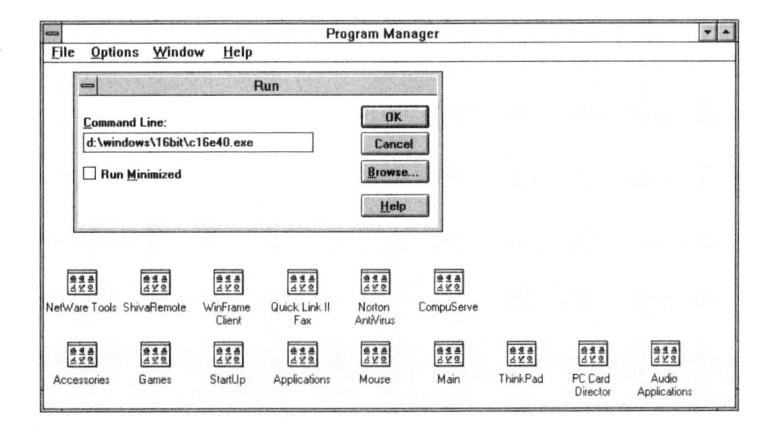

**FIG. B.1**
You can use the File, Run command from the Program Manager menu to start the installation program.

2. In a few seconds, the installation program prompts you to confirm that you are about to install Netscape Communicator on your PC (see Figure B.2) and that you want to continue. Answer Yes to continue with the installation. For the next minute or so, depending on the speed of your computer, the installation program begins extracting the files it needs (contained in the file n16e40.exe) to install Netscape Communicator on your PC (see Figure B.3). Be patient; this is a normal part of the installation.

**FIG. B.2**
At the start of the installation, you are prompted to make sure you want to install Netscape Communicator.

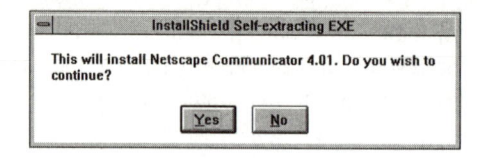

**FIG. B.3**
The installation program first extracts the files it needs to complete the installation.

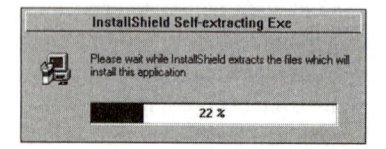

3. The next screen (see Figure B.4) prompts you to make sure no other programs are running in Windows. Click Next to continue with the installation.

   **NOTE** If, for any reason, you need to stop the installation before the installation is completed, click Cancel. It appears on most of the installation screens.

4. Next, you are prompted to select the type of setup you want to perform for this installation (see Figure B.5). The choices are Typical and Custom. The Typical choice has pre-selected the most often used components under Windows 3.1. The Custom choice allows you to select what options you want installed.

   If you are new to using Netscape, go ahead and select the Typical choice for now. If, after running Netscape Communicator for a while, you discover an option you would like to use that was not installed during this installation, you can always re-run this installation program, select Custom, and select any option not included in the Typical setup. For now, make sure the option button next to Typical is selected.

   Next, you are prompted to select the destination directory. This is the directory where Netscape Communicator is installed on your computer. The installation program suggests you install the program in directory C:\NETSCAPE\COMM. If you select to install Netscape Communicator in C:\NETSCAPE, you will install Netscape Communicator over your previous version of Netscape (if you have a previously installed version). This installation arrangement is perfectly OK. The advantage in installing Netscape Communicator over a previous version of Netscape is that all of your previous configuration settings and bookmarks are picked up by the new installation. The disadvantage in

http://www.quecorp.com

installing over a previous version of Netscape is that you are not able to use the previous version.

**FIG. B.4**
The installation program needs to have complete control of all files on your computer which might need to be updated.

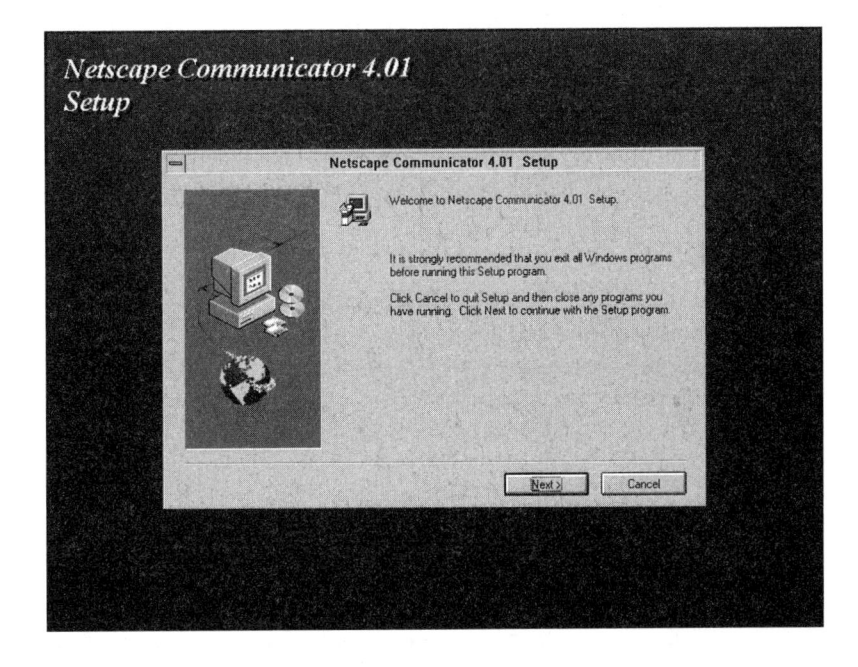

**FIG. B.5**
The installation program offers you the choice of performing a Typical or Custom setup.

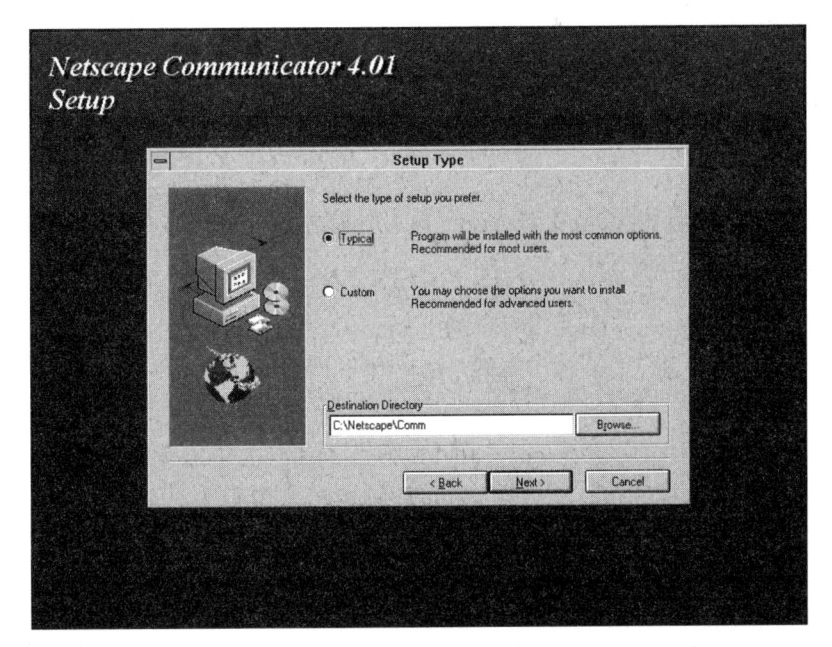

## Appendix B  Installing Netscape Communicator for Windows 3.1

> **CAUTION**
>
> If you have a previous version of Netscape on your computer and you select a different directory to install Netscape Communicator into, the two versions combined use more than 40M of disk space on your computer.

Select the directory you want to install Netscape Communicator into (the default is C:\NETSCAPE\COMM). Select Next to continue with the installation.

> **CAUTION**
>
> If you do not have Microsoft Video for Windows installed, the installation program warns you that the program is required to run Netscape Communicator and asks if you want to stop the installation and install Video for Windows. You can safely continue with the installation and install Video for Windows after the installation. If you do not have Video for Windows, you can download a copy from one of the Netscape FTP sites at **ftp://ftp.netscape.com/pub/navigator/3.01/windows/wv1160.exe**.

5. Next, the installation program prompts you for the program group folder into which it creates the program icons for Netscape Communicator (see Figure B.6). The default selection allows the program to create a new program folder, Netscape Communicator. You can, however, elect to place the Netscape Communicator icons into one of your existing program group folders. If you are new to Netscape, go ahead and select the default choice and have the installation program create a new program group folder. If you decide later that you want to move the Netscape Communicator icons into another folder, you can simply drag the icons into another folder from Program Manager. After you make your decision, select Next to continue with the installation.

> **NOTE**  Netscape will continue to produce Communicator versions and components beyond the present 4.0. To keep you updated, Netscape offers a SmartUpdate feature allowing you to tune your present version of Communicator in less time than it would take to completely reinstall a newer program.
>
> In Navigator, click on the Software Update command under the Help menu. You will see the SmartUpdate web page where Netscape will tell you what version you are presently using and, if applicable, what version you could be running. If you need to update, simply click Begin SmartUpdate and the program will automatically begin downloading and installing the new components. ■

6. The next screen merely confirms the installation choices you have made so far (see Figure B.7). Look over the configuration choices displayed and, if you see any errors or any settings you want to change, select the Back button to go back to any of the previous screens and change the selection. When you are ready to continue with the installation, select Install.

http://www.quecorp.com

## Beginning the Installation 695

**FIG. B.6**
During the installation, you can select the Program Group folder you want your Netscape Communicator icons to be placed into.

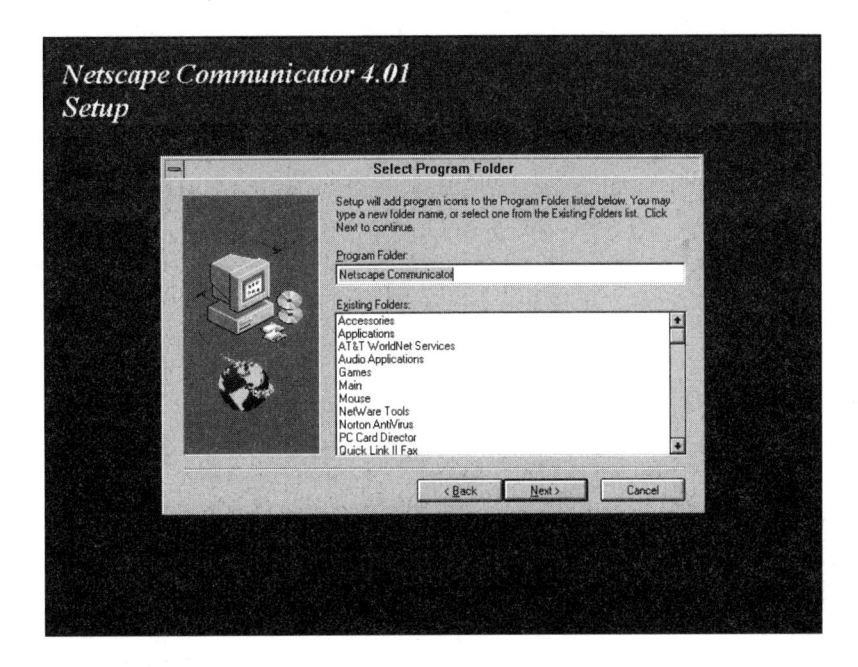

**FIG. B.7**
Before the actual installation begins, you get a chance to review the choices you've made so far.

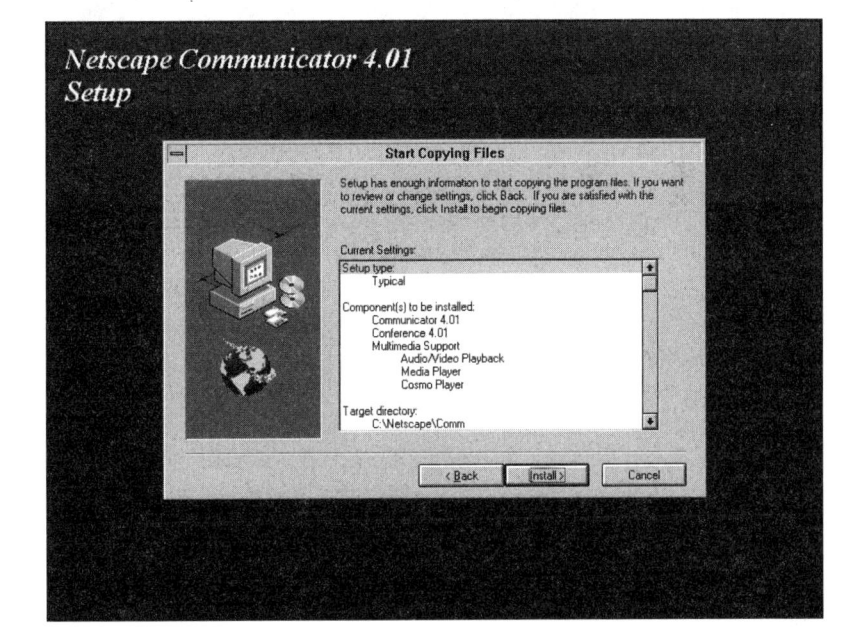

7. The installation program now begins to copy files to the destination directory you previously selected (see Figure B.8). This process can take several minutes, so just sit back and relax.

**FIG. B.8**
The installation program spends the next minute or two copying files to your destination directory.

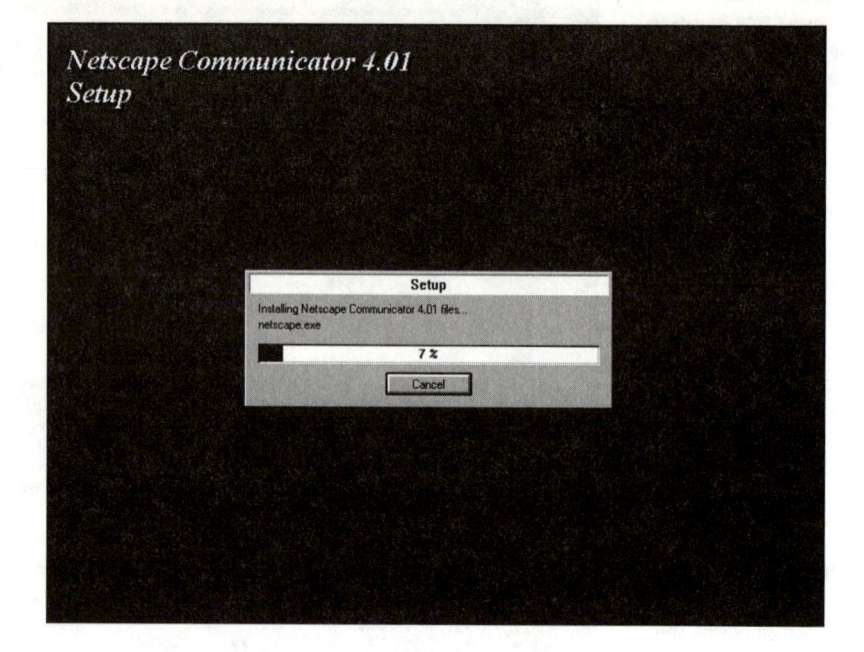

8. When the installation program has completed copying files to your designated destination directory, the program finally prompts you to view a README file (see Figure B.9).

    The README file contains last minute information that Netscape did not have time to include in instruction manuals or Help files.

9. The installation program displays a prompt, telling you that the installation of Netscape Communicator is complete and that you can now run any of the various Netscape Communicator applications by clicking the icons in the Program Group folder (see Figure B.10). Select OK to continue.

10. Finally, the installation program prompts you to restart your PC. Select Yes, I Want to Restart My Computer Now. Select OK to restart your PC (see Figure B.11).

    If you look in Program Manager after your PC restarts, you see that you now have another Program Group folder containing the icons for Netscape Communicator (see Figure B.12).

**FIG. B.9**
The README file often contains late information that the manufacturer was not able to add to the documentation.

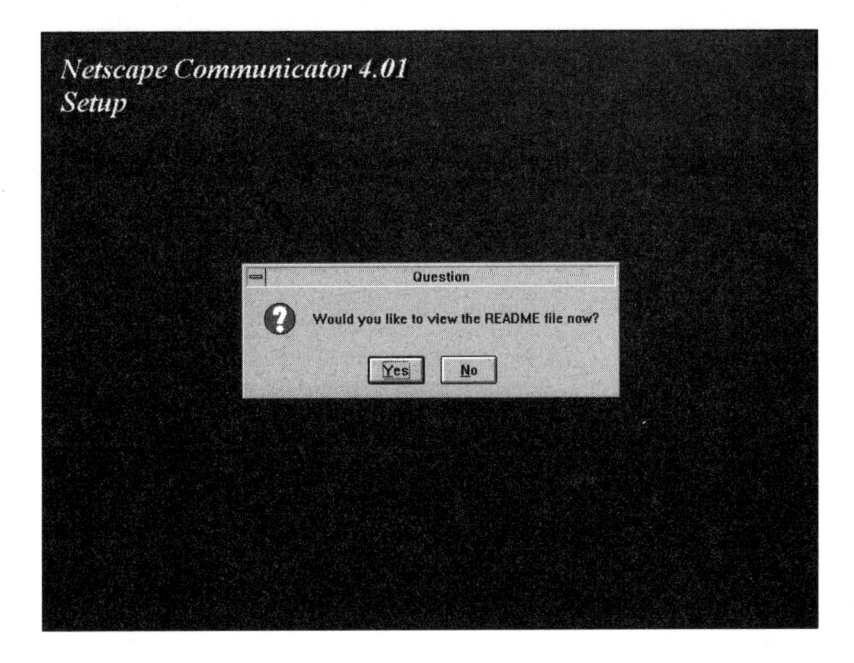

**FIG. B.10**
You will get this prompt when you successfully install Netscape Communicator.

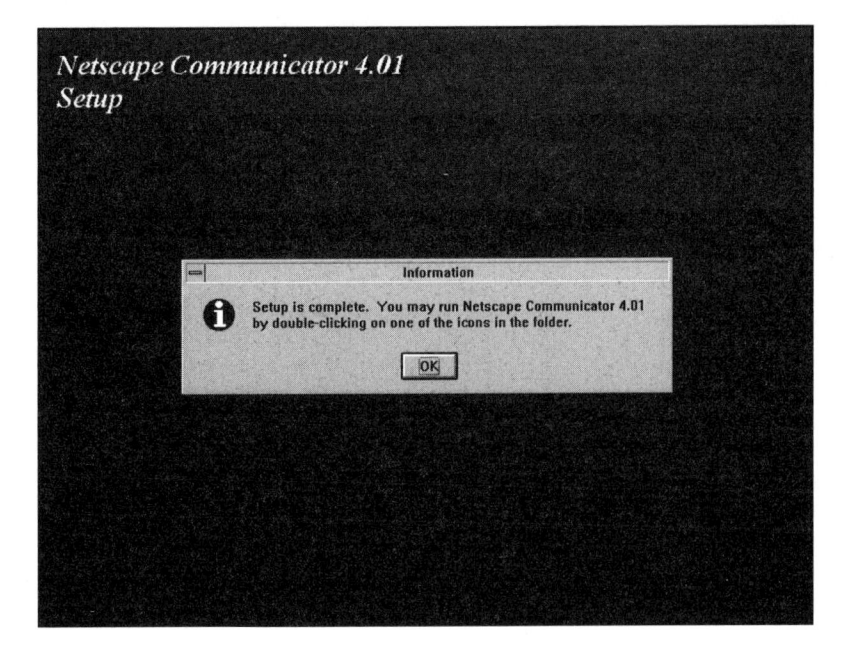

**FIG. B.11**
After the installation you will need to restart your computer before you can run Netscape.

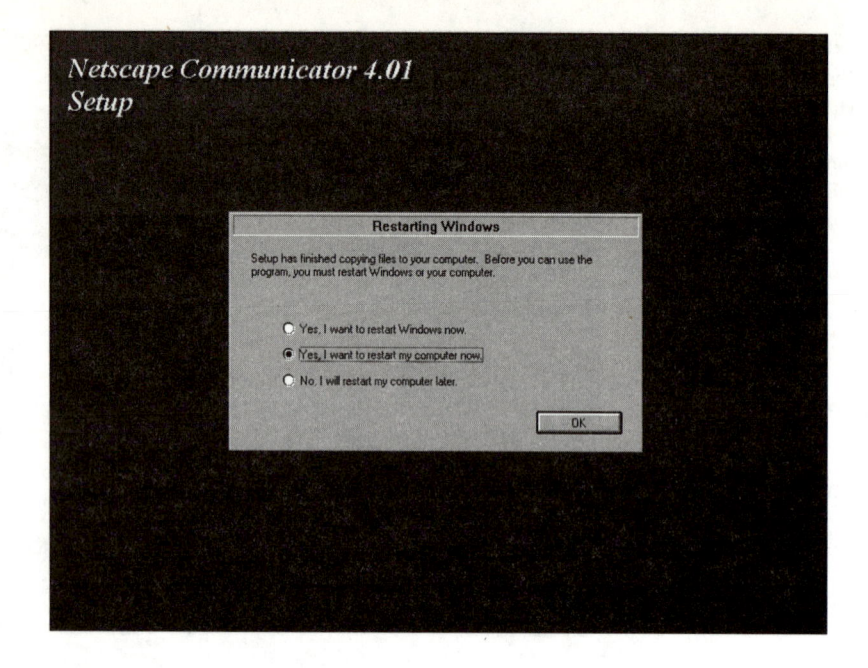

**FIG. B.12**
The installation program creates the Netscape Communicator program group in your Windows Program Manager.

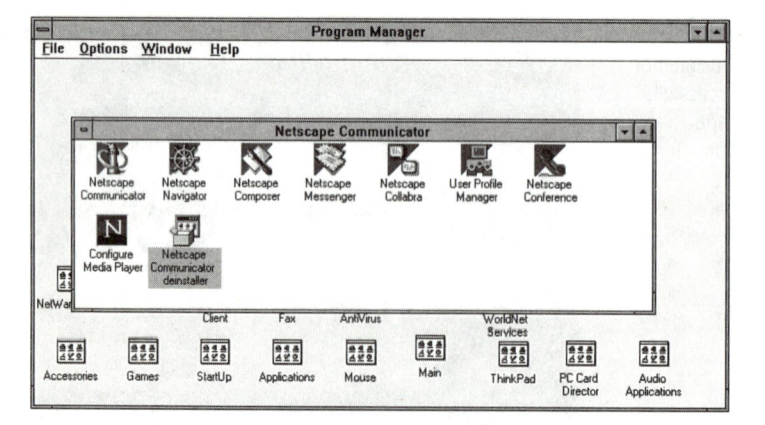

# Creating Your First User Profile

A new feature in Netscape Communicator is the capability to create multiple user profiles. A user profile is tantamount to a container that holds configuration information, bookmarks, and e-mail messages for individual users. If you share your computer with others who will be also using Netscape Communicator, you can now create separate profiles for each user, and each user can configure Netscape Communicator according to his or her own preferences.

http://www.quecorp.com

> **CAUTION**
> Netscape does not provide any degree of security in user profiles. This means that there is nothing to prevent one user from viewing or using another user's profile.

Before you can use Netscape Communicator for the first time, you need to create at least one user profile. Here's how to create your first user profile:

> **CAUTION**
> Make sure you are connected to the Internet either through your service provider or through a network connection. The utility to create a new user profile does not operate if you are not connected to the Internet.

1. Make sure you are connected to the Internet either through your service provider or through a network connection.
2. Double-click the Netscape Communicator icon in Program Manager to open the Netscape Communicator program group folder (see Figure B.13).

**FIG. B.13**
The Netscape Communicator program group folder in Program Manager is where you find the Setup New User Profile utility program.

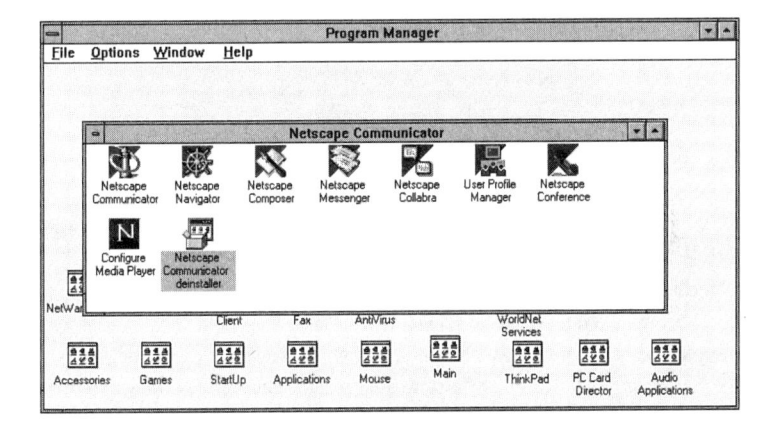

3. Double-click the User Profile Manager icon to start the user profile utility program. In a few seconds, the opening screen appears (see Figure B.14).
4. Select New to begin creating your profile. After you read the disclaimer screen, select Next to advance to the first user input screen (see Figure B.15) where you enter your name and e-mail address. Select Next to advance to the next screen.
5. At the next screen, you can change the name of the profile if you prefer to use a profile name other than the user account name in your e-mail address (see Figure B.16). You can also change the directory where your profile is stored.

**FIG. B.14**
This is the first screen you see when you start the Profile Manager utility.

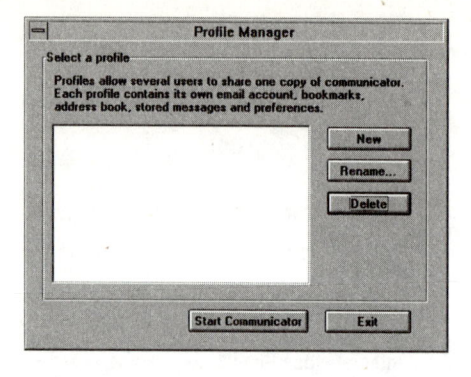

**FIG. B.15**
Your profile is created around the e-mail address you enter here.

> **CAUTION**
> The only really good reason to change the profile name and the directory where Netscape stores your profile is if you create two profiles with similar names. For example, if I create a profile for my two service provider user accounts, gagrimes@city-net.com and gagrimes@bellatlantic.net, Netscape attempts to name both profiles gagrimes and attempts to store both profiles in directory c:\netscape\users\gagrimes. The end result is that the second profile over-writes the first. To prevent the second profile from over-writing the first profile, I rename the second profile gagrime2, and I have the second profile stored in directory c:\netscape\users\gagrime2.

Select Next to continue with the creation of your user profile.

**NOTE** If you don't have the information requested for your mail and news servers and IDs, don't worry. You can enter the information later in one of the Netscape Communicator components. Just accept the default values entered by the profile manager. ■

6. At the next screen, enter information for sending e-mail, that is, your name, e-mail address, and the name of your outgoing (SMTP) mail server (see Figure B.17). Select Next to continue.

http://www.quecorp.com

**FIG. B.16**
You can name your profile any name you want and select the directory where your profile will be stored.

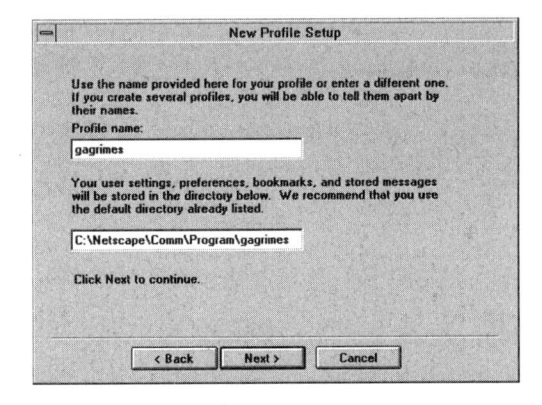

**FIG. B.17**
If you intend to send e-mail make sure you correctly enter the requested information.

7. At the next screen, enter information for receiving e-mail, that is, your mail server user name and the name of your incoming mail server (see Figure B.18). Select Next to continue.

**FIG. B.18**
You will not be able to receive e-mail if you do not enter the information about yourself and the incoming mail server correctly.

8. Next, enter information about your news server, specifically the name of your news server, its designated port number, and whether the server is secure (see Figure B.19).

**FIG. B.19**
If you intend to access newsgroups, you need to correctly enter the news server information.

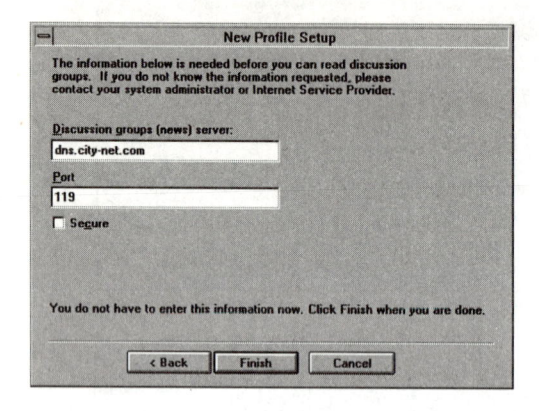

9. Select Finish to continue. After your profile is created, the Profile Manager automatically starts Netscape Communicator.

# Testing Netscape with Your New User Profile

Now that you've successfully installed Netscape Communicator and created your first user profile, you can start Netscape Communicator for the first time to test your installation and new user profile. The major application in the Netscape Communicator suite is Netscape Navigator, your Web browser.

To start Netscape and begin testing your new user profile:

1. Double-click the Netscape Navigator icon in the Netscape Communicator program group folder. In a few seconds, the user license agreement appears on the screen. After reading the license agreement, select Accept to agree to the license agreement and start Netscape Navigator (see Figure B.20).

> **CAUTION**
> If this is a new installation of Netscape Communicator and you are not upgrading from a previous version, you get several warning screens stating that certain files and settings (for example, bookmark files and mail and news settings, and so on) cannot be found. Don't be alarmed. These are merely files and settings that you haven't created yet. Answer OK to continue.

**FIG. B.20**
When you start Netscape Navigator by default it displays the Netscape home page.

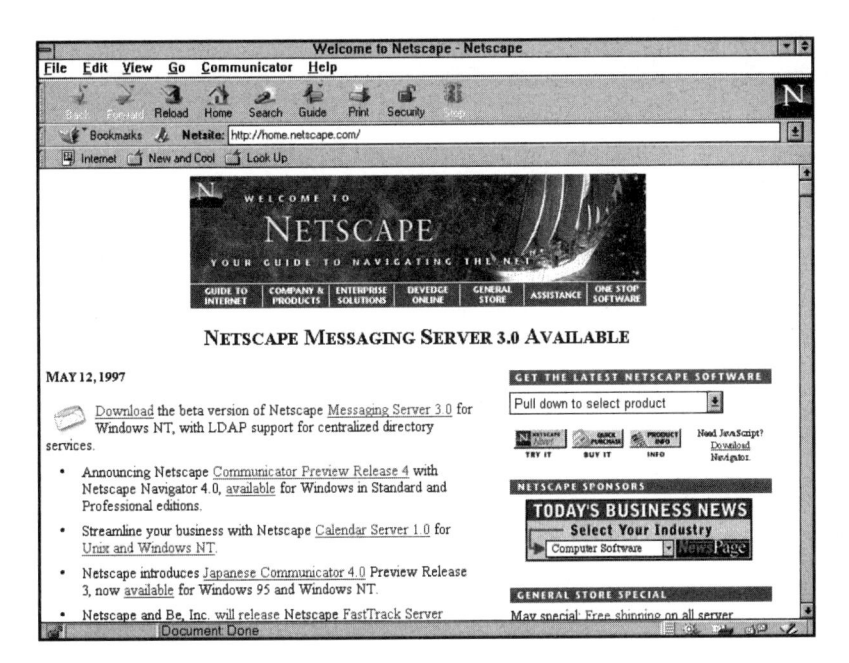

## Configuring Netscape

The final step in installing Netscape Communicator is tending to a few configuration settings. In previous versions of Netscape, there was a host of configuration screens and settings to deal with. In Netscape Communicator, many of those user settings have been configured for you to the most commonly used default settings. What remains are just a few simple settings dealing mainly with mail and discussion (newsgroup) settings.

### Configuring Mail and Discussion Settings

Before you can use the Messenger application in Netscape Communicator to send and receive e-mail messages or Netscape Collabra to read and post messages to a newsgroup, you need to set a few configuration parameters.

Before you begin, make sure you have gotten the following information from your service provider or network systems administrator:

- Your e-mail user name and address
- The name of your incoming e-mail server or post office, the type of incoming mail server, either POP3 (Post Office Protocol 3) or IMAP (Internet Message Access Protocol) server, and, if IMAP, your mail directory location

### Appendix B  Installing Netscape Communicator for Windows 3.1

- The name of your outgoing e-mail server, also referred to as your SMTP (Simple Mail Transfer Protocol) server
- Whether your service provider or network administrator requires you to remove from the mail server e-mail messages that you have read
- Whether your mail server supports encrypted passwords
- The name of your discussion (news) server

With your mail and discussion configuration information in hand, you're now ready to begin configuring Netscape Communicator.

To finish setting configuration options in Netscape:

1. If Netscape Navigator is not up and running from when you earlier started the Web browser, restart Netscape Navigator by selecting the Netscape Navigator icon.

2. In Netscape Navigator, select Edit, Preferences, Mail & Groups from the menu bar to open the Preferences dialog box. Click the plus sign (+) in front of Mail & Groups to open the folder (see Figure B.21).

**FIG. B.21**
You make your mail and discussion configuration settings in the Mail & Groups section of the Preferences dialog box.

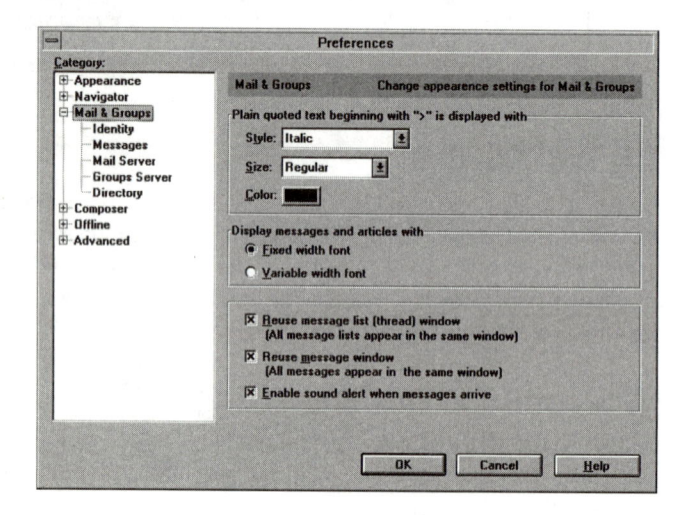

3. Select Identity to open the Identity section (see Figure B.22).

4. In the Your name text box, enter your name as you want it to appear on your e-mail messages addressed to others. In my case, I entered Galen A. Grimes.

5. In the E-mail Address text box, enter your e-mail address. This is the address others use to send you e-mail. In my case, I entered **gagrimes@city-net.com**.

6. In the Reply-to Address (Only Needed if Different from E-mail Address) text box, enter a reply to address if you want users to respond to your e-mail messages by sending their replies to an address different than your previously entered e-mail address. In my case, because I want all of my e-mail messages to be sent to my e-mail address, I left this text box blank.

http://www.quecorp.com

**FIG. B.22**
Enter information about yourself in the Identity section.

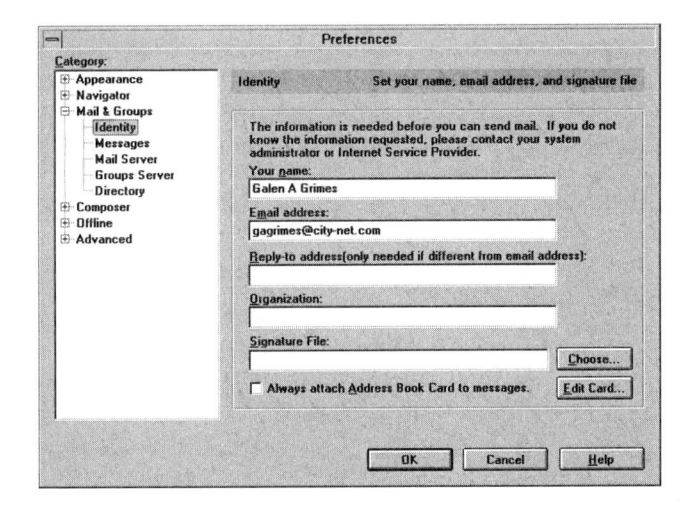

7. In the Organization text box, you can (optionally) enter the name of your company if you are using your company's e-mail system.

8. In the Signature File text box, you can specify a file to be appended to the end of your e-mail messages. Signature files are short witticisms, phrases, or sentences added to the end of e-mail messages, and are often used to convey short witty sayings or make personal or philosophical comments. If you have a signature file that you want to use, enter the drive/path/ and file name of your signature file. If you are not sure what directory your signature file is located in, you can use the Browse button to browse through your hard disk to find it. If you're not sure what a signature file is, leave the text box blank. After you've started receiving e-mail, sooner or later you will receive a message with a signature file tacked on.

9. If you also want to attach your Personal Address Book card to your outgoing e-mail messages, select the check box Always Attach Personal Address Book Card to Outgoing Messages. If you want to edit your personal Address Book Card, select Edit Card to open your personal address book (see Figure B.23).

**FIG. B.23**
Netscape Messenger will allow you to attach a copy of your personal address book card to all of your outgoing e-mail messages.

**NOTE** Your personal address book is the address book of names and e-mail addresses of people you correspond with. Netscape includes an entry for you as you enter your e-mail configuration information. Besides entries for name and e-mail address, you can also enter normal contact information (for example, company, phone numbers, address, and so on).

Now select Messages to open the Messages section (see Figure B.24).

**FIG. B.24**
You specify in the Messages section how you want Messenger to handle your messages.

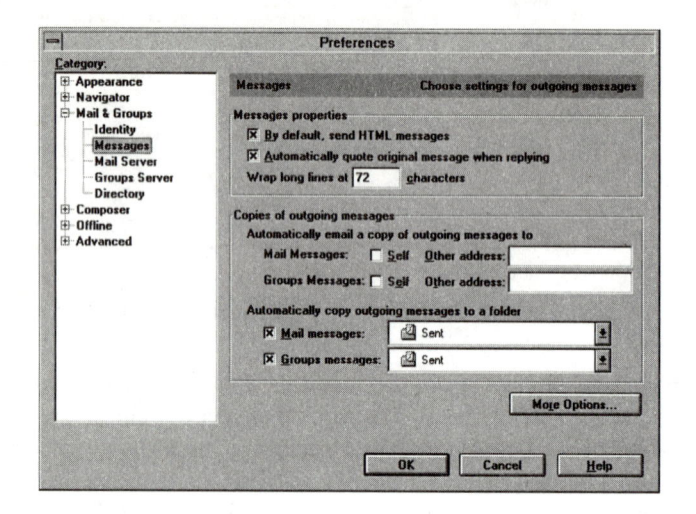

To configure Netscape Messenger on how you want your messages handled:

1. In the Message properties section, enter a check mark if you want to send HTML messages by default, otherwise your messages are sent as plain text. Because most other e-mail programs do not display HTML, you might want to leave this choice blank for now.

2. Enter a check mark if you want to quote the original message when you are replying to a message. When you quote the original message, it makes it easier for the person receiving the reply to remember what the original message was about.

3. If you want each line of text to wrap at a length other than 72 characters, enter the new value here.

4. If you want or need to keep copies of your outgoing e-mail messages, decide in the next section whether you want your copies sent to yourself or someone else. If you are the only one who needs a copy of your outgoing messages, you might just want to copy the message copies to a folder rather than e-mail them to yourself.

5. Select the More Options button to display the More Messages Preferences dialog box (see Figure B.25).

6. In the first section, leave the default setting to expand addresses against names and nicknames because this allows you to enter both regular names and nicknames in your address book.

**FIG. B.25**
The More Messages Preferences dialog box allows you to specify additional parameters for sending messages.

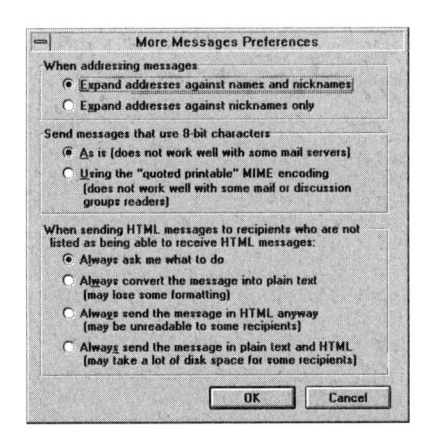

7. In the middle section on how to send 8-bit character messages, again leave the default value. If you need to change this setting because someone you sent a message to can't read the message, that person usually lets you know and you can return to this dialog box and change this setting.

8. And, in the final section, if you checked on the previous screen to send HTML Messages by default, then you need to decide how to handle an HTML message that is sent to someone you know who can't read HTML messages. The default value of Always ask me what to do is probably the safest choice.

9. Select OK to save your settings and close the More Messages Preferences dialog box.

Now select Mail Server to enter information about your mail server and how you want it to handle your mail messages (see Figure B.26).

**FIG. B.26**
To send and receive e-mail you need to configure Netscape Messenger with information about your Mail Server.

To configure Messenger to communicate with your mail server:

1. Enter or change your mail server user name.
2. In the Outgoing (SMTP) Mail Server text box, enter the name of the outgoing (SMTP) mail server you got from your service provider or network systems administrator. In my case, I entered **dns.city-net.com**.
3. In the Incoming Mail Server text box, enter the name of the incoming mail server you got from your service provider or network systems administrator. In my case, the name of my outgoing and incoming mail server are the same, so once again I entered **dns.city-net.com**.
4. In the Mail Server Type section, select the option button that corresponds to the type of incoming mail server your service provider or network systems administrator has implemented, either POP3 or IMAP. Also select where your messages are stored after you read them. Message storage location can depend on the policies of your service provider or network systems administrator.
5. Select More Options to display the More Mail Server Preferences dialog box (see Figure B.27).

**FIG. B.27**
The More Mail Server Preferences dialog box has additional preferences.

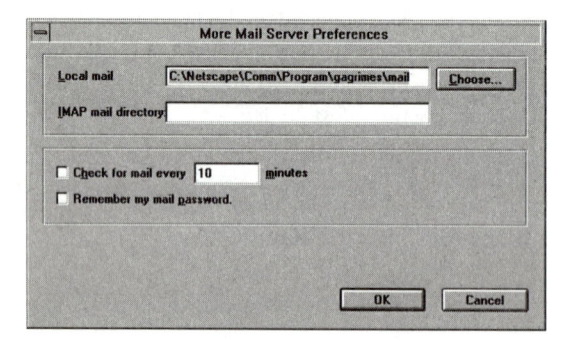

6. In the Local Mail Directory text box, do not change this directory entry unless you have a very good reason for changing it. This entry was set by the user profile utility.
7. In the IMAP Mail Directory text box, enter the information provided by your service provider or network systems administrator.
8. If you want Netscape messenger to automatically check your mailbox for new mail, select the check box Check for mail every [ ] minutes and enter a number for the number of minutes between checks. If you want Netscape Messenger to check your mailbox every 30 minutes, enter 30 in the blank.
9. If you want Netscape Messenger to remember your mail server logon password, select the check box Remember my mail password. Remember that, because Netscape does

not provide any security for user profiles, if you have Netscape Messenger remember your mail password and you share your computer, it is possible for another user to access your e-mail.

10. Unless you have a good reason to change the Netscape Messenger MAPI server setting, leave it on the default value of Always.

11. Select OK to save your settings and close the More Mail Server Preferences dialog box.

If you also plan to access newsgroups using Netscape Collabra, you need to enter information in the Groups Server section on your service provider's discussions (news) server (see Figure B.28).

**FIG. B.28**
The Groups Server section on the Preferences dialog box is where you enter information on your discussion (news) server.

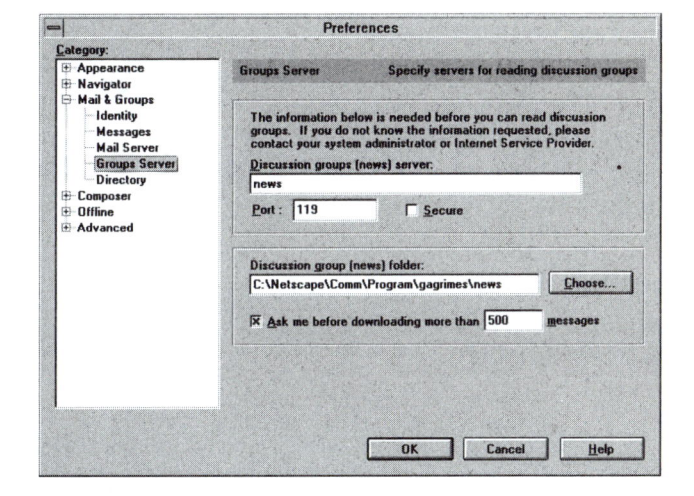

1. In the Discussion Groups (news) Server text box, enter the name of your service provider's discussions (news) server. In my case, I entered **dns.city-net.com**.

2. In the Discussion Group (news) Folder text box, do not change this directory entry unless you have a very good reason for changing it. This entry was set by the user profile utility.

3. For now, leave the setting to have Netscape Communicator notify you when downloading more than 500 messages. This is a warning Netscape Communicator provides whenever you attempt to access a large newsgroup, which can be time consuming, especially if you have a slow dial-up Internet connection.

4. Select OK to save your configuration settings and close the Preferences dialog box.

Now select Directory to enter information about the e-mail search directories you will use (see Figure B.29).

**FIG. B.29**
The final section of the Mail & Groups preferences allows you to control the order of the directory search engines used in Messenger.

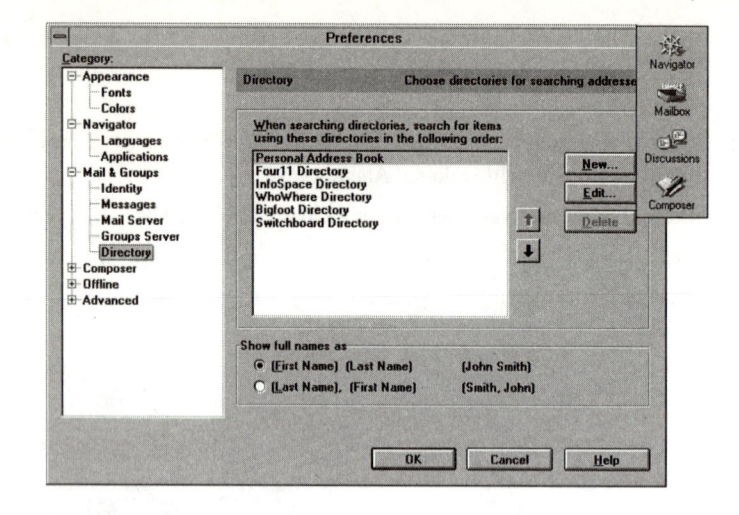

To change the order of the directory search engines Messenger will use when searching for an e-mail address:

1. Unless you are already very familiar with the directory search engines listed here, you should probably not rearrange the order.
2. You can also specify the order in which names are listed in your address book, last name first or first name first.
3. Select OK to save your Preference settings and close the dialog box.

As you become more familiar with Netscape Communicator, you might decide to make additional changes, but, for now, these are the only configuration settings you are required to make to use Netscape Communicator to send mail and access newsgroups. ●

http://www.quecorp.com

APPENDIX C

# Installing Communicator for Windows 95

*by Galen Grimes*

**P**ractically since its release, Windows 95 has literally become the platform of choice for accessing the Internet. Windows 95 comes complete with all the basic tools you need for Internet access, and you can easily configure the necessary Windows 95 Internet components in under 20 minutes.

Add to this that just about every Internet program, tool, and utility is first released as a 32-bit Windows 95 application, and you can easily see why the popularity of Windows 95 and the Internet have nourished each other.

Even if you haven't mastered all of the intricacies of Windows 95, you should have no problem installing Netscape Communicator. The entire installation should take no longer than 20 to 30 minutes, including the small amount of program configuration you need to perform for mail and discussion. ■

- **Computer requirements**
  Learn the minimum computer hardware requirements for installing Netscape Communicator to operate under Windows 95.

- **Installation decisions**
  How to install Netscape Communicator and what decisions you have to make if you are new to using Netscape, new to the Internet, and this is your first Web browser installation.

- **Upgrading to Netscape Communicator**
  How to install Netscape Communicator over a previous Netscape installation and how to preserve and carry over your previous settings and options.

## Installation Requirements

Before you begin, you need to make sure your computer is properly configured to run Netscape Communicator and Windows 95. The minimum configuration you should have for running Netscape Communicator with Windows 95 is the following:

- 486/25MHz processor
- 8M of RAM
- VGA graphics card and monitor
- 14.4Kbps modem

While this configuration runs both Windows 95 and Netscape Communicator, you may be frustrated with the performance of the minimum requirements. A more realistic minimum configuration probably looks something like this:

- 486/66MHz processor
- 16M of RAM
- VGA or SVGA graphics card and color monitor
- 28.8Kbps modem

**NOTE** If your computer meets the hardware requirements specified in this appendix and you can connect to the Internet, then your computer is ready to install Netscape Communicator and you do not need any additional software.

## Beginning the Installation

Because you will be installing Netscape Communicator to run under Windows 95, you need to make sure you are installing the 32-bit version (Windows 95 version) of the program and not the 16-bit version. The 16-bit version (Windows 3.1 version) runs under Windows 95, but you do not get the same level of performance because the 16-bit version is not optimized to take advantage of the more advanced memory features in Windows 95.

Locate the file c32e40.exe. If you are installing Netscape Communicator from a purchased CD, this file is located in directory x:\Windows\32bit (x:\ represents the drive configured as your CD-ROM drive). If your CD-ROM drive is configured as drive D:\, then the file you run to install Netscape Communicator is D:\Windows\32bit\c32e40.exe. If you do not have a CD-ROM drive and instead downloaded c32e40.exe, locate the directory where you saved the downloaded file.

Before you begin the installation program, make sure you exit any programs you have running in Windows 95. The installation program writes to and updates some of your common Windows system files. If you have other programs running, the installation program might not have complete access to update these common system files. Also, at the end of the installation, you need to restart your computer and Windows 95, which means you have to exit all programs to perform the restart.

http://www.quecorp.com

To begin installing Netscape Communicator, follow these steps:

1. If you are installing Netscape Communicator from a CD, from the Windows taskbar, select Start, Run and enter **d:\windows\32bit\c32e40.exe** to start the installation program (see Figure C.1). Click OK to start the program.

**FIG. C.1**
The Run dialog box is one way you can start the installation program.

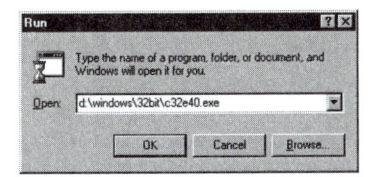

2. In a few seconds, the installation program prompts you to confirm that you are about to install Netscape Communicator on your PC and asks you if you want to continue. Answer Yes to continue with the installation. For the next minute or so, depending on the speed of your computer, the installation program begins extracting the files it needs (contained in the file c32e40.exe) to install Netscape Communicator on your PC (see Figure C.2). Be patient; this is a normal part of the installation.

**FIG. C.2**
The installation program first extracts the files it needs to complete the installation.

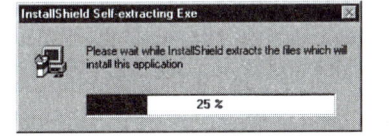

3. The next screen prompts you to make sure no other programs are running in Windows. Select Next to continue with the installation.

   **N O T E** If, for any reason, you need to stop the installation before the installation is complete, select the Cancel button that appears on most of the installation screens. ■

4. Next, you are prompted to select the type of setup you want to perform for this installation and the directory where the program will be installed on your hard disk (see Figure C.3). The choices are Typical and Custom. The Typical choice has pre-selected the most often used components under Windows 95. The Custom choice allows you to select what options you want installed.

   If you are new to using Netscape, go ahead and select the Typical choice for now. If, after running Netscape Communicator for a while, you discover an option you want to use that was not installed during this installation, you can always re-run this installation program, select Custom, and select any option not included in the Recommended setup. For now, make sure the option button next to Typical is selected.

**FIG. C.3**
Two of the first choices you need to make are whether to perform a Typical or Custom setup and where Netscape Communicator will be installed.

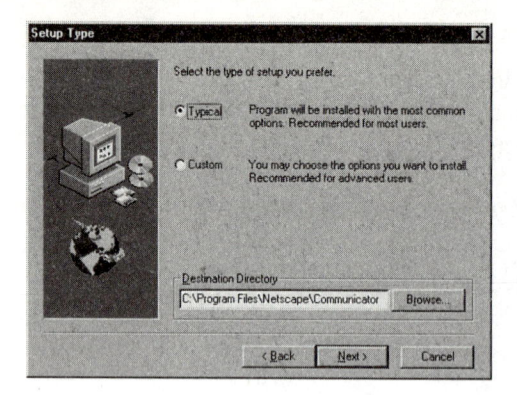

5. Next, you are prompted to select the destination directory. This is the directory where Netscape Communicator will be installed on your computer. The installation program suggests you install the program in directory C:\Program Files\Netscape\Communicator.

   If you are upgrading from Netscape 3.0, you may notice that Netscape Communicator is not being installed over that version. Netscape 3.0 was installed (or should have been installed) into C:\Program Files\Netscape\Navigator. If you accept the suggested location for Netscape Communicator, you then have two versions of Netscape installed on your computer, which allows you to compare the two versions and decide if you are ready to upgrade from Netscape 3.0 to Netscape Communicator. When you are ready to continue, click Next.

6. The installation program briefly checks to make sure you have enough free disk space on the drive you designated for the installation.

7. The installation program then prompts you for the program group folder into which it creates the program icons for Netscape Communicator (see Figure C.4).

   The default selection allows the program to create a new program folder, Netscape Communicator. You can, however, place the Netscape Communicator icons into one of your existing program group folders. If you are new to Netscape, go ahead and accept the default choice and have the installation program create a new program group folder. If you decide later that you want to move the Netscape Communicator icons into another folder, you can simply drag the icons into another folder. After you make your decision, click Next to continue with the installation.

   **N O T E** Netscape will continue to produce Communicator versions and components beyond the present 4.0. To keep you updated, Netscape offers a SmartUpdate feature allowing you to tune your present version of Communicator in less time than it would take to completely reinstall a newer program.

   In Navigator, click the Software Update command under the Help menu. You will see the SmartUpdate web page where Netscape will tell you what version you are presently using and, if applicable, what version you could be running. If you need to update, simply click Begin SmartUpdate and the program will automatically begin downloading and installing the new components.

http://www.quecorp.com

Beginning the Installation | 715

**FIG. C.4**
During the installation, you can select the program group folder you want your Netscape Communicator icons to be placed into.

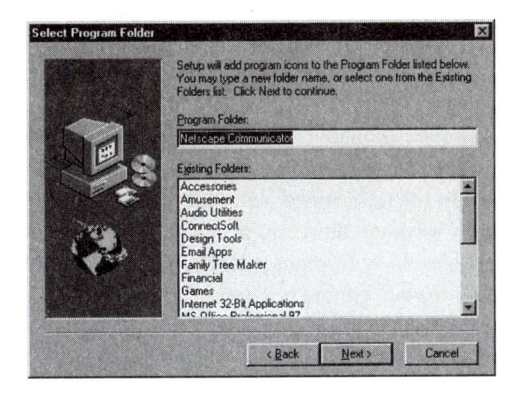

8. The next installation screen merely confirms the installation choices you have made thus far (see Figure C.5). Look over the configuration choices displayed and, if you see any errors or see any settings you want to change, click the Back button to go back to any of the previous screens and change the selection.

**FIG. C.5**
Before the actual installation begins, you get a chance to review the choices you've made so far.

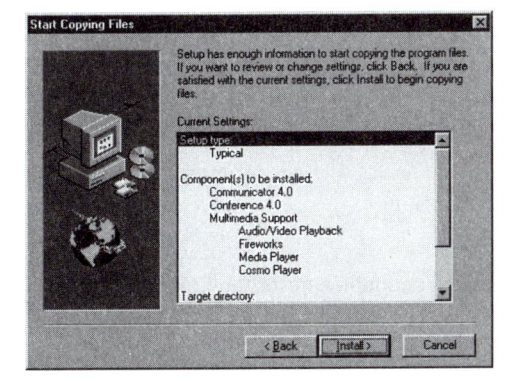

9. When you are ready to continue with the installation, click Install. The installation program now begins to copy files to the destination directory you previously selected. This process can easily take five minutes or more depending on the speed of your computer. During this time, the installation program is copying files for each of the various Netscape Communicator components as well as several plug-ins that are included with Netscape Communicator.

10. When the installation program has finished copying files to your designated destination directory, the program asks you if you want to read the README file. The README file is a file containing last minute information or changes to the program. If you want to read the README file, select Yes, and the installation program opens the README file in Windows Notepad. When you finish reading the README file, select File, Exit to close Notepad and resume the installation. If you do not want to read the README file, select No to continue.

Part VII
App C

11. Finally, the installation program informs you that the installation is complete and that you can run Netscape Communicator by double-clicking the icons in the Netscape Communicator folder. Click OK to continue.

12. The final prompt from the installation program tells you to restart your computer. When you restart your computer, the installation program copies some files to your Windows system directory and to the designated Netscape Communicator directory; the files copied to your Windows system directory are only run when Windows is first started. Click Yes, I Want to Restart My Computer Now and then click OK to restart your computer. If, for some reason, you do not want to restart your computer now, select No, I Will Restart My Computer Later and then OK. Just remember to restart your PC before you attempt to run Netscape Communicator for the first time.

# Creating Your First User Profile

A new feature in Netscape Communicator is the capability to create multiple user profiles. A user profile contains configuration information, bookmarks, and e-mail messages for individual users. If you share your computer with others who will also use Netscape Communicator, you can now create separate user profiles for each person, and each person can configure Netscape Communicator according to his or her own preferences.

> **CAUTION**
> Netscape Communicator does not provide any degree of security around user profiles. This means that there is nothing to prevent one user from viewing or using another user's profile or the information, such as e-mail messages, contained in a user profile.

Before you can use Netscape Communicator for the first time, you need to create at least one user profile. To create your first user profile, follow these steps:

1. From the taskbar, select Start, Programs, Netscape Communicator, Utilities and then select the User Profile Manager icon to start the user profile utility program. In a few seconds, the opening screen appears (see Figure C.6).

**FIG. C.6**
Before you can use Netscape Communicator for the first time you have to create at least one user profile.

http://www.quecorp.com

Creating Your First User Profile   717

2. The next screen (see Figure C.7), which appears when you select New, explains the purpose of creating user profiles and what information and settings are controlled by the profiles. Click Next to advance to the first user input screen (see Figure C.8) where you enter your name and e-mail address. Select Next to advance to the next screen.

**FIG. C.7**
The User Profile Manager first explains its purpose and why you need to create profiles.

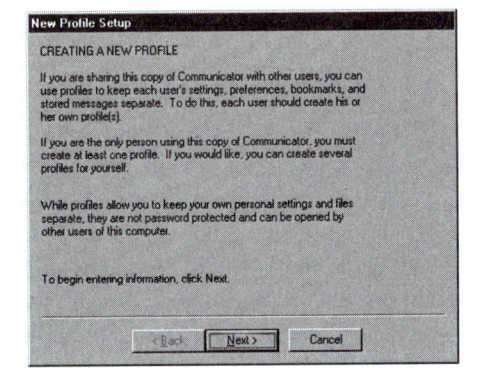

**FIG. C.8**
On the first user input screen, enter your name and e-mail address.

3. At the next screen, you can change the name of the profile if you prefer to use a profile name other than your e-mail address. You can also change the directory where your profile is stored (see Figure C.9).

> **CAUTION**
> The only good reason to change the profile name and the directory where Netscape stores your profile is if you create two profiles with similar names. For example, if I create a profile for my two service provider user accounts, gagrimes@city-net.com and gagrimes@bellatlantiLB.net, Netscape attempts to name both profiles gagrimes and attempts to store both profiles in directory c:\netscape\users\gagrimes. The end result is that the second profile over-writes the first. To prevent the second profile from over-writing the first profile, I rename the second profile gagrime2 and have the second profile stored in directory c:\netscape\users\gagrime2.

**FIG. C.9**
You don't have to accept the default values for the profile name or the directory where it is stored.

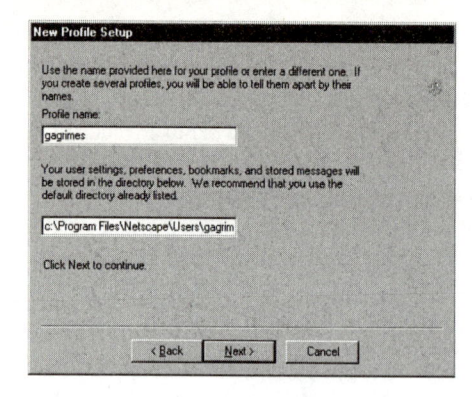

Select Next to continue with the creation of your user profile.

4. On the next screen, you need to enter information for e-mail and newsgroups. If you want to change your name as it will appear on your e-mail messages, do so now. The e-mail address you entered previously should appear in the e-mail address field. Finally, enter the name of your outgoing (SMTP) mail server. In my case, I enter dns.city-net.com. If you do not know the name of your outgoing mail server, contact your systems administrator or service provider (see Figure C.10).

**FIG. C.10**
You also need to enter information for use in mail and discussion newsgroups.

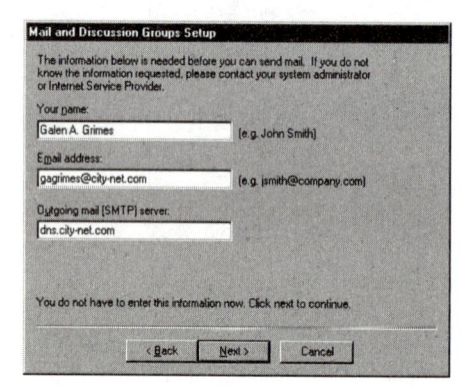

**N O T E** Don't worry if you don't have all of the information requested for your mail and news servers. You can enter this information later in either Netscape Navigator or Netscape Messenger.

5. Next, you need to enter information for incoming mail. Enter your mail server user name. In most cases, this is the name portion of your e-mail address (the potion before the @). In my case, my e-mail address is **gagrimes@city-net.com** so my mail server user name is gagrimes (see Figure C.11). You also need to enter the name of your incoming mail server and specify whether the mail server is POP3 or IMAP. Your systems administrator or service provider can supply you with this information. Select Next to continue.

**FIG. C.11**
You cannot send or receive mail unless you enter information on your mail servers.

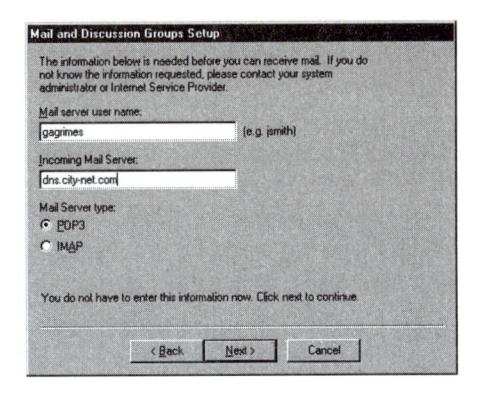

6. Next, enter the name of your News (NNTP) server, its port designation, and whether the server is secure. Again, your systems administrator or service provider can supply you with this information (see Figure C.12). Click Finish to save your profile.

**FIG. C.12**
If you want to participate in news (discussion) groups, you must enter the name of a news server.

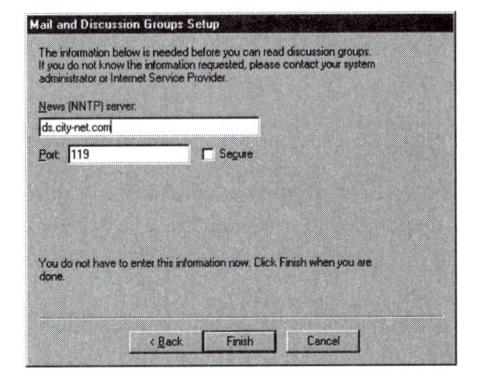

## Testing Netscape with Your New User Profile

Now that you've successfully installed Netscape Communicator and created your first user profile, you can now start using Netscape Communicator for the first time to test your installation and new user profile. The major application in the Netscape Communicator suite is Netscape Navigator, your Web browser; so let's start with Netscape Navigator first. After you create your first user profile, Netscape Navigator should start automatically.

> **CAUTION**
> If this is a new installation of Netscape Communicator and you are not upgrading from a previous version, you get several warning screens stating that certain files and settings (for example, bookmark files and mail and news settings, and so on) cannot be found. Don't be alarmed. These are merely files and settings that you haven't created yet. Merely answer OK to continue.

# Configuring Netscape Communicator Mail and Discussion Settings

The final step in installing Netscape Communicator is tending to a few configuration settings. In previous versions of Netscape, there was a host of configuration screens and settings to deal with. In Netscape Communicator, many of those user settings have been configured for you to the most commonly used default settings. What remains are just a few simple settings dealing mainly with mail and discussion (newsgroup) settings.

Before you can use the Messenger application in Netscape Communicator to send and receive e-mail messages, or use Netscape Collabra to read and post messages to a newsgroup, you need to set a few configuration parameters.

Before you begin, make sure you have gotten the following information from your service provider or network systems administrator:

- Your e-mail user name and e-mail address
- The name of your incoming e-mail server or post office, the type of incoming mail server, either POP3 (Post Office Protocol 3) or IMAP (Internet Message Access Protocol) server, and, if IMAP, your mail directory location
- The name of your outgoing e-mail server, also referred to as your SMTP (Simple Mail Transfer Protocol) server
- Whether your service provider or network administrator requires you to remove from the mail server e-mail messages that you have read
- Whether your mail server supports encrypted passwords
- The name of your discussion (news) server

With your mail and discussion configuration information in hand, you're now ready to begin configuring Netscape Communicator.

To begin configuring Netscape Communicator, follow these steps:

1. If Netscape Navigator is not up and running from when you earlier started the Web browser, restart Netscape Navigator by selecting the Netscape Navigator icon.
2. In Netscape Navigator, select Edit, Preferences, Mail & Groups from the menu bar to open the Preferences dialog box. Click the plus sign (+) in front of Mail & Groups to open the folder (see Figure C.13).
3. Select Identity to open the Identity section (see Figure C.14).
4. In the Your Name text box, enter your name as you want it to appear on your e-mail messages addressed to others. In my case, I entered **Galen A. Grimes**.
5. In the E-mail Address text box, enter your e-mail address. This is the address others use to send you e-mail. In my case, I entered **gagrimes @ city-net.com**.
6. In the Reply to address (only needed if different from e-mail address) text box, enter a reply to address if you want users to respond to your e-mail messages by sending their

replies to an address different than your previously entered e-mail address. In my case, because I want all of my e-mail messages to be sent to my e-mail address, I left this text box blank.

**FIG. C.13**
You make your mail and discussion configuration settings in the Mail & Groups section of the Preferences dialog box.

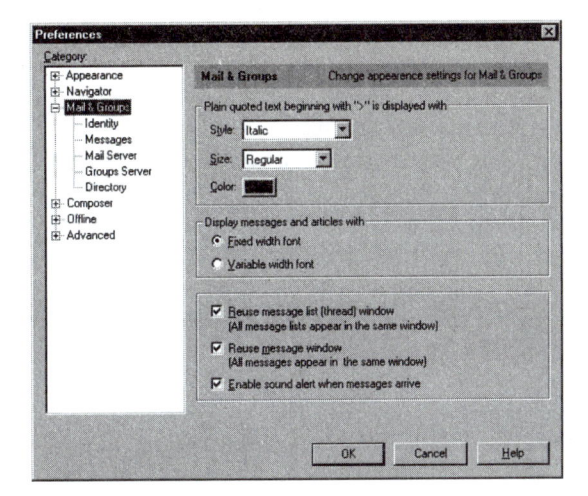

**FIG. C.14**
You enter information about yourself in the Identity section.

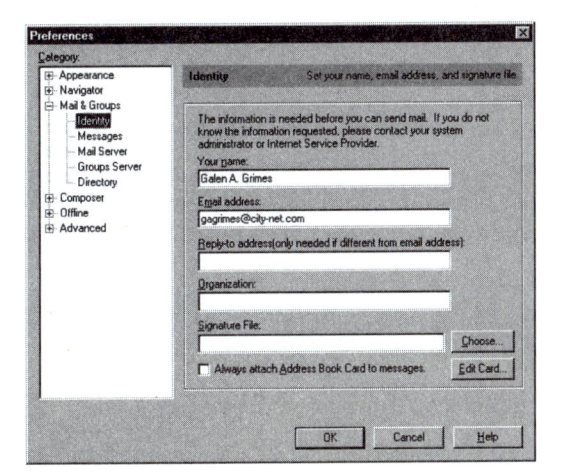

7. In the Organization text box, you can (optionally) enter the name of your company if you are using your company's e-mail system.
8. In the Signature File text box, you can specify a file to be appended to the end of your e-mail messages. Signature files are often used to convey short witty sayings or make personal or philosophical comments. If you have a signature file that you want to use, enter the drive/path/ and file name of your signature file. If you are not sure what directory your signature file is located in, you can use the Browse button to browse through your hard disk to find it. If you're not sure what a signature file is, leave the text

box blank. After you've started receiving e-mail, sooner or later you will receive a message with a signature file tacked on.

9. If you also want to attach your Personal Address Book card to your outgoing e-mail messages, select the check box Always attach Address Book Card to messages. If you want to edit your personal Address Book Card, select Edit Card to open your personal address book.

> **NOTE** Your personal address book is the address book of names and e-mail addresses of people you correspond with. Netscape includes an entry for you as you enter your e-mail configuration information. Besides entries for name and e-mail address, you can also enter normal contact information (for example, company, phone numbers, address, and so on).

## Configuring Netscape Messenger to Handle Incoming Messages

Select Messages to open the Messages section (see Figure C.15).

**FIG. C.15**
You specify in the Messages section how you want Messenger to handle your messages.

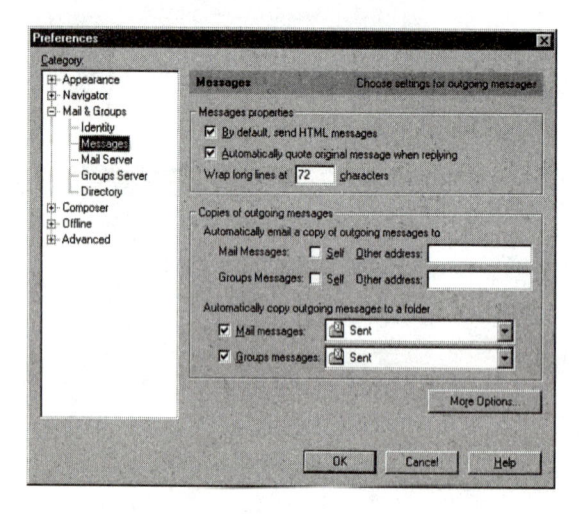

To configure Netscape Messenger to handle your messages, follow these steps:

1. In the Message properties section, enter a check mark if you want to send HTML messages by default; otherwise your messages are sent as plain text. Because most other e-mail programs do not display HTML, you might want to leave this choice blank for now.

2. Enter a check mark if you want to quote the original message when you are replying to a message. When you quote the original message, it makes it easier for the person receiving the reply to remember what the original message was about.

3. If you want each line of text to wrap at a length other than 72 characters, enter the new value in the appropriate text box, requesting a text length value.

Configuring Netscape Communicator Mail and Discussion Settings | 723

4. If you want or need to keep copies of your outgoing e-mail messages, decide in the next section whether you want your copies sent to yourself or to someone else. If you are the only one who needs a copy of your outgoing messages, you might want to copy the message copies to a folder rather than e-mail them to yourself.

5. Select the More Options button to display the More Messages Preferences dialog box (see Figure C.16).

**FIG. C.16**
The More Messages Preferences dialog box allows you to specify additional parameters for sending messages.

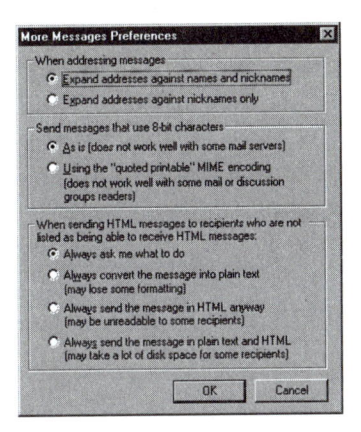

6. In the first section, leave the default setting to expand addresses against names and nicknames because this allows you to enter both regular names and nicknames in your address book.

7. In the middle section on how to send 8-bit character messages, again leave the default value. If you need to change this setting because someone you sent a message to can't read the message, that person will usually let you know and you can return to this dialog box and change this setting.

8. And, in the final section, if you checked on the previous screen to send HTML Messages by default, then you need to decide how you want to handle an HTML message you create to send to someone you know can't read HTML messages. The default value of Always Ask Me What to Do is probably the safest choice.

9. Select OK to save your settings and close the More Messages Preferences dialog box.

Now select Mail Server to enter information about your mail server and how you want it to handle your mail messages (see Figure C.17).

## Configuring Netscape Messenger to Handle Outgoing Mail

To configure Netscape Messenger to handle your outgoing mail, follow these steps:

1. Enter or change your mail server user name.

2. In the Outgoing (SMTP) Mail Server text box, enter the name of the outgoing (SMTP) mail server you got from your service provider or network systems administrator. In my case, I entered **dns.city-net.com**.

# Appendix C  Installing Communicator for Windows 95

3. In the Incoming mail server text box, enter the name of the incoming mail server you got from your service provider or network systems administrator. In my case, the name of my outgoing and incoming mail server are the same, so again I entered **dns.city-net.com**.

4. In the Mail server type section, select the radio button that corresponds to the type of incoming mail server your service provider or network systems administrator has implemented, either POP3 or IMAP. Also select where your messages will be stored after you read them. Message storage location can depend on the policies of your service provider or network systems administrator.

5. Select More to display the More Mail Server Preferences dialog box (see Figure C.18).

**FIG. C.17**
The Mail Server preferences section is where you enter information about your mail servers.

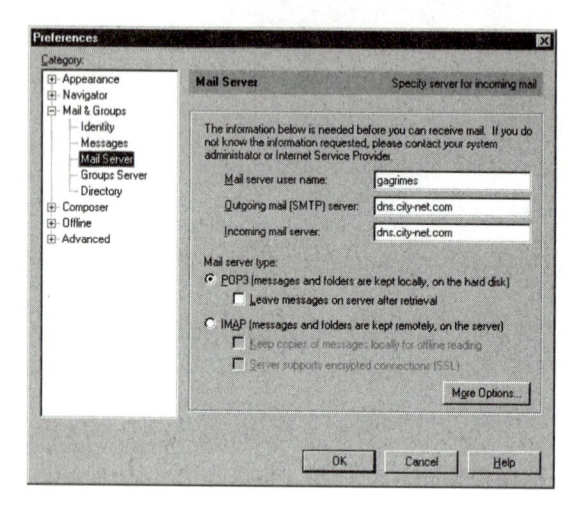

6. In the Local mail directory text box, do not change this directory entry unless you have a very good reason for changing it. This entry was set by the user profile utility.

7. In the IMAP mail directory text box, enter the information provided by your service provider or network systems administrator.

8. If you want Netscape messenger to automatically check your mailbox for new mail, select the check box Check for mail every [ ] Minutes and enter a number for the number of minutes between checks. If you want Netscape Messenger to check your mailbox every 30 minutes, enter **30** in the blank.

9. If you want Netscape Messenger to remember your mail server logon password, select the check box Remember my mail password. Remember that, because Netscape does not provide any security for user profiles, if you share your computer and you have Netscape Messenger remember your mail password, it is possible for another user to access your e-mail.

10. If you use applications that are capable of sending out e-mail messages, select the Use Netscape Messenger from MAPI-based applications option.

http://www.quecorp.com

Configuring Netscape Communicator Mail and Discussion Settings | 725

11. Click OK to save your settings and to close the More Mail Server Preferences dialog box.

If you also plan to access newsgroups using Netscape Collabra, you need to enter information in the Groups Server section on your service provider's discussions (news) server (see Figure C.19).

**FIG. C.18**
Select the More Mail Server Preferences dialog box to specify how often you want Messenger to check for new mail.

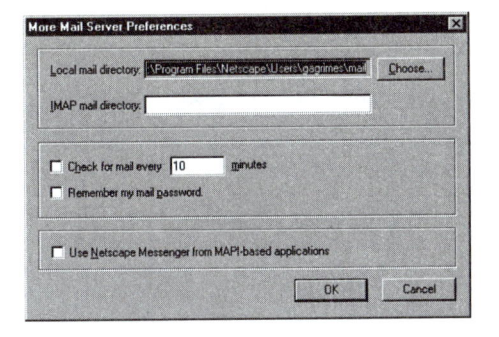

**FIG. C.19**
The Groups Server section on the Preferences dialog box where you enter information on your discussion (news) server.

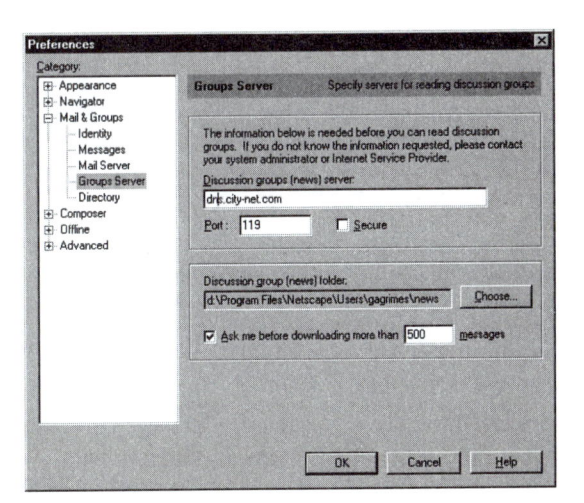

## Configuring Netscape Collabra to Access Newsgroups

To configure Netscape Collabra so that you can access discussion groups, follow these steps:

1. In the Discussion groups (News) server text box, enter the name of your service provider's discussions (news) server. In my case, I entered **dns.city-net.com**.

2. In the Discussion group (News) folder text box, do not change this directory entry unless you have a very good reason for changing it. This entry was set by the user profile utility.

# Appendix C  Installing Communicator for Windows 95

3. For now, leave the setting to have Netscape Communicator notify you when downloading more than 500 messages. This is a warning Netscape Communicator provides whenever you attempt to access a large newsgroup, which can be time consuming, especially if you have a slow dialup Internet connection.

4. Click OK to save your configuration settings and close the Preferences dialog box.

Now select Directory to enter information about the e-mail search directories you will be using (see Figure C.20).

**FIG. C.20**
The final section of the Mail & Groups preferences allows you to control the order of the directory search engines used in Messenger.

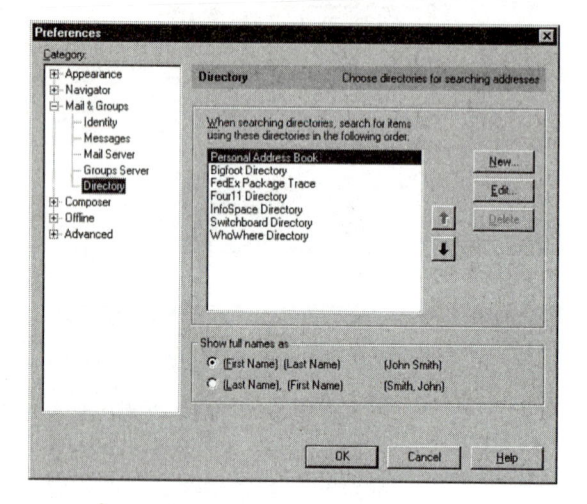

To control the order of the directory search engines that Messenger uses, perform these steps:

1. Unless you are already very familiar with the directory search engines listed here, you should probably not rearrange the order.

2. You can also specify the order in which names are listed in your address book—last name first or first name first.

3. Select OK to save your Preference settings and close the dialog box.

As you become more familiar with Netscape Communicator you might decide to make additional changes, but, for now, these are the only configuration settings you are required to make to use Netscape Communicator to send mail and access newsgroups. ●

# APPENDIX D

# Installing Communicator for Macintosh

*by Ted Lesley*

Each Macintosh sold includes networking software and, with the advent of popular interest in the Internet and Internet software. With the prevalence of the Apple in academia and the sciences, the Macintosh community quickly embraced the Internet and the early iterations of Internet software were first written for the Macintosh.

Installing Netscape Communicator is a snap on the Mac and will probably take you no longer than ten minutes. ■

**Computer Requirements**
What the minimum computer hardware requirements are for installing Netscape Communicator to your Mac.

**Installation Decisions**
How to install Netscape Communicator and what decisions you will have to make if you are new to using Netscape, new to the Internet, and this is your first Web browser installation.

**Upgrading to Netscape Communicator**
How to install Netscape Communicator over a previous Netscape installation and how to preserve and carry over your previous settings and options.

# Installation Requirements

Before we begin, we first need to make sure that your computer is properly configured to run Netscape Communicator. Probably the minimum configuration you should have for running Netscape Communicator is:

- An 040 Mhz CPU
- 8M of RAM
- A monitor
- A 14.4 Kbps modem

While this configuration will run both the system and Netscape Communicator, I can almost guarantee you won't like the performance. A more realistic minimum configuration will probably look something like this:

- A PowerPC Mac
- 16M of RAM
- A color monitor
- A 28.8Kbps modem or faster Internet connection

**NOTE** If your computer meets the hardware requirements specified in this appendix and you can connect to the Internet, your Mac is ready to install Netscape Communicator and you won't need any additional software.

# Beginning the Installation

Because you will be installing Netscape Communicator to either a PowerPC Mac or a non-PowerPC Mac, you will need to decide whether to install Navigator for either CPU or the install dedicated to both.

If you specifically install either the PPC (PowerPC) or the non-PPC (040 or 030) version, less disk space is used on your hard disk. If you install the Communicator that can be used on either platform (commonly referred to as fat binary), it will use more of your disk space. The fat binary program takes up more space because it includes more programming code.

---

### How to Get the Latest and Greatest Software from Netscape

Remember that you can always get the most recent version of Netscape products directly from the Netscape Web and FTP sites. Start with **http://home.netscape.com/download/index.html** and then select the software you want for the kind of Mac you have.

---

Locate the file **communicator_complete_PPC.bin** and download it.

Before you run the Installer, make sure you quit any programs that are already open. The Installer will create a folder and install some extensions into your System Folder. If you have other programs running, the Installer will offer to automatically quit any open programs. Also, at the end of the installation you should restart your Mac.

1. Open the folder named **Netscape Installer** and double-click the **Netscape Installer** program (see Figure D.1).

**FIG. D.1**
Double-clicking the Netscape Installer application will start the ball rolling.

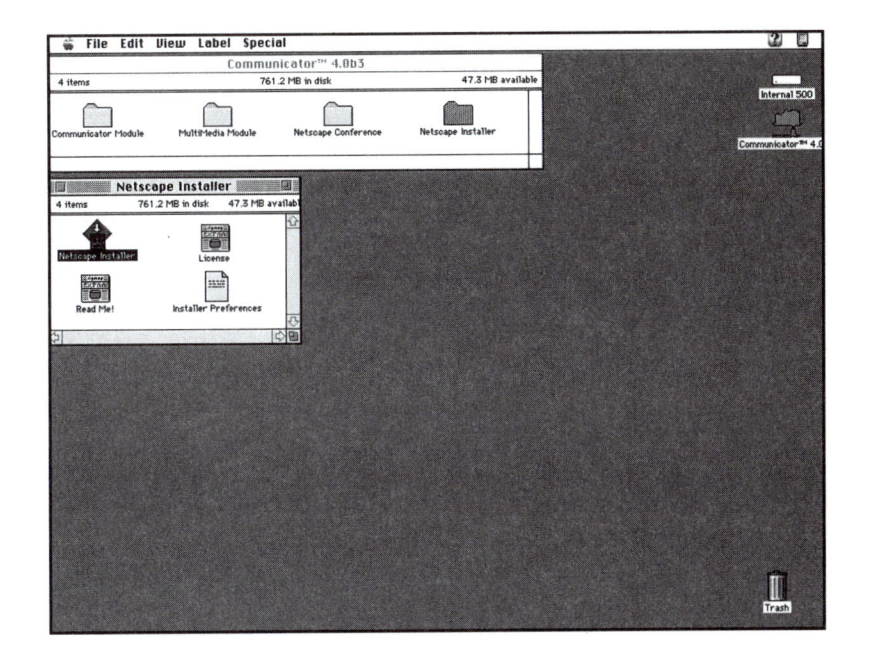

2. Next the Installer will prompt you to confirm that you are about to install Netscape Communicator on your Mac and want to continue. Click **Continue**.

3. Now click **Accept** at the next dialog box to acknowledge and acquiesce to the Netscape Software Licensing Agreement. You may print it out before you read it, but if you click **Decline**, you will be canceling the installation of this software.

4. After you read and print the combination release/installation notes, click **OK** to continue.

**NOTE** If you need to stop the installation for any reason before the installation is complete, select the Cancel button that appears on the Netscape Installer.

5. You will then be prompted to select the type of setup you want to perform for this installation, the hard drive selected for the install, and, if you prefer, the folder where the program will be installed on your hard disk (see Figure D.2). The choices are **Easy Install** and **Custom Install**. The **Easy Install** choice has been preselected and includes the most common components.

The **Custom Install** choice enables you to select what options you want installed. If you are new to using Netscape, go ahead and select the **Easy Install** choice for now. If after running Netscape Communicator for a while you discover an option you would like to use which was not installed during this installation, you can always rerun this installation program, select **Custom Install**, and select any option not included in the Recommended setup. For now, make sure **Easy Install** is selected.

**FIG. D.2**
Two of your first choices are an Easy or Custom Install and where to put Netscape Communicator.

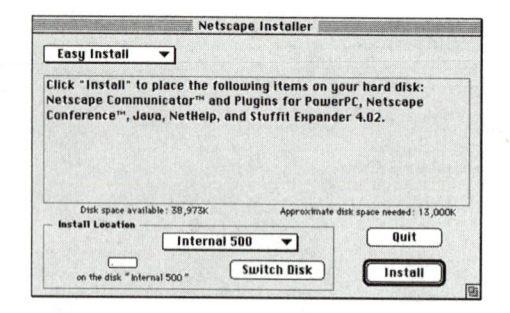

6. The next dialog box (see Figure D.3) will prompt you to confirm that no other programs stay open while the installation takes place. You are also reminded that restarting your Mac after installation is a good thing. Click **Continue** to do so.

**FIG. D.3**
Ensuring that no other applications are running minimizes the risk of other programs interfering with the installation.

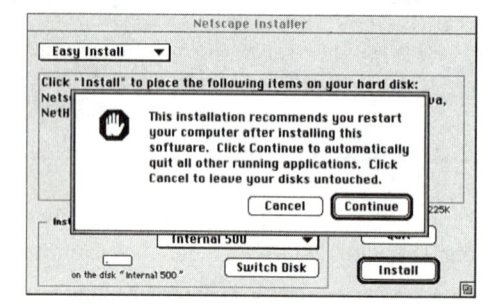

7. The installation program will briefly check to make sure you have enough free disk space on the drive you designated for the installation.
8. The Installer now begins to copy files to the destination directory you previously selected (see Figure D.4). This process will take less than three minutes on a PowerPC Mac. During this time the Installer is copying files for each of the various Netscape Communicator components, as well as several plug-ins included with Netscape Communicator.

**FIG. D.4**
The Installer will spend the next few seconds copying files to the destination.

9. Finally, the installation program will inform you that the installation is completed and will suggest that you restart your Mac before you run Netscape Communicator (see Figure D.5). Select **Restart** to do so.

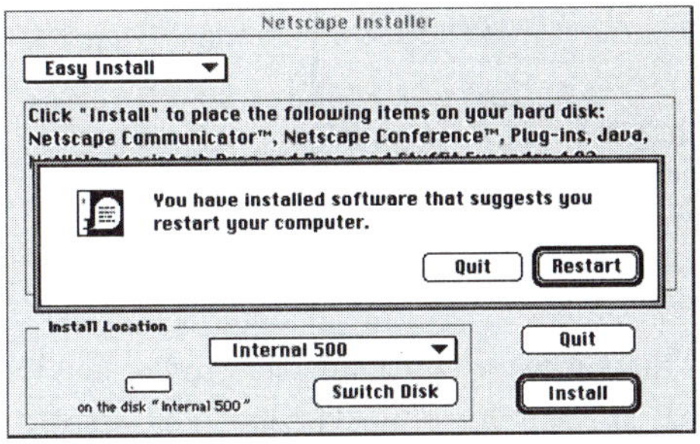

**FIG. D.5**
The Installer will inform you that the installation is completed.

N O T E   You need to restart your computer before starting Netscape Communicator for the first time because the Installer copies some files to your System Folder as well as the designated Netscape Communicator folder, and the files copied to the System Folder only run when your Mac is first started. Select **Restart** to restart your computer. If for some reason you do not want to restart your computer now, select **Quit**. Just remember to restart your Mac before you attempt to run Netscape Communicator for the first time.

## Creating Your First User Profile

A new feature in Netscape Communicator is the capability to create multiple user profiles. A user profile contains configuration information, bookmarks, and e-mail messages for individual users. If you share your computer with others who will be also using Netscape Communicator, you can now create separate user profiles for each person, and each person can configure Netscape Communicator according to his or her own preferences.

> **CAUTION**
> Netscape Communicator does not provide any degree of security around user profiles. This means that there is nothing to prevent one user from viewing or using another user's profile or the information, such as e-mail messages, contained in a user profile.

When you use Netscape Communicator for the first time, you will need to create at least one user profile. Here's how to create your first user profile:

1. From inside the Netscape Communicator Folder, double-click the Netscape Communicator icon to start the program. In a few seconds the user profile utility opening screen appears (see Figure D.6).

**FIG. D.6**
The opening screen of the user profile utility. The User Profile Manager first explains its purpose and why you need to create profiles.

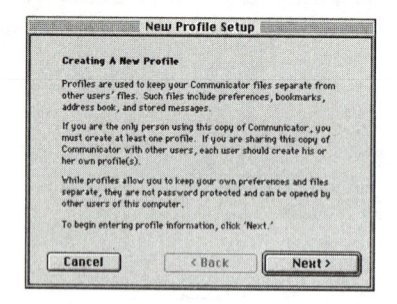

2. This screen explains the purpose of creating user profiles and what information and settings are controlled by the profiles. Select **Next** to advance to the first user input screen (see Figure D.7), where you will enter your name and e-mail address. Select **Next** to advance to the next screen.

**FIG. D.7**
On the first user input screen, enter your name and e-mail address.

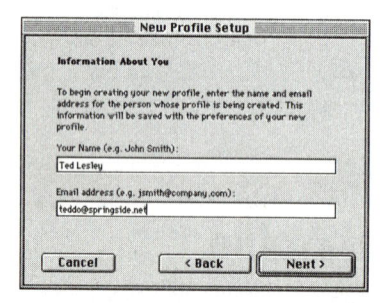

3. At the next screen you can change the directory where your profile will be stored (see Figure D.8).

**NOTE** The only really good reason to change the folder where Netscape will store your profile is to create a profile on removable storage (like a jaz or zip disk) that you can take with you. For example, if I create a profile on a removable cartridge, I can take that profile with me to home, school and work and keep my Communicator environment consistent.

4. Select **Finish** to save your profile.

**FIG. D.8**
You can change the folder where your profile will be stored on your Mac.

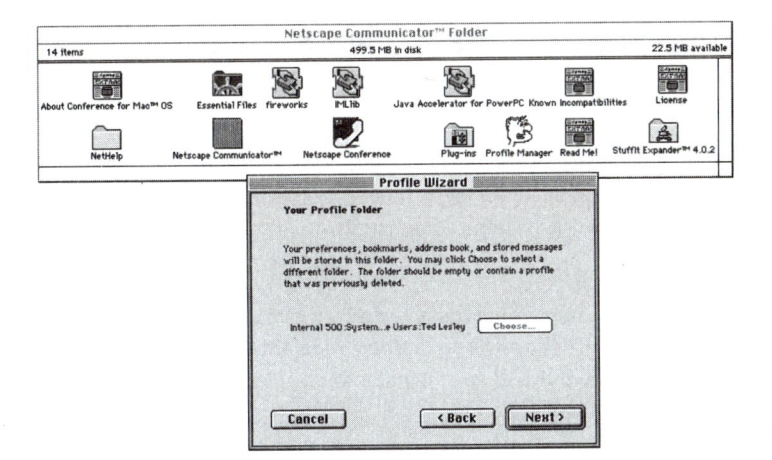

## Testing Netscape with Your New User Profile

Now that you've successfully installed Netscape Communicator and created your first user profile, you can now start using Netscape Communicator for the first time to test it. The major application in the Netscape Communicator suite is Netscape Navigator, your Web browser. So we will start with Netscape Navigator first. After you create your first user profile, Netscape Navigator should start automatically.

> **NOTE** Netscape will continue to produce Communicator versions and components beyond the present 4.0. To keep you updated, Netscape offers a SmartUpdate feature allowing you to tune your present version of Communicator in less time than it would take to completely reinstall a newer program.
>
> In Navigator, click the Software Update command under the Help menu. You will see the SmartUpdate Web page where Netscape will tell you what version you are presently using and, if applicable, what version you could be running. If you need to update, simply click Begin SmartUpdate and the program will automatically begin downloading and installing the new components.

## Configuring Netscape

The final step in installing Netscape Communicator is tending to a few configuration settings. In previous versions of Netscape there was a host of configuration screens and settings to deal with. In Netscape Communicator, many of those user settings have been configured for you to the most commonly used default settings. What remain are just a few simple settings dealing mainly with mail and discussion (newsgroup) settings.

## Configuring Mail and Discussion Settings

Before you can use the Messenger application in Netscape Communicator to send and receive e-mail messages, or use Netscape Collabra to read and post messages to a newsgroup, you need to set a few configuration parameters.

Before you begin, make sure you have gotten the following information from your service provider or network systems administrator:

- Your e-mail user name and e-mail address
- The name of your incoming e-mail server or post office, the type of incoming mail server, either POP3 (Post Office Protocol 3) or IMAP (Internet Message Access Protocol) server, and if IMAP, your mail directory location
- The name of your outgoing e-mail server, also referred to as your SMTP (Simple Mail Transfer Protocol) server
- Whether your service provider or network administrator requires you to remove from the mail server e-mail messages that you have read
- Whether your mail server supports encrypted passwords
- The name of your discussion (news) server

With your mail and discussion configuration information in hand, you're now ready to begin configuring Netscape Communicator.

1. If Netscape Navigator is not still up and running from when you earlier started the Web browser, restart Netscape Navigator by selecting the Netscape Navigator icon.

2. In Netscape Navigator choose **Edit, Preferences, Mail & Groups** to open the Preferences dialog box. Click the triangle in front of Mail & Groups to open the folder (see Figure D.9).

**FIG. D.9**
You make your mail and discussion configuration settings in the Mail & Groups section of the Preferences dialog box.

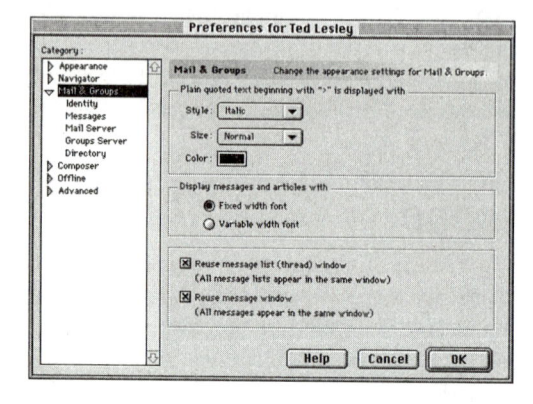

3. Select **Identity** to open the Identity section (see Figure D.10).

**FIG. D.10**
You enter information about yourself in the Identity section.

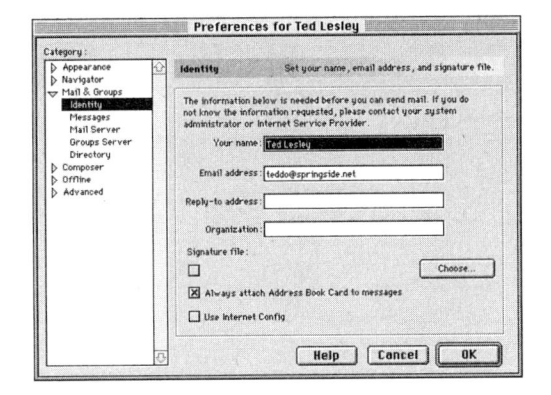

4. In the textbox labeled Your name, enter **your name** as you want it to appear on your e-mail messages addressed to others. In my case I entered **Ted Lesley**.
5. In the textbox labeled E-mail address, enter your e-mail address. This is the address others will use to send you e-mail. In my case I entered **teddo@springside.net**.
6. In the textbox labeled Reply to address (only needed if different from e-mail address), enter a **Reply-to address** if you want users to respond to your e-mail messages by sending their replies to an address different than your previously entered e-mail address. In my case, I left this textbox blank because I want all of my e-mail messages to be sent to my e-mail address.
7. In the textbox labeled Organization, you can (optionally) enter the **name of your company** if you are using your company's e-mail system.
8. You may select a **Signature file** to specify a file to be appended to the end of your e-mail messages. Signature files are often used to convey short witty sayings, or make personal or philosophical comments. If you have a signature file that you want to use, choose the folder and name of your signature file. If you're not sure what a signature file is, leave the checkbox unchecked. After you've started receiving e-mail, sooner or later you will receive a message with a signature file tacked on.
9. If you also want to attach your Personal Address Book card to your outgoing e-mail messages, select the checkbox Always attach Personal Address Book Card to outgoing messages. If you want to edit your personal Address Book Card, select **Edit Card** to open your personal address book.

**NOTE** Your personal address book is the address book of names and e-mail addresses of people you correspond with. Netscape will include an entry for you as you enter your e-mail configuration information. Besides entries for name and e-mail address, you can also enter normal contact information (e.g., company, phone numbers, address, etc.).

Now select Messages to open the **Messages** section (see Figure D.11).

**FIG. D.11**
You specify in the Messages section how you want Messenger to handle your messages.

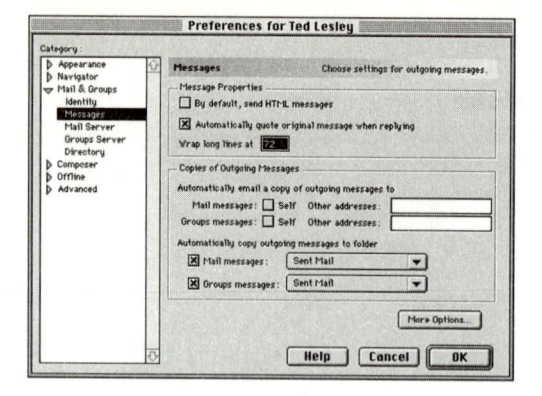

1. In the Message properties section, check the box if you want to send HTML messages by default, or otherwise your messages will be sent as plain text. Because most other e-mail programs do not display HTML, you should leave this choice blank for now.
2. Check the box if you want to quote the original message when you are replying to a message. When you quote the original message, it makes it easier for the person receiving the reply to remember what the original message was about.

> **CAUTION**
>
> Quoting the entire message can create long chains of mail that become more of a nuisance than a communication. A better strategy is to only quote the pertinent parts of the message. Your recipients will prefer this and pay more attention to the purpose of your communiqué.

3. If you want or need to keep copies of your outgoing e-mail messages, decide in the next section whether you want your copies sent to yourself or to someone else. If you are the only one who needs a copy of your outgoing messages, you may just want to copy the message copies to a folder rather than e-mail them to yourself.
4. Select the **More Options** button to display the More Messages Preferences dialog box (see Figure D.12).

**FIG. D.12**
The More Messages Preferences dialog box allows you to specify additional parameters for sending messages.

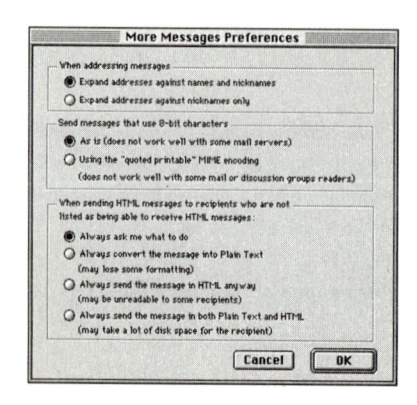

http://www.quecorp.com

5. In the first section, leave the default setting to expand addresses against names and nicknames, because this will allow you to enter both regular names and nicknames in your address book.

6. In the middle section on how to send 8-bit character messages, again leave the default value. If you need to change this setting because someone can't read a message from you, that person will usually let you know and you can return to this dialog box and change this setting.

7. And in the final section, if on the previous screen you selected to send HTML Messages by default, then you will need to decide how you want to handle an HTML message you create to someone who can't read HTML messages. The default value of Always ask me what to do is probably the safest choice.

8. Click **OK** to save your settings and close the More Messages Preferences dialog box.

Now select **Mail Server** to enter information about your mail server and how you want it to handle your mail messages (see Figure D.13).

**FIG. D.13**
The Mail Server preferences section is where you enter information about your mail servers.

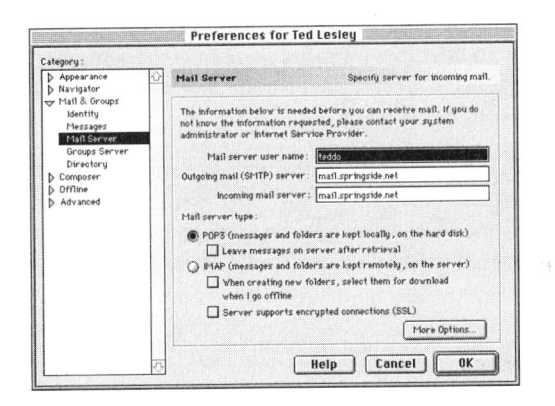

1. Enter or change your mail server user name. This is also referred to as your account name.

2. In the textbox labeled **Outgoing (SMTP) mail server**, enter the name of the outgoing (SMTP) mail server you got from your service provider or network systems administrator. In my case I entered **mail.springside.net**.

3. In the textbox labeled **Incoming mail server**, enter the name of the incoming mail server you got from your service provider or network systems administrator. In my case the name of my outgoing and incoming mail server are the same, so once again I entered **mail.springside.net**.

4. In the section labeled **Mail server type**, select the option button which corresponds to the type of incoming mail server your service provider or network systems administrator has implemented, either **POP3** or **IMAP**. Also select where your messages will be stored after you have read them. Message storage location may depend on the policies of your service provider or network systems administrator.

5. Select **More** to display the More Mail Server Preferences dialog box (see Figure D.14).

**FIG. D.14**
The More Mail Server Preferences dialog box has additional mail server preferences.

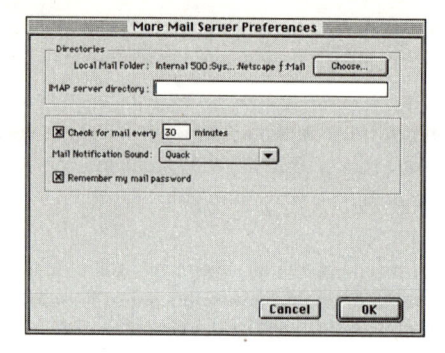

6. In the textbox labeled **Local mail folder**, do not change this directory entry unless you have a very good reason for changing it. This entry was set by the user profile utility.

7. In the textbox labeled **IMAP server directory**, enter the information provided by your service provider or network systems administrator.

8. If you want Netscape messenger to automatically check your mailbox for new mail, select **Check for mail every [ ] minutes**, and enter a number for the number of minutes between checks. If you want Netscape Messenger to check your mailbox every 30 minutes, enter **30** in the blank.

9. If you'd like to hear a particular sound when your mail arrives, choose the sound from the Mail Notification Sound pop-up.

10. If you want Netscape Messenger to remember your mail server logon password, select **Remember my mail password**. Remember, though, that if you share your computer, Netscape does not provide any security for user profiles. If you have Netscape Messenger remember your mail password, it is possible for another user to access your e-mail.

11. Click **OK** to save your settings and close the More Mail Server Preferences dialog box.

If you also plan to access newsgroups Using Netscape Collabra, you will need to enter information in the **Groups Server** section on your service provider's discussions (news) server (see Figure D.15).

**FIG. D.15**
The Groups Server section on the Preferences dialog box where you enter information on your discussion (news) server.

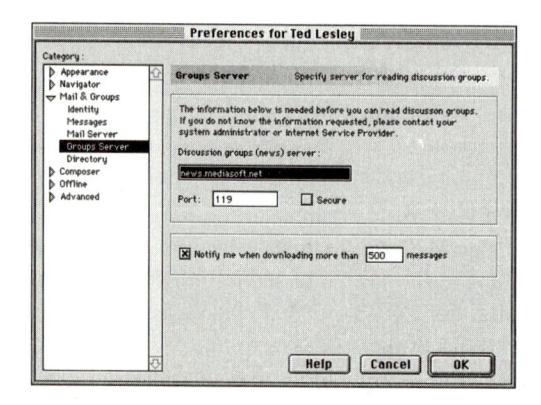

1. In the textbox labeled **Discussion groups**, enter the name of your service provider's discussions (news) server. In my case I entered **news.mediasoft.net**.
2. In the textbox labeled **Discussion group (news) folder**, do not change this unless you have a very good reason for changing it. This entry was set by the user profile utility.
3. For now leave the setting to have Netscape Communicator notify you when downloading more than 500 messages. This is a warning Netscape Communicator will provide whenever you attempt to access a large newsgroup because accessing large newsgroups can be time-consuming, especially if you have a slow dial-up Internet connection.
4. Click **OK** to save your configuration settings and close the Preferences dialog box.

Now return to the preferences dialog box and select Directory from the Main & Groups list to enter information about the e-mail search directories you will be using (see Figure D.16).

**FIG. D.16**
The final section of the Mail & Groups preferences enables you to control the order of the directory search engines used in Messenger.

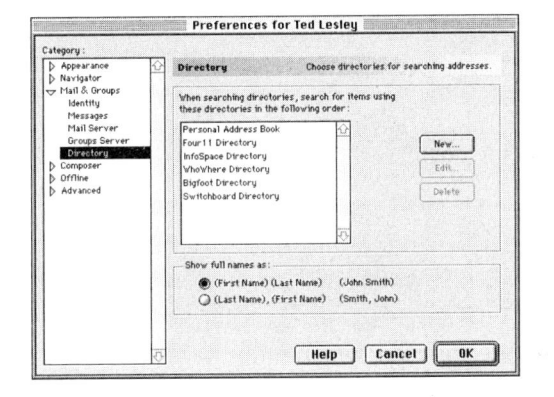

1. Unless you are already very familiar with the directory search engines listed here, you should probably not rearrange the order.
2. You can also specify the order in which names are listed in your address book: last name first or first name first.
3. Select **OK** to save your Preference settings and close the dialog box.

These are all of the mail and discussion configuration settings you need to make for now. As you become more familiar with Netscape Communicator you may decide to make additional changes, but for now these are the only configuration settings you are required to make to use Netscape Communicator to send mail and access newsgroups. ●

APPENDIX E

# Installing Communicator for UNIX

*by Allen Hutchison*

**N**etscape Communicator on a UNIX system is fundamentally the same as it is on a Windows or Macintosh system.

One of the major differences between the different versions of Communicator lies in how the application is installed. While both the Windows and Mac versions of Communicator have GUI install tools, the UNIX version is text-based. ■

- **Hardware requirements**
  Learn what the minimum computer hardware requirements are for installing Netscape Communicator to operate under UNIX.

- **Installation decisions**
  Learn how to install Netscape Communicator and what decisions you have to make if you are new to using Netscape, new to the Internet, and this is your first Web browser installation.

- **Upgrading to Netscape Communicator**
  Learn how to install Netscape Communicator over a previous Netscape installation and how to preserve and carry over your previous settings and options.

## Hardware Requirements

You must have a graphics workstation to install and use Netscape Communicator. You must have a desktop UNIX workstation such as a PC running Linux, an IBM RS/6000, or a Sun Workstation, to name a few. Not to belabor the obvious, but an ASCII terminal will not work. If you aren't sure whether your workstation can run Netscape, ask your local system administrator.

> **NOTE** If you are connected to the UNIX system from a Windows PC using X Terminal emulation software such as Reflection X or Hummingbird Exceed, it is best if you use the Windows version of Netscape. The PC version of Communicator takes better advantage of your PC hardware and you will have more plug-ins and helper applications available to you.

The current downloadable copies of Netscape for UNIX are compressed using a program named gzip. This program might not be present on your UNIX system. You can find a copy of the gunzip program at the URL **ftp://ftp.netscape.com/pub/**. (The same directory applies if you are getting the software with manual FTP). As with Netscape itself, get the version for your particular system.

> **NOTE** Your UNIX system must be connected to the Internet. It is beyond the scope of this chapter to cover the details of making this connection. Your system administrator has the details you need to reach the outside world, especially if there is a firewall of some kind protecting your local network from the barbarians outside the gates.

## Obtaining the Netscape Binaries

Some UNIX vendors include Netscape with their operating system installation media, most notably recent releases of AIX for the IBM RS/6000 and Caldera Linux. While what is provided is not likely to be the latest release of Netscape Communicator, it does provide a starting point for getting onto the Internet where you can purchase or download the latest version of the software. Again, check with your system administrator. You might have another World Wide Web browser installed on your system, such as NCSA Mosaic. If not, do not lose hope. Most UNIX systems have all of the utilities you need to acquire Netscape.

> **CAUTION**
> Before you can begin the acquisition and installation of Netscape, make sure that you have enough free disk space to work with. Depending on your system type, this could be as much as 25M or more. You need to create a directory to hold the installation file and the temporary files that will be produced during installation.

Figure E.1 shows the terminal window as it appears after you have entered the `ftp` command from the UNIX shell prompt and logged into Netscape's anonymous FTP server.

http://www.quecorp.com

## Obtaining the Netscape Binaries | 743

**FIG. E.1**
The password should be your complete Internet electronic mailing address, like flintsone@bedrock.com or rubble@stoneage.edu.

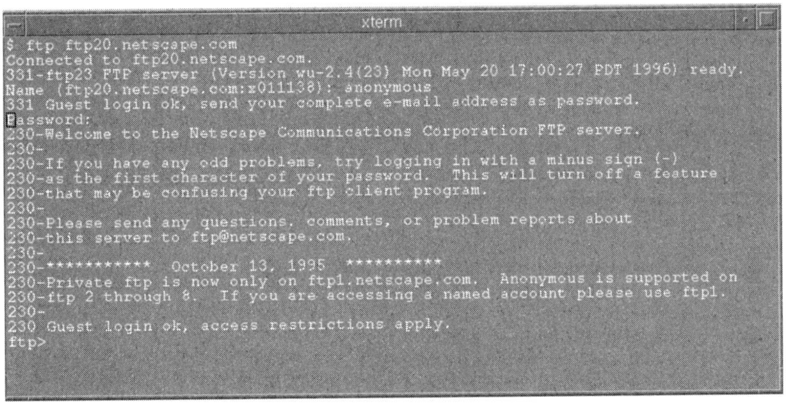

Figure E.2 shows the actual download from the Netscape FTP server. You need to cd (change directory) to the directory containing the version of Netscape Communicator you want, which, by the time you read this, might be a different version than what is shown in the figure. The file names can be quite long, so you might want to use a copy and paste operation with your mouse instead of actually typing the file name. And note that the command binary has been issued explicitly. While many systems automatically adjust to the data, it isn't universal so it's better to be safe than sorry. After the download is complete, you just type **bye** to exit from the FTP program.

**FIG. E.2**
An example of the FTP download process from Netscape's site.

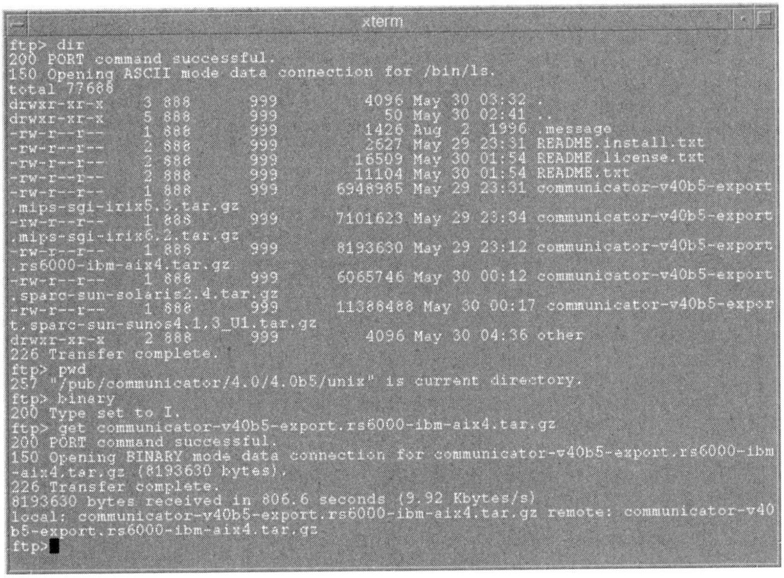

# Downloading Communicator Using Netscape Navigator

If you have an older version of Netscape already running on your system or some other World Wide Web browser, you can use it to get the newest release of Netscape Communicator. Start up your browser, then type in the URL **ftp://ftp.netscape.com/pub/**. This takes you to the top of the tree under which the various versions of Netscape for different machines and operating systems are found. The one you want will be there somewhere.

The file names are too long to be displayed completely in the main window, so watch the status line as you move the mouse pointer down the list to see the full names and click the one for your system. Figure E.3 shows what a typical screen looks like with Netscape Navigator version 3, and Figure E.4 is the Netscape progress indicator showing that the file transfer is being performed.

**FIG. E.3**
This is what you will see if you are using a Web browser to ftp the Communicator binaries.

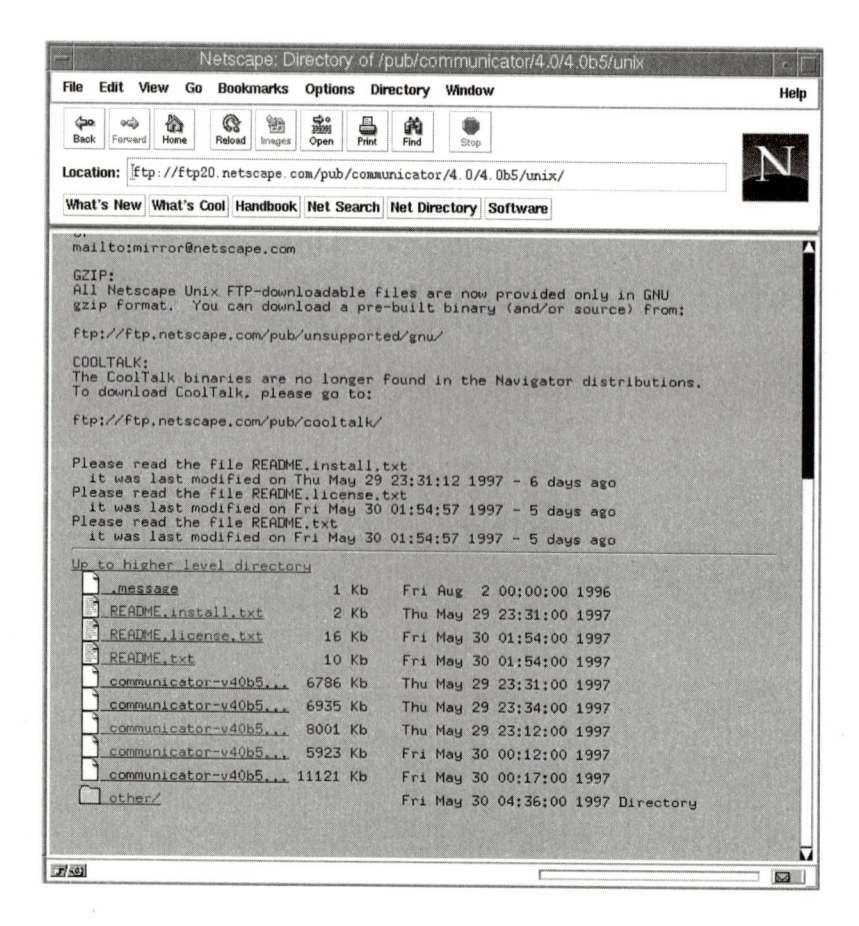

**FIG. E.4**
Here is an example of the status bar you will see when downloading with Navigator.

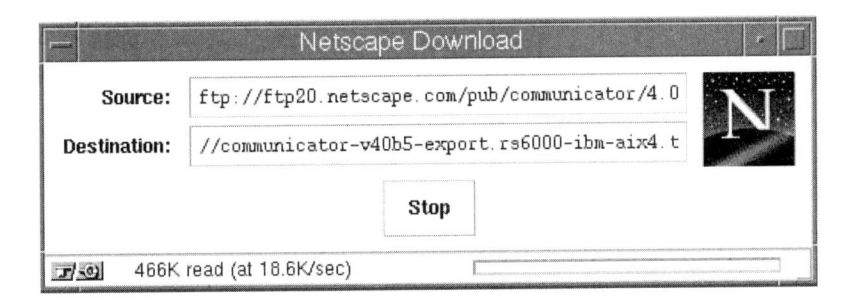

You can also locate the file you want from Netscape's home page at **http://home.netscape.com** (or click the big N in the upper-right corner of the Netscape window). This gives you a series of menus and selection boxes that let you specify your operating system, language (such as English or French), and continent. Besides being able to download the evaluation version of Netscape, you have the option of using a credit card to purchase the official version containing additional features.

# Installing Netscape from an Archive File

Once you have obtained the Communicator binaries, either by downloading them or getting them from a CD, you will need to install the program.

Use the following steps to install Netscape from the archive file you downloaded from Netscape's FTP or Web site:

1. Create a temporary directory to hold the files that you will be downloading by using the mkdir command. For example:

   ```
   $ mkdir temp
   ```

2. Make the new directory your current directory by using the cd command:

   ```
   $ cd temp
   ```

3. Use gunzip to uncompress the file you have downloaded:

   ```
   $ gunzip -v communicator-v40-export.rs6000-ibm-aix4.tar.gz
   ```

4. Unpack the installation files with the following:

   ```
   $ tar xvf communicator-v40-export.rs6000-ibm-aix4.tar
   x README.install, 2627 bytes, 6 media blocks.
   x ns-install, 9024 bytes, 18 media blocks.
   x vreg, 26538 bytes, 52 media blocks.
   x ifc11.jar, 1017192 bytes, 1987 media blocks.
   x iiop10.jar, 460452 bytes, 900 media blocks.
   x jae40.jar, 481711 bytes, 941 media blocks.
   x java40.jar, 2266654 bytes, 4428 media blocks.
   x jio40.jar, 802334 bytes, 1568 media blocks.
   x jsd10.jar, 31447 bytes, 62 media blocks.
   x policyMoz40P1.jar, 4327 bytes, 9 media blocks.
   x nethelp-v40.nif, 281996 bytes, 551 media blocks.
   x netscape-v40.nif, 5981281 bytes, 11683 media blocks.
   ```

Now you have a directory containing the software you want to install. The next step is to run the install program. Most likely, you want to install Communicator in a public directory for the enjoyment of everyone who uses the computer.

# Installing Netscape from a CD-ROM

If you have purchased a copy of Netscape Communicator on a CD-ROM, you need to extract the installation files into a temporary directory on your hard disk. To do this, you must mount the CD-ROM onto a directory on your system. On most UNIX systems, this must be performed by the system administrator. The device name of the CD-ROM drive varies with each version of UNIX and type of hardware connection involved. Your system administrator knows the names of the devices on his systems.

> **NOTE** Netscape will continue to produce Communicator versions and components beyond the present 4.0. To keep you updated, Netscape offers a SmartUpdate feature allowing you to tune your present version of Communicator in less time than it would take to completely reinstall a newer program.
>
> In Navigator, click on the Software Update command under the Help menu. You will see the SmartUpdate web page where Netscape will tell you what version you are presentlky using and, if applicable, what version you could be running. If you need to upadate, simply click Begin SmartUpdate and the program will automatically begin downloading and installing the new components ■

After the CD-ROM is mounted, you will find a directory tree organized by operating system type. Rather than produce a separate CD-ROM for each version of UNIX, Netscape Communications produces a single CD that contains the software for a variety of hardware platforms and their versions of UNIX. Look at the directory of the CD-ROM for a subdirectory that matches your system. Then extract the version you need into your temporary directory. This process will look just like it does when you download the software from the Internet. See Listing E.1 for an example.

**Listing E.1   Example of Temp File**

```
$ cd /tmp/netscape
$ tar xvf /cdrom/aix4/netscape.tar
x README.install, 2627 bytes, 6 media blocks.
x ns-install, 9024 bytes, 18 media blocks.
x vreg, 26538 bytes, 52 media blocks.
x ifc11.jar, 1017192 bytes, 1987 media blocks.
x iiop10.jar, 460452 bytes, 900 media blocks.
x jae40.jar, 481711 bytes, 941 media blocks.
x java40.jar, 2266654 bytes, 4428 media blocks.
x jio40.jar, 802334 bytes, 1568 media blocks.
x jsd10.jar, 31447 bytes, 62 media blocks.
x policyMoz40P1.jar, 4327 bytes, 9 media blocks.
x nethelp-v40.nif, 281996 bytes, 551 media blocks.
x netscape-v40.nif, 5981281 bytes, 11683 media blocks.
```

And now, whether the software was downloaded or extracted from a CD-ROM, you're ready for the final installation steps. Note that, in the working directory containing the installation files, there is some sort of README file, probably named README.install. Read this file; some of the final installation steps might have changed, and this file has the latest word.

In Listing E.2, the instruction is basically to execute a shell script that has been provided called ns-install. The script asks a few questions, suggesting the answers which you are able to override with your own preferences.

**Listing E.2  ns-install**

```
$ ./ns-install
==================================================================
         NETSCAPE Platform-Independent Software Installation
                    For Communicator release 40
            Copyright (c) 1997 by Netscape Communications Corp.
==================================================================
Please specify the directory path under which the software will be
installed.  The default directory is /usr/local/netscape.
Location for Communicator software [/usr/local/netscape]:
Installing Communicator files...
Installing Communicator Java files...
Installing Communicator Help files...
Registering Communicator 40...
The Netscape Communicator software installation is complete.
$
```

After this is finished, Netscape is ready to run as-is on most systems. You might want to change the PATH assignment in your login profile to include the directory containing the Netscape programs. Depending on your login shell, this might be as simple as adding a line containing the following to your .profile:

PATH=$PATH:/usr/local/netscape

For best results, exit your current X Window session and start it again to take advantage of the changes made. Then, just type **netscape** from a terminal window.

> **NOTE**  The first time you run Netscape on your workstation, you see some extra windows with the title Netscape: Error. These windows are informational and shouldn't cause alarm.

> **CAUTION**
> If you are running this version of Communicator over a previous version, don't worry. Netscape has made sure that all of your old settings are taken care of. Old versions of Netscape Navigator stored user information in a directory called .netscape in the user's home directory. The new versions of Communicator use the same directory.

# Index

## Symbols

! (exclamation point) denoting important definitions, style sheets, 570
(+) plus signs, subscribing to newsgroups, 75
- (dashes), style sheets, 606
/*, style sheet comments, 605
: (colons), style sheets, 603
; (semicolons)
   JavaScript, 656
   style sheets, 603
<!-, -> tags, HTML code comments, 463
@import url statement, style sheets, 562
{} (braces)
   JavaScript, 655
   style sheets, 603
16-bit version install for Windows 3.1, 691
32-bit version of Communicator, 712
3270 terminals and IBM Host On-Demand, 392

## A

A (anchor) tags
   attributes
      HREF, 470
      NAME, 475
      links, 470
      onMouseOut attribute, 662
      onMouseOver attribute, 662
About Plug-ins command (Help menu), 634
about: location help feature, 142
ABOVE attribute, LAYER tags, 575, 586
ABSBOTTOM property, ALIGN attribute, 646
ABSMIDDLE property, ALIGN attribute, 646
absolute links, 470-471
absolute positioned elements, 566
access rights and privileges
   Calendar, 386
   Directory Server, 673
accounts for e-mail, mail server addresses, 55
ACTION attribute, FORM tags, 544
active links, color options, 455
ActiveX controls, ScriptActive plug-in, 197
Add Channel button, Netcaster, 407
adding
   columns to tables, 292
   graphics to Web pages, 284-286
   rows to tables, 292

Address Books, 231-235
   address cards, 331
      adding, 238-239
      changing, 235, 239
      creating, 235
      deleting, 235, 239-240
   Bcc: (blind carbon copy), 243
   Conference phone calls, 308
   directories, 240-242
   fields, displaying, 236
   Help menu commands, 234
   mailing lists, 241-242
   Netscape Conference calling, 243-244
   searches
      LDAP directories, 237-238
      names, 237
      nicknames, 237
   sending mail, 242-243
   sorting, 235-236
   toolbar, 234-235, 238
Address Book command (Communicator menu), 234
address lookups, Phonebook (Conference), 98
addresses
   FTP site uploads for Web pages, 90
   IP, Internet connections, 686
   mail servers, e-mail accounts, 55
   preferences for e-mail, 334
   search preferences, 337
   writing e-mail, 58
Adobe Acrobat Reader, PDF files viewing, 197

ADSL (Asymmetric Digital Subscriber Line), 681
advanced options for frames, 512-516
Advanced panel preferences, 111, 342-347
advanced searches for newsgroups, 254
Advanced/Cache panel, frequently visited site update settings, 127
Agenda, Calendar, 370-371
    adding entries, 377-380
    entering scheduling data, 371-373
    entry settings options, 375
    invitation responses, 381-382
    task entries, 383
    updating Host Agenda, 373
    updating offline Agenda, 373
AIFF files, LiveAudio playback, 188
ALIGN attribute
    APPLET tag, 646
    EMBED tag, 630
    IMG tag, 481
    OBJECT tag, 647-648
alignment options
    e-mail messages, 226
    tables, 291
    text, style sheets, 620
ALINK= keyword, BODY tags, 455
ALT attribute
    APPLET tags, 646
    IMG tags, 481
    OBJECT tags, 648
alternative text for non-graphical browsers, 284, 480-481
Amazon.com Web site, online shopping example, 171
amplification options, Conference microphone and speaker options, 309
anchor (A) tags, 470
anchors, named anchors as internal link references, 289
anonymous FTP, 139
API (Applications Programming Interface), 31
APPC (Advanced Program to Program Communication), 390
Appearance panel
    program launch options, 110, 320-324
    toolbar options, 320-324
Apple, see Macintosh
APPLET tags, 645
    alternative content, 646-647
    attributes, 646
    passing parameters, 646
applets, 642-644
    APPLET tag, 645-647
        alternative content, 646-647
        attributes, 646
        passing parameters, 646
    applications, compared, 642
    ButtonOnFly, 651
    bytecodes, 642
    fly-over buttons example, 650-651
    Java, 183-184
    JavaScript, 654
    JIT (Just in Time) compilation, 642
    Navigator Ticker example, 649-650
    OBJECT tag, 647-648
        alternative content, 648
        attributes, 647-648
        passing parameters, 648
    plug-ins, compared, 643
    security certification, 365, 643
    Virtual Library, 649
applications
    helper, 185
    Java applet comparisons, 642
    switching, 48-49
Applications panel, helper app options, 110
APPN (Advanced Peer to Peer Networking), 390
ARCHIVE attribute, APPLET tag, 646
archive files, installing UNIX version of Communicator, 745-746
AREA tags
    attributes, 533
    imagemaps, 532
articles in newsgroups, 246-248
    browsing, 256-266
    encoded, 262
    opening in separate window, 263
    posting articles, 266-269
    reading, 256-266
        offline, 269-271
    replies, 264-265
    saving, 263
        file attachments, 265-266
    signatures, 268
    threads, 262
    viewing options, 263
AS/400 IBM Host On-Demand, 391
asterisk (*) wild card, frame sizing, 506
attaching style sheets
    embedding, 601-602
    importing, 603
    inline (on-the-fly), 602
    linking, 600-601
attachment values for backgrounds, style sheets, 609
attachments
    e-mail
        files, 219-221
        graphics, 226-228
        Web pages, 220-221
    newsgroup articles
        saving, 265-266
        sending, 268
Attendant, Conference Internet phone calls, 310
attributes
    A tags, 475
    AREA tags, 533
    CLASS, 604-605
    EMBED tags, 630
    FORM tags
        ACTION, 544
        ENCTYPE, 545
        METHOD, 544
    FRAME tags
        FRAMEBORDER, 515
        NORESIZE, 510
        SCROLLING, 510
        SRC, 508
        TARGET, 511
    FRAMESET tags
        COLS, 504
        ROWS, 505
    IMG SRC tags, 526
    IMG tags, 479
        ALIGN options, 481
        ALT, 481
        BORDER, 483

HEIGHT, 482
HSPACE, 482-483
VSPACE, 482-483
WIDTH, 482
INPUT tags
    CHECKBOX, 550
    HIDDEN, 552
    PASSWORD, 549
    RADIO, 551
    RESET, 552
    SUBMIT, 553
    TEXT, 549
    TYPE, 549
LANGUAGE, SCRIPT tags, 658
LAYER tags, 575
    ABOVE, 586
    BACKGROUND, 580
    BELOW, 586
    BGCOLOR, 580
    HEIGHT, 578
    LEFT, 576, 583
    RIGHT, 576
    TOP, 576, 583
    VISIBILITY, 591
    WIDTH, 578
    Z-INDEX, 584
LiveAudio, 636-637
MAP tags, 532
OBJECT tags, 631-632, 647-648
OnChange, SELECT tags, 662
onMouseOut, A tags, 662
onMouseOver, A tags, 662
OPTION tags, 548
QuickTime plug-in, 638-639
SELECT tags, 547
STYLE, 602
TEXTAREA tags, 546

AU files, LiveAudio playback, 188

**audio**
    adding, 634-636
    alerts for e-mail, 331
    codecs, Conference options, 305
    LiveAudio, 634-636
    playback options, 188
    sound cards, configuring for Conference use, 97

AUDIO parameter, IBM Host On-Demand connection page, 401

auto-search feature, 137

AUTO_CONNECT parameter, IBM Host On-Demand connection page, 401

AUTOLOAD attribute, LiveAudio, 636

**automatic**
    address completion, 123
    image loading, turning off, 126
    page loading with Server Push and Client Pull, 165
    saving, 80
    update option, 343

**Automatically Load Images option, Advanced panel, 342**

**AUTOPLAY attribute, QuickTime plug-in, 638**

**autoscroll pages, 165**

**AUTOSTART attribute, LiveAudio, 636**

AVI files, LiveVideo playback, 190

# B

B tags, bold text, 445-446

**Back button**
    forms, 179
    Navigation toolbar, 29, 44

**back display option, Netcaster, 422**

**BACKGROUND attribute, LAYER tags, 575, 580**

**background images, loading into Whiteboard, 315-316**

**background-attachment property, style sheets, 607-609**

**background-color property, style sheets, 607**

**background-image property, style sheets, 607-608**

**background-position property, style sheets, 607-610**

**background-repeat property, style sheets, 607-609**

**backgrounds**
    layer options, 580-581
    style sheets, 607-610
        attachment values, 609
        coloring, 607
        images, 608
        positioning, 609-610
        repeat values, 608-609
    Web pages, 286

**bandwidth, user considerations, 638**

base installation, Windows 3.1 Communicator, 691

BASELINE property, ALIGN attribute, 646

baseline value, vertical-align paragraph property for style sheets, 626

BCC (blind carbon copying), e-mail messages, 62, 243

BELOW attribute, LAYER tags, 575, 586

BGCOLOR attribute, LAYER tags, 575, 580

BIG tags, 450

binaries, Netscape UNIX versions, 742

Blank Page startup option, 325

blind carbon copy (Bcc:), 243

BLINK tags, 448

blink value, text-decoration property for style sheets, 624-625

BLOCKQUOTE tags, 450, 566

blue headings examples, 564

BODY BGCOLOR=> tag, 454

body section of HTML documents, 437

BODY tags, 437, 464
    ALINK= keyword, 455
    LINK= keyword, 454
    TEXT= keyword, 454
    VLINK= keyword, 455

bold e-mail messages, 222

bold text, 445

Bongo (Marimba), Castanet channels creation, 428

Bookmark button, Personal toolbar, 157-159

bookmark folders
    designating folders as such, 158
    Edit Bookmarks window, 153
    organizing, 154

Bookmark QuickFile button, Location toolbar, 146

bookmark.htm file, 151

bookmarks, 45, 145-147
    adding, 154-155
    deleting, 154-155
    Description field options, 156-157
    drag-and-drop method, 147-149

duplicates, 159
editing, 154-155
Find function, 156-157
History List, 149
lists
   item separators, 153
   merging, 160
   multiple, 160-161
organizing, 151-155
selecting multiple, 155
sorting, 156
tricks and tips, 158-160
troubleshooting missing, 147
updating, 161
view options, 156

**Bookmarks command, 234**

**Bookmarks Quickfile button (Location toolbar), 45**

**BORDER attribute**
EMBED tags, 630
IMG tags, 483
OBJECT tags, 631, 648

**borderless frames, 515-516**

**borderless tables, formatting HTML documents, 291**

**borders, style sheets, 610-611**
coloring, 614
grouping, 612
sizing, 613-614
troubleshooting, 615
values, 614

**bottom keyword, background-position property for style sheets, 610**

**BOTTOM property, ALIGN attribute, 646**

**bottom value, vertical-align paragraph property for style sheets, 626**

**box properties, style sheets**
borders, 610
margins, 610
padding, 610-612, 616
sizing, 611-613

**bps (bits per second), 680**

**BR tags, 280, 283, 442-443**

**braces ({})**
JavaScript, 655
style sheets, 603

**brainstorming sessions with Whiteboard, 104**

**browsers**
HotJava, 642
JavaScript, executing functions, 657
style sheets
   non-supporting, 606
   *see also* style sheets
text-only, alternative text, 284
*see also* Web browsers

**BrowserWatch Web site, 639**

**browsing**
newsgroup articles, 256-266
   discussion folder options, 262-263
collaboratively, 103-104, 313
offline, 429

**Business Cards, Conference, 98, 306**

**business discussion on the Internet via Conference, 96**

**ButtonOnFly**
class, 650
Java applet listing, 651
Web site, 650

**By City command (View menu), 233**

**By Company command (View menu), 233**

**By E-mail Address command (View menu), 233**

**By Name command (View menu), 233**

**By Nickname command (View menu), 233**

**By Type command (View menu), 233**

**bytecodes, Java, 642**

# C

**c32e40.exe file, 712**

**CABBASE parameter, IBM Host On-Demand connection page, 401**

**cable modems, 681**

**cache**
Netcaster options, 415
update options for frequently visited sites, 127

**Cache panel, 343-344**

**Cache subpanel, page caching options, 111**

**Calendar, 369**
Agendas, 370-371
   adding entries, 377-380
   entering scheduling data, 371-373
   entry settings options, 375
   In-Tray view, 370
   updating Host Agenda, 373
   updating offline Agenda, 373
configuring, 374-376
Daily Note function, 384-385
In-Tray, 385-386
invitation responses, 381-382
notification settings, 374
online mode, 371
reminders for activities, 379
resource scheduling options, 371
starting, 370-371
task entries, 383
task list, 383
toolbar, 376-377
user access rights, 386

**Calendar Server, 669, 674**

**Call command (File menu), 233**

**calling, Netscape Conference Address Book, 243-244**

**Canvas Size options, White Board, 317**

**capitalization**
text-transform, style sheets, 624-625
variant property, style sheets, 623

**capturing screen shots for Whiteboard, 317**

**Card Properties command (Edit menu), 233**

**cards, address, 235-236**

**cascading style sheets, 562-565, 600**
hiding tags from non-capable browsers, 564
overriding, 605

**Cascading Style Sheets Level 1,** *see* style sheets

**Castanet cookies and logging options, Netcaster, 420**

**Catalog Server, 669, 672**

**CC (carbon copying) e-mail messages, 61**

cell options in tables, 295
center keyword, background-position property for style sheets, 610-612
CENTER property, ALIGN attribute, 646
CENTER tags, 449
centering text, 449
Certificate Authorities, 359-361
Certificate Server, 669, 675
certificates for security, 356-362
CGI (Common Gateway Interface) scripts, 538-539
   Content MIME types, 541
   dynamic, 542
   examples, 541-543
   forms integration examples, 553-556
   input processing example program, 553-554
   public domain references, 558
   requirements for using, 540
   troubleshooting, 542
   URLs, 540
CGI programs, server-side imagemaps, 522
cgi-bin directory, 540
Channel Finder
   More Channels option, 413
   Netcaster, 407, 412-416
Channel Finder Web site, 413
channels, Netcaster, 36, 426-427
   adding to My Channels menu, 417
   Castanet, 428
   deleting, 418
   previewing, 407
   quitting, 409
   updating in Netcaster, 418
   viewing offline, 429
   *see also* Webtops
Channels panel, Netcaster properties, 418
characters
   character sets for font display, 120
   formatting, HTML documents, 278-280
   spacing properties, style sheets, 619
      letter-spacing, 619, 625
      line-height, 625

      line-spacing, 619
      white-space, 619, 625
      word-spacing, 619, 625
Chat Tool, 311-312
chatting via Text Chat, 102
check boxes, forms, 178
Check Spelling button, Composer toolbar, 275
CHECKBOX attribute, INPUT tags, 550
child layers, 587
CICS (Customer Information Control System), Communicator integration, 390
circle value, list-style-type property, 619
circular areas, imagemaps, 533
CLASS attribute, style sheets, 604-605
classes
   ButtonOnFly, 650
   defining styles, 604-605
   definitions using CSS syntax, 565
CLASSES property, STYLE tags, 565-566
CLASSID attribute, OBJECT tags, 631, 648
clear property, floating elements in style sheets, 618
ClearHelp() function, 598
clearing
   History List, 135
   Whiteboard
      graphics, 105
      screen, 315
Client Pull, 165
client-side imagemaps, 521-522
CLIP attribute, LAYER tags, 575
Close command (File menu), 233
Close the Webtop button, Netcaster, 422
closing mini browser windows, 113
CNET Web site, 605
CODE attribute, APPLET tags, 646

code example for HTML documents, 463-464
code for HTML documents
   editing, 278
   viewing, 276-278
CODEBASE attribute
   APPLET tag, 646
   OBJECT tag, 648
CODETYPE attribute, OBJECT tag, 648
Collaborative Browsing, 103, 313
collaborative Web browsing, 103-104
Collabra, 19-21
   browsing newsgroup articles, 262-263
   checking for new newsgroups, 254
   configuring
      Macintosh version, 738
      Windows 3.1 version, 703-710
      Windows 95 install, 725
   discussion folders, sorting options, 263
   Location toolbar, 73
   Message Center, 249-256
   multiple news servers, 255-256
   Navigation toolbar, 73
      Next button, 75-76
      Subscribe button, 74
   new features, 32-33
   newsgroup articles
      encoded, 262
      saving, 263
      signatures, 268
      viewing options, 263
   newsgroup searches, 253-254
   newsreading, 245
   Offline Work mode, 271
   posting articles to newsgroups, 266-269
   reading newsgroup articles, 256
      reading offline, 269-271
   setup, 72
   subscribing to newsgroups, 252-253
   unsubscribing from newsgroups, 253
   *see also* newsgroups
Collabra Discussions command (Communicator menu), 233

**Collabra Server, 669, 674**

**collapsing Messenger folders, 211**

**colons (:), style sheets, 603**

**Color Index Web site, 456**

**color options**
  active links, 455
  hexadecimal values, 455-456
  HTML-coded e-mail messages, 223
  links, 454
  text, 453-454
  visited links, 455

**color property, style sheets, 620-621**

**COLOR= keyword, FONT tags, 453**

**colors**
  backgrounds
    layers, 580
    style sheets, 607
  borders, style sheets, 611, 614
  link options, 287-288
  table options, 291

**Colors panel**
  screen display options, 121
  screen, text and link color options, 323-324
  text, link and background display options, 110

**COLS attribute**
  FRAMESET tags, 504
  TEXTAREA tags, 546

**columns**
  adding to tables, 292
  formatting, 293-296
  Message List, resizing, 200

**Comm... messages, IBM Host On-Demand OIA, 399-400**

**command-line options for Communicator, 132**

**commands**
  Communicator menu (Address Book), 233-234
  Edit menu
    Find in Page, 125
    Preferences, 72, 80
    Select All, 125
  Edit menu (Address Book), 233
  Edit menu (Composer), 84
  Edit menu (Navigator), 41
  File menu (Address Book), 232-233
  File menu (Composer), 88

  File menu (Navigator), 42
  Go menu, 44
  Help menu (Address Book), 234, 634
  Insert menu (Composer), 85
  View menu, 126-128
  View menu (Address Book), 233

**commenting**
  HTML, hiding scripts, 659
  style sheets, 605-606
  Web page code, 463

**Communicator**
  command-line options, 132
  configuring
    Macintosh version, 733-739
    Windows 95 e-mail options, 720-726
  Dynamic Fonts feature, 323
  FTP smart resume, 139
  hotkeys for starting other components, 119
  IBM Host On-Demand, 389
  installing
    Macintosh verison, 727
    UNIX systems, 741
    UNIX version from archive files, 745-746
    Windows 95 version, 713-716
  Message Composition window, 58
  Navigator integration with other tools, 117-120
  new features, 28
    Collabra, 32-33
    Component bar, 28-29
    Composer, 33-34
    Conference, 34-35
    HTML, 31
    Java, 32
    Location toolbar, 30
    Messenger, 32-33
    Navigation toolbar, 29
    Netcaster, 35-37
    OLE application integration, 32
    plug-ins, 31
    Preferences dialog box, 37
    Security Advisor window, 37
    toolbars, 29
  OLE integration, 198
  plug-ins, 186-194
  Preferences dialog box options settings, 110
  Preferences options, 319
  starting Netcaster, 418
  user profiles

  Macintosh install, 731-732
  Windows 95 install, 716-719
  Windows 3.1 version
    configuring, 703-710
    installing, 689, 691
    testing user profiles, 702
    user profiles, 698-702
  Windows 95 version
    install, 712
    user profiles, 719

**Communicator menu commands (Address Book)**
  Address Book, 234
  Bookmarks, 234
  Collabra Discussions, 233
  Conference, 96, 234
  History, 234
  Java Console, 234
  Message Center, 234
  Messenger Mailbox, 233
  Navigator, 233
  Page Composer, 234
  Security Info, 234
  Show Component Bar, 234

**companies and intranets, 15-17**

**company page startup option, 325**

**compilers, 656**

**complete installation, Windows 3.1 Communicator, 691**

**Component bar, 28-29**
  display options, 122
  Navigator window, 113
  status bar, 136
  switching applications, 49

**component elements of URLs, 469**

**Composer, 21-22**
  Composition toolbar, 81
  configuring for publishing Web pages, 90
  cutting and pasting, 125
  Formatting toolbar, 81
  HTML documents
    adding graphics, 284-286
    character formatting, 278
    editing, 278
    headings, 282
    indenting text, 281
    links, 287-290
    lists, 282
    paragraph formatting, 280-284
    preformatting text, 283
    previewing, 275-276

tables, 290-296
text alignment, 281
white space, 283
word searches, 274
new features, 33-34
plug-ins, 296-299
preferences panel, 338-339
setup, 80-81
spelling checker, 274-275
toolbar, 275

**composing e-mail messages, 58-63**

**Composition dialog box, 241**

**Composition toolbar, 81**
Find button, HTML document word searches, 274
Insert/Make Link, 87
Inserting Image, 85
Save button, 88

**compressing folders to remove files from system, Messenger, 216**

compression
File Exchange, 313
JPEG files, 478

**Conference, 22, 34-35, 95, 235**
Address Book, 243-244
address lookups, 98
amplification options for microphone and speaker, 309
audio codec options, 305
Business Card information, 306
Business Cards, 98
Chat Tool, 311-312
Collaborative Browsing, 313
Collaborative Browsing button, 103
configuring, 303-307
Dial button, 101
Direct Address field, 308
Do Not Disturb mode, 101, 309
Echo Suppression field, 305
File Exchange button, 312-313
firewall options, 306
Hang Up button, 101
incoming phone calls, 310
making phone calls, 100-102, 307-310
microphone sound level output settings, 99
Silence Sensor, 100
Speed Dial button, 308
starting, 96-97
telephony software, 301
troubleshooting calls, 305
Voice Mail messages, 309
Whiteboard, 104-105, 314-317

**Conference command (Communicator menu), 96, 234**

**Conference Setup Wizard, 97-100**

**Conference toolbar, Text Chat button, 102**

**Configuration program, Media Player, 189**

configuring
Calendar, 374-376
Collabra
Macintosh version, 738
Windows 3.1 version, 703-710
Windows 95 install, 725
Communicator
e-mail options for Windows 95, 720-726
for Windows 3.1, 703-710
Macintosh version, 733-739
Composer, publishing Web pages, 90
Conference, 303-307
Dial-Up Networking, 683
mail servers, Messenger for Windows 3.1, 708
Messenger, 54-55, 199
Macintosh version, 734-739
Windows 3.1 version, 706-707
Windows 95 install, 722-725
multiuser environments, 350-352
TCP/IP network properties, 685-687

**conflicts in scheduling, checking with Calendar, 377**

**Connection icon, 687**

**connection speeds, Conference, 304**

connections
IBM Host On-Demand, 396-401
online access, 680-682
troubleshooting e-mail, 66

**console controls, LiveAudio plug-in, 188**

**containers,** *see* **tags**

**content varieties in Netcaster channels, 426**

**Contents button, NetHelp, 141**

**contextual selectors (HTML tags), 604**

**CONTROLLER attribute, QuickTime plug-in, 638**

controls, layers, 654

**CONTROLS attribute, LiveAudio, 636**

conversations on the Internet
Conference, 96
Text Chat, 102

cookies
disabling, 175
Netcaster options , 420
online shopping, 175
preference settings, 343

**CoolTalk, 34**

**COORDS attribute, AREA tags, 533**

copying
e-mail messages, 213-214
Navigator options, 125
outgoing e-mail, 334

**copyright laws, 633**

**Cosmo VRML viewer plug-in, 193**

**Cryptographic Modules, 365**

**CSS**
files, linking style sheets, 601
syntax
blue headings, 564
class definition, 565
overriding style sheet tags, 565

**Ctrl+5 hotkeys, starting Conference, 97**

**Ctrl+B keys, bold text, 280**

**Ctrl+I keys, italic text, 280**

**Ctrl+U keys, underline text, 280**

**cumulative text sizing, 453**

**Custom Install**
Macintosh Communicator install, 729
Windows 95 version, 713

customizing
Messenger, 199
toolbars, Appearance panel options, 320-324

cutting
Composer options, 125
text, 84

CyberDungeon Web site, frames example, 181-182

## D

Daily Note function, Calendar, 384-385

dashes (-), style sheets, 606

DATA attribute, OBJECT tag, 631

DEBUG parameter, IBM Host On-Demand, 398, 401

debugging CGI scripts, 542

decimal value, list-style-type property, 619

declarations, style sheets, 603

defaults
   links on imagemaps, 534-535
   settings, viewing Web pages, 120-123

defining classes using CSS syntax, 565

defining mapped areas for imagemaps, 529

definition definition, DL tags, 460

definition lists, 459-461

definition term, DL tags, 460

Delete command (Edit menu), 233

deleting
   Address Book address cards, 239-240
   Bookmark buttons from Personal toolbar, 157
   bookmarks, 154-155
   channels from Netcaster, 418
   e-mail messages, 214
   e-mail recipients, 63
   Messenger folders, 213
   text, 83
   Web page links, 287
   Whiteboard graphics, 105

Description field options, bookmarks, 156-157

design elements of Webtops, 423-425

designing
   imagemaps, 525
   Web pages with frames, 504

desktop shortcut icon, launching applications automatically, 132

destination directories, Communicator install for Windows 3.1, 692

destination directory, Windows 95 Communicator install, 714

DevEdge Web site, 669

Dial button, Conference, 101

Dial-Up Adapter, PPP Internet connections, 684

dial-up Internet connection, 681

Dial-Up Networking, configuring, 683

dialog boxes
   Composition, 241
   Image Properties, 85
   New Card, 238
   Preferences, 41, 80
   Select Addresses, 243
   Subscribe to Discussion Groups, 74

digital certificates
   user certificates, 357
   Web Sites' Certificates, 359

Direct Address field, Conference, 308

directories
   Address Book
      address cards, 240-242
      searching, 237-238
   cgi-bin, 540
   Communicator install for Windows 3.1, 692
   destination, Windows 95 Communicator install, 714
   FTP links, 472
   graphics storage, 480
   LDAP directory, searching, 235
   paths of HTML documents in URLs, 469
   UNIX version install, 745

Directory panel, preferences, 337-338

Directory Server, 669, 672-673

disabling cookies, 175

disc value, list-style-type property, 619

discussion folders
   browsing newsgroup articles, 262-263
   Navigation toolbar buttons, 261
   reading newsgroup articles, 256
   sorting options, 263

discussion groups, preferences, 54, 337

discussions on the Internet
   via Conference, 96
   via Text Chat, 102

Disk Space subpanel, 111

display options
   fonts, 322-323
   Navigation toolbar, 322
   Netcaster, 414, 419
   toolbars, 122-123
   Web tops, 423

displaying Address Book fields, 236

DIV tags, 568, 602

dividing lines, HTML documents, 283

dividing screen space via frames, 504

DL tags, 460, 464

DLS (Dynamic Lookup Service) Server
   Conference call routing, 98
   Conference connections, 303

DNS (Domain Name Server) servers, 686-688

Do Not Disturb mode, Conference, 101, 309

documents HTML, 21-22 *see also* Web pages

domain names, servers, 124

Download panel, preferences, 341

downloading
   bandwidth considerations, 638
   Composer plug-ins, 298
   FTP site options, 138
   JavaScript, 661
   JDK (Java Development Kit), 644
   plug-ins, 639
   timing options for Netcaster, 414
   Video for Windows, 694
   Web pages, Navigator control tools, 126-127

Windows 3.1 Communicator version, 691
**dragging and dropping**
bookmarking, 147-149
text, 84
**drop caps in text, 453**
**drop-down menus, Next button (Navigation toolbar), 75-76**
**dumb terminals, IBM Host On-Demand, 392**
**duplicating bookmarks, 159**
**dynamic CGI scripts, 542**
**Dynamic Fonts, Web page display options, 121, 323, 571**
**Dynamic HTML, 31**

# E

e-mail, 18-19
  accounts, mail server addresses, 55
  adding recipients to messages, 62-63
  Address Book, see Address Book
  addressing preferences, 334
  alignment options with HTML code, 226
  attachments
    files, 219-221
    graphics, 226
    Web pages, 220-221
  carbon copying, 61-62
  checking messages, 55-57
  compressing folders to remove files from system, 216
  Conference address setup, 98
  configuring
    Windows 3.1 version, 703-710
    Windows 95 Communicator, 720-726
  copying outgoing messages, 334
  deleting recipients, 63
  directory of e-mail FAQs, 19
  emptying Trash, 215
  folders, 210-215
    deleting, 213
    filing messages, 213
    moving, 211
    renaming, 212
  fonts, HTML options, 222
  grouping messages into threads, 205-209
  headings, HTML options, 224-225
  HTML formatting options, 64-65
  Internet headers, hiding, 204-205
  links
    with graphics, 228
    with HTML code, 226
  messages
    adding graphics, 226-228
    adding HTML codes, 221-223
    copying, 213-214
    deleting, 214
    sorting, 201
    viewing only new, 202
  Messaging Server options, 673
  Netiquette, 60
  new features, 32-33
  Personal Address Book cards, 705
  preferences, 54
  quoting prior messages, 69
  reading messages, 56-57
  responses, 67-70
  S/MIME encryption and digital signatures, 364-365
  saving newsgroup messages, 76
  searches for messages, 217-218
    filters, 218-219
  sending messages, 64-66,
    Address Book options, 242-243
    at later time, 66
  signature files
    Communicator for Windows 3.1, 705
    Windows 95 install, 721
  sound alerts, 331
  spell-checking, 63
  threads
    expanding and reading, 207
    ignoring, 209
    viewing, 206
    watched threads, 208
  troubleshooting connections, 56
  see also Messenger
**EBCDIC (Extended Binary Coded Decimal Interchange Code), 392**
**Echo Suppression field, Conference, 305**
**Edit Bookmarks window, bookmark folders, 153**
**Edit menu commands**
Find in Page, 125
Preferences, 72, 80
Select All, 125
**Edit menu commands (Address Book)**
Card Properties, 233
Delete, 233
Preferences, 233
Redo, 233
Search Directory, 233
Undo, 233
**Edit menu commands (Composer), 84**
**Edit menu commands (Navigator), 41**
**editing**
bookmarks, 154-155
frames from Navigator, 118
HTML, 80-81, 278
tables, 292-293
text, 83-84
Web pages from Navigator, 118
**electronic malls, 170**
**elements of forms, 177**
Back button, 179
check boxes, 178
Mailto: option, 179
option buttons, 178
Password fields, 178
Reset button, 179
Select, 179
Submit buttons, 178
text fields, 177
**EM tags, 446**
**EMBED tag**
attributes, 630
audio options, 635-636
plug-ins, 630-631
**embedding**
audio, 635
FONT tags, 453
lists within lists, 461
plug-ins, 629
style sheets, 601-602
video, 636-637
**emptying Trash, Messenger options, 215**
**encoded newsgroup articles, 262**
**encoding schemes for character sets, 121**

encoding schemes for language use, 322

encryption handling with Certificate Server, 675

ENCTYPE attribute, FORM tags, 545

ENDTIME attribute, LiveAudio, 636

Enterprise Server, 669-672

entries, adding to Calendar Agendas, 377-380

Entries You've Accepted folder, Calendar, 385

Entries You've Refused folder, Calendar, 385

Entries You've Sent Out folder, Calendar, 385

entry settings options, Calendar Agendas, 375

equivalent standard keys for IBM Host On-Demand function keys, 396

Eraser tool, Whiteboard, 316

erasing Whiteboard graphics, 105

etiquette in newsgroups, 77-78

evaluation programs for Netscape servers, 671

event handler plug-ins, 299

events, JavaScript
  connecting scripts, 659-661
  handling, 656-657

exchanging files, 102-103

Exit command (File menu), 233

expanding
  Messenger folders, 211
  My Channels list, Netcaster, 408

# F

family property, fonts (style sheets), 621

FAQs
  e-mail, 19
  UseNet, 20
  WWW, 15

FastTrack Server, small-scale Web page server, 675-676

fields, Address Book, 236

file attachments to newsgroup articles
  saving, 265-266
  sending, 268

File Exchange, 102-103, 312-313

File menu commands (Address Book) 232-233

File menu commands (Composer), 88

File menu commands (Navigator), 42

File menu Frame option commands, 183

file names, URLs, 124

file support display options, 327-330

files
  bookmark.htm, 151
  c32e40.exe, 712
  e-mail attachments, 219-221
  graphics formats, 477-478
  HTML document names in URLs, 469
  IBM Host On-Demand connection defaults, 400
  Interlaced GIF imagemaps, 524
  Log files, Chat Tool, 311
  opening, 42
  Progressive JPEG imagemaps, 524
  README
    Communicator install for Windows 3.1, 696
    UNIX version install updates, 747
    Windows 95 Communicator install, 715
  security, applets, 643
  sharing, 102-103

Fill style indicator, Whiteboard, 316

filters, searching e-mail messages, 218-219

Find button
  HTML document word searches, 274
  NetHelp, 141

Find function, bookmarks, 156-157

Find in Page command (Edit menu), 125

finding plug-ins, 639

firewalls
  Conference settings options, 306
  Proxy Server, 673

fixed background-attachment Values, style sheets, 609

fixed-width fonts, 323

flexibility in frames, 501

floating elements, style sheets
  clear property, 618
  example, 617
  values, 616

Floating Toolbox, White Board, 317

fly-over buttons example, Java, 650-651

fly-over help with layers, 596

fly-over text displays, links, 661-662

folders
  bookmarks
    deleting, 155
    designating folders as such, 158
    Edit Bookmarks window, 153
    organizing, 154
  Messenger, 210-215
    compressing to remove from system, 216
    deleting, 213
    expanding or collapsing, 211
    filing messages, 213
    moving, 211
    renaming, 212
    searches for messages, 217-218
  plug-ins, 628
  saving newsgroup messages, 76
  Trash, emptying, 215

font display options panel, 322-323

font properties, style sheets, 619-623
  color property, 620-621
  family, 619-621
  size, 619-622
  style, 620-623
  variant, 620, 623
  weight, 620, 623

**FONT tags, 451-453**
  embedding, 453
  keywords, 451-453
**fonts**
  e-mail HTML options, 222
  fixed-width, 323
  names, 621
  relative sizing, 451
  variable-width, 323
**Fonts panel**
  font display options, 110
  screen display font options, 120-121
**footers**
  options for printing Web pages, 116
  Web pages, 443
**FORM tags, 544-545**
**formatting**
  HTML documents, 278-283
    borderless table options, 291
    character options, 278-280
    paragraphs, 280-284
  HTML
    options for e-mail, 64
    tags, 451-456
  style sheets properties, 620
    color, 620
    text-decoration, 620, 624
    text-transform, 620, 624-625
  tables, rows and columns, 293-296
**Formatting toolbar, HTML document paragraph options, 280**
**Formatting toolbar (Composer), 81**
**forms, 538, 543-553**
  buttons for layers, 569
  CGI script integration examples, 553-556
  data processing methods, 555
  elements
    Back button, 179
    check boxes, 178
    Password fields, 178
    option buttons, 178
    Mailto: option, 179
    Reset button, 179
    Select, 179
    Submit buttons, 178
    text fields, 177
  input processing example program, 553-554
  JavaScript navigation, 662-663
  parsing data, 555

  registration options, 168
  requests from Web servers, 168
  searches, 168
  security issues, 556-557
  shopping options, 170-177
    cookies, 175
    security, 176-177
  Submit buttons, troubleshooting, 178
  tags, TEXTAREA, 179
  URLs, https secure URL type, 557
  validating, JavaScript, 654
  Web pages, 167-179
**Forward button (Navigator toolbar), 29**
**FRAME tags, 508-510**
  FRAMEBORDER attribute, 515
  NORESIZE attribute, 510
  SCROLLING attribute, 510
  SRC attribute, 508
  TARGET attribute, 511
**FRAMEBORDER attribute**
  EMBED tag, 630
  FRAME tags, 515
**frames, 180-183, 498-512**
  accommodating non-frames-abled browsers, 515
  advanced options, 512-516
  borderless, 515-516
  editing from Navigator, 118
  limitations and advantages, 502-503
  links, 511
  multiple, 512
  navigation options, 182, 500
  organizing data, 501
  pixel counts for sizing, 505-506
  resizing, 182
  saving, 115
  tic-tac-toe example, 513-514
  viewing information, 129
  within frames, 514-515
**FRAMESET tags, 504-505**
**Freehand tool, Whiteboard, 316**
**frequently visited site update settings, Advanced/Cache panel, 127**
**front display option, Netcaster, 422**
**FTP (File Transfer Protocol), 472**
  downloading Netscape binaries, 742

  FTP server
    UNIX version downloads, 743
    uploading Web pages to ISPs, 90
  FTP sites
    file uploads, 139
    Monster FTP Sites List, 139
    Navigator options, 138-139
  FTP smart resume, 139
  links, 472
**full duplex mode, sound cards, 303**
**full-page plug-ins, 629**
**function key options with IBM Host On-Demand, 392, 396**
**functions**
  ClearHelp(), 598
  JavaScript, 655
    executing, 657
    Message(), 660
    MyFunction(), 660
    OpenURL(), 662
  OnLink(), 598
  Right, moving layers right, 594
  ToggleFirst(), hiding or showing layers, 591
  Up, moving layers upward, 594

# G

**Gamelan Web site, 649, 661**
**gas gauge area, status bar, 135**
**gateways, IBM Host On-Demand connectivity, 394**
**GET METHOD, forms data processing, 555**
**GIF animations, turning off, 126**
**GIF Construction Set Web site, 638**
**GIF files (Graphics Interchange Format), 477**
**Go menu commands, 44**
**Go to next page on Webtop icon, Netcaster, 421**
**Go to previous page on Webtop icon, Netcaster, 421**
**Gopher, 12**
  links, 472
  sites, 140

graphics, 476
    adding to e-mail messages, 226-228
    adding to Web pages, 284-286
        alignment options, 285
        margins, 286
        text wrapping options, 285
    alternative text for non-graphical browsers, 480-481
    automatic loading, turning off, 126
    backgrounds, 286, 608
    copyright laws, 633
    GIF files, 477
    imagemaps, 519, 523-524
    JPEG files, 478
    layer backgrounds, 581
    links, 484-485
    lists, style sheets, 618
    loading into Whiteboard, 104, 315-316
    saving, 125
GRAPHICS parameter, IBM Host On-Demand connection page, 401
grouping e-mail messages into threads, 205-209
grouping layers, 588
Groups Server Preferences panel, 336-337
Guide button, Navigator toolbar, 137

## H

H.323 phone communication standard, 305
H1...H6 tags, 438, 464
half duplex mode, sound cards, 303
Hang Up button, Conference, 101
hardware requirements, UNIX install, 742
hash symbol (#), named targets, 476
he3270en.htm file, IBM Host On-Demand connection defaults, 400
HEAD tags, 437, 463
headers, options for printing Web pages, 116

headings
    e-mail messages, 224-225
    HTML documents, 282, 437-438
height, box properties for style sheets, 611-613
HEIGHT attribute
    APPLET tag, 646
    EMBED tag, 630
    IMG tags, 482
    LAYER tags, 575, 578
    OBJECT tag, 631, 648
Help, Netcaster, 420
Help button (Navigator toolbar), 49
Help menu commands
    About Plug-ins, 634
    Address Book, 234
help options with layers, 596
helper applications, 185, 328
hexadecimal color values, 456
HIDDEN attribute
    EMBED tag, 630
    INPUT tags, 552
Hide Address Book Toolbar command (View menu), 233
hiding
    Internet headers for e-mail, 204-205
    layers, 591-593
    scripts, JavaScript, 658-659
    status bar, 136
    style sheets, 606
        style sheet tags from browsers, 564
    Web tops, 423
highlighting successive links with Tab key, 123
History command, (Communicator menu), 234
History List, 133-135
    bookmarks, 149
    clearing, 135
    multiple selections, 134
    window preference settings, 324-325
home pages
    Netscape automatic setup, 124
    settings, 41-42
    startup option, 325
horizontal (x) background-position property, style sheets, 609-610

host names as URL component, 469
hot text
    e-mail links, 474
    Web page links, 470
HotJava, 642
hotkeys for starting other Communicator components, 119
HR tags, 443
HREF attribute
    A tags, 470
    QuickTime plug-in, 638
HSPACE attribute
    APPLET tag, 646
    EMBED tag, 630
    IMG tags, 482-483
    OBJECT tag, 631, 648
HTML (HyperText Markup Language)
    adding to e-mail messages, 221-223
    BR tags, 280, 283
    code example, 463-464
    commenting, 463
        hiding scripts, 659
    documents, 21-22
    Dynamic HTML, 31
    editor, 80-81
    formatting options for e-mail, 64-65
    links, coding process, 470-471
    new features, 31
    overview of coding process, 435
    style sheets
        Cascading Style Sheets, 31
        embedding, 601-602
        importing, 603
        inline (on-the-fly), 602
        JavaScript-accessible Style Sheets, 31
        linking, 600-601
    tags, 31
        <!-, ->, 463
        A, 470, 662
        APPLET, 645
        B, 445-446
        BIG, 450
        BLINK, 448
        BLOCKQUOTE, 450, 566
        BODY, 437, 464
        BODY BGCOLOR=>, 454
        BR, 442-443
        CENTER, 449
        DIV, 568, 602
        DL, 460, 464

EM, 446
EMBED, 630-631
FONT, 451-453
FORM, 544-545
formatting options, 451-456
FRAME, 508-510
FRAMESET, 504-505
H1...H6, 438, 464
HEAD, 437, 463
HR, 443
I, 446-447
ILAYER, 578
IMG, 479-483
INPUT, 549-553, 660
inserting into documents, 276
LAYER, 566, 573
LH, 458
LI, 458
LINK, 601
LINK REL, 562
MAP, 532
NOBR, 443
NOFRAMES, 515
NOLAYER, 589
OBJECT, 631-633, 647-648
OL, 458
OPTION, 547
P, 441
paragraph, 440-445
PARAM, 632, 646
PRE, 444
S, 448
SCRIPT, 658
SELECT, 547-549, 662
SMALL, 450
SPAN, 566, 602
STRONG, 446
STYLE, 563, 601
STYLE TYPE, 564
SUB, 450
SUP, 450
TEXTAREA, 545
TITLE, 436-438, 463
TT, 450
U, 447
UL, 458
word break, 443
viewing source code for pages, 128

**HTML documents**
backgrounds, 286
dividing lines, 283
editing, 278
formatting, 278-283
borderless table options, 291
character, 278-280
paragraphs, 280-284
graphics, 284-286
alignment options, 285
margins, 286
text wrapping options, 285
headings, 282
indenting text, 281
inserting tags into documents, 276
layers, 573
background graphics or colors, 580-581
fly-over help options, 596
hiding, 591-593
moving with scripts, 594-596
multiple layers, 582-587
nesting, 587-589
ordering options for layer stacking, 585
overlapping layers, 583
positioning, 576-578
showing, 591-593
sizing options, 578
special effects with scripts, 589-596
stacking order options, 584
links
changing, 287
color options, 287-288
internal links, 288-290
named anchors, 289
removing, 287
lists, 282
non-breaking spaces, 283
opening, troubleshooting, 93
plug-ins, 296-298
preformatting text, 283
previewing, 275-276
publishing, 89
configuring Composer, 90
uploading to ISP, 89
spelling checker, 274
tables, 290-296
borderless, 291
cell spanning, 295
editing, 292-293
formatting rows and columns, 293-296
row and column options, 292
text
alignment options, 281
display alternatives for graphics, 284-285
viewing source code, 276-278
white space, 283
word or phrase searches, 274
*see also* Web pages

**HTML editor, new features, 33-34**

**HTTP (HyperText Transfer Protocol), 469, 667**

**https secure URL type, 557**

**hyperlinks**
color options, 454
*see also* links

**hypertext links,** *see* **links**

# I

**I tags, italic text, 446-447**

**IBM Host On-Demand, 389**
connections, 396-401
debug logs, 398
function keys, 392
equivalent standard keys, 396
gateways, TN3270E Server, 394
MVS (Multiple Virtual Storage), 393
OIA (Operator Information Area), 393
message definitions, 398-400
OS/390, 393
overview of process, 394-402
quitting sessions, 402
starting sessions, 401-402
VM (Virtual Machine), 393

**IBM RS/6000 Communicator install, 742**

**ID attribute, OBJECT tag, 632, 648**

**Identity panel preferences, 331-333**

**ignoring e-mail threads, 209**

**ILAYER tags, 578**

**Image Properties dialog box, 85**

**image property for lists, style sheets, 618**

**imagemaps, 166, 519, 523-532**
adding to Web page, 525-526
AREA tags, 532
circular areas, 533
client-side, 521-522
default links, 534-535
designing, 525
HTML code example, 531
Interlaced GIF or file format, 524

## imagemaps

links, 43-44
mapping, Map This! program, 527
overlapping, 534
overview of process, 520-521
polygon areas, 533
Progressive JPEG file format, 524
rectangular areas, 533
selecting graphic for use, 523-524
server-side, 522-523
testing, 535
text alternatives, 535

**images, 476**
adding to e-mail messages, 226-228
adding to Web pages
alignment options, 285
margins, 286
text wrapping options, 285
automatic loading, turning off, 126
backgrounds, 286
style sheets, 608
file formats, 477-478
inserting in Web pages, 84-85
loading into Whiteboard, 104, 315-316
mapping for imagemaps, 526-532
saving, 125

**Images button (Navigation toolbar), 30**

**IMG tags, 479-483**
ALIGN attributes, 481
ALT attribute, 481
BORDER attribute, 483
HEIGHT attribute, 482
HSPACE attribute, 482-483
SRC attribute, 479
USEMAP attribute, 526
VSPACE attribute, 482-483
WIDTH attribute, 482

**Import command (File menu), 232**

**@import keyword, style sheets, 603**

**@import url statement, style sheets, 562**

**! important definitions, style sheets, 570**

**importing**
bookmark lists, 160
style sheets, 603

**In-Tray, Calendar, 385-386**

**In-Tray view, Agenda, 370**

**incoming Internet phone calls with Conference, 310**

**incremental searches for newsgroups, 253**

**indenting text**
HTML documents, 281
style sheets, 620

**Index button, NetHelp, 141**

**indexes of links, named targets, 475**

**inheritance**
lists, 618
style sheets, 604

**initial caps in text, 453**

**inline**
images, 476
JavaScript, 656
style sheets (on-the-fly), 602
DIV tag, 602
organization, 602
SPAN tag, 602

**INPUT tags, 549-553, 660**

**Insert menu Image command (Composer), 85**

**inserting**
images, 84-85
links, 87
plug-ins
alternative content, 632-633
EMBED tag, 630-631
OBJECT tag, 631-633

**insertion point, moving, keyboard shortcuts, 82-83**

**inside value, list-style-position property, 618**

**Installer, Communicator install on Apple machines, 729**

**installing**
Communicator
for Windows 3.1, 689, 691
Macintosh verison, 727
UNIX verison from archive files, 745-746
Windows 95 version, 712-713
Composer plug-ins, 298
Dial-Up Networking, 683
helper applications for file support, 328
Netscape Communicator for UNIX systems, 741
TCP/IP, 685

**integrating applications into Web pages with Java, 183**

**interactive collaboration, 95**

**Interlaced GIF files, imagemaps, 524**

**internal links**
named anchors, 289
Web pages, 288

**International Users command (Help menu), 234**

**Internet, 12**
access options, Proxies panel, 344
ISP connection options, 681
newsgroups, top-level categories, 247
online access connections, 680-682
origin, 12
phone calls via Conference, 100-102
telephone options with Conference, 301

**Internet Explorer, 14**

**Internet headers for e-mail, hiding, 204-205**

**interpreted language**
compiled language comparison, 656
JavaScript, 656

**interpreters, 656**

**InterVU Web site, 196**

**intranets, 15**

**invitation responses, Calendar, 381-382**

**IP addresses, 686-688**

**ISPs (Internet Service Providers)**
IP addresses, 686
mail server accounts, 55
online connection options, 681-682
passwords, 682
uploading new Web sites, 89-90
User IDs, 682

**italic e-mail messages, 222**

**italic style property, fonts (style sheets), 622-623**

**italic text, 447**

**ITS' Web site, 649**

## J

**Java, 183-184, 642**
  applets
    APPLET tag, 645-647
    applications, compared, 642
    ButtonOnFly, 651
    creating, 644
    fly-over buttons example, 650-651
    JavaScript, 654
    Navigator Ticker example, 649-650
    OBJECT tag, 647-648
    preference settings, 342
    plug-ins, compared, 643
    security, 643
    security certification, 365
    Virtual Library, 649
  bytecodes, 642
  HotJava, 642
  JIT compilation (Just in Time compilation), 642
  new features, 32

**Java Console, viewing Java applet information, 130, 234**

**Java Development Kit (JDK), downloading, 644**

**JavaScript, 184-185, 654**
  associating scripts, 654
  blue headings example, 564
  downloading, 661
  events, handling, 656-657
  forms
    navigation, 662-663
    validation, 654
  functions, 655
    executing, 657
    Message(), 660
    MyFunction(), 660
    OpenURL(), 662
  inline, 656
  interpreted language, 656
  Java applets, 654
  JScript, 654
  layer controls, 654
  layers, 570-571
  links, fly-over text displays, 661-662
  on-the-fly Web pages, 654
  preferences, 342
  script example, 655-656
  scripts
    adding, 658
    connecting events, 659-661
    hiding, 658-659

  layer options, 589-596
  organizing, 658
  security certification, 365
  statements, 656

**JavaScript-accessible Style Sheets (JASS), 31**

**Javasoft Web site, 644**

**JDK (Java Development Kit), downloading, 644**

**JIT compilation (Just in Time compilation), 642**

**JPEG files (Joint Photographers Expert Group), 478**

**JScript Web site, 654**

## K

**Kbps (kilobits per second), 680**

**key combinations**
  Ctrl+5 keys, starting Conference, 97
  starting other Communicator components, 119

**keyboard shortcuts**
  moving insertion point, 82-83
  opening files, 42
  redoing changes, 84
  undoing changes, 84

**keywords**
  BODY tags
    ALINK=, 455
    LINK=, 454
    TEXT=, 454
    VLINK=, 455
  bottom, background-position property, 610
  center, background-position property, 610-612
  FONT tags
    COLOR=, 453
    SIZE=, 451
  @import, style sheets, 603
  left, background-position property, 609-610
  OL tags, TYPE=, 459
  right, background-position property, 609-610
  top, background-position property, 609-610
  *see also* attributes

**kiosk mode, 133**

## L

**LAM files, Media Player playback, 189**

**LANGUAGE attribute, SCRIPT tag, 658**

**language character sets for font display, 120**

**language encoding schemes, 322**

**language preferences, 326-327**

**Languages panel, Web page language options, 110**

**large font size, 622**

**Last Page Visited startup option, 325**

**launch options for Communicator, 321**

**launching, Conference, 96-97**
  *see also* starting

**Layer indicator, Whiteboard, 316**

**Layer object**
  methods, 591
  properties, 590

**LAYER tags, 566, 573**
  ABOVE attribute, 586
  BACKGROUND attribute, 580
  BELOW attribute, 586
  BGCOLOR attribute, 580
  HEIGHT attribute, 578
  LEFT attribute, 576, 583
  RIGHT attribute, 576
  TOP attribute, 576, 583
  VISIBILITY attribute, 591
  WIDTH attribute, 578
  Z-INDEX attribute, 584

**layers, 566-568, 573**
  backgrounds
    colors, 580
    graphics, 581
  child, 587
  fly-over help options, 596
  form buttons, 569
  hiding or showing, 591-593
  JavaScript controls, 654
  JavaScript examples, 570-571
  methods, 591
  moving with scripts, 594-596
  multiple layers, 582-587
  nesting, 587-589
  ordering options for layer stacking, 585

## layers

overlapping layers, 583
parent, 587
positioning, 576-578
properties, 590
reference layers, 589
simple example, 574-581
sizing, 578-579
special effects with scripts, 589-596
stacking options with Z-INDEX, 568
stacking order options, 584
visibility property, 569

**layout display options, Netcaster, 419**

**LDAP (Lightweight Directory Access Protocol), searching directories, 237-238, 670**

**leading, style sheets, 625**

**LEFT attribute, LAYER tags, 575-576, 583**

**left keyword, background-position property, style sheets, 609-610**

**LEFT property, ALIGN attribute, 646**

**legacy IBM applications and Communicator, 389**

**letter numbering for lists, 459**

**letter-spacing property, style sheets, 619, 625**

**LH tags, 458**

**LI tags, 458**

**license agreement, Windows 3.1 Communicator version, 702**

**limitations and advantages of frames, 502-503**

**line breaks, 442**

**line-height property, style sheets, 625**

**line-spacing property, style sheets, 619**

**line-through value, text-decoration property, style sheets, 624**

**LINK REL tags, 562**

**LINK= keyword, BODY tags, 454**

**LINK tags, style sheets, 601**

links, 43-44, 468-469
  absolute, 470-471
  bookmarking, 149
  color options, 121, 323-324, 454
    active links, 455
    visited links, 455
  e-mail messages
    graphics as links, 228
    with HTML code, 226
  fly-over text displays, 661-662
  frames, 511
  FTP, 472
  Gopher, 472
  graphics, 484-485
  highlighting with Tab key, 123
  hot text, 470
  HTML coding process, 470-471
  HTML documents
    changing, 287
    color options, 287
    internal links, 288
    named anchors, 289
    removing, 287
  imagemap defaults, 534-535
  inserting, 87
  mailto:, 473-474
  named targets, 475
  relative, 470
  style sheets, 600-601
  unvisited link color options, 324
  URLs, 468
  UseNet, 473
  visited link color options, 324
  Web pages, shortcuts, 124
  Web tops, 424

**Linux Communicator install, 742**

**list headers, 458**

**lists**
  definition, 459-461
  HTML documents, 282
  nested, 461-462
  numbered, 458-459
  style sheets, 618-619
    image property, 618
    inheritance, 618
    position property, 618
    type property, 619
  unordered, 458
  Web pages, 456-461

**LiveAudio plug-in, 634-636**
  audio playback options, 188
  console controls, 188

**LiveScript,** *see* **JavaScript**

**LiveVideo plug-in, 637**
  troubleshooting playback, 190
  video playback, 189

**LiveWire Pro 3.0, 669**

**local files, URLs, 125**

**location selection for meetnigs with Calendar, 379**

**Location toolbar, 112**
  Bookmark QuickFile button, 30, 146
  Bookmarks Quickfile button, 45
  Collabra, 73
  display options, 122
  jumping to a location, 42
  opening Web pages, 114
  search options, 137

**Log File window, 102**

**Log files, Chat Tool, 311**

**logging options, Netcaster, 420**

**logical formatting tags, 446**

**logins, IBM Host On-Demand, 401**

**long-distance phone service via the Internet, 301**

**LOOP attribute, QuickTime plug-in, 638**

**lower-alpha value, list-style-type property, 619**

**lower-roman value, list-style-type property, 619**

**lowercase value, text-transform, style sheets, 625**

## M

**Macintosh**
  Communicator install, 727
    Collabra configuration, 738
    configuration, 733-739
    Messenger configuration, 734-739
    user profile testing, 733
    user profiles, 731
  plug-ins, folders, 628

**Macromedia**
  Shockwave for Director plug-in, 197
  Web site, 197

**Magnavox Web site, imagemaps example, 520**

**Mail & Groups panel, preference settings, 330-338**

Mail Server, 669
    addresses, e-mail accounts, 55
    Macintosh Messenger
        configuration, 737
    Messenger configuration for
        Windows 3.1, 708
    preferences, 335
mailing lists, 19-21, 235, 241-242
mailto: option
    forms, 179
    links, 473-474
mainframe integration, 390
MAP tags, 532
mapping images for imagemaps, 526-532
margins, style sheets, 610-611, 615
Marimba Bongo and Castanet, Netcaster integration, 427-428
Marimba Web site, 428
markup tools, Whiteboard, 105, 316-317
    Eraser tool, 316
    Fill style indicator, 316
    Freehand tool, 316
    Layer indicator, 316
    Oval tools, 316
    Rectangle tools, 316
    Text tool, 317
MAYSCRIPT attribute, APPLET tags, 646
Media Player plug-in, 189-194
Media Server, 669, 674
medium font size, 622
meeting planning with Calendar, 377
Member Services command (Help menu), 234
memory
    Cache panel preferences, 343-344
    security, applets, 643
menu bar
    Navigator window, 111-113
    Netcaster, 417-421
menu option plug-ins, 299
menus
    Collabra discussion folder options, 256
    Message Center options, 249

merging bookmark lists, 160
Message Center, 249-256
    Messenger folders, 210
    Navigation toolbar, 252
    newsgroup articles, 256
        reading offline, 269
        replies, 266
    tracking multiple news servers, 255
Message Center command (Communicator menu), 234
Message Composition window, 58
message definitions, IBM Host On-Demand, 398-400
Message List
    columns, resizing, 200
    filing messages in folders, 213
    sorting messages, 201
    viewing only new e-mail, 202
message pane, sizing options, 202-203
Message() function (JavaScript), 660
messages
    e-mail
        adding recipients, 62-63
        carbon copying, 61
        checking, 55
        composing, 58-63
        deleting recipients, 63
        HTML formatting options, 64-65
        quoting prior messages, 69
        reading, 56-57
        responses, 67-70
        sending, 64-66
        spell-checking, 63
    newsgroup articles, 262-263
    see also e-mail
Messages properties panel, 333
Messaging Server, 669, 673
Messenger, 18-19
    adding graphics to messages, 226-228
    adding HTML codes to messages, 221-223
    alignment options with HTML codes, 226
    attachments
        files, 219-221
        Web pages, 220-221
    checking messages, 55-57
    composing e-mail messages, 58-63

compressing folders to remove files from system, 216
configuring, 54-55
    Macintosh version, 734-739
    Windows 3.1 version, 703-710
    Windows 95 install, 722-725
copying messages, 213-214
customizing, 199
deleting messages, 214
e-mail, 51
emptying Trash, 215
filters, 218-219
folders, 210-215
    deleting, 213
    expanding or collapsing, 211
    filing messages, 213
    moving, 211
    renaming, 212
fonts, HTML options, 222
headings, HTML options, 224-225
Internet headers for e-mail, hiding, 204-205
links with graphics, 228
links with HTML codes, 226
Message List, sorting messages, 201
message pane, sizing options, 202-203
new features, 32-33
opening, 53
reading e-mail messages, 56-57
searches for messages, 217-218
subfolders, 210-211
threads
    expanding and reading, 207
    grouping messages, 205-209
    ignoring, 209
    viewing, 206
    watched, 208
viewing only new e-mail, 202
see also e-mail
Messenger Mailbox command (Communicator menu), 233
METHOD attribute, FORM tags, 544
methods, layers, 591
microphone amplification options, Conference, 99, 309
Microsoft, 14
    Active Desktop compared to Netcaster, 431
    Video for Windows, 694
middle positioning of layers, 577-578

MIDDLE property, ALIGN attribute, 646

middle value, vertical-align paragraph property, style sheets, 626

MIDI files, LiveAudio playback, 188

MIME types (Multipurpose Internet Mail Extensions)
  CGI script Content-types, 541
  file support options, 328

mini browser windows, 113

missing bookmarks, troubleshooting, 147

modems
  cable modems, 681
  online connection options, 680-681

moderated newsgroups, 246-248

Monster FTP Sites List, 139

More Channels option, Channel Finder, 413

Mosaic, 13

movie playback, QuickTime plug-in, 191-192

moving
  insertion point, keyboard shortcuts, 82-83
  layers with scripts, 594-596
  Message List columns, 200
  Messenger folders, 211
  text, 84
  through VRML worlds, 193

MPEG files
  LiveVideo playback, 189
  third-party plug-ins, 196

multimedia, 627-628
  adding, 633-634
  audio
    adding LiveAudio, 634-636
    LiveVideo, 637-638
    bandwidth considerations, 638
    copyright laws, 633
    playback options, 197
  plug-ins, 628-629
  see also plug-ins
  video
    adding, 636-639
    QuickTime plug-in, 638

multimedia handling, Media Server, 674

MULTIPLE attribute, SELECT tags, 547

multiple bookmark lists, 160-161

multiple frames, 512

multiple layers, 582-587

multiple links, removing, 287

multiple news servers, 255-256

multiple selections in History List, 134

multiple user profiles, 131-132, 350
  Macintosh Communicator install, 731-732
  Windows 3.1 Communicator version, 700
  Windows 95 Communicator install, 716-719

multiple windows, 113

multiuser environments, 350

music LiveAudio playback, 188
  see also audio

MVS (Multiple Virtual Storage), IBM Host On-Demand, 393

My Address Book Card command (View menu), 233

My Channels list, Netcaster, 408

My Channels menu
  adding channels, 417
  Netcaster, 416

MyFunction() function (JavaScript), 660

# N

NAME attribute
  A tags, 475
  APPLET tag, 646
  EMBED tag, 630
  LAYER tags, 575
  MAP tags, 532
  SELECT tags, 547
  TEXTAREA tags, 546

named anchors, internal links, 289

named targets, Web pages, 475

names
  Address Book, searching, 237
  fonts, 621

navigation
  button bars, Web pages, 517
  Cosmo VRML viewer plug-in options, 193
  forms, JavaScript, 662-663
  frames, 182
  tips and tricks, 123-125

Navigation toolbar, 111
  Back button, 44
  Collabra, 73-76
  discussion folder buttons, 261
  display options, 122, 322
  Message Center, 252
  Reload button, 126
  Stop button, 126
  Subscribe button, 252

navigational imagemaps, 166

navigational uses for frames, 500

Navigator, 40
  copying, 125
  displaying bookmarks, 151
  downloading
    control tools, 126-127
    UNIX version of Communicator, 744
  editing
    frames, 118
    Web pages, 118
  FTP site options, 138-139
  Gopher sites, 140
  History List, 133-135
  home page settings, 41-42
  integration with other Communicator tools, 117-120
  kiosk mode, 133
  NetHelp, 141
  OLE integration, 198
  opening multiple windows, 113
  pop-up menu, 136
  status bar
    Component bar, 136
    gas gauge area, 135
    security icon, 135
  Telnet sites, 140
  transfer status for Web pages, 128
  user profiles, 131
  see also Communicator

Navigator command (Communicator menu), 233

Navigator panel
  Clear History button, 135
  home page address options, 110
  preference and settings options, 324-330

Navigator Ticker example (Java), 649-650
Navigator toolbar
  Guide button, 137
  Help button, 49
  Search button, 47
Navigator window
  component bar, 113
  menu bar, 111-113
  Netcaster, 416
  status bar, 113
NCompass Web site, 197
nested lists, 461-462
nesting layers, 587-589
Net Etiquette command (Help menu), 234
Netcaster, 35-37, 405
  Add Channel button, 407
  cache options, 415
  Channel Finder, 407, 412-416
  channels, 426-427
    adding for favorite sites, 426
    previewing, 407
    quitting, 409
    viewing offline, 429
  Channels panel properties, 418
  compared to Microsoft Active Desktop, 431
  deleting channels, 418
  download timing options, 414
  layout display options, 419
  Marimba Castanet integration, 427-428
  menu bar, 417-421
  My Channels list, expanding, 408
  My Channels menu, 416-417
  Navigator window, 416
  NetHelp, 420
  offline browsing options, 429
  onscreen viewing options, 407
  risk classifications for Java applets, 431
  Security panel, 420
  security permissions, 430-431
  starting, 406-410
    with Communicator, 418
  Toolbar, 421-422
  updating channels, 418
  Webtop view, 416
  Web tops, 422-425
  window display options, 414
NetHelp, 49, 141-143, 420
Netiquette, 60

Netscape
  automatic home page setup, 124
  Composer plug-ins, 297-298
  plug-ins, 186-194
Netscape Conference, Address Book calling, 95, 243-244
Netscape DevEdge Web site, frames example, 180-181
Netscape FTP server, UNIX version downloads, 743
Netscape LiveWire Pro 3.0, 669
Netscape Message Center, 249-256
Netscape Messenger e-mail, 51
Netscape Navigator, downloading UNIX version of Communicator, 744
Netscape ONE Web site, 669
Netscape plug-ins Web site, 194
Netscape servers, 667-668, 671
Netscape Web site, 641, 668
  home page, 40
  intranet study, 17
  JavaScript Guide Web site, 653
Network News Transfer Protocol (NNTP), 20
New Card command (File menu), 232
New Card dialog box, 238
New command (File menu), 232
New Entries folder, Calendar, 385
new features, 28
  Collabra, 32-33
  Component bar, 28-29
  Composer, 33-34
  Conference, 34-35
  HTML, 31
  Java, 32
  Location toolbar, 30
  Messenger, 32-33
  Navigation toolbar, 29-30
  Netcaster, 35-37
  OLE application integration, 32
  Personal (Custom) toolbar, 30
  plug-ins, 31
  Preferences dialog box, 37
  Security Advisor window, 37
  toolbars, 29

New List command (File menu), 232
new user newsgroups, 247-248
news servers, 55, 247, 669
news.announce.newusers newsgroup, 248
Newscaster, 23-25
newsgroups
  articles
    browsing, 256-266
    discussion folder options, 262-263
    encoded, 262
    opening in separate window, 263
    posting articles, 266-269
    reading, 256-266
    reading offline, 269-271
    replies, 264-265
    saving, 263
    saving file attachments, 265-266
    sending file attachments, 268
    signatures, 268
    threads, 262
    viewing options, 263
  availability, troubleshooting, 247
  checking for new, 254
  Collabra Server options, 674
  discussion folders, sorting options, 263
  etiquette, 77-78
  info and assistance for new users, 247-248
  links, 473
  news.announce.newusers, 248
  organization, 246-247
  reading messages, 75-76
  replying, 77
  saving messages in mail folders, 76-77
  searches, 253-254
  setup, 72
  shortcuts, 253
  subscribing, 73-78, 252-253
  top-level categories, 247
  tracking multiple news servers, 255-256
  types, 246
  unsubscribing, 253
  UseNet, 246-248
newsreaders, 245
Next button (Navigation toolbar), Collabra, 75-78

nicknames in Address Book,
  searching, 237
no break tags, 443
no-repeat background-repeat
  values, style sheets, 609
NOBR tags, 443
NOFRAMES tags, 515
NOLAYER tags, 589
non-breaking spaces, HTML
  documents, 283
non-graphical browsers,
  alternative text, 284
NORESIZE attribute, FRAME
  tags, 510
normal style property, fonts,
  style sheets, 622-623
normal value, white-space
  property, style sheets, 625
note function, Calendar,
  384-385
notification settings, Calendar,
  374
Notification utility, checking for
  new e-mail, 67
nowrap value, white-space
  property, style sheets, 625
ns-install shell script, UNIX
  version install, 747
numbered lists, 458-459

# O

Oak, *see* Java
OBJECT tag, 647-648
  alternative content, 648
  attributes, 631-632, 647-648
  audio, 635-636
  passing parameters, 648
  plug-ins, 631-632
    alternative content, 632-633
    PARAM tag, 632
objects, Layer, 590-591
oblique style property, fonts,
  style sheets, 622-623
offline Agendas, Calendar, 370
offline browsing, 429
Offline panel, 111, 340-342
Offline Work mode, Collabra,
  271

OIA (Operator Information
  Area), IBM Host On-Demand,
  393, 398-400
OL tags, 458-459
OLE (Object Linking and
  Embedding)
  applications, 32
  Navigator integration, 198
on-the-fly style sheets (inline),
  602
  DIV tag, 602
  JavaScript, 654
  organization, 602
  SPAN tag, 602
onBlur event, JavaScript, 660
OnChange attribute, SELECT
  tag, 662
onChange event, JavaScript,
  660
onClick event, JavaScript, 660
onFocus event, JavaScript, 660
online access connections,
  680-682
online forms, 167
online mode, Calendar, 371
online shopping, 170-177
  cookies, 175
  security, 176-177
OnLink() function, 598
onMouseOut attributes, A tag,
  662
onMouseOut event, JavaScript,
  660
onMouseOver attributes, A tag,
  662
onMouseOver event, JavaScript,
  660
onSelect event, JavaScript, 660
onSubmit event, JavaScript,
  660
Open a Navigator button,
  Netcaster, 422
Open Page command (File
  menu), 42
opening
  files, 42
  Messenger, 53
  multiple Navigator windows,
    113
  newsgroup articles in separate
    window, 263

Web pages, 114-115
  troubleshooting, 93
OpenURL() function,
  JavaScript, 662
option buttons, forms, 178
OPTION tags
  attributes, 548
  form data entry, 547
Options menu, Whiteboard,
  317
order forms online, 170
ordering options for layer
  stacking, 585
organization domain names,
  124
organization of newsgroups,
  246-247
organizing
  bookmark folders, 154
  bookmarks, 151-155
  data with frames, 501
  JavaScript scripts, 658
OS/390 and IBM Host
  On-Demand, 393
Outbox, sending e-mail at later
  time, 66
outside value, list-style-position
  property, 618
Oval tools, Whiteboard, 316
overlapping imagemaps, 534
overlapping layers, 583
overline value, text-decoration
  property, style sheets, 624
overriding cascading style
  sheets, 605
overriding style sheet tags, 565
overview of HTML coding
  process, 435

# P

P tags, 441
padding style sheets, 610-612,
  616
padlock icons, secure server
  indicator, 176
Page Composer command
  (Communicator menu), 234
Page Info command (View
  menu), 128

page options for printing Web pages, 115
Page Source command (View menu), 128
pages (Web pages)
    audio, 634-636
    backgrounds, style sheets, 607-610
    creating, 81
    home page settings, 41-42
    images, inserting, 84-85
    links, inserting, 87
    on-the-fly, 654
    plug-ins, 629
    saving, 88
    style sheets
        cascading, 600
        embedding, 601-602
        importing, 603
        inline (on-the-fly), 602
        linking, 600-601
    style sheets, see style sheets
    text, 82-84
    video, 636-639
    see also Web pages
PAGEX attribute, LAYER tags, 575
PAGEY attribute, LAYER tags, 575
PALETTE attribute, EMBED tag, 630
paragraph formatting, HTML documents, 280-284
paragraph properties
    style sheets, 620, 625-626
    text-align, 620
    text-indent, 620
    text-indent property, 626
    vertical-align, 620-621, 626
paragraph tags, 440-445
PARAM tag, 632, 646
parameter options, IBM Host On-Demand, 400-401
parent directories, links, 471
parent layers, 587
parsing forms data, 555
passing parameters
    APPLET tag, 646
    OBJECT tag, 648
PASSWORD attribute, INPUT tags, 549
Password fields, forms, 178

passwords
    e-mail accounts, 55
    ISP connections, 682
    private key, 361-362
pasting
    options, Composer, 125
    text, 84
pathnames, URLs, 124
PAUSEBUTTON property, CONTROLS attribute, 636
PDF files, viewing with Adobe Acrobat Reader plug-in, 197
permissions, Netcaster security options, 430-431
Personal (Custom) toolbar, 30
Personal Address Book cards
    Communicator for Windows 3.1, 705
    Macintosh Messenger install, 735
    Windows 95 e-mail configuration, 722
Personal Note Pad, 102
personal page startup option, 325
Personal toolbar
    adding page shortcuts, 134
    Bookmark button, 157-159
    display options, 122
phone calls via Conference, 100-102
phone service via the Internet, 301, 307-310
Phonebook, Conference call user address lookups, 98
phrases, HTML document searches, 274
physical formatting tags, 446
PIMs (Personal Information Managers), see Calendar
Piper Studios Web site, frames example, 500
pixel counts for frame sizing, 505-506
playback options, multimedia, 197
PLAYBUTTON property, CONTROLS attribute, 636
PLAYEVERYFRAME attribute, QuickTime plug-in, 638
plug-ins, 186-197, 296-299, 628-629

Adobe Acrobat Reader, PDF files viewing, 197
alternative content, 632-633
Composer, 297-298
Cosmo VRML viewer, 193
embedded, 629
finding, 639
folders, 628
full-page, 629
inserting
    EMBED tag, 630-631
    OBJECT tag, 631-633
Java applets, compared, 643
LiveAudio, audio playback options, 188
LiveVideo, video playback, 189
Media Player, 189-194
new features, 31
packaged with Netscape, 186-194
PreVU, MPEG playback, 196
QuickTime, movie playback, 191
RealAudio, 195
ScriptActive, ActiveX controls options, 197
Shockwave for Director, 197
SuiteSpot servers, 671
third-party, 194-196
Plug-Ins Plaza Web site, 195
plug-ins Web site, 639
PLUGINSPAGE attribute, EMBED tag, 630
plus signs (+), subscribing to newsgroups, 75
polygon areas, imagemaps, 533
pop-up menu, 136-137
POP3 protocol, e-mail accounts, 55
positioned elements, 566
    stacking with Z-INDEX, 568
    visibility property, 569
positioning
    backgrounds, 609-610
    layers, 576-578
    lists, 618
POST METHOD, forms data processing, 555
posting articles to newsgroups, 266-269
PowerPC Communicator install, 728-731
PPP (Point-to-Point Protocol), 683-685, 688

**PRE tags, 444**
**pre value, white-space property, style sheets, 625**
**preferences**
  Address Book Cards, 331
  Advanced panel, 342-347
  automatic update option, 343
  Cache panel memory options, 343-344
  Calendar options, 374
  Collabra setup, 72
  Composer, 80-81
  Composer panel options, 338-339
  Composer Publishing panel, 339
  Cookies options, 343
  Directory panel, 337-338
  Discussion groups, 337, 347
  Download panel, 341
  e-mail
    address searches, 337
    storage options, 347
  file support display options, 327-330
  Groups Server panel, 336-337
  History window, 325
  HTML font display options, 322
  Identity panel, 331-333
  Java applets, 342
  JavaScript options, 342
  language, 326-327
  link colors, 323
  Mail & Groups panel, 330-338
  Mail Server panel, 335
  Messages properties panel, 333
  Navigation toolbar, 322
  Navigator, 41
  Offline panel, 340-342
  options, 319
  program launch at startup options, 321
  Proxies panel, 344
  publishing Web pages, 90
  screen colors, 323
  signature files, 331-333
  style sheets, 342
  text colors, 323
  viewing Web pages, 120-123
**Preferences command (Edit menu), 80, 233**
**Preferences dialog box, 41, 80**
  Communicator options settings, 110
  new features, 37
**preformatted text options, 444**
**preformatting text, HTML**

documents, 283
**previewing**
  HTML documents, 275-276
  Netcaster channels, 407
  Web page printouts, 116
**PreVU plug-in, MPEG playback, 196**
**Print the Webtop icon, Netcaster, 421**
**printing Web pages, 115-117**
**private key passwords, 361-362**
**Product Information and Support command (Help menu), 234**
**Profile Manager, user profiles, 131**
**Prog 755 message, IBM Host On-Demand OIA, 400**
**program group folders**
  Communicator install, 694
  Windows 95 Communicator install, 714
**Program Manager, Communicator install for Windows 3.1, 691**
**programs, CGI, 539**
**progressive enlarging of text, 453**
**Progressive JPEG files, imagemaps, 524**
**properties**
  CONTROLS attribute, 636
  layers, 590
  style sheets
    background-attachment, 607-609
    background-color, 607
    background-image, 607-608
    background-position, 607
    background-position property, 609-610
    background-repeat, 607-609
    character spacing (text), 619, 625
    fonts, 619-623
    formatting, 620, 624-625
    list-style-image property, 618
    list-style-position property, 618
    list-style-type property, 619
    paragraphs, 620, 625-626
    text, 619-620

STYLE tags
  CLASSES, 565-566
  visibility, 568-570
**property names, declarations, style sheets, 603**
**protocols**
  as URL component, 469
  e-mail accounts, 55
**Proxies panel, Internet access options, 344**
**Proxies subpanel, 111**
**Proxy Server, Internet firewalls, 669, 673**
**public domain CGI references, 558**
**public key cryptography, 357**
**Publicly Accessible Mailing Lists Web site, 19**
**Publishing panel, Composer preferences, 339**
**publishing Web pages, 89-93**
  configuring Composer, 90
  uploading to ISP, 89
**push-oriented Internet content options with Netcaster, 412**

# Q

**QuickTime plug-in**
  attributes, 638-639
  movie playback, 191
  QuickTime VR, 192
**quitting**
  IBM Host On-Demand, 402
  Netcaster channels, 409
  newsgroups, 253
**quoted text, 450**
**quoting prior e-mail messages, 69**

# R

**RADIO attribute, INPUT tags, 551**
**raised caps in text, 453**
**reading**
  e-mail messages, 56-57
    threads, 207
  files, security applets, 643

newsgroup articles, 256-266
  offline, 269-271
**README files**
  Communicator install for
    Windows 3.1, 696
  UNIX version install updates,
    747
  Windows 95 Communicator
    install, 715
**RealAudio plug-in, 195-196**
**recipients**
  adding to e-mail messages, 58,
    62-63
  deleting from e-mail messages,
    63
**Rectangle tools, Whiteboard,
  316**
**rectangular areas, imagemaps,
  533**
**recursive frames, 514-515**
**Redo command (Edit menu),
  233**
**reference layers, 589**
**referencing bookmarks,
  146-147**
**registration forms, 168**
**relative font sizes, 451**
**relative links, 470**
**relative positioned elements,
  566**
**Reload button, Navigation
  toolbar, 126**
**reminders for Calendar
  activities, 379**
**removing Web page links, 287**
**renaming Messenger folders,
  212**
**replacing text, 83**
**replies**
  e-mail messages, 67
  newsgroup articles, 77, 264-265
**requests with forms, 168**
**requirements**
  Communicator install, Windows
    3.1, 690
  Conference setup, 302-303
  IBM Host On-Demand, 394-395
  Macintosh install, 728
  UNIX install, 742
  using CGI, 540
  Windows 95 install, 712

**RESET attribute, INPUT tags,
  552**
**Reset button, forms, 179**
**resizing**
  frames, 182
  Message List columns, 200
**resources, scheduling options
  with Calendar, 371**
**responding to e-mail, 67-70**
**return receipts, e-mail, 64**
**revealing layers, 591-593**
**RIGHT attribute, LAYER tags,
  576**
**Right function, moving layers
  right, 594**
**right mouse button pop-up
  menu, 136-137**
**RIGHT property, ALIGN
  attribute, 646**
**risk classifications for Netcaster
  Java applets, 431**
**Roman numerals for lists, 459**
**ROT13-encoded newsgroup
  articles, 262**
**rows, adding to tables,
  292-296**
**ROWS attribute**
  FRAMESET tags, 505
  TEXTAREA tags, 546
**rules, style sheets, 603**
  declarations, 603
  selectors (HTML tags), 603-604

# S

**S tags, 448**
**S/MIME, e-mail encryption and
  digital signatures, 364-365**
**Save As command (File menu),
  233**
**Save Image As command, 125**
**saving**
  automatically, 80
  frames, 115
  graphics, 125
  newsgroup articles, 263
    file attachments, 265-266
  newsgroup messages, 76-77
  Web pages, 88, 114-115
    without viewing, 159

**scheduling conflict checking,
  Calendar Agenda, 377**
**scheduling information,
  Calendar Agenda, 371-373**
**screen**
  capture options, Whiteboard,
    317
  color options, 323-324
  display font options, Fonts
    panel, 120-121
**SCRIPT tag, 658**
**ScriptActive plug-in, ActiveX
  controls options, 197**
**scripts, 538-543**
  Content MIME types, 541
  dynamic, 542
  examples, 541-543
  hiding or showing layers,
    591-593
  input processing example
    program, 553-554
  JavaScript, 184-185
    adding, 658
    connecting events, 659-661
    hiding, 658-659
    organizing, 658
  moving layers, 594-596
  ns-install shell script, UNIX
    version install, 747
  public domain references, 558
  special layer effects, 589-596
  troubleshooting, 542
  URLs, 540
**SCROLLING attribute, FRAME
  tags, 510**
**SDK (Software Development
  Kit), 35**
**Search button (Navigation
  toolbar), 30, 47, 137**
**Search Directory command
  (Edit menu), 233**
**search engine startup page
  option, 325**
**Search History List option, 135**
**searches**
  Address Book
    LDAP directories, 237-238
    names, 237
    nicknames, 237
  bookmarks, 157
  Calendar scheduling options,
    377
  e-mail
    addresses, 337
    messages, 217-218

## searches

LDAP directory, 235
Location toolbar options, 137
newsgroups, 253-254
plug-ins, 639
Search button options, 137
sites, 47
with forms, 168
words or phrases, 274

**section tags, 437**

**secure e-mail services with Messaging Server, 673**

**secure server indicator, padlock icons, 176**

**security, 349**
applets, 643
Certificate Authorities, 359-361
forms, 556-557
JavaScript certification, 365
Netcaster permissions, 430-431
private key passwords, 361-362
Proxy Server firewalls, 673
user certificates, 357
Web pages, viewing data for current page, 130
Web Sites' Certificates, 359

**Security Advisor window, 37**

**security button, 352-354**

**Security command (Help menu), 234**

**security icon, status bar, 135**

**Security Info command (Communicator menu), 234**

**Security Info option, 354**

**Security panel, Netcaster, 420**

**Select Addresses dialog box, 243**

**Select All command (Edit menu), 125**

**Select element, forms, 179**

**SELECT tags, 547-549, 662**

**SELECTED attribute, OPTION tags, 548**

**selecting multiple bookmarks, 155**

**selectors (HTML tags)**
contextual, 604
grouping, 604
style sheets, 603
*see also* tags

**semicolons (;)**
JavaScript, 656
style sheets, 603

**Send Mail/Post News window, 58**

**sending**
e-mail messages, 64-66
Address Book, 242-243
files, 102

**SEPARATE_WINDOW parameter, IBM Host On-Demand, 401**

**separators for bookmark lists, 153**

**Server Push, 165**

**server-side imagemaps, 522-523**

**servers**
DLS Server, 303
Conference call routing, 98
domain names, 124
FTP, uploading Web pages to ISPs, 90
SuiteSpot, 668-671
Web servers, requests with forms, 168

**setup**
Collabra, 72
Composer, 80-81

**SHAPE attribute, AREA tags, 533**

**sharing files, 102-103, 312**

**Shockwave for Director plug-in, 197**

**shopping with forms, 170-177**
cookies, 175
security, 176-177

**shortcut keys, text formatting, 280** *see also* **key combinations**

**shortcuts**
launching applications automatically, 132
newsgroups, 253
Web page links, 124

**Show Component Bar command (Communicator menu), 234**

**Show or hide the Web top button, Netcaster, 422**

**showing layers, 591-593**

**signature files**
configuring for Messenger, 735
e-mail, 705, 721
newsgroup article postings, 268

preferences, 331-333

**Silence Sensor, Conference, 100, 305**

**Silicon Graphics Web site, VRML information and plug-ins, 194**

**simple layer example, 574**

**SIZE attribute, SELECT tags, 547**

**size property (fonts), style sheets, 619-620**

**SIZE= keyword, FONT tags, 451**

**sizing**
borders, 613-614
box properties, 611-613
fonts, 121, 622
frames, 504
HTML-coded e-mail messages, 223
layers, 578-579
message pane, 202-203
text, FONT tags, 451

**small font size, 622**

**SMALL tags, 450**

**small-scale Web page distribution 675-676**

**SMALLCONSOLE property, CONTROLS attribute, 636**

**smaller font size, 622**

**SMTP (Simple Mail Transfer Protocol), 720**

**SMTP mail servers**
configuring
Macintosh version, 737
Windows 3.1 version, 708
Windows 95 version, 718-720

**SNA (Systems Network Architecture), 390**

**SNMP (Simple Network Management Protocol), 670**

**Software Updates command (Help menu), 234**

**Sort... commands (View menu), 233**

**sorting**
Address Book, 235-236
bookmarks, 156
discussion folder, 263
Message List messages, 201

sound
    alerts, mail messages, 331
    playback options, LiveAudio plug-in, 188
    see also audio
sound cards
    Conference requirements, 302
    configuring for Conference use, 97
sound level output settings, Conference microphone, 99
source code
    editing for HTML documents, 278
    viewing for HTML documents, 276-278
source code example for HTML documents, 463-464
spamming, 60
SPAN tags, 566, 602
speaker amplification options, Conference, 309
special layer effects with scripts, 589-596
Speed Dial button, Conference, 308
speeds of throughput for modems, 680
spell-checking, 63, 274-275
square value, list-style-type property, 619
SRC attribute
    EMBED tags, 631
    FRAME tags, 508
    IMG tags, 479
    LAYER tags, 575
SSL (Secure Sockets Layer), 675
    encryption handling with Certificate Server, 675
    public key transmission security, 363-364
stacking options for layers with Z-INDEX, 568
stacking order for layers, 584
starting
    Calendar, 370-371
    Conference, 96-97
    IBM Host On-Demand, 401-402
    Messenger, 53
    Netcaster, 406-410, 412, 418
STARTTIME attribute, LiveAudio, 636

statements, JavaScript, 656
static IP addresses, Internet connections, 686
status bar
    Component bar, 136
    gas gauge area, 135
    hiding, 136
    Navigator, 135-136
    Navigator window, 113
    security icon, 135
Stop Animations command (View menu), 126
Stop button, Navigation toolbar, 126
Stop Page Loading command (View menu), 126
STOPBUTTON property, CONTROLS attribute, 636
storage options, e-mail and discussion group messages, 347
streaming audio
    Media Player plug-in, 189
    Media Server, 674
strikethrough text, 448
STRONG tags, 446
STYLE attribute, 602
style property, fonts, style sheets, 620-623
style sheets (Web pages), 31, 562-565, 599
    backgrounds, 607-610
    box properties, 610-616
        borders, 610-615
        margins, 610-612, 615
        padding, 610-612, 616
        sizing, 611-613
    cascading, 31, 600, 605
    CLASS attribute, 604-605
    commenting, 605-606
    conflicting, 600
    embedding, 601-602
    floating elements
        clear property, 618
        example, 617
        values, 616
    hiding, 606, 564
    @import url statement, 562
    ! important definitions, 570
    importing, 603
    inheritance, 604
    inline (on-the-fly), 602
    JavaScript-accessible Style Sheets (JASS), 31
    linking, 600-601

    lists, 618-619
    overriding tags, 565
    preference settings, 342
    rules, 603-604
    text properties, 619-620, 625
STYLE tags, 563, 601
    CLASSES property, 565-566
    visibility property, 568-570
STYLE TYPE tags, 564
SUB tags, 450
Subarea SNAs, 391
subdirectories, relative links, 470
subfolders, Messenger, 210-211
SUBMIT attribute, INPUT tags, 553
Submit buttons, forms, 178
    online shopping example, 172
    troubleshooting, 178
subscribing to newsgroups, 252-253
subscript text, 450
SuiteSpot servers, 668-671
Sun Workstations, Communicator install, 742
SUP tags, 450
super reload option for site update checking, 127
superscript text, 450
switching between applications, 48-49
Symantec Café Web site, 644
system fonts for screen displays, 121
system requirements, Conference, 302-303

# T

T1/T3 lines, Internet connections, 681
Tab key, highlighting successive links, 123
tables, 290-296, 516-517
    cell spanning, 295
    color options, 291
    editing, 292-293
    formatting rows and columns, 293-296
    row and column options, 292

tags, *see* HTML tags
talking on the Internet
    Conference, 96
    Text Chat, 102
TARGET attribute, FRAME tags, 511
target layers, 589
task entries, Calendar, 383
task list, Calendar, 383
TCP/IP (Transmission Control Program/Internet Protocol), 688
    configuring network properties, 685-687
    e-mail connections, 66
    installing, 685
telephone service via the Internet, dialing Conference calls, 307-310
Telnet sites, 140
temp files for UNIX version install, 746
Template Studio Web site, 661
templates
    cascading style sheets, 562-565
    new features, 34
    Web pages, 464
terminal processing options with IBM Host On-Demand, 392
test drive programs for Netscape servers, 671
testing
    imagemaps, 535
    user profiles
        Macintosh Communicator install, 733
        Windows 3.1 Communicator version, 702
        Windows 95, 719
TESTTOP property, ALIGN attribute, 646
text
    adding to Web pages, 82-84
    blinking, 448
    bold, 445
    centering, 449
    color options, 323-324, 453-454
    deleting, 83
    display alternatives for graphics, 284-285
    drop caps, 453
    formatting options, 445

indentation options for HTML documents, 281
italic, 447
moving, 84
preformatted options, 444
progressive enlarging, 453
quoted, 450
redoing changes, 84
replacing, 83
sizing options, 451
strikethrough, 448
style sheet properties, 619-620
    character spacing, 619, 625
    fonts, 619-623
    formatting, 620, 624-625
    paragraphs, 620, 625-626
subscript, 450
superscript, 450
table alignment options, 294
typewriter-style, 450
underlined, 447
undoing changes, 84
text alternatives for imagemaps, 535
TEXT attribute, INPUT tags, 549
Text Chat, 102
text editors, editing HTML documents, 278
text fields, forms, 177
Text Properties (listing), 623
Text tool, Whiteboard, 317
text wrapping
    graphics options, 285
    list-style-position property, 618
text-align paragraph property, 620
text-based chatting with Chat Tool, 311
text-bottom value, vertical-align paragraph property, 626
text-decoration property, 620, 624
text-indent paragraph property, 620, 626
text-only browsers, alternative text, 284
text-top value, vertical-align paragraph property, 626
text-transform property, 620, 624-625
TEXT= keyword, BODY tag, 454

TEXTAREA tag, forms, 179
TEXTAREA tags, 545-546
third-party plug-ins, 194-196
threads
    expanding and reading, 207
    grouping e-mail messages, 205-209
    ignoring, 209
    newsgroup articles, 262-263
    viewing, 206
    watched, 208
throughput for modems, 680
thumbnails, 479
tic-tac-toe board frame example, 501, 513-514
title section of HTML documents, 437
TITLE tags, 436-438, 463
TN3270 emulation and IBM Host On-Demand, 392
TN3270_SERVER_PORT parameter, IBM Host On-Demand, 401
TN3270E Server gateway, IBM Host On-Demand, 394
ToggleFirst() function, hiding or showing layers, 591
toolbars
    Address Book, 234-235
    Address Book Toolbar, 238
    Calendar, 376-377
    Composition, 85, 88
    Cosmo VRML viewer plug-in, 194
    customizing, 320-324
    display options, 122-123
    Location, 45, 73, 112, 146
    Navigation, 111
        Back button, 29, 44
        Collabra, 73
        display options, 322
        Forward button, 29
        Images button, 30
        new features, 29
        Reload button, 126
        Stop button, 126
    Netcaster, 421-422
    new features, 29
    Personal, 112
        adding page shortcuts, 134
        Bookmark button, 157, 159
Tool Tips, 142
TOP attribute, LAYER tags, 575-576, 583

top keyword, background-position property, 609-610
TOP property, ALIGN attribute, 646
top value, vertical-align paragraph property, 626
top-level newsgroup categories, 247
tracking tasks with Calendar, 383
transfer status for Web pages, 128
Trash, emptying in Messenger, 215
trial programs for Netscape servers, 671
troubleshooting
 borders, style sheets, 615
 CGI scripts, 542
 Conference calls, 305
 e-mail connections, 56, 66
 encoded newsgroup articles, 262
 LiveVideo playback, 190
 missing bookmarks, 147
 newsgroup availability, 247
 OIA messages for IBM Host On-Demand, 398
 opening Web pages, 93
 Submit buttons on forms, 178
TT tags, 450
turning off automatic image loading, 126
turning off GIF animations, 126
TYPE attribute
 EMBED tag, 631
 INPUT tag, 549
 OBJECT tag, 632
type property, lists, 619
TYPE= keyword, OL tags, 459
types of newsgroups, 246
typewriter-style text, 450
Typical install setup for Windows 3.1, 692
Typical installation option Windows 95 version, 713

# U

U tags, 447
UL tags, 458

underline value, text-decoration property, 624
underlined e-mail messages, 222
underlined text, 447
Undo command (Edit menu), 233
UNITS attribute, EMBED tag, 631
UNIX systems
 directories, cgi-bin, 540
 installing Netscape Communicator
  from archive files, 741
  from CD-ROM, 746-747
  ns-install shell script, 747
  temp file example, 746
 plug-ins folder, 628
 uploading Web pages to ISPs, 89
unordered lists, 458
unsubscribing from newsgroups, 253
unvisited links, color options, 121, 324
Up function, moving layers upward, 594
updating
 bookmarks, 161
 channels in Netcaster, 414, 418, 423
 Host Agenda, Calendar, 373
 offline Agenda, Calendar, 373
upgrades
 from Netscape 3.0, 714
 UNIX version updates, 744
uploading
 files to FTP sites, 139
 new Web sites to ISP, 89-90
upper-alpha value, list-style-type property, 619
upper-roman value, list-style-type property, 619
uppercase value, text-transform, 624-625
URLs (Uniform Resource Locators), 124-125
 as links, 468
 automatically completing addresses, 123
 background-image property (style sheets), 608
 CGI scripts, 540
 component elements, 469

file names, 124
forms handling scripts, 544
FTP links, 472
Gopher links, 472
https secure URL type, 557
local files, 125
Location field options, Netcaster, 417
mailto: links, 473
pathnames, 124
registering with ISP, 90
sending with e-mail Web page attachments, 221
server domain names, 124
UseNet links, 473
USEMAP attribute, IMG SRC tags, 526
UseNet
 Collabra newsreader options, 245
 Collabra Server options, 674
 etiquette, 77-78
 links, 473
 reading messages, 75-78
UseNet newsgroups, 246-248
 Collabra setup, 72
 FAQs, 20
 new users, 248
 news.announce.newusers, 248
 reading articles, 256-266
 replies to articles, 264
 replying, 77
 saving messages in mail folders, 76-78
 subscribing, 73-78
 types, 246
user access rights, Calendar, 386
user certificates, 357
User IDs, ISP connections, 682
user interfaces, Webtop design, 424
user privileges with Directory Server, 673
user profiles
 Macintosh Communicator install, 731-732
 multiple profiles, 131-132, 350
 Windows 3.1 Communicator version, 698-702
 Windows 95 Communicator install, 716-719
user tracking with Directory Server, 672-673
uses of Web forms, 167-170

## V

validating forms, 654
VALUE attribute, OPTION tags, 548
values
   borders, 614
   clear property, 618
   declarations, 603
   floating elements, 616
   list-style-position property, 618
   list-style-type property, 619
   text-decoration property, 624
   text-transform, 624-625
   white-space property, 625
variable-width fonts, 323
variant property, fonts, 623
vertical (y), background-position property, 609-610
vertical-align paragraph property, 620-621, 626
video
   adding, 636-639
   bandwidth considerations, 638
   LiveVideo attributes, 637-639
   QuickTime plug-in attributes, 638-639
Video for Windows files, LiveVideo playback, 189
video playback
   LiveVideo plug-in, 189
   QuickTime plug-in, 191
videoconferencing with Conference, 96
View menu commands, 126-128
View menu commands (Address Book), 233
View menu options, Whiteboard, 317
viewing
   bookmarks, 156
   Calendar notes, 385
   frames information, 129
   HTML document source code, 276-278
   Java applet information, 130
   Netcaster channels offline, 429
   newsgroup articles, 263
   security information, 354
   threads, 206
   Web pages
      HTML source code, 128

   preferences and default settings, 120-123
   security data, 130
Virtual Library Web site, 649
VISIBILITY attribute, LAYER tags, 575, 591
visibility property, STYLE tags, 568-570
visited link color options, 324
visited links, color options, 121, 455
Visual J++ Web site, 644
VLINK= keyword, BODY tags, 455
VM (Virtual Machine), IBM Host On-Demand, 393
voice files, LiveAudio playback, 188
Voice Mail messages with Conference, 309
VOLUME attribute, LiveAudio, 636
VOLUMEBUTTON property, CONTROLS attribute, 636
VRML (Virtual Reality Modeling Language) plug-ins, 193
VSPACE attribute
   APPLET tag, 646
   EMBED tag, 631
   IMG tags, 482-483
   OBJECT tag, 632, 648
VTAM (Virtual Telecommunications Access Method), 391

## W

W3C (World Wide Web Consortium), 21, 561
W3C recommendation Web site, 599
W3C Web site, 631
watched e-mail threads, 208
watermarks, background-image property, 608
WAV files, LiveAudio playback, 188
Web Developer magazine Web site, 628

Web pages
   active links, color options, 455
   adding to Netcaster channels, 426
   attaching to e-mail, 220-221
   audio, adding, 634-636
   automated loading with Server Push and Client Pull, 165
   automatic image loading, turning off, 126
   automatically completing addresses, 123
   autoscroll, 165
   backgrounds, 286
   blinking text, 448
   bold text, 445
   centering text, 449
   code comments, 463
   color options, 455-456
   dividing lines, 283
   downloading Navigator control tools, 126-127
   Dynamic Font display options, 121
   dynamic fonts, 571
   editing from Navigator, 118
   Enterprise Server distribution, 671-672
   font sizing options, 121
   FONT tags, 453
   footers, 443
   formatting, 278-283
   forms, 167-179, 538, 543-553
   frames, 180-183, 498, 503-512
      accommodating non-frames abled browsers, 515
      borderless, 515-516
      design issues, 504
      limitations and advantages, 502-503
      multiple, 512
      navigation options, 182
      recursive, 514-515
   frequently visited site update settings, 127
   GIF animations, turning off, 126
   graphics, 284-286, 476
      alignment options, 285
      alternative text for non-graphical browsers, 480-481
      as links, 484-485
      margins, 286
      text wrapping options, 285
   headings, 282, 438
   home pages, Netscape automatic setup, 124
   horizontal rule lines, 443

HTML code example, 463-464
imagemaps, 166, 519, 523-532
  adding, 525-526
  circular areas, 533
  default links, 534-535
  mapping, 526-532
  overlapping, 534
  polygon areas, 533
  rectangular areas, 533
  selecting graphic for use, 523-524
  testing, 535
italic text, 447
Java applets, 183-184
JavaScript, 184-185
layers, 566-568, 573
  background graphics or colors, 580-581
  fly-over help options, 596
  hiding or showing, 591-593
  moving with scripts, 594-596
  multiple layers, 582-587
  nesting, 587-589
  ordering options for layer stacking, 585
  overlapping layers, 583
  positioning, 576-578
  sizing options, 578
  special effects with scripts, 589-596
  stacking order options, 584
links, 468
  absolute, 470-471
  changing, 287
  color options, 121, 287, 454
  frames, 511
  FTP, 472
  Gopher, 472
  internal links, 288
  mailto:, 473-474
  named anchors, 289
  named targets, 475
  relative, 470
  removing, 287
  shortcuts, 124
  UseNet, 473
lists, 282, 456-461
  definition, 459-461
  nested, 461-462
  numbered, 458-459
  unordered, 458
mini browser windows, 113
named targets, 475
navigation button bars, 517
non-breaking spaces, 283
on-the-fly, 654
online cataloging via Catalog Server, 672

opening, 114-115
  troubleshooting, 93
paragraph tags, 440-445
plug-ins, 186-197, 296-298, 629
preformatting text, 283
printing, 115-117
publishing, 89-93
quoted text, 450
saving, 114-115
  without viewing, 159
screen display font options, 120-121
scripts, 538
searches, 137
security, viewing data for current page, 130
strikethrough text, 448
style sheets, 562-565
subscript text, 450
super reload option for site update checking, 127
superscript text, 450
tables, 290-296, 516-517
  borderless, 291
  cell spanning, 295
  editing, 292-293
  formatting rows and columns, 293-296
  row and column options, 292
templates, 464
text
  alignment options, 281
  color options, 453-454
  display alternatives for graphics, 284-285
  drop caps, 453
  indentation options, 281
  preformatted options, 444
  progressive enlarging, 453
  relative font sizing, 451
  sizing options with FONT tags, 451
thumbnails, 479
toolbar display options, 122-123
transfer status, 128
typewriter-style text, 450
underlined text, 447
URLs, 124-125
video, 636-639
viewing
  HTML source code, 128
  preferences and default settings, 120-123
visited link color options, 455
white space, 283
word break tags, 443

**Web Phonebook, Conference phone calls, 308**

**Web search engine startup page option, 325**

**Web servers**
  domain names, 124
  requests with forms, 168
  secure server indicator, 176

**Web sites**
  adding to Netcaster channels, 426
  bookmarking, 146-147
  Channel Finder, 413
  dynamic fonts, 571
  forms, 538, 543-553
  graphics, 476
  imagemaps, 519, 523-532
  integration examples of forms and CGI scripts, 553-556
  layers, 566-568
  links, 468
  named targets, 475
  navigation button bars, 517
  plug-ins, 186-197
  scripts, 538
  searches, 137
  shopping with forms, 170-177
  style sheets, 562-565
  tables, 516-517

**Web Sites Certificates, 359**

**Web top view, Netcaster, 416**

**Web tops, 406, 422-425**
  design elements, 423-425
  display options, 423
  hiding, 423
  updating, 423
  user interface design, 424
  *see also* channels

**weight property, fonts, 620**

**white space, HTML documents, 283**

**white-space property, 619, 625**

**Whiteboard, 104-105, 314-317**
  Canvas Size options, 317
  capturing screen shots, 317
  clearing screen, 315
  Floating Toolbox, 317
  loading background images, 315-316
  markup layer, 105
  markup tools, 316-317
  Options menu, 317
  View menu options, 317

**WIDTH attribute**
  APPLET tag, 646-648
  EMBED tag, 631
  IMG tags, 482

## 778 | WIDTH attribute

LAYER tags, 575, 578
OBJECT tag, 632, 648-651

**width options for tables, 291**

**widths, borders, 611**

**wild card asterisk (*), frame sizing, 506**

**windows**
Conference, 97
Edit Bookmarks, 153
History, 324-325
Log File, 102
Navigator, 111-113
NetHelp, 141-143
opening multiple, 113
Personal Note Pad, 102
Text Chat, 102

**Windows**
plug-ins folder, 628
shortcuts, 253

**Windows 3.1**
configuring Communicator, 703-710
installing Communicator, 689, 691

**Windows 95**
Collabra configuration, 725
Dial-Up Networking configuration, 683
installing Communicator, 712-716
Internet connections, 680-682
Messenger configuration, 722-725
OLE applications, 32
PPP connections, 683-685

**Windows NT, OLE applications, 32**

**Winsock, Windows 3.1 Communicator install, 690**

**Wizards, Conference Setup, 97-100**

**word break tags, 443**

**word-spacing, style sheets, 625**

**word-spacing property, style sheets, 619**

**words, HTML document searches, 274**

**World Wide Web Consortium (WC3), 21, 561**

**World Wide Web Consortium (WC3) Web site, 21**

**WRAP attribute, TEXTAREA tags, 546**

**wrapping text, list-style-position property, 618**

**writing**
e-mail, recipient addresses, 58
files, security applets, 643

**WWW (World Wide Web)**
collaborative Web browsing, 103-104
FAQs (frequently asked questions), 15
online access connections, 680-682

# X

x (horizontal), background-position property, 609-610

X <-o-> message, IBM Host On-Demand OIA, 399

X message, IBM Host On-Demand OIA, 398

X SYSTEM message, IBM Host On-Demand OIA, 399

# Y-Z

y (vertical), background-position property, 609-610

Yahoo! Web site, searches with forms, 41, 168

Z-INDEX attribute, LAYER tags, 568, 575, 584

zooming Web page areas for print preview, 116

# Complete and Return this Card for a *FREE* Computer Book Catalog

Thank you for purchasing this book! You have purchased a superior computer book written expressly for your needs. To continue to provide the kind of up-to-date, pertinent coverage you've come to expect from us, we need to hear from you. Please take a minute to complete and return this self-addressed, postage-paid form. In return, we'll send you a free catalog of all our computer books on topics ranging from word processing to programming and the internet.

Mr. ☐   Mrs. ☐   Ms. ☐   Dr. ☐

Name (first) _____ (M.I.) ___ (last) _____
Address _____
City _____ State ___ Zip _____
Phone _____ Fax _____
Company Name _____
E-mail address _____

## 1. Please check at least (3) influencing factors for purchasing this book.

Front or back cover information on book ........ ☐
Special approach to the content ..................... ☐
Completeness of content ............................... ☐
Author's reputation ....................................... ☐
Publisher's reputation ................................... ☐
Book cover design or layout .......................... ☐
Index or table of contents of book ................ ☐
Price of book ................................................. ☐
Special effects, graphics, illustrations ............ ☐
Other (Please specify): _____ ☐

## 2. How did you first learn about this book?

Saw in Macmillan Computer Publishing catalog ........ ☐
Recommended by store personnel ................ ☐
Saw the book on bookshelf at store ............... ☐
Recommended by a friend ............................ ☐
Received advertisement in the mail .............. ☐
Saw an advertisement in: _____ ☐
Read book review in: _____ ☐
Other (Please specify): _____ ☐

## 3. How many computer books have you purchased in the last six months?

This book only ....... ☐      3 to 5 books ........ ☐
2 books .................. ☐      More than 5 ......... ☐

## 4. Where did you purchase this book?

Bookstore ...................................................... ☐
Computer Store ............................................ ☐
Consumer Electronics Store ......................... ☐
Department Store ......................................... ☐
Office Club ................................................... ☐
Warehouse Club ........................................... ☐
Mail Order .................................................... ☐
Direct from Publisher ................................... ☐
Internet site .................................................. ☐
Other (Please specify): _____ ☐

## 5. How long have you been using a computer?

☐ Less than 6 months      ☐ 6 months to a year
☐ 1 to 3 years              ☐ More than 3 years

## 6. What is your level of experience with personal computers and with the subject of this book?

| | With PCs | With subject of book |
|---|---|---|
| New | ☐ | ☐ |
| Casual | ☐ | ☐ |
| Accomplished | ☐ | ☐ |
| Expert | ☐ | ☐ |

Source Code ISBN: 0-7897-0980-5

## 7. Which of the following best describes your job title?

- Administrative Assistant ☐
- Coordinator ☐
- Manager/Supervisor ☐
- Director ☐
- Vice President ☐
- President/CEO/COO ☐
- Lawyer/Doctor/Medical Professional ☐
- Teacher/Educator/Trainer ☐
- Engineer/Technician ☐
- Consultant ☐
- Not employed/Student/Retired ☐
- Other (Please specify): _____ ☐

## 8. Which of the following best describes the area of the company your job title falls under?

- Accounting ☐
- Engineering ☐
- Manufacturing ☐
- Operations ☐
- Marketing ☐
- Sales ☐
- Other (Please specify): _____ ☐

## 9. What is your age?

- Under 20 ☐
- 21-29 ☐
- 30-39 ☐
- 40-49 ☐
- 50-59 ☐
- 60-over ☐

## 10. Are you:

- Male ☐
- Female ☐

## 11. Which computer publications do you read regularly? (Please list)

_____
_____
_____
_____
_____
_____
_____

**Comments**: _____

*Fold here and scotch-tape to mail.*

---

**BUSINESS REPLY MAIL**
FIRST-CLASS MAIL PERMIT NO. 9918 INDIANAPOLIS IN

POSTAGE WILL BE PAID BY THE ADDRESSEE

ATTN MARKETING
MACMILLAN COMPUTER PUBLISHING
MACMILLAN PUBLISHING USA
201 W 103RD ST
INDIANAPOLIS IN 46290-9042

NO POSTAGE NECESSARY IF MAILED IN THE UNITED STATES

# Check out Que® Books on the World Wide Web
## http://www.quecorp.com

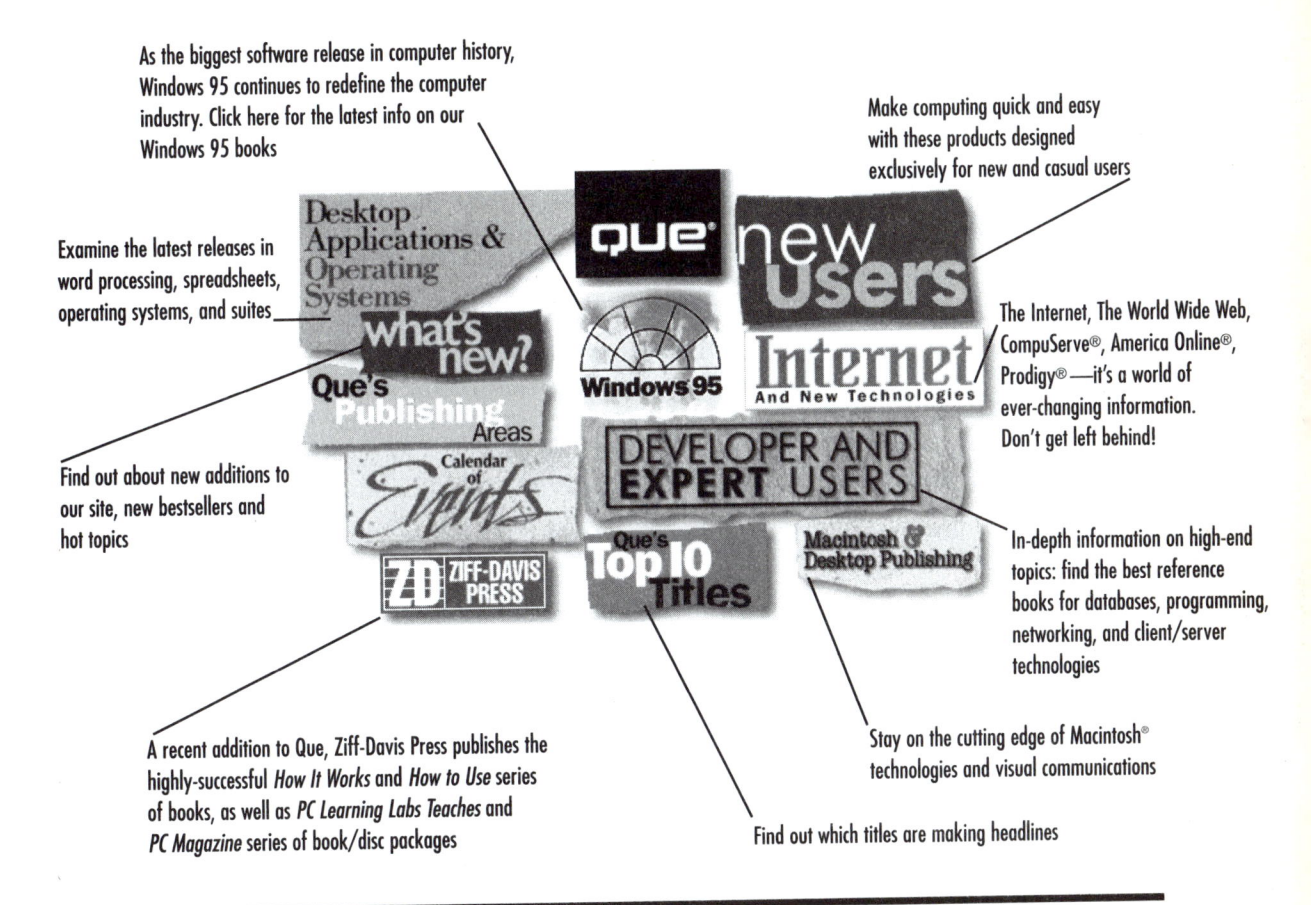

As the biggest software release in computer history, Windows 95 continues to redefine the computer industry. Click here for the latest info on our Windows 95 books

Make computing quick and easy with these products designed exclusively for new and casual users

Examine the latest releases in word processing, spreadsheets, operating systems, and suites

The Internet, The World Wide Web, CompuServe®, America Online®, Prodigy® —it's a world of ever-changing information. Don't get left behind!

Find out about new additions to our site, new bestsellers and hot topics

In-depth information on high-end topics: find the best reference books for databases, programming, networking, and client/server technologies

A recent addition to Que, Ziff-Davis Press publishes the highly-successful *How It Works* and *How to Use* series of books, as well as *PC Learning Labs Teaches* and *PC Magazine* series of book/disc packages

Stay on the cutting edge of Macintosh® technologies and visual communications

Find out which titles are making headlines

---

With 6 separate publishing groups, Que develops products for many specific market segments and areas of computer technology. Explore our Web Site and you'll find information on best-selling titles, newly published titles, upcoming products, authors, and much more.

- Stay informed on the latest industry trends and products available
- Visit our online bookstore for the latest information and editions
- Download software from Que's library of the best shareware and freeware

Copyright © 1997, Macmillan Computer Publishing-USA, A Viacom Company

MACMILLAN COMPUTER PUBLISHING USA
A VIACOM COMPANY

# Technical Support:

If you need assistance with the information in this book or with a CD/Disk accompanying the book, please access the Knowledge Base on our Web site at **http://www.superlibrary.com/general/support**. Our most Frequently Asked Questions are answered there. If you do not find the answer to your questions on our Web site, you may contact Macmillan Technical Support **(317) 581-3833** or e-mail us at **support@mcp.com**.